12 MONTHS FREE ACCESS WITH THIS TEXT!

Boone & Kurtz Xtra!
Contemporary Marketing 2005

Congratulations! Your purchase of
this new textbook includes complimentary
access to the Boone & Kurtz Xtra! Web Site
(http://boonextra.swlearning.com).
This site offers a robust set of online
multimedia learning tools, including:

Xtra! Quizzing
Flash Chapter Review Presentations
Krispy Kreme Continuing Case Video
Marketing Plan Worksheets
Applying Marketing Concepts Exercises

Tear-Out Card Missing?

If you did not buy a new textbook, the
tear-out portion of this card may be missing
or the serial number on this card may not be valid.
Serial numbers can be used only once to register
for access to Boone & Kurtz Xtra! and are not
transferable. You can choose to either buy a new
book or purchase access to the Boone & Kurtz Xtra!
site at http://boonextra.swlearning.com

THOMSON
✳
SOUTH-WESTERN

xtra!

SERIAL NUMBER

SC-000BIFCW-XBCM

HOW TO REGISTER YOUR SERIAL NUMBER

1. Launch a web browser and go to
   http://boonextra.swlearning.com
2. Click the "register" button to enter your
   serial number.
3. Enter your serial number exactly as it appears
   here and create a unique User ID, or enter an
   existing User ID if you have previously registered
   for a South-Western product.
   and create a password (or enter
   password, if you have previously
   a different product via a serial
   ubmit.

**Record your User ID and password
in a secure location.**

5. Once registered, follow the link to enter the
   product, or return to the URL above and
   select the "enter" button; have your User ID
   and password handy.

   Note: The duration of your access to the
   product begins when registration is complete.

contact 1-800-423-0563 or email **tl.support@thomson.com**

D1208467

Contemporary Marketing 2005

DOUGHNUTS

COFFEE

COLLECTIBLES

MARKETING

STORES

PRICE
PRODUCT
DISTRIBUTION
PROMOTION

Louis E. Boone
University of South Alabama

David L. Kurtz
University of Arkansas

THOMSON
™
SOUTH-WESTERN

Australia · Canada · Mexico · Singapore · Spain · United Kingdom · United States

Contemporary Marketing 2005
Louis E. Boone and David L. Kurtz

VP/Editorial Director:
Jack W. Calhoun

VP/Editor-in-Chief:
Michael P. Roche

Publisher:
Melissa Acuña

Senior Acquisitions Editor:
Steve Hazelwood

Senior Developmental Editor:
Rebecca von Gillern

Marketing Manager:
Nicole Moore

Production Editor:
Chris Hudson

Media Developmental Editor:
Kristen Meere

Media Production Editor:
Karen Schaffer

Manufacturing Coordinator:
Diane Lohman

Production House:
LEAP/GGS

Printer:
QuebecorWorld
Dubuque, Iowa

Senior Design Project Manager:
Michelle Kunkler

Internal Designer:
Knapke Design
Cincinnati, Ohio

Cover Designer:
WHIZBANG
Cincinnati, Ohio

Cover Revisions:
Ramsdell Design
Cincinnati, Ohio

Photography Manager:
Deanna Ettinger

Photo Researcher:
Terri Miller

*To the two million students around the globe who began their marketing studies using **Contemporary Marketing** in their classes*

and

to the Text and Academic Authors Association, which awarded **Contemporary Marketing** *the William Holmes McGuffey Award for Excellence and Longevity, the first basic marketing text to receive this prestigious award.*

Boone&Kurtz

Dear Fellow Principles of Marketing Instructor:

As the new ads at fast-food giant McDonald's say, "I'm lovin' it." You are likely to echo this marketing tag line because you finally have a chance to offer your students an up-to-the-minute textbook so complete, so well written, and accompanied by teaching/learning materials that serve as industry benchmarks for quality and completeness. Even better is the fact that students can purchase a new copy of the text for about the same price as a used copy of last year's hardcover version.

Contemporary Marketing 2005 contains every chapter and every page of the hardcover edition and is updated to include important business and marketing developments occurring since publication of the original version. In fact, with the additional integrated case and video on the clothing and entertainment company FUBU, there's even more here than in the hardcover version.

You'll love the size of our test bank—at more than 4,000 test questions categorized by chapter objectives, it's easily the largest and best in the market. You'll also be pleased with our customer service; a special *Instructor's Manual* supplement on the Web site (http://boone.swlearning.com) identifies every change in every chapter and shows how to integrate them into your class notes.

Your students will rave about the free audio reviews that accompany the text. The four CDs allow students to review classroom reading assignments anywhere, anytime. Students can listen to them while exercising, in their car, or even while walking across campus on their way to class.

To give *Contemporary Marketing 2005* a fresh new feel, we added extensive coverage of

- How the 99-cent-per-downloaded-song services supplied by firms like Apple Computer, Blockbuster, and Wal-Mart are assisting the troubled music industry by resolving the conflict between music lovers fed up with high CD prices and the recording industry so determined to stop illegal downloading that they have resorted to filing lawsuits against 12-year-olds
- The impact of the recent FTC "Do Not Call" rule on telemarketing and the drive to put a lid on spam
- The 2005 increase in the number of EU members from 15 to 25
- How food marketers are responding to growing concerns about obesity—the new version of tobacco worries
- Why Canada is the country of choice for buying prescription drugs
- Why Lowe's is growing by focusing on a new target market: women
- How Dell has expanded beyond servers and personal computers into computer games, plasma TVs, and music downloads in response to the trend toward digital convergence
- The soaring popularity of hybrid cars

You and your students will be able to use our highly acclaimed Web site (http://boone.swlearning .com) to perform many assignments and conduct research. It's easy to use and contains invaluable features.

We're delighted to bring you the industry's best marketing text. We're sure that you—and your students—will agree.

Sincerely,

Gene Boone

Louis E. Boone

Dave Kurtz

David L. Kurtz

It's as current as today's headlines. A hallmark of any Boone & Kurtz text is its focus on how marketing concepts apply to today's business issues. And instructors who have used earlier editions of this text in their classes already know that when students ask questions like

- "Why is the recording industry in such trouble that it is filing lawsuits against 12-year-olds?"

- "Why did the telemarketers stop calling me? And can whomever was responsible help me rid my life of spam?"

- "Will all of these news stories about the growing problem of obesity—especially among kids—mean major problems for the fast-food industry?"

- "My other business text says there are 15 members of the European Union. But Boone & Kurtz say the number is actually 25. Who is correct?"

The questions will be discussed—and answered correctly—in *Contemporary Marketing 2005*. After all, the book's position as the benchmark in measuring overall quality has been

> ## Lead, follow, or get out of the way.
>
> Anonymous

recognized by fellow authors who voted it the first marketing text to receive the prestigious McGuffey Award for Textbook Excellence.

But *CM 2005* goes far beyond overall accuracy and quality. Instructors have come to expect additional qualities from a Boone & Kurtz text: complete, easy to understand coverage of all relevant topics in a lively, engaging writing style that makes students forget that they are reading a college-level textbook. And when students ask

- "Why is it impossible for a principles of marketing text to cover the subject in less than 600 pages?" and

- "Are there any textbooks out there that include high-quality coverage of the importance of business ethics?"

You can simply point to the class text. After all, from the very first edition, *Contemporary Marketing* has been a book of firsts. No introductory marketing text in print has been used by as many students—either in the U.S. or abroad. And the best continues to get better.

Contemporary Marketing Firsts

Previous users will recognize the significant improvements and up-to-the-minute currency of *Contemporary Marketing 2005* as the latest installment of a trend we established back in the first edition—to lead the principles of marketing market with new "firsts." We know that keeping several steps ahead of the competition is the way we became the best-selling basic marketing text. We plan to keep it that way.

Consider our record of providing instructors and students with "firsts":

- The FIRST marketing text written specifically for the student—rather than the professor—featuring a clear, concise style that students readily understand and enjoy.

- The FIRST marketing text based on marketing research, written the way instructors actually teach the course.

- The FIRST marketing text to integrate computer applications—and later, Internet assignments—into each chapter.

- The FIRST marketing text to employ extensive pedagogy—such as opening vignettes and boxed features—to breathe life into the exciting concepts and issues of marketing.

- The FIRST marketing text to offer end-of-chapter cases written by the authors and then filmed by professional producers who include text concepts in each chapter video.

- The FIRST marketing text to offer early services, international, and marketing planning chapters and to thoroughly integrate these topics throughout with literally hundreds of examples.

- The FIRST marketing text to utilize multimedia technology to integrate all components of the principles of marketing ancillary program, videos, overhead transparencies, and PowerPoint® CD-ROMs for both instructors and students—enabling instructors to custom create lively lecture presentations.

- The FIRST marketing text to include an entire, separate chapter on relationship marketing and customer relationship management (CRM).

- The FIRST marketing text to include coverage of category management—the fast-growing industry trend in product management—in Chapter 12 and to include it as part of the chapter title.

Key Features of Contemporary Marketing 2005

Contemporary Marketing 2005 is packed full of innovations. Here are some new and exciting features of the 2005 edition.

Major Expansion of Marketing Ethics

In the wake of the recent crisis in business ethics, business programs in colleges and universities are examining their curricula and evaluating the extent and quality of their coverage of ethical issues. A number of universities, including Rutgers University and Ohio State University, are either adding new courses or expanding existing elective courses in ethics. Still others advocate the integration of ethics throughout the courses that comprise their business core curriculum. Many of the latter are currently engaged in extensive review of course contents to determine the adequacy of current coverage.

Contemporary Marketing 2005 provides instructors and students with a thorough treatment of ethical issues affecting marketing, both from a macro perspective and in relation to specific aspects of marketing. The value of marketing ethics is introduced in Chapter 1 and then followed with a detailed analysis in Chapter 3, which focuses specifically on ethical and social responsibility issues. Topics discussed in this chapter include ethical problems in marketing research, product decisions, pricing, distribution, and promotional strategy.

Chapter 5 analyzes the ethical issues surrounding online marketing and the Internet. Topics examined here include copyright issues and a lengthy discussion of privacy issues and the potential misuse of customer information by e-commerce firms. The importance of acting in an ethical manner as a key to developing effective marketing relationships is discussed in Chapter 6. A separate section in Chapter 18 examines advertising ethics and ethical issues in sales promotion and public relations. Ethical issues in personal selling are examined in a separate section in Chapter 19.

Every chapter includes a special experiential feature called **Solving an Ethical Controversy.** This feature is designed to facilitate class debates on current ethical issues. Each begins with a brief background and is followed by a series of pro and con points designed to elicit class discussion of the issues. Examples of this feature in *CM 2005* include:

- "The National Do Not Call List: Friend or Foe?" (Ch. 19)
- "Wi-Fi and the Invasion of Privacy" (Ch. 1)
- "Is the Fox Guarding the Henhouse? The Alcohol Industry's 'Drink Responsibly' Promotions" (Ch. 3)
- "Is the Web Spying on You?" (Ch. 5)
- "Minority Marketing Campaigns Miss Their Target" (Ch. 8)
- "What to Do about Pop-Up Ads?" (Ch. 18)
- "Secret Costs of Shelf Space" (Ch. 15)
- "Should Marketing Promotions Target Children?" (Ch. 17)

Current Events and Their Impact on Marketing

The impact of largely uncontrollable environmental factors—the beginning of an economic recovery following months of lingering recession, the continuing costs—monetary and human—of the Iraqi war, the recent SARS epidemic, and continuing terrorist attacks around the globe—are a part of almost every chapter. The Chapter 13 opening vignette, "Airlines Fight for Their Lives," describes the problems encountered by airline marketers in their efforts to stimulate sales during a period in which both vacationers and business travelers decided to minimize air travel in favor of driving vacations and videoconferencing.

The threat of terrorism continues to impact marketing in various ways, and its shadow can be found in most chapters. New laws passed to reduce consumer security concerns and lessen the threat to marketers are introduced in the legal environment section of Chapter 3. Several new **Marketing Hits** are included in this new edition, such as:

- "The U.S. Military Turns to Private-Sector Logistics" (Ch. 15)

Marketing Miss

SARS Threatens Economic Growth in China

Background. No one outside China really saw it coming. By the time the outbreak of the respiratory illness known as SARS— severe acute respiratory syndrome—became world news, it had already spread from southern China to Hong Kong and on to

Although the SARS epidemic began in Southeast Asia, it quickly claimed more than 800 lives and impacted commerce globally. This global impact is described in detail in the following features:

- "SARS Threatens Economic Growth in China" (Ch. 4)
- "How Wal-Mart Battled SARS Overseas" (Ch. 10)

A New, More Strategic Focus

"More strategic, less descriptive." In response to numerous instructors who made complaints about the overly descriptive nature of the typical principles of marketing text, the new 2005 edition of *Contemporary Marketing* has made significant changes. First, the marketing planning chapter has been relocated so that it can be assigned much earlier in the term, helping to equip students with a solid foundation of strategic thinking. In addition, a new section on strategic implications of marketing concepts discussed in each chapter has been included in every chapter in the new edition. Two new appendices, **Developing a Marketing Plan** and **Financial and New-Product Analysis,** provide additional strategic tools for the reader.

Two Cases for Every Chapter

Many reviewers of the previous edition requested alternative cases to provide more flexibility for different assignments from one academic term to the next. The new 2005 edition includes two case assignments for every chapter. For example, Case 1.1, "Dracula Park Wants YOU," is accompanied by Video Case 1.2, "How Burton Snowboards Built a Sport—and a Customer Base." The second case in each chapter is accompanied by a professionally created video to augment the written case materials.

Krispy Kreme Doughnuts: An Exciting New Continuing Video Case

Each Part of the new *CM 2005* is linked with a continuing case featuring one of the major recent marketing successes: the rapid expansion of Krispy Kreme beyond its southeastern origins to new markets throughout the United States and Canada, and beyond North America. A special seven-segment video was created specifically for *Contemporary Marketing 2005* to add to the written cases for each Part. This continuing case video is in addition to the 19 videos available with the newly written video cases at the end of each chapter.

FUBU: For Us, By Us: A New Integrated Case and Video Alternative

Contemporary Marketing 2005 provides added flexibility for instructors who want to make use of more than one comprehensive case by providing an alternative to the Krispy Kreme continuing case and video. FUBU is an all-new, custom-produced case that gives the instructor a

choice of using different cases for different sections of the class or from one class term to the next. The case and accompanying video detail the story of FUBU, the brainchild of several young African American entrepreneurs whose modest beginnings include making clothing in their homes before sky-rocketing to the top of the niche fashion trade. The video demonstrates that entrepreneurship is one career path in which age doesn't matter—and the sky's the limit if you find the right niche, product, and marketing strategy. Included with the instructor support materials on the Web site (http:// boone.swlearning.com) is a summary of the video, as well as answers to the case questions.

Every Chapter Has a Video Case!

Professionally written and produced, the new video case package provides intriguing, relevant, and current real-world insights into the modern marketplace. Tied directly to chapter concepts, the videos highlight how real-world organizations struggle with the challenges of the 21st century marketplace. Each video is supported by a written case with applications questions. They include:

VC-14   VIDEO CASE 11.2   FOSSIL IS A REMINDER OF GOOD TIMES

VIDEO CASE 11.2 — Fossil Is a Reminder of Good Times

Twenty million dollars for a one-week vacation on the U.S.–Russian space station? If you had $20 million to burn—and someone had just perfected time travel—you might put your money down on a quick trip back 50 years ago. What a trip: seeing your grandparents as youngsters and raving at all those retro fashions. And if you checked out the watches they wore then, you'd notice that watches were considered jewelry. They were expensive, often jewel bedecked, and usually sold at retail jewelry stores.

But then along came Timex—and market segmentation came to visit the watch industry and never left. Timex was inexpensive, highly utilitarian, almost disposable, and possessed an ... TV and print ads ... king and keeps on ... latively low-priced ... comers were care- ... ity. In fact, the dif- ... nds permitted their ... urchasing different ... continued to be fea- ... s such as Cartier, ... d Rolex. Such

But Fossil wasn't content to make and sell just one watch. Instead, the company wanted to create and market watches of different designs to match the different tastes of everyone, all at affordable prices. So the firm developed several lines of Fossil watches. Among the more than 500 styles of Fossil watches available today you can find watches for men, women, and children—even watches for collectors. If you're an Elvis fan, you're in luck: You can pick up a Fossil watch commemorating the 25th anniversary of his death for about $95. If you're hung up on Batman, a *Batman Dark Knight* model will set you back $125 (but hurry; it's part of a limited edition of 2,000). You can even join the Fossil Collectors' Club to get monthly updates on new and upcoming Fossil collectible items.

Fossil also offers specialty watches like the Kaleido, which comes in several models at prices ranging from $65 to $75. With the touch of a button, the Kaleido dial changes colors just like a kaleidoscope. Of course, conservative customers can set the dial color to remain constant as well. If you want the dial numbers in Chinese characters, you can purchase the Chinese Tic for about $65. And for the more technologically advanced watch buyers, Fossil offers two new high-tech models: the Wrist PDA and th... The Wrist PDA, used as a companion to ... nal dat...

VC-2   VIDEO CASE 1.2   HOW BURTON SNOWBOARDS BUILT A SPORT—AND A CUSTOMER BASE

VIDEO CASE 1.2 — How Burton Snowboards Built a Sport—and a Customer Base

No one would deny that Jake Burton is an innovative guy. But he's quick to dispel the myth that he invented snowboarding or snowboards. He points out that the snowboard—a single board that looks and operates like a cross between a skateboard and a surfboard that athletes ride down snow-covered mountains—has been around since the 1920s. And Jake himself experimented with the Snurfer, a precursor to the snowboard, as a kid. But the Snurfer—a short, fat ski with a rope tied to the tip that the rider would hold like a rein in one hand—was marketed more like a toy, on the order of a snow tube or one-person toboggan. Certainly, no one thought of Snurfing as a full-blown sport.

No one, that is, except Jake Burton. Burton had grown up skiing, and after graduating from college in 1977 with a degree in economics, he moved from New York to Vermont to follow a hunch. "I felt like [snowboarding] could be a sport, but it wasn't a sport for the company that was manufacturing [Snurfers]," he recalls. So he set out to do two things simultaneously: build the boards and the market. "I was blindly optimistic," he says. In addition to developing a new product, he needed to develop the market for that product. He had to find a way to show people h... ds would create util-...

had to develop a third type of marketing relationship, one with distributors and dealers.

Today, Burton Snowboards, which is still based in Burlington, Vermont, is both the pioneer and the world leader in the development and sale of snowboards and related products. Burton markets its snowboards and accessory gear through a network of about 3,000 dealers around the world. The company continues to develop relationships with consumers by staging promotions featuring demonstrations at ski resorts—about 400 demos around the world per year, according to vice president and director of sales, Dave Schmidt. These events are conducted by Burton representatives who show up at a resort, unload Burton products, and let people try them for free. In addition, for the past 20 years the firm has sponsored a number of snowboarding competitions—including the U.S. Open for snowboarding—as another effective technique for developing relationships with its customers. Finally, Burton's Learn-to-Ride (LTR) program teaches snowboarding to anyone who wants to learn from instructors. The program includes lessons taught by certified American Association of Snowboard instructors ... rton equipment specifically designed for begi... ...vents and programs enhance Burton's

Additional Features of the New 2005 Edition

Contemporary Marketing 2005 is packed full of innovations. Here are some of the exciting new features:

 NEW! The rapid growth of the African-American and Hispanic-American market segments is discussed in detail in the market segmentation chapter and in the Marketing Hits feature, "Procter & Gamble Taps the Hispanic Market," in Chapter 9.

REVISED! The relationship marketing chapter has been completely revised to include coverage of customer relationship management (CRM).

 NEW! Category management, a major organizational development among firms with extensive product lines, is discussed in detail in Chapter 12. Its importance is communicated in the new chapter title, "Category and Brand Management, Product Identification, and New-Product Planning."

EARLY COVERAGE! "Planning a Career in Marketing" has been completely rewritten and moved to the front of the textbook. In an environment characterized by limited jobs for entry-level business graduates, it offers practical insights to help students prepare for a successful business career.

REVISED! The materials at the end of each chapter have been completely revised. A new Summary of Chapter Objectives replaces the Achievement Check Summary to provide improved summary materials. New Projects and Teamwork Exercises have been included, and all of the 'netWork assignments are new.

 NEW! All opening vignettes, Marketing Hits, and Marketing Misses are new to this edition.

 NEW! Two important promotional innovations—guerilla marketing and product placement—are included in Chapter 17. The Marketing Hits feature in this chapter focuses on Code Red, a recent Pepsi success story of guerilla marketing in action.

Unparalleled Resource Package

Like the eleven editions before it, *Contemporary Marketing 2005* is filled with innovations. The result: the most powerful marketing package available.

Boone & Kurtz lead the market with precedent-setting learning materials and we continue to improve on our signature package features—equipping students and instructors with the most comprehensive collection of learning tools, teaching materials, and innovative resources available. As expected, the new 2005 edition delivers the most extensive, technologically advanced, user-friendly package on the market.

For the Professor

Test Bank and ExamView® Testing Software

Providing over 4,000 total questions, the test bank fills every need you have in testing your students on the chapter contents. Each chapter of the test bank is organized following the chapter objectives, and every question is categorized by type of question (including application, comprehension, and knowledge-based multiple choice, true/false, and essay) and text page reference. The ExamView Testing Software is a Windows-based software program that is both easy to use and attractive. You won't believe that testing software has come this far!

Instructor's Manual

Completely revised! Each chapter of the IM now begins with an introduction to the chapter and a concise guide to changes in the new 2005 edition (2005 edition changes can be found on the Instructor's Resource section of the Web site). Following this easy transition guide, instructors will find a complete set of teaching tools. Each chapter contains the following teaching tools:

- Annotated chapter objectives: a quick summary of each objective for the instructor that also shows how it relates to the rest of the chapter materials.

- Detailed lecture outline that includes suggestions for use of other appropriate support materials for each lecture. These support materials include additional examples, articles, activities, discussion suggestions, transparencies, and PowerPoint presentation slides.

In addition, the Instructor's Manual includes complete solutions to all the end-of-chapter questions, teamwork projects, 'netWork assignments, cases, and video cases.

Media Instructor's Manual

This Media Instructor's Manual includes everything you'll need to help you use all of the media products that accompany *Contemporary Marketing 2005* to the fullest. Each chapter includes a comprehensive guide for incorporating each of the media elements available for this text:

- The 19 video cases

- The seven Krispy Kreme continuing case segments, each related to a different Part in the text

- Web site resources

- E-lectures

- The PowerPoint presentation

Transparency Acetates with Teaching Notes

More than 200 full-color transparency acetates are available to support *Contemporary Marketing 2005*. The transparencies consist of important figures and ads from the text as well as special content acetates outlined specifically for *Contemporary Marketing 2005*. Included with the transparency acetates is a complete set of teaching notes describing how best to use them in a classroom lecture or discussion.

PowerPoint Presentation Software

After reviewing competitive offerings, the authors are convinced that the *Contemporary Marketing 2005* PowerPoint Presentation is clearly one of the best you'll find. It provides a complete teaching experience for instructors and a memorable learning experience for students. Each chapter of the presentation contains chapter objectives, the main concepts of the chapter outlined and explained after each chapter objective, many figures from the text to enhance student learning, and embedded Web links and video links that give students a strong, complete visual presentation of the chapters' main concepts. Each chapter ends with a clearly presented summation of the chapter objectives and key concepts from the chapter.

Instructor's Resource CD-ROM

It's so easy to organize your support materials when they're all in one place! New with this edition of the text is an Instructor's Resource CD-ROM that contains all of the key instructor supplements: Instructor's Manual, Test Bank, ExamView Testing Software, PowerPoint Presentation, and Media Instructor's Manual.

WebTutor® Advantage on Blackboard® and/or WebCT™

WebTutor Advantage puts you ahead of the game in providing online course management for you and online learning for your students. It contains all of the interactive study guide components that you could ever want and many valuable technology-oriented additions you never thought you'd get!
    Included in our WebTutor Advantage offerings for *Contemporary Marketing 2005* are:

- Chapter Objectives
- A Chapter Outline
- Chapter Flashcards
- Electronic Lectures (E-Lectures)
- Applying Marketing Concepts—Critical Thinking Exercises
- Chapter Quizzing
- Quizbowl, a Jeopardy-style Learning Game
- Video Cases with Questions
- Threaded Discussion Questions for Online Discussions
- Links to the Text Web Site: **http://boone.swlearning.com**

Video Cases

Would this be *Contemporary Marketing 2005* without a custom video package containing a new video case for every chapter in the text? Of course not! And these videos will exceed your every expectation. Each of the 19 videos was professionally produced and is tied directly to the key concepts in each chapter. Each video case is new and highlights marketers as tiny as lobster marketer Ipswich Shellfish and as large as toy maker Fisher-Price. Each gives students a glimpse into how marketers actually work, strategize, and meet challenges in the real world. The video-creation process begins with written cases prepared by the authors and contained in the text. Each is a significant improvement over corporate public relations–type cases used by competing texts.
    Guides to the video cases can be found in the Media Instructor's Manual. Answers to the discussion and applications questions can be found in both the Instructor's Manual and the Media Instructor's Manual.

FUBU Integrated Case

This brand new integrated case follows the firm's target market and each of the marketing mix elements and can be assigned as a single project or after each element of the marketing mix is taught. FUBU, the ultra-hip clothing and entertainment company, is the subject, but this video case should get your student's creative juices going!

Krispy Kreme Continuing Video Case

This brand-new feature has been created for the new edition. The written and video case elements are divided into seven sections and related to each Part in *Contemporary Marketing*. The cases appear all together at the end of the text. The continuing case relates the Parts of the text to the story of this dynamic and creative North Carolina company and its use of marketing concepts to enhance its phenomenal recent success in expanding beyond its southeastern roots to new markets throughout the U.S., Canada, Australia, Great Britain, and beyond.

The written case segments created by the authors include learning concepts and discussion questions. Answers to these questions can be found in the Instructor's Manual and in the Media Instructor's Manual.

For the Student

Study Guide

Completely updated for the new edition, the Study Guide contains the following features for each chapter in the text:

- A Chapter Overview that briefly discusses the chapter objectives
- A complete Chapter Outline
- A Self Quiz
- A set of Critical Thinking Questions

Each chapter ends with a Surfing the Net section in which students are provided with online resources related to the chapter concepts.

Audio Chapter Reviews on CD-ROM

Every new copy of *Contemporary Marketing 2005* now comes with an audio review! These audio chapter reviews are provided on CD-ROM for student use. Listen to them while you're exercising, listen to them while you're walking around campus. Heck! Listen to them on the way to class as a preview of what you'll be learning that day! Just listen to them, because they'll supply you with a good summary of the chapter objectives and the major concepts in the chapter. Step to the head of the class, because they'll get you prepared in a completely new way!

Xtra!

Provided free with each new copy of the text, Xtra! gives you just a little bit more than you imagined! This online product provides you with access to additional learning tools including: the Krispy Kreme Continuing Video Case, the PowerPoint Presentation, a Marketing Plan with related exercises, and Xtra! quizzing that you won't get anywhere else!

Boone & Kurtz Web Site

The Boone & Kurtz Web site contains a complete array of supplementary materials for both instructors and students. Instructors will find many ways to enhance their courses using the Instructor's Resource section, where they will find all of the major text supplements in electronic format for viewing or downloading.

Students will find a Web site designed specifically for *Contemporary Marketing 2005* that includes Student Resources, NewsRoom, and Personal Development sections, and an Interactive Study Center.

- The **Student Resource** section consists of downloadable files for the PowerPoint Presentation as well as information about study aids that can help you ace your course.

- The **Personal Development Center** includes extensive information on career development and business ethics, as well as a special feature on time management. This feature includes advice and guidelines on effectively managing your work and leisure time as a student.

- The **Interactive Study Center**, a dynamic online learning center, consists of Chapter Objectives, Crossword Puzzles, Interactive Quizzes, Marketing Topics, and more, including:

  - **InfoTrac® Exercises.** The InfoTrac database gives students direct access to the real world of marketing through academic journals, business and popular magazines, newspapers, and a vast assortment of government publications. InfoTrac Exercises created for use with our text provide learning exercises related to specific articles or industries, as well as giving guidance on how to conduct original research based on materials found in InfoTrac.

  - **Internet Applications.** These online marketing applications allow you to apply chapter concepts to real-world exercises.

Cadotte: Experiencing Marketing at the Marketplace

This simulation will challenge students to make tough marketing decisions in a competitive, fast-paced market where the customers are demanding and the competition is working hard to increase market share. Theory comes alive as students learn to manage a new business venture, improve customer satisfaction, increase profits, and capture dominant market share.

http://boone.swlearning.com

ACKNOWLEDGMENTS

We are grateful for the many suggestions and contributions of dozens of people who teach the introductory marketing course on a regular basis and are in the best position to comment on what works best—and what doesn't work at all. Every recommendation made a difference in the creation of the new 2005 edition. Our special thanks go out to Focus Group attendees at Summer Educators Conference of the American Marketing Association at the recent Washington, D.C., meetings:

Elise Sautter
New Mexico State University

Oscar Deshields, Jr.
California State University–Northridge

Brian Larson
Widener University (PA)

Rama Yelkur
University of Wisconsin–Eau Claire

Michael Tsiros
University of Miami (FL)

Chick Kasouf
Worcester Polytechnic Institute (MA)

Michael Little
Virginia Commonwealth University

David Urban
Virginia Commonwealth University

Janet Parish
University of Alabama

Sue Mantel
University of Toledo

Don Roy
Middle Tennessee State University

Bill Kehoe
University of Virginia

Guangping (Walter) Wang
Pennsylvania State University

A large number of marketing colleagues made major contributions to the previous edition. Our special thanks go out to:

Keith Absher
University of North Alabama

Alicia T. Aldridge
Appalachian State University

Amardeep Assar
City University of New York

Tom F. Badgett
Angelo State University

Joe K. Ballenger
Stephen F. Austin State University

Michael Bernacchi
University of Detroit Mercy

David Blanchette
Rhode Island College

Barbara Brown
San Jose State University

Reginald E. Brown
Louisiana Tech University

Marvin Burnett
St. Louis Community College–Florissant

Scott Burton
University of Arkansas

Howard Cox
Fitchberg State University

James Coyle
Baruch College

William Demkey
Bakersfield College

Michael Drafke
College of DuPage

Joanne Eckstein
Macomb Community College

John Frankel
San Juan College

Robert Georgen
Trident Technical College

Robert Googins
Shasta College

Arlene Green
Indian River Community College

Joel Haynes
State University of West Georgia

Mabre Holder
Roane State Community College

Andrew W. Honeycutt
Clark Atlanta University

Dr. H. Houston
California State University–Los Angeles

John Howe
Santa Ana College

Tom Jensen
University of Arkansas

Stephen C. King
Keene State College

Kathleen Krentler
San Diego State University

Laddie Logan
Arkansas State University

Kent Lundin
College of the Sequoias

Patricia Macro
Madison Area Tech College

Frank Markley
Arapahoe Community College

Tom Marshall
Owens Community College

Dennis C. Mathern
The University of Findlay

Lee McGinnis
University of Nebraska

Michael McGinnis
Pennsylvania State University

Norma Mendoza
University of Arkansas

Mohan Menon
University of South Alabama

Anthony Miyazaki
University of Miami

Jerry W. Moorman
Mesa State College

Linda Morable
Richland College

Diane Moretz
Ashland University

Eugene Moynihan
Rockland Community College

Margaret Myers
Northern Kentucky University

Nita Paden
Northern Arizona University

George Palz
Erie Community College–North

George Prough
University of Akron

Warren Purdy
University of Southern Maine

Salim Qureshi
Bloomsburg University

Thomas Read
Sierra College

Joel Reedy
University of South Florida

Dominic Rella
Polk Community College

Ken Ridgedell
Southeastern Louisiana University

Lillian Roy
McHenry County College

Arthur Saltzman
California State–San Bernardino

Elise T. Sautter
New Mexico State University

Jonathan E. Schroeder
University of Rhode Island

Farouk Shaaban
Governors State University

John Sondey
South Dakota State University

James Spiers
Arizona State University

David Starr
Shoreline Community College

Bob Stassen
University of Arkansas

Sue Taylor
Belleville Area College

Lars Thording
Arizona State University–West Campus

Rajiv Vaidyanathan
University of Minnesota

Charles Vitaska
Metro State College of Denver

Cortez Walker
Baltimore City Community College

Roger Waller
San Joaquin Delta College

Mary M. Weber
Emporia State University

Vicki L. West
Southwest Texas State University

Elizabeth White
Orange County Community College

David Wiley
Anne Arundel Community College

William Wilkinson
Governors State University

James Williams
Richard Stockton College of New Jersey

Mary Wolfindarger
California State University– Long Beach

Joyce Wood
North Virginia Community College

Earlier reviewers of *Contemporary Marketing* include:

Keith Absher
Kerri L. Acheson
Zafar U. Ahmed
M. Wayne Alexander
Bruce Allen
Linda Anglin
Allen Appell
Paul Arsenault
Dub Ashton
Amardeep Assar
Tom F. Badgett
Joe K. Ballenger
Wayne Bascom
Richard D. Becherer
Tom Becker
Richard F. Beltramini
Robert Bielski
Carol C. Bienstock
Roger D. Blackwell
Jocelyn C. Bojack
Michele D. Bunn
James Camerius
Les Carlson
John Carmichael
Robert Collins
Elizabeth Cooper-Martin
Deborah L. Cowles
Howard B. Cox
Jacob Chacko
John E. Crawford
Michael R. Czinkota

Kathy Daruty
Grant Davis
Gilberto de los Santos
Carol W. DeMoranville
Fran DePaul
Gordon Di Paolo
John G. Doering
Jeffrey T. Doutt
Sid Dudley
John W. Earnest
Philip E. Egdorf
Michael Elliot
Amy Enders
Bob Farris
Lori Feldman
Sandra M. Ferriter
Dale Fodness
Gary T. Ford
Michael Fowler
Edward Friese
Sam Fullerton
Ralph M. Gaedeke
G.P. Gallo
Nimish Gandhi
Sheryl A. Gatto
Robert Georgen
Don Gibson
David W. Glascoff
James Gould
Donald Granbois
John Grant

Paul E. Green
William Green
Blaine Greenfield
Matthew Gross
Robert F. Gwinner
Raymond M. Haas
John H. Hallaq
Cary Hawthorn
E. Paul Hayes
Hoyt Hayes
Betty Jean Hebel
Debbora Heflin-Bullock
John (Jack) J. Heinsius
Sanford B. Helman
Nathan Himelstein
Robert D. Hisrich
Ray S. House
George Housewright
Donald Howard
Michael D. Hutt
Gregory P. Iwaniuk
Don L. James
James Jeck
Candida Johnson
David Johnson
Eugene M. Johnson
James C. Johnson
Harold H. Kassarjian
Bernard Katz
Stephen K. Keiser
Michelle Keller

J. Steven Kelly
James H. Kennedy
Charles Keuthan
Maryon King
Randall S. Kingsbury
Donald L. Knight
Linda S. Koffel
Philip Kotler
Terrence Kroeten
Russell Laczniak
Martha Laham
L. Keith Larimore
Edwin Laube
Ken Lawrence
Francis J. Leary, Jr.
Mary Lou Lockerby
James Lollar
Paul Londrigan
David L. Loudon
Dorothy Maass
James C. Makens
Lou Mansfield
Warren Martin
James McCormick
Carl McDaniel
Michael McGinnis
James McHugh
Faye McIntyre
H. Lee Meadow
Mohan Menon
William E. (Gene) Merkle
John D. Milewicz
Robert D. Miller
Laura M. Milner
Banwari Mittal
Harry J. Moak
J. Dale Molander
John F. Monoky
James R. Moore
Thomas M. Moran

Susan Logan Nelson
Colin F. Neuhaus
Robert T. Newcomb
Jacqueline Z. Nicholson
Tom O'Connor
Robert O'Keefe
Sukgoo Pak
Eric Panitz
Dennis D. Pappas
Constantine Petrides
Barbara Piasta
Dennis D. Pitta
Barbara Pletcher
Carolyn E. Predmore
Arthur E. Prell
Bill Quain
Rosemary Ramsey
Thomas C. Reading
Gary Edward Reiman
Glen Riecken
Arnold M. Rieger
C. Richard Roberts
Patrick J. Robinson
William C. Rodgers
William H. Ronald
Bert Rosenbloom
Barbara Rosenthal
Carol Rowery
Ronald S. Rubin
Don Ryktarsyk
Rafael Santos
Duane Schecter
Dennis W. Schneider
Larry J. Schuetz
Bruce Seaton
Howard Seigelman
Jack Seitz
Steven L. Shapiro
F. Kelly Shuptrine
Ricardo Singson

Norman Smothers
Carol S. Soroos
James Spiers
Miriam B. Stamps
William Staples
David Steenstra
Bruce Stern
Robert Stevens
Kermit Swanson
G. Knude Swenson
Cathy Owens Swift
Clint B. Tankersley
Ruth Taylor
Donald L. Temple
Vern Terpstra
Ann Marie Thompson
Howard A. Thompson
John E. Timmerman
Frank Titlow
Rex Toh
Dennis H. Tootelian
Fred Trawick
Richard Lee Utecht
Rajiv Vaidyanathan
Toni Valdez
Peter Vanderhagen
Dinoo T. Vanier
Gayle D. Wasson
Donald Weinrauch
Fred Weinthal
Susan B. Wessels
John J. Whithey
Debbora Whitson
Robert J. Williams
Nicholas C. Williamson
Cecilia Wittmayer
Van R. Wood
Julian Yudelson
Robert J. Zimmer

We would also like to express our appreciation to our research and editorial assistants Jeanne Bartimus, Karen Hill, and Mikhelle Taylor. Their untiring efforts on our behalf are most appreciated.

In addition, we applaud the contributions of the high-quality instructors who participated in making the *Contemporary Marketing* supplements an outstanding and innovative teaching and learning package:

Douglas Hearth
University of Arkansas

Stephen M. Peters
Walla Walla Community College

Tom O'Connor
The University of New Orleans

Dona Hightower
UpStream Press

Finally, this book would never have become a reality without the outstanding efforts of the South-Western/Thomson editorial, production, and marketing teams. Our Acquisitions Editor Steve Hazelwood, Developmental Editor Rebecca von Gillern, Marketing Manager Nicole Moore, and Production Editor Chris Hudson all did a wonderful job. We also thank Karen Hill at Elm Street Press for her contributions to making this exciting new 2005 edition.

Louis E. Boone & David L. Kurtz

About the Authors

Gene Boone was born about the time World War II began and had a relatively quiet childhood until 1956 when he received a 45 rpm RCA Victor recording of "Heartbreak Hotel" by Elvis Presley. Within a year he had discovered Buddy Holly, Little Richard, and Chuck Berry—and he wanted more. So he decided to combine high school with a two-year gig as a part-time DJ at a local radio station. Talk about soft jobs! Play music you wanted to hear and get paid for it. Play lists didn't exist in those days, and as long as irate listeners didn't call in and demand that the station manager fire you, you could play anything you liked. A diverse group of fellow DJs introduced him to artists who were quickly added to his growing list of favorites: blues greats John Lee Hooker and B.B. King; the haunting, poetry-like songs of Simon & Garfunkel; the unique vocal blending of the Everly Brothers, whose work impacted the groups who led the British Invasion of the 1960s; and the riveting, soulful music by the son of an Arkansas cotton farmer—a man named Johnny Cash.

But few people spend a lifetime career spinning tunes at a small-time radio station, and, following graduation, he started looking for something fun that paid a bit more. College professor sounded like a cool occupation that would keep him indoors and, perhaps, help him meet women (assuming they considered tweed jackets attractive). Nobody told him until it was too late that it was going to take another eight years in college to achieve his ambition—eight more years!—but he struggled through it. He's happy he did because he was able to affect (at least a little) the lives of thousands of his young, middle age, and older students in a half-dozen universities throughout the United States, as well as in Australia, England, and Greece. These gigs proved to be almost as much fun as the first.

But his love of music, which had never died, was rekindled during an evening section of a Principles of Marketing class several decades ago at the University of Southern Mississippi in which one of his students—sitting on the back row—would soon make music that linked him forever to tequila-flavored drinks and talking tropical birds. Short in stature and soft-spoken, Jimmy Buffett hardly looked the part of a pop music star, but over the decades he consistently demonstrated just how much he had learned about marketing in that fall semester course.

During his high-school days, no one in Salisbury, Maryland, would have mistaken **Dave Kurtz** for a scholar. In fact, he was a mediocre student, so bad that his father felt he might convince him that an educated life was preferable to a series of day jobs by finding him a succession of back-breaking summer jobs. Thankfully, most of them have been erased from his memory, but a few linger, including picking peaches, loading watermelons on trucks headed for market, and working as a pipe fitter's helper. The work made him physically strong, but had zero impact on his academic standing. Worse yet, it made him no better than average as a high-school athlete in football and track.

But a four-year stint at Davis & Elkins College in Elkins, West Virginia, turned him around. Excellent instructors like Dr. Gloria Payne helped get Dave on a sound academic footing. His grade point average soared—enough to get him accepted by the Graduate School at the University of Arkansas, where he met Gene Boone. After graduate school, the two became career coauthors, with 48 books between them.

Today, Dave is back teaching at the University of Arkansas after duty tours in Ypsilanti, Michigan, Seattle, and Melbourne, Australia. He is the proud grandfather of five "perfect" kids and a sportsman with a golfing handicap too high to mention. Dave, his wife, Diane, and his two Yorkies named Daisy and Lucy live in Rogers, Arkansas, where he holds a university professorship at the University of Arkansas in nearby Fayetteville.

Contents in Brief

Contents

Part 2
Managing Technology and Information to Achieve Marketing Success 129

Chapter 5
E-Commerce: Electronic Marketing and the Internet for Dot.com and Brick-and-Mortar Marketers 130

Chapter Overview 132

Chapter 6
Relationship Marketing and Customer Relationship Management (CRM) 162

Opening Vignette
Behind the Scenes: The Decisions Leading to New Movies 193

Solving an Ethical Controversy
Dumpster Diving at Unilever 197

Marketing Miss
Why the Latest Federal Census Failed to Count Arab Americans 201

Marketing Hit
Collecting Qualitative Research Online 209

Chapter 7
Marketing Research, Decision-Support Systems, and Sales Forecasting 192

Part 3
Market Segmentation and Customer Behavior 221

Chapter 8
Market Segmentation, Targeting, and Positioning 222

Chapter 12
Category and Brand Management, Product Identification, and New-Product Planning 344

Part 5
Pricing Strategy 373

Opening Vignette
Airlines Fight for Their Lives 375

Marketing Hit
How Much Is Electricity Worth to You? 378

Marketing Hit
How PepsiCo Is Making a Killing with Aquafina Bottled Water 384

Solving an Ethical Controversy
What's a Fair Price for Prescription Drugs? 388

Chapter 16
Direct Marketing and Marketing Resellers:
Retailers and Wholesalers 464

Part 7
Promotional Strategy 493

Chapter 17
Integrated Marketing Communications 494

Opening Vignette
Transforming the Sales Force at IBM 567

Marketing Hit
Sales Pro Bounces Back 572

Solving an Ethical Controversy
The National Do Not Call List: Friend or Foe? 573

Marketing Hit
Selling SAP Software in a Rotten Economy 580

Chapter 19
Personal Selling and Sales-Force Management 566

Planning a Career in Marketing

At this point, you should be congratulated on your decision to take this course. After all, marketing is a pervasive element in our lives. In one form or another, it reaches every person. As you begin this course, you should be aware of three important facts about marketing.

Marketing Costs Are a Big Component of Your Total Budget

Approximately 50 percent of the total costs of products you buy are marketing costs. In short, half of the $20 you pay for that chart-topping compact disc goes not for the plastic disc, protective sleeve, paper jacket, or the physical act of burning the tracks onto the disk, but for marketing costs. The same is true of your purchase of a new flat-screen monitor for your desktop, your first DVD player, and the $22,000 price tag on that PT Cruiser you want so badly.

But costs alone do not indicate the value of marketing. The high living standard your family, friends, and you enjoy in large part is a function of our nation's efficient marketing systems. When considered in this perspective, the costs of marketing seem more reasonable. For example, marketing expands overall sales, thereby spreading fixed production costs over more units of output and reducing total output costs.

Marketing Provides an Opportunity to Contribute to Society as Well as to an Individual Company

Marketing decisions affect everyone's welfare. How much quality should be built into a product? Will people buy a safer product if it costs twice as much as the current version? Should every community adopt recycling programs? Because ethics and social responsibilities are critical factors for marketers in a business environment tarnished by both ethical and legal failings of a number of well-known companies and their leaders, it is essential that marketers strive to exceed customer and government expectations of ethical behavior. Reading the *Solving an Ethical Controversy* exercises included in every chapter will increase your awareness of the role of high ethical standards in every dimension of marketing and allow you to examine the not always black-and-white ethical issues such as prescription drug pricing, online privacy, advertising to children, promotion of liquor and tobacco products, and invasive practices such as spam, pop-up ads, and telemarketing.

Not only does marketing influence numerous facets of our daily lives, decisions regarding marketing activities affect everyone's welfare. Opportunities to advance to more responsible decision-making positions come sooner in marketing than in most occupations. This combination of challenges and opportunities has made marketing one of the most popular fields of academic study.

A recent survey by executive recruiter Korn/Ferry International revealed that the best route to the top of the corporate ladder begins in a company's marketing division. Three of every eight CEOs are

Briefly Speaking

If I had my life to live over again, I would elect to be a trader of goods rather than a student of science. I think barter is a noble thing.

*Albert Einstein
(1879–1955)
American physicist*

Colon polyps. Stop them before they go bad.

Colon cancer almost always starts with a polyp. Get the polyp early and stop colon cancer before it even starts. And that's for both men and women. Just get a test from your doctor. 1-800-ACS-2345 or cancer.org

Colon cancer. Get the test. Get the polyp. Get the cure.

Managers of not-for-profit organizations like The American Cancer Society use on-staff specialists and outside agencies to develop marketing strategies designed to strengthen commitments to early detection of all types of cancer. In addition to communicating the overall mission, promotional messages like this are intended to prompt concerned readers to make donations to the organization.

chosen from a company's marketing division because the growing global economy demands proven market leaders in winning the fight to increase a firm's worldwide market shares. Finance, which had long dominated as the top career path for senior executives, fell to third place, and executives who had completed international assignments—many of the assignments being marketing related—came in second.

You May Choose a Career in Marketing

When asked about their conception of an ideal entry-level job following graduation, most students mention salary and opportunity for professional growth and advancement. While compensation is almost always an issue, the 21st century job seeker also wants to feel recognized for his or her achievements, be assigned new responsibilities, and work in continuous-learning environments. Many will also include as an important issue working for a family-friendly organization that offers a high quality of life.

Of the many career paths chosen by business graduates, marketing is the single largest employment category in the U.S. labor force, and job growth in the field is expected to accelerate. The U.S. Bureau of Labor Statistics estimates that the number of jobs in marketing, advertising, and public relations management will grow much faster through 2010 than the average for all occupations. Every successful organization—profit-seeking or not-for-profit—recognizes the necessity of effective marketing in accomplishing its goal of providing customer satisfaction by hiring highly motivated, professionally educated marketing specialists to design and implement these customer-driven programs.

Marketing-related occupations account for 25 to 30 percent of jobs in the typical highly industrialized nation. History has shown that the demand for effective marketers is not affected by cyclical economic fluctuations.

Your Quest for a Successful, Rewarding Career

Selecting a career may be the most important decision you will ever make. That's why *Contemporary Marketing* begins by discussing the best way to approach career decisions and how to prepare for an *entry-level position*—your first permanent employment after leaving school. We then look at a range of marketing careers and discuss employment opportunities in fields related to each major part of the text.

Entry-level positions have been more difficult to find recently. As the economy suffered after September 11, 2001, so did the job market. As a result, students have to be even more creative in their employment searches. But, as you know, creativity has never been in short supply on the nation's campuses.

Today, economic conditions are improving, and job prospects are brighter for most students. Still, you need to do everything you can to enhance your career opportunities. You've already taken an important first step by enrolling in a class using this textbook.

During the next few months, you will be introduced to all of the key functional areas of marketing. As you learn about marketing concepts, you will also be able to identify areas of employment that you may wish to pursue.

Education will improve your prospects of finding and keeping the right job. Last year, the average full-time employee 18 or older with a high school diploma earned just under $23,000. By contrast, the average employee with a bachelor's degree earned $40,000-plus annually—one and three-fourths more than the pay of the high school grad. Applying yourself in class, expanding your experiences through career-directed volunteer efforts, part-time and summer jobs, and effective internships—and selecting the right major—will put you well on your way to improving these salary statistics when you launch your career.

In addition to taking classes, try to gain related experience either through a job and/or by participating in campus organizations. Internships, carefully selected summer and part-time jobs, and volunteer activities on campus and in your community can also give you invaluable hands-on experience while you pursue your education. During the tight job market of the recent recession when youth unemployment has soared to 12 percent and even college-educated young people with little or no job experience have had difficulty in securing job offers, these work experiences will often set you apart from other job seekers in the eyes of recruiters.[1] They are invaluable for traditional students who entered college immediately following graduation from high school and who possess little or no work experience.

This career-focused Prologue provides you with a brief look at the trends and opportunities available for future marketers in an increasingly diversified professional field. It describes essential elements of an effective résumé and discusses the latest trends in electronic job searches. Finally, it provides a listing of primary marketing information sources that contain answers to many of the questions typically asked by applicants. This information will provide valuable career-planning assistance in this and other future courses, whether your career plans involve marketing or you decide to major in another field.

Many of the marketing positions you read about throughout the text are described here. Specifically, the job summaries describe the job and the responsibilities and duties that are typically required as well as the usual career path for each of the eight marketing-related positions.

Marketing your skills to a prospective employer is much the same as marketing a product to a consumer. Increasingly, job seekers are selling their skills online, eliminating the intermediary and leveling the playing field between applicant and potential employer. The greatest challenge for online job seekers is learning how to market themselves.

Despite the vast databases and fancy tools of the giant career sites such as Monster.com and CareerMosaic (**http://www.careermosaic.com**), which may receive hundreds of thousands of visits each day, savvy job seekers often find their time better spent zeroing in on niche boards offering more focused listings. For example, sales applicants can check out Salesgiant.com.

In many instances, students desiring interviews with specific employers or in certain geographical locations will go directly to the employer's or region's Web site to learn of available positions. Most employers include an employment site as part of their home page. Some offer virtual tours of what it is like to work for the firm. For example, the Enterprise Rent-a-Car Web site features profiles of young assistant managers as they perform daily work activities.

After spending $1.8 million in a single year to hire between 12,000 and 14,000 people, Lockheed Martin decided to make better use of its corporate Web site in recruiting job candidates. The defense contractor hired the same number of new employees during 2002, but its cost-cutting approach made it possible to fill its vacancies and spend only $750,000 on boards.[2]

Your online job search can focus on positions in a specialized field or location, or these positions can be posted on meta-sites like Monster.com with few if any particular limitations on company or location. In either case, the key to getting the job you want is letting the market know who you are and what you can do. While few college graduates are hired directly based on their response to an online listing, this approach is often an important first step in zeroing in on specific employers of interest and then soliciting interviews that may lead to subsequent job offers.

As you begin your career, you will apply many of the principles and concepts discussed in the text, including how to do the following: target a market, capitalize on brand equity, position a product, and use marketing research techniques. Even in jobs that seem remote from the marketing discipline, this knowledge will help you stay focused on the most important aspect of business: the consumer.

An ideal job is one that makes you want to go to work every morning. It's working at something you enjoy and for which you get rewarded handsomely for performing at your typically superior level.

Briefly Speaking

True terror is to wake up one morning and discover that your high school class is running the country.

Kurt Vonnegut, Jr.
(b. 1922)
American author

6FigureJobs.com is just one of the 3,000-plus online career sites available for use by online job seekers.

Standing Out from the Crowd of Job Seekers

In a tight job market, employers can afford to be choosy in deciding which applicants will make the cut, be interviewed, and, possibly, be offered a position. And often the applicant's accumulated job and leadership experiences will be key decision criteria in determining whether he or she is given serious consideration as a potential employee.

Students often choose to continue their studies following graduation and pursue an MBA degree or enter a master's program specially suited to their career goals. For example, students interested in a marketing research career may decide to study for a specialized master's degree in this field offered by a growing number of universities. A student who wishes to extend formal education in a specialized degree program should seek advice on specific programs from instructors who teach in that area. For example, a marketing research professor is likely to have information on master's programs in that field at different universities.

Other activities that enhance your personal worth are internships and volunteering. Internships have been described as a critical link in bridging the theory–practice educational gap. They help to carry students between the academic present and the professional future. They provide students with an opportunity for learning how classroom theory is applied in real-world business environments.

An internship is a partnership between the student, the university, and the agency or internship site. All of these parties assume definite responsibilities, perform specific functions, and achieve benefits as a result of their involvement. In addition, internships can serve as critical networking and job-hunting tools. In some instances, internships are precursors for specific employment opportunities, allowing students to demonstrate technical proficiency while providing cost-effective employee training for the company or not-for-profit organization.[3]

Excellent sources of information about the nation's outstanding internships can be found at your local bookstore. One particularly useful publication by Mark Oldman and Samer Hamadeh is *America's Top 100 Internships,* published annually by Villard Books in New York.

Your Résumé

Writing a résumé is a task that almost every job seeker dislikes—and one that is often postponed until the last minute. "After all," the thinking usually goes, "I won't be involved in interviewing for another year." However, this task is made less daunting with the help of your faculty advisor or career counselor, a growing number of books and articles on résumé writing, and numerous computer software packages that require little more than filling in the blanks.

A résumé is probably the most important document that a job seeker can provide to a potential employer because it frequently is the only written record of credentials available with which an evaluation and the selection of a job candidate can be made. It is a concise summary of academic, professional, and personal accomplishments that makes focused statements about the job applicant.

Three basic formats are used in preparing a résumé. *Chronological résumés* arrange informa-

---

Résumé Blunders

The following list of errors appeared in job résumés, applications, and cover letters received by Robert Half, the late founder of Accountemps:

- "I have worked in a fairy wide range of industries."

- "Great eye for derail."

- "I have incredibly entertaining hair."

- "I am accustomed to being in the hot seat."

- "EDUCATION: Some."

tion in reverse chronological order, emphasizing job titles and organizations and describing responsibilities held and duties performed. This format highlights continuity and career growth. A *functional résumé* accents accomplishments and strengths, placing less emphasis on job titles and work history, and often omits job descriptions. A functional résumé prepared by a recent graduate is shown in Figure 1. Some applicants use a *combined résumé* format, which emphasizes skills first, followed by employment history. This format highlights a candidate's potential and suits students who often have little experience directly related to their desired positions.

Most résumés include full names as well as mail and e-mail addresses. If the username of your e-mail address is "MachoDude" or "SnowboardDoll," replace it with one related to your real name or location to convince employers to take you seriously.

A statement of career objectives typically follows. Academic information is provided next, followed by experience and work history. Applicants with limited work histories and no internship experiences typically focus on relevant personal activities and interests. Any and all professional and extracurricular activities, as well as academic, work, and internship experiences, should be included on your résumé. Most résumés close with lists of references.

Whether yours is a traditional résumé on paper or posted on an Internet résumé listing, the important thing to remember in creating an effective résumé is to present the most relevant information in a clear, concise manner that emphasizes your best attributes.

Jorge Paz
Two Seaside Drive, Apt. 3A
Los Angeles, CA 90026
215-555-7092
JPAZ@hotmail.com

Objective
Joining a growth-oriented company that values highly productive employees. Seeking an opportunity that leads to senior merchandising position.

Professional Experience
Administration
Management responsibilities in a major retail buying office included coordinating vendor relation efforts. Supervised assistant buyers.

Category Management
Experience in buying home improvement and sport, recreation, and fitness categories.

Planning
Leader of a team charged with reviewing the company's annual vendor evaluation program.

Problem Solving
Successfully developed a program to improve margins in the tennis, golf, and fishing product categories.

Work Experience
Senior Buyer
Southern California Department Stores   2000–Present

Merchandiser
Pacific Discount Stores, a division of Southern California
Department Stores   1998–2000

Education
Bachelor of Science degree in business
Double major in marketing and retailing
California State University–San Bernardino   1994–1998

Computer Skills
Proficient with IBM-compatible computers and related software, including spreadsheets, graphics, desktop publishing, and word processing.
Packages: Excel, Lotus 1-2-3, Harvard Graphics, PowerPoint, Microsoft Word 7.0

Familiar with Adobe PageMaker and the Macintosh.

Language Skills
Fluent in speaking and writing Spanish.

FIGURE 1
Functional Résumé

Cover Letter

An employer is typically first introduced to a job applicant through a cover letter. Like gift wrapping on a present, a cover letter should attract attention and interest about what is inside and should be addressed to a specific person. The cover letter must provide specifically targeted information, state the particular position you are applying for, where you learned about the position, and why you are interested in it. It should also describe attributes of your personality, such as dependability, responsibility, energy level, and technical skills, without sounding overly boastful or arrogant.

Next, your cover letter should specifically state when you will follow up with a phone call or letter. Your cover letter then should close with an expression of appreciation for being considered for the position. Make certain that your cover letter is neat and grammatically correct, since employers often use it to evaluate written communication skills. Finally, sign the letter in blue or black ink.

Mark your calendar and follow up your cover letter and résumé when you stated you would. If you indicated that you would call, then use this opportunity to ask any additional questions and set a possible date for an interview.

Letters of Recommendation

Letters of recommendation serve as testimonials to your performance in academic and work settings. The best references provide information relevant to the desired industry or marketing specialty, as well as opinions of your skills, abilities, and character. References may be obtained from former or current

Briefly Speaking

A résumé is a balance sheet without any liabilities.

Robert Half (1918–2001) American personnel agency executive

Briefly Speaking

employers, supervisors from volunteer experiences, professors, and others who can attest to your academic and professional competencies.

An effective letter of recommendation typically contains the following elements:

1. Statement of the length and nature of the relationship between the writer and the job candidate.

2. Description of the candidate's academic and career growth potential.

3. Review of important achievements.

4. Evaluation of personal characteristics (what kind of colleague the candidate will make).

5. Summary of the candidate's outstanding strengths and abilities.

Because letters of recommendation take time and effort, it helps to provide a résumé and any other information relevant to the recommendation, along with a stamped, addressed (typed) envelope. When requesting letters of recommendation, you should allow ample time for your references to compose them—as long as a month is not unusual.

In addition to including a cover letter, résumé, and letters of recommendation, candidates should include photocopies of transcripts, writing samples, or other examples of work completed. For example, if you are applying for a position in public relations, advertising, or sports marketing, you may want to include examples of professional writing, graphics, and audio/visual tapes and DVDs to support written evidence of your credentials. Research and service projects that resulted in published or unpublished articles may also enhance your portfolio.

Tips for Preparing an Electronic Résumé

- Use a plain font. Use a standard serif typeface, such as Courier, Times, Arial, Univers, or Futura. Simplicity is key.
- Use 11- to 14-point type sizes.
- Keep your line length to no more than 65 characters (letters, spaces, and punctuation).
- Do not use graphics, bullets, lines, bold, italics, underlines, or shading.
- Use capital letters for your headings.
- Justify your text to the left.
- Use vertical and horizontal lines sparingly. Lines may blur your type.
- Omit parentheses and brackets, even around telephone numbers. These can blur and leave the number unreadable.
- Use white paper and black type.
- Use a laser-quality printer.
- Print on one side of the paper only.
- Don't compress space between letters. Use a second page rather than pack everything into one page and have it scan unclearly.
- Do not staple pages of a résumé together.
- Use industry buzzwords. Keyword searches often look for industry jargon.
- Place your name as the first text on the résumé. Do not put anything else on that line.
- Fax résumés on the *fine mode* setting. It is much easier to read than the *standard mode* setting.
- Do not fold your résumé. A crease makes scanning—and retrieving—difficult.
- If you are sending your résumé in the body of an e-mail transmission, do not distinguish between pages, as the full e-mail will download into the database as one sheet.
- Don't send a résumé as an e-mail attachment unless you are specifically instructed to do so. Many employers discard unsolicited attachments.

Dealing with Automated Systems

Employers are quickly moving to automated (paperless) résumé processing and applicant-tracking systems. As a result, if you prepare a technology-compatible résumé and cover letter, you'll enjoy an edge over applicants whose résumés and cover letters can't be added to the firm's database. Also, remember that résumés are often transmitted electronically. Figure 2 contains a number of tips for creating an effective, technology-compatible résumé.

Employers who review electronic résumés and those posted on some of the 3,000 Web sites currently carrying job postings frequently save time by using computers to search for keywords in job titles, job descriptions, or résumés to narrow the search. In fact, *manager* is the number one word for which companies search. Regardless of the position you seek, the key to an effective electronic résumé is to use exact words and phrases, emphasizing nouns rather than the action verbs you are likely to use in a printed résumé. For example, a company looking for a marketing account manager with experience in Lotus 1-2-3, Microsoft Word, and

FIGURE 2
Tips for Preparing an Electronic Résumé

SOURCE: Mary Dixon Werdler, "Translate Your Résumé for Electronic Eyes," http://www.jobweb.com, accessed February 1, 2002. © National Association of Colleges and Employers. Used by permission.

Microsoft Excel programs is likely to conduct computer searches for only those résumés that include the job title and the three software programs.

Learning More about Job Opportunities

You should carefully study the various employment opportunities you have identified. Obviously, you will like some more than others, but you should examine a number of factors when assessing each job possibility:

1. Actual job responsibilities
2. Industry characteristics
3. Nature of the company
4. Geographic location
5. Salary and opportunities for advancement
6. How the job is likely to contribute to your long-range career opportunities

Too many job applicants consider only the most striking features of a job, perhaps its location or the salary offer. However, a comprehensive review of job openings should provide a balanced perspective of the overall employment opportunity, including both long-run and short-run factors.

Job Interviews

The first objective of your job search is obtaining an interview with a prospective employer. This interview demands considerable planning and preparation on your part. You want to enter the interview equipped with a good understanding of the company, its industry, and its competitors. Prepare yourself by researching the following basic information about the firm:

- When was the company founded?
- What is its current position in the industry?
- What is its financial status?
- In which markets does it compete?
- How is the firm organized?
- Who are its competitors?
- How many does it employ?
- Where are its production facilities and office located?
- Does it have a written code of ethics? How is it administered?

This information is useful in several ways. First, knowing so much about the firm should give you a feeling of confidence during the interview. Second, it can help you avoid making an unwise employment decision. Third, it may help you to impress an interviewer, who may well try to determine how much you know about the company as a means of evaluating your interest level. A job applicant who fails to make an effort to obtain such information often risks elimination from further consideration.

But where do you find this company information? First, your college's or university's career center is likely to have detailed information on prospective employers. Your marketing and business professors may also provide tips. In addition, the university's reference librarian can direct you to sources to use in investigating a firm. Also, you can write directly to the company. Most medium- and large-sized companies maintain informative Web sites; others publish career brochures. Finally, ask friends and relatives for input. Either they or people they know may have had experience with the company.

Interviewers usually cite poor communication as the main reason for an unsuccessful job interview. The job seeker either is inadequately prepared for the interview or lacks confidence. Remember that

> **Briefly Speaking**
>
> The future belongs to those who believe in the beauty of their dreams.
>
> *Eleanor Roosevelt (1884–1962) First Lady of the United States (1933–1945)*

the interviewer will certainly make a determination of whether you can communicate directly based on the question-and-answer sequence that comprises this meeting. You should be specific in answering and asking questions, and you should clearly and positively express your concerns. The questions that interviewers ask most often include the following:

- "Why do you want this job?"
- "Where do you see yourself ten years from now?"
- "What are your strengths?"
- "What are your weaknesses?"
- "Why should I hire you?"

It is important to know the name of the person (or persons) who will conduct the interview, what the interviewer's regular job responsibilities are, and who will make the final hiring decisions. In many cases the people who conduct initial job interviews work in the human resources division of their company. These interviewers typically make recommendations to line managers about which applicants appear most suitable for the vacancy. Line managers who head the units in which the applicant would be employed will get involved later in the hiring process. Some hiring decisions result from joint interviews conducted by both human resources personnel and the immediate supervisor of the prospective employee. Most often, however, immediate supervisors make the decision alone or in combination with input from senior employees in the department who will be colleagues of the new hire. Rarely does the human resources department have sole hiring authority.

In a typical format, the interviewer talks little during the interview. This approach, referred to as an *open-ended interview,* forces you to talk about yourself and your career goals. If you appear unorganized, the interviewer may eliminate you on that basis alone. When faced with this type of interview, be sure to express your thoughts clearly and keep the conversation on target. Talk for about 10 minutes, then ask some specific question of the interviewers. (Come prepared with questions to ask.) Listen carefully to the responses. Remember that if you prepare for a job interview, it will become a mutual exchange of information.

A successful first interview will probably result in an invitation to return for another interview. In some cases, this invitation will include a request to take a battery of tests. Most students do very well on these tests because they have had plenty of practice during the previous years in class!

It is not uncommon for applicants to receive an attractive job offer only after being rejected one or more times previously. Students at an Arizona university once pooled their rejection letters from would-be employers, reviewed them, and then voted on the company that had written the worst rejection letter. Here are excerpts from the five finalists:

- "After most careful consideration of your qualifications and background, we are unable to identify anything you can do for us . . . "
- "We're certain you could be more useful someplace else . . . "
- " . . . but we're sure you will find something you can do."
- "My conscience doesn't allow me to encourage you . . . "
- "Unfortunately, we have to be selective . . . "[4]

Employment Decisions

Employers still considering you to be a viable job candidate now know a lot about you. You should also know a lot about the company. The primary purpose of further interviews is to determine whether you can work effectively within the organization.

If you continue to create a positive impression during subsequent interviews, you may be offered a position with the firm. Again, your decision to accept the offer should depend on how well the opportunity matches your career objectives. Make the best entry-level job decision you can, and learn from it. Learn your job responsibilities as quickly and thoroughly as possible; then start looking for ways to improve your performance and that of your employer.

TABLE 1   Text Chapters Describing Responsibilities of Different Marketing Positions

Marketing Position	*Contemporary Marketing* Chapter(s) Most Directly Related to the Marketing Position
Marketing, Advertising, Product, and Public Relations Managers	Chapters 1–2 (marketing)
	Chapters 11–12 (product)
	Chapters 17–18 (advertising and public relations)
Sales Representatives and Sales Managers	Chapter 19
Advertising Specialists	Chapters 17–18
Public Relations Specialists	Chapters 17–18
Purchasing Agents and Managers	Chapter 10
Retail and Wholesale Buyers and Merchandise Managers	Chapter 16
Marketing Research Analysts	Chapter 7
Logistics: Material Receiving, Scheduling, Dispatching, and Distributing Occupations	Chapter 15

Marketing Positions

The basic objective of any firm is to market its goods or services. Marketing responsibilities vary among organizations and industries. In a small firm, the owner or president may assume many of the company's marketing responsibilities. A large firm needs a staff of experienced marketing, advertising, and public relations managers to coordinate these activities. Some typical marketing positions are described in the following sections. Table 1 identifies the text chapters directly related to the responsibilities of each position. Note also that specific titles of different marketing positions may vary among firms. For example, the person holding the senior marketing position in a company may hold such titles as vice president of marketing, marketing director, or marketing manager. Job descriptions and typical career paths of eight major marketing positions are included in Table 2.

TABLE 2   Job Descriptions and Career Paths for Eight Major Marketing Positions

MARKETING, ADVERTISING, PRODUCT, AND PUBLIC RELATIONS MANAGERS

Marketing management spans a range of positions, including vice president of marketing, marketing manager, sales manager, product manager, advertising manager, promotion manager, and public relations manager. The vice president directs the firm's overall marketing policy, and all other marketers report through channels to this person. Sales managers direct the efforts of sales professionals by assigning territories, establishing goals, developing training programs, and supervising local sales managers and their personnel. Advertising managers oversee account services, creative services, and media services departments. Promotion managers direct promotional programs that combine advertising with purchase incentives designed to increase the sales of the firm's goods or services. Public relations managers are responsible for communicating with the firm's various publics, conducting publicity programs, and supervising the specialists who implement these programs.

JOB DESCRIPTION
As with senior management positions in production, finance, and other areas, top marketing management positions often involve long hours and extensive travel. Work under pressure is also common. For sales managers, job transfers between headquarters and regional offices may disrupt one's personal life. Approximately 460,000 marketing, advertising, product, and public relations managers are currently employed in the U.S. The Bureau of Labor Statistics estimates for the first decade of this century show strong growth of 168,000 new positions in these categories, the seventh-largest growth category.[5]

CAREER PATH
A degree in business administration, preferably with a concentration in marketing, is usually required for these positions. In highly technical industries, such as computers, chemicals, and electronics, employers typically prefer bachelor's degrees in science or engineering combined with master's degrees in business administration. Liberal arts students can also find many opportunities, especially if they have business minors. Most

TABLE 2   *continued*

managers are promoted from positions such as sales representatives, product or brand specialists, and advertising specialists within their organizations. Skills or traits that are most desirable for these jobs include high motivation levels, maturity, creativity, resistance to stress, flexibility, and the ability to communicate persuasively.

SALES REPRESENTATIVES AND SALES MANAGERS

Millions of items are bought and sold every day. The people in the firm who carry out this activity may have a variety of titles—sales representative, account manager, manufacturer's representative, sales engineer, sales agent, retail salesperson, wholesale sales representative, and service sales representative. Sales managers are typically selected from people in the current sales force who have demonstrated that they possess the managerial skills needed to lead teams of sales representatives. In addition, many organizations require that all marketing professionals spend some time in the field to experience the market firsthand and to understand the challenges faced by front-line personnel.

JOB DESCRIPTION

Salespeople are usually responsible for developing prospective client lists, meeting with current and prospective customers to discuss the firm's products, and then following up to answer questions and supply additional information. By knowing the business needs of each customer, the sales representative can identify products that best satisfy these needs. Following a customer purchase, they are likely to revisit their customers to ensure that the products are meeting the customers' needs and to explore further business opportunities or referrals provided by satisfied buyers. Some sales of technical products involve lengthy interactions. In these cases, a salesperson may work with several clients simultaneously over a large geographical area. Those responsible for large territories may spend most of their workdays on the phone, receiving and sending e-mail messages, or on the sales floor. Recent compensation data revealed that top-level professional salespeople received total annual pay of $140,000 on average, a nine-percent increase over the previous year—even in the midst of a recession.[6]

Work as a sales representative or sales manager can be rewarding for those who enjoy interacting with people, those invigorated by competition, and those who feel energized by the challenge of expanding sales in their territories. Successful sales professionals—both individual sales reps and sales managers—should be goal-oriented, persuasive, self-motivated, and independent. In addition, patience and perseverance are important qualities.

CAREER PATH

The background needed for a sales position varies according to the product line and market. Most professional sales jobs require a college degree, and many companies run their own formal training programs that can last up to two years for sales representatives in technical industries. This training may take place in a classroom, in the field with a mentor, or most often using a combination of both methods. Sales managers are usually promoted from the field; they are likely to include successful sales representatives who exhibit managerial skills and promise. Sales management positions begin at a local or district level, then advance to positions of increased authority and responsibility such as area, regional, national, and international sales manager.

Many newly graduated marketing majors begin their careers in advertising agencies. These members of the Joker Ad Agency were responsible for a notable anti-AIDS campaign.

ADVERTISING SPECIALISTS

Most companies, especially firms serving consumer markets, maintain small groups of advertising specialists who serve as liaisons between the marketer and its outside advertising agencies. The leader of this liaison function is sometimes called a *marketing communications manager.* Positions in an advertising agency include specialists in account services, creative services, and media services. Account services functions are performed by account executives, who work directly with clients. An agency's creative services department develops the themes and presentations of the advertisements. This department is supervised by a creative director, who oversees the copy chief, art director, and their staff members. The media services department is managed by a media director, who oversees the planning group that selects media outlets for ads.

JOB DESCRIPTION

Advertising can be one of the most glamorous and creative fields in marketing. Because the field combines the best of both worlds—that is, the tangible and scientific aspects of marketing along with creative artistry—advertising attracts people with a broad array of abilities.

TABLE 2   *continued*

CAREER PATH

Most new hires begin as assistants or associates for the position they hope to acquire, such as copywriter, art director, and media buyer. Often, a newly hired employee must receive two to four promotions before becoming manager of these functions. College degrees in liberal arts, graphic arts, communications, psychology, or sociology, in addition to marketing training, are preferred for entry-level positions in advertising.

PUBLIC RELATIONS SPECIALISTS

Specialists in public relations strive to build and maintain positive relationships with various publics. They may assist management in drafting speeches, arranging interviews, overseeing company archives, responding to information requests, and handling special events, such as sponsorships and trade shows, that generate promotional benefits for the firm.

JOB DESCRIPTION

While public relations specialists normally work a standard 40-hour week, they will occasionally rearrange their normal schedules to meet deadlines or prepare for major events. Occasionally, they are required to be on the job or on call around the clock to respond to an emergency or crisis. About 110,000 public relations specialists are currently employed in the U.S., two-thirds of them in service industries. Public relations positions tend to be concentrated in large cities near major press services and communications facilities. However, this centralization is changing with the increased popularity of new communications technologies, such as satellite uplinks, wireless technologies, and the Internet, which allow more freedom of movement. Most public relations consulting firms are concentrated in New York, Los Angeles, Chicago, and Washington, D.C.

Essential characteristics for a public relations specialist include creativity, initiative, good judgment, and the ability to express thoughts clearly and simply—both verbally and in writing. An outgoing personality, self-confidence, and enthusiasm are also recommended traits.

CAREER PATH

A college degree combined with public relations experience, usually gained through one or more internships, is considered excellent preparation for public relations. Many entry-level public relations specialists hold degrees with majors in advertising, marketing, public relations, or communications. New employees in larger organizations are likely to participate in formal training programs; those who begin their careers at smaller firms typically work under the guidance of experienced staff members. Entry-level positions carry such titles as research assistant or account assistant. A potential career path includes a promotion to account executive, account supervisor, vice president, and eventually senior vice president.

PURCHASING AGENTS AND MANAGERS

In the 21st century business world the two key marketing functions of buying and selling are performed by trained specialists. Just as every organization is involved in selling its output to meet the needs of customers, so too must all companies make purchases of goods and services required to operate their businesses and turn out items for sale.

Modern technology has transformed the role of the purchasing agent. The transfer of routine tasks to computers now allows contract specialists, or procurement officers, to focus on products, suppliers, and contract negotiations. The primary function of this position is to purchase the goods, materials, component parts, supplies, and services required by the organization. These agents ensure that suppliers deliver quality and quantity levels that match the firm's needs; they also secure these inputs at reasonable prices and make them available when needed.

Purchasing agents must develop good working relationships both with colleagues in their own organizations and with suppliers. As the popularity of outsourcing has increased, the selection and management of suppliers have become critical functions of the purchasing department. In the government sector, this role is dominated by strict laws, statutes, and regulations that change frequently.

JOB DESCRIPTION

Purchasing agents can expect a standard work week with some travel to suppliers' sites, seminars, and trade shows. Over 600,000 people are employed in purchasing positions in the U.S., most of them in manufacturing and government.

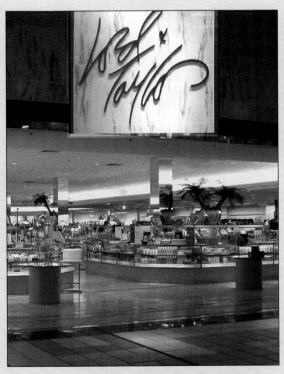

Thousands of retailers such as May Department Stores—parent of such widely known and highly regarded retailers as Lord & Taylor, Robinsons-May, Filene's, Foley's, Kaufmann's, Famous-Barr, and Hecht's—employ hundreds of thousands of college graduates who have decided on a career in retailing.

TABLE 2   *continued*

CAREER PATH

Organizations prefer college-educated candidates for entry-level jobs in purchasing. Strong analytical and communication skills are required for any purchasing position. New hires often begin their careers by enrolling in extensive company training programs in which they learn procedures and operations. Training may include assignments dealing with production planning. Professional certification is becoming an essential criterion for advancement in both the private and the public sectors. A variety of associations serving the different categories of purchasing confer certifications on agents, including Certified Purchasing Manager, Professional Public Buyer, Certified Public Purchasing Officer, Certified Associate Contract Manager, and Certified Professional Contract Manager.

RETAIL AND WHOLESALE BUYERS AND MERCHANDISE MANAGERS

Buyers working for retailers and wholesale businesses purchase goods for resale. Their goal is to find the best possible merchandise at the lowest prices. They also influence the distribution and marketing of this merchandise. Successful buyers must understand what appeals to consumers and what their establishments can sell. Product bar codes and point-of-purchase terminals allow organizations to accurately track goods that are selling and those that are not; buyers frequently analyze this data to improve their understanding of consumer demand. Buyers also check competitors' prices and sales activities and watch general economic conditions to anticipate consumer buying patterns.

JOB DESCRIPTION

Approximately 260,000 people are currently employed in the U.S. as retail and wholesale buyers and merchandise managers. These jobs often require substantial travel, as many orders are placed on buying trips to shows and exhibitions. Effective planning and decision- making skills are strong assets in this career. In addition, the job involves anticipating consumer preferences and ensuring that the firm keeps needed goods in stock. Consequently, the people filling these positions must possess such qualities as resourcefulness, good judgment, and self-confidence.

CAREER PATH

Most retail and wholesale buyers begin their careers as assistant buyers or trainees. Larger retailers seek college-educated candidates, and extensive training includes job experience in a variety of positions. Advancement often comes when buyers move to departments or new locations with larger volumes—or become merchandise managers to coordinate or oversee the work of several buyers.

MARKETING RESEARCH ANALYSTS

These marketing specialists provide information that assists marketers in identifying and defining opportunities. They generate, refine, and evaluate marketing actions and monitor marketing performance. Marketing research analysts devise methods and procedures for obtaining needed, decision-oriented data. Once they compile data, analysts evaluate it and then make recommendations to management.

JOB DESCRIPTION

Firms that specialize in marketing research and management consulting employ the majority of the nation's marketing research analysts. These positions are often concentrated in larger cities, such as New York, Los Angeles, and Chicago. Those who pursue careers in marketing research must be capable of working accurately with detail, display patience and persistence, work effectively both independently and with others, and operate objectively and systematically. Significant computer and analytical skills are essential for success in this field.

CAREER PATH

A bachelor's degree with an emphasis in marketing provides sufficient qualifications for many entry-level jobs in marketing research. Because of the importance of quantitative skills and the need for competence in using analytical software packages, this education should include courses in calculus, linear algebra, statistics, sampling theory and survey design, computer science, and information systems. Students should try to gain experience in conducting interviews or surveys while still in college. A master's degree in business administration or a related discipline is advised for improving advancement opportunities.

LOGISTICS: MATERIAL RECEIVING, SCHEDULING, DISPATCHING AND DISTRIBUTING OCCUPATIONS

Logistics offers a myriad of career positions. Job titles under this broad heading include material receiving, scheduling, dispatching, materials management executive, distribution operations coordinator, distribution center manager, and transportation manager. The logistics function includes responsibilities for production and inventory planning and control, distribution, and transportation.

TABLE 2   *continued*

JOB DESCRIPTION
Approximately 3.8 million people are currently employed in logistics positions in the U.S., including material receiving, scheduling, dispatching, and distribution. These positions demand good communication skills and the ability to work effectively under pressure.

CAREER PATH
Computer skills are highly valued in these jobs. Employers look for candidates with degrees in logistics and transportation. However, graduates in marketing and other business disciplines may succeed in this field.

Additional Information Sources

A wealth of helpful career information is continually updated for you at the Boone & Kurtz Web site: http://boone.swlearning.com. You'll find a complete *Marketing Careers* section located under the heading *Marketing Topics* on the left-hand navigation bar. Here you'll learn more about marketing careers and be able to locate currently posted job opportunities. The site provides a vast number of career resources such as links to job sites, career guidance sites, U.S. newspaper job ads, and company information. It also provides ways for researching cities of special interest to you.

In addition, the *Personal Development* section of the Web site contains career guidance tips, including interviewing techniques and résumé writing advice. The site is updated regularly.

Part 1

Designing Customer-Oriented Marketing Strategies

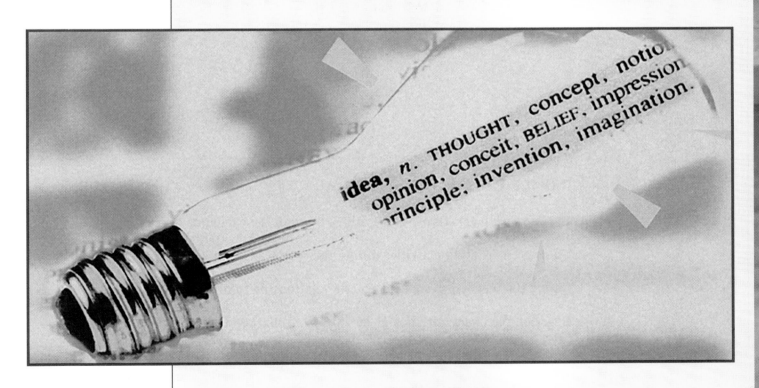

1

Customer-Driven Marketing

Chapter Objectives

1 Explain how marketing creates utility through the exchange process.

2 Contrast marketing activities during the four eras in the history of marketing.

3 Define the marketing concept and its relationship to marketing myopia.

4 Describe the characteristics of not-for-profit marketing.

5 Describe the five types of nontraditional marketing.

6 Outline the changes in the marketing environment due to technology.

7 Explain the shift from transaction-based marketing to relationship marketing.

8 Identify the universal functions of marketing.

9 Demonstrate the relationship between ethical business practices and marketplace success.

iTunes Strikes a Chord with Consumers

Music fans everywhere have spoken. They want better music, better recordings of the music, and access to their favorite songs at a fair price. These fans are important customers to the music industry. Without them, there would be no industry. Still, for years the record company giants have been criticized by music lovers who believe they pay exorbitant—and unjustifiable—prices for compact disks products—$16 per CD is pretty steep for most folks. However, industry spokespeople claim that prices are legitimate.

Greater tension arose over this issue several years ago when computer technology made downloading music possible, and some people began accessing their music for free, first via Napster and later via Kaaza and similar sites. An estimated 60 million computer users currently participate in the illegal practice of file-sharing. The record companies cried foul and sued the Web sites that helped distribute copyrighted music files. Later the Recording Industry Association of America issued subpoenas to colleges and Internet service providers for the names and addresses of more than 950 computer owners—including college students—suspected of piracy and stealing millions of dollars in potential revenues.

Despite the fact that the industry—including recording artists themselves—was losing revenues and that free distribution of copyrighted music is illegal, the record companies' actions did nothing to win back its customers. In fact, a number of recording artists publicly supported consumers, and some stars such as Jimmy Buffett and Pearl Jam left their record companies to start their own labels in an effort to control product, price, and distribution—and create value for their fans. "We're just starting to appreciate the freedom and see where it can take us," says Pearl Jam's manager, Kelly Curtis. This freedom also allows artists to fill a desire expressed by fans who say, "I'd be happy to pay if I could pick and choose so that I wouldn't have to pay so much money for so much junk. I'd pay as much as a dollar a song if I can choose the songs."

Enter Steve Jobs. He's been around a long time, but he's never been associated with the music industry—until now. The cofounder and CEO of Apple Computer announced his latest venture, the iTunes Music Store. Initially available to Apple Macintosh users, the Internet music store allows consumers to purchase and download a song for 99 cents, with almost no restrictions on how or where the song is played. There's no monthly fee, as opposed to sites like Pressplay

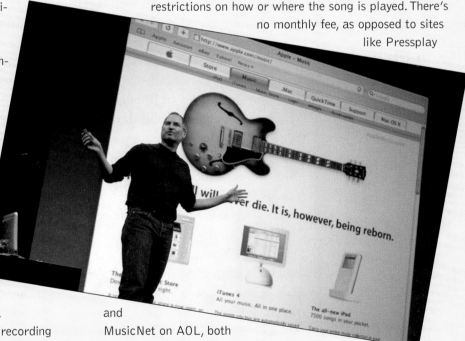

and MusicNet on AOL, both of which charge $9.95. And it's legal. Jobs and a few Apple colleagues spent nearly a year and a half negotiating deals with such companies as Universal, Warner, BMG, EMI, and Sony Music; he also demonstrated his idea to artists such as the Eagles and Sheryl Crow. He won them over. When iTunes was launched, more than 2 million song tracks were downloaded within the first two weeks. When iTunes expanded beyond its audience of Macintosh users (only 3% of all computer users) to include people with Windows-based computers, industry analysts predicted that revenues could reach $500 million per year.

Apple addresses many of the needs consumers express that other legitimate downloading sites and music suppliers have not, and it hopes these features will create loyal customers in a highly competitive market. First, there is no monthly charge to subscribe to the service—just the 99 cents it costs to download each tune. Second, for 99 cents consumers can actually buy the tune, rather than rent it for a period of time. A song won't disappear from a customer's screen after a designated period the way rented tunes do. Third, music buffs can pick and choose the songs they want, rather than having to buy an entire CD. If iTunes succeeds, Steve Jobs may turn out to be a very unlikely rock star.[1]

Chapter Overview

Briefly Speaking

Increasingly, the center of the marketing universe is the customer. It's the customer who sets the rules and the marketer who responds.

Robert Wientzen
CEO, Direct
Marketing Association

- "They're the best."
- "I always eat there."
- "I only fly with that airline."
- "I buy my electronics at that store."

These words are music to a marketer's ears. Customer loyalty is the watchword of 21st century marketing. But today, individual consumers and business purchasers have so many goods and services from which to choose—and so many different ways to purchase them—that marketers must continually seek out new—and better—ways to attract and keep customers, as Apple Computer has done with its new iTunes Music Store. Advances in communications technology allow information to be exchanged between buyers and sellers faster, cheaper, and through more media channels than ever before, including broadcast media, print, telecommunications, online computer services, and the Internet. Companies can now offer consumers more product choices and more places to buy. Today's savvy shoppers can visit a brick-and-mortar shopping mall, hire a personal shopper, order from catalogs, watch television home shopping channels, and browse virtual stores accessed through online services.

The technology revolution is changing the rules of marketing during this first decade of the 21st century. The combined power of telecommunications and computer technology creates inexpensive, global networks that transfer voice messages, text, graphics, and data within seconds. These sophisticated technologies create new types of products, and they also demand new approaches to marketing existing products. Communications technology contributes as well to the globalization of today's marketplace, where businesses manufacture, buy, and sell across national borders. You can eat a Big Mac or drink Coca-Cola almost anywhere in the world; your DVD or CD player was probably manufactured in China or Korea. Both Mercedes-Benz and Hyundai sport utility vehicles are assembled in Alabama, while many Volkswagens are imported from Mexico. Products and components routinely cross international borders, but successful global marketing also requires knowledge to tailor products to regional tastes. An Asian food store in Austin, Texas, may also sell popular Hispanic foods such as tortillas to satisfy local tastes of shoppers who like both.

Rapidly changing business landscapes create new challenges for companies, whether they are giant multinational firms or small boutiques, profit-oriented or not-for-profit. Organizations must react quickly to shifts in consumer tastes, competitive offerings, and other market dynamics. Fortunately, information technologies give organizations fast, new ways to interact and develop long-term relationships with their customers and suppliers. In fact, such links have become a core element of marketing today.

Every company must serve customer needs—create customer satisfaction—to succeed. Two customer satisfaction researchers described its value this way: "Customer satisfaction has come to represent an important cornerstone for customer-oriented business practices across a multitude of companies operating in diverse industries."[2] Marketing strategies provide the tools by which businesspeople identify and analyze customers' needs and then inform these customers about how the company can meet those needs. Tomorrow's market leaders will be companies who can effectively harness the vast amounts of customer feedback and respond with solutions to their needs.

This new edition of *Contemporary Marketing* focuses on the strategies that allow companies to succeed in today's interactive marketplace. This chapter sets the stage for the entire text, examining the meaning of customer-driven marketing and its importance for all organizations. Initial sections describe the development of marketing, from early times to today's focus on relationship marketing and its contributions to society. Later sections introduce the technology revolution, the universal functions of marketing, and the relationship between ethical business practices and marketplace success.

Briefly Speaking

We're always looking to see what we can do to make our customers' lives easier or save them money. It pervades every part of the company.

Michael Dell
(b. 1965)
founder and CEO,
Dell

What Is Marketing?

Production and marketing of goods and services are the essence of economic life in any society. All organizations perform these two basic functions to satisfy their commitments to society, their customers, and their owners. They create a benefit that economists call **utility**—the want-satisfying power of a good or service. Table 1.1 describes the four basic kinds of utility—form, time, place, and ownership.

Form utility is created when the firm converts raw materials and component inputs into finished goods and services. By combining glass, plastic, metals, circuit boards, and other components, Toshiba creates a television set and Sony makes a camcorder. With fabric, thread, wood, springs, and down feathers, Ethan Allen produces a sofa. MTV's hit television comedy show *The Osbournes*—starring heavy metal superstar Ozzy Osbourne, his wife, and their teenagers pink-haired Kelly and spiky-haired Jack—starts with writers, artists, actors, scripts, a director, producers, technical crew, and a sound stage.[3] Although the marketing function determines consumer and audience preferences, the organization's production function is responsible for the actual creation of form utility.

Marketing creates time, place, and ownership utilities. Time and place utility occur when consumers find goods and services available when and where they want to purchase them. Overnight courier services like FedEx and Airborne Express emphasize time utility; vending machines focus on providing place utility for people buying newspapers, snacks, and soft drinks. The transfer of title to goods or services at the time of purchase creates ownership utility.

The Osbourne family portrait shown in Figure 1.1 illustrates the result of a combination of efforts by both production and marketing to achieve this marketplace success. While production is responsible for creating form utility, marketing's ability to create time, place, and ownership utility also contributes to the success of this rock 'n' roll sitcom. The choice of cable channel MTV as the delivery vehicle is particularly appropriate in reaching the *The Osbournes'* core audience of teenagers and young adults.

All organizations must create utility to survive. Designing and marketing want-satisfying goods, services, and ideas are the foundation for the creation of utility. Organizations recently have begun to elevate the function of

1

Explain how marketing creates utility through the exchange process.

Marketing Dictionary

utility Want-satisfying power of a good or service.

TABLE 1.1   Four Types of Utility

Type	Description	Examples	Organizational Function Responsible
Form	Conversion of raw materials and components into finished goods and services	Citibank checking account; Nissan Pathfinder; Ramen Noodles (nutrition for students who are hungry, broke, and can't— or won't—cook)	Production*
Time	Availability of goods and services when consumers want them	One-hour photographs; LensCrafters eyeglass guarantee; U.S. Priority Mail	Marketing
Place	Availability of goods and services at convenient locations	Soft-drink machines outside gas stations; on-site day care; ATM machines in shopping malls	Marketing
Ownership (possession)	Ability to transfer title to goods or services from marketer to buyer	Retail sales (in exchange for currency or credit-card payment)	Marketing

*Marketing provides inputs related to consumer preferences, but the actual creation of form utility is the responsibility of the production function.

marketing in their hierarchies; top marketing executives may be promoted to senior vice presidential positions. But where does the process start? In the toy industry, manufacturers try to come up with items that children will want to play with—creating utility. But that's not as simple as it sounds. At the Toy Fair held each February in New York, retailers pore through the different booths of manufacturers and suppliers, looking for the next Barbie or scooter—trends that turn into classics, generating millions of dollars of revenues over the years. They also try to identify which toys will be the hottest items for the coming year; often figures or games tied to the latest film release in the *Star Wars*, *Hobbit*,

FIGURE 1.1
Production and Marketing at the Osbourne Household: Generating a Surprise Cable TV Success by Creating Form, Time, Place, and Ownership Utility

and *Harry Potter* series. If their decisions are on target, everyone wins—retailers, manufacturers, and children. But if parents and kids don't buy what the retailers stock in their stores, everyone loses.[4] If a toy creates utility, manufacturers and retailers have created customers.

In general, how does an organization create a customer? Professors Joseph Guiltinan and Gordon Paul explain it this way:

Essentially, "creating" a customer means identifying needs in the marketplace, finding out which needs the organization can profitably serve, and developing an offering to convert potential buyers into customers. Marketing managers are responsible for most of the activities necessary to create the customers the organization wants. These activities include:

- Identifying customer needs

- Designing goods and services that meet those needs

- Communicating information about those goods and services to prospective buyers

- Making the goods or services available at times and places that meet customers' needs

- Pricing goods and services to reflect costs, competition, and customers' ability to buy

- Providing for the necessary service and follow-up to ensure customer satisfaction after the purchase[5]

A Definition of Marketing

The word *marketing* encompasses such a broad scope of activities and ideas that settling on one definition is often difficult. Ask five people to define it, and five different definitions are likely to follow. Continuous exposure to advertising and personal selling leads most respondents to link marketing and selling or to think that marketing activities start once goods and services have been produced. But marketing also involves analyzing customer needs, securing information needed to design and produce goods or services that match buyer expectations, and creating and maintaining relationships with customers and suppliers. It applies not only to profit-oriented firms but also to thousands of not-for-profit organizations that offer goods and services.

Today's definition takes all these factors into account. **Marketing** is the process of planning and executing the conception, pricing, promotion, and distribution of ideas, goods, services, organizations, and events to create and maintain relationships that will satisfy individual and organizational objectives.

The expanded concept of marketing activities permeates all organizational functions. It assumes that the marketing effort will proceed in accordance with ethical practices and that it will effectively serve the interests of both society and the organization. The concept also identifies the marketing variables—product, price, promotion, and distribution—that combine to provide customer satisfaction. In addition, it assumes that the organization begins by identifying and analyzing the consumer segments that it will later satisfy through its production and marketing activities. In other words, the customer, client, or public determines the marketing program. The concept's emphasis on creating and maintaining relationships is consistent with the focus in business on long-term, mutually satisfying sales, purchases, and other interactions with customers and suppliers. Finally, it recognizes that marketing concepts and techniques apply to not-for-profit organizations as well as to profit-oriented businesses.

Today's Global Marketplace

Several factors have forced countries to extend their economic views to events outside their own national borders. First, international agreements are being negotiated in attempts to increase trade among nations. Second, the growth of electronic commerce and related computer technologies brings previously isolated countries into the marketplace for buyers and sellers around the globe. Third, the interdependence of the world's economies is a reality since no nation produces all of the raw materials and finished goods purchased by its citizens or

Marketing Dictionary

marketing Process of planning and executing the conception, pricing, and distribution of ideas, goods, services, organizations, and events to create and maintain relationships that will satisfy individual and organizational objectives.

consumes all of its output without some exporting to other countries. Evidence of this interdependence is illustrated by the introduction of the euro as a common currency to facilitate trade among the nations of the European Union and the creation of trade alliances such as NAFTA.

A recession in Europe affects business strategies in North America and the Pacific Rim. To remain competitive, companies must continually search for the most efficient manufacturing sites and most lucrative markets for their products. Marketers now find tremendous opportunities serving customers not only in traditional industrialized nations but also in Latin America and emerging economies in eastern Europe and Asia, where rising standards of living create increased customer demand for the latest goods and services.

Expanding operations beyond the U.S. market gives domestic companies access to 6 billion international customers. This explains why over 80 percent of Coca-Cola sales are generated outside the United States. Japan alone accounts for nearly 20 percent of Coke's profit.[6] For Colgate-Palmolive, a whopping 70 percent of its revenue comes from abroad, and three-fourths of Exxon's revenues are from non–U.S. customers.

Service firms also play a major role in today's global marketplace. The New York Stock Exchange, illustrated in Figure 1.2, advertises itself as the "gateway to the global economy." Although the organization is based in New York City, investors trade over $50 billion worldwide every day over the exchange.[7] Manpower Temporary Services, a worldwide firm that provides temporary and permanent workers in a broad range of jobs, earns almost 70 percent of its profits from foreign contracts. Technology products are also popular U.S. exports. Compaq's Digital Equipment subsidiary sells two-thirds of its computer products outside the United States, while Apple Computer generates half its revenues from non–U.S. sales.

The U.S. is also an attractive market for foreign competitors because of its size and the high standard of living that American consumers enjoy. Companies like Nissan, Sony, and Sun Life of Canada operate production, distribution, service, and retail facilities in the U.S. Foreign ownership of U.S. companies has increased as well. Pillsbury and MCA are two well-known firms with foreign parents. Even American-dominated industries like computer software must contend with foreign competition. While U.S. firms still hold about 75 percent of the market, European companies are quickly gaining market share. They currently supply about 18 percent of the $100 billion worldwide market for packaged software.

FIGURE 1.2
The New York Stock Exchange: "Gateway to the Global Economy"

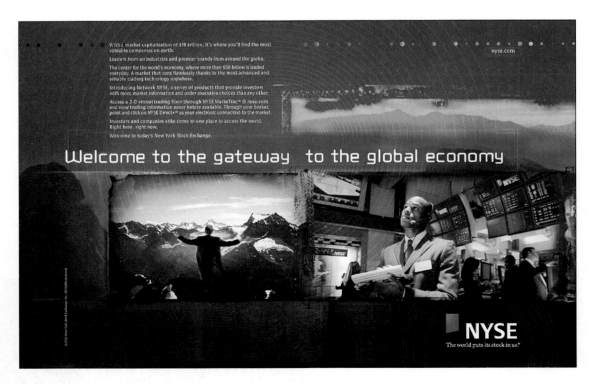

In many cases, global marketing strategies are almost identical to those used in domestic markets. Rather than creating a different promotional campaign for each country where they sell Pringles potato chips, Procter & Gamble marketers used the same ad—with spectacular results. Nearly everything in the U.S.-made ads was the same—the rap music themes, the young people dancing, and the tag line, "Once you pop, you can't stop." As a result, P&G had to boost production to handle the global demand.[8]

In other instances, domestic marketing strategies may need significant changes to adapt to unique tastes or different cultural and legal requirements abroad. It is often difficult to standardize a brand name on a global basis. The Japanese, for example, like names of flowers or girls for their car models, such as Bluebird, Bluebonnet, Violet, and Gloria. Americans, on the other hand, prefer rugged outdoorsy names like Mountaineer, Explorer, Sierra, and Yukon.[9]

Four Eras in the History of Marketing

2

Contrast marketing activities during the four eras in the history of marketing.

The essence of marketing is the **exchange process,** in which two or more parties give something of value to each other to satisfy felt needs. In many exchanges, people trade money for tangible goods, such as CDs, clothes, or cars. In others, they trade for intangible services like child care, haircuts, or concerts. In still others, people may donate funds or time for a cause, such as a Red Cross blood drive, a new gymnasium for a church or school, or a campaign to clean up the environment.

Although marketing has always been a part of business, its importance has varied greatly. Figure 1.3 identifies four eras in the history of marketing: (1) the production era, (2) the sales era, (3) the marketing era, and (4) the relationship era.

The Production Era

Prior to 1925, most firms—even those operating in highly developed economies in western Europe and North America—focused narrowly on production. Manufacturers stressed production of quality products and then looked for people to purchase them. The history of Pillsbury provides an excellent example of a production-oriented company. The late Robert J. Keith, who was once the company's chief executive officer, described Pillsbury during its early years:

> We are professional flour millers. Blessed with a supply of the finest North American wheat, plenty of water power, and excellent milling machinery, we produce flour of the highest quality. Our basic function is to mill high-quality flour, and, of course, we must hire [salespeople] to sell it, just as we hire accountants to keep our books.[10]

The prevailing attitude of this era held that a good product (one with high physical quality) would sell itself. This **production orientation** dominated business philosophy for decades; indeed, business success was often defined solely in terms of production victories.

The production era did not reach its peak until the early part of the 20th century. Henry Ford's mass-production line exemplifies this orientation. Ford's slogan, "They [customers] can have any color they want, as long as it's black," reflected the prevalent attitude toward marketing. Production shortages and intense consumer demand ruled the day. It is easy to understand how production activities took precedence.

The essence of the production era resounds in a statement made over 100 years ago by the philosopher Ralph Waldo Emerson: "If a man writes a better book, preaches a better sermon, or makes a better mousetrap than his neighbor, though he builds his house in the woods, the world will make a beaten path to his door." However, a better mousetrap is no guarantee of success, and marketing history is full of miserable failures despite better mousetrap designs.

Marketing Dictionary

exchange process Activity in which two or more parties give something of value to each other to satisfy perceived needs.

production orientation Business philosophy stressing efficiency in producing a quality product, with the attitude toward marketing that "a good product will sell itself."

FIGURE 1.3
Four Eras of
Marketing History

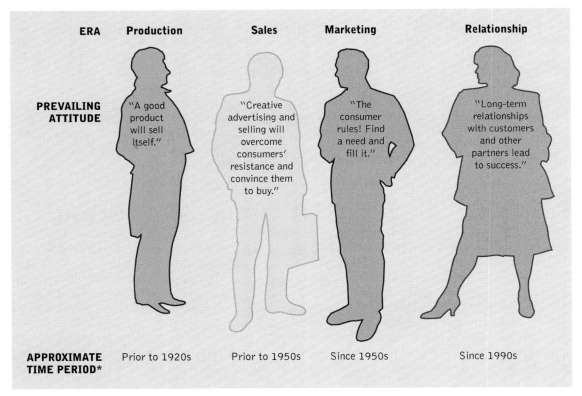

*In the United States and other highly industrialized economies

In fact, over 80 percent of new products fail. Inventing the greatest new product is not enough. That product must also solve a perceived marketplace need. Otherwise, even the best-engineered, highest-quality product will fail. Even the horseless carriage took a while to catch on. People were afraid of motor vehicles, which spit out exhaust, stirred up dust on dirt roads, got stuck in mud, and tied up horse traffic. Besides, at the wild speed of seven miles per hour, they caused all kinds of accidents and disruption. It took savvy marketing by some early salespeople—and eventually a widespread perceived need—to change people's minds about the product.[11]

The Sales Era

Production techniques in the United States and Europe became more sophisticated, and output grew from the 1920s into the early 1950s. Thus, manufacturers began to increase their emphasis on effective sales forces to find customers for their output. In this era, firms attempted to match their output to the potential number of customers who would want it. Companies with a **sales orientation** assume that customers will resist purchasing goods and services not deemed essential and that the task of personal selling and advertising is to convince them to buy.

Although marketing departments began to emerge from the shadows of production, finance, and engineering during the sales era, they tended to remain in subordinate positions. Many chief marketing executives held the title of sales manager. Here is how Pillsbury described itself during the sales era:

We are a flour-milling company, manufacturing a number of products for the consumer market. We must have a first-rate sales organization which can dispose of all the products we can make at a favorable price. We must back up this sales force with consumer advertising and marketing intelligence. We want our sales representatives and our dealers to have all the tools they need for moving the output of our plants to the consumer.[12]

But selling is only one component of marketing. As Harvard University marketing professor Theodore Levitt has pointed out, "Marketing is as different from selling as chemistry is from alchemy, astronomy from astrology, chess from checkers."[13]

88
86
88
94

The Marketing Era

Personal incomes and consumer demand for goods and services dropped rapidly during the Great Depression of the early 1930s, thrusting marketing into a more important role. Organizational survival dictated that managers pay close attention to the markets for their goods and services. This trend ended with the outbreak of World War II, when rationing and shortages of consumer goods became commonplace. The war years, however, created only a pause in an emerging trend in business: a shift in the focus from products and sales to satisfying customer needs.

Emergence of the Marketing Concept

The marketing concept, a crucial change in management philosophy, can be explained best by the shift from a **seller's market**—one in which there were more buyers for fewer goods and services—to a **buyer's market**—one in which there were more goods and services than people willing to buy them. When World War II ended, factories stopped manufacturing tanks and ships and started turning out consumer products again, a type of activity that had, for all practical purposes, stopped in early 1942.

The advent of a strong buyer's market created the need for **consumer orientation** in businesses. Companies had to market goods and services, not just produce and sell them. This realization has been identified as the emergence of the marketing concept. The recognition of this concept and its dominant role in business dates from 1952, when General Electric heralded a new management philosophy:

> [The concept] introduces the [marketer] at the beginning rather than at the end of the production cycle and integrates marketing into each phase of the business. Thus, marketing, through its studies and research, will establish for the engineer, the designer, and manufacturing [person], what the customer wants in a given product, what price he [or she] is willing to pay, and where and when it will be wanted. Marketing will have authority in product planning, production scheduling, and inventory control, as well as in sales, distribution, and servicing of the product.[14]

Marketing would no longer be regarded as a supplemental activity performed after completion of the production process. Instead, the marketer would play a leading role in product planning. Marketing and selling would no longer be synonymous terms.

The fully developed **marketing concept** is a *company-wide consumer orientation* with the objective of achieving long-run success. All facets of the organization must contribute first to assessing and then to satisfying customer wants and needs. Marketers are not the only people working on this. Accountants in the credit office and engineers designing products also play important roles. Focusing on the objective of achieving long-run success differentiates the concept from policies of short-run profit maximization. Since the firm's continuity is an assumed component of the marketing concept, company-wide consumer orientation will lead to greater long-run profits than managerial philosophies geared toward reaching short-run goals.

A strong market orientation—the extent to which a company adopts the marketing concept—generally improves market success and overall performance. It also has a positive effect on new-product development and the introduction of innovative products. Companies that implement market-driven strategies are better able to understand their customers' experiences, buying habits, and needs. These companies can, therefore, design products with advantages and levels of quality compatible with customer requirements. Customers more quickly accept the new products. This is the beginning of customer-driven marketing.

Marketing Dictionary

sales orientation Business assumption that consumers will resist purchasing nonessential goods and services with the attitude toward marketing that only creative advertising and personal selling can overcome consumers' resistance and convince them to buy.

seller's market Market in which there are more buyers for fewer goods and services.

buyer's market Market in which there are more goods and services than people willing to buy them.

consumer orientation Business philosophy incorporating the marketing concept that emphasizes first determining unmet consumer needs and then designing a system for satisfying them.

marketing concept Company-wide consumer orientation with the objective of achieving long-run success.

The Relationship Era

The fourth era in the history of marketing emerged during the last decade of the 20th century, and continues today into the 21st century. Organizations now carry the marketing era's customer orientation one step further by focusing on establishing and maintaining relationships with both customers and suppliers. This effort represents a major shift from the traditional concept of marketing as a simple exchange between buyer and seller. **Relationship marketing,** by contrast, involves long-term, value-added relationships developed over time with customers and suppliers. Strategic alliances and partnerships among manufacturers, retailers, and suppliers often benefit everyone. Ryder System—owner of those yellow rental trucks—has made alliances with such firms as Delphi Automotive, America's largest auto parts supplier, and Toyota Tsusho America, which provides iron, steel, and textiles to automotive companies. Ryder and Toyota formed a joint venture called TTR Logistics, in which Toyota Tsusho provides the materials and Ryder manages the flow and warehousing of other materials such as plastics and wires.[15] Ryder expects the alliance to generate $22 million in its first year and hundreds of millions in the future. Participants in collaborative relationships generate an estimated 25 percent more sales than independent firms. Teaming up with potential buyers of their products also reduces the risks of new-product introductions. The concept of relationship marketing, which is the current state of customer-driven marketing, is discussed in detail later in this chapter.

Converting Needs to Wants

Every consumer must acquire goods and services on a continuing basis to fill certain needs. Everyone must satisfy the fundamental needs for food, clothing, shelter, and transportation by purchasing things or, in some instances, temporarily using rented property and hired or leased transportation. By focusing on the benefits resulting from these goods and services, effective marketing converts needs to wants. A need for clothing may be translated into a desire (or want) for designer clothes. The need for a vacation may become the desire to take a Caribbean cruise or to backpack in the Rocky Mountains.

As easier-to-use software has enabled millions of nontechnical consumers to operate personal computers, and as falling retail prices make these computers affordable to most households, computers have become fixtures in many schools, offices, and homes. Thousands of tiny and large PC makers have pushed prices below $1,000, and this once-prestigious possession has been reduced to a commodity. Best Buy, the electronics discount retailer shown in Figure 1.4, has achieved major sales success during

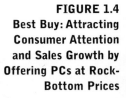

FIGURE 1.4
Best Buy: Attracting Consumer Attention and Sales Growth by Offering PCs at Rock-Bottom Prices

TABLE 1.2 **Avoiding Marketing Myopia by Focusing on Benefits**

Company	Myopic Description	Marketing-Oriented Description
Verizon	"We are a telephone company."	"We are a communications company."
JetBlue Airways	"We are in the airline business."	"We are in the transportation business."
Merrill Lynch	"We are in the stock brokerage business."	"We are in the financial services business."
Nintendo	"We are in the video game business."	"We are in the entertainment business."

the past five years by offering PCs from companies like HP for less than $600 and e-machines for under $400. Because computers are now viewed as a common household need, much like a television or a cell phone, retailers and manufacturers must find new ways to compete for consumer attention.

Companies that adopt the marketing concept focus on providing solutions to customer problems. They stress product benefits rather than features to show the added value that customers will receive from the product. Auto marketers emphasize powerful engines, ABS brakes, and air bags as safety benefits, while office products dealers promote reliable, high-speed copiers and printers for the time savings and low maintenance costs they offer to business purchasers.

Avoiding Marketing Myopia

The emergence of the marketing concept has not been devoid of setbacks. One troublesome problem led Theodore Levitt to coin the term marketing myopia. According to Levitt, **marketing myopia** is management's failure to recognize the scope of its business. Product-oriented rather than customer-oriented management endangers future growth. Levitt cites many service industries—dry cleaning, electric utilities, movies, and railroads—as examples of marketing myopia.

To avoid marketing myopia, companies must broadly define organizational goals oriented toward consumer needs. This approach can help a company stand out from others in highly competitive environments, such as the communications industry. The evolution of AT&T in the information age has created the largest telecommunications company in the U.S. and a world leader in communication services.

AT&T has undergone drastic changes since the demise of the regulated telephone monopoly in 1984. It began by focusing on offering long-distance service but gradually escaped the myopic view of itself as merely a telephone company. In the decades since deregulation, AT&T added Internet, wireless, cable, and local telephone services, transforming itself into a much broader role as a provider of communication services. Intense competition coupled with declining long-distance rates prompted AT&T to divide into separate companies so that specific marketing and other specialists could devote their creative efforts to become market leaders in each product category.[16]

Revlon founder and president Charles Revson understood the need for a broader focus on benefits rather than on products. As Revson described it, "In our factory we make perfume; in our advertising we sell hope." Table 1.2 illustrates how firms in a number of other industries have overcome myopic thinking by developing broader marketing-oriented business ideas that focus on consumer need satisfaction.

Marketing Dictionary

relationship marketing Long-term, value-added relationships developed over time with customers and suppliers.

marketing myopia Management's failure to recognize the scope of its business.

Extending the Traditional Boundaries of Marketing

Today's organizations—both profit-oriented and not-for-profit—recognize universal needs for marketing and its importance to their success. During a television commercial break, viewers might be exposed to an advertisement for a Subaru Outback, an appeal to help children in foreign countries, a message by a political candidate, and a 30-second music-oriented ad featuring Britney Spears for a soft drink—all in the space of about two minutes.

Marketing in Not-for-Profit Organizations

The more than 1 million not-for-profit organizations across the U.S. employ nearly 15.1 million people and generate revenues of more than $620 billion each year.[17] In addition, 109 million volunteers do $255 billion worth of work every year.[18] That makes not-for-profit organizations big business.

Not-for-profit organizations operate in both public and private sectors. Federal, state, and local government units and agencies derive revenues from tax collection to pursue service objectives that are not keyed to profitability targets. The U.S. Department of Defense, for example, protects the nation from foreign aggression; a state's department of natural resources regulates conservation and environmental programs; the local animal-control officer enforces ordinances that protect people and animals.

The private sector has an even more diverse array of not-for-profit organizations, including art institutes, the University of Miami football team, labor unions, hospitals, private schools, the American Cancer Society, and the YMCA. Some, like University of Miami's football team, may generate surplus revenues that can pay for other athletic activities, but the organization's primary goal is to win football games.

In some not-for-profit organizations, adopting the marketing concept means forming a partnership with a for-profit company to promote the not-for-profit's message or image. The organization Save the Children Federation—which provides food, clothing, and shelter to impoverished children around the world—has 27 licensees, or for-profit companies that use the name of the organization on various products, and donate portions of the proceeds to Save the Children. Discount retailer T.J. Maxx recently introduced a line of clothing called Save the Children in a five-year licensing deal. Pepsi ran a holiday promotion offering greeting cards with children's artwork on them, donating $1 from each purchase to Save the Children. Licensing fees and royalties raise about $2 million a year for the organization.[19]

Generally, the alliances formed between not-for-profit organizations and commercial firms benefit both. The reality of operating with multimillion-dollar budgets requires not-for-profit organizations to maintain a focused business approach. Consider some current examples:

- McDonald's Ronald McDonald House Charities work with several local and national not-for-profit organizations to help critically ill children and their families through difficult times.

- The fight against breast cancer has generated donations from many organizations, including the U.S. Postal Service, Avon, JCPenney, and Ford Motor Co., among others.

- The Children's Miracle Network, a $172 million organization that raises money for children's hospitals across the country, gets about $70 million from contributions from corporations like Wal-Mart, Toys "R" Us, and Delta Air Lines.

- General Motors throws its charitable funding behind the United Negro College Fund.

The diversity of not-for-profit organizations suggests the presence of numerous organizational objectives other than profitability. In addition to organizational goals, not-for-profit organizations differ from profit-seeking firms in other ways.

Characteristics of Not-for-Profit Marketing

4
Describe the characteristics of not-for-profit marketing.

The most obvious distinction between not-for-profit organizations and for profit—commercial—firms is the financial *bottom line*, business jargon that refers to the overall profitability of an organization. For-profit organizations measure profitability in terms of sales and revenues, and their goal is to generate revenues above and beyond their costs in order to make money for all stakeholders involved, including employees, shareholders, and the organization itself. Not-for-profit organizations hope to generate just as much revenue to support their causes, whether it is feeding children, preserving wilderness, or helping single mothers find work. Historically, not-for-profits have had less exact goals and marketing objectives than for-profit firms, but in recent years many of these groups have recognized that in order to succeed, they must develop more cost-effective ways to provide services, and they must compete with other organizations for donors' dollars. Marketing can help them accomplish these tasks.

There are other distinctions between the two types of organizations as well, which influence marketing activities. Like profit-seeking firms, not-for-profit organizations may market tangible goods and/or intangible services. The Chicago Art Institute offers items in its gift shop and through direct-mail catalogs (tangible goods), as well as the special exhibits and educational classes (intangible services). But profit-seeking businesses tend to focus their marketing on just one public—their customers. Not-for-profit organizations, however, must often market to multiple publics, which complicates decision making regarding the correct markets to target. Many deal with at least two major publics—their clients and their sponsors—and often many other publics, as well. Political candidates, for example, target both voters and campaign contributors. A college targets prospective students as clients of its marketing program, but it also markets to current students, parents of students, alumni, faculty, staff, local businesses, and local government agencies.

A customer or service user of a not-for-profit organization may wield less control over the organization's destiny than would be true for customers of a profit-seeking firm. The children who are fed and sheltered by Save the Children, Childreach, and other such organizations have less influence on the organization's direction than do affluent American children who buy CDs at the local mall. Not-for-profit organizations also often possess some degree of monopoly power in a given geographic area. An individual contributor might object to United Way's inclusion of a crisis center among its beneficiary agencies, but that agency still receives a portion of the person's total contribution.

In another potential problem, a resource contributor—whether it is a cash donor, a volunteer, or someone who provides office space—may try to interfere with the marketing program in order to promote the message that he or she feels is relevant. Or a donor might restrict a contribution in certain ways that make it difficult for the organization to use. During a capital campaign to raise funds for a new science center, a college alumnus might make a restricted gift to the college theater instead.

Nontraditional Marketing

5
Describe the five types of nontraditional marketing.

As marketing has gained acceptance as a generic activity, its application has broadened far beyond its traditional boundaries. In some cases, broader appeals focus on causes, events, individuals, organizations, and places in the not-for-profit sector. In other instances, they encompass diverse groups of profit-seeking individuals, activities, and organizations. Table 1.3 lists and describes five major categories of nontraditional marketing: person marketing, place marketing, cause marketing, event marketing, and organization marketing.

Person Marketing

One category of nontraditional marketing, **person marketing,** refers to efforts designed to cultivate the attention, interest, and preferences of a target market toward a celebrity or authority figure. Celebrities can be real people; Olympic skier Picabo Street promotes

Marketing Dictionary

person marketing Marketing efforts designed to cultivate the attention, interest, and preference of a target market toward a person (typically a political candidate or celebrity).

TABLE 1.3   Categories of Nontraditional Marketing

Type	Brief Description	Examples
Person marketing	Marketing efforts designed to cultivate the attention and preference of a target market toward a person	Celebrity Britney Spears; athlete Tiger Woods; political candidates
Place marketing	Marketing efforts designed to attract visitors to a particular area; improve consumer images of a city, state, or nation; and/or attract new business	Georgia: Experience the Soul of Georgia; Belize: Catch the Adventure; Tennessee: Sounds Good to Me
Cause marketing	Identification and marketing of a social issue, cause, or idea to selected target markets	"Welfare to Work. It works." "Friends don't let friends drive drunk."
Event marketing	Marketing of sporting, cultural, and charitable activities to selected target markets	NASCAR Pepsi 400; American Cancer Society Relay for Life
Organization marketing	Marketing efforts of mutual-benefit organizations, service organizations, and government organizations that seek to influence others to accept their goals, receive their services, or contribute to them in some way	U.S. Army: An Army of One. United Way brings out the best in all of us. Tech Corps: America needs to know.

Chapstick; former boxing great George Foreman can be seen in Meineke muffler ads as well as commercials for his indoor barbecue grill; actor Jason Alexander runs around the television screen carrying buckets of Kentucky Fried Chicken. Celebrities can be fictional characters, such as Snoopy, who encourages people to buy MetLife insurance. Or they can be widely recognized authority figures, such as former presidential candidate Bob Dole—who spoke out for cancer awareness and promoted Viagra. Campaigns for political candidates and the marketing of celebrities are examples of person marketing. In political marketing, candidates target two markets: They attempt to gain the recognition and preference of voters and the financial support of donors.

FIGURE 1.5
City Harvest:
Generating Increased
Public Awareness and
Contributions from
Person Advertising

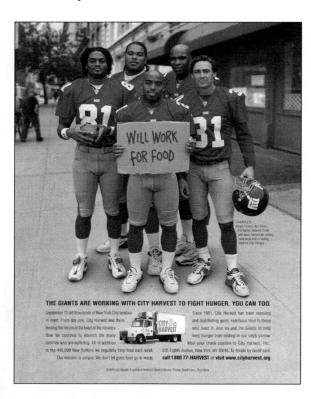

The big winners among celebrity endorsers are professional athletes. Basketball legend Michael Jordan earns as much as $40 million each year endorsing such products as Oakley sunglasses and Hanes underwear; tennis stars Venus and Serena Williams have agreements with Avon and other companies; and golfer Tiger Woods lends his celebrity to products ranging from Nike to American Express.[20] Sometimes, professional athletes lend their names and images to ads promoting not-for-profit organizations, like the one in Figure 1.5. Five New York Giants football players posed for this advertisement for City Harvest, an organization that picks up fresh food from restaurants and supermarkets and distributes it to those in need.

Jimmy Buffett is the most unlikely sort of celebrity. His only top-ten single hit the charts back in 1977. But here in the 21st century, he is packing in thousands of concertgoers who make his summer tours one of the top draws each year. His hard-core fans, known as Parrot Heads, often show up in full tropical attire—foam parrot hats, green and yellow grass skirts, and coconut-shell bras.

The fans are eager to participate in an illusion—those landlocked pillars of their community pretending they are finally going to cash in their chips and set sail for uncharted waters. And the man they have come to see is Jimmy Buffett. They spend over $50 million a year on his concert tickets, albums, books, T-shirts, trinkets, and food. The Buffett "brand" is carved from over 30 albums, eight movies, a clothing line, a series of Margaritaville Cafes, a custom record label, three best-selling novels, and hundreds of gift-shop trinkets.

Buffett works hard at perpetuating this image. He launched a Web site to sell his merchandise and was among the first stars to land a corporate sponsor—Corona Beer. His books, including *Tales from Margaritaville* and *A Pirate Looks at Fifty*, add to the carefree, beach-bum lifestyle legend. In addition, he gives freely to environmental causes, donating $1 from every concert ticket to local causes of the cities where he tours. He has served as chairman of the Save the Manatee society. Buffett's three-decades-long career is a textbook example of how to cross-market books, music, restaurants, and retailing.[21]

Top-grossing entertainer Jimmy Buffett practices person marketing with a combination of CD releases, concert tours, restaurants, and merchandise sales.

Place Marketing

Another category of nontraditional marketing is **place marketing,** which attempts to attract customers to particular areas. Cities, states, and countries publicize their tourist attractions to lure vacation travelers. They also promote themselves as good locations for businesses. Place marketing has become more important in the world economy, where localities compete for economic advantage, increased employment, trade, and investment. Organizations as varied as the San Diego Zoo, the Alamo in San Antonio, state bureaus of tourism and conventions, and the Seattle Port Authority apply place marketing techniques to attract visitors, residents, and new businesses to their areas. Their strategies include promoting positive images; marketing special attractions like The Great Wall of China, India's Taj Mahal, and Niagara Falls; highlighting efficient transportation infrastructures and communication systems; and stressing the quality of available education, low crime rates, clean air and water, and cultural and recreational opportunities. Place marketing also fills promotional messages with positive perceptions of visitors as well as people who live in the area. Iraq hopes to attract visitors to view its ancient treasures, as "Marketing Hits" describes.

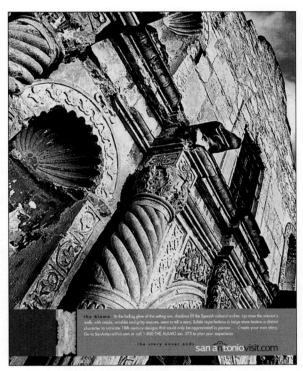

To entice more visitors to its historic city, the San Antonio Convention & Visitors Bureau uses promotions such as this striking photo of the Alamo, the 18th century mission that ranks as one of the most recognized structures in the U.S.

Cause Marketing

A third category of nontraditional marketing, **cause marketing,** refers to the identification and marketing of a social issue, cause, or idea to selected target markets. Cause marketing covers a wide range of issues, including literacy, physical fitness, gun control, family planning,

Marketing Hit

Is An Iraqi Vacation in Your Future?

Background. Who would think of Iraq as a vacation spot? Perhaps those with family ties to the still-dangerous, war-ravaged nation. But what about the average tourist? Actually, today's travelers seem to be drawn toward trips that offer adventure or a dose of reality. Each year, thousands of thrill seekers visit Antarctica, and the base camp at Mt. Everest is swollen with climbers who hope to reach the summit of the world's highest mountain.

The Challenge. How could the new Iraqi government—and travel companies—attract visitors to a war-torn nation that is still perceived by the rest of the world to be dangerous, poor, and without easily accessible points of interest? Southern Iraq contains one of the world's greatest treasures: Mesopotamia, often called the cradle of civilization, where Sumerians built the world's first cities 5,000 years ago. The wheel first appeared here, as did the written word. If marketers could reach potential tourists with this message—along with assurances that travel in Iraq would be comfortable and safe—it could become a desperately needed new source of income for the impoverished country.

The Marketing Strategy. One of the first things that officials accomplished after the recent war ended was reopening Baghdad International Airport. At first, the airport hosted just three round-trip flights a day. But Northwest Airlines quickly proposed adding flights between Baghdad and Detroit, where there is a large Iraqi population. Businesses also began to send employees back and forth to Iraq as well. In addition, archeologists and museum curators worked tirelessly to retrieve and account for ancient artifacts that may have been damaged or looted during the chaos of war. Meanwhile,

continued on next page

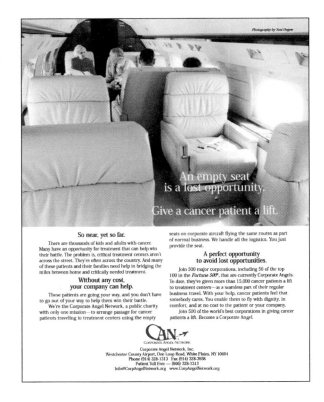

Corporate Angel Network supports cancer patients who need to travel for their treatment.

prison reform, control of overeating, environmental protection, elimination of birth defects, child-abuse prevention, and punishment of drunk drivers.

An increasingly common marketing practice is for profit-seeking firms to link their products to social causes. The San Francisco Giants baseball team dedicates several dates each season to raising awareness—and funds—for a worthy cause. In one recent season, the team used several game days at their home park to focus on AIDS research, blood donations, and prevention of domestic violence. The team also sponsors book and food drives.[22] The Coca-Cola Co. sponsors TigerJam, Tiger Woods's annual fundraiser, which can run the company as much as $1 million. Other corporate sponsors of the event who spend as much as $100,000 include American Airlines, Williams Energy, Cirque du Soleil, Southern Wine and Spirits, and NetJets. The proceeds from the event go to the Tiger Woods Foundation, which supports various youth organizations.[23]

Surveys show strong support for cause-related marketing by both consumers and company employees. Two-thirds of those surveyed say they are more likely to switch to a civic-minded brand or retailer if price and quality are equal. The top three issues consumers would like marketers to address are public education, crime, and the environment.[24] Of course, supporting good causes is good publicity for corporations.

Event Marketing

Event marketing refers to the marketing of sporting, cultural, and charitable activities to selected target markets. It also includes the sponsorship of such events by firms seeking to increase public awareness and bolster their images by linking themselves and their products to the events. Sports sponsorships have gained effectiveness in increasing brand recognition, enhancing image, boosting purchase volume, and increasing popularity with sports fans in demographic segments corresponding to sponsor business goals.

Likely sponsors for the 2004 Summer Olympics in Athens include beer marketers, a major credit-card company, an auto maker, and a fast-food franchise. Such global events are effective in attracting huge audiences that include prime targets for these firms' offerings.

Some people might say that the premier sporting event is the World Series. Others might argue that it's the Super Bowl. But there is a special place in everyone's heart for the Olympics, both summer and winter. Countries the world over compete for the privilege of hosting the games. Television networks bid for the right to cover them. Marketers pour millions into special campaigns tied to the events. Home Depot and UPS, which proudly count a number of athletes among their own employees, create advertisements featuring Olympians such as speed skater Derek Parra. Hallmark recently sponsored the 2002 Winter Games in Salt Lake City and plans to continue its sponsorship of the U.S. Olympic team through the 2006 Games in Turin, Italy. In addition to a flurry of TV commercials, the giant card marketer offered Olympic visitors at Salt Lake City the opportunity to send a complimentary greeting card with a unity theme free of charge to friends or family members and furnished the flower bouquets presented to medalists. Hallmark marketers chose the Olympics carefully as an event to sponsor. "When you look at the values of the Olympics—celebration, support, family being behind everyone—all the emotional elements of the Games fit quite neatly with Hallmark," explained Kylie Watson-Wheeler, director of advertising at Hallmark.[25]

Marketing Hit

agencies and businesses in all sectors began to rebuild the economy and the society. Wireless communications was expected to replace the largely destroyed telephone system. A recovering economy would help make Iraq a more desirable destination.

The Outcome. As people begin to trickle back to this damaged nation—adventurers wanting to visit a nation closed to most tourists since the 1991 Gulf War, businesspeople, those with Iraqi heritage—they will discover the treasures that Iraq has harbored all along. Iraq won't be home to the next Club Med or Disney theme park, but it may once again shine as the home of the most ancient civilization of all.

SOURCES: Samantha Levine, "The Red Eye to Baghdad?" *U.S. News & World Report*, July 21, 2003, p. 12; Andrew Lawler, "Saving Iraq's Treasures," *Smithsonian*, June 2003, p. 42; Sue Kirchoff, "Iraq's History of Commerce, Culture Key to Rebuilding," *USA Today*, April 10, 2003, p. B1.

Organization Marketing

The category of nontraditional marketing called **organization marketing** involves attempts to influence others to accept the goals of, receive the services of, or contribute in some way to an organization. Organization marketing includes mutual-benefit organizations (churches, labor unions, and political parties), service organizations (colleges and universities, hospitals, and museums), and government organizations (military services, police and fire departments, and the U.S. Postal Service).

As cultural organizations encounter declining public funding for the arts and rising competition from other entertainment forms, they respond by actively marketing their programs. Like profit-seeking businesses, the Detroit

Marketing Dictionary

event marketing   Marketing of sporting, cultural, and charitable activities to selected target markets.

organization marketing   Marketing by mutual-benefit organizations, service organizations, and government organizations intended to influence others to accept their goals, receive their services, or contribute to them in some way.

FIGURE 1.6
Request for Donations
to Help the Relief
Efforts Related to
September 11, 2001

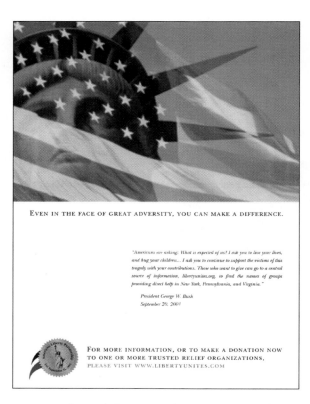

EVEN IN THE FACE OF GREAT ADVERSITY, YOU CAN MAKE A DIFFERENCE.

"Americans are asking: What is expected of us? I ask you to live your lives, and hug your children... I ask you to continue to support the victims of this tragedy with your contributions. Those who want to give can go to a central source of information, libertyunites.org, to find the names of groups providing direct help in New York, Pennsylvania, and Virginia."

President George W. Bush
September 20, 2001

FOR MORE INFORMATION, OR TO MAKE A DONATION NOW
TO ONE OR MORE TRUSTED RELIEF ORGANIZATIONS,
PLEASE VISIT WWW.LIBERTYUNITES.COM

Museum of Art must generate funds to cover its operating expenses. Revenues come from a number of sources, including individual donations, memberships, government grants, gift-shop sales, and special fund-raising drives. The organization also has a Web site and uses such business techniques as marketing research, advertising, and publicity. Special events, such as a recent exhibition of one of the largest number of works ever exhibited in the U.S. by the Dutch Post-Impressionist master Vincent van Gogh, provide added value to museum members and attract thousands of occasional and first-time visitors who may become members.

Organization marketers don't just make appeals for money. They must also reassure donors that the money is being handled correctly and ethically. After the tragedy of the September 11 terrorist attacks, millions wanted to donate funds to charities and relief organizations in an effort to help the victims and their families recover. In fact, so much money flowed into organizations that it became a huge task for administrators to identify who should receive the money and to distribute it in a manner that everyone deemed fair. Even the American Red Cross suffered some damage to its reputation when it announced that some of the $500 million collected would be kept in reserve for possible future terrorist attacks and other disasters. But within weeks of the announcement, the organization reversed its stance and agreed that all the contributions would be directed to victims and relief efforts related to September 11.[26] The advertisement in Figure 1.6 emphasizes that donors can trust these organizations to handle their contributions correctly; a quote from President George W. Bush lends the ad credibility.

Critical Thinking and Creativity

The challenges presented by today's complex and technologically sophisticated marketing environment require critical-thinking skills and creativity from marketing professionals. *Critical thinking* refers to the process of determining the authenticity, accuracy, and worth of information, knowledge, claims, and arguments. Critical thinkers do not take information at face value and simply assume that it is accurate; they analyze the data themselves and develop their own opinions and conclusions.

Creative government bureaucracy might sound like an oxymoron, but it is an accurate description of the U.S. Mint since Philip N. Diehl became director. After years of fighting entrenched political resistance, Diehl was able to transform this $1 billion government agency into a close approximation of a private sector, profit-seeking business. The organization chart was reorganized, jobs were redesigned and positions added, state-of-the-art computerized information systems were installed, bureaucratic workers were trained to become customer-responsive employees, and new products were introduced. The 50-state quarter program, launched during Diehl's tenure, proved highly successful. The Mint decided to release five quarters a year, through 2008, each featuring a different state. As a result, kids— and adults—are clamoring to collect the new quarters as they are released. Despite slowdowns in consumer purchases during the recent economic downturn, these creative changes contributed in a big way in bringing about a government agency that shines, as they say, like a brand-new penny.[27]

Creativity is a human activity that produces original ideas or knowledge, frequently by testing combinations of ideas or data to produce unique results. It is an extremely valuable skill for marketers. Creativity helps them to develop novel solutions to perceived marketing problems. Creativity has been a part of human endeavor since the beginning of time. Leonardo da Vinci conceived his idea for a hel-

FIGURE 1.7
Demonstrating Duke Energy's Creativity and Ability to Become a Global Energy Leader

icopter after watching leaves twirl in the wind. Swiss engineer George de Mestral, noticing that burrs stuck to his wool socks because of their tiny hooks, invented Velcro. Many people think that creativity is the domain of only the young. But famed architect I. M. Pei designed the Rock and Roll Hall of Fame in Cleveland when he was 78 years old. Tom Peters, who wrote the business and marketing best-seller *In Search of Excellence* at age 40, launched a five-book series at age 57. "Creativity is being in one setting and seeing something strange someplace else," he says. "To me, books on butterflies or baseball are more legitimate in terms of thinking about business strategy issues than books on business strategy."[28] Peters' remark is particularly applicable to the creation of promotional messages. Figure 1.7 demonstrates the use of creativity to communicate that Duke Energy has the power to become a global energy leader, no matter which way the wind blows.

The Technology Revolution in Marketing

As we move through the opening decade of the 21st century, we also enter a new era in communication, considered by some as unique as the 15th-century invention of the printing press or the first radio and television broadcasts early in the 20th century. *Technology* is the business application of knowledge based on scientific discoveries, inventions, and innovations. Interactive multimedia technologies such as computer networks, video conferencing, online services and the Internet, interactive kiosks, CD-ROM catalogs, and personal digital assistants (PDAs) have revolutionized the way people store, distribute, retrieve, and present information. Computer networks and other telecommunications technologies link employees, suppliers, and customers in different locations through the Internet or in-house intranets.

These technological advances are revolutionizing marketing. Companies can reach specific groups of customers in a variety of ways: from hotels' in-house television channels targeting guests to toll-free telephone numbers and in-store videos with point-of-purchase product demonstrations. Now that half

6

Outline the changes in the marketing environment due to technology.

SIRIUS// 100 STREAMS OF SATELLITE RADIO

commercials_OFF
music_ON

SIRIUS it's_ON

Satellite radio giants Sirius and XM offer subscribers 100 commercial-free channels of music, news, talk, and sports for their cars at about the same price that cable viewers pay to tune in weekly installments of *The Sopranos* and similar fare on HBO. Market growth is being aided by the growing number of automakers who offer this feature in their new models.

of all U.S. households have personal computers, online services and the Internet offer a new medium over which companies can market products and offer customer service. Marketing and sales departments can quickly access vast databases with information about customers and their buying patterns. They can develop targeted marketing campaigns and zoned advertising programs for consumers located within a certain distance from a store and even within specific city blocks.

Shoppers can visit kiosks in shopping malls that feature video displays, discount coupons, and product information for a variety of merchants. They can browse through a CD-ROM product catalog on their computers or conduct specific searches to quickly find desired items. Surfing the Web or online services is another way to get product information and order merchandise from catalogs. Firms can quickly update this information at minimal costs. Online retail spending in the U.S. is growing at an astounding rate—from $7.8 billion in 1998 to $100 billion in 2003. Consumers' willingness to spend online is growing—as is the amount they spend on each visit, despite the sluggish economy. More women are now shopping online than men, and shoppers are now looking for a greater range of products. "In the past, online shopping was all about books, videos, and music," observes Rob Solomon of Yahoo! "Now shoes, watches, and all sorts of apparel items are moving into the top categories."[29] Still, the most popular items at MSN's eShop include digital cameras, personal digital assistants, and MP3 players. All of these changes represent opportunities for marketers.

Interactive Marketing

Interactive media technologies combine computers and telecommunications resources to create software that users can direct themselves. They allow people to digitize reports and drawings and transmit them, quickly and inexpensively, over phone lines, coaxial cables, or fiber-optic cables. People can subscribe to personalized news services that deliver article summaries on specified topics directly to their fax machines or computers. They can telecommunicate via e-mail, voice mail, fax, videoconferencing, and computer networks; pay bills using online banking services; and use online resources to get information about everything from investments to a local retailer's special sale, day-care facilities, and local entertainment activities for the upcoming weekend.

Companies are now using interactivity in their marketing programs. **Interactive marketing** refers to buyer-seller communications in which the customer controls the amount and type of information received from a marketer. This technique provides immediate access to key product information when the consumer wants it. Interactive techniques have been used for more than a decade; point-of-sale brochures and coupon dispensers are a simple form of interactive advertising. Want to go skiing tomorrow? Log on to the Web site of your favorite mountain and you may be offered a coupon for a free lift ticket. Want to try a new restaurant? Check the Web site for a coupon offering a free appetizer. Interactive marketing also includes two-way electronic communication using a variety of media such as the Internet, CD-ROMs, and virtual reality kiosks.

Interactive marketing allows marketers and customers to customize their communication. Customers may come to companies for information, creating opportunities for one-to-one marketing. Interactive marketing can also allow many-to-many exchanges, where consumers can communicate with one another using e-mail or electronic bulletin boards. These electronic conversations establish innovative relationships between users and the technology, providing customized information based on users' interests and levels of understanding. Interactive technologies support almost limitless exchanges of information.

One of the busiest areas of interactive marketing is online auctions and name-your-own-price vendors. Ebay, the online auction house, connects sellers and buyers directly—millions of them daily. Consumers who want to name their own price for airline tickets, hotel rooms, cruises, and rental cars can do so at a variety of sites. Budget Car Rental was the first in the car rental industry to establish an interactive price bidding feature, the BidBudget program. Online bidders simply fill out a form indicating the desired dates and airport pickup location, preferred car type, contact information, a major credit-card number, and the price they are willing to pay. Budget notifies the bidder within 24 hours whether a bid is accepted and offers a money-back guarantee up to 48 hours before the pick-up time.[30]

Interactive promotions put the customer in control. Consumers can easily get tips on product usage and answers to customer service questions, they can also tell the company what they like or dislike about a product, and they can just as easily click the exit button and move on to another area. As interactive promotions grow in number and popularity, the challenge will be attracting and holding consumer attention.

The Internet

Most of today's discussion of interactive marketing centers on the Internet. The **Internet** is an all-purpose global network composed of some 50,000 different networks around the globe that, within limits, lets anyone with access to a personal computer send and receive images and text anywhere.

The Internet provides an efficient way to find and share information, but until the last decade, most people outside universities and government agencies found it difficult to use and learn. This changed in 1993 with the advent of browser technology that provides point-and-click access to the **World Wide Web (WWW** or **Web).** The Web is actually an interlinked collection of graphically rich information sources within the larger Internet. Web sites provide hypermedia resources, a system allowing storage of and access to text, graphics, audio, and video in so-called pages linked to each other in a way that integrates these different media elements. When a user clicks on a highlighted word or picture (icon), the browser converts the click to computer commands and brings the requested new information—text, photograph, chart, song, or movie clip—to the user's computer.

Compared with traditional media, the hypermedia resources of the Web offer a number of advantages. Data moves in seconds, without the user noticing that several computers in different locations combine to fulfill a request. Interactive control allows users to quickly access other information resources through related pages, either at the same or other sites, and easily navigate through documents. Because it is dynamic, Web site sponsors can easily keep information current. Finally, multimedia capacities increase the attractiveness of these documents.

Broadband

Broadband technology—an always-on Internet connection that runs at a speed of 200 kilobytes per second or higher—can deliver large amounts of data at once, making online marketing even faster and easier than it was a few years ago. Consumers can access Web pages and sites can process credit card purchases much quicker via broadband. The number of households with broadband connections is increasing rapidly, as people grow impatient with the old, slower "dial-up" Internet connections. By 2003, more than 18 million U.S. households (nearly 30 percent of all online U.S. households) used a broadband Internet connection, even though subscription costs remained about double that of traditional dial-up connections. "These technologies are going to be moving from novelties to integrated tools," predicts Glenn McClanan, director of broadband initiatives for Edmunds .com, a California-based auto shopping information site that offers free downloads of informational video clips.[31]

Wireless

More and more consumers now have *wireless* Internet connections for their laptop computers and personal digital assistants, which is both a

Marketing Dictionary

interactive marketing Buyer-seller communications in which the customer controls the amount and type of information received from a marketer.

Internet All-purpose global network of 50,000 different networks that, within limits, lets anyone with access to a personal computer send and receive images and text anywhere.

World Wide Web (WWW or **Web)** Interlinked collection of graphically rich information sources within the larger Internet.

broadband technology Extremely high speed, always-on Internet connection.

challenge and an opportunity for marketers. By 2003, the number of U.S. consumers with these connections had passed the 30 million mark, a 100 percent increase in a single year. Although wireless advertising is still in its infancy, industry watchers predict that wireless ad revenues will reach $700 million by 2005.[32] This high-tech form of advertising has been slower to catch on with marketers because of the relatively high cost—$40 to $50 per thousand impressions, compared with $2 to $3 for a banner ad on the Web. But wireless ads offer tremendous potential to target certain audiences. And since these ads appear by themselves on a PDA user's screen, they command more attention than a banner ad would. Currently, wireless carriers put a limit on how much wireless advertising they allow, for fear of alienating their own customers if they are bombarded with unneeded—and unwanted—information. Also, the speed of data transfer via wireless Internet service is not quite where it needs to be in order to handle this type of communication on a regular basis. But marketers would do well to prepare for this next generation of advertising.

Interactive Television Service

Interactive Television (iTV) service is another new technology for marketers and consumers alike to embrace. Interactive television service is a package that includes a return path for viewers to interact with programs or commercials by clicking their remote controls. The 18 million U.S. TV viewers who have iTV can request additional information about products or actually purchase them without having to dial their phones. Companies such as Ford have already incorporated iTV into their marketing programs.[33]

How Marketers Use the Web

The Web offers marketers a powerful, yet affordable way to reach customers across town or overseas, at almost any time, with interactive messages. The online techniques that companies use to market their businesses fall into four broad categories: virtual storefronts, interactive brochures, online newsletters, and customer service tools.

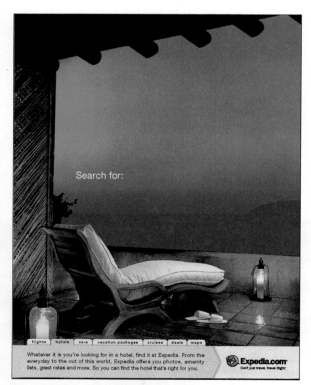

The Web is a powerful, affordable way to reach consumers anywhere, anytime.

- The virtual storefront allows customers to view and order merchandise. Amazon.com and eBay are two of the largest such sites. Web stores can be stand-alone operations or grouped in cybermalls with links to 30 to 100 participating retailers. The Internet service provider Yahoo! operates such a mall.

  After the initial rush to establish a virtual storefront, many retailers are backing off because they have discovered that their customers are either not interested in shopping for their products online or their product offerings just don't lend themselves to online shopping. Ames Department Stores learned that customers would rather run into the store to pick up the small items it sells; Ikea reasoned that the shipping costs it would have to charge to send its furniture items to online shoppers would undermine the store's low prices. Such companies instead set up Web sites that act as information clearinghouses, providing in-depth product information. Shoppers can ask questions and get online answers, and companies can hold virtual meetings (online conferences) and sponsor discussion groups. Not-for-profit organizations use this tool as well. The World Wildlife Fund (WWF) maintains a Web site that provides information about the organization and its conservation activities. With 4.7 million supporters and a global network active in over 100 countries, WWF's primary mission is to protect nature. Site visitors can obtain membership information and learn about publications, fund-raising campaigns, educational programs, and current conservation issues facing the world today.

'net-x

How marketers use the Web. Commerce Net promotes itself as "the premier global industry consortium for companies using, promoting, and building electronic solutions on the Internet." Review the Web site (**http://www.commerce.net**) and then prepare a list of three to five specific pieces of information to use in a class discussion on the topic "How Marketers Use the Web."

- Interactive brochures that provide company and product information are popular Internet marketing applications. These range from simple, one-page electronic flyers to multimedia presentations. When American Airlines' travelers need information, they can simply log on to AA.com to get instant access to their AAdvantage account, browse programs and services, make reservations, and check out special benefits available to them as members of American's frequent flyer programs.

- Online newsletters provide current news, industry information, and contacts and links for internal and external customers. *Web Commerce Today*, a monthly online newsletter, helps merchants plan, design, manage, and promote retail or business-to-business Web stores.

- The Web is also a customer service tool. Consumers can order catalogs, refer to lists of frequently asked questions with answers, place orders online, and send questions to company representatives. For instance, they can access many Kraft Foods Web sites, such as jell-o.com, to obtain information on Kraft's many products, learn new recipes, ask questions about cooking, and even buy merchandise online.

A colorful, dynamic, user-friendly Web site is not enough to ensure cyberspace success. The online marketer must convince potential customers to visit the site. A common method of generating traffic is to advertise on heavy-traffic sites like directories and search engines such as Yahoo! and AOL.

The Web is probably the most significant innovation affecting marketing and business in the past 50 years. Properly used, it should prove an indispensable tool in promoting connections, building associations, delivering information, and creating online communities.

However, to date, few companies have made money on the Internet—and many have lost a bundle. The primary beneficiaries have been firms marketing Net-related goods or services—for example, computer networking equipment; software such as access, browser, Web page authoring, and e-mail programs; consultants and Web page creators; Internet access and online service providers like PsiNet, Netcom, America Online, and CompuServe; and companies offering sites where businesses can advertise.

As fast as the first tidal wave of Internet-based companies—dot.coms—rose, it crashed, drowning most of the firms that thought they were going to ride the wave to riches. Even companies that became household names, like Pets.com and eToys, fell victim to the flood. The online auction house eBay was the only major online merchant to show a profit, while Monster.com and E*Trade survived but remained in the red. As the Web evolves, marketers need to explore its capabilities and learn the best ways to use it effectively in combination with other distribution channels and communications media. Among the questions marketers need to ask are the following:

- What types of goods and services can be successfully marketed on the Web?

- What characteristics make a successful Web site?

- Does the Internet offer a secure way to process customer orders?

- How will Internet sales affect traditional store-based and non-store retailing and distribution?

- What is the best use of this technology in a specific firm's marketing strategy: promotion, image building, or sales?

The importance of the Internet is reflected throughout this text, and as forthcoming chapters discuss specific marketing topics, we will revisit the Internet and its related technologies to look for answers to the preceding questions.

7

Explain the shift from transaction-based marketing to relationship marketing.

From Transaction-Based Marketing to Relationship Marketing

As marketing progresses through the 21st century, a significant change is taking place in the way companies interact with customers. The traditional view of marketing as a simple exchange process, or *transaction-based marketing*, is being replaced by a different, longer-term approach. Traditional marketing strategies focused on attracting customers and closing deals. Today's marketers realize that, although it's important to attract new customers, it's even more important to establish and maintain a relationship with them so they become loyal repeat customers. These efforts must expand to include suppliers and employees, as well.

As defined earlier in this chapter, relationship marketing refers to the development, growth, and maintenance of long-term, cost-effective exchange relationships with individual customers, suppliers, employees, and other partners for mutual benefit. It broadens the scope of external marketing relationships to include suppliers, customers, and referral sources. In relationship marketing, the term *customer* takes on a new meaning. Employees serve customers within an organization as well as outside it; individual employees and their departments are customers of and suppliers to one another. They must apply the same high standards of customer satisfaction to intradepartmental relationships as they do to external customer relationships. Relationship marketing recognizes the critical importance of internal marketing to the success of external marketing plans. Programs that improve customer service inside a company also raise productivity and staff morale, resulting in better customer relationships outside the firm.

Relationship marketing gives a company new opportunities to gain a competitive edge by moving customers up a loyalty hierarchy from new customers to regular purchasers, then to loyal supporters of the firm and its goods and services, and finally to advocates who not only buy its products but recommend them to others, as shown in Figure 1.8.

By converting indifferent customers into loyal ones, companies generate repeat sales. As pointed out earlier in this chapter, the cost of maintaining existing customers is far below the cost of finding new ones, and these loyal customers are profitable ones. In fact, creating loyal customers can mean the difference between flying and remaining grounded. Air travel plummeted in the aftermath of September 11, 2001, causing the nation's air carriers to suffer tremendous losses, despite a federal bail-out. While most airlines chose the cost-cutting path, eliminating onboard meals and in-flight movies, closing ticket offices and airport clubs, and suspending any construction projects, Continental decided to push ahead. CEO Gordon M. Bethune reasoned that cabin comforts and customer service, part of building relationships with passengers, were more important than making a couple of extra bucks from each passenger. Understanding and acknowledging passenger safety concerns, Continental added security checkpoints and self-service check-in kiosks. The airline offered free in-flight movies and free drinks at its airport clubs—which it kept open. Bethune authorized more than a month of overtime pay to construction workers in order to complete an expanded terminal at Newark International Airport, which was vital to Continental's presence in the New York area. Then Continental launched a commuter-train service, making it easier for New York passengers to get to the new terminal. Within a couple of months, the results of this relationship building were evident. While all the big U.S. airlines incurred billions in losses during those difficult times, Continental's losses were minimal compared with its competitors. And by the end of the year, its planes carried a higher percentage of passengers than those of its rivals, who had grounded many of their nearly empty flights.[34]

Programs to encourage customer loyalty are not new. Frequent purchaser rewards for everything from clothing to groceries are popular examples. Firms in the service industries are among the leaders in building such relationships. Visa teams up with Holiday Inn resorts and hotels during peak vaca-

FIGURE 1.8
Converting New Customers to Advocates

tion months. Holiday Inn advertisements target families, offering a "kids eat free, stay free" program. In addition, travelers who use their Visa cards to stay at one of over 1,000 participating hotels receive a Kids' Activity Book with valuable coupons. Customers who use their Holiday Inn Visa for any purchase receive points for upgrades and free nights at Holiday Inns.

Effective relationship marketing relies heavily on information technologies such as computer databases that record customers' tastes, price preferences, and lifestyles. This technology helps companies become one-to-one marketers who gather customer-specific information and provide individually customized goods and services. The firms target their marketing programs to appropriate groups, rather than having to rely on mass-marketing campaigns. Companies who study customer preferences and react accordingly gain distinct competitive advantages.

Developing Partnerships and Strategic Alliances

Relationship marketing does not apply just to individual consumers and employees, however. It also affects a wide range of other markets, including business-to-business relationships with the firm's suppliers and distributors as well as other types of corporate partnerships. In the past, companies have often viewed their suppliers as adversaries against whom they must fiercely negotiate prices, playing one off against the other. But this attitude has changed radically, as both marketers and their suppliers discover the benefits of collaborative relationships.

The formation of **strategic alliances**—partnerships that create competitive advantages—is also on the rise. These take many forms, from product development partnerships that involve shared costs for research and development and marketing to vertical alliances in which one company provides a product or component to another firm who then distributes or sells it under its own brand. Starbucks follows its customers' tastes by forming alliances with other businesses. Several years ago, the coffee giant made a deal with Dreyer's Ice Cream to create five coffee-flavored ice creams. Then it formed an alliance with PepsiCo to create the leading bottled coffee drink, Frappuccino. Shoppers can find Starbucks products in Marriott's airport hotels, Albertson's supermarkets, and Barnes & Noble bookstore cafes—all the result of strategic alliances. These partnerships now rake in an additional $20 million a year in earnings for Starbucks.[35]

Not-for-profit organizations often make use of strategic alliances in order to raise awareness and funds for their causes. In Figure 1.9, Stride Rite and Save the Children have teamed up in a combined effort to increase shoe sales and raise money for needy children.

Relationship building begins early in marketing, beginning with high-quality products and continuing with excellent customer service during and after purchase. It also includes programs that encourage repeat purchases and foster customer loyalty. Marketers may try to rebuild damaged relationships with these practices also, as "Marketing Misses" explains.

Briefly Speaking

I get by with a little help from my friends.

John Lennon (1940–1980) and Paul McCartney (b. 1942) English songwriters

There are moments when the choices you make count a little more.

stride rite.

You can help us help the kids who have the least. For every pair of this special footwear sold, Stride Rite will make a donation to Save the Children.

Save the Children.

FIGURE 1.9
Stride Rite and Save the Children: Working Together to Market Shoes and Raise Money for Needy Children

Marketing Dictionary

strategic alliance Partnership formed to create or maintain a competitive advantage.

8

Identify the universal functions of marketing.

Marketing Miss

Americans Take the French out of Fries

Background. When pre–Iraq war tensions between the U.S. and France intensified, a sign appeared in a government cafeteria: "Now Serving . . . In All House Office Buildings Freedom Fries." Soon, "freedom fries"—instead of french fries—were being served at public eateries around the country. Then along came "liberty dressing" instead of French dressing. And millions of Americans began boycotting everything French—from wine to Perrier—to express their support for American troops in Iraq and their displeasure with the French government's antiwar stance.

The Marketing Problem. Two sets of marketers had a problem to solve during this boycott: those who offered authentically French products and those whose product names only sounded French. Owners of French restaurants, makers of French wines, and French companies such as Dannon and L'Oréal suffered from the boycott. But consumers also mistook Estée Lauder, Grey Poupon, and Yoplait to be French in origin— these companies are actually American. The French Government Tourist Office estimated a $500 million loss in American tourism business. "We're going to talk directly to the American people," said Robin Massee, a tourism spokeswoman for France.

The Outcome. The French Government Tourist Office conducted surveys, which showed that more than 66 percent of Americans who changed their travel plans to

continued on next page

Costs and Functions of Marketing

Firms must spend money to create time, place, and ownership utilities. Numerous attempts have been made to measure marketing costs in relation to overall product costs, and most estimates have ranged between 40 and 60 percent of total costs. On the average, one-half of the costs involved in a product, such as a Subway sandwich, an ounce of Safari perfume, a pair of Steve Madden shoes, or even a European vacation, can be traced directly to marketing. These costs are not associated with fabrics, raw materials and other ingredients, baking, sewing, or any of the other production functions necessary for creating form utility. What, then, does the consumer receive in return for this 50 percent marketing cost? What functions does marketing perform?

As Figure 1.10 reveals, marketing is responsible for the performance of eight universal functions: buying, selling, transporting, storing, standardizing and grading, financing, risk taking, and securing marketing information. Some functions are performed by manufacturers, others by retailers, and still others by marketing intermediaries called *wholesalers*.

Buying and selling, the first two functions shown in Figure 1.10, represent *exchange functions*. *Buying* is important to marketing on several levels. Marketers must determine how and why consumers buy certain goods and services. To be successful, they must try to understand consumer behavior. In addition, retailers and other intermediaries must seek out products that will appeal to their customers. Since they generate time, place, and ownership utilities through these purchases, marketers must anticipate consumer preferences for purchases to be made several months later. *Selling* is the second half of the exchange process. It involves advertising, personal selling, and sales promotion in an attempt to match the firm's goods and services to consumer needs.

Transporting and storing are *physical distribution functions*. *Transporting* involves the physical movement of goods from the seller to the purchaser. Storing involves warehousing goods until they are needed for sale. Manufacturers, wholesalers, and retailers all typically perform these functions.

The final four marketing functions—standardizing and grading, financing, risk taking, and securing marketing information—are often called *facilitating functions* because they assist the marketer in performing the exchange and physical distribution functions. Quality and quantity control *standards* and grades, frequently set by federal or state governments, reduce the need for purchasers to inspect each item. Specific tire sizes, for example, permit buyers to request needed sizes and to expect uniform sizes.

Financing is another marketing function because buyers often need access to funds in order to finance inventories prior to sales. Manufacturers often provide financing for their wholesale and retail customers. Some types of wholesalers perform similar functions for their retail customers. Finally, retailers frequently permit their customers to buy on credit.

The seventh function, *risk taking*, is part of most ventures. Manufacturers create goods and services based on research and their belief that consumers need them. Wholesalers and retailers acquire inventory based on similar expectations of future consumer demand. Entrepreneurial risk takers accommodate these uncertainties about future consumer behavior when they market goods and services.

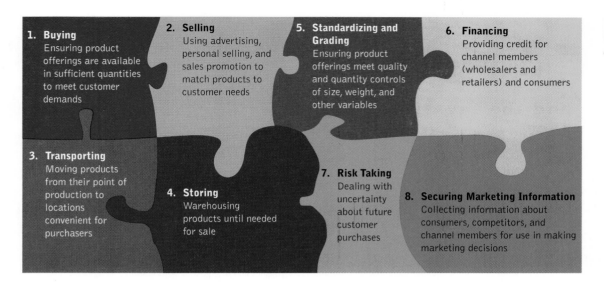

FIGURE 1.10
Eight Universal Marketing Functions

1. **Buying**
Ensuring product offerings are available in sufficient quantities to meet customer demands

2. **Selling**
Using advertising, personal selling, and sales promotion to match products to customer needs

3. **Transporting**
Moving products from their point of production to locations convenient for purchasers

4. **Storing**
Warehousing products until needed for sale

5. **Standardizing and Grading**
Ensuring product offerings meet quality and quantity controls of size, weight, and other variables

6. **Financing**
Providing credit for channel members (wholesalers and retailers) and consumers

7. **Risk Taking**
Dealing with uncertainty about future customer purchases

8. **Securing Marketing Information**
Collecting information about consumers, competitors, and channel members for use in making marketing decisions

The final marketing function involves *securing marketing information.* Marketers gather information to meet the need for decision-oriented input about customers—who they are, what they buy, where they buy, and how they buy. By collecting and analyzing marketing information, marketers also try to understand why consumers purchase some goods and services and reject others.

Ethics and Social Responsibility: Doing Well by Doing Good

While most companies do their best to abide by an ethical code of conduct, sometimes organizations and their leaders fall short. In recent years, headlines have publicized unethical conduct by several well-known businesses. In 1999, Microsoft Corp., which owns more than 90 percent of the PC operating-systems software market, was convicted of violating antitrust laws by abusing its monopoly to stifle competition and harm consumers. In late 2001, the Texas-based energy giant Enron collapsed, taking with it the retirement savings of its employees and investors. Enron's accounting firm, Arthur Andersen, was accused of shredding documents related to the fall of the company. And in 2002, chemical manufacturer Monsanto was convicted not only of polluting water sources and soil in a rural Alabama area for decades, but of ignoring evidence its own scientists had gathered indicating the extent and severity of the pollution.

Despite these and other alleged breaches of ethical standards, most businesspeople do follow ethical practices. Over half of all major corporations now offer ethics training to employees, and most corporate mission statements include pledges to protect the environment, contribute to communities, and improve workers' lives. Unfortunately though, in some cases, only media attention and pressure from consumers

right wrong   Solving an Ethical Controversy

Wi-Fi and the Invasion of Privacy

Wi-Fi—wireless Internet access—is one of the hottest new products. Some say this technology will transform everyday life in the 21st century. Individual consumers and businesspeople can now connect to the Internet via wireless technology at breakneck speeds, which is prompting companies like Dell, HP, Intel, Sony, and Toshiba to equip their laptops, PDAs, and other devices for it. So-called *hot* spots—now numbering 29,000 in the U.S. alone—are being added to attract customers in outlets ranging from Starbucks and Borders bookstores to McDonald's and Omni Hotels. But as always, when a new technology arrives, people question its side effects, in this case the security of wireless networks and the issue of privacy.

Does Wi-Fi contribute to the invasion of individual and business privacy?

PRO
1. The high speed of connection allows a greater number of users to interact simultaneously—and a greater potential for theft of information such as credit card numbers and Social Security numbers.

2. Most average users do not yet know how to secure their wireless connections to prevent hackers from gaining access.

CON
1. A Wi-Fi connection is no less secure than a traditional Internet connection or a phone call in which a consumer verbally supplies a credit card number to a sales representative.
2. Security systems are constantly being developed and will only improve as Wi-Fi technology is used more frequently by the general public.

Summary

Wi-Fi technology still has its glitches, including "dead" spots where service is not available and the potential for security vulnerabilities. Consumers and businesses who adopt Wi-Fi will have to become educated in its strengths and weaknesses, as well as in ways to protect themselves from vulnerability, until security measures catch up with the technology.

SOURCES: Nick Wingfield, "Wi-Fi Moochers," *The Wall Street Journal*, July 31, 2003, pp. B1, B2; Sky Dayton and David Worrell, "Wireless Wealth," *Entrepreneur*, July 2003, p. 92; Mark Anderson, "When It Comes to Wi-Fi, You Ain't Surfed Nothing Yet," *Fortune*, June 23, 2003, p. 134; Matthew Boyle, "The Wi-Fi Revolution," *Fortune*, May 12, 2003, pp. 86-92.

9

Demonstrate the relationship between ethical business practices and marketplace success.

motivate companies to implement social responsibility programs. The tobacco industry paid for an antismoking commercial during the 2002 Super Bowl, but the agreement to do so was part of a $205 billion settlement with 46 state attorneys general in 1998.[36]

These programs often produce such benefits as improved customer relationships, increased employee loyalty, marketplace success, and improved financial performance. The National Basketball Association has a partnership with Reading Is Fundamental, in which the NBA holds NBA Reading Month and produces and airs public service announcements for reading. This socially responsible program helps develop relationships with the general public.[37] Timberland Co., the New Hampshire–based manufacturer of boots and other outdoor clothing featured in Figure 1.11, is well-known for its high ethical standards and socially responsible programs. The company donates large sums of money to charities each year, and its employees are given paid time off to volunteer for their favorite organizations—from the animal shelter to the local preschool.

Many companies of all types and sizes sponsor community-based programs. Phillips Petroleum expresses its commitment to reducing air pollution by reducing sulfur emissions in its refining processes. In its communications to shareholders, employees, customers, and the general public, the energy giant stresses its belief that not only does the human race benefit, but so do animals and vegetation.[38]

Because ethics and social responsibility are important topics to marketers, each chapter in this book includes a critical thinking box called "Solving an Ethical Controversy." This chapter's controversy deals with new wireless networking technology and the loss of privacy.

FIGURE 1.11
Timberland: Reminding Readers of Everyone's Capabilities

Strategic Implications of Marketing in the 21st Century

Unprecedented opportunities have emerged out of electronic commerce and computer technologies in business today. These advances and innovations have allowed organizations to reach new markets, reduce selling and marketing costs, and enhance their relationships with customers and suppliers. Business-to-business e-commerce has grown into a global market thanks to the Internet.

As a new universe for consumers and organizations is created, it demands new marketing approaches to meet changing environments and avoid being left behind in a desolate business world. Profit-seeking and not-for-profit organizations must broaden the scope of their activities to prevent myopic results in their enterprises.

As we begin the rapid journey on a course paved by information technology that leads to a global economy, many aspects of business will become extinct while others will be born. It seems everything is electronic these days: marketing, communications, entertainment, the economy, commerce, and business in general. While some have predicted the demise of traditional marketing and brick-and-mortar retailing, the majority feel that the world of electronic commerce will not eliminate but enhance the systems that exist today.

Marketers must be aware of today's customer-oriented environment and employ computer technologies to satisfy individual needs. One outcropping of this new electronic era is mass customization—providing unique product offerings to match the specific needs of individual buyers while also retaining the production efficiencies of mass-produced items. Five key trends that will influence consumer behavior include an environment ranging from do-it-yourself, no-service to full-service organizations; a strong emphasis on healthy, better-for-you purchases; more leisure activities with less effort and physical exertion; a shift to entrepreneurship; and a search for goods and services that save time in a multi-tasking society.

Marketers must understand that although consumers are empowered with unlimited accessibility to information, they still require quality and satisfaction in the products they purchase. Marketers must overcome barriers facing one-to-one interactive relations with their customers, be faster than the competition, and be able to adapt to changes when necessary. The future is in the Internet, using data, voice, optical, and wireless communications to help bring buyers and sellers together. After all, communication is the basis of all marketing activities.

Summary of Chapter Objectives

1. Explain how marketing creates utility through the exchange process.

Utility is the want-satisfying power of a good or service. Four basic kinds of utility exist: form, time, place, and ownership. Form utility is created when a firm converts raw materials and component inputs into finished goods and services. Marketing creates time, place, and ownership utilities.

2. Contrast marketing activities during the four eras in the history of marketing.

During the production era, the prevailing attitude was that quality products would sell themselves. In the sales era, the emphasis was on convincing people to buy. The marketing concept emerged during the marketing era, in which there was a companywide focus on consumer orientation with the objective of achieving long-term success. The relationship era focuses on establishing and maintaining relationships with customers and suppliers. Relationship marketing involves long-term, value-added relationships.

3. Define the marketing concept and its relationship to marketing myopia.

The marketing concept is a companywide consumer orientation with the objective of achieving long-run success. To many marketers, it means "Find a need and fill it—profitably." Marketing myopia is management's failure to recognize a company's scope of business.

4. Describe the characteristics of not-for-profit marketing.

Not-for-profit organizations operate in both public and private sectors. The biggest distinction between not-for-profits and commercial firms is the bottom line—whether the firm is judged by its profitability levels. A customer or service user of a not-for-profit organization may have less control over the organization's destiny than do customers of a profit-seeking firm. Not-for-profits often lack a clear organizational structure, but are conservative about spending.

5. Describe the five types of nontraditional marketing.

Person marketing focuses on efforts to cultivate the attention, interest, and preferences of a target market toward a celebrity or authority—celebrities from the world of entertainment or sports and political candidates. Place marketing attempts to attract visitors, potential residents, and businesses planning to relocate to a particular destination. Cause marketing identifies and markets a social issue, cause, or idea. Event marketing promotes sporting, cultural, charitable, or political activities. Organization marketing attempts to influence others to accept the organization's goals or services and contribute to it in some way.

6. Outline the changes in the marketing environment due to technology.

Technology by itself now constitutes one of the major elements of the marketing environment. Interactive marketing, the Internet, broadband, wireless, and iTV are all technological advances that can be used by marketers. These new technologies have spawned new industries and products, created new advertising opportunities, redefined competition, significantly impacted marketing mix decisions, and resulted in increased government supervision.

7. Explain the shift from transaction-based marketing to relationship marketing.

Relationship marketing represents a dramatic change in buyer-seller interactions from the previous transaction-based marketing that focused on a single transaction. The new focus on relationships gives a company new opportunities to gain a competitive edge by moving customers up a loyalty hierarchy from new customers to regular purchasers, then to loyal supporters and advocates. By converting new customers to loyal ones, companies generate repeat sales. Effective relationship marketing relies heavily on information technologies. It can also rely on developing strategic partnerships and alliances.

8. Identify the universal functions of marketing.

Marketing is responsible for eight universal functions, divided into three categories: (1) exchange functions (buying and selling); (2) physical distribution (transporting and storing); and

(3) facilitating functions (standardization and grading, financing, risk taking, and securing market information).

9. Demonstrate the relationship between ethical business practices and marketplace success.

Although some firms conduct themselves unethically in order to profit in the short run, programs that promote ethical behavior and social responsibility usually produce increased employee loyalty and a better public image for a firm. This image should also pay off in customer growth, since many buyers want to associate themselves—and be customers of—firms that exhibit high ethical standards and employ socially responsible corporate citizens.

Marketing Terms You Need to Know

utility 5	buyer's market 11	place marketing 17	World Wide Web 23
marketing 7	consumer orientation 11	cause marketing 17	broadband technology 23
exchange process 9	marketing concept 11	event marketing 18	strategic alliance 27
production orientation 9	relationship marketing 12	organization marketing 19	
sales orientation 10	marketing myopia 13	interactive marketing 22	
seller's market 11	person marketing 15	Internet 23	

Other Important Marketing Terms

bottom line 15	Interactive Television (iTV) 24	physical distribution
critical thinking 20	transaction-based	function 28
creativity 20	marketing 26	facilitating function 28
wireless technology 23	exchange function 28	

Review Questions

1. Identify the types of utility created by marketing. What types are created in each example?
   a. weekend mountain bike rental outlet
   b. one-hour photo developers
   c. Disney World
   d. Azalea Trail annual 10k race
   e. factory outlet shopping mall
2. Relate the definition of marketing to the concept of the exchange process.
3. How does relationship marketing expand the marketing concept? Why does marketing myopia occur?
4. Describe the major characteristics of not-for-profit marketing.
5. Which type of nontraditional marketing does each of the following illustrate?
   a. President Bush's efforts to attract enough voters to win reelection as president

   b. A two-page magazine ad with a photograph of Las Vegas
   c. A poster informing music lovers of an upcoming concert
   d. A recruitment ad for the National Guard
   e. A radio ad advising teenagers not to drink
6. What is the relationship between critical thinking and creativity?
7. In what ways is technology revolutionizing marketing?
8. How does the development of partnerships and alliances help create a competitive advantage through the building of relationships?
9. How do the exchange, physical distribution, and facilitating functions relate to each other?
10. How can organizations use ethical and socially responsible programs to gain a competitive edge in the marketplace?

Projects and Teamwork Exercises

1. Research a company that has been around awhile, such as Ford Motor Co., BellSouth, General Electric, or Kellogg, and write a brief description of what the firm's marketing focus would have been during each of these eras: production, sales, marketing, and relationship. (Teams can also work together by having a different person write the description of each era.)

2. Choose a company that interests you from the following list, or select one of your own. Research the company in the library or on the Internet to learn what seems to be the scope of its business. Write a brief description of the company's scope of business as it is now—and what it could be in five years, as you imagine it.

   General Mills
   Bank of America
   Marriott Hotels
   IBM

3. Choose a not-for-profit organization, such as the Environmental Protection Agency, United Way, American Heart Association, or the Metropolitan Opera, and design a cause or organization ad promoting its message.

4. Team up with one or more classmates to form a strategic alliance. Each group represents an organization—one to be for-profit, the other to be not-for-profit. Identify what business your organization is in, and formulate a plan for an advertisement, event, or some other promotion that would benefit both organizations.

5. Divide into two groups to discuss the ethical or socially responsible conduct of an organization that interests you: Arthur Andersen, the American Red Cross, Enron, Ford Motor Co., Patagonia, or Timberland. Research the organization on the Internet to come up with information to use in your debate.

'net Work

http://www.chrysler.com

http://www.ford.com

http://www.gm.com

http://www.honda.com

http://www.toyota.com

http://www.philips.com

http://www.patagonia.com

http://www.starbucks.com

1. Using the Net to market a product. All of the major automakers have Web sites. (Some examples are listed at the left.) Visit the Web sites of at least three. Compare and contrast how each uses the Web to market its products. Which of the three sites did you find to be the most effective? Defend your selection.

2. Operating globally. Philips, the Dutch electronics giant, is a global marketer. Visit the company's Web site to learn more about its global marketing efforts. Make a list of three interesting marketing facts that you learned about Philips.

3. Cause marketing. Locate a Web site for a company that supports a social cause in which you are interested. For example, Patagonia's Web site includes detailed descriptions of the company's environmental efforts. Starbucks' Web site contains information about the company's social efforts, including using its business to aid developing countries and depressed urban areas in the U.S. Write a brief report in which you identify the company, the social cause you researched, the effectiveness of the information presented, and your assessment of the fit between the marketer and the social cause being addressed.

Note: Internet Web addresses change frequently. If you don't find the exact sites listed, you may need to access the organization or company's home page and search from there.

CASE 1.1   Dracula Park Wants YOU

Need a vacation? Something you can really sink your teeth into? Ignore those ads for adventure trips to the Himalayas, for cruises to the Bahamas, for spring break in Florida. Romanian tourism minister Dam Matei Agathon wants to convert your need for a vacation into the desire to visit Transylvania—Dracula Park, in particular. Lest you think this $31.5 million park is on par with Dollywood or the upcoming theme park dedicated to the King (Elvis Presley), this development is no phantom—it's a serious venture. Romania wants tourists, and the country is banking on one of its most famous "residents" to draw people there. "We know the border between interesting and ridiculous," assures Marius Stoian, the tourism ministry's man in charge of the park. This park may be person and place marketing at its most extreme.

Officials hope the park will breathe new life into Romania's tourism industry. Many Americans have few associations with this Eastern European land beyond the ruinous regime of Nicolae Ceauşescu during the 1980s and, of course, Dracula. In addition, Transylvania has excellent name recognition among vampire enthusiasts.

Before Romania could show a single fang, the government had to buy the rights to Dracula's image from Universal Studios in Hollywood. That's because Dracula, the fictional character created by Irish novelist Bram Stoker in 1897, actually achieved fame through Universal's 1930s films based on his exploits, starring Bela Lugosi. Hollywood agreed, and construction on Dracula Park began near Sighisoara, a southern Transylvanian town of 37,000 believed to be the birthplace of Vlad Dracula.

What will visitors encounter during a visit to Dracula Park? Dracula Castle, of course—nestled among the oldest oaks in Europe. But park plans also include a sports arena and golf course, a theater, rides (like the Dracula carousel), a house of horrors, and a house of mirrors. Oh, and the Institute for Vampirology. "The center for vampirology will be there," says a spokesman for the local mayor's office. "A little train will connect it all." Tourism minister Dam Matei Agathon expands a bit: "We'll have Draculas who will walk, speak, fly, land." But it won't be ridiculous at all.

Agathon had to do a bit of marketing just to convince Romanians that this was a good idea. For a century, Romania has rejected the Bram Stoker and Hollywood versions of the vampire. Instead, they celebrated the historical vampire, Vlad Tepes, son of Vlad Dracul, as a heroic count who fought off Turkish invaders and brought law and order to this area of southeastern Europe in the 1400s. Vlad used wooden stakes to impale his foes, earning him a harsh reputation and the nickname Vlad the Impaler. "But he wasn't a vampire," says Sighisoara mayor Dorin Danesan. "That's silly." But Agathon, Danesan, and other Romanian officials recognized an opportunity to boost the economy of their tiny nation. "There's big money in Dracula all over the world—except in Romania," says Agathon. "I realized I had a world-renowned marketing icon that I could wrap in a ribbon and sell. So I came up with the idea of Dracula Park." Danesan agrees. "This myth, this legend, we must use."

Danesan predicts that the park will create at least 3,000 new jobs when it opens in 2004 and estimates that more than 1 million tourists will visit each year, generating $12 million in revenues. At the Dracula Bar and Grill, which is located in Vlad Dracul's old house, the curator of the current local museum, Adriana Antihi, is serious about the opportunities that the park will bring. "We respect Vlad Tepes for what he did," she explains, "and some people here are frightened that the park will be too full of kitsch. But we could use $300,000 for a new heating system in the museum." Even scholars are interested in the park. Raymond McNally, a professor of East European history at Boston College, is eager to visit. "It will be tricky for Romanians who treat Dracula as a national hero to define him as a vampire," he concedes. "But if you think the average tourist is going to Transylvania to find out about an obscure ruler from the 15th century, you've got to be kidding. For if you destroy the myth, you destroy the interest." And if you do that, the whole thing seems even sillier.

Questions for Critical Thinking

1. What kind(s) of utility does Dracula Park create?
2. What types of strategic alliances might Romania's ministry of tourism make in marketing Dracula Park?
3. Suggest a slogan for Dracula Park that focuses on person and/or place marketing, as well as converting needs to wants.

SOURCES: "Dracula Park Project Launched," "Romania Eyes Tourist Boom from Dracula Theme Park," and "Romanian Government Intends to Buy Dracula's Image from Hollywood," from the Dracula Park Web site, http://www.draculand.com, accessed January 21, 2003; Jayne Clark, "Dracula Theme Park Goes for the Jugular," USA Today, April 12, 2002, p. D4; Roger Thurow, "The Vampire Strikes Back: Romania Wants Bigger Cut of Dracula," The Wall Street Journal, October 30, 2001, p. A1.

VIDEO CASE 1.2   How Burton Snowboards Built a Sport—and a Customer Base

The written case on Burton Snowboards appears on page VC-2. The recently filmed Burton Snowboards video is designed to expand and highlight the concepts in this chapter and the concepts and questions covered in the written video case.

2

Strategic Planning and the Marketing Process

Chapter Objectives

1 Distinguish between strategic planning and tactical planning.

2 Explain how marketing plans differ at various levels in an organization.

3 Identify the steps in the marketing planning process.

4 Describe the concept of SWOT analysis and its major elements.

5 Discuss how a strategy can be implemented through marketing plans.

6 Identify the basic elements of a marketing strategy.

7 Describe the environmental characteristics that influence strategy decisions.

8 Explain how the strategic business unit concept, the market share/market growth matrix, the market attractiveness/business strength matrix, and spreadsheet analysis can be used in marketing planning.

Curves for Women: Strength in Numbers

Forget the fancy gyms with personal trainers, juice bars, saunas, and Olympic-size pools. They take precious time out of a busy woman's day—she may be juggling kids, a job, school, home, and other obligations—which means she hardly ever gets to the gym anyway. And they're expensive—far too pricey for a family already spending money on children's braces, saving for college tuition, and paying the mortgage. Instead, think of a quick workout, no frills, women in T-shirts and shorts (instead of multicolored Spandex), and low cost. Think Curves.

Curves International operates more than 5,000 Curves for Women fitness centers in all 50 U.S. states, Canada, and 6 other countries, making it the largest fitness franchise company in the world. It is also the fastest-growing franchise in the world, period. Curves specializes in the 30-minute, no-nonsense individual workout on 8 to 12 exercise machines—no Tae Bo classes, no aqua-aerobics, no yoga. The registration fee runs between $40 and $70, with a monthly fee of between $29 and $49, depending on where the center is located. These fees add up to a yearly cost of $388 to $658, compared with the thousands people spend at fancier gyms each year. No guys are allowed; the workouts are designed especially for women, and many of the franchises are owned by women who understand their customers.

The tremendous popularity and growth of Curves has marketers paying attention to what the company has done right. "A few years ago, this company called Curves started showing up on our lists," notes Maria Anton, executive editor of *Entrepreneur*. "We said, 'Whoa, where did this company come from?'" Much of the company's success comes from developing the right marketing plan at the right time. "They've carved out

a niche within the population that has never been served," explains Bill Howland, director of research for the International Health, Racquet, and Sports Association. "[Curves] has broken through the perception that you have to be fit, coordinated, and thin to go to a gym." Instead, Curves's 1 million members are women who want to lose a few pounds, get in better shape, and have more energy. While other workout centers cater to a market segment that demands luxury, Curves focuses on a larger segment—women with little time or money to spend on exercise routines. Whereas other fitness centers offer a wide variety of classes, workouts, and services, Curves offers only one. And while other franchises may cost hundreds of thousands or more—with enormous monthly fees afterward—a Curves franchise can be purchased for under $20,000 and a $395 monthly fee.

Curves cofounders Gary and Diane Heavin carved out their strategic plan in Houston, where Gary had already made and lost his first million by the age of 26. He had owned several traditional gyms and hit serious financial trouble when he tried to expand the company too quickly. So, when he and Diane launched the Curves chain, they took steps to keep costs down and grow at a rate that they could afford. The average Curves gym occupies only 1,200 square feet—other gyms may occupy ten times that much—and can turn a profit with as few as 200 members. The small space means that a Curves franchise can be located in a storefront in a strip mall, which not only costs a lot less than building a new freestanding building but also affords easy access to women who are doing other errands. Instead of focusing on fancy, expensive equipment and luxuries that take up more space and dollars, Curves owners emphasize personal attention to their customers. They create an atmosphere of fun for their clients—and also generates profits.

The Curves marketing philosophy is echoed by its franchise owners. "There really isn't somewhere [else] in town where you can get exercise, be done and gone in a half-hour," says Christy Bosanek, who owns a franchise in Yuba City, California. "Women need something that's easy to do and that's quick and fun, too." The cycle of workout stations, which provides stretch-

ing, aerobics, and strength training, helps women achieve their desired results, and the music system fills the workout area with exercise-motivating music interspersed with instructions to move to the next station.

The Heavins' planning appears to have paid off. Their company—which is still privately held—now accounts for 25 percent of all gyms in the U.S. and rakes in about $750 million a year. Although Curves faces competition from other gyms that have developed a similar formula, and some franchise owners worry that the company is growing so fast they may be competing against each other, the Heavins understand that their company's greatest strength lies in the women who own the franchises and the women who patronize them. "The fact is, I like to go," says one customer. That's the best kind of endorsement there is.[1]

Chapter Overview

- Given the success of recent retro models, should we add a similar model to our line of cars?

- Our lines of detergent are not moving according to the marketing plans. Should we seek lower entry-level price points from our vendors?

- Recent marketing research shows we are not reaching our customer target—women aged 30 to 50 with household incomes over $60,000. Should we reconsider our advertising agency pick?

These are strategic issues that marketers face every day. The marketplace changes continually in response to changes in consumer tastes and expectations, technological developments, competitors' actions, economic trends, and political and legal events, as well as product innovations and pressures from channel members. Although the causes of these changes often lie outside a marketer's control, effective planning can anticipate many of these changes. In fact, effective planning often means the difference between success and failure, something that the founders of Curves understand well.

This chapter provides an important foundation for thinking about all aspects of marketing by demonstrating the necessity for effective planning and gathering reliable information. These activities provide a structure within which a firm can take advantage of its unique strengths. Marketing planning identifies the markets a company can best serve as well as the most appropriate mix of approaches to satisfy the customers in those markets. This chapter examines marketing planning. Later, Chapter 7 discusses marketing research, the way marketers use the information they gather to make decisions, and sales forecasting—all of which are based on planning.

What Is Marketing Planning?

Everyone plans. We plan which courses we want to take, which movie we want to see, which outfit to wear to a party. We plan where we want to live, what career we want to pursue. Businesspeople engage in planning as well. **Planning** is the process of anticipating future events and conditions, and of determining the best way to achieve organizational objectives. Of course, before marketing planning can even begin, an organization must define its objectives. Planning is a continuous process that includes identifying objectives and then determining the actions through which a firm can attain these objectives. The planning process creates a blueprint for marketers, executives, production staff, and everyone else in the organization to follow for achieving organizational objectives. It also defines checkpoints so that people within the organization can compare actual performance with expectations to indicate whether current activities are moving the organization toward its objectives.

Marketing planning—implementing planning activities devoted to achieving marketing objectives—establishes the basis for any marketing strategy. Product lines, pricing decisions, selection of appropriate distribution channels, and decisions relating to promotional campaigns all depend on plans formulated within the marketing organization.

An important trend in marketing planning centers on relationship marketing. You will recall from Chapter 1 that this term refers to a firm's attempt to develop long-term, cost-effective links with individual customers and suppliers for mutual benefit. Good relationships with customers can arm a firm with vital strategic weapons. Many companies now include relationship-building goals and strategies in their plans. Nordstrom, the Seattle-based chain of fashion specialty retail stores illustrated in Figure 2.1, is legendary for its relationship marketing; in fact, the company has focused most of its marketing efforts in that direction. Sales staff routinely send thank-you notes to customers; they call customers when sought-after items arrive in the store; they answer the telephone within three rings; they lead customers to fitting rooms instead of just pointing them in the right direction. None of this activity takes place at random; it is all part of a plan to develop strong relationships with customers, and it works. Building relationships with consumers online requires planning, as well. On the company's Web site, keywords (words that customers have typed in to do a search) are analyzed to figure out what customers are looking for, in order to make the site easier for shoppers to navigate.[2]

Relationship marketers frequently maintain databases to track customer preferences. These marketers may also manipulate spreadsheets, discussed later in the chapter, to answer what-if questions related to prices and marketing performance.

Strategic Planning versus Tactical Planning

Planning is often classified on the basis of its scope or breadth. Some extremely broad plans focus on long-range organizational objectives that will significantly affect the firm for a period of five or more years. Other, more targeted plans cover the objectives of individual business units over shorter periods of time. The "Marketing Hit" box describes how McDonald's is using both strategic and tactical planning to win back customers.

FIGURE 2.1 Nordstrom's: Famous for Strong Customer Relationships

Briefly Speaking

Someone's sitting in shade today because someone planted a tree a long time ago.

Warren E. Buffett (b. 1930) American investor

1

Distinguish between strategic planning and tactical planning.

Marketing Dictionary

planning Process of anticipating future events and conditions, and of determining the best way to achieve organizational goals.

marketing planning Implementing planning activities devoted to achieving marketing objectives.

Marketing Hit

McDonald's Looks Beyond the Tactic of Price

Background. For several years, McDonald's has relied on price as a tactic to sell more burgers, fries, and shakes. But the price wars backfired. Instead of building brands and loyal customers, the 99-cent specials turned fast food into a commodity. People who want the cheapest food buy the cheapest thing on any menu.

The Challenge. McDonald's marketers know that they have to develop new strategies and tactics to win over a new generation of Ronald McDonald fans—and win back a generation that has strayed to competitors. A recent survey showed that food flavor, faster service, cleaner restaurants, and more upscale food offerings were most important to consumers. Nutrition and appeal to children ranked fairly low on the scale.

The Strategy. McDonald's marketers have already developed several ideas for attracting more diners. They've begun to position burgers and fries as "indulgence" foods or snacks instead of advertising them as a regular diet, and they are offering salads, which appeal to women. CEO Jim Cantalupo is on a crusade to improve service and cleanliness in restaurants, make menus simpler, and jazz up the flavor of McDonald's food. In addition, some restaurants now offer design-your-own deli sandwiches. In France, McDonald's is trying an experiment—redecorating in chic motifs, showing music videos, and offering local specialty sandwiches. Finally, there's the new advertising slogan—"I'm Lovin' It."

The Outcome. McDonald's new look is a hit in France, where marketers are "upgrading the experience, making McDonald's a

continued on next page

Strategic planning can be defined as the process of determining an organization's primary objectives and then adopting courses of action that will eventually achieve these objectives. This process includes, of course, allocation of necessary resources. The word *strategy* dates back to a Greek term meaning "the general's art." Strategic planning has a critical impact on a firm's destiny because it provides long-term direction for its decision makers.

Strategic planning is complemented by **tactical planning,** which guides the implementation of activities specified in the strategic plan. Unlike strategic plans, tactical plans typically address shorter-term actions that focus on current and near-future activities that a firm must complete to implement its larger strategies.

Mistakes in strategic decisions and in tactical planning are usually costly. Once-trendy Gap has been criticized for the past couple of years for some goofy styles—like flared capri pants—that shoppers aren't buying. Sales have dropped dramatically, but the company has continued with plans for expansion and long-term leases, making it difficult to cut costs. The company's long-term debt has mushroomed to $2 billion, damaging Gap's credit and stock ratings. The company's bankers and investors are not happy with the situation. "They'll have to give up something," says Gerald Hirschberg, an analyst at Standard & Poor's.[3]

Planning at Different Organizational Levels

2

Explain how marketing plans differ at various levels in an organization.

Planning is a major responsibility for every manager, so managers at all organizational levels devote portions of their workdays to planning. However, the amount of time spent on planning activities and the types of planning typically vary.

Top management—the board of directors, chief executive officers (CEOs), chief operating officers (COOs), and functional vice presidents, such as chief marketing officers—spend greater proportions of their time engaged in planning than do middle-level and supervisory-level managers. Also, top managers usually focus their planning activities on long-range strategic issues. In contrast, middle-level managers—such as advertising directors, regional sales managers, and marketing research managers—tend to focus on operational planning, which includes creating and implementing tactical plans for their own departments. Supervisors often engage in developing specific programs to meet goals in their areas of responsibility. Table 2.1 summarizes the types of planning undertaken at various organizational levels.

To be most effective, the planning process includes input from a wide range of sources—employees, suppliers, and customers. Monica Luechtefeld, head of Office Depot's online business, obtains information and feedback from a variety of people, in a variety of ways. She calls on customers and potential customers in person to learn what they might need or want. She communicates with purchasing managers, who are typically the people in companies who buy office equipment, supplies, and services. She studies customer-satisfaction surveys and e-mails. "I learn the most from the ones that challenge me," Luechtefeld comments. One thing she discovered from reading the surveys is that her customers care more about how easy the Office Depot Web site is to use than they do about cutting-edge technology. Based on this knowledge, she badgered Office Depot's tech staff to design an online network that even the most inexperienced customer could use.[4]

TABLE 2.1   Planning at Different Management Levels

Management Level	Types of Planning Emphasized at This Level	Examples
Top Management		
Board of directors Chief executive officer (CEO) Chief operating officer (COO) Divisional vice presidents	Strategic planning	Organization-wide objectives; fundamental strategies; long-term plans; total budget
Middle Management		
General sales manager Marketing research manager Advertising director	Tactical planning	Quarterly and semiannual plans; divisional budgets; divisional policies and procedures
Supervisory Management		
District sales manager Supervisors in staff Marketing departments	Operational planning	Daily and weekly plans; unit budgets; departmental rules and procedures

Steps in the Marketing Planning Process

3

Identify the steps in the marketing planning process.

The marketing planning process begins at the corporate level with the development of objectives. It then moves to develop procedures for accomplishing those objectives. Figure 2.2 shows the basic steps in the process. First, a company must define its mission. It then determines its objectives, assesses its resources, and evaluates environmental risks and opportunities. Guided by this information, marketers then formulate a marketing strategy, implement the strategy through operating plans, and gather feedback to monitor and adapt strategies when necessary.

Defining the Organization's Mission

The planning process begins with activities to define the firm's **mission,** the essential purpose that differentiates the company from others. The mission statement specifies the organization's overall goals and operational scope and provides general guidelines for future management actions. Adjustments in this statement reflect changing business environments and management philosophies.

Bass Pro Shops was founded in 1972 by tournament bass fisherman John L. Morris because he couldn't find a consistent source for the top-quality bass fishing gear he needed to pursue his sport. Since then, the company has been serving the more than 35 million U.S. anglers—nearly 70 percent of whom are men.

Marketing Hit

destination restaurant," says Denis Henniquen, CEO of the company's French unit. McDonald's marketers elsewhere hope their efforts will pay off in the same way. If consumers in the U.S. begin to think of McDonald's as a sit-down restaurant instead of just a drive through window, McDonald's marketers will be lovin' it.

SOURCES: Theresa Howard, "McDonald's Salads Lure Women," *USA Today*, June 16, 2003, p. B7; Bruce Horovitz, "Fast-Food Chains to Tempt Gourmet Palates," *USA Today*, June 3, 2003, p. 2B; Carol Matlack and Pallavi Gogoi, "What's This? The French Love McDonald's?" *BusinessWeek*, January 13, 2003, p. 50.

Marketing Dictionary

strategic planning   Process of determining an organization's primary objectives and adopting courses of action that will achieve these objectives.

tactical planning   Planning that guides the implementation of activities specified in the strategic plan.

mission   Essential purpose that differentiates one company from others.

FIGURE 2.2
The Marketing Planning Process

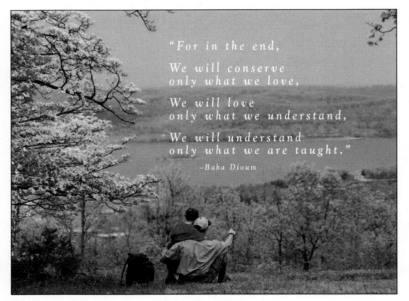

"For in the end,

We will conserve
only what we love,

We will love
only what we understand,

We will understand
only what we are taught."

—Baba Dioum

This Bass Pro Shops ad promotes not only outdoor recreation but also environmental conservation.

The company sells everything for freshwater and saltwater fishing—from rods, reels, and flies to apparel. They also sell a complete line of hunting, camping, and biking equipment and casual clothing. The company's mission statement is as follows: "To be the leading merchant of outdoor recreational products, inspiring people to love, enjoy, and conserve the great outdoors."[5]

Bass Pro Shops' mission is more than selling fishing gear; it is to inspire people to enjoy outdoor recreational activities and to preserve the natural environment. To that end, the company has made major contributions to, and has been honored by, various wildlife conservation organizations and causes, including a $100,000 commitment to the National Fish and Wildlife Foundation a couple of years ago. In addition, the company's Outdoor World retail stores, located in states across America, try to offer visitors a true "outdoor environment" while they are shopping for products.

Determining Organizational Objectives

An organization lays out its basic objectives, or goals, in its mission statement. These objectives in turn guide development of supporting marketing objectives and plans. Soundly conceived objectives should state specific intentions (for example, generate a 12 percent increase in profits over last year, attain a 20 percent share of the market by 2008, or increase sales 15 percent over last year). In addition, these objectives should specify the time periods for specific achievements.

Assessing Organizational Resources and Evaluating Environmental Risks and Opportunities

The third step of the marketing planning process involves a back-and-forth assessment of an organization's strengths, weaknesses, and available opportunities. Organizational resources include the capabilities of the firm's production, marketing, finance, technology, and employees. An organization's planners pinpoint its strengths and weaknesses. Strengths help them to set objectives, develop plans for meeting those objectives, and take advantage of marketing opportunities. Malden Mills, maker of Polarfleece and Polartec fabrics, can identify several strengths: 200 percent growth in the past decade; customers in more than 50 countries; U.S. factory operations; high visibility, with appearances in *People*, on *Dateline*, and in the Lands' End catalog; and customer *and* employee retention above 95 percent. Its weaknesses include the high cost of manufacturing in the U.S.; a devastating factory fire; and an increase in competition.[6]

Chapter 3 will discuss environmental factors that affect marketing opportunities. Environmental effects can emerge both from within the organization and from the external environment. For example, the World Wide Web has transformed the way people communicate and do business.

Polartec and Polarfleece: Featured in Catalogs Like Lands' End

SWOT Analysis

An important strategic planning tool, the **SWOT analysis,** helps planners to compare internal organizational strengths and weaknesses with external opportunities and threats. (SWOT is an acronym for **s**trengths and **w**eaknesses, **o**pportunities, and **t**hreats.) This form of analysis provides managers with a critical view of the organization's internal and external environments and helps them to evaluate the firm's fulfillment of its basic mission.

A company's strengths reflect its *core competencies*—what it does well. Core competencies are capabilities that customers value and competitors find difficult to duplicate.[7] As Figure 2.3 shows, matching an internal strength with an external opportunity produces for the organization a situation known as leverage. Marketers face a problem when environmental threats attack their organization's weaknesses. Planners anticipate constraints when internal weaknesses or limitations prevent their organization from taking advantage of opportunities. These internal weaknesses can create vulnerabilities for a company—environmental threats to its organizational strength.

4

Describe the concept of SWOT analysis and its major elements.

The Strategic Window

Professor Derek Abell has suggested the term **strategic window** to define the limited periods during which the key requirements of a market and the particular competencies of a firm best fit together.[8] The view through a strategic window shows planners a way to relate potential opportunities to company capabilities. Such a view requires a thorough analysis of (1) current and projected external environmental conditions, (2) current and projected internal company capabilities, and (3) how, whether, and when the firm can feasibly reconcile environmental conditions and company capabilities by implementing one or more marketing strategies.

Apple Computer took advantage of a strategic window when it introduced its new iMac, which contains its new operating system, the Mac OS X. The new computer appears in the ad in Figure 2.4, which shows a highly streamlined machine that allows users to perform a number of cutting-edge tasks, including getting the most out of their digital cameras. When a digital camera is plugged into iMac's USB port, software called iPhoto automatically imports the photos, catalogs them, stores them, and displays them on the computer screen. Apple planners noted that while people were buying digital cameras, they were having trouble storing, sending, and displaying the photos. So they leapt through the strategic

Marketing Dictionary

SWOT analysis   Analysis that helps planners compare internal organizational strengths and weaknesses with external opportunities and threats.

strategic window   Limited periods during which the key requirements of a market and the particular competencies of a firm best fit together.

FIGURE 2.3
SWOT Analysis

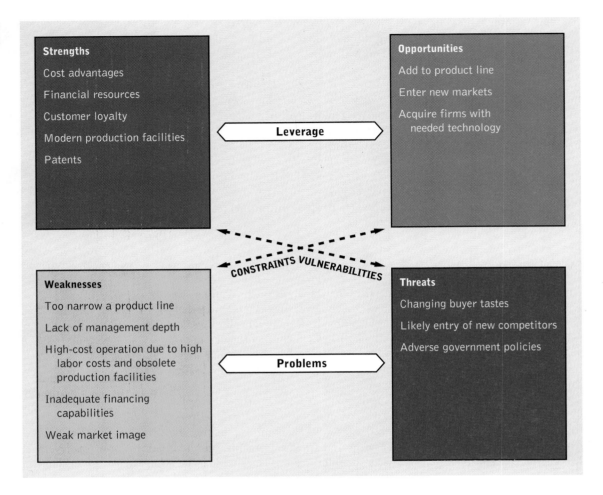

Strengths

Cost advantages

Financial resources

Customer loyalty

Modern production facilities

Patents

Opportunities

Add to product line

Enter new markets

Acquire firms with needed technology

Leverage

CONSTRAINTS VULNERABILITIES

Weaknesses

Too narrow a product line

Lack of management depth

High-cost operation due to high labor costs and obsolete production facilities

Inadequate financing capabilities

Weak market image

Threats

Changing buyer tastes

Likely entry of new competitors

Adverse government policies

Problems

FIGURE 2.4
Apple Computer's
New iMac

The new iMac.

15" LCD flat screen. 800-MHz G4. CD/DVD-burning SuperDrive. Like nothing before. From $1,299.

window with a software product—iPhoto—linked to the capabilities of its new hardware product—the iMac.

Formulating a Marketing Strategy

Opportunity analysis culminates in the formulation of marketing objectives designed to achieve overall organizational objectives and to help planners develop a marketing plan. The marketing plan revolves around a resource-efficient, flexible, and adaptable marketing strategy.

A marketing strategy is an overall, company-wide program for selecting a particular target market and then satisfying consumers in that market through a careful balance of the elements of the marketing mix—product, price, distribution, and promotion—each of which is a subset of the overall marketing strategy.

Implementing a Strategy through Marketing Plans

5

Discuss how a strategy can be implemented through marketing plans.

In the two final steps of the marketing-planning process, marketers use operating plans to put the marketing strategy into action; then they monitor performance to ensure that objectives are being achieved. Sometimes strategies need to be modified if the product's or company's actual performance is not in line with expected results.

Consider what happened at Cisco Systems. Just a couple of years ago, the company was riding high on the wave of a surging economy. Deregulation of the U.S. telecommunications industry, along with a healthy stock market and the boom of the Internet, propelled Cisco and hundreds of other companies into a whole new industry and economy. Cisco's core business is selling software and hardware used in powering Internet networks. But Cisco's bold strategy of pursuing new service providers as customers turned out to be the wrong move. As each of these new companies began to stumble and fall, Cisco suffered a loss. By now, not only have these companies slowed their spending on products that Cisco provides, but many have also simply gone under. Meanwhile, Cisco ignored or alienated some of the larger, "old economy" phone companies. In addition, planners were overly optimistic about the demand for Cisco's equipment, and the company was stuck with inventory it couldn't sell. Today, Cisco is focusing its attention on the more established telecommunications companies and is dedicating more sales and technical support staff to give better service to a smaller number of customers. The strategy now is to focus on helping existing phone companies develop value-added services that their own corporate customers desire. Senior Vice President William Nuti says, "We're going to get back to basics in terms of listening to our customers and responding to what their needs are."[9]

As Cisco's experience shows, the overall strategic marketing plan serves as the basis for a series of operating plans necessary to move the organization toward accomplishing its objectives. Marketing planning affects activities discussed throughout this text, including analysis and selection of a target market and development of a marketing mix designed to satisfy that market.

Elements of a Marketing Strategy

Although the product at the center of a marketing campaign may consist of a tangible good or an intangible service, cause, event, person, place, or organization, success in the marketplace always depends on an effective marketing strategy. The basic elements of a marketing strategy consist of (1) the target market and (2) the marketing mix variables of product, distribution, promotion, and price that combine to satisfy the needs of the target market. The outer circle in Figure 2.5 lists environmental characteristics that provide the framework within which marketing strategies are planned.

The Target Market

A customer-driven organization begins its overall strategy with a detailed description of its *target market:* the group of people toward whom the firm decides to direct its marketing efforts, and ultimately its goods and services. For instance, Kohl's serves a target market consisting of consumers purchasing for themselves and their families. Other companies, such as Boeing, market most of their products to business buyers like American Airlines and government purchasers. Still other firms provide goods and services to retail and wholesale buyers. In every instance,

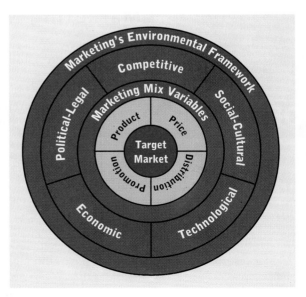

**FIGURE 2.5
Elements of a Marketing Strategy and Its Environmental Framework**

however, marketers should pinpoint their target markets as specifically as possible. Although the concept of actually dividing markets into segments is discussed in more detail in Chapter 8, it's important to understand the idea of targeting a market from the outset. Consider the following examples:

- Just My Size targets plus-size women (who account for over half of U.S. women) by designing casual wear, lingerie, hosiery, and jeans in sizes 16 and up.

- Build-a-Bear Workshop is a unique retailer in that it provides a setting for people of all ages to make their own stuffed bears. Founder Maxine Clark jokingly says her target market is aged 3 to 103.[10]

- The target market for Overseas Adventure Travel is well-educated, healthy individuals with household incomes over $50,000 who want a high-adventure vacation experience. When the Cambridge, Massachusetts–based travel company started 20 years ago, its target market was people in their twenties and thirties; today, OAT focuses on older customers who are retired, have the time and money to travel, and want adventure. The company now offers shorter trips with more amenities.

Diversity plays an ever-increasing role in targeting markets. According to the U.S. Census Bureau, the rapidly growing Hispanic population in the U.S. is now surpassing African Americans. The census reports about 35 million Hispanics in America, an increase of 58 percent in one decade; the African American population is roughly the same. "It's a little surprising," notes Hans Johnson, demographer with the Public Policy Institute of California in San Francisco. "But still, we've known the trends for some time. We know eventually Hispanics will become the largest minority group in the United States."[11] With this phenomenal growth, marketers would be wise to pay attention to these and other markets—including women, seniors, and children of baby boomers—as they develop goods and services to offer to consumers. Food manufacturers like General Mills and Bestfoods have enlisted the help of consultants to help them understand and develop products for the Hispanic market. Under their advice, the division that produces General Mills's Trix cereal sponsored a 17-city tour of an all-Hispanic circus, Trix Circo Mundial. Similarly, Bestfoods's grocery division took several of its brands that were already popular in the Hispanic market (including Mazola and Best Foods Mayonnaise) to Fiesta Broadway, an annual festival in Los Angeles.[12]

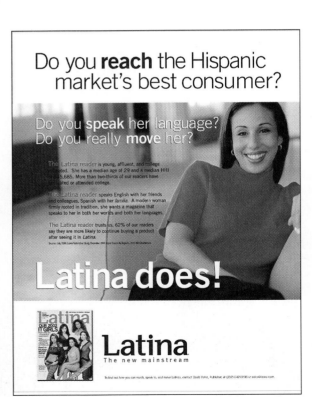

Hispanics are now the largest minority group in the U.S. A growing number of marketers use magazines such as *Latina* to reach this audience.

Marketing Mix Variables

After marketers select a target market, they direct their company's activities toward profitably satisfying that segment. Although they must manipulate thousands of variables to reach this goal, marketing decision making can be divided into four strategies: product, pricing, distribution, and promotion strategies. The total package forms the **marketing mix**—the blending of the four strategic elements to fit the needs and preferences of a specific target market. While the fourfold classification is useful to study and analyze, remember that the marketing mix can—and should—be an ever-changing combination of variables to achieve success.

Figure 2.5 illustrates the focus of the marketing mix variables on the central choice of the target market. In addition, decisions about product, price, distribution, and promotion are affected by the environmental factors in the outer circle of the figure. The environmental variables may play a major role in the success of a marketing program, and marketers must consider their probable effects.

Product Strategy

In marketing, the word *product* means more than a good, service, or idea. Product is a broad concept that also encompasses the satisfaction of all consumer needs in relation to a good, service, or idea. So **product strategy** involves more than just deciding what goods or services the firm should offer to a group of consumers. It also includes making decisions about customer service, package design, brand names, trademarks, patents, warranties, the life cycle of a product, positioning the product in the marketplace, and new product development. Figure 2.6 illustrates some of these elements. The ad for Lean Cuisine emphasizes Stouffer's ability to provide high quality, healthful food fast, as a way for the consumer to "do something good for yourself." The product is aimed at the busy person who wants to eat well but doesn't have time to cook. The ad even provides a Web address for consumers to learn more about Stouffer's Lean Cuisine foods. Lean Cuisine is a well-known, trademarked brand, and the packaging includes a photograph of a tasty-looking meal.

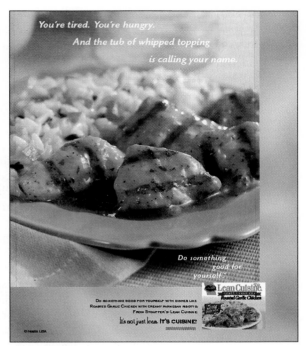

FIGURE 2.6
Stouffer's Lean Cuisine: Low-Fat, Easy-to-Prepare Meals in Attractive Packaging

The growing number of female business travelers has prompted the travel industry to modify its offerings by adding a number of services designed to increase satisfaction among women hotel guests. Based on suggestions by Wyndham Hotels & Resorts' Advisory Board of Women Business Travelers, the chain added a number of features in its product strategy:

- special amenities such as loofah mitts and skirt hangers in hotel rooms

- networking tables set aside in hotel restaurants for solo travelers who prefer to eat with others

- a warning call five minutes before room-service delivery to alert guests before a meal is delivered

- jogging partners and chilled bottled water, fresh fruit, and plush towels upon return from a run.

This strategy lets Wyndham offer improved customer satisfaction for this growing market. As recently as 1970, women accounted for only 1 percent of all business travelers; today the number has grown to 50 percent.[13]

Some companies adopt the *first-mover strategy*, which is exactly that—being the first company to offer a product in a market. This strategy hopes to link that company's goods or services permanently in customers' minds when they consider what to buy. The strategy can work if you are Kimberly-Clark and you own the trademark to Kleenex, or if you happen to be Microsoft and manage to get your operating system onto just about every personal computer. But being the first mover

Marketing Dictionary

marketing mix   Blending of the four strategic elements—product, pricing, distribution, and promotion—to fit the needs and preferences of a specific target market.

product strategy   Decisions about what goods or services a firm will offer its customers; also includes decisions about customer service, packaging, brand names, and the like.

into a market can have its pitfalls. If a company invests too much money too fast in a product for a new market, it can end up with a flop, which is what happened to Apple Computer with its pioneering handheld computer, Newton. Yes, there was a new market for handheld computers, but Apple failed to consider a variety of factors and set too-high performance goals for the Newton, too soon.[14]

Distribution Strategy

Marketers develop **distribution strategies** to ensure that consumers find their products in the proper quantities at the right times and places. Distribution decisions involve modes of transportation, warehousing, inventory control, order processing, and selection of marketing channels. Marketing channels are made up of institutions such as retailers and wholesalers—all those involved in a product's movement from producer to final consumer.

Technology is opening new channels of distribution in many industries. For example, software, a product made of digital data files, is ideally suited to electronic distribution. Major players like Microsoft and IBM already distribute their programs and upgrades directly over the Internet. Electronic commerce holds great promise for providing quick response to purchasers while markedly reducing prices by slashing packaging and shipping costs, cutting out many intermediaries, and allowing online shoppers to look for the best prices from both domestic and international suppliers.

Distribution is the perfect place for many companies to form alliances. Sony's music division formed an agreement with Universal Music Group to form Duet, an online music service that will make thousands of songs available to consumers over the Internet—without the royalty issues confronted by Napster. Georgia-Pacific Group, best known for manufacturing paper goods, formed an alliance with Amazon.com to exclusively provide the corrugated boxes for shipping books.[15]

FIGURE 2.7
Combining Promotions in One Advertisement

Promotional Strategy

Promotion is the communication link between sellers and buyers. Organizations use varied ways to send messages about their goods, services, and ideas. They may communicate messages directly through salespeople or indirectly through advertisements and promotions. Figure 2.7 shows a new promotion for Oreo cookies that have a new center that turns blue when dunked in milk. Sometimes firms face an ethical decision about whether to continue a relationship with a spokesperson, as discussed in the "Solving an Ethical Controversy" box.

In developing a promotional strategy, marketers blend the various elements of promotion to communicate most effectively with their target market. Many companies use an approach called *integrated marketing communications (IMC)* to coordinate all promotional activities so that the consumer

right wrong

Solving an Ethical Controversy

What If Your Celebrity Spokesperson Is Martha Stewart?

When it comes to featuring well-known spokespeople in a marketing campaign, image is everything. A company that signs up a celebrity to promote its good or services—from Tour de France champion Lance Armstrong to NBA star LeBron James—expects that individual to represent the firm's products in a positive manner. Many of these contracts include a so-called morals clause, permitting the firm to cancel the agreement in the event of legal misdeeds or antisocial behavior. Because a celebrity spokesperson naturally appears in the media for other reasons, the marketer wants those appearances to be as positive as its own advertisements. What happens, then, when an internationally known celebrity spokesperson like Martha Stewart—whose home decorating products have been featured by the financially troubled Kmart—is indicted in a stock trading scandal?

Should a company distance itself from a celebrity spokesperson whose image has been tarnished?

PRO
1. Kmart has the financial responsibility to distance itself from Stewart, even though the company may not terminate its contract with her, because its performance is tied to the sales of Stewart's products. "The controversy does seem to be impacting the [Kmart] franchise as sales dip," writes one industry analyst.
2. Martha Stewart's continued association with Kmart could damage Kmart's image, causing consumers to shop at competing stores instead. A damaged reputation could take Kmart marketers years to repair.

CON
1. In the U.S., a person is considered innocent until proven guilty, so Kmart should support Stewart until the conclusion of any legal proceedings. In addition, as long as Kmart has a contract with Stewart, the firm must meet its obligations.
2. Consumers should be able to make their own choices about whether to support Stewart and whether to buy her products.

SUMMARY

Martha Stewart stepped down as chairman and CEO of her own company, Martha Stewart Living Omnimedia, when she was formally charged by federal prosecutors with lying to regulators. A Kmart spokesperson stated that the company planned to continue airing television commercials in which Stewart appeared, while Stewart tried to rally public support by posting her side of the story on her Web site.

SOURCES: Anne D'Innocenzio, "Martha Stewart Company Profits Plunge," *Mobile Register*, August 12, 2003, p. B6; Jyoti Thottam, "Why They're Picking on Martha," Time, June 16, 2003, pp. 44-46; Nanette Byrnes, "Propping Up the House That Martha Built," *Business Week*, June 16, 2003, p. 38; Bruce Horovitz, "Stewart Uploads Her Cause to Web Site," *USA Today*, June 6, 2003, p. B1.

---

receives a unified and consistent message. Consumers might receive newsletters, e-mail updates, discount coupons, catalogs, invitations to company-sponsored events, and any number of other types of marketing communications about a product.

Pricing Strategy

One of the most difficult areas of marketing decision making, **pricing strategy,** deals with the methods of setting profitable and justifiable prices. It is closely regulated and subject to considerable public scrutiny.

One of the many factors that influence a marketer's pricing strategy is competition.

Marketing Dictionary

distribution strategy   Planning that ensures that consumers find their products in the proper quantities at the right times and places.

promotion   Communication link between buyers and sellers.

pricing strategy   Methods of setting profitable and justifiable prices.

Marketing Hit

Wal-Mart in the Neighborhood

Background. Wal-Mart is a retail superpower. Even though the company became the nation's largest grocer recently, with sales of more than $53 billion, it is still looking for expansion opportunities—both in the U.S. and abroad.

The Challenge. Despite the success of its Supercenters, Wal-Mart has experienced some backlash. Communities complain about increased traffic, packed store aisles, and empty retail buildings when traditional Wal-Mart outlets were replaced by Supercenters.

The Strategy. The company is implementing a new marketing strategy based on attractively designed Neighborhood Markets that sell a combination of food and pharmacy products with such conveniences as self-checkout, honor-system coffee and baked goods, drive-through prescription service, and half-hour film processing. Neighborhood Markets are located in regions with Supercenters to capitalize on the existing distribution system, while offering customers the added convenience of a shorter trip to a local store.

The Outcome. A total of 53 Neighborhood Markets are now open, with plans for more. The combination of everyday low prices and convenience may just be the answer to customers' shopping needs.

SOURCES: "Our Retail Divisions," Wal-Mart Web site, http://www.walmartstores.com, accessed January 18, 2004; Michael Liedtke, Anita French, "Wal-Mart Sales, Profit Healthy," *Morning News*, August 14, 2003, pp. 1B, 2B; "Wal-Mart Supercenters Face California Resistance," *The Miami Herald*, July 21, 2003, http://www.miami.com/mld/miamiherald/business; Patricia Callahan and Ann Zimmerman, "Price War in Aisle 3," *The Wall Street Journal*, May 27, 2003, pp. B1, B16; Jerry Useem, "One Nation Under Wal-Mart," *Fortune*, March 3, 2003, pp. 64–78.

The computer industry has become all too familiar with price cuts by both current competitors and new market entrants. After years of steady growth, the market has become saturated with low-cost computers, driving down profit margins even farther. Big PC makers such as Dell and IBM are trying to compensate by focusing more on business customers. Meanwhile, start-ups like eMachines are giving the large competitors a run for their money. EMachines prices its computers at least $100 lower than competing models—from $399 to $699 after a $75 rebate. Customers have responded, placing the company at the number 3 spot at retail, right behind Hewlett-Packard and Compaq.[16]

While price wars are well-known in industries such as air travel and automobile manufacturing, price fixing is another type of practice altogether. It is both illegal and unethical. For example, A. Alfred Taubman, the former head of the elite Sotheby's auction house, was convicted of price fixing—by meeting secretly with Sir Anthony Tennant, the former chairman of Christie's auction house, to set identical rates for sellers' commissions, which would effectively cut out fair pricing competition. After the guilty verdict was announced, jury foreman Mike D'Angelo said, "You've got to have competition. Competition is what makes the world go around."[17]

The Marketing Environment

Marketers do not make decisions about target markets and marketing mix variables in a vacuum. They must take into account the dynamic nature of the five dimensions of the marketing environment shown back in Figure 2.5: competitive, political-legal, economic, technological, and social-cultural factors. Environmental concerns have led to new regulations concerning air and water pollution. Automobile engineers, for instance, have turned public concerns and legal issues into opportunities by developing hybrid cars. These new models are fueled by dual energy: a gasoline engine and an electric motor. Toyota was the first to enter the market with its Prius, which depends primarily on the electric motor but includes a backup gasoline engine. The Prius currently sells in Japan for about $19,000. Changes in the legal environment regarding automobile emissions alerted automobile designers to make these changes. By accommodating future needs of consumers and meeting the more stringent legal requirements, they created a new market segment. It did not take long for competitors to follow Toyota's lead. Honda's new VV model, a hybrid version of the Civic, runs primarily on its gasoline engine with the electric motor as its secondary energy source. Honda plans to hit the showrooms with a vehicle that offers a lower price and better gas mileage. Nissan and Fuji Heavy Industries also have models on the drawing boards for launches scheduled within the next two years. European and U.S. automakers, however, have not jumped at the chance to enter the race with their version of a hybrid car. Ford and DaimlerChrysler plan to have their versions ready by 2005.[18] However, U.S. automakers may have missed the boat when it comes to maintaining the competitive advantage against foreign rivals in the manufacture of popular trucks and SUVs.

Businesses are increasingly looking to foreign shores for new growth markets. General Mills has been manufacturing everything from cereal to snack foods for decades. But when the company wanted to expand overseas, instead of starting from scratch it decided to partner with Nestlé in a venture called Cereal Partners Worldwide. General Mills was the cereal expert and Nestlé already had a presence in Europe. So far, the strategy has been successful. Since its formation, CPW has expanded its operations into 75 different markets and captured 21 percent of the international cold cereal business.[19]

Technology has changed the marketing environment as well, partly with the advent of the Internet. Throughout this text, you will encounter examples of the way the Internet and other technological developments are continuously altering the way firms do business. And as technology forces these changes, other aspects of the environment must respond. Naturally, there are legal disputes over who owns which innovations. Amazon.com recently won a court battle barring its rival Barnes & Noble.com from using Amazon's patented "one-click" checkout system, which allows shoppers to place their orders with a single click of the mouse instead of re-keying in billing information when they are ready to complete a sale.

Interestingly, technology moves much more quickly than patenting procedures, which can leave some businesses behind. Amazon founder and chief executive Jeff Bezos has suggested that software and Internet patents should have a shorter life span than other patents—perhaps because of the rapid changes in technology—and that they should be open to public comment before being issued. "I now believe it's possible that the current rules governing business methods and software patents could end up harming all of us," says Bezos.[20]

Two other important characteristics in the contemporary marketing environment include cultural diversity and ethical concerns. Every chapter in this book contains detailed examples that explore the impact of these factors, like the ones in the section in this chapter on targeting markets. The "Solving an Ethical Controversy" boxes in each chapter discuss in detail one ethical issue.

The marketing environment provides a framework for all marketing activity. Marketers consider environmental dimensions when they develop strategies for segmenting and targeting markets, and when they study consumer and organizational buying behavior. Wal-Mart marketers gauged the environment before launching Neighborhood Markets (see the "Marketing Hits" box).

Tools for Marketing Planning

As growing numbers of companies have discovered the benefits of effective marketing planning, they have developed planning tools to assist in this important function. This section discusses four specific tools: the strategic business unit concept, the market share/market growth matrix, the market attractiveness/business strength matrix, and spreadsheet analysis.

Strategic Business Units (SBUs)

Although a relatively small company may offer only a few items to its customers, a larger organization frequently produces and markets numerous offerings to widely diverse markets. Top managers at these larger firms need some method for spotting promising product lines that warrant investments of additional resources, as well as those lines that they should weed out from the firm's product portfolio. This is where the concept of an SBU comes in.

Strategic business units (SBUs) are key business units within diversified firms. Each SBU has its own managers, resources, objectives, and competitors. A division, product line, or single product may define the boundaries of an SBU. Each SBU pursues its own distinct mission, and each develops its own plans independently of other units in the organization.

Strategic business units focus the attention of company managers so that they can respond effectively to changing consumer demand within limited markets. Companies redefine their SBUs as market conditions dictate. An example of this redefinition is Maine-based outfitter L.L. Bean, a longtime family-run

7

Describe the environmental characteristics that influence strategy decisions.

8

Explain how the strategic business unit concept, the market share/market growth matrix, the market attractiveness/business strength matrix, and spreadsheet analysis can be used in marketing planning.

Briefly Speaking

Success is simply a matter of luck. Ask any failure.

Earl Wilson
(1907–1987)
American newspaper
columnist

Marketing Dictionary

strategic business unit (SBUs)   Key business units within diversified firms.

enterprise. In fact, its current president, Leon Gorman, is a grandson of L.L. himself and has run the company since 1967. To counter recent sagging sales, Gorman reorganized the company's hierarchical management structure to create SBUs that focus on specific merchandise areas, such as men's and women's clothing, hunting and fishing product lines, travel clothing and accessories, and home furnishings. The catalog shown in Figure 2.8 features the SBU of women's outdoor and fitness clothing.[21]

Market Share/Market Growth Matrix

To evaluate their organization's strategic business units, marketers need some type of portfolio performance framework. A widely used framework was developed by the Boston Consulting Group. This **market share/market growth matrix** places SBUs in a four-quadrant chart that plots market share—the percentage of a market that a firm controls—against market growth potential. The posi-

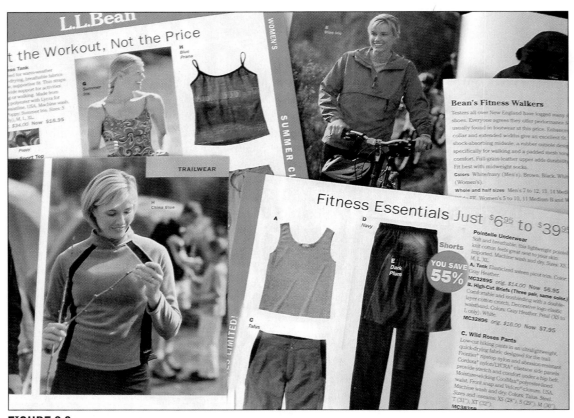

FIGURE 2.8
Women's Outdoor & Fitness: An SBU of L.L. Bean

FIGURE 2.9
Market Share/Market Growth Matrix

tion of an SBU along the horizontal axis indicates its market share relative to those of competitors in the industry. Its position along the vertical axis indicates the annual growth rate of the market. After plotting all of a firm's business units, planners divide them according to the matrix's four quadrants. Figure 2.9 illustrates this matrix by labeling the four quadrants cash cows, stars, dogs, and question marks. Firms in each quadrant require a unique marketing strategy.

Stars represent units with high market shares in high-growth markets. These products or businesses are high-growth market leaders. Although they generate considerable income, they need inflows of even more cash to finance further growth. Microsoft's Windows operating system requires ongoing expenditures on research and development to stay current, but the outlay pays off by maintaining the company's dominant position in the global personal computer market. It is estimated that Microsoft spent $500 million in marketing and launch costs alone to present its new Windows XP to the world.[22]

Cash cows command high market shares in low-growth markets. Marketers for such an SBU want to maintain this status for as long as possible. The business produces strong cash flows, but instead of investing heavily in the unit's own promotions and production capacity, the firm can use this cash to finance the growth of other SBUs with higher growth potentials.

Question marks achieve low market shares in high-growth markets. Marketers must decide whether to continue supporting these products or businesses since question marks typically require considerably more cash than they generate. If a question mark cannot become a star, the firm should pull out of the market and target other markets with greater potential. Early Toyota and Honda minivans actually failed because they were too small for Americans.[23] With design adjustments, they became the staple of the average American family.

Dogs manage only low market shares in low-growth markets. SBUs in this category promise poor future prospects, and marketers should withdraw from these businesses or product lines as quickly as possible.

Marketing Dictionary

market share/market growth matrix   Framework that places SBUs in a chart that plots market share against market growth potential.

For example, after Stroh's beer sales had languished for several years, managers finally decided to sell the company to Miller and Pabst.[24]

Market Attractiveness/Business Strength Matrix

Another model that can aid marketing planning is the **market attractiveness/business strength matrix,** a portfolio analysis technique that rates SBUs according to the attractiveness of their markets and their organizational strengths, as illustrated in Figure 2.10. Market attractiveness criteria include market share, growth, size, and stability; potential profitability; extent of government regulation; potential environmental and social impacts; and competitive conditions.[25] Managers must also take into account the organization's specific strengths and areas of competence, including its financial resources, image, relative cost advantages, customer base, and technological capabilities, along with the skills of its personnel.

Based on these criteria, managers create composite evaluations of SBUs. The most promising units in the upper-left area of the matrix offer strong business positions in attractive markets. These initiatives should receive the most company support. Those in the lower-right corner, on the other hand, offer little potential since they hold weak business positions in unattractive markets. Managers may choose to reduce funding for these operations or discontinue them altogether. In between, other SBUs rank from low to medium on market attractiveness and business strength. Decisions about allocating resources to these borderline SBUs depend on the strengths and weaknesses of the firm's entire business portfolio.

Planners apply this matrix when they are analyzing both their company's core competencies and their industry's environments. Using a matrix like this can help them direct investments to more profitable areas.

Evaluating the Matrix Approach to Planning

The market share/market growth matrix emphasizes the importance of creating market offerings that will help a company gain a competitive advantage. It also acknowledges changes in successful SBUs as they move through their life cycles. A successful product or business typically begins as a question mark, then becomes a star, and eventually drops into the cash-cow category, generating surplus funds that finance the firm's new stars.

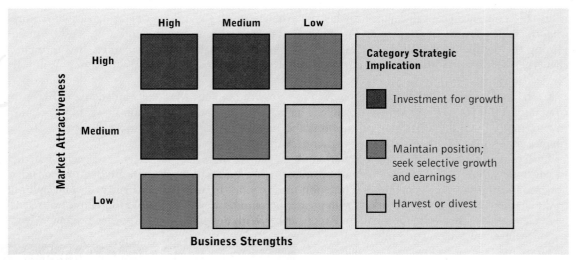

FIGURE 2.10
Market Attractiveness/Business Strength Matrix

The market attractiveness/business strength matrix is a useful tool for identifying SBUs with the greatest and least potential. It can also help managers identify a firm's need for new sources of growth while indicating its most and least attractive markets.

Spreadsheet Analysis

Spreadsheet analysis lays out a rigid grid of columns and rows that organize numerical information in a standardized, easily understandable format. It helps planners to answer what-if questions. Electronic spreadsheets, such as the popular Microsoft Excel, are the computerized equivalent of an accountant's hand-prepared worksheet.

Spreadsheet analysis helps planners anticipate marketing performance given specified sets of circumstances. For example, a spreadsheet might project the outcomes of different pricing decisions for a new product, as shown in Table 2.2.

In this example, the item will be sold for $10 per unit and can be produced for $5 in variable costs. The total fixed costs of $310,000 include $100,000 for manufacturing-overhead outlays, such as salaries, general office expenses, rent, utilities, and interest charges; $120,000 for marketing expenditures; and $90,000 for research and development to design the product. The spreadsheet calculation, using the basic model on line 1, reveals that the product would have to achieve sales of 62,000 units to break even.

But what if someone convinces other members of the marketing team to increase marketing expenditures to $230,000? In line 2 of Table 2.2 the $120,000 marketing expenditure changes to $230,000, and the newly calculated break-even point is 84,000 units. As soon as an amount in one or more cells changes, the software automatically recalculates all affected amounts.

Line 3 of Table 2.2 demonstrates the impact of a reduction in variable costs to $4 (perhaps the result of switching to lower-cost materials) coupled with a $1 reduction in the product's selling price. The new break-even point is 62,000 units.

This figure demonstrates the ease with which a marketing manager can use a computer spreadsheet program to determine the potential results of alternative decisions. More complex spreadsheets may include 50 or more columns of data and formulas but can complete new calculations as quickly as the manager changes the variables.

TABLE 2.2   How Spreadsheet Analysis Works

Fixed Costs				Per-Unit Variable Cost	Sales Price	Break-Even Point
Manufacturing	**Marketing**	**R & D**	**Total**			
$100,000	$120,000	$90,000	$310,000	$5	$10	62,000
$100,000	$230,000	$90,000	$420,000	$5	$10	84,000
$100,000	$120,000	$90,000	$310,000	$4	$9	62,000

Marketing Dictionary

market attractiveness/business strength matrix   Portfolio analysis technique that rates SBUs according to the attractiveness of their markets and their organizational strengths

spreadsheet analysis   Analysis that lays out a rigid grid of columns and rows that organize numerical information in a standardized, easily understandable format.

Strategic Implications of Marketing in the 21st Century

Never before has planning been as important to marketers as the 21st century speeds ahead with technological advances. Marketers need to plan carefully, accurately, and quickly if their companies are going to gain a competitive advantage in today's global marketplace. They need to define their organization's mission and understand the different methods for formulating a successful marketing strategy. They must consider a changing, diverse population and the boundaryless business environment created by the Internet. They must be able to evaluate when it's best to be first to get into a market, and when it's best to wait. They need to recognize when they've got a star and when they've got a dog; when to hang on and when to let go. As daunting as this seems, planning can reduce the risk and worry of bringing new goods and services to the marketplace.

Summary of Chapter Objectives

1. Distinguish between strategic planning and tactical planning.

Strategic planning is the process of identifying an organization's primary objectives and adopting courses of action toward these objectives. Tactical planning guides the implementation of the activities specified in the strategic plan.

2. Explain how marketing plans differ at various levels in an organization.

Top management spends more time engaged in strategic planning than do middle- and supervisory-level managers, who tend to focus on narrower, tactical plans for their departments. Supervisory managers are more likely to engage in developing specific plans designed to meet the goals for their areas of responsibility.

3. Identify the steps in the marketing planning process.

The basic steps in the marketing planning process are mission definition, determination of organizational objectives, assessment of organizational resources and evaluation of environmental risk and opportunities, formulation of a marketing strategy, implementation of the marketing strategy, and monitoring and adaptation.

4. Describe the concept of SWOT analysis and its major elements.

SWOT (strengths, weaknesses, opportunities, and threats) analysis focuses on the relationship between an organization's internal strengths and weaknesses and external opportunities and

threats. A company can best gain a competitive advantage when its internal strength coincides with an external opportunity. Likewise, problems can arise when a threat occurs against an organization's weakness.

5. Discuss how a strategy can be implemented through marketing plans.

Marketers use operating plans to implement the marketing strategy that has already been developed, then monitor the results and the performance of the company or product to make sure that the objectives are being achieved.

6. Identify the basic elements of a marketing strategy.

Development of a marketing strategy is a two-step process: (1) selecting a target market and (2) designing an effective marketing mix to satisfy the chosen target. The target market is the group of people toward whom a company decides to direct its marketing efforts. The marketing mix blends four strategy elements to fit the needs and preferences of a specific target market. These elements are: product strategy, distribution strategy, promotional strategy, and pricing strategy.

7. Describe the environmental characteristics that influence strategy decisions.

The five dimensions of the marketing environment are competitive, political-legal, economic, technological, and social-cultural. In addition, marketers must be aware of growing cultural diversity and ethical concerns.

8. **Explain how the strategic business unit concept, the market share/market growth matrix, the market attractiveness/business strength matrix, and spreadsheet analysis can be used in marketing planning.**

The SBU focuses the attention of company managers so they can respond effectively to changing consumer demand within certain markets. The two matrixes help marketers identify a product's share of the market and the attractiveness of a market as it is related to a business' strength in that market. Spreadsheet analysis helps planners anticipate marketing performance given specified sets of circumstances.

Marketing Terms You Need to Know

planning 39	SWOT analysis 43	promotion 48	market share/market growth
marketing planning 39	strategic window 43	pricing strategy 49	matrix 52
strategic planning 40	marketing mix 46	strategic business units	market attractiveness/business
tactical planning 40	product strategy 47	(SBUs) 51	strength matrix 54
mission 41	distribution strategy 48		spreadsheet analysis 55

Other Important Marketing Terms

core competencies 43	target market 45	first-mover strategy 47

Review Questions

1. List three differences that distinguish strategic planning from tactical planning.
2. Summarize in one or two sentences a strategic plan that a top manager in an organization might be involved with. Then state in a sentence or two a related tactical plan that a middle-level manager might focus on.
3. How does SWOT analysis help marketers in planning?
4. What are the basic elements of a marketing strategy?
5. Why is identifying a target market so important to a company?
6. Identify the four strategy elements in the marketing mix, and give an example of each element for *one* of the following organizations: General Mills, Procter & Gamble, the U.S. Army, or Dell.
7. Identify the dimensions of the marketing environment. Explain briefly how each one is important to the marketing planner.
8. What are the quadrants of a market share/market growth matrix? Explain what each one means.
9. Why do marketers use the matrix approach to planning? Can you think of any situations in which it wouldn't be appropriate? Explain.
10. How would spreadsheet analysis help marketers for Burton Snowboards decide whether to bring out a new model of snowboard for the next winter season?

Projects and Teamwork Exercises

1. Choose a company whose goods and services are familiar to you. With at least one other classmate, formulate a mission statement for that company.
2. Prepare a case history of strategic planning for a leading company that interests you. Include successes as well as failures, where applicable. Present your case history to the class.
3. While Kmart has filed for bankruptcy, Kohl's is expanding into new regions. Find out more about Kohl's to prepare a presentation explaining why this is a good strategic window in which to expand.
4. Research one of the following companies (or select one of your own) and identify the firm's target market(s). Note that a large company might have more than one target market. Write a brief proposal for a marketing strategy to reach that market. Suggested firms:
   - American Express
   - Ralph Lauren
   - UPS
   - Boeing
   - Best Buy
5. Team up with one or more classmates to research companies on the Web, looking for firms that have created successful SBUs like L.L. Bean's outdoor and fitness department, which is aimed at women. Then create an advertisement for one of those SBUs.

'net Work

http://www.amgen.com

1. Mission statements. Locate and print out two company mission statements. Most medium-sized and large businesses and not-for-profit organizations publish mission statements on their Web sites. For instance, Amgen's mission statement can be found at **http://www.amgen.com**. Bring your printouts to class and be prepared to explain the major components of each during the discussion of the first step of the planning process.

http://www.homedepot.com
http://www.lowes.com

2. SWOT Analysis. Visit the Web sites of Home Depot and Lowe's. At both sites, access company information. Prepare a SWOT table for the two companies similar to the one shown in the chapter.

http://www.ge.com

3. Market share/market growth matrix. Most companies can be organized into strategic business units. Visit General Electric's Web site and list GE's major divisions. Then, using the market share/market growth matrix shown in Figure 2.10, try to classify each of GE's divisions in terms of market attractiveness and business strengths. Which units did you classify as "stars"?

Note: Internet Web addresses change frequently. If you don't find the exact sites listed, you may need to access the organization or company's home page and search from there.

CASE 2.1

Every Company Needs a Disaster Plan

"Plan for the worst." It sounds like something a worrywart would say, or maybe an advertisement for disaster insurance or even a funeral parlor. Most of us don't like to think about the worst, in either our personal or professional lives. But September 11, 2001, brought home in a tragic way how important it is for companies to plan for disaster. When the twin towers of the World Trade Center collapsed, thousands of lives were lost. Although of far less importance, Morgan Stanley estimates that $500 million in computing equipment was destroyed, along with the information contained in it. The information itself was, in many ways, more valuable than the equipment.

Some companies were prepared, with sophisticated strategies for storing and backing up their data. In fact, Steve Duplessie, senior analyst at the Enterprise Storage Group of Milford, Massachusetts, estimates that because of good planning, 95 percent of the companies that were located in the buildings would completely recover their programs and data. But in other locations—in businesses that were both directly and indirectly affected by the tragedy—companies suffered losses that in some cases drove them out of business. "Disaster recovery was secondary for most enterprises," explains Duplessie. "Now it's at the forefront of everybody's concerns." A study done by the University of Texas revealed that only 6 percent of companies that sustain some kind of catastrophic data loss survive.

Managers must include planning for disasters such as this in their strategic and tactical planning. First, they must identify the data that is absolutely necessary to run their businesses; maybe it is a list of clients, or perhaps it includes information about suppliers. Then they should research methods for ensuring that the necessary data are protected even under the most unthinkable conditions—such as a catastrophic fire. One way to achieve this protection is to keep backup tapes of data and store them in vaults in another location, such as the ones managed by Iron Mountain of Boston. If disaster strikes, these tapes can be shipped to a recovery site like the ones run by Sungard in Pennsylvania or Comdisco in Illinois. But what if this simple type of backup isn't sophisticated enough? Financial institutions often use a "mirroring" technique that backs up data in real time; this method, however, is much more expensive. Ken Rubin of Iron Mountain cites a third method that is more sophisticated than the first and less expensive than the second: "electronic vaulting," which provides continuous back-up and data recovery via the Web.

What about paper documents? Everyone heard stories about the blizzard of paper that drifted into the streets of New York after the collapse of the towers. Rubin says that as much as 80 percent of a company's data is inactive and could actually be stored immediately off-site, keeping only the 20 percent that is necessary to the daily running of the firm. But it is up to planners to decide which information falls into which category. And even companies that have adequate recovery strategies are re-evaluating their planning. Steve Tall of Fiduciary Trust, which was located in the towers and sustained catastrophic human and economic loss, says that even though his company was up and running shortly afterward because it had stored much of its data at a Comdisco site, his managers are adjusting their disaster recovery plans. "It's absolutely accurate to say we're going back to rewrite our plans," he notes. And like every other manager, Tall hopes those plans never have to be put to use.

Questions for Critical Thinking

1. Describe an action that might be considered part of a strategic plan for disaster recovery in a financial institution. Describe two actions that might be considered part of a tactical plan.
2. How might a SWOT analysis help in the development of a disaster recovery plan?

SOURCES: Eric J. Savitz, "Read This, Then Go Back up Your Data," *Fortune/CNET Tech Review*, Winter 2002, pp. 28–29; Bob Tedeschi, "Picking up the Pieces," *Smart Business*, December 1, 2001, http://www.smartbusinessmag.com; "Disaster Planning Saves Wall Street," *BBC News*, September 13, 2001, http://www.bbc.co.uk.

VIDEO CASE 2.2

Caribou Coffee Brews Up a Fine Cup of Strategy

The written case on Caribou Coffee appears on page VC-3. The recently filmed Caribou Coffee video is designed to expand and highlight the concepts in this chapter and the concepts and questions covered in the written video case.

3

The Marketing Environment, Ethics, and Social Responsibility

Chapter Objectives

1 Identify the five components of the marketing environment.

2 Explain the types of competition marketers face and the steps necessary for developing a competitive strategy.

3 Describe how government and other groups regulate marketing activities and how marketers can influence the political-legal environment.

4 Outline the economic factors that affect marketing decisions and consumer buying power.

5 Discuss the impact of the technological environment on a firm's marketing activities.

6 Explain how the social-cultural environment influences marketing.

7 Describe the role of marketing in society and identify the two major social issues in marketing.

8 Identify the four levels of the social responsibility pyramid.

Hybrids Are Hot

We all love to say we want cleaner air and less pollution from motor vehicles. But when it's time to hop in the car, we don't think twice about it—we'd never give up the freedom we have with our automobile. We don't carpool unless it's absolutely necessary. And if an SUV fits in the budget (and the garage), we'll buy one—regardless of whether we really need the four-wheel drive.

But what if we could contribute to cleaner air without changing our habits? Toyota, Honda, Ford, and General Motors have created a slick new product: the hybrid vehicle, which runs on a combination of electric and gasoline power. It's not one of those quirky battery cars that dies in the middle of the road. It doesn't have to be plugged in, because the battery recharges itself as you drive, and the power is evenly distributed between a gasoline engine and electric motor. When you get low on gas, you fill up the tank just like any other car. Well, there is one difference: hybrids get more than 50 miles per gallon. Got your attention?

Traditionally, the auto industry hasn't always received high marks for social responsibility when it comes to fuel efficiency and air pollution; instead, automakers have been dragged into compliance with federal and state laws. Nor has it been able to come up with a "green" product that meets consumers' needs and preferences when it comes to design, convenience, and price—until now. To be fair, the marketing environment has made this kind of progress grueling. The auto industry is extremely competitive; regulations are strict; the economy affects how much consumers can or will spend on new vehicles and gasoline; and until now, the technology simply wasn't refined enough. Although the effort to market the original battery-powered cars was admirable, and certainly generated good publicity for

auto manufacturers, there was no way consumers would accept those vehicles.

Now you can buy a hybrid that's a lot more like the vehicle you're used to. In fact, Toyota (including Lexus), Honda, and Ford have launched hybrids that are based on some of consumers' favorite models. There's a hybrid Ford Escape and a hybrid based on the Lexus RX330, the model that combines car and SUV features. There's even a hybrid Honda Civic. And the new version of Toyota's Prius is larger, gets more miles per gallon than its predecessor, and can accelerate from 0 to 60 mph in a little more than 10 seconds, which is comparable to the popular Camry.

Is there a market for these new cars? Many experts say yes. One factor is the price of gasoline—as prices have pushed higher, consumers are more interested in fuel economy. "The trend was coming before, but fuel prices are accelerating it a bit," explains one Honda dealer, who says that he has done so well with the new hybrid Civic that he could sell 15 or 20 of them per month instead of the 4 or 5 that Honda allots him.

The government is helping, too. Currently, consumers can claim a $2,000 tax deduction for the purchase of a hybrid. Still, there's a price to pay for the new technology—the Toyota Prius runs about $20,500, which is about $5,000 more than Toyota's Corolla. And the technology itself is still new, which raises questions about the cost of maintaining the vehicles down the road. Toyota backs its Prius batteries with a 150,000-mile warranty—and its vehicles are well known for their longevity—but no one knows for certain how long the new cars will last.

By creating a fuel-efficient vehicle that is also practical and meets the needs of consumers, car makers are acting as good corporate citizens. They are behaving ethically by giving motorists the ability to reduce air pollution. They are obeying laws regarding fuel emissions. And eventually, these new cars may even be profitable. Although both automakers and motorists need to be willing to accept change, marketers are striving to convey the message that consumers don't need to sacrifice any of their expectations for new vehicles. Toyota division general manager Don Esmond says that the new Lexus hybrid will be like "a hot fudge sundae with fewer calories," meaning that it will perform in every way like a traditional Lexus but burn less gasoline. Ford's marketing tag line for the new hybrid Escape is that the truck will ask for "no compromises" from its purchasers. That's a tough promise, but one that just might work.[1]

Chapter Overview

Change is a fact of life for all people, including marketers. Introducing change to one of the world's largest industries isn't easy, and introducing change that is socially responsible can be even harder. But that's what auto manufacturers are trying to do with the launch of hybrids.

While some change may be the result of crises, more often it is gradual. For example, not a video rental outlet could be found in America in 1975, but by 2003, over 21,000 were open for business—with as much shelf space devoted to DVDs as to videotapes. During the same period, computer retail outlets exploded in number, increasing twelve-fold. Mobile phones replaced car phones—and transformed from plain gray into a rainbow of colors and styles. Beauty salons reinvented themselves as day spas. The prosperity of recent years led consumers to outsource their domestic drudgery, contributing to growth in industries ranging from restaurants and hotels to amusement parks and lawn-care services.

In addition to planning for change, marketers must set goals to meet concerns of customers, employees, shareholders, and members of the general public. Industry competition, legal constraints, the impact of technology on product designs, and social concerns are some of the many important factors that shape the business environment. All potentially have impact on a firm's goods and services. Although external forces frequently are outside the marketing manager's control, decision makers must still consider those influences together with the variables of the marketing mix in developing—and occasionally modifying—marketing plans and strategies that take these environmental factors into consideration.

This chapter begins by describing five forces in marketing's external environment—competitive, political-legal, economic, technological, and social-cultural. Figure 3.1 identifies them as the foundation for making decisions involving the four marketing mix elements and the target market. These forces provide the frame of reference within which all marketing decisions are made. The second focus of this chapter is marketing ethics and social responsibility. This section describes the nature of marketers' responsibilities, both to business and to society at large.

FIGURE 3.1
Elements of the Marketing Mix within an Environmental Framework

Environmental Scanning and Environmental Management

Marketers must carefully and continually monitor crucial trends and developments in the business environment. **Environmental scanning** is the process of collecting information about the external marketing environment to identify and interpret potential trends. The goal is to analyze the information and decide whether these trends represent opportunities or threats to the company. The firm is then able to determine the best response to a particular environmental change.

All across America, consumers have discovered that there is money to be made in online auctions. Bidding on everything from Beanie Babies to sports memorabilia, over a third of all U.S. online retail customers made at least one online auction purchase during the first four years of the 21st century. With over 2 million registered users, eBay is the industry giant among approximately 1,000 auction Web sites. Yet the Federal Trade Commission links almost half of all scams on the Web to online auctions. Counterfeit items, failure to deliver (or pay for) products sold at auction, and manipulation of bids by sellers are common complaints. Even though eBay claims that fraud accounts for a minuscule 1 in every 3,000 transactions, the company takes steps to overcome consumer fears. It offers free insurance coverage for transactions up to $200. Rival Auction Universe provides up to $3,000 of insurance for $19.95.[2]

Environmental scanning is a vital component of effective **environmental management.** Environmental management involves marketers' efforts to achieve organizational objectives by predicting and influencing the competitive, political-legal, economic, technological, and social-cultural environments. In the political-legal environment, managers who are seeking modifications of regulations, laws, or tariff restrictions may join political action

1

Identify the five components of the marketing environment.

Marketing Dictionary

environmental scanning   Process of collecting information about the external marketing environment in order to identify and interpret potential trends.

environmental management   Attainment of organizational objectives by predicting and influencing the competitive, political-legal, economic, technological, and social-cultural environments.

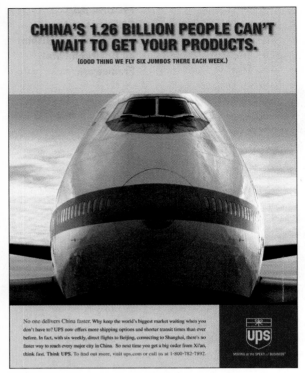

CHINA'S 1.26 BILLION PEOPLE CAN'T WAIT TO GET YOUR PRODUCTS.

(GOOD THING WE FLY SIX JUMBOS THERE EACH WEEK.)

No one delivers China faster. Why keep the world's biggest market waiting when you don't have to? UPS now offers more shipping options and shorter transit times than ever before. In fact, with six weekly, direct flights to Beijing, connecting to Shanghai, there's no faster way to reach every major city in China. So next time you get a big order from Xi'an, think fast. Think UPS. To find out more, visit ups.com or call us at 1-800-782-7892.

Environmental management played a major role in United Parcel Service's receipt of the air package delivery rights between the U.S. and China. Today, UPS offers the fastest delivery of packages between the two countries—with direct six-times-a-week flights to Beijing.

committees (PACs) to lobby legislators or contribute to the campaigns of sympathetic politicians. After a multimillion-dollar lobbying campaign that lasted more than 18 months, the U.S. Department of Transportation granted United Parcel Service (UPS) a new air route into China, the most recent member of the World Trade Organization. The route is potentially worth $300 million in annual revenues.[3]

For many domestic and international competitors, competing with established industry leaders frequently involves *strategic alliances*—partnerships with other firms in which the partners combine resources and capital to create competitive advantages in a new market. A recent alliance between MasterCard International and Dallas-based Hotel Reservations Network allows cardholders to book rooms online and take advantage of exclusive offers and rebates. MasterCard benefits from extra exposure in the network's print and online advertising. Amazon marketers decided to jump-start their move into online auctions by forming an alliance with Sotheby's, the world's largest international auction house for fine art. Amazon benefits from the instant credibility associated with Sotheby's name, along with access to its clients. Sotheby's gains entry into the market for lower-end collectibles.[4]

Strategic alliances are especially common in international marketing, where partnerships with local firms provide regional expertise for a company expanding its operations abroad. Members of such alliances share risks and profits. Alliances are essential in countries such as China and Mexico, where local laws require foreign firms doing business there to work with local companies.

Through successful research and development efforts, firms may influence changes in their own technological environments. A research breakthrough may lead to reduced production costs or a technologically superior new product.

While the dynamic marketing environment may exceed the confines of the firm and its marketing mix components, effective marketers continually seek to predict its impact on marketing decisions and to modify operations to meet changing market needs. Even modest environmental shifts can alter the results of those decisions.

The Competitive Environment

As organizations vie to satisfy customers, the interactive exchange creates the **competitive environment**. Marketing decisions by each individual firm influence consumer responses in the marketplace. They also affect the marketing strategies of competitors. As a consequence, decision makers must continually monitor competitors' marketing activities—their products, channels, prices, and promotional efforts.

Few organizations enjoy *monopoly* positions as the sole supplier of a good or service in the marketplace. Utilities, such as natural gas, electricity, water, and cable TV service, have traditionally accepted considerable regulation from local authorities who controlled such marketing-related factors as rates, service levels, and geographic coverage. In exchange, the utilities gained exclusive rights to serve a particular group of consumers. The *deregulation movement* of the past three decades has ended total monopoly protection for most utilities. Today's shoppers can choose from alternative cable TV and Internet providers, cell phone and long-distance telephone carriers, and even gas and electric utilities. The constant stream of solicitations from long-distance telephone companies provides almost daily evidence of increased competition in this formerly monopolized industry.

Some marketers, such as pharmaceutical firms Merck and Pfizer, are able to achieve temporary monopolies from patents on drugs they invest millions to develop. When the Food and Drug Administration approves a new antiarthritis drug, improved blood pressure medicine, or even a pill to stimulate hair growth, the manufacturers are typically granted exclusive rights to produce and market the product during the life of the patent. By being first to market and holding on to their leadership positions, some firms have achieved virtual monopolies. De Beers owns more than 70 percent of the diamond market; Intel has the lion's share of the market for microprocessors; four out of five flights out of Charlotte, N.C., are operated by U.S. Airlines; and baseballs made by Rawlings Sporting Goods are practically the only game in town.[5]

Through industry megamergers, often on a global scale, some companies seek to dominate markets without ceding the controls that regulated monopolies forfeit. As a result of mergers, the auto, tobacco, accounting, and telecommunications industries are all dominated by just three or four giants. Rather than seeking sole dominance of a market, corporations increasingly prefer to share the pie with just a few rivals. Referred to by economists as an *oligopoly*, this industry structure of a limited number of sellers in an industry where high start-up costs form barriers to keep out new competitors deters newcomers from breaking into markets, while ensuring that corporations remain innovative. In the ongoing antitrust trial, Microsoft Corp. is fighting allegations that it first attempted to create an oligopoly by sharing the Internet browser market with Netscape Communications. When Netscape balked, Microsoft allegedly attempted to destroy the fledgling Internet company.[6]

THE WAY BOB DEVOURED HIS BURGER, YOU'D THINK NO ONE TOLD HIM IT'S MEATLESS WITH 70% LESS FAT.*

*Than a ground beef hamburger.   www.bocaburger.com

OKAY, NO ONE TOLD HIM.   Boca Burgers ALL AMERICAN   THE TASTE WILL CHANGE YOU.

Although Kraft's Boca Burgers brand targets the market niche of shoppers choosing meatless dishes, it still competes directly with other menu options in the packaged foods category. Boca Burgers is the subject of Case 3.1 on page 95.

Types of Competition may be demonstrated.

Marketers face three types of competition. The most *direct* form occurs among marketers of similar products, as when a Shell station opens across the street from BP or Marathon. Telecommunications giant Motorola, battered by Finland's Nokia when the market for cell phones exploded, recently fought back with

2

Explain the types of competition marketers face and the steps necessary for developing a competitive strategy.

Marketing Dictionary

competitive environment   Interactive process that occurs in the marketplace among marketers of directly competitive products, marketers of products that can be substituted for one another, and marketers competing for the consumer's purchasing power.

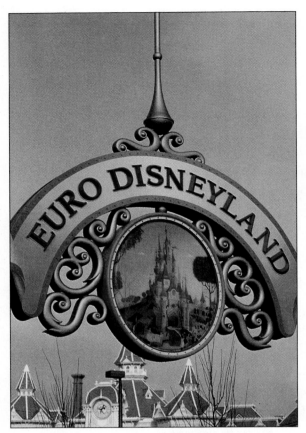

Euro Disneyland competes for vacation dollars. The resort mingles Disney-style fun with attractions that are distinctly European—including daredevil stunts in a mock car race through a model of Saint-Tropez.

the release of a new line of sleek and stylish phones that serve as fashion accessories as well as communication devices. Motorola hopes that its aggressive design offensive, coupled with the launch of its new 3G handsets—an innovative technology that offers instant access to the Internet—will win back lost market share. In the race for teen dollars, chain store Hot Topic is beating out youth retailers like Gap and American Eagle. Offering funky fashions and oddball gifts—like the glow-in-the-dark tongue ring—the store caters to tastes of almost a fifth of high-school students who consider themselves "alternative." Located in easy-to-access suburban malls, Hot Topic keeps in touch with customers' fashion choices, inviting comments and suggestions. Buyers also check out cutting-edge trends at rock concerts and rave parties.[7]

A second type of competition is *indirect* and involves products that are easily substituted. In the business document delivery industry, overnight express mail services and messenger services compete with e-mail and voice mail. In the fast-food industry, pizza competes with chicken, hamburgers, and tacos. In transportation, Greyhound bus lines compete with auto rental services, airlines, and train services. Unable to compete directly with substitute transportation services, Amtrak decided to team up with their cruise ship and airline competitors by offering custom-designed vacation packages. With a single phone call, Amtrak can make travel arrangements to get vacationers where they want to go by air, land, and sea.

Six Flags and Universal Studios amusement parks—the traditional hot spots for family vacations—now compete with outdoor adventure trips. One of every two U.S. adults now substitutes a tranquil week at the beach or a trip to Disney World for something more adventurous—thrill-filled experiences such as skydiving, white-water rafting, or climbing Mount Rainier. A decade after it was slammed for ignoring local culture and travel habits in its Disneyland Paris theme park, Walt Disney Co. opened a more Eurocentric resort nearby. The new Euro Disney park combines traditional Hollywood-style entertainment with features that are distinctly European. Restaurants, theaters, rides, and montages are all designed to appeal to the multiple indigenous cultures throughout Europe.[8]

A change such as a price increase or an improvement in a product's attributes can also affect demand for substitute products. A major drop in the cost of solar energy would not only increase the demand for solar power but also adversely affect the demand for such energy sources as heating oil, electricity, and natural gas.

The final type of competition occurs among all organizations that compete for consumers' purchases. Traditional economic analysis views competition as a battle among companies in the same industry (direct competition) or among substitutable goods and services (indirect competition). Marketers, however, are aware that all firms compete for a limited amount of discretionary buying power. Competition in this sense means that a PT Cruiser competes with a Colorado ski vacation. For the buyer's entertainment dollar, a Korn compact disc competes with two tickets to a San Antonio Spurs' game.

Because the competitive environment often determines the success or failure of a product, marketers must continually assess competitors' marketing strategies. New product offerings with technological advances, price reductions, special promotions, service requirements, or other competitive variations must be monitored. Then, marketers must decide whether to adjust one or more marketing mix components to compete with the new market entry.

Developing a Competitive Strategy

Every firm's marketers must develop an effective strategy for dealing with the competitive environment. One company may compete in a broad range of markets in many areas of the world. Another may specialize in particular market segments, such as those determined by customers' geographical location, age, or income characteristics. Determining a *competitive strategy* involves answering the following three questions:

1. Should we compete?

2. If so, in what markets should we compete?

3. How should we compete?

The answer to the first question depends on the firm's resources, objectives, and expected profit potential. A firm may decide not to pursue or continue operating a potentially successful venture that does not mesh with its resources, objectives, or profit expectations. Semiconductor manufacturer Texas Instruments shed its defense electronics business unit, which makes missile sensors and radar and night-vision systems, to an aircraft company where this unit was a better fit. In a recent move to spin off Medco, its profitable pharmacy-benefits-management subsidiary, Merck cited its needs to concentrate on its core business—the development of breakthrough medicines.[9]

Answering the second question—In what markets should we compete?—requires marketers to acknowledge their firm's limited resources (sales personnel, advertising budgets, product development capability, and the like). They must accept responsibility for allocating these resources to the areas of greatest opportunity.

Some companies gain access to markets or new technologies through acquisitions and mergers. The merger of Hewlett-Packard and Compaq created an $87 billion company, an instant world leader in PCs, computer servers, handheld devices, and printers. Moreover, the elimination of overlapping units was expected to trim operating costs by $2.5 billion a year. The emergence of international petroleum giant ChevronTexaco through the merger of the world's two leading oil companies resulted in annual savings of at least $1.2 billion—and the opportunity to create breakthrough technologies by combining strengths and expertise.[10]

Answering the third question—How should we compete?—requires marketers to make product, pricing, distribution, and promotional decisions that give the firm a competitive advantage in the marketplace. Firms can compete on a variety of bases, including product quality, price, and customer service. For example, retailer Neiman Marcus has gained a competitive advantage by providing superior customer service, while retailer Target competes by providing quality goods at low prices. As Figure 3.2 shows, the ultra-hip clothing company FUBU has an extensive Web site. FUBU brings a competitive edge to the hip-hop clothing market by offering shoppers the ability to purchase their clothing online, but supports the retail sales of the company's signature stores by also directing online shoppers to the nearest FUBU clothing retailer in their area of the country.

Time-Based Competition

With increased international competition and rapid changes in technology, a steadily growing number of firms are using time as a strategic competitive weapon. **Time-based competition** is the strategy of developing and distributing goods and services more quickly than competitors. The flexibility and responsiveness of time-based competitors enables them to improve product quality, reduce costs, and expand product offerings to satisfy new market segments and enhance customer satisfaction.

Time was a key factor that recently won Lockheed Martin Aeronautics the biggest Defense Department contract ever—$200 billion to build a new fleet of supersonic stealth fighter planes. By collaborating via the Internet with more than 80 suppliers scattered worldwide using a complex system of Web software tools, the Lockheed proposal won over government procurement specialists by demonstrating its ability to get the first plane in the air in just four years.[11]

In the computer industry, time-based competition is critical. Consumer demands for speed push developers to work on several generations of their technology simultaneously. In the mid-1990s, high-speed 3-D graphics capability came at a cost exceeding $300,000 and was reserved for high-tech applications such as medical imaging or flight simulations. Today,

Marketing Dictionary

time-based competition   Strategy of developing and distributing goods and services more quickly than competitors.

FIGURE 3.2
The Internet: Important Sales Component of FUBU's Competitive Strategy

3

Describe how government and other groups regulate marketing activities and how marketers can influence the political-legal environment.

far more sophisticated graphics programs are available on Sony's PlayStation 2 or Microsoft's Xbox for less than $200. Less than five years ago, a new PC typically came with 20 gigabytes of storage; now a single drive has a terabyte—or 1,000 gigabytes. That's enough space to hold about 400 movies. The speed at which changes occur in the Internet arena is so great that marketers count time in "Internet years," actually time periods of only several weeks or months.[12]

The Political-Legal Environment

Before you play the game, learn the rules! It is absurd to start playing a new game without first understanding the rules, yet some businesspeople exhibit a remarkable lack of knowledge about marketing's **political-legal environment**—the laws and their interpretations that require firms to operate under certain competitive conditions and to protect consumer rights. Ignorance of laws, ordinances, and regulations or noncompliance with them can result in fines, embarrassing negative publicity, and expensive civil damage suits.

The existing U.S. legal framework was constructed on a piecemeal basis, often in response to issues that were important at the time individual laws were enacted. Businesspeople need considerable diligence to understand its relationship to their marketing decisions. Numerous laws and regulations affect those decisions, many of them vaguely stated and inconsistently enforced by a multitude of different authorities.

Regulations enacted at the federal, state, and local levels affect marketing practices, as do the actions of independent regulatory agencies. These requirements and prohibitions touch on all aspects of marketing decision making—designing, labeling, packaging, distribution, advertising, and promotion of goods and services. To cope with the vast, complex, and changing political-legal environment, many large firms maintain in-house legal departments; small firms often seek professional advice from outside attorneys. All marketers, however, should be aware of the major regulations that affect their activities.

Government Regulation

No it for 3rd Test

The history of U.S. government regulation can be divided into four phases. The first phase was the antimonopoly period of the late 19th and early 20th centuries. During this era, major laws such as the Sherman Antitrust Act, Clayton Act, and Federal Trade Commission Act were passed to maintain a competitive environment by reducing the trend toward increasing concentration of industry power in the hands of a small number of competitors. Laws enacted more than 100 years ago still affect business in the 21st century.

The recent Microsoft case is a good example of antitrust legislation at work. The U.S. Justice Department accused the software powerhouse of predatory practices designed to crush competition. By bundling its own Internet Explorer browser with its Windows operating system (which runs 90 percent of the world's personal computers), Microsoft grabbed significant market share from rival Netscape. It also bullied firms as large as America Online to drop

Sony's PlayStation 2 brings sophisticated technology to the fingertips of game players. PlayStation 3, now in development, promises even better performance.

Netscape Navigator in favor of the Microsoft browser. Microsoft's supporters countered that consumers have clearly benefited from the integrated features in Windows. Its bundling decisions were simply efforts to offer customer satisfaction through added value. As one critic joked, "In the U.S. government's fight with Bill Gates, I'm for the federal government. I always like to root for the little guy."[13]

The second phase, aimed at protecting competitors, emerged during the Depression Era of the 1930s, when independent merchants felt the need for legal protection against competition from larger chain stores. Among the federal legislation enacted was the Robinson-Patman Act. The third regulatory phase focused on consumer protection. Although the objective of consumer protection underlies most laws—with good examples including the Sherman Act, FTC Act, and Federal Food and Drug Act—many of the major consumer-oriented laws have been enacted during the past 40 years. The fourth phase, industry deregulation, began in the late 1970s and continues to the present. During this phase, government has sought to increase competition in such industries as telecommunications, utilities, transportation, and financial services by discontinuing many regulations and permitting firms to expand their service offerings to new markets.

The newest regulatory frontier is cyberspace. Federal and state regulators are investigating ways to police the Internet and online services. For example, the FTC has devoted a Web site to publicizing *e-fraud*, schemes such as meta-tags that falsely lure browsers to sites they have not requested or start-your-own business scams. Another popular con is to send consumers a check, apparently with no strings attached. When the check is cashed the consumer has signed up for a long-term Internet access agreement, usually with an unreliable and overpriced operator. Although the federal government has been slow to regulate spam—junk e-mail—many states have enacted legislation and many more have introduced bills to

Marketing Dictionary

political-legal environment   Component of the marketing environment consisting of laws and interpretations of laws that require firms to operate under competitive conditions and to protect consumer rights.

protect consumers and punish offenders. Yet the effectiveness of state campaigns is limited. The Internet is, after all, global, not local.[14]

Privacy and child protection issues are another difficult enforcement challenge. With the passage of the Children's Online Privacy Protection Act, Congress took the first step in regulating what children are exposed to on the Internet. The primary focus is a set of rules regarding how and when marketers need to get parental permission before obtaining marketing research information from children over the Web.

Many Internet marketers are taking proactive steps to protect the consumer. Microsoft is developing technology that lets people automatically skip sites that do not meet their privacy standards. Citigroup has teamed up with the U.S. Secret Service to develop a pilot program to combat identity theft.[15]

Table 3.1 lists and briefly describes the major federal laws affecting marketing. Legislation covering specific marketing practices, such as product development, packaging, labeling, product warranties, and franchise agreements, is discussed in later chapters.

Marketers must also monitor state and local laws that affect their industries. Many states, for instance, allow hard liquor to be sold only in liquor stores; such laws limit the distribution of low-alcohol cocktails made with rum, vodka, whiskey, and bourbon. California's stringent regulations for automobile emissions require special pollution control equipment on cars sold in the state.

Government Regulatory Agencies

Federal, state, and local governments have established regulatory agencies to enforce laws. At the federal level, the Federal Trade Commission (FTC) wields the broadest powers of any agency to influence marketing activities. It has the authority to enforce laws regulating unfair business practices and can take action to stop false and deceptive advertising. The Federal Communications Commission regulates communication by wire, radio, and television. Other federal regulatory agencies include the Food and Drug Administration, the Consumer Products Safety Commission, the Federal Power Commission, and the Environmental Protection Agency.

The FTC uses several procedures to enforce laws. It may issue a consent order through which a business accused of violations can agree to voluntary compliance without admitting guilt. If a business refuses to comply with an FTC request, the agency can issue a cease-and-desist order, which gives a final demand to stop an illegal practice. Firms often challenge cease-and-desist orders in court. The FTC can require advertisers to provide additional information about products in their advertisements, and it can force firms using deceptive advertising to correct earlier claims with new promotional messages. In some cases, the FTC can require a firm to give refunds to consumers misled by deceptive advertising.

The FTC and U.S. Justice Department can stop mergers if they believe the proposed acquisition will reduce competition by making it harder for new companies to enter the field. In recent years, these agencies have taken a harder line on proposed mergers, especially in the computer, telecommunications, financial services, and health-care sectors.

Removing regulation also changes the competitive picture considerably. Following deregulation of the telecommunications and utilities industries, suppliers no longer have exclusive rights to operate within a territory. Natural gas utilities traditionally competed with electric companies to supply homeowners and businesses with energy needs. Because of deregulation, they now also compete with other gas companies. Customers of KN Energy in southeastern Wyoming can choose from among 12 competing gas companies, some of which deliver gas through out-of-state pipelines. Deregulation also allows new opportunities for start-up companies. GreenMountain.com differentiates itself as an environmentally conscious energy supplier, claiming to offer a cleaner electricity product. Moreover, its 100,000 customers, mostly in California and Pennsylvania, earn discounts whenever they engage in environmentally beneficial activities, such as walking to work instead of driving.[16]

Restructuring of the utility industry after 90 years of monopoly will affect many different sectors. If power costs drop the expected 20 percent due to deregulation of the generation process, businesses and individuals will have more money to spend on other things. Competition will improve efficiency in what had become a complex and inefficient market. Consolidation of the industry will increase due to mergers between utility companies.

TABLE 3.1   Major Federal Laws Affecting Marketing

Date	Law	Description
A. Laws Maintaining a Competitive Environment		
1890	Sherman Antitrust Act	Prohibits restraint of trade and monopolization; identifies a competitive marketing system as national policy goal
1914	Clayton Act	Strengthens the Sherman Act by restricting such practices as price discrimination, exclusive dealing, tying contracts, and interlocking boards of directors where the effect "may be to substantially lessen competition or tend to create a monopoly"
1914	Federal Trade Commission Act (FTC)	Prohibits unfair methods of competition; establishes the Federal Trade Commission, an administrative agency that investigates business practices and enforces the FTC Act
1938	Wheeler-Lea Act	Amends the FTC Act to outlaw additional unfair practices; gives the FTC jurisdiction over false and misleading advertising
1950	Celler-Kefauver Antimerger Act	Amends the Clayton Act to include major asset purchases that will decrease competition in an industry
2001	Air Transportation Safety and System Stabilization Act	Enacted in response to terrorist attacks that crippled the airline industry; granted airlines $5 million in cash and $10 million in loan guarantees to keep them in business
B. Laws Regulating Competition		
1936	Robinson-Patman Act	Prohibits price discrimination in sales to wholesalers, retailers, or other producers; prohibits selling at unreasonably low prices to eliminate competition
1993	North American Free Trade Agreement (NAFTA)	International trade agreement between Canada, Mexico, and the United States designed to facilitate trade by removing tariffs and other trade barriers among the three nations
C. Laws Protecting Consumers		
1906	Federal Food and Drug Act	Prohibits adulteration and misbranding of foods and drugs involved in interstate commerce; strengthened by the Food, Drug, and Cosmetic Act (1938) and the Kefauver-Harris Drug Amendment (1962)
1970	National Environmental Policy Act	Establishes the Environmental Protection Agency to deal with various types of pollution and organizations that create pollution
1971	Public Health Cigarette Smoking Act	Prohibits tobacco advertising on radio and television
1972	Consumer Product Safety Act	Created the Consumer Product Safety Commission, which has authority to specify safety standards for most products
1998	Children's Online Privacy Protection Act	Empowers FTC to set rules regarding how and when marketers must obtain parental permission before asking children marketing research questions
2000	Cybersquatting Law	Bans the bad-faith purchase of domain names that are identical or confusingly similar to existing registered trademarks
2001	Electronic Signature Act	Gives electronic signatures the same legal weight as handwritten signatures
2001	Aviation Security Act	Requires airlines to take extra security measures to protect passengers, including the installation of cockpit doors, improved baggage screening, and increased security training for airport personnel
D. Laws Deregulating Specific Industries		
1978	Airline Deregulation Act	Grants considerable freedom to commercial airlines in setting fares and choosing new routes
1980	Motor Carrier Act and Staggers Rail Act	Significantly deregulates trucking and railroad industries by permitting them to negotiate rates and services
1996	Telecommunications Act	Significantly deregulates the telecommunications industry by removing barriers to competition in local and long-distance phone and cable and television markets

The latest round of deregulation brought the passage of the Telecommunications Act of 1996. This law removed barriers between local and long-distance phone companies and cable companies. It allowed the so-called "Baby Bells"—the seven regional Bell operating companies—to offer long-distance service; at the same time, long-distance companies—such as AT&T, MCI, and Sprint, which control over 90 percent of this market—were able to offer local service. Satellite television providers such as DISH and DirectTV and cable companies like Comcast and Time Warner Cable can offer phone service, and phone companies can get into the cable business. The change promises huge rewards for competitive winners. Just capturing 20 percent of the local calling market, for example, is worth $15 billion to $20 billion per year to AT&T.

However, deregulation is not without its critics. Although the previous decade witnessed a flurry of moves by state authorities to deregulate utilities, California's near disaster from their recent deregulatory moves prompted dozens of states to postpone further consideration of deregulations. Following allegations of financial malpractice at Houston's Enron Corp.—once the poster child of deregulation—the courts recently decided to split the bankrupt company apart and sell it off in pieces. Skyrocketing prices due to gas shortages led the Georgia legislature to try to reform the state's deregulated gas market. One bill would re-regulate prices under state rules; another would create a state-regulated supplier to which consumers could switch from privately owned, unregulated gas companies.[17]

Other Regulatory Forces

Public and private consumer interest groups and self-regulatory organizations are also part of the legal environment. Consumer interest organizations have mushroomed in the past 25 years, and today hundreds of groups operate at national, state, and local levels. The National Coalition Against Misuse of Pesticides seeks to protect the environment. People for Ethical Treatment of Animals (PETA) opposes the use of animals for product testing. Other groups attempt to advance the rights of minorities, elderly Americans, and other special-interest causes. The power of these groups has also grown. Pressure from antialcohol groups has resulted in proposed legislation requiring health warnings on all alcohol ads and stricter regulations of alcoholic beverage advertising.

Self-regulatory groups represent industries' attempts to set guidelines for responsible business conduct. The Council of Better Business Bureaus is a national organization devoted to consumer service and business self-regulation. The Council's National Advertising Division (NAD) is designed to promote truth and accuracy in advertising. It reviews and advocates voluntary resolution of advertising-related complaints between consumers and businesses. If NAD fails to resolve a complaint, an appeal can be made to the National Advertising Review Board, which is composed of advertisers, ad agency representatives, and public members. In addition, many individual trade associations set business guidelines and codes of conduct and encourage members' voluntary compliance. The alcoholic beverage industry is trying to educate teens about underage drinking, as described in "Solving an Ethical Controversy."

In an effort to protect consumer privacy and curb unwanted mail or phone solicitations, the Direct Marketing Association (DMA) recently approved new rules requiring customers to be notified if information about them—including their name and address—was being shared with other marketers. Companies must also tell consumers that they have the option not to have their information shared. The new rules apply to nearly 4,500 DMA member firms and include 2,600 Internet companies, catalogs, banks, financial institutions, publishers, not-for-profits, and book and music clubs.

As mentioned earlier, regulating the online world poses a challenge. Favoring self-regulation as the best starting point, the FTC sponsored a Privacy Initiative for consumers, advertisers, online companies, and others as a way to develop voluntary industry privacy guidelines. The Interactive Services Association is also working on its own privacy standards.

Controlling the Political-Legal Environment

Most marketers comply with laws and regulations, since noncompliance can scar a firm's reputation and hurt profits. Yet most also fight regulations they consider unjust. The regional Bell operating companies filed lawsuits to protect their turf against competition from long-distance carriers and cable companies, while GTE claimed the deregulation of local phone service was unconstitutional. Other companies have jumped in to take advantage of new opportunities. Furst Group, a long-distance

Solving an Ethical Controversy

right / wrong

Is the Fox Guarding the Henhouse? The Alcohol Industry's "Drink Responsibly" Promotions

The old public service announcements that pleaded with young TV watchers not to drink until they were 21 probably fell on deaf ears, even when the message was delivered by the likes of former NFL quarterback Dan Marino and others. Those announcements were a convenient break during which to fix a snack or call a friend. No one would have guessed that eventually the alcohol beverage industry itself would jump into the ring with its own "Drink Responsibly" advertising campaign, with commercials as slick and expensive to produce as the ads for their own products. During the last 15 years, the beer industry alone has poured more than $500 million into advertising against underage drinking, along with support for designated drivers, care cabs, and scanners for fake ID cards. Some people applaud this effort at social responsibility, while critics contend that the industry is actually behaving unethically and shouldn't be in the business of looking as though they condemn the consumption of their own products.

Is the alcoholic beverage industry's "Drink Responsibly" advertising campaign socially responsible?

PRO

1. If the ads get kids' attention, they are worth it. Combined education efforts by groups such as Mothers Against Drunk Driving (MADD), school programs, and the alcoholic beverage industry have had positive results.
2. The "Drink Responsibly" ad campaign is only part of an overall education effort by the industry that includes providing resources for teachers, parent-student discussion groups, server training at bars and restaurants, safe ride vouchers, and the like.

CON

1. Instead of showing the "Drink Responsibly" ads, the alcoholic beverage industry should stop marketing its products on television—which is mostly watched by children and teens—altogether.
2. Since it is illegal for teens and school-age children to be drinking at all, they should not be viewing "Drink Responsibly" ads.

SUMMARY

In the last 15 years, alcoholic beverage consumption among students between 6th and 12th grade has dropped significantly. In addition, alcohol-related traffic deaths have decreased 50 percent in the last 20 years. However, binge drinking among college students has increased over the last decade. Industry critics worry about the mixed message that the "Drink Responsibly" campaign sends to young viewers. Yet in one poll, 89 percent of respondents said that they believed the industry's participation in these ads was appropriate.

SOURCES: Mike Beirne, "In the Name of Responsibility," *Brandweek*, May 12, 2003, pp. 32-36; Nat Ives, "A Campaign for Drinking," *The New York Times*, April 17, 2003, accessed at the Advertising Educational Foundation, www.aef.com; Alexander Conant, "Everybody Isn't Doing It," *The Badger Herald Online*, April 11, 2002, www.badgerherald.com.

phone company with no lines or equipment, buys blocks of long-distance time from major carriers at greatly reduced rates and resells it by the minute at a discount. Now the regional Bells and long-distance carriers are competing aggressively to keep their customers. They are also working with *switchless resellers* like Furst to retain small business customers that they would otherwise lose.

Consumer groups and political action committees within industries may try to influence the outcome of proposed legislation or change existing laws by engaging in political lobbying or boycotts. Lobbying groups frequently enlist the support of customers, employees, and suppliers to assist their efforts.

The Economic Environment *the depression of 1930's*

The overall health of the economy influences how much consumers spend and what they buy. This relationship also works the other way. Consumer buying plays an important role in the economy's health; in fact, consumer outlays perennially make up some two-thirds of overall economic activity.

4

Outline the economic factors that affect marketing decisions and consumer buying power.

Since all marketing activity is directed toward satisfying consumer wants and needs, marketers must understand how economic conditions influence consumer purchasing behavior.

Marketing's **economic environment** consists of forces that influence consumer buying power and marketing strategies. They include the stage of the business cycle, inflation and deflation, unemployment, income, and resource availability.

Stages in the Business Cycle

Historically, the economy has tended to follow a cyclical pattern consisting of four stages: prosperity, recession, depression, and recovery. No depressions have occurred in the U.S. since the 1930s, and many economists argue that society is capable of preventing future depressions through intelligent use of various economic policies. Good decision making should ensure that a recession would give way to a period of recovery, rather than sinking further into depression.

Consumer buying differs in each stage of the *business cycle*, and marketers must adjust their strategies accordingly. In times of prosperity, consumer spending maintains a brisk pace and buyers are willing to spend more for premium versions of well-known brands. Marketers respond by expanding product lines, increasing promotional efforts and expanding distribution to raise market share, and raising prices to widen profit margins. Figure 3.3 illustrates how marketers appeal to shoppers' desires to indulge themselves with luxury items during prosperous times—such as the TAG Heuer watch embedded with "alter ego diamonds."

During the recent recession, consumers shifted their buying patterns to emphasize basic, functional products that carry low price tags. They limited travel, restaurant meals, entertainment, and convenience purchases, preferring to spend money on video rentals and home cooking. In recessionary periods, sales of lower-priced brands of grocery and household-goods products and private-label goods rise. To compete, marketers consider lowering prices, eliminating marginal products, improving customer service, and increasing promotional outlays to stimulate demand. They may also launch value-priced products likely to appeal to cost-conscious buyers.

FIGURE 3.3

Spending for Luxury Products Increases during Times of Prosperity

Consumer spending sinks to its lowest level during a depression. The last true depression in the U.S. occurred during the 1930s. Although a severe depression could occur again, most experts see it as a slim possibility. Through its monetary and fiscal policies, the federal government attempts to control extreme fluctuations in the business cycle that lead to depression.

In the recovery stage, the economy emerges from recession and consumer purchasing power increases. But while consumers have money to spend, caution often restrains their willingness to buy. During the recovery of the early 1990s, for instance, U.S. consumers paid down their car loans and bank loans and borrowed less on their credit cards. With lower principal and interest payments, they actually had higher levels of disposable income to spend; however, they continued to spend cautiously. Usually, as a recovery strengthens, consumers become more indulgent, buying more convenience products and higher-priced goods and services.

In the 1990s, the U.S. economy surpassed the performance of the previous quarter-century. The nation experienced strong productivity growth, as measured by the gross domestic product (GDP), low inflation, a strong labor market, and profits that more than doubled. Sales of new single-family homes and cars were up, reflecting an increasing confidence in the economy. These major purchases had a ripple effect in related sectors, such as home appliances, furnishings, and lawn care. Not only did consumers spend more, but they also charged more purchases. As the economy showed signs of slowdown in 2001, growth stalled. In attempts to cut costs and hold on to profits, corporations made massive layoffs. Telecommunications company Motorola shed a third of its worldwide workforce. Consumer debt rose faster than income, delinquent credit-card payments reached new highs, and personal bankruptcy filings increased fivefold over the previous year.[18] By 2003, following federal interest rate cuts and tax cuts aimed at stimulating the economy, the worst was over.

Recovery remains a difficult stage for businesses just climbing out of a recession since it requires them to earn profits while trying to gauge uncertain consumer demand. Many cope by holding down costs. Some trim payrolls and close branch offices. Others cut back on business travel budgets. DaimlerChrysler pared spending on airline tickets by two-thirds during a single year. Teleconferencing and videoconferencing took the place of nonessential travel. Some industries struggle more than others during recovery periods. Among the hardest hit after the recent recession were the airline and lodging industries and the nation's major theme parks. Not only were consumers reluctant to fly following the terrorist attacks of September 11, but they viewed such services as travel and entertainment as unnecessary luxuries.[19]

Despite the recent slowdown, economic growth is expected to continue at an annual rate of 3 percent for the remainder of this decade. Inflation should continue to level off, and the standard of living will rise. During the first decade of this century, established industries such as finance, media, wholesale, and retail will change dramatically and new industries will be created at an astounding pace.

Business cycles, like other aspects of the economy, are complex phenomena that seem to defy the control of marketers. Success depends on flexible plans that can be adjusted to satisfy consumer demands during the various business cycle stages.

Inflation and Deflation ✓

A major constraint on consumer spending, which can occur during any stage of the business cycle, is *inflation*—rising prices caused by some combination of excess demand and increases in the costs of raw materials, component parts, human resources, or other factors of production. Inflation devalues money by reducing the products it can buy through persistent price increases. These rising prices increase marketers' costs, such as expenditures for wages and raw materials, and the resulting higher prices may therefore negatively affect sales. U.S. inflation hit a heart-stopping high in 1979 of 13.3 percent.

If inflation is so bad, is its opposite, *deflation*, better? At first, it might seem so. Falling prices mean that products are more affordable. But deflation can be a long and damaging downward spiral, causing a freefall in business profits, lower returns on most investments, and widespread job layoffs. The last time that the U.S. experienced significant deflation was in the Great Depression of the 1930s. During the recent recession economists worried about deflation, as interest rates declined and some product prices declined. Still, other than the cost of energy and food prices, which can fluctuate wildly, inflation is rising at about a 1 percent rate annually, in part due to the rising cost of services—which make up 60 percent of the consumer price index. Productivity gains have also helped keep U.S. prices in neutral, with neither inflation nor deflation a significant threat.

Unemployment

Unemployment is defined as the proportion of people in the economy who do not have jobs and are actively looking for work. Unemployment rises during recessions and declines in the recovery and prosperity stages of the business cycle. Like inflation, unemployment affects marketing by modifying consumer behavior.

Marketing Dictionary

economic environment Factors that influence consumer buying power and marketing strategies, including stage of the business cycle, inflation, unemployment, income, and resource availability.

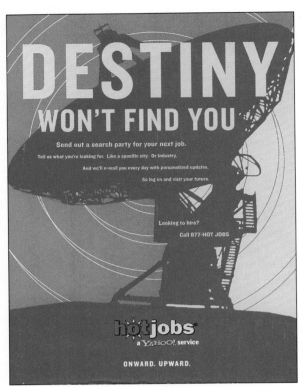

HotJobs.com is one of the major firms that help job seekers and employers find each other online.

Unless unemployment insurance, personal savings, and union benefits effectively offset lost earnings, unemployed people have relatively little income to spend. Even if these protections completely compensate people for lost earnings, their buying behavior is still likely to change. Instead of buying, they may choose to build their savings.

The relationship between unemployment and stages in the business cycle was illustrated the past dozen years. After peaking near 8 percent during the recession of 1992, it declined steadily since then in the midst of the extended period of prosperity from the mid-1990s to the early years of this century, reaching a low of 3.9 percent in 2001. It crept back up to the 6 percent mark when the nation experienced a double blow of an economic downturn combined with the terrorist attacks.[20] Since that time, unemployment has declined in the wake of an improved economy.

Internet job boards are cutting into the job-search market once controlled by matchmaking agencies and newspaper advertising. The Web now accounts for about 15 percent of employment advertising, up from only 2 percent just three years ago. Thousands of large and medium-sized employers include an "Available Positions" section on their Web sites. Online recruiters like HotJobs.com and Monster.com are both popular with job seekers and growing rapidly. HotJobs.com, one of the big success stories in online recruiting, is a regular advertiser on annual Super Bowl telecasts. It maintains a database of more than 9.8 million registered job seekers—and has in excess of 70,000 job listings.[21]

Income

Income is another important determinant of marketing's economic environment because it influences consumer buying power. By studying income statistics and trends, marketers can estimate market potential and develop plans for targeting specific market segments. For example, U.S. household incomes have grown in recent years. Coupled with a low rate of inflation, this increase has boosted purchasing power for millions of consumers. A rise in income represents a potential for increasing overall sales. However, marketers are most interested in *discretionary income*, the amount of money people have to spend after buying necessities such as food, clothing, and housing.

Changes in average earnings powerfully affect discretionary income. Historically, periods of major innovation have been accompanied by dramatic increases in living standards and rising incomes. During the first half of the 20th century—a period of unprecedented innovations in transportation from the railroads to supersonic jets—real per-capita incomes tripled and even quadrupled, fueled by rising productivity. The 21st century could see similar income gains with the growth of electronic technologies. Some predictions indicate a 9 percent rise in real wages, a more than 50 percent rise in corporate earnings, and interest rates below 4 percent. These rapidly climbing income rates could lead to a 25 percent growth in the overall economy.

Resource Availability

Resources are not unlimited. Shortages—temporary or permanent—can result from several causes, including lack of raw materials, component parts, energy, or labor. A continuing concern of both business executives and government officials is the nation's dependence on imported oil and the risk that these imports might be curtailed by exporting countries attempting to influence U.S. foreign policy. Also, brisk demand may bring in orders that exceed manufacturing capacity or outpace the response time required to gear up a production line. Regardless of the cause, shortages require marketers to reorient their thinking.

One reaction is **demarketing,** the process of reducing consumer demand for a product to a level that the firm can reasonably supply. Oil companies publicize tips on how to cut gasoline consumption and utility companies encourage homeowners to install more insulation to reduce heating costs. Many cities discourage central business-district traffic by raising parking fees and violation penalties and promoting mass transit and carpooling.

A shortage presents marketers with a unique set of challenges. They may have to allocate limited supplies, a sharply different activity from marketing's traditional objective of expanding sales volume. Shortages may require marketers to decide whether to spread limited supplies over all customers or limit purchases by some customers so that the firm can completely satisfy others.

Marketers today have also devised ways to deal with increased demand for fixed amounts of resources. Reynolds Metal Co. addresses the dwindling supply of aluminum through its recycling programs, including cash-paying vending machines. Such "reverse" vending machines allow people to insert empty cans into the machines and receive money, stamps, and/or discount coupons for merchandise or services.

The International Economic Environment

In today's global economy, marketers must also monitor the economic environment of other nations. Just as in the U.S., a recession in Europe or Japan changes buying habits. Changes in foreign currency rates compared with the U.S. dollar also affect marketing decisions. The strong dollar and the problems in Asia hurt companies such as BP Amoco, whose foreign sales fell nearly 20 percent in just two years. Even beverage giant Coca-Cola Co. is not immune. With 75 percent of its operating profit generated overseas, currency fluctuations risk damaging overall performance. Rival PepsiCo gets only a fifth of its earnings from international sales.[22]

For the most part, however, U.S. companies have posted higher revenue gains in overseas operations. Technology companies are the biggest beneficiaries. Combined, Lucent Technologies, Dell, and Seagate Technology accounted for well over $12 billion in sales from outside the U.S.

In China, where the market for cell phones shows growth at the phenomenal rate of 50 percent while demand in Europe slows down, technology companies foresee a similarly explosive market for wireless Internet access. A recent partnership between Chinese Internet commerce platform Best-of-China.com, Motorola, IBM/China, direct marketer R. R. Donnelley, and Internet company Roundpoint seeks to enable e-commerce opportunities for businesses and Internet consumers. The alliance will create an Internet gateway into China.[23]

The Technological Environment

The **technological environment** represents the application to marketing of knowledge in science, inventions, and innovations. Technology leads to new goods and services for consumers; it also improves existing products, offers better customer service, and often reduces prices through new, cost-efficient production and distribution methods. Technology can quickly make products obsolete—e-mail, for example, quickly eroded the market for fax machines—but it can just as quickly open new marketing opportunities.

As we discussed in Chapter 1, technology is revolutionizing the marketing environment, transforming the way companies promote and distribute goods. Technological innovations create not just new products and services but also entirely new industries. Among the new businesses developing as a result of the Internet are Web-page designers, new types of software firms, interactive advertising agencies, and companies like VeriSign that allow customers to make secure financial transactions over the Web. Industrial and medical use of lasers, superconductor transmission of electricity, wireless communications products, seeds and plants enhanced by biotechnology, and genetically engineered proteins that fight disease are just a few more examples of technological advances.

Phillips Petroleum Co. has revamped its manufacturing operations with new software applications. A new planning and optimization

5
Discuss the impact of the technological environment on a firm's marketing activities.

Marketing Dictionary

demarketing Process of reducing consumer demand for a good or service to a level that the firm can supply.

technological environment Applications to marketing of knowledge based on discoveries in science, inventions, and innovations.

FIGURE 3.4
The Toyota Prius: One of the First Hybrid Automobiles Available for U.S. Auto Buyers

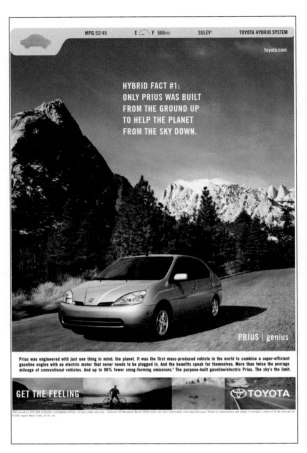

program, designed to help refinery operations comply with stiff federal environmental regulations that took effect in 2004, also cut supply chain and manufacturing costs.[24]

Technology can sometimes address social concerns. In response to pressure from the World Trade Organization and the U.S. government, Japanese automakers were first to use technology to develop more fuel-efficient vehicles and reduce dangerous emissions with offerings like the Toyota Prius and a hybrid version of the Honda Civic. A new wave of "hybrid vehicles" that combine a conventional gasoline engine with a battery-powered electric motor will be released in 2005 by the Big Three automakers. Ford Motor Co.'s hybrid Escape sport-utility vehicle (SUV) promises up to 40 mpg in the city and DaimlerChrysler is offering a hybrid Durango SUV. In 2004, General Motors launched a hybrid powertrain for its big pickups and SUVs.[25] Figure 3.4 shows the Prius, Toyota's successful hybrid vehicle capable of achieving up to 52 miles per gallon in highway driving.

Industry, government, colleges and universities, and other not-for-profit institutions all play roles in the development of new technology—but not always with the best results. Energy-efficiency improvements for home appliances, mandated by Congress, will do little to help the environment or give consumers value for the money. For instance, after 2006, all new air-conditioning systems must be designed to meet higher efficiency standards. The systems will save consumers money only if they are used at maximum capacity for 18 years, even though the average American moves every 7 years and, depending on climate, turns on the air conditioning only in the summertime. Even worse, most homeowners will have to install new ductwork and interior walls to fit the new units. Rather than take on this expense, they're likely to just keep fixing existing appliances, negating the energy savings initiative.[26]

Research and development efforts by private industry represent a major source of technological innovation. Pfizer, a U.S.-based global pharmaceutical company, discovers, develops, manufactures, and markets innovative medicines, spending billions each year on research. Among its most publicized breakthroughs are the cholesterol-lowering drug Lipitor, which ranks as the biggest-selling prescription drug in the U.S.; Viagra, a revolutionary treatment for erectile dysfunction; and Trovan, one of the most prescribed antibiotics in the U.S. Pfizer Animal Health develops animal vaccines, feed additives, and the first arthritis medication in the U.S. specifically for dogs. To maximize the strength of its product lines, Pfizer invests nearly $3 billion in research and development annually. Its U.S. sales force, which doubled in just three years, has ranked number one in overall quality for the last four years.

Another major source of technology is the federal government, including the military. Air bags originated from Air Force ejection seats, digital computers were first designed to calculate artillery trajectories, and the microwave oven is a derivative of military radar systems. The technology and styling behind Hummer trucks, featured in Figure 3.5, comes from U.S. military vehicles.

Although the United States has long been the world leader in research, competition from rivals in Japan and Europe is intense. While U.S. companies spearheaded the technologies behind personal computers, networking systems, and the Internet, Japanese firms capitalized on their ability to transfer those technologies into commercial products. For instance, Sony and JVC commercialized videocassette recorders—an American technology—into one of the most successful new products of the past two decades. Chinese companies, which traditionally operated as subcontractors for U.S. firms, are working to build their own international brands—much like current Japanese competitors did 30 years ago.[27]

FIGURE 3.5
Adapting Military Technology and Styling to Create a Successful Product for the Consumer Market

Applying Technology

The technological environment must be closely monitored for a number of reasons. For one, creative applications of new technologies not only give a firm a definite competitive edge but can also benefit society. Kenmore's energy-efficient refrigerator uses less energy than a light bulb, while delivering all custom features and the sleek styling buyers require. As the message from the Council for Biotechnology Information in Figure 3.6 explains, advances in biotechnology help Hawaiian crop farmers resist viruses—and increase production.

Marketers who monitor new technology and successfully apply it may also enhance customer service. Breakthroughs in electronic communications have brought consumers the convenience of in-home shopping and 24-hour banking at automated teller machines and via the Internet. Some restaurants provide faster service by equipping serving staff with palmtop computers that transmit patrons' orders to the kitchen staff.

When boutique online brokers such as Ameritrade, E*Trade Group, and Scott created a new market of small Internet traders, Merrill Lynch & Co, Wall Street's largest brokerage firm, decided to get in on the act. Transferring its reputation for financial services expertise to its online capabilities, Merrill Lynch was able to compete on price with discount rival Charles Schwab Corp., charging a fraction of the cost of its traditional

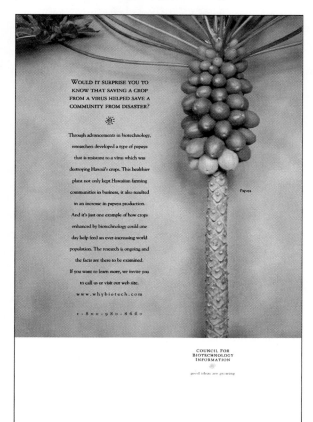

FIGURE 3.6
How Biotechnology Advances Reduce Prices, Increase Production, and Benefit Hawaii's Economy

transaction fees. However, online trading has fallen dramatically since 2001 as the stock market was buffeted by the blows of recession and widespread investor concerns following the collapse of Enron and other former high-flyers. The resulting slowdown took its toll on brokerages that did not enjoy the protection of a larger umbrella organization.[28]

As Merrill Lynch learned, implementing technology involves considerable expense, and there is no guarantee of unbridled success. Subsequent chapters discuss in more detail how companies apply technologies—such as databases, electronic data interchange, and interactive promotional techniques—to create a competitive advantage.

6

Explain how the social-cultural environment influences marketing.

The Social-Cultural Environment

As a nation, the U.S. is becoming older, more affluent, and more culturally diverse. The birthrate is falling, and subculture populations are rising. People express concerns about the environment, buying ecologically friendly products that reduce pollution. They value the time at home with family and friends, watching videos and eating microwavable snacks. These aspects of consumer lifestyles help to shape marketing's **social-cultural environment**—the relationship between marketing and society and its culture.

To remain competitive, marketers must be sensitive to society's demographic shifts and changing values. These variables affect consumers' reactions to different products and marketing practices. College students—the core market for new releases on compact disc or DVD—have found new ways to get hold of popular music and movies. While Napster, the song-swapping service that allowed friends to trade pirated music over the Web, has been silenced by litigation, a wave of new products that promise "free" entertainment have recently flooded the market. Microsoft, Sony, TiVo, and others offer devices that can download video through high-speed Net connections. A software program, Morpheus, enables video piracy via PC and claims over 20 million users. In response, five major film studios—MGM, Sony, Paramount, Warner Bros., and Universal—recently initiated Moviefly, a joint venture through which they will deliver movies via the Internet. The move may have lasting impact on the buying behavior of movie fans.[29]

Creative marketers of products for the U.S. population of the 21st century must take into consideration all the segments of their market. In addition to its original Quaker Oats and its spin-off brands targeted to children, Quaker now offers a product targeted specifically to women. Figure 3.7 shows the company's new Nutrition for Women offering, which promises a breakfast fortified with calcium, iron, and all the vitamins women need to stay healthy.

Another social-cultural consideration is the increasing importance of cultural diversity. The U.S. is a mixed society composed of

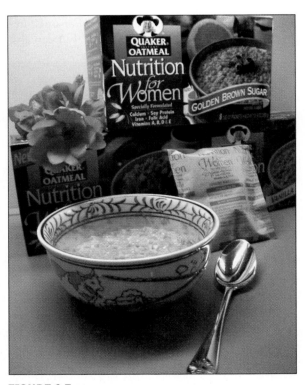

FIGURE 3.7
Nutrition for Women: A New Breakfast Alternative from Quaker Oats Designed Especially for Women

various submarkets, each with its unique values, cultural characteristics, consumer preferences, and purchasing behaviors. Advertising firm Dieste Harmel specializes in targeting the Hispanic market. When research showed that Hispanic consumers ate only half as many salty snacks as non-Hispanic consumers, Dieste went to work. The resulting campaign featured two Latin music stars and created a fun, party atmosphere around the client's product, Doritos. Sales shot up by 25 percent. Even better, a campaign tie-in showcased Pepsi, whose sales in Hispanic markets tripled.[30]

The social-cultural context often exerts a more pronounced influence on marketing decision making in the international sphere than in the domestic arena. Learning about cultural and societal differences among countries is paramount to a firm's success abroad. Marketing strategies that work in the U.S. often fail when directly applied in other countries, and vice versa. In many cases, marketers must redesign packages and modify products and advertising messages to suit the tastes and preferences of different cultures.

French firm Alcatel badly misjudged the effects of its recent marketing campaign in the U.S. Its ads featuring the late Martin Luther King, Jr., not only raised eyebrows but some tempers as well. Chapter 4 explores the social-cultural aspects of international marketing.

Consumerism anti-firm movement

Changing societal values have led to **consumerism,** defined as a social force within the environment that aids and protects the buyer by exerting legal, moral, and economic pressures on business. Today everyone—marketers, industry, government, and the public—is acutely aware of the impact of consumerism on the nation's economy and general well-being.

In recent years, marketers have witnessed increasing consumer activism. No organization or industry is immune. Marketers of canned tuna have been criticized for promoting sales of tuna caught by nets that also trap and kill dolphins. Private airport security firms have been replaced by federal employees in response to heightened concerns over the threat of terrorist attacks. Protesters oppose moves to allow oil drilling in the Alaska wildlife refuge. Boycotts, another means through which consumers make their objections known, have increased in recent years to include companies from almost every industry: Nike, McDonald's, Disney, Monsanto, and British Airways have all been targeted in recent years. Even the threat of a boycott can bring results.

But firms do not always give in to consumer demands. The economic system cannot work if excessive demands prevent firms from achieving reasonable profit objectives. This choice between pleasing consumers and remaining viable defines one of the most difficult dilemmas facing society, as the "Marketing Miss" box describes. Given these constraints, what should buyers have the right to expect from the competitive marketing system?

The most frequently quoted answer came from a speech made by President John F. Kennedy in 1962. While this list does not

Marketing Miss

Why Consumers Are Crossing the Border to Fill Their Prescriptions

Background. There's no escaping the fact that U.S. prescription drug prices are often the most expensive in the world. As a result, consumers are doing what they've always done—finding the best deals. Many have discovered that drug prices in Canada are much lower than in the U.S., so they are making the trip—by car, by phone, by computer.

The Marketing Problem. Losing customers to Canada naturally upsets U.S. pharmaceutical companies and retail drugstores. But a free market says that if one drugstore offers a 90-day supply of a drug for $100 less than another, the consumer can make his or her own choice. The Food & Drug Administration (FDA) says it "cannot guarantee the safety of Canadian drugs." Drug manufacturers justify their domestic prices by pointing out their need to recoup high R&D costs inherent in new drugs. But these arguments haven't deterred U.S. consumers, particularly senior citizens, who are frustrated by the high cost of prescriptions in the U.S.

The Outcome. Some small U.S. drugstores have actually profited from the problem by providing fax machines, phones, and computers for consumers to use to purchase their

continued on next page

Marketing Dictionary

social-cultural environment   Component of the marketing environment consisting of the relationship between the marketer and society and its culture.

consumerism   Social force within the environment designed to aid and protect the consumer by exerting legal, moral, and economic pressures on business and government.

Marketing Miss

prescriptions directly from Canada. However, the FDA has begun warning these pharmacies, as well as insurance companies that are willing to cover some of the imported drugs, that they are violating federal law. The U.S. House and Senate are working on a law to allow reimportation of certain prescription drugs. Still, there has been no long-term solution to the problem.

Lessons Learned. The issue of the cost of prescription drugs in the U.S. remains unresolved. But consumers have spoken: they want high-quality drugs at fair prices, and they will go wherever possible to obtain them.

SOURCES: Tony Pugh, "Prescription Drug Bill Unlikely to Become Law," *Pioneer Press*, August 3, 2003, **http://www.twincities.com**; Robert Novak, "Drug Company Backlash Hits Fever Pitch in Congress," *Chicago Sun-Times*, July 17, 2003, **http://www.suntimes.com**; Julie Appleby, "Stores Pop Up to Help Seniors Buy Canadian Drugs," *USA Today*, April 9, 2003, p. B1; Thomas M. Burton, "The FDA Begins Cracking Down on Cheaper Drugs from Canada," *The Wall Street Journal*, March 12, 2003, p. A1.

amount to a definitive statement, it offers good rules of thumb that explain basic **consumer rights:**

1. *The right to choose freely.* Consumers should be able to choose from among a range of goods and services.

2. *The right to be informed.* Consumers should be provided with enough education and product information to enable them to be responsible buyers.

3. *The right to be heard.* Consumers should be able to express their legitimate displeasure to appropriate parties—that is, sellers, consumer assistance groups, and city or state consumer affairs offices.

4. *The right to be safe.* Consumers should be assured that the goods and services they purchase are not injurious with normal use. Goods and services should be designed in such a way that the average consumer can use them safely.

These rights have formed the conceptual framework of much of the legislation passed in the first 40 years of the consumer rights movement. However, the question of how best to guarantee them remains unanswered. Sometimes, state or federal authorities step in. California's "lemon law" gives car dealers only three chances to repair a defective auto. Following the terrorist attacks of September 11, airlines were immediately required to install titanium cockpit doors. Food labeling regulations force disclosure of such details as expiration date, ingredients, and nutritional values on packaged foods. Though not required to do so, fast-food chain Subway now includes similar information on its menus. Often, marketers such as Subway who see a genuine consumer benefit in their products use advertising to communicate it. Recently, the FDA, which already permitted marketers to advertise the disease-fighting benefits of foods rich in dietary fiber, allowed marketers of foods with more than 51 percent whole-grain ingredients to make the same claims. General Mills's whole-grain cereals Cheerios, Total, and Wheaties can now promise consumers health benefits for breakfast—a diet high in whole-grain foods and low in fat may reduce the risk of heart disease and certain cancers.[31]

The social-cultural environment for marketing decisions at home and abroad is expanding in scope and importance. Today, no marketer can initiate a strategic decision without considering the society's norms, values, culture, and demographics. Understanding how these variables affect decisions is so important that some firms have created a new position—typically, manager of public policy research—to study the changing societal environment's future impact on their organizations. And consumer groups are finding that sometimes progress can be made more quickly if they work with marketers, instead of against them, as the "Marketing Hits" box on page 84 explains.

7

Describe the role of marketing in society and identify the two major social issues in marketing.

read

Ethical Issues in Marketing

The five environments described so far in this chapter do not completely capture the role that marketing plays in society and the consequent effects and responsibilities of marketing activities. Because marketing is closely connected with various public issues, it invites constant scrutiny by the public. Moreover, since marketing acts as an interface between an organization and the society in which it operates, marketers often carry much of the responsibility for dealing with social issues that affect their firms.

Marketing operates in an environment external to the firm. It reacts to that environment and, in turn, is acted upon by environmental influences. Relationships with customers, employees, the government, vendors, and society as a whole form the basis of the social issues that confront contemporary marketers. While these concerns often grow out of the exchange process, they produce effects coincidental to the primary sales and distribution functions of marketing. Marketing's relationship to its

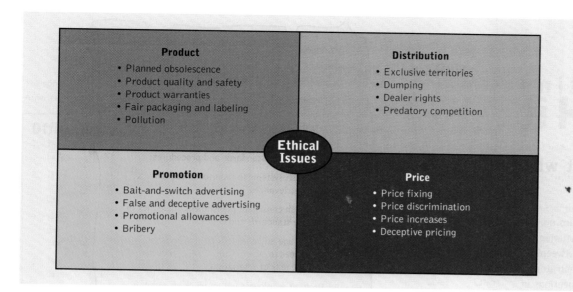

FIGURE 3.8
Ethical Questions in Marketing

external environment has a significant effect on the firm's eventual success. It must continually find new ways to deal with the social issues facing the competitive system.

The diverse social issues that marketers face can be divided into two major categories: marketing ethics and social responsibility. While the overlap and classification problems are obvious, this simple framework provides a foundation for systematically studying these issues.

Environmental influences have directed increased attention toward **marketing ethics,** defined as the marketer's standards of conduct and moral values. Ethics concern matters of right and wrong: the responsibility of individuals and firms to do what is morally right. As Figure 3.8 shows, each element of the marketing mix raises its own set of ethical questions. Before any improvements to the marketing system can be made, each of them must be evaluated.

Increased recognition of the importance of marketing ethics is evident from the more than 600 full-time corporate ethics officers in firms ranging from Dun & Bradstreet, Dow Corning, and Texas Instruments to even the Internal Revenue Service. The Federal Sentencing Guidelines for Organizations provides a framework for evaluating misconduct in business activities, such as fraud or price fixing. The sentencing guidelines act as an incentive for corporations to implement effective ethics compliance programs—if they are hauled into court, the existence of such a program can help reduce fines or sentences. A step-by-step framework for building an effective program is shown in Figure 3.9.

When Tyson Foods paid $6 million to settle accusations that it made illegal gifts to build political favor, the company was also required to set up an ethics compliance program. However, since then, Tyson has had a checkered ethical track record, facing allegations of violating antipollution laws and child labor laws and of racial discrimination in its hiring practices. Recently, six Tyson employees were indicted on charges of accepting false immigration documents and smuggling illegal workers into the U.S.[32]

Ensuring ethical practices means promising customers and business partners not to sacrifice quality and fairness for profit. In exchange, organizations hope for increased customer loyalty toward their brands. Yet issues involving marketing ethics are not always clear-cut. The issue of cigarette advertising, for example, has divided the ranks of advertising executives. Is it right for advertisers to promote a product that, while legal, has known health hazards?

For years, charges of unethical conduct have plagued the tobacco industry. In the largest civil settlement in U.S. history, tobacco manufacturers agreed to pay $206 billion to 46 states. Four

Marketing Dictionary

consumer rights   As stated by President Kennedy in 1962, the consumer's right to choose freely, to be informed, to be heard, and to be safe.

marketing ethics   Marketers' standards of conduct and moral values.

Social Responsibility in Marketing

As several of the examples in this chapter demonstrate, companies can benefit from their contributions to society and at the same time minimize the negative impact they have on the natural and social environment. **Social responsibility** demands that marketers accept an obligation to give equal weight to profits, consumer satisfaction, and social well-being in evaluating their firm's performance. They must recognize the importance of relatively qualitative consumer and social benefits as well as the quantitative measures of sales, revenue, and profits by which firms have traditionally measured marketing performance.

8

Identify the four levels of the social responsibility pyramid.

Social responsibility allows for easier measurement than marketing ethics. Government legislation can mandate socially responsible actions. Consumer activism can also promote social responsibility by business. Actions alone determine social responsibility, and a firm can behave responsibly, even under coercion. Government requirements may force firms to take socially responsible actions in matters of environmental policy, deceptive product claims, and other areas. Also, consumers, through their power to repeat or withhold purchases, may force marketers to provide honest and relevant information and fair prices. Ethically responsible behavior, on the other hand, requires more than appropriate actions; ethical intentions must also motivate those actions. The four dimensions of social responsibility—economic, legal, ethical, and philanthropic—are shown in Figure 3.11. The first two dimensions have long been recognized, but ethical obligations and the need for marketers to be good corporate citizens have increased in importance in recent years.

The locus for socially responsible decisions in organizations has always been an important issue. Who should accept specific accountability for the social effects of marketing decisions? Responses range from the district sales manager to the marketing vice president, the firm's CEO, and even the board of directors. Probably the most valid assessment holds that all marketers, regardless of their stations in the organization, remain accountable for the social aspects of their decisions.

FIGURE 3.11
The Four-Step Pyramid of Corporate Social Responsibility

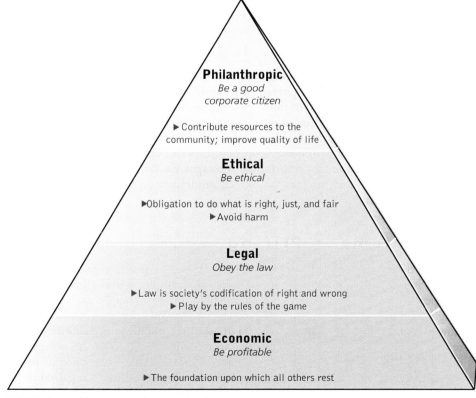

SOURCE: Reprinted from *Business Horizons.* Used with permission.

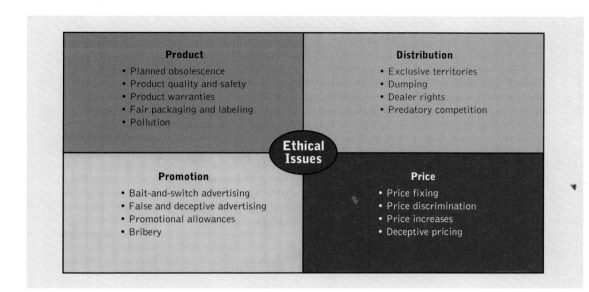

FIGURE 3.8
Ethical Questions in Marketing

external environment has a significant effect on the firm's eventual success. It must continually find new ways to deal with the social issues facing the competitive system.

The diverse social issues that marketers face can be divided into two major categories: marketing ethics and social responsibility. While the overlap and classification problems are obvious, this simple framework provides a foundation for systematically studying these issues.

Environmental influences have directed increased attention toward **marketing ethics,** defined as the marketer's standards of conduct and moral values. Ethics concern matters of right and wrong: the responsibility of individuals and firms to do what is morally right. As Figure 3.8 shows, each element of the marketing mix raises its own set of ethical questions. Before any improvements to the marketing system can be made, each of them must be evaluated.

Increased recognition of the importance of marketing ethics is evident from the more than 600 full-time corporate ethics officers in firms ranging from Dun & Bradstreet, Dow Corning, and Texas Instruments to even the Internal Revenue Service. The Federal Sentencing Guidelines for Organizations provides a framework for evaluating misconduct in business activities, such as fraud or price fixing. The sentencing guidelines act as an incentive for corporations to implement effective ethics compliance programs—if they are hauled into court, the existence of such a program can help reduce fines or sentences. A step-by-step framework for building an effective program is shown in Figure 3.9.

When Tyson Foods paid $6 million to settle accusations that it made illegal gifts to build political favor, the company was also required to set up an ethics compliance program. However, since then, Tyson has had a checkered ethical track record, facing allegations of violating antipollution laws and child labor laws and of racial discrimination in its hiring practices. Recently, six Tyson employees were indicted on charges of accepting false immigration documents and smuggling illegal workers into the U.S.[32]

Ensuring ethical practices means promising customers and business partners not to sacrifice quality and fairness for profit. In exchange, organizations hope for increased customer loyalty toward their brands. Yet issues involving marketing ethics are not always clear-cut. The issue of cigarette advertising, for example, has divided the ranks of advertising executives. Is it right for advertisers to promote a product that, while legal, has known health hazards?

For years, charges of unethical conduct have plagued the tobacco industry. In the largest civil settlement in U.S. history, tobacco manufacturers agreed to pay $206 billion to 46 states. Four

Marketing Dictionary

consumer rights   As stated by President Kennedy in 1962, the consumer's right to choose freely, to be informed, to be heard, and to be safe.

marketing ethics   Marketers' standards of conduct and moral values.

Marketing Hit

Alliances Win Out when Activism Fails

Background. When protests turn ugly, even those who set out to defend consumer rights get bad press. Violent clashes between big business and overzealous demonstrators at recent international economic meetings in Canada, Italy, and Seattle led some activist groups to rethink their methods.

The Challenge. Greenpeace, whose high-pressure tactics once stormed the headlines, recently launched a unit that works hand in hand with corporations to develop and market environmentally responsible "green" technologies. Through its green marketing unit, Greenpeace has reinvented itself as marketing partner to companies whose environmental practices it so publicly decries.

The Strategy. Working alongside German manufacturers, Greenpeace campaigned to replace environmentally dangerous refrigerants with Greenfreeze, a hydrocarbon-based alternative. Greenpeace linked scientists and engineers with industrialists to develop the product, lobbied government for speedy certification, won development funds, and struck joint-venture deals with appliance makers and factories throughout Europe.

The Outcome. The Greenpeace initiative demonstrates that what can't be won through protests in the streets may be achieved by stepping inside the boardroom. Similarly, a recent partnership between New York's Environmental Defense organization and its one-time combatant McDonald's resulted in dramatic reductions in the fast-food giant's waste output. A contest sponsored by the Natural Resources Defense Council spurred innovative designs for super-efficient appliances.

SOURCES: "Sorting Out 'Green' Advertising Claims," Federal Trade Commission, accessed January 15, 2003, http://www.ftc.gov; "Time to Regroup," *BusinessWeek*, August 6, 2001, pp. 26–28; Cathy L. Hartman and Edwin R. Stafford, "Enviro Groups Entering Marketing Fray," *Marketing News*, July 30, 2001, p.15.

1. Appoint a senior-level ethics compliance officer.

2. Set up an ethics code capable of detecting and preventing misconduct.

3. Distribute a written code of ethics to employees, subsidiaries, and associated companies and require all business partners to abide by it.

4. Conduct regular ethics training programs to communicate standards and procedures.

5. Establish systems to monitor misconduct and report grievances.

6. Establish consistent punishment guidelines to enforce standards and codes.

7. Encourage an open-door policy, allowing employees to report cases of misconduct without fear of retaliation.

8. Prohibit employees with a track record of misconduct from holding positions with substantial discretionary authority.

9. Promote ethically aware and responsible managers.

10. Continually monitor effectiveness of all ethics-related programs.

FIGURE 3.9
Ten Steps for Corporations to Improve Standards of Business Ethics

SOURCE: Adapted from O. C. Ferrell, John Fraedrich, and Linda Ferrell, *Business Ethics* (Boston, MA: Houghton Mifflin, 2002), pp. 179–184.

other states—Florida, Minnesota, Mississippi, and Texas—had separate settlements totaling another $40 billion. The settlement frees tobacco companies from state claims for the cost of treating sick smokers. For their part, cigarette makers can no longer advertise on billboards or use cartoon characters in ads, nor can they sell non-tobacco merchandise containing tobacco brands or logos. A University of Michigan study credits the lawsuits and the resulting advertising restrictions—especially the elimination of the teen-oriented Joe Camel campaign—with recently reducing teen smoking by up to 9 percent in a single year. Aggressive state-run antismoking campaigns, paid for out of the tobacco settlements, was another key factor. However, researchers reported a fourfold rise in smoking among college students over a recent 5-year period. Consumer groups are also pointing their fingers at cigarette marketers. Says one analyst, "Tobacco is still a highly profitable business and companies are going to remain competitive with each other. You may not be able to put up a 50-foot sign on the street, but you can still send it in the mail to smokers. I would expect to see more emphasis on direct-to-consumer marketing."[33]

People develop standards of ethical behavior based on their own systems of values, which help them deal with ethical questions in their personal lives. However, the workplace may generate serious conflicts when individuals discover that their ethical beliefs are not necessarily in line with those of the employer. For example, while employees may think that shopping

Workplace Ethics Quiz

The spread of technology into the workplace has raised a variety of new ethical questions, and many old ones still linger. Compare your answers with those of other Americans surveyed on page 95.

Office Technology

1. Is it wrong to use company e-mail for personal reasons?
    ❑Yes   ❑No

2. Is it wrong to use office equipment to help your children or spouse do schoolwork?
    ❑Yes   ❑No

3. Is it wrong to play computer games on office equipment during the workday?
    ❑Yes   ❑No

4. Is it wrong to use office equipment to do Internet shopping?
    ❑Yes   ❑No

5. Is it unethical to blame an error you made on a technological glitch?
    ❑Yes   ❑No

6. Is it unethical to visit pornographic Web sites using office equipment?
    ❑Yes   ❑No

Gifts and Entertainment

7. What's the value at which a gift from a supplier or client becomes troubling?
    ❑$25   ❑$50   ❑$100

8. Is a $50 gift to a boss unacceptable?
    ❑Yes   ❑No

9. Is a $50 gift from the boss unacceptable?
    ❑Yes   ❑No

10. Of gifts from suppliers: Is it OK to take a $200 pair of football tickets?
    ❑Yes   ❑No

11. Is it OK to take a $120 pair of theater tickets?
    ❑Yes   ❑No

12. Is it OK to take a $100 holiday food basket?
    ❑Yes   ❑No

13. Is it OK to take a $25 gift certificate?
    ❑Yes   ❑No

14. Can you accept a $75 prize won at a raffle at a supplier's conference?
    ❑Yes   ❑No

Truth and Lies

15. Due to on-the-job pressure, have you ever abused or lied about sick days?
    ❑Yes   ❑No

16. Due to on-the-job pressure, have you ever taken credit for someone else's work or idea?
    ❑Yes   ❑No

SOURCE: *The Wall Street Journal,* October 21, 1999, p. B1, from Ethics Officer Association, Belmont, Massachusetts; Leadership Group, Wilmette, Illinois; surveys sampled a cross-section of workers at large companies and nationwide.

FIGURE 3.10
Test Your Workplace Ethics

online during lunch break using a work computer is fine, the company may decide otherwise. The quiz in Figure 3.10 highlights other everyday ethical dilemmas.

How can these conflicts be resolved? In addition to individual and organizational ethics, individuals may also be influenced by a third basis of ethical authority—a professional code of ethics that transcends both organizational and individual value systems. A professional peer association can exercise collective oversight to limit a marketer's individual behavior.

Any code of ethics must anticipate the variety of problems that marketers are likely to encounter. While promotional matters tend to receive the greatest attention, ethical considerations also influence marketing research, product strategy, distribution strategy, and pricing.

Ethical Problems in Marketing Research

Invasion of personal privacy has become a critical issue in marketing research. The proliferation of databases, the selling of address lists, and the ease with which consumer information can be gathered through Internet technology have all increased public concern. The issue of privacy will be explored in greater detail in Chapter 5. From an ethical standpoint, a marketing research practice that is particularly problematic is the promise of cash rewards or free offers in return for marketing information that can then be sold to direct marketers. Consumers commonly disclose their demographic information in return for an e-mail newsletter or a favorite magazine. Recently, California-based marketing research company Free-PC.com offered consumers a new desktop PC in exchange for revealing personal

Briefly Speaking

There's no incompatibility between doing the right thing and making money.

William Clay Ford, Jr. (b. 1958) CEO, Ford Motor Co.

information, such as age, income, and spending habits. Says Jupiter Media Metrix analyst Rob Leathern, "Consumers are very schizophrenic. They want their privacy, but they're willing to give out information for entry into an online sweepstakes."[34]

Privacy issues have grown as rapidly as companies on the Web, and consumers are fighting back. Following a recent investigation by the Federal Trade Commission (FTC) into its consumer research practices, online advertiser DoubleClick.com paid out $1.8 million to settle federal and state class-action suits. In addition, DoubleClick will send out more than 300 million consumer-privacy banner ads, inviting consumers to learn more about protecting their privacy online.[35]

Several agencies, including the FTC, offer assistance for Internet consumers. To find information on how to stop junk mail and telemarketing calls, a good place to start is at **http://www.ftc.gov/privacy**. The Direct Marketing Association also offers services, such as the Mail, Telephone, and E-Mail Preference Services, to help consumers get their names removed from marketers' targeted lists. UnlistMe.com and Junkbusters are free Web services that also help consumers remove their names from direct mail and telemarketing mailing lists.

Ethical Problems in Product Strategy

Product quality, planned obsolescence, brand similarity, and packaging questions are of critical importance to the success of a brand. Not surprisingly, competitive pressures have forced some marketers into packaging practices that may be considered misleading, deceptive, or unethical. Larger packages help gain shelf space and consumer exposure in the supermarket. Oddly sized packaging makes price comparisons difficult. Bottles with concave bottoms give the impression that they contain more liquid than they actually do. Are these practices justified in the name of competition or can they be considered deceptive? Growing regulatory mandates appear to be narrowing the range of discretion in this area.

Product endorsement is another area that raises ethical concerns. To convince consumers of quality, product-packaging prominently displays "seals of approval," such as the Good Housekeeping Seal of Approval or the American Heart Association seal. The seals do not promise that the product is the best one on the market nor even that it has been tested against competing brands. Yet since they can be purchased for fees ranging from $10,000 to $1 million, is their use misleading?[36]

Ethical Problems in Distribution Strategy

Two ethical issues influence a firm's decisions regarding channel strategy:

1. What is the appropriate degree of control over the channel?

2. Should a company distribute its products in marginally profitable outlets that have no alternative source of supply?

The question of channel control typically arises in relationships between manufacturers and franchise dealers. For example, should an automobile dealership, a gas station, or a fast-food outlet be coerced to purchase parts, materials, and supplementary services from the parent organization?

The second question concerns marketers' responsibility to serve unsatisfied market segments even if the profit potential is slight. Should marketers serve retail stores in low-income areas, serve users of limited amounts of the firm's product, or serve a declining rural market? These problems are difficult to resolve because they often involve individuals rather than broad segments of the general public. An important first step is to ensure that the firm consistently enforces its channel policies.

Ethical Problems in Promotional Strategy

Promotion is the component of the marketing mix that gives rise to the majority of ethical questions. Personal selling has always been a target of criticism. Early traders, pack peddlers, drummers, and today's used-car salespeople have all been accused of marketing malpractices that range from exaggerating product merits to outright deceit. Gifts and bribes are common ethical abuses.

In the realm of brand advertising, the means through which marketers target specific demographic groups sometimes falls short of ethical standards. A recent campaign for Merisant's top brand, Equal, for example, targets the artificial sweetener to aging baby boomers with weight or health problems such as diabetes. The campaign, running in such magazines as *Diabetes Digest* and *Voice of the Diabetic*, features custom-created dessert recipes using Equal as a sugar alternative. Critics question the wisdom of persuading people who need to avoid sugar to indulge in cakes and cookies.[37]

The pharmaceutical industry has frequently attracted attention for its questionable advertising practices. Increasingly, television advertising directed at consumers suggests that viewers take a proactive role in family health care by requesting that their doctors prescribe the medications they see advertised. Opponents allege that such advertising puts undue pressure on physicians to prescribe costly branded drugs rather than nondrug remedies or over-the-counter alternatives. Not only may consumer-driven prescriptions lead to unnecessary or even harmful drug use, but it also ratchets up the cost of insurance coverage. The pharmaceutical industry argues that direct-to-consumer advertising educates patients while leaving physicians in control of treatment.[38]

The methods pharmaceutical advertisers use to target doctors has also sounded ethical alarms. Stories are rife of prominent advertisements in medical journals and company-paid seminars in popular vacation spots intended to influence prescription decisions. Recently, an intense campaign by Genzyme Corp. sought to persuade doctors to recommend its $12-a-day-drug Renagel to counter excess phosphorus levels common in kidney-dialysis patients. The alternative? Over-the-counter Tums, at $1-a-day or less. Competitors allege that advertisements for Renagel unfairly claim that calcium-based compounds like Tums cause a condition akin to hardening of the arteries. So far, there is no hard evidence that Tums can aggravate the problem—nor that the costly Renagel can remedy it. Sales of Renagel doubled in 2002, making it one of the year's hottest biotechnology stocks.[39]

Pfizer talks directly to consumers, recommending that they ask their doctors about cholesterol-lowering Lipitor.

As the effectiveness of the Internet as an advertising medium increases, marketers have run afoul of regulations that protect the rights of consumers to full disclosure of product information. For instance, the U.S. Department of Transportation recently investigated five Internet travel agencies who failed to disclose a fuel-surcharge in ticket prices they advertised on the Web. Since marketers have only seconds to communicate their messages on the Web before consumers click to a new site, the length and placement of disclosures is also at issue. While it may be easiest for consumers to see disclosure statements if they are at the very top of the Web page, advertisers prefer to save that prominent spot for interest-grabbing promotional messages. So far, the Federal Trade Commission has not made any hard rules but instead has offered guidelines on how to make disclosures convenient for consumers to find.[40]

Ethical Problems in Pricing

Pricing is probably the most regulated aspect of a firm's marketing strategy. As a result, most unethical price behavior is also illegal. Schering-Plough Corp., for example, is under investigation for offering pharmaceuticals at no cost or at extremely deep discounts to managed-care plans that include Schering-Plough drugs on HMO lists of drugs for which companies are reimbursed.[41] Some aspects of pricing, however, are still open to ethics abuses. For example, should some customers pay more for merchandise if distribution costs are higher in their areas? Do marketers have an obligation to warn customers of impending price, discount, or return policy changes? All these concerns must be dealt with in developing a professional ethic for pricing products. The ethical issues involved in pricing for today's highly competitive and increasingly computerized markets are discussed in greater detail in Chapters 13 and 14.

Social Responsibility in Marketing

As several of the examples in this chapter demonstrate, companies can benefit from their contributions to society and at the same time minimize the negative impact they have on the natural and social environment. **Social responsibility** demands that marketers accept an obligation to give equal weight to profits, consumer satisfaction, and social well-being in evaluating their firm's performance. They must recognize the importance of relatively qualitative consumer and social benefits as well as the quantitative measures of sales, revenue, and profits by which firms have traditionally measured marketing performance.

Social responsibility allows for easier measurement than marketing ethics. Government legislation can mandate socially responsible actions. Consumer activism can also promote social responsibility by business. Actions alone determine social responsibility, and a firm can behave responsibly, even under coercion. Government requirements may force firms to take socially responsible actions in matters of environmental policy, deceptive product claims, and other areas. Also, consumers, through their power to repeat or withhold purchases, may force marketers to provide honest and relevant information and fair prices. Ethically responsible behavior, on the other hand, requires more than appropriate actions; ethical intentions must also motivate those actions. The four dimensions of social responsibility—economic, legal, ethical, and philanthropic—are shown in Figure 3.11. The first two dimensions have long been recognized, but ethical obligations and the need for marketers to be good corporate citizens have increased in importance in recent years.

The locus for socially responsible decisions in organizations has always been an important issue. Who should accept specific accountability for the social effects of marketing decisions? Responses range from the district sales manager to the marketing vice president, the firm's CEO, and even the board of directors. Probably the most valid assessment holds that all marketers, regardless of their stations in the organization, remain accountable for the social aspects of their decisions.

8

Identify the four levels of the social responsibility pyramid.

**FIGURE 3.11
The Four-Step
Pyramid of
Corporate Social
Responsibility**

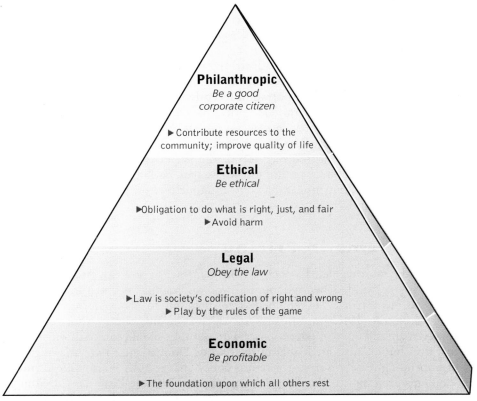

SOURCE: Reprinted from *Business Horizons.* Used with permission.

Marketing's Responsibilities

The concept of business's social responsibility traditionally has concerned managers' relationships with customers, employees, and stockholders. Managers felt responsible for providing quality products at reasonable prices for customers, adequate wages and decent working environments for employees, and acceptable profits for stockholders. Only occasionally did the concept extend to relations with the government and rarely with the general public.

Today, corporate responsibility has expanded to cover the entire societal framework. A decision to temporarily delay the installation of a pollution-control device may satisfy the traditional sense of responsibility. Customers would continue to receive an uninterrupted supply of the plant's products, employees would not face layoffs, and stockholders would still receive reasonable returns on their investments. Contemporary business ethics, however, would not accept this choice as socially responsible.

Similarly, a firm that markets foods with low nutritional value may satisfy the traditional concept of responsibility, but such behavior is questionable in contemporary perspective. This is not to say that all firms should distribute only foods of high nutritional value; it means merely that the previous framework for evaluation is no longer considered comprehensive in terms of either scope or time.

Contemporary marketing decisions must consider the entire societal framework, not only in the U.S. but throughout the world. Recently, apparel manufacturers and retailers have come under fire for buying from foreign suppliers who force employees to work in dangerous conditions or who violate child-labor laws. Drug companies, for example, that refuse to allow the development of low-cost versions of their patented drugs to combat epidemics like AIDS, malaria, or tuberculosis have been accused of ignoring the global reach of corporate responsibility. Merck's pricing policy for a year's supply of its AIDS-fighting drugs ranges from $6,000 in rich countries to $600 in less-developed nations.[42] Marketers must also take into account the long-term effects of their decisions and the well-being of future generations. Manufacturing processes that negatively impact the environment or that use up natural energy resources are easy targets for criticism.

There are several methods through which marketers can help their companies behave in socially responsible ways. Chapter 1 discussed cause marketing as just one channel through which companies can promote social causes. Socially responsible marketing involves campaigns that encourage people to adopt socially beneficial behaviors, whether they be safe driving, eating more nutritious food, or improving the working conditions of people half a world away. Not only can campaigns like these help society, but they can affect the firm's bottom line as well.

Home Depot is one of thousands of firms addressing philanthropic responsibilities by giving back to the communities in which it operates through *volunteerism*. In this ad, the firm's CEO and his Atlanta-based associates are working on a Habitat for Humanity project to build homes for the community's neediest citizens.

Marketing Dictionary

social responsibility   Marketing philosophies, policies, procedures, and actions that have the enhancement of society's welfare as a primary objective.

FIGURE 3.12
Iron Eyes Cody:
Teaching Generations
of Americans to
Become Concerned
About Their
Environment

SOURCE: Advertisement created by Marstellar Inc. for the Ad Council. Reprinted by permission of the Ad Council.

Marketing and Ecology

Ecology—the relationship between organisms and their natural environments—has become a driving force in influencing the ways in which businesses operate. Many industry and government leaders rank the protection of the environment as the biggest challenge for today's corporations. From water pollution, garbage disposal, and acid rain to depletion of the ozone layer and global warming, environmental issues are global. They influence all areas of marketing decision making from product planning to public relations, spanning such topics as planned obsolescence, pollution control, recycling waste materials, and resource conservation.

In creating new-product offerings that respond to consumer demands for convenience by offering extremely short-lived products, such as disposable diapers, ballpoint pens, razors, and cameras, marketers occasionally find themselves accused of intentionally offering products with limited durability—in other words, of practicing *planned obsolescence.* In addition to convenience-oriented items, other products become obsolete when rapid changes in technology allow for better alternatives. In the software industry, upgrades that make still-new products obsolete are the name of the game. While companies insist that upgrades are inevitable to meet increasingly sophisticated consumer demands, opponents have countered that new releases are frequently only polished versions of existing technologies, intended to stimulate sales.[43]

Public concern about pollution of such natural resources as water and air affects some industries, such as pharmaceuticals or heavy-goods manufacturing, more than others. However, the marketing system annually generates billions of tons of packaging materials such as glass, metal, paper, and plastics that add to the world's growing piles of trash and waste. Recycling such materials for reuse is another important aspect of ecology. Recycling can benefit society by saving natural resources and energy as well as by alleviating a major factor in environmental pollution—waste disposal.

The impact of powerful, highly creative promotional messages on changing consumer attitudes was never demonstrated more powerfully than in Figure 3.12. First introduced over 30 years ago by advertising agency Marstellar Inc. for the Ad Council, the industry's public service group, a Native American—the very symbol of dignity and respect for the natural world—is brought to tears by pollutants in the air, water, and land. The message made the image of Iron Eyes Cody, the tear-shedding model for the ad, an advertising icon and shamed Americans into accepting responsibility for their environment.[44]

Lawmakers in California, Massachusetts, Nebraska, and South Carolina have proposed legislation to force manufacturers to take back "e-waste"—used PCs and other technology products that contain toxic chemicals. When electronics end up in landfills, the chemicals inside them can poison groundwater, posing health risks. Manufacturers claim that recycling is prohibitively expensive and will likely add about $20 to the cost of a PC.[45]

As the saying goes, one person's trash is another's treasure. Yokohama Metals mines used cell phones, digging out the gold, platinum, and silver embedded there. It takes 125,000 phones to produce a single gold bar worth $10,000. Swedish-owned Metech International turns discarded computer hardware into gold. In just one year, the firm recovered 120,000 ounces of gold worth $35 million, as well as other precious metals including silver, platinum, and palladium.[46]

The disposal of nuclear waste is an ongoing public safety issue. Nevada recently lost its long fight against government plans to open a national storage site in the bowels of isolated Yucca Mountain, about 100 miles outside Las Vegas. The September 11 terrorist attacks gave supporters of the proposed national repository an unexpected boost. Housed at more than 100 power plants nationwide, radioactive materials pose a considerable national security risk—as possible terrorist targets. Supporters of the

Briefly
Speaking

Air pollution is turning Mother Nature prematurely gray.

*Irv Kupcinet (b. 1912)
American newspaper
columnist*

Nevada storage site also argue that Yucca Mountain is critical to building America's nuclear-power capacity—the means through which the nation may one day meet its own energy needs.[47]

Many companies respond to consumers' growing concern about ecological issues through **green marketing**—production, promotion, and reclamation of environmentally sensitive products. In the green marketing revolution of the early 1990s, marketers were quick to tie their companies and products to ecological themes. Yet recent trends demonstrate that consumers will not pay more at the checkout to support the environment. After finding that 70 percent of baby food shoppers prefer the convenience of plastic, Gerber Products Co. recently traded glass jars for plastic packaging. A recent poll revealed that more than 40 percent of shoppers say that they won't buy green products because they don't work as well as their competitors.[48]

The nuclear-storage depository at Yucca Mountain, Nevada, has already cost taxpayers $4 billion.

Strategic Implications of Marketing in the 21st Century

Management of the nation's businesses is affected by and must respond to a large number of important trends that are shaping business in the 21st century. The marketing decisions they make will influence and be influenced by changes in the competitive, political-legal, economic, technological, and social-cultural environments. Marketing ethics and social responsibility will continue to play important roles in business transactions in your hometown and around the globe.

As the Internet and the rapid changes in technology that it represents are fully absorbed into the competitive environment in coming years, competition will become even more intense than it is today. Respondents to a recent survey report that competitive forces will come from every sector of business. A full third believe the most serious competition will come from U.S. companies who are not yet listed in the Fortune 500. Thirty percent expect foreign marketers to pose the most formidable competitive threat. By a larger than four-to-one majority, most CEOs believe that expanding their markets is a more important priority than increasing their share of current markets.[49]

Much of the competition will result from innovations in technology and scientific discoveries. Business in the 21st century will be propelled by information technologies and sustained by creativity and entrepreneurial activity. Biotechnology— an industry whose

Marketing Dictionary

green marketing   Production, promotion, and reclamation of environmentally sensitive products.

growth was fueled in response to terrorist threats of bio-war in 2001—is still in its infancy. It is expected to explode in the next decade. Scientists will be able to create materials atom by atom, replicating much that nature can do and more.

In the 20th-century economy, the major industrial sectors included retail, financial services, and manufacturing. But today, those old sectors frequently do not fit the networked economy. The idea of what it means to be a retail company will change in five years when a billion people are logged on to the Internet. The bundling of services on the Internet will bypass many of the financial services we take for granted today. For example, when a 14-year-old buys a digital CD off the Internet, digital cash will be transferred from her hard drive to that of the recording artist, thereby eliminating the need for a bank or credit-card company. Money will eventually be relegated to encrypted numbers on disk drives and digital wallets.

Dynamic growth cannot be left entirely to self-regulation. The next ten years will produce a plethora of rules and regulations to control the marketing environments that will force businesses to change aspects of their operations. For example, new legislation to control dangerous emissions that deplete the ozone layer will lead to energy-efficient manufacturing processes and a new wave of alternative energy automobiles.

Consumers will feel the impact of environmental changes in every aspect of their lives. The new century is ushering in new generations of consumers who expect high-quality, low-cost products readily available on demand. Every company will be forced to build relationships to attract and retain loyal customers to succeed.

Underlying all the changes in the business environments and marketing mix elements is a requirement for companies to act ethically and in socially responsible ways. Marketers will have to go beyond what is legally right and wrong by integrating ethical behavior in all of their actions. Forward-looking companies will reap the benefits tomorrow of socially responsible behavior today.

Summary of Chapter Objectives

1. Identify the five components of the marketing environment.

The five components of the marketing environment are (1) *the competitive environment*—the interactive process that occurs in the marketplace as competing organizations seek to satisfy markets; (2) *the political-legal environment*—the laws and interpretations of laws that require firms to operate under competitive conditions and to protect consumer rights; (3) *the economic environment*—environmental factors resulting from business fluctuations and resulting variations in inflation rates and employment levels; (4) *the technological environment*—applications to marketing of knowledge based on discoveries in science, inventions, and innovations; and (5) *the social-cultural environment*—the component of the marketing environment consisting of the relationship between the marketer and society and its culture.

2. Explain the types of competition marketers face and the steps necessary for developing a competitive strategy.

Three types of competition exist: (1) direct competition among marketers of similar products; (2) competition among goods or services that can be substituted for one another; and (3) competition among all organizations that vie for the consumer's purchasing power. To develop a competitive strategy, marketers must answer the following questions: (1) Should we compete? The answer depends on the firm's available resources and objectives as well as its expected profit potential; (2) If so, in what markets should we compete? This question requires marketers to make product, pricing, distribution, and promotional decisions that give their firm a competitive advantage; (3) How should we compete? This question requires marketers to make the technical decisions involved in setting a comprehensive marketing strategy.

3. Describe how government and other groups regulate marketing activities and how marketers can influence the political-legal environment.

Marketing activities are influenced by federal, state, and local laws that require firms to operate under competitive conditions and to protect consumer rights. Government regulatory agencies such as the Federal Trade Commission enforce these laws and develop procedures for identifying and correcting unfair marketing practices. Public and private consumer interest groups and industry self-regulatory groups also affect marketing activities. Marketers may seek to influence public opinion and legislative actions through advertising, political action committees, and political lobbying.

4. Outline the economic factors that affect marketing decisions and consumer buying power.

The primary economic factors are: (1) the stage in the business cycle, (2) inflation, (3) unemployment, (4) income, and (5) resource availability. All are vitally important to marketers because of their effects on consumers' willingness to buy and consumers' perceptions regarding changes in the marketing mix variables.

5. Discuss the impact of the technological environment on a firm's marketing activities.

The technological environment consists of applications to marketing of knowledge based on discoveries in science, inventions, and innovations. This knowledge can provide marketing opportunities: it results in new products and improves existing ones, and it is a frequent source of price reductions through new production methods or materials. Technological applications also pose a threat, since they can make existing products obsolete overnight. The technological environment demands that marketers continually adapt to change, since its scope of influence reaches into consumers' lifestyles, competitors' products, industrial user's demands, and government regulatory actions.

6. Explain how the social-cultural environment influences marketing.

The social-cultural environment relates to the attitudes of members of society toward goods and services as well as pricing, promotion, and distribution strategies. It influences the general readiness of society to accept new marketing ideas. It also has an impact on legislation regulating business and marketing. While the social-cultural environment affects all domestic marketing decisions, it is an even more prevalent force in influencing international marketing strategy. Society demands that business be concerned with the quality of life. Consumerism is the social force within the environment designed to aid and protect the consumer by exerting legal, moral, and economic pressures on business. Consumer rights include the following: (1) the right to choose freely, (2) the right to be informed, (3) the right to be heard, and (4) the right to be safe.

7. Describe the role of marketing in society and identify the two major social issues in marketing.

Marketing operates in an environment external to the firm, building relationships with customers, employees, vendors, the government, and society as a whole. These relationships have a significant effect on the relative degree of success the firm achieves. The two critical social issues in marketing are marketing ethics and social responsibility. Marketing ethics describes the marketer's standards of conduct and moral values. Social responsibility is the marketer's acceptance of the obligation to consider profit, consumer satisfaction, and societal well being of equal value when evaluating the performance of the firm.

8. Identify the four levels of the social responsibility pyramid.

The four dimensions of social responsibility are (1) *economic*—to be profitable, the foundation upon which the other three levels of the pyramid rest; (2) *legal*—to obey the law, society's codification of right and wrong; (3) *ethical*—to do what is right, just, and fair and to avoid wrongdoing; (4) *philanthropic*—to be a good corporate citizen, contributing to the community and improving quality of life.

Marketing Terms You Need to Know

environmental scanning 63
environmental management 63
competitive environment 64
time-based competition 67

political-legal environment 68
economic environment 74
demarketing 76
technological environment 77

social-cultural environment 80
consumerism 81
consumer rights 82
marketing ethics 83

social responsibility 88
green marketing 91

Other Important Marketing Terms

strategic alliance 64
monopoly 64
deregulation movement 64

oligopoly 65
competitive strategy 67
switchless reseller 73

business cycle 74
inflation 75
unemployment 75

discretionary income 76
planned obsolescence 90

Review Questions

1. Briefly describe each of the five components of the marketing environment. Give an example of each.
2. Explain the types of competition marketers face. What steps must they complete to develop a competitive strategy?
3. Government regulation in the U.S. has evolved in four general phases. Identify each phase and give an example of laws enacted during that time.
4. Give an example of a federal law affecting:
   a. product strategy
   b. pricing strategy
   c. distribution strategy
   d. promotional strategy
5. Explain the methods the Federal Trade Commission uses to protect consumers. Which of these methods seems the most effective to you?
6. What major economic factors affect marketing decisions? How does each of these forces produce its effect?
7. Identify the ways in which the technological environment and the social-cultural environment affect marketing activities. Cite examples of both.
8. What are the two major social issues in marketing? Give an example of each.
9. Describe the ethical problems related to:
   a. marketing research
   b. product strategy
   c. distribution strategy
   d. promotional strategy
   e. pricing strategy
10. Identify each of the four dimensions of social responsibility. Which two dimensions have emerged most recently?

Projects and Teamwork Exercises

1. Find examples of how marketers in your community might meet each of the following responsibilities:
   a. economic
   b. legal
   c. ethical
   d. philanthropic
2. Classify the following laws as (a) assisting in maintaining a competitive environment, (b) assisting in regulating competitors, (c) regulating specific marketing activities, or (d) deregulating industries. Justify your classifications and identify the marketing mix variable(s) most affected by each law.
   a. Children's Online Privacy Protection Act
   b. Robinson-Patman Act
   c. Airline Security Act
   d. Telecommunications Act
3. Should the U.S. impose regulations on advertising of alcoholic beverages? Working in small groups, have one team present the argument for regulation and the other present the counterargument.
4. Cite two examples of instances in which the technological environment has produced positive benefits for marketers. Give two instances of the harmful affect of the technological environment on a firm's marketing operations.
5. Identify a critical social issue confronting your local community. In teams, research all sides of the issue via newspapers, the Internet, or through contacting local activist groups and reviewing their literature. How does this issue affect marketers in your area? Provide specific examples. Describe your findings in either a written or an oral presentation.

'net **W**ork

http://www.ftc.gov

http://www.fcc.gov

1. Federal regulation. Two important federal regulatory agencies are the Federal Trade Commission (FTC) and Federal Communications Commission (FCC). Visit both Web sites and familiarize yourself with the content of each site specifically dealing with consumer protection and marketing. Prepare a brief report summarizing your findings.

http://www.green
marketing.com

2. Green marketing. Visit the following Web site (http://www.greenmarketing.com) and click on "Green Marketing: Opportunity for Innovation." According to the author, seven strategies are available in successful green marketing. What are they? Identify two or three companies that have followed a successful green marketing strategy.

http://www.coopamerica.org

http://www.afl-cio.org*

3. Consumer boycotts. Several organizations publish lists of products on their Web sites that they are urging consumers to boycott for a variety of reasons. Go to the two Web sites listed here and select two lists: one you feel you can support and one you feel you cannot support. Include justifications for your support, or lack of support, to each boycott listed.

*(Click on "Worker Friendly Products" and follow links to section on current boycotts.)

Note: Internet Web addresses change frequently. If you don't find the exact sites listed, you may need to access the organization or company's home page and search from there.

CASE 3.1 — Boca Burgers: The Taste Will Change You

Veggie smoothie? Fat-free bagel sandwich? Another tuna and celery salad? In our health-conscious society, what's a meat lover to do? A generation ago, people ate with gusto, but today's consumers, young and old, watch their diets, cut back on fat, and will even pay more for heart-healthy ingredients. This major lifestyle shift has opened opportunities for marketers who could whip up a magical formula—low on fat, but high on taste.

Boca Burgers was the brainchild of a restaurateur who noticed that more of his neighbors were cooking up veggie burgers—and grimacing as they swallowed. Inspired, he set out to create a meatless burger that tasted good. Big and juicy, blended with herbs and spices, and ready to grill, Boca delivers a good-for-you burger—without sacrificing taste or texture.

Boca Burgers offer more fiber but fewer calories and less fat and cholesterol. They have just as much protein as regular burgers. The protein comes from soy, considered the healthiest possible source. Since the product is meatless, there is no risk of contamination from *E. coli* or bovine diseases. The burgers are easy to cook and—best of all—the taste and texture satisfy even the most ardent meat lover.

Boca Burgers rapidly gained distribution in retail grocery chains, natural foods stores, and food services channels nationwide. The company made sure its product was not relegated to the vegan shelf, since it was developed to appeal to nonvegetarians making healthy diet choices. The clever byline, "The Taste Will Change You," propelled the product into the mainstream. The product line was quickly expanded to include alternatives for ground beef, the meatless way to enjoy tacos, chili, or lasagna. Breakfast links and patties and Boca Tenders & Nuggets soon followed. Strongly aligned with consumers' desires for healthy food choices, Boca raced to the top of the fast-growth meat-alternatives category.

In 2000, Boca won the attention of Kraft Foods, the nation's largest packaged goods company. With revenues of over $40 million—twice its sales from the previous year—the product line gave Kraft a lead position in a category set for exponential growth in coming years. The latest addition, Boca Rising Crust Pizza, is expected to solidify Boca's market dominance.

Boca Burgers were recently tested for genetically modified ingredients—and then added to a growing list of gene-spliced foods that may have ill effects on health and the environment. However, with its stellar track record for responding to consumer needs, Boca is ready to meet the challenges ahead.

Questions for Critical Thinking

1. Discuss the societal factors that helped Boca Burgers enter into the fiercely competitive packaged foods market.
2. What regulatory controls or other checks and balances influence the marketing of goods in the packaged foods industry?

SOURCES: Ameet Sachdev, "Group Lists Kraft Foods Containing Biotech Grains," *Chicago Tribune*, February 2, 2002, [no page no.]; Sonia Reyes, "Meatless Market," *Brandweek*, January 28, 2002, p. 2; Joel. R. Cooper, "Boca: A Burger Like No Other," *The Medical Reporter*, http://medicalreporter.health.org, accessed March 21, 2002; and "Kraft Foods Acquires High-Growth Boca Burger, Inc." Kraft Foods, Inc.—Newsroom, January 18, 2000. See also http://www.bocaburger.com.

VIDEO CASE 3.2 — Equal Exchange: Fair Pay Is Fair Play

The written case on Equal Exchange appears on page VC-4. The recently filmed Equal Exchange video is designed to expand and highlight the concepts in this chapter and the concepts and questions covered in the written video case.

Ethics Quiz Answers

Quiz is on page 85.

1. 34% said personal e-mail on company computers is wrong
2. 37% said using office equipment for schoolwork is wrong
3. 49% said playing computer games at work is wrong
4. 54% said Internet shopping at work is wrong
5. 61% said it's unethical to blame your error on technology
6. 87% said it's unethical to visit pornographic sites at work
7. 33% said $25 is the amount at which a gift from a supplier or client becomes troubling, while 33% said $50, and 33% said $100
8. 35% said a $50 gift to the boss is unacceptable
9. 12% said a $50 gift from the boss is unacceptable
10. 70% said it's unacceptable to take the $200 football tickets
11. 70% said it's unacceptable to take the $120 theater tickets
12. 35% said it's unacceptable to take the $100 food basket
13. 45% said it's unacceptable to take the $25 gift certificate
14. 40% said it's unacceptable to take the $75 raffle prize
15. 11% reported they lied about sick days
16. 4% reported they have taken credit for the work or ideas of others

Chapter 4

13 pages

4

Global Dimensions of Marketing

Chapter Objectives

1 Describe the importance of international marketing from the perspectives of the individual firm and the nation.

2 Identify the major components of the environment for international marketing.

3 Outline the basic functions of GATT, WTO, NAFTA, the proposed FTAA, and the European Union.

4 Compare the alternative strategies for entering international markets.

5 Differentiate between a global marketing strategy and a multidomestic marketing strategy.

6 Describe the alternative marketing mix strategies used in international marketing.

7 Explain the attractiveness of the U.S. as a target market for foreign marketers.

Joining the Club: Ten New Members Enter the European Union

At first, the club was designed to be small: six European countries that decided to combine their economies and trade policies into a single, more powerful and effective union. The club wasn't formed in the 21st century, or even the 1990s; the original European Economic Community was established nearly a half-century ago back in 1957. This community continued to grow through the fall of the Berlin Wall in 1989, the Treaty of European Union (EU) in 1993, and the introduction of euro banknotes and coins in 2002. At that time, there were 15 members of the club. Then in 2004, 10 new members were accepted into the EU, including the Mediterranean island nations of Cyprus and Malta and 8 others from Eastern and Central Europe—countries such as the Czech Republic, Estonia, Hungary, Lithuania, and Poland. The club has now grown to the point that it's no longer small—and many experts debate how it should be governed and by whom as well as its likely impact on global marketing.

By far, the EU is the granddaddy of multinational trade agreements, surpassing even North America's NAFTA, which also expects to accept new members in the future. The removal of trade barriers; a seamless flow of investments, imports, and exports; and smooth movement of workers from one nation to another are all benefits of the EU agreements. These agreements also dovetail well with boundaryless transactions created by the Internet and e-commerce. But the transition has not always been easy. Labor laws and infrastructures differ among the nations, not to mention languages. When the euro experienced devaluation—a reduction in value—all the countries were affected, instead of one. And as more cultures—with varying values, customs, road systems, communication networks, business hours, and consumer tastes and preferences—join the union, its business and marketing environment grows more and more complex.

Because of these complexities, EU member officials met for 12 months to draft a new, single constitution that would replace the network of treaties that formed the union. Not surprisingly, differences arose; France called for a powerful, full-time EU president, while smaller countries worried that such an organization would silence their voices. In the end, a team, or shared, presidency seems likely.

Meanwhile, U.S. officials have been watching the progress of the EU closely, acknowledging the union as a strong institution that plays an essential role "as a force for democracy, prosperity, and a force for stability throughout Europe and well beyond Europe."

Despite some growing pains, the EU continues to be a powerful economic force in the global economy, in part because its requirements for admission include a stable, democratic government and the existence of a functioning market economy. All new members must demonstrate that their governments respect human rights and can cope with changes in the business environment. By 2005, the 10 new members had begun integrating their separate economies into those of the rest of the EU. Technology will continue to help these and other transitions take place, as broadband access to the Internet offers rapid, inexpensive, and permanent online communications that are unlikely to be easily disrupted. By the time these countries are fully integrated into the EU, the union will be the world's largest trading bloc, with a single market of 500 million consumers. Optimists predict that the union will boost the economies of all its member nations and help promote stable governments and peace. "Accession of 10 new member states will bring an end to the divisions in Europe," says Romano Prodi, the Italian president of the executive European Commission. "For the first time in history, Europe will become one because unification is the free will of its people."[1]

Chapter Overview

Briefly Speaking

Hong Kong will take your breath away.

Tourism ad headline commissioned before the SARS outbreak and cancelled soon afterwards

U.S. and foreign companies, including those based in the European Union, are crossing national boundaries in unprecedented numbers in search of new markets and profits. International trade now accounts for at least 25 percent of the U.S. gross domestic product (GDP), compared with 5 percent thirty years ago. As Figure 4.1 shows, ten nations account for more than 70 percent of U.S. imports and almost two-thirds percent of U.S. exports.

International trade can be divided into two categories: **exporting,** marketing domestically produced goods and services abroad, and **importing,** purchasing foreign goods and services. International trade is vital to a nation and its marketers for several reasons. It expands markets, makes production and distribution economies possible, allows companies to explore growth opportunities in other nations, and makes them less dependent on economic conditions in their home nations. Many also find that global marketing and international trade can help them meet customer demand, reduce costs, and provide valuable information on potential markets around the world.

For North American marketers, international trade is especially important because the U.S. and Canadian economies represent a mature market for many products. Outside North America, however, it is a different story. Economies in many parts of sub-Saharan Africa, Asia, Latin America, Europe, and the Middle East are growing rapidly. This opens up new markets for U.S. products as consumers in these areas have more money to spend and as the need for American goods and services by foreign companies expands. Exports of high-tech products account for more than one-fourth of U.S total exports worldwide—the largest segment at a whopping $181 billion. International trade also builds employment. The world's 50 largest businesses keep 7.3 million people gainfully employed.[2] Your next job, in fact, might involve global marketing, since export-related jobs play an important role in the U.S. economy.

International marketers carefully evaluate the marketing concepts described in earlier chapters. However, transactions that cross national borders involve additional considerations. For example, different laws, varying levels of technological capability, economic conditions, cultural and business norms, and consumer preferences often require new strategies. Companies that want to market their products worldwide must reconsider each

US has a balance payment defect. We import more than we export.

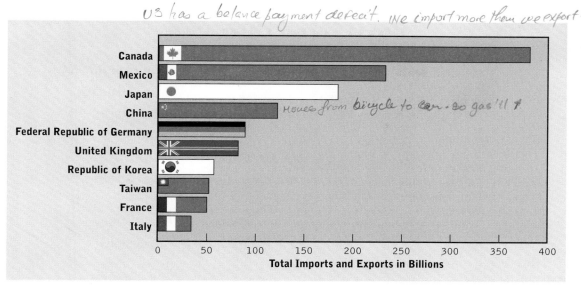

FIGURE 4.1
Top Ten U.S. Trading Partners

Moves from bicycle to car. so gas '11 ↑

Read about Soccer

SOURCE: U.S. Census Bureau, "Top Ten Countries with Which the U.S. Trades." Downloaded from **http://www.census.gov**, May 29, 2002.

of the marketing variables (product, price, distribution, and promotion) in terms of the global marketplace. To succeed in global marketing, today's marketers answer questions such as: How do our products fit into a foreign market? How can we turn potential threats into opportunities? Which strategic alternatives will work in global markets?

Many of the answers to these questions can be found by studying techniques used by successful international marketers. This chapter first considers the importance and characteristics of the global marketplace. It then examines the international marketing environment, the trend toward multinational economic integration, and the steps that most firms take to enter the global marketplace. Next, the importance of developing an international marketing mix is discussed. The chapter closes with a look at the U.S. as a target market for foreign marketers.

The US is the world nkt importer. We Import more than we export. We have a Bal payment surplus. ~~deficit~~ or money goes down over other currencies. V loose power over cur money.

The Importance of Global Marketing 201

1 Describe the importance of international marketing from the perspectives of the individual firm and the nation.

As the list of the world's 10 largest corporations shown in Table 4.1 reveals, half of them are head-quartered in the U.S. For most U.S. companies—both large and small—global marketing is rapidly becoming a necessity. The demand for foreign products in the fast-growing economies of Asia and other Pacific Rim nations offers one example of the benefits of thinking globally. In a recent year, U.S. exports to Asia rose 37 percent to about $200 billion—almost twice its exports to Europe. This surge is partly because Asian consumers believe American goods are higher quality and a better value than those made in their own countries. International marketers recognize how the slogan "Made in the USA" yields tremendous selling power throughout the world. As a result, overseas sales are important revenue sources for many U.S. firms.

Over the last 15 years, U.S. exports have grown an average of 10 percent each year, with the number one export during this time period being agricultural products. Other products included among the top five U.S. exports were electrical machinery, computers and office equipment, general industrial machinery, and

Marketing Dictionary

exporting   Marketing domestically produced goods and services in foreign countries.

importing   Purchasing foreign goods, services, and raw materials.

In the 70's Ford car was 100% made in the US, But now if 80% of the car is made here itsconsideres as American.

TABLE 4.1   The World's 10 Largest Marketers

Rank	Company	Country of Origin
1	Wal-Mart Stores	United States
2	ExxonMobil	United States
3	General Motors	United States
4	British Petroleum	Britain
5	Ford Motor Co.	United States
6	DaimlerChrysler	Germany
7	Royal Dutch/Shell	Britain/Netherlands
8	General Electric	United States
9	Toyota Motor	Japan
10	Citicorp	United States

Pepsi + Coke r Multiple Companies

SOURCE: Paola Hjelt, "Fortune Global Hundred," *Fortune,* July 22, 2002.

motor vehicle parts. Among the leading U.S. firms in terms of the portion of their revenues generated from exports were Boeing, Intel, Motorola, Caterpillar, and Sun Microsystems.

Wal-Mart currently ranks as the biggest retailer in the U.S., Canada, and Mexico. And although it recently passed longtime leaders ExxonMobil and General Motors as America's largest corporation, its sights are clearly aimed at global dominance. The retail giant is currently devoting billions of dollars in expansion efforts abroad in Great Britain, the European mainland, Japan, and South America. After some early stumbles with foreign languages, customs, and regulations, the Bentonville, Arkansas–based company is beginning to gain its stride overseas, planning at least 120 new store openings annually during the next few years. "As a global organization, they've become more savvy," says Ira Kalish, director of global retail intelligence at PricewaterhouseCoopers.[3]

The rapid globalization of business and the boundless nature of the Internet have made it possible for every marketer to become an international marketer. However, as the opening vignette illustrates, becoming an Internet international marketer is not necessarily easy. While larger firms have the advantage of more resources and wider distribution systems, smaller companies can build Web sites for as little as a few hundred dollars and can bring products to market quickly. Beth and Lou Drucker began their wedding supplier referral service in 1996 with $3,000. Recently, the couple took their business online at **http://NewYorkMetroWeddings.com**. The site was an instant hit and remains so, with about 300,000 visitors per month. In one 12-month period, the company tripled in size.[4]

Just as some firms depend on foreign and Internet sales, others rely on purchasing raw materials abroad as input for their domestic manufacturing operations. A North Carolina furniture manufacturer may depend on purchases of South American mahogany, while 21st century furniture retailers are taking advantage of increased Chinese-made styling and quality and their traditionally low prices. The top five U.S. imports are computers and office equipment, crude oil, clothing, telecommunications equipment, and agricultural products. Over the past 15 years, U.S. imports have grown about 7 percent annually.

Service and Retail Exports

In addition to agricultural products and manufactured goods, the U.S. is also the world's largest exporter of services and retailing. Of the approximately $210 billion in annual U.S. service exports, over half comes from travel and tourism—money spent by foreign nationals visiting the U.S. Tourism is the third-largest U.S. industry, contributing $430 billion to its economy each year, and is responsible for creating more than $6 billion in travel and tourism-related jobs. With 102 million tourists per year, the

U.S. ranks second only to China in visitors. By 2020, tourists will spend $2 trillion during their international travels. Vacation marketers look to attract and serve customers on a global basis. Hilton Hotels' HHonors program allows travelers to earn hotel points and airline miles for the same stay at any Hilton or affiliate—including Doubletree, Homewood Suites, and Conrad hotels—around the world. If customers book their trip online, they earn 1,000 bonus points toward upgrades and free stays.[5]

The most profitable U.S. service exports are business and technical services, such as engineering, financial, computing, legal services, and entertainment. Worldwide Internet services revenues grew an enormous 71 percent to almost $8 billion during a recent 12-month period. Even more surprising is that the growth is expected to continue at a 60 percent annual rate. The U.S. continues to be the largest market for Internet service providers.[6]

The financial services industry, already a major presence outside North America, is expanding globally via the Internet. Nearly half of the world's active Web population visits a finance Web site at least once a month, with online stock trading and banking leading the way. And more than one of every four Europeans with Internet access currently banks online. By 2005, nearly 60 million French, German, British, Italian, and Spanish consumers will bank online.[7] A glance at the increasing number of foreign companies listed on the New York Stock Exchange illustrates the importance of global financial services.

A number of global service exporters are household names in the U.S.: American Express, AT&T, Citicorp, Disney, and Allstate Insurance. Many earn a substantial percentage of their revenues from international sales. Others are smaller firms, such as the many software firms that have found overseas markets receptive to their products. Still others are non-profit organizations such as the United States Postal Service, which is attempting to increase overall revenues by operating a worldwide delivery service, as illustrated in Figure 4.2. The service competes with for-profit firms like DHL, UPS, and Federal Express.

The entertainment industry is another major service exporter. Movies, TV shows, and music groups often travel to the ends of the earth to find their audience. Almost a century of exposure to U.S.-made films, television programs, and—more recently—music video clips have made international viewers more familiar with American culture and geography than

The global coverage and international reputation of the Hilton name combine to generate additional sales revenues both in the U.S. and around the world as both business and vacation travelers from the U.S. and other countries select accommodations for their stays. Hilton's affiliated hotels offer different services to meet specific traveler needs and the Hilton HHonors frequent-stay card seeks to enhance customer loyalty through rewards for heavy users.

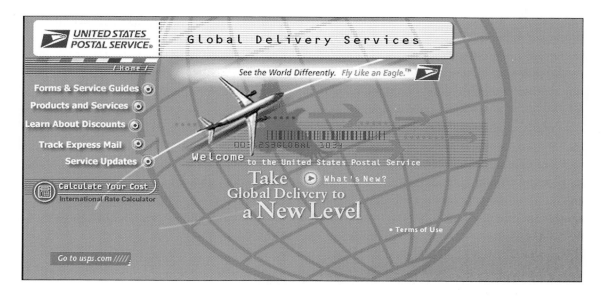

FIGURE 4.2
The U.S. Postal Service's Global Delivery Service: Increasing Revenues by Offering High-Speed International Delivery Service

any other nation on earth. However, some markets are more receptive to American entertainment than others, depending on their own culture and language barriers. India and some Asian countries have their own entertainment industries, complete with stars, and are not necessarily interested in American products. Still, when Warner Bros. released *Lethal Weapon 4* in Hong Kong, it hired a popular local heavy metal band to create a promotional music video in the hope of attracting viewers to the movie.

American retailers ranging from Victoria's Secret, Foot Locker, and The Gap to Office Depot, Toys "R" Us, and Costco, are opening stores around the world at rapid paces. U.S. retailers do especially well in Asia, where consumers like the convenience and wide selection of American-made products. They are also attracted to products associated with American lifestyles. Seattle-based Recreational Equipment Inc. (REI) recently opened a Tokyo store featuring an indoor rock-climbing wall and in-store Starbucks coffee shop. A footwear test trail lets Japanese customers try out hiking boots and trail running shoes; the Kids' Camp area will let children have fun in a "play" campsite; and a family of life-sized bronze bears welcomes shoppers to the new store.[8]

During the last three decades, U.S. fast-food franchises have been opening outlets in foreign countries at a phenomenal rate. To meet local demands for U.S. pizza styles in Brazil, Tricon Global opened 60 Pizza Hut restaurants there by 2003. Pizza Hut competitor Domino's countered by opening 48 new outlets there. McDonald's currently operates over 6,000 outlets internationally in 91 countries. Domino's Pizza now serves its pies to customers in 1,200 outlets in 46 countries. Arby's parent company, Florida-based Triarc Restaurant Group, operates over 3,000 outlets in the U.S. and has recently signed an agreement with Sybra Restaurants UK to take the roast-beef sandwich chain to London. Over 100 Arby's restaurants are expected to open in the U.K. during the next 10 years.[9]

Benefits of Going Global

Besides generating additional revenue, firms expand their operations outside their home country to gain other benefits, including new insights into consumer behavior, alternative distribution strategies, and advance notice of new products. By setting up foreign offices and production facilities, marketers may learn new marketing techniques and gain invaluable experience.

Global marketers are typically well-positioned to compete effectively with foreign competitors. A major key to achieving success in foreign markets is a firm's ability to adapt its products to local preferences. It's important for a fast-food marketer to know that Venezuelans like their fries with mayonnaise, not ketchup; Chileans want an avocado on their burger instead of a tomato; and Europeans prefer the word "light" to "diet" on their cola drinks.[10]

Another method used by international marketers before entering foreign markets is to conduct transcontinental product testing. Procter & Gamble is a veteran of global marketing but only recently began to develop truly global products. Swiffer, a lightweight mop with disposable cleaning cloths that use static electricity to attract dust and dirt, was successfully test marketed in Cedar Rapids, Iowa, and in Sens, France, before its global launch. As one P&G spokesperson explained, "The more that we truly explore consumers on a global basis, the more we find that they're really more alike than they are dissimilar."[11]

Since firms must perform the marketing functions of buying, selling, transporting, storing, standardizing and grading, financing, risk taking, and obtaining market information in both domestic and global markets, some may question the wisdom of treating international marketing as a distinct subject. After all, international marketing is marketing; a firm performs the same functions and works toward the same objectives in domestic or international marketing. As the chapter will explain, however, both similarities and differences influence strategies for international and domestic marketing.

The International Marketplace

Today, it is rare to find a U.S. firm that never ventures outside its domestic market. Even if it focuses almost entirely on the domestic market, which is huge in its own right, it may look overseas for raw materials or component parts or it may face foreign competition in its home market. Those who venture abroad may find the international marketplace far different than the domestic one they are accustomed to. Market sizes, buyer behavior, and marketing practices all vary. To be successful, international marketers must do their homework, capitalize on similarities, and carefully evaluate all market segments in which they expect to compete.

Market Size

From the dawn of civilization until the 1800s, world population grew to about 1 billion people. It almost doubled by 1900, and today over 6 billion people inhabit the planet. According to Census Bureau projections, world population will increase to nearly 8 billion by 2025. Ninety-six percent of the increase in world population occurs in less-developed regions such as Africa, Asia, and Latin America. Population growth rates in affluent countries, however, have slowed to 0.4 percent annually—one-fifth the annual growth of less-developed countries. What this all means is that, over the next quarter-century, firms will have to adapt their goods and services to meet the needs and wants of growing numbers of young consumers in developing countries.

One-fifth of the world's population—1.2 billion people—lives in China. Africa is growing fastest at 2.8 percent a year, followed by Latin America at 1.9 percent and Asia at 1.7 percent. Average birth rates are dropping around the world due to family planning efforts, but death rates are declining even more rapidly and people are living longer. Although African birth rates are still high—6 children per woman—European birth rates have fallen considerably, with couples averaging only 1 or 2 children.[12] All of this information is important to marketers as they try to target these markets for their goods and services.

The global marketplace is increasingly an urban one. Today, almost 50 percent of its people live in large cities. As a result, city populations are swelling: 39 cities currently have a population of 5 million or more. Mexico City, whose population of 18 million ranks it as the world's largest city, is expected to grow to 31 million by 2010. Increased urbanization will expand the need for transportation, housing, machinery, and services.

The growing size and urbanization of the international marketplace does not necessarily mean all foreign markets offer the same potential. Another important influence on market potential is a nation's economic development stage. In a subsistence economy such as Nepal, most people engage in agriculture and earn low incomes, supporting few opportunities for international trade of any magnitude. In a newly industrialized country, such as Brazil or South Korea, growth in manufacturing creates demand for consumer products and industrial goods such as high-tech equipment. Industrial nations, including the U.S., Japan, and countries in western Europe, trade manufactured goods and services among themselves and export to less-developed countries. Although these wealthy countries account for just a small percentage of the world's population, they produce over half of its output.

As a nation develops, an increasingly affluent, educated, and cosmopolitan middle class emerges. India's middle class includes nearly 300 million people, a number larger than the entire U.S. population. India's processed-food producers and marketers are now facing global competition as a result of economic reforms and market liberalization. But marketers in India must overcome an underdeveloped **infrastructure,** the underlying foundation for modern life and efficient marketing that includes transportation and communications networks, banking, utilities, and public services. In addition, cultural differences and language barriers frequently exist. On the other end of the scale is Japan, a highly industrialized, educated country with a sophisticated infrastructure that includes such high-speed transportation modes as the bullet trains shown in Figure 4.3. However, in both cases, significant opportunities can be found through joint ventures and strategic alliances.

International marketers see much growth in middle-income households occurring in the booming East Asian economies such as China, Thailand, Singapore, South Korea, and Hong Kong, as well as in Mexico, South America, and sub-Saharan Africa. These new middle-class consumers have both the desire for consumer goods, including luxury and leisure goods and services, and money to pay for them.

Buyer Behavior

Buyer behavior differs among nations and often among market segments within a country. Marketers must carefully match their marketing

Marketing Dictionary

infrastructure   A nation's basic system of transportation networks, communication systems, and energy facilities.

FIGURE 4.3
High-Speed Bullet Trains: Sophisticated Transportation Component of the Japanese Infrastructure

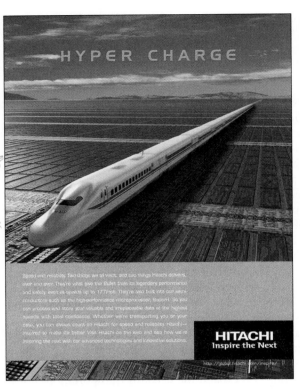

strategies to local customs, tastes, and living conditions. Even the Coca-Cola Co. can't go to the bank on its name alone in foreign countries. That's because, although Americans consume an average of 872 servings of soft drinks a year, Germans drink only 344 and Chinese a mere 23.[13] Still, Coke commands about half of the global soft-drink market and generates 60 percent of its sales from international markets by varying its product emphasis in different parts of the world. In Japan, it heavily promotes Leaf, a new canned-tea product that has become a hot seller there. The reason for the shift: Soft drinks make up only 20 percent of nonalcoholic beverage sales in Japan.[14]

Meanwhile, Coke's rival PepsiCo is concentrating much of its efforts on the snack foods that its Frito-Lay division produces. In Mexico, the firm's Sabritas brand snacks have captured 81 percent of the salty snack market. PepsiCo plans to export its Mexican marketing strategy—which includes installing colorful "Power of One" displays of Pepsi products in small neighborhood groceries—to other developing nations such as China and India. PepsiCo marketers recognize that to be successful in these countries where personal incomes are low, they must attract consumers by keeping prices low and increasing the availability of snack foods and soft drinks.[15]

In some instances, international marketers succeed in changing local buyer behavior by introducing new marketing strategies that have been well-received in other countries. Johnson & Johnson (J&J) recently debuted RoC, a 40-year-old French line of skincare products, in an attempt to leverage its strong European brand in the U.S. market. J&J marketers are positioning RoC as a major alternative to both the mass-market brand of L'Oréal and prestige department-store brands such as Clinique.[16]

Failure to adapt to local preferences can create costly problems. The French discount retailer Promodes recently expanded into other countries such as Turkey, only to discover that almost everything—from the atmosphere in its huge hypermarkets to the color of meat—had to be modified to meet the specific expectations of Turkish consumers. Shoppers there don't like the large, orderly, brightly lit Promodes store that was recently opened in Mersin, Turkey. They prefer the clutter of their own retail chain, Cetinkaya, which places metal baskets filled with inexpensive goods that customers can dig through to find bargains, like they would at a traditional open-air market. They also want fresh beef to have a light pink color. If it is too dark, they won't buy it. Promodes managers know that they are going to have to make some adjustments if the French discounter is going to be successful in Turkey.[17]

Differences in buying patterns require marketing executives to complete considerable research before entering a foreign market. Sometimes the marketer's own organization or a U.S.-based research firm can provide needed information. In other cases, only a foreign-based marketing research organization can tell marketers what they need to know. Regardless of who conducts the research, investigators must focus on six different areas before advising a company to enter a foreign market:

1. *Demand.* Do foreign consumers need the company's good or service?

2. *Competitive environment.* How do supplies currently reach the market?

3. *Economic environment.* What is the state of the nation's economic health?

4. *Social-cultural environment.* How do cultural factors affect business opportunities?

5. *Political-legal environment.* Do any legal restrictions complicate entering the market?

6. *Technological environment.* To what degree are technological innovations used by consumers in the market?

The International Marketing Environment

is Target good Mktg to get to the est?

As in domestic markets, the environmental factors discussed in Chapter 3 have a powerful influence on the development of international marketing strategies. Marketers must pay close attention to economic, social-cultural, political-legal, and technological influences as they venture abroad.

International Economic Environment

A nation's size, per-capita income, and stage of economic development determine its prospects as a host for international business expansion. Nations with low per-capita incomes may be poor markets for expensive industrial machinery but good ones for agricultural hand tools. These nations cannot afford the technical equipment that powers an industrialized society. Wealthier countries may offer prime markets for many U.S. industries, particularly those producing consumer goods and services and advanced industrial products.

In India, for example, the median annual household income is only $480. Economic reforms have improved the country's standard of living somewhat, but most Indians have very few Western conveniences. Only 2 percent own cars, 4 percent have running hot water, and 7 percent have phones. Color television and refrigerator ownership run a bit higher at 12 percent.

Successful marketing in India requires an understanding of how the economy affects Indian consumers. Both rich and poor Indians practice frugal buying habits and spend as little as possible at one time. They prefer small packages with low prices, even though larger packages may offer more economical purchases. Even the wealthy are price-conscious consumers. Nestlé S.A. improved its market penetration in India by reducing package sizes and then pricing more than half of its food products under 25 rupees (about 70 cents). For example, sales of Maggi instant noodles tripled after Nestlé reduced the price from 19 cents to 14 cents a package. Recycling, a way of life for many Indians, is another issue U.S. marketers must keep in mind before entering the Indian marketplace. Although that country is the world's largest market for razor blades, disposable razors sell very poorly because the idea of throwing them away mystifies typical Indians.[18]

Infrastructure, discussed earlier in the chapter, is another important economic factor to consider when planning to enter a foreign market. An inadequate infrastructure may constrain marketers' plans to manufacture, promote, and distribute goods and services in a particular country. People living in countries blessed by navigable waters often rely on them as inexpensive, relatively efficient alternatives to highways, rail lines, and air transportation. Thai farmers use their nation's myriad rivers to transport their crops. Their boats even become retail outlets in so-called floating markets like the one located outside the capital city of Bangkok.

Marketers expect developing economies to have substandard utility and communications networks. China encountered numerous problems in establishing a 21st-century communications industry infrastructure. The Chinese government's answer was a huge investment in wireless technology. China's cell phone market is the largest in the world now. In one year alone, 60 million cell phones were sold there, and the number will grow to 200 million subscribers by 2010. But Chinese cell phone users pay only a nickel a minute, one of the cheapest rates in the world.[19] And China suffered another economic setback—SARS (see the "Marketing Miss" box on page 107). The South Korean business recruitment message shown in Figure 4.4 is based on the reality that people who live in most newly industrialized countries have established a strong enough infrastructure to begin attracting customers from around the world.

Changes in exchange rates can also complicate international marketing. An **exchange rate** is the price of one nation's currency in terms of another country's currency. Fluctuations in exchange rates can make a nation's currency more valuable or less valuable compared with those of other nations. Argentina plunged into a deep recession for several years, during which it devalued its currency, the peso, which was previously tied to the U.S. dollar. This made Argentina

2

Identify the major components of the environment for international marketing.

Marketing Dictionary

exchange rate   Price of one nation's currency in terms of other countries' currencies.

FIGURE 4.4
South Korea: A Newly Industrialized Nation with a Sophisticated Infrastructure, Employee Skills, and Sufficient Per-Capita Incomes Needed to Attract New Businesses and International Retailers

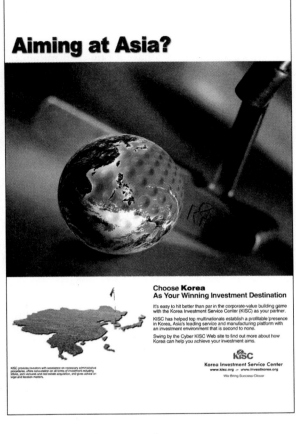

and some of its neighbors a less attractive trade partner for many international businesses.[20]

In 2002, the European Union introduced a new, uniform currency called the euro. The long-range idea behind the new currency is that switching to a single currency will actually strengthen Europe's competitiveness in the global marketplace.[21] Russian and many eastern European currencies are considered *soft currencies* that cannot be readily converted into such hard currencies as the dollar, euro, or Japanese yen. International marketers doing business in these countries may resort to barter, accepting such commodities as oil or timber as payment for exports. U.S. currency continues to be one of the strongest in the world; in fact, demand for American dollars is higher than ever.

International Social-Cultural Environment

Before entering a foreign market, marketers should study all aspects of that nation's culture, including language, education, religious attitudes, and social values. Indian executives are accustomed to interrupting each other. Europeans feel as if they are being treated like children when asked to wear name tags. Israelis prefer fast-paced meetings, without small talk. Malaysian and Japanese managers expect six-second pauses for silence during negotiations. Italians, Germans, and French believe that it is manipulative to soften someone up before offering criticism.[22] The "Marketing Hit" box on page 109 describes how Starbucks caters to the tastes of consumers abroad.

Language plays an important role in international marketing. Table 4.2 lists the world's eight most frequently spoken languages. Marketers must make sure not only to use the right language for a country but also ensure that the message is translated and conveys the intended meaning. Abbreviations and slang words and phrases may also cause misunderstandings when marketing abroad. Among the most humorous—and disastrous—language faux pas by marketers are the following:

- The mailbox icon used for e-mail messages is confusing to most Europeans. To them it looks like a loaf of bread.

- Clocks are out as gifts in China. They're considered by Chinese to be symbols of death.

- Speaking of death, Koreans refer to the Pentium IV chip as the "chip of death."

- Kentucky Fried Chicken's "finger lickin' good" slogan translates literally to "eat your fingers off" in China.

- The "Bakin" brand logo used on some Nike shoes proved offensive in several Muslim countries because it resembles the word *Allah* in Arabic.

- The well-known baby-food brand Gerber translates as "vomit" in French.[23]

International Technological Environment

More than any innovation since the telephone, Internet technology has made it possible for both large and small firms to be connected to the entire world. The Internet transcends political, economic, and

---

Briefly
Speaking

An Argentine is an Italian who speaks Spanish and thinks he is British.

Lydia Chavez
(b. 1952)
American journalist
and educator

TABLE 4.2   The World's Most Frequently Spoken Languages

Rank	Language	Number of Speakers
1	Chinese (Mandarin)	1.2 billion
2	English	478 million
3	Hindi	437 million
4	Spanish	392 million
5	Russian	284 million
6	Arabic	225 million
7	Portuguese	184 million
8	French	125 million

SOURCE: Reported in "Vital Statistics," *U.S. News & World Report,* July 2, 2001, p. 9.

cultural barriers, reaching to every corner of the globe. The Internet has helped traditional brick-and-mortar retailers add new e-commerce alternatives. It also assists developing nations in becoming competitive with industrialized nations.

Consider the following facts regarding the Internet:

- The world's online population currently stands at more than 300 million, with the most users in North America and the fewest in the Middle East.

- Business-to-consumer e-commerce grew $120 billion in 2004.

- Advertising on the Web already surpasses $4 billion.

- By 2005, more than 700 million Internet users will be non-English-speaking; only 250 million will be English-speaking Internet users.[24]

The Internet is truly a global medium that allows seamless communications and business transactions between individual consumers and multinational companies. It is critical that 21st-century marketers understand how the Web is reshaping social and cultural values.

Technology presents challenges for international marketers that extend beyond the Internet and other telecommunications innovations. A major issue involving food marketers competing in Europe is genetic reengineering. Although U.S. grocery shelves are filled with foods grown with genetically modified organisms (GMOs), most Americans do not know they are eating GMO foods, since no labeling disclosures are required. In Britain and other European countries, the story is quite different. Referred to in these countries as "Frankenfoods," activists are pushing for labeling laws to inform shoppers that these foods are "not naturally grown" or to ban them altogether. Marketers of agricultural commodities and packaged goods are already taking actions in response to these concerns. Gerber recently reformulated its baby foods to remove all ingredients containing GMOs.[25]

Marketing Miss

SARS Threatens Economic Growth in China

Background. No one outside China really saw it coming. By the time the outbreak of the respiratory illness known as SARS—severe acute respiratory syndrome—became world news, it had already spread from southern China to Hong Kong and on to Canada. Besides trying to contain the illness itself, Chinese officials, especially President Hu Jintao, had to figure out how to contain the massive economic damage to the country resulting from the epidemic.

The Marketing Problem. China quickly came under fire throughout the world—and from its own citizens—for its slow response to the SARS outbreak. In addition, people stopped traveling to mainland China as well as Hong Kong and other Asian destinations such as Singapore and Malaysia, all of which were hit by the deadly disease. Foreign investors closed their wallets, movie theaters and restaurants were shuttered, and the annual Canton Trade Fair was cut short with only one-fifth of the business deals that usually take place during the fair. International economists carved 2 percentage points off their projections for China's annual growth. Turning the economy—and the country's health—around would be an enormous task.

The Outcome. It has taken China much longer than its own officials originally hoped to get itself back on track. With a temporarily unstable economy, the credibility of the Chinese government suffered. Powerful groups like the World Health Organization placed temporary warnings against travel to Hong Kong and South China. But even during the height of the outbreak, creative busi-

continued on next page

Marketing Miss

nesspeople find ways through the tangle. For instance, business deals were temporarily shifted to Western countries, or via the Web and videoconferencing with Chinese firms.

Lessons Learned. As word of mouth of the initial cover-up of the SARS problem spread around the world, public opinion turned against China. If government officials had publicized the problem and even asked for help from health organizations, not only might lives have been saved, but businesses and the overall economy might not have suffered as greatly.

SOURCES: Charles Hutzler and Peter Wonacott, "SARS Outbreak Is Threatening China's Stability," *The Wall Street Journal*, April 30, 2003, p. A13; Dexter Roberts, "Epidemics & Economics," *BusinessWeek*, April 28, 2003, pp. 44–47; Allen Wan, "SARS Infects Business Worldwide," CBS.*MarketWatch.com*, April 20, 2003, **http://www.CBS.MarketWatch.com**.

The global reach of the Internet and the size of the Asian marketplace are the main reasons for the startling speed at which marketers are adopting this innovation and using it to their advantage.

Briefly Speaking

The new trade routes of the [21st century] are laser flashes and satellite beams. The cargo is not silk or spices, but technology, information, and ideas.

*Renato Ruggiero
(b. 1930)
Italian-born director
general, World Trade
Organization*

International Political-Legal Environment

Global marketers must continually stay abreast of laws and trade regulations in each country in which they compete. Some laws, such as *les Soldes* (the Sales) in France, are uncommon to U.S. marketers. By law, retail sales can be held only twice a year—in January or February and again during autumn. At least 30 percent of French clothing sales occur during these two sales seasons.[26]

Political conditions often influence international marketing, as well. Political unrest in places like the Middle East, Afghanistan, Africa, eastern Europe, and South America sometimes results in acts of violence, such as destruction of a firm's property. As a result, many Western firms have set up internal *political risk assessment* (PRA) units or turned to outside consulting services to evaluate the political risks of the marketplaces in which they operate. In addition, the fall of communism and the transformation of state-dominated industries into privately owned and managed profit-seeking enterprises has been accompanied by a trend toward freer trade among nations.

The political environment also involves labor conditions in different countries. Chinese officials do not respond well to labor unrest, particularly when it spills into the streets in protest. As recently as 1998, government officials jailed labor activist Zhang Shangguang for ten years for "endangering state security." A year later, 1,000 miners blocked a railway over delayed pay, and 2,000 retired steelworkers barricaded a road after their pensions were cut. In 2002, tens of thousands of factory workers surrounded government buildings, demanding that city officials resign because of unpaid employment benefits and back pay. Protests like these seem to provoke the government's old tactics of rounding people up, arresting them, silencing them with bribes, and the like. All of this makes for an uncertain climate for foreign businesses and investors. Still, many choose to pursue their investment in such a large potential market. The situation "hasn't deterred us," says Michael Dell, founder and CEO of Dell Computer Corp. "We [understand] the risk."[27]

The legal environment for U.S. firms operating abroad results from three forces: (1) international law, (2) U.S. law, and (3) legal requirements of host nations. International law emerges from the treaties, conventions, and agreements that exist among nations. The U.S. has many *friendship, commerce, and navigation (FCN) treaties* with other governments. These agreements set terms for various aspects of commercial relations with other countries, such as the right to conduct business in the treaty partner's domestic market. Other international business agreements concern worldwide standards for various products, patents, trademarks, reciprocal tax treaties, export control, international air travel, and international communication.

Since the 1990s, Europe has pushed for mandatory *ISO (International Standards Organization) 9000 certification*—internationally recognized standards that ensure a company's goods and services meet established quality levels. Today, many U.S. companies follow these certification standards as well. The International Monetary Fund, another major player in the international legal environment, lends foreign exchange to nations that require it to conduct international trade. These agreements facilitate the whole process of world marketing. However, there are no international laws for corporations, only for governments. So marketers include special provisions in contracts, such as which country's courts have jurisdiction.

The second dimension of the international legal environment, U.S. law, includes various trade regulations, tax laws, and import/export requirements that affect international marketing. One important law, the Export Trading Company Act of 1982, exempts companies from antitrust regulations so they can form export groups that offer a variety of products to foreign buyers. The law seeks to make it easier for foreign buyers to connect with U.S. exporters. A controversial 1996 law, the Helms-Burton Act, tried to impose trade sanctions against Cuba. Under this law, U.S. corporations and citizens can sue foreign companies and their executives for using expropriated U.S. assets to do business in Cuba. The Foreign Corrupt Practices Act, which makes it illegal to bribe a foreign official in an attempt to solicit new or repeat sales abroad, has had a major impact on international marketing. The act also mandates that adequate accounting controls be installed to monitor internal compliance. Violations can result in a $1 million fine for the firm and a $10,000 fine and five-year imprisonment for the individuals involved. This law has been controversial, mainly because it fails to clearly define what constitutes bribery. The 1988 Trade Act amended the law to include more specific statements of prohibited practices.

Finally, legal requirements of host nations affect foreign marketers. International marketers generally recognize the importance of obeying legal requirements since even the slightest violation could set back the future of international trade. As discussed in the opening vignette, marketers must navigate a maze of international and foreign laws pertaining to conducting business on the Internet. Sometimes foreign governments allow practices that are not accepted worldwide, as discussed in the "Solving an Ethical Controversy" box. Most European laws governing e-commerce have to do with consumer privacy. The U.S. and European Commission are still at odds over whose consumer privacy laws should reign supreme.[28]

A number of European countries have also enacted stringent laws restricting marketing aimed at children. Sweden limits all TV and radio marketing

Marketing Hit

Planet Starbucks Expands Its Orbit

Background. Some Wall Street analysts call Starbucks the last great growth story. Despite the recent recession, the company's stock rose more than 2,200 percent over the last decade—eclipsing such giants as Wal-Mart, Coca-Cola, and Microsoft in total returns. One survey called it the fastest-growing brand in the world.

The Challenge. So many Starbucks shops are already operating in the U.S. that, to maintain its revenue growth rate of 20 percent a year, Starbucks has to reach out overseas. Starbucks already has about 1,300 shops abroad, but the company has grand goals for worldwide expansion. Starbucks still has to confront its own premium prices, sluggish economies in major markets such as Japan, and well-established coffee companies in Europe.

The Strategy. Starbucks is aiming for a younger, hipper consumer crowd overseas than it does in the U.S. In Austria, 20-something consumers view Starbucks as new and cool. "The coffeehouses in Vienna are nice, but they are old. Starbucks is hip," says a newspaper business editor. Young consumers in Tokyo like the sweeter taste of Starbucks coffee. Industry watchers predict that French consumers will like the taste as well—but France is a maze of business and labor regulations. Starbucks has also installed high-speed wireless Internet service in more than 1,000 shops both in the U.S. and in Europe. Customers can sip coffee while checking their e-mail or downloading multimedia presentations. Finally, although U.S. Starbucks stores are company owned, the firm has formed joint ventures and licenses with other

continued on next page

to children age 12 and under, and direct marketing to children under 16. The British Codes of Advertising and Sales Promotion specify that marketing to children may not encourage them to eat or drink near bedtime, or to replace regular meals with snacks or candy. Most European countries also restrict the use of famous cartoon or comic characters, actors, athletes, or other celebrities to attract children to products.[29]

Legal requirements of host countries can create unexpected hurdles. Under new city laws in Beijing, China's capital city, all companies must remove advertising signs that have been posted in pavement or on rooftops. That includes McDonald's famous golden arches, which have risen above Beijing for the past decade. McDonald's has been a huge success in Beijing, particularly with children and teens. But middle-aged and elderly Chinese citizens often view the fast-food chain as a victory of capitalism over traditional Chinese cooking. And city officials, intent on sprucing up Beijing's image by the time it hosts the 2008 Summer Olympics, have decided that the arches "are not in harmony with the surroundings and affect the architectural ambience." Cai Weiqian, deputy general manager of Beijing McDonald's, is concerned about the effects of the new regulation on his business. "Seventy percent of our business comes from people who see our signs," he argues. "Fast food is an instant consumption, and sign-boards are important to attract customers." But a Chinese official in the public relations office of Beijing McDonald's demurs. "We are a law-abiding company. Since the city government has adjusted its rules, we will follow the new regulations."[30]

Trade Barriers *+ the Price.*

Assorted trade barriers also affect global marketing. These barriers fall into two major categories: **tariffs**—taxes levied on imported products—and administrative, or nontariff, barriers. Some tariffs impose set taxes per pound, gallon, or unit; others are calculated according to the value of the imported item. Administrative barriers are more subtle than tariffs and take a variety of forms such as customs barriers, quotas on imports, unnecessarily restrictive standards for imports, and export subsidies. Because the GATT and WTO agreements (discussed later in the chapter) eliminated tariffs on many products, countries frequently use nontariff barriers to boost exports and control the flows of imported products. The U.S. and other nations are constantly negotiating tariffs and other trade agreements. Recently, the U.S. signed an agreement with Vietnam—a quarter century after the war between the two countries ended—under which Vietnamese goods and services can now be sold in U.S. markets under the same low tariffs that most U.S. trade partners enjoy.[31]

Protective Tariffs *× was called protective agency.*

The U.S. has long been the champion of free trade throughout the world, but recently with shrinking economies of industrialized foreign nations and a growing number of developing countries that are struggling to stabilize their economies, U.S. legislators have been pressured to protect domestic industries from troubles abroad. But moves designed to protect business at home are frequently a double-edged sword. They also frequently end up penalizing domestic consumers, since prices typically rise under protectionist regulations. For example, the U.S. recently slapped a 30 percent import tax on frozen orange juice concentrate; duties on imported glassware, porcelain, and china as high as 38 percent; rubber boots and shoes, 20 percent; luggage, 16 percent; and canned tuna, 12.5 percent. While this may or may not create a competitive environment for domestic producers, it seldom reduces product prices for the consumer.

Tariffs can be classified as either revenue or protective tariffs. *Revenue tariffs* are designed to raise funds for the importing government. Most early U.S. government revenue came from this source. *Protective tariffs*, which are usually higher than revenue tariffs, are designed to raise the retail price of an imported product to match or exceed that of a similar domestic product. Some countries use tariffs in a selective manner to discourage certain consumption practices and thereby reduce access to their local markets. For example, the U.S. has tariffs on luxury items like Rolex watches and Russian caviar.

right wrong Solving an Ethical Controversy

China's Credibility in the World Marketplace Is Plagued by Piracy

Twenty-first-century pirates look like ordinary people. They stand on street corners and quietly whisper, "Watches, CDs, DVDs" to passersby. Theoretically, this could happen anywhere in the world, but the place where it is most prevalent is China. In fact, piracy of all kinds of goods, from shampoo to software CDs, is big business in China. And that's a real problem for the nation most recently admitted to the WTO. Because of a political-legal environment that turns a blind eye to piracy, China's credibility in the marketplace may be on the line.

Should China be held responsible for the practice of making and selling counterfeit goods within its borders?

PRO
1. If the practice of counterfeiting is not stopped, trade between China and other countries will ultimately suffer. Companies such as Procter & Gamble, Gillette, Bestfoods, Yamaha, Nike, Microsoft, and Epson have discovered fake products in China bearing their names.

2. Piracy can harm consumers as well. DaimlerChrysler discovered fake brake disks, windshields, and shock absorbers for its Mercedes cars being made and sold in China.

CON
1. China isn't the only place where counterfeiting takes place. According to the Software & Information Industry Association, Vietnam actually has a higher piracy rate.
2. Piracy will actually die out by itself, as consumers become more educated and prefer the higher quality of the genuine goods.

Summary

Although authorities claim to have launched raids on counterfeit manufacturers and sellers, the problem is still rampant throughout China. One cosmetics vendor explains the situation by holding up a bottle of Procter & Gamble's Rejoice shampoo and saying, "This one smells much sweeter, so we can sell it for more." But she continues, "Of course, the fakes sell much better. They're so much cheaper."

SOURCES: Ted Anthony, "If West Can Make It, Chinese Will Fake It," *Mobile Register,* April 21, 2002, p. A2; Reuters Limited, "U.S. Says China Lags on Piracy," *Wired News,* January 23, 2002, http://www.wired.com; Steve Friess, "Product Piracy Poses Biggest Threat to China's Economic Status," *USA Today,* June 28, 2001, p. B6.

Recently, the U.S. government placed a 19.3 percent protective percent tariff on softwood timber imported from Canada because it believes that Canada subsidizes its lumber industry to the point that prices are too low for American timber companies to compete. Some experts predicted that the tariff would add about $1,500 to the cost of building a new home, but U.S. lumber companies welcomed the tariff, saying that it would help level the playing field.[32]

In 1988, the U.S. passed the Omnibus Trade and Competitiveness Act to remedy what it perceived as unfair international trade conditions. Under the so-called Super 301 provisions of the law, the U.S. can now single out countries that unfairly impede trade with U.S. domestic businesses. If these countries do not open their markets within 18 months, the law requires retaliation in the form of U.S. tariffs or quotas on the offenders' imports into this country.

Some nations limit foreign ownership in the business sectors. In the U.S., for example, non-U.S. citizens cannot own more than 25 percent of the voting stock in a U.S.-based airline; they cannot hold controlling interest in a U.S. television station or network; nor can they fish for mackerel—the only fish in surplus in U.S. waters.[33] Tariffs also can be used to gain bargaining clout with other countries, but they risk adversely affecting the fortunes of domestic companies.

In recent years, scores of trading nations have agreed to abolish tariffs on 500 high-technology products such as computers, software, calculators, fax machines, and related goods. Elimination of such tariffs means as much as $100 million in annual savings to communication giants like IBM.

Marketing Dictionary

tariff Tax levied against imported goods.

Administrative Barriers

In addition to direct taxes on imported products, governments may erect a number of other barriers ranging from special permits and detailed inspection requirements to quotas on foreign-made items to stem the flow of imported goods—or halt them altogether. European shoppers pay about twice the price for bananas that North American shoppers pay. The reason for these high prices? Through a series of import license controls, Europe allows fewer bananas to be imported than people want to buy. Even worse, the European countries set up a system of quotas designed to support banana growing in former colonies in Africa and Asia, which hurt imports from Latin American countries.

Other forms of trade restrictions include import quotas and embargoes. **Import quotas** limit the number of units of products in certain categories that can cross a country's border. The quota is supposed to protect domestic industry and employment and to preserve foreign exchange, but it doesn't always work that way. Since the late 1950s, the U.S. has had quotas affecting the apparel industry—whether they involve certain textiles or the manufacturing of the clothes themselves. However, foreign companies often find loopholes in the quota systems and wind up not only with huge profits but also plenty of jobs for their own workers. Hong Kong billionaire William Fung makes no apologies for his company's success through quotas. "Everybody got rich through holding quotas," he says. "The U.S. artificially restricted supply. So when demand rises, prices rise. That's the quota premium."[34]

The ultimate quota is the embargo—a complete ban on the import of a product. Since 1960, the U.S. has maintained an embargo against Cuba in protest of Fidel Castro's dictatorship and policies such as expropriation of property and disregard for human rights. Not only do the sanctions prohibit Cuban exports (cigars and sugar are the island's best-known products) to enter the country, but they also apply to companies that profit from property that Cuba's communist government expropriated from Americans following the Cuban revolution.[35] However, many leading U.S. executives oppose the embargo. They know that they are losing the opportunity to develop the Cuban market while foreign rivals establish production and marketing facilities there.

Other administrative barriers include *subsidies*. Airbus, the French, German, British, and Spanish aircraft consortium, often comes under attack from U.S. trade officials because it is so heavily subsidized. The Europeans, on the other hand, argue that Boeing and Lockheed Martin benefit from research done by NASA, the Pentagon, and other U.S. agencies. And still another way to block international trade is to simply create so many regulatory barriers that it is almost impossible to reach target markets. The European Union, for example, enforces more than 2,700 different sets of trade requirements by states, counties, cities, and insurance providers. Indian law contains even more complex requirements.

Foreign trade can also be regulated by exchange control through a central bank or government agency. *Exchange control* means that firms that gain foreign exchange by exporting must sell foreign currencies to the central bank or other foreign agency and importers must buy foreign currencies from the same organization. The exchange control authority can then allocate, expand, or restrict foreign exchange according to existing national policy.

Dumping

The practice of selling a product in a foreign market at a price lower than what it commands in the producer's domestic market is called *dumping*. Critics of free trade often argue that foreign governments give substantial support to their own exporting companies. Government support may permit these firms to extend their export markets by offering lower prices abroad. In retaliation for this kind of interference with free trade, the U.S. adds import tariffs to products that foreign firms dump on U.S. markets to bring their prices in line with those of domestically produced products. That is the current situation in the U.S. steel industry. However, businesses often complain that charges of dumping must undergo a lengthy investigative and bureaucratic procedure before the government assesses import duties. U.S. firms that claim dumping threatens to hurt their business can file a complaint with the U.S. International Trade Commission (ITC), which tends to reject about half the claims it receives.

Multinational Economic Integration

A noticeable trend toward multinational economic integration has developed since the end of World War II. Multinational economic integration can be set up in several ways. The simplest approach is to establish a **free-trade area** in which participating nations agree to the free trade of goods among themselves, abolishing all tariffs and trade restrictions. A *customs union* establishes a free-trade area plus a uniform tariff for trade with nonmember nations. A *common market* extends a customs union by seeking to reconcile all government regulations affecting trade. Despite the many factors in its favor, not everyone is enthusiastic about free trade, particularly Americans who think their jobs may be affected. So it is important to consider both sides of the issue. Although productivity and innovation are said to grow more quickly with free trade, American workers face pay-cut demands and potential job loss as more companies move their operations overseas.[36]

GATT and the World Trade Organization *3 Trade barriers*

The **General Agreement on Tariffs and Trade (GATT),** a 117-nation trade accord that has sponsored several rounds of major tariff negotiations, substantially reducing worldwide tariff levels, celebrated its *U have more free trade* 50th birthday in 1997. In 1994, a seven-year series of GATT conferences, called the Uruguay Round, culminated in one of the biggest victories for free trade in decades. The new accord's partial opening of trade helped the U.S. economy grow by $1 trillion and created some 2 million new jobs.

The Uruguay Round cut average tariffs by one-third, or more than $700 billion. Among its major victories are the following:

- Reduction of farm subsidies, which opened new markets for U.S. exports

- Increased protection for patents, copyrights, and trademarks

- Inclusion of services under international trading rules, creating opportunities for U.S. financial, legal, and accounting firms

- Phasing out import quotas on textiles and clothing from developing nations, a move that benefits U.S. retailers and consumers because quotas increase clothing prices by $15 billion

A key outcome of the GATT talks was establishment of the **World Trade Organization (WTO),** a 136-member organization that succeeds GATT. The WTO oversees GATT agreements, mediates disputes, and continues the effort to reduce trade barriers throughout the world. Unlike GATT, WTO decisions are binding. *GATT falls on under WTO Exam.*

To date, however, the WTO has made only slow progress toward its major policy initiatives—liberalizing world financial services, telecommunications, and maritime markets. Trade officials have not agreed on the direction for the WTO. Its activities have focused more on complaint resolution than on removing global trade barriers. The U.S. has been the most active plaintiff in WTO dispute courts. Recently, the WTO announced a decision about U.S. tax breaks for companies like Microsoft and Boeing, which have significant operations overseas, essentially granting the European Union permission to impose billions of dollars in punitive tariffs on U.S. imports. However, both the European Union and the U.S. immediately engaged in discussions to resolve the situation and avert a trade war, which would have been harmful to both.[37] *is good for the world*

Big differences between developed and developing areas create a major roadblock to WTO progress. These conflicts became apparent at the first WTO meeting in Singapore in the late 1990s. Asian nations want trade barriers lifted on their manufactured goods, but they also want to protect their own telecommunications

Briefly Speaking

WE ARE ALL AMERICANS

Headline in the French newspaper Le Monde *following the September 11, 2001, terrorist attacks*

3

Outline the basic functions of GATT, WTO, NAFTA, the proposed FTAA, and the European Union.

EU used to call EC european community.
Rule on one country is the rule of the other country.
Comparative advantage. expl Labor cost is expensive on the USA than China.

Marketing Dictionary

import quota   Trade restriction that limits the number of units of certain goods that can enter a country for resale.

free-trade area   Region in which participating nations agree to the free trade of goods among themselves, abolishing tariffs and trade restrictions.

General Agreement on Tariffs and Trade (GATT)   International trade accord that has helped reduce world tariffs.

World Trade Organization (WTO)   Organization that replaces GATT and oversees agreements and makes binding decisions in mediating disputes, and reducing trade barriers.

'net =x

companies. In addition, they oppose monitoring of corruption and labor practices by outsiders. The U.S. wants free trade for telecommunications, more controls on corruption, and establishment of international labor standards. Europe wants standard rules on foreign investments and removal of profit repatriation restrictions but is not as concerned with worker rights.

China is the world's largest nation with an economy that has grown 10 percent annually for the last two decades. As a market, it holds the promise of enormous potential for exporters. But China's exports show less than a 2 percent annual growth as a result of the multitude of barriers and red tape that make it extremely difficult for foreign firms to operate there. Recently, however, the release of trade rights allowed new enterprises to engage in importing and exporting, and the nation was admitted to the WTO.

The NAFTA Accord

A heated controversy continues almost a decade after the passage of the **North American Free-Trade Agreement (NAFTA),** an agreement between the U.S., Canada, and Mexico that removes trade restrictions among the three nations over a 14-year period. Proponents claim that NAFTA has been good for the American economy; critics charge that U.S. and Canadian workers have lost their jobs to cheap Mexican labor. The NAFTA accord brings together more than 415 million people and a combined gross domestic product of $7.9 trillion, making it by far the world's largest free-trade zone.

The NAFTA accord was approved despite serious concerns about job losses from the relatively high-wage industries in the U.S. and Canada as manufacturers relocated their production facilities in lower-wage Mexico. However, NAFTA supporters point out that imports of components and intermediate goods that require further refinements before becoming part of products "Made in the USA" actually hold down the cost of U.S.-made output and support local jobs. And even though imports of such products as autos assembled in Mexico have risen, these vehicles now include a high percentage of components manufactured in the U.S.[38]

To date, NAFTA seems to have succeeded in promoting greater trade between the U.S. and Mexico, and actually boosted jobs and cut inflation without hurting wages. Canada has long been the United States' leading trade party. In recent years, however, Mexico passed Japan as our No. 2 trade partner—despite the fact that Japan's GDP is 10 times larger than that of Mexico.

But nine of every ten dollars in Mexican exports are shipped to the U.S., and its recent recession has had an impact on the Mexican economy. Exports of electronics, textiles, chemicals, and auto parts dropped sharply. Not surprisingly, Mexico's unskilled labor is now more expensive than China's, so companies are looking to Asia for production facilities. Despite the fact that China was admitted to the WTO, Mexico lagged in forming a bilateral trade agreement with that country.[39]

Recently, the U.S. signed a free trade agreement with Chile—the first between the U.S. and a South American country—which went into effect January 1, 2004. It immediately eliminated tariffs on more than 85 percent of trade between the two nations. Other trade barriers will be phased out over a 12-year period. Total trade between the U.S. and Chile amounts to roughly $6.5 billion annually. This pact is a step toward a comprehensive Free Trade Area of the Americas.

The Free Trade Area of the Americas

NAFTA was actually the first step toward creating a **Free Trade Area of the Americas (FTAA),** stretching the length of the entire Western Hemisphere, from the Bering Strait to Cape Horn, encompassing 34 countries, a population of 800 million, and a combined gross domestic product of more than $11 trillion. The FTAA would be the largest free-trade zone on earth and would offer low or nonexistent tariffs, streamlined customs, and no quotas, subsidies, or other barriers to trade. Figure 4.5 identifies

SOURCE: Data from Economist Intelligence Unit, Inter-American Development Bank, found in "Betting on Free Trade," *BusinessWeek,* April 23, 2001, p. 62.

the countries expected to be members of the proposed FTAA, their levels of economic output, and recent levels of foreign trade. The Bush administration is a staunch supporter of the FTAA, which still has many hurdles to overcome as countries wrangle for conditions that are most favorable to them. Caterpillar Inc., the largest manufacturer of earth-moving equipment in the world, stands to gain a hefty slice of the profit pie. Removal of tariffs and customs delays are expected to increase sales of construction equipment as much as $4.5 billion over the first ten years.[40]

The European Union

The best-known example of a multinational economic community is the **European Union (EU).** Twenty-five countries belong to the EU: Finland, Sweden, Denmark, United Kingdom, Ireland, Netherlands, Belgium, Germany, Luxembourg, France, Austria, Italy, Greece, Spain, Portugal, Hungary, Poland, the Czech Republic, the Slovak Republic, Slovenia, Estonia, Latvia, Lithuania, Malta, and Cyprus. With a total population of approximately 500 million people, the EU forms a huge common market.

The goal of the EU is to eventually remove all barriers to free trade among its members, making it as simple and painless to ship products between England and Spain as it

Marketing Dictionary

North American Free-Trade Agreement (NAFTA)   Accord removing trade barriers among Canada, Mexico, and the United States.

Free Trade Area of the Americas (FTAA)   Proposed free trade area stretching the length of the entire Western hemisphere and designed to extend free trade benefits to additional nations in North, Central, and South America.

European Union (EU)   Customs union that is moving in the direction of an economic union by adopting a common currency, removing trade restrictions, and permitting free flow of goods and workers throughout the member nations.

**FIGURE 4.6
Why Marketers
Decide to Go Global**

What Drives Globalization?

Technology Advances — 8%
Reduced Trade Barriers — 10%
Enhanced Customer Responsiveness — 8%*
Globalization of Competitors — 16%
New Customers in Emerging Markets — 27%*
Globalization of Customers — 31%*

Change driven by the customer = 66%

SOURCE: Data from "Shaping the Value Chain for Outstanding Performance," PricewaterhouseCoopers survey of 200 leading European businesses, found in *Fortune*, special advertising section, June 26, 2000, p. S8.

is between New Jersey and Pennsylvania. Also involved is the standardization of regulations and requirements that businesses must meet. Instead of having to comply with 25 sets of standards and 25 different currencies, companies will have fewer to deal with. This simplification should lower the costs of doing business in Europe by allowing firms to take advantage of economies of scale.

In some ways, the EU is making definite progress toward its economic goals. We have already seen that it is drafting standardized eco-labels to certify that products are manufactured according to certain environmental standards, as well as creating guidelines governing marketers' uses of customer information. Marketers can also protect trademarks throughout the entire EU with a single application and registration process through the Community Trademark (CTM), which simplifies doing business and eliminates having to register with each member country. It is, however, sometimes difficult to obtain approval for trademark protection.

Yet marketers still face challenges when selling their products in the EU. Customs taxes differ, and there is no uniform postal system. Mail between countries is extremely slow. In fact, the Federation of European Direct Marketing is pushing for modernization and integration of postal systems. Using one toll-free number for several countries will not work, either, because each country has its own telephone system for codes and numbers. Furthermore, when the euro was introduced by the European Union, three EU nations decided to retain their own national currencies, at least temporarily.

Mexico has successfully negotiated a trade agreement with the EU that makes it easier for European companies to set up their operations in Mexico, which benefits EU companies by giving them the same privileges enjoyed by the U.S. and Canada and brings new investors to Mexico. "The agreement places Mexico in a privileged position," says Mexican Undersecretary of Commerce Luis de la Calle.[41]

Going Global

As we move further into the 21st century, globalization will affect almost every industry and every individual throughout the world. Traditional marketers who decide to take their firms global may do so because they already have strong domestic market shares or their target market is too saturated to offer any substantial growth. Sometimes, by evaluating key indicators of the marketing environment, marketers can move toward globalization at an optimal time. A critical task facing international marketers is developing strategies for successfully entering new foreign markets. Figure 4.6 identifies six reasons that companies cite for going global.

Most large firms already participate in global commerce, and many small businesses recognize the need to investigate whether to market their products overseas. It is not an easy step to take, requiring careful evaluation and preparation.

First Steps in Deciding to Market Globally

The first step toward successful global marketing is to secure top management's support. Without the enthusiasm and support of senior executives, export efforts are likely to fail. The advocate for going global must explain and promote the potential of foreign markets and facilitate the global marketing process.

TABLE 4.3   Sources for Analyzing Foreign Markets

Source	Description
U.S. Department of Commerce	Maintains the National Trade Data Bank (market reports on foreign demand for specific products), produces catalogs and video shows and participates in trade shows.
Tradepoint USA	A not-for-profit service with print and online resources. Its Internet service, I-Trade, offers country data, international news, the National Trade Data Bank, and other reports.
The Green Book	Published by the American Management Association, this guide lists all market research firms and those with international capabilities.
Esomar	The European Society of Opinion and Market Research maintains a worldwide listing by company.
U.S. State Department	Offers commercial guides compiled by local embassies to almost every country in the world.

The next important step is to research the export process and potential markets. Burt Cabanas, CEO of Texas-based Benchmark Hospitality, which develops and manages conference centers, hotels, and resorts, explains the consequences of failing to research a market when going global: "We went into Thailand initially without doing research and that was a mistake. We made many assumptions about how we would do marketing in ways that were a few degrees off target. We were told by U.S. companies that if we were going to do business in Thailand, we should be in Bangkok, and we spent a tremendous amount of time getting a presence there. We then found out we could have been just as successful outside the city. Taking someone else's word for it rather than doing the research set us back a year and a half."[42] Benchmark Hospitality has since expanded to Japan and the Philippines and is now researching six additional markets in foreign countries.

The U.S. Department of Commerce sponsors a toll-free hotline that describes the various federal export programs that are currently available. Trade counselors at 68 district offices offer export advice, computerized market data, and names of contacts in over 60 countries. Some services are free, while others are available at a reasonable cost. Table 4.3 describes five important resources for marketers who want to analyze foreign markets.

Strategies for Entering International Markets

Once marketers have completed their research, they may choose from among three basic strategies for entering international markets: importing and exporting; contractual agreements like franchising, licensing, and subcontracting; and international direct investment. As Figure 4.7 shows, the level of risk and the firm's degree of control over international marketing increase with greater involvement. Firms often use more than one of these entry strategies. L.L. Bean subcontracts with a Japanese company to handle its product returns, and it also maintains a direct investment in several Japanese retail outlets in partnership with Matsushita.

A firm that brings in goods produced abroad to sell domestically or to be used as components in its products is an importer. In making import decisions, the marketer must assess local demand for the product, taking into consideration such factors as the following:

- ability of the supplier to maintain agreed-to quality levels

- capability of filling orders that might vary considerably from one order to the next

- response time in filling orders

- total costs—including import fees, packaging, and transportation—in comparison with costs of domestic suppliers

4

Compare the alternative strategies for entering international markets.

FIGURE 4.7
Levels of Involvement in International Marketing

Exporting, another basic form of international marketing, involves a continuous effort in marketing a firm's merchandise to customers in other countries. Many firms export their products as the first step in reaching foreign markets. Success in exporting often encourages them to try other entry strategies.

First-time exporters can reach foreign customers through one or more of three alternatives: export-trading companies, export-management companies, or offset agreements. An export-trading company (ETC) buys products from domestic producers and resells them abroad. While manufacturers lose control over marketing and distribution to the ETC, it helps them export through a relatively simple and inexpensive channel, in the process providing feedback about the overseas market potential of their products.

The second option, an export-management company (EMC), provides the first-time exporter with expertise in locating foreign buyers, handling necessary paperwork, and ensuring that its goods meet local labeling and testing laws. However, the manufacturer retains more control over the export process when it deals with an EMC than if it were to sell the goods outright to an export-trading company. Smaller firms can get assistance with administrative needs such as financing and preparation of proposals and contracts from large EMC contractors.

The final option, entering a foreign market under an offset agreement, teams a small firm with a major international company. The smaller firm essentially serves as a subcontractor on a large foreign project. This entry strategy provides new exporters with international experience, supported by the assistance of the primary contractor in such areas as international transaction documentation and financing.

Contractual Agreements

As a firm gains sophistication in international marketing, it may enter contractual agreements that provide several flexible alternatives to exporting. Both large and small firms can benefit from these methods. Franchising and foreign licensing, for example, are good ways to take services abroad. Subcontracting may set up either production facilities or services. Sponsorships are another form of international contractual marketing agreements. When Nintendo CEO Hiroshi Yamauchi bought the Seattle Mariners baseball team a decade ago, skeptics worried about the wisdom of selling "America's pastime" to another nation. But the relationship, which includes sponsorships as well as foreign licensing deals, has been beneficial to Seattle, Major League Baseball, and Japanese baseball fans, who are as passionate about the sport as American fans are. "It's been great for everybody," says baseball commissioner Bud Selig. Major League Baseball has pursued sponsorship deals in Japan with Kirin Brewery Co. and Sumitomo Forestry Co., who have paid out millions to use the Major League Baseball logo in their marketing. In addition, Major League Baseball has a five-year deal with the Japanese television networks for international rights to broadcast the games.[43]

Franchising

A **franchise** is a contractual arrangement in which a wholesaler or retailer (the franchisee) agrees to meet the operating requirements of a manufacturer or other franchiser. The franchisee receives the right to sell the products and use the franchiser's name, as well as a variety of marketing, management, and other services. As mentioned earlier, fast-food companies such as McDonald's have been active franchisers around the world.

One advantage of franchising is risk reduction by offering a proven concept. Standardized operations typically reduce costs, increase operating efficiencies, and provide greater international recognizability. However, the success of an international franchise depends on its willingness to balance standard practices with local customer preferences. McDonald's, Pizza Hut, and Domino's are all expanding into India with special menus that feature lamb, chicken, and vegetarian items, in deference to Hindu and Muslim customers who do not eat beef and pork.

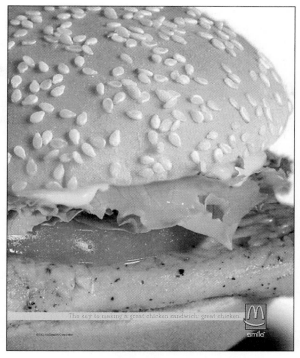

Foreign Licensing

A second method of going global through the use of contractual agreements is **foreign licensing,** as described in the example about the Seattle Mariners. Such an agreement grants foreign marketers the right to distribute a firm's merchandise or use its trademark, patent, or process in a specified geographic area. These arrangements usually set certain time limits, after which agreements are revised or renewed.

Licensing offers several advantages over exporting, including access to local partners' marketing information and distribution channels and protection from various legal barriers. Because licensing does not require capital outlays, many firms, both small and large, regard it as an attractive entry strategy. Like franchising, licensing allows a firm to quickly enter a foreign market with a known product or concept. The arrangement also may provide entry into a market that government restrictions close to imports or international direct investment.

As every international traveler knows, Oak Brook, Illinois–headquartered McDonald's has expanded its franchised fast-food operations around the globe. The "smile" logo of the firm's Golden Arches ranks among the world's ten most valuable brands.

Subcontracting

A third strategy for going global through contractual agreements is *subcontracting,* in which the production of goods or services is assigned to local companies. Using local subcontractors can prevent mistakes involving local culture and regulations. Manufacturers might subcontract with a local company to produce their goods or use a foreign distributor to handle their products abroad or provide customer service. Manufacturing within the country can provide protection from import duties and may be a lower-cost alternative that makes it possible for the product to compete with local offerings. Sears subcontracts with local manufacturers in Mexico and Spain to produce many of the products—especially clothing—sold in its department stores.

International Direct Investment

Another strategy for entering global markets is international direct investment in foreign firms, production, and marketing facilities. As the world's largest economy, the U.S.'s foreign direct investment inflows and outflows—total of American firm investments abroad and foreign firm investments in the U.S.—are nearly 32 percent greater than Germany's and 100 percent greater than Japan's, its two largest competitors. By the beginning of this century, U.S. direct investment abroad was nearly $2.2 trillion, with a high number of acquisitions in the United Kingdom, the Netherlands, and Canada. On the other hand, foreign direct investment in the U.S. had grown to over $2.1 trillion. Three of every four dollars of foreign investment in the U.S. came from Europe and Canada.[44]

Marketing Dictionary

franchise   Contractual arrangement in which a wholesaler or retailer agrees to meet the operating requirements of a manufacturer or other franchiser.

foreign licensing   Agreement that grants foreign marketers the right to distribute a firm's merchandise or to use its trademark, patent, or process in a specified geographic area.

Although high levels of involvement and high-risk potential are characteristics of investments in foreign countries, firms choosing this method often have a competitive advantage. Direct investment can take several forms. A company can acquire an existing firm in a country where it wants to do business, or it can set up an independent division outside its own borders with responsibility for production and marketing in a country or geographic region. Recently, European firms have been acquiring U.S. companies as a way to enter the American marketplace. Vodafone Group and Deutsche Telekom bought AirTouch Communications and VoiceStream for a combined $114 billion. Purchases like this open up the wide American market to European firms.[45]

Foreign sales offices, overseas marketing subsidiaries, and foreign offices and manufacturing facilities of U.S. firms all involve direct investment. Motorola has had offices in Israel since 1964 and continues to strengthen its presence in the Middle East. Currently, Motorola has more than 5,000 employees in its manufacturing, design, and marketing facilities in Israel, which generate $1.3 billion in revenue for the company. "The market in Israel in the last ten years shows great potential, and it is very active in the communications area," says Yardena Astel of Motorola Israel. More than 40 percent of the Israeli population has a cell phone, which is far greater than the 20 percent of Americans.[46]

Companies may also engage in international marketing by forming joint ventures, in which they share the risks, costs, and management of the foreign operation with one or more partners. These partnerships join the investing companies with nationals of the host countries. While some companies choose to open their own facilities overseas, others share with their partners. Service companies often find that joint ventures provide the most efficient way to penetrate a market.

Although joint ventures offer many advantages, foreign investors have encountered problems in several areas throughout the world, especially in developing economies. Lower trade barriers, new technologies, lower transport costs, and vastly improved access to information means that many more partnerships will be involved in international trade.

From Multinational Corporation to Global Marketer

A **multinational corporation** is a firm with significant operations and marketing activities outside its home country. Examples of multinationals include General Electric, Siemens, and Mitsubishi in heavy electrical equipment, and Timex, Seiko, and Citizen in watches. Some companies, like Tyco International, are widely diversified in both the industries and the countries they serve. Tyco, whose headquarters are in New Hampshire, has 220,000 employees in more than 100 countries in fields that include medical products, fire safety, fiber optics, and even commercial lending. Despite recent cutbacks resulting in some layoffs, Tyco is looking to strengthen its international presence by selecting directors from Europe and Asia to serve on its board.[47]

Since they first became a force in international business in the 1960s, multinationals have evolved in some important ways. First, these companies are no longer exclusively U.S. based. Today it is as likely for a multinational to be based in Japan, Germany, or Great Britain as in the U.S. Second, multinationals no longer think of their foreign operations as mere outsourcing appendages that carry out the design, production, and engineering ideas conceived at home. Instead, they encourage constant exchanges of ideas, capital, and technologies among all the multinational operations.

Multinationals often employ huge foreign workforces relative to their American staffs. Over half of all Ford and IBM personnel are located outside the U.S. These workforces are no longer seen merely as sources of cheap labor. On the contrary, many multinationals center technically complex activities in locations throughout the world. Texas Instruments does much of its research, development, design, and manufacturing in East Asia. In fact, it is increasingly common for U.S. multinationals to bring product innovations from their foreign facilities back to the States.

Multinationals have become global corporations that reflect the interdependence of world economies, the growth of international competition, and the globalization of world markets. An increasing number of acquisitions include U.S. multinationals as targets for takeover. In one recent year, Germany's Deutsche Bank acquired Bankers Trust; British Petroleum took over Amoco; and Chrysler became part of Germany's Daimler-Benz.

Developing an International Marketing Strategy

[handwritten: other foreign country takes the US as their target Mkt. what USA has, and other countries don't and want. US has a large Population. we have a large level of discretionary income. US has a Stable Gt. US Federal Reserve System also is a strong Part for USA.]

5
Differentiate between a global marketing strategy and a multidomestic marketing strategy.

[handwritten: These n reasons y the US is a target 4 Intl Mkters. The US is a very cool controllable Mkt. w/ a large level of discretionary Income.]

In developing a marketing mix, international marketers may choose between two alternative approaches: a global marketing strategy or a multidomestic marketing strategy. A **global marketing strategy** defines a standard marketing mix and implements it with minimal modifications in all foreign markets. This approach brings the advantage of economies of scale to production and marketing activities. Procter & Gamble (P&G) marketers follow a global marketing strategy for Pringles potato chips, their leading export brand. P&G sells one product with a consistent formulation in every country. Unlike Frito-Lay's Cheetos snacks, which come in flavors geared to local tastes, P&G meets 80 percent of worldwide demand with only six flavors of Pringles. The brand relies on one package design throughout the world. This standardized approach saves money since it allows large-scale production runs and reinforces the brand's image. Also, similar advertising around the world builds brand awareness by featuring the slogan, "Once you pop, you can't stop." P&G intends all of these tactics to build strong global brand equity for Pringles.

A global marketing perspective can effectively market some goods and services to segments in many nations that share cultures and languages. This approach works especially well for products with strong, universal appeal, such as McDonald's, luxury items like Rolex watches, and high-tech brands like Microsoft. Global advertising outlets, such as international editions of popular consumer and business magazines and international transmissions of such TV programs as CNN, MTV, and the CNBC financial network, help marketers deliver a single message to millions of global viewers. International satellite television channels such as StarTV reach 260 million Asian viewers through a host of sports, news, movie, music, and entertainment channels programmed in eight languages.

A global marketing strategy can be highly effective for luxury products that target upscale consumers everywhere. Marketers of diamonds and luxury watches, for instance, typically use advertising with little or no copy—just a picture of a beautiful diamond or watch with the name discreetly displayed at the bottom.

A major benefit of a global marketing strategy is its low cost to implement. Most firms, however, find it necessary to practice market segmentation outside their home markets and tailor their marketing mixes to fit the unique needs of customers in specific countries. This **multidomestic marketing strategy** assumes that differences between market characteristics and competitive situations in certain nations require firms to customize their marketing decisions to effectively reach individual marketplaces. (This strategy is sometimes mistakenly called *multinational* marketing. In fact, a multinational corporation may combine both strategies in its international marketing plans.)

Many marketing experts feel that most products demand multidomestic marketing strategies to give them realistic global marketing appeals. Cultural, geographic, language, and other differences simply make it impractical to try to send one message to many countries. Specific situations may allow them to standardize some parts of the marketing process but customize others. Pillsbury wanted to offer its Progresso brand of Italian-style foods to markets in nations outside the U.S. But Pillsbury marketers discovered that in some South American countries, "progress" could mean many different things, including financial services. So they came up with a made-up name, Frescarini, meaning "fresh dough and pasta," to use as the global brand name.[48]

Marketers of luxury watches such as Rolex rely on the images of exclusiveness and extremely high quality to deliver a universal message.

Marketing Dictionary

multinational corporation Firm with significant operations and marketing activities outside its home country.

global marketing strategy Standardized marketing mix with minimal modifications that a firm uses in all of its domestic and foreign markets.

multidomestic marketing strategy Application of market segmentation to foreign markets by tailoring the firm's marketing mix to match specific target markets in each nation.

FIGURE 4.8
Alternative International Product and Promotional Strategies

		Product Strategy		
		Same Product	**Product Adaptation**	**New Product**
Promotion Strategy	**Same Promotion**	**Straight Extension** Wrigley's gum Coca-Cola Eastman Kodak cameras and lm	**Product Adaptation** Campbell's soup Exxon gasoline	**Product Invention** Nonelectric sewing machines Manually operated washing machines
	Different Promotion	**Promotion Adaptation** Bicycles/motorcycles Outboard motors	**Dual Adaptation** Coffee Some clothing	

6

Describe the alternative marketing mix strategies used in international marketing.

International Product and Promotional Strategies *or*

4 P's work the same way.

International marketers can choose from among five strategies for selecting the most appropriate product and promotion strategy for a specific foreign market—straight extension, promotion adaptation, product adaptation, dual adaptation, and product invention. As Figure 4.8 indicates, the strategies center on whether to extend a domestic product and promotional strategy into international markets or adapt one or both to meet the target market's unique requirements.

A firm may follow a one-product, one-message straight extension strategy as part of a global marketing strategy, like Pepsi Cola's. This strategy permits economies of scale in production and marketing. Also, successful implementation creates universal recognition of a product for consumers from country to country.

Other strategies call for product adaptation, promotion adaptation, or both. While bicycles, motorcycles, and outboard motors primarily form part of the market for U.S. recreational vehicles, they may represent important basic transportation modes in other nations. Consequently, producers of these products may adapt their promotional messages even if they sell the product without changes. Coca-Cola executives in Atlanta have recently loosened their grip on the company's international marketing efforts in order to adapt to local markets around the world. "We used to make TV commercials in Atlanta for China," notes CEO Douglas Daft. "That's not appropriate."[49]

Sometimes, international marketers must change both the product and the promotional message in a dual adaptation strategy to meet the unique needs of specific international markets. As part of its overall efforts to adapt to local markets, Coca-Cola developed new drink flavors. In Turkey, the firm now offers a pear-flavored drink, while in Germany consumers are treated to a berry-flavored Fanta. Both new drinks are designed to appeal to the tastes of people in those countries.[50]

Finally, a firm may select product invention to take advantage of unique foreign market opportunities. To match user needs in developing nations, an appliance manufacturer might introduce a hand-powered washing machine even though such products became obsolete in industrialized countries years ago.

Although Chapter 12 discusses the idea of branding in greater detail, it is important to note here the importance of a company's recognizable name, image, product, or even slogan around the world. Figure 4.9 identifies the world's ten most valuable brands, as rated by Interbrand. Other than Mercedes and Nokia, all are brands owned by U.S.-based companies.[51]

International Distribution Strategy

Distribution is a vital aspect of overseas marketing. Marketers must set up proper channels and anticipate extensive physical distribution problems. Foreign markets may offer poor transportation systems and warehousing facilities—or none at all. International marketers must adapt promptly and efficiently to these situations in order to profit from overseas sales.

A distribution decision involves two steps. First, the firm must decide on a method of entering the foreign market. Second, it must determine how to distribute the product within the foreign market through that entry channel.

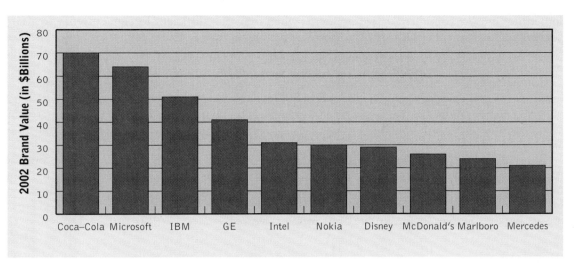

FIGURE 4.9
The World's 10 Most Valuable Global Brands

SOURCE: Data from Interbrand Corp., J.P. Morgan Chase & Co.; found in "The Best Global Brands," *BusinessWeek*, August 5, 2002, p. 93.

Distribution decisions balance many factors, including the nature of the firm's products, consumer tastes and buying habits, market competition, and transportation options. Even though music may be considered a universal language, U.S.-based global Internet music company SonicNet believes that the traditional MTV one-world-sound approach turned off as many viewers as it served. After all, young people do not share the same lifestyles and cultures. SonicNet's strategy involves working with foreign partners who supply rock, pop, rap, and other music video clips, live concerts, and breaking news to local cyberspace surfers. For example, it turned to telecommunications provider Swisscom to create German, French, and Italian editions of its Web-based music entertainment programming. MTV has responded by increasing its focus on country-specific artists and video DJs to address more specifically the music interests of viewers in different countries. But by developing local language editions that reflect that area's taste in music, SonicNet has also succeeded in growing local audiences all around the world for advertisers.[52]

Pricing Strategy

Pricing can critically affect the success of an overall marketing strategy for foreign markets. Considerable competitive, economic, political, and legal constraints often limit pricing decisions. Global marketers can succeed if they thoroughly understand these requirements.

Companies must adapt their pricing strategies to local markets and change them when conditions change. Until recently, foreign shipments carried premium prices without assurance that the package would be delivered on time in good condition—or even delivered at all. After the air-freight and overnight-delivery services boomed in the 1980s, delivery became more reliable but costs were exorbitant to many areas. To compete in this crowded market without losing market share, the United States Postal Service (USPS) began advertising International Express Mail services to over 175 countries at set delivery rates. Global Priority Mail, for example, provides prompt delivery to over 30 key business countries for as little as $3.75.

An important development in pricing strategy for international marketing has been the emergence of commodity marketing organizations that seek to control prices through collective action. The Organization of Petroleum Exporting Countries (OPEC) is a good example of this kind of collective export organization, but many others exist.

Countertrade

In a growing number of nations, the only way a marketer can gain access to foreign markets is through **countertrade**—a form of exporting in which a firm barters products rather than selling them for cash. Less-developed nations

Marketing Dictionary

countertrade   Form of exporting whereby goods and services are bartered rather than sold for cash.

sometimes impose countertrade requirements when they lack sufficient foreign currency to attain goods and services they want or need from exporting countries. These countries allow sellers to exchange their products only for domestic products as a way to control their balance-of-trade problems.

Countertrade became popular two decades ago, when companies wanted to conduct business in eastern European countries and the former Soviet Union. Those governments did not allow exchanges of hard currency, so this form of barter facilitated trade. PepsiCo made one of the largest countertrades ever when it exchanged $3 billion worth of Pepsi Cola for Russian Stolichnaya vodka, a cargo ship, and tankers from the former Soviet Union.

Estimating the actual volume of countertrade as percentage of world trade is difficult, but the American Countertrade Association puts the figure at about 25 percent. Countertraders include large multinational firms like General Electric and PepsiCo. Almost half of the *Fortune* 500 companies now practice countertrade in response to increasing global competition. Although countertrade is still growing at about 10 percent a year, its rate of increase has slowed.

7

Explain the attractiveness of the U.S. as a target market for foreign marketers.

The U.S. as a Target for International Marketers

Foreign marketers regard America as an inviting target. It offers a large population, high levels of discretionary income, political stability, a generally favorable attitude toward foreign investment, and a relatively well-controlled economy.

Among the best-known industries in which foreign manufacturers have established U.S. production facilities is automobiles. Most of the world's leading auto companies have built assembly facilities in the U.S.: Honda, Hyundai, and Mercedes-Benz in Alabama, BMW in South Carolina, Toyota in Kentucky, Nissan in Tennessee, and Honda in Mississippi and Ohio.

Many foreign executives are transforming their companies' mission statements to reflect their move toward globalization. Fusao Sekiguchi, president and CEO of Venture Safenet, a Japanese firm that provides professional engineers to companies on a temporary basis, wants to expand his company's reach around the world. "With the chance of developing this company profile, I am also in hope of sharing useful business hints with investors who are interested in the Japanese human resource market, as well as looking forward to all the opportunities of expanding my business to a global scale," he writes in an open letter on the firm's Web site.[53] Sekiguchi expanded his reach to America when the racehorse he owned, Fusaichi Pegasus, won the 2000 Kentucky Derby.

As we discussed earlier, foreign investment continues to grow in the U.S. Foreign multinationals will probably continue to invest in U.S. assets as they seek to produce goods locally and control distribution channels. Major U.S. companies owned by foreign firms include Columbia Pictures and Universal Studios, owned by Sony Corp. (Japan); Pillsbury, Heublein, Pearle Vision, and Pet Inc., owned by Grand Metropolitan (United Kingdom); and Maybelline and Cosmair cosmetics, owned by L'Oréal (a French subsidiary of the Swiss conglomerate Nestlé SA); and Citgo Petroleum, owned by Petróleos de Venezuela (Venezuela). European firms poured $250 billion into the U.S. in one recent 12-month period, accounting for 80 percent of all direct foreign investment.[54]

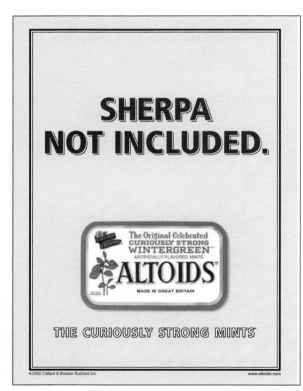

The huge U.S. success of strongly flavored Altoids mints explains why British marketer Callard & Bowser-Suchard views America as an attractive market. The product's packaging, in traditional—even old-fashioned—tins, also contributes to the image of a brand of mints totally different from current U.S. product offerings.

Strategic Implications of Marketing in the 21st Century

This first decade of the new century is marking a new era of truly global marketing, where nearly every marketer can become a global marketer. The previous eras of domestic markets are largely being relegated to niche marketing. The Internet has played a major role in these changes in the traditional marketing practices of the last century. Marketers in both small, localized firms and giant businesses need to reevaluate the strengths and weaknesses of current marketing practices and realign their plans to meet the new demands of the information age.

Marketers are the pioneers in bringing new technologies to developing nations. Their successes and failures will determine the direction global marketing will take and the speed with which they will be embraced. Actions of international marketers will influence every component of the marketing environments: competitive, economic, social-cultural, political-legal, and technological.

The greatest competitive advantages will belong to those marketers who capitalize on the similarities of their target markets and adapt to the differences. In some instances, the actions of marketers today help determine the rules and regulations of tomorrow.

Marketers need flexible and broad views of an increasingly complex customer. Goods and services will become more customized as they are introduced in foreign markets. New and better products in developing markets will create and maintain relationships for the future. Specialization will once again be a viable business concept.

Marketing has just entered a new frontier of limitless opportunities. Much like the first voyages into space, the world looks more different than anyone could have ever imagined. The impact of the Web and other new computer and communications technologies will be discussed in greater detail in the next chapter.

Summary of Chapter Objectives

1. Describe the importance of international marketing from the perspectives of the individual firm and the nation.

International marketing expands a company's market, allows firms to grow, and makes them less dependent on their own country's economy for success. Companies find that global marketing and international trade can help them meet customer demand, reduce certain costs, provide information on markets around the world, and increase employment.

2. Identify the major components of the environment for international marketing.

The major components of the international environment are economic, social-cultural, and political-legal.

3. Outline the basic functions of GATT, WTO, NAFTA, the proposed FTAA, and the European Union.

The General Agreement on Tariffs and Trade is a 117-nation accord that has substantially reduced tariffs. The World Trade Organization oversees GATT agreements, mediates disputes, and tries to reduce trade barriers throughout the world. The North American Free Trade Agreement removes trade restrictions among Canada, Mexico, and the U.S. The proposed Free Trade Area of the Americas is a free trade area covering the entire Western hemisphere. The European Union is a customs union whose goal is to remove all barriers to free trade among its members.

4. Compare the alternative strategies for entering international markets.

Several strategies are available to marketers, including exporting, importing, franchising, foreign licensing, subcontracting, and direct investment.

5. Differentiate between a global marketing strategy and a multidomestic marketing strategy.

A global marketing strategy defines a standard marketing mix and implements it with minimal modifications in all foreign markets. A multidomestic marketing strategy requires firms to customize their marketing decisions to reach individual marketplaces.

6. Describe the alternative marketing mix strategies used in international marketing.

Product and promotional strategies include the following: straight extension, promotion adaptation, product adaptation, dual adaptation, and product invention. Marketers may also choose among distribution, pricing, and countertrade strategies.

7. Explain the attractiveness of the U.S. as a target market for foreign marketers.

The U.S. has a large population, high levels of discretionary income, political stability, a favorable attitude toward foreign investment, and relatively controlled economic ills.

Marketing Terms You Need to Know

exporting 98
importing 98
infrastructure 103
exchange rate 105
tariff 110
import quota 112

free-trade area 113
General Agreement on
    Tariffs and Trade
    (GATT) 113
World Trade Organization
    (WTO) 113

North American Free-Trade
    Agreement (NAFTA) 114
Free Trade Area of the
    Americas (FTAA) 114
European Union (EU) 115
franchise 118

foreign licensing 119
multinational corporation 120
global marketing strategy 121
multidomestic marketing
    strategy 121
countertrade 123

Other Important Marketing Terms

political risk assessment
    (PRA) 108
friendship, commerce, and
    navigation (FCN)
    treaties 109

ISO (International Standards
    Organization) 9000
    certification 109
revenue tariff 110
protective tariff 110

embargo 112
subsidy 112
exchange control 112
dumping 112
customs union 113

common market 113
subcontracting 119

Review Questions

1. Why is international trade important for North American marketers? Why is it important for marketers in developing and newly industrialized nations?
2. How does the international marketplace differ from the domestic marketplace? What are the six different areas that marketers must study before advising their company to enter a foreign market?
3. Explain each of the three forces that drive the legal environment for U.S. firms operating abroad.
4. Identify the two major categories of trade barriers to global marketing. Give an example of each.
5. Describe briefly the following trade agreements:
   a. GATT
   b. WTO
   c. NAFTA
   d. FTAA
   e. European Union

6. Describe importing and exporting as strategies for entering international markets.
7. Define *franchising, foreign licensing,* and *subcontracting.* Which might be the best strategy for a chain of moderately priced hotels to enter a foreign market?
8. Distinguish between a global marketing strategy and a multidomestic marketing strategy. What are the pros and cons of each?
9. What is countertrade? Why is the practice growing in popularity?
10. Why is the U.S. an attractive target for foreign marketers?

Projects and Teamwork Exercises

1. Imagine that you and a classmate are marketers for one of the following companies: AT&T, Amazon.com, Starbucks, Apple Computer, Burger King (or select one of your own). Decide whether your company will expand internationally by entering the market in either Mexico, India, or China.

Then write a brief outline describing the issues that your company must consider, based on the six areas of demand, competition, economy, political-legal, social-cultural, and technology.

2. Suppose you work for Domino's Pizza, which already has 3,000 outlets in more than 46 countries. With a classmate, identify a country that Domino's has not yet reached and write a brief plan for entering that country's market. Then create a print ad for that market (you can write the ad copy in English). It may be helpful to visit Domino's Web site for some ideas.

3. Assume that you are a marketer for a recognizable company like IBM, Old Navy, or Nike. Decide whether you think a global marketing strategy or a multidomestic strategy would be better for your product. Then create a print ad for your product, reflecting your decision.

4. Beijing, China's capital city, is slated to host the 2008 Summer Olympics. By yourself or with a classmate, identify a company that might benefit from promoting its goods or services at the Beijing Olympics. Describe which strategy you would use: straight extension, product or promotion adaptation, dual adaptation, or product invention.

5. Imagine that you are a consultant for one of the following businesses. Write a proposal to the marketers for that company that could help the firm enter the U.S. market.
   a. A chain of Japanese restaurants
   b. A chain of European theme parks
   c. A South American music producer
   d. The manufacturer of Australian outdoor clothing and gear

'net Work

1. **Importance of global marketing.** Go to the Web site of *Fortune* magazine and click on "Global 500." Choose five non-U.S. companies listed among the top 50 that you would like to know more about and find the following information: http://www.fortune.com
   a. name of company and global rank
   b. industry
   c. location of headquarters (country)
   d. number of employees
   e. total revenues (in U.S. dollars)
   f. a brief description of how the firm showcases its global presence on its Web site

2. **World Trade Organization (WTO).** Visit the Web site of the World Trade Organization to learn more about the organization. Answer the following questions: http://www.wto.org
   a. What is the overall purpose of the WTO?
   b. How is membership in the WTO obtained?
   c. Which countries have most recently become members of the WTO?
   d. What are some of the benefits of WTO membership?

3. **International product strategies.** Visit the Web site of a major U.S.-based international consumer products company (such as Gillette, PepsiCo, or Procter & Gamble). Review the site carefully and prepare two lists. The first list should consist of approximately five differences in the product or promotional strategies you found between the company's products sold in the U.S. and those sold in other countries. In the second list, record about five similarities among product and promotional strategies used by the company in different countries. Be prepared to discuss your findings in class.

Note: Internet Web addresses change frequently. If you don't find the exact sites listed, you may need to access the organization or company's home page and search from there.

CASE 4.1

It's a Small World: Disney Says Going Global Is Crucial

When Walt Disney Co.'s chairman Michael Eisner visited Paris with his wife in 1988, he vowed that his company would become a powerful force in Europe—and around the world. "We must be in television in all countries," he declared to the board of directors when he returned. A dozen years after that declaration, Disney is hardly a worldwide household presence, despite the global appeal of Mickey Mouse. Currently, Eisner acknowledges that his company still generates 80 percent of its $23.4 billion revenues in the U.S. True, there is a Euro Disney park located in Paris, and two in Tokyo, and the company just reached agreement for a Hong Kong Disneyland. But these efforts hardly match those of other U.S. consumer giants such as Coca-Cola, McDonald's, or Gillette. It took Disneyland Paris a decade to catch on, though it is now popular and profitable. The newly opened Euro Disneyland, located next door, is much more Eurocentric—and highly successful. And visitors are beginning to flock to the Tokyo parks, perhaps in part because of the new DisneySea. The two parks recorded a total of 22 million guests last year. But the world's second-largest media and entertainment firm (after AOL Time Warner) still isn't a formidable force around the world.

Michael Johnson, the newly appointed head of Walt Disney International, intends to change that. He plans to boost the proportion of Disney's international revenue to 30 percent over the next five years. "I want to rebuild this company overseas and reformat it," he says. But in doing so, perhaps Johnson and his colleagues should examine why the company does not have a stronger position overseas. In developing nations such as China and India, where citizens have little disposable income, each person spends about 10 to 15 cents a year on Disney products. Recent years have seen a $159 million decline in Disney's worldwide licensing revenues. And while Time Warner's Cartoon Network is viewed in 54 million foreign homes, Disney Channel subscribers account for only 4.7 percent of the cable

and satellite market in Europe, Asia, and Latin America. In addition, Disney has had a long tradition of managing foreign operations from its California headquarters, instead of letting overseas managers operate with the authority to make decisions that pertain to their own markets.

Johnson and Peter Murphy, the company's chief strategic officer, will need to examine a variety of issues regarding the international environment, from economic to social-cultural, from the sizes of different markets—such as the European Union and China—to individual buying behavior. Still, Disney has negotiated a deal in its favor in Hong Kong. In the agreement, Disney gets a 43 percent stake in the new park for its $314 million investment, while the local government pays out $2.9 billion in low-interest loans, land, and infrastructure improvements in return for the other 57 percent. It's an arrangement that everyone can live with. "The opportunities are definitely there," says Johnson. Even Mickey Mouse himself would hope so.

Questions for Critical Thinking

1. Identify one or two issues about each of the four environmental factors—economic, social-cultural, technological, and political-legal—in *either* Europe or China that Disney marketers should examine as they refocus their international marketing program.
2. Do you think Disney should adopt a global marketing strategy or a multidomestic marketing strategy to promote its products overseas? Why?

SOURCES: "Visitors to Tokyo Disney Theme Parks up 27 Percent Last Fiscal Year," *Dow Jones News Service,* April 1, 2002, http://biz.yahoo.com; David Teather, "Magic Kingdom under Siege," *Guardian Unlimited,* January 15, 2002, http://www.guardian.co.uk; "Disney in Global Push," *BBC News,* June 8, 2001, http://news.bbc.co.uk; Mark Lacter, "Mickey Stumbles at the Border," *Forbes,* June 12, 2000, p. 58.

VIDEO CASE 4.2   Fallon Worldwide: Going Global, Targeting Local

The written case on Fallon Worldwide appears on page VC-5. The recently filmed Fallon Worldwide video is designed to expand and highlight the concepts in this chapter and the concepts and questions covered in the written video case.

Krispy Kreme Continuing Case for Part 1 appears on page KK-2.

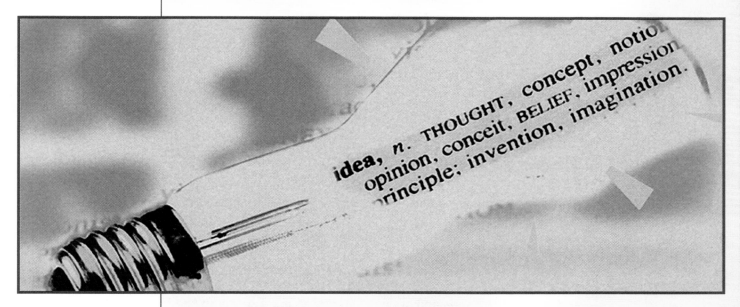

5

E-Commerce: Electronic Marketing and the Internet for Dot.com and Brick-and-Mortar Marketers

Chapter Objectives

1 Define e-commerce and give examples of each function of the Internet.

2 Describe how marketers use the Internet to achieve their firm's objectives.

3 Explain how online marketing benefits organizations, marketers, and consumers.

4 Identify the goods and services marketed most often on the Internet.

5 Identify the primary online marketing channels.

6 Explain how marketers use interactive tools as part of their online marketing strategies.

7 Discuss how an effective Web site can enhance customer relationships.

8 Describe how to measure the effectiveness of online marketing efforts.

How the Web Has Changed Marketing Forever

A few years ago, it was easy to believe that e-commerce wasn't all its believers and promoters had hyped it up to be. The economy, along with tech stocks, had taken a major tumble. Companies were afraid to spend on technology; consumers, fearful that the next wave of job cuts might include their own, were afraid to spend on anything— online or offline. As businesses, investors, and consumers struggled to climb out of the economic sinkhole in which they'd been trapped, a single fact emerged: online marketing wasn't dead. In fact, it was very much alive. While it's true that the Web didn't deliver on some of the promises made by its earlier promoters, it survived the U.S. economic downturn and made a comeback.

A major reason for the survival of e-commerce is that consumers never abandoned it. Instead, they used it to change the way entire industries conduct their marketing and business practices. Music buffs now share 35 billion song files each year, which has forced the music industry to rethink how it will deliver its products to the public. While there has been controversy over various solutions to the problem, the fact is that the traditional music business must adapt to this change. The movie industry is not far behind. Travel has undergone an Internet makeover as well. Expedia.com is now the largest leisure travel agency in the world, but its success has come at a price to some brick-and-mortar travel agencies that have been forced to close their doors. A major factor in Dell's ranking as the leading computer maker is that it built its sales and manufacturing efforts around the Internet. Financial institutions, from mortgage companies to stock brokerage firms have discovered the power of the Internet. Online-based LendingTree is growing at a rate of 70 percent a year, while E*Trade is posting its largest profits ever. E*Trade is no longer just an online brokerage; it is now the 62nd largest bank in the U.S.

What do online consumers expect from their e-commerce experience? According to a survey conducted by *Channel Intelligence*, 89 percent want low prices, and 78 percent want a convenient return policy. Seven in ten want a retailer's Web site to be easy to use and generally visit sites represented by brand names and good reputations. Two-thirds of the respondents say that shipping rates and methods are also very important. In other words, consumers who shop the Internet want good prices, convenience, and reliability—just like brick-and-mortar consumers do.

Although a large number of online business-to-business (B2B) exchanges failed during the economic downturn, many companies have not given up; in one year during the economic recovery, $3.9 trillion worth of B2B e-commerce transactions took place worldwide. Company spending on various e-business projects actually increased during the tech recession, but firms spent their money more carefully than they had before. Kinko's boosted its spending, but targeted it toward specific projects, such as one with Microsoft in which people could send documents from Microsoft programs over the Internet to Kinko's for professional-quality copying.

E-commerce has already moved into the next generation of development. "It will take visionary leadership to keep investing in this environment," says Krishna Kolluri, head of a networking-equipment start-up called Neoteris. "But if you're standing still, you're losing a step every day."[1]

Chapter Overview

Dramatic changes in global economies and societies in the last ten years have grabbed the attention of almost every person in every industry, from banking and air travel to communications. Marketing now holds the key to creating a competitive advantage. Demographic and lifestyle changes have transformed homogenous mass markets into personalized, one-on-one interactions. Deregulation, rapid technological changes, and the relative stability of its economy has made the U.S. the world leader in e-commerce.

During the past ten years, marketing has become the cutting-edge tool for success on the Internet. Profit-seeking organizations are not the only benefactors of the Internet; organizations of all kinds are beginning to emphasize marketing's role in achieving set goals. Colleges and universities, charities, museums, symphony orchestras, and hospitals now employ the marketing concept discussed in Chapter 1: providing customers the goods and services they want to buy when they want to buy them. Marketing continues to perform its function of bringing buyers and sellers together; it just does it faster and more efficiently than ever before.

With just a few ticks of the clock and a few clicks of a mouse, the Internet revolutionizes every aspect of life. New words have emerged, such as software, Internet, extranet, and intranet; and old words have new meanings never imagined a few years ago: Web, Net, surfer and server, banner and browsers, online and offline. E-commerce has turned virtual reality into reality. With a computer and a telephone, a virtual marketplace is open twenty-four hours, seven days a week to provide almost anything anywhere to anyone, including clothes, food, information, entertainment, and medicine. You can do your banking, make travel reservations, send out a résumé online, or even buy a car—perhaps at a lower price than you could in person.

Internet marketers can reach individual consumers or target organizations worldwide through a vast array of computer and communications technologies. In just a few short years, almost a half million companies large and small have been connected to electronic marketing channels. Goods and services sold to consumers total close to $50 billion per year.[2]

This chapter examines the nature of electronic commerce and explores the many ways it is transforming marketing. After defining e-commerce and e-marketing, this chapter proceeds with a discussion of the Internet and the World Wide Web. It further explains the transition of industrial economies to electronic economies, the benefits online marketing provides, and the challenges it presents. The chapter also looks at the buyers and sellers who populate the Web and how marketers build online relationships with customers. Next, the chapter discusses the various digital marketing tools and the ways marketers use Web sites to achieve organizational goals. Finally, it examines the promises and challenges associated with online marketing.

What Is Electronic Commerce?

1

Define e-commerce and give examples of each function of the Internet.

A number of terms have been used to describe marketing activities that take place on the Internet or through such electronic tools as computer modems, telephones, fax machines, and CD-ROMs. Among the most popular is **electronic commerce (e-commerce)**—targeting customers by collecting and analyzing business information, conducting customer transactions, and maintaining online relationships with customers by means of telecommunications networks. E-commerce provides a foundation for launching new businesses, extending the reach of existing companies, and building and retaining customer relationships.

The component of e-commerce of particular interest to marketers is **electronic marketing (e-marketing),** the strategic process of creating, distributing, promoting, and pricing goods and services to a target market over the Internet or through such **digital tools** as fax machines, computer modems, telephones, and CD-ROMs. E-marketing is the means by which e-commerce is achieved. It encompasses such activities as:

- Ordering a best-seller from Barnes & Noble with the expectation that it will arrive within a few days.

- Placing a bid for a vintage Rolex watch on eBay.

- Purchasing downloaded copies of *New York Times* and *The Economist*'s articles on European retailing to use as source material for a research paper.

The application of these electronic tools to 21st century marketing has the potential to greatly reduce costs and increase customer satisfaction by increasing the speed and efficiency of marketing interactions. Just as e-commerce is a major function of the Internet, e-marketing is an integral component of e-commerce.

A closely related but somewhat narrower term than e-marketing is online marketing. While electronic marketing can involve noncomputer digital technologies ranging from fax machines to telephones, online marketing refers to marketing activities that connect buyers and sellers electronically through interactive computer systems.

Regardless of what you are selling or buying, what kind of business you are in, or whether your company has hundreds of employees or just you, e-commerce offers almost limitless opportunities. However, the traditional marketing strategies, such as pricing and distribution, inventory, advertising, promotion, and customer service, must still be dealt with. Each organization needs to develop new business models that adapt to the large volumes of traffic inherent with online transactions. New communities of buyers and sellers are created through e-commerce. In ways not thought of just a few years ago, organizations are utilizing Internet technology to set up businesses and successfully conduct trade over the Web.

E-commerce offers countless opportunities for marketers to reach consumers. This radical departure from traditional bricks-and-mortar operations provides the following benefits to contemporary marketers, as shown in Table 5.1.

- *Global reach.* The Net eliminates the geographic protections of local business. Car dealers selling online, for example, have attracted buyers from hundreds of miles away.

- *One-to-one marketing (personalization).* Only a handful of Dell computers are waiting for customers at any one time. The production process begins when an order is received and ends a day or two later when the PC is shipped to the customer.

- *Interactive marketing.* Customers and suppliers negotiate prices online in

Marketing Dictionary

electronic commerce (e-commerce)   Targeting customers by collecting and analyzing business information, conducting customer transactions, and maintaining online relationships with customers by means of computer networks.

electronic marketing (e-marketing)   Strategic process of creating, distributing, promoting, and pricing goods and services to a target market over the Internet or through digital tools.

digital tools   Electronic technologies used in e-commerce, including fax machines, computer modems, telephones, and CD-ROMs.

TABLE 5.1   E-Commerce Capabilities

Capability	Description	Example
Global reach	The ability to reach anyone connected to a PC anywhere in the world.	Major car makers, such as Ford, Nissan, and Volvo, use the Web to reach car buyers around the world.
One-to-one marketing	Creating products to meet customer specifications, also called personalization.	Customers can order customized clothing—from jeans to shirts to shoes—online.
Interactive marketing	Buyer-seller communications through such channels as the Internet, CD-ROMs, toll-free telephone numbers, and virtual reality kiosks.	Intouch Group's iStations are interactive kiosks placed in retail music stores that allow customers to listen to 30-second music clips before they purchase compact discs.
Right-time marketing	The ability to provide a good or service at the exact time needed.	FedEx customers can place service orders online and track shipments 24 hours a day.
Integrated marketing	Coordination of all promotional activities to produce a unified, customer-focused promotional message.	Nike marketers use the familiar Swoosh logo and "Just Do It" slogan in both online and offline promotions.

much the same manner as they do at a local flea market or car dealership. The result is the creation of an ideal product at the right price that satisfies both parties.

■ *Right-time marketing.* Web companies, such as Amazon.com and Buy.com, can provide products when and where customers want them.

■ *Integrated marketing.* The Internet enables the coordination of all promotional activities and communication to create a unified, customer-oriented promotional message.

In addition to the benefits listed here, there is increasing evidence that an effective online presence improves the performance of traditional brick-and-mortar operations. For instance, a study by e-commerce research firm Jupiter Media Metrix found that half of customers use a retailer's Web site primarily for research before buying a product in the retailer's physical store.[3]

Interactivity and E-Commerce

The e-commerce approach to buying and selling has been embraced by millions worldwide because it offers substantial benefits over traditional marketing practices. The two-way, back-and-forth communications enable marketers to supply the precise items desired by their customers. At the same time, purchasers can continue to refine their product specifications to create an opportunity that fills their precise needs.

One of the largest e-tailers is Amazon.com. It uses a concept called **interactive marketing.** This approach, which consists of buyer-seller communications in which the customer controls the amount and type of information received from a marketer, has been used by marketers for over a decade. Point-of-sale brochures and coupon dispensers located in supermarkets are simple forms of interactive marketing. However, when digital tools such as the Internet are included in interactive marketing efforts, the results are infinitely improved for the seller and buyer alike.

Say, for example, you want to buy an espresso machine. If you have a computer, Amazon.com has you covered. You don't have to get in the car and drive to the mall. Just visit Amazon.com, where you can search by brand or price, compare features, and read customer ratings. With a few mouse clicks, your order is placed and will be shipped to you. You can even track the status of your shipment online. But Amazon.com doesn't stop there. You can sign in with Amazon.com, permanently registering your shipping information and credit card information. Based on your past purchases and personal preferences, Amazon.com will even send you personalized recommendations of new products. The company wants you to feel that your shopping experience is as personal as it would have been at a brick-and-mortar store.

The Internet

Although two-way communications between buyers and sellers describe most personal sales and have been taking place electronically since the invention of the telephone, the Golden Age of interactivity began a few decades ago. Its beginnings can be traced to the creation of the **Internet (Net),** a global collection of computer networks linked together for the purpose of exchanging data and information. The Net originally served scientists and government researchers, but it has since evolved into a multi-faceted and popular medium of communication for individual households and business users. Users can exchange data with other computer users around the world in such formats as text, graphic images, audio, and video.

Even in small, niche markets, the Internet helps build e-commerce capabilities. For instance, Neoforma, a California-based medical supplies distributor, markets its products globally through its Web sites. Among some of its best customers are foreign governments—such as the government of Oman. If this small company had depended only on traditional marketing efforts, it would have had a difficult time serving international markets.[4]

Growth of the Internet

In less than 10 years, the Internet has grown from a mere 18 million American users to over 173 million today. The number of Americans online is expected to rise to over 200 million by 2006.[5] This growth has opened more channels for consumers to find a wide array of information. The appeal of the new approach to shopping is obvious. E-commerce shifts the balance of power to the buyer. The online shopper knows that an alternative supplier is just a click away. Consumers today can easily compare prices on such products as new or used automobiles, notebook computers, and airline tickets. Travel sites, for instance, can search through hundreds of airfares, hotel rates, and cruise packages, finding you the best deals.

Intranets and Extranets

Internet technologies provide a platform for **intranets,** internal corporate networks that allow employees within a firm to communicate with each other and gain access to corporate information. **Extranets,** on the other hand, are corporate networks that allow communication between a firm and selected customers, suppliers, and business partners outside the firm. Companies that use both extranets and intranets benefit even further from online communication. Intelsat, which operates global communications satellites, has an extranet called Intelsat Business Network (IBN). The more than 2,300 users of IBN log on from 400 organizations to check the availability of satellite capacity, view satellite maps, download corporate documents, and participate in discussion groups. Users can personalize their IBN account so that it shows information about only the services they use.

The World Wide Web

The Internet provides an efficient way to find and share information, but initially, most people outside of universities and government agencies found it difficult to use. This changed in the mid-1990s, when Tim Bernes-Lee at the

Marketing Dictionary

interactive marketing   Buyer-seller communications in which the customer controls the amount and type of information received from a marketer through such channels as the Internet, CD-ROMs, interactive toll-free telephone numbers, and virtual reality kiosks.

Internet (Net)   Worldwide network of interconnected computers that lets anyone with access to a personal computer send and receive images and data anywhere.

intranets   Internal corporate network that allows employees within an organization to communicate with each other and gain access to corporate information.

extranets   Secure network accessible through a Web site by external customers or organizations for electronic commerce. It provides more customer-specific information than a public site.

European Center for Nuclear Research in Geneva, Switzerland, developed the *World Wide Web.* Originally thought of as an internal document-management system, the Web quickly grew to become a collection of tens of thousands of interlinked computers, called Web servers, that function together within the Internet. These computers are located all over the world and rely on high-speed Internet circuits and software to allow users to hop from server to server, providing the illusion that the Web is one big computer. The Web, along with the development of specialized software called Web browsers—such as Netscape and Microsoft Internet Explorer—made the Internet accessible to millions.

The Web can handle so much information in so many different media that it has become the premier means for marketers to reach consumers in their target markets. Close to 50 percent of all online households make a purchase through the Web. Millions of other visitors, though not actually buying online, use the Web to help them make purchasing decisions.

How do people use the Web? Figure 5.1 illustrates how a typical consumer might spend time online during a day. Many of these interactions occur as a means of communicating—such as sending electronic mail or posting messages on electronic bulletin boards. Still other interactions involve gathering information—about airfares, gifts for friends or family members, a new home, a mortgage, or a credit card. Still other interactions—such as L.L. Bean clothing purchases or an order for printer supplies from Staples—would be considered electronic commerce. The Web's entertainment function might be performed reading reviews of a best-selling book on Amazon.com or watching a trailer for an upcoming movie.

Four Web Functions

As Figure 5.2 shows, there are four primary functions of the Web: communication, information, entertainment, and e-commerce. Let's consider the role of each in contemporary marketing.

Communication

For both households and businesses, one of the most popular applications of the Internet in the U.S. is e-mail. In fact, e-mails now outnumber regular mail by over ten to one. Its popularity is easy to understand: E-mail is simple to use, travels quickly, and can be read at the receiver's convenience. Also, files—such as Microsoft Office documents—can be easily sent as attachments to e-mail messages.

A more recent adaptation of e-mail is **instant messaging.** With this application, when someone sends a message, it is immediately displayed on the recipient's computer screen. As sender and recipient reply to one another, they can communicate in real time. However, unlike regular e-mail messages, instant messages have to be relatively short—a few sentences at the most.

Other popular ways to communicate are chat rooms and bulletin boards. These methods provide a forum in which a group of people can share information. When someone sends a message, it is displayed for all to see. Users join chat sessions, or messages on bulletin boards, on topics that interest them. The resulting online communities are not only personally satisfying but an important force for

FIGURE 5.1
A Typical Day
on the Web

11:30 A.M. American Airlines (http://www.aa.com) sends you an e-mail with a special rate on your usual business route.

9 A.M. At the of ce, you're running low on fax paper. Order it from Of ce Depot at http://www.of cedepot.com.

8 A.M. The kids need new clothes. You order jeans and jackets from Lands' End at http://www.landsend.com.

12 P.M. Amazon.com (http://www.amazon.com) sends you an e-mail telling you the new John Grisham thriller is now available. You click on the site and order the book.

2 P.M. You remember that your aunt's birthday is next week. At the InternetMall.com site, http://www.internetmall.com, you nd the perfect gift.

4:30 P.M. You are thinking of moving to another town but don't have time to drive by every home the Realtor has to show. So you check the listings at http://www.realtor.com.

7 P.M. You want to see how mortgage rates are doing and apply for a platinum Visa. So you log on to your bank at http://www.bankone.com to get the information you need.

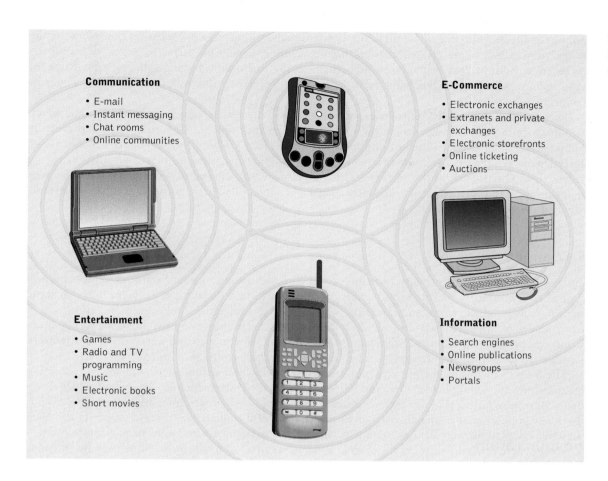

FIGURE 5.2
Four Functions of the Internet

Communication
- E-mail
- Instant messaging
- Chat rooms
- Online communities

E-Commerce
- Electronic exchanges
- Extranets and private exchanges
- Electronic storefronts
- Online ticketing
- Auctions

Entertainment
- Games
- Radio and TV programming
- Music
- Electronic books
- Short movies

Information
- Search engines
- Online publications
- Newsgroups
- Portals

business. Many companies sponsor such communication as part of their overall customer service. For instance, Symantec's Web site contains several bulletin boards. When a customer has a question or a problem with one of Symantec's products, he or she can send an e-mail directly to Symantec. A technician or customer support representative replies by e-mail to the customer. The original question, as well as the answer, are automatically posted on the appropriate bulletin board. Visitors to the Symantec Web site can search the bulletin boards by entering various key words.

Information

For many users, getting information is one of the main reasons they go online. Internet users can begin by consulting commercial search engines—such as Google or AskJeeves—which search for information on topics entered by the user. Or they may visit the online editions of publications like the *Los Angeles Times* or *Forbes*. Government sites provide a wealth of free data in the public domain. Another fast-growing area of the Internet consists of sites providing online educational services. Over one-third of U.S. colleges now offer some sort of accredited degree online.

Entertainment

Internet users find lots of entertainment online, including everything from concert Webcasts to online gaming. Online providers of entertainment can offer competitive prices, speed, and boundless services. Games, radio programming, short movies, and music clips are available

Marketing Dictionary

instant messaging E-mail service that allows for the immediate exchange of short messages between online users.

online, sometimes for free, with the costs borne by advertising on the Web site. Sometimes entire songs, movies, and books are available on the Net. Online gaming has attracted a great deal of interest recently. Both Microsoft and Sony are betting heavily that online gaming is the next big thing for video games. Microsoft's Xbox game console, for instance, has an Ethernet port making it a snap to connect to the Internet.

The availability of free content poses some ethical and business issues, including copyright issues. For instance, a federal judge ordered Video Pipeline to stop posting streaming clips and creating online previews of Disney films, ruling that such actions may violate Disney's copyrights. The judge agreed with Disney's contention that while Video Pipeline had the company's permission to sell video clips to brick-and-mortar retailers, Video Pipeline wasn't allowed to disseminate the same content online.[6] However, copyright and other legal and ethical issues are unlikely to chase entertainment off the Internet.

E-Commerce

Today e-commerce is the primary function of the Web. According to recent statistics, almost 80 percent of all Web sites are devoted to some aspect of e-commerce.[7] Almost every organization has some sort of Web presence, from multinational corporations to individual entrepreneurial ventures, and from sellers of goods to service providers. Organizations ranging from the not-for-profit Nature Conservancy to world-famous Tiffany's are vying for space on the Web and for consumers' attention. Upscale retailer Nordstrom recently created the world's largest online shoe store.

The Web facilitates marketing activities, including buying and selling goods and services, building relationships, increasing market size, and reducing the costs of intermediaries. This chapter focuses on the e-commerce function of the Internet since it fuels the growth of electronic marketing. The Web is the most popular area of the Internet, with more than 400 million users worldwide.[8] As the Web becomes easier to use and attracts more participants, it will become a pervasive part of modern life.

Most people generally think of the Web as a giant cybermall of retail stores selling millions of goods online. However, service providers are also important participants in e-commerce. These include providers of financial services. Brick-and-mortar banks—such as Bank of America—and brokerage firms—such as Charles Schwab—have greatly expanded their online services. In addition, many new online service providers are rapidly attracting customers who want to do more of their own banking and investment trading on whatever time and day that suits them. Figure 5.3 illustrates some of the benefits of banking online. Airlines, too, have discovered the power of the Web. Southwest Airlines, for example, generates over $1 billion annually from online ticket sales.

The Web also provides tremendous opportunities for business-to-business e-commerce. Over one-quarter of all B2B transactions are estimated to take place online, amounting to almost $1 trillion. This penetration of e-commerce is predicted to increase to more than 40 percent of B2B sales by 2006.[9] These sales are spread out across many businesses. The number of U.S. businesses engaged in B2B e-commerce is expected to grow to more than 90 percent within a year or two.[10] Cisco Systems, IBM, and Intel are among the firms that generate billions of dollars in revenues online each year.

FIGURE 5.3
The Benefits of Online Banking

Name	What It Did	Why It Failed
iHarvest.com	Company offered a browser plug-in that allowed users to store copies of Web pages.	Both Netscape and Internet Explorer already have the same feature; why would anyone pay for something they could get for free?
Furniture.com	Online furniture store.	Since UPS and FedEx wouldn't ship large, bulky items—like furniture—products were shipped using much more expensive common carriers; shipping costs often exceeded cost of product.
Kozmo.com	Single movie rental service; movies messengered to your front door.	Costs overwhelmed revenues; no way the business model could make money.
SwapIt.com	People could trade in used CDs and video games, receiving "swap-it bucks" that they could use to buy other people's used CDs and videos.	Could make money only on shipping and handling charges; people mostly "sold" CDs and videos no one else wanted to buy.
MySpace.com	Gave away free disk space on company servers for people and businesses to store files.	Tried to make money by selling ads; when that didn't work, the company started charging for the service. Only 6,000 out of the company's 9 million customers were willing to pay for the service.

SOURCE: "Fiercely Stupid," *Newsweek,* March 25, 2002, p. 52. Article excerpted from Philip Kaplan, *F'd Company,* New York: Simon and Schuster, 2002.

FIGURE 5.4
Some Notorious Dot.Com Busts

Needless to say, however, not every e-commerce idea worked out. The online landscape is littered with dozens of dot.com failures. Figure 5.4 describes some of the most notorious dot.com busts.

Accessing the Internet

In the same way an explorer relies on a compass and a map to seek out a desired destination, marketers and their customers must depend on navigation instruments to locate Web sites and find information in a database. The basic pathway for going online is through an **Internet service provider (ISP).** An ISP, such as Earthlink and Prodigy, provides individuals and organizations with direct access to the Internet. ISP giants such as America Online (AOL) let the user access the Internet through their own specially designed online sites. Such sites can be thought of as doors opening to a giant communication center called the Internet.

The early gateways for Internet access were *search engines.* Over time, these Internet entrances became portals by adding to their site contents, shopping services, and software applications like e-mail and online calendars. In addition to AOL, Earthlink, and Prodigy, major portals include MSN, Terra Lycos, and Yahoo! A more recent trend is the creation of portals built around specific services or communities. These include ESPN, CNN.com, and CBS Market Watch. Their aim is to draw in Web surfers and keep their interest with specific types of content or transactions.

In addition to serving as gateways for Internet access, portals are pushing to become the grand entrance for consumer business. At present, most portal revenue comes from advertising. Online shopping generates only a small percentage of portal site revenue, but this percentage is increasing. For instance, with around 25 million subscribers, AOL is the world's largest commercial online service. Its virtual shopping mall consists of over 400 merchant partners who pay rent for "real estate" on AOL's shopping pages.

Marketing Dictionary

Internet service provider (ISP)   Organization that provides access to the Internet via a telephone, satellite TV service, or cable TV network.

E-Commerce and the Economy

The last years of the 20th century and the early years of the 21st century witnessed the change from a century-old industrial economy to its electronic successor—an economy based on the Internet and other related online technologies. Many people see e-commerce as the fuel for the rest of the 21st century. Since the Web first opened for commercial activity in 1993, e-commerce has become a leading force in changing the way the world lives and breathes. It is estimated that in the U.S. e-commerce is currently over 2 percent of GDP. This figure is expected to increase to over 5 percent by 2006. The Web is now being explored by small, previously unheard-of companies as well as large, multinational corporations. Consider the following successes:

- Catalog retailer Lands' End's Web site generates more than $200 million a year in sales, or over 15 percent of the firm's total sales; three years earlier, online sales amounted to less than five percent of total sales.

- Startup airline JetBlue sells over half of its tickets online, the highest of any airline.

- Dell is the world's largest maker of personal computers. The Internet accounts for well over half of the company's $30 billion in annual sales.

- After learning that a significant number of the nation's 3 million farmers use the Internet, Ben Zaitz created Farms.com, an online cattle and farm equipment auction site, as well as a general source of agricultural information. Annual sales are approaching $5 million, and the firm was recently cited by *Forbes* magazine as one of the top B2B e-commerce sites.[11]

2

Describe how marketers use the Internet to achieve their firm's objectives.

But conducting business on the Net is more than just creating a Web site. State-of-the-art graphics and pages of information do not spell success any more than fancy business cards or company brochures do. A Web site must provide a platform for communication between organizations, customers, and suppliers. Businesses now hold auctions for utilities, banks partner with computer companies, and authors sell directly to their readers. New businesses and new ways of conducting business on the Web have contributed to overall economic growth. The following sections in this chapter illustrate the explosion of business-to-business (B2B) transactions. B2B e-commerce has grown to over $800 billion and is expected to top $2.4 trillion by 2005. By some estimates, B2B transactions amount to over 80 percent of e-commerce.[12]

Business-to-Business Online Marketing

CSX's Web site is nothing flashy. No fancy graphics, catchy songs, or state-of-the-art video clips—just lots of practical information, and that's just fine with the railroad's customers. The site enables customers to obtain price quotes, schedule shipments, and examine a map of the railroad's network to see where their shipments are at any given moment. This information is vital to CSX's business customers, who access the site hundreds of thousands of times each month.

Unlike the business-to-consumer (B2C) segment of the online market, B2B interactions involve professional buyers and sellers—people whose performances are evaluated by their purchasing and selling decisions. Consequently, B2B online marketing usually does not need the same glitz and glamour as the B2C segment.

Although most people are familiar with such B2C online marketers as eBay and Amazon.com, these transactions are dwarfed by their B2B counterparts, which are buying and selling both business services and commodities like paper, plastics, and chemicals. The earliest B2B e-commerce usually consisted of a company setting up a Web site and offering products to any buyer willing to make online purchases. More recently, businesses are buying and selling through **electronic exchanges,** Web-based marketplaces that cater to a specific industry's needs. An example of an electronic exchange is FreeMarkets, where suppliers compete for the business of organizational buyers who might be purchasing anything from gears to printed circuit boards. FreeMarkets was founded by Glen Meakem, a former General Electric executive. Meakem understood that manufacturers spend roughly $5 trillion each year on industrial parts and that the purchase process is usually very inefficient. He developed a system whereby suppliers promise to deliver parts on standardized schedules, with identical payment terms and inventory arrangements. The only variable is price. FreeMarkets consults with buyers and screens suppliers so that, by the time an auction takes place, each is familiar with the process. The auction itself usually takes less than an hour. FreeMarkets has proven quite popular, and large manufacturing firms such as General Motors, United Technologies, Raytheon, Emerson Electric, and Quaker Oats regularly participate. H.J. Heinz Company concluded that its relationship with FreeMarkets saved the company at least $50 million.[13]

As noted earlier, B2B e-commerce totals over $800 billion worldwide and is expected to grow to over $2.4 trillion by 2005. The U.S. is expected to remain the largest market for B2B e-commerce over the next few years, with transactions increasing at an annual rate of around 68 percent. However, B2B e-commerce is expected to grow even faster in Western Europe (increasing at an annual rate of 91 percent) and the Asia-Pacific region, where B2B e-commerce transactions are expected to increase at an annual rate of over 100 percent by 2005.[14]

Durable goods manufacturers alone account for almost half of all B2B e-commerce sales. Wholesalers of business products such as office supplies, electronic goods, and scientific equipment are a close second in B2B e-commerce market share. Even though they still provide many of their services in person, professionals such as doctors, attorneys, and accountants are finding new ways to use the Internet to reach existing and potential clients as well as communicate with others in their fields.

Companies large and small have developed the systems and software necessary to make B2B online marketing a reality. Many have even created new business units to serve the needs of customers and suppliers online. Jet-engine maker Pratt & Whitney created a special Web site that collects detailed performance records from its customers to help determine when engine service is required.[15] In addition, a whole new industry has been created to design and manage e-commerce sites for companies who wish to outsource these tasks. While there are many small, start-up companies in this industry, larger, more established firms also have a significant presence. IBM, for instance, provides e-commerce services to hundreds of other companies. In a recent year, e-commerce services generated almost $30 billion in revenue, or more than a third of IBM's total revenue.[16]

Many firms are also finding entirely new markets for their goods and services—markets that either did not exist or were inaccessible without the benefits of the Internet. Network Associates, for example, limited the marketing of its products to the U.S. for years because marketers believed their products were too expensive for foreign consumers. That all changed a few years ago when a Spanish bank downloaded a product from the firm's Web site. No additional marketing expenses were involved, and the message reached the right customers thousands of miles away.[17]

An important objective of both online and offline marketing is to distinguish a firm and its products from competitive offerings. Purchasing managers for companies can search the Web looking for the best deals on everything from office supplies to steel, selecting from hundreds of different vendors. But what about the vendors themselves? How do they position themselves on the Web so that corporate buyers notice them, let alone make a purchase? A first step is to list themselves with the major search engines—such as Terra Lycos and Google. But that is not enough. A single search for an item— say laser printer supplies—could yield thousands of sites, some of which might not even be relevant. Marketers also need to list their firms with Internet yellow pages such as Verizon's SuperPages.com, which operate just like their printed counterparts. A purchasing manager can look up "laser printer supplies" at the SuperPages.com Web site and get listings of relevant sites. Many industries have their own online references, such as the *Thomas Register of American Manufacturers*.

Successful online B2B marketers serve their customers by thinking like a buyer. They interview their regular customers to find out how these customers use the Internet and where they find information they need in making purchase decisions. This information can be used to devise strategies to attract new customers and improve relationships with existing ones.

Benefits of B2B Online Marketing

The advantages of business-to-business online marketing strategies over traditional methods are only beginning to be realized. Online marketers can find new markets and customers.

Marketing Dictionary

electronic exchanges   Online marketplaces that bring buyers and seller together.

They also produce cost savings in every aspect of the marketing strategy as electronic marketing replaces the traditional bricks-and-mortar approach. Some argue that the cost savings from B2B online marketing can add at least a couple of points to the typical firm's profit margin.[18] Finally, online marketing greatly reduces the time involved in reaching target markets. Many business writers label e-commerce as easy commerce, since online marketing tools allow the direct exchange of information, such as order fulfillment and customer service, in a seamless fashion without involvement of marketing intermediaries. Communicating with suppliers, customers, and distributors over the Web is much more cost-effective and efficient than letters, phone calls, faxes, and personal sales calls that were the conventional methods of the pre-Internet era.

The number of Web sites increases daily, with most of the growth being new corporate sites. A home page creates a company's online storefront where consumers go for product and corporate information. A Web site should capture the personality of the company and serve as an effective public relations tool. The Web enhances an organization's operations by reducing distances and removing time zones. Both not-for-profit and profit-seeking organizations are enjoying these benefits. For instance, MunicipalNet Inc. is a growing e-procurement business based in Boston. It focuses on services to state and local governments, and the businesses that supply them. The city of Evanston, Illinois, recently put its procurement process online using the services of MunicipalNet Inc. According to Chad Walton, the city's purchasing manager, one advantage of e-procurement is that "it lessens the cost of responding to solicitations from the city for businesses, which in turn should translate to lower costs for us as well." Both sides, he believes, can save time and money by cutting out some of the red tape from the process. MunicipalNet can also help governments set up Web sites at which citizens can register cars, pay taxes, or look for government jobs. By one estimate, 15 percent of federal, state, and local taxes will be collected online by 2006.[19]

Online Consumer Marketing

Just as e-commerce is a major function of the Internet, online marketing is an integral component of e-commerce. Lands' End used to generate virtually all of its orders by telephone. A few years ago the company decided to turn to online marketing to boost sales and reduce costs. With ads such as the one shown in Figure 5.5, Lands' End marketers alert consumers to its new online services, such as its virtual model that allows consumers to "try on" clothes before they buy. Online customers can communicate with customer service representatives in real time. Two customers can even shop on the site simultaneously—just as if they were shopping together in a brick-and-mortar store. As the following sections explain, both consumers and marketers alike enjoy the benefits of online marketing.

Online marketing is inherently interactive marketing. While it obviously expands the reach of marketers in connecting with consumers, to be effective it must be part of an overall marketing strategy before it can create value for customers. A point to remember is that just as quickly as a firm can rise to become a star in cyberspace, if its online site is not launched properly and operated efficiently, it can just as quickly burn out.

Consumers who shop online can point to a number of advantages to online marketing. Figure 5.6 shows the results of a recent survey in which consumers were asked why they seek out or avoid online transactions.

The benefits online shoppers obtain from Web purchases fall into three categories: lower prices, convenience, and personaliza-

FIGURE 5.5
Lands' End Web Site

FIGURE 5.6
Determinants of Online Purchasing Behavior

MOTIVATORS		DETRACTORS	
Save money	75%	Privacy/security	53%
Convenience	50%	Poor navigation	35%
Better selection	48%	No brand recognition	24%
Fun	29%	Higher prices	20%
Avoiding crowds/salespeople	11%	Can't see or touch	20%

tion. Marketers should ensure that their Web sites offer consumers these basic advantages over traditional shopping experiences. In addition, Web sites should be easy to navigate, offer a high level of security and privacy, and provide information that consumers can use in making product comparisons and purchase decisions. Moreover, it is important for e-tailers to listen to their customers and be willing to make changes to their Web sites. Online auction site eBay—perhaps the most successful B2C e-commerce firm—has a history of responding quickly to customer needs and concerns. Its approach to e-commerce is profiled in the "Marketing Hits" box.

3

Explain how online marketing benefits organizations, marketers, and consumers.

Lower Prices

Many products actually cost less online. Many of the best deals on airfares and hotels, for instance, can often be found at travel sites on the Internet. Visitors to BN.com—the online store of bookseller Barnes & Noble—find many bestsellers are discounted by up to 40 percent. At the brick-and-mortar stores bestsellers are marked down by only 30 percent. It comes as no surprise to anyone who has ever searched the Web for the best price for software or a newly issued CD that three out of four Web shoppers cited lower prices as a primary motivation for shopping online.

The Web is an ideal method for savvy shoppers to compare prices from dozens—even hundreds—of sellers. Online shoppers can compare features and prices at their leisure, without being pressured by a salesperson or having to conform to the company's hours of operation. Say, for instance, you're in the market for a new computer monitor. One of the newer e-commerce tools, **bots,** aid consumers in comparison shopping. Bots—short for robots—are search programs that check hundreds of sites, gather and assemble information, and bring it back to the sender. At the

Marketing Dictionary

bot   Search program that checks hundreds of sites, gathers and assembles information, and brings it back to the sender.

Listening to Your Customers

Background. The online auction site eBay is perhaps the most successful of all B2C e-commerce firms. From its beginning in September 1995, the company's growth has been nothing short of amazing. Revenues have grown from less than $10 million to over $1 billion today. Even more impressive, and unlike many e-commerce companies, eBay has a record of profitability to match its revenue growth. It is far and away the most frequently visited e-commerce site on the Internet. During a recent month, eBay recorded over 56 million visitors worldwide, ranking it right below popular search engine Google and various U.S. government Web sites. Meg Whitman, eBay's CEO, was second on a recent *Fortune* magazine list of the most powerful U.S. businesswomen.

The Challenge. The company runs on a very simple business model. Sellers pay a fee to list everything from baseball cards to automobiles to vacation time shares, and eBay also collects a percentage of each item sold. Every auction has a set of ground rules, including minimum bids and bidding period. Buyers can search the list of auctions—and there are around 7 million ongoing auctions at any one point in time—by category and key words. By most measures, eBay has approximately an 80 percent share of the online auction market.

The Marketing Strategy. While eBay's concept is fairly simple, what sets the company apart is the degree to which it listens to its customers. Simply put, eBay has mastered, as well as any company, the communications power of the Net. Customers sound off directly to management, and eBay carefully tracks customer habits so that new services can be tailored to what customers

continued on next page

CNET Web site, you can specify the type and size of monitor you're looking for and the Web site displays a list of the highest-ranked monitors along with the e-tailer offering the best price on each. The Web site even ranks the e-tailers by customer experience and tells you whether or not a particular model is in stock.

Convenience

A second important factor in prompting online purchases is shopper convenience. Cybershoppers can order goods and services from around the world at any hour of the day or night. Many e-tailers allow customers to register their credit-card and shipping information for quick use in making future purchases. Registered customers are asked to type in a password when they place another order. E-tailers typically send an e-mail message confirming an order, its shipping date, and the amount charged to the buyer's credit card. Online order tracking is also commonplace today.

Many Web sites offer customized products to match individual customer requirements. Nike offers online shoppers the opportunity to customize a running shoe, personalizing such features as the outsole, the amount of cushioning, and the width. The personalized shoe costs about $10 more than buying it off the shelves. Consumers are also able to personalize men's and women's dress pants and men's dress shirts at Landsend.com.[20]

Personalization

While electronic marketing often operates with little or no human interaction, cyberspace marketers know how important personalization is to the quality of the shopping experience. Customer satisfaction is greatly affected by the marketer's ability to offer service tailored to many customers. But each person expects a certain level of customer service. Consequently most leading online retailers currently offer customized features on their Web sites.

The early years of e-commerce saw Web marketers casting their nets broadly in an effort to land as many customers as possible. Today, the emphasis has turned toward one-to-one marketing, creating loyal customers who are likely to make repeat purchases. How does personalized marketing work online? Say you buy a book at Amazon.com and register with the site. The site will welcome you back for your next purchase by name. Using special software that analyzes your previous purchases, it will also suggest several other books you might like. You even have the option of receiving periodic e-mails from Amazon.com informing you of new products.

Benefits of Online Consumer Marketing

Many of the same benefits achieved by B2B online marketers are also realized by marketers of consumer products who rely on the Web in their businesses. As Figure 5.7 indicates, marketers can use their Web sites to build strong relationships, reduce costs, increase efficiency, create a more level playing field, and achieve a global presence.

Relationship Building

Building relationships with consumers is crucial to the success of both offline and online marketing. As an earlier section explained, personalization is an important component of online relationship building. If a shop-

FIGURE 5.7
Benefits of Business-to-Consumer Online Marketing

per visits a Web site that sells accessories and buys a dress and a purse, the next time she visits the site, she may be greeted with an attractive ad showing a belt or shoes that can be coordinated with her previous purchase. In this way, marketers create a one-on-one shopping experience that often leads to customer satisfaction and repeat purchases. Brand loyalty forms a part of many offline relationships that can be transferred to online sites. In fact, customers expect Web sites to emulate the traditional brick-and-mortar retail world. They like being greeted when they enter a store or a Web site.

Small businesses, with even smaller budgets, can use the Internet to find customers in unexpected places and build relationships with them. Rick Brown, president of Newspaper Collectors Society of America, holds online auctions to sell historic papers to collectors. A few years ago, he sold a 19th-century receipt from a drugstore in Canton, Maine. Ordinarily, this would not be a big seller, but it proved highly desirable to residents of Canton who were establishing a local historical society. Another antiques dealer had difficulty at first selling a 1903 bicycle-parts catalog from France, but it sold quickly after French collectors discovered Brown's Web site (now at **http://www.historybuff.com**).[21] Once customers have received quick and efficient service from online dealers, they often return in search of other rare objects for which they might be looking.

Customer service is the key to building strong customer relationships, in both traditional and online marketing. Because the Web has the power to create two-way communications between companies and their customers instantly, many people get a good feeling about shopping online, believing that someone is on the other end with immediate answers to their questions and solutions to their problems. Unfortunately, this is too often not the case. Consumers sometimes report waiting hours and even days for a reply; others get no reply at all. A recent survey by Jupiter Media Metrix found that the online travel industry needs to improve customer service if it is going to continue to grow. A majority of respondents, 79 percent, said that they would be less likely to use an online travel site again after a dissatisfying customer service experience.[22]

Increased Efficiency

For large corporations and small businesses, sales made entirely through a Web site have a much greater profit margin than sales from traditional channels such as catalogs, retail outlets, or phone centers. However, even if the sale does not close online, marketers who educate their customers online ultimately save money because salespeople no longer have to spend their time answering routine questions.

Marketing Hit

really want. Here are some examples of what has made eBay the "people's company":

■ Shortly after one seller suggested eBay speed up auctions, the company introduced its "buy it now" feature that allowed bidders to end an auction at a set price. Almost 40 percent of listings use it, and the program has helped attract more mainstream buyers and sellers. Auctions close nearly a day faster today than they did earlier.

■ Soon after reviewing customer comments on bulletin boards suggesting methods for rating buyers and sellers, eBay set up a method that allows people to give each other ratings on every transaction. Only sellers with good ratings are allowed to remain on eBay. This greatly enhances the confidence of buyers, a key to future success.

■ After sellers requested training to improve their auctions, eBay created a series of classes in several major cities. Sellers who complete courses at eBay University typically double their activity on eBay within a month.

■ After noticing random car sales, eBay created a separate site for auto sales and car parts—called eBay motors. Currently over $1 billion worth of autos and parts sell on eBay each year. It is one of the company's fastest-growing categories.

The Outcome. With all of the success, however, has come challenges. System outages occasionally plague eBay. Security and fraud are always concerns for online auctions. Given its size and prominence, eBay seems to be an inviting target for hackers. And a host of rivals—including Yahoo!, Amazon.com, AOL, and even Microsoft—are taking aim at eBay.

SOURCES: CyberAtlas Web traffic statistics, accessed from the CyberAtlas Web site, **http://cyberatlas.internet.com**, April 1, 2002; Rachel Konrad, "From Beanie Babies to a Bigger, Better eBay," CNET News, **http://www.cnet.com**, accessed April 1, 2002; Robert Hof, "The People's Company," *Business Week,* December 3, 2001, pp. EB15–EB21.

Cost Reductions

Marketers have found that e-commerce can markedly reduce the costs of starting and operating a business. Scott Smith, manager of inventory at Ace Hardware, says that since his company installed a Web-enabled collaborative-commerce program, the cost of picking goods off warehouse shelves has fallen about 18 percent and receiving costs dropped by 20 percent.[23]

A More Level Playing Field

Minority business owners believe that the anonymity provided them by the Internet has allowed them to succeed on their own merits in a world where discrimination still exists. Roosevelt Gist, an African-American car dealership owner, often had white customers who would ask for another salesperson when he would approach them. Today, Gist is still in the car business but in cyberspace. He runs AutoNetwork.com, an online forum for researching, buying, and selling cars. The site hosts over 40,000 visitors a month, none of whom have had the chance to prejudge Gist on the basis of race.[24]

Online Marketing Is International Marketing

Another advantage to both online consumer and business-to-business marketers is the Internet's global reach, enabling inexpensive communication with consumers in faraway places. A U.S. marketer who wants to contact consumers in Australia, for example, may find express mail or long-distance telephone rates prohibitive, but the low cost and speed of such online marketing tools as fax machines and e-mail make global marketing a reality. Thirty percent of Australian households have computers, and the typical Australian spends more time accessing Web pages than anyone except Americans.

Culture can prove to be a barrier that hampers online marketing overseas, however. Marketers, particularly those in Asia, face such barriers. Today, most e-commerce sites are still in English, which often restricts access by Asian consumers. Although Asia contains a significant portion of the world's population and the number of Internet users there is increasing, the region still only accounts for less than 20 percent of Internet users worldwide. (The U.S. and Canada make up over one-third of all Internet users worldwide.)[25] Finally, many Asian consumers are less familiar and comfortable with catalog or telephone purchases than are U.S. and Canadian shoppers. Consequently, they are more reluctant to accept online shopping as a safe and secure way of purchasing products.

Even though over 50 million Europeans are online, they use the Internet for shopping much less than American consumers. The European wired set is much more likely to value the Internet as a way to work from home, catch up on local politics, choose vacation destinations, and take courses. Even in Norway, Sweden, and Denmark, where Net penetration is Europe's highest at around half of all households, e-commerce takes a back seat to such uses as e-mail and information services.[26]

As noted in earlier chapters, business is becoming increasingly global. E-commerce allows companies like Pacific Internet and Europe Online to create a regional framework for business transactions. Pacific Internet joined with Internet Initiative and Sumitomo (both based in Japan) and the Hong Kong Supernet, using Hong Kong and Singapore as hubs. Figure 5.8 lists a sampling of international Web sites that call the world their domestic market. Marketers must not forget that although the Internet has no geographical boundaries, countries do. Issues of infrastructure, economy, and politics all come into play when marketers try to enter international markets. While astute marketers think globally, they should also remember that e-commerce is a local experience in each country.

Even though e-commerce is growing rapidly, global online commerce still lags behind the pace of online marketing in the U.S. Web advertising revenues in Europe will not reach current U.S. levels for at least another five years. Some countries have infrastructure barriers. For instance, most telephone calls in Europe, including local calls, are metered and charged

http://www.starmedia.com	Spanish- and Portuguese-language StarMedia Network; launched in November 1998 in the United States.
http://www.uol.com.br	Universo Online, the largest portal serving Brazilians.
http://www.sina.com.tw	Sinanet.com, which targets the approximately 60 million Chinese living outside China and Taiwan.
http://www.sify.com	Sify.com, offering users of Indian ancestry "all the India you want to know."

FIGURE 5.8
Examples of Companies with Global Web Sites

based on the length of the call, which makes it much more expensive for European consumers to spend time on the Internet if they use a dial-up connection. Moreover, a smaller percentage of Europeans use broadband connections to get online compared with Americans and Canadians.[27] Nevertheless, marketers should recognize the tremendous potential of international Internet markets, and many are scrambling to expand their international online presence. For instance, eBay has over 20 different country-specific Web sites.

Security and Privacy Issues of E-Commerce

Consumers worry that information about them will become available to others without their permission. In fact, marketing research indicates that privacy is the top concern of Internet users and may be an impediment to the growth of e-commerce.[28] For example, concern about the privacy of credit card numbers has led to the use of secure payment systems. To add to those security systems, e-commerce sites require passwords as a form of authentication—that is, to determine that the person using the site is actually the one authorized to have access to the account. More recently, **electronic signatures** have become a way to enter into legal contracts, such as home mortgages and insurance policies, online. With an e-signature, an individual obtains a form of electronic identification and installs it in his or her Web browser. Signing the contract involves looking up and verifying the buyer's identity with this software.

Thanks to automatic data collection methods, Web users leave electronic trails of personal information about their buying and viewing habits. The way that companies use cookies has the potential both to make visits to the Web site more convenient and to invade computer users' privacy. DoubleClick abandoned a plan to merge its data on Web use with a database of catalog orders, which would have given the company the ability to target online advertising to individual consumers based on their shopping habits.[29] Similarly, Amazon.com received such bad press over its plan to publicize customer shopping information by company or group, called Purchase Circles, that it now allows customers to request removal of their names. With over 23 million customers, Amazon's customer database is one of the largest, and keeping its customers happy is critical to its success.[30]

Most consumers want assurances that any information they provide won't be sold to others without their permission. In response to these concerns, online merchants have been taking steps to protect consumer information. For example, many Internet companies have signed on with Internet privacy organizations like TRUSTe, shown in Figure 5.9. By displaying the TRUSTe logo on their Web sites, they indicate that they have promised to disclose how they collect personal data and what they do with the information. Prominently displaying a privacy policy is an effective way to build customers' trust.

A policy is only as good as the company publishing it, though. Consumers have no assurances about what happens if a company is sold or goes out of business. Now-defunct Toysmart.com promised customers that it would never share their personal data with a third party. But when the company landed in bankruptcy court, it considered selling its database, one of its most valuable assets. And Amazon.com has told customers openly that if it or part of its business is purchased at some point, its database would be one of the transferred assets.[31] With these concerns, it is no wonder that some companies are profiting

**FIGURE 5.9
TRUSTe: Ensuring Internet Privacy**

Marketing Dictionary

electronic signature   Electronic approval of a document that has the same status as a written signature.

by selling software designed to protect privacy. For example, a program called Freedom enables the user to set up an anonymous online identity. Another package called PersonaValet allows users to determine which personal data to reveal when they visit Web sites that have installed software that works with PersonaValet.[32]

Such privacy features may become a necessary feature of Web sites if consumer concerns continue to grow. They also may become legally necessary. Already in the U.S., the Children's Online Privacy Protection Act (COPPA) requires that Web sites targeting children younger than 13 years of age obtain "verifiable parental consent" before collecting any data that could be used to identify or contact individual users, including names and e-mail addresses. Congress has also begun considering laws to protect the privacy of adult users. The "Solving an Ethical Controversy" box debates whether or not additional legislation is needed to protect the privacy of Internet users.

Who Are the Online Buyers and Sellers?

As the growth of e-commerce continues, it becomes easier to use and much broader in its appeal to consumers. Over the past couple of years, online spending has more than doubled. Leading the charge were two primary groups of consumers: people who had never bought online before and consumers over the age of 50. These shoppers spent an average of around $125 per online purchase during a recent holiday period.[33] The actual and projected growth in online consumer spending is shown in Figure 5.10.

Online Buyers

The U.S. Department of Commerce has identified the demographics of Internet users—the target market for e-commerce marketers. The heaviest Internet users make $75,000 or more a year and live in urban areas; conversely, low-income rural dwellers account for less than 3 percent of Internet users. States with the highest percentage of Internet users include Alaska, New Hampshire, Washington, Utah, and Colorado. Americans of Asian and Pacific Island origin are the racial group most likely to use the Internet. In fact, they are twice as likely as African Americans and Hispanics to own PCs and three times more likely to be online. About 75 percent of employed people use the Internet at work, and more than 87 percent of college graduates do so. Over half of all people currently looking for jobs go online to send out résumés and check for job openings.[34]

While the typical Internet user is still relatively young and affluent, there is evidence that online demographics are changing. According to Jupiter Media Metrix, tomorrow's online shoppers will be older and less affluent. As the number of online shoppers doubles over the next five years, the new shoppers will more likely be over 35 and have annual household incomes of between $30,000 and $75,000. Marketers must adapt to these changing demographics. Ken Cassar of Jupiter puts it this

FIGURE 5.10
Actual and Projected Online Consumer Spending

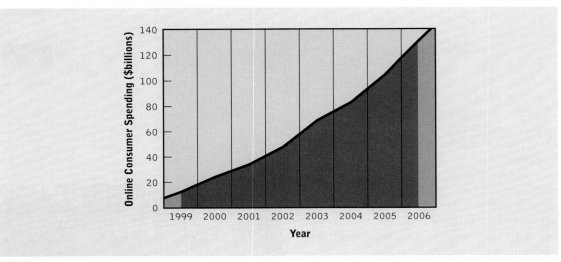

SOURCES: CyberAtlas and U.S. Department of Commerce.

right wrong

Solving an Ethical Controversy

Is the Web Spying on You?

Cable television company Comcast attracted a lot of publicity, most of it negative, when the company revealed that it was tracking the Internet habits of over 1 million individual users. Comcast was recording which Web sites users checked out, for how long, and in what sequence. The company claimed that it was just gathering data for research into how to better serve its high-speed Internet subscribers. Following comments of a couple of members of Congress that such research "might violate federal laws," Comcast quickly announced that it was discontinuing the practice. Around the same time, Internet company DoubleClick settled several class-action lawsuits. The suits alleged that the company was violating state and federal laws by secretly collecting personal data on users and combining it with information about their Web habits. As part of the settlement, DoubleClick agreed to give users clear notice and choice anytime it wanted to collect user data. The controversy surrounding Comcast and DoubleClick helped fuel renewed debate over the privacy of Internet users and raised the question whether additional federal legislation is needed. While a survey by the Progress and Freedom Foundation found that Web sites collect less data than they did two years ago, 96 percent of Web sites still collect user data.

Are Additional Laws Needed to Protect the Privacy of Internet Users?

PRO

1. Internet service providers and other Internet companies can collect and store massive amounts of personal information about users. Users never know exactly what information is being collected, nor when it is being collected. And currently there is no means for determining whether Internet companies are actually following their own privacy policies.
2. Existing federal and state privacy laws don't prohibit Internet companies from tracking where users go on the Web and storing that information.

CON

1. Current laws adequately protect user privacy because they make it illegal for firms to misrepresent their privacy policies or fail to disclose "material" practices, such as the sale of customer information. And law enforcement agencies occasionally subpoena usage information during criminal probes.
2. No evidence exists that Internet companies are quietly passing on "material" customer information to outside entities.

Summary

Just about everyone agrees that user privacy will remain a major issue with the Internet and that, unless privacy issues are adequately addressed, the growth of e-commerce could suffer. Beyond that there is much less agreement among privacy advocates, the Internet industry, and government about what to do next. The key is to strike a balance between Web users, Internet companies, and law-enforcement agencies. According to legal experts the best thing for companies to do is to prominently display their privacy policies, fully and clearly disclosing what type of user information they collect and store, and who, outside the company, might have access to the information. AT&T, for instance, has an entire Web page devoted to its privacy policy.

SOURCES: Electronic Privacy Information Center, accessed from the center's Web site, http://www.epic.org, March 30, 2002; Stefanie Olsen, "DoubleClick Nearing Privacy Settlements," CNET News, http://www.cnet.com, accessed March 30, 2002; Stephenie Steitzer, "Web Sites Cut Back on Personal Data Collected Online," *The Wall Street Journal*, March 28, 2002, p. B7; Jeffry Bartash, "Internet Privacy Debate Intensifies," CBS Market Watch, http://cbs.marketwatch.com, accessed February 15, 2002.

way: "The next generation of online shoppers will be quite a bit different. . . . They will be more representative of middle-class America. Retailers who want to appeal to these new shoppers must constantly study the changing composition of their customer base."[35]

Marketers must also continually be aware of the ways in which e-commerce is actually changing customers. For one thing, online marketing reaches people who do not normally watch television and read magazines. For another, online marketing is educating consumers in ways that traditional marketing cannot—by offering more information (often personalized) more rapidly than a retail salesperson, product brochure, or 30-second television commercial. Customers are more knowledgeable—and sometimes more demanding—than they used to be. Once consumers discover how easy it is to learn about wines at winespectator.com, they may be disappointed with the wine-shopping experience in a supermarket.

FIGURE 5.11
What's Selling
on the Internet

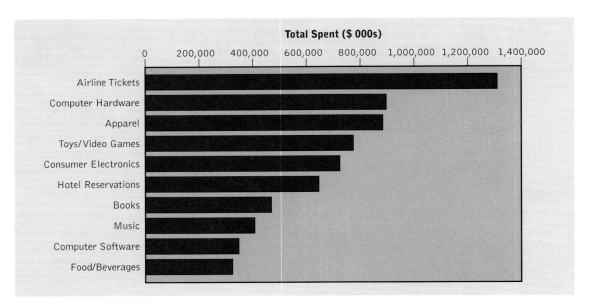

The data shown are for a recent two-month holiday shopping period.
SOURCE: NRF/Forrester Online Retail Index, accessed from the CyberAtlas Web site, http://cyberatlas.internet.com, April 19, 2002.

Online Sellers

Realizing that customers would have little or no opportunity to rely on many of the sense modes—smelling the freshness of direct-from-the-oven bread, touching the soft fabric of a new cashmere sweater, or squeezing fruit to assess its ripeness—early online sellers focused on offering products that consumers were familiar with and tended to buy frequently, such as books and music. Other popular early online offerings included computer hardware and software, and airline tickets.

Figure 5.11 lists the ten most popular goods and services sold online during a recent two-month holiday shopping period. While airline tickets and computer hardware remained the most popular items sold online, apparel and food and beverages also rank in the top ten. Moreover, online sales of apparel, food and beverages, and other products Web sellers initially avoided selling are growing faster than online sales of books and music.

A study by Jupiter Media Metrix predicts that apparel, prescription drugs, and home products will be hot online sellers in the years ahead. Once women become a larger share of Internet users, online apparel sales are likely to climb. And as the population of online users over 55 grows, so will the online sales of prescription drugs. Jupiter also predicts that kitchen products, small appliances, and large appliances—which typically are bought more often by women and older consumers—will experience strong growth over the next five years. According to Ken Cassar of Jupiter, "With the online shopping population expected to change dramatically, retailers must adopt a proactive merchandising strategy, anticipating changes in their customer base rather than reacting to changes in sales patterns. In order to measure these changes, retailers must track transaction data, survey customers, analyze the evolving customer base and quickly make appropriate changes."[36] Yet, online sellers must find ways for their legitimate marketing messages to reach buyers (see the "Marketing Miss" box on page 152).

4

Identify the goods and services marketed most often on the Internet.

Interactive Online Marketing Channels

Both manufacturers and marketing intermediaries frequently turn to online channels to market their goods and services. Want Dell to build a notebook computer that meets your computing needs? Click on **http://www.dell.com**. Need a student loan? Click on **http://www.lendingtree.com**. Looking for a better deal on car insurance? Click on **http://www.progressive.com**.

Each of these marketers—and thousands more like them—has turned to online marketing as a faster, less expensive, and more efficient alternative to the traditional approach of setting up brick-and-mortar retail stores. As Figure 5.12 shows, businesses deciding to market their products online can do so through one or a combination of primary online alternatives: company Web sites, online advertisements on other sites, and online communities. Other interactive marketing links include Web kiosks, smart cards, and virtual coupons and samples.

Company Web Sites

Virtually all online marketers have their own Web site that offers general information, electronic shopping, and promotions such as games, contests, and online coupons. Type in the firm's Internet address, and the Web site's home page will appear on your computer screen.

Two types of company Web sites exist. Many firms have established **corporate Web sites** to increase their visibility, promote their goods and services, and provide information for other interested parties. Rather than selling products directly, these sites attempt to build customer goodwill and assist channel members in their marketing efforts. For example, the Web site for Levi's jeans offers product information and a chance to view recent commercials. Consumers who want to actually buy jeans can link to the Web sites of retailers such as Kohl's and JCPenney.

Although marketing Web sites often include information about company history, products, locations, and financial information, their goal is to increase purchases by site visitors. For instance, Starbucks's Web site contains all of the information traditionally found on a corporate Web site, but it also includes an online store selling everything from coffee to espresso machines. Many marketing Web sites try to engage consumers in interactions that will move them closer to a demonstration, trial visit, purchase, or other marketing outcome. Some marketing Web sites, such as Sony.com, are quite complex. Visitors can link to pages for Sony Pictures Entertainment (with movie trailers and sweepstakes), Sony Music (audio and video clips plus news about recordings), and Sony Online Entertainment (online games plus information about games and gaming systems), among other possibilities.

Electronic Storefronts and Cybermalls

Clicking on **http://www.jcpenney.com** takes you on a virtual visit to the store. This **electronic storefront** is just what its name implies—an online store where customers can view and order merchandise much like shopping at brick-and-mortar retail establishments. The JCPenney online shopper is offered a store finder, electronic forms for ordering a catalog or subscribing to promotional e-mail, a gift registry, thousands of inventory items, and secure online shopping. The shopper has the option of having purchases delivered or picking them up at the local JCPenney store.

Whether a supplement to existing brick-and-mortar retail outlets or as a virtual replacement, electronic storefronts can offer marketers a number of advantages. These include the ability to expand operations in different cities, states, or countries without the major capital investments typically required for such growth. Also there is evidence that an electronic storefront can enhance the performance of brick-and-mortar operations. In addition, virtual stores provide great flexibility since the business is open 24 hours a day, thus removing time-zone barriers. Inventory locations can be centralized and orders can be filled promptly. Moreover, the image of the electronic storefront is controlled by the quality, creativity, and originality of the Web site and the ability of the Web marketers to offer customer satisfaction.

As noted in the chapter's opening vignette, online shopping got off to a rocky start. Many of the original e-tailers went out of business and those that survived learned some hard lessons about how to satisfy customers. While many of the surviving e-tailers have successful brick-and-mortar operations, a few exist only in cyberspace.

FIGURE 5.12 Online Marketing Channels

Company Web Sites	Online Communities
– corporate Web sites	– online forums
– marketing Web sites	– newsgroups
– virtual storefronts	– electronic bulletin boards
– cybermalls	

Advertisements on Other Web Sites	Other Interactive Marketing Links
– banner ads	– interactive kiosks
– pop-up windows	– smart cards
	– virtual coupons and samples

5

Identify the primary online marketing channels.

Marketing Dictionary

corporate Web sites   Web site that seeks to build customer goodwill and supplement other sales channels rather than to sell goods and services.

electronic storefront   Online store where customers can view and order merchandise much like window shopping at traditional retail establishments.

Marketing Miss

Jam That Spam

Background. A few years ago, spam—junk e-mail—was nothing more than an annoyance to businesses and consumers who use the Internet to communicate and conduct business. Today, however, spam accounts for 50 percent of Internet traffic. That number amounts to 1,000 mailings a year for every man, woman, and child on the Net. It's even worse for business, where an estimated 75 percent of all e-mails consist of spam, costing businesses about $10 billion per year in lost productivity among workers. Worse yet, it only costs a sender about $100 to buy a list of 150 million e-mail addresses. Spam is filling up in boxes so fast that it sometimes causes computer systems to crash, losing valuable messages in the process.

The Marketing Problem. Marketers naturally wanted to be the first to use this new medium to reach as many potential customers as possible, but a few of them have overdone it. "Spam is the scourge that benefits almost no one," notes David Baker, vice president for legal and public policy for Earthlink. Spammers have discovered how to send their e-mails from false addresses, under false names, so they cannot be traced easily. Yet marketers who send legitimate e-mails to existing and potential customers say that 15 percent of their messages aren't getting through because of blocking software or because recipients are simply deleting everything in their in-boxes. Servers such as Earthlink and America Online are suing spammers, and antispam activists have been pushing Congress to ban unsolicited e-mail altogether, as it did faxes a decade ago. While no one argues that spam must somehow be controlled—or eliminated—legitimate marketers want to be able to get their messages through to customers.

continued on next page

A common approach is to group electronic storefronts into **cybermalls,** some of which can link as many as 400 participating online retailers. Like concrete shopping malls, cybermalls typically feature a popular national retailer with high customer traffic as an anchor tenant. Other stores included in the mall are selected to produce a good match of merchandise offerings for the shopper. The operators of cybermalls charge each individual storefront operator a fee—either a flat monthly charge or a sliding scale depending on the number of visits to the storefront. Cybermalls are also operated by the major Internet portals and ISPs. In fact the world's largest cybermall is operated by AOL.

Advertising on Other Web Sites

Rather than relying completely on their Web sites to attract buyers, online marketers frequently expand their reach in the marketplace by placing ads on sites their prospective customers are likely to visit. *Banner ads,* the most common form of Internet advertising, are typically small, strip messages placed in high-visibility areas of frequently visited Web sites. *Pop-up ads* are separate windows that pop up. Examples of both types of ads are shown in Figure 5.13.

Many online marketers advocate using a variety of online and offline advertising combined with other forms of interactive promotion for better results. Lands' End created its "My Virtual Model" interactive tool to give customers a way of "trying on" clothes and accessories while sitting at their computers. The customer enters some basic information—such as height, weight, and hair color—and the software creates a customized model. The model can even be saved for future use. The firm's marketers also use banners placed on popular Web sites and portals to target its customer base.

FIGURE 5.13
Example of Banner Ad and Pop-up Ad

Online Communities

In addition to such direct channels as marketing merchandise through a firm's Web site, many firms use Internet forums, newsgroups, electronic bulletin boards, and Web communities that appeal to people who share common interests. All of these take advantage of the communication power of the Internet which, as noted earlier in the chapter, is still a main reason people go online. Members congregate online and exchange views and information on topics of interest. These communities may be organized for commercial or noncommercial purposes.

Online communities can take several forms, but all offer specific advantages to users and marketers alike. Online forums, for instance, are Internet discussion groups located on commercial online services. Users log in and participate by sending comments and questions or receiving information from other forum members. Forums may operate as electronic bulletin boards, as libraries for storing information, or even as a type of classified ad directory. Marketers often use forums to ask questions and exchange information with customers. Adobe, which designs such software as Acrobat and Photoshop, operates a "user-to-user" forum on its Web site as a support community for its customers. Customers who share common personal and professional interests can congregate, exchange industry news and practical product tips, share ideas, and—equally important—create publicity for Adobe products.

Newsgroups are noncommercial Internet versions of forums. Here people post and read messages on specific topics. Tens of thousands of newsgroups are on the Internet, and the number continues to rise. **Electronic bulletin boards** are specialized online services that center on a specific topic or area of interest. For instance, white-water rafters might check online bulletin boards to find out about the latest equipment, new places to raft, or current rafting conditions on particular waterways. While newsgroups resemble two-way conversations, electronic bulletin boards are more like announcements. Marketers often place banner or pop-up ads on newsgroups and electronic bulletin boards.

Online communities are not limited to consumers. They also facilitate business-to-business marketing. Participating in extranets or business communities like Farms.com helps small businesses develop relationships that transcend the former limits of their real-world, local communities. Using the Internet to build communities helps companies find other organizations to benchmark against, including suppliers, distributors, and competitors that may be interested in forming an alliance. Business owners who want to expand internationally frequently seek advice from other members of their online community.

Other Interactive Marketing Links

A variety of high-tech interactive tools are used by today's marketers to reach targeted market segments. These buyer-seller links include interactive kiosks, smart cards, and virtual coupons and samples. **Web kiosks** are freestanding computers, often located in retail showrooms or shopping centers. They are versatile multimedia devices that deliver information on demand. Shoppers can stop by a kiosk and get

Marketing Miss

The Outcome. Currently, Internet service providers are stuck with the problem of spam—investing in software to block it, suing spammers, answering complaints from angry customers. Software companies have rushed to create more and more sophisticated blocking programs and tools ranging from simple text filters to "smart" programs that calculate whether a message is wanted or unwanted. Some states have jumped ahead of Congress, enacting laws against spam. Virginia now requires jail time for spammers who use false identities or send 10,000 copies of an identical e-mail message. Meanwhile, the push for antispam legislation has met resistance from civil liberties groups. "Users at least need to know what's being filtered and why," says a member of one such group.

Lessons Learned. If marketers hadn't rushed headlong to the Internet, if some hadn't latched on to the idea of sending hundreds of thousands of unsolicited messages to consumers' computers, e-mail might now be an efficient, lucrative medium for marketers to reach customers. Instead, the medium is mired in lawsuits, a technology race, and politics. But the companies producing antispam software have found a niche. "Antispam vendors will win the arms race," predicts Marten Nelson of Ferris Research.

SOURCES: Stephen Baker, "Where Danger Lurks," *BusinessWeek*, August 25, 2003, pp. 114-118; Stephen H. Wildstrom, "Hitting Spammers Where It Hurts," *BusinessWeek*, May 19, 2003, p. 20; Lorraine Woellert et al., "Slamming Spam," *BusinessWeek*, May 12, 2003, p. 40.

Marketing Dictionary

cybermall   Group of virtual stores planned, coordinated, and operated as a unit for online shoppers.

electronic bulletin board   Specialized online service that provides information on a specific topic or area of interest.

Web kiosk   Small, free-standing computer, often located in a store, that provides consumers with Internet connections to a firm and its goods and services.

6

Explain how marketers use interactive tools as part of their online marketing strategies.

discount coupons or product information. Web kiosks are a marriage of traditional kiosks and Internet connections. Officially dubbed "in store, Web-assisted selling," the goal of these kiosks is to keep customers from leaving empty-handed and provide new levels of selection, especially for customers who may not otherwise have Internet access.

Some Web kiosks can even take the place of online shopping. For instance, all Best Buy stores have a "Computer Creation Station," a Web kiosk that lets customers design their own PC, with or without the assistance of a salesperson. The customer's custom-built PC is usually ready within a week and can be picked up at the store or sent to the customer's home or business. Best Buy's Computer Creation Station allows it to compete with direct sellers of custom-made computers, such as Dell and Gateway.

Another e-commerce innovation involves **smart cards**—plastic cards similar to credit cards that are embedded with computer chips that store personal and financial information. To buy an item, the card is inserted into a card scanner or reader, which electronically debits the purchase amount. The card can be "reloaded" periodically with cash from a checking or savings account. Smart cards were the first step toward electronic currency—a system of exchange in which a consumer can set up accounts at Web sites and transfer money into the accounts.

Although smart cards have been popular in Europe and Asia for years, they have been slower to catch on in the U.S. A few years ago, American Express began offering Blue—one of the first smart credit cards. American Express marketed Blue as a card that provided an added layer of security when shopping on the Web. Each card contains a unique digital certificate that acts much like a key. Those who want extra security online can swipe their cards through a special reader attached to their PCs. After the cardholder enters a PIN, the certificate is read, and the necessary information to complete the purchase is transmitted securely. Blue also contains a magnetic strip so it can be used like an ordinary credit card.

Recently, many traditional direct marketing companies began going online with *virtual coupon* and *online sample* offerings. Customers can find virtual coupons on their PCs by such criteria as business name, location, and keyword and can download them on a home computer. Online consumers can also register to have coupons e-mailed directly to them. ValPak Direct Marketing Systems, a longtime leader in the paper coupon industry, now offers the online equivalent at its Web site, **http://www.valpak.com**.

Other Web sites offer free product samples. Members of FreeSampleClub (accessible at **http://www.sunflowergroup.com**) complete interactive profiles that include information such as age, family data, and pet ownership. Based on the profiles, the system creates a personal sample menu from merchants who are targeting that profile. Members click on their choices and receive products within a week.

7

Discuss how an effective Web site can enhance customer relationships.

Creating an Effective Web Presence

One of the preliminary tasks of starting a business or entering a new market is performing marketing research. Marketers evaluate every proposed e-commerce venture to ensure it benefits the firm by cutting costs, improving customer satisfaction, and increasing revenues. To have a successful e-commerce business, it is also essential that marketing activities remain customer-oriented. Other areas that must be assessed include the competitive environment and the costs of updating the firm's technological infrastructure. An effective Internet strategy should create sustainable shareholder value by increasing profits, accelerating growth, reducing time-to-market for products, improving customer service, and improving the public perception of the organization.

Building an Effective Web Site

Most Web experts agree: "It is easier to build a bad Web site than a good one." To be effective, a firm's strategies must focus on building relationships through the use of company Web sites. Because of the high costs associated with going online, marketers must get the highest possible return on their Web site investments. Building an effective Web site involves three basic steps: establish a mission for the company's site, identify the purpose of the site, and satisfy customer needs and wants through a clear site design.

Briefly Speaking

The 'Net is a waste of time, and that's exactly what's right about it.

*William Gibson
(b. 1948)
American writer*

The first step is to establish a mission for the site. A site mission involves the creation of a statement that explains the organization's overall goals. Without a mission to guide decision makers, the technology will be aimless. Dell describes its mission in three clicks: to make it easier for customers to do business with them, to reduce the cost of business for Dell and its customers, and to enhance Dell's relationship with it customers.[37]

Next, marketers must identify the purpose of the site. Is it primarily to provide information or entertainment, or is it intended to solely connect buyers and sellers? Priceline.com, which auctions such things as airline tickets and hotel rooms, operates by the phrase "Name your price" and prominently displays this phrase throughout its Web site. Visitors know exactly what they are supposed to do. In addition, marketers should educate themselves—not so much about the details of technology but about how Web sites enhance customer communications and how those communications benefit the company.

Marketers should also be clear about how the purpose of the site fits in with the company's overall marketing strategy. For instance, Mattel, well-known for producing toys such as Barbie, Cabbage Patch dolls, and Matchbox cars, sells most of its products in toy stores and toy departments of other retailers, like Target and Wal-Mart. The company wants an Internet presence, but it would cut the retailers out of this important source of revenue if it sold toys online to consumers. Mattel cannot afford to lose the goodwill and purchasing power of these giant retailers. So the company sells only specialty products online, such as the pricey American Girl dolls, that are not carried in most retail stores.

Finally, identifying customer needs and wants is critical to marketers both online and offline. However, online marketers must consider how their strategies will need to be adjusted to continue satisfying customers through online transactions. Well-designed Web sites are straightforward, provide security and privacy, and, most important, are easy to navigate. Successful sites follow accepted Internet conventions and familiar screen layouts so customers will not get lost on the site. They also use the right color combinations. Many organizations outsource their Internet services entirely, from building Web sites to designing intranets and extranets.

Managing a Web Site

Once a site is up and running, it has to be managed effectively. Marketers must update the site frequently, flagging new merchandise and services, and eliminating items that did not sell well and references to past events. Some marketers recommend avoiding dates on site pages so the site always appears current. Web site management involves constant attention not only to content but to technical presentation. Frequent software updates may be necessary to take advantage of new technologies that permit increasing levels of customer interaction. Marketers should keep track of costs associated with Web sites. Profitability has still been erratic. If costs exceed revenues, marketers need to reevaluate whether the site is meeting expected goals or whether changes need to be implemented to boost the site's effectiveness.

Amazon.com, one of the world's largest e-tailers, found profitability elusive. Consequently, it kept tinkering with its Web site. It expanded its offerings from books and music to electronics, toys, and housewares. Amazon.com was also the first commercial site to use software that could analyze a customer's purchases and suggest other related items—a terrific way of targeting a market. In order to keep up with future technology needs, Amazon.com acquired Junglee Corporation, a developer of comparison-shopping technologies, and PlanetAll, a computerized register of customer information ranging from addresses to birthdays. Amazon.com marketers use this personalized marketing tool to send e-mail reminders to customers.

8

Describe how to measure the effectiveness of online marketing efforts.

Measuring Effectiveness of Online Marketing

How does a company gauge the return from investing in a Web site? Measuring the effectiveness of a Web site is a tricky process and often depends on the purpose of the Web site. Figure 5.14 lists some measures of effectiveness. Profitability is relatively easy to measure in firms

Marketing Dictionary

smart card   Multipurpose card embedded with computer chips that store personal and financial information, such as credit card data, health records, and driver's license number.

FIGURE 5.14
Measures of Web Site Effectiveness

| Profitability | Web site traffic counts | Click-through rates | Conversion rates | Research studies |

that generate revenues directly from online product orders, advertising, or subscription sales. However, a telephone order resulting from an ad on a Web site still shows the sale as a phone sale, not a Web site sale, even though the order originated at the site.

For many companies, revenue is not a major Web site objective. Only about 15 percent of large companies use their Web sites to generate revenue; the rest use them to showcase their products and to offer information about their organizations. For such companies, success is measured by increased brand awareness and brand loyalty, which presumably translates into greater profitability offline.

Some standards guide efforts to collect and analyze traditional consumer purchase data, such as how many Ohio residents bought new Honda Accords the previous year, watched HBO's award-winning *The Sopranos,* or tried Arby's deli-style sandwiches. Still, the Internet presents several challenges for marketers. Although information sources are getting better, it is difficult to be sure how many people use the Internet, how often, and what they actually do online. Some Web pages display counters that measure the number of visits. However, the counters can't tell whether someone has spent time on the page or skipped over it on the way to another site, or whether that person is a first-time or repeat viewer.

Advertisers typically measure the success of their ads in terms of **click-through rate,** meaning the percentage of people presented with a banner ad who click on it, thereby linking to a Web site or a pop-up page of information related to the ad. Recently, the average click-through rate has been declining to about half of 1 percent of those viewing an ad. This rate is much lower than the 1.0 to 1.5 percent response rate for direct-mail advertisements. Low click-through rates have made Web advertising less attractive than it was when it was novel and people were clicking on just about anything online. Selling advertising has therefore become a less reliable source of e-commerce revenues.[38]

As e-commerce gains popularity, new models for measuring its effectiveness are being developed. A basic measurement is the **conversion rate,** the percentage of Web site visitors who make purchases. A conversion rate of 3 to 5 percent is average by today's standards.[39] A company can use its advertising cost, site traffic, and conversion rate data to find out the cost to capture each customer. For instance, a company that spends $10,000 to attract 5,000 visitors to a Web site with a 4 percent conversion rate is obtaining 200 transactions, .04 × 5,000. It spent $10,000 for those 200 transactions, so the advertising cost is $50 per transaction, meaning each of those customers cost $50 to acquire through the advertising campaign.

E-commerce businesses are trying to boost their conversion rates by ensuring their sites download quickly, are easy to use, and deliver on their promises. For instance, Lexmark International turned to Web consultants WebCriteria to help it improve the overall performance of its Web site. Analysis of the traffic on Lexmark.com indicated that visitors used the site primarily for product and pre-sales support. The site was large and difficult to navigate. WebCriteria assisted Lexmark.com by simplifying the site and better enabling customers to reach their goals. According to Patti Lybrook of Lexmark.com, "We're in constant change mode. We are constantly monitoring and updating the site design."[40]

Besides measuring click-through and conversion rates, companies can study samples of consumers. Research firms such as PC-Meter and Relevant Knowledge recruit panels of computer users to track Internet site performance and evaluate Web activity. This service works in much the same way that television rating firm AC Nielsen—a major marketing research firm—monitors television audiences. The WebTrends service provides information on Web site visitors, including where they come from, what they see, and how many "hits," or visits to the site, are logged during different times of the day. Other surveys of Web users investigate their brand awareness and their attitudes toward Web sites and brands.

Strategic Implications of Marketing in the 21st Century

The future is bright for marketers who continue to take advantage of the tremendous potential of e-commerce. Online channels that seem cutting edge today will be eclipsed within the next decade by newer technologies, some of which haven't even been invented yet. First and foremost, e-commerce empowers consumers. For instance, already a significant percentage of car buyers show up at a dealership armed with information on dealer costs and option packages—information they obtained online. And the percentage of informed car buyers is only going to increase. This trend isn't about being market led or customer focused; it is about consumer control. Some argue that the Internet represents the ultimate triumph of consumerism.

Since the end of World War II, there has been a fundamental shift in the retailing paradigm from Main Street to malls to superstores. Each time the paradigm shifted, a new group of leaders emerged. The old leaders often missed the early warning signs because they were easy to ignore. When the first Wal-Mart Stores and Home Depots appeared, how many really understood what the impact of superstores and category killers would be on supply chain management? Similarly, marketers must understand the potential impact of the Web.

Initially some experts predicted the death of traditional retailing. This hasn't happened yet, and it may never happen. Rather, what has occurred has been a marketing evolution for organizations that embrace Internet technologies as essential parts of their marketing strategies. E-commerce is fueled by information; marketers who effectively use the wealth of data available will not only survive but thrive in cyberspace.

Summary of Chapter Objectives

1. Define e-commerce and give examples of each function of the Internet.

E-commerce involves targeting customers by collecting and analyzing business information, conducting customer transactions, and maintaining online relationships with customers by means of computer networks such as the Internet. The four main functions of the Internet are communications (such as e-mail), information (searching commercial and government sites), entertainment (such as online music), and e-commerce (such as selling products on a company Web site).

2. Describe how marketers use the Internet to achieve their firm's objectives.

A Web site can provide a platform for communication between organizations, customers, and suppliers. It can distinguish a firm and its merchandise from competitive offerings. The Web site can be used to interview customers to find out how they use the Internet and where they find information needed to make purchase decisions. This information can be used to devise strategies to attract new customers and improve relationships with existing ones.

3. Explain how online marketing benefits organizations, marketers, and consumers.

Online marketers can find new markets and customers who could not have been served adequately using traditional techniques. They also produce cost savings in every area of the

Marketing Dictionary

click-through rate   The percentage of people presented with a Web banner ad who click on it.

conversion rate   The percentage of visitors to a Web site who make a purchase.

marketing mix. Online marketing greatly reduces the time involved in reaching target markets. Online marketing tools allow the direct exchange of information in a seamless fashion without involvement of marketing intermediaries. The benefits online shoppers obtain from Web purchases include lower prices, convenience, and personalization. Marketers can use their Web sites to build strong relationships, reduce costs, increase efficiency, and achieve a global presence.

4. Identify the goods and services most often sold on the Internet.

Traditionally, online users tended to live in urban areas, earn more than $75,000 per year, and have college degrees. However, in recent years the typical Internet user has gotten older and less affluent. Also, as many women shop online as men. All of these trends mean that the typical online shopper is looking more and more like the average consumer. The most popular goods and services sold online include airline tickets, computer hardware, and apparel. As the demographics of online shoppers change so too will the mix of items sold online. For instance, as the average age of Internet users rises, so will the online sales of prescription drugs.

5. Identify the primary online marketing channels.

The primary online marketing channels include company Web sites, online advertisements on other Web sites, and online communities. Company Web sites can be either corporate sites (containing general product and financial information) or marketing sites (sites that enable e-commerce). Online advertisements on other Web sites consist of either banner ads or pop-up ads. Both types of advertisements contain links to the firm's Web site. Online communities consist of online forums, electronic bulletin boards, and newsgroups.

6. Explain how marketers use interactive tools as part of their online marketing strategies.

Marketers reach targeted segments of their markets using a variety of interactive tools. Web kiosks deliver information and coupons on demand. Smart cards are used as a form of electronic currency for payment. Virtual coupons and online sample offerings can be downloaded from Web sites to home computers.

7. Discuss how an effective Web site can enhance customer relationships.

An effective Web site is customer oriented and follows three basic steps: Establish a mission for the company's site, identify the purpose of the site, and satisfy customer needs and wants through clear site design. Well-designed Web sites are straightforward, provide security and privacy, and are easy to navigate. Sites must also be carefully maintained and should be kept up to date. Marketers should always be aware of the cost of a Web site relative to the revenue it generates.

8. Describe how to measure the effectiveness of online marketing efforts.

Some of the first steps online marketers use to measure the effectiveness of their Web efforts included counting hits and page views. More sophisticated measures of Web site effectiveness include click-through rates and conversion rates. Click-through rates are the number of viewers that click on the link. The conversion rate calculates the advertising cost per visitor.

Marketing Terms You Need to Know

electronic commerce (e-commerce) 133	Internet (Net) 135	electronic exchanges 140	electronic bulletin boards 153
electronic marketing (e-marketing) 133	intranet 135	bots 143	Web kiosk 153
digital tools 133	extranet 135	electronic signatures 147	smart card 154
interactive marketing 134	instant messaging 136	corporate Web sites 151	click-through rate 156
	Internet service provider (ISP) 139	electronic storefront 151	conversion rate 156
		cybermall 152	

Other Important Marketing Terms

World Wide Web 136	banner ads 152	virtual coupons 154
search engine 139	pop-up ads 152	online sample offerings 154

Review Questions

1. Define e-commerce. Explain the five advantages of e-commerce to contemporary marketers.
2. What is interactive marketing? Give an example.
3. List the four functions of the Internet. Give an example of each function.
4. Explain how online marketing benefits the following organizations:
   a. National Audubon Society

b. The local chapter of USA Cycling
c. Voodoo dolls designed by the Voodoo Cultural Center in New Orleans
d. General Electric

5. Discuss the differences between B2C and B2B online marketing. What is an electronic exchange?

6. List the advantages for both firms and consumers from online shopping. Are security and privacy impediments to online shopping?

7. Which products sell best online? How are the demographics of online shoppers changing?

8. List the interactive marketing channels. Explain the difference between a corporate Web site and a marketing Web site.

9. What are the keys to building an effective Web site? Discuss how to properly manage an existing Web site.

10. What is the difference between a click-through rate and a conversion rate? If an e-commerce Web site costs $1 million to develop, attracts 750,000 visitors, and has a conversion rate of 5 percent, what is the advertising cost per transaction?

Projects and Teamwork Exercises

1. How can marketers use the concept of community to add value to their products? Give an example of each of the types of communities discussed in the chapter.

2. Working with a small group, assume your group is a designer of e-commerce Web sites. Identify a local company that operates with little or no online presence. Outline a proposal that explains the benefits to the firm of either going online or significantly expanding its online presence. Sketch out what the firm's Web site should look like and the functions it should perform.

3. Suggest ways in which a Web marketer might reduce consumer reluctance to purchase products that are perishable or that consumers typically like to touch, feel, or smell before buying.

4. How are the profiles of online buyers and sellers changing? What are some of the strategic implications of these shifts to online marketers?

5. Working with a partner, identify and visit 10 different e-commerce Web sites. Which of these sites, in your opinion, has the highest and lowest conversion rates? Explain your choices. Suggest some ways in which the conversion rates of all 10 sites could be improved.

'net **W**ork

http://www.landsend.com

http://www.eddiebauer.com

1. Online shopping experience. Assume the role of a consumer who wishes to purchase a pair of jeans over the Internet. Two leading online clothing retailers are Lands' End and Eddie Bauer. Visit both retailers and learn enough about each site so you can describe them to a friend. Be prepared to identify the site you'd recommend and why.

http://www.cnn.com

http://www.foxsports.com

http://www.bestbuy.com

2. Three Web functions. Locate a Web site that you consider to be an outstanding example of each of the three Web functions described in the chapter—information, entertainment, and e-commerce. For example, http://www.cnn.com is an information site; http://www.foxsports.com is an entertainment site; and http://www.bestbuy.com is an e-commerce site. Write a brief review of the Web site you selected for each function.

http://www.google.com

http://www.ecommerce times.com/

3. Security and privacy issues. As the chapter described, security and privacy concerns are critical factors in building a relationship online. Using the Web sites listed, or a search engine (such as Google), research the current status of laws and regulation dealing with online security and privacy issues.

Note: Internet Web addresses change frequently. If you don't find the exact sites listed, you may need to access the organization or company's home page and search from there.

CASE 5.1   The Evolution of E*Trade

Online banking continues to grow rapidly. The number of customers performing such banking functions as checking account balances, transferring money, and paying bills is expected to triple over the next five years. Hundreds of banks offer online banking services today, including both Internet-only banks and traditional brick-and-mortar banks. At the same time, changes in banking laws have allowed banks to enter new businesses, such as investment and insurance. Conversely, investment firms and insurance companies can now offer banking services.

E*Trade was founded in 1996 and was one of the first Internet-only brokerage firms. E*Trade offered small, individual investors access to relevant information and stock market news 24 hours a day, 7 days a week from the convenience of their personal computers. E*Trade also charged much less to buy and sell securities than traditional brick-and-mortar brokerage firms. E*Trade's business surged, and today it is the second-largest online brokerage firm in the country. However, along with success has come increased competition from established brokerage firms such as Charles Schwab and Merrill Lynch. E*Trade's growth rate slowed and its profitability declined. Management decided it was time to diversify into other financial services. But where to start?

The opportunity presented itself in early 2000. E*Trade purchased struggling Internet Bank Telebanc Financial Corporation for $1.6 billion. Now E*Trade could offer its customers not only brokerage services but a full range of banking services as well. Without the expense of brick-and-mortar branches, E*Trade Bank, as it became known, could offer customers lower fees and higher rates on deposits. With a few mouse clicks, customers could complete virtually all of their banking transactions 24 hours a day, 7 days a week.

Initially, however, there was one major stumbling block. E*Trade Bank didn't have any ATM machines of its own. Its customers could still use other banks' ATM machines, but they usually had to pay a fee. E*Trade overcame that problem when it purchased the nation's third-largest ATM network. Now E*Trade Bank customers have access to over 9,600 no-fee ATM machines located throughout the country. The company's Web site provides a guide to ATM locations and proclaims, "Find an E*Trade ATM near you and never pay an ATM fee again!" Today, E*Trade Bank has almost 500,000 accounts and over $5.5 billion in deposits.

E*Trade appears to be on track toward its goal of becoming the nation's first Internet-based financial services company. The company recently acquired a large stake in E-Loan, Inc., an online mortgage lender. E*Trade has opened financial emporiums and discount-store kiosks where customers can do everything from check stock prices to apply for a home-equity loan. Plans are in the works to begin offering credit cards and insurance. The company is also expanding its wireless services. At some point, customers will be able to use their handheld devices or cell phones to conduct a wide range of financial transactions. The company has even rebranded itself as E*Trade Financial.

While the future looks bright for E*Trade Financial, don't count out the traditional brick-and-mortar financial service companies just yet. Fleet Financial Bank of Massachusetts, for example, is aggressively expanding its ATM network and online services and has taken specific aim at the online banks. The brick-and-mortar banks also have one major advantage over online banks: actual people customers can talk to. Many banking experts believe that online banks such as E*Trade Bank will eventually have to offer human help. One puts it this way, "Every once in a while, you need to talk to someone."

Questions for Critical Thinking

1. Why did E*Trade expand into banking and other financial services? Do you agree or disagree with the observation that eventually online banks will have to offer the level of personal service that brick-and-mortar banks offer customers? What factors did you consider when choosing your current bank?
2. The benefits of online shopping, to both consumers and companies, were discussed in the chapter. Use E*Trade as an example to illustrate each of these benefits. Do you currently conduct any of your banking business online? If so, what kinds of banking transactions do you perform online? If not, why not?

SOURCES: Christian Berthelsen, "E*Trade Puts on Banking Glitz," *San Francisco Chronicle*, http://www.sfgate.com, April 22, 2002; E*Trade Financial Web site, http://www.etrade.com, accessed April 22, 2002; John Helyar, "At E*Trade Growing Up Is Hard to Do," *Fortune*, March 18, 2002, pp. 88–90; Beth Healy, "Reinventing ATMs: Online Brokerage Challenges Banks with Hip Brand, New Services," *Boston Globe*, http://www.boston.com, accessed March 16, 2002.

VIDEO CASE 5.2   Tower Records Uses Bricks—and Clicks—to Survive Troubled Times

The written case on Tower Records appears on page VC-6. The recently filmed Tower Records video is designed to expand and highlight the concepts in this chapter and the concepts and questions covered in the written video case.

6

Relationship Marketing and Customer Relationship Management (CRM)

Chapter Objectives

1 Contrast transaction-based marketing with relationship marketing.

2 Identify and explain each of the core elements of relationship marketing.

3 Explain the steps in the development of a marketing relationship and how they lead to enhanced customer satisfaction.

4 Explain customer relationship management (CRM) and the role of technology in building customer relationships.

5 Describe the buyer-seller relationship in business-to-business marketing.

6 Compare the different types of business partnerships and explain how they contribute to relationship marketing.

7 Describe how relationship marketing incorporates national account selling, electronic data interchange, vendor-managed inventories, and collaborative planning, forecasting, and replenishment techniques.

8 Identify and evaluate the most common measurement and evaluation techniques within a relationship marketing program.

Dylan's Candy Bar Sweetens Relationships

When the father of your new business partner wants to give you advice, you might listen just to be polite. But when your new business partner is Dylan Lauren—and her father is Ralph Lauren, head of the fashion empire—you really pay attention to what he has to say. That's what Jeff Rubin did after mutual friends introduced the young entrepreneur and candy lover to fellow candy buff Dylan Lauren. The two hit it off and decided they wanted to start their own business together. Rubin had already experienced success with his own family's chain of bulk candy stores and had created FAO Schweetz, a candy store inside each of the famous FAO Schwarz toy stores. FAO Schweetz was so popular that it accounted for almost 8 percent of Schwarz's total sales. Warner Bros., Sony, and Toys 'R' Us approached him to discuss carrying his products, and the enduring relationships resulted in candy concepts tailored to each of those customer's needs. But Dylan's dad had some advice—and a bit of a warning—for Rubin. "You haven't really created anything that's yours, that you own," said Ralph. "I don't create Bloomingdale's shirts, I create Polo Ralph Lauren to be sold in Bloomingdale's. You need to create your own brand and identity that you can place in these stores and stop creating brands for [other] people."

Rubin took Lauren's advice to heart. While Dylan Lauren used her knowledge of trends and styles to develop a unique brand, Rubin relied on the relationships he had already established in the candy industry. Together they came up with Dylan's Candy Bar, a 10,000 square foot candy boutique in Manhattan. "I was able to use all my connections in the business to go after M&Ms/Mars, who created 16 colors of Skittles only available at Dylan's Candy Bar," recalls Rubin. "Hershey's created 10 colors of Hershey Kisses available only at Dylan's Candy Bar, and Double Bubble created Double Bubble bath soap and shampoo only available at Dylan's Candy Bar. I've been able to do that with so many vendors."

When Rubin works with a candy manufacturer to develop new flavors or innovative products, he asks for exclusive distribution rights, which helps set Dylan's Candy Bar apart from other stores and also strengthens the shop's bond with manufacturers. Recently, he approached Dorval Trading Co. with an idea to make a three-foot version of its Sour Power Belts—powder-coated, chewy candy strips that are usually nine inches long. "My reaction was, 'Absolutely,'" notes Roberta Cappel, president of Dorval. "I believe in Dylan's and the exposure that the brand gets there." At Dylan's, each manufacturer has its own booth showcasing its wares—reminiscent of FAO Schwarz's store—within-a-store—so that the candies aren't lost in bins or on poorly lit shelves. Candy makers love the arrangement, as do shoppers, who know exactly where to find their favorites.

Who are Dylan's customers? Plenty of celebrities have been spotted hovering over the sweet treats—word has it that Spike

Lee likes Jolly Ranchers while Jerry Seinfeld has a taste for old-fashioned Bit O' Honey. Kelly Ripa is partial to green Swedish Fish and Serena Williams loves her Laffy Taffy. Plenty of tourists and local residents shop at Dylan's as well; Rubin estimates that 8,000 customers visit the store on a busy day. Dylan's also assembles gift baskets for corporate customers. Dylan's does cater to people who are willing to spend a bit more to indulge themselves in sweets; the average sale is about $14.50, compared with $4.25 in a mall-based candy store.

"This is the most expensive candy store in the world," claims Rubin. But customers don't seem to mind. They love the atmosphere, enjoy finding their old favorites or trying exclusive varieties, and don't mind paying for the experience. Manufacturers love the exposure they get in an upscale, popular store. Dylan's has become so popular that its owners are planning new stores in trendy Florida and Texas locations. Clearly, Rubin knows how to manage his business relationships; in fact, you could say he's a real sweetheart.[1]

Chapter Overview

As the success of Dylan's Candy Bar demonstrates, marketing revolves around relationships, not only with customers but with everyone involved in creating a product and bringing it to market. The shift away from **transaction-based marketing,** which focuses on short-term, single exchanges, to customer-focused relationship marketing is one of the most important trends in marketing today. Companies recognize that they cannot prosper simply by identifying and attracting new customers; to succeed, they must build loyal, mutually beneficial relationships with existing customers, suppliers, distributors, and employees. This strategy benefits the bottom line, because retaining customers costs much less than acquiring new ones.

Building and managing long-term relationships between buyers and sellers is the hallmark of relationship marketing. **Relationship marketing** is the development, growth, and maintenance of cost-effective, high-value relationships with individual customers, suppliers, distributors, retailers, and other partners for mutual benefit over time. Emerging from and closely linked to relationship marketing, **customer relationship management (CRM)** is the combination of strategies and tools that drive relationship programs, reorienting the entire organization to a concentrated focus on satisfying customers. It leverages technology as a means to manage customer relationships and to integrate all stakeholders into a company's product design and development, manufacturing, marketing, sales, and customer service processes.

Building long-term relationships with consumers and other businesses involves four basic elements. First, database technology helps a company to identify current and potential customers with selected demographic, purchase, and lifestyle characteristics. Second, through database marketing, the firm analyzes this information and can modify its marketing mix to deliver differentiated messages and customized marketing programs to individual consumers. Third, through relationship marketing, the firm is able to monitor each relationship. The company can calculate the cost of attracting one new customer and figure out how much profit that customer will generate during the relationship. The company is also able to assess the customer's level of satisfaction or dissatisfaction with its service. Information is fed back to the firm, which is then able to seek ways to add value to the buyer-seller transaction so that the relationship will continue. Finally, customer relationship management uses intimate knowledge of customers and customer preferences

Briefly Speaking

In every instance we found that the best-run companies stay as close to their customers as humanly possible.

Thomas J. Peters
(b. 1942)
American business
writer

FIGURE 6.1
Forms of Buyer-Seller Interactions on a Continuum from Conflict to Integration

to orient every part of the organization, including its external partners, toward building a unique company differentiation that is based on strong, unbreakable bonds with customers. Sophisticated technology and the Internet are the tools that make that happen.[2]

As Figure 6.1 illustrates, relationship marketing emphasizes cooperation rather than conflict between all of the parties involved. This ongoing collaborative exchange creates value for both parties and builds customer loyalty. Customer relationship management goes a step further, integrating the customer's needs into all aspects of the firm's operations and its relationships with suppliers, distributors, and strategic partners. It combines people, processes, and technology with the long-term goal of maximizing customer value through mutually satisfying interactions and transactions.[3]

This chapter begins by examining the reasons organizations are moving toward relationship marketing and customer relationship management, exploring the impact this move has on producers of goods and services and their customers.

The Shift from Transaction-Based Marketing to Relationship Marketing

Since the Industrial Revolution, most manufacturers have run production-oriented operations. They have focused on making products and then promoting them to customers in the hope of selling enough to cover costs and earn profits. The emphasis has been on individual sales or transactions.

In transaction-based marketing, buyer and seller exchanges are characterized by limited communications and little or no ongoing relationships. The primary goal is to entice a buyer to make a purchase through such inducements as low price, convenience, or packaging. The goal is simple and short term: Sell something—now.

Some marketing exchanges remain largely transaction based. In residential real estate sales, for example, the primary goal of the agent is to make a sale and collect a commission. While the agent may seek to maintain the appearance of an ongoing, buyer-seller relationship, in most cases, the possibility of future transactions is limited. The best an agent can

1

Contrast transaction-based marketing with relationship marketing.

Marketing Dictionary

transaction-based marketing   Buyer and seller exchanges characterized by limited communications and little or no ongoing relationship between the parties.

relationship marketing   Development and maintenance of long-term, cost-effective relationships with individual customers, suppliers, employees, and other partners for mutual benefit.

customer relationship management (CRM)   Combination of strategies and tools that drive relationship programs, reorienting the entire organization to a concentrated focus on satisfying customers. Leveraging technology, CRM integrates all stakeholders into a company's product design and development, manufacturing, marketing, sales, and customer service processes.

hope for is to represent the seller again in a subsequent real-estate deal that may be several years down the line or, more likely, to gain positive referrals to other buyers and sellers. To a lesser extent, automobile purchases are transaction-based—many customers shop around for each new car rather than buy from one dealer exclusively.

Today, many organizations are trying an alternate approach. Relationship marketing looks at customers as equal partners in buyer-seller transactions. By motivating customers to enter a long-term relationship in which they repeat purchases or buy multiple brands from the firm, marketers are able to obtain a clearer understanding of customer needs. This process leads to improved products or customer service, which pays off through better sales and lower marketing costs.

The move from transactions to relationships is reflected in the changing nature of the interactions between customers and sellers. In transaction-based marketing, exchanges with customers are generally sporadic, often disrupted by conflict. As interactions become relationship oriented, however, conflict changes to cooperation, and infrequent contacts between buyers and sellers become ongoing exchanges. Firms now understand they must do more than simply create products and then sell the items. With so many goods and services to choose from, customers look for added value from their marketing relationships.

As a means of providing added value through superior service, Enterprise Rent-A-Car set up each of its 4,800 branch offices worldwide as a separate entrepreneurial entity. Employees were encouraged to find new ways to boost customer referrals and retention. Personalized service scores big. If a customer forgets her driver's license, an agent will take her home to pick it up. If the license has expired, Enterprise will take her to obtain a new one. Recently, Enterprise revenue grew at twice the rate of rival companies.[4]

Internal Marketing

The concept of customer satisfaction is usually discussed in terms of *external customers*—people or organizations that buy or use a firm's goods or services. But, as noted in Chapter 1, marketing in organizations concerned with quality must also address *internal customers*—employees or departments within the organization whose success depends on the work of other employees or departments. A person processing an order for a new piece of equipment is the internal customer of the salesperson who completed the sale, just as the person who bought the product is the salesperson's external customer. Although the order processor might never directly encounter an external customer, his or her performance can have a direct impact on the overall value the firm is able to deliver.

Internal marketing involves managerial actions that enable all members of an organization to understand, accept, and fulfill their respective roles in implementing a marketing strategy. Good internal customer satisfaction helps organizations to attract, select, and retain outstanding employees who appreciate and value their role in the delivery of superior service to external customers. Consider how National City Corp. enriched the banking experience for its customer base. A dual approach involved upgrading the bank's services to better suit customer needs in tandem with a major employee training program. The retraining was intended not only to stem staff turnover but to reduce defections by customers. Within the first year, 3,000 employees—a tenth of the workforce—graduated from National City Institute, a training program that focused on service. New hires now receive three weeks of training rather than three days. Salary increases and major investments in technology also served to boost employee morale. National City credits its customer-focused initiative with reducing turnover by 20 percent.[5]

An organizational culture that is steeped in customer orientation enables employees to achieve the firm's objectives—when employees are loyal, some of that loyalty rubs off on customers. When terrorist attacks on the World Trade Center coated New York's J&R Music World with grit and dust, forcing the retailer to close its doors for six weeks, all 800 employees were kept on at full pay. Recognizing that its employees are its biggest asset, J&R sought to maintain sales levels by cutting prices and adding free shipping rather than eliminating jobs. Many customers responded by deciding to wait to buy music until the store reopened.[6]

Employee knowledge and involvement are important goals of internal marketing. Companies that excel at satisfying customers typically place a priority on keeping employees informed about corporate goals, strategies, and customer needs. Employees must also have the necessary tools to address cus-

Briefly Speaking

The team that trusts—their leader and each other—is more likely to be successful.

*Mike Krzyzewski
(b. 1947)
Duke basketball coach*

tomer requests and problems in a timely manner. As we discussed in Chapter 5, companywide intranets aid the flow of communications between departments and functions. Several companies—like Harley-Davidson—also include key suppliers on their intranets as a means of speeding and easing communication of all aspects of business from product design to inventory control.

Employee satisfaction is another critical objective of internal marketing. Employees can seldom, if ever, satisfy customers when they themselves are unhappy. Dissatisfied employees are likely to spread negative word-of-mouth messages to relatives, friends, and acquaintances, and these reports can affect purchasing behavior. Satisfied employees buy their employer's products, sending a powerful message to customers. In an industry in which 100 percent employee turnover is common, The Container Store—which sells home organizers such as bins and shelving—boasts a level as low as 15 percent. Almost half of new hires come from employee referrals. Says CEO Kip Tindell, "A funny thing happens when you take the time to educate your employees, pay them well, and treat them as equals. You end up with extremely motivated and enthusiastic people." The Container Store credits its people-management strategies with sustaining sales increases of up to 25 percent each year.[7] The "Marketing Hits" box discusses another example of the power of positive employee attitudes—at U.S. Cellular.

Relationship Marketing

In rapidly increasing numbers, producers of goods and services have shifted away from transaction-based systems of marketing to longer-term, more customer-focused relationship systems. Table 6.1 summarizes the differences between the narrow focus of transaction marketing and the much broader view that relationship marketing takes.

Every marketing transaction involves a relationship between the buyer and seller. In a transaction-based situation, the relationship may be quite short in duration and narrow in scope. Few if any social relationships may develop. For example, a traveler running low on gas in an unfamiliar town will likely stop at the first gas station she encounters, regardless of whether it carries ExxonMobil, her preferred brand. When the driver gets back home, however, she is likely to return to her previous practice of buying at ExxonMobil. In short, the single emergency transaction is unlikely to affect future gasoline purchase patterns.

The customer-seller bonds developed in a relationship marketing situation, on the other hand, last longer and cover a much broader scope than those developed in transaction marketing. Customer contacts are generally more frequent. A companywide emphasis on customer service contributes to customer satisfaction. Figure 6.2 shows the need to blend quality and customer service with traditional elements of the marketing mix. When a company integrates customer service and quality with marketing, the result is a relationship marketing orientation.[8]

Relationship marketing creates a new level of interaction between buyers and sellers. Rather than focusing exclusively on attracting new customers, marketers have discovered that it pays to retain customers they already have. Moreover, customers who are satisfied with one of the firm's brands may be persuaded to try others. Consider the popularity of TV's new wave of celebrity chefs. Once confined to restaurant kitchens, the people who create great meals are

Marketing Hit

U.S. Cellular Spins Superior Service into Sales

Background. In the cell phone industry, the race for customers has reached a frantic pace. Marketers shell out millions to sign up new accounts, offering rock-bottom rates and free gadgetry that slash profit margins. Yet most companies lose an astounding 40 percent of those high-cost new customers each year. Bouncing from one provider to the next, customers complain that service goes downhill once contracts are signed.

The Strategy. U.S. Cellular, a wireless telecommunications company serving rural and medium-sized markets, sought to break its industry's money-losing cycle—instead of competing for new accounts, it focused on keeping existing customers happy. Identifying a link between improved employee relations and superior service, the company initiated an intensive training program to stem employee turnover, improve morale, and dramatically increase customer-retention rates. Six-week training sessions centered around solving problems and "making the customer smile." Using an array of tools such as surveys and focus groups, U.S. Cellular monitors and continually improves customer relationships.

The Outcome. Within 18 months, U.S. Cellular trimmed customer turnover by more than a sixth, achieving the lowest rate in the

continued on next page

Marketing Dictionary

internal marketing   Managerial actions that help all members of the organization understand and accept their respective roles in implementing a marketing strategy.

Marketing Hit

industry. With over 3.3 million customers, it is now the dominant carrier in most of its markets.

Lessons Learned. In a maturing industry, growth is more likely to come from enhancing existing customer relationships than from seeking new buyers. Excellent customer service starts with sound internal relationships—employees quickly communicate a sense of loyalty to customers.

SOURCES: Cordell Hauglie, "Promises to Employees? Culture Branding," *Performance Improvement,* Vol. 41, No. 1, accessed at the International Society Performance Improvement Web site, **http://www.ispi.org,** January 2002; Wendy Cole, "Suddenly Loyalty Is Back in Business," *Time Bonus Section, Your Business,* December 2001, p. Y13; Vince Vittore, "Mr. Big Mouth," *Telephony,* February 7, 2001, p. 34; Michael H. Mescon and Timothy S. Mescon, "Building on the Basics Helps to Create a Winner," *Atlanta Business Chronicle,* December 18, 2000.

TABLE 6.1   Comparing Transaction-Based Marketing and Relationship Marketing Strategies

Characteristic	Transaction Marketing	Relationship Marketing
Time orientation	Short-term	Long-term
Organizational goal	Make the sale	Emphasis on retaining customers
Customer service priority	Relatively low	Key component
Customer contact	Low to moderate	Frequent
Degree of customer commitment	Low	High
Basis for seller-customer interactions	Conflict manipulation	Cooperation; trust
Source of quality	Primarily from production	Companywide commitment

SOURCE: Adapted from Martin Christopher, Adrian Payne, and David Ballantyne, *Relationship Marketing.* Oxford, UK: Butterworth-Heineman Ltd., 1993, p. 4.

beginning to leverage their success by becoming their own brands. Chefs like Emeril LaGasse, Wolfgang Puck, and a host of others first connected with national audiences through TV's Food Network. In lively in-the-kitchen demonstrations, LaGasse quickly developed an easy camaraderie with mass audiences with whom he shared food, tastes, and a sense of humor. Then, like fellow chefs, he leveraged that intimate relationship with viewers by offering multiple lines of products under his name. From franchise restaurants, cookbooks, and cookware to spices, marinades, and packaged meals, top chefs have built extensive businesses around their on-air personalities. Customers are enticed with free recipes on the chef's Web sites, where they can buy knives, gift sets, gift certificates, clothing, and other

FIGURE 6.2 Relationship Marketing Orientation

FIGURE 6.3
Celebrity Chefs: Offering Multiple Products to a Core Base of Customers

branded merchandise online. Figure 6.3 shows how celebrity chefs Paul Prudhomme and Charlie Trotter count on their mass appeal to bring more and more products to the same core customers who watch their shows.[9]

Basic Foundations of Modern Buyer-Seller Relationships

Relationship marketing depends on the development of close ties between the buyer—whether an individual or a company—and the seller. This section considers the core elements of the buyer-seller relationship and how promises form the basis of relationship marketing.

Promises in Relationship Marketing

Relationship marketing is based on promises from organizations that go beyond obvious assurances that potential customers expect. A network of promises—outside the organization, within the organization, and between buyer and seller interactions—determines whether a marketing encounter will be positive or negative and will either enhance or detract from an ongoing buyer-seller relationship.[10]

Making Promises

Most firms make promises to potential customers through *external marketing.* As discussed earlier in the book, this term refers to the marketing efforts that a company directs toward customers, suppliers, and other parties outside the organization. These promises communicate what a customer can expect from the firm's goods or services.

For example, the NBC television network might run an advertisement for its upcoming coverage of the National Basketball Association finals, touting the great games, great coverage, and great

2

Identify and explain each of the core elements of relationship marketing.

FIGURE 6.4
**Making a Promise
to Customers**

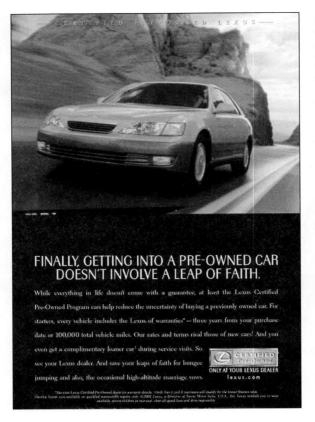

entertainment viewers will experience if they tune in. In this ad, the network would make a promise to its potential viewers and advertisers about what to expect and what the network would deliver. Similarly, in Figure 6.4, Lexus promises customers that its pre-owned vehicles come with a solid warranty that even includes a loaner when their car is in for service.

External marketing goes beyond advertising, however. Special sales promotions, the physical design of a business facility, its cleanliness and comfort, and the service process all provide other ways that companies make promises to potential customers. Tucson Electric Power Co., the electric utility for Tucson, Arizona, recently started a guaranteed cost and comfort program. Building contractors submit their plans to the utility, make recommended design and equipment changes, and undergo regular inspections during construction. In return, Tucson Electric promises flat heating and cooling costs for three years—regardless of jumps in the price of electricity or the owners' carelessness. Tucson Electric has guaranteed large custom-built homes and modest Habitat for Humanity houses. The guarantee results in upgraded building standards, competitive energy rates for consumers, and long-term customers for Tucson Electric.[11]

The promises that companies communicate to potential customers must be both realistic and consistent with one another. A firm that makes unrealistic promises can create a disappointed customer who may not buy the product again. For example, an infomercial for a new weight-loss product promises to work quickly. If after six weeks and considerable expense, you have not lost any weight, you are likely to be very disappointed.

Enabling Promises

A company can follow through on promises made to potential customers by external marketing only if it enables these promises through internal marketing. Internal marketing includes recruiting talented employees and providing them with the tools, training, and motivation they need to do their jobs effectively. The firm's structure itself must facilitate rather than hinder the provision of quality offerings. Efficient systems and processes, empowered front-line workers, and flat organizational hierarchies all contribute to a company's ability to provide quality goods and services.

It takes FedEx's entire 200,000-plus workforce to keep its promise to deliver 3.3 million packages to 210 countries—"Absolutely, Positively Overnight." The company invests over $100 million a year in training every employee how to play his or her role in meeting its high-speed, high-performance guarantee. Career development, leadership training, succession planning, organizational development, executive development, and safety training all work toward enabling FedEx's finely tuned, internal-marketing network.[12]

Keeping Promises

Every customer interaction with a business reaches the moment of truth when a product is provided to the customer. This action was defined in Chapter 1 as the exchange process. This exchange, the third stage in the buyer-seller relationship following external and internal marketing, defines the point at which a company keeps its promises.

The exchange also provides the place where long-term relationships develop between buyers and sellers. Positive encounters help to build long-term relationships, with the added benefit of possible positive word-of-mouth recommendations from satisfied customers to other potential customers. On the other hand, a company that fails to keep its promises at the exchange point in the marketing process may destroy any hope of continuing buyer-seller relationships. Even a single negative encounter can have a devastating effect.

The Relationship Marketing Continuum

Like all other interpersonal relationships, buyer-seller relationships function at a variety of levels. As an individual or firm progresses from the lowest level to the highest level on the continuum of relationship marketing, as shown in Table 6.2, the strength of commitment between the parties grows. The likelihood of a continuing, long-term relationship, as well, grows. Whenever possible, marketers want to move their customers along this continuum, converting them from Level 1 purchasers, who focus mainly on price, to Level 3 customers, who receive specialized services and value-added benefits that may not be available from another firm.[13]

First Level—Focus on Price

Interactions at the first level of relationship marketing are the most superficial and the least likely to lead to a long-term relationship. In the most prevalent examples of this first level, relationship marketing efforts rely on pricing and other financial incentives to motivate customers to enter into buying relationships with a seller. General Motors MasterCard rewards cardholders with credits for every dollar charged toward purchases of GM products. McDonald's sometimes offers two Big Macs for the price of one. CleanSweep Homewood Suites offers a "spring cleaning" weekend away. Guests who take a suite for four days receive coupons from ServiceMaster Clean and MerryMaids so that their homes are spotless when they return.[14]

Although these programs can be attractive to users, they may not create long-term buyer relationships. Because the programs are not customized to the needs of individual buyers, they are easily duplicated by competitors. When McDonald's runs its two-for-one special on Big Macs, there is a chance that Burger King will respond with a similar offer on its Whopper sandwiches. Within three years after American Airlines introduced its AAdvantage frequent-flyer program, some 23 other airlines enacted similar programs. The lesson here is that it takes more than a low price or other financial incentive to create a long-term relationship between buyer and seller.

3

Explain the steps in the development of a marketing relationship and how they lead to enhanced customer satisfaction.

TABLE 6.2 **Three Levels of Relationship Marketing**

Characteristic	Level 1	Level 2	Level 3
Primary bond	Financial *Exte AA card*	Social	Structural *Exam*
Degree of customization	Low	Medium	Medium to high
Potential for sustained competitive advantage	Low	Moderate	High
Examples	American Airlines' AAdvantage program	Harley-Davidson's Harley Owners Group (HOG)	Federal Express's PowerShip Program

SOURCE: Adapted from information in Leonard L. Berry, "Relationship Marketing of Services—Growing Internet, Emerging Perspectives," *Journal of the Academy of Marketing Science,* Fall 1995, p. 240.

A collaboration between Priority Club Rewards and Visa allows guests who choose participating hotels for a second stay to gain their choice of double points or double miles.

Although its owners' club has only 1,000 members, Indian's top brand, American Spirit, appeals to the bike-rider's desire for individuality. This distinctly American product enjoys a cult status similar to that of Harley-Davidson.

Second Level—Social Interactions

As buyers and sellers reach the second level of relationship marketing, their interactions develop on a social level—one that features deeper and less superficial links than the financially motivated first level. Sellers have begun to learn that social relationships with buyers can be very effective marketing tools. Customer service and communication are key factors at this stage.

The NFL builds on its already loyal fan bases through e-mail newsletters that reach 1.5 million subscribers. Not only are they customized for each of its 31 league teams, but they are even tailored toward each fan's special interests or favorite players. By monitoring the "click-through" behavior of avid fans, NFL marketers tailor merchandising to appeal to them.[15]

Third Level—Interdependent Partnership

At the third level of relationship marketing, relationships are transformed into structural changes that ensure buyer and seller are true business partners. As buyer and seller work more closely together, they develop a dependence on one another that continues to grow over time.

Although car manufacturers do not sell through the Internet, their Web strategies are structured to develop leads and provide support for dealers. By advertising on independent research sites like Kelley Blue Book (http://www.kbb.com) or Carmax.com (http://www.carmax.com), manufacturers such as Saturn entice browsers to their sites. Since there is no chance of being cornered by a salesperson before they are ready to buy, some customers find Web research a less stressful process than walking into a showroom. At the carmaker's site, customers can configure the exact car they want to buy, feature by feature. Saturn offers price and affordability calculators that help buyers figure out monthly payments. From there, Saturn buyers can find their local dealer and continue the sales process there at the price quoted on the Web site. DaimlerChrysler posts dealer inventory on its site, allowing buyers to find a perfect match for their dream car. Within the first few months of its "dealer inventory transparency" program, 70,000 people sent price requests to dealers—and almost a fifth of visitors to the site ended up buying a DaimlerChrysler vehicle.[16]

Through their Web strategies, Saturn and DaimlerChrysler strengthen relationships with dealers. Not only does this type of collaboration lead directly to increased sales through dealerships, but it enhances the entire buying experience, increasing customer satisfaction.

Enhancing Customer Satisfaction

Marketers monitor customer satisfaction through various methods of marketing research discussed in more detail in Chapter 7. As part of an ongoing relationship with customers, marketers must continually measure and improve how well they meet customer needs. As Figure 6.5 shows, three main steps are involved in this process: understanding customer needs, obtaining customer feedback, and instituting an ongoing program to ensure customer satisfaction.

Understanding Customer Needs

Knowledge of what customers need, want, and expect is a central concern of companies focused on building long-term relationships. This information is also a vital first step in setting up a system to measure *customer satisfaction*. Marketers must carefully monitor the characteristics of their product that really matter to customers. They also must remain constantly alert to new elements that might affect satisfaction.

Satisfaction can be measured in terms of the gaps between what customers expect and what they perceive they have received. Such gaps can produce favorable or unfavorable impressions. A product may be better than expected or worse than expected. To avoid unfavorable gaps, marketers need to keep in touch with the needs of current and potential customers. They must look beyond traditional performance measures and explore the factors that determine purchasing behavior in order to formulate customer-based missions, goals, and performance standards.

Obtaining Customer Feedback

The second step in measuring customer satisfaction is to compile feedback from customers regarding present performance. Increasingly, marketers try to improve customers' access to their companies by including toll-free 800 numbers or Web site addresses in their advertising. Most firms rely on reactive methods of collecting feedback. Rather than solicit complaints, they might, for example, monitor Usenet and other online discussion groups as a means of tracking customer comments and attitudes about the value received. Some companies hire mystery shoppers, who visit or call businesses posing as customers, to evaluate the service they receive. Their unbiased appraisals are usually conducted semiannually or quarterly to monitor employees, diagnose problem areas in customer service, and measure the impact of employee training.

FIGURE 6.5
Three Steps to Measure Customer Satisfaction

Briefly Speaking

If we are going to be leaders, we're going to have to make decisions with maybe 75 percent of the facts that we'd like to have. If you wait for 95 percent, you are going to be a follower.

Lawrence A. Weinbach Chairman and CEO, Unisys

HomeMadeSimple, a Web site sponsored by packaged-goods giant Procter & Gamble, counts on input from customers as a means of improving relationships with users of its products. The site features an ideas forum and a monthly poll, both providing direct customer feedback on such brands as Febreze, Dawn, and Swiffer. A monthly e-newsletter is responsive to customer comments and shares ideas on using P&G products.[17]

Any method that makes it easier for customers to complain benefits a firm and may be considered a blessing in disguise. Customer complaints offer firms the opportunity to overcome problems and prove their commitment to service. Customers often have greater loyalty to a company after a conflict has been resolved than if they had never complained at all.

Many organizations also use proactive methods to assess customer satisfaction, including visiting, calling, or mailing out written surveys to clients to find out their level of satisfaction. Xerox gathers information by mailing approximately 60,000 customer satisfaction surveys per month to its customers, and AT&T's Universal Credit Card division calls 2,500 customers every month to measure quality in the company's nine most important areas of service performance. Pizza Hut calls 50,000 customers each week to ask about their experiences at the restaurant chain's units. Many car dealers call or send surveys to customers asking them to rate the service they received, either in a purchase situation or service visit.

Building Buyer-Seller Relationships

Marketers of consumer goods and services have discovered that they must do more than simply create products and then sell them. With a dizzying array of products to choose from, many customers are seeking ways to simplify both their business and personal lives, and relationships provide a way to do this.

One reason consumers form continuing relationships is their desire to reduce choices. Through relationships, they can simplify information gathering and the entire buying process as well as decrease the risk of dissatisfaction. They find comfort in brands that have become familiar through their ongoing relationships with companies. Such relationships may lead to more efficient decision making by customers and higher levels of customer satisfaction.

A key benefit to consumers in long-term, buyer-seller relationships is the perceived positive value they receive. Relationships add value through increased opportunities for frequent customers to save money through discounts, rebates, and similar offers; via special recognition from the relationship programs; and through convenience in shopping. Figure 6.6 shows how retailer L.L. Bean seeks to encourage buyers to spend more—by offering free coupon dollars and monogramming to its best customers.

Marketers should also understand why consumers end relationships. Computerized technologies and the Internet have made consumers better informed than ever before by giving them unprecedented abilities to compare prices, products, and customer service. If they perceive that a competitor's products or customer service are better, customers may switch loyalties. Many consumers dislike feeling that they are locked into a relationship with one company, and that is reason enough for them to try a competing item next time they buy. Some customers simply become bored with their current providers and decide to sample the competition.

**FIGURE 6.6
The Benefits of
Becoming a
High-Value
Customer**

How Marketers Keep Customers

One of the major forces driving the push from transaction-based marketing to relationship marketing is the realization that retaining customers is far more profitable than losing them. Customers usually enable a firm to generate more profits with each additional year of the relationship. In fact, one marketing expert notes that a 5 percent gain in customer retention can pay off with an 80 percent increase in profits.[18]

A good example of this is the Marriott Rewards program, which now boasts 17 million members. Members spend an average of 2.5 times more at Marriott hotels than nonmembers and account for 40 percent of Marriott's total sales. Marriott has three elite levels in the program: Silver, Gold, and Platinum. Each offers special benefits and perks for Marriott's most frequent guests. Marriott Rewards is just one way in which the company seeks to invest in even stronger relationships from its high-value customers. Figure 6.7 illustrates another recent Marriott Rewards offer—visitors who stay for any three weekend nights get one weekend night free. Marriott periodically offers similar promotions to add value to the program and retain these important customers.[19]

An example of **frequency marketing,** programs like Marriott's reward top customers with cash, rebates, merchandise, or other premiums. Buyers who purchase an item more often earn higher rewards. Frequency marketing focuses on a company's best customers with the goal of increasing their motivation to buy even more of the same or other products from the seller.

Many different types of companies use frequency programs, from fast-food restaurants to retail stores, telecommunications companies, and travel firms. Popular programs include airline frequent-flyer programs, such as United Airlines' Mileage Plus, and retail programs, such as Hallmark's Gold Crown Card.

The Internet is proving a fertile medium for frequency-marketing initiatives. Borrowing from the airlines' frequent-flyer model, Harrah's Casino has created a Web-based program to reward frequent gamblers. Loyalty cards are swiped on the casino floor to monitor time spent at slot machines or card tables and to total up the sums gambled. A Web site allows members to view their points and learn how to earn more benefits as they gamble their way up to platinum or diamond status. The program is also able to identify which so-called "high-rollers" yield the highest profits.[20]

In addition to frequency programs, companies use **affinity marketing** to retain customers. Each of us holds certain things dear. Some may feel strongly about Eastern Michigan University, while others admire the New York Yankees. These symbols, along with an almost unending variety of others, are subjects of affinity programs. An affinity program is a marketing effort sponsored by an organization that solicits involvement by individuals who share common interests and activities. With affinity programs, organizations create extra value for members and encourage stronger relationships.

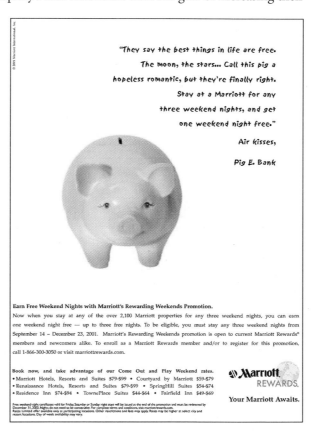

FIGURE 6.7
Rewards for High-Frequency Customers

Affinity credit cards are a popular form of this marketing technique. The sponsor's name appears prominently in promotional materials, on the card itself, and on monthly statements. For example, the National Association for Female Executives, a professional networking organization, offers qualified members a Gold Visa or MasterCard with no first-year fee and with low interest rates. A not-for-profit organization such as a charity or educational institution, such as the Smithsonian Institution, may sponsor a card if the issuer donates a percentage of user purchases to the group. Not all affinity programs involve credit cards. KETC, the St. Louis public television station, thanks members who contribute more than $50 annually with a diner's card that entitles them to discounts at participating restaurants.

Database Marketing

The use of information technology to analyze data about customers and their transactions is referred to as **database marketing.** The results form the basis of new advertising or promotions targeted to carefully identified groups of customers. Database marketing is a particularly effective tool for building relationships because it allows sellers to sort through huge quantities of data from multiple sources on the buying habits or preferences of thousands or even millions of customers. Companies are then able to track buying patterns, develop customer relationship profiles, customize their offerings and sales promotions, and even personalize customer service to suit the needs of targeted groups of customers. Properly used, databases can help companies in several ways, including these:

- Identifying their most profitable customers
- Calculating the lifetime value of each customer's business
- Creating a meaningful dialogue that builds relationships and encourages genuine brand loyalty
- Improving customer retention and referral rates
- Reducing marketing and promotion costs
- Boosting sales volume per customer or targeted customer group

Where do organizations find all the data that fill these vast marketing databases? Everywhere! Credit card applications, software registration, and product warranties all provide vital statistics of individual customers. Cash register scanners, customer opinion surveys, and sweepstakes entry forms may offer not just details of name, address, and income, but information on preferred brands and shopping habits. Web sites offer free access in return for personal data, allowing companies to amass increasingly rich marketing information. DaimlerChrysler recently developed a partnership with videogame maker Terminal Reality to create a new game that incorporates "cheats"—special codes players need to win. To find the codes, players need to log on to the DaimlerChrysler Web site. The personal details they provide—name, address, income, and other data—are captured for future database marketing use. In its recent Rocket Cash sweepstakes promotion for Sprite, The Coca-Cola Company used a hand-held touch-screen device to swipe the driver's licenses of teens and young adults gathered at rock concerts and other popular events. Not only was the firm able to capture names, addresses, and other valuable data, they also instantly verified the ages of all sweepstakes entrants.[21]

Interactive television promises to deliver even more valuable data—information on real consumer behavior and attitudes toward brands. Linked to digital television, sophisticated set-top boxes like TiVo and Replay TV are already able to collect vast amounts of data on television viewer behavior, organized in incredible detail. Once the technology makes its way into more homes, marketers will have firsthand knowledge of what kind of programming and products their targeted customers want. In addition, rather than using television to advertise to the masses, they will be able to talk directly to those viewers most interested in their products. At a click of a button, viewers will be able to skip ads, but they'll also be able to click to a full-length infomercial on any brand that captures their interest.[22]

As database marketing has become more complex, a variety of software tools and services will enable marketers to target consumers more and more narrowly while enriching their communications to selected groups. *Application service providers* (*ASPs*) assist marketers in capturing, manipulating, and analyzing masses of consumer data. For example, retail chain Blinds to Go, Inc., based in Iselin, New Jersey, uses an online service to sort and query customer information from 120 stores for use in direct marketing campaigns. Customer-specific purchasing records and buying-frequency data are immediately accessible via secure Internet connections. The Legal Aid Society for Washington Fund uses an ASP to manage extensive donor profile information, maximizing the effectiveness of personalized fundraising campaigns.[23]

Customer Relationship Management

4

Explain customer relationship management (CRM) and the role of technology in building customer relationships.

Emerging from relationship marketing, customer relationship management (CRM) is the combination of strategies and technologies that empowers relationship programs, reorienting the entire organization to a concentrated focus on satisfying customers. Made possible by technological advances, it leverages technology as a means to manage customer relationships and to integrate all stakeholders into a company's product design and development, manufacturing, marketing, sales, and customer service processes.

CRM represents a shift in thinking for everyone involved with a firm—from the CEO down through and encompassing all other key stakeholders, including suppliers, dealers, and other partners. All recognize that solid customer relations are fostered by similarly strong relationships with other major stakeholders.[24] Since CRM goes well beyond traditional sales, marketing, or customer services functions, it requires a top-down commitment and must permeate every aspect of a firm's business. Technology makes that possible, allowing firms—regardless of size and no matter how far-flung their operations—to manage activities across functions, locations, and among their internal and external partners.

CRM software systems are capable of making sense of the vast amounts of customer data that technology allows firms to collect. After several years of trying to patch together its existing technology to automate functions like customer service and sales lead management, IBM decided to seek a CRM solution. A custom-created software application was implemented at IBM's 26 customer service centers and connected employees worldwide. The impact was huge and immediate: Most customer inquiries were quickly and efficiently resolved, and the number of abandoned calls fell dramatically. Since customer service personnel spent significantly less time with each call, IBM was able to handle the same volume of calls with 450 fewer people.[25] Great Plains software by Microsoft, featured in Figure 6.8, is an example of widely used customer relationship management software. With Great Plains, Microsoft enables companies of all sizes to serve customers better, faster, and with ease.

Another key benefit of customer relationship management systems is that they are able to simplify complex business processes while keeping the best interests of customers at heart. Biotechnology company Amgen runs about 100 new drug trials each year, involving thousands of doctors and patients and hundreds of clinics. "Protocols" or rules for administering the drugs were so complicated that a third of doctors who signed up for a trial refused to participate again. On top of that, Amgen's system of paying doctors was abysmally inefficient. The result was a huge loss in terms of both money and knowledge, as doctors and patients defected from the trials. As part of its commitment to CRM, Amgen worked with Siebel Systems to create software that would make it easy for customers—in this case, physicians—to manage drug trials. The software is able to keep digital logs of each protocol, as well as each patient's progress. Not only is Amgen able to receive more reliable test results, but physicians get paid faster and are more willing to take part in new trials. Moreover, administration for the trials takes Amgen staff only a fifth of the time it took in the past. Here, a commitment to improve relationships with doctors has led to improved efficiency and real cost savings.[26]

Yet software solutions are just one component of a successful CRM initiative. Like Dylan's Candy Bar, whose successes are described at the beginning of this chapter, and Green Hills Farms, the subject of the end-of-chapter case, the most effective companies approach customer relationship management as a complete business strategy, in which people, processes,

Marketing Dictionary

database marketing Use of software to analyze marketing information, identifying and targeting messages toward specific groups of potential customers.

FIGURE 6.8
Great Plains Software:
A Customer
Relationship
Software Solution

and technology are all organized around delivering superior value to customers. Successful CRM systems share the following qualities:

- They are results driven. It is important that the firm decide on specific goals and benefits before attempting to implement a CRM strategy.

- They are implemented from the top down. The CEO and senior-level executives must be committed to changing the firm to a new focus on customers.

- They require investment in training. Remember that firms do not nurture customer relationships—their people do. Training must be companywide so that everyone knows that the firm is transforming itself. Training must also upgrade the skill sets of employees so that they are able to handle new tools.

- They communicate effectively across functions. Effective customer relationship management depends on cross-disciplinary teams that work together to solve customer problems. It shouldn't make any difference whether the customer interacts with the company directly through the sales force, over the Web, or indirectly through a reseller (or is accessing all of these channels simultaneously).

- They are streamlined. A concentrated focus on the customers allows firms to weed out wasteful business practices. If any function or process does not help the firm better serve its customers, it probably is not necessary. Streamlining also eliminates the need for costly customization when it comes to creating software solutions.

- They involve end users in creation of software solutions. Input from employees, suppliers, distributors, and any other partners who will use the systems is essential. It not only ensures that the systems meet the needs of all those who will implement them, but it encourages everyone to support the transition to customer relationship management.

- They constantly seek improvement. By tracking and measuring results, firms are able to continuously improve relationships with customers.[27]

Once the groundwork has been laid, technology solutions drive firms toward a clearer understanding of each customer and his or her needs.

Tom Siebel, who founded one of the first companies to develop CRM systems, credits customer relationship management with saving his sales-automation software firm. In 2000, Siebel Systems held a 70 percent share of its core market. Sales had doubled for the seventh straight year and were set to double again in 2001. A month before the recent recession began, Siebel's up-to-the-minute data on pending sales, gathered from 1,500 field agents, showed customers backing out of deals at an unprecedented rate. With a few clicks of his mouse, Siebel was able to see that this was no mere coincidence—all across the nation, companies were tightening their belts. To Siebel, there was just one possible explanation—the high-tech sector was about to crash. Within hours, Siebel's sales teams were visiting key accounts, closing as many deals as possible. Siebel changed the focus of the company from an aggressive growth strategy to a survival plan. He cut off three underperforming business units, laid off employees, slashed travel, marketing, and hiring budgets, and even cut executive salaries by 20 percent. When recession hit, Silicon Valley reeled and hundreds of dot.coms went under. Siebel Systems stayed financially healthy.[28]

Buyer-Seller Relationships in Business-to-Business Markets

Customer relationship management and relationship marketing are not limited to consumer goods and services. Building strong buyer-seller relationships is a critical component of business-to-business marketing as well.

Business-to-business marketing involves an organization's purchase of goods and services to support company operations or the production of other products. Buyer-seller relationships between companies involve working together to provide advantages that benefit both parties. These advantages might include lower prices for supplies, quicker delivery of inventory, improved quality and reliability, customized product features, and more favorable financing terms.

A **partnership** is an affiliation of two or more companies that assist each other in the achievement of common goals. Partnerships cover a wide spectrum of relationships from informal cooperative purchasing arrangements to formal production and marketing agreements. Such links can involve a single function or activity of production and marketing—for example, distribution—or all functions, such as product development, manufacturing, and marketing of a new product. In business-to-business markets, partnerships form the basis of relationship marketing.

A variety of common goals motivate firms to form partnerships. Companies may want to protect or improve their positions in existing markets, gain access to new domestic or international markets, or quickly enter into new markets. Expansion of a product line—to fill in gaps, broaden the product line, or differentiate the product—is another key reason for joining forces. Other motives include sharing resources, reducing costs, warding off threats of future competition, raising or creating barriers to entry, and learning new skills. "Solving an Ethical Controversy" describes the rocky partnership between video-rental giant Blockbuster and the major film studios.

Choosing Business Partners

How does an organization decide which companies to select as partners? The first priority is to locate firms that can add value to the relationship—whether through financial resources, contacts, extra manufacturing capacity, technical know-how, or distribution capabilities. The greater the value added, the greater the desirability of the partnership. In many cases, the attributes of each partner complement those of the other; each firm brings something to the relationship that

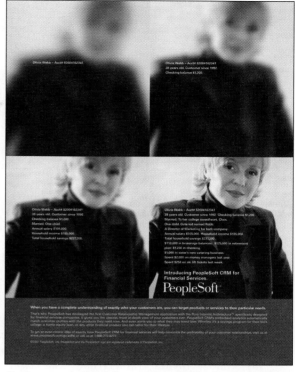

Customer relationship management technology offers marketers more information than traditional customer databases can provide.

5
Describe the buyer-seller relationship in business-to-business marketing.

Marketing Dictionary

partnership   Affiliation of two or more companies that assist each other in the achievement of common goals.

right wrong
Solving an Ethical Controversy

When Strategic Alliances Turn Sour

In 1997, choked by the high cost of new movie releases, Blockbuster entered an alliance with the major Hollywood studios. In exchange for getting each video at half price, Blockbuster would pay 40 percent of rental revenues to the studios. Lower cost coupled with broader selection strengthened Blockbuster's market position—sales leaped by 14 percent annually. The alliance was a moneymaker for the studios, too—a revenue stream worth $14 billion a year. Hinting at plans to phase out the video rental-sharing agreement, Blockbuster refused to extend it to DVDs, estimated to account for half of Blockbuster's revenues by 2003.

Angered at being excluded from the home-viewing market for DVDs, Hollywood fought back by pricing new releases low enough to encourage movie fans to buy rather than rent. This strategy invites retailers like Wal-Mart to slice into Blockbuster's rental revenues.

The battle is set to move to the Internet. Moviefly.com, an alliance between five major studios, will deliver movies on demand over the Web. Walt Disney Company is planning its own on-demand strategy. Recently, Blockbuster muscled its way into a licensing deal with Universal to create its own video-on-demand channel. When Universal balked, Blockbuster refused to stock two of Universal's new releases. A day later, Universal signed. Though this deal eventually fell apart, Blockbuster is not likely to let itself be shut out in the future. If a studio wants Blockbuster to carry its movies, the price is a license to distribute over the Internet as well.

Is Blockbuster exploiting its position as a near-monopolist by playing hardball with its partners?

PRO

1. Movies-on-demand could quickly erode Blockbuster's dominance. The company has as much right to license those rights as anyone else.
2. Blockbuster's core asset is its customers—the company knows the rental preferences of more than 52 million movie-viewers. By working with Blockbuster, the studios can provide better service and selection.

CON

1. The studios own the movie content—they should be free to choose the terms on which they license it.
2. If the studios are not the first to exploit Internet distribution, they risk losing out by having others spread their content.

Summary

The studios need video rental revenues, so for now they need Blockbuster, too. Delivery of movies over the Internet is still a long way off. If they want to benefit from Blockbuster's customer relationships, a continuing alliance is in the studios' favor.

SOURCES: "About Us," Blockbuster Web site, http://www.blockbuster.com, accessed January 15, 2003; John Gorham, "The Player," *Forbes*, September 3, 2001, pp. 60–61; Ron Grover, "Hollywood vs. Blockbuster, Now on DVD," *BusinessWeek*, August 23, 2001, http://www.businessweek.com; "Blockbuster vs. the Studios," *BusinessWeek*, August 19, 2001, http://www.businessweek.com.

---

the other party needs but cannot provide on its own. Some partnerships join firms with similar skills and resources, however, perhaps motivated to reduce costs.

Organizations must share similar values and goals for a partnership to succeed in the long run. Walt Disney Records forged a partnership with Kellogg Cereals that builds sales of Disney CDs while moving newer cereal brands like Mickeys' Magix, Buzz Blasts, and Hunny B's off grocery store shelves. Free on-the-pack sampler CDs encourage families to buy the cereals, and $2-off coupons for full-length CDs spur sales at Disney. Since both marketers target the same group of customers—families with young children—the ongoing campaign succeeds in generating excitement for two distinct products in a single promotion.[29]

6

Compare the different types of business partnerships and explain how they contribute to relationship marketing.

Types of Partnerships

Companies form four key types of partnerships in business-to-business markets: buyer, seller, internal, and lateral partnerships. The following section briefly examines each category.

In a *buyer partnership,* a firm purchases goods and services from one or more providers. For example, a company may contract with a certified public accountant (CPA) to conduct annual audits of its accounting system and to file federal and state income tax returns. Another company might purchase pens, pencils, and other office supplies exclusively from Office Depot.

When a company assumes the buyer position in a relationship, it has a unique set of needs and requirements that vendors must meet to make the relationship successful over a long period of time. While buyers want sellers to provide fair prices, quick delivery, and good quality, a lasting relationship often requires more effort. To induce a buyer to form a long-term partnership, a supplier must also be responsive to the purchaser's unique needs. If the buyer has a rush job that must be done in one hour, a vendor will score highly if it can perform. Similarly, buyers want reliable partners. Suppose a caterer contracts with a new food broker to provide ingredients for a major charity fund-raising dinner. The supplier, however, fails to perform satisfactorily. The caterer is not likely to use this food broker again, and no relationship results.

Seller partnerships set up long-term exchanges of goods and services in return for cash or other valuable consideration. Sellers, too, have specific needs as partners in ongoing relationships. Most prefer to develop long-term relationships with their partners. Sellers also want prompt payment.

The importance of *internal partnerships* is widely recognized in business today. The classic definition of the word *customer* as the buyer of a good or service is now more carefully defined in terms of external customers. However, customers within an organization also have their own needs. In a company that manufactures cell phones, the unit that assembles the phones is a customer of the firm's purchasing department. In essence, the manufacturing plant "buys" cell phone parts from the purchasing department, and the purchasing department supplies these parts to the plant. In this partnership, the purchasing department must continue to fulfill the needs of manufacturing by selecting vendors that can provide the parts needed with the price, quality, and time-frame characteristics specified by manufacturing. Similarly, the payroll department is a customer of all company employees; data processing is a customer of the accounting department; and a supervisor may be considered the customer of his or her employees.

Internal partnerships are the foundation of an organization and its ability to meet its commitments to external entities. If the purchasing department selects a parts vendor that fails to ship on the dates required by manufacturing, production will halt, and phones will not be delivered to customers as promised. As a result, external customers will likely seek other, more reliable suppliers. Without building and maintaining internal partnerships, an organization will have difficulty meeting the needs of its external partnerships.

Lateral partnerships include strategic alliances with other companies or with not-for-profit organizations, and research alliances with universities and colleges. The relationship is focused on external entities—such as customers of the partner firm—and involves no direct buyer-seller interactions. Strategic alliances are discussed in a later section of this chapter.

Improving Buyer-Seller Relationships in Business-to-Business Markets

Organizations that know how to find and nurture partner relationships, whether through informal deals or contracted partnerships, can enhance revenues and increase profits. Partnering often leads to lower prices, better products, and improved distribution, resulting in higher levels of customer satisfaction. Partners who know each other's needs and expectations are more likely to satisfy them and forge stronger long-term bonds.

In the past, business relationships were conducted primarily in person, over the phone, or by mail. Today, businesses are using the latest electronic, computer, and communications technology to link up. E-mail, the Internet, and other telecommunications services allow businesses to communicate anytime and anyplace. Chapter 5 discussed the business role of the Internet in detail. The following sections explore other ways that buyers and sellers cooperate in business-to-business markets.

7

Describe how relationship marketing incorporates national account selling, electronic data interchange, vendor-managed inventories, and collaborative planning, forecasting, and replenishment techniques.

National Account Selling

Some relationships are more important than others due to the large investments at stake. Large manufacturers like Procter & Gamble pay special attention to the needs of major retailers such as Wal-Mart, Target, and others, which sell many millions of dollars of products each year. Manufacturers use a technique called *national account selling* (discussed in detail in Chapter 19) to serve their largest, most profitable customers. The cluster of vendor offices in northwestern Arkansas—near Wal-Mart's home office—suggests how national account selling might be implemented.

The advantages of national account selling are many. By assembling a team of individuals to serve just one account, the seller demonstrates the depth of its commitment to the customer. The buyer-seller relationship is strengthened as both collaborate to find solutions that are mutually beneficial. Finally, cooperative buyer-seller efforts can bring about dramatic improvements in both efficiency and effectiveness for both partners. These improvements find their way to the bottom line in the form of decreased costs and increased profits.[30]

Business-to-Business Databases

As noted earlier, databases are indispensable tools in relationship marketing. They are also essential in building business-to-business relationships. Using information generated from sales reports, scanners, and many other sources, sellers can create databases that help to guide their own efforts and those of buyers who resell products to final users. Quaker Oats teamed with San Francisco–based ThirdAge Media, which operates an Internet site geared to older adults, to build a database of health information. The Heart Smart Challenge offered 1,500 ThirdAge members a free bowl of oatmeal every day for a month in exchange for information on their cholesterol levels. Quaker tracked and tabulated the responses and used them in a promotional campaign documenting the link between good nutrition and cardiovascular health. At the same time, ThirdAge acquired valuable data about the health and interests of its members.[31]

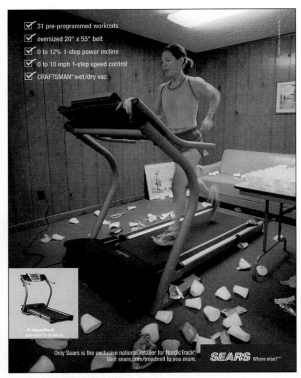

- ☑ 31 pre-programmed workouts
- ☑ oversized 20" x 55" belt
- ☑ 0 to 12% 1-step power incline
- ☑ 0 to 10 mph 1-step speed control
- ☑ CRAFTSMAN® wet/dry vac

Only Sears is the exclusive national retailer for NordicTrack. Visit sears.com/treadmill to see more. *SEARS* Where else?™

Sears's relationship with its vendors allows for improved inventory control and cost savings across its 900 stores.

Electronic Data Interchange

Technology has transformed the ways in which companies control their inventories and replenish stock. Gone are the days when a retailer would notice stocks were running low, call the vendor, check prices, and reorder. Today's **electronic data interchanges (EDIs)** automate the entire process. EDI involves computer-to-computer exchanges of invoices, orders, and other business documents. It allows firms to reduce costs and improve efficiency and competitiveness. Retailers like Wal-Mart, Dillard's, and Lowe's all require vendors to use EDI as a core **quick-response merchandising** tool. Quick response merchandising is a just-in-time strategy that reduces the time merchandise is held in inventory, resulting in substantial cost savings. An added advantage of EDI is that it opens new channels for gathering marketing information that is helpful in developing long-term business-to-business relationships.

Vendor-Managed Inventory

The proliferation of electronic data interchange and the constant pressure on suppliers to improve response time has led to another way for buyers and sellers to do business. **Vendor-managed inventory (VMI)** has replaced buyer-managed inventory in many instances. It is an inventory management system in which the seller—based on an existing agreement with the buyer—determines how much of a product a buyer needs and automatically ships new supplies to that buyer.[32]

Supply chain management. Visit the Web site of Ecomworld (**http://www.ecomworld.com**), the online resource for B2B commerce. Choose the link for "supply chain management," and select three or more facts about supply chain management that you can contribute during a classroom discussion on the topic.

Sears collaborates with its appliance vendors to manage inventory in its 900 stores nationwide. Supply-chain management software collects data both from Sears's vendor network and across multiple stores. The application alerts Sears to any potential shortages or overstocks before they have a chance to create a problem. Since vendors also have access to information in the system, they have the opportunity to resolve possible issues, thereby maintaining good relationships with the buyer. While the system currently manages only Sears's appliance vendor relationships, the company expects that if rolled out to Sears's entire vendor network, it could result in inventory savings of tens of millions of dollars.[33]

Some firms, such as Wal-Mart, have modified VMI to an approach called collaborative planning, forecasting, and replenishment (CPFAR). This is a planning and forecasting technique involving collaborative efforts by both purchasers and vendors. Ford Motor Company's sophisticated system manages not just inventory levels of auto parts but factors in transportation routes to assembly plants, freight costs, and many other variables.[34]

Managing the Supply Chain

Good relationships between businesses require careful management of the **supply chain** (sometimes called the *value chain*), which is the entire sequence of suppliers that contribute to the creation and delivery of a product. This process affects both upstream relationships between the company and its suppliers and downstream relationships with the product's end users. Figure 6.9 illustrates the supply chain for Dell. Raw materials go into making subassemblies. When Dell receives an order, these subassemblies are put together into a finished computer that is then shipped to the buyer. The first two steps shown in Figure 6.9 are Dell's upstream relationships, and the final two steps are its downstream relationship with its customers.

Effective supply-chain management can provide an important competitive advantage for a business marketer that results in the following:

- Increased innovation
- Decreased costs
- Improved conflict resolution within the chain
- Improved communication and involvement among members of the chain

FIGURE 6.9
The Dell Supply Chain

Raw Materials

Subassemblies

Finished Goods Assembled to Order in the Channel

Final Demand

SOURCES: Charles H. Fine, "The Primary of Chains," *Supply Chain Management Review*, Spring 1999, p. 80. Excerpt from Charles H. Fine, *Clockspeed: Winning Industry Control in the Age of Temporary Advantage* (Perseus Books, 1998).

Marketing Dictionary

electronic data interchange (EDI)   Computer-to-computer exchanges of invoices, orders, and other business documents.

quick response merchandising   Just-in-time strategy that reduces the time a retailer must hold merchandise in inventory, resulting in substantial cost savings.

vendor-managed inventory (VMI)   Inventory management system in which the seller—based on an existing agreement with a buyer—determines how much of a product is needed.

supply (value) chain   Sequence of suppliers that contribute to the creation and delivery of a good or service.

Several software applications and services are available that promise to simplify the supply chain for companies large and small.

By coordinating operations with the other companies in the chain, boosting quality, and improving its operating systems, a firm can improve speed and efficiency. Because companies spend considerable resources on goods and services from outside suppliers, cooperative relationships can pay off in many ways.[35]

Business-to-Business Alliances

Strategic alliances are the ultimate expression of relationship marketing. Recall from Chapter 1 that a *strategic alliance* is a partnership formed to create a competitive advantage. These more formal long-term partnership arrangements improve each partner's supply-chain relationships and enhance flexibility in operating in today's complex and rapidly changing marketplace. The size and location of strategic partners is not important. Strategic alliances include businesses of all sizes, of all kinds, and in many locations; it is what each partner can offer the other that is important.

Companies can structure strategic alliances in two ways. Alliance partners can establish a new business unit in which each takes an ownership position. In such a joint venture, one partner might own 40 percent, while the other owns 60 percent. Alternatively, the partners may decide to form a cooperative relationship that is less formal and does not involve ownership—for example, a joint new-product design team. The cooperative alliance can operate more flexibly and can change more easily as market forces or other conditions dictate. In either arrangement, the partners agree in advance on the skills and resources, such as those listed in Table 6.3, that each will bring into the alliance to achieve their mutual objectives and gain a competitive advantage.

Companies form many types of strategic alliances today. Some create horizontal alliances between firms at the same level in the supply

---

TABLE 6.3   Resources and Skills That Partners Contribute to Strategic Alliances

RESOURCES		SKILLS
Patents	Customer base	Marketing skills
Product lines	Marketing resources	• Innovation and product development
Brand equity	• Marketing infrastructure	• Positioning and segmentation
Reputation	• Sales force size	• Advertising and sales promotion
• For product quality	Established relationship with:	Manufacturing skills
• For customer service	• Suppliers	• Miniaturization
• For product innovation	• Marketing intermediaries	• Low-cost manufacturing
Image	• End-use customers	• Flexible manufacturing
• Companywide	Manufacturing resources	Planning and implementation skills
• Business unit	• Location	R&D skills
• Product line/brand	• Size, scale economies, scope economies, excess capacity, newness of plan and equipment	Organizational expertise, producer learning, and experience effects
Knowledge of product-market		
	Information technology and systems	

SOURCE: Adapted from P. Rajan Varadarajan and Margaret H. Cunningham, "Strategic Alliances: A Synthesis of Conceptual Foundations," *Journal of the Academy of Marketing Science,* Fall 1995, p. 292.

chain; others define vertical links between firms at adjacent stages. The firms may serve the same or different industries. Alliances can involve cooperation among rivals who are market leaders or between a market leader and a follower.

Strategic alliances can also be domestic or international. SkyTeam is an international airline network that includes Delta Airlines, Aeromexico, Alitalia, Air France, CSA Czech Airlines, and Korean Air. A recent global advertising campaign, "Caring Hands," is built around the consumer and focuses on amenities offered to passengers.[36]

Evaluating Customer Relationship Programs

Service is to exceed the expectation of the customers.

8

Identify and evaluate the most common measurement and evaluation techniques within a relationship marketing program.

One of the most important measures of relationship marketing programs, whether in consumer or business-to-business markets, is the **lifetime value of a customer:** the revenues and intangible benefits such as referrals and customer feedback that a customer brings to the seller over an average lifetime, less the amount the company must spend to acquire, market to, and serve the customer. Long-term customers are usually more valuable assets than new ones, because they buy more, cost less to serve, refer other customers, and provide valuable feedback. The "average lifetime" of a customer relationship depends on industry and product characteristics. Customer lifetime for a consumer product like microwave pizza or breath mints may be very short, while that for a computer system will last longer.

For a simple example of a lifetime value calculation, assume that a Chinese takeout restaurant determines that its average customer buys dinner twice a month at an average cost of $25 per order over a lifetime of five years. That business translates this calculation to revenues of $600 per year and $3,000 for five years. The restaurant can calculate and subtract its average costs for food, labor, and overhead to arrive at the per-customer profit. This figure serves as a baseline against which to measure strategies to increase the restaurant's sales volume, customer retention, or customer referral rate.

Another approach is to calculate the payback from a customer relationship, or the length of time it takes to break even on customer acquisition costs. Assume that an Internet-service provider spends $75 per new customer on direct mail and enrollment incentives. Based on average revenues per subscriber, the company takes about three months to recover that $75. If an average customer stays with the service 32 months and generates $800 in revenues, the rate of return is nearly 11 times the original investment. Once the customer stays past the payback period, the provider should make a profit on that business.

In addition to lifetime value analysis and payback, companies use many other techniques to evaluate relationship programs, including:

- Tracking rebate requests, coupon redemption, credit-card purchases, and product registrations

- Monitoring complaints and returned merchandise and analyzing why customers leave

Marketing Hit

Improving Internet Research by Measuring Relationships, Not Just Eyeballs

Background. Since the emergence of the Internet, e-marketers have struggled to find the best system to measure performance. A popular technique was to count "eyeballs"—the number of site hits, or visits. A simple formula gave each eyeball a value. Sites selling products or charging for access were assessed in terms of sales per customer. For no-cost sites like Yahoo!, ad revenue was the key indicator.

The Challenge. In the recent recession, Amazon still spent more per customer than it made, while tumbling ad revenues rattled even high-traffic sites like Yahoo! A decline in the growth of Internet usage meant marketers needed new ways to turn their millions of eyeballs into long-term profits.

The Strategy. By finding out more about site visitors—what they do on the Web and what they want from it—marketers can devise ways to make their visits more rewarding. Yahoo! now offers premium services targeted to a small but lucrative part of its vast audience. Armed with knowledge of the preferences of high-frequency visitors, other sites have diversified their revenue streams to include ads, sponsorships, products, premium services, and licenses—all geared around a core of loyal customers.

continued on next page

Exam

Marketing Dictionary

lifetime value of a customer   Revenues and intangible benefits, such as referrals and customer feedback, that a customer brings to the seller over an average lifetime, less the amount the company must spend to acquire, market to, and service the customer.

Marketing Hit

The Outcome. The more e-marketers offer customers, the better their chances of keeping them. By counting relationships rather than eyeballs, they are able to cross-market multiple products to a loyal site audience.

SOURCES: "ISPs Diversifying Services to Meet Demand," CyberAtlas Web site, **http://www.cyberatlas.internet.com**, accessed April 2, 2002; Kara Swisher, "What Matters? Relationships, Not Eyeballs," *The Wall Street Journal*, August 6, 2001, p. B1; Erick Schonfeld, "How Much Are Your Eyeballs Worth?" *Fortune*, February 21, 2000, pp. 197–204.

- Reviewing reply cards, comment forms, and surveys
- Monitoring "click-though" behavior on Web sites to identify why customers stay and why they leave

These tools give the organization information about customer priorities so that managers can make changes to their systems, if necessary, and set appropriate, measurable goals for relationship programs.

A hotel chain may set a goal of improving the rate of repeat visits from 44 percent to 52 percent. A mail-order company may want to reduce time from 48 to 24 hours to process and mail orders. If a customer survey reveals late flight arrivals as the number-one complaint of an airline's passengers, the airline might set an objective of increasing the number of on-time arrivals from 87 percent to 93 percent.

Companies large and small are able to implement technology to aid in measuring the value of customers and the return on investment from expenditures developing customer relationships. They are able to choose from among a growing number of software products, many of which are tailored to specific industries or that are flexible enough to suit companies of varying sizes. The "Marketing Hits" box on the previous page explains how e-marketers have tried to pin down the value of their Internet customers.

Strategic Implications of Marketing in the 21st Century

Clearly, a focus on relationship marketing helps companies create better ways to communicate with customers and to develop long-term relationships. A company's relationship marketing efforts challenge managers to develop strategies that closely integrate customer service, quality, and marketing functions. This goal usually requires changes in organizational philosophy, structure, and processes in order to be effective. By leveraging technology—both through database marketing and through customer relationship management applications—companies are able to compare the costs of acquiring and maintaining customer relationships with the profits received from these customers. This information allows managers to evaluate the potential returns from investing in relationship marketing programs.

Relationships are not limited to customers but are a way of doing business with partners—including vendors, suppliers, and other companies—outside the firm. Partners can structure relationships in many different ways to improve performance, and these choices will vary for consumer and business markets. In business-to-business relationships such as vendor-retailer partnerships, it is especially important to build shared trust. This goal may require both parties to provide detailed financial information—data some may prefer to keep confidential. However, as the Dylan's Candy Bar case at the beginning of the chapter demonstrates, successful partnerships start with the premise that both parties need to make reasonable profits, and cooperation can pay off in lower costs and higher sales for all concerned.

Summary of Chapter Objectives

1. Contrast transaction-based marketing with relationship marketing.

Transaction-based marketing refers to buyer-seller exchanges characterized by limited communications and little or no ongoing relationships between the parties. The primary goal is to entice a buyer to make a purchase based on such reasons as low price, convenience, or packaging. Relationship marketing is the development and maintenance of long-term, cost-effective relationships with individual customers, suppliers, employees, and other partners for mutual benefit. Its primary goal is to create a bond with the partners that has much broader scope than a simple buyer-seller transaction.

2. Identify and explain each of the core elements of relationship marketing.

The core elements of relationship marketing are the three promises that form the basis of the relationship. Most companies make promises to potential customers through external marketing. Enabling those promises requires that the company have in place an internal system that makes it possible to carry them out. By keeping its promises, the company is able to begin a relationship with the customer, based on the customer knowledge of satisfactory products received.

3. Explain the steps in the development of a marketing relationship and explain how they lead to enhanced customer satisfaction.

As an individual or organization moves into a marketing relationship, the strength of commitment between the parties proceeds through three primary levels. First, purchasers focus mainly on price. Interactions are superficial and are unlikely to lead to a long-term relationship. As the buyer and seller reach the second level, their interactions develop on a social basis, one that features deeper and less superficial links than financial motivation. The third level of relationship marketing involves structural changes that make buyer and seller true partners in business. As they work more closely together, they develop a dependence on one another that continues to grow over time.

At each level, marketers can use several techniques to measure and enhance customer satisfaction. Based on positive and negative customer feedback garnered through toll-free customer comment lines or Web sites, surveys, or other methods, marketers can improve both products and customer service. Several companies use such techniques as customer rewards, frequent buyer programs, and affinity programs to increase satisfaction and retain customers over the long term. Also, database marketing helps firms focus on improving levels of satisfaction among their most valuable customer groups.

4. Explain customer relationship management (CRM) and the role of technology in building customer relationships.

Customer relationship management is the combination of strategies and technologies that empowers relationship programs, reorienting the entire organization to a concentrated focus on satisfying customers. Made possible by technological advances, it leverages technology as a means to manage customer relationships and to integrate all stakeholders into a company's product design and development, manufacturing, marketing, sales, and customer service processes. CRM allows firms to manage vast amounts of data from multiple sources to improve overall customer satisfaction. The most effective companies approach CRM as a complete business strategy in which people, processes, and technology are all organized around delivering superior value to customers.

5. Describe the buyer-seller relationship in business-to-business marketing.

By developing buyer-seller relationships, companies work together for their mutual benefit. Advantages may include lower prices for supplies, faster delivery of inventory, improved quality or reliability, customized product features, or more favorable financing terms. Business partnerships cover a wide spectrum of relationships, but partners usually share similar values and goals that help the alliance endure over time.

6. Compare the different types of business partnerships and explain how they contribute to relationship marketing.

Companies form four basic types of relationships in business-to-business markets. In a buyer partnership, a firm purchases goods and services from one or more providers. When a company assumes the buyer position, it has a unique set of needs and requirements that the other firm must meet to make the relationship successful over a long period of time. Seller partnerships set up long-term exchanges of goods and services in return for cash or other valuable consideration. Sellers, too, have their own unique needs as partners in ongoing relationships. Internal partnerships form the foundation of an organization and its ability to meet its commitments to external entities. Lateral partnerships might include strategic relationships between firms and their competitors, global alliances, alliances with not-for-profit organizations, and research alliances with government organizations.

Partnerships form the basis of relationship marketing by enabling a firm to achieve long-term, cost-effective bonds with its employees, customers, suppliers, distributors, and even competitors.

7. Describe how relationship marketing incorporates national account selling, electronic data interchange, vendor-managed inventories, and collaborative planning, forecasting, and replenishment techniques.

Contemporary businesses use the latest electronic, computer, and communications technology to network with internal and external customers. National account selling assists firms in forming a strong commitment with key buyers, resulting in improvements in efficiency and effectiveness for both parties. The use of electronic data interchanges allows firms to reduce costs and improve efficiency and competitiveness. Vendor-managed inventory is a system in which sellers can automatically restock to previously requested levels. By contrast, the collaborative planning, forecasting, and replenishment (CPFAR) approach bases plans and forecasts on collaborative seller-vendor efforts.

All these techniques help form strong bonds and build long-term relationships among buyers and sellers. A common goal of maximizing profits and increasing competitiveness helps sepa-rate firms act together to achieve market efficiencies which, in turn, better serve the end customer.

8. Identify and evaluate the most common measurement and evaluation techniques within a relationship marketing program.

The effectiveness of relationship marketing programs can be measured using several methods. In the lifetime value of a customer, the revenues and intangible benefits that a customer brings to the seller over an average lifetime, less the amount the company must spend to acquire, market to, and service the customer, are calculated. With this method, a company may determine its costs to service each customer and develop ways to increase profitability. Payback method calculates how long it takes to break even on customer acquisition costs. Other measurements include tracking rebates, coupons, and credit card purchases; monitoring complaints and returns; and reviewing reply cards, comment forms, and surveys. These tools give the organization information about customer priorities so that managers can make changes to their systems and set measurable goals.

Marketing Terms You Need to Know

transaction-based
    marketing 164
relationship marketing 164
customer relationship
    management (CRM) 164
internal marketing 166

frequency marketing 175
affinity marketing 175
database marketing 176
partnership 179
electronic data interchange
    (EDI) 182

quick response
    merchandising 182
vendor-managed inventory
    (VMI) 182
supply (value) chain 183

lifetime value of a
    customer 185

Other Important Marketing Terms

external customer 166
internal customer 166
employee satisfaction 167
external marketing 169

customer satisfaction 173
interactive television 176
application service providers
    (ASPs) 176

business-to-business
    marketing 179
buyer partnership 180
seller partnership 181

internal partnership 181
lateral partnership 181
national account selling 182
strategic alliance 184

Review Questions

1. Trace the evolution from transaction-based to relationship marketing and explain why relationship marketing is appropriate for today's marketing environment.
2. Distinguish between external customers and internal customers. Cite examples of each.
3. Briefly describe the three types of promises that form the basis of relationship marketing. Give an example of each.
4. Explain the role of customer feedback in achieving customer satisfaction. What are the primary methods of securing such feedback?
5. Explain affinity programs, frequent buyer programs, and database marketing. How are these concepts used to build relationships with consumers?

6. Explain customer relationship management. Describe the elements that an effective CRM system requires and the role of technology in customer relationship management programs.
7. Summarize the reasons why businesses form partnerships. Identify the four types of business partnerships.
8. Define supply-chain management and strategic alliances. How do these concepts build relationships and provide competitive advantages?
9. What are national account selling, EDI, VMI, and CPFAR? Explain their roles in relationship marketing.
10. What are the major techniques by which companies can measure and evaluate the effectiveness of their relationship marketing programs? Why should a company calculate the lifetime value of a customer?

Projects and Teamwork Exercises

1. First set up teams. Then have each team select an organization in your area and devise a relationship marketing strategy that could help it improve customer relations. How could your relationship marketing strategy increase customer-retention rates and find new customers?

2. A hotel chain's database has information on guests that includes demographics, number of visits, and room preferences. Describe how the chain can use this information to develop several relationship marketing programs. How can it use a more general database to identify potential customers and to personalize its communications with them?

3. Select a local business enterprise. Find out as much as you can about its customer base, marketing strategies, and internal functions. Consider whether a customer relationship management focus would help the enterprise's competitive position. Argue your position in class.

4. Find examples of a strategic alliance in current business magazines. In pairs, analyze the partners' motives for forming the alliance, their place in the supply chain, and the benefits to each member. Compare your findings with other pairs of students.

5. Find an example of an operational supply chain. Draw, label, and explain this supply chain.

'net Work

http://www.microsoft
.com/education

1. Relationship marketing. Microsoft provides a great deal of assistance to educators and students who use the company's products. Visit the Web site listed at the left and make a list of five resources Microsoft has available for educators and students using Microsoft Office software.

http://www.frequency
marketing.com

2. Loyalty marketing programs. Visit the Web site listed here. Review the goods and services offered to assist in the development of frequency marketing programs. Then, locate Web sites that offer coupons or other rewards to frequent visitors. Write a brief summary of what you found.

http://www.ecomworld
.com/portals/CRM

3. Customer relationship marketing. Go to http://www.ecomworld.com/portals/CRM and select five facts about customer relationship marketing that you will be prepared to present during a classroom discussion of the topic or as a hand-in assignment.

Note: Internet Web addresses change frequently. If you don't find the exact sites listed, you may need to access the organization or company's home page and search from there.

CASE 6.1

Green Hills Farms: Leveraging Loyalty to Compete with Giants

In the retail grocery business, horror stories abound of mom-and-pop stores eaten alive when chains like Safeway come to town. Yet Green Hills Farms, started as a summer farm stand in Syracuse, New York, over 60 years ago, has won out against the supermarket giants. Its secret? Customer relationships.

Green Hills was an independent grocery store facing fierce competition. CEO Gary Hawkins needed to find ways to keep customers, but he was not convinced that conventional promotions could help. The trouble was, they were built around products and prices, not around customers.

Take the popular free-turkey-at-Thanksgiving campaigns. Retailers typically lose about $10,000 by selling turkeys below cost to anyone who walks in the door. The theory is that turkey buyers will shop for other holiday items as well, increasing sales volume at the checkout. Hawkins was skeptical of mass promotions like these, suspecting that they attracted store-hopping bargain-hunters rather than motivating regular customers to spend more. He also distrusted loyalty programs—if cards offer the same benefits to everyone, how can they possibly reward top shoppers?

When Hawkins established his own loyalty program, he decided to do things differently. His first promotion offered a free turkey—but it was presented as a reward, not a giveaway. Using loyalty cards to track purchases, he promised farm-fresh turkeys to everyone who spent more than $500 in the 10 weeks before Thanksgiving. While the store lost some customers, Hawkins was amazed to see that profits went up. Quite simply, the promotion motivated loyal customers to increase spending—and the bargain-hunters went elsewhere.

From that point on, Hawkins determined to focus on top shoppers rather than target anyone with a loyalty card. By analyzing purchasing data, Green Hills segmented its 15,000 customers into four tiers—Diamonds, Rubies, Pearls, and Opals. Diamonds spent over $100 per week on groceries, while Rubies spent $50 or more. Hawkins quickly found that it was difficult to get customers to move up the ranks—there is no way to get low-income shoppers to spend more. Instead, he zeroed in on the 1,300 customers in his top two categories.

When shoppers sign up at Green Hills, they immediately get $15 back for the first $100 spent. Throughout the year, top spenders are rewarded with regular discounts off total purchases. The store gives free turkeys, Christmas trees, and prizes, too. By constantly mining its database, Green Hills tailors stock to suit the preferences of its most profitable customers. In-the-mail flyers to top-shopper zip codes—rather than mass-market advertising in newspaper circulars—cut down on marketing costs while attracting more ideal customers.

When two new competitors moved into town on the same day, Green Hills appealed to loyal customers for support. Each received a custom-created gift basket, with a gift certificate for his or her favorite department. The store held its ground—and even saw sales increase.

Within the first year of offering its loyalty program, Green Hills saw a 20 percent increase in the number of customers spending $500 or more. Moreover, while most supermarkets lose 70 percent of new customers by their third visit, Green Hills boasts retention rates of over 80 percent. Better still, it keeps an astonishing 96 percent of its high-margin top shoppers.

Green Hills really knows its best customers. The experience it offers shoppers is as close as it can be to the one-to-one relationship Hawkins's grandmother nurtured with her farmstand customers all those years ago.

Questions for Critical Thinking

1. Is it possible to convert bargain hunters into loyal customers? Explain.
2. In what ways can Green Hills Farms be said to be a one-to-one marketer?

SOURCES: "Customer Loyalty Answer Man," *Sage Online*, Vol. 3, No. 1, http://www.sagemag.com, accessed April 5, 2002; and "Integrated Solutions for Retailers," *Integrated Solutions Magazine*, February 2002, http://www.ismretail .com, accessed April 5, 2002; Susan Greco, "The Best Little Grocery Store in America," *Inc.*, June 2001, pp. 54–61.

VIDEO CASE 6.2

Dunkin' Donuts and Hill, Holliday: A Recipe for Good Relationships

The written case on Dunkin' Donuts and Hill, Holliday appears on page VC-8. The recently filmed Dunkin' Donuts and Hill, Holliday video is designed to expand and highlight the concepts in this chapter and the concepts and questions covered in the written video case.

7

Marketing Research, Decision-Support Systems, and Sales Forecasting

Chapter Objectives

1 Describe the development of the marketing research function and its major activities.

2 List and explain the steps in the marketing research process.

3 Differentiate between the types and sources of primary and secondary data.

4 Explain the different sampling techniques used by marketing researchers.

5 Identify the methods by which marketing researchers collect primary data.

6 Discuss the challenges of conducting marketing research in global markets.

7 Outline important uses of computer technology in marketing research.

8 Identify the major types of forecasting methods and explain the steps in the fore-casting process.

Behind the Scenes: The Decisions Leading to New Movies

No product gets more hype than a new movie. In fact, you often feel like you've seen the film even before it has been released. But aside from the preparation that goes into advertising a movie, many more marketing decisions are made before the movie is finally "wrapped" and ready for the screen. These decisions involve more than who will write the screenplay, who will star in the film, where it will be shot, and who the production crew will be. They involve what brands of clothing the actors will wear on screen, what model of cars they will drive, what types of restaurants they might eat in, and their hairstyles or hair color. Decisions involve alternative plot turns and endings; sometimes two or more entirely different conclusions are filmed. These decisions might even include the color of a superhero's pants.

To make the right decisions, film-industry marketers use methods of communicating with and obtaining feedback from their customers— the movie-going public. That feedback can be crucial to a film's success. Since studios routinely spend tens of millions of dollars to bring a film to market, success—or failure—can rock a studio and the careers of those who work in the industry. Take the color of the Incredible Hulk's pants. Before *The Hulk* was complete, director Ang Lee happened to mention publicly that the Hulk might not be wearing his traditional purple pants—the ones so familiar to his comic-book fans. When the news got out, comic-book Web sites were ablaze with angry fans' comments. Changes were quickly made, and when the film opened first in Great Britain, the fictional hero was wearing his purple pants.

Movie marketing research—finding out what consumers want—also takes place in a much more organized fashion. Instead of the traditional practice of waiting until the movie is complete and showing it to test audiences, marketers now involve the audience right from the start. During filming, focus groups are invited to view particular scenes and supply feed-

back on everything from wardrobe to plot; sometimes they may even be asked to choose their favorite among alternative endings. Movie companies can either conduct the testing themselves or hire firms that specialize in this type of marketing research. Although this effort seems the perfect way to ensure a hit, directors caution that testing will only work if it is used carefully. "I think of movies as an art form, and ultimately what makes movies work is an intensely personal vision," explains director Anthony Minghella. In other words, if several hundred people contribute their feedback to a film, the movie may become watered down or lose its focus and intensity—and may very well turn into a flop. And some industry executives worry that a "mole" might attend a screening and feed secrets—or a damaging negative opinion— to the media or other movie companies. But others argue that the enormous cost of movie production justifies the use of focus groups as a way to reduce the risk of failure. "When you are investing $30 to $80 million in a product, you want to make sure the product has a defined audience and is enjoyed by the audience," says Scott Neeson of 20th Century Fox. Some producers have moved toward screening parts of films to smaller audiences, even just family and friends, in order to avoid leaks to the press.

Movie marketers also rely on the Internet for their research, sometimes receiving more information than they bargained for, as in the case of the Incredible Hulk's pants. It was responses from Web sites devoted to comic-book heroes like SuperHeroHype.com and DarkHorizons.com that warned Lee and Marvel studios they'd be in trouble with fans if the Hulk's pants were changed.

Briefly Speaking

You can give people responsibility and authority, but without information they are helpless. Knowledge is the ultimate power tool.

Bill Gates (b. 1954)
Cofounder, Microsoft Corp.

Chapter Overview

The makers of *The Hulk* responded quickly to fans' angry feedback about the superhero's attire. Monitoring fan Web sites is a form of marketing research. Marketers must not only solve problems as they arise but also anticipate and prevent those that may occur in the future. To avoid surprises and to make the best decisions possible, the right information in sufficient quantities is required in choosing effective solutions.

Marketing research is the process of collecting and using information for marketing decision making. Data comes from a variety of sources. Some results from well-planned studies designed to elicit specific information. Other valuable information comes from sales force reports, accounting records, and published reports. Still other data emerges from controlled experiments and computer simulations. Marketing research, by presenting pertinent information in a useful format, aids decision makers in analyzing data and in suggesting possible actions.

This chapter deals with the marketing research function, which is closely linked with the other elements of the marketing planning process. The chapter also explains how marketing research techniques are used to make accurate sales forecasts, a critical component of the strategic plan.

Information collected through marketing research underlies much of the material on market segmentation in Chapter 8. Clearly, the marketing research function is the primary source of the information needed in making effective marketing decisions.

The Marketing Research Function

Before looking at how marketing research is conducted, we must first examine its historical development, the people and organizations it involves, and the activities it entails. Since an underlying purpose of the research is to find out more about consumers, it is clear that research is central to effective customer satisfaction and customer relationship programs. Media technologies such as the Internet and virtual reality are opening up new channels through which researchers can tap into consumer information.

1

Describe the development of the marketing research function and its major activities.

Development of the Marketing Research Function

More than a century has passed since N. W. Ayer conducted the first organized marketing research project in 1879. A second important milestone in the development of marketing research occurred 32 years later, when Charles C. Parlin organized the nation's first commercial research department at Curtis Publishing Company.

Parlin got his start as a marketing researcher by counting soup cans in Philadelphia's garbage. Here is what happened. Parlin, an ad salesman, was trying to sell space in the *Saturday Evening Post* to the Campbell Soup Company. Campbell Soup resisted, believing that the *Post* reached primarily working-class readers, who preferred to make their own soup. Campbell Soup was targeting higher-income people who could afford to pay for the convenience of soup in a can. To prove Campbell wrong, Parlin began counting soup cans in the garbage collected from different neighborhoods. His research revealed that working-class families bought more soup than wealthy ones, who had servants to cook for them. Campbell Soup soon became a *Saturday Evening Post* client. It is interesting to note that garbage remains a good source of information for marketing researchers today. Prior to the recent cutbacks in food service, some airlines studied the leftovers from onboard meals to determine what to serve passengers.

Most early research gathered little more than written testimonials from purchasers of firms' products. Research methods became more sophisticated during the 1930s as the development of statistical techniques led to refinements in sampling procedures and greater accuracy in research findings.

In recent years, advances in computer technology have significantly changed the complexion of marketing research. Besides accelerating the pace and broadening the base of data collection, computers have aided marketers in making informed decisions about problems and opportunities. Simulations, for example, allow marketers to evaluate alternatives by posing what-if questions. Marketing researchers at many consumer goods firms simulate product introductions through computer programs to determine whether to risk real-world product launches or even to subject products to test marketing.

Who Conducts Marketing Research?

The size and organizational form of the marketing research function is usually tied to the structure of the company. Some firms organize research units to support different product lines, brands, or geographic areas. Others organize their research functions according to the types of research they need performed, such as sales analysis, new-product development, advertising evaluation, or sales forecasting.

Many firms depend on independent marketing research firms.[2] These independent organizations might handle just part of a larger study, such as conducting consumer interviews. Firms can also contract out entire research studies.

Marketers usually decide whether to conduct a study internally or through an outside organization based on cost. Another major consideration is the reliability and accuracy of the information collected by an outside organization. Because collecting marketing data is what these outside organizations do full time, the information they gather is often more thorough and accurate than that collected by inexperienced in-house staff. A marketing research firm can provide technical assistance and expertise not available within the contracting firm. Interaction with outside suppliers also helps to ensure that a researcher does not conduct a study only to validate a favorite personal theory or preferred option.

Marketing research companies range in size from sole proprietorships to national and international firms such as A. C. Nielsen, Information Resources Inc., and Arbitron. Recently, the 25 largest marketing research firms earned total revenues of $8.8 billion—an increase of almost 9 percent from the year before. Almost 50 percent of these revenues were generated outside the firms' home countries.[3]

Marketing research suppliers can be classified as syndicated services, full-service suppliers, or limited-service suppliers, depending on the primary thrust of their methods. Some full-service organizations are also willing to take on limited-service activities.

Syndicated Services

An organization that regularly provides a standardized set of data to all customers is called a *syndicated service*. Mediamark Research Inc., for example, operates a syndicated product research service based on personal interviews with adults regarding their exposure to advertising media. Clients include advertisers, advertising agencies, magazines, newspapers, broadcasters, and cable TV networks.

FIGURE 7.1
Full-Service Marketing Research Firm

Full-Service Research Suppliers

An organization that contracts with clients to conduct complete marketing research projects is called a *full-service research supplier*. Roper Starch Worldwide, shown in Figure 7.1, is a full-service

Marketing Dictionary

marketing research   Process of collecting and using information for marketing decision making.

A commissioned survey into the fragrance-selection habits of shoppers revealed that younger buyers like "scratch and sniff" strips.

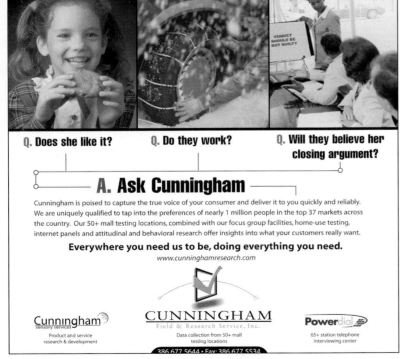

FIGURE 7.2
Research to Help Assess Levels of Customer Satisfaction

firm specializing in brand strategies and in building customer loyalty. A full-service supplier becomes the client's marketing research arm, performing all of the steps in the marketing research process (discussed later in this chapter).

Limited-Service Research Suppliers *Read.*

A marketing research firm that specializes in a limited number of activities, such as conducting field interviews or performing data processing, is called a *limited-service research supplier*. Working almost exclusively for clients in the movie industry, The National Research Group specializes in rating entertainment facilities through input from moviegoers. The firm also prepares studies to help clients develop advertising strategies and to track awareness and interest. Syndicated services can be considered a type of limited-service research supplier. Vertis Direct Marketing Services recently commissioned specialty research on the fragrance industry. A telephone survey of 2,000 adults showed that shoppers like to try out scents before buying them. The survey concluded that scent strips that accompany fragrance ads in magazines appeal to 75 percent of Generation Y noses.[4] The "Solving an Ethical Controversy" box describes one other group that conducts marketing research—competitive analysis teams, better known as corporate spies.

Customer Satisfaction Measurement Programs

In their marketing research, firms often focus on tracking the satisfaction levels of current customers. But some companies have gained valuable insights by tracking the dissatisfaction that leads customers to abandon certain products for those of competitors. Some customer defections are only partial; customers may remain somewhat satisfied with a business but not completely satisfied. Such attitudes could lead them to take their business elsewhere. Studying the underlying causes of customer defections, even partial defections, can be useful for identifying problem areas that need attention. Cunningham Field & Research Service, Inc., featured in Figure 7.2, promises to use a variety of research methods to find out exactly how satisfied consumers will be with a firm's products.

The Marketing Research Process

As discussed earlier, businesspeople rely on marketing research to provide the information they need to make effective decisions regarding their firm's current and future activities. The chances of making good decisions improve when the right information is provided at the right time during decision making. To achieve this goal, marketing researchers often follow the six-step process shown in Figure 7.3 on page 198. In the initial

right / wrong
Solving an Ethical Controversy

Dumpster Diving at Unilever

Like nine out of ten large corporations, Procter & Gamble systematically gathers data on competing brands. Using methods ranging from database searches to schmoozing with rivals' employees, it's typical for top organizations to spend $1 million a year to track competitive moves. The information feeds into future decision making, affecting product releases, sales strategies, and pricing. While some methods such as wiretapping, computer hacking, or bribery are clearly illegal, other intrusive techniques are not.

When executives in P&G's hair-care business hired subcontractors to snoop on archrival Unilever, its competitive analysis system spun out of control. The P&G operatives rifled through dumpsters looking for stray documents that would reveal the strategies behind Unilever brands. The spies hit the jackpot and secreted away information on product rollouts, profit margins, selling prices, and more.

In a surprise move akin to shutting the stable door once the horse has bolted, P&G—whose policy manual specifically prohibits dumpster diving—came clean, voluntarily alerting Unilever to its findings. Three managers were fired, and after prolonged negotiations, a settlement was reached. While details were not disclosed, the deal included $10 million in cash. Also, a third-party audit of P&G's hair-care business ensured that no trash-can secrets could be used for competitive advantage.

Did Procter & Gamble Go Too Far in Collecting Competitive Information?

PRO

1. P&G broke no laws. The only policies violated were those outlined in the company's own code of ethics.
2. Corporate espionage is standard practice—more than 60 percent of companies systematically collect information on competitors.

CON

1. There's a big difference between analyzing competitive strategies and stealing from garbage cans. P&G stepped over the line.
2. Even after blowing the whistle, P&G continued to withhold sensitive information. Initially, P&G offered Unilever two pilfered documents, but as many as 50 later came to light.

Summary

It's not enough to have a formal ethics code—companies must constantly monitor the activities of employees and contractors to ensure that guidelines are strictly enforced. While the Unilever incident may lead P&G to crack down on rogue operators, it is unlikely to alter the company's policy of collecting competitive intelligence.

SOURCES: Cliff Peale, "Spying on Rival Costs P&G $10M," *The Cincinnati Enquirer,* April 19, 2002, http://enquirer.com; Louis Lavelle, "The Case of the Corporate Spy," *BusinessWeek,* November 26, 2001, pp. 56–58; "Settlement in Shampoo Spy Case," *BBC News,* September 6, 2001, http://news.bbc.co.uk; Andy Serwer, "P&G's Covert Operation," *Fortune,* September 17, 2001, pp. 42–44.

---

stages, researchers define the problem, conduct exploratory research, and formulate a hypothesis to be tested. Next, they create a design for the research study, followed by the collection of data. Finally, researchers interpret and present the research information. The following sections take a closer look at each step of the marketing research process.

2

List and explain the steps in the marketing research process.

Define the Problem

A popular anecdote advises that well-defined problems are half-solved. A well-defined problem permits the researcher to focus on securing the exact information needed for the solution. Clearly defining the question that research needs to answer increases the speed and accuracy of the research process.

Researchers must carefully avoid confusing symptoms of a problem with the problem itself. A symptom merely alerts marketers that they have a problem. For example, suppose that a maker of frozen pizzas sees its market share drop from 8 percent to 5 percent in six months. The loss of market share is a symptom of a problem the company must solve. To define the problem, the firm must look for the underlying causes of its market share loss.

There's always trying research in every [handwritten]

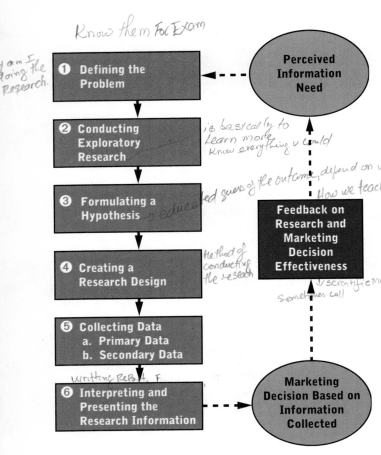

Know them For Exam [handwritten]

Y am I doing the Research [handwritten]

is basically to Learn more. Know everything u could [handwritten]

educated guess of the outcome, depend on ur exploration res [handwritten]

How we teach [handwritten]

Method of conducting the research [handwritten]

v scientific method Sometimes call [handwritten]

writing Report, F [handwritten]

FIGURE 7.3
The Marketing Research Process

A logical starting point in identifying the problem might be to evaluate the firm's marketing mix elements and target market. Suppose, for example, a firm has recently changed its promotional strategies. Research might then seek to answer the question "What must we do to improve the effectiveness of our marketing mix?" The firm might also look at possible environmental changes. Perhaps a new competitor entered the firm's market. Decision makers will need information to help answer the question "What must we do to distinguish our company from the new competitor?"

Tom Stemberg, CEO of office-supply retailer Staples, values marketing research so highly that he often does his own. Stemberg makes a habit of visiting a different competitor's store at least once a week. During these visits, he pushes himself to answer what he views as the most important question: In what ways are they doing a better job than Staples? Stemberg views every shopping visit as an opportunity to learn from his competition.[5]

Once u define the Problem now. [handwritten]

Conduct Exploratory Research

Once a firm has defined the question it wants to answer, researchers can begin exploratory research. **Exploratory research** seeks to discover the cause of a specific problem by discussing the problem with informed sources both within and outside the firm and by examining data from other information sources. The pizza firm, for example, might talk with its wholesalers, retailers, and customers. Executives might also ask for input from the sales force or look for overall market clues.

Staples chairman Stemberg enlists family members as undercover researchers. When a new Office Depot store opened in south Florida, for example, Stemberg asked his mother-in-law to investigate its competitive potential by buying items, noting how long delivery took, and then reporting on the ease of returning these items. She obtained even more valuable insights into the efficiency of the new store's delivery operations by talking to the experts—delivery truck drivers.[6]

In addition to talking with employees, exploratory research can include evaluation of company records, such as sales and profit analyses, and available competitive data. Marketing researchers often refer to internal data collection as situation analysis. The term *informal investigation* is often used for exploratory interviews with informed persons outside the researchers' firms.

Using Internal Data

Marketers can find valuable data in their firm's own internal records. Typical sources of internal data are sales records, financial statements, and marketing cost analyses. Marketers analyze sales performance records to gain an overall view of company efficiency and to find clues to potential problems. Easily prepared from company invoices or a computer database system, this sales analysis can provide important details to management. The study typically compares actual and expected sales based on a detailed sales forecast by territory, product, customer, and salesperson. Once the sales quota—the level of expected sales to which actual results are compared—has been established, it is a simple process to compare actual results with expected performance.

Other possible breakdowns for sales analysis separate transactions by customer type, product, sales method (mail, telephone, or personal contact), type of order (cash or credit), and order size. *Sales analysis* is one of the least expensive and most important sources of marketing information available to a firm.

Accounting data, as summarized in the firm's financial statements, can be another good tool for identifying financial issues that influence marketing. Using ratio analysis, researchers can compare performance in current and previous years against industry benchmarks. These exercises may hint at possible problems, but only more detailed analysis would reveal specific causes of indicated variations.

A third source of internal information is marketing cost analysis—evaluation of expenses for tasks such as selling, warehousing, advertising, and delivery to determine the profitability of particular customers, territories, or product lines. Firms most commonly examine the allocation of costs to products, customers, and territories or districts. Marketing decision makers then evaluate the profitability of particular customers and districts on the basis of the sales produced and the costs incurred in generating those sales.

Like sales performance and financial research, marketing cost analysis is most useful when it provides information linked to other forms of marketing research. A later section of this chapter will address how computer technologies can accomplish these linkages and move information among a firm's units.

Formulate a Hypothesis

After defining the problem and conducting an exploratory investigation, the marketer needs to formulate a *hypothesis*—a tentative explanation for some specific event. A hypothesis is a statement about the relationship among variables that carries clear implications for testing this relationship. It sets the stage for more in-depth research by further clarifying what researchers need to test.

Not all studies test specific hypotheses. However, a carefully designed study can benefit from the rigor introduced by developing a hypothesis before beginning data collection and analysis.

Create a Research Design

To test hypotheses and find solutions to marketing problems, a marketer creates a *research design*, a master plan or model for conducting marketing research. In designing a research project, marketers must be sure that the study will measure what they intend to measure. A second important research design consideration is the selection of respondents. Marketing researchers use sampling techniques (discussed later in the chapter) to determine which consumers to include in their studies.

Some of the nation's biggest food companies employ a sample research design to test new products. They offer items to Wal-Mart first. The nation's largest retailer doesn't charge producers a fee—called a *slotting fee*—to stock their merchandise. Then, if the item sells at Wal-Mart, other retailers will take notice and drop their slotting fees.[7]

Collect Data

Marketing researchers gather two kinds of data: secondary data and primary data. **Secondary data** is information from previously published or compiled sources. Census data is an example.

Because 'TOP SECRET' always looks good on your resume.

Get the kind of high-tech training that always shows up on employers' radar. To learn more, log on the Life Accelerator at navy.com or call 1-800-USA-NAVY.

NAVY accelerate your life.

Improvements in retention and reduction of attrition in recent years have helped the U.S. Navy to raise the bar on their recruitment requirements. The Navy, among other organizations, uses advertising to deliver messages emphasizing the positive impact of high-tech military training on future civilian job prospects.

Briefly Speaking

Getting the facts is the key to good decision making. Every mistake that I made—and we all make mistakes—came because I didn't take the time. I didn't drive hard enough. I wasn't smart enough to get the facts.

*Charles F. Knight
(b. 1936)
Chairman, Emerson Electric*

3

Differentiate between the types and sources of primary and secondary data.

Marketing Dictionary

exploratory research Process of discussing a marketing problem with informed sources both within and outside the firm and examining information from secondary sources.

secondary data Previously published information.

FIGURE 7.4
The Research Report and Presentation: Linking the Study and the Research User

Primary data refers to information collected for the first time specifically for a marketing research study. An example of primary data is statistics collected from a survey that asks current customers about their preferences for product improvements.

Secondary data offers two important advantages: (1) It is almost always less expensive to gather than primary data, and (2) researchers usually must spend less time to locate and use secondary data. A research study that requires primary data may take three to four months to complete, while a researcher can often gather secondary data in a matter of days.

Secondary data does have limitations that primary data does not. First, published information can quickly become obsolete. A marketer analyzing the population of various areas may discover that the most recent census figures are already out of date because of rapid growth and changing demographics. Second, published data collected for an unrelated purpose may not be completely relevant to the marketer's specific needs. For example, census data will not reveal the brand preferences of consumers in a particular region.

Although research to gather primary data can cost more and take longer, the results can provide richer, more detailed information than secondary data offers. The choice between secondary and primary data is tied to cost, validity, and effectiveness. In reality, many marketing research projects combine secondary and primary data to fully answer marketing questions. This chapter examines specific methods for collecting both secondary and primary data in later sections.

Interpret and Present Research Information

The final step in the marketing research process is to interpret the findings and present them to decision makers in a format that allows management to make effective judgments. Figure 7.4 illustrates possible differences between marketing researchers and their audiences in interpretations of research results due to differing backgrounds, levels of knowledge, and experience.

Marketing researchers and research users must cooperate at every stage in the research process. Too many studies go unused because management fears restrictions on the results after hearing lengthy discussions of research limitations or unfamiliar terminology. Marketing researchers must remember to direct their reports toward management and not to other researchers. They should spell out their conclusions in clear and concise terms that can be put into action. Reports should confine technical details of the research methods to an appendix, if they are included at all. By presenting research results to all key executives at a single sitting, researchers can ensure that everyone will understand the findings. Decision makers can then quickly reach consensus on what the results mean and what actions are to be taken.[8]

Marketing Research Methods

Clearly, data collection is an integral part of the marketing research process. One of the most time-consuming parts of collecting data is determining what method the marketer should use to obtain the data. This section discusses the most commonly used methods by which marketing researchers find both secondary and primary data.

Secondary Data Collection

Secondary data comes from many sources. The overwhelming quantity of secondary data available at little or no cost challenges researchers to select data that is pertinent.

Secondary data consists of two types: internal and external data. Internal data, as discussed earlier, includes sales records, product performance reviews, sales force activity reports, and marketing cost reports. External data comes from a variety of sources, including government records, syndicated research services, and industry publications. Computerized databases provide access to vast amounts of data from both inside and outside an organization. The following sections on government data, private data, and online sources focus on databases and other external data sources available to marketing researchers.

Government Data

The federal government is the nation's most important source of marketing data. Census data provides the most frequently used government statistics. A census of population is conducted every ten years and is made available at no charge in local libraries, on computer disks, and through the Internet. The Bureau of the Census also conducts a periodic census of housing, population, business, manufacturers, agriculture, minerals, and governments.

The census of population contains a wealth of valuable information for marketers. It breaks down the population by very small geographic areas, making it possible to determine population traits by city block or census tract in large cities. It divides the populations of nonmetropolitan areas into block-numbering areas (BNAs). The BNAs and census tracts are important for marketing analysis because they highlight populations with similar traits, avoiding diversity within political boundaries such as county lines. This data helps marketers such as local retailers and shopping center developers to gather vital information about customers in an immediate neighborhood without spending time or money to conduct comprehensive surveys. The Census Bureau uses a variety of statistical techniques to group households into homogeneous clusters of people who have similar lifestyles and spending habits, who listen to similar kinds of programming, and who watch similar television shows.[9]

Marketing researchers find even more valuable resources in the government's computerized mapping database called the TIGER system, for Topographically Integrated Geographic Encoding and Referencing system. This system combines topographic features such as railroads, highways, and rivers with census data such as household income figures. TIGER data is available on DVD, making the Census Bureau one of the first federal agencies to use the technology to publish huge amounts of digital data. The DVDs contains both database management software and mapping software, making TIGER data highly accessible to marketers.[10]

Marketers often get other information from the federal government, such as the following:

- *Monthly Catalog of the United States Government Publications* and *Statistical Abstract of the United States,* published annually

- *Survey of Current Business,* updated monthly

- *County and City Data Book,* typically published every three years, providing data on each county and city of over 25,000 residents

Even with the wealth of information available from the Census Bureau, the data gathered is not necessarily comprehensive, as the "Marketing Misses" box explains.

Marketing Miss

Why the Latest Federal Census Failed to Count Arab Americans

Background. The first place to look for market statistics is the U.S. Census. But for marketers seeking data on an important U.S. ethnic group such as Arab Americans, the census is woefully inadequate.

The Marketing Problem. The problem is that the census does not include "Arab American" as an ethnic category. Asian Americans can identify their ethnicity as Indian, Chinese, Filipino, Japanese, Korean, or Vietnamese. Even Pacific Islanders choose from four subcategories. Yet the census offers not a single classification for people of Middle Eastern descent, who must either opt for "white" or "some other race."

The Outcome. The racial categorization is particularly misleading, since not everyone of Middle Eastern descent is Arabic. Iranians, for example, are Caucasian. Nor are all Arabs from the Middle East. While some people try to pinpoint their ethnicity by stating that they are Muslim, the Census Bureau, as a matter of policy, suppresses those answers. In fact, data on religion serves only to complicate the matter further. Muslims are a complex group, coming from more than 25 countries in Europe, Asia, Africa, and the Middle East.

Lessons Learned. There are few reliable estimates of U.S. Arab and Muslim populations and even less data on how and where they live. But the Council for American-

continued on next page

Marketing Dictionary

primary data Information collected for the first time.

Marketing Miss

Islamic Relations puts the U.S. Muslim population at between 4 and 8 million. The Arab American Institute suggests a total of more than 3 million Arab Americans, with high population densities in Chicago, Detroit, Los Angeles, New Jersey, and New York.

SOURCES: Shibley Telhami, "Arab and Muslim America," *The Brookings Review*, Winter 2002, pp. 14–15; Nicholas Kulish, "Why the Census of 2000 Failed to Count Arabs," *The Wall Street Journal*, September 26, 2001, p. B1; D'Vera Cohn and Sarah Cohen, "Statistics Portray Settled, Affluent Mideast Community," *The Washington Post*, November 20, 2001, p. A4; and "American Religious Identification Survey," *Aris Report No. 2*, October 2001, The Graduate Center, City University of New York, **http://www.gc.cuny.edu**.

State and city governments serve as additional important sources of information on employment, production, and sales activities. In addition, university bureaus of business and economic research frequently collect and disseminate valuable information.

Private Data *o have to pay b4 get it.*

Many private organizations provide information for marketing decision makers. A trade association may be an excellent source of data on activities in a particular industry. Gale Publishing's *Encyclopedia of Associations*, available in many libraries, can help marketers to track down trade associations that may have data pertinent to their company. Also, the advertising industry continuously collects data on audiences reached by various media.

Business and trade magazines also publish a wide range of valuable data. Ulrich's *Guide to International Periodicals*, another common library reference, can point researchers in the direction of trade publications that conduct and publish industry-specific research. General business magazines can also be good sources. *Sales & Marketing Management*, for instance, publishes an annual *Survey of Media Markets* that combines statistics for population, effective buying income (EBI), and retail sales into buying power indexes that indicate each market's ability to buy.

Since few libraries carry specialized trade journals, the best way to gather data from them is either directly from the publishers or through online periodical databases like Dialog's *ABI/Inform*, available at many libraries, or CompuServe's *Knowledge Index*. Increasingly, trade publications maintain Web home pages that allow archival searches. Larger libraries can often provide directories and other publications that can help researchers find secondary data. For instance, Find/SVP's *FindEx, the Directory of Market Research Reports, Studies, and Surveys* lists a tremendous variety of completed research studies that are available for purchase.

Several national firms offer information to businesses by subscription. *Roper Starch Worldwide* is a global database service with consumer attitudes, lifestage, and behavior information for 30 countries. Roper also provides *Starch Readership Reports* that measure more than 20,000 ads in 400 magazines.

Electronic systems that scan UPC bar codes speed purchase transactions, and they also provide data for inventory control, ordering, and delivery. Scanning technology is widely used by grocers and other retailers, and marketing research companies, such as A. C. Nielsen and Information Resources Inc., store this data in commercially available databases. These scanner-based information services track consumer purchases of a wide variety of UPC-coded products. Retailers can use this information to target customers with the right products at the right time.

A. C. Nielsen SalesNet uses the Internet to deliver scanner data quickly to clients. Data is processed as soon as it is received from supermarkets and is then forwarded to market researchers so they can perform more in-depth analysis. At the same time, Nielsen representatives summarize the data in both graphic and spreadsheet form and post it on the Internet for immediate access by clients. Recently, retail giant Wal-Mart decided to withhold its scanner data from research services. Nielsen, backed by rival stores, responded by refusing to sell any scanner data to the world's largest retailer.[11]

Online Sources of Secondary Data

The tools of cyberspace sometimes simplify the hunt for secondary data. Hundreds of databases and other sources of information are available online, both through the Internet and through commercial services such as America Online. A well-designed, Internet-based marketing research project can cost less yet yield faster results than offline research. For instance, Lego needed to make a quick decision on rereleasing some of its classic sets. The company posted a bulletin board at Lego.com, inviting its 2 million monthly visitors to share opinions and to comment on their favorite Lego classics. Using software from Recipio, results were gathered and analyzed in real time. Within two weeks, the company had the information it needed. Almost 40 percent of respondents aged 18 and under—Lego's "sweet spot"—

'net Ξx

Online information sources. Marketers make regular use of several online information sources for their research needs. These sources fall into two general categories: statistical sources and indexes. Statistical sources contain a variety of data that may be of assistance in marketing research. For example, examine the *Statistical Abstract of the United States,* the online version of which can be accessed at **http://www.census.gov/prod/www/statistical-abstract-us.html**. Go to the Web site and access the most recent year you can find. Click on "Population" and answer the following questions:

a. What is the current population of the United States?

b. Which age groups grew the fastest over the past 12 months?

c. What is the projected U.S. population in 2014?

d. Which age groups are expected to grow the fastest over the next 10 years? (Note: In order to access data you will need Adobe Acrobat Reader. If you don't already have Adobe Acrobat Reader, you may download a free copy at **http://www.adobe.com**).

By contrast, an index is a list of publications that are accessed through keyword searches. Many colleges and universities have either Lexis-Nexis or ProQuest for use by faculty and students. If your institution has one or both, search the database for articles pertaining to marketing research. Print out the abstracts of two articles you find to be the most interesting.

---

favored rereleasing Guarded Inn and Metroliner. Within six weeks Metroliner sales topped the annual sales of comparable Lego sets.[12]

A recent survey reported that more than 70 percent of marketing research firms conduct some form of Internet research, up from 50 percent a year earlier. Today, industry experts estimate that about half of all marketing research could easily be done online.[13]

The Internet has spurred the growth of research aggregators—companies that acquire, catalog, reformat, segment, then resell premium research reports that have already been published. Aggregators put valuable data within reach of marketers who lack the time or the budget to commission custom research. Since Web technology makes their databases easy to search, aggregators are able to compile detailed, specialized reports quickly and cost-effectively.[14]

Internet search tools such as Google and Yahoo! can find specific sites that are rich with information. Discussion groups may also provide information and insights that can help answer some marketing questions. Additionally, a post to a chat room or newsgroup may draw a response that uncovers previously unknown sources of secondary data. Usenet, the largest newsgroup network, boasts 500 million messages posted since 1995. Unlike chat-room postings, these opinions are unsolicited and uncensored. Online services like Survey.com and PlanetFeedback gather data from multiple sources, organized according to demographic, industry, product, or multiple other characteristics. A quick search through PlanetFeedback alerted Procter & Gamble to complaints that the tape on its Pampers brand diapers came loose too easily. The company was able to fix the problem before it had thousands of annoyed parents.[15]

Researchers must, however, carefully evaluate the validity of information they find on the Internet. People without in-depth knowledge of the subject matter may post information in a newsgroup. Similarly, Web pages might contain information that has been gathered using questionable research methods. The saying *caveat emptor* (buyer beware) should guide Internet searches for secondary data.

Sampling Techniques

Before undertaking a study to gather primary data, researchers must first identify which participants to include in the study. **Sampling** is the process of selecting survey respondents or research participants. It is one of the most

Marketing Dictionary

sampling   Process of selecting survey respondents or other research participants.

important aspects of research design because if a study fails to involve consumers who accurately reflect the target market, the research will likely yield misleading conclusions.

The total group of people that the researcher wants to study is called the *population* or *universe*. For a political campaign study, the population would be all eligible voters. For research about a new cosmetics line, it might be all women in a certain age bracket. The sample is a representative group from this population. Researchers rarely gather information from a study's total population, resulting in a census. Unless the total population is small, the costs of a census are too high.

Samples can be classified as either probability samples or nonprobability samples. A **probability sample** is one that gives every member of the population a chance of being selected. Types of probability samples include simple random samples, stratified samples, and cluster samples.

In a *simple random sample*, every member of the relevant universe has an equal opportunity of selection. The draft lottery of the Vietnam era is an example. The days of the year were drawn and set into an array. The placement of a person's birthday in this list determined his likelihood of being called for service. In a *stratified sample*, randomly selected subsamples of different groups are represented in the total sample. Stratified samples provide efficient, representative groups for such studies as opinion polls, in which groups of individuals share various divergent viewpoints. In a *cluster sample*, researchers select areas (or clusters) from which they draw respondents. This cost-efficient type of probability sample may be the best option where the population cannot be listed or enumerated. A good example is a marketing researcher identifying various U.S. cities and then randomly selecting supermarkets within those cities to study.

In contrast, a **nonprobability sample** is an arbitrary grouping that does not permit the use of standard statistical tests. Types of nonprobability samples are convenience samples and quota samples. A *convenience sample* is a nonprobability sample selected from among readily available respondents. Broadcast news "on-the-street" interviews are a good example. Marketing researchers sometimes use convenience samples in exploratory research but not in definitive studies. A *quota sample* is a nonprobability sample that is divided to maintain representation for different segments or groups. It differs from a stratified sample, in which researchers select subsamples by some random process; in a quota sample, they hand-pick participants. An example would be a survey of owners of imported autos that includes two Hyundai owners, six Honda owners, four Volvo owners, and so on.

4

Explain the different sampling techniques used by marketing researchers.

5

Identify the methods by which marketing researchers collect primary data.

Primary Research Methods

Marketers use a variety of methods for conducting primary research. The principal methods for collecting primary data are observation, surveys, and controlled experiments. The choice among these methods depends on the issues under study and the decisions that marketers need to make. In some cases, researchers may decide to combine techniques during the research process.

Observation Method

In observational studies, researchers view the overt actions of the subjects. Marketers trying to understand how consumers actually behave in certain situations find observation to be a useful technique. Observation tactics may be as simple as counting the number of cars passing by a potential site for a fast-food restaurant or checking the license plates at a shopping center to determine where shoppers live. Research companies like Ipsos, featured in Figure 7.5, use observation methods to create psychological and sociological profiles of potential market segments.

Technological advances provide increasingly sophisticated ways for observing consumer behavior. The television industry relies on data from people meters, which are electronic remote-control devices that record the TV-viewing habits of individual household members to measure the popularity of TV shows. Traditional people meters require each viewer to punch a button each time he or she turns on the TV, changes channels, or leaves the room.

Marketers have long worried that some viewers do not bother to push people meter buttons at appropriate times, skewing research findings. In response, Arbitron recently tested a portable people meter (PPM) that participants keep with them at all times. Throughout the day, the PPM picks up and stores codes embedded in radio and TV programming. At night, the participant puts the PPM into a docking station, from which the data is uploaded to Arbitron. The PPM even has a built-in motion detector to ensure that it is not abandoned midtest.[16]

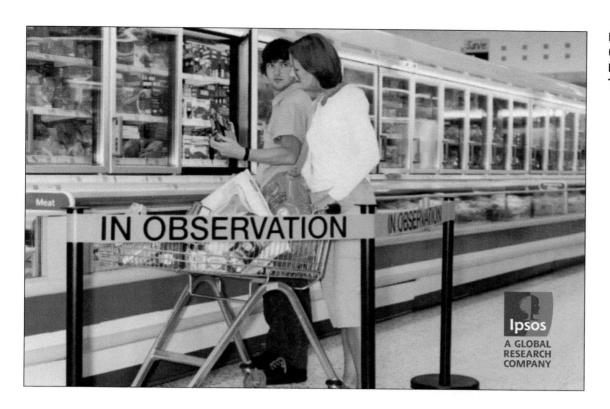

FIGURE 7.5
Observation Methods
Leading to Profiles of
Target Segments

Videotaping consumers in action is also gaining acceptance as a research technique. Cookware manufacturers may videotape consumers cooking in their own kitchens to evaluate how they use their pots and pans. A toothbrush manufacturer asked marketing research firm E-Lab to videotape consumers brushing their teeth and using mouthwash in its quest to develop products that would leave behind the sensation of cleanliness and freshness.

When French electronics maker Thomson developed a new digital technology for storing, accessing, and playing music, the company also hired E-Lab to study how, when, and where people listen to music. To get the information, E-Lab researchers issued beepers to consumers. At certain times of the day, E-Lab researchers beeped study participants and asked them to make a note of the music they were listening to, who chose it, and their mood. Researchers also followed people as they moved around their homes, recording where they kept their stereos and how they organized their music collections.[17]

In an effort to understand what makes teenagers tick, advertising agency Bates USA mailed disposable cameras to 36 teens around the U.S. and asked them to document their favorite possessions, locations, and people. Back came snapshots of everything imaginable, including (literally) a kitchen sink. One ninth-grader photographed her hockey stick and enclosed a note explaining that making the hockey team was her way of showing she was as good an athlete as her brothers. Bates senior vice president Janice Figueroa notes that information like this is valuable because it goes beyond mere statistics, which document that more girls are participating in sports, and reveals these girls' underlying motivations. Athletics may actually relate to self-confidence—a powerful motivator that marketers can use.[18]

Ethnography—also known as interpretive research or "going native"—is a method of observational research that has attracted considerable interest in recent years. Developed by social anthropologists as a method for explaining behavior that operates below the level of conscious thought, ethnography can provide insights into consumer behavior and the ways in which consumers interact with brands. Ethnography is often used to interpret consumer behavior within a foreign culture, where language, ideals, values, and expectations are all subject to different cultural influences.[19]

Marketing Dictionary

probability sample Sample that gives every member of the population a chance of being selected.

nonprobability sample Arbitrary grouping that produces data unsuited for most standard statistical tests.

Survey Method

Observation alone cannot supply all of the desired information. Researchers must ask questions to get information on attitudes, motives, and opinions. It is also difficult to get exact demographic information—such as income levels—from observation. To discover this information, researchers can use either interviews or questionnaires.

Telephone Interviews

Telephone interviews are a quick and inexpensive method for obtaining a small quantity of relatively impersonal information. Simple, clearly worded questions are easy for interviewers to pose over the phone and are effective at drawing appropriate responses. Telephone surveys have relatively high response rates, especially with repeated calls; calling a number once yields a response rate of 50 to 60 percent, but calling the same number five times raises the response rate to 85 percent. To maximize responses and save costs, some researchers use computerized dialing and digitally synthesized voices that interview respondents.

However, phone surveys have several drawbacks. Most importantly, about 44 percent of all people now invited to take part in them refuse, compared with only 15 percent 20 years ago. Their reasons include concern for data privacy, a negative association of phone surveys with telemarketing, and the lack of financial rewards for participating.[20]

Many respondents are hesitant to give personal characteristics about themselves over the telephone. Results may be biased by the omission of typical households where adults are off working during the day. Other households, particularly market segments such as single women and physicians, are likely to have unlisted numbers. While computerized random dialing can give access to unlisted numbers, it is restricted in several states.

The popularity of caller-ID systems to screen unwanted calls is another obstacle for telephone researchers. Some legal experts believe caller-ID violates the caller's right to privacy; in one case, the Pennsylvania state courts ruled it unconstitutional. Still, state laws on caller-ID vary. Some require vendors to offer a blocking service to callers who wish to evade the system.

Other obstacles restrict the usefulness of telephone surveys abroad. In areas where telephone ownership is rare, survey results will be highly biased. Telephone interviewing is also difficult in countries that lack directories or where call volumes congest limited phone line capacity.

Personal Interviews

The best means for obtaining detailed information about consumers is usually the personal interview since the interviewer can establish rapport with respondents and explain confusing or vague questions. Although slow and expensive to conduct, personal interviews offer a flexibility and a return of detailed information that often offsets the limitations of mail questionnaires. Marketing research firms can conduct interviews in rented space in shopping centers, where they gain wide access to potential buyers of the merchandise they are studying. These locations sometimes feature private interviewing space, videotape equipment, and food-preparation facilities for taste tests. Interviews conducted in shopping centers are typically called *mall intercepts*. Downtown retail districts and airports provide other valuable locations for marketing researchers.

Focus Groups

Marketers also gather research information through the popular technique of focus groups. A **focus group** brings together 8 to 12 individuals in one location to discuss a subject of interest. Unlike other interview techniques that elicit information through a question-and-answer format, focus groups usually encourage a general discussion of a predetermined topic. Focus groups can provide quick and relatively inexpensive insight into consumer attitudes and motivations. Within days of the September 11 terrorist attacks, Southwest Airlines was able to roll out a campaign that reflected the changed mood of the American public. Focus groups were a key technique used to quickly evaluate consumer attitudes toward the airlines in the wake of the attacks.

In a focus group, the leader, or moderator, typically explains the purpose of the meeting and suggests an opening topic. The moderator's main purpose, however, is to stimulate interaction among group members to encourage their discussion of numerous points. The moderator may occasionally interject questions as catalysts to direct the group's discussion. The moderator's job is difficult, requiring preparation and group facilitation skills.

Focus group sessions often last one or two hours. Researchers usually record the discussion on tape, and observers frequently watch through a one-way mirror. Some research firms also allow clients to view focus groups in action through videoconferencing systems.

Marketers use focus groups for a variety of purposes. In Figure 7.6, C&R Research conveys a projective technique that might be used with a focus group to find out how brands of toothpaste are perceived by customers. Teenage Research Unlimited conducts focus groups for a variety of clients to explore aspects of adolescent life. The research firm has found that indirect questions can be the best way to elicit information from teens. For instance, the moderator may display a cartoon drawing of a young woman and ask focus group participants to describe her clothes, accessories, and favorite magazines and music. Rather than inquiring into fast-food preferences directly, the moderator might ask participants to match a list of restaurants with the celebrities most likely to eat at each one. Another favorite ploy, especially for gaining insight into modern teen fashion trends, is to ask teens to pretend they are costume designers for a hit TV show and describe how they would dress the show's characters. Recently, Teen Research Unlimited launched its first syndicated online product, Omnibuzz, a monthly teen survey. Each sample of 850 respondents is weighted to match the national teen population in terms of gender, region, and ethnicity. Questions are custom-designed to meet client needs and results are survey results are available within three weeks.[21]

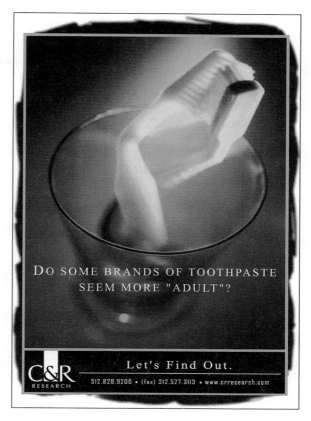

FIGURE 7.6
Focus Groups: Insights into Consumer Perceptions

Focus groups are a particularly valuable tool for exploratory research, developing new product ideas, and preliminary testing of alternative marketing strategies. They can also aid in the development of well-structured questionnaires for larger-scale research.

Focus groups do have some drawbacks, however. Some researchers fear that the focus group setting is sterile and unnatural and may not produce honest responses to questions. Participants may, for example, feel a need to identify with other members of the group and so provide less-than-truthful answers. Other researchers feel that the sample sizes are too small to be truly representative of larger population groups. Still others question the consistency of the interviewing process.[22]

Researchers are finding ways to re-create the focus group environment over the Internet. With experienced moderators who have the technical skills to function fluently online, it is possible to gain valuable qualitative information at a fraction of the cost it takes to run a traditional focus group session.

Research firm Greenfield Online used an online focus group to test reactions to a redesigned Web site for Captain Morgan Original Spiced Rum. Participants "gathered" in Greenfield's private chat room. A moderator posed questions and responded to answers on one side of a split screen, while participants typed their comments on the other side. How can researchers tell if online participants are being truthful? Greenfield staff members cross-checked participants' answers to earlier screening questionnaires against the information they entered later when they registered for the database. The company then cross-checked a second time before the focus group began and found substitutes for respondents whose answers appeared inconsistent.

Marketing Dictionary

focus group   Marketing research procedure that typically brings together 8 to 12 individuals to discuss a given subject.

FIGURE 7.7
Benefits of Online
Focus Groups

FocusVision Worldwide in Figure 7.7 advertises some of the benefits Internet-based focus groups can offer. FocusVision technology promises to enable clients to view focus group sessions around the world through videoconferencing and Internet videostreaming. Multiple camera systems, picture-in-picture enhancements, and simultaneous language translation deliver reliable, qualitative data saving staff travel time and expenses. The "Marketing Hits" box further explains how researchers are hosting real-time focus groups over the Internet.

Mail Surveys

Although personal interviews can provide very detailed information, cost considerations usually prevent an organization from using personal interviews in a national study. A mail survey can be a cost-effective alternative. Mail surveys also provide anonymity that may encourage respondents to give candid answers.

Mail surveys help marketers track consumer attitudes through ongoing research. Corning conducts a semiannual survey of consumers to measure customer awareness and satisfaction and to gather information for new-product development. Mail surveys can also provide demographic data that may be helpful in market segmentation.

Mail questionnaires do, however, have several limitations. First, response rates are typically much lower than for personal interviews. Because researchers must wait for respondents to complete and return questionnaires, mail surveys also usually take a long time to conduct. A third limitation, questionnaires cannot answer unanticipated questions that occur to respondents as they complete the forms. Complex questions may not be suitable for a mail questionnaire. Finally, unless they gather additional information from nonrespondents, researchers must worry about bias in the results stemming from differences between respondents and nonrespondents.

Researchers try to minimize these limitations by paying careful attention in developing and in pretesting questionnaires. Researchers can boost response rates by keeping questionnaires short and by offering incentives to respondents who complete and return the survey documents.

Fax Surveys

The low response rates and long follow-up times associated with mail surveys have spurred interest in the alternative of faxing survey documents. In some cases, faxes may supplement mail surveys; in others, it may be the primary method for contacting respondents.

Online Surveys and Other Internet-Based Methods

The growing population of Internet users has spurred researchers to conduct online surveys. Using the Web, they are able to speed the survey process, increase sample sizes, ignore geographic boundaries, and dramatically reduce costs. While a standard research project can take up to eight weeks to complete, a thorough online project may take two weeks or less. Less intrusive than telephone surveys, online research allows participants to respond at their leisure. The novelty and ease of answering online may even encourage higher response rates. Additional questions and longer responses have only a slight effect, if any, on an online study's cost, enabling researchers to gather detailed information through surveys. Furthermore, since online research is already in digital form, it generally requires less preparation—such as retyping into a database—before analysis.[23]

Businesses are increasingly including questionnaires on their Web pages to solicit information about consumer demographics, attitudes, and comments and suggestions for improving goods and services or improving marketing messages. Circuit City's online survey aims to gather feedback from customers regarding their in-store shopping experiences. It takes just minutes to complete, and participants are automatically registered to win cash prizes in Circuit City's Customer Satisfaction Sweepstakes.[24]

Marketers are also experimenting with electronic bulletin boards as an information-gathering device. On a password-protected Web site, moderators pose questions to selected respondents—usually just 15 to 25—over a predetermined period of time. Respondents have the chance to try out a product and are able to submit feedback at their leisure. Unlike focus group sessions, there are no group dynamics, so some researchers feel that responses are more truthful. Bulletin boards are particularly effective when targeting respondents who are unable to commit to real-time group sessions or for topics that are highly sensitive or complex.[25]

The growth of the Internet is creating a need for new research techniques to measure and capture information about Web-site visitors. At present, no industrywide standards define techniques for measuring Web use. Some sites ask users to register before accessing the pages; others merely keep track of the number of "hits" or number of times a visitor accesses a page. Marketers have tried to place a value on a site's "stickiness" (longer-lasting site visits) as a means of measuring effectiveness. Others use "cookies," which are electronic identifiers deposited on viewers' computers, to track click-through behavior—the paths users take as they move through the site. However, since some consumers change their Internet service providers frequently, cookies have lost some of their effectiveness.

Some software can monitor the overall content that a person is viewing and display banner advertisements likely to be of interest. For example, a search using the keyword "car" might call up a banner ad for General Motors or Ford. CMG Information Services offers a service called Engage.Knowledge, which collects profiles of Web users from numerous sites and organizes the data into 800 categories, including sports and hobbies. Researchers can use this information to develop marketing strategies. The popularity of video games has led to the emergence of a new advertising platform, "advergames." YaYa LLC streams three-dimensional console-quality games over the Internet. A promotional e-mail, for example, invites users to play a Honda-sponsored racing game, driving a replica of a new-model car through an exciting virtual racetrack. A marketing research tool in disguise, players must register before starting their engines—submitting details of their age, address, occupation, and hobbies. They are rewarded with free entry into a contest to win a Honda CR-V. Four out of five users register—and many pass the game along to friends. Of course, Honda gains market data on a key demographic group—potential young car buyers. [26]

The Experimental Method

The least-used method for collecting primary data is the *controlled experiment.* A marketing research experiment is a scientific investigation in which a researcher controls or manipulates a test group (or groups) and compares the results with those of a control group that did not receive the experimental controls or manipulations.

The most common use of this method by marketers is *test-marketing*, or introducing a new product in a specific area and then observing its degree of success. Up to this point, a product development team may have gathered

Marketing Hit

Collecting Qualitative Research Online

Background. The Internet delivers unbeatable cost and time savings in gathering quantitative data. Yet because of the clear advantages of working face to face with participants, companies have been slow to trust the Web to deliver qualitative results.

The Challenge. Marketers who accept online focus groups as a viable research methodology gain not only economy and speed but a bigger pool of qualified candidates. For example, physicians and senior executives are reluctant to join traditional focus groups because of time or travel commitments, but they may be willing to log into online sessions.

The Strategy. Greenfield Online won over its *Fortune* 500 client base by giving compelling demonstrations of focus group software at key trade shows. Another company, iTracks, offers demos, re-creating a focus-group environment on the Web. Regardless of technology, researchers agree that it is critical to back up the software with moderators skilled in qualitative techniques. They must also be able to rein in dominant participants and know when to draw reluctant subjects aside into online interview rooms for follow-up questions. To elicit honest responses, moderators must be able to interpret subtle signals from participants. Delays in typing responses, for example, may indicate hesitation. As the software improves, audio clips, video clips, and real-time videostreaming enable moderators to get behind a one-way mirror, observing the body language of participants.

continued on next page

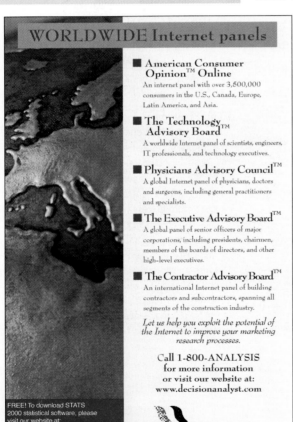

Research companies offer a broad range of services that harness Internet technology to deliver research results on a global scale.

feedback from focus groups. Other information may have come from shoppers' evaluations of competing products. Test-marketing is the first stage at which the product performs in a real-life business environment.

Test-marketing introduces a new product supported by a complete marketing campaign to a selected city or TV coverage areas. Marketers look for a location with a manageable size, where residents match their target market's demographic profile. After the test has been under way for a few months and sales and market share in the test market have been calculated, marketers can estimate the product's likely performance in a full-scale rollout.

After September 11, Hollywood test-marketed upcoming movies in an attempt to gauge the psychological effects of the tragedy on moviegoers. In recruited screenings, viewers were asked whether they saw anything offensive in movies that featured acts of terrorism or scenes filmed in Manhattan. Based on test-market responses, studios decided whether to release their new films, delay them, or reshoot offending scenes.[27]

Anheuser-Busch test-marketed its low-carbohydrate Michelob Ultra in Denver, Tucson, and central Florida. Enthusiastic response led to an earlier-than-expected national rollout. Teasers ads, featuring the famous Michelob red ribbon, promise that the new brand will make diet-conscious consumers "look at beer in a whole new light."[28]

Some firms omit test-marketing and move directly from product development to full-scale production. These companies cite four problems with test-marketing:

1. Test-marketing is expensive. A firm can spend more than $1 million, depending on the size of the test-market city and the cost of buying media to advertise the product.

2. Competitors quickly learn about the new product. By studying the test market, competitors can develop alternative strategies.

3. Some products are not well-suited to test-marketing. Few firms test-market long-lived, durable goods such as cars because of the major financial investments required for their development, the need to establish networks of dealers to distribute the products, and requirements for parts and servicing.

Companies that decide to skip the test-marketing process can choose several other options. A firm may simulate a test-marketing campaign through computer-modeling software. By plugging in data on similar products, it can develop a sales projection for a new product. Another firm may offer an item in just one U.S. region or in another country, adjusting promotions and advertising based on local results before going to other geographical regions. Another option may be to limit a product's introduction to just one retail chain in order to carefully control and evaluate promotions and results.

Conducting International Marketing Research

As corporations expand globally, they need to gather correspondingly more knowledge about consumers in other countries. Although marketing researchers follow the same basic steps for international studies as for domestic ones, they do face some different challenges.

U.S. organizations can tap many secondary resources as they research global markets. One major information source is the U.S. government, particularly the Department of Commerce. The Commerce Department regularly publishes two useful reports, *Foreign Economic Trends and Their Implications for the United States* (semiannual) and *Overseas Business Reports* (annual), that discuss marketing activities in more than 100 countries. The Department of State offers commercial guides to almost every country in the world, compiled by the local embassies. Other government sources include state trade offices, small business development centers, and U.S. embassies in various nations.

When conducting international research, companies have to be prepared to deal with both language issues—communicating their message in the most effective way—and cultural issues—capturing local citizens' interests while avoiding missteps that could unintentionally offend them. Companies also need to take a good look at a country's business environment, including political and economic conditions, local trade regulations, and the potential for short- and long-term growth. Many marketers recommend tapping local researchers to investigate foreign markets.

Businesses may need to adjust their data collection methods for primary research in other countries because some methods do not easily transfer across national frontiers. Face-to-face interviewing, for instance, remains the most common method for conducting primary research outside the U.S.

While mail surveys are a common data collection method in developed countries, they are useless in many other nations because of low literacy rates, unreliable mail service, and a lack of address lists. Telephone interviews may also not be suitable in other countries, especially those where many people do not have phones.

Marketers sometimes use foreign countries as test markets prior to global product rollouts. Citicorp chose Japan to test the use of mobile phones for electronic commerce because of the high penetration of cellular technology in that country.[29]

Businesses entering new markets often contract with marketing research firms based in the countries they want to study. Also, a growing number of international research firms offer experience in conducting global studies. For example, through alliances between leading U.S. and European research companies, NOP World offers access to integrated information from multiple sources. As Figure 7.8 shows, clients receive custom research specific to industries ranging from automotive and healthcare to finance and high-tech.

6

Discuss the challenges of conducting marketing research in global markets.

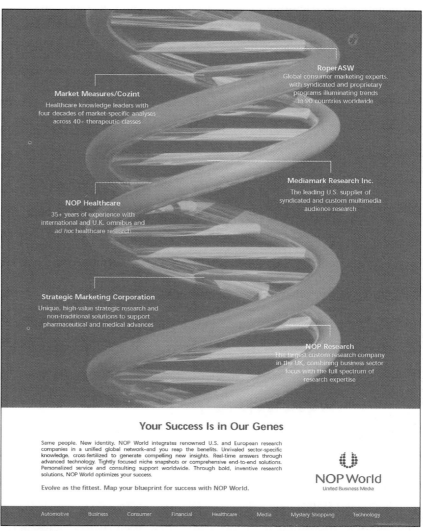

FIGURE 7.8
Marketing Research on a Global Scale

Computer Technology in Marketing Research

In a world of rapid change, the ability to quickly gather and analyze business intelligence can create a substantial strategic advantage. As noted earlier, computer databases provide a wealth of data for marketing research, whether they are maintained outside the company or designed specifically to gather important facts about its customers. Chapter 6 explored how companies are leveraging internal databases and customer relationship management technology as a means of developing long-term relationships with customers. This section addresses three important uses of computer technology related to marketing research—the marketing information system (MIS), marketing decision support system (MDSS), and data mining.

7

Outline important uses of computer technology in marketing research.

The Marketing Information System (MIS)

In the past, many marketing managers complained that their information problems resulted from too much rather than too little information. Reams of data were difficult to use, not always relevant, and almost impossible to find. Modern technological advances have made constraints like these obsolete.

A *marketing information system (MIS)* is a planned, computer-based system designed to provide decision makers with a continuous flow of information relevant to their areas of responsibility. A component of the organization's overall management information system (also often called an *MIS*), a marketing information system deals specifically with marketing data and issues.

A well-constructed MIS serves as a company's nerve center, continually monitoring the market environment—both inside and outside the organization—and providing instantaneous information. Marketers are able to store data for later use, classify and analyze that data, and retrieve it easily when needed.

The Marketing Decision Support System (MDSS)

A *marketing decision support system (MDSS)* consists of software that helps users quickly obtain and apply information in a way that supports marketing decisions. Taking MIS one step further, it allows managers to explore and make connections between such varying information as the state of the market, consumer behavior, sales forecasts, competitors' actions, and environmental changes. An MDSS can create simulations or models to illustrate the likely results of changes in marketing strategies or market conditions.

While an MIS provides raw data, an MDSS develops this data into business intelligence—information useful for decision making. For example, an MIS might provide a list of product sales from the previous day. The manager could use an MDSS to transform this raw data into graphs illustrating sales trends or reports estimating the impacts of specific decisions, such as raising prices or expanding into new regions.

Data Mining

Data mining is the process of searching through customer files to detect patterns. The data is stored in a huge database called a data warehouse. Software for the marketing decision support system is often associated with the data warehouse and is used to mine data. Once marketers identify patterns and connections, they use this intelligence to check the effectiveness of strategy options.

Data mining is an efficient way to sort through huge amounts of data and to make sense of that data. It helps marketers create customer profiles, pinpoint reasons for customer loyalty or the lack thereof, analyze the potential returns on changes in pricing or promotion, and forecast sales. Wal-Mart, for example, mines its point-of-sale data for insights into shoppers' buying habits. By examining data, the retailer can tell which products are purchased together and drive up sales of both items through store placement or special offers.[30]

Advances in data mining applications allow for real-time analysis of data flows. NonObvious Relationship Awareness (NORA) software from Systems Research & Development (SRD) was devised to help casinos identify nonobvious relationships between data from multiple sources. For example, using real-time analysis, the software might discover that a job applicant shares a telephone number with a known criminal and issue an immediate alert to the hiring manager. Given an unexpected boost due to the September 11 terrorist attacks, NORA recently received funding from the CIA to create plug-ins that would help identify potential terrorists. Using streaming technology that scans data in real time, the software might discover that a passenger buying a ticket at an airline counter recently purchased controlled explosive materials. An alert would go out before the passenger could board a plane.[31]

Sometimes the associations revealed by data mining can be unexpected as well as enlightening. Camelot Music Holdings identified a group of customers aged 65-plus who tended to buy lots of classical music, jazz tunes, and movies. Surprisingly, though, Camelot found that a large percentage of them were also buying rap and alternative music. Further analysis of the data revealed that they were buying gifts for their grandchildren.[32]

Sales Forecasting

A basic building block of a marketing plan is a **sales forecast,** an estimate of a firm's revenue for a specified future period. Sales forecasts play major roles in new-product decisions, production scheduling, financial planning, inventory planning and procurement, distribution, and human-resource planning. An inaccurate forecast may lead to incorrect decisions in each of these areas. Marketing research techniques are used to deliver effective sales forecasts. A sales forecast is also an important tool for marketing control because it sets standards against which to measure actual performance. Without such standards, no comparisons can be made.

Planners rely on short-run, intermediate, and long-run sales forecasts. A short-run forecast usually covers a period of up to one year, an intermediate forecast covers one to five years, and a long-run forecast extends beyond five years. Although sales forecasters practice dozens of techniques to divine the future—ranging from computer simulations to studying trends identified by futurists—their methods fall into two broad categories: qualitative and quantitative forecasting.

Qualitative forecasting techniques rely on subjective data that reports opinions rather than exact historical data. *Quantitative forecasting* methods, by contrast, use statistical computations such as trend extensions based on past data, computer simulations, and econometric models. As Table 7.1 shows, each method has benefits and limitations. Consequently, most organizations combine techniques.

8

Identify the major types of forecasting methods and explain the steps in the forecasting process.

Qualitative Forecasting Techniques

Planners apply qualitative forecasting methods when they want judgmental or subjective indicators. Qualitative forecasting techniques include the jury of executive opinion, Delphi technique, sales force composite, and survey of buyer intentions.

Jury of Executive Opinion

The technique called the **jury of executive opinion** combines and averages the outlooks of top executives from such areas as finance, production, marketing, and purchasing. Top managers bring the following capabilities to the process: experience and knowledge about situations that influence sales, open-minded attitudes toward the future, and awareness of the bases for their judgments. This quick and inexpensive method generates good forecasts for sales and new-product development. It works best for short-run forecasting.

Delphi Technique

Like the jury of executive opinion, the **Delphi technique** solicits opinions from several people, but it also gathers input from experts outside the firm, such as university researchers and scientists, rather than relying completely

Marketing Dictionary

sales forecast   Estimate of company revenue for a specified future period.

jury of executive opinion   Qualitative sales forecasting method that considers the sales expectations of various executives.

Delphi technique   Qualitative sales forecasting method that gathers and redistributes several rounds of anonymous forecasts until the participants reach a consensus.

TABLE 7.1   Benefits and Limitations of Various Forecasting Techniques

TECHNIQUES	BENEFITS	LIMITATIONS
Qualitative Methods		
Jury of executive opinion	Opinions come from executives in many different departments; quick; inexpensive	Managers may lack sufficient knowledge and experience to make meaningful predictions
Delphi technique	Group of experts can accurately predict long-term events such as technological breakthroughs	Time-consuming; expensive
Sales force composite	Salespeople have expert customer, product, and competitor knowledge; quick; inexpensive	Inaccurate forecasts may result from low estimates of salespeople concerned about their influence on quotas
Survey of buyer intentions	Useful in predicting short-term and intermediate sales for firms that serve only a few customers	Intentions to buy may not result in actual purchases; time-consuming; expensive
Quantitative Methods		
Market test	Provides realistic information on actual purchases rather than on intent to buy	Alerts competition to new product plans; time-consuming; expensive
Trend analysis	Quick; inexpensive; effective with stable customer demand and environment	Assumes the future will continue the past; ignores environmental changes
Exponential smoothing	Same benefits as trend analysis, but emphasizes more recent data	Same limitations as trend analysis, but not as severe due to emphasis on recent data

on company executives. It is most appropriately used to predict long-run issues, such as technological breakthroughs, that could affect future sales and the market potential for new products.

The Delphi technique works as follows: A firm selects a panel of experts and sends each a questionnaire relating to a future event. After combining and averaging the answers, the firm develops another questionnaire based on these results and sends it back to the same people. The process continues until it identifies a consensus of opinion. Although firms have successfully used Delphi to predict future technological breakthroughs, the method is both expensive and time-consuming.

Sales Force Composite

The **sales force composite** technique develops forecasts based on the belief that organization members closest to the marketplace—those with specialized product, customer, and competitor knowledge—offer the best insights concerning short-term future sales. It typically works from the bottom up. Management consolidates salespeople's estimates first at the district level, then at the regional level, and finally nationwide to obtain an aggregate forecast of sales that reflects all three levels.

The sales force composite approach has some weaknesses, however. Since salespeople recognize the role of their sales forecasts in determining sales quotas for their territories, they are likely to make conservative estimates. Moreover, their narrow perspectives from within their limited geographic territories may prevent them from considering the impact on sales of trends developing in other territories, forthcoming technological innovations, or the major changes in marketing strategies. Consequently, the sales force composite gives the best forecasts in combination with other techniques.

Survey of Buyer Intentions

A *survey of buyer intentions* gathers input through mail-in questionnaires, online feedback, telephone polls, and personal interviews to determine the purchasing intentions of a representative group of present and potential customers. This method suits firms that serve limited numbers of customers. This method often proves impractical for those with millions of customers. Also, buyer surveys gather useful information only when customers willingly reveal their buying intentions. Moreover, customer intentions do not necessarily translate into actual purchases. These surveys may help a firm to predict short-run or intermediate sales, but they employ time-consuming and expensive methods.

Quantitative Forecasting Techniques

Quantitative techniques attempt to eliminate the subjectiveness of the qualitative methods. They include such methods as market tests, trend analysis, and exponential smoothing.

Market Tests   *NO*

One quantitative technique, the *market test*, frequently helps planners in assessing consumer responses to new-product offerings. The procedure typically begins by establishing a small number of test markets to gauge consumer responses to a new product under actual marketplace conditions. Market tests also permit experimenters to evaluate the effects of different prices, alternative promotional strategies, and other marketing mix variations by comparing results among different test markets.

Verizon Communications recently conducted a limited test in the Boston area to find out whether it could increase overall revenues from pay phones by charging 10 cents rather than 50 cents for a one-minute call. Verizon wanted to see if it could win back business from cell phones if the price was right.[33]

The primary advantage of market tests is the realism that they provide for the marketer. On the other hand, these expensive and time-consuming experiments may also communicate marketing plans to competitors before a firm introduces a product to the total market.

Trend Analysis

Trend analysis develops forecasts for future sales by analyzing the historical relationship between sales and time. It implicitly assumes that the collective causes of past sales will continue to exert similar influence in the future. When historical data is available, planners can quickly and inexpensively complete trend analysis. Software programs can calculate the average annual increment of change for the available sales data. This average increment of change is then projected into the future to come up with the sales forecast. So, if the sales of a firm have been growing $15.3 million on average per year, this amount of sales could be added to last year's sales total to arrive at next year's forecast.

Of course, trend analysis cannot be used if historical data is not available, as in new-product forecasting. Also, trend analysis makes the dangerous assumption that future events will continue in the same manner as the past. Any variations in the determinants of future sales will cause deviations from the forecast. In other words, this method gives reliable forecasts during periods of steady growth and stable demand. If conditions change, predictions based on trend analysis may become worthless. For this reason, forecasters have applied more sophisticated techniques and complex, new forecasting models to anticipate the effects of various possible changes in the future.

Exponential Smoothing

A more sophisticated method of trend analysis, the **exponential smoothing** technique, weighs each year's sales data, giving greater weight to results from the most recent years. Otherwise, the statistical approach used in trend analysis is applied here. For example, last year's sales might receive a 1.5 weight, while sales data from two years ago could get a 1.4 weighting. Exponential smoothing is considered the most commonly used quantitative forecasting technique.

Marketing Dictionary

sales force composite   Qualitative sales forecasting method based on the combined sales estimates of the firm's salespeople.

trend analysis   Quantitative sales forecasting method that estimates future sales through statistical analyses of historical sales patterns.

exponential smoothing   Quantitative forecasting technique that assigns weights to historical sales data, giving the greatest weight to the most recent data.

Strategic Implications of Marketing in the 21st Century

Marketing research can help an organization develop effective marketing strategies. Approximately 75 percent of new products eventually fail to attract enough buyers to remain viable. Why? A major reason is the seller's failure to understand market needs.

Consider, for example, the hundreds of dot-com companies that have gone under. A characteristic shared by all of those failing businesses is that virtually none of them were founded on sound marketing research. Very few used marketing research techniques to evaluate product potential and even fewer studied consumer responses after the ventures were initiated. While research might not have prevented every dot-com meltdown, it may have helped a few of those businesses survive the waning economy in which they were launched.[34]

Marketing research ideally matches new products to potential customers. Marketers also conduct research to analyze sales of their own and competitors' products, to gauge the performance of existing products, to guide the development of promotional campaigns and product enhancements, and to develop and refine products. All of these activities enable marketers to fine-tune their marketing strategies and reach customers more effectively and efficiently.

Marketing researchers have at their disposal a broad range of techniques with which to collect both quantitative and qualitative data on customers, their lifestyles, behaviors, attitudes, and perceptions. Vast amounts of data can be rapidly collected, accessed, interpreted, and applied to improve all aspects of business operations. Because of customer relationship management technology, that information is no longer generalized to profile groups of customers—it can be analyzed to help marketers understand each and every customer.

Summary of Chapter Objectives

1. Describe the development of the marketing research function and its major activities.

Marketing research, or the collection and use of information in marketing decision making, started when Charles C. Parlin, an advertising space salesperson, counted empty soup cans in Philadelphia's trash in an effort to convince the Campbell Soup Company to advertise in the *Saturday Evening Post*. Today, the most common marketing research activities are (1) determining market potential, market share, and market characteristics; and (2) conducting sales analyses and competitive product studies. Most large companies now have internal marketing research departments. However, outside suppliers still remain vital to the research function. Some perform the complete research task, while others specialize in a limited area or provide specific data services.

2. List and explain the steps in the marketing research process.

The marketing research process can be divided into six specific steps: (1) defining the problem, (2) conducting exploratory research, (3) formulating hypotheses, (4) creating a research design, (5) collecting data, and (6) interpreting and presenting the research information. A clearly defined problem focuses on the researcher's search for relevant decision-oriented information. Exploratory research refers to information gained outside the firm. Hypotheses, tentative explanations of specific events, allow researchers to set out specific research designs—that is, the series of decisions that, taken together, comprise master plans or models for the conduct of the investigations. The data-collection phase of the marketing research process can involve either or both primary (original data) and secondary data (previously published data). After the data is collected, researchers must interpret and present it in a way that will be meaningful to management.

3. Differentiate between the types and sources of primary and secondary data.

Primary data can be collected by the firm's own researchers or by independent marketing research companies. Three principal methods of primary data collection are: observation, survey, or experiment. Secondary data can be classified as either internal or external. Sources of internal data include sales records, product evaluation, sales force reports, and records of marketing costs. Sources of external data include the government and private sources, such as business magazines. Both external and internal data can also be obtained from computer databases.

4. Explain the different sampling techniques used by marketing researchers.

Samples can be categorized as either probability samples or nonprobability samples. A probability sample is one in which every member of the population has an equal chance of being selected. Probability samples include simple random samples, in which every item in the relevant universe has an equal opportunity to be selected; stratified samples, which are constructed such that randomly selected subsamples of different groups are represented in the total sample; and cluster samples, in which geographic areas are selected from which respondents are drawn. A nonprobability sample is arbitrary and does not allow application of standard statistical tests. Nonprobability sampling techniques include convenience samples, in which readily available respondents are picked, and quota samples, which are divided so that different segments or groups are represented in the total sample.

5. Identify the methods by which marketing researchers collect primary data.

Observation data is gathered by observing consumers via devices such as people meters or videotape. Survey data can be collected through telephone interviews, mail or fax surveys, personal interviews, focus groups, or through a variety of online methods. Telephone interviews provide over half of all primary marketing research data. They give the researcher a fast and inexpensive way to get small amounts of information, but generally not detailed or personal information. Personal interviews are costly, but allow researchers to get detailed information from respondents. Mail surveys are a means of con-

ducting national studies at a reasonable cost; their main disadvantage is potentially inadequate response rates. Focus groups elicit detailed, qualitative information that provides insight not only into behavior but into consumer attitudes and perceptions. Online surveys and other online methods can yield fast responses but face obstacles such as the adequacy of the probability sample. The experimental method creates verifiable statistical data through the use of test and control groups to reveal actual benefits from perceived benefits.

6. Discuss the challenges of conducting marketing research in global markets.

Many resources are available to help U.S. organizations research global markets. Government resources include the Department of Commerce, state trade offices, Small Business Development Centers, and foreign embassies. Private companies, such as marketing research firms and companies that distribute research from other sources, are another resource. Electronic networks offer online international trade forums, in which marketers can establish global contacts.

7. Outline important uses of computer technology in marketing research.

Important uses of computer technology in marketing research include: (1) a marketing information systems (MIS)—a planned, computer-based system designed to provide managers with a continuous flow of information relevant to their specific decision-making needs and areas of responsibility; (2) a marketing decision support system (MDSS)—a marketing information system component that links a decision maker with relevant databases and analysis tools; and (3) data mining—the process of searching through consumer information files or data warehouses to detect patterns that guide marketing decision making.

8. Identify the major types of forecasting methods and explain the steps in the forecasting process.

There are two categories of forecasting methods: (1) Qualitative methods are more subjective since they are based on opinions rather than exact historical data. They include the jury of executive opinion, the Delphi technique, the sales force composite, and the survey of buyer intentions. (2) Quantitative methods employ statistical computations such as trend analysis and exponential smoothing.

Marketing Terms You Need to Know

marketing research 194	sampling 203	sales forecast 213	trend analysis 215
exploratory research 198	probability sample 204	jury of executive opinion 213	exponential smoothing 215
secondary data 199	nonprobability sample 204	Delphi technique 213	
primary data 200	focus group 206	sales force composite 214	

Other Important Marketing Terms

syndicated service 195	research design 199	quota sample 204	marketing decision support
full-service research	slotting fee 199	ethnography 205	system (MDSS) 212
supplier 195	population (universe) 204	mall intercept 206	data mining 212
limited-service research	simple random sample 204	controlled experiment 209	qualitative forecasting 213
supplier 196	stratified sample 204	test-marketing 209	quantitative forecasting 213
sales analysis 198	cluster sample 204	marketing information system	survey of buyer intentions 214
hypothesis 199	convenience sample 204	(MIS) 212	market test 215

Review Questions

1. Outline the development and current status of the marketing research function. What role did Charles Parlin play in the development of marketing research?
2. List and explain the various steps in the marketing research process. Trace a hypothetical study through the various stages of this process.
3. Distinguish between primary and secondary data. When should researchers collect each type of data?
4. Compare and contrast sales analysis and marketing cost analysis. What roles does each play in marketing research?
5. Explain the differences between probability and non-probability samples. Identify the various types of each.
6. Distinguish among surveys, experiments, and observational methods of primary data collection. Cite examples of each method.
7. Define and give an example of each of the methods of gathering survey data. Under what circumstances should researchers choose a specific approach?
8. Discuss international marketing research. How does this process compare with domestic marketing research?
9. Distinguish among marketing information systems, marketing decision support systems, and data mining. Cite examples of each.
10. Compare the major sales forecasting methods. Explain the steps for the most typical method.

Projects and Teamwork Exercises

1. A. C. Nielsen offers data collected by optical scanners from the United Kingdom, France, Germany, Belgium, the Netherlands, Austria, Italy, and Finland. This scanner data tracks sales of UPC-coded products in those nations. In small teams, imagine that you are Nielsen clients in the United States. One team might be retail chain, another an Internet company, and still another a toy manufacturer. Discuss the types of marketing questions this data might help you answer. Share your list with other teams.
2. Set up two class teams to debate the use of the Internet to research new domestic markets. What other research options are available?
3. Today, one in three new homes sold in America is likely to be a manufactured home. Newly-built manufactured homes are better built using higher-quality materials than those of the past. As a result, the market for manufactured homes has grown to include more affluent buyers. Alabama-based Southern Energy Homes tries to appeal to upscale buyers by custom-building its homes according to customer specifications. What type of data and information should Southern Energy gather through its ongoing marketing intelligence to predict demand for its products? Would primary or secondary methods work best? Name some specific secondary sources of data that Southern Energy might study to find useful business intelligence.
4. Discuss some of the challenges McDonald's Corp. might face in conducting marketing research in potential new international markets. What types of research would you recommend the company use in choosing new countries for expansion?
5. Which sales forecasting technique(s) are most appropriate for each of the following products? Prepare your arguments in pairs or teams:
   a. Post Shredded Wheat breakfast cereal
   b. No Doubt rock group
   c. Kinko's copy shops
   d. *Rolling Stone* magazine

'net **W**ork

1. Census data. Visit the Bureau of the Census Web site. Assume you're considering launching a new business in your local community but want to conduct some marketing research before making extensive time and financial commitments. Prepare a list of the statistical reports that may assist you in this task.

http://www.census.gov

2. Private data. Visit the following Web site, http://www.nielsen-netratings.com. Answer the following questions:

a. According to the most recent daily statistics, how many people are typically online? What was the average time spent online?

b. Based on weekly statistics reported on the site, identify the top three online advertisers for the most recent week.

c. According to either daily or weekly statistics, which Web sites are the most popular?

http://www.nielsen-netratings.com

3. Guidelines for conducting focus groups. Go to the Web site listed. Review the basics of conducting a focus group interview, including how to run a focus group and techniques for getting more out of this research approach. Prepare a written report summarizing your findings.

http://www.mapnp.org/library/grp_skll/focusgrp/focusgrp.htm

Note: Internet Web addresses change frequently. If you don't find the exact sites listed, you may need to access the organization or company's home page and search from there.

CASE 7.1

Using Demand Management Software to Predict What Customers Want and When

In an era when marked-down items account for more than a third of retail sales, it pays to know which items are likely to be hot sellers—and which are destined to end up in discount bins. Demand management software now offers businesses large and small just the crystal ball they need to keep inventory in check.

Demand management applications tell companies what will sell when, allowing them to control inventory, keep fast-selling products in stock, and sell, whenever possible, at full price. Attuned to factors such as regional climate readings, economic trends, and geographic variances, the software can predict spikes and dips in demand, whether for snow gear in Minnesota or swimsuits in Hawaii.

Consider the experience of Dal-Tile International. Using software from Demantra, the company quickly figured out that fully 95 percent of its sales of angle-corner bathroom tiles were to customers on the West Coast. The tilemaker was able to divert the lion's share of inventory to California, cutting costs, minimizing returns—and saving its product from the bargain-price shelf.

Large firms, too, are incorporating demand software into their supply chains. Hyundai's parts division credits demand software with reducing delivery time by a fifth while trimming staffing costs. Fairchild Semiconductor's global system integrates four business groups in Asia, Europe, and North America, connecting thousands of employees and aligning data from hundreds of sources, delivered in multiple languages. Similarly, O'Reilly Auto Parts, with 850 stores nationwide, uses the software to shift inventory according to seasonal demands.

As with any technology, the rule "garbage-in, garbage-out" applies to demand software. The technology depends on obtaining honest, reliable data from salespeople, marketing analysts, customers, and countless other sources. Since so many factors—such as market conditions and competitive strategies—influence demand, any system requires constant adaptation. And then there are glitches in the software itself—Unilever was left with a glut of $400,000 worth of smoked sausages when its pilot program went askew, while Nike blames a 33 percent shortfall in earnings estimates on a flaw in its demand software.

Questions for Critical Thinking

1. What are the potential benefits of forecasting technologies to customer-driven companies, large and small?
2. A partner at PricewaterhouseCoopers, while praising the virtues of demand management systems, offered the following caveat: "One of the problems with demand software is that you can't test the tools in the laboratory. The only way to know whether they will work is to put live data into them." Is costly demand forecasting technology worth the risks?

SOURCES: "What Is the Demand Management Process?" http://www.demand solutions.com, accessed January 15, 2003; Chana R. Schoenberger, "The Weakest Link," *Forbes*, October 1, 2001, pp. 114–115; Tim Wilson, "Accuracy's in Demand," *Industry Week*, July 19, 2001; Doug Bartholomew, "MES Provides Vital Link," *Industry Week*, May 21, 2001, pp. 55–57.

VIDEO CASE 7.2

Fisher-Price: Marketing Research Is More than Child's Play

The written case on Fisher-Price appears on page VC-9. The recently filmed Fisher-Price video is designed to expand and highlight the concepts in this chapter and the concepts and questions covered in the written video case.

Krispy Kreme Continuing Case for Part 2 appears on page KK-4.

Part 3

Market Segmentation and Customer Behavior

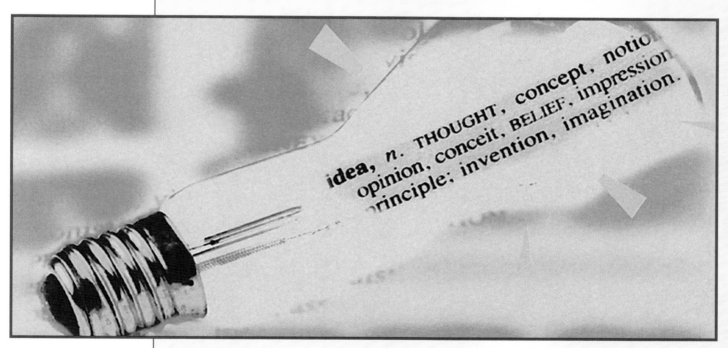

8

Market Segmentation, Targeting, and Positioning

Chapter Objectives

1 Identify the essential components of a market.

2 Outline the role of market segmentation in developing a marketing strategy.

3 Describe the criteria necessary for effective segmentation.

4 Explain each of the four bases for segmenting consumer markets.

5 Identify the steps in the market segmentation process.

6 Discuss four basic strategies for reaching target markets.

7 Summarize the types of positioning strategies.

8 Explain the reasons for positioning and repositioning products.

Torrid Taps the Teen Market

Teens represent a blazing hot market for consumer-oriented businesses. They spend $155 billion each year in the U.S. alone, and that's not counting the family purchases they may influence, including groceries, TV sets and computers, autos, and vacations. According to Teen Research Unlimited, the average U.S. teen spends about $116 per week. If that seems like a lot, you aren't mistaken. Marketers have begun to pay attention to this group of consumers because of their considerable appetites for consumer goods. "All brands recognize it's important to get them [teens] early because they're already starting to formulate their own opinions," notes Melisa Wolfson, president of a California-based teen marketing agency.

Experts in understanding and targeting the teen market offer advice to marketers who want to reach these consumers: Never have a "when I was a teen" attitude—it's an instant turnoff. See teens as they are now, but don't make blanket generational statements about them. Don't try to shove a brand message at teens, and don't underestimate their intelligence.

One company that has followed the rules—and then made its own—is Torrid, a hot chain of boutiques that teenage girls think is really cool. Torrid—a division of Hot Topic—knows a few things about teens. First, they come in all shapes and sizes. Second, they want to wear up-to-the-minute styles. Third, they want to feel good about themselves. But Torrid is different from other stores because the chain specializes in a particular segment of the teen fashion market: plus-size girls. Before Torrid, teen girls who were size 14 or more had very little choice in what to wear. Hot Topic CEO Betsy McLaughlin saw a need and decided to fill it.

At any of Torrid's stores, teen customers can try on clothes in just about any style—punk, club, gothic, even retro lounge. They can pick up lingerie, cosmetics, belts, handbags, shoes, and body jewelry. They can buy candles, teen magazines, even collectible action figures. In fact, they could probably live quite comfortably at Torrid. Boutique marketers assure consumers that all of their fashion ideas come straight from current music videos, concerts, and music magazines, so when customers choose at Torrid they know it's on the cutting edge of style. In addition, shoppers get advice on how to make the most of their looks. "Accessorize, accessorize, accessorize!" exclaims McLaughlin, with jewelry, handbags, and shoes. The Torrid philosophy encourages plus-size girls to choose clothing that fits well and shows off their best features, instead of hiding under boxy or oversized items.

Although Torrid has only been around for a few years, it's a hit with teens—and their parents. McLaughlin enjoys special satisfaction in this success because she was a plus-size teen who struggled to find clothes. "There was no place for me to shop," she recalls. Hot Topic plans to open more Torrid boutiques soon, as more teens and parents write to McLaughlin requesting stores near them.[1]

Chapter Overview

Each of us is unique. We come from different backgrounds, have different household makeups, different interests and goals. Even best friends may shop at different stores, attend different sporting or cultural events, take different courses. Consider teen clothing, as we did in the opening vignette. A wide variety of fashions are available–from 1970s retro, to urban hip hop, to gothic, to glamour. Marketers offer clothes in a kaleidoscope of colors and many different sizes, all to satisfy consumers' varied needs and to tempt window shoppers to become buyers. Your taste in clothing relates to your interests, your family and friends, your income–even the city and state where you live. Plus-size teens constitute a certain portion of teen consumers, too, as Torrid knows well. All of these factors make up a market. A **market** is composed of people or institutions with sufficient purchasing power, authority, and willingness to buy. And marketers must use their expertise to understand the market for a good or service, whether it's tickets for a baseball game—or a T top.

Most markets likely include consumers with different lifestyles, backgrounds, and income levels. It is unusual for a single marketing mix strategy to attract all sectors of a market. By identifying, evaluating, and selecting a target market to pursue, marketers are able to develop more efficient and effective marketing strategies. The **target market** for a product is the specific segment of consumers most likely to purchase a particular product.

As Chapter 4 illustrated, marketing now takes place on a global basis more than ever, incorporating many target markets. To identify those markets, marketers must determine useful ways for segmenting different populations and communicating with them successfully. This chapter discusses useful ways to accomplish this, explaining the steps of the market segmentation process, and surveying strategies for reaching target markets. Finally, it will look at the role of positioning in developing a marketing strategy.

1

Identify the essential components of a market.

Types of Markets

Products are usually classified as either consumer products or business products. **Consumer products** are those bought by ultimate consumers for personal use. **Business products** are goods and services purchased for use either directly or indirectly in the production of other goods and services for resale. Most goods and services purchased by individual consumers—books, cleaning services, and clothes, for example—are considered consumer products. Rubber and raw cotton are examples of items generally purchased by manufacturers and are, therefore, classified as business products. Goodyear buys rubber to manufacture tires; textile manufacturers such as Burlington Industries convert raw cotton into cloth.

Sometimes a single product can serve different uses. Tires purchased for the family car constitute consumer products; but tires purchased by General Motors to be mounted during production of its Chevy Suburban truck are business products because they become part of another product destined for resale. (Some marketers add another term, *commercial products,* for business products like legal services that do not contribute directly to the production of other goods.) If you want to determine the classification of items, just think about who is going to buy the product and why (or how it will be used). Chapters 8 and 9 focus on segmentation and buying behavior in consumer markets. Chapter 10 will cover business-to-business markets.

Market segmentation. Visit the Ford Motor Company Web site (http://www.ford.com) and review the various makes and models offered by Ford. (Remember, Ford also owns such well-known makes as Jaguar and Volvo.) Prepare a table listing market segments in the first column under the heading "Segment," and in the second column the makes and models offered by Ford aimed at that segment of the car-buying market. Discuss your findings.

Def N break the Mrkt down into segments, variable then Target areas they r interested, + Position then 4 P's.

The Role of Market Segmentation

2

Outline the role of market segmentation in developing a marketing strategy.

In today's business world, the diversification of people causes too many variables in consumer needs, preferences, and purchasing power to attract all consumers within a single marketing mix. That's not to say that firms must actually change products to meet the needs of different market segments—although they often do—but they must attempt to identify the factors that affect purchase decisions and then group consumers according to the presence or absence of these factors. Finally, they adjust marketing strategies to meet the needs of each group.

Consider cars. Unlike a century ago, when Henry Ford pronounced that customers could order any color of car they liked—as long as it was black—there is a make, model, and color for every taste and budget. But auto manufacturers need to adjust their messages for different markets. And smart marketers are looking toward markets that show growth, such as the U.S. Hispanic population.[2] African Americans, the second-largest U.S. racial or ethnic group, are also an attractive market for automakers. Chevrolet emphasizes its long-standing relationship with African Americans in the advertisement featured in Figure 8.1.

The division of the total market into smaller, relatively homogeneous groups is called **market segmentation.** Both profit-oriented and not-for-profit organizations practice market segmentation.

Criteria for Effective Segmentation

3

Describe the criteria necessary for effective segmentation.

Segmentation doesn't automatically guarantee success in the marketing arena; instead, it is a tool for marketers to use. Effectiveness depends on the following four basic requirements.

First, the market segment must present measurable purchasing power and size. A perfect example is women. With jobs, incomes, and decision making power, women consumers represent a hefty amount of purchasing power. According to some experts, women make up half the potential market for many new electronic products.[3]

Second, marketers must find a way to promote effectively to and serve the market segment. Since women are more likely than men to think twice about a technology purchase—and often care about style and color as well as functionality—marketers need to find different ways to appeal to women. Catherine Markman, director of Evins Communications' technology division, asserts that nearly any electronic device could be sold to women with the right kind of marketing.[4]

Third, marketers must then identify segments that are sufficiently large to give them good profit potential. As mentioned earlier, citizens of Hispanic descent make up one of the

Marketing Dictionary

market Group of people or institutions with sufficient purchasing power, authority, and willingness to buy.

target market Specific segment of consumers most likely to purchase a particular product.

consumer products Products bought by ultimate consumers for personal use.

business products Goods and services purchased for use either directly or indirectly in the production of other goods and services for resale.

market segmentation Division of the total market into smaller, relatively homogeneous groups.

**FIGURE 8.1
Chevrolet's Attempt to
Attract African
American Consumers**

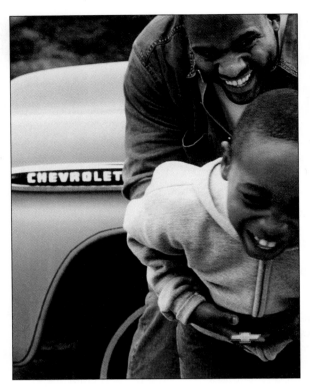

fastest-growing populations in the U.S. Forty-two percent of the population of New Mexico and 32 percent of California's and Texas's populations are Hispanic.[5] General Mills pays special attention to this market not only with advertising and promotion but also with Betty Crocker products targeted for Hispanic tastes. Some of these foods include *arroz con leche* (rice pudding) and *flan* (caramel custard), as illustrated in Figure 8.2. "We developed these products with the Latino palate in mind," says Michelle Freedman, marketing manager. "Our strategy is now to put more resources behind ethnic-specific products." Kraft and Nabisco also sell similar products such as Kraft's Jell-O American Flan and Nabisco's Royal Flan.[6]

And fourth, the firm must aim for segments that match its marketing capabilities. Targeting a large number of niche markets can be an expensive, complex, and inefficient strategy; so smaller firms may decide to stick with a particular niche, or target market. Zephwear.com creates footwear for children's and youth sports teams. Its special appeal is that consumers can go online to design their own logo cards that slide inside a plastic insert in the tongue flap of each shoe. Kids love it, and the cost of this customization is low to the company; it is also part of the firm's marketing strategy. Furthermore, the shoes themselves are relatively inexpensive at about $35 a pair.[7]

**FIGURE 8.2
Betty Crocker Food
Products Targeted for
Hispanic Tastes**

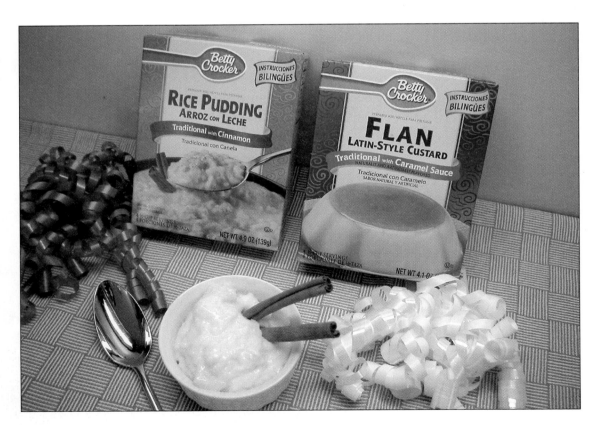

Segmenting Consumer Markets

Market segmentation attempts to isolate the traits that distinguish a certain group of consumers from the overall market. An understanding of the group's characteristics—such as age, sex, geographical location, income, and expenditure patterns—plays a vital role in developing a successful marketing strategy. In most cases, marketers seek to pinpoint a number of factors affecting buying behavior in the target segment. For example, toy manufacturers such as Ideal, Hasbro, Mattel, and Kenner consider not only birthrate trends but also changes in income levels and expenditure patterns to successfully market their products. In trying to attract new students, colleges and universities are affected by the number of graduating high-school seniors and also by changing attitudes toward the value of a college education and trends in enrollment of older adults. Also, few, if any, marketers identify totally homogeneous segments, in which all potential customers are alike; they always encounter some differences among members of a target group.

The four common bases for segmenting consumer markets are geographic segmentation, demographic segmentation, psychographic segmentation, and product-related segmentation. These segmentation approaches can give important guidance for marketing strategies, provided they identify significant differences in buying behavior.

4

Explain each of the four bases for segmenting consumer markets.

Geographic Segmentation

Marketers have practiced **geographic segmentation**—dividing an overall market into homogeneous groups on the basis of their locations—for hundreds of years. Geographic location does not ensure that all consumers in a location will make the same buying decisions, but this segmentation approach does help in identifying some general patterns. The 288 million people who live in the U.S. are not scattered evenly across the country. Instead, they are concentrated in major metropolitan areas. New York City is the largest U.S. city, with 8 million citizens. Los Angeles, Chicago, Houston, and Philadelphia follow. The states with the most residents are California (34 million), Texas (21 million), New York (19 million), Florida (16 million), and Illinois (12 million). By contrast, only about 1 million citizens live in New Hampshire, with about half that in Vermont.[8]

As discussed in Chapter 4, a look at the worldwide population distribution illustrates why so many firms are pursuing customers around the globe. As in the U.S., many of these people live in urban environments. The two metropolitan areas with the world's largest populations, Tokyo and Mexico City, dwarf New York City.

Population size alone, however, may not be reason enough for a business to expand into a specific country. Businesses also need to look at a wide variety of economic variables. Some businesses may decide to cluster together countries that share similar population and product-use patterns instead of treating each country as an independent segment. This grouping is taking place with greater frequency throughout the European Union as the currency and trade laws are unified.

While population numbers indicate the overall size of a market, other geographic indicators such as job growth can also give useful guidance to marketers, depending on the type of products they sell. Food companies might look for geographic segments with large populations because food is an essential product used by everyone. Automobile manufacturers, on the other hand, might segment geographic regions by household income because it is an important factor in the purchase of a new car.

Geographic areas also vary in population-migration patterns. The U.S., for example, has traditionally been a mobile society. About one of every six Americans moves each year. However, this figure is down from one out of five a few decades ago. The slowdown has resulted from changes such as increased home ownership.

U.S. census data also indicates two major population shifts: migration toward the Sunbelt states of the Southeast and Southwest and toward the West. Researchers expect this trend to continue. Between now and 2020, the states expected to experience the fastest population growth are Nevada, Hawaii, California, and Washington.[9]

As people migrate from one geographic area to another, regional consumer tastes often change. Catfish, a longtime staple in the diet of

Marketing Dictionary

geographic segmentation   Dividing an overall market into homogeneous groups based on their locations.

the southern U.S., is now popular in all parts of the country. By contrast, cornbread and other popular southern recipes using cornmeal are considered exotic in Great Britain, where cornmeal is available mainly through health-food stores.

The move from urban to suburban areas after World War II created a need to redefine the urban marketplace. This trend radically changed cities' traditional patterns of retailing and led to disintegration in many downtown shopping areas. It also rendered traditional city boundaries almost meaningless for marketing purposes.

In an effort to respond to these changes, the government now classifies urban data using three categories.

- A *Metropolitan Statistical Area (MSA)* is a freestanding urban area with a population in the urban center of at least 50,000 and a total MSA population of 100,000 or more. Buyers in MSAs exhibit social and economic homogeneity. They usually border on nonurbanized counties. Examples include Rochester, New York; Odessa-Midland, Texas; and Kalamazoo-Battle Creek, Michigan.[10]

- The category of *Consolidated Metropolitan Statistical Area (CMSA)* includes the country's 25 or so urban giants such as Detroit-Ann Arbor-Flint, Michigan; Los Angeles-Riverside-Orange County, California; and Philadelphia-Wilmington-Atlantic City. (Note that in the third example, three states are involved—Pennsylvania, Delaware, and New Jersey.)[11] A CMSA must include two or more Primary Metropolitan Statistical Areas, discussed next.

- A *Primary Metropolitan Statistical Area (PMSA)* is an urbanized county or set of counties with social and economic ties to nearby areas. PMSAs are identified within areas of 1-million-plus populations. Olympia, Washington, is part of the Seattle-Tacoma-Bremerton PMSA. Bridgeport, Connecticut, is part of the New York-Northern New Jersey-Long Island PMSA and Riverside-San Bernardino, California, is a PMSA within the Los Angeles-Riverside-Orange County PMSA.[12]

Using Geographic Segmentation

BEAUTIFUL GARDENS.
(GREEN THUMB NOT REQUIRED.)

That's because our Garden Club Select plants are carefully chosen by our Garden Club experts for their outstanding performance, resilience, disease resistance and number of blooms. Many are also available in exclusive colors and are backed by our one year plant guarantee*. For a garden that can't miss, stop by Lowe's and see one of our Certified Nursery Specialists.

Call toll-free 1-877-61-LOWES today to join the Lowe's Garden Club!

LOWE'S
Improving Home Improvement

EVERYDAY LOW PRICES. GUARANTEED!*

Suburbanites spend the most on lawn and garden products.

Demand for some categories of goods and services can vary according to geographic region, and marketers need to be aware of how these regions differ. Most major brands get 40 to 80 percent of their sales from what are called *core regions;* elsewhere in the national marketplace, such a product is essentially a specialty brand.

Residence location within a geographic area is an important segmentation variable. City dwellers often get along fine without automobiles, whereas those who live in the suburbs or the country depend on their vehicles. Also, those who live in the suburbs spend more on lawn and garden care products than people in the city.

Climate is another important segmentation factor. Consumers in chilly, northern states, for example, eat more soup than residents in warmer, southern markets. But here's a surprise—they also eat a great deal of ice cream!

Geographic segmentation provides useful distinctions when regional preferences or needs exist. A consumer might not *want* to invest in a snowblower or flood insurance but may *have* to because of the location of his or her home. But it's important for marketers not to stop at geographic location as a segmentation method, because distinctions among consumers also exist within a geographic location. Consider those who relocate from one region to another for work or family reasons. They may bring along with them their preferences from other parts of the country. In one recent year, 19 percent of those who relocated moved to another state.[13] Using multiple segmentation variables will probably be a much better strategy for targeting a specific market.

Geographic Information System (GIS)

At Domino's Pizza, Super Bowl Sunday is more than a sporting event—it is also the company's single biggest sales day of the year. As the pro football teams face off, Domino's tackles its own challenge: planning and executing timely delivery of more than 900,000 pizzas to residences throughout the country. Domino's has built its reputation as the number-one pizza delivery company in the world, which means that its delivery system must be as streamlined and efficient as possible.

Companies like Domino's traditionally obtained much of their geographic data for deliveries from statistical databases and reports. These sources do provide valuable information, but not in a format that is quick and easy to use. So Domino's invested in a geographic information system. Once used mainly by the military, a **geographic information system (GIS)** simplifies the job of analyzing marketing information by placing data in a spatial format. The result is a geographic map overlaid with digital data about consumers in a particular area.

Thanks to its GIS, Domino's delivery drivers can map in advance the best route to reaching each customer's address. Managers use the GIS to pinpoint the best locations for stores, based on purchase data and driving distances, and identify areas that are promising candidates for new stores. The system also helps them to allocate inventory more efficiently.[14]

The earliest geographic information systems were prohibitively expensive for all but the largest companies. Recent technological advances, however, have made GIS software available at a much lower cost, increasing usage among smaller firms. Like Domino's, a growing number of companies benefit from using a GIS to locate new outlets, assign sales territories, and plan distribution centers and delivery routes. Marketing researchers agree, however, that firms have not yet realized the full potential of GIS technology.

Demographic Segmentation

The most common method of market segmentation—**demographic segmentation**—defines consumer groups according to demographic variables such as gender, age, income, occupation, education, household size, and stage in the family life cycle. This approach is also sometimes called *socioeconomic segmentation*. Marketers review vast quantities of available data to complete a plan for demographic segmentation. One of the primary sources for demographic data in the U.S. is the Bureau of the Census. Marketers can obtain many of the Census Bureau's statistics online at **http://www.census.gov**. The following discussion considers the most commonly used demographic variables.

Segmenting by Gender

Gender is an obvious variable that helps to define the markets for certain products. When segmenting by gender, marketers need to be sure they are targeting consumers correctly. As discussed earlier, women now make up about half the potential market for consumer electronics. Furthermore, during a recent holiday season, a significant percentage of women indicated that computers topped their gift wish list. But a survey conducted by the Consumer Electronics Marketing Association (CEMA) revealed that typical marketing of most technical products leaves women cold. According to Angela Gunn, a columnist for *Yahoo! Life*, women make a distinction between "appliance" technology and "accessory" technology. When shopping for an electronic appliance such as a high-end entertainment center, women want to shop around, learn the specifications, and get the best price. But when it comes to an accessory like a cell phone, color counts.[15]

Some companies market the same product successfully to both genders. Gillette markets its disposable razor Slim Twist in two colors— one for men, one for women—but it's the same razor nonetheless. "The only difference is the color," says a company product specialist.[16]

Other marketers may start by targeting one gender and then later switch to both. In fact, Gillette began producing men's razors first

Marketing Dictionary

geographic information system (GIS)   System that places data in a spatial format, on a map.

demographic segmentation   Dividing an overall market into homogeneous groups based on variables such as gender, age, and income.

Oprah Winfrey lends her support to Oxygen Media.

and then added a women's razor in 1915. While the disposable razors remain unisex in design, the nondisposables have distinctive features for each gender. The women's razors typically have larger handles and moisturizers behind the blade, whereas men's are smaller and do not contain lubricants.[17]

Even if marketers think they have targeted a gender market correctly, a product may not reach its audience. After a splashy launch, the cable-TV and Web site operator Oxygen Media failed to catch its breath—or its audience. Oxygen proclaimed that it would offer an intelligent media outlet for women and an online community of women with common interests. But initially, the project fizzled, partly because the station couldn't penetrate enough cable systems. After a year or so of languishing, Oxygen debuted on an important cable system in New York City, delivering the kinds of programs it had promised in the beginning, and reaching its target market—women. Prominent women such as Oprah Winfrey lent their support to the cable channel, and it began to turn around.[18]

Segmenting by Age

Many firms identify market segments on the basis of consumers' ages. In fact, they develop some products specifically to meet the needs of people in certain age groups. Gerber Food focuses on food for infants and toddlers. Del Webb Corp. creates Sun Cities retirement communities. Warner-Lambert developed Halls Juniors cough drops for children 5 years and over. Age distribution and projected changes in each age group are important to marketers because consumer needs and wants differ notably among age groups.

Clothing retailer Limited Too targets girls between the ages of 8 and 17 by offering hip clothes and accessories that appeal to the age bracket—including fashion jewelry, glitter cosmetics, and room decorations. The company offers a range of discounts and promotions, including an offer of $5 off any purchase when a customer brings in a current report card with all passing grades. The catalog often shows groups of girls engaged in activities as friends—whether it's sports, trips to the beach, or sleepovers.

Sociologists attribute some of these differences to the *cohort effect*—the tendency of members of a generation to be influenced and bound together by significant events occurring during their key formative years, roughly 17 to 22 years of age. These events help to define the core values of the age group that eventually shape consumer preferences and behavior. Marketers have already labeled people who were in the 17–22 age bracket at the time of the terrorist attacks the *9/11 Generation*. Clearly, this group's previous priorities and values have changed. How the cohort effect for the 9/11 Generation will play out in later years remains uncertain—at least in a marketing sense.

Now let's look at two age groups whose unique characteristics have proved to be of particular importance to marketers: the boomers and the seniors. Let's start with the boomers.

Baby Boomers

So-called *baby boomers*—people born from 1946 until 1965—are a popular segment to target because of their numbers. Nearly 42 percent of U.S. adults were born in this period. The values of this age group were influenced both by the Vietnam War era and the career-driven era that followed.

There is no doubt that baby boomers are a lucrative market. Experts predict that baby boomers over the age of 50 will have a total disposable income of $1 trillion within the next few years, which is why businesses are trying to woo this group. Members of the group, however, do not always behave as expected, complicating segmentation and targeting strategies. For instance, although pundits have predicted the demise of movie theaters, boomers are flocking to the cinema in record numbers.

Different subgroups within this generation also complicate segmentation and targeting strategies. Some boomers put off starting families until their 40s, while others of their age have already become

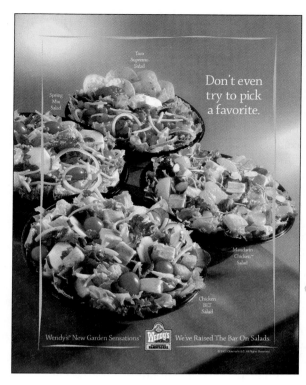

Don't even
try to pick
a favorite.

Taco
Supremo
Salad

Spring
Mix
Salad

Mandarin
Chicken
Salad

Chicken
BLT
Salad

Wendy's® New Garden Sensations™ | We've Raised The Bar On Salads.

Menus at fast-food restaurants such as Wendy's, Burger King, and Arby's have changed as their marketing efforts have focused more on adults and less on children. Increased emphasis on healthy dining has prompted fast-food restaurants to depend less on high-calorie, high-fat mainstays such as fries and burgers.

GI generation called seniors
BB 1964-1965 Baby boomers

Marketing Miss

Targeting the Senior Set

Background. Seniors now account for one-third of the U.S. population. Yet, more important to marketers is that they control nearly three-quarters of disposable income. They buy 2 of every 5 new cars sold and most travel sales. As the baby-boom generation ages, the senior market will only grow larger.

The Marketing Problem. For decades, senior consumers have been ignored by many marketers, who have focused on younger consumers. Many marketers believe that older consumers are too set in their ways to switch brands or try new products. Recently, however, they have realized their mistake and have attempted to reach this market with ads featuring older consumers and products designed to meet their needs. L'Oréal cosmetics launched an ad campaign featuring 50-something model Dayle Haddon promoting its products, and Toyota aired commercials with former mountaineer, Sir Edmund Hillary, who is in his 80s.

The Outcome. Some firms experienced a backlash as they discovered that, while seniors appreciate the attention, they don't necessarily want age mentioned in ads. "People don't want to see who they really are," argues Scott Gilbert, an ad agency executive. "They want to see who they want to be." So, many marketers now focus on product features and benefits instead of messages that remind consumers of their age. Still, some older consumers say they like viewing ads that feature people their own age. "All you see is teeny-bopper models, although I know some darn good-looking 50- and 60-year-olds," says one senior who owns her own restaurant.

continued on next page

grandparents. Boomer grandparents are healthier and more physically active than their own grandparents were, and they expect to take an active role in their grandchildren's lives. When buying toys, for instance, they often purchase items that focus on a shared experience—games they can play with their grandchildren or craft sets they can assemble together.

Nostalgic references that remind baby boomers of their own childhood and adolescence are a popular way to target this segment. Retro toys such as Sock Monkey, a stuffed-sock simian, are big sellers at home-furnishings retailer Restoration Hardware. The catalog merchant even sells frames for record-album covers so that boomers can decorate their homes with their favorite old album covers, as shown in Figure 8.3.

Seniors   *1900   1999- 28 y@ more of life.*

Marketers also recognize a trend dubbed *the graying of America.* By 2025, Americans who are over age 65 will make up nearly 20 percent of the population. As Americans continue to live longer, the median age of the U.S. population has dramatically increased. The current median age is now 35.2 years, up from 32.8 years a decade ago.[19] And the average life expectancy in the U.S. has increased for both genders—to age 74 for men and to age 79 for women.[20] In addition, people aged 65 can expect to live an average of nearly 18 more years—to age 83.[21] It is believed that these increases in life spans are due to better medicines, healthier lifestyles, and lower infant mortality rates.[22] And instead of settling down to quiet pursuits, some seniors are opting for adventure travel trips to places like Nepal and South America.

In the U.S., heads of households aged 55-plus control about three-quarters of the country's total financial assets. Their discretionary incomes and rates of home ownership are higher than those of any other age group. These statistics show why many marketers should target this group (see the "Marketing Miss" box). Some refer to these prosperous consumers as WOOFS—Well-Off Older Folks. Although many seniors live on modest,

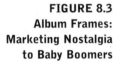

Marketing Miss

Lessons Learned. Ignoring an entire market segment translates to lost opportunities. Not only are sales lost, but the opportunity to build relationships is sacrificed as well. Smart marketers will pay attention to the senior market and communicate the types of messages they want to receive.

SOURCES: Chuck Nyren and Brent Green, "50+ Marketing by Senioragency's Jean-Paul Tréguer," *Suite101.com*, June 13, 2003, www.suite101.com; Chuck Nyren, "Advertising to Baby Boomers: Mentioning Age," *Suite101.com*, May 19, 2003, http://www.suite101.com; Michael McCarthy, "Some Consumers Want Ads for a Mature Audience," *USA Today*, November 19, 2002, pp. B1, B2.

fixed incomes, those who are well-off financially have both time and money to spend on leisure activities such as travel and golf. They may also be looking to purchase and furnish a retirement home.

One privilege that seniors have looked forward to since the 1950s is the senior discount—whether it's at McDonald's or on the ski slopes. But in today's slower economy, with more and more people entering the senior age group, companies are rolling back those discounts. Airlines, ski resorts, and travel companies have curtailed or discontinued senior discounts. Cable TV provider AT&T Broadband recently axed its 10 percent discount for Florida seniors. Some public utilities are reevaluating their senior discount policies. Philadelphia Gas Works estimates that it could save as much as $18 million a year if it cuts out its 20 percent senior discount. But not all marketers agree with this money-saving approach, because seniors make up such a large, affluent group. "There's a saying that today's seniors clip coupons and drive Cadillacs—they'll spend money, but only if they get a good deal," explains Sharon Brooks, an expert in senior marketing. "Discounts are still a very attractive marketing tool."[23]

Segmenting by Ethnic Group

According to the Census Bureau, America's racial and ethnic makeup is changing. Because of comparatively high immigration and birthrates among some minority groups, the Census Bureau projects that by 2050, nearly half of the population will belong to nonwhite minority groups. Figure 8.4 shows the breakdown of minority populations in the U.S. in 2002.

The three largest and fastest-growing racial/ethnic groups are Hispanics, African Americans, and Asian Americans. From a marketer's perspective, it is important to note that spending by these groups is rising at a faster pace than for U.S. households in general.

Hispanics and African Americans are currently the largest racial/ethnic minority groups in the U.S.—some 13 percent of the U.S. population

FIGURE 8.3
Album Frames: Marketing Nostalgia to Baby Boomers

each. African-American numbers are projected to grow to 45 million by 2020.[24] But the Hispanic population's growth rate is four times that of the African-American population and nine times the growth rate for whites. During the 1990s, nearly 2 million people immigrated to the U.S. from Mexico alone. Census projections predict that Hispanics will continue to widen their lead over African Americans through 2020.[25]

Many marketers have focused their efforts on the Hispanic population in the U.S. during the last few years, from fast-food restaurants to toy manufacturers. Food manufacturers and supermarkets such as General Mills, Bestfoods, and Pathmark have not only tailored certain products to Hispanic tastes, they have sponsored

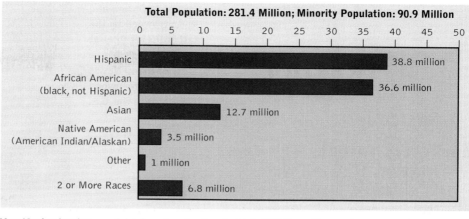

Total Population: 281.4 Million; Minority Population: 90.9 Million

Hispanic	38.8 million
African American (black, not Hispanic)	36.6 million
Asian	12.7 million
Native American (American Indian/Alaskan)	3.5 million
Other	1 million
2 or More Races	6.8 million

Note: Numbers have been rounded. Information taken from the July 1, 2002, Census Bureau estimates.
SOURCE: Data from the U.S. Census Bureau, in Haya El Nasser, "Census Numbers Show Jump from 2000 Tally," *USA Today*, June 19, 2003, pp. 1A, 2A.

FIGURE 8.4
Breakdown of U.S. Minority Populations

cultural events designed to draw Hispanics into the marketplace. Last year Bestfoods grocery division took several of its best-selling brands to Fiesta Broadway in Los Angeles. Integrating with its parent company's sponsorship of Major League Soccer (a popular sport among the Hispanic population), promotion of the foods featured soccer themes and interactive games.[26] Knorr Foods has sponsored sweepstakes contests as one way of making its products better known in the Hispanic community. As shown in Figure 8.5, the grand-prize winner won a trip for four to the Bahamas.

Although Asian Americans and Pacific Islanders represent a smaller segment than either the African-American or Hispanic populations, they are the second-fastest-growing segment of the U.S. population. The Census Bureau estimates that this group will grow to 23 million by 2020. Asian Americans are an attractive target for marketers because they also have the fastest-growing income. Their average income per household is considerably higher than that of any other ethnic group, including whites.[27]

The Asian-American population is concentrated in fewer geographic areas than are other ethnic markets. A particularly high concentration of Asian Americans live in California. Companies can lower their costs of reaching Asian-American consumers by advertising in appropriate local markets rather than on a national scale. Honda's first Asian-American advertising campaign, called "Calligraphy," was launched in Los Angeles.[28]

Another important minority group is Native Americans, whose current population numbers about 4 million. Native American groups have begun to establish economic and political clout, which marketers take seriously. One way these groups have gained economic power is through the establishment of entertainment centers like Foxwoods—a huge resort and casino in Connecticut that is owned and operated by the Mashantucket Pequot Tribal Nation (*Pequot* means "the fox people").

FIGURE 8.5
Marketing to the Hispanic Community through Contests

Marketing Hit

Marketers Target Alternative Households

Background. It's a market too big to ignore. Sixty percent of gay-male households and 50 percent of lesbian households have annual incomes above $60,000, nearly $20,000 above the national average. And many of these households have more disposable income than traditional households.

The Challenge. To reach this segment, marketers must identify the needs and preferences of alternative households. It may be only a matter of tweaking the advertising, or it may mean developing new goods and services.

The Strategy. Orbitz and Subaru both recognized that their gay and lesbian customers liked their products, so these firms designed ad campaigns aimed directly at this segment. Subaru created ads featuring tennis star Martina Navratilova. Orbitz not only aired TV commercials aimed at gay travelers, the firm set up a "micro" site targeting them, offering airline and hotel specials. Other firms recognized that gay consumers have their own needs. American Express now has financial advisers who offer estate planning and guardianship guidance to gay couples.

The Outcome. Firms that market to alternative households are building relationships with a large market segment that has money to spend. "Going on TV is the ultimate sign that you're a gay-friendly company," says Jeffrey Marsh, president of Orbitz.

SOURCES: Claire Atkinson, "Marketers Warm Up to Gay Audience," *Advertising Age*, August 4, 2003, pp. 4, 26; Jayne Clark, "In New TV Commercial, Orbitz Has Gay Travelers in Its Sights," *USA Today*, August 1, 2003, p. D1; Gene Koretz, "Do Gays Have Higher Incomes?" *BusinessWeek*, April 21, 2003, p. 30; Christine L. Romero, "Valley Hosts Gay Chambers," *The Arizona Republic*, April 10, 2003, pp. D1, D2.

Foxwoods Casino and Resort, owned by the Mashantucket Pequot Tribal Nation, is one of many Native American–owned casinos in the U.S.

Thousands of tourists visit Foxwoods each year to stay in the 1,400 guest rooms and suites, play golf, enjoy live entertainment, and gamble.[29] The entertainment centers that Native Americans own often are economic dynamos in some of the more rural locations in which they operate.

Researchers have identified differences in consumer preferences, motivations, and buying habits among different ethnic and racial segments. Increasingly, businesses are targeting their marketing strategies to more closely match those differences. All three of the major greeting-card manufacturers have launched ethnically oriented card lines. Chapter 9 will take a closer look at how ethnic and racial culture affects consumer behavior.

U.S. residents now have the option of identifying themselves as more than one racial category. Marketers need to be aware of this change. In some ways, it benefits marketers by making racial statistics more accurate. On the other hand, marketers may find it difficult to compare the new statistics with data from earlier censuses. For example, families previously reported as African American or white could now be classified as both, causing them to be tabulated separately from the exclusively African-American or white totals. It remains to be seen how the new approach will affect market segmentation by ethnic groups. See the "Solving an Ethical Controversy" box on page 236 for a discussion of minority marketing campaigns.

Segmenting by Family Life Cycle Stages

Still another form of demographic segmentation employs the stages of the *family life cycle*—the process of family formation and dissolution. The underlying theme of this segmentation approach is that life stage, not age per se, is the primary determinant of many consumer purchases. As people move from one life stage to another, they become potential consumers for different types of goods and services.

An unmarried person setting up an apartment for the first time is likely to be a good prospect for inexpensive furniture and small home appliances. This consumer probably must budget carefully, ruling out expenditures on luxury items. On the other hand, a young, single person who is still living at home will probably have more money to spend on goods such as sporting and entertainment equipment, personal-care items, and clothing. As couples marry, their consumer profiles change. Couples without children are frequent buyers of personalized gifts, power tools, furniture, and homes. Eating out and travel may also be part of their lifestyles.

The birth of a first child changes any couple's consumer profile considerably; parents must buy cribs, changing tables, baby clothes, baby food, car seats, and similar products. Parents usually spend less on the children who follow the first because they have already bought many essential items for the first child. Today, the average woman gives birth to two children (as opposed to four children in 1905), and she usually has her children at a later age—about 35, as opposed to 22 in the early part of the last century. Whether or not she works outside the home, she and her spouse probably have more disposable income than they would have had a century ago.[30]

In the U.S., there are about 8 million divorced men and 11 million divorced women.[31] Divorce can dramatically alter an individual's consumer profile. As the household breaks up, the partners may need new household items at the same time that their income levels drop.

Marketers at Dodge are targeting mothers, whose lives are increasingly hectic—whether they work inside or outside the home.

"Empty nesters"—married couples whose children have grown up and moved away from home—are an attractive life-cycle segment for marketers. Empty nesters may also have the disposable incomes necessary to purchase premium products. These couples may struggle to maintain a four-bedroom home and a half-acre lawn, making them customers for lawn-care and home-care services, as well as townhouses or condominiums. Later, these people may become customers for retirement centers, supplemental medical insurance, and hearing aids. They are also a prime target market for travel and leisure products.

One trend noted by researchers in the past decade is an increase in the number of grown children who have returned home to live with their parents. Some of these grown children bring along families of their own.

Segmenting by Household Type

The first U.S. census in 1790 found an average household size of 5.8 persons. By 1960, this number had fallen to 3.4 persons, and today that number is below 3. The U.S. Department of Commerce cites several reasons for the trend toward smaller households: lower fertility rates, young people's tendency to postpone marriage or to never marry, the increasing tendency among younger couples to limit the number of children or to have no children at all, the ease and frequency of divorce, and the ability and desire of many young singles and the elderly to live alone.

An important U.S. trend over the past decades has been the decline of the so-called traditional family, consisting of two parents and their children living in one household. In 1900, 4 of 5 Americans lived within these families; today, only 50 percent do. Meanwhile, three other segments—single-parent families, single-person households, and nonfamily group households—have increased dramatically during the same time period. Conversely, the numbers of large, extended families living together has fallen dramatically—from 50 percent to 10 percent.[32]

While the percentage of married-couple families has fallen, the number of unmarried individuals living together has risen. Consequently, the Bureau of the Census created another category, *POSSLQ*, an acronym for unmarried "persons of the opposite sex in the same living quarters," to describe this trend. In addition, there has been a rise in the number of gay and lesbian couples establishing homes. Companies from auto manufacturers to media outlets have been scrambling to attract loyal customers from within this market, which represents more than $450 billion in buying power. When research showed that lesbian women had a high rate of purchasing its Outback vehicles, Subaru marketers began to tailor its marketing efforts toward lesbians.[33] The "Marketing Hit" box discusses the gay and lesbian segment further.

Finally, one of the most actively pursued market segments are DINKs—dual-income couples with no kids. With high levels of spendable income, such couples are big buyers of gourmet foods, luxury items, and travel.

Briefly Speaking

It's the right thing to do for our employees. We want all our associates to feel that they are valued and treated with respect—no exceptions.

Mona Williams (b. 1953) Wal-Mart vice-president of communications (on the company's decision to include gays and lesbians in its antidiscrimination policy) right wrong

Solving an Ethical Controversy

Minority Marketing Campaigns Miss Their Target

Most marketers already know the stats: Ethnic minorities make up one-fourth of the U.S. population, and that percentage will grow to one-half by the year 2050. Ethnic consumers spend more than $460 billion a year on retail purchases. At least five new 2003-2004 network TV programs featured Hispanics in feature roles. Yet marketers seem uncertain how to reach a diverse audience. Some groups accuse entire industries—like the auto industry—of ignoring ethnic preferences. Until recently, very few ads have been targeted at a specific minority audience. But some marketing experts argue that factors like household income, age, and gender are actually more important predictors of shopping behavior.

Are marketers failing to serve the ethnic consumer market in the U.S.?

PRO

1. Firms are not developing messages targeted specifically to diverse groups of consumers. "[Advertisers] take the same message they put in *Time* and *Life* and slap it in *Ebony, Essence,* or *Vibe*," says Kevyn Lewis of the multicultural advertising agency GlobalHue.

2. The Association of Hispanic Advertising Agencies reports that auto manufacturers, pharmaceutical companies, financial institutions, computer manufacturers, and travel/entertainment firms devote only about 3 percent of their total marketing budgets to Hispanics—the fastest-growing minority segment.

CON

1. In the big picture, "consumers of a specific socioeconomic group have similar shopping attitudes—regardless of race," notes Christopher M. Kelley of Forrester Research. This means that marketers should focus on demographics instead of race.
2. Corporations are already turning to advertising agencies that are owned and staffed by minorities in order to create messages for specific audiences.

SUMMARY

More companies are adopting a multicultural approach to marketing. "It's respect of culture, of African Americans and their buying power and choices," says Kevyn Lewis. "If we do our job right, African Americans or Hispanics will see things in the spot that [others] might not be sensitive to."

SOURCES: "The New Majority Marketing to Minorities," *Small Business Administration,* www.sba.gov; accessed August 12, 2003; "Retailers Need to Remedy Ethnic Marketing, Recommends Forrester Research," *Business Wire,* June 10, 2003, http://yahoo.com/bw; Karl Greenberg, "Respect," *Brandweek,* April 14, 2003, pp. 28-32.

Segmenting by Income and Expenditure Patterns

Part of the earlier definition of *market* described people or institutions with purchasing power. Not surprisingly, then, a common basis for segmenting the consumer market is income. For instance, marketers often target geographic areas known for the high incomes of their residents. *Sales & Marketing Management* magazine conducts a periodic *Survey of Buying Power,* which lists metropolitan markets by income. Metropolitan markets that rise dramatically in effective buying income often make promising targets for income-related segmentation. Cessna targets consumers and business owners who are wealthy enough to purchase their own aircraft, as shown in Figure 8.6.

Engel's Laws

How do expenditure patterns vary with income? Over a century ago, Ernst Engel, a German statistician, published what became known as *Engel's laws*—three general statements based on his studies of the impact of household income changes on consumer spending behavior. According to Engel, as family income increases, the following will take place:

1. A smaller percentage of expenditures go for food.

2. The percentage spent on housing and household operations and clothing remains constant.

3. The percentage spent on other items (such as recreation and education) increases.

Are Engel's laws still valid? Newer studies say essentially yes, with a few exceptions. Researchers note a steady decline in the percentage of total income spent on food, beverages, and tobacco as income increases. Although high-income families spend greater absolute amounts on food items, their purchases represent declining percentages of their total expenditures as compared with low-income families. The second law remains partly accurate since the percentage of expenditures for housing and household operations remains relatively unchanged in all but the very lowest income groups. The percentage spent on clothing, however, rises with increased income. The third law is also true, with the exception of medical and personal-care costs, which appear to decline as a percentage of increased income.

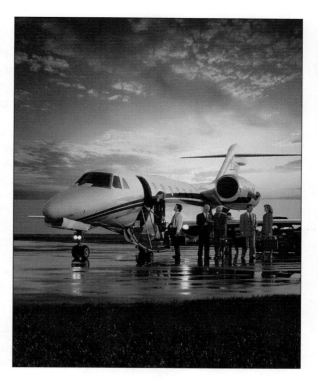

FIGURE 8.6
Targeting Wealthier Consumers and Business Owners

Engel's laws provide the marketing manager with useful rules about the types of consumer demand that evolve with increased income. These laws can also help marketers to evaluate a foreign country as a potential target market.

Demographic Segmentation Abroad

Marketers often face a difficult task in obtaining the data necessary for demographic segmentation abroad. Many countries do not operate regularly scheduled census programs. For instance, the most recent count of the Dutch population is now over two decades old. Germany skipped counting from 1970 to 1987, and France conducts a census about every seven years. By contrast, Japan and Canada conduct censuses every five years; however, the mid-decade assessments are not as complete as the end-of-decade counts.

Also, some foreign data includes demographic divisions not found in the U.S. census. Canada collects information on religious affiliation, for instance. On the other hand, some of the standard segmentation data for U.S. markets are not available abroad. Many nations do not collect income data. Great Britain, Japan, Spain, France, and Italy are examples. Similarly, family life cycle data is difficult to apply in global demographic segmentation efforts. Ireland acknowledges only three marital statuses—single, married, and widowed—while Latin American nations and Sweden count their unmarried cohabitants.

One source of global demographic information is the International Programs Center (IPC) at the U.S. Bureau of the Census. The IPC provides a searchable online database of population statistics for many countries on the Census Bureau's Web page. Another source is the United Nations, which sponsors national statistical offices that collect demographic data on a variety of countries. In addition, private marketing research firms can supplement government data.

Psychographic Segmentation AIO's (Activities / Interest / Opinions)

Marketers have traditionally referred to geographic and demographic characteristics as the primary bases for dividing consumers into homogeneous market segments. Still, they have long recognized the

Actualizers		**High Resources**
Self-confident.		
Enjoy the "finer things."		
Receptive to new products and technologies.		
Skeptical of advertising.		
Frequent readers of a wide variety of publications.		

Principle Oriented	**Status Oriented**	**Action Oriented**
Fulfilleds	**Achievers**	**Experiencers**
Value knowledge.	Image-conscious.	Action-oriented.
Little interest in image	Relatively affluent.	Follow fashion and fads.
or prestige.	Attracted to premium	Spend much of
Like educational and	products.	disposable income on
public affairs	Average TV watchers.	socializing.
programming.		Buy on impulse.
Read widely and often.		Listen to rock music.
Believers	**Strivers**	**Makers**
Traditional.	Image-conscious.	Self-sufficient, hands on.
Family-oriented.	Limited discretionary	Shop for comfort,
Buy American.	incomes, but carry	durability, value.
Slow to change habits.	credit balances.	Unimpressed by luxuries.
Look for bargains.	Spend on clothing and	Read auto, home
Watch TV more than	personal-care products.	mechanics, fishing
average.	Prefer TV to reading.	magazines.

Strugglers		
Restricted consumption.		
Concerned with security and safety.		
Brand loyal.		
Trust advertising.		
Watch TV often.		**Low Resources**

FIGURE 8.7
VALS2 Network

need for fuller, more lifelike portraits of consumers in developing their marketing programs. As a result, psychographic segmentation can be a useful tool for gaining sharper insight into consumer purchasing behavior.

What Is Psychographic Segmentation?

Psychographic segmentation divides a population into groups that have similar psychological characteristics, values, and lifestyles. *Lifestyle* refers to a person's mode of living; it describes how an individual operates on a daily basis. Consumers' lifestyles are composites of their individual psychological profiles, including their needs, motives, perceptions, and attitudes. A lifestyle also bears the mark of many other influences, such as family, job, social activities, and culture.

The most common method for developing psychographic profiles of a population is to conduct a large-scale survey that asks consumers to agree or disagree with a collection of several hundred AIO statements. These *AIO statements* describe various activities, interests, and opinions. The resulting data allows researchers to develop lifestyle profiles. Marketers can then develop a separate marketing strategy that closely fits the psychographic makeup for each lifestyle segment.

Marketing researchers have conducted psychographic studies on hundreds of goods and services, ranging from beer to air travel. Hospitals and other health-care providers use such studies to assess consumer behavior and attitudes toward health care in general, to learn the needs of consumers in particular marketplaces, and to determine how consumers perceive individual institutions. Many businesses turn to psychographic research in an effort to learn what consumers in various demographic and geographic segments want and need.

VALS2   Not For Test

A quarter century ago, the research and consulting firm SRI International developed a psychographic segmentation system called VALS. The name stands for "values and lifestyles," and the original VALS scheme categorized consumers by their opinions regarding social issues. A decade later, SRI revised the system to link it more closely with consumer-buying behavior. The revised system, VALS2, is based on two key concepts: resources and self-motivation. VALS2 divides consumers into eight psychographic categories. Figure 8.7 details the profiles for these categories and their relationships.

The VALS network chart in the figure displays differences in resources as vertical distances, while self-orientation is represented horizontally. The resource dimension measures income, education, self-confidence, health, eagerness to buy, and energy level. Self-orientations divide consumers into three groups: principle-oriented consumers who have a set of ideas and morals—principles—that they live their lives by; status-oriented consumers who are influenced by what others think; and action-oriented consumers who seek physical activity, variety, and adventure.

SRI has created several specialized segmentation systems based on this approach. GeoVALS, for instance, estimates the percentage of each VALS type in each U.S. residential zip code. JapanVALS was developed to help companies understand Japanese consumers, and iVALS focuses on Internet sites and users.[34]

SRI uses the VALS2 segmentation information in conjunction with marketers in consulting projects and on a subscriber basis. Product, service, and media data are available by VALS-types from companies' databases.

Several other commercially available psychographic profile systems offer their own insights to marketers. One is MONITOR, available from Yankelovich Partners.[35] A newer syndicated psychographic service, from marketing research firm Odyssey, focuses on the psychographics of people who use new technologies, such as the Internet.

Psychographic Segmentation of Global Markets

As JapanVALS suggests, psychographic profiles can cross national boundaries. Roper Starch Worldwide, a marketing research firm, recently surveyed 7,000 people in 35 countries. From the resulting data, Roper identified six psychographic consumer segments that exist in all 35 nations, although to varying degrees:

- *Strivers,* the largest segment, value professional and material goals more than the other groups. One-third of the Asian population and one-fourth of Russians are strivers. They are slightly more likely to be men than women.

- *Devouts* value duty and tradition. While this segment comprises 22 percent of all adults, they are most common in Africa, the Middle East, and developing Asia. They are least common in Western Europe and developed Asian countries. Worldwide, they are more likely to be female.

- *Altruists* emphasize social issues and societal well-being. Comprising 18 percent of all adults, this group shows a median age of 44 and a slightly higher percentage of women. Altruists are most common in Latin America and Russia.

- *Intimates* value family and personal relationships. They are divided almost equally between males and females. One-fourth of people in America and Europe are intimates, but only 7 percent of consumers in developing Asia fall into this category.

- *Fun seekers,* as you might guess from their name, focus on personal enjoyment and pleasurable experiences. They comprise 12 percent of the world's population, with a male-female ratio of 54 to 46. Many live in developed Asia.

- *Creatives,* the smallest segment, account for just 10 percent of the global population. This group seeks education, technology, and knowledge, and their male-female ratio is roughly equal. Many creatives live in Western Europe and Latin America.

Roper researchers note that some principles and core beliefs apply to more than one psychographic segment. For example, consumers in all 35 countries cite "family" as one of their five most important values, and "protecting the family" ranks as one of the top 10.[36]

Using Psychographic Segmentation

Psychographic profile systems like those of Roper and SRI can paint useful pictures of the overall psychological motivations of consumers. These profiles produce much richer descriptions of potential target markets than other techniques can achieve. The enhanced detail aids in matching a company's image and product offerings with the types of consumers who use its products.

Identifying which psychographic segments are most prevalent in certain markets helps marketers plan and promote more effectively. Often, segments overlap. For instance, the advertisement for MasterCard in Figure 8.8 would be attractive both to altruists and intimates.

Psychographic segmentation is a good supplement to segmentation by demographic or geographic variables. For example, marketers may have access to each consumer type's media preferences in network television, cable television, radio format, magazines, and newspapers. Psychographic studies may then refine the picture of segment characteristics to give a more elaborate lifestyle profile of the consumers in the firm's target market.

Marketing Dictionary

psychographic segmentation   Division of a population into groups that have similar psychological characteristics, values, and lifestyles.

FIGURE 8.8
Using Psychographic Segmentation

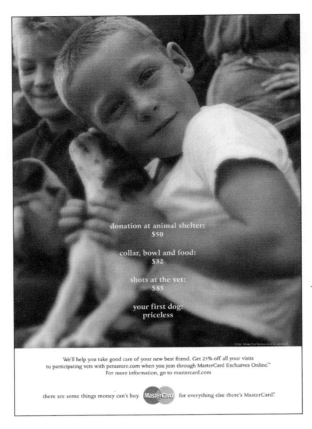

donation at animal shelter:
$50

collar, bowl and food:
$32

shots at the vet:
$85

your first dog:
priceless

We'll help you take good care of your new best friend. Get 25% off all your visits to participating vets with petassure.com when you join through MasterCard Exclusives Online.™ For more information, go to mastercard.com

there are some things money can't buy. **MasterCard** for everything else there's MasterCard.®

Product-Related Segmentation

Product-related segmentation involves dividing a consumer population into homogeneous groups based on characteristics of their relationships to the product. This segmentation approach can take several forms:

1. Segmenting based on the benefits that people seek when they buy a product

2. Segmenting based on usage rates for a product

3. Segmenting according to consumers' brand loyalty toward a product

Segmenting by Benefits Sought

This approach focuses on the attributes that people seek in a good or service and the benefits they expect to receive from that good or service. It groups consumers into segments based on what they want a product to do for them.

Consumers who quaff Starbucks' premium coffees, for example, are not just looking for a dose of caffeine. They are willing to pay extra to savor a pleasant experience, one that makes them feel pampered and appreciated. Women who use Maybelline cosmetics want to look their best and be able to put their makeup on quickly. People who feed their pets Iams believe that they are giving their animals the best tasting, healthiest pet food.

Even if a business offers only one product line, however, marketers must remember to consider product benefits. Two people may buy the same product for very different reasons. A box of Arm & Hammer baking soda could end up serving as a refrigerator freshener, a toothpaste substitute, an antacid, or a deodorizer for a cat's litter box.

Segmenting by Usage Rates

Marketers may also segment a total market by grouping people according to the amounts of a product that they buy and use. Markets can be divided into heavy-user, moderate-user, and light-user segments. The *80/20 principle* holds that a big percentage of a product's revenues—roughly 80 percent—comes from a relatively small, loyal percentage of total customers—perhaps 20 percent. The 80/20 principle is sometimes referred to as "Praedo's Law." While the percentages need not exactly equal these figures, the general principle often holds true: Relatively few heavy users of a product can account for much of its consumption.

Depending on their goals, marketers may target heavy, moderate, or light users as well as nonusers. A company may attempt to lure heavy users of another product away from their regular brands to try a new brand. Nonusers and light users may be attractive prospects because other companies are ignoring them. Usage rates can also be linked to other segmentation methods such as demographic and psychographic segmentation.

Some advertisers, such as cosmetics companies, segment by the benefits consumers seek by using their products.

✳ Segmenting by Brand Loyalty

A third product-related segmentation method groups consumers according to the strength of the brand loyalty they feel toward a product. Despite its nearly 250-year history, the Irish brewer Guinness needed to update the way consumers viewed its brand. So the company revamped its outmoded visitors' center in Dublin, Ireland, to attract more tourists and locals. The new Guinness Storehouse features everything from historic exhibits to a fully stocked gift shop, where loyal Guinness guzzlers can purchase all kinds of company paraphernalia. "The goal was for Storehouse to evolve, adapt, and grow up," explains the company's director of marketing and strategic planning, Ralph Ardill. "Places like Storehouse bring consumers and employees together and open the doors to the community."[37]

A classic example of brand loyalty segmentation is airline frequent-flyer programs. Originally targeted at heavy users—business travelers—frequent-flyer programs now help to tie even occasional travelers to specific airlines. The success of these programs has resulted in similar efforts in the hotel industry, bookstores, and elsewhere. Other companies attempt to segment their market by developing brand loyalty over a period of time, through consumers' stages of life, as shown by Oral-B toothbrushes in Figure 8.9.

FIGURE 8.9
Creating Brand Loyalty through Different Life Stages

The Market Segmentation Process

To this point, the chapter has discussed various bases on which companies segment markets. How does a marketer decide which segmentation base to use? As Figure 8.10 shows, marketers follow a five-step decision process.

Stage I: Identify Market Segmentation Process

5
Identify the steps in the market segmentation process.

Segmentation begins when marketers determine the bases on which to identify markets. They follow two methods for achieving this goal. In the first, management-driven method, segments are predefined by managers based on their observation of the behavioral and demographic characteristics of likely users. The market-driven method defines segments by asking customers which attributes are important to them, and then clusters responses to identify potential segments. Both methods try to develop segments that group customers who respond similarly to specific marketing-mix alternatives. For example, Procter & Gamble cannot simply target Crest toothpaste to large families. Management must first confirm that most large families are concerned about preventing tooth decay and will be receptive to the Crest marketing offer.

Sometimes marketers have trouble isolating a preferred segment, or may serve several overlapping segments. Sears serves a variety of segments—families, men or women, children, and seniors. So the company isolates its segments by running a series of advertisements in the same

Marketing Dictionary

product-related segmentation Division of a population into homogeneous groups based on characteristics of their relationships to the product.

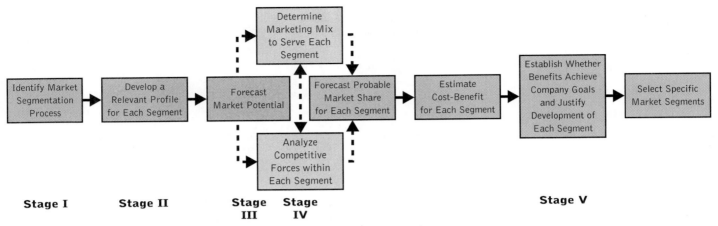

Stage I   Stage II   Stage   Stage   Stage V
                                   III   IV

SOURCE: M. Dale Beckman and John M. Rigby, *Foundations of Marketing*, 7th Edition (Toronto: Nelson, 2001).

FIGURE 8.10
Market Segmentation Decision Process

format, but showcasing different products, like the ad in Figure 8.11. While this ad focuses on household appliances, another features women's shoes and Samsonite luggage; still another centers on power tools.

Stage II: Develop a Relevant Profile for Each Segment

After identifying promising segments, marketers should understand the customers in each one. This in-depth analysis of customers helps managers to accurately match customers' needs with the firm's marketing offers. The process must identify characteristics that both explain the similarities among customers within each segment and account for differences among segments.

The task at this stage is to develop a profile of the typical customer in each segment. Such a profile might include information about lifestyle patterns, attitudes toward product attributes and brands, product-use habits, geographic locations, and demographic characteristics.

FIGURE 8.11
Sears Targets a Variety of Consumer Segments

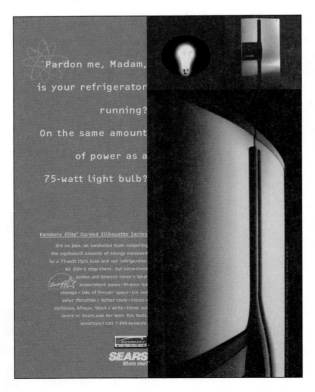

Stage III: Forecast Market Potential

In the third stage, market segmentation and market opportunity analysis combine to produce a forecast of market potential within each segment. Market potential sets the upper limit on the demand that competing firms can expect from a segment. Multiplying by market share determines a single firm's maximum sales potential. This step should define a preliminary go or no-go decision from management since the total sales potential in each segment must justify resources devoted to further analysis.

An example of a segment that shows tremendous market potential is U.S. children ages 4 to 12. Aggregate spending by consumers in this age group or on their behalf doubled every decade between the 1960s and 1980s and tripled during the 1990s to reach its current level of $24 billion a year. Thirty years ago children spent most of their money on candy. Today, only one-third is spent on food and beverages; the rest goes toward clothing, movies, games, and toys.

Clothing retailers, noting this trend, have opened new stores that specialize in fashions for this age segment. An example is the Limited Too, which now has more than 300 stores nationwide as well as a catalog and Web site. Competitors Abercrombie & Fitch and Gymboree have also opened separate outlets for preteens.

Stage IV: Forecast Probable Market Share

Once market potential has been estimated, a firm must forecast its probable market share. Competitors' positions in targeted segments must be analyzed and a specific marketing strategy must be designed to reach these segments. These two activities may be performed simultaneously. Moreover, by settling on a marketing strategy and tactics, a firm determines the expected level of resources it must commit, that is, the costs that it will incur to tap the potential demand in each segment.

Kinko's currently has more than 1,100 photocopying outlets in Asia, Australia, Europe, and North America. The company used to be viewed (and used to view itself) as simply a copy shop at which customers could get quick turnaround for their reports, flyers, or manuscripts. But Gary Kusin, CEO of the company, made a trip around the U.S. to talk to his customers and learned that they are now looking "more for ongoing business partners. They want to know that they can partner with us for digital solutions for bigger jobs." So Kusin and his managers needed to figure out how to meet these needs and capture as much of this segment of the market as possible. "Right now," he says, "the biggest service we can sell is competence: the ability to listen to our customers, to understand their problems, and to apply our knowledge to come up with creative solutions."[38]

Stage V: Select Specific Market Segments

The information, analysis, and forecasts accumulated throughout the entire market segmentation decision process allows management to assess the potential for achieving company goals and to justify committing resources in developing one or more segments. Demand forecasts together with cost projections determine the profits and the return on investment (ROI) that the company can expect from each segment. Marketing strategy and tactics must be designed to reinforce the firm's image, yet keep within its unique organizational capabilities.

At this point in the analysis, marketers weigh more than monetary costs and benefits; they also consider many difficult-to-measure but critical organizational and environmental factors. The firm may lack experienced personnel to launch a successful attack on an attractive market segment. Similarly, a firm with 60 percent of the market faces possible legal problems with the Federal Trade Commission if it increases its market concentration. This assessment of both financial and nonfinancial factors is a difficult but vital step in the decision process.

Strategies for Reaching Target Markets

Considerable marketing efforts are dedicated to developing strategies that will best match the firm's product offerings to the needs of particular target markets. An appropriate match is vital to the firm's marketing success. Marketers have identified four basic strategies for achieving consumer satisfaction: undifferentiated marketing, differentiated marketing, concentrated marketing, and micromarketing.

6

Discuss four basic strategies for reaching target markets.

Undifferentiated Marketing

A firm may produce only one product or product line and promote it to all customers with a single marketing mix; such a firm is said to practice **undifferentiated marketing,** sometimes called *mass marketing*. Undifferentiated marketing was much more common in the past than it is today.

While undifferentiated marketing is efficient from a production viewpoint, the strategy also brings inherent dangers. A firm that attempts to satisfy everyone in the market with one standard product may suffer if competitors offer specialized units to smaller segments of the total market and better satisfy individual segments. In fact, firms that implement strategies of differentiated marketing, concentrated marketing, or micromarketing may capture enough small segments of the market to defeat another competitor's strategy of undifferentiated marketing.

Differentiated Marketing

Firms that promote numerous products with differing marketing mixes designed to satisfy smaller segments are said to practice **differentiated marketing.** By providing increased satisfaction for each of many target markets, a company can produce more sales by following a differentiated marketing strategy than undifferentiated marketing would generate. Oscar Mayer, a marketer of a variety of meat products, practices differentiated marketing. It increased its sales by introducing a new product—Lunchables—aimed at children. In general, however, differentiated marketing also raises costs. Production costs usually rise because additional products and variations require shorter production runs and increased setup times. Inventory costs rise because more products require added storage space and increased efforts for record keeping. Promotional costs also rise because each segment demands a unique promotional mix.

Despite higher marketing costs, however, an organization may be forced to practice differentiated marketing to remain competitive. The travel industry now recognizes the need to target smaller groups of travelers with specialized interests. Elderhostel, for instance, targets seniors with specialized trips that may focus on history, hiking, golf, cooking, or other special interests. Old Sturbridge Village in Massachusetts targets people who are interested in American history.

(Sport Utility Vehicle SUV's)

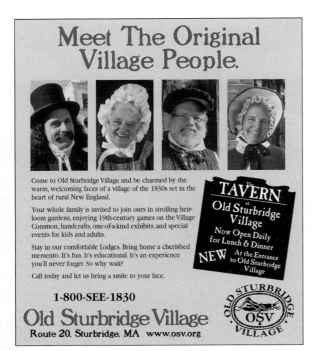

Old Sturbridge Village museum in Massachusetts targets individuals who are interested in American history.

Concentrated Marketing

Rather than trying to market its products separately to several segments, a firm may opt for a concentrated marketing strategy. With **concentrated marketing** (also known as *niche marketing*), a firm focuses its efforts on profitably satisfying only one market segment. This approach can appeal to a small firm that lacks the financial resources of its competitors and to a company that offers highly specialized goods and services. The Petco chain appeals to most owners of small animals—fish, cats, dogs, hamsters, birds—with its array of pet care products and accessories. But a small, Boston-based firm called anguswear.com targets a much narrower audience with tiny cashmere dog sweaters (at $56 apiece), fragrances, and custom-made wooden sleigh beds (for $1,000).[39]

Magazine publishers have discovered that niche markets can be highly lucrative. New niche publications *Jane* and *O* (Oprah Winfrey's magazine) are making the wider-audience magazines reevaluate their strategies. And although conventional wisdom has always declared that young men didn't care about magazines, *Maxim, FHM,* and *Stuff* have been hugely successful during their first few years. Highly specialized spin-offs such as *Sports Illustrated Women* and *Travel & Leisure Golf* are doing better than their more generalized parents.[40]

But along with its benefits, concentrated marketing has its dangers. Since the strategy ties a firm's growth to a specific segment, sales can suffer if new competitors appeal successfully to the same target. Furthermore, errors in forecasting market potential or customer buying habits lead to severe problems, particularly if the firm has spent substantially on product development, advertising, and promotion. "Segmentation can take a marketer only so far before it begins to lose its effectiveness," says Bruce Hall, partner and vice president of marketing research for Howard Merrell & Partners, a marketing and advertising agency in Raleigh, North Carolina.[41]

Micromarketing

The fourth targeting strategy, still more narrowly focused than concentrated marketing, is **micromarketing,** which involves targeting potential customers at a very basic level, such as by zip code, specific occupation, or lifestyle. Ultimately, micromarketing can target even individuals themselves. The salesperson at your favorite clothing boutique may contact you when certain merchandise that she thinks you might like arrives at the store. The Internet may allow marketers to make micromarketing even more effective. By tracking specific demographic and personal information, marketers can send e-mail directly to individual consumers who are most likely to buy their products. If you purchase a book via Amazon.com, the company will offer to send you e-mail notices about other books that may be of interest to you.

But micromarketing, like niche marketing, can turn out to be too much of a good thing if companies spend too much time, effort, and marketing dollars to unearth a market that is too small and specialized to be profitable. In addition, micromarketing may cause a company to lose sight of other, reachable markets. "It may be that only 5 percent to 6 percent of a particular [direct marketing] list may fit the true target criteria, but one cannot rule out the other 94 or 95 percent, because it's still difficult to predict a full range of human behavior," notes marketing researcher Bruce Hall.[42]

Selecting and Executing a Strategy

Although most organizations adopt some form of differentiated marketing, no single, best choice suits all firms. Any of the alternatives may prove most effective in a particular situation. The basic determinants of a market-specific strategy are (1) company resources, (2) product homogeneity, (3) stage in the product life cycle, and (4) competitors' strategies.

A firm with limited resources may have to choose a concentrated marketing strategy. Small firms may be forced to select small target markets because of limitations in their financing, sales force, and promotional budgets. On the other hand, an undifferentiated marketing strategy suits a firm selling items perceived by consumers as relatively homogeneous. Marketers of grain, for example, sell standardized grades of generic products rather than individual brand names. Some petroleum companies implement undifferentiated marketing to distribute their gasoline to the mass market.

The firm's strategy may also change as its product progresses through the stages of the life cycle. During the early stages, undifferentiated marketing might effectively support the firm's effort to build initial demand for the item. In the later stages, however, competitive pressures may force modifications in products and in the development of marketing strategies aimed at segments of the total market.

The strategies of competitors also affect the choice of a segmentation approach. A firm may encounter obstacles to undifferentiated marketing if its competitors actively cultivate smaller segments. In such instances, competition usually forces each firm to adopt a differentiated marketing strategy.

Having chosen a strategy for reaching their firm's target market, marketers must then decide how best to position the product. The concept of **positioning** seeks to put a product in a certain position, or place, in the minds of prospective buyers. Marketers use a positioning

Marketing Dictionary

undifferentiated marketing   Marketing strategy to produce a single product and market it to all customers; also called *mass marketing*.

differentiated marketing   Marketing strategy to produce several products and promote them with different marketing mixes designed to satisfy smaller segments.

concentrated marketing   Focusing marketing efforts on satisfying only one market segment; also called *niche marketing*.

micromarketing   Targeting potential customers at a basic level, such as zip code.

positioning   Placing a product in a certain position in the minds of prospective buyers.

Some marketers position their products directly against those of major competitors.

 7

Summarize the types of positioning strategies.

8

Explain the reasons for positioning and repositioning products.

strategy to distinguish their firm's offerings from those of competitors and to create promotions that communicate the desired position.

To achieve this goal, marketers follow a number of positioning strategies. Possible approaches include positioning a product according to the following categories:

1. *Attributes*—Jeep wants you to "think of it as a 4,000-lb. guardian angel."

2. *Price/quality*—Rolex watches are high-quality, high-priced timepieces; Timex watches are low priced but long lasting.

3. *Competitors*—Formula 409 claims that "409 Is Better."

4. *Application*—Crest Whitestrips "reveal your whiter smile."

5. *Product user*—Visa's ads target consumers who are concerned about the security of making purchases on line.

6. *Product class*—Wendy's has "raised the bar on salad."

Whatever the strategy they choose, marketers want to emphasize a product's unique advantages and to differentiate it from competitors' options. Companies may even promote similar products by stressing different advantages. Managers at Sprint, for instance, feel that their long-distance carrier's prices offer a competitive advantage over AT&T's. So Sprint ads tend to stress price and value. Meanwhile, marketers for AT&T think that their company has a positive image with customers based on its longevity and experience in telecommunications. AT&T ads, therefore, often emphasize reliability and the high quality of its overall service.

A *positioning map* provides a valuable tool in helping managers position products by graphically illustrating consumers' perceptions of competing products within an industry. Marketers can create a competitive positioning map from information solicited from consumers or from their accumulated knowledge about a market. A positioning map might present two different characteristics—price and perceived quality—and show how consumers view a product and its major competitors based on these traits. The hypothetical positioning map in Figure 8.12 compares selected retailers based on possible perceptions of their prices and quality of their offerings.

Sometimes, changes in the competitive environment force marketers to *reposition* a product—changing the position it holds in the minds of prospective buyers relative to the positions of competing products. Repositioning may become necessary even for highly successful products. Disney used to pitch its Disney World and Disneyland parks as great places for family vacations. As successful as that positioning was, in recent years the company began to advertise its parks as great places for empty nesters to take a second honeymoon. Bayer aspirin used to get by on its reputation for relieving headaches; now the company is allowed to advertise the aspirin's usefulness in reducing the chances of potential heart attacks. By repositioning their products, these companies reach new markets that they might not otherwise have tapped.

FIGURE 8.12
Hypothetical Competitive Positioning Map for Selected Retailers

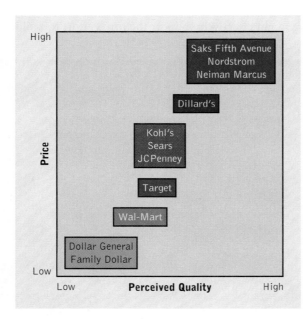

Strategic Implications of Marketing in the 21st Century

To remain competitive, today's marketers must be able to accurately identify potential customers for their goods and services. They can use a variety of methods to accomplish this, from segmenting markets by gender to segmenting by geographic location. The trick is to figure out the best combination of methods for segmentation to identify the most lucrative, long-lasting potential markets. Marketers must also be able to remain flexible, responding to markets as they change—for instance, following a generation as it ages or reaching out to new generations by revamping or repositioning products.

The greatest competitive advantage will belong to firms that can pinpoint and serve markets without segmenting them to the point where they are too small or specialized to garner profits. "In the broadest possible sense, one wants to develop a sense of the key target audience in terms that reach beyond the basic demographics but not so far as to be beyond the ability of media to reach that audience," explains strategic media consultant Jane Hendrickson. "The trick, ideally, is that you end up with a cluster, a target, that you actually can reach and communicate with in some fashion."[43] Marketers who can reach and communicate with the right customers have a greater chance of attracting and keeping those customers than those who are searching for the wrong customers, in the wrong place.

Summary of Chapter Objectives

1. Identify the essential components of a market.

A market consists of people and organizations with the necessary purchasing power, willingness, and authority to buy. Consumer products are purchased by the ultimate consumer for personal use. Business products are purchased for use directly or indirectly in the production of other goods and services. Certain products may fall into both categories.

2. Outline the role of market segmentation in developing a marketing strategy.

Market segmentation is the process of dividing a total market into several homogeneous groups. It is used in identifying a target market for a product or service. Segmentation is the key to deciding a marketing strategy.

3. Describe the criteria necessary for effective segmentation.

Effectiveness of segmentation depends on these four basic requirements: (1) The segment must have measurable purchasing power and size; (2) marketers can find a way to promote to and serve the market; (3) marketers must identify segments large enough for profit potential; and (4) the firm can target a number of segments that match its marketing capabilities.

4. Explain each of the four bases for segmenting consumer markets.

Consumer markets may be divided on the basis of geographic, demographic, psychographic, or product-related segmentation approaches. Geographic segmentation divides the overall market into homogeneous groups according to population locations. Demographic segmentation classifies the market into groups based on characteristics such as age, gender, and income level. Psychographic segmentation uses behavioral profiles developed from analyses of consumers' activities, opinions, interests, and lifestyles to identify market segments. Product-related segmentation involves dividing a population into groups based on characteristics of the consumer's relationship to the product, including benefits, usage rates, and brand loyalty.

5. Identify the steps in the market segmentation process.

Market segmentation is the division of markets into relatively homogeneous groups. Segmentation follows a five-step sequence: (1) identifying the bases on which to segment markets; (2) developing user profiles; (3) forecasting the overall market potential; (4) estimating market share; and (5) selecting specific market segments.

6. Discuss four basic strategies for reaching target markets.

Four strategies are (1) undifferentiated marketing, which uses a single marketing mix; (2) differentiated marketing, which pro-duces numerous products, each with its own mix; (3) concentrated marketing, which directs all the firm's marketing resources toward a small segment; and (4) micromarketing, which targets potential customers at basic levels, such as zip code or occupation.

7. Summarize the types of positioning strategies.

Positioning strategies include positioning a product or service according to attributes, price/quality, competitors, application, product user, and product class.

8. Explain the reasons for positioning and repositioning products.

Positioning helps create a memorable impression of a product in a consumer's mind and is used to differentiate a product from competitors' products. Changes in the competitive environment may require repositioning in order to maintain or even grab more of the market share.

Marketing Terms You Need to Know

market 224
target market 224
consumer products 224
business products 224
market segmentation 225
geographic segmentation 227

geographic information system (GIS) 229
demographic segmentation 229
psychographic segmentation 238

product-related segmentation 240
undifferentiated marketing 244
differentiated marketing 244
concentrated marketing 244

micromarketing 245
positioning 245

Other Important Marketing Terms

metropolitan statistical area (MSA) 228
consolidated metropolitan statistical area (CMSA) 228

primary metropolitan statistical area (PMSA) 228
cohort effect 230
9/11 Generation 230
baby boomers 230

family life cycle 234
POSSLQ 235
Engel's laws 236
AIO statements 238
VALS2 238

80/20 principle 240
positioning map 246
repositioning 246

Review Questions

1. What is the difference between a market and a target market? Give an example of the target market for each of the following:
   a. *Newsweek* magazine
   b. John Deere tractors
   c. Maybelline cosmetics
   d. Toys "R" Us

2. Explain how a truck could be both a consumer product and a business product.
3. Identify the four main criteria for effective market segmentation.
4. In what situations might marketers best use geographic segmentation? Identify at least one product or service for which geographic segmentation would be appropriate, and explain why.

Frito-Lay markets Cheetos snacks *without* cheese flavoring in Asia because consumers there prefer steak-flavored and cuttlefish-flavored snacks. What type of segmentation strategy is Frito-Lay employing in its Asian markets?

What market segmentation basis would you recommend for each of the following products, and why?

a. Colorado Avalanche hockey team

b. iPod digital music players

c. Subway fat-free sandwiches

Explain the difference between undifferentiated marketing and differentiated marketing. What are some of the benefits and drawbacks to each?

What are the four basic determinants of a market-specific strategy? Explain each determinant.

As a marketer, how might you position each of the following products?

a. Kraft Macaroni & Cheese

b. Tiffany's

c. Wal-Mart

d. Hyundai autos

Canyon Ranch is an exclusive fitness resort with locations in Tucson, Arizona, and the Berkshire Mountains of western Massachusetts. Peak-season weekly rates often exceed $5,000 per person. The fee covers use of the fitness facility, programs, and meals. Discuss possible segmentation and positioning strategies for Canyon Ranch's programs.

Projects and Teamwork Exercises

1. Choose your favorite sport, either as a participant or as a spectator. Identify the different market segments for your sport. Then write a brief plan for selecting a segmentation strategy for your sport.

2. Find an advertisement that uses product-related segmentation as part of its strategy for reaching consumers. Present the ad to the class, identifying specific aspects of the ad such as segmenting by benefits sought, segmenting by usage rates, or segmenting by brand loyalty.

3. Identify a product that you or someone you know uses that is either niche marketed or micromarketed. Do you believe that the product could actually reach a wider audience? Why or why not?

4. With a partner, comb through various media to find an example of each type of positioning for goods or services. Discuss your finds with the rest of the class.

5. With a partner, choose a product that you believe might benefit from repositioning—whether it's a favorite food (such as pizza or tacos), a form of entertainment (such as a theme park or radio station), or a type of automobile or some electronic equipment. Identify ways in which marketers might reposition the product.

'net Work

http://www.oldnavy.com

http://www.rei.com

http://www.williams-sonoma.com

http://www.nielsen-net ratings.com

http://www.sric-bi.com/ VALS/

1. Market segmentation. Visit the Web sites listed and determine how each business has segmented its market. Has the firm used geographic, demographic, psychographic, product-related approaches, or a combination of two or more, to segment its market?

2. Demographic segmentation. Go to Nielsen/Net Ratings Web site and review a recent report on the most popular Web site destinations for college students. Visit three of these sites and describe the features that you think make them appealing to college students.

3. Psychographic categories. After reading the chapter, you may already have an idea of which of the eight VALS2 categories you fall into. Either to confirm your guess or to determine precisely which type you are, go to http://www.sric-bi.com/VALS/ and choose the "VALS Survey" link. Complete the survey and submit it. Then read the information concerning your type. Write a brief summary and discuss whether or not you agree with the results.

Note: Internet Web addresses change frequently. If you don't find the exact sites listed, you may need to access the organization or company's home page and search from there.

CASE 8.1   Getting Ahead by Clipping Kids' Heads

It's not a market that you'd necessarily think of right off the top of your head: kids' haircuts. True, the American hair care industry is substantial at $45 billion in annual revenues, but it is fragmented into many segments and competitors. Of the 350,000 salons currently operating in the U.S., 4 of 5 are small businesses and the other 20 percent are chains such as Supercuts.

Some of these chains have salons that are for kids only. About a decade ago, Cartoon Cuts opened in Fairfax, Virginia, to cut kids' hair only (Mom and Dad have to go elsewhere). Today, the company has 16 salons and $4.5 million a year in sales. Kids' Hair Inc. launched a similar business in Minnesota and is still going strong with ten stores and $2 million in sales. More recently, operations like Snip-its and Cool Cuts 4 Kids have made a hit with the younger set, and still more kids' salons are opening every month. Many of the start-ups are regional outfits, although the founder of Cool Cuts envisioned a national chain from the outset (the company has 25 salons and revenues of $4 million).

Marketing research shows that until about age eight, kids' haircuts are largely their parents' decisions. So Snip-its welcomes both children and parents, although the focus is clearly on the kids. Proprietary cartoon characters welcome the children and guide them through their haircuts, but the company has a "parent's chair" at every station so that mom or dad can direct the stylist with regard to length or style of the cut. In addition, there is a place for siblings and others to relax and play as well.

Kids' salons have special issues to deal with, particularly boredom and fear. Young children are often afraid of the scissors-wielding stylist, and they don't like to sit still in the chair. Siblings need to be kept busy as well. For that reason, these new salons make extra efforts to deal with these issues, whether it is providing toys and other amusements for waiting siblings or the "parent's chair" as Snip-its does. In addition, the cost of haircuts for the whole family can seem staggering if everyone visits at once. So the Treehouse organization offers family discount packages.

Salons also face the issue of attracting a new generation of customers and developing loyalty over the years. That's why Snip-its owner Joanna B. Meiseles takes the long view of her business and her customers. Instead of using someone else's characters to populate her salon, she created her own Snip-its characters. Why? "I had this idea that I would have more equity if Snip-its were a brand," she explains. "The kids would see the characters . . . and when they thought about hair care, they would think of Snip-its."

Questions for Critical Thinking

1. What market segments do children's hair salons actually serve? Identify them and explain your answer.
2. With such a small market share of the overall hair care market, do you think it is a good idea for business owners to focus only on kids? Why or why not?

SOURCES: Snip-its, http://www.snipits.com, accessed January 4, 2003; "Salon Makes Waves in Children's Hair Cutting," *Foster's Online*, February 21, 2002, http://www.fosters.com; Thea Singer, "Little Clippers," *Inc.*, July 2001, pp. 25–28.

VIDEO CASE 8.2   Annie's Homegrown: A Natural Success

The written case on Annie's Homegrown appears on page VC-10. The recently filmed Annie's Homegrown video is designed to expand and highlight the concepts in this chapter and the concepts and questions covered in the written video case.

9

13 pages of Reading

Consumer Behavior

Chapter Objectives

1 Differentiate between customer behavior and consumer behavior.

2 Explain how marketers classify behavioral influences on consumer decisions.

3 Describe cultural, group, and family influences on consumer behavior.

4 Explain each of the personal determinants of consumer behavior: needs and motives, perceptions, attitudes, and self-concept theory.

5 Discuss the difference between high-involvement and low-involvement purchase decisions.

6 Outline the steps in the consumer decision process.

7 Differentiate among routinized response behavior, limited problem solving, and extended problem solving by consumers.

Russell Simmons: How Star Power Can Influence Consumers

13

We're surrounded by media stars whose images, words, and actions influence the decisions consumers make every day when they buy products. We see ads featuring such notables as actor James Earl Jones for Verizon, cyclist Lance Armstrong for the U.S. Postal Service, and baseball star Barry Bonds for Baldwin pianos. These celebrities hope to influence consumers to purchase the goods and services offered by the organizations paying for the ads.

Russell Simmons is more than a star, though. Some might call him a phenomenon. Many people know him as the founder of Def Jam Records and the Phat Farm clothing label, but Simmons's influence carries far beyond those brands. Simmons represents certain cultural ideals and values, tastes, and preferences—among African Americans in particular but also among young consumers in general. His image as a business success and a contributor to his community make him a role model and an opinion leader for product purchasers. For instance, he recently launched a new company called RUSH Visa, which offers a debit card designed to help struggling consumers establish credit. Simmons-Latham Media is an entertainment company focusing on African American filmmakers and actors. Def Con 3 is a line of energy drinks from which a portion of the profits go to Simmons's handpicked charities and causes, including the Hip-Hop Summit Action Network. In addition, Simmons is a vocal advocate and financial sponsor for various causes, ranging from political candidates to education funding to reparations for descendants of slaves.

Still, Def Jam and Phat Farm are Simmons's two largest business endeavors. Although he sold the Def Jam label to Vivendi Universal, he is still chairman of the company, and many of its followers consider him to be its soul, dubbing him the "godfather of hip hop." Through Def Jam, Simmons wants to bring hip-hop into the mainstream, beyond a purely African American market. Already he is succeeding—scores of young music buffs of varying backgrounds listen to and follow hip-hop. He's even made it to Broadway—his show, "Russell Simmons' Def Poetry Jam on Broadway," won a Tony award. Meanwhile, Phat Farm has brought the hip-hop look to young consumers. Simmons knows that young African American consumers want to look like their hip-hop heroes, so the clothes

reflect that style. They make wearers feel like they belong to a special group—a feeling likely to influence future purchases as well. Not surprisingly, Phat Farm clothes, ranging from baseball caps and backpacks to jeans and jackets, have been selling like crazy. Phat Farm helped create a whole new category of apparel—urban wear—that has spawned competition from hip-hop stars P. Diddy and Jay-Z, who now have their own labels, called Sean Jean and RocaWear. Russell Simmons is more than a successful entrepreneur. He is a trendsetter whose opinion is valued by many demographic groups. "Russell could be someone who represents the imperative and ideology of a generation," predicts Bill Stephney, a music industry veteran.[1]

Chapter Overview

1

Differentiate between customer behavior and consumer behavior.

Why do people buy one product over another? Answering this question is the goal of every marketer. The answer directly affects every aspect of the marketing strategy, from product development to pricing and promotion. Discovering that answer requires an understanding of customer behavior, the process by which consumers and business-to-business buyers make purchase decisions. **Customer behavior** includes both individual consumers who buy goods and services for their own use and organizational buyers who purchase business products.

A variety of influences affect both individuals buying items for themselves and professional buyers purchasing products for their firms. This chapter focuses on individual purchasing behavior, which applies to all of us. **Consumer behavior** is the process through which the ultimate buyer makes purchase decisions, from toothbrushes to autos to vacations. Chapter 10 will shift the focus to business buying decisions.

2

Explain how marketers classify behavioral influences on consumer decisions.

The study of consumer behavior builds on an understanding of human behavior in general. In their efforts to understand why and how consumers make buying decisions, marketers borrow extensively from the sciences of psychology and sociology. The work of psychologist Kurt Lewin, for example, provides a useful classification scheme for influences on buying behavior. (The same concept also sheds light on motivation theory discussed in your management courses.) Lewin's proposition is:

$$B = f(P,E)$$

This statement means that behavior (B) is a function (f) of the interactions of personal influences (P) and pressures exerted by outside environmental forces (E).

This statement is usually rewritten to apply to consumer behavior as follows:

$$B = f(I,P)$$

Consumer behavior (B) is a function (f) of the interactions of interpersonal influences (I)—such as culture, friends, classmates, coworkers, and relatives—and personal factors (P)—such as attitudes, learning, and perception. In other words, inputs from others and an individual's psychological makeup both affect his or her purchasing behavior. Before looking at how consumers make purchase decisions, we first consider how both interpersonal and personal factors affect consumers.

Interpersonal Determinants
of Consumer Behavior

= other individual

You don't make purchase decisions in a vacuum. You might not be consciously aware of it yet, although you will be after this course, but every buying decision you make is influenced by something, whether it's external or internal. This section focuses on external, interpersonal influences. Consumers often decide to buy goods and services based on what they believe others expect of them. They may want to project positive images to peers or to satisfy the unspoken desires of family members. Marketers recognize three broad categories of interpersonal influences on consumer behavior: cultural, social, and family influences.

Cultural Influences

3

Describe cultural, group, and family influences on consumer behavior.

Culture can be defined as the values, beliefs, preferences, and tastes handed down from one generation to the next. Culture is the broadest environmental determinant of consumer behavior. Marketers need to understand its role in consumer decision making, both in the U.S. and abroad. They must also monitor trends in cultural values as well as recognize changes in these values.

Marketing strategies and business practices that work in one country may be offensive or ineffective in another. Strategies may even have to be varied from one area of a country to another. Sears has 30 of its stores in areas of the U.S. with large Asian populations, so the retailer has created a promotional campaign to coincide with the Asia Moon Festival, a traditional harvesting celebration. While the retail giant reports success with the effort, one major challenge is the diversity of Asian languages. "The main countries [of origin for Asian-American consumers] are China, Korea, Vietnam, Japan, and the Philippines," says Gilbert Davila, vice president of multicultural and relationship marketing, "and they all speak different languages." So Sears has to focus on promotions that rely less on language and more on cultural similarities, like traditional dance performances featuring puppets depicting animals and mythological creatures.[2]

It is also important to recognize the concept of *ethnocentrism*, or the tendency to view your own culture as the norm, as it relates to consumer behavior. Marketers must remember that each culture they are trying to reach views its own values, beliefs, and customs as the norm.

Core Values in U.S. Culture

While some cultural values change over time, basic core values do not. The work ethic and the desire to accumulate wealth are two such core values in American society. Even though the typical family structure and family members' roles have changed in recent years, American culture still emphasizes the importance of family and home life. This value has been further strengthened in the wake of the events of September 11, as illustrated by the Stouffer's ad for its Slowfire Classics in Figure 9.1. Stouffer's slogan even reflects this core value: "Nothing comes closer to home."

Other core values include education, individualism, freedom, youthfulness, activity, humanitarianism, efficiency, and practicality. Each of these values influences consumer behavior. As Figure 9.2 emphasizes, Target hopes to attract customers with its pharmacy campaign for St. Jude's Children's Hospital. One percent of each pharmacy purchase goes to the internationally recognized children's hospital.

Values that change over time also have their effects. The Internet has created a generation of sophisticated, globally aware teens who have access to a greater diversity of information and products. They also have considerable purchasing power. Sony recognizes the importance of

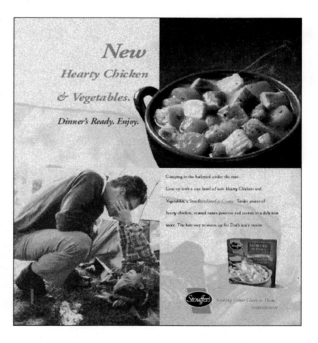

**FIGURE 9.1
Reflecting Core Values in Contemporary Advertising**

New
Hearty Chicken & Vegetables.
Dinner's Ready. Enjoy.

Stouffer's

Marketing Dictionary

customer behavior Buying behavior of individual consumers as well as organizational buyers.

consumer behavior Buying behavior of individuals who will use the goods and services they purchase.

culture Values, beliefs, preferences, and tastes handed down from one generation to the next in a society.

**FIGURE 9.2
Humanitarianism:
A Core Value for
Many Americans**

this group and plans to make extra efforts to build loyal consumers among them. One strategy is to use a comprehensive consumer database to make frequent contact with teens. According to the company's Consumer Segment Marketing Division's mission, the goal is to "develop an intimate understanding of Sony's end consumers . . . from cradle to grave."[3]

International Perspective on Cultural Influences

Cultural differences are particularly important for international marketers. Marketing strategies that prove successful in one country often cannot extend to other international markets because of cultural variations. Europe is a good example, with nine different languages and a wide range of lifestyles and product preferences. Even though the continent is becoming a single economic unit, cultural divisions continue to define multiple markets.

Sometimes cultural differences can work to a marketer's advantage. Hog farmers Dale and Lisa Siebrecht have been able to make a profit during a time when more than half of Iowa's pork producers have gone out of business. The Siebrechts decided to begin raising Berkshire hogs, which are big and slow-growing (and thus unappealing to large corporate farming operations) because the meat produced by this breed of hog is fat, sweet, and juicy—and preferred by Japanese consumers. With the reduction of trade barriers and new CryoVac packaging, an improved sealant that keeps meat fresh for the long trip from Iowa to Tokyo, the Siebrechts can get their product to market quickly, much to the delight of Japanese importers.[4]

Subcultures

Cultures are not homogeneous entities with universal values. Each culture includes numerous **subcultures**—groups with their own distinct modes of behavior. Understanding the differences among subcultures can help marketers develop more effective marketing strategies.

The U.S., like many nations, is composed of significant subcultures that differ by ethnicity, nationality, age, rural versus urban location, religion, and geographic distribution. The Southwestern lifestyle emphasizes casual dress, outdoor entertaining, and active recreation. Mormons refrain from buying or using tobacco and liquor. Orthodox Jews purchase and consume only kosher foods. Understanding these and other differences among subcultures contributes to successful marketing of goods and services.

As Chapter 8 indicated, America's ethnic mix is changing. By 2050, marketers will no longer easily spot the "typical" American. Ethnic and racial minority groups will constitute much larger percentages of the population. Marketers will need to be sensitive to these changes and to the differences in shopping patterns and buying habits among ethnic segments of the population. Businesses will no longer succeed by selling one-size-fits-all products; they will need to consider consumer needs, interests, and concerns when developing their marketing strategies.

Nearly one-third of Hispanic Americans are younger than age 17, and many are "bilingual and bicultural in their day-to-day lives and able to choose the best of what each world has to offer," says Monica Gadsby, director of Hispanic media for Starcom Worldwide. According to Starcom's Internet-based surveys of this group, they tend to watch general-market television during the day with their friends but Spanish-language programs with their families in the evening. So, Univision Communications, the leading Spanish-language broadcaster in the U.S., developed a prime-time miniseries called *Sonadoras*, which was a huge success among teens and young adults. Now the network is working on several more such series.[5]

Marketing concepts may not always cross cultural boundaries without changes. For example, new immigrants may not be familiar with cents-off coupons and contests. Marketers may need to provide specific instructions when targeting such promotions to these groups.

According to the U.S. Census Bureau, the three largest and fastest-growing U.S. ethnic subcultures are Hispanics, African Americans, and Asians. Figure 9.3 shows the proportion of the U.S. population made up of minority groups. While no ethnic or racial subculture is entirely homogeneous, researchers have found that each of these three ethnic segments have identifiable consumer behavior profiles.

African-American Consumers

A recent study shows African-American buying power rose 73 percent during the past ten years, compared with 57 percent for U.S. consumers in general. The growing African-American market offers a tremendous opportunity for marketers who understand its buying patterns.

Family structures may differ for African-American consumers. The median age of the typical African-American household is about five years younger than that of the average white family. This creates differences in preferences for clothing, music, cars, and many other products. Also, African-American households are twice as likely as non–African-American households to be headed by women who make the majority of the purchase decisions.

Successful firms try to reach African-American consumers through various approaches. For example, the Ariel/Schwab Black Investor Survey, sponsored in part by Charles Schwab & Co., Inc., revealed that many African-American investors feel insecure about their investment knowledge and do not fully trust financial advisors. Adding to the credibility issue is a perceived lack of African-American

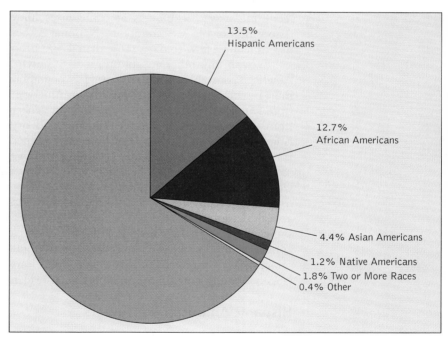

Note: Percentages have been rounded.
SOURCE: Data from the U.S. Census Bureau, in Haya El Nasser, "Census Numbers Show Jump from 2000 Tally," *USA Today*, June 19, 2003, pp. 1A, 2A.

FIGURE 9.3
Ethnic and Racial Minorities as a Percentage of the Total U.S. Population

Marketing **Dictionary**

subcultures   Groups with their own distinct modes of behavior.

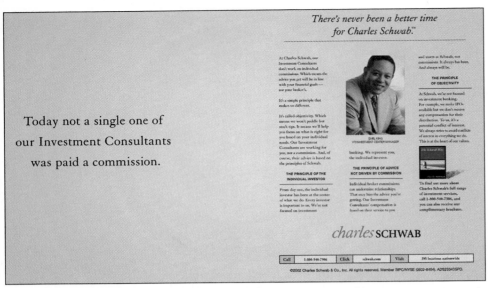

Today not a single one of our Investment Consultants was paid a commission.

The rising affluence and growing numbers of African Americans prompted Charles Schwab & Co., Inc., to better serve this important market segment by offering services such as retirement workshops at many of their nationwide offices.

financial professionals. Perhaps as a result, African Americans tend to invest more conservatively than other groups. They are more likely to choose real estate and life insurance as investments and are less likely to put their money in the stock market. However, the latest survey found that the number of high-income African Americans who invest in the stock market is up 30 percent since 1998, while stock ownership among whites rose only 4 percent.

Schwab used this information to design programs specifically for African Americans and believes that these programs helped to increase the percentage of African Americans in the stock market. The company teamed up with the Coalition of Black Investors to sponsor nationwide investment seminars at beginner, intermediate, and advanced levels. Schwab is also actively recruiting new stockbrokers at conferences hosted by professional groups, such as the National Association of Black Accountants, National Association of Black MBAs, and Blacks in Government, just to name a few. To date, more than 4,500 people have attended Schwab's seminars.[6]

As with any other subculture, it is important for marketers to avoid approaching all African-American consumers in the same way; demographic factors such as age, language, and educational level must be considered as well. Some African Americans are recent immigrants, while others are descended from families who have lived in the U.S. for generations. They are members of all economic groups—from the well-to-do to poverty stricken. John Bryant founded Operation Hope after the 1992 Los Angeles riots in an effort to attract banks and other businesses to South Central Los Angeles to revitalize the area and the minorities—including African Americans—who lived there. Because of the organization's efforts, today two Starbucks coffee shops and a Sony Theater operate in the neighborhood, where one of every four movie tickets sold are purchased by African Americans. Still other African Americans occupy the upper levels of economic class. Oprah Winfrey's *O, The Oprah Magazine,* reaches a wealthier group of readers (including both African Americans and whites) than does her daily talk show, whose advertisers include Procter & Gamble, Sears, and Wal-Mart. *O* readers earn an average annual income of $63,000 and generally prefer brands like Lexus, Donna Karan, and Coach. The magazine, which is produced in partnership with Hearst Publishing, enjoyed the most successful magazine launch ever and now has 2.5 million regular readers and more than $140 million a year in revenues.[7]

Hispanic-American Consumers

As the experience of Procter & Gamble shows in the "Marketing Hits" box, marketers face several challenges in appealing to Hispanic consumers. The 35 million Hispanics in the U.S. are not a homogeneous group. They come from a wide range of countries, each with its own culture. Some 64 percent come from Mexico, about 15 percent from Central and South America, 10.5 percent from Puerto Rico, and approximately 4.7 percent from Cuba. Cultural differences among these segments often affect consumer preferences.

The term "Hispanic" is a broad concept that includes a wide spectrum of national identities. "There are white, black, and brown Hispanics," notes Esteban Torres, a former Congressman from California. "You are what you think you are." Even the word *Hispanic* is not universal; Puerto Ricans and Dominicans in New York and Cubans in South Florida refer to themselves as Hispanic, but many Mexican and Central Americans in the Southwest U.S. prefer to be called Latinos.

More important than differences in national origin are differences in *acculturation,* or the degree to which newcomers have adapted to U.S. culture. Acculturation plays a vital role in consumer behavior.

For instance, marketers should not assume that all Hispanics understand Spanish. By the third generation after immigration, most Hispanic Americans speak only English.

Hispanics can be divided into three major acculturation groups:

- *Largely unacculturated Hispanics* (about 28 percent of the U.S. Hispanic population) were typically born outside the U.S. and have lived in the country for less than 10 years. They tend to have the lowest income of the three groups and depend almost exclusively on Spanish-language media.

- *Partially unacculturated Hispanics* (approximately 59 percent) were born in the U.S. or have lived there for more than 10 years. Most are bilingual, speaking English at work and Spanish at home. Many are middle income, and marketers can reach them through both Spanish- and English-language media.

- *Highly acculturated Hispanics* (13 percent) enjoy the highest income of the three groups. Usually born and raised in the U.S., they are English speaking but retain many Hispanic cultural values and traditions.

Research indicates several other important points:

- The Hispanic market is large and fast growing. Already the U.S. is home to the fifth-largest Hispanic population in the world; only the populations of Argentina, Colombia, Mexico, and Spain are bigger.

- Hispanics tend to be young, with a median age of 25 compared with a median age of 35 for the general U.S. population.

- Hispanic consumers are geographically concentrated in the following states: California, Florida, New Mexico, New York, and Texas. In fact, 42 percent of New Mexico's population is Hispanic. Almost half of all Hispanics living in the U.S. reside in five cities: Chicago, Los Angeles, Miami, New York, and San Francisco.

Hispanics tend to have larger households than non-Hispanics, making them good customers for products sold in bulk. They spend more on their children than do parents in other subcultures, especially on clothing. Hispanics also place great importance on keeping in touch with relatives in other countries, making them excellent customers for long-distance phone service, air travel, and wire transfers of money. In addition, Hispanics make more visits to pizza and chicken chain restaurants than do general-market consumers and bring along with them a larger group of family members and friends. "Fast-food marketers think about this segment more and more as the opportunity for growth lies within this fast-growing segment," says Andy Barish, a restaurant analyst with Robertson Stephens. "They've barely scratched the surface right now."[8]

Asian-American Consumers

Marketing to Asian Americans presents many of the same challenges as reaching Hispanics. Like Hispanics, Asian Americans are spread among culturally diverse groups, many retaining their own languages. The Asian-American subculture actually consists of more than two dozen ethnic groups, including Chinese, Filipinos, Indians, Japanese, Koreans, and Vietnamese. Each group brings its own language, religion, and value system to purchasing decisions. As mentioned earlier in the chapter, Sears has been working on

Marketing Hit

Procter & Gamble Taps the Hispanic Market

Background. Focusing marketing efforts on a specific subculture can generate significant opportunities for firms that are willing to take the time and effort to learn about its consumers and try to serve them. The Hispanic market is one of the nation's largest subcultures, accounting for about 13 percent of the U.S. population. Marketing powerhouse Procter & Gamble (P&G) is one of the companies that has decided to invest dollars and personnel in reaching this market.

The Challenge. Procter & Gamble wanted to establish a presence within the Hispanic population to attract consumers among this group. Marketers needed to understand members of this subculture, including their shopping patterns and buying habits.

The Strategy. P&G located the headquarters for its new U.S. Hispanic marketing unit in San Juan, Puerto Rico. Staffed with about 65 people, the office plays the leading role in initiating the development and promotion of products such as Downy Tropical Bloom fabric softener to the Hispanic market. In addition, the company has circulated its semiannual promotional magazine *Avansando con tu Familia* (Getting Ahead with Your Family) throughout the U.S. P&G marketers have also reworked the slogans for Cover Girl cosmetics and Pampers diapers to attract Hispanic shoppers.

The Outcome. Progress is slow but steady, and the unit in Puerto Rico has proved advantageous. Graciela Eleta de Cacho, general manager of the unit, admits that while results are mixed, her company is the first to make such a bold move, allowing the unit to focus entirely on multicultural marketing.

SOURCES: "Overview and Facts," Procter & Gamble Web site, http://www.pg.com, accessed January 10, 2003; Jack Neff and Laurel Wentz, "Diversity Drive," *Advertising Age,* May 21, 2001, pp. 3, 28; Eduardo Porter and Emily Nelson, "P&G Reaches Out to Hispanics," *The Wall Street Journal,* October 13, 2000, p. B1.

Being aware of subcultures is critical to marketing success. Sears's promotions for the Asia Moon Festival are tailored to the makeup of the local community where its stores are located—whether they are Mandarin, Cantonese, Vietnamese, or Korean.

attracting Asian-American consumers to its stores by conducting promotions in conjunction with the Asia Moon Festival. Depending on the cultural makeup of the community surrounding a particular Sears store, the company advertises the Festival in Mandarin, Cantonese, Vietnamese, or Korean. The programs within each store are conducted in English. Sixty-eight Chinese language newspapers and 20 magazines are currently published in the U.S.; 34 Vietnamese newspapers and 45 magazines; 46 Korean newspapers and 16 magazines; 37 Filipino newspapers and 18 magazines; and 20 Japanese newspapers and 18 magazines.[9]

Regardless of which Asian subgroup they target, marketers should take care to avoid sounding patronizing; in fact, this advice holds true for any subculture. In addition, Asian-American consumers like gift-with-purchase promotions; again, this is true of many other groups. But marketers should be careful to select gifts that are appropriate. Sears gives out traditional pastries called moon cakes in Chinese communities during its Moon Festival promotion. In other Asian communities, shoppers receive decorative lanterns. "It's a celebration," says Sears vice president of multicultural and relationship marketing Gilbert Davila. "We always run out of gifts."[10]

Social Influences *sociology*

Every consumer belongs to a number of social groups. A child's earliest group experience comes from membership in a family. As children grow older, they join other groups such as friendship groups, neighborhood groups, school groups, and organizations such as Girl Scouts and Little League. Adults are also members of various groups, at work and in the community.

Group membership influences an individual's purchase decisions and behavior in both overt and subtle ways. Every group establishes certain norms of behavior. *Norms* are the values, attitudes, and behaviors that a group deems appropriate for its members. Group members are expected to comply with these norms. Members of the National Rifle Association, Nature Conservancy, American Medical Association, and local country club tend to adopt their organization's norms of behavior. Norms can even affect nonmembers. Individuals who aspire to membership in a group may adopt its standards of behavior and values.

Differences in group status and roles can also affect buying behavior. *Status* is the relative position of any individual member in a group; *roles* define behavior that members of a group expect of individuals who hold specific positions within that group. Some groups (such as Rotary Club or Lion's Club) define formal roles, and others (such as friendship groups) impose informal expectations. Both types of groups supply each member with both status and roles; in doing so, they influence that person's activities—including his or her purchase behavior.

The Internet provides an opportunity for individuals to form and be influenced by new types of groups. Usenet mailing lists and chat rooms allow groups to form around common interests. Some of these online "virtual communities" can develop norms and membership roles similar to those found in real-world groups. For example, to avoid criticism, members must observe rules for proper protocol in posting messages and participating in chats.

The Asch Phenomenon

Groups often influence an individual's purchase decisions more than is realized. Most people tend to adhere in varying degrees to the general expectations of any group that they consider important, often without conscious awareness of this motivation. The surprising impact of groups and group norms on individual behavior has been called the *Asch phenomenon*, named after social psychologist S. E. Asch, who through his research first documented characteristics of individual behavior.

Asch found that individuals would conform to majority rule, even if that majority rule went against their beliefs. The Asch phenomenon can be a big factor in many purchase decisions, from major choices such as buying a house or car to deciding whether to buy a pair of shoes on sale.

Reference Groups

Non-contact of reference groups. = Team

Discussion of the Asch phenomenon raises the subject of **reference groups**—groups whose value structures and standards influence a person's behavior. Consumers usually try to coordinate their purchase behavior with their perceptions of the values of their reference groups. The extent of reference-group influence varies widely among individuals. Strong influence by a group on a member's purchase requires two conditions:

1. The purchased product must be one that others can see and identify.

2. The purchased item must be conspicuous; it must stand out as something unusual, a brand or product that not everyone owns.

Reference-group influence would significantly affect the decision to buy a Jaguar, for example, but it would have little or no impact on the decision to purchase a loaf of bread. The status of the individual within a group produces three subcategories of reference groups: a membership group to which the person actually belongs, such as a political party, an aspirational group with which the person desires to associate, and a dissociative group with which the individual does not want to be identified.

Children are especially vulnerable to the influence of reference groups. They often base their buying decisions on outside forces—what they see on television, popular choices among friends, fashionable products among adults. Advertising, especially endorsements by celebrities, can have much bigger impacts on children than on adults, in part because children want so badly to belong to aspirational groups.

Reference-group influences appear in other countries, as well. Many young people in Japan aspire to American culture and values. Buying products decorated with English words and phrases—even if inaccurate—helps them to achieve this feeling.

Social Classes

Research augmented many years ago by sociologist W. Lloyd Warner identified six classes within the social structures of both small and large U.S. cities: the upper-upper, lower-upper, upper-middle, and lower-middle classes, followed by the working class and lower class. Class rankings are determined by occupation, income, education, family background, and residence location. Note, however, that income is not always a primary determinant; pipe fitters paid at union scale earn more than many college professors, but their purchase behavior may be quite different. Thus, marketers are likely to disagree with the old adage that "a rich man is a poor man with more money."

Family characteristics, such as the occupations and incomes of one or both parents, have been the primary influences on social class. As women's careers and earning power have increased over the past few decades, marketers have begun to pay more attention to their position as influential buyers.

People in one social class may aspire to a higher class and therefore exhibit buying

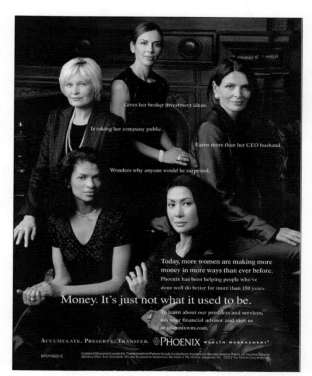

Dual-income households and increases in the number of highly paid and high-profile professional women have made female household members more influential in U.S. social class rankings.

Marketing Dictionary

reference groups Groups whose value structures and standards influence a person's behavior.

FIGURE 9.4
A Product for Those Aspiring to a Higher Social Class

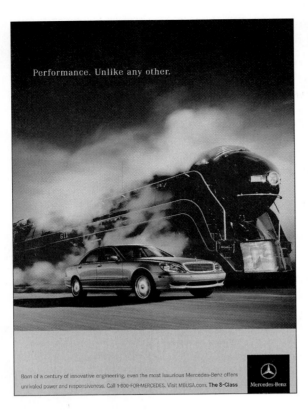

Performance. Unlike any other.

Born of a century of innovative engineering, even the most luxurious Mercedes-Benz offers unrivaled power and responsiveness. Call 1-800-FOR-MERCEDES. Visit MBUSA.com. **The S-Class**

Mercedes-Benz

behavior common to that class rather than to their own. For example, middle-class consumers often buy items they associate with the upper classes. Although the upper classes themselves account for a very small percentage of the population, many more consumers treat themselves to prestigious products, such as designer clothing or luxury cars, as illustrated in Figure 9.4.

Opinion Leaders Exam.

In nearly every reference group, a few members act as **opinion leaders.** These trendsetters are likely to purchase new products before others in the group and then share their experiences and opinions via word of mouth. As others in the group decide whether to try the same product, they are influenced by the reports of opinion leaders.

Generalized opinion leaders are rare; instead, individuals tend to act as opinion leaders for specific goods or services based on their knowledge of and interest in those products. Their interest motivates them to seek out information from mass media, manufacturers, and other sources and, in turn, transmit this information to associates through interpersonal communications. Opinion leaders are found within all segments of the population.

Information about goods and services sometimes flows from the Internet, radio, television, and other mass media to opinion leaders and then from opinion leaders to others. In other instances, information flows directly from media sources to all consumers. In still other instances, a multistep flow carries information from mass media to opinion leaders and then on to other opinion leaders before dissemination to the general public. Figure 9.5 illustrates these three types of communication flow.

Some opinion leaders influence purchases by others merely through their own actions, which is particularly true in the case of fashion decisions. When actress Sarah Jessica Parker began wearing a horseshoe necklace studded with diamonds during her television series *Sex in the City,* the necklace style suddenly became the rage among women and girls of all ages. Jewelry manufacturers reproduced the necklace in a variety of materials, ranging from platinum and diamonds to silvertone metal and crystals.

Family Influences Exam

Most people are members of at least two families during their lifetimes—the ones they are born into and those they eventually form later in life. The family group is perhaps the most important determinant of consumer behavior because of the close, continuing interactions among family members. Like other groups, each family typically has norms of expected behavior and different roles and status relationships for its members.

The traditional family structure consists of a husband, wife, and children. However, according to the U.S. Census

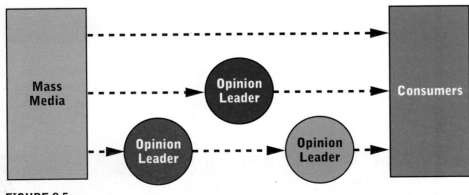

FIGURE 9.5
Alternative Channels for Communications Flow

Bureau, this structure has been steadily changing over the last century. In 1900, 80 percent of households were headed by married couples; today, only 53 percent are. A century ago, half of all households consisted of extended families, with six or more people living under one roof; today, only 10 percent of such households exist. Today, three of every five married women and 69 percent of single women work outside the home, as compared with 6 percent of married women and 44 percent of single women in the year 1900.[11] These statistics have important implications for marketers, because they indicate a change in who makes buying decisions. Still, marketers describe the role of each spouse in terms of these four categories:

1. *Autonomic role* is when the partners independently make equal numbers of decisions. Personal-care items would fall into the kinds of purchase decisions each would make for themselves.

2. *Husband-dominant role* is when the husband makes most of the decisions. Life insurance is a typical example.

3. *Wife-dominant role* is when the wife makes most of the decisions. Children's clothing is a typical wife-dominant purchase.

4. *Syncratic role* is when both partners jointly make most decisions. The purchase of a house or car usually follows a syncratic pattern.

The emergence of the two-income family has changed the role of women in family purchasing behavior. In the 1950s and early 1960s, women exercised only limited control of family purchasing decisions. A woman might make buying decisions about groceries and household items, but she was likely to defer to her husband on larger expenditures. Today, however, women have more say in large-ticket family purchases such as automobiles and computers. Studies of family decision making have also shown that households with two wage earners are more likely than others to make joint purchasing decisions.

Men's roles are also changing. More and more men are now major food purchasers, shopping either alone or with their spouse. Members of two-income households often do their shopping in the evening and on weekends.

Shifting family roles have created new markets for time-saving goods and services. The desire to save time is not new. As early as 1879, Heinz advertised its ready-made ketchup "for the blessed relief of mother and other women of the household"—but it has taken on new urgency as growing numbers of parents juggle multiple roles: raising families, building careers, and managing household operations. This time crunch explains the growing market for home-meal replacement, as more and more grocery stores prepare and sell complete meals to go. As Figure 9.6 shows, Oscar Mayer offers precooked bacon for people who want old-fashioned comfort food quickly.

Busy consumers are looking for ways to save shopping and purchase time as well. Internet and catalog shopping are natural time-savers for frantic families, but brick-and-mortar stores are catching on as well. Banks, fast-food

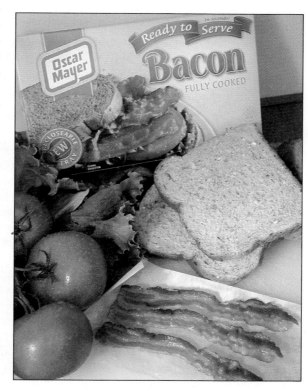

FIGURE 9.6
Oscar Mayer's Appeal to Busy Families

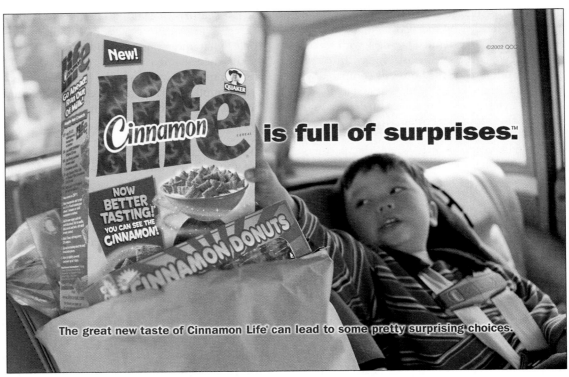

Children often influence what their parents buy. Cereal is a classic example.

restaurants, and even drugstores have completely changed the way they serve today's families by adding drive-through windows and call-ahead services.[12]

Children and Teenagers in Family Purchases

As parents have become busier, they have delegated some family purchase decisions to children, specifically teenagers. Children learn about the latest products and trends because they watch so much television and cruise the Internet, often becoming the family experts on what to buy. As a result, children have gained sophistication and assumed new roles in family purchasing behavior.

Children and teenagers represent a huge market—over 50 million strong—and they influence what their parents buy, from cereal to automobiles. According to James McNeal, a retired professor from Texas A&M University, children had an influence on an estimated $290 billion in family spending in a recent year. "That's kids actually pointing fingers and making demands," he says. But there's also the "nag factor," in which youngsters had an indirect impact on another $320 billion of household spending. "The real story of kids' market power is not their spending," says John Geraci, vice president of youth research at Harris Interactive. "It's their influence on the household."[13]

The Nickelodeon cable network is a favorite advertising outlet for marketers trying to reach parents through the younger set, in addition to reaching kids themselves. Recently Nickelodeon partnered with Gateway, Ford, and even Embassy Suites Hotels, which began offering a "Nick Trip Pack" with a disposable camera, travel journal, and *Rugrats* "Tommy" doll. In just one month, hotel visits tied directly to the advertising campaign boosted weekend bookings by 34 percent.[14] Even after they grow up, children continue to play roles in family consumer behavior, often by recommending products to their parents. Advertisers try to influence these relationships by showing adult children interacting with their parents.

Of course, children have their own purchasing power as well. In one recent year, children between the ages of 4 and 12 spent $29 billion of their own allowances, baby-sitting and odd-jobs earnings, and handouts from parents on various goods and services.[15]

Personal Determinants
of Consumer Behavior

Individual (handwritten) *Read* (handwritten)

Consumer behavior is affected by a number of internal, personal factors, in addition to interpersonal ones. Each individual brings unique needs, motives, perceptions, attitudes, learned responses, and self-concepts to buying decisions. This section will look at how these factors influence consumer behavior.

Needs and Motives

Individual purchase behavior is driven by the motivation to fill a need. A **need** is an imbalance between the consumer's actual and desired states. Someone who recognizes or feels a significant or urgent need then seeks to correct the imbalance. Marketers attempt to arouse this sense of urgency, that is making a need "felt," and then influence consumers' motivation to satisfy their needs by purchasing specific products.

Motives are inner states that direct a person toward the goal of satisfying a felt need. The individual takes action to reduce the state of tension and return to a condition of equilibrium.

Maslow's Hierarchy of Needs *Exam* (handwritten)

Psychologist A. H. Maslow developed a theory that characterized needs and arranged them in a hierarchy to reflect their importance. Maslow identified five levels of needs, beginning with physiological needs and progressing to the need for self-actualization. A person must at least partially satisfy lower-level needs, according to his theory, before higher needs can affect behavior. In developed countries, where relatively large per-capita incomes allow most people to satisfy the basic needs on the hierarchy, higher-order needs may be more important to consumer behavior. Table 9.1 illustrates products and marketing themes designed to satisfy needs at each level.

**FIGURE 9.7
Pepperidge Farm's
Direct Appeal to
Physiological Needs**

Physiological Needs

Needs at the most basic level concern essential requirements for survival, such as food, water, shelter, and clothing. Pepperidge Farm French Toast Swirl Bread, shown in Figure 9.7, appeals to physiological needs by stating in its advertisements that, "It doesn't go with breakfast. It is breakfast."

Safety Needs

Second-level needs include security, protection from physical harm, and avoidance of the unexpected. To gratify these needs, consumers may buy mutual fund shares, disability insurance, or security devices. State Farm Insurance appeals to these needs by saying, "Like a good neighbor State Farm is there."

Marketing Dictionary

need   Imbalance between a consumer's actual and desired states.

motive   Inner state that directs a person toward the goal of satisfying a need.

Know it 4 exam   Motivitional Model.

TABLE 9.1   Marketing Strategies Based on Maslow's Hierarchy of Needs

Bottom

Physiological Needs	Products	Vitamins, herbal supplements, medicines, food, exercise equipment, fitness clubs
	Marketing themes	Church's Fried Chicken—"Gotta love it."; Campbell's Healthy Request Soups—"M'm! M'm! Good! . . . and Healthy!"; Bausch & Lomb—"See the wonder."
Safety Needs	Products	Cars and auto accessories, burglar alarm systems, retirement investments, insurance, smoke and carbon-monoxide detectors, medicines
	Marketing themes	Fireman's Fund Insurance—"License to get on with it."; American General Financial Group—"Live the life you've imagined." Shell Oil—"Count on Shell."; Bayer—"Changing the world with great care."; Volvo—"Protect the body. Ignite the soul."
Belongingness *R social needs*	Products	Beauty aids, entertainment, clothing, cars
	Marketing themes	Dell Computer—"Hey Dude, you're getting a Dell."; Blue Ridge Knives—"Follow the leader."; Lawson Software—"Leading-edge technology without the attitude."; Egift online retailer—"Great gifts for everyone . . . starting with you."
Esteem Needs	Products	Clothing, cars, jewelry, liquors, hobbies, beauty spa services
	Marketing themes	Saks Fifth Avenue—"Defining Style."; Van Cleef & Arpels—"The pleasure of perfection."; Accutron watches—"Perhaps it's worthy of your trust."; Jenn-Air kitchen appliances—"The sign of a great cook."
Self-Actualization *What is the reason of being on earth.*	Products	Education, cultural events, sports, hobbies, luxury goods, technology, travel
	Marketing themes	Gatorade—"Is it in you?"; Baccarat Crystal—"Beauty has its reasons."; Grand Lido Resorts—"Lost and found for the soul."; Gauthier jewelry—"Wear art."

TOP

FIGURE 9.8
Olive Garden's Appeal to Social and Belongingness Needs

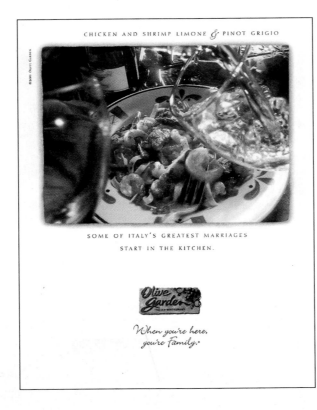

CHICKEN AND SHRIMP LIMONE & PINOT GRIGIO

SOME OF ITALY'S GREATEST MARRIAGES
START IN THE KITCHEN.

When you're here, you're Family.

Social/Belongingness Needs

Satisfaction of physiological and safety needs leads a person to attend to third-level needs—the desire to be accepted by people and groups important to that individual. To satisfy this need, people may join organizations and buy goods or services that make them feel part of a group. The ad for Olive Garden restaurants in Figure 9.8 actually appeals to two needs—physiological (food) and social/belongingness. The ad's tagline is "When you're here, you're family."

Esteem Needs

The desire for a sense of accomplishment and achievement, to gain the respect of others, and even to exceed the performance of others is a universal human trait that emerges after lower-order needs are satisfied.

Self-Actualization Needs

At the top rung of Maslow's ladder of human needs is people's desire to realize their full potential and to find fulfillment by fully expressing their talents and capabilities. Companies specializing in exotic adventure vacations aim to satisfy consumers' needs for self-actualization. Other travel providers, such as Smithsonian Study Tours, offer specialized educational trips that appeal to consumers' desires for a meaningful experience as well as a vacation. Elderhostel tailors similar trips for baby boomers and seniors. These trips usually involve an informal course of study—whether it's cooking, history, anthropology, or golf.

Maslow noted that a satisfied need no longer motivates a person to act. Once the physiological needs are met, the individual moves on to pursue satisfaction of higher-order needs. Consumers are periodically motivated by the need to relieve thirst and hunger, but their interests soon return to focus on satisfaction of safety, social, and other needs in the hierarchy.

Critics have pointed out a variety of flaws in Maslow's reasoning. For example, some needs can be related to more than one level. However, the hierarchy of needs continues to occupy a secure place in the study of consumer behavior.

Perceptions

Perception is the meaning that a person attributes to incoming stimuli gathered through the five senses—sight, hearing, touch, taste, and smell. Certainly a buyer's behavior is influenced by his or her perceptions of a good or service. Only recently have researchers come to recognize that people's perceptions depend as much on what they want to perceive as on the actual stimuli. It is for this reason that Saks Fifth Avenue and Godiva chocolates are perceived so differently from Wal-Mart and Hershey, respectively.

A person's perception of an object or event results from the interaction of two types of factors:

1. Stimulus factors—characteristics of the physical object such as size, color, weight, and shape

2. Individual factors—unique characteristics of the individual, including not only sensory processes but also experiences with similar inputs and basic motivations and expectations

Perceptual Screens

The average American today is constantly bombarded by marketing messages. According to the Food Marketing Institute, a typical supermarket now carries 30,000 different packages, each serving as a miniature billboard vying to attract consumers' attention. Over 6,000 commercials a week are aired on network TV. Prime-time TV shows carry more than 15 minutes of advertising every hour. Thousands of businesses have set up World Wide Web sites to tout their offerings. Marketers have also stamped their messages on everything from popcorn bags in movie theaters to airsickness bags on planes.

This unceasing marketing clutter has caused consumers to ignore many promotional messages. People respond selectively to attend only to messages that manage to break through their *perceptual screens*—the mental filtering processes through which all inputs must pass.

All marketers struggle to determine which stimuli evoke responses from consumers. They must learn how to capture a customer's attention long enough to read an advertisement, listen to a sales representative, or react to a point-of-purchase display. In general, marketers seek to make a message stand out and to gain the attention of prospective customers. One way marketers can draw attention to their messages is through appeals to consumers' fears, as the "Solving an Ethical Controversy" box discusses.

One way to break through clutter is to run large ads. Doubling the size of an ad in printed media increases its attention value by about 50 percent. Advertisers use color to make newspaper ads contrast with the usual black-and-white graphics, providing another effective way to penetrate the reader's perceptual screen. Other methods for enhancing contrast include arranging a large amount of white space around a printed area or placing white type on a dark background. Vivid illustrations and photos can also help to break through clutter in print ads.

The psychological concept of closure also helps marketers create a message that stands out. Closure is the human tendency to perceive a complete picture from an incomplete stimulus. Advertisements that allow consumers to do

Marketing Dictionary

perception Meaning that a person attributes to incoming stimuli gathered through the five senses.

right wrong Solving an Ethical Controversy

Marketing to Consumers' Fears

You've seen the ads. A 40-year-old woman dying of lung cancer; a bereaved husband. A tough guy with a frying pan and an egg warning, "This is your brain. This is drugs. This is your brain on drugs." A videotape of a child at a birthday party, with a tagline noting the date of the child's death caused by a drunk driver. All of these ads are intended to use fear to change consumer attitudes about the products they buy or the behaviors they engage in. In Canada, warning labels on cigarette packs have become increasingly graphic and specific.

Should marketers use fear tactics to change consumers' perceptions and attitudes about products?

PRO

1. Any strategy that will convince consumers to change their attitudes about purchasing or using dangerous or unhealthful products is ethical.
2. "We need health warning labels that cut through Big Tobacco's advertising spin," says Rep. Marty Meehan of Massachusetts. In Canada, 43 percent of smokers say the new labels have made them consider quitting. (It should also be noted that Canada has a higher tax on tobacco.)

CON

1. Consumers should be able to buy and use the products they want without interference, as long as the products and their behavior are legal.
2. Shock advertising doesn't work with some consumers. "The goal of health warnings should be to inform adults, not to repel or humiliate adults for legal choices they are making," says Philip Morris spokesperson Michael Pfeil.

Summary

Warnings and advertisements that use fear in an attempt to change consumers' perceptions and attitudes are a common strategy not only for public service notices like those just described but also for the insurance, financial, health, and other industries. Educated consumers must decide whether to respond to these tactics as they make their purchasing decisions.

SOURCES: Michael D. Shear, "VA Fires Up Teen Anti-Smoking Effort," *The Washington Post*, April 3, 2002, p. B8; Gordon Fairclough, "Study Backs Graphic Cigarette Warnings," *The Wall Street Journal*, January 10, 2002, p. B6; Wayne Drash, "Anti-Tobacco Ads Target Deadly Product," *CNN.com*, February 19, 2001, http://www.cnn.com.

The bright, vivid, swirling colors make this ad stand out and increase the likelihood that it will be noticed by readers.

this often succeed in breaking through perceptual screens. During a Kellogg campaign promoting consumption of fruit with cereal, the company emphasized the point by replacing the letters *ll* in Kellogg with bananas. In a campaign featuring a 25-cent coupon offer, Kellogg reinforced the promotional idea by replacing the letter *o* in the brand name with the image of a quarter.

Word-of-mouth marketing can be a highly effective way of breaking through consumers' perceptual screens. Take the early *Harry Potter* books. Although the series featuring the orphaned English schoolboy who is sent to wizardry school is now a huge international success, early popularity of the first two books was based on word of mouth. Before American marketers even got wind of the bespectacled young wizard from England, kids were requesting the books at their local bookstores, reading them, and passing them along to friends.

A new tool that marketers are exploring is the use of virtual reality. Some companies have created presentations based on virtual reality that display marketing messages and information in a three-dimensional format. Eventually, experts predict, consumers will be able to tour resort areas via virtual reality before booking their trips or to walk through the interiors of homes they are considering buying via virtual reality. Virtual

Virtual reality and consumer behavior. Go to the Web site listed. At this site you can engage in the same basic shopping activities that are available at many e-commerce sites. Spend some time browsing at this site, and identify some features that qualify it as a "virtual reality" shopping mall. Explain which steps of the consumer decision process this virtual reality shopping mall helps consumers complete.

http://www.world-of-shops.co.uk/USA/2DMALLUSA/2DMALLUSA.htm

reality technology may allow marketers to penetrate consumer perceptual filters in a way not currently possible with other forms of media.

With selective perception at work screening competing messages, it is easy to see the importance of marketers' efforts in developing brand loyalty. Satisfied customers are less likely to seek information about competing products. Even when competitive advertising is forced on them, they are less apt than others to look beyond their perceptual filters at those appeals. Loyal customers simply tune out information that does not agree with their existing beliefs and expectations.

Subliminal Perception

Almost 50 years ago, a New Jersey movie theater tried to boost concession sales by flashing the words *Eat Popcorn* and *Drink Coca-Cola* between frames of actress Kim Novak's image in the movie *Picnic*. The messages flashed on the screen every five seconds for a duration of one three-hundredth of a second each time. Researchers reported that these messages, though too short to be recognizable at the conscious level, resulted in a 58 percent increase in popcorn sales and an 18 percent increase in Coke sales. After the findings were published, advertising agencies and consumer protection groups became intensely interested in *subliminal perception*—the subconscious receipt of incoming information.

Subliminal advertising is aimed at the subconscious level of awareness to circumvent the audience's perceptual screens. The goal of the original research was to induce consumer purchases while keeping consumers unaware of the source of the motivation to buy. All later attempts to duplicate the test findings, however, have been unsuccessful.

Although subliminal advertising has been universally condemned as manipulative, it is exceedingly unlikely that it can induce purchasing except by people already inclined to buy. Three reasons ensure that this fact will remain true:

1. Strong stimulus factors are required just to get a prospective customer's attention.

2. Only a very short message can be transmitted.

3. Individuals vary greatly in their thresholds of consciousness. Messages transmitted at the threshold of consciousness for one person will not be perceived at all by some people and will be all too apparent to others. The subliminally exposed message, "Drink Coca-Cola," may go unseen by some viewers, while others may read it as "Drink Pepsi-Cola," "Drink Cocoa," or even "Drive Slowly."

Despite early fears, research has shown that subliminal messages cannot force receivers to purchase goods that they would not consciously want without the messages.

In recent years, subliminal communication has spread to programming for self-help tapes. These tapes play sounds that listeners hear consciously as relaxing music or ocean waves; subconsciously, imperceptibly among the other sounds, they hear thousands of subliminal messages. Americans spend millions of dollars a year on subliminal tapes that are supposed to help them stop smoking, lose weight, or achieve a host of other goals. Unfortunately, the National Research Council recently concluded that the subliminal messages do little to influence personal behavior.

Attitudes

Perception of incoming stimuli is greatly affected by attitudes. In fact, a consumer's decision to purchase an item is strongly based on his or her attitudes about the product, store, or salesperson.

Attitudes are a person's enduring favorable or unfavorable evaluations, emotions, or action tendencies toward some object or data. As they form over time through individual experiences and group contacts, attitudes become highly resistant to change.

Because favorable attitudes likely affect brand preferences, marketers are interested in determining consumer attitudes toward their offerings. Numerous attitude-scaling devices have been developed for this purpose.

Exam Attitude Components *h*

An attitude has cognitive, affective, and behavioral components. The *cognitive* component refers to the individual's information and knowledge about an object or concept. The *affective* component deals with feelings or emotional reactions. The *behavioral* component involves tendencies to act in a certain manner. For example, in deciding whether to shop at a warehouse-type food store, a consumer might obtain information about what the store offers from advertising, trial visits, and input from family, friends, and associates (cognitive component). The consumer might also receive affective input by listening to others about their shopping experiences at this type of store. Other affective information might lead the person to make a judgment about the type of people who seem to shop there—whether they represent a group with which he or she would like to be associated. The consumer may ultimately decide to buy some canned goods, cereal, and bakery products there but continue to rely on his regular supermarket for major food purchases (behavioral component).

All three components maintain a relatively stable and balanced relationship to one another. Together they form an overall attitude about an object or idea.

Changing Consumer Attitudes

Since a favorable consumer attitude provides a vital condition for marketing success, how can a firm lead prospective buyers to adopt such an attitude toward its products? Marketers have two choices: (1) attempt to produce consumer attitudes that will motivate purchase of a particular product or (2) evaluate existing consumer attitudes and then make the product features appeal to them.

If consumers view an existing good or service unfavorably, the seller may choose to redesign it or offer new options. American automakers have struggled for years to change consumers' attitudes about the way American cars are built, perform, and look. General Motors has spent decades—and millions—working to overcome quality problems, and has succeeded in many areas. But "hard quality"—making sure things don't break—is only a step toward changing consumers' attitudes. "Hard quality is simply not enough to be competitive," says William Shikany, a GM quality specialist. "Perceived quality is vital." Although GM's new Cadillac Escalade SUV is selling well, the Lexus LX470 SUV is doing better, even though the Lexus is a smaller, less powerful vehicle than the Escalade and costs more. Why? Lexus invested more in the look and feel of the vehicle's interior, which makes it look and feel like a more luxurious truck than the Escalade. Under a new "perceived quality" initiative, General Motors will be upgrading the interiors of several of its models, including the Escalade.[16]

FIGURE 9.9
Attempts to Change Consumer Attitudes Concerning the Use of Steak Sauce

Modifying the Components of Attitude

Attitudes frequently change in response to inconsistencies among the three components. The most common inconsistencies result when new information changes the cognitive or affective components of an attitude. Marketers can work to modify attitudes by providing evidence of product benefits and by correcting misconceptions. The makers of A1 steak sauce, shown in Figure 9.9, want consumers to think about their sauce as a necessity to meals, not just an optional condiment. Marketers may also attempt to change attitudes by getting buyers to engage in new behavior. Free samples, for instance, can change attitudes by getting consumers to try a product.

Sometimes new technologies can encourage consumers to change their attitudes. Many people, for example, are reluctant to purchase clothing by mail-order mainly because they are afraid it will not fit properly. To address these concerns, e-retailer Lands' End (now part of Sears) introduced a "personal model" feature on its Web site. Women who visit the site answer a series of questions about height, body proportions, and hair color, and the software creates a three-dimensional figure reflecting their responses. Consumers can then adorn the electronic model with Lands' End garments to get an idea of how various outfits might look on them. Of course, for the electronic model to be correct, women must enter information about their bodies accurately, instead of simply relying on their perception of themselves.

Marketers may rely on new innovations to help change components of consumer attitudes. The Ortho Biotech Products ad in Figure 9.10 attempts to change the attitude of cancer patients that chemotherapy will cause anemia or make them feel tired by offering a new drug, Procrit, to counteract this particular side effect of their treatment.

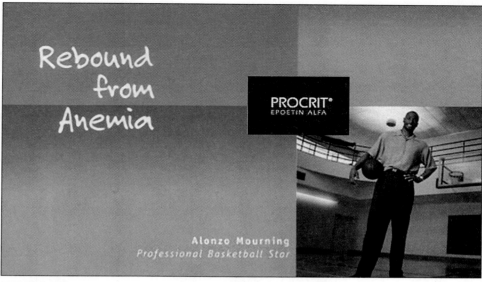

FIGURE 9.10
Ortho Biotech Products, the Maker of Procrit, Using Persuasive Advertising to Change Attitudes about Anemia

Learning *Read For Exam*

Marketing is concerned as seriously with the process by which consumer decisions change over time as with the current status of those decisions. **Learning,** in a marketing context, refers to immediate or expected changes in consumer behavior as a result of experience. The learning process includes the component of *drive*, which is any strong stimulus that impels action. Fear, pride, desire for money, thirst, pain avoidance, and rivalry are examples of drives. Learning also relies on a *cue*, that is, any object in the environment that determines the nature of the consumer's response to a drive. Examples of cues are a newspaper advertisement for a new Thai restaurant—a cue for a hungry person—and a Shell sign near an interstate highway—a cue for a motorist who needs gasoline.

A *response* is an individual's reaction to a set of cues and drives. Responses might include such reactions as purchasing Frontline flea and tick prevention for pets, dining at Pizza Hut, or deciding to enroll at a particular community college or university.

Reinforcement is the reduction in drive that results from a proper response. As a response becomes more rewarding, it creates a stronger bond between the drive and the purchase of the product, likely increasing future purchases by the consumer. Reinforcement is the rationale that underlies frequent-buyer programs, which reward repeat purchasers for their loyalty. These programs may offer points for premiums, frequent-flyer miles, and the like. The OneWorld ad in Figure 9.11 demonstrates a frequent-flyer program for eight participating airlines. Members that earn miles on one of the airlines can redeem the miles on any of the other seven, reinforcing the customer's choice of those airlines.

Briefly Speaking

A man who carries a cat by the tail learns something he can learn in no other way.

*Mark Twain
(1835–1910)
American author*

Marketing Dictionary

attitudes Person's enduring favorable or unfavorable evaluations, emotions, or action tendencies toward some object or data.

learning Immediate or expected changes in consumer behavior as a result of experience.

**FIGURE 9.11
Reinforcement
Provided for Loyalty
to the OneWorld
Frequent-Flyer
Program**

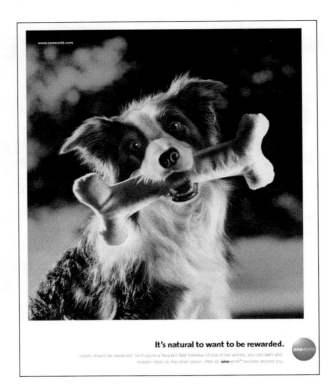

It's natural to want to be rewarded.

Applying Learning Theory to Marketing Decisions

Learning theory has some important implications for marketing strategists, particularly those involved with consumer packaged goods. Marketers must find a way to develop a desired outcome such as repeat purchase behavior gradually over time. *Shaping* is the process of applying a series of rewards and reinforcements to permit more complex behavior to evolve over time.

Both promotional strategy and the product itself play a role in the shaping process. Marketers want to motivate consumers to become regular buyers of a certain product. Their first step in getting consumers to try the product might be to offer a free-sample package that includes a substantial discount coupon for the next purchase. This example uses a cue as a shaping procedure. If the product performs well, the purchase response is reinforced and followed by another inducement—the coupon.

The second step is to entice the consumer to buy the item with little financial risk. The discount coupon enclosed with the free sample prompts this action. Suppose the package that the consumer purchases has still another, smaller discount coupon enclosed. Again, satisfactory product performance and the second coupon provide reinforcement.

The third step is to motivate the person to buy the item again at a moderate cost. A discount coupon accomplishes this objective, but this time the purchased package includes no additional coupon. The only reinforcement comes from satisfactory product performance.

The final test comes when the consumer decides whether to buy the item at its true price without a discount coupon. Satisfaction with product performance provides the only continuing reinforcement. Repeat purchase behavior is literally shaped by effective application of learning theory within a marketing strategy context.

Self-Concept Theory

The consumer's **self-concept**—a person's multifaceted picture of himself or herself—plays an important role in consumer behavior. Say a young woman views herself as bright and ambitious, headed for a successful marketing career. She'll want to buy good clothes and jewelry to reflect that image of herself. Say an older man views himself as young for his age—he may purchase a sports car and stylish clothes to reflect his self-concept.

The concept of self emerges from an interaction of many of the influences—both personal and interpersonal—that affect buying behavior. The individual's needs, motives, perceptions, attitudes, and learning lie at the core of his or her conception of self. In addition, family, social, and cultural influences affect self-concept.

The self-concept has four components: real self, self-image, looking-glass self, and ideal self. The *real self* is an objective view of the total person. The *self-image*—the way an individual views himself or herself—may distort the objective view. The *looking-glass self*—the way an individual thinks others see him or her—may also differ substantially from the self-image because people often choose to project different images to others than their perceptions of their real selves. The *ideal self* serves as a personal set of objectives, since it is the image to which the individual aspires. In purchasing goods and services, people are likely to choose products that move them closer to their ideal self-images. Marketers appeal to the components of self-concept all the time. Nowhere is this more apparent than in the health and beauty industry, which constantly appeals to consumers' ideal self, as discussed in the "Marketing Hits" box.

The Consumer Decision Process

Consumers complete a step-by-step process in making purchasing decisions. The length of time and the amount of effort they devote to a particular purchasing decision depend on the importance of the desired good or service to the consumer.

5

Discuss the difference between high-involvement and low-involvement purchase decisions.

Purchases with high levels of potential social or economic consequences are said to be *high-involvement purchase decisions*. Buying a new car or deciding where to go to college are two examples of high-involvement decisions. Routine purchases that pose little risk to the consumer are *low-involvement decisions*. Purchasing a candy bar from a vending machine is a good example.

Consumers generally invest more time and effort in buying decisions for high-involvement products than in those for low-involvement products. A home buyer will visit a number of homes, compare asking prices, apply for a mortgage, have the selected house inspected, even have friends or family members visit the home before signing the final papers. Few buyers invest that much effort in choosing between Nestlé's and Hershey's candy bars. Believe it or not, though, they will still go through the steps of the consumer decision process—but on a more compressed scale.

6

Outline the steps in the consumer decision process.

Figure 9.12 shows the six steps in the consumer decision process. First, the consumer recognizes a problem or unmet need and then searches for goods or services that will fill that need and evaluates the alternatives before making a purchase decision. The next step is the actual purchase act. After completing the purchase, the consumer evaluates whether he or she made the right choice. Much of marketing involves steering consumers through the decision process in the direction of a specific item.

Consumers apply the decision process in solving problems and taking advantage of opportunities. Such decisions permit them to correct differences between their actual and desired states. Feedback from each decision serves as additional experience in helping guide subsequent decisions.

Problem or Opportunity Recognition

During the first stage in the decision process, the consumer becomes aware of a significant discrepancy between the existing situation and a desired situation. Perhaps the consumer realizes that there is no food in the refrigerator when he or she would rather have a full refrigerator. By identifying the problem—an empty refrigerator—the consumer can begin to prepare for a possible solution, such as a trip to the grocery store. Sometimes, the problem is more specific. The consumer might have a full refrigerator but no mustard or mayonnaise with which to make sandwiches. This problem requires a solution, as well.

Suppose the consumer is unhappy with a particular purchase—say, a brand of cereal. Or maybe he or she just wants a change from the same old cereal every morning. This is the recognition of another type of problem or opportunity—the desire for change.

What if our consumer just got a raise at work? He or she might want to try some of the

Marketing Hit

Botox Marketers Want Consumers to Like What They See

Background. Marketers know that the health and beauty industry in this country is huge. But what if consumers could look in the mirror and see their ideal selves—without expensive or invasive surgery, and without slathering on layers of makeup? Allergan, the maker of Botox, which has been approved by the FDA to treat frown lines by injection, is hoping that the 29 million middle-aged American women (and at least a few million middle-aged men) who have household incomes above $50,000 will plunk down some of their discretionary income for a quick treatment that promises to take away lines and wrinkles.

The Challenge. Botox has been around for a while in different medical settings, but it is also widely known as a poison if eaten in contaminated foods. So Allergan must figure out how to attract its target market.

The Strategy. Allergan has launched a $50 million consumer advertising campaign to attract women with both the means and the desire to achieve their ideal self. The ads run in magazines such as *People, The New Yorker, Vogue,* and *In Style*—all magazines that reflect the way readers want to see themselves, as well as reference groups to which they may want to belong. In a couple of years, Allergan will begin to target men, who currently account for only about 12 percent of Botox sales. All told, Allergan

continued on next page

Marketing Dictionary

self-concept Person's multifaceted picture of himself or herself.

SOURCE: Roger Blackwell, Paul W. Miniard, and James F. Engel, *Consumer Behavior,* 10th Edition (Mason, OH: South-Western, 2004).

FIGURE 9.12
Integrated Model of the Consumer Decision Process

plans to saturate the media with advertisements; the company claims that 90 percent of its target audience will see both print and television ads at least ten times in the coming year.

The Outcome. The outcome of Allergan's efforts is still unclear, but some industry watchers believe that Botox sales could reach $1 billion within a few years. "The market," says Allergan marketing strategist Tom Albright, "could be much bigger than a lot of people have ever thought."

SOURCES: David Noon and Jerry Adler, "The Botox Boom," *Newsweek,* May 13, 2002, pp. 50-58; Michael McCarthy, "Botox Maker Plans $50 Million Ad Campaign," *USA Today,* April 29, 2002, p. B1; "FDA Approves Botox to Treat Frown Lines," *FDA Talk Paper,* April 15, 2002, http://www.fda.gov.

prepared gourmet take-home dinners offered by the local supermarket. These dinners are more expensive than the groceries our consumer has purchased in the past, but now they are within financial reach. The marketer's main task during this phase of the decision-making process is to help prospective buyers identify and recognize potential problems or needs. This task may take the form of advertising, promotions, or personal sales assistance. A supermarket employee might suggest appetizers or desserts to accompany our grocery shopper's gourmet take-home dinner.

Search Read

During the second step in the decision process, the consumer gathers information about the attainment of a desired state of affairs. This search identifies alternative means of problem solution. High-involvement purchases may elicit extensive information searches, while low-involvement purchases require little search activity.

The search may cover internal or external sources of information. Internal search is a mental review of stored information relevant to the problem situation. Maybe the consumer recalls past experiences with or observations of a certain type of product. Or perhaps it is just recollection of a commercial or magazine advertisement. On an external search, the consumer gathers information from outside sources, which may include family members, friends, associates, store displays, sales representatives, brochures, and product-testing publications such as *Consumer Reports.* The Internet has become a popular source of information as well. Since conducting an external search requires time and effort, consumers often use an internal search to make purchase decisions.

The search identifies alternative brands for consideration and possible purchase. The number of alternatives that a consumer actually considers in making a purchase decision is known in marketing as the **evoked set.** In some searches, consumers already know of the brands that merit further consideration; in others, their external searches develop such information. The actual number of brands included in the evoked set vary depending on both the situation and the person. For example, an immediate need might limit the evoked set, while someone who has more time to make a decision might expand the evoked set to choose from a broader range of options.

Consumers now choose among more alternative products than ever before. This variety can confuse and complicate the analysis necessary to narrow the range of choices for consumers. Instead of comparing one or two brands, a consumer often faces a dizzying array of brands and sub-brands. Products that once included only one or two categories—regular coffee versus decaffeinated—are now available in many different forms—cappuccino, latte, tall skinny latte, flavored coffee, espresso, and iced coffee, just to name a few possibilities.

Marketers try to influence buying decisions during the search process by providing persuasive information about their goods or services in a format useful to consumers. As discussed earlier, marketers encounter a difficult challenge in breaking through the clutter that distracts customers. The marketer must find creative ways to get into a consumer's evoked set of alternatives.

Evaluation of Alternatives *Read*

The third step in the consumer decision process is to evaluate the evoked set of options identified during the search step. Actually, it is difficult to completely separate the second and third steps since some evaluation takes place as the search progresses; consumers accept, discount, distort, or reject incoming information as they receive it.

The outcome of the evaluation stage is the choice of a brand or product in the evoked set or possibly a decision to renew the search for additional alternatives, should all those identified during the initial search prove unsatisfactory. To complete this analysis, the consumer must develop a set of evaluative criteria to guide the selection. **Evaluative criteria** are the features that a consumer considers in choosing among alternatives. These criteria can either be objective facts (government tests of an automobile's miles-per-gallon rating) or subjective impression (a favorable view of DKNY clothing). Common evaluative criteria include price, brand name, and country of origin. Evaluative criteria can also vary with the consumer's age, income level, social class, and culture. Auto shoppers planning to select one of the so-called "retro" cars introduced in recent years may include such popular models as the Chrysler PT Cruiser, Ford Thunderbird, or the recent entry by BMW of the British Morris MiniCar popularized in the *Austin Powers* movies. The T-Bird has proven so popular that Ford dealers frequently ask buyers to sign a pledge not to resell the vehicle for at least six months.

Marketers attempt to influence the outcome of this stage in three ways. First, they try to educate consumers about attributes that they view as important in evaluating a particular class of goods. They also identify which evaluative criteria are important to an individual and attempt to show why a specific brand fulfills those criteria. Finally, they try to induce a customer to expand the evoked set to include the product being marketed.

A travel agent might ask a client about the family's budget and recreational preferences. The agent might also explain the differences between two destinations that the client had not considered, pointing out important considerations, such as weather and activities. Finally, the agent might suggest other destinations or resorts, increasing the client's range of choices.

Purchase Decision and Purchase Act

The search and alternative evaluation stages of the decision process result in the eventual purchase decision and the act of making the purchase. At this stage, the consumer has evaluated each alternative in the evoked set based on his or her personal set of evaluative criteria and narrowed the alternatives down to one.

The consumer then decides the purchase location. Consumers tend to choose stores by

Marketing Dictionary

evoked set   Number of alternatives that a consumer actually considers in making a purchase decision.

evaluative criteria   Features that a consumer considers in choosing among alternatives.

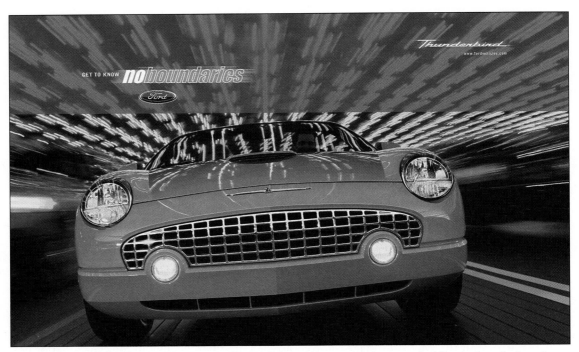

To provide a favorable impression in consumers, Ford demonstrates the appeal of its sleek, redesigned retro-style Thunderbird. The new style has struck a chord with consumers—even with a $40,000-plus sticker price, dealers have a hard time keeping up with demand.

considering such characteristics as location, price, assortment, personnel, store image, physical design, and services. In addition, store selection is influenced by the product category. Some consumers choose the convenience of in-home shopping via telephone or mail order rather than traveling to retail stores to complete transactions. Marketers can smooth the purchase decision and purchase act phases by helping customers arrange for financing or delivery.

Postpurchase Evaluation

The purchase act produces one of two results. The buyer feels either satisfaction at the removal of the discrepancy between the existing and desired states or dissatisfaction with the purchase. Consumers are generally satisfied if purchases meet their expectations.

Sometimes, however, consumers experience some postpurchase anxieties, called **cognitive dissonance.** This psychologically unpleasant state results from an imbalance among a person's knowledge, beliefs, and attitudes. A consumer may experience dissonance after choosing a particular automobile over several other models when some of the rejected models have desired features that the chosen one does not provide.

Dissonance is likely to increase (1) as the dollar values of purchases increase, (2) when the rejected alternatives have desirable features that the chosen alternatives do not provide, and (3) when the purchase decision has a major effect on the buyer. In other words, dissonance is more likely with high-involvement purchases than with those that require low involvement. The consumer may attempt to reduce dissonance by looking for advertisements or other information to support the chosen alternative or by seeking reassurance from acquaintances who are satisfied purchasers of the product. The individual may also avoid information that favors a rejected alternative. Someone who buys a Toyota is likely to read Toyota advertisements and avoid Nissan and Honda ads.

Marketers can help buyers to reduce cognitive dissonance by providing information that supports the chosen alternative. Automobile dealers recognize the possibility of "buyer's remorse" and often follow up purchases with letters or telephone calls from dealership personnel offering personal attention to any customer problems. Advertisements that stress customer satisfaction also help to reduce cognitive dissonance.

A final method of dealing with cognitive dissonance is to change product options, thereby restoring the cognitive balance. The consumer may ultimately decide that one of the rejected alternatives would have been the best choice and vows to purchase that item in the future. Marketers may capitalize on this with advertising campaigns that focus on the benefits of their products or with taglines that say something like, "If you're unhappy with them, try us."

7

Differentiate among routinized response behavior, limited problem solving, and extended problem solving by consumers.

Classifying Consumer Problem-Solving Processes

As mentioned earlier, the consumer decision processes for different products require varying amounts of problem-solving efforts. Marketers recognize three categories of problem-solving behavior: routinized response, limited problem solving, and extended problem solving.[17] The classification of a particular purchase within this framework clearly influences the consumer decision process.

Routinized Response Behavior

Consumers make many purchases routinely by choosing a preferred brand or one of a limited group of acceptable brands. This type of rapid consumer problem solving is referred to as **routinized response behavior.** A routine purchase of a regular brand of soft drink is an example. The consumer has already set evaluative criteria and identified available options. External search is limited in such cases, which characterize extremely low-involvement products.

Limited Problem Solving

Consider the situation in which the consumer has previously set evaluative criteria for a particular kind of purchase but then encounters a new, unknown brand. The introduction of a new shampoo is an example of a **limited problem-solving** situation. The consumer knows the evaluative criteria for the product, but he or she has not applied these criteria to assess the new brand. Such situations demand moderate amounts of time and effort for external searches. Limited problem solving is affected by the number of evaluative criteria and brands, the extent of external search, and the process for determining preferences. Consumers making purchase decisions in this product category are likely to feel involvement in the middle of the range.

Extended Problem Solving

Extended problem solving results when brands are difficult to categorize or evaluate. The first step is to compare one item with similar ones. The consumer needs to understand the product features before evaluating alternatives. Most extended problem-solving efforts involve lengthy external searches. High-involvement purchase decisions usually require extended problem solving.

Marketing Dictionary

cognitive dissonance Imbalance among a person's knowledge, beliefs, and attitudes.

routinized response behavior Type of rapid consumer problem solving in which the consumer has already set evaluative criteria and identified available options.

limited problem solving Situation in which the consumer knows the evaluative criteria for a product, but has not applied the criteria to assess a new brand.

extended problem solving Situation that results when brands are difficult to categorize or evaluate, and usually involves lengthy external searches.

Strategic Implications of Marketing in the 21st Century

Marketers who plan to succeed with today's consumers will understand how their potential market behaves. Consider the new generation spawned by the tragic events of September 11 and the ensuing war on terrorism, during which consumers tended to engage in cocooning, or staying close to home.

Cultural influences will play a big role in marketers' relationships with consumers, particularly as firms attempt more and more to conduct business on a global or international scale, but also as they try to reach diverse populations in the U.S. Since 40 percent of U.S. consumers fit a niche that does *not* include the white, heterosexual, middle-class consumers who were once defined as the marketing mainstream, marketers must pedal hard to catch up with the 70 million U.S. residents who identify with other racial, ethnic, social, or economic groups.[18]

In addition, family characteristics are changing—more women are in the workforce, people are working longer—which forecasts a change in the way families make purchasing decisions. Perhaps the most surprising shift in family spending is the amount of power—and money—children and teenagers now wield in the marketplace. These young consumers are becoming more and more sophisticated, and in some cases know more about certain products, like electronics, than their parents do, and very often influence purchase decisions. This holds true even with high-involvement purchases like the family auto. "In [an automobile] showroom, kids will run to the vehicle they like," says Jim Townsend, brand manager for Ford's Windstar minivan. "And if they run to your vehicle, you know you'll be sitting close to the deal."[19]

Marketers will constantly work toward changing or modifying components of consumers' attitudes about their products in order to gain a favorable attitude and purchase decision. Finally, they will refine their understanding of the consumer decision process in order to use their knowledge to design effective marketing strategies.

Summary of Chapter Objectives

1. Differentiate between customer behavior and consumer behavior.

The term *customer behavior* refers to both individual consumers and organizational buyers. By contrast, *consumer behavior* refers to the buyer behavior of individual consumers only.

2. Explain how marketers classify behavioral influences on consumer decisions.

The behavioral influences on consumer decisions are classified as either personal or interpersonal. These categories resulted from the work of Kurt Lewin, who developed a general model of behavior that can be adapted to consumer behavior.

3. Describe cultural, group, and family influences on consumer behavior.

Cultural influences, such as the work ethic or the desire to accumulate wealth, are those that come from society. Core values may vary from culture to culture. Group or social influences include social class, opinion leaders, and reference groups with which consumers may want to be affiliated. Family influences may come from parents, grandparents, teenagers, or children.

4. Explain each of the personal determinants of consumer behavior: needs and motives, perceptions, attitudes, and self-concept theory.

A need is an imbalance between a consumer's actual and desired states. A motive is the inner state that directs a person toward the goal of satisfying a need. Perception is the meaning that a person attributes to incoming stimuli gathered through the five senses. Attitudes are a person's enduring favorable or unfavorable evaluations, emotions, or action tendencies toward something. In self-concept theory, a person's view of himself or herself plays a role in purchasing behavior. In purchasing goods and services, people are likely to choose products that move them closer to their ideal self-images.

5. Discuss the difference between high-involvement and low-involvement purchase decisions.

Purchases with high levels of potential social or economic consequences are called high-involvement purchase decisions. Examples include buying a new car or home. Routine purchases that pose little risk to the consumer are called low-involvement

purchase decisions. Choosing a candy bar or a newspaper are examples.

6. Outline the steps in the consumer decision process.

The consumer decision process consists of six steps: problem or opportunity recognition, search, alternative evaluation, purchase decision, purchase act, and postpurchase evaluation. The time involved in each stage of the decision process is determined by the nature of the individual purchases.

7. Differentiate among routinized response behavior, limited problem solving, and extended problem solving by consumers.

Routinized response behavior refers to repeat purchases made of the same brand or limited group of items. Limited problem solving occurs when a consumer has previously set criteria for a purchase, but then encounters a new brand or model. Extended problem solving results when brands are difficult to categorize or evaluate. High-involvement purchase decisions usually require extended problem solving.

Marketing Terms You Need to Know

customer behavior 254	opinion leaders 262	learning 271	routinized response
consumer behavior 254	need 265	self-concept 272	behavior 277
culture 255	motive 265	evoked set 274	limited problem solving 277
subculture 256	perception 267	evaluative criteria 275	extended problem solving 277
reference groups 261	attitudes 270	cognitive dissonance 276	

Other Important Marketing Terms

ethnocentrism 255	Asch phenomenon 260	response 271	low-involvement purchase
acculturation 258	perceptual screen 267	reinforcement 271	decision 273
norms 260	subliminal perception 269	shaping 272	
status 260	drive 271	high-involvement purchase	
roles 260	cue 271	decision 273	

Review Questions

1. What is the difference between customer behavior and consumer behavior? Give an example of each.
2. What is culture, and how does it influence consumer buying behavior? Why is it important for marketers to avoid ethnocentrism in their marketing efforts?
3. Identify the three main U.S. subcultures. What are some of the key factors that marketers should keep in mind when targeting each of these subcultures?
4. Identify and describe briefly the four major social influences on consumer behavior. Then describe a recent pur-

chase you made, as it pertains to one or more of those influences.
5. How has the changing family structure altered family influences on consumer purchasing decisions? In what ways do children and teenagers influence family purchases?
6. Identify and describe briefly Maslow's hierarchy of needs. How can marketers use this hierarchy to create successful marketing efforts?
7. What are perceptual screens? What strategies might marketers use to break through them?
8. What are the three components to an attitude? What strategies might marketers use to change a consumer's attitude toward a product?

9. Differentiate between high-involvement purchase decisions and low-involvement purchase decisions. Then identify each of the following as high or low:
   a. shampoo
   b. computer
   c. magazine
   d. car
   e. snack food
   f. entertainment system
10. Identify and describe briefly the six steps in the consumer decision process. Cite an example of each step.

Projects and Teamwork Exercises

1. Choose a classmate to be your partner. Separately, list what you think the core values for your culture are. Then compare your two lists. Which values are similar? Which are different? What influences do you think have created the differences?

2. Think about your participation in family purchases. How much influence do you have on your family's decisions? Has this influence changed over time? Why or why not? Describe your experience with a recent family purchase to the class.

3. With another student, create a one-page advertisement using stimuli such as color or size designed to evoke a response from consumers. Present your ad to the class for their response. Do they think it is effective? Why or why not?

4. Select a print advertisement and identify its cognitive, affective, and behavorial components, as well as your attitude toward the advertisement. Present the advertisement and discuss it with your class.

5. Find an advertisement that makes use of the self-concept theory to promote its product. Write a brief description of how the ad plays on self-image, looking-glass self, or the ideal self to promote the product, or present your findings to the class.

'net Work

http://www.riaa.org/
MD-Cons-4.cfm

1. Hispanic consumers. Visit the Web site listed here. It reports the results of a survey of Hispanic music consumers. List five interesting facts that you can use in a class discussion of cultural influences and consumer behavior.

http://www.gm.com

http://www.honda.com

2. Maslow's hierarchy of needs. Automobiles are often considered to be products that satisfy three needs: safety, belongingness, and esteem needs. Go to at least four automobile manufacturer Web sites (examples include http://www.gm.com and http://www.honda.com) and find examples of features at the sites that focus on meeting each of these three needs.

http://www.zdnet.com/
computershopper

http://www.dell.com

3. Consumer decision process. Assume you're in the market for a new computer. Go to a Web site such as http://www.zdnet.com/computershopper or http://www.dell.com, where you can shop for a computer online. Specify your requirements, search for your options, and print out the results. Prepare a report in which you list the evaluative criteria you used. Also, identify the computer you would choose and summarize your opinion about using the Internet to help you make a purchase decision.

Note: Internet Web addresses change frequently. If you don't find the exact sites listed, you may need to access the organization or company's home page and search from there.

CASE 9.1 | CVS and Walgreen Cater to Consumer Convenience

We consumers are a bundle of contradictions. Through our purchasing decisions, we indicate to marketers that we want to slow down and enjoy a simpler, more relaxed life. But we also want to minimize the time we spend on certain tasks, like shopping. We want to zip through the bank line, the fast-food line, the grocery express line. Now, pharmacies like CVS, Walgreen, and Rite Aid are catering to our need for speed and convenience by adding drive-through windows—presumably so we can rush home to enjoy more quality time with our families.

Of its 4,100 stores located nationwide, CVS has installed drive-through windows in nearly 1,200. The windows largely serve pharmacy customers—those who are there simply to pick up prescriptions, which account for about 63 percent of the chain's business. The company plans continued expansion with 400 new stores, all of which will have the drive-through option.

Walgreen began adding drive-through windows to its stores about ten years ago, and currently about 25 percent of prescriptions are picked up at the windows. But Todd Frank, a real estate manager for the company, observes that, when people have a number of items to purchase, they prefer to walk into the store. "They like the store better because of the options," he explains. In other words, it is actually more convenient for consumers to make purchase decisions when they can evaluate products and choose among them in the store.

Both companies have discovered that the drive-through set-up works best with free-standing stores, which are larger and have more surrounding space, than those that are located in shopping centers, which tend to be smaller and subject to more congestion. In other words, if the drive-through window doesn't add to convenience, consumers won't use it. In fact, in a survey conducted by Ortho Biotech, the number one reason consumers choose a pharmacy is convenience to home. This means that the 21,000 consumers surveyed want to be able to reach the pharmacy quickly and easily, make their purchases, and leave as soon as possible. "Our research has shown people don't like to go beyond one mile for their pharmacy needs, and they want it to be quick and convenient," says Todd Andrews, director of communications for CVS.

So far, 64 percent of Walgreen stores, 36 percent of Rite Aid stores, and 29 percent of CVS stores nationwide have drive-through windows, largely devoted to prescription purchases. If we consumers keep behaving the way we have been in the past few years, there are likely to be many more of those in the near future.

Questions for Critical Thinking

1. How might marketers use learning theory to attract consumers to pharmacy drive-through windows?
2. By their nature, pharmacies are local stores. What challenges might CVS's or Walgreen's marketers face in serving their customers in African-American, Hispanic, or Asian neighborhoods?

SOURCES: Jodi Spiegel Arthur, "Chains Seek to Go it Alone," *The Intelligencer,* April 2, 2002, http://www.phillyburbs.com; Carole Paquette, "Drive-Throughs: They're Not Just for Banks and Fast Food," *Mobile Register,* April 22, 2001, p. 2J; Ken Alltucker, "Pharmacies Jockeying for Drive-Through Room," *The Cincinnati Enquirer,* February 10, 2001, http://enquirer.com; "Chain Stores again Rank as Most Popular Consumer Choice," *Drug Store News,* October 16, 2000, http://www.findarticles.com.

VIDEO CASE 9.2   WBRU Sounds Good to Listeners

The written case on WBRU Radio appears on page VC-11. The recently filmed WBRU Radio video is designed to expand and highlight the concepts in this chapter and the concepts and questions covered in the written video case.

10

Business-to-Business (B2B) Marketing

Chapter Objectives

1 Explain each of the components of the business market.

2 Describe the major approaches to segmenting business-to-business markets.

3 Identify the major characteristics of the business market and its demand.

4 Describe the major influences on business buying behavior.

5 Outline the steps in the organizational buying process.

6 Classify organizational buying situations.

7 Explain the buying center concept.

8 Discuss the challenges of marketing to government, institutional, and international buyers.

How Wal-Mart Battled SARS Overseas

You wouldn't necessarily speak of SARS and Wal-Mart in the same breath, but the global retailing giant found itself mentioned in the same sentence with Severe Acute Respiratory Syndrome far too many times for comfort a few years ago. That's because the initial outbreak of SARS began in China, where Wal-Mart has long-standing relationships with suppliers for many of the products it sells.

Wal-Mart spends about $12 billion per year in China, purchasing everything from wooden furniture to cargo pants. Before the SARS outbreak, Wal-Mart marketers and buyers made an average of 500 trips to China each year to work out product details such as specifications for the width of a shoe or the height of a coffee table. These trips, which involved face-to-face meetings with suppliers, were an important part of building strong relationships along the supply chain. But the outbreak of SARS forced travel restrictions between the U.S. and China, as well as Singapore, Hong Kong, and Vietnam, where Wal-Mart also has supply connections.

How did Wal-Mart handle the crisis? Since its business-to-business relationships are so important, company executives knew they had to find a way to maintain these contacts without putting any Wal-Mart employees at risk for contracting SARS. First, the company turned to technology to assist in communication. Using e-mail, videoconferencing, digital photography, and computer-assisted design, Wal-Mart's product buyers communicated their requirements to Chinese suppliers. With computer-aided design, product designs and modifications could be shared via the Internet, while live discussions could take place through videoconferencing. Second, in an ambitious undertaking, Wal-Mart invited hundreds of Chinese suppliers to a Dallas showroom to exhibit their goods and engage in contract negotiations. To protect U.S. workers from possible infection by Chinese representatives, Wal-Mart asked the traveling vendors to enter the U.S. ten days before the Dallas buying session, which was enough time to determine that sellers were not contagious. Most agreed to the request; those who did not were not admitted to the session.

Despite a few glitches, the improvised system worked well. "We are pretty pleased with the results," noted Andrew Tsuei, Wal-Mart's vice president for worldwide sourcing. During the crisis and its aftermath, the Bentonville, Ark.-based retail giant made no reduction in the amount of goods it purchased from China.

Wal-Mart did not ignore another relationship during the SARS outbreak—its 26 retail stores in China. The company instituted a program called "Leading Group of the Control and Prevention of SARS," headed by the general manager in each store. Under the program, all bulk food was sold in packages; associates in the food sections wore gloves and gauze masks; each store was thoroughly cleaned and disinfected every day;

and tips about SARS prevention were offered to customers as they entered the door. These measures helped maintain—and strengthen—Wal-Mart's relationship with its Chinese customers, employees, communities, and suppliers.

Wal-Mart has continued to use many of the business tools it developed during the SARS crisis. Why? Electronic communications are much less expensive than overseas travel. Sending Wal-Mart marketers and buyers to Asia several times each year is an expensive, time-consuming undertaking, so Wal-Mart has upgraded its Bentonville television studio with special cameras and lighting. Teams in China and the U.S. can now review fabric samples, toys, and furniture designs simultaneously via high-quality videoconferencing. And many Wal-Mart buyers have discovered that they prefer viewing products in a setting that better represents an actual Wal-Mart store than in a factory located 10,000 miles away. "We found a lot of value doing it here," says Ken Eaton, senior vice president of Wal-Mart's global procurement division. In the end, some of the challenges posed by the SARS crisis resulted in improvements to Wal-Mart's business-to-business marketing.[1]

Chapter Overview

Although the average person is well aware of the consumer market, the business-to-business marketplace is, in fact, significantly larger. U.S. companies pay more than $300 billion each year just for office and maintenance supplies. Government agencies inflate the business-to-business market even further; the Department of Defense budget for 2003 was almost $390 billion.[2] Whether conducted through face-to-face transactions, via telephone, or over the Internet—as the opening vignette describes—every day business marketers deal with complex purchasing decisions involving multiple decision makers. They range from simple reorders of previously purchased goods or services to complex buys for which materials are sourced from all over the world.

As you will recall from Chapter 9, attitudes, perceptions, family and social influences, and other factors affect consumer buying behavior. This chapter will discuss buying behavior in the business or organizational market. **Business-to-business**, or **B2B, marketing** deals with organizational purchases of goods and services to support production of other products, to facilitate daily company operations, or for resale.

Nature of the Business Market

Firms generally sell fewer standardized products to organizational buyers than to ultimate consumers. Customer service is extremely important to buying organizations. Advertising plays a much smaller role in the business market than in the consumer market. Business marketers advertise primarily to enhance their company images and the images of their products and to attract new prospects, who are then contacted directly by salespeople. Personal selling plays a much bigger role in business markets than in consumer markets, distribution channels are shorter, customer relationships tend to last longer, and purchase decisions can involve multiple decision makers. Table 10.1 shows significant differences between B2B and consumer-goods marketing.

Like final consumers, an organization purchases products to fill needs. However, its primary need—meeting the demands of its own customers—is similar from firm to firm. A manufacturer buys raw materials to create the company's product, while a wholesaler or retailer buys products to resell. Companies also buy services from other businesses. Institutional purchasers such as government agencies and nonprofit organizations buy things to meet the needs of their constituents.

TABLE 10.1   Comparing Business-to-Business Marketing and Consumer Marketing

	BUSINESS-TO-BUSINESS MARKETING	CONSUMER MARKETING
Product	Relatively technical in nature, exact form often variable, accompanying services very important	Standardized form, service important but less than for business products
Price	Competitive bidding for unique items, list prices for standard items	List prices
Promotion	Emphasis on personal selling	Emphasis on advertising
Distribution	Relatively short, direct channels to market	Product passes through a number of intermediate links en route to consumer
Customer Relations	Relatively enduring and complex	Comparatively infrequent contact, relationship of relatively short duration
Decision-Making Process	Diverse group of organization members makes decision	Individual or household unit makes decision

Environmental, organizational, and interpersonal factors are among the many influences in B2B markets. Budget, cost, and profit considerations all play parts in business buying decisions. In addition, the business buying process typically involves complex interactions among many people. An organization's goals must also be considered in the B2B buying process.[3] Later sections of the chapter will explore these topics in greater detail.

Some firms focus entirely on business markets. For instance, Hoechst sells chemicals to manufacturers, who use them in a variety of products. Advanced Micro Devices makes flash memory chips for the cellular phone and Internet-provider markets. Manpower Inc., provides temporary personnel services to firms that need extra workers. Computer Associates, Oracle, and Sybase are software vendors specializing in business applications. Chevy Express, featured in Figure 10.1, markets vans designed to meet the needs of businesses.

Other firms sell to both consumer and business markets. The J. M. Smucker Co., for example, sells jellies and preserves to consumers and also sells filling mixes to companies that manufacture yogurt and dessert products. Netscape, best known for selling its Navigator Web browser to consumers, actually gets about 80 percent of its revenues from corporate customers. It offers a complete line of sophisticated networking software for companies like 3M and Chrysler. Similarly, Eastman Kodak sells film to consumers, and it also sells photofinishing paper, chemicals, and services to wholesale photofinishing companies.

Note also that marketing strategies developed in consumer marketing are often appropriate for the business sector, too. As the "Marketing Hits" box demonstrates, final

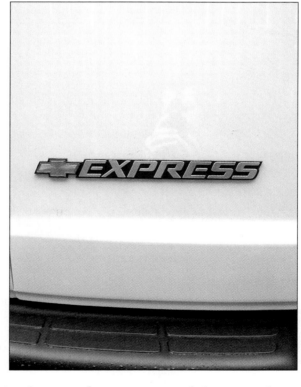

FIGURE 10.1
The Chevy Express: Catering to the Business-to-Business Market

Marketing Dictionary

business-to-business marketing (B2B)   Organizational purchases of goods and services to support production of other products, for daily company operations, or for resale.

Marketing Hit

A Duck Rules the Roost in B2B Insurance Marketing

Background. For years, the B2B sector was considered pretty old-fashioned when it came to marketing. While consumer companies looked to innovative advertising and promotions to win and keep customers, their counterparts in the B2B sector relied on personal relationships with organizational buyers. Most firms would scoff at the idea that marketing icons like the Marlboro Man or newcomers like the Geico Gecko could boost B2B sales. But that was before AFLAC, a provider of supplementary medical insurance to businesses, decided to borrow a tried-and-tested consumer strategy.

The Challenge. AFLAC, a U.S. company, entered the global health insurance market early and was better known in Japan than on its home turf. In fact, the company is Japan's largest foreign insurer, easing the concerns of the ever-health-conscious Japanese. Believing that end-users influence insurance-buying decisions, AFLAC sought to increase its name recognition among the American public.

The Strategy. Enter a little white duck with the bright yellow beak and blue bib, frantically quacking "Aaaaa-flaaack" every time it hears mention of insurance. An award-winning television campaign—styled after the very best consumer advertising—jolted AFLAC out of U.S. obscurity and into prime time. Following the ads, nine out of ten people recognized the company's name, and U.S. sales increased by a third. A second round of commercials, aired during the Winter Olympic Games, secured the duck its place in American pop culture. At AFLAC's Web site, browsers can shop for a plush toy and spin-off "duck gear"—proceeds go to the AFLAC Cancer Center.

The Outcome. Branding campaigns can be as powerful in the B2B sector as they are in

continued on next page

---

consumers are often the end-users of products sold into the business market and, as explained later in the chapter, can influence the buying decision.

1

Explain each of the components of the business market.

The B2B market is diverse. Transactions can range from orders as small as a box of paper clips or copy-machine toner for a home-based business to transactions as large as thousands of parts for an automobile manufacturer or massive turbine generators for an electric power plant. Businesses are also big purchasers of services, such as telecommunications, computer consulting, and transportation services. Four major categories define the business market: (1) the commercial market, (2) trade industries, (3) government organizations, and (4) institutions.

Components of the Business Market

The **commercial market** is the largest segment of the business market. It includes all individuals and firms that acquire products to support, directly or indirectly, the production of other goods and services. When Lufthansa buys aircraft built by the European consortium Airbus Industrie, when Sara Lee purchases wheat to mill into flour for an ingredient in its cakes, and when a plant supervisor orders light bulbs and cleaning supplies for a factory in Tennessee, these transactions all take place in the commercial market. Some products aid in the production of other items (the new airplane). Others are physically used up in the production of a good or service (the wheat). Still others contribute to the firm's day-to-day operations (the maintenance supplies). The commercial market includes manufacturers, farmers, and other members of resource-producing industries; construction contractors; and providers of such services as transportation, public utilities, financing, insurance, and real-estate brokerage.[4]

Briefly Speaking

We call them naked chickens just because they are naked.

Dr. Avigdor Cahaner, on the new breed of featherless chicken he developed to save on plucking costs

The second segment of the organizational market, *trade industries*, includes retailers and wholesalers, known as *resellers*, who operate in this sector. Most resale products, such as clothing, appliances, sports equipment, and automobile parts, are finished goods that the buyers sell to final consumers. In other cases, the buyers may complete some processing or repackaging before reselling the products. For example, retail meat markets may carry out bulk purchases of sides of beef and then cut individual pieces for their customers. Lumber dealers and carpet retailers may purchase in bulk and then provide quantities and sizes to meet customers' specifications. In addition to resale products, trade industries buy such things as computers, display shelves, and other products they need to operate their businesses. These goods, as well as maintenance items, and specialized services such as scanner installation, newspaper inserts, and radio advertising all represent organizational purchases. Chapter 16 provides detailed discussions of the trade industries.

Government organizations, the third category of the business market, include domestic units of government—federal, state, and local—as well as foreign governments. This important market segment makes a wide variety of purchases, ranging from highways to social services. The primary motivation of government purchasing is to provide some form of public benefit, such as national defense or pollution control.

Institutions, both public and private, are the fourth component of the business market. This category includes a wide range of organizations, such as hospitals, churches, skilled care centers, colleges and universities, museums, and not-for-profit agencies. Some institutions—state universities, for instance—must rigidly follow standardized purchasing procedures, while others have less formal buying practices. Business-to-business marketers often benefit by setting up separate divisions to sell to institutional buyers.

B2B Markets— The Internet Connection

While consumers' use of Internet markets receives the bulk of public attention, about 70 percent of all Internet sales are, in fact, B2B transactions. Internet-based trade hit $2.4 trillion in 2004.[5] Many business-to-business marketers have set up private portals that allow their customers to buy needed items. Service and customized pages are accessed through passwords provided by B2B marketers. Online auctions and virtual marketplaces offer other ways for buyers and vendors to connect with each other over the Internet. Figure 10.2 shows the composition of B2B online sales.

FIGURE 10.2 Composition of B2B Online Sales

SOURCE: Giga Information Group.

Differences in Foreign Business Markets

Business markets in other countries may differ due to variations in government regulations and cultural practices. Some business products need modifications to succeed in foreign markets. In Australia, Japan, and Great Britain, for instance, motorists drive on the left side of the road. Modifications need to be made to automobiles to accommodate such differences. As another example, the electrical wiring of a European building differs from that of a building in the United States. Again, modifications are necessary.

Business marketers must be willing to adapt to local customs and business practices when operating in foreign markets. They should also research cultural preferences. Factors as deceptively simple as the time of a meeting and methods of address for associates can make a difference. A company even needs to consider what ink colors to use for documents because colors can have different meanings in different countries.

Segmenting B2B Markets

2

Describe the major approaches to segmenting business-to-business markets.

Like consumer markets, business-to-business markets include wide varieties of customers. By applying market segmentation concepts to groups of business customers, a firm's marketers can develop a strategy that best suits a particular segment's needs. The overall process of segmenting business markets resembles consumer market segmentation, but it divides markets based on different criteria, usually organizational characteristics and product applications. Among the major ways to segment business markets are demographics (size, geographic location), customer type, end-use application, and purchasing situation.[6]

Marketing Dictionary

commercial market   Individuals and firms that acquire products to support, directly or indirectly, production of other goods and services.

FIGURE 10.3
Targeting the Small
Business Segment

BREAK OUT

Go beyond black and white. Get stunning color that's
surprisingly affordable with the Xerox Phaser 8200 printer.
There's a new way to look at it.

Now every idea you hatch can look brilliant. Starting at only $1499,* the Phaser® 8200 color printer delivers rich, vibrant color and crisp black and white prints up to 1200 dpi — all at a surprisingly low cost per page. Just as attractive as its low cost is its high speed. With an industry-leading first-page-out of only 9 seconds and 16 ppm full color, the Phaser 8200 is faster than 90% of today's office printers.* What's more, it's just one of a full line of office printers designed to help your business break out and sparkle. For more information, call 1-877-362-6567, ext.1886 or visit xerox.com/officeprinting/egg1886

THE DOCUMENT COMPANY
XEROX.

Segmentation by Demographic Characteristics

As with consumer markets, demographic characteristics define useful segmentation criteria for business markets. For example, firms can be grouped by size, based on sales revenues or number of employees. Marketers may develop one strategy to reach *Fortune* 500 corporations with complex purchasing procedures and another strategy for small firms where decisions are made by one or two people. Despite the dot-com bust, small businesses—especially firms with fewer than 100 employees—constitute a major market for B2B companies. This fast-growing segment of about 20 million firms offers tremendous potential.[7] To win their business, American Express created its Small Business Services unit, providing information and assistance for entrepreneurs and small business owners. The ability to print fast, high-quality color is a desired goal in business, regardless of the size of the business. Xerox targets all business users, with an emphasis on small business, with ads like the one in Figure 10.3.

Segmentation by Customer Type

Another useful segmentation approach groups prospects according to type of customer. Marketers can apply this concept in several ways. They can group customers by broad categories—manufacturer, service provider, government agency, not-for-profit organization, wholesaler, or retailer—and also by industry. These groups may be further divided using other segmentation approaches discussed in this section.

Customer-based segmentation is a related approach often used in the business-to-business marketplace. Organizational buyers tend to have much more precise product requirements than ultimate consumers do. As a result, business products often fit narrower market segments than consumer products do. This fact leads some firms to design business goods and services to meet detailed buyer specifications, creating a form of market segmentation.

North American Industrial Classification System (NAICS)

In the 1930s, the U.S. government set up a uniform system for subdividing the business marketplace into detailed segments. The Standard Industrial Classification (SIC) system standardized efforts to collect and report information on U.S. industrial activity.

SIC codes divided firms into broad industry categories: agriculture, forestry, and fishing; mining and construction; manufacturing; transportation, communication, electric, gas, and sanitary services; wholesale trade; retail trade; finance, insurance, and real-estate services; public administration; and nonclassifiable establishments. The scheme assigned each major category within these classifications its own two-digit number. Three-digit and four-digit numbers further subdivided each industry into smaller segments.

For almost 70 years, B2B marketers used SIC codes as a tool for segmenting markets and identifying new customers. The system, however, became outdated with implementation of the North American Free Trade Agreement (NAFTA). Each NAFTA member—the United States, Canada, and

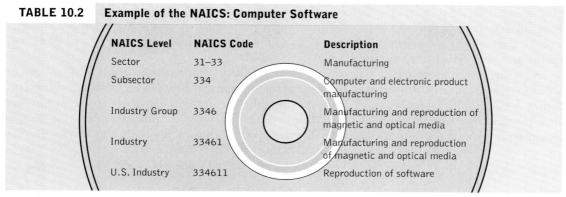

TABLE 10.2 Example of the NAICS: Computer Software

NAICS Level	NAICS Code	Description
Sector	31–33	Manufacturing
Subsector	334	Computer and electronic product manufacturing
Industry Group	3346	Manufacturing and reproduction of magnetic and optical media
Industry	33461	Manufacturing and reproduction of magnetic and optical media
U.S. Industry	334611	Reproduction of software

SOURCE: Reprinted from http://www.census.gov/epcd/www/naics.html, downloaded October 2, 2002.

Mexico—had its own system for measuring business activity. The new North American Free Trade Area required a joint classification system that would allow marketers to compare business sectors among the member nations. In effect, marketers required a segmentation tool they could use across borders.

Established in 1999 and updated every five years, the **North American Industrial Classification System (NAICS)** replaces the SIC and provides more detail than was previously available. NAICS created new service sectors to better reflect the economy of the 21st century. They include information; health care and social assistance; and professional, scientific, and technical services.

Table 10.2 demonstrates the more detailed NAICS system for software. NAICS uses six digits, compared with the four digits used in the SIC. The first five digits are fixed among the members of NAFTA. The sixth digit can vary among U.S., Canadian, and Mexican data. In short, the sixth digit accounts for specific data needs of the member nation.[8]

Briefly Speaking

Poor Mexico. So far from God and so close to the United States.

Porfirio Diaz (1830–1915) President of Mexico

Segmentation by End-Use Application

A third basis for segmentation, **end-use application segmentation,** focuses on the precise way in which a business purchaser will use a product. For example, a printing equipment manufacturer may serve markets ranging from a local utility to a bicycle manufacturer to the U.S. Department of Defense. Each end use of the equipment may dictate unique specifications for performance, design, and price. Praxair, a supplier of industrial gases, for example, might segment its markets according to user. Steel and glass manufacturers might buy hydrogen and oxygen, while food and beverage manufacturers need carbon dioxide. Praxair also sells krypton, a rare gas, to companies that produce lasers, lighting, and thermal windows. Many small- and medium-sized companies also segment markets according to end-use application. Instead of competing in markets dominated by large firms, they concentrate on specific end-use market segments.

Segmentation by Purchasing Situation

Yet another approach to dividing business markets centers on the purchasing situation. As a later section of the chapter explains, organizations use more complicated purchasing procedures than those of consumers. Firms also structure their purchasing functions in specific ways, and for some business marketers, this may be the best way to segment the market. Some companies designate centralized purchasing departments to serve the entire firm, while others allow each unit to handle its own buying. A supplier may deal with one purchasing agent or several decision makers at various levels. Each of these structures results in different buying behavior.

When the buying situation is important to marketers, they typically consider whether the

Marketing Dictionary

customer-based segmentation Dividing a business-to-business market into homogeneous groups based on buyers' product specifications.

North American Industrial Classification System (NAICS) Classification used by NAFTA countries to categorize the business marketplace into detailed market segments.

customer has made previous purchases or if this is the customer's first order. For example, IBM's Integrated Systems Solutions Corp. subsidiary might use a different marketing approach to sell to Lucent Technologies, an existing customer of its computer support services, than to a potential new customer who is unfamiliar with its offerings.

Increasingly, businesses that have developed customer relationship management (CRM) systems are able to segment customers in terms of the stage of the relationship between the business and the customer. A B2B company, for example, might develop different strategies for newly acquired customers than it would for existing customers to which it hopes to cross-sell new products. Similarly, building loyalty among satisfied customers requires a different approach than developing programs to "save" at-risk customer relationships.[9] CRM was covered in more depth in Chapter 6.

3

Identify the major characteristics of the business market and its demand.

Characteristics of the B2B Market

Businesses that serve both B2B and consumer markets must understand the needs of their customers. However, several characteristics distinguish the business market from the consumer market: (1) geographic market concentration, (2) the sizes and numbers of buyers, (3) purchase decision procedures, and (4) buyer-seller relationships. The next sections will consider how these traits influence business-to-business marketing.

Geographic Market Concentration

As noted in the previous section, the U.S. business market is more geographically concentrated than the consumer market. Manufacturers converge in certain regions of the country, making these areas prime targets for business marketers. For example, the Midwestern states that make up the East North Central region—Ohio, Indiana, Michigan, Illinois, and Wisconsin—lead the nation in industrial concentration, followed by the Middle Atlantic and the South Atlantic regions.

Certain industries locate in particular areas in order to be close to customers. Firms may choose to locate sales offices and distribution centers in these areas to provide more attentive service. For example, the Washington, D.C., area is favored by companies that sell to the federal government. One survey showed that federal spending on goods and services accounted for about one of every four new jobs created in the Washington, D.C., area.[10]

In the automobile industry suppliers of components and assemblies frequently build plants close to their customers. Ford recently established a first-of-its-kind campus for suppliers, located near its Chicago assembly plant. The campus will allow suppliers to produce or assemble products in close proximity to the plant, reducing costs, controlling parts inventory, and increasing flexibility.[11] Other industries establish facilities near power sources (chemical plants near Niagara Falls) or populations of skilled workers (high-tech firms in California's Silicon Valley).

As Internet-based technology continues to improve, allowing companies to transact business even with distant suppliers, business markets may become less geographically concentrated. Much of government spending, for example, is now directed through the Internet.

Sizes and Numbers of Buyers

In addition to geographic concentration, the business market features a limited number of buyers. Marketers can draw on a wealth of statistical information to estimate the sizes and characteristics of business markets. The federal government is the largest single source of such statistics. Every five years it conducts both a Census of Manufacturers and a Census of Retailing and Wholesaling, which provide detailed information on business establishments, output, and employment. Many government units and trade organizations also operate Web sites that contain helpful information.

Many buyers in limited-buyer markets are large organizations. The international market for jet engines is dominated by three manufacturers: United Technology's Pratt & Whitney unit, General Electric, and Rolls-Royce. These firms sell engines to Boeing and the European consortium, Airbus Industrie. These aircraft manufacturers compete for business from passenger airlines like Delta

Airlines, British Airways, KLM, and Singapore Airlines, along with cargo carriers such as Federal Express and United Parcel Service. The case at the end of the chapter describes the intense rivalry between two companies in the limited-buyer market for small regional passenger jets.

Trade associations and business publications provide additional information on the business market. Private firms such as Dun & Bradstreet publish detailed reports on individual companies. This data serves as a useful starting point for analyzing a business market. Finding data in such a source requires an understanding of the NAICS, which identifies much of the available statistical information.

The Purchase Decision Process

To market effectively to other organizations, businesses must understand the dynamics of the organizational purchase process. Suppliers who serve business-to-business markets must work with multiple buyers, especially when selling to larger customers. Decision makers at several levels may influence final orders, and the overall process is more formal and professional than the consumer purchasing process. Purchases typically require a longer time frame because B2B involves more complex decisions. Suppliers must evaluate customer needs and develop proposals that meet technical requirements and specifications. Also, buyers need time to analyze competing proposals. Often, decisions require more than one round of bidding and negotiation, especially for complicated purchases.

Buyer-Seller Relationships

An especially important characteristic of B2B marketing is the relationship between buyers and sellers. Such relationships are more intense than consumer relationships, and they require better communication among the organizations' personnel.

As Chapter 6 explained, relationship marketing involves developing long-term, value-added customer relationships. A primary goal of business-to-business relationships is to provide advantages that no other vendor can provide—for instance, lower price, quicker delivery, better quality and reliability, customized product features, or more favorable financing terms. For the business marketer, providing these advantages means expanding the company's external relationships to include suppliers, distributors, and other organizational partners. For example, John Deere & Co. has built strong relationships with its worldwide network of 5,000 dealerships that sell the company's agricultural products to farmers. Deere recently created a new distribution system that electronically connects the dealers' sales reports to a centralized warehouse that replenishes products as the dealers need them.

Close cooperation, whether through informal contacts or under terms specified in contractual partnerships and strategic alliances, enables companies to meet buyers' needs for quality products and customer service. This holds true both during and after the purchase process. Goodyear, which equips law enforcement vehicles with its Goodyear Eagle tires, uses its advertising to promote its customers' objectives, thus building the buyer-seller relationship.

Close buyer-seller relationships help companies in good times—and in bad. The "Solving an Ethical Controversy" box demonstrates how a crisis can derail even the most long-standing B2B ties.

Evaluating International Business Markets

Business purchasing patterns differ from one country to the next. Researching these markets poses a particular problem for B2B marketers. Of course, as explained earlier, NAICS is correcting this problem in the NAFTA countries.

In addition to quantitative data such as the size of the potential market, companies must also carefully weigh its qualitative features. This involves considering cultural values, work styles, and generally the best ways to enter overseas markets. For example, after winning a campaign to fly its aircraft into China, international

Marketing Dictionary

end-use application segmentation   Segmenting a business-to-business market based on how industrial purchasers will use the product.

Solving an Ethical Controversy

right wrong

The Failed Relationship between Ford and Bridgestone/Firestone

The Ford-Firestone debacle severed a B2B relationship that dated back to a handshake deal between Henry Ford and Harvey Firestone to put tires on the early Model T. The troubles began with a recall of tires manufactured in South America and quickly escalated into a full-blown crisis. More than 200 deaths were blamed on defective tires, whose treads appeared to "unpeel" on the road, leading to a high incidence of rollover crashes involving the Ford Explorer. At first, both companies were slow to react, but soon accusations flew fast and furious. A recall of 6.5 million tires drew public attention away from the Explorer, putting the heat on Firestone. Ford then announced a voluntary recall of a further 13 million tires at the staggering cost of $3 billion. Outraged that a partner company would recall its product, Firestone fought back, claiming that the Explorer was "defectively designed"—it did not matter what kind of tires the SUV was riding on.

Should alliance partners stick together during a crisis?

PRO

1. Regardless of who knew what and when, Ford and Firestone should have presented a united front since they were jointly responsible for putting the Explorer—and its tires—on the road.

2. If they are to battle hundreds of pending lawsuits, it makes sense for Ford and Firestone to come to a truce rather than keep pointing fingers.

CON

1. Companies are responsible only for their own roles in the products they make. The tire was designed to Ford's specifications, so why should Firestone take the blame?

2. Firestone warned Ford that low tire pressure would detract from safety performance, but Ford insisted on keeping to the initial tire pressure specifications. Firestone could have averted the crises by refusing to supply tires it suspected were defective—even if that meant risking the alliance.

Summary

Although the courts refused to uphold a class-action suit on behalf of Ford Explorer owners, it could be years before all lawsuits are settled. While Firestone's CEO stepped down after the first headlines erupted, Ford ousted CEO Jacques Nasser later. New chief William Ford, great-grandson of the company's founder, made steps toward repairing the rift, fighting to avoid a multimillion-dollar legal battle that could severely damage both companies.

SOURCES: David Kiley, "Bridgestone, Ford Fight Ruling," *USA Today*, April 18, 2002, accessed at http://story.news.yahoo.com; "Judge Declares Mistrial in Firestone Case," Reuters Limited, April 5, 2002; Mark Truby, "Firestone, Ford May Mend Fences," *The Detroit News*, November 1, 2001, http://www.detnews.com.

---

shipper UPS promoted the introduction of its first flights with media briefings, TV advertising, print and billboard ads, and direct mail. The messages are delivered using Chinese characters that represent such attributes as speed and reliability. The company's Web site uses Mandarin.

Liftomatic Materials Handling, a small company that makes equipment to handle barrels on factory floors, estimates that the Chinese market accounts for a quarter of its revenue. The company found that the Chinese are unwilling to invest in new products without having seen them demonstrated, so Liftomatic depends heavily on in-person or video demonstrations. Trade shows, print advertising, and a Chinese-enabled Web site all aim to improve communications between the American company and its Chinese customers.[12]

In today's international marketplace, companies often practice **global sourcing,** which involves contracting to purchase goods and services from suppliers worldwide. This practice can result in substantial cost savings. FedEx, for example, estimates that it saves over 30 percent on the prices of computer hardware and software by soliciting bids worldwide. Applica is a business-to-business company that manufactures small appliances such as irons and hair dryers for large retailers like Wal-Mart. Applica uses Internet-based technology to link sales data from Wal-Mart directly to the factory floor in Mexico, where irons are made to order. By connecting manufacturing operations directly with customer sales, Applica is able to slash inventories while producing in low-cost regions of the world.[13]

Global sourcing requires companies to adopt a new mind-set; some must even reorganize their operations. Among other considerations, businesses sourcing from multiple multinational locations should streamline the purchase process and minimize price differences due to labor costs, tariffs, taxes, and currency fluctuations.

Business Market Demand

The previous section's discussion of business market characteristics demonstrated considerable differences between marketing techniques for consumer and business products. Demand characteristics also differ in these markets. In business markets, the major categories of demand include derived demand, joint demand, volatile demand, and inventory adjustments.

Derived Demand

The term **derived demand** refers to the linkage between consumer demand for a company's output and its purchases of business products such as machinery, components, supplies, and raw materials. For example, demand for microprocessor chips within a computer's central processing unit is derived from the demand for personal computers from both business and individual consumers. Worldwide slowdowns in sales of personal computers have reduced demand for chips. Dell attempts to offset fluctuations in demand by keeping its inventories low and by using falling prices resulting from reduced demand to drive down the cost of computer components, including chips. Dell then passes these savings along to its customers in the form of lower PC prices, thus stimulating sales. Recently, Intel slashed prices of its high-end Pentium 4 processors in half, due to drastically lower demand and excess capacity.[14] Advertisements like the one in Figure 10.4 seek to increase demand.

While demand for computer chips has decreased, demand for embedded chips—microprocessors built into other consumer devices ranging from rice cookers to automobiles—has not. For every personal computer shipped, companies ship approximately 30 toasters, pagers, watches, and other items that rely on built-in chips. As businesses and consumers become increasingly security-conscious, smart cards that store personal information, including passwords, frequent flyer miles, and more, represent a potentially huge new market for embedded chips.[15]

Organizational buyers purchase two general categories of business products: capital items and expense items. Derived demand ultimately affects both. Capital items are long-lived business assets that must be depreciated over time. (Depreciation is an accounting term that refers to charging a portion of a capital item's cost as a deduction against the company's annual revenue for purposes of determining its net income.) Examples of capital items include major installations such as new plants, office buildings, and computer systems.

FIGURE 10.4 Microprocessors: An Example of Derived Demand

Expense items, in contrast, are items consumed within short time periods. Accountants charge the cost of such products against income in the year of purchase. Examples of expense items include the supplies necessary to operate the business, ranging from paper clips to machine lubricants.

Joint Demand

Another important influence on business market demand is **joint demand,** which results when the demand for one business product is related to the demand for another business product used in combination with the first item. For example, both coke and iron ore are required to make pig iron. If the coke supply falls, the drop in pig iron production will immediately affect the demand for iron ore.

Another example is the joint demand for electrical power and large turbine engines. If consumers decide to conserve power, demand for new power plants drops, as does the demand for components and replacement parts for turbines.

Volatile Demand

Derived demand creates volatility in business market demand. As an example, assume that the sales volume for a chain of gasoline stations is increasing at an annual rate of 5 percent. Now suppose that the demand for this gasoline brand slows to a 3 percent annual increase. While not a dramatic drop, this slowdown might convince the firm to keep its current gasoline pumps and replace them only when market conditions improved. In this way, even modest shifts in consumer demand for a gasoline brand would greatly affect the pump manufacturer. This disproportionate impact of changes in consumer demand on business market demand is referred to as the *accelerator principle.*

Inventory Adjustments

Adjustments in inventory and inventory policies can also affect business demand. Assume that manufacturers in a particular industry consider a 60-day supply of raw materials to be the optimal inventory level. Now suppose that economic conditions or other factors induce these firms to increase their inventories to a 90-day supply. The change will bombard the raw-materials supplier with new orders.

Further, innovative *just-in-time (JIT)* inventory policies seek to boost efficiency by cutting inventories to absolute minimum levels and by requiring vendors to deliver inputs as the production process needs them. JIT allows companies to better predict which supplies they will require and the timing for when they will need them, markedly reducing their costs for production and storage. While JIT inventory and delivery systems suffered disruptions following the September terrorist attacks, the overall benefits in supply chain savings outweigh the adverse impact of delays to shipments resulting from cross-border conflicts or other international crises.[16] Widespread implementation of JIT has had a substantial impact on organizations' purchasing behavior. Firms that practice JIT tend to order from relatively few suppliers. In some cases, JIT may lead to *sole sourcing* for some items—in other words, buying a firm's entire stock of a product from just one supplier. Electronic data interchange (EDI) and quick-response inventory policies have produced similar results in the trade industries.

The latest inventory trend, *JIT II*, leads suppliers to place representatives at the customer's facility to work as part of an integrated, on-site customer-supplier team. Suppliers plan and order in consultation with the customer. This streamlining of the inventory process improves control of the flow of goods.

The Make, Buy, or Lease Decision

Before a company can decide what to buy, it should decide whether to buy at all. Organizational buyers must figure out the best way to acquire needed products. In fact, a firm considering the acquisition of a finished good, component part, or service has three basic options:

1. Make the good or provide the service in-house.
2. Purchase it from another organization.
3. Lease it from another organization.

Manufacturing the product itself, if the company has the capability to do so, may be the best route. It may save a great deal of money if its own manufacturing division does not incur costs for overhead that an outside buyer would otherwise charge.

On the other hand, most firms cannot make all of the business goods they need. Often, it would be too costly to maintain the necessary equipment, staff, and supplies. Therefore, purchasing from an outside vendor is the most common choice. Companies can also look outside their own plants for goods and services that they formerly produced in-house, a practice called *outsourcing* that the next section will describe in more detail.

In some cases, however, a company may choose to lease inputs. This option spreads out costs compared with lump-sum costs for up-front purchases. The company pays for the use of equipment for a certain time period. For example, a small business may lease a copy machine for a few years, making monthly payments. At the end of the lease term, the firm can buy the machine at a prearranged price or replace it with a different model under a new lease. This option can provide useful flexibility for a growing business, allowing it to easily upgrade as its needs change.

Companies can also lease sophisticated computer systems and heavy equipment. For example, some airlines prefer to lease airplanes rather than buy them outright because short-term leases allow them to adapt quickly to changes in passenger demand.

The Rise of Outsourcing

Packaged goods giant Procter & Gamble recently announced plans to hire an outside firm to handle parts of its back-office operations, a deal that could be worth approximately $8 billion over 10 years. The top candidate was Affiliated Computer Services (ACS). By farming out such operations as finance and accounting, human resources, and information technology—functions that employ over 8,000 people—P&G can concentrate its efforts on what it does best: manufacturing and marketing top consumer brands. At the same time, P&G can take advantage of the technological and professional expertise of ACS.[17]

In their rush to improve efficiency, firms look outside for just about everything from mailroom management, customer service, human resources, and accounting, to information technology, manufacturing, and distribution.

Outsourcing allows firms to concentrate their resources on their core business. It also allows access to specialized talent or expertise that does not exist within the firm. The most frequently outsourced business functions include information technology, human resources, and facilities management. Many hospitals and managed-care organizations spend more than a third of their IT budgets on outsourced consulting and support services.[18] The ad in Figure 10.5 highlights the benefits of outsourcing even complex office functions, such as payroll administration.

About 60 percent of all outsourcing is done by North American–based companies. However, the practice is rapidly becoming commonplace in Asia and Europe; European firms' expenditures for outsourcing are growing by an impressive 34 percent annually.

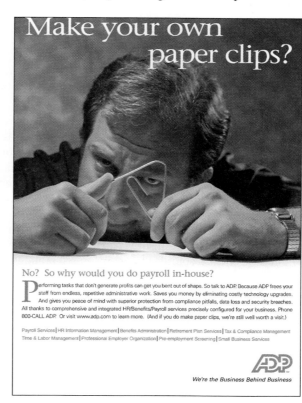

FIGURE 10.5
Benefits of Outsourcing Services

Marketing Dictionary

joint demand Demand for a business product that depends on the demand for another business product used in combination with the first item.

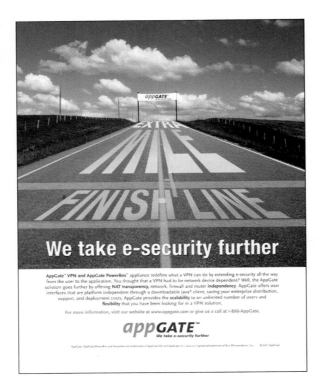
Heightened awareness of security following the terrorist attacks of September 11 led companies like Sun Microsystems to focus on e-security as a reason why businesses should outsource computer networking systems. The ad in Figure 10.6 promises improved firewall protection as well as reliability and flexibility.

Outsourcing can be a smart strategy if a company chooses a vendor that can provide high-quality products and perhaps at a lower cost than could be achieved on the company's own. This priority allows the outsourcer to focus on its core competencies. Successful outsourcing requires companies to carefully oversee contracts and manage relationships. Some vendors now provide performance guarantees to assure their customers that they will receive high-quality services that meet their needs.

Problems with Outsourcing

Outsourcing is not without its downside. Many companies discover that their cost savings average closer to 10 percent than the 20 to 40 percent that vendors sometimes promise. Also, companies who sign multiyear contracts may find that their savings drop after a year or two. When proprietary technology is an issue, outsourcing raises security concerns. Similarly, companies that are protective of customer data and relationships may think twice about entrusting functions like customer service to outside sources.

In some cases, outsourcing can reduce a company's ability to respond quickly to the marketplace or it can slow efforts in bringing new products to market. Suppliers who fail to deliver goods promptly or provide required services can adversely affect a company's reputation with its customers. General Electric had to delay the introduction of a new washing machine because of a contractor's production problems. Similarly, Southern Pacific Rail had problems with an outsourced computer network.

Another major danger of outsourcing is the risk of losing touch with customers. When Telecom giant Sprint realized that customer data from its outsourced technology providers was not being put to work fast enough, the company decided to pull the plug on its outside vendors. In their place, customized customer relationship management (CRM) software was able to pull data on more than 10 million business accounts, saving Sprint $1 million in the first year.[19]

Outsourcing is a controversial topic with unions, especially in the auto industry, as the percentage of component parts made in-house has steadily dropped. Outsourcing can create conflicts between nonunion outside workers and in-house union employees, who fear job loss from outsourcing. Management initiatives to outsource jobs can lead to strikes and plant shutdowns. Even if it does not lead to disruption in the workplace, outsourcing can have a negative impact on employee morale and loyalty.

The Business Buying Process

Suppose that CableBox Inc., a hypothetical manufacturer of cable television decoder boxes, decides to upgrade its manufacturing facility with $1 million in new automated assembly equipment. Before approaching equipment suppliers, the company must analyze its needs, determine goals that the project should accomplish, develop technical specifications for the equipment, and set a budget. Once it receives vendors' proposals, it must evaluate them and select the best one. But what does *best* mean in this context? The lowest price or the best warranty and service contract? Who in the company is responsible for such decisions?

Clearly, the business buying process is more complex than the consumer decision process described in Chapter 9. Business buying takes place within a formal organization's budget, cost, and profit considerations. Furthermore, B2B and institutional buying decisions usually involve many people with complex interactions among individuals and organizational goals. To understand organizational buying behavior, business marketers require knowledge of influences on the purchase decision process, the stages in the organizational buying model, types of business buying situations, and techniques for purchase decision analysis.

4

Describe the major influences on business buying behavior.

Influences on Purchase Decisions

B2B buying decisions react to various influences, some external to the firm and others related to internal structure and personnel. In addition to product-specific factors such as purchase price, installation, operating and maintenance costs, and vendor service, companies must also consider broader environmental, organizational, and interpersonal influences.

Environmental Factors

Environmental conditions such as economic, political, regulatory, competitive, and technological considerations influence business buying decisions. For example, CableBox may wish to defer purchases of the new equipment in times of slowing economic activity. During a recession, sales to cable companies might drop because households hesitate to spend money on cable service. The company would look at the derived demand for its products, possible changes in its sources of materials, employment trends, and similar factors before committing to such a large capital expenditure.

Political, regulatory, and competitive factors also come into play in influencing purchase decisions. For example, passage of a law freezing cable rates would affect demand, as would an introduction of a less expensive decoder box by a competitor. Finally, technology plays a role in purchase decisions. For example, cable-ready televisions decreased demand for set-top boxes, and smaller, more powerful satellite dishes have cut into the market for cable TV, reducing derived demand. CableBox can benefit from technological advances, too. As more homes want fast Internet connections, adding cable modems to its product line may present a growth opportunity.

Organizational Factors

Successful business-to-business marketers understand their customers' organizational structures, policies, and purchasing systems. A company with a centralized procurement function operates differently than one that delegates purchasing decisions to divisional or geographic units. Trying to sell to the local store when head office merchandisers make all the decisions would clearly waste salespeople's time. Buying behavior also differs among firms. For example, centralized buying tends to emphasize long-term relationships, while decentralized buying focuses more on short-term results. Personal selling skills and user preferences carry more weight in decentralized purchasing situations than in centralized buying.

How many suppliers should a company patronize? Because purchasing operations spend over half of each dollar their companies earn, consolidating vendor relationships can lead to large cost savings. However, a fine line separates maximizing buying power from relying too heavily on a few suppliers. Many companies engage in *multiple sourcing*—purchasing from several vendors. Spreading orders ensures against shortages if one vendor cannot deliver on schedule. However, dealing with many sellers can be counterproductive and take too much time. Each company sets its own criteria for this decision.

Interpersonal Influences

Many people may influence B2B purchases, and considerable time may be spent obtaining the input and approval of various organization members. Both group and individual forces are at work here. When committees handle buying, they must spend time to gain majority or unanimous approval. Also, each individual buyer brings to the decision process her individual preferences, experiences, and biases.

Business marketers should know who will influence buying decisions in an organization for their products and should know each of their priorities. To choose a supplier for an industrial press, for example, a purchasing manager and representatives of the company's production, engineering, and quality control departments may jointly decide on a supplier. Each of these principals may have a different point of view that the vendor's marketers must understand.

Boise Cascade in collaboration with a training and consulting company ran an innovative marketing campaign to encourage organizations to use its catalog and online service as a single source for office supplies. A color flyer was included with its direct-mail catalog, which reached 300,000 potential business buyers. The flyer was designed to appeal to Boise's end users—administrative assistants, a group typically composed of women aged 18 to 54 with a high-school diploma. A focal point of the campaign was an online personality assessment that had been developed using cues that would be popular with this demographic group. The quiz allowed catalog users to gain a better understanding of themselves and their coworkers by "color-typing" themselves, then gave tips on how best to work with other color types. The flyer was so popular that administrative assistants passed it around the office, along with the Boise catalog—creating an informal network of people who influenced the purchase of office supplies. In addition, an interactive quiz on the Boise Web site won more new customers through pass-along e-mails.[20]

To effectively address the concerns of all people involved in the buying decision, sales representatives must be well-versed in the technical features of their products. They must also interact well with employees of the various departments involved in the purchase decision. Sales representatives for medical products, for example, are frequent visitors to hospitals and surgery centers, where they discuss their product line with clinical staff and demonstrate new devices.

The Role of the Professional Buyer

Most organizations attempt to make their purchases through systematic procedures employing professional buyers. In the trade industries, these buyers, often referred to as *merchandisers*, are responsible for securing needed products at the best possible prices. Unlike ultimate consumers, who incorporate periodic buying decisions with other activities, a firm's purchasing department devotes all of its time and effort in determining needs, locating and evaluating alternative suppliers, and making purchase decisions.

Purchase decisions for capital items vary significantly from those for expense items. Firms often buy expense items routinely with little delay. Capital items, however, involve major fund commitments and usually undergo considerable review.

One way in which a firm may attempt to streamline the buying process is through *systems integration*, or centralization of the procurement function. One company may designate a lead division to handle all purchasing. Another firm may choose to designate a major supplier as the systems integrator. This vendor then assumes responsibility for dealing with all of the suppliers for a project and for presenting the entire package to the buyer. In trade industries, this vendor is sometimes called a *category captain.*

A business marketer may set up a sales organization to serve national accounts that deals solely with buyers at geographically concentrated corporate headquarters. A separate field sales organization may serve buyers at regional production facilities.

As noted earlier in the chapter, corporate buyers often use the Internet to identify supplier sources. They view online catalogs and Web sites to compare vendors' offerings and to obtain product information. Some use Internet exchanges to extend their supplier networks.

By bringing together far-flung businesses to compete online, Internet exchanges are able to save businesses money as well as locate quality suppliers. The "Marketing Misses" box demonstrates that there is a downside to entrusting the buyer-seller relationship to Internet intermediaries.

Model of the Organizational Buying Process

5

Outline the steps in the organizational buying process.

An organizational buying situation requires a sequence of activities similar to the six-step consumer decision model presented in the previous chapter. Figure 10.7 illustrates an eight-stage model of a complex organizational buying process. The additional steps arise because business purchasing introduces new complexities that do not affect consumers. Not every buying situation will follow these precise steps, but this model presents a useful overview of the general process.

Stage 1: Anticipate or Recognize a Problem/Need/Opportunity and a General Solution

Both consumer and business purchase decisions begin when the recognition of problems, needs, or opportunities triggers the buying process. Perhaps a firm's computer system has become outdated or a sales representative demonstrates a new good or service that could improve the company's performance.

Companies may decide to hire an outside marketing specialist when their sales stagnate. This was the case for a large building-products manufacturer, which had traditionally sold its products through a catalog mailed to approximately 45,000 building contractors. When its mail-order business stalled, the purchasing manager interviewed several marketing firms, including Milwaukee-based Hunter Business Direct, to create new ways for the company to increase sales.[21]

Stage 2: Determine the Characteristics and Quantity of a Needed Good or Service

The problem described in Stage 1 translated into a service opportunity for Hunter Business Direct. To stimulate the manufacturer's sales, Hunter executive vice president Mark Peck suggested a database marketing strategy.

Peck quickly assembled a marketing team, consisting of employees from both Hunter and the manufacturer's marketing department, to determine what was needed. The team ranked the manufacturer's customers into 10 groups according to total sales. Peck decided to focus on the top three groups, a total of approximately 1,000 contracting businesses. Customers in the top 10 percent of this group placed an average of 18 orders per year, approximately $20,000 per order; the other 90 percent averaged about six orders per year at $5,500 each.

Stage 3: Describe Characteristics and the Quantity of a Needed Good or Service

After determining the characteristics and quantity of needed products, B2B buyers must translate these ideas into detailed specifications. For his manufacturer client, Peck prepared a detailed proposal that described how Hunter would implement a database

Marketing Miss

The Failure of B2B Exchanges

Background. Web-enabled procurement promised to revolutionize B2B purchasing. Internet exchanges, specializing in everything from auto parts to electronic components, devised a system of real-time competitive bidding to give buyers access to multiple suppliers while forcing prices downward.

The Problem. Internet exchanges—the equivalent of online intermediaries—sought to save B2B companies the labor-intensive tasks of seeking out reliable suppliers, comparing bids, and finalizing deals. Zetheus, for example, offered one-stop shopping for commercial real estate, attempting to replace a

continued on next page

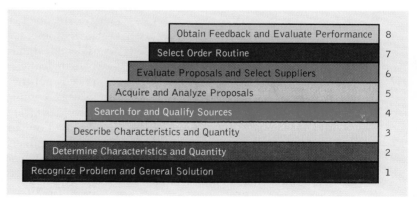

Obtain Feedback and Evaluate Performance	8
Select Order Routine	7
Evaluate Proposals and Select Suppliers	6
Acquire and Analyze Proposals	5
Search for and Qualify Sources	4
Describe Characteristics and Quantity	3
Determine Characteristics and Quantity	2
Recognize Problem and General Solution	1

SOURCE: Based on Michael P. Hutt and Thomas W. Speh, *Business Marketing Management*, 8th Edition (Mason, OH: South-Western Publishing, 2004).

FIGURE 10.7
Stages in the B2B Buying Process

marketing program for his client. His goals were to increase the frequency of target customers' orders, the amount they ordered, and the number of repeat purchases.

Depending on the type of purchase, a company's technical personnel can play an important role in this early stage of the B2B buying process. For instance, a quality control engineer might establish certain specifications for a product that only a few suppliers could meet. This type of decision could have a big impact on the ultimate evaluation and selection of vendors.

Stages 2 and 3 apply mostly to organizations rather than individual consumers. While consumers may perform these steps, they would use a much more superficial analysis.

Stage 4: Search for and Qualify Potential Sources

Both consumers and businesses search for good suppliers of desired products. The choice of a supplier may be relatively straightforward; the manufacturer's purchasing manager decided within a few days to hire Hunter Business Direct.

Other searches may involve more complex decision making. A company that wants to buy a group life and health insurance policy, for example, must weigh the varying provisions and programs of many different vendors.

Stage 5: Acquire and Analyze Proposals

The next step is to acquire and analyze suppliers' proposals, which are generally submitted in writing. If the buyer is a government or public agency, this stage of the purchase process may involve competitive bidding. During this process, each marketer must develop its bid, including a price, that will satisfy the criteria determined by the customer's problem, need, or opportunity. While competitive bidding is less common in the business sector, a company may follow the practice to purchase nonstandard materials, complex products, or products that are made to its own specifications.

Stage 6: Evaluate Proposals and Select Suppliers

Next in the buying process, buyers must compare vendors' proposals and choose the one that seems best suited to their needs. Proposals for sophisticated equipment, such as a large computer networking system, can include considerable differences among product offerings, and the final choice may involve tradeoffs.

Price is not the only criterion for the selection of a vendor. Relationship factors like communication and trust may also be important to the buyer. Other issues include reliability, delivery record, time from order to delivery, quality, and order accuracy. As the ad in Figure 10.8 suggests, reducing the headaches and delays of business travel in the security-conscious post–September 11 world is the reason businesses might invest in the Cessna Turbo.

Recently, United Airlines broke its decades- long pact with The Coca-Cola Company and decided to switch to Pepsi as its inflight soft-drinks supplier. While the financial package was a key motivator, the two companies also explored ways in which the partnership could benefit their businesses. Marketing sessions for flight attendants and soft-drink promotions with air tickets as prizes are among the strategies designed to strengthen the relationship between PepsiCo and United.[22]

Stage 7: Select an Order Routine

Once a supplier has been chosen, buyer and vendor must work out the best way to process future purchases. Ordering routines can vary considerably. Most orders will, however, include product descriptions, quantities, prices, delivery terms, and payment terms. Today, companies have a variety of options for submitting orders: written documents, phone calls, faxes, or electronic messages (EDI).

Stage 8: Obtain Feedback and Evaluate Performance

At the final stage, buyers measure vendors' performances. Sometimes this judgment may involve a formal evaluation of each supplier's product quality, delivery performance, prices, technical knowledge, and overall responsiveness to customer needs. At other times, vendors may be measured according to whether they have lowered the customer's costs or reduced its employees' workloads.

In general, large firms are more likely to use formal evaluation procedures, while smaller companies lean toward informal evaluations. Regardless of the method used, buyers should tell vendors how they are going to be evaluated.

Returning to the example of Hunter Business Direct, evaluation of the database marketing program showed it was highly successful. During the first six months of the program, 380 of the targeted customers purchased supplies from the manufacturer. The number of orders they placed rose by an impressive 112 percent, and the average size of individual orders also increased. Hunter's client spent approximately $50,000 to implement the program but increased its revenues by nearly $3 million.[23]

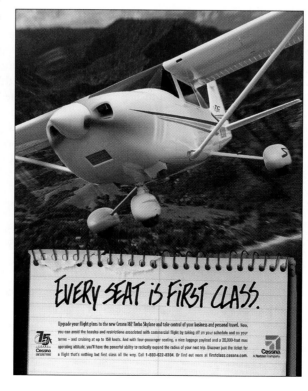

FIGURE 10.8
Price—Not Always the Key Criterion in Selecting a Supplier

Classify organizational buying situations.

Classifying Business Buying Situations

As discussed earlier, business buying behavior responds to many purchasing influences such as environmental, organizational, and interpersonal factors. This buying behavior also involves the degree of effort that the purchase decision demands and the levels within the organization where it is made. Like consumer behavior, marketers can classify organizational buying situations into three general categories, ranging from least to most complex: (1) straight rebuying, (2) modified rebuying, and (3) new-task buying. Business buying situations may also involve reciprocity. The following sections look at each type of purchase by a company like CableBox.

Straight Rebuying

The simplest buying situation is a *straight rebuy*, a recurring purchase decision in which an existing customer places a new order for a familiar product that has performed satisfactorily in the past. This organizational buying situation occurs when a purchaser likes the product and the terms of the sale. Therefore, the purchase requires no new information. The buyer sees little reason to assess other options and so follows a routine repurchase format. A straight rebuy is the business market equivalent of routinized response behavior in the consumer market.

Purchases of low-cost items such as paper clips and pencils for an office are typical examples of straight rebuys. If the products and their prices and terms satisfy the organization, it will treat future purchases as straight rebuys from the current vendor. For instance, CableBox probably has an account with an office supply firm that provides prompt service.

A marketer who wants to ensure continuing straight rebuys should concentrate on maintaining a good relationship with the buyer by providing excellent service and delivery performance. Competitors will then find it difficult to present unique sales proposals that would break this chain of repurchases.

Modified Rebuying

In a *modified rebuy*, a purchaser is willing to reevaluate available options. The decision makers see some advantage in looking at alternative offerings using established purchasing guidelines. They might take this step if a marketer allows a straight rebuy situation to deteriorate because of poor service or delivery performance. Perceived quality and cost differences can also provoke modified rebuys. Modified rebuys resemble limited problem solving in consumer markets.

B2B marketers want to induce current customers to make straight rebuys by responding to all of their needs. Competitors, on the other hand, try to induce buyers to make modified rebuys by raising issues that will convince these buyers to reconsider their decisions. Suppose that CableBox wants to upgrade its computer equipment to optimize business performance. In addition to requesting proposals from its current supplier, IBM, the firm might investigate other computer manufacturers such as Dell and Hewlett-Packard by using an analytic software such as ProClarity. Figure 10.9 shows an ad for ProClarity in which the copy is very brief but the emphasis is on making good decisions quickly. Each vendor will promote its computers' technological advantages and other unique features.

New-Task Buying

The most complex category of business buying is *new-task buying*—first-time or unique purchase situations that require considerable effort by the decision makers. The consumer market equivalent of new-task buying is extended problem solving. A recent copy-intensive ad from Hewlett-Packard gave a detailed explanation of how Hewlett-Packard will help solve the problem of information storage, despite the complexities of shrinking budgets, reduced staff, and the difficulties of predicting future storage needs.

A new-task buy often requires a purchaser to carefully consider alternative offerings and vendors. For example, a company entering a new field must seek suppliers of component parts that it has never before purchased. If CableBox was to decide to manufacture cable modems, it would have to buy new equipment and component parts. This new-task buying would require several stages, each yielding a

FIGURE 10.9
Reducing the Complexity of New-Task Buying

ProClarity Corporation delivers analytic software and services that accelerate the speed at which organizations make informed decisions to optimize business performance. ProClarity has been delivering innovative analytic solutions to Global 3000 companies since 1995. ProClarity ensures maximum return on investment and widespread user adoption by delivering solutions tailored around business processes and decision-making workflows. Headquartered in Idaho, with regional sales offices in Europe and Asia-Pacific, ProClarity currently supports over 500 customers globally including, AT&T, CompUSA, Ericsson, Hewlett-Packard, Nordstrom, and Verizon.. (PRNewsFoto/ProClarity Corporation)

decision of some sort. These decisions would include developing product requirements, searching out potential suppliers, and evaluating proposals. Information requirements and decision makers can complete the entire buying process, or they may change from stage to stage.

Reciprocity

Reciprocity—a practice of buying from suppliers that are also customers—is a controversial practice in a number of organizational buying situations. For example, an office equipment manufacturer may favor a particular supplier of component parts if the supplier has recently made a major purchase of the manufacturer's products. Reciprocal arrangements traditionally have been common in industries featuring homogeneous products with similar prices, such as the chemical, paint, petroleum, rubber, and steel industries.

Reciprocity suggests close links among participants in the organizational marketplace. It can add to the complexity of B2B buying behavior for new suppliers who are trying to compete with preferred vendors. Although buyers and sellers enter into reciprocal agreements in the U.S., both the Justice Department and the Federal Trade Commission view them as attempts to reduce competition.

Outside the U.S., however, governments may take more favorable views of reciprocity. Business-to-business buyers in Canada, for instance, see it as a positive, widespread practice. In Japan, close ties between suppliers and customers are common.

Analysis Tools

Two tools that help professional buyers in improving purchase decisions are value analysis and vendor analysis. **Value analysis** examines each component of a purchase in an attempt to

Marketing Dictionary

reciprocity   Policy to extend purchasing preference to suppliers that are also customers.

value analysis   Systematic study of the components of a purchase to determine the most cost-effective approach.

either delete the item or replace it with a more cost-effective substitute. For example, airplane designers have long recognized the need to make planes as light as possible. Value analysis supports using DuPont's synthetic material Kevlar in airplane construction because it weighs less than the metals it replaces. The resulting fuel savings are significant for the buyers in this marketplace.

Vendor analysis carries out an ongoing evaluation of a supplier's performance in categories such as price, EDI capability, back orders, delivery times, liability insurance, and attention to special requests. In some cases, vendor analysis is a formal process. Some buyers use a checklist to assess a vendor's performance. A checklist quickly highlights vendors and potential vendors that do not satisfy the purchaser's buying requirements.

7

Explain the buying center concept.

The Buying Center Concept

Read

The buying center concept provides a vital model for understanding organizational buying behavior. A company's **buying center** encompasses everyone who is involved in any aspect of its buying action. For example, a buying center may include the architect who designs a new research laboratory, the scientist who works in the facility, the purchasing manager who screens contractor proposals, the chief executive officer who makes the final decision, and the vice president for research who signs the formal contracts for the project. Buying-center participants in any purchase seek to satisfy personal needs, such as participation or status, as well as organizational needs.

A buying center is not part of a firm's formal organizational structure. It is an informal group whose composition and size vary among purchase situations and firms.

Buying Center Roles

Buying-center participants play different roles in the purchasing decision process. Users are the people who will actually use the good or service. Their influence on the purchase decision may range from negligible to extremely important. Users sometimes initiate purchase actions by requesting products, and they may also help to develop product specifications. Users, for example, often influence the purchase of office equipment. Steelcase promotes its Montage brand of affordable office furniture by featuring the end user prominently in its ads, as shown in the ad in Figure 10.10.

FIGURE 10.10
End Users: Buying Center Participants

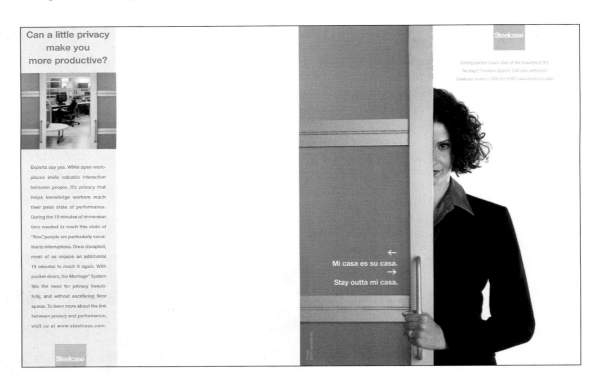

Gatekeepers control the information that all buying center members will review. They may exert this control by distributing printed product data or advertisements or by deciding which salespeople will speak to which individuals in the buying center. For example, a purchasing agent might allow some salespeople to see the engineers responsible for developing specifications but deny others the same privilege.

Influencers affect the buying decision by supplying information to guide evaluation of alternatives or by setting buying specifications. Influencers are typically technical staff such as engineers or quality control specialists. Sometimes a buying organization hires outside consultants, such as architects, who influence its buying decisions.

The *decider* actually chooses a good or service, although another person may have the formal authority to do so. The identity of the decider is the most difficult role for salespeople to pinpoint. For example, a firm's buyer may have the formal authority to buy, but the firm's chief executive officer may actually make the buying decision. A decider might be a design engineer who develops specifications that only one vendor can meet.

The *buyer* actually has the formal authority to select a supplier and to implement the procedures for securing the good or service. The buyer often surrenders this power to more influential members of the organization, though. The purchasing manager often fills the buyer's role and executes the administrative functions associated with a purchase order.[24]

B2B marketers face a critical task of determining the specific role and the relative decision-making influence of each buying-center participant. Salespeople can then tailor their presentations and information to the precise role that an individual plays at each step of the purchase process. Business marketers have found that their initial—and, in many cases, most extensive—contacts with a firm's purchasing department often fail to reach the buying-center participants who have the greatest influence, since these people may not work in that department at all.

Consider the selection of meeting and convention sites for trade or professional associations. The primary decision maker could be an association board or an executive committee, usually with input from the executive director or a meeting planner; the meeting planner or association executive might choose meeting locations, sometimes with input from members; finally, the association's annual-meeting committee or program committee might make the meeting location selection. Because officers change annually, centers of control may change from year to year. As a result, destination marketers and hotel operators are constantly assessing how an association makes its decisions on conferences.

International Buying Centers

Two distinct characteristics differentiate international buying centers from domestic ones. First, marketers may have trouble identifying members of foreign buying centers. In addition to cultural differences in decision-making methods, some foreign companies lack staff personnel. For example, in less-developed countries, line managers may make most purchase decisions.

Second, a buying center in a foreign company often includes more participants than U.S. companies involve. International buying centers employ from one to 50 people, with 15 to 20 participants being commonplace. Global B2B marketers must recognize and accommodate this greater diversity of decision makers.

International buying centers can change in response to political and economic trends. Many European firms, for instance, once maintained separate facilities in each European

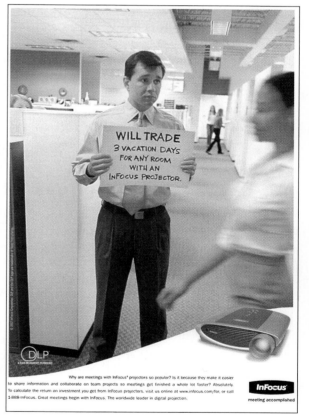

The end user may sometimes feel left out of the buying decision.

Marketing Dictionary

vendor analysis Assessment of supplier performance in areas such as price, back orders, timely delivery, and attention to special requests.

buying center Participants in an organizational buying action.

nation in order to avoid tariffs and customs delays. When the European Community lowered trade barriers between member nations, however, many companies closed distant branches and consolidated their buying centers. The Netherlands has been one of the beneficiaries of this trend.

Team Selling

To sell effectively to all members of a firm's buying center, many vendors use *team selling*, combining several sales associates or members of the organization to assist the lead sales representative in reaching all those who influence the purchase decision. Fibre Containers, a company that sells corrugated paperboard for making boxes, considers team selling particularly helpful in building chemistry between the buyer and seller. If a salesperson learns, for example, that a prospect's two biggest concerns are box design and payment schedules, a meeting that includes the head designer and the director of finance can help develop a relationship of trust.[25]

Team selling may be extended to include members of the seller firm's own supply network into the sales situation. Consider, for example, the case of small resellers of specialized computer applications whose clients require high levels of product knowledge and access to training. By working with its supply network, for example by forming alliances with suppliers to provide training or ongoing service to end-clients, resellers are able to offer a higher degree of support.

Developing Effective Business-to-Business Marketing Strategies

A business marketer must develop a marketing strategy based on a particular organization's buying behavior and on the buying situation. Clearly, many variables affect organizational purchasing decisions. This section will examine three market segments whose decisions present unique challenges to B2B marketers: units of government, institutions, and international markets. Finally, it will summarize key differences between consumer and business marketing strategies.

8

Discuss the challenges of marketing to government, institutional, and international buyers.

Challenges of Government Markets

Government agencies—federal, state, and local—together make up the largest customer in the U.S. Over 85,000 government units buy a wide variety of products, including office supplies, furniture, concrete, vehicles, grease, military aircraft, fuel, and lumber, to name just a few.

To compete effectively, business marketers must understand the unique challenges of selling to government units. One challenge results because government purchases typically involve dozens of interested parties who specify, evaluate, or use the purchased goods and services. These parties may or may not work within the government agency that officially handles a purchase.

Government purchases are also influenced by social goals, such as minority subcontracting programs. Government entities such as the U.S. Postal Service strive to maintain diversity in their suppliers, often making a special effort to purchase goods and services from small firms and companies owned by minorities and women. The government also relies on its prime suppliers to subcontract to minority businesses.[26]

Contractual guidelines create another important influence in selling to government markets. The government buys products under two basic types of contracts: fixed-price contracts, in which seller and buyer agree to a set price before finalizing the contract, and cost-reimbursement contracts, in which the government pays the vendor for allowable costs, including profits, incurred during performance of the contract. Each type of contract has advantages and disadvantages for B2B marketers. While the fixed-price contract offers more profit potential than the alternative, it also carries greater risks from unforeseen expenses, price hikes, and changing political and economic conditions.

Government Purchasing Procedures

Many U.S. government purchases go through the General Services Administration (GSA), a central management agency involved in such areas as procurement, property management, and information resources management. The GSA buys goods and services for its own use and for use by other government agencies. In its role as, essentially, the federal government's business manager, it purchases billions of dollars worth of products. The Defense Logistics Agency (DLA) serves the same function for the Department of Defense.

By law, most federal purchases must be awarded on the basis of bids, or written sales proposals, from vendors. As part of this process, government buyers develop specifications—detailed descriptions of needed items—for prospective bidders. U.S. government purchases must comply with the Federal Acquisition Regulation (FAR), a 30,000-page set of standards originally designed to cut red tape in government purchasing. FAR standards have been further complicated by numerous exceptions issued by various government agencies. Numerous additional restrictions are designed to prevent overspending, corruption, and favoritism. Recent reforms have attempted to speed purchasing and increase flexibility. They include an increased reliance on fast, easy-to-use, prenegotiated contracts with multiple vendors; elimination of detailed specifications for readily available commercial products; paperwork reduction; and the use of government-issued credit cards to make small buys.[27]

As an indicator of the government's success in making its acquisition system more responsive and effective, consider the following sample of what the GSA purchased for the New York and Pentagon relief efforts within just days of the September 11 attacks: 65,000 protective suits, 5,000 face masks, 3,000 respirators, 400 vehicles, 250 cell phones, 2,000 computers, 300 fax machines, and more than 1,200 items of office equipment.[28]

State and local government purchasing procedures resemble federal procedures. Most states and many large cities have created buying offices similar to the GSA. Detailed specifications and open bidding are common at this level as well. Many state purchasing regulations typically give preference to in-state bidders. For example, the state of Ohio allows a 5 percent preference to businesses with a presence in that state. The preference increases the price upon which the out-of-state bid is evaluated by 5 percent. (This regulation does not apply to bordering states.)

Government spending patterns may differ from those in private industry. Because the federal government's fiscal year runs from October 1 through September 30, many agencies spend much of their procurement budgets in the fourth quarter (July 1 to September 30). They hoard their funds to cover unexpected expenditures, and if they encounter no such problems, they find themselves with money to spend in late summer. Companies understand this system and keep their eyes on government bulletins, so they can bid on the listed agency purchases, which often involve large amounts of money.

Online with the Federal Government

Like their colleagues in the private sector, government procurement professionals are streamlining purchasing procedures with new technology. Rather than paging through piles of paper catalogs and submitting handwritten purchase orders, government buyers now prefer online catalogs that help them to compare competing product offerings. In fact, vendors find business with the government almost impossible unless they embrace electronic commerce.

Vendors can sell products to the federal government through three electronic options. Web sites provide a convenient method of exchanging information for both parties. Government buyers locate and order products, paying with a federally issued credit card, and the vendors deliver the items within about a week. Another route is through government-sponsored electronic ordering systems, which help to standardize the buying process. GSA Advantage, shown in Figure 10.11, allows federal employees to order products directly over the Internet at the preferred government price. The Electronic Posting System sends automatic notices of opportunities to sell to the government to more than 29,000 registered vendors. The Phoenix Opportunity System, set up by the Commerce Department, provides a similar service for minority-owned companies. A pilot program at the Treasury is testing an electronic check-payment system to speed up the settling of vendor invoices.[29]

Despite these advances, many government agencies remain less sophisticated than private-sector businesses. The Pentagon, for instance, is still coping with procurement procedures that were developed over the last 50 years. However, it is introducing a streamlined approach to defense contracting that reduces the time necessary to develop specifications and select suppliers. Spurred by the

FIGURE 10.11
Goods and Services
Sold Online to the
U.S. Government

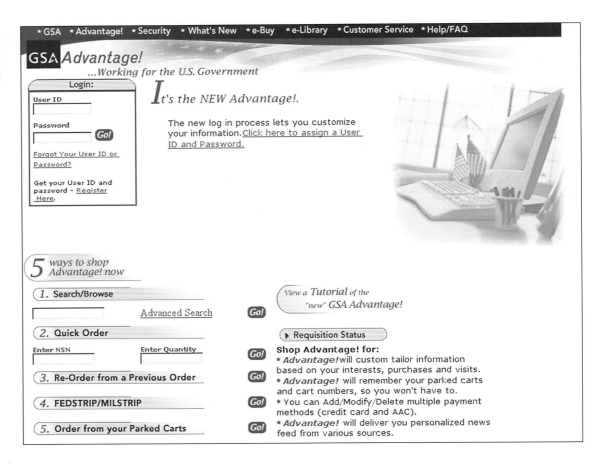

events of September 11, the Department of Defense is taking a lead role reinventing the federal procurement system. The government expenditures on upgrading technology are expected to grow by 65 percent by 2007.[30]

Challenges of Institutional Markets

Institutions constitute another important market. Institutional buyers include a wide variety of organizations, such as schools, hospitals, libraries, foundations, clinics, churches, and not-for-profit agencies.

Institutional markets are characterized by widely diverse buying practices. Some institutional purchasers behave like government purchasers because laws and political considerations determine their buying procedures. Many of these institutions, such as schools and prisons, may even be managed by government units. Other, privately managed institutions may, however, implement buying procedures that resemble those of private companies.

Buying practices can differ even between institutions of the same type. For instance, in a small hospital, the chief dietitian may approve all food purchases, while in a larger medical facility, food purchases may go through a committee consisting of the dietitian and a business manager, purchasing agent, and cook. Other hospitals may belong to buying groups, perhaps health maintenance organizations or local hospital cooperatives. Still others may contract with outside firms to prepare and serve all meals.

Within a single institution, multiple-buying influences may affect decisions. Many institutions, staffed by professionals such as physicians, nurses, researchers, and instructors, may also employ purchasing managers or even entire purchasing departments. Conflicts may arise among these decision makers. Professional employees may prefer to make their own purchase decisions and resent

EDS aids the U.S. Chamber of Commerce in upgrading its infrastructure.

giving up control to the purchasing staff. This conflict can force a business marketer to cultivate both professionals and purchasers. For instance, a sales representative for a pharmaceutical firm must convince physicians and nurses of the value to patients of a certain drug while simultaneously convincing the hospital's purchasing department that the firm offers superior prices, delivery schedules, and service.

Group purchasing is an important factor in institutional markets since many institutions join cooperative associations to pool purchases for quantity discounts. Universities may join the Education and Institutional Purchasing Cooperative; hospitals may belong to regional associations; and chains of profit-oriented hospitals like HCA Healthcare can also negotiate quantity discounts. Central headquarters staff usually handles purchasing for all members of such a chain.

Diverse practices in institutional markets pose special challenges for B2B marketers. They must maintain flexibility in developing strategies for dealing with a range of customers, from large cooperative associations and chains to medium-sized purchasing departments and institutions to individuals. Buying centers can work with varying members, priorities, and levels of expertise. Discounts and effective distribution functions play important roles in obtaining—and keeping—institutions as customers.

Challenges of International Markets

To sell successfully in international markets, business marketers must consider buyers' attitudes and cultural patterns within areas where they operate. In Asian markets, for example, a firm must maintain a local presence to sell products. Personal relationships are also important to business deals in Asia. Companies that want to expand globally often need to establish joint ventures with local partners.

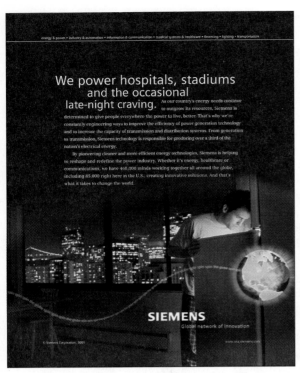

Munich, Germany–based Siemens provides power generation technology to institutional customers, including hospitals and public stadiums.

International marketers must be poised to respond to shifts in cultural values. Consider Taiwan. Government laws mandated that advertisers had to use the official language of Beijing, Mandarin, instead of Taiwan's native dialect. However, as Taiwan has renewed its efforts to break free of Chinese rule, a rise in patriotism has brought the native Taiwanese culture back to the fore. In response, advertisers such as Japan's Kirin Brewery quickly developed new ads with Taiwanese songs and dialog. Booksellers are asking their suppliers to locate works on Taiwanese history; music stores are seeking recordings by native artists; and art stores are ordering record numbers of posters featuring Taiwan's former world champion Little League baseball players.[31]

Local industries, economic conditions, geographic characteristics, and legal restrictions must also be considered in international marketing. For instance, many local industries in Spain specialize in food and wine; therefore, a maker of forklift trucks might market smaller vehicles to Spanish companies than to German firms, which require bigger, heavier trucks to serve the needs of that nation's large automobile industry.

Remanufacturing—production to restore worn-out products to like-new condition—can be an important marketing strategy in a nation that cannot afford to buy new products. Developing countries often purchase remanufactured factory machinery, which costs 35 to 60 percent less than new equipment.

Foreign governments represent another important business market. In many countries, the government or state-owned companies dominate certain industries, such as construction and other infrastructure sales. Additional examples include airport and highway construction, telephone system equipment, and computer networking equipment. Sales to a foreign government can involve an array of regulations. For example, many governments, like that of the U.S., limit foreign participation in their defense programs. Joint ventures and countertrade are common, as are local content laws, which mandate domestic production of a certain percentage of a business product's components.

Strategic Implications of Marketing in the 21st Century

To develop marketing strategies into the organizational sector, marketers must first understand the buying practices that govern the segment they are targeting, whether it is the commercial market, trade industries, government, or institutions. Similarly, when selling to a specific organization, strategies must take into account the many factors that influence purchasing. B2B marketers must identify people who play the various roles in the buying decision. They must also understand how these members interact with one another, other members of their own organizations, and outside vendors. Marketers must be careful to direct their marketing efforts to their organization, to broader environmental influences, and to individuals, who operate within the constraints of the firm's buying center.

Summary of Chapter Objectives

1. Explain each of the components of the business market.

The business, or so-called B2B, market is divided into four segments: the commercial market, trade industries, governments, and institutions. The commercial market consists of individuals and firms that acquire products to be used, directly or indirectly, to produce other goods and services. Trade industries are organizations, such as retailers and wholesalers, that purchase for resale to others. The primary purpose of government purchasing, at federal, state, and local levels, is to provide some form of public benefit. The fourth segment, institutions, includes a diverse array of organizations, such as hospitals, schools, museums, and not-for-profit agencies.

2. Describe the major approaches to segmenting business-to-business markets.

Business markets can be classified according to multiple criteria: (1) demographic segmentation—divides the market into homogeneous groups based on factors such as the size of the firm, the number of employees, or growth potential; (2) customer-based segmentation—divides a business market into homogeneous groups based on product specifications needed; (3) end-use application segmentation—divides a business market into homogeneous groups based on precisely how industrial purchasers will use a product; and (4) purchasing situation segmentation—divides a business market into homogeneous groups based on the status of the supplier-buyer relationship such as new accounts and repeat customers.

3. Identify the major characteristics of the business market and its demand.

The major characteristics of the business market are geographic concentration, relatively few buyers, and complex buying behavior. Organizational buyer behavior tends to be more complex than consumer buying behavior for several reasons: (1) many people may exert influence in business purchases; (2) organizational buying may be handled by committees, which makes it more time-consuming; (3) some organizations engage in multiple sourcing; and (4) organizational buyers are influenced by both rational considerations (cost, quality, delivery, reliability) and emotional needs (status, fear, recognition) that are not involved in individual consumer buying.

Business market demand is characterized by derived demand, joint demand, volatile demand, and inventory adjustments. Derived demand means that the demand for business products is linked to the demand for consumer goods and services. Joint demand refers to the relationship of the demand for some business products that are used jointly. Changes in inventory policy, such as just-in-time inventory management, can also have significant effects on business demand.

4. Describe the major influences on business buying behavior.

B2B buying behavior tends to be more complex than individual consumer behavior. More people and time are involved, and buyers often seek several alternative supply sources. The systematic nature of organizational buying is reflected in the use of purchasing managers to direct such efforts. Major organizational purchases may require elaborate and lengthy decision-making processes involving many people. Purchase decisions typically depend on combinations of such factors as price, service, certainty of supply, and product efficiency.

5. Outline the steps in the organizational buying process.

The organizational buying process consists of eight general stages: (1) anticipate or recognize a problem/need/opportunity and a general solution; (2) determine characteristics and quantity of needed good or service; (3) describe characteristics and quantity of needed good or service; (4) search for and qualify potential sources; (5) acquire and analyze proposals; (6) evaluate proposals and select supplier(s); (7) select a routine order; and (8) obtain feedback and evaluate performance.

6. Classify organizational buying situations.

Organizational buying situations differ. A straight rebuy is a recurring purchase decision in which a customer purchases an item that has performed satisfactorily again. In a modified rebuy, a purchaser is willing to reevaluate available options. New-task buying refers to first-time or unique purchase situations that require considerable effort on the part of the decision makers.

7. Explain the buying center concept.

The buying center includes everyone who is involved in some fashion in an organizational buying action. There are five buying center roles: users, gatekeepers, influencers, deciders, and buyers.

8. Discuss the challenges of marketing to government, institutional, and international buyers.

A government purchase typically involves dozens of interested parties who may or may not be part of the government agency that is officially handling the purchase. Social goals and programs influence government purchases. Many U.S. government purchases are directed by complex contractual guidelines and often require detailed specifications and a bidding process.

Institutional markets are challenging because of their diverse buying influences and practices. Group purchasing is an important factor, since many institutions join cooperative associations to get quantity discounts. An institutional marketer must be flexible enough to develop strategies for dealing with a range of customers. Discounts and effective distribution play an important role.

An effective international business partner must be aware of a buyer nation's attitudes and cultural patterns. Other important factors include economic conditions, geographic character-

istics, legal restrictions, and local industries. In many countries, certain industries, such as construction and other infrastructure sales, are likely to involve government representatives. A big challenge in international marketing involves identifying and communicating with potential customers.

Marketing Terms You Need to Know

business-to-business (B2B) marketing 284
commercial market 286
customer-based segmentation 288

North American Industrial Classification System (NAICS) 289
end-use application segmentation 289

global sourcing 292
derived demand 293
joint demand 294
reciprocity 303
value analysis 303

vendor analysis 304
buying center 304

Other Important Marketing Terms

trade industry 286
reseller 286
accelerator principle 294
just-in-time (JIT)/just-in-time II (JIT II) 294

sole sourcing 294
outsourcing 295
multiple sourcing 297
systems integration 298
straight rebuy 302

modified rebuy 302
new-task buying 302
gatekeeper 305
influencer 305
decider 305

buyer 305
team selling 306
remanufacturing 310

Review Questions

1. Outline the four components of the business market. Cite examples of each.
2. Contrast organizational buying behavior and consumer purchasing behavior. What are the primary differences and similarities?
3. What are the characteristics of the commercial market? Show how each characteristic affects the marketing strategies of firms serving that market.
4. What is NAICS? How do the NAFTA partners use NAICS?
5. Give examples of the effects on B2B markets of derived demand, volatile demand, joint demand, inventory adjustments, and the accelerator principle.
6. What is outsourcing? Explain the advantages and disadvantages of this practice.
7. Discuss the major influences on organizational purchasing. Cite examples of each.
8. Describe the roles in a buying center. Identify the person in an organization who would most likely play each role. How is team selling used in buying-center situations?
9. In what ways is the government market similar to other organizational markets? How does it differ?

10. Describe major characteristics of institutional and international markets. How might these characteristics affect marketing strategy?

Projects and Teamwork Exercises

1. In small teams, research the buying process through which your school purchases needed products. Compare this process with the chapter's discussion of institutional markets.
2. Choose a commercial product and analyze its foreign market potential. Report your findings to other teams in the class.
3. In pairs, investigate the qualifications needed to be a purchasing manager in an industry located in your area. Discuss these qualifications in class.
4. Research the debate and later cancellation of the proposed Crusader artillery system. Relate what you learned to the concepts presented in this chapter.
5. Investigate Canada's Department of Supply and Services. What function does the department perform? What is the comparable agency in the U.S. government?

'net W ork

1. **North American Industrial Classification System (NAICS).** To familiarize yourself with the North American Industrial Classification System (NAICS), visit http://www.naics.com/search.htm. Enter the following keywords: *bicycles, locks, music,* and *coffee.* Several five-digit NAICS codes will be displayed for each keyword. Select one five-digit U.S. industry code from each keyword list. Next, go to http://www.census.gov/epcd/www/naics.html and interpret each five-digit U.S. industry code (sector, sub sector, industry group, and industry).

2. **Outsourcing.** Visit one or more of the listed Web sites to learn more about outsourcing. Record three specific points from your research that you can report on during a class discussion on this topic.

3. **Government purchasing programs.** Assume you run a business and are interested in expanding into the government market by selling your merchandise to the Pennsylvania Department of Transportation. Visit the listed Web site and review how to do business with the Commonwealth of Pennsylvania's Department of Transportation.

Note: Internet Web addresses change frequently. If you don't find the exact sites listed, you may need to access the organization or company's home page and search from there.

http://www.naics.com/search.htm

http://www.census.gov/epcd/www/naics.html

http://www.outsourcing-journal.com

http://www.outsourcing.com

http://www.outsourcing-suppliers.com

http://www.outsourcing-jobs.com

http://www.dot.state.pa.us/internet/secinet.nsf/frmpage2doingbusiness

CASE 10.1   Bombardier vs. Embraer: Trade War at 30,000 Feet

Montreal-based Bombardier, a pioneer in the regional jet category, had been manufacturing small passenger planes for decades before Embraer took to the skies. Within five years, the upstart Brazilian company toppled Bombardier's monopoly position, snaring major deals with its lighter, less expensive fleet of jets. Embraer even snagged a $230 million contract to deliver six jets to InterCanadian Airlines—its first order from Canada. This sale and others depended on low-cost loans from the Brazilian government.

As the small-jet market grew at a rate of 10 percent a year, an intense rivalry between Embraer and Bombardier accelerated into an international dogfight. Accusing Brazil of illegal subsidies, Canada triggered an investigation by the World Trade Organization into Brazil's ProEx financing program. The program allows the government to provide financing so that Brazilian companies can compete at international market rates. Since Brazil is a developing nation, it is tough to get competitive credit terms. ProEx can take as much as $2 million off the price of an $18 million jet, enabling Embraer to compete on price.

Before the WTO could resolve the situation, Bombardier tapped loans from the Canadian government to finance sales to Northwest Airlines and Air Wisconsin. The money came from an account reserved for purchases that protect national interests, and the deals were shielded from Canada's public disclosure laws. Brazil immediately counterattacked, accusing Canada of blatantly flouting global trade rules. While the WTO backed Brazil's use of ProEx loans, Canada was blasted for offering unfair subsidies. Despite the ruling, Canada has vowed to continue financing aircraft deals, insisting that it is providing exactly the same financing help that Brazil offers to win contracts for Embraer.

An emerging market for 70- to 90-seat passenger planes—smaller than full-sized jets but bigger than Bombardier's or Embraer's regional fleets—is set to add fuel to the dispute. Both firms are racing to get their first midsize planes into the skies. For the first time, they will compete with Boeing and Airbus Industrie, which are also manufacturing jets for this market. Similarly, increased demand for corporate jets represents another key market both companies are targeting.

Questions for Critical Thinking

1. What is your assessment of the competition between Bombardier and Embraer? Are Brazil and Canada competing fairly or not?

2. As Boeing and Airbus enter the regional jet market with their own 90-seat passenger planes, how is this emerging market likely to change? What strategies might Bombardier and Embraer follow to strengthen their positions?

SOURCES: John Croft, "Embraer Cuts Output, Revels in WTO Win," *Aviation Week & Space Technology*, April 1, 2002, pp. 38–39; Christopher Bowe, "Bombardier May Sell Jets to Avolar" and Thierry Ogier, "Embraer Lands $1bn Corporate Jet Order," *Financial Times*, December 14, 2001, http://www.ft.com; James Cox, "Trade War at 30,000 Feet," *USA Today*, March 19, 2001, p. B1.

VIDEO CASE 10.2   UPS Delivers for Its Business Customers

The written case on UPS appears on page VC-12. The recently filmed UPS video is designed to expand and highlight the concepts in this chapter and the concepts and questions covered in the written video case.

Krispy Kreme Continuing Case for Part 3 appears on page KK-6.

Part 4

Product Strategy

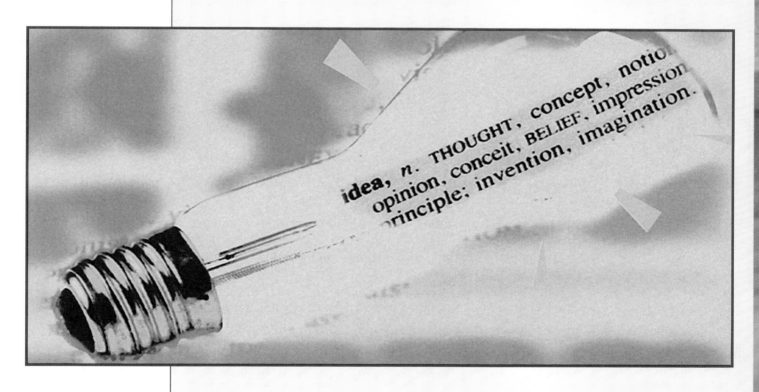

11

Product Strategies

Chapter Objectives

1 Define the term *product* and distinguish between goods and services.

2 List the classifications of consumer goods and services, and briefly describe each category.

3 Describe each of the types of business goods and services.

4 Discuss how total quality management (TQM) is implemented.

5 Explain the role benchmarking plays in achieving continuous improvement.

6 Explain why firms develop lines of related products rather than marketing individual items.

7 Identify the major product mix decisions that marketers must make.

8 Explain the concept of the product life cycle and how a firm can extend a product's life cycle.

Porsche Peppers Its Product Offerings with Cayenne

Even if you aren't a car nut, it's hard to imagine a Porsche as anything other than a sleek two-seater rocketing down the highway, weaving in and out of light traffic. It's also hard to imagine a Porsche costing anything less than six figures, although several of them do, including the Boxster, priced at $43,000 to $53,000. We think instead of the top of the line, like the 911 Turbo ($116,200) or the Carrera GT2 ($181,700). But the German sports car manufacturer wants you to stretch your imagination to include a new picture: the Porsche SUV. Porsche has expanded its line of automobiles to include one that, it hopes, upscale consumers feel they need—instead of an often impractical, sporty little number that takes up space in the garage and doesn't hold two kids and a dog. "No one on Earth *needs* a Porsche sports car," quips Fred Schwab, who recently retired as CEO of Porsche Cars North America. The new vehicle is called the Cayenne—as in cayenne pepper— and Porsche is banking that consumers will find it just as spicy as the other cars in its line.

Porsche is a special company, not just for the cars it makes, but because it has $5 billion in revenues and is still an independent firm. So far, it hasn't yet been gobbled up by any of the larger auto manufacturers. During a recent year its net profits amounted to over 6 percent of sales, compared with the auto industry in general, which averaged less than 1.5 percent. Porsche has a reputation among car lovers for producing the highest-quality sports cars, not clunky family vehicles. So why would the firm risk its image by offering a new product that at first glance doesn't seem to fit the rest of the line? "We need the revenue, and so do our dealers," explains Schwab. "It's no exaggeration to say that if the Cayenne were to flop, the company's independence could be in serious question."

Although Porsche has continued to offer strong designs, it cannot last forever without innovation. A new vehicle model that fits the lifestyle and preferences of auto buyers is a bet that Porsche marketers are willing to make. When it came time to choose a new model, management voted unanimously for the SUV. Hans Riedel, vice president of marketing and sales for Porsche describes the vote this way. "It was simple. Could we develop the Porsche of SUVs? Yes. Does the Porsche of sedans make any sense? No."

In fact, research told marketers that 40 percent of Porsche sports car owners also own an SUV—until now, made by other manufacturers. In addition, marketers believe that consumers who are on the fence will be better able to justify a Porsche purchase if they consider that the Cayenne, priced between $56,000 and $90,000, can carry five people instead of only two.

Some Porsche purists don't like the idea of an SUV with the Porsche name on it. "They are losing integrity in the marque for the sake of a few sales," complains one customer who owns a

Many ideas. Singular experience.

Cayenne. The next Porsche.

It is pure Porsche. In a most unexpected form.

PORSCHE

1996 Porsche 911. But since its launch, the Cayenne has been a hit. Within the first few months, Porsche sales were up 26 percent, while sales of the 911 were down 23 percent. This may be because the Cayenne is new; but it also appeals to a broader range of consumers. And while it doesn't look like the typical Porsche, it's still got that Porsche engine, which may mean you'll soon see Mom, Dad, the kids and the dog cruising down the open highway.[1]

Chapter Overview

Briefly Speaking

Competition brings out the best in products and the worst in people.

*David Sarnoff
(1891–1971)
Founder and president
of RCA*

We've discussed how marketers conduct research to determine their markets, how customers behave during the purchasing process, and how firms expand their horizons overseas. Now our attention shifts to a company's **marketing mix,** the blend of four elements of a marketing strategy—product, price, distribution, and promotion—to satisfy the target market. This chapter focuses on how firms select and develop the goods and services they offer. Planning efforts begin with the choice of goods or services to offer. The other variables of the marketing mix—pricing discussions, distribution channels, and promotional plans—must accommodate the product strategy selected.

Marketers develop strategies to promote both goods and services in the same manner. Any such program begins with investigation, analysis, and selection of a particular target market, and it continues with the creation of a marketing mix designed to satisfy that segment. But whereas the designs of tangible goods and intangible services both intend to satisfy consumer wants and needs, their marketing efforts may be vastly different.

This chapter examines both the similarities and the differences in marketing goods and services. It then presents basic concepts—classifications of products, development of product lines, and the product life cycle—that marketers apply in developing successful products. Finally, the chapter discusses product deletion and product mix decisions.

What Is a Product?

At first, you might think of a product as an object you hold in your hand. But that doesn't take into account the idea of a service as a product. Nor does it consider the idea of what the product is used for. So a television is more than a black box with a screen and a remote control. It's really a means of providing entertainment—your favorite movies or shows. And if something goes wrong with the TV, you can call a repair person to fix it for you—that service is also a product. Marketers acknowledge this broader conception of product; they realize that people buy *want satisfaction* rather than objects. You might feel a need for a television in order to satisfy a want for entertainment. You might not know a lot about how the machine itself works, but you understand the results.

Marketers think in terms of a product as a compilation of package design and labeling, brand name, warranty, and customer-service activities that add value for the customer. Consequently, a **product** is a bundle of physical, service, and symbolic attributes designed to satisfy a customer's wants and needs.

1

Define the term *product* and distinguish between goods and services.

MKt MIX

FIGURE 11.1
Goods-Services
Continuum

Pure Good   Car   Dinner in an Exclusive Restaurant   **Pure Service**   Cinema Complex

What Are Goods and Services?

Services are products. A general definition identifies **services** as intangible tasks that satisfy the needs of consumer and business users. But you can't hold a service in your hand the way you can **goods,** which are tangible products that customers can see, hear, smell, taste, or touch like the television just described. Most service providers cannot transport or store their products; customers simultaneously buy and consume these products, like haircuts, car repairs, and visits to the dentist. One way to distinguish services from goods is the *goods-services continuum,* as shown in Figure 11.1.

This spectrum helps marketers to visualize the differences and similarities between goods and services.[2] A car is a pure good, but the dealer may also offer repair and maintenance services or include the services in the price of a lease. Cinema complexes provide pure services, but they also sell goods such as soft drinks and popcorn. The car falls at the pure-good extreme of the continuum because the customer values the repair service less than the car itself, just as movie patrons consider refreshments less important than the entertainment that the theater provides. In the middle range of the continuum, dinner at an exclusive restaurant has equally important good and service components. Customers derive satisfaction not only from the food and beverages but also from services rendered by the restaurant's staff.

You can begin to see how diverse services can be. In fact, they are more diverse than pure goods. Services can be distinguished from goods in several ways:

1. *Services are intangible.* Services do not have physical features that buyers can see, hear, smell, taste, or touch prior to purchase. Service firms essentially ask their customers to buy a promise.

2. *Services are inseparable from the service providers.* Consumer perceptions of a service provider become their perceptions of the service itself. A good haircut will give you the perception that your hairstylist is excellent; a bad haircut will give the opposite perception.

3. *Services are perishable.* Providers cannot maintain inventories of their services. During times of peak demand, prices may rise, only to fall drastically when demand declines. For instance, hotels often raise room rates during special events and lower them to normal levels after the end of the events.

4. *Companies cannot easily standardize services.* However, many firms are trying to change this. Most fast-food chains promise that you'll get your meal within a certain number of minutes. Hotel chains often use the same room decor or offer the same dining menu at all of their hotels.

5. *Buyers often play roles in the development and distribution of services.* Service transactions frequently require interaction between buyer and seller at the production and distribution stages. Marriott International uses a customer management software program to interact with customers and

Marketing Dictionary

marketing mix   Blend of four elements of a marketing strategy—product, price, distribution, and promotion.

product   Bundle of physical, service, and symbolic attributes designed to satisfy a customer's wants and needs.

service   Intangible task that satisfies the needs of consumer and business users.

good   Tangible product that customers can see, hear, smell, taste, or touch.

coordinate their visits to Marriott hotels. Several weeks in advance of a visit, a Marriott planning coordinator may contact a visitor to ask whether he or she wants to play golf, eat at certain restaurants, or attend a concert. When the guest arrives, the arrangements have been made.[3]

6. *Service quality shows wide variations.* New York City's posh Le Cirque and your local Pizza Hut are both restaurants. Their customers, however, experience considerably different cuisine, physical surroundings, service standards, and prices.

Always keep in mind that often a product blurs the distinction between services and goods, as when a service provides a good. Avis is a service that provides rental cars, which are goods. Pearle Vision Centers provide eye examinations—services through optometrists—while Pearle sells eyeglasses and contact lenses (goods).

Importance of the Service Sector

You would live a very different life without service firms to fill many needs. You could not place a telephone call, log on to the Internet, flip a switch for electricity, or even take a college course if organizations did not provide such services. During an average day, you probably use many services without much thought, but these products play an integral role in your life.

The service sector makes a crucial contribution to the U.S. economy. Consider that there are more than 1 million retail trade establishments in the U.S., and they produce almost $2.5 trillion annually in sales receipts. While there are fewer finance and insurance service firms—approximately 400,000—their annual sales of over $2.2 billion come close to the retail figure.

Services account for four out of five jobs in the U.S. While manufacturing firms employ a total of 17 million Americans, many more people work for a service provider. The biggest service employers are retail—more than 14 million employees—and health care—more than 13 million employees.[4]

Services also play a crucial role in the international competitiveness of U.S. firms. While the U.S. runs a continuing trade deficit in goods, it has maintained a trade surplus in services for every year since 1970. This trade surplus continues to rise from its current total of roughly $70 billion. Some economists think that more precise measurements of service exports would reveal an even larger surplus.

Observers cite several reasons for the growing economic importance of services, including consumer desire for speed and convenience and technological advances that allow firms to fulfill this demand. Services that involve wireless communications, data backup and storage, and even meal preparation for busy families are on the rise. In the wake of a weak economy and poor stock market performance, consumers are looking to financial advisors for help in managing their investments.

Most service firms emphasize marketing as a significant activity for two reasons. First, the growth potential of service transactions represents a vast marketing opportunity. Second, increased competition is forcing traditional service industries to emphasize marketing in order to compete in the marketplace.

Classifying Goods and Services for Consumer and Business Markets

A firm's choices for marketing a good or service depend largely on the offering itself and on the nature of the target market. Product strategies differ for consumer and business markets. Consumer products are those destined for use by ultimate consumers, while business or B2B products (also called *industrial* or *organizational products*) contribute directly or indirectly to the output of other products for resale. Marketers further subdivide these two major categories into more specific categories, as discussed in this section.

It is important to note that some products fall into both categories. A case in point is prescription drugs. Traditionally, pharmaceutical companies marketed prescription drugs to doctors, who then made the purchase decision for their patients by writing the prescription. Thus, the medications could be classified as a business product. However, many drug companies now advertise their products in

consumer-oriented media, including magazines and television. In fact, in a recent year,
pharmaceutical giant Merck & Co. spent a
whopping $135.5 million on advertising for its
anti-inflammatory drug Vioxx, which included
TV spots featuring Olympic figure-skating
champion Dorothy Hamill.[5] As patients
begin to behave more like customers, they may
request prescriptions for certain medications
they have seen advertised in the media, making
a classification of consumer product more
appropriate.

Types of Consumer Products

Several classification systems divide consumer
goods and services in different ways. One basic
distinction focuses on the buyer's perception of
a need for the product. *Unsought products* are
marketed to consumers who may not yet recognize any need for them. Examples of
unsought products are life insurance and
funeral services. Figure 11.2 takes this classification to another level by suggesting to pet
owners that they need veterinary insurance for
their pets.

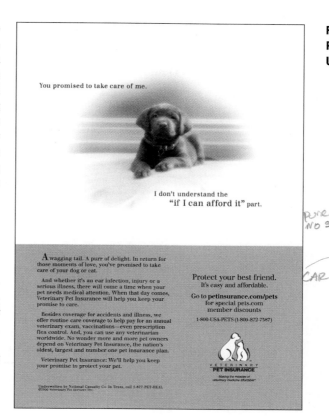

FIGURE 11.2
Pet Insurance: An Unsought Product

In contrast, most consumers recognize their own needs for various types of consumer purchases.
The most common classification scheme divides consumer goods and services into three groups: convenience, shopping, and specialty. These categories are based on customers' buying behavior. Figure
11.3 illustrates samples of these three categories, together with the unsought classification.

2

List the classifications
of consumer goods and
services, and briefly
describe each category.

Convenience Products B2C

Convenience products refer to goods and services that consumers want to purchase frequently, immediately, and with minimal effort. Milk, bread, and soft drinks are examples of these products, as are
chewing gum, candy, and most vending-machine items. Convenience services include 24-hour quick-
stop stores, walk-in hair salons, copy shops, and dry cleaners.

Marketers further subdivide the convenience category into impulse items, staples, or emergency
items:

- *Impulse goods and services* are purchased on the spur of the moment, such as a visit to a car
wash or a pack of gum tossed in at the register. Some marketers have even come up with
ways to make impulse shopping on the Internet attractive. Marc Malaga, founder of
GiftBaskets.com, a site that provides gift and food baskets, flowers, and other gifts, decided
to set up a special Gift Emergency Center on his Web site's home page. The Emergency
Center allows customers to purchase gift baskets that will be sent the same day, which actually encourages impulse buying. "People might be coming to the site for one thing, and
then they see they can send something the same or next day, so they may choose to buy it,"
Malaga explains.[6]

- *Staples* are convenience goods and services that consumers constantly replenish to maintain a ready inventory—for
instance, gasoline and dry cleaning.

Marketing Dictionary

convenience products Goods and services that consumers want to purchase frequently, immediately, and with minimal effort.

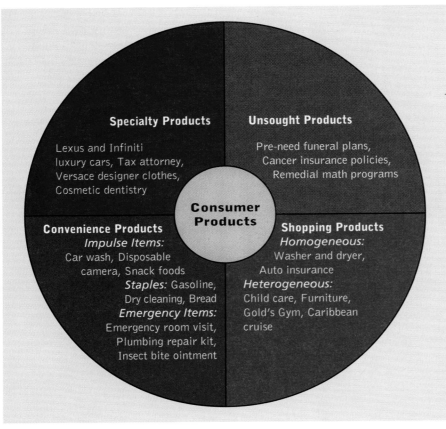

FIGURE 11.3
Classification of Consumer Products

■ *Emergency goods and services* are bought in response to unexpected and urgent needs. An ice scraper purchased during a snowstorm and a visit to a hospital emergency room to treat a sprained ankle are examples.

Since consumers devote little effort to these purchase decisions, marketers must strive to make these exchanges as convenient as possible. Store location can boost a convenience product's visibility. Marketers compete vigorously for prime locations, which can make all the difference between a consumer choosing one gas station, vending machine, or dry cleaner over another. In addition, location *within* a store can make the difference between success and failure of a product, which is why manufacturers fight so hard for the right spot on supermarket shelves. Typically, the larger and more powerful grocery manufacturers get the most visible spots. For instance, Kraft Foods has eight or ten special displays in many supermarkets. Brands like Miracle Whip, Ritz crackers, Philadelphia cream cheese, Kool-Aid, and Oreo cookies all belong to Kraft—and enjoy prime shelf space. But visibility to consumers comes at a price, often through a practice called *slotting allowances*, money paid to retailers to guarantee prominent display. The standard slotting price for a new product in a major supermarket can run as much as $25,000, which could put a small manufacturer of one product line, say yogurt or salsa, out of business before it even gets started. For this reason, the Federal Trade Commission (FTC) has begun to look at the practice of paying for shelf space. "The practice raises questions about whether the big dog not only eats first, but also decides who gets the table scraps," notes U.S. Senator Christopher Bond (Missouri), the ranking member of the Senate Small Business Committee.[7]

Shopping Products

In contrast to their purchases of convenience items, consumers buy **shopping products** only after comparing competing offerings on such characteristics as price, quality, style, and color. Shopping products typically cost more than convenience purchases. This category includes tangible items such as clothing, furniture, and appliances and services such as child care, home remodeling, auto repairs, and insurance. The purchaser of a shopping product lacks complete information prior to the buying trip and gathers information during the buying process.

Several important features distinguish shopping products: physical attributes, service attributes such as warranties and after-sale service terms, prices, styling, and places of purchase. A store's name and reputation have considerable influence on people's buying behavior. The personal selling efforts of salespeople provide important promotional support.

Buyers and marketers treat some shopping products, such as refrigerators and washing machines, as homogeneous products. To the consumer, one brand seems largely the same as another. Marketers may try to differentiate homogeneous products from competing products in several ways. They may emphasize price and value, or they may attempt to educate buyers about less obvious features that contribute to a product's quality, appeal, and uniqueness. In Figure 11.4, Elkay attempts to distinguish its sinks from those of other manufacturers by focusing on design and customization.

Other shopping products seem heterogeneous because of basic differences among them. Examples include furniture, physical-fitness training, vacations, and clothing. Differences in features often separate competing heterogeneous shopping products in the minds of consumers. Perceptions of style, color, and fit can all affect consumer choices.

Specialty Products a Mazoriity CAR

Specialty products offer unique characteristics that cause buyers to prize those particular brands. They typically carry high prices, and many represent well-known brands. Examples of specialty goods include Hermès scarves, Gucci leather goods, Ritz-Carlton resorts, Tiffany jewelry, and Rolls-Royce automobiles. Specialty services include professional services such as financial, legal, and medical services.

Purchasers of specialty goods and services know just what they want—and they are willing to pay accordingly. These buyers begin shopping with complete information, and they refuse to accept substitutes. Because consumers are willing to exert considerable effort to obtain specialty products, producers can promote them through relatively few retail locations. In fact, some firms, like Hermès, a designer and maker of exclusive scarves, ties, and other accessories, intentionally limit the range of retailers that carry their products to add to their cachet. In addition, the location of these shops, such as New York or Paris, adds to the mystique of the product.

Both highly personalized service by sales associates and image advertising help marketers to promote specialty items. Because these products are available in so few places, advertisements frequently list the locations or give toll-free telephone numbers that provide customers with this information.

It is important to note that in recent years some makers of specialty products, such as Coach handbags and Donna Karan clothing, have broadened their market by selling some of their goods through company-owned discount outlets. These stores attract consumers who want to own specialty items but who cannot or do not wish to pay the high prices usually associated with these goods.

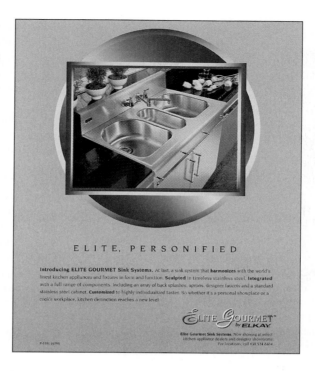

FIGURE 11.4
Distinguishing One Shopping Product from Another

Applying the Consumer Products Classification System

The three-way classification system of convenience, shopping, and specialty goods and services helps to guide marketers in developing a marketing strategy. Consumer behavior patterns differ for the three types of purchases. For example, classifying a new food item as a convenience product leads to insights about marketing needs in branding, promotion, pricing, and distribution decisions. Table 11.1 summarizes the impact of this classification system on the development of an effective marketing mix.

The classification system, however, also poses a few problems. The major obstacle in implementing this system results from the suggestion that all goods and services must fit within one of the three categories. Some fit neatly into one category, but others share characteristics of more than one category.

For example, how would you classify the purchase of a new automobile? Before classifying the expensive good, which is sold by brand and handled by a few exclusive dealers in each city as a specialty product, consider other characteristics. Most new car buyers shop

Marketing Dictionary

shopping products   Products that consumers purchase after comparing competing offerings.

specialty products   Products that offer unique characteristics that cause buyers to prize those particular brands.

Hermès, an exclusive designer of accessories such as ties, scarves, belts, and purses, enhances its product image by limiting the sale of its specialty products to a few stores in prestigious locations.

extensively among competing models and dealers before deciding on the best deal. Consider a continuum representing degrees of effort expended by consumers. At one end of the continuum, they casually pick up convenience items; at the other end, they search extensively for specialty products. Shopping products fall between these extremes. In addition, car dealers may offer services, both during and after the sale, that play a big role in the purchase decision. On this continuum, the new car purchase might appear between the categories of shopping and specialty products but closer to specialty products.

A second problem with the classification system emerges because consumers differ in their buying patterns. One person may make an emergency visit to the dentist because of a toothache, while another may extensively compare prices and office hours before selecting a dentist. But one buyer's impulse purchase does not make dental services a convenience item. Marketers classify goods and services by considering the purchase patterns of the majority of buyers.

Types of Business Products B2B

3

Describe each of the types of business goods and services.

Business buyers are professional customers. Their job duties require rational, cost-effective purchase decisions. For instance, General Mills applies much of the same purchase decision process to buy flour that Pillsbury does.

The classification system for business products emphasizes product uses rather than customer buying behavior. Business products generally fall into one of six categories for product uses: installations,

TABLE 11.1   Marketing Impact of the Consumer Products Classification System

B2C	Convenience Products	Shopping Products	Specialty Products
Consumer Factors			
Planning time involved in purchase	Very little	Considerable	Extensive
Purchase frequency	Frequent	Less frequent	Infrequent
Importance of convenient location	Critical	Important	Unimportant
Comparison of price and quality	Very little	Considerable	Very little
Marketing Mix Factors			
Price	Low	Relatively high	High
Importance of seller's image	Unimportant	Very important	Important
Distribution channel length	Long	Relatively short	Very short
Number of sales outlets	Many	Few	Very few; often one per market area
Promotion	Advertising and promotion by producer	Personal selling and advertising by both producer and retailer	Personal selling and advertising by both producer and retailer

accessory equipment, component parts and materials, raw materials, supplies, and business services.[8] Figure 11.5 illustrates the six types of business products.

Installations *Not a exam*

The specialty products of the business market are called **installations.** This classification includes major capital investments for new factories and heavy machinery, and for telecommunications systems. Purchases of Boeing 737s for Air New Zealand and locomotives for Burlington Northern are considered installations.

Since installations last for long periods of time and their purchases involve large sums of money, they represent major decisions for organizations. Negotiations often extend over several months and involve numerous decision makers. Vendors often provide technical expertise along with tangible goods. Representatives who sell custom-made equipment work closely with buying firms' engineers and production personnel to design the most satisfactory products possible.

Price typically does not dominate purchase decisions for installations. A purchasing firm buys such a product for its efficiency and performance over its useful life. The firm also wants to minimize breakdowns. Downtime is expensive because the firm must pay employees while they wait for repairs on the machine.

FIGURE 11.5
Classification of Business Products

Installations are major investments often designed specifically for the purchasers. Effective operation may also require considerable training of the buyer's workforce along with significant after-sale service. As a result, marketers of these systems typically emphasize highly trained sales representatives, often with technical backgrounds. Advertising, if the firm employs it at all, emphasizes company reputation and directs potential buyers to contact local sales representatives.

Most installations are marketed directly from manufacturers to users. Even a one-time sale may require continuing contacts for regular product servicing. Some manufacturers prefer to lease extremely expensive installations to customers rather than selling the items outright and assign personnel directly to the lessees' sites to operate or maintain the equipment.

Accessory Equipment *NOT 4 EX*

Only a few decision makers may participate in a purchase of **accessory equipment**—capital items that typically cost less and last for shorter periods than installations.

Although quality and service exert important influences on purchases of accessory equipment, price may significantly affect these decisions. Accessory equipment includes products such as hand tools, portable drills, small lathes, and laptop computers. Although these products are considered capital investments and buyers depreciate their costs over several years, their useful lives generally are much shorter than those of installations.

Resolution revolution.

The new Z65. At 4800 x 1200 dpi, it's the ultimate photo printer.

The revolution is here and the Z65 is ready to rule. Just imagine what industry-leading 5.8 megapixels and a microscopic drop size will do for your digital images. Crisp, razor-sharp color. Amazingly lifelike skin tones. Lighting fast speeds of up to 21 pages per minute. Add to that outstanding paper handling capabilities and the Z65 delivers output that's everything you can imagine. And more.

LEXMARK
Passion for printing ideas

Marketing these products requires continuous representation and dealing with the widespread geographic dispersion of purchasers. To cope with these market characteristics, a wholesaler—often called an industrial distributor—contacts potential customers in its own geographic area. Customers usually do not need technical assistance, and a manufacturer of accessory equipment often can sell its products effectively through wholesalers.

Advertising is an important component in the marketing mix for accessory equipment. Lexmark's ad for its Z65 Photo printer in Figure 11.6 emphasizes the machine's speed, the quality of copies it produces, and potential savings to the business customer. Note that Lexmark sells a variety of computer printers and related products. Lexmark develops and manufacturers its own devices, thereby speeding product cycles.

Component Parts and Materials

Whereas business buyers use installations and accessory equipment in the process of producing their own final products, **component parts and materials** represent finished business products of one producer that actually became part of the final products of another producer. Milwaukee-based Johnson Controls has supplied automobile seats to car manufacturers for years. Now the company has teamed up with Philips Electronics to deliver in-car DVD entertainment systems. The products made and sold by these two firms become part of the completed autos sold by the auto manufacturers.[9] Some fabricated materials, such as flour, undergo further processing before becoming part of finished products. Textiles, paper pulp, and chemicals are also examples of component parts and materials.

Purchasers of component parts and materials need regular, continuous supplies of uniform-quality products. They generally contract to purchase these items for set periods of time. Marketers commonly emphasize direct sales, and satisfied customers often become regular buyers. Wholesalers sometimes supply fill-in purchases and handle sales to smaller purchasers.

Raw Materials

Farm products, such as beef, cotton, eggs, milk, poultry, and soybeans, and natural products, such as coal, copper, iron ore, and lumber, constitute **raw materials.** These products resemble component parts and materials in that they actually become part of the buyers' final products.

Most raw materials carry grades determined according to set criteria, assuring purchasers of the receipt of standardized products of uniform quality. As with component parts and materials, vendors commonly market raw materials directly to buying organizations, typically according to contractual terms. Wholesalers are increasingly involved in purchasing raw materials from foreign suppliers.

Price is seldom a deciding factor in a raw materials purchase since terms are often set at central markets, determining virtually identical exchanges among competing sellers. Purchasers buy raw materials from the firms they consider best able to deliver the required quantities and qualities.

Supplies

If installations represent the specialty products of the business market, operating supplies are its convenience products. **Supplies** constitute the regular expenses that a firm incurs in its daily operations. These expenses do not become part of the buyer's final products.

Supplies are also called *MRO items* because they fall into three categories: (1) maintenance items, such as brooms, filters, and light bulbs; (2) repair items, such as nuts and bolts used in repairing equipment; and (3) operating supplies, such as fax paper, Post-it notes, and pencils.

A purchasing manager regularly buys operating supplies as a routine job duty. Wholesalers often facilitate sales of supplies due to the low unit prices, the small order size, and the large number of potential buyers. Since supplies are relatively standardized, heavy price competition frequently keeps costs under control. However, a business buyer spends little time making decisions about these products. Exchanges of products frequently demand simple telephone or EDI orders or regular purchases from a sales representative of a local wholesaler.

Business Services

The **business services** category includes the intangible products that firms buy to facilitate their production and operating processes. Examples of business services are financial services, leasing and rental services that supply equipment and vehicles, insurance, security, legal advice, and consulting. Many service providers sell the same services—telephone, gas, and electric, for example—to both consumers and organizational buyers, although service firms may maintain separate marketing groups for the two customer segments.

Organizations also purchase many adjunct services that assist their operations but are not essentially a part of the final product. Akamai Technologies serves customers such as CNN.com and MarthaStewart.com by helping their Web pages avoid bottlenecks on the Internet. Akamai accomplishes this by developing alliances with other hardware and software vendors and ISPs in order to provide an entire spectrum of Internet business services.[10] When so many businesses lost their computer data in the attacks on New York's World Trade Center, firms began to turn to data storage companies such as StorageNetworks, advertised in Figure 11.7, to protect valuable data.

Price often strongly influences purchase decisions for business services. The buying firm must decide whether to purchase a service or

Marketing Dictionary

component parts and materials Finished business products of one producer that actually become part of the final products of another producer.

raw materials Natural resources such as farm products, coal, copper, or lumber, which become part of a final product.

supplies Maintenance and repair items and operating supplies used in a firm's daily operations that do not become a part of the final product.

business services Intangible products that firms buy to facilitate their production and operating processes.

FIGURE 11.7
Business Services:
A Storage
Management
Solution

provide that service internally. This decision may depend on how frequently the firm needs the service and the specialized knowledge required to provide it.

Purchase decision processes vary considerably for different types of business services. For example, a firm may purchase window-cleaning services through a routine and straightforward process similar to that for buying operating supplies. By contrast, a purchase decision for highly specialized environmental engineering advice requires complex analysis and perhaps lengthy negotiations similar to those for purchases of installations. This variability of the marketing mix for business services and other business products is outlined in Table 11.2.

The buying and selling of business products often involves alliances among different types of firms. As mentioned earlier, Johnson Controls formed a relationship with Philips Electronics in order to deliver in-car DVD systems. Akamai Technologies has relationships with 750 hardware and software vendors in order to provide services to its customers. Equity Office Properties, a real estate firm that leases offices and buildings to businesses, has formed partnerships with other companies to offer its tenants telecom services, full-service business suites including mailrooms and copy centers, office furniture, and fitness clubs.[11]

TABLE 11.2   Marketing Impact of the Business Products Classification System

FACTOR	INSTALLATIONS	ACCESSORY EQUIPMENT	COMPONENT PARTS AND MATERIALS	RAW MATERIALS	SUPPLIES	BUSINESS SERVICES
Organizational Factors						
Planning time	Extensive	Less extensive	Less extensive	Varies	Very little	Varies
Purchase frequency	Infrequent	More frequent	Frequent	Infrequent	Frequent	Varies
Comparison of price and quality	Quality very important	Quality and price important	Quality important	Quality important	Price important	Varies
Marketing Mix Factors						
Price	High	Relatively high	Low to high	Low to high	Low	Varies
Distribution channel length	Very short	Relatively short	Short	Short	Long	Varies
Promotion method	Personal selling by producer	Advertising	Personal selling	Personal selling	Advertising by producer	Varies

Quality as a Product Strategy

Read

No matter how a product is classified, nothing is more frustrating to a customer than having a new item break after just a few uses, or having it not live up to expectations. The portable phone that hisses static at you unless you stand still, the seam that rips out of the new jacket, the plastic wrap that tears or sticks to itself instead of to the bowl of leftovers, aren't life-altering experiences, but they do leave an impression of poor quality that likely will lead you to make different purchases in the future. Then there's the issue of quality in service—the department store that seems to have no salespeople or the computer help line that leaves you on hold for 20 minutes.

Quality is a key component to a firm's success in a competitive marketplace, so few aspects of product strategy have attracted as much attention during the past two decades as the quality of the firm's output. The result of these efforts to create and market goods and services equal to any in the world has been a movement referred to as **total quality management (TQM)**. It asks all employees in a firm to continually improve products and work processes with the goal of achieving customer satisfaction and world-class performance. In a total quality organization, marketers develop products that people want to buy; engineers design items to work the way customers want to use them; production workers build quality into everything they produce; salespeople deliver what they promise customers; information systems' experts apply technology to ensure that customer orders are filled correctly and on time; and financial specialists help to determine prices that give customers value.

The quality movement started in the U.S. during the 1920s as an attempt to improve product quality by improving the manufacturing process itself. Walter Shewhart, a physicist at AT&T Bell Laboratories, pioneered an innovative approach called *statistical quality control*, which employed statistical techniques to locate and measure quality problems on production lines. W. Edwards Deming, a statistician who worked with Shewhart, helped to popularize Shewhart's quality control methods in the U.S. and abroad. Deming encouraged managers to view their organizations as systems that direct the knowledge and skills of all employees toward improving quality. Managers are responsible for communicating the goals of total quality management to all staff members and for encouraging workers to improve themselves and take pride in their work.

Of course, achieving maximum quality is easier said than done. At one electric utility, the top 350 business customers are served by six people in the customer service department. The next level of 700 customers are served by six more employees, and the "bottom" layer of 30,000 customers are handled by just two customer service representatives. At this company, it's almost impossible to provide top-quality service.[12] To achieve quality, support must come from top management in the form of resources and staff.

Worldwide Quality Programs

During the 1980s, the quality revolution picked up speed in U.S. corporations. The campaign to improve quality found leadership in large manufacturing firms like Ford, Xerox, and Motorola that had lost market share to Japanese competitors. Smaller companies that supplied parts to large firms then began to recognize quality as a requirement for success. Today, a commitment to quality has spread to service industries, not-for-profit organizations, government agencies, and educational institutions.

As part of the national quality improvement campaign, Congress established the Malcolm Baldrige National Quality Award in 1987 to recognize excellence in quality management. Named after late Secretary of Commerce Malcolm Baldrige, the award is the highest national recognition for quality that a U.S. company can receive. The award works toward promoting quality awareness, recognizing quality achievements of U.S. companies, and publicizing successful quality strategies.

The quality movement is very strong in European countries. The European Union's *ISO 9002* (for- *Exam* merly ISO 9000) standards define international criteria for quality management and quality assurance. These standards were developed by the International Standards Organization in Switzerland to ensure consistent quality among products manufactured and sold throughout the nations of the European Union (EU).

4

Discuss how total quality management (TQM) is implemented.

Marketing Dictionary

total quality management (TQM)   Movement that asks all employees in a firm to continually improve products and work processes with the goal of achieving customer satisfaction and world-class performance.

FIGURE 11.8
The Benchmarking Process

Many European companies now require suppliers to complete ISO certification as a condition of doing business with them. To become ISO certified, a company must undergo an on-site audit that includes an inspection of the firm's facilities to ensure that documented quality procedures are in place and that all employees understand and follow those procedures. Meeting ISO requirements is an ongoing process, typically covering a 14-month period, during which periodic audits verify conformance. Once granted certification, the firm must frequently ensure that its suppliers are also ISO certified. ISO 9002 is clearly a basic requirement for firms doing business in Europe. Competitors in non-EU countries, concerned over the threats of exclusion from this huge market, have moved quickly to implement ISO 9002 standards.

The Role of Benchmarking in Quality

5

Explain the role benchmarking plays in achieving continuous improvement.

Many quality-conscious businesspeople rely on an important tool called *benchmarking* to set performance standards. This method for creating a world-class marketing operation seeks to identify how business leaders achieve superior marketing performance levels in their industries and to develop a system for continuously comparing and measuring performance against outstanding performers. The technique involves learning how the world's best goods and services are designed, produced, and marketed. The purpose of benchmarking is to achieve superior performance that results in a competitive advantage in the marketplace.

A typical benchmarking process involves three main activities: identifying processes that need improvement, comparing internal processes against similar activities of industry leaders, and implementing changes for better quality. As Figure 11.8 shows, the process continuously repeats itself since vigilant companies continue to search for and identify areas that need improvement, even after implementing changes. This ongoing devotion helps these firms to ensure that they remain market leaders.

Benchmarking requires two types of analyses: internal and external. Before a company can compare itself with another, it must first analyze its own activities to determine strengths and weaknesses. This establishes a baseline for comparison. External analysis involves gathering information about the benchmark partner to find out why the partner is perceived as the best. A comparison of the results of the analysis provides an objective basis for making improvements.

FIGURE 11.9
Chevy Blazer: Improved Quality as a Result of Benchmarking

In recent years, General Motors has used benchmarking and other strategies to dramatically improve quality and productivity in its auto manufacturing processes. CEO Rick Wagoner relied on a successful program called Work Out, developed by General Electric. (Note that benchmarking can take place across different industries.) Wagoner renamed the program Go Fast and began to use it to reengineer manufacturing processes and break through logjams in decision making. At Go Fast meetings, engineers, designers, and other managers discuss how to fix defects in manufacturing and engineering, helping GM to improve the quality of its processes and automobiles, as illustrated in Figure 11.9. In just a couple of years, managers have held thousands of Go Fast meetings and trained 25,000 employees in the quality improvement process.[13]

Development of Product Lines

Few firms today market only one product. A typical firm offers its customers a **product line,** that is, a series of related products. The Clorox Company has many product lines, one of which is the Glad Products line, illustrated in Figure 11.10. Other items in the line include freezer, sandwich, and food storage bags; food wraps; ovenware; and containers.[14]

By developing comprehensive product lines as opposed to concentrating solely on individual products, firms benefit in four ways. The motivations for marketing full product lines include the desire to grow, optimal use of company resources, enhancing the company's position in the market, and exploiting the product life cycle. Large companies such as Clorox have the resources to develop and market an entire mix of product lines, which may or may not be related to one another. The following paragraphs examine each of the first three reasons. The final reason, exploiting the product life cycle, is discussed in the next section, which focuses on strategic implications of the product life cycle concept.

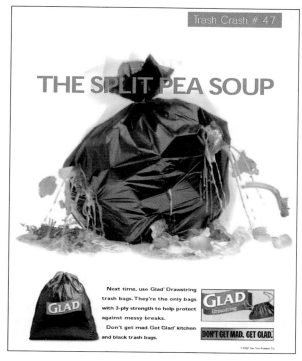

FIGURE 11.10
Promoting One Item in Glad's Product Line

Desire to Grow

A company limits its growth potential when it concentrates on a single product, even though the company may have started that way, as retailer L.L. Bean did with its single style of work boots called Maine Hunting Shoes. Now the company sells a complete line of work boots for men, women, and children, not to mention other types of boots, along with apparel, outdoor and travel gear, home furnishings, and even products for pets. In 2002 the company, which has grown into a large mail-order and online retailer with a flagship store in Freeport, Maine, celebrated its 90th anniversary. It is unlikely that the company would have grown to its current size if Leon Leonwood Bean had stuck to manufacturing and selling a single style of his Maine Hunting Shoes.[15]

6

Explain why firms develop lines of related products rather than marketing individual items.

Enhancing the Company's Position in the Market

A company with a line of products often makes itself more important to both consumers and marketing intermediaries than a firm with only one product. A shopper who purchases a tent often buys related camping items. As just described, L.L. Bean now offers a wide range of products so that consumers can completely outfit themselves for outdoor activities or travel. They can purchase hiking boots, sleeping bags and tents, duffel bags, and clothing for their adventures. Few would know about Bean if the company only sold its original boots. Business buyers often expect a firm that manufactures a particular product to offer related items as well.

Optimal Use of Company Resources

By spreading the costs of its operations over a series of products, a firm may reduce the average production and marketing costs of each product. Hospitals have taken advantage of idle facilities by adding a variety of outreach services. Many now operate health and fitness centers that, besides generating profits themselves, also feed customers into other hospital services. For example, a blood pressure check at the fitness center might result in a referral to a staff physician.

Marketing Dictionary

product line Series of related products offered by one company.

7

Identify the major
product mix decisions
that marketers must
make.

The Product Mix *Not Exam*

A company's **product mix** is the assortment of product lines and individual product offerings that the company sells. The right blend of product lines and products allows a firm to maximize sales opportunities within the limitations of its resources. Marketers typically measure product mixes according to width, length, and depth.

Product Mix Width *NEx*

The width of a product mix refers to the number of product lines the firm offers. As Table 11.3 shows, Clorox offers a broad line of retail consumer products in the U.S. market. Clorox also has products designed for professional users. Some ten different product lines are offered: laundry additives; household cleaners; automotive care; charcoal; insecticides; bags, wraps, and containers; cat litter; dressings and sauces; water filtration; and home fireplaces. Contrast this width with that of Colgate-Palmolive: oral care, personal care, household surface cleaners, fabric care, and pet food.

Product Mix Length *Not Ex*

The length of a product mix refers to the number of different products a firm sells. Table 11.3 shows 42 separate Clorox products ranging from Clorox and Formula 409 to Armor All, Black Flag, and Hidden Valley dressings. By comparison, Colgate-Palmolive offers only nine major brands in the U.S. market. Some of Colgate's leading brands are Colgate, Palmolive, Mennen, Ajax, and Fab. The firm has other brands targeted at selected foreign markets.

Product Mix Depth *Not Exam*

Depth refers to variations in each product that the firm markets in its mix. For instance, Clorox sells Glad, Glad-Lock, and Gladware in its bags, wraps, and containers line. Formula 409 and Formula 409

TABLE 11.3   Clorox's Mix of U.S. Retail Consumer Products

Laundry Additives	Automotive Care	Bags, Wraps, and Containers	Dressings and Sauces
Clorox	Armor All	Glad	Hidden Valley
Clorox 2	No. 7	Glad-Lock	K.C. Masterpiece
Stain Out	Rain Dance	Gladware	Kitchen Bouquet
Household Cleaners	Rally	**Cat Litter**	**Water Filtration**
Clorox toilet bowl cleaner	**Charcoal**	EverClean	Brita
Clorox Clean-Up	Kingsford	EverFresh	**Home Fireplace**
Formula 409	BBQ Bag	Jonny Cat	Crackling HearthLogg
Formula 409 carpet cleaner	Match Light	Scoop Away	HearthLogg
Liquid-Plumr	**Insecticides**	Fresh Step	StarterLogg
Lestoil	Black Flag	Fresh-Step Scoop	
Pine Sol	Roach Motel	Perfomax	
Soft Scrub	Combat		
S.O.S.			

SOURCE: *Clorox Company Annual Report*, p. 21, accessed at Clorox Web site, http://www.clorox.com, June 11, 2002.

carpet cleaner are included among its household-cleaners line. Similarly, Colgate-Palmolive offers Hill's Prescription Diet and Hill's Science Diet in its pet food line.

To evaluate a firm's product mix, marketers look at the effectiveness of all three elements—width, length, and depth. Has the firm ignored a viable consumer segment? It may improve performance by increasing product line depth to offer a product variation that will attract the new segment. Can the firm achieve economies of scale in its sales and distribution efforts by adding complementary product lines to the mix? If so, a wider product mix may seem appropriate. Does the firm gain equal contributions from all products in its portfolio? If not, it may decide to lengthen or shorten the product mix to increase revenues.

Product Mix Decisions *Exam*

Establishing and managing the product mix has become an increasingly important marketing task. In the 1980s, many large firms added depth, length, and width to their product mixes without fully considering the consequences of expansion. Recently many of these same firms had to contend with unprofitable product lines and products. Retailers could not carry the full range of this merchandise, and consumers felt overwhelmed by their choices. A number of companies decided to eliminate poor sellers and focus on a few key products.

Other firms, however, seek to expand their product mixes. This is especially true for newer and smaller firms seeking to grow. Often, firms purchase product lines from other companies that want to narrow their product mixes. Other firms expand their offerings by acquiring entire companies through mergers or acquisitions. Recently, Sears, Roebuck & Company acquired the mail-order firm Lands' End in order to re-establish its general mail-order presence. Sears originally started as a mail-order firm, but stopped publishing its "Big Book" in recent years. Instead of starting it back up again, the firm decided to acquire Lands' End. Some firms, like Swiss Army, must expand their mix out of necessity, as described in the "Solving an Ethical Controversy" box.

A firm should assess its current product mix for another important reason: to determine the feasibility of a line extension. A *line extension* develops individual offerings that appeal to different market segments while remaining closely related to the existing product line. Coach, a manufacturer of luxury leather handbags, belts, wallets, and briefcases, recently decided to extend its offerings to include such products as leather and wood director's chairs, leather headbands, and leather picture frames. Chic pet owners can even purchase leather dog collars and jackets for their canine friends. Coach's decision to expand its product mix came from a reassessment of its entire mission. "Once we redefined ourselves from a house of leather to a lifestyle accessories brand, everything else fell into place," explains CEO Lew Frankfort.[16]

The marketing environment also plays a role in a marketer's evaluation of a firm's product mix. In the case of Coach, the social-cultural environment had shifted so that consumers were looking for more casual, contemporary styles than Coach had been offering. In addition, the company wanted to attract younger customers. "I received a wake-up call that the classic world of Coach needed transformation," said Frankfort.[17]

Careful evaluation of a firm's current product mix can also help marketers in making decisions about brand management and new-product introductions. Chapter 12 will examine the importance of branding, brand management, and the development and introduction of new products.

8

Explain the concept of the product life cycle and how a firm can extend a product's life cycle.

The Product Life Cycle *Read*

Products, like people, pass through stages as they age. Successful products progress through four basic stages: introduction, growth, maturity, and decline. This progression, known as the **product life cycle,** is depicted in Figure 11.11 on page 335, along with examples of products that currently fit into each stage. Notice that the product life cycle concept applies to products or product

Marketing Dictionary

product mix   Assortment of product lines and individual product offerings that a company sells.

product life cycle   Progression of a product through introduction, growth, maturity, and decline.

right wrong

Solving an Ethical Controversy

Swiss Army Looks in New Directions

It's the hallmark of many sports enthusiasts: the Swiss Army knife. The knife has had an unshakable reputation for decades for being able to solve every outdoor problem the hiker, hunter, or camper might encounter. Its quality has never been in doubt; neither has its intended use. But when airport security measures were tightened after September 11, 2001, Connecticut-based Swiss Army Brands suffered a huge blow. Not only had leisure travel—including adventure and outdoor travel—dropped off dramatically, but the knives were no longer allowed aboard commercial flights, and the duty-free airport stores that sold the knives were no longer allowed to stock them.

Should companies like Swiss Army be forced to develop alternative product lines and marketing strategies for their products because of changing airport security rules?

PRO

1. Public safety takes precedence, and passengers currently may pack their pocketknives in their check-through luggage, which cannot be accessed until the destination has been reached.
2. Companies like Swiss Army Brands could actually work with the airlines and airport officials to develop safe products and marketing strategies for those products.

CON

1. New security rules should make some allowance for items like shaving equipment and small pocketknives, whose intended use is clearly benign and which could not seriously harm another person.
2. Companies like Swiss Army Brands should receive some kind of compensation for the business they have lost because the losses are outside their control and are related to national security interests.

Summary

Swiss Army Brands is already working on developing new products, from outdoor apparel to a bladeless pocket tool. Peter Gilson, CEO of the company, says that it is also important to educate consumers about packing away their pocketknives in check-through luggage. Finally, the company has begun to focus on its line of watches—also a mature product—which could turn out to be its strongest product in the next few years. "Our goal is to own the world market for moderately priced Swiss watches," says Sue Rechner, head of the Swiss Army watch division.

SOURCES: "In the News," Swiss Army Brands Web site, http://www.swissarmy.com, accessed January 15 2003; Gary Strauss, "Swiss Army Forced to Get Resourceful," *USA Today*, November 1, 2001, p. 3B; Sharon L. Crenson, "Knives Permitted Aboard Planes," *The Boston Globe*, November 12, 2001, http://www.boston.com.

---

categories within an industry, not to individual brands. Also, some products may move rapidly through the product life cycle, while others pass slowly through the four stages.

Introductory Stage

During the early stages of the product life cycle, a firm works to stimulate demand for the new market entry. Products in the introductory stage often bring new technical features to a product category. Since the product is unknown to the public, promotional campaigns stress information about its features. Additional promotions directed toward distribution channel members try to induce these members to carry the product. In this phase, the public becomes acquainted with the item's merits and begins to accept it.

Technical problems are common during the introductory stage as companies fine-tune product design. This is especially true of new technologies, such as the wireless Web. When it was introduced, the idea of using wireless phones and hand-held computers to check e-mail and perform other tasks on the Internet sounded like a sure hit. But the reality proved to be less promising. The equipment was hard for the average consumer to figure out, connections were often cut, and tiny handheld screens were just too hard too read. In addition, services that were once free began to carry charges. Although Sprint and Verizon claimed to have 1 million and 750,000 wireless Web subscribers respectively only months

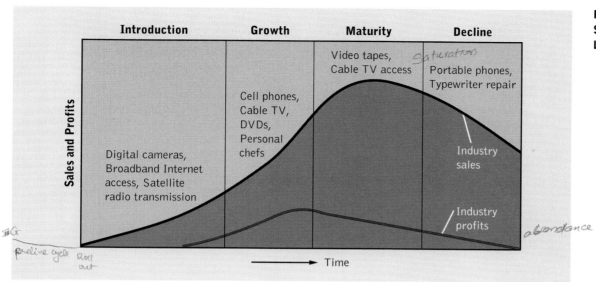

**FIGURE 11.11
Stages in the Product
Life Cycle**

after beginning to offer the services, industry watchers noted that the companies had raised consumers' expectations too high, too early, and could not yet deliver the level of service that they promised.[18]

Financial losses are common during the introductory stage as the firm incurs considerable costs associated with heavy promotion and extensive research-and-development costs. However, by finding the correct formula for consumer trial and acceptance during the introductory stage, a business lays the groundwork for future profits, as Research in Motion did (see "Marketing Hits" box). Firms can then focus on recovering their costs and on beginning to earn profits as the new product moves into the second phase of its life cycle—the growth stage.

Growth Stage

Sales volume rises rapidly during the growth stage as new customers make initial purchases and early buyers repurchase the product, such as DVD players, as described in the "Marketing Hits" box on page 337. Word-of-mouth reports and mass advertising encourage hesitant buyers to make trial purchases. The growth stage usually begins when a firm starts to realize substantial profits from its investment.

However, the growth stage may also bring new challenges for marketers. Inevitably, success attracts competitors, who rush into the market with similar offerings. An item that built enviable market share during the introductory stage may suddenly lose sales to competitive products. To compete effectively, a firm may need to make improvements and changes to a product during this stage. Additional spending on promotion and distribution may also be necessary.

Maturity Stage

Sales of a product category continue to grow during the early part of the maturity stage, but eventually they reach a plateau as the backlog of potential customers dwindles. By this time, many competitors have entered the market, and the firm's profits begin to decline as competition intensifies.

At this stage in the product life cycle, differences between competing products diminish as competitors discover the product and promotional characteristics most desired by customers. Available supplies exceed industry demand for the first time. Companies can increase their sales and market shares only at the expense of competitors, so the competitive environment becomes increasingly important.

In the maturity stage, heavy promotional outlays emphasize any differences that still separate competing products, and brand competition intensifies. Some firms try to differentiate their products by focusing on attributes such as quality, reliability, and service. The 70-year-old Zippo Manufacturing Company found itself head-to-head against competition in the form of disposable lighters, so the com-

Marketing Hit

Customers Pick BlackBerries

Background. During the 1990s, Palm Computing wowed consumers with their innovative, handheld computer called the Palm Pilot. As often happens with new products, competitors soon appeared on the scene. One in particular, Canada-based Research in Motion, served up a new version of the handheld called the BlackBerry.

The Challenge. In order to succeed, Research in Motion (RIM) had to determine how to lure customers away from Palm to try its BlackBerry instead.

The Strategy. RIM sought out businesses who could benefit from having their employees use the wireless BlackBerry to send, retrieve, and display e-mail no matter where they were in the world. The company promoted the BlackBerry as simple to use even for technophobes, and it made sure those claims were true.

The Outcome. During its introductory stage, RIM sold about 500,000 BlackBerry computers to a variety of companies ranging from law firms to large corporations. Although the sales numbers weren't huge, the BlackBerry quickly developed a following via word-of-mouth from user to potential user—perhaps the most effective kind of advertising. "Not many cult brands evolve into national labels," reported *Forbes* magazine, which then went on to name the BlackBerry as one that has.

SOURCES: Research in Motion Web site, http://www.blackberry.net, accessed May 16, 2002; Walter S. Mossberg, "Palm's New Hand-Held Goes *Mano a Mano* with a BlackBerry," *The Wall Street Journal,* January 31, 2002, p. B1; Eileen Glanton, "Making It Big," *Forbes.com,* April 16, 2001, http://www.forbes.com.

---

pany decided to rejuvenate its product by investing in a new ad campaign with the tagline, "Zippo. For Real," as illustrated in Figure 11.12. Zippo marketers wanted consumers to consider the quality and value of its long-lasting product, as opposed to its throwaway competitors. "We wanted to equate that long-lasting relationship with other things in life," explained Bill Garrison, group creative director for the Blattner Brunner advertising agency that developed the new campaign.[19]

As competition intensifies, competitors tend to cut prices to attract new buyers. Although a price cut may seem the easiest method for boosting purchases, it is also one of the simplest moves for competitors to duplicate. Reduced prices decrease revenues for all firms in the industry, unless the lower prices stimulate enough new purchases to offset the loss in revenue on each unit sold. Interestingly, Zippo decided not to reduce its prices. Consumers can purchase a Zippo lighter for around $12.95 for conventional models, or splurge for a collectible style at $3,000. Competing disposables run around $2.[20]

Decline Stage

In the final stage of a product's life, innovations or shifts in consumer preferences bring about an absolute decline in industry sales. The color television replaced original black and white TVs; now high-definition TV is nipping at the heels of conventional color TVs. Dial telephones became touch-tone phones, which evolved to portable phones, which are now increasingly being replaced by cell phones. Notice that the decline stage of an old product often coincides with the growth stage for a new entry.

As sales fall, profits for the product category decline, sometimes actually becoming negative. This change forces firms to cut prices further in a bid for the dwindling market. Companies gradually drop the declining items

FIGURE 11.12
Investing in Retaining Market Share by Extensive Promotion during the Maturity Stage

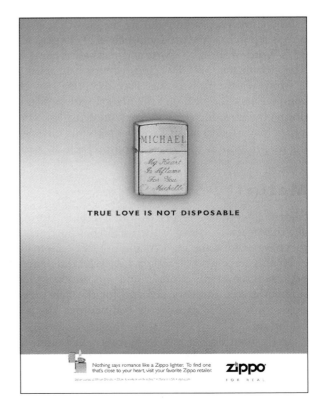

TRUE LOVE IS NOT DISPOSABLE

Nothing says romance like a Zippo lighter. To find one that's close to your heart, visit your favorite Zippo retailer.

Zippo
FOR REAL

from their product lines and search for alternatives. The next section discusses potential strategies for actually extending the life cycle of a product.

The traditional product life cycle differs from fad cycles. Fashions and fads profoundly influence marketing strategies. *Fashions* are currently popular products that tend to follow recurring life cycles. Women's apparel and accessories provide the best examples. After more than a decade out of fashion, the miniskirt became stylish again recently. Small, wire-rimmed sunglasses, popular during the late 1960s, became fashionable again decades later. Often the fashion is reintroduced with a different name. Bell-bottom pants that were popular in the 1960s and 1970s are now called flares; diamond tennis bracelets (made fashionable by tennis star Chris Evert) are now referred to as line bracelets.

In contrast, *fads* are fashions with abbreviated life cycles. Most fads experience short-lived popularity and then quickly fade, although some maintain residual markets among certain segments. The average clothing fad is popular for a few months, after which customers abandon it for the next fad.

Strategies for Managing the Product Life Cycle

A variety of factors in the marketing environment, including the strength or weakness of the economy, increased competition, and technological innovation can affect the way a product moves through its life cycle. Knowledge of the life cycle itself can provide useful guidance for marketing strategy decisions. Marketers can anticipate that sales and profits will assume a predictable pattern throughout the life cycle stages, so they can shift promotional emphasis from product information in the early stages to brand promotion in the later ones. Such insight helps marketers to focus on maximizing sales and profits at each stage through appropriate promotional efforts.

At the introductory stage, a firm's marketing efforts should emphasize the goal of stimulating demand. The focus then shifts to cultivating selective demand in the growth period. Extensive market segmentation helps to maintain momentum in the maturity period. During the decline stage, the emphasis returns to increasing primary demand. Chapter 12 will cover new-product strategies in more detail.

Extending the Product Life Cycle

Marketers usually try to extend each stage of the life cycles for their products as long as possible. They can often accomplish this goal if they take action early in the maturity stage. Product life cycles can stretch indefinitely as a result of decisions designed to increase the frequency of use by current customers, increase the number of users for the product, find new uses, or change package sizes, labels, or product quality.

Increasing Frequency of Use

During the maturity stage, the sales curve for a product category reaches a maximum point as the competitors exhaust the supply of potential customers who previously had not made purchases. However, if current customers buy more frequently than they formerly did, total sales will rise even though no new buyers enter the market.

Marketing Hit

DVD Sales Rocket through the Growth Stage

Background. Usually, it takes marketers awhile to introduce a product to the market and spread the word about its benefits. When the product represents a whole new category, it may take even longer. But in the case of the DVD player and all of its related products, the introductory phase seems to have been short and sweet. Growth is the name of the game.

The Challenge. In the first four years of its existence, the DVD player has been purchased by 31 million Americans—a much quicker adoption of a new product than occurred with the CD player, which took about seven years to reach the growth stage. Now marketers need to figure out how to continue the growth.

The Strategy. To encourage growth, companies have kept the prices of both the players and the disks low—$20 for a disk, $100 for a player. They have made as many movies available for rent on DVD as possible. In one recent year, consumers spent more than $6 billion buying or renting their favorite movies on DVD. "DVD is our engine of growth," notes Steve Beeks, president of Artisan Home Entertainment. And at prices under $100, consumers aren't worried about how long the players themselves will last.

The Outcome. As consumers rush to pick up the latest DVDs, the Hollywood studios, Blockbuster, and retailers like Wal-Mart and Best Buy are duking it out for the dollars. Retailers offer the disks at rock-bottom prices to attract customers, which means less money for Hollywood, which normally gets a cut of rental fees from Blockbuster and other rental stores. But because only 34

continued on next page

Marketing Hit

percent of American households own DVD players, there is still a huge market to tap. In the end, everyone wins.

SOURCES: Eric Hellweg, "Who Wins as DVD Sales Soar?" *Business 2.0*, June 26, 2002, **http://www. business2.com**; Bruce Orwall, Martin Peers, and Ann Zimmerman, "Disc Jockeying," *The Wall Street Journal*, February 5, 2002, p. A1; Ronald Grover, "DVDs Are Turning into a Solid Gold Hit," *BusinessWeek*, January 21, 2001, p. 8.

For instance, consumers buy some products during certain seasons of the year. Marketers can boost purchase frequency by persuading these people to try the product year-round. Many ski resorts advertise the advantages of visiting their areas during the summer—for the scenery, hiking, and golf. Marketers may try to connect the use of seasonal holiday products to additional occasions throughout the year. During the summer months, Butterball—traditionally known for its Thanksgiving turkeys—advertises "turkey on the grill." And Mars Incorporated comes out with special-edition M&Ms for different holidays, including Halloween and Easter.

Increasing the Number of Users

A second strategy for extending the product life cycle seeks to increase the overall market size by attracting new customers who previously have not used the product. Marketers may find their products in different stages of the life cycle in different countries. This difference can help firms to extend product growth. Items that have reached the maturity stage in the U.S. may still be in the introductory stage somewhere else.

In recent years, the Walt Disney Company has spent time and money on advertising its theme parks to attract adults, in addition to young families. Television commercials portray empty nesters taking off to Disney World for a second honeymoon once their children are grown. And the dairy industry's "Got Milk?" campaign is aimed at all sorts of nontraditional milk drinkers—anyone other than children or pregnant women—in an attempt to increase the number of people who drink milk.

Finding New Uses

Still another strategy for extending a product's life cycle is to identify new uses for it. New applications for mature products include oatmeal as a cholesterol-reducer, mouthwash as an aid in treating and preventing plaque and gum disease, and antacids as a calcium supplement. The Web sites of some manufacturers such as Kraft Foods provide information on new recipes and uses for their products.

Changing Package Sizes, Labels, or Product Quality

Many firms try to extend their product life cycles by introducing physical changes in their offerings. Food marketers have brought out small packages designed to appeal to one-person households and extra large containers for customers who want to buy in bulk. Other firms offer their products in convenient packages for use away from home or for use at the office.

The wine industry is well-known for relying on packaging and labeling to attract consumers to its mature products. Upstate New York–based Constellation Brands, the fourth largest winemaker in the world—E. & J. Gallo is the largest—recently introduced a line of fruit-flavored wines under its Arbor Mist label. The wines, such as a Chardonnay with a peach flavor, come in gently curved, frosty bottles that have attracted a whole new group of wine drinkers, according to some retailers.[21]

New "M&M's" Speckled Egg-Shaped Candies for Easter.

In addition to promoting "contests" to select new M&M colors, Mars offers holiday versions of its M&Ms candy.

Product Deletion Decisions

To avoid wasting resources promoting unpromising products, marketers must sometimes prune product lines and eliminate marginal products. Marketers typically face this decision during the late maturity and early decline stages of the product life cycle. Periodic reviews of weak products should justify either eliminating or retaining them.

A firm may continue to carry an unprofitable item in order to provide a complete line for its customers. For example, while most grocery stores lose money on bulky, low-unit-value items such as salt, they continue to carry these items to meet shopper demand.

Shortages of raw materials sometimes prompt companies to discontinue production and marketing of previously profitable items. Alcoa discontinued making its brand of aluminum foil due to such a shortage. A firm may even drop a profitable item that fails to fit into its existing product line. Some of these products return to the market carrying the names of other firms that purchase the brands from the original manufacturers. One marketer tried to build an entire business on this idea. Ian R. Wilson founded Aurora Foods in 1995, persuading investors that he could make a hit by buying up a dozen "orphan" food brands—items that other food companies no longer wanted—such as Mrs. Butterworth's syrup, Mrs. Paul's frozen fish, and Lender's frozen bagels. But it turned out that the market had already turned away from many of these products for a variety of reasons; for instance, consumers were gravitating away from frozen bagels and toward fresh-baked ones. In addition, supermarkets grant shelf space based on the current strength of brands, and these products had already declined to the point that their originators had chosen to delete them by selling them to Aurora, which later began to falter.[22]

Some food industry experts do say that products deleted by their original companies might sell well on the Internet. A Web site called hometownfavorites.com currently offers 400-some products, including Brer Rabbit Molasses and My-T-Fine Pudding. Shelf space for these products is not a problem, and the site can offer these products to a loyal following.[23]

9 essential nutrients in every easy-to-open bottle.

got milk?

For more than a decade, the dairy industry has featured celebrities wearing a milk "moustache" in its advertising efforts.

Strategic Implications of Marketing in the 21st Century

Marketers who want their businesses to succeed will continue to develop new goods and services to satisfy their customers. They will engage in continuous improvement activities, including benchmarking when necessary. And they will continually evaluate their company's mix of products. Corning, the number-one glassmaker in the U.S., is a good example of such a firm. Corning has long had a tradition of inventing new manufacturing processes that produce top-quality items at low cost. This constant quest is true of its fiber-manufacturing process, in which Corning currently holds 40 to 50 percent of worldwide sales. The company also relies on constant innovation for growth. In one recent year, 84 percent of Corning's revenues came from products that had not existed four years before. In fact, company officials like to say that their goal is to keep making Corning's own products obsolete, instead of constantly coming up with new items in the product line designed to anticipate and fulfill customers' needs.[24]

Just like the marketers at Corning, marketers everywhere are constantly developing new and better products that fit their firm's overall strategy. They will come up with ways to extend the lives of certain products and will be able to recognize and delete those that no longer meet expectations.

Summary of Chapter Objectives

1. Define the term *product* and distinguish between goods and services.

Marketers define a *product* as the bundle of physical, service, and symbolic attributes designed to satisfy customers' wants and needs. Goods are tangible products that customers can see, hear, smell, taste, or touch. Services are intangible tasks that satisfy the needs of customers.

2. List the classifications of consumer goods and services, and briefly describe each category.

Consumer products—both goods and services—are classified as convenience products (frequently purchased items), shopping products (products purchased after comparison), and specialty products (those that offer unique characteristics that consumers prize).

3. Describe each of the types of business goods and services.

Business products are classified as installations (major capital investments), accessory equipment (capital items that cost less and last for shorter periods than installations), component parts and materials (finished business products of one producer that become part of the final products of another producer), raw materials (natural resources such as lumber, beef, or cotton), supplies (the regular expenses that a firm incurs in daily operations), and business services (the intangible products that firms buy to facilitate their production and operating processes).

4. Discuss how total quality management (TQM) is implemented.

Total quality management (TQM) asks all employees in a firm to continually improve products and work processes to achieve customer satisfaction and world-class performance. Marketers develop products that people want; engineers design items to work properly; product workers build quality into products;

salespeople deliver on promises; information systems staff fill orders correctly; and financial people set fair prices.

5. Explain the role benchmarking plays in achieving continuous improvement.

Benchmarking helps firms achieve superior performance by allowing them to (1) identify processes that need improvement, (2) compare internal processes to similar activities of industry leaders, and (3) implement changes for better quality.

6. Explain why firms develop lines of related products rather than marketing individual items.

Companies usually produce several related products rather than individual ones to achieve the objectives of growth, optimal use of company resources, and increased company importance in the market, and to make optimal use of the product life cycle.

7. Identify the major product mix decisions that marketers must make.

Marketers must decide the right width, consistency, length, and depth of product lines. Width is the number of product lines. Consistency is the similarity of product lines in use, distribution, and target markets. Length is the number of products a company sells. Depth refers to the number of variations of a product available in a product line.

8. Explain the concept of the product life cycle and how a firm can extend a product's life cycle.

The product life cycle outlines the stages that a product goes through, including introduction, growth, maturity, and decline. Marketers can extend the product life cycle by increasing frequency of use or users, finding new uses for the product, or changing package size, label, or quality.

Marketing Terms You Need to Know

marketing mix 318
product 318
service 319
good 319
convenience products 321

shopping products 322
specialty products 323
installations 325
accessory
    equipment 325

component parts and
    materials 326
raw materials 326
supplies 327
business services 327

total quality management
    (TQM) 329
product line 331
product mix 332
product life cycle 333

Other Important Marketing Terms

goods-services continuum 319
unsought products 321
slotting allowances 322

MRO items 327
ISO 9002 329
benchmarking 330

line extension 333
fashion 337
fad 337

Review Questions

1. What is a product? Differentiate between goods and services.
2. Identify and describe briefly the three major classifications of consumer products. Which category would each of the following occupy?
   a. soft drink
   b. gasoline
   c. Rolex watch
   d. winter coat
   e. Godiva chocolates
   f. DVD player
3. Identify and describe briefly the six different types of business products. Give an example of each.
4. Explain the concept of quality or continuous improvement. Why is it important in today's marketplace?
5. What is a product line? Why do companies usually develop at least one product line?
6. Describe a product mix. How do marketers typically measure product mixes?
7. What strategies do marketers use to expand their product mixes? Cite an example of each strategy.
8. Describe the four stages of the product life cycle. Identify a product currently in each of the stages.
9. In what ways can marketers extend the life cycle of a product? Give an example of each approach.
10. Why is it just as important for marketers to identify the point at which a product should be deleted as it is to identify when to introduce or extend the life of a product? Cite an example of a recent product deletion decision.

Projects and Teamwork Exercises

1. Locate an advertisement that catches your attention. Then describe where you believe the product falls on the goods-services continuum and explain why. Be sure to include the product features that you think belong in the goods category and the services category.
2. Make a list of all the goods and services you purchase in a week. Then classify them. Which types of purchases do you make the most? Which do you make the least?
3. Choose a good that you have purchased or are interested in purchasing. Visit the manufacturer's Web site to learn more about the processes that go into bringing the product to market. Then list as many businesses products—goods and services—as you think the company might rely on to get your product to market.
4. With a classmate, visit the Web site of a company that interests you—say, Burton snowboards, Sony, Donna Karan, or Kellogg's. Identify at least one of the company's product lines. Together, come up with a plan for extending the line. Describe the strategy you would recommend for extending the line, as well as new products that might be included.
5. With a classmate, choose a product that you believe has reached either the maturity or decline stage—say, portable phones, personal computers, or sport-utility vehicles. Together, come up with a possible strategy for extending the life cycle of your product and present your plan to the class.

'netWork

http://www.iso.ch

1. ISO. Visit the International Organization for Standardization (ISO) Web site. After reviewing the material on the site, prepare a brief report explaining how ISO standards are developed, the ISO structure, and criteria for ISO membership.

http://www.blackand
decker.com

2. Product mix. Go to the Web site of Black and Decker or another company of your choosing. Make a list of the company's mix of U.S. retail consumer products. Classify these products as being either convenience products, shopping products, or specialty products. Choose two products from your list. Which phase of the product life cycle do you think these products are currently in? Defend your answer.

http://www.pricing-
advisor.com

3. Pricing strategy for services. After browsing the Professional Pricing Society's Web site, list three ways this organization could help a service provider in its pricing decisions.

Note: Internet Web addresses change frequently. If you don't find the exact sites listed, you may need to access the organization or company's home page and search from there.

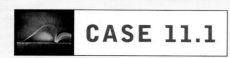

CASE 11.1 Satellite Radio: A New Product Hits the Air Waves

Everyone who drives knows the frustration: You tune into your favorite radio station, only to have the sound become choppy and then fade to a hiss moments later as you drive out of the station's range. In fact, two companies, Sirius Satellite and XM Satellite Radio, are banking on the fact that you've had this experience. They've come up with a new product to satisfy your listening needs: satellite radio, offering commercial-free programming for a monthly fee. In the first sixth months after its introduction, this new service got a lot of valuable publicity. But so far, consumers aren't lining up to retrofit their cars with radios costing $179 and up, along with the cost of antennas, installation, and monthly fees. Still, marketers and business analysts believe that this new product is a coming trend.

If the cost of installing a special radio, along with $10 to $15 a month for listening, turns you off, most consumers agree that satellite radio is a low priority on their list of most-wanted features in a car. Even if you are purchasing a new car, 52 percent of your peers would say that satellite radio is not at all important as a vehicle option. But 32 percent of these consumers, according to one survey, say that it is somewhat important. And marketers at Sirius and XM Satellite, as well as electronics manufacturers Sony, Kenwood, and Clarion, are counting on the fact that satellite radio will become increasingly important to consumers as time passes. You might say that satellite radio is an unsought product—many consumers don't yet know that they need it. Or you might simply call it a solution to an existing problem, in which technology has come to the rescue.

Currently, both major competitors—Sirius Satellite Radio and XM Satellite Radio—offer 100 commercial-free radio channels, covering just about every genre of radio you can think of, from country to classical. In addition, news, talk, entertainment, and specialty programs are usually in the mix. Sirius offers 60 commercial-free channels devoted to music, plus CNBC, NPR, Radio Disney, and other popular channels. XM devotes 71 channels to music, 36 of them free of ads. XM also partners with CNN, ESPN, and USA Today. The digital sound that comes from satellite transmissions is of much higher quality than traditional radio broadcasts.

XM has the early competitive edge, having launched its service first. The company claimed to have more than 30,000 paying subscribers within the first six months of operation. Sirius's launch lagged behind because of management changes and launched several months later, but a winner can't be picked in this race until both services have been on air for awhile. They will have to compete with each other as well as newer entries to the market. They'll have to wrestle with the high cost of the new hardware, coaxing consumers to purchase radios, accessory equipment, and new cars with the satellite option. But innovations in music technology nearly always win in the end. If they didn't, we'd still be cranking up the old Victrola.

Questions for Critical Thinking

1. If you consider Sirius's and XM's product line to be their offering of channels, what strategies might marketers use to create a line extension? What strategies might they use to expand the product mix?
2. What actions would you advise marketers of satellite radio to take to move their product successfully into the growth stage?

SOURCES: Stephen H. Wildstrom, "Tech Steals a March on the Hit Parade," *BusinessWeek,* April 8, 2002, p. 20; Larry Armstrong, "Tuning in to Pay Radio," *BusinessWeek,* March 25, 2002, p. 110; Earle Eldridge, "Drivers Tune in Satellite Radio," *USA Today,* January 24, 2002, p. 16B; Edward C. Baig, "Satellite Radio Is a Turn-On," *USA Today,* January 16, 2002, p. 3D.

VIDEO CASE 11.2 Fossil Is a Reminder of Good Times

The written case on Fossil appears on page VC-14. The recently filmed Fossil video is designed to expand and highlight the concepts in this chapter and the concepts and questions covered in the written video case.

12

Category and Brand Management, Product Identification, and New-Product Planning

Chapter Objectives

1 Explain the benefits of category and brand management.

2 Identify the different types of brands.

3 Explain the strategic value of brand equity.

4 Discuss how companies develop strong identities for their products and brands.

5 Describe the strategies for new product development.

6 Describe the consumer adoption process.

7 List the stages in the process for developing new products.

8 Discuss the relationship between product safety and product liability.

PepsiCo: The New Health Food Company?

When North Carolina pharmacist Caleb Bradham founded his company more than 100 years ago, his goal was to peddle a cure for the stomach upset known as dyspepsia. He hardly could have predicted that his remedy for indigestion would turn into a global empire. Nor could he have imagined that the evolved version of his drink—Pepsi—would turn into one of the most recognized brands in the world. PepsiCo, now headquartered in Purchase, N.Y., earns an estimated $3.5 billion on revenues of $25 billion per year. It offers a wide range of beverages, from soft drinks like Pepsi and Sierra Mist, to power drinks like Gatorade, to real fruit juices like Tropicana. When the company acquired Frito-Lay, it became a giant in the snack industry as well, with popular snacks such as Fritos, Doritos, and those orange powder-coated favorites, Cheetos. A few years ago, PepsiCo bought Quaker Oats for a whopping $13.4 billion, adding more famous brands to its stable.

Although the power of all these brands continues to fatten PepsiCo's wallet, the company—and others like it such as Kraft Foods and McDonald's—has received heavy criticism for helping to fatten America's waistline. With 64 percent of U.S. adults and 15 percent of children overweight according to the Centers for Disease Control, pressure is intense on the purveyors of snack foods and beverages to come out with more healthful products. This is particularly true for young people, whose eating habits become ingrained early on. Food manufacturers are finding themselves hit where it hurts: in the bottom line. For instance, the Los Angeles unified school district, which represents 750 institutions, recently announced that it would no longer sell soft drinks in its vending machines and lunch rooms. Other school districts have taken similar actions, and many are discussing banning fatty and salty snacks as well. With the FDA ruling that food manufacturers must add the content of trans fats to their nutrition labels by January 1, 2006, food manufacturers are under pressure to come up with more healthful foods for consumers.

Three years before the FDA deadline for the new labeling, PepsiCo had already reduced or eliminated the trans fats in snacks such as Doritos, Tostitos, and Cheetos, and it had begun adding the trans fat line on its nutrition labels. Also, researchers in the snack division have developed new products such as Vegetable Rice Puffs (whose brand name admittedly doesn't have the ring of a Frito or a Dorito), to create chips made with rice and tomatoes that contain only 3 grams of fat per serving. Meanwhile, the beverage division is concocting new drinks, although those products are kept under tight wraps because of competition. "Pepsi is looking at and will be testing beverages we've never heard of. Think dairy. Think grain. Think fiber," says John Sicher, editor of *Beverage Digest*. It sounds like Pepsi may be returning to its roots. The new Pepsi may be a health drink, after all—a brew to settle an upset stomach.[1]

Briefly Speaking

Obesity is becoming as large a factor as tobacco once was.

Dr. Vincent Kerr
(b. 1950)
Ford Motor Co. director of healthcare management (on healthcare spending by corporations)

Brands play a huge role in our lives. We try certain brands for all kinds of reasons, on recommendations from friends or because we remember colorful advertisements. We develop loyalty to certain brands and product lines through category management for varying reasons as well—quality of a product, price, and habit are a few examples. This chapter examines the way companies make decisions about developing and managing the products and product lines that they hope will become necessities to consumers. Developing and marketing a product and product line are costly propositions. To protect its investment and maximize the return on it, a business and category manager must carefully nurture both existing and new products.

This chapter focuses on two critical elements of product planning and strategy. First, it looks at how firms build and maintain identity and competitive advantage for their products through branding. Second, it focuses on the new product planning and introduction process, often influenced greatly by a category manager. Effective new product planning and meeting the profit responsibility that a category manager has for a product line require careful preparation. The needs and desires of consumers change constantly, and the successful companies are those that manage to keep up with—or stay just ahead of—those changes. Even marketers at PepsiCo had to plan their strategy to respond to consumer demand for more healthful food and beverages, developing new products to suit customer tastes.

Managing Brands for Competitive Advantage

1

Explain the benefits of category and brand management.

Think of the last time you went shopping for groceries. As you moved through the store, chances are your recognition of various brand names influenced many of your purchasing decisions. Perhaps you chose Colgate toothpaste over competitive offerings or loaded Heinz ketchup into your cart instead of the store brand. Walking through the snack food aisle, you might have reached for Smartfood popcorn or Lay's potato chips without much thought.

Marketers recognize the powerful influence on customer behavior that creating and protecting a strong identity for products and product lines has. Branding is the process of creating that identity. A **brand** is a name, term, sign, symbol, design, or some combination that identifies the products of one firm while differentiating these products from competitors' offerings. For decades, brawny Mr. Clean has represented the cleansing strength of his household cleaner. Even as new scents and colors are added to the product line, the image of Mr. Clean is clearly represented on every bottle, as illustrated in Figure 12.1.

As you read this chapter, consider how many brands you are aware of—both those you are loyal to and those you have never tried, or have tried and abandoned. Table 12.1 shows some selected brands, brand names, and brand marks. Buyers respond to branding by making repeat purchases of the same product because they identify the item with the name of its producer. One buyer might derive satisfaction from an ice cream bar with the brand name Dove; another might derive the same satisfaction from one with the name Ben & Jerry's.

Brand Loyalty

is everything in Mktg.

Read 4 exam

Brands achieve widely varying consumer familiarity and acceptance. While a snowboarder might insist on a Burton snowboard, the same consumer might show little loyalty to particular brands in another product category such as tissues. Marketers measure brand loyalty in three stages: brand recognition, brand preference, and brand insistence.

Brand recognition is a company's first objective for newly introduced products. Marketers begin the promotion of new items by trying to make these items familiar to the public. Advertising offers one effective way for increasing consumer awareness of a brand. McDonald's introduced its new Premium Salads with advertisements such as the one in Figure 12.2, which shows an enticing fresh salad with the McDonald's Golden Arches below it.

Other strategies for creating brand recognition include offering free samples or discount coupons for purchases. Once consumers have used a product, seen it advertised, or noticed it in stores, it moves from the unknown to the known category, which increases the probability that those consumers will purchase it.

At the second level of brand loyalty, **brand preference,** buyers rely on previous experiences with the product when choosing that product, if available, over competitors' products. Recently, several competitors in the meat industry have launched major advertising campaigns designed to create brand preference for their precooked entrees. Although the meat industry historically has not enjoyed the benefits of branding that other food categories have, "We're convinced this is the future, and it may be a $1 billion category in the next five years," predicts Jim Schloss of one of Smithfield Foods' subsidiaries. Tyson Fresh Meats, the country's leading beef processor, is promoting its new line of precooked pork and beef under the brand name Thomas E. Wilson. The product line, which includes an Italian-seasoned pork roast, achieved the number one brand spot in all refrigerated entrees in its test markets. The firm followed its test marketing with a national advertising campaign.[2]

Brand insistence, the ultimate stage in brand loyalty, leads consumers to refuse alternatives and to search extensively for the desired merchandise. A product at this stage has achieved a monopoly position with its consumers. Although many firms try to establish brand insistence with all consumers, few achieve this ambitious goal. Companies that offer specialty or luxury goods and services, such as Tiffany diamonds or Rothschild wine,

FIGURE 12.1
Promoting a Well-Known Brand

The freshness of the seasons. The strength of Mr. Clean.

Mr. Clean now brings you Seasons' Freshness. An antibacterial cleaner with four great scents.
Spring Garden, Summer Citrus, Sparkling Apple and Invigorating Breeze.
They'll remind you of your favourite season. Any time of the year.

TABLE 12.1	Selected Brands, Brand Names, and Brand Marks
Brand type	Dr. Pepper or Canada Dry ginger ale
Private brand	Sam's Choice beverage (Wal-Mart) or ACE brand tools
Family brand	RAID insect sprays or Progresso soups
Individual brand	Tide or Clorox
Brand name	Life or Cheese Nips
Brand mark	Colonel Sanders for KFC or Mr. Peanut for Planters

1ˢᵗ Exam.

Marketing Dictionary

brand   Name, term, sign, symbol, design, or some combination that identifies the products of one firm while differentiating them from the competition's.

brand recognition   Consumer awareness and identification of a brand.

brand preference   Consumer reliance on previous experiences with a product to choose that product again.

brand insistence   Consumer refusals of alternatives and extensive search for desired merchandise.

Marketing Miss

Mustaches Fail to Attract Milk Drinkers

Background. More than a decade ago, the dairy industry realized its product needed a boost. Milk drinkers were on the decline as more consumers chose soft drinks and other beverages instead. Consumers viewed milk as a generic product—white, chocolate, or strawberry, in a plastic or cardboard jug, something for babies, boring.

The Marketing Problem. Industry marketers decided to create a "brand" based on a certain image—and the famous milk mustache campaign was launched. Ads featured celebrities from every corner of the sports and entertainment world—each designed to accomplish two goals: create a recognizable brand for a generic product and stimulate more demand for that product.

The Outcome. Ten years later, the general public was certainly more aware of milk—no one could miss those mustaches. But those mustaches weren't very attractive, no matter who was wearing them. And milk consumption was still declining—consumers drank only 20 gallons of milk a year, compared with 54 gallons of soft drinks.

Lessons Learned. Creating a brand for a generic product is an excellent idea, but it may not change consumers' habits. Since milk consumption by kids is still declining, the dairy industry is trying a new tactic: offering dairy drinks in flavors such as amaretto, strawberry, banana, peach, and seasonal flavors like blueberry. Maybe this time, they'll skip the mustache.

SOURCES: National Milk Mustache Web site, http://www.whymilk.com, accessed January 15, 2004; Lisa McLaughlin, "This Moo's for You," *Time*, September 22, 2003, p. 47; Jeff Manning, "Got Milk? A Decade of Lessons Pours In," *Brandweek*, June 2, 2003, p. 24.

FIGURE 12.2
Salads: A New Line of McDonald's Food Offerings

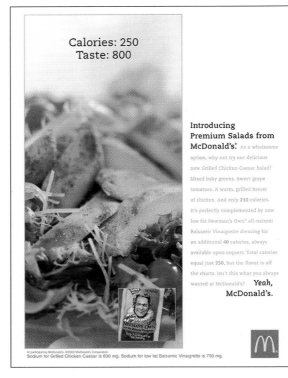

are more apt to achieve this status than those that offer mass goods and services.

Types of Brands

2

Identify the different types of brands.

Companies that practice branding classify brands in many ways: private, manufacturer's (national), family, and individual brands. In making branding decisions, firms weigh the benefits and disadvantages of each type of brand.

Some firms, however, sell their goods without any efforts at branding. These items are called **generic products.** They are characterized by plain labels, little or no advertising, and no brand names. Common categories of generic products include food and household staples. These no-name products were first sold in Europe at prices as much as 30 percent below those of brand name products. This product strategy was introduced in the U.S. a quarter century ago. The market shares for generic products increase during economic downturns but subside when the economy improves. However, many consumers do request generic substitutions for certain brand-name prescriptions at the pharmacy whenever possible. Sometimes marketers try to create a brand for a generic product (see the "Marketing Miss" box).

Manufacturers' Brands versus Private Brands

Manufacturers' brands, also called *national brands*, define the image that most people form when they think of a brand. A **manufacturer's brand** refers to a brand name owned by a manufacturer or other producer. Well-known manufacturers' brands include Kodak, Pepsi Cola, and Heinz. In contrast, many large wholesalers and retailers place their own brands on the merchandise they market. The brands offered by wholesalers and retailers are usually called *private brands* (or private labels). Although some manufacturers refuse to produce private label goods, most regard such production as a way to reach additional market segments. Wal-Mart offers many private label products at its stores, including its Sam's Choice cola. In addition, Information Resources Inc. estimates that Wal-Mart accounted for three-quarters of the private-label sales growth in nonfood categories in one recent year.[3]

Private brands and generic products expand the number of alternatives available to consumers. As Figure 12.3 illustrates, True Value hardware stores sells its own brand of paint called E-Z Kare. Sears sells its own brands under the names of Craftsman, Kenmore, Diehard, and Canyon River Blues. Shaw's supermarkets have their own Signature line of groceries.

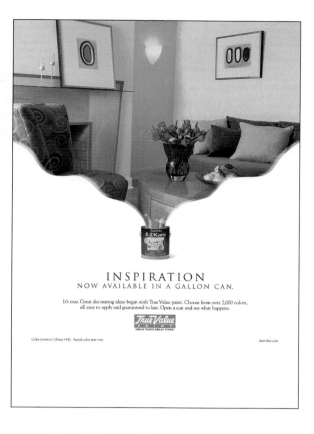

The growth of private brands has paralleled that of chain stores in the U.S., most of the growth occurring since the 1930s. Manufacturers not only sell their well-known brands to stores but also put the store's own label on these products. Such leading manufacturers as Westinghouse, Armstrong Rubber, and Heinz generate ever-increasing percentages of their total incomes by producing goods for sale under retailers' private labels.

One arena in which private label branding is gaining new ground is personal computers. After watching sales of big-name PCs stumble, retailers such as Best Buy and RadioShack have begun stocking their shelves with their own private-label computers—and watching them sell. Best Buy started by selling a line of PCs designed for teenagers who mostly play games. The PCs come in fluorescent colors instead of black or silver, and the kids are attracted to them. The computers are just as expensive as brand-name PCs, but they do come with fancy components. Ted Waitt, founder of Gateway, refers to Best Buy as one of his biggest competitors. "Best Buy moved a lot of those [private label] products very quickly," he notes. "They can drive a lot of share with that model."[4]

Captive Brands

The nation's major discounters—such as Wal-Mart, Target, and Kmart—have come up with a spin-off of the private-label idea. So-called *captive brands* are national brands that are sold exclusively by a retail chain. Captive brands typically provide better profit margins than private labels. Kmart's captive brands include Martha Stewart paints, linens, and home furnishings. Similarly, Wal-Mart sells General Electric small appliances, even though these items are actually made by other manufacturers.

Family and Individual Brands

A **family brand** is a single brand name that identifies several related products. For example,

Marketing Dictionary

generic products Products characterized by plain labels, no advertising, and no brand names.

manufacturer's brand Brand name owned by a manufacturer or other producer.

family brand Single brand name that identifies several related products.

KitchenAid markets a complete line of appliances under the KitchenAid name, and Johnson & Johnson offers a line of baby powder, lotions, plastic pants, and baby shampoo under one name. All Pepperidge Farm products, from bread to rolls to cookies, carry the Pepperidge Farm name.

A manufacturer may instead choose to market a product under an *individual brand,* which uniquely identifies a product itself, rather than promoting it under the name of the company or under an umbrella name covering similar items. Lever Brothers, for example, markets Aim, Close-Up, and Pepsodent toothpastes; All and Wisk laundry detergents; Imperial margarine; Caress, Dove, Lifebuoy, and Lux bath soaps; and Shield and Lever 2000 deodorant soaps. PepsiCo's Quaker Oats unit markets Aunt Jemima breakfast products, Gatorade beverages, and Celeste Pizza. Individual brands cost more than family brands to market because the firm must develop a new promotional campaign to introduce each new product to its target market. Distinctive brands are extremely effective aids in implementing market segmentation strategies, however.

On the other hand, a promotional outlay for a family brand can benefit all items in the line. For example, a new addition to the Kool-Aid line, shown in Figure 12.4, gains immediate recognition as part of the well-known family brand. Family brands also help marketers to introduce new products to both customers and retailers. Since supermarkets stock thousands of items, they hesitate to add new products unless they are confident they will be in demand.

Family brands should identify products of similar quality, or the firm risks harming its overall product image. If Rolls Royce marketers were to place the Rolls name on a low-end car or a line of discounted clothing, they might severely tarnish the image of the luxury car line. Conversely, Lexus, Infiniti, and Mercedes-Benz put their names on luxury sport-utility vehicles to capitalize on their reputations and to enhance the acceptance of the new models in a competitive market.

Individual brand names should, however, distinguish dissimilar products. PepsiCo's Quaker Oats division markets dog food under the Ken-L Ration brand name and cat food under Puss 'n Boots. Kimberly-Clark markets two different types of diapers under its Huggies and Pull-Ups names. Procter & Gamble offers fruit drinks under its Sunny Delight name, laundry detergent under Cheer, and dishwasher soap under Cascade.

**FIGURE 12.4
An Addition to a
Family Brand—
Kool-Aid Jammers**

Brand Equity

As individuals, we often like to say that our strongest asset is our reputation. The same is true of organizations. A brand can go a long way toward making or breaking a company's reputation. A strong brand identity backed by superior quality offers important strategic advantages for a firm. First, it increases the likelihood that consumers will recognize the firm's product or product line when they make purchase decisions. Second, a strong brand identity can contribute to buyers' perceptions of product quality. Branding can also reinforce customer loyalty and repeat purchases. A consumer who tries a brand and likes it will likely look for that brand on future store visits. All of these benefits contribute to a valuable form of competitive advantage called brand equity.

Brand equity refers to the added value that a certain brand name gives to a product in the marketplace. Brands with high equity confer financial advantages on a firm because they often command comparatively large market shares and consumers may pay little attention to differences in prices. Studies have also linked brand equity to high profits and stock returns.

In global operations, high brand equity often facilitates expansion into new markets. Currently, Coca-Cola is the most valuable—and most recognized—brand in the world.[5] Similarly, Disney's brand equity allows it to market its goods and services in Europe and Japan—and now China. What makes a global brand powerful? According to Interbrand Corp., a division of Omnicom Group, which measures brand equity in dollar values, a strong brand is one that has the power to increase a company's sales and earnings. A global brand is generally defined as one that sells at least 20 percent outside of its home country, as Coca-Cola does. Interbrand's top ten global brands include Microsoft, Disney, McDonald's, and AT&T.[6]

The global advertising agency Young & Rubicam (Y&R) developed another brand equity system called the *Brand Asset Valuator*. Y&R interviewed more than 90,000 consumers in 30 countries and collected information on over 13,000 brands to help create this measurement system. According to Y&R, a firm builds brand equity sequentially on four dimensions of brand personality. These four dimensions are differentiation, relevance, esteem, and knowledge:

- *Differentiation* refers to a brand's ability to stand apart from competitors. Brands like Porsche and Victoria's Secret stand out in consumers' minds as symbols of unique product characteristics.

- *Relevance* refers to the real and perceived appropriateness of the brand to a big consumer segment. A large number of consumers must feel a need for the benefits offered by the brand. Brands with high relevance include AT&T and Hallmark.

- *Esteem* is a combination of perceived quality and consumer perceptions about the growing or declining popularity of a brand. A rise in perceived quality or in public opinion about a brand enhances a brand's esteem. But negative impressions reduce esteem. Brands with high esteem include Starbucks and Honda.

- *Knowledge* refers to the extent of customers' awareness of the brand and understanding of what a good or service stands for. Knowledge implies that customers feel an intimate relationship with a brand. Examples include Jell-O and Band-Aid.[7]

Brand equity can actually be assisted by outside organizations that endorse a product. The Good Housekeeping Seal signifies to consumers that a product has been tested by a staff of independent evaluators at *Good Housekeeping* who are willing to apply the Good Housekeeping Consumers' Refund or Replacement Policy to the product.[8] Although not all advertisers in *Good Housekeeping* magazine have received the seal, many have. Figure 12.5 showcases the advertisers who had received the seal in a recent year. Consumers

**FIGURE 12.5
Brands That Have Received the Good Housekeeping Seal**

Marketing Dictionary

brand equity   Added value that a brand name gives to a product in the marketplace.

who are familiar with the seal—which is a brand itself—often feel more comfortable purchasing products that have been tested by an independent organization.

Unfortunately, even brands with high equity can lose their luster for a variety of reasons. It may be because of perceived or real defects in a product that become public knowledge, as in the case of the Bridgestone/Firestone tires installed on Ford's Explorer SUVs. Or it may be because of a court battle, as in the case of Microsoft's antitrust struggles. In fact, although Microsoft sits in the number two spot on Interbrand's list of most valuable global brands, some analysts assert that it could easily have soared to the top spot without the court battles.[9]

The Role of Category and Brand Management *Read*

Because of the tangible and intangible value associated with strong brand equity, marketing organizations invest considerable resources and effort in developing and maintaining these dimensions of brand personality. Traditionally, companies assign the task of managing a brand's marketing strategies to a *brand manager*. Recently, companies have been reevaluating the effectiveness of brand management and changing the system in a variety of ways. General Motors has decided to eliminate brand managers in favor of marketing director positions, largely because of duplication. The company found that it was spending time, money, and effort in separate divisions to come up with essentially the same car.[10]

Today, major consumer goods companies have adopted a strategy called **category management**, in which a category manager oversees an entire product line. Unlike traditional product managers, category managers have profit responsibility for their product group. These managers are assisted by associates usually called "analysts." Part of this shift was initiated by large retailers, who realized they could benefit from the marketing muscle of large grocery and household goods producers like Kraft and Procter & Gamble.

As a result, producers began to focus their attention on in-store merchandising instead of mass-market advertising. A few years ago, Kraft reorganized its sales force so that each representative was responsible for a retailer's needs, instead of pushing a single brand. Kraft now has a "customer manager" for each major grocery chain in a city or region. Technology also plays a role in Kraft's strategy. A software application called Three-Step Category Builder allows managers to tear apart a product category, analyze all its related data, and create a new management plan in two days. The software presents the plan in a few easy-to-read charts that the manager can show to the retailer. "It shouldn't take more than 15 minutes to explain," says Christopher Hogan, technology chief of Kraft's sales division. Kraft then recommends everything from which products the retailer should carry to where they should be positioned.[11]

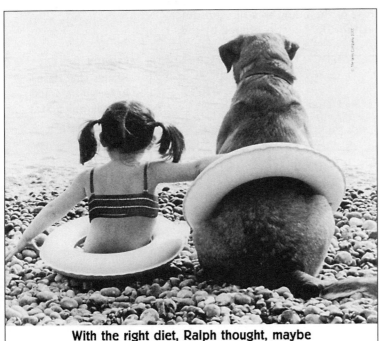

With the right diet, Ralph thought, maybe he could lose those love handles.

Like people, dogs can have weight issues too. Iams Less Active Formula turns fat into energy to help trim unnecessary pounds. Gradually.

The result? More healthy years for your dog. And perhaps, a little less embarrassment at the beach.

Contact us at www.iams.com or 1-800-525-4267

IAMS
Good for Life

Iams identifies its products with a paw print on every package.

Product Identification

Organizations identify their products in the marketplace with brand names, symbols, and distinctive packaging. Almost every product that is distinguishable from another gives buyers some means of identifying it.

Sunkist Growers, for instance, stamps its oranges with the name Sunkist. Iams stamps a paw print on all of its pet food packages. For nearly 100 years, Prudential Insurance Co. has used the Rock of Gibraltar as its symbol. Choosing how to identify the firm's output represents a major strategic decision for marketers.

4

Discuss how companies develop strong identities for their products and brands.

Brand Names and Brand Marks

What's in a name? According to researchers, a name plays a central role in establishing brand and product identity. The American Marketing Association defines a **brand name** as the part of the brand consisting of words or letters that form a name that identifies and distinguishes the firm's offerings from those of its competitors. The brand name is, therefore, the part of the brand that people can vocalize. Firms can also identify their brands by brand marks. A *brand mark* is a symbol or pictorial design that distinguishes a product. In Figure 12.6, "French's" is the brand name of the mustard; the red flag and white lettering are the brand mark that distinguish this mustard from those made by other companies.

Effective brand names are easy to pronounce, recognize, and remember. Short names, such as Nike, Ford, and Bounty, meet these requirements. Marketers try to overcome problems with easily mispronounced brand names by teaching consumers the correct pronunciations. For example, early advertisements for the Korean car maker Hyundai explained that the name rhymes with *Sunday*.

A brand name should also give buyers the correct connotation of the product's image. The name Lunchables for Oscar Mayer's prepackaged lunches suggests a convenient meal that can be eaten anywhere. Discover suggests a credit card that allows treasure hunting. Chevy's Trail Blazer represents adventure and ruggedness.

A brand name must also qualify for legal protection. The Lanham Act of 1946 states that registered trademarks must not contain words or phrases in general use, such as *automobile* or *suntan lotion*. These generic words actually describe particular types of products, and no company can claim exclusive rights to them.

Marketers feel increasingly hard-pressed to coin effective brand names, as multitudes of competitors rush to stake out brand names for their own products. Some companies register names before they have products to fit the names in order to stop competitors from using them.

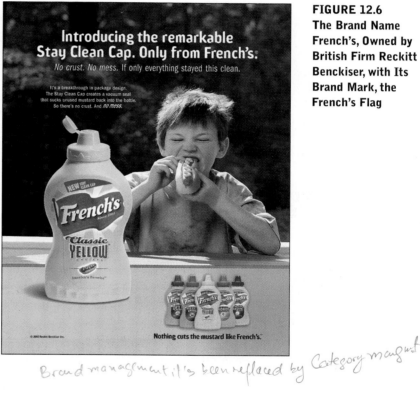

Introducing the remarkable
Stay Clean Cap. Only from French's.
No crust. No mess. If only everything stayed this clean.

It's a breakthrough in package design.
The Stay Clean Cap creates a vacuum seal
that sucks unused mustard back into the bottle.
So there's no crust. And *no mess.*

NEW STAY CLEAN CAP
French's Since 1904
Classic
YELLOW
MUSTARD
America's Favorite™

Nothing cuts the mustard like French's.™

FIGURE 12.6
The Brand Name French's, Owned by British Firm Reckitt Benckiser, with Its Brand Mark, the French's Flag

Brand management it's been replaced by Category mangmt

When a class of products becomes generally known by the original brand name of a specific offering, the brand name may become a descriptive generic name. If this occurs, the original owner loses exclusive claim to the brand name. The generic names nylon, aspirin, escalator, kerosene, and zipper started as brand names. Other generic names that were once brand names include cola, yo-yo, linoleum, and shredded wheat.

Marketers must distinguish between brand names that have become legally generic terms and those that seem generic only in many consumers' eyes. Consumers often adopt legal brand names as descriptive names. Jell-O, for instance, is a brand name owned exclusively by

Marketing Dictionary

category management Product management system in which a category manager—with profit and loss responsibility—oversees a product line.

brand name Part of a brand consisting of words or letters that form a name that identifies and distinguishes a firm's offerings from those of its competitors.

'net Ex

Leveraging a brand name. Visit the Web site of John Deere & Co. (http://www.deere.com) and Harley-Davidson (http://www.h-d.com) and list several ways in which both companies are attempting to leverage their brand names.

General Foods, but many consumers casually apply it as a descriptive name for gelatin desserts. Similarly, many people use the term Kleenex to refer to facial tissues. English and Australian consumers use the brand name Hoover as a verb for vacuuming. Xerox is such a well-known brand name that people frequently—though incorrectly—use it as a verb to mean photocopying. To protect its valuable trademark, Xerox Corp. has created advertisements explaining that Xerox is a brand name and registered trademark and should not be used as a verb.

Trademarks

Businesses invest considerable resources in developing and promoting brands and brand identities. The high value of brand equity encourages firms to take steps in protecting the expenditures they invest in their brands.

A **trademark** is a brand for which the owner claims exclusive legal protection. A trademark should not be confused with a trade name, which identifies a company. The Coca-Cola Company is a trade name, but Coke is a trademark of the company. Some trade names duplicate companies' brand names. For example, Stride Rite is the children's shoe brand name of Stride Rite Corporation.

Protecting Trademarks

Trademark protection confers the exclusive legal right to use a brand name, brand mark, and any slogan or product name abbreviation. It designates the origin or source of a good or service. The multicolored butterfly for MSN shown in Figure 12.7 is a trademarked symbol.

Frequently, trademark protection is applied to words or phrases, such as *Bud* for Budweiser or *the Met* for the New York Metropolitan Opera. For example, the courts upheld Budweiser's trademark in one case, ruling that an exterminating company's slogan "This Bug's for You" infringed on Budweiser's rights.

FIGURE 12.7 The Butterfly Trademark Used by MSN

Firms can also receive trademark protection for packaging elements and product features such as shape, design, and typeface. U.S. law has fortified trademark protection in recent years. The Federal Trademark Dilution Act of 1995 gives a trademark holder the right to sue for trademark infringement even if other products using its brand are not particularly similar or easily confused in the minds of consumers. The infringing company does not even have to know that it is diluting another's trademark. The act also gives a trademark holder the right to sue if another party imitates its trademark.

The Internet may be the next battlefield for trademark infringement cases. Some companies are attempting to protect their trademarks by filing infringement cases against companies using similar Internet addresses.

Trade Dress *Read*

Visual cues used in branding create an overall look sometimes referred to as *trade dress*. These visual components may be related to color selections, sizes, package and label shapes, and similar factors. For example, McDonald's golden arches, Merrill Lynch's bull, and the yellow of Shell's seashell are all part of these products' trade dress. A combination of visual cues may also constitute trade dress. Consider a Mexican food product that uses the colors of the Mexican flag: green, white, and red. The leaping jaguar figure that adorns the front of a Jaguar as well as brand name is part of the trade dress for Jaguar cars.

Trade dress disputes have led to numerous courtroom battles. In one widely publicized case, Kendall-Jackson Vineyards and Winery sued Ernest & Julio Gallo Winery Inc., claiming that the bottle design used for Gallo's Turning Leaf Chardonnay was too similar to its Kendall's Vintner's Reserve chardonnay bottle. Kendall-Jackson lost in court, but this case suggests the importance that firms assign to trade dress.[12]

Developing Global Brand Names and Trademarks

International marketers face a particularly acute problem in selecting brand names and trademarks; an excellent brand name or symbol in one country may prove disastrous in another. Iranian detergent producer Paxan Corp., for example, might have a hard time marketing its laundry detergent Barf to English-speaking countries. (In Iran, *barf* means "snow.")[13] A firm marketing a product in multiple countries must also decide whether to use a single brand name for universal promotions or tailor names to individual countries. Yum! Brands has decided its name speaks for itself everywhere as the "Marketing Hits" box describes. Most languages contain *o* and *k* sounds, so *okay* has become an international word. Most languages also have a short *a*; so Coca-Cola, Kodak, and Texaco work as effective brands abroad. Figure 12.8 shows the most popular global brand names, as reported by marketing research company ACNielsen.

Trademarks that are effective in their home countries may do less well in other cultures. Perhaps the world's most dubious brand name at the moment is attached to a line of clothing recently launched by one of Osama bin Laden's relatives, Yeslam Binladin. Yeslam Binladin applied for trademark protection for the "Bin Ladin" clothing label in Switzerland several months before the tragedies of September 11, 2001. In spite of the events, he decided to push ahead with his line. Yeslam is from a

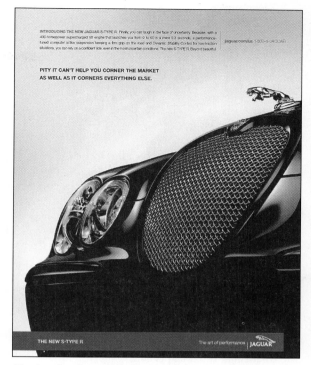

The leaping jaguar figure is part of Jaguar's distinctive and distinguished trade dress.

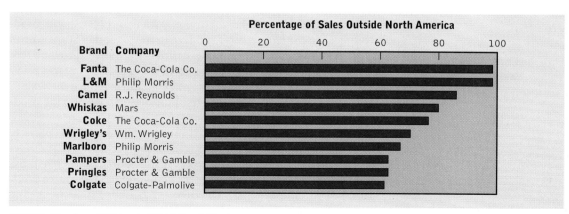

SOURCE: Data from ACNielsen in "Which Brands Travel Best?" *Time,* November 26, 2001, p. B10.

FIGURE 12.8
The World's Most Popular Brands

Marketing Dictionary

trademark   Brand for which the owner claims exclusive legal protection.

Yum! Creates Customer Mania

Background. Developing a global brand takes skill, creativity, energy, and guts—along with experience and understanding of local customers and preferences. Yum! Brands Inc. believes its employees have all of those qualities, regardless of which of the company's restaurants they work for—Kentucky Fried Chicken, Pizza Hut, Taco Bell, Long John Silver's, or A&W All American Food.

The Challenge. A difficult economy, the war with Iraq, and the 9/11 terrorist attacks all contributed to flat or sluggish sales at restaurants. So marketers at Yum! Brands, which used to be called Tricon, began looking for ways to strengthen and grow its brands together internationally.

The Strategy. Despite an uncertain business environment, Yum! Brands continued to open more restaurants around the world. Currently, it operates about 33,000 in more than 100 countries, making it the largest restaurant company in the world. Recently, the company launched a major marketing effort involving nearly all of its workers. Called Customer Mania, more than 725,000 employees—known as Customer Maniacs— are being trained to enhance every customer's restaurant experience, from food quality to excellent service. In addition, the change of name from Tricon to Yum! Brands "reflects the unique fun and recognition culture we are driving across our global company." Company marketers want every customer to think "Yum!" after a visit to one of its restaurants, whether in Tokyo or Topeka. The acquisition of restaurant chains Long John Silver's and A&W All-American Food—which often operate under the same roof—has allowed the company to grow its

continued on next page

different branch of the family (the surnames are spelled slightly differently), and the Saudi family is well respected in the Middle East, where it controls a $5 billion construction conglomerate, the Saudi Binladin Group. So Yeslam hopes to counteract negative impressions of the Bin Ladin brand name with a positive one. The clothing line will appear first in the Arab world, then in Europe, and much later in the U.S. Yeslam wants to donate a portion of the profits from the clothing line to a charitable foundation in Switzerland. Gaining worldwide acceptance for the label will be an uphill battle. "It's not that the sins of the fathers should fall on the shoulders of the children, or that one brother should be blamed for the actions of another," explains Mario Boselli, head of Italy's fashion trade organization. "But I can't see how someone could ever try to exploit this type of notoriety."[14]

Packaging

is a product decision, purpose to protect the product but it does a lot more than that.

A firm's product strategy must address questions about packaging. Like its brand name, a product's package can powerfully influence buyers' purchase decisions.

Firms are applying increasingly scientific methods to their packaging decisions. Rather than experimenting with physical models or drawings, more and more package designers work on special computer graphics that create three-dimensional images of packages in thousands of colors, shapes, and typefaces. Another computer system helps firms design effective packaging by simulating the displays shoppers see when they walk down supermarket aisles. Companies conduct marketing research to evaluate current packages and to test alternative package designs. Kellogg, for example, tested its Nutri-Grain cereal package—as well as the product itself—before launching the product into the market.

A package serves three major objectives: (1) protection against damage, spoilage, and pilferage; (2) assistance in marketing the product; and (3) cost effectiveness. Let's briefly consider each of these objectives.

Protection against Damage, Spoilage, and Pilferage

The original objective of packaging was to offer physical protection for the merchandise. Products typically pass through several stages of handling between manufacturing and customer purchases, and a package must protect the contents from damage. Furthermore, packages of perishable products must protect the contents against spoilage in transit and in storage until purchased by the consumer. The American Plastics Council developed an advertising campaign to promote the benefits of using plastics in food packaging, asserting that plastic bottles, wraps, and containers reduce the chance of food contamination and that tamper-resistant plastic seals provide product safety assurance.

Fears of product tampering have forced many firms to improve package designs. Over-the-counter medicines are sold in tamper-resistant packages covered with warnings informing consumers to not purchase merchandise without protective seals intact. Many grocery items and light-sensitive products are packaged in tamper-resistant containers as well. Products in glass jars, like spaghetti sauce and jams, often come with vacuum-depressed buttons in the lids that pop up the first time the lids are opened.

Likewise, many packages offer important safeguards for retailers against pilferage. Shoplifting and employee theft cost retailers several billion dollars each year. To limit this activity, many packages feature oversized cardboard backings too large to fit into a shoplifter's pocket or purse. Efficient packaging that protects against damage, spoilage, and theft is especially important for international marketers, who must contend with varying climatic conditions and the added time and stress involved in overseas shipping.

Assistance in Marketing the Product

The proliferation of new products, changes in consumer lifestyles and buying habits, and marketers' emphasis on targeting smaller market segments have increased the importance of packaging as a promotional tool. Many firms are addressing consumer concerns about protecting the environment by designing packages with minimal amounts of biodegradable and recyclable materials. To demonstrate serious concern regarding environmental protection, Procter & Gamble, Coors, McDonald's, BP Chemical, and other firms have created ads that describe their efforts in developing environmentally sound packaging.

In a grocery store where thousands of different items compete for notice, a product must capture the shopper's attention. Marketers combine colors, sizes, shapes, graphics, and typefaces to establish distinctive trade dress that sets their products apart from the products of their competitors. Packaging can help to establish a common identity for a group of items sold under the same brand name. Like the brand name, a package should evoke the product's image and communicate its value. Some companies patent their package designs, which may play crucial roles in consumers' brand insistence.

Packages can also enhance convenience for the buyers. Pump dispenser cans, for example, facilitate the use of products ranging from mustard to insect repellent. Squeezable bottles of honey and ketchup make the products easier to use and store. Packaging provides key benefits for convenience foods such as meals and snacks packaged in microwavable containers, juice drinks in aseptic packages, and frozen entrees and vegetables packaged in single-serving portions. Beverage manufacturers have gone to great lengths to accommodate the needs of consumers. First, scientists videotaped consumers drinking from bottles, then made plaster molds of their hands. Researchers discovered that an average gulp took in 6.44 ounces of fluid and that half the people studied would rather sip liquid through a pop-up top than guzzle it from an open container. The results are new, sleeker, hourglass-shaped bottles that are easy to grip and drink from. Within six months of introducing its new bottles, Gatorade saw a 25 percent jump in sales. "We think of our bottles as sports equipment," explains a Gatorade marketing manager. Other beverage producers, including Dannon, Nestlé, and Snapple, have developed similar, ergonomically designed bottles; these companies claim a double-digit increase in sales, as well.[15]

Some firms increase consumer utility with packages designed for reuse. Empty peanut butter jars and jelly jars have long doubled as drinking glasses. Parents can buy bubble bath in animal-shaped plastic bottles suitable for bathtub play. Packaging is a major component in Avon's overall marketing strategy. The firm's decorative, reusable bottles have even become collectibles.

Cost-Effective Packaging

Although packaging must perform a number of functions for the producer, marketers, and consumers, it must do so at a reasonable cost. Sometimes changes in the packaging can make packages both cheaper and better for the environment. Compact disc manufacturers, for instance, once packaged music CDs in two containers, a disk-sized plastic box inside a long, cardboard box that fit into the record bins in the stores. Consumers protested against the waste of the long boxes, and the recording industry finally agreed to eliminate the cardboard outer packaging altogether. Now CDs come in just the plastic cases, and stores display them in reusable plastic holders to discourage theft.

Labeling

Labels were once a separate element that was applied to a package; today, it is an integral part of a typical package. Labels perform both promotional and informational functions. A **label** carries an item's brand name or symbol, the name and address of the manufacturer or distributor, information about the product's composition and size, and recommended uses. The right label can play an important role in attracting consumer attention and encouraging purchase.

Consumer confusion and dissatisfaction over such incomprehensible descriptions as giant economy size, king size, and family size led to the passage of the Fair Packaging and Labeling Act in 1966. The act requires that a label offer adequate information concerning the package contents and that a package design facilitate value comparisons among competing products.

The Nutrition Labeling and Education Act of 1990 imposes a uniform format in which food manufacturers must disclose nutritional information about their products. In addition, the Food and Drug Administration (FDA) has mandated design standards for nutritional labels that provide clear guidelines to consumers about food products. The FDA has also tightened definitions for loosely used terms like light, fat free, lean, and extra lean, and it mandates that labels list the amounts of fat, sodium, dietary fiber, calcium, vitamins, and other components in typical servings. The fast-food industry has long been plagued with labeling challenges. Not long ago, McDonald's faced a new one. For over a decade, the company has advertised that its famous french fries were cooked in "100 percent vegetable oil." However, in a recent statement, the company admitted that some additional flavoring used in the fries contains "a miniscule amount of beef extract." Several consumers who are vegetarians subsequently filed suit against the company in Seattle, alleging that McDonald's had engaged in deceptive marketing practices in its labeling. The lawsuit sought financial compensation and class-action status for all vegetarian consumers who have eaten McDonald's fries since 1990 thinking that they were receiving nonanimal foods.[16]

Labeling requirements differ elsewhere in the world. In Canada, for example, labels must give information in both French and English. The type and amount of information required on labels also varies among nations. International marketers must carefully design labels to conform to the regulations of each country in which they operate and market their merchandise.

The *Universal Product Code (UPC)* designation is another very important aspect of a label or package. Introduced in 1974 as a method for cutting expenses in the supermarket industry, UPCs are numerical bar codes printed on packages. Optical scanner systems read these codes, and computer systems recognize items and print their prices on cash register receipts. Virtually all packaged grocery items carry the UPC bars. While UPC scanners are costly, they permit both considerable labor savings over manual pricing and improved inventory control. The Universal Product Code is also a major asset for marketing research. However, many consumers feel frustrated when only a UPC is placed on a package without an additional price tag, because they do not always know how much an item costs if the price labels are knocked off the shelf.

Co-Branding and Co-Marketing

Co-branding joins together two strong brand names, perhaps owned by two different companies, to sell a product. The automotive world is packed with co-branded vehicles. A quick tour of car dealerships would reveal The North Face edition of the Chevy Avalanche, the Eddie Bauer edition of the Ford Explorer, the Lexus special Coach edition of the ES 300 sedan, and even the Bugs Bunny Chevrolet Venture minivan, complete with video screen. Subaru of America has also teamed up with L.L. Bean Inc. in a multiyear co-branding agreement that makes Subaru the official car of the outdoor retail giant, featured at L.L. Bean stores and in its catalogs. For its part, L.L. Bean has become the official outfitter to Subaru, which will sell Bean's outdoor clothing with Subaru branding at Subaru auto dealerships. Subaru currently sponsors events such as the Subaru Gorge Games in Oregon, in which L.L. Bean will participate. "L.L. Bean is a natural partner for Subaru, as both companies provide outdoor enthusiasts with products that enhance their lives," says Bill Cyphers, vice president for marketing at Subaru.[17]

In a co-marketing effort, two organizations join together to sell their products in an allied marketing campaign. Perhaps you've seen a Reebok logo on a college campus scoreboard or stopped in at the Burger King booth at the campus food court. More and more schools are forming co-marketing relationships with commercial firms, including brands such as Nike, Powerade, Coca-Cola, Fidelity Investments, and Barnes & Noble. The University of Massachusetts even has a relationship with the Boston Celtics. Although these relationships are becoming increasingly common, it has been a decade since Boston University opened a food court with vendors such as Burger King and Starbucks, and negotiated with Barnes & Noble to add the bookseller's logo to the name of the Boston University bookstores. Both the food court—whose revenues doubled from $2.5 million to $5.2 million in one year—and the bookstore have been huge successes. The practice has its critics, but so far students seem to appreciate having access to the brands they like.[18]

Brand Extensions

Some brands become so popular that companies carry these products over to unrelated products in pursuit of marketing advantages. The strategy of attaching a popular brand name to a new product in an unrelated product category is known as **brand extension.** Readers should not confuse this practice with *line extensions,* which refers to new sizes, styles, or related products. A brand extension, in contrast, carries over from one product nothing but the brand name. In establishing brand extensions, companies hope to gain access to new customers and markets by building on the equity already established in their existing brands.

The Bic brand of ballpoint pens became popular, after which the late French entrepreneur Marcel Bich launched his successful line of Bic disposable razors and Bic utility lighters. But brand extensions run considerable risk of brand dilution, as Bich discovered. Brand dilution occurs when a firm introduces too many brand extensions, some of which might not succeed. You've probably never even heard of "fannyhose," a Bic brand of hosiery launched in the 1970s, or Bic sailboards. But Bich's biggest blunder was probably Parfum Bic, a drugstore fragrance introduced in 1989 with a $20 million marketing campaign. The perfume sat on the shelves for so long that Bich finally pulled it out of the stores a year later, taking an $11 million loss.[19]

Brand Licensing

A growing number of firms have authorized other companies to use their brand names. This practice, known as *brand licensing,* expands a firm's exposure in the marketplace, much as a brand extension does. The brand name's owner also receives an extra source of income in the form of royalties from licensees, typically from 4 to 8 percent of wholesale revenues.

Major League Baseball has long been engaged in successful brand licensing. Hats, trading cards, and electronic games—not to mention baseballs, bats, and gloves with the MLB logo—have all been popular at retail outlets. Rawlings makes the baseballs, Russell Athletic and Majestic Apparel make clothing, Topps produces trading cards, and New Era puts out headwear. Altogether there are about 20 top licensees currently working with the MLB organization.[20]

Brand experts note several potential problems with licensing, however. Brand names do not transfer well to all products. If a licensee produces a poor-quality product or an item ethically incompatible with the original brand, the arrangement could damage the reputation of the brand.

New Product Planning

As its offerings enter the maturity and decline stages of the product life cycle, a firm must add new items to continue to prosper. Regular additions of new products to the firm's line helps to protect it from product obsolescence.

New products are the lifeblood of any business, and survival depends on a steady flow of new entries. Some new products may implement major technological breakthroughs.

Marketing Dictionary

label   Branding component that carries an item's brand name or symbol, the name and address of the manufacturer or distributor, information about the product, and recommended uses.

brand extension   Strategy of attaching a popular brand name to a new product in an unrelated product category.

Opinion lea [handwritten]

right wrong   Solving an Ethical Controversy

Whose Idea Is It Anyway?

History is filled with stories of people who invented today's essential products without ever getting credit—figuratively or literally—for their ideas. Charles Babbage is now generally credited with coming up with the modern computer, but he didn't die a celebrity or a millionaire. Tim Berners-Lee invented HyperText Transport Protocol (HTTP), the telecommunications protocol that made it possible for the World Wide Web to be constructed over the Internet. Although he takes credit for the invention, his slice of the financial pie is minuscule. Then there's Douglas Engelbart, who came up with the computer mouse as well as the first Windows-type software in the 1950s and 1960s while working for McDonnell Douglas. He received an honorarium of $10,000 for his mouse idea when the patent expired in 1984.

Should inventors receive greater compensation for their ideas, especially when their inventions catch on decades later?

PRO

1. Inventors such as those described deserve much greater compensation than they have received because their ideas have created so much wealth for others.

2. Many experts believe that ideas now drive our economy—and they should be compensated for them.

CON

1. There is no way to know if or when a new idea will catch on—if every inventor were compensated like a millionaire, companies could not stay in business.
2. Companies are the ones that actually make the financial outlay to bring products to market, so they—not individual inventors—should be able to dictate compensation.

Summary

Many companies as well as universities still have policies that prohibit inventors from commercializing their ideas and striking it rich on their own. Venture capitalist Ira Ehrenpreis of Technology Partners stands firm: "Ideas aren't proprietary. Execution is." But inventors, many of whom are maverick souls anyway, may revolt against such policies. If they go on "strike," a lack of new products may force companies to open their pocketbooks a little more generously.

SOURCES: "Douglas Carl Engelbart," *Bootstrap Alliance*, http://www.bootstrap.org, accessed January 15, 2003; "The Electronic Labyrinth: Douglas Engelbart," Institute for the Advanced Technology in the Humanities, University of Virginia, http://www.iath.virginia.edu, accessed January 10, 2003; Richard Todd, "The Man Who Didn't Get Rich," *Worth*, May 2001, pp. 96–101, 127.

Cannibalize is when v open to many store one Product taking away from another Product. [handwritten]

Other new products simply extend existing product lines. In other words, a new product is one that either the company or the customer has not handled before. Only about 10 percent of new product introductions bring truly new capabilities to people who are completely unfamiliar with them. But who should get credit for product innovations? The "Solving an Ethical Controversy" box discusses this issue.

Product Development Strategies

5

Describe the strategies for new product development.

A firm's strategy for new product development varies according to its existing product mix and the match between current offerings and the firm's overall marketing objectives. The current market positions of products also affect product development strategy. Figure 12.9 identifies four alternative development strategies: market penetration, market development, product development, and product diversification.

A *market penetration strategy* seeks to increase sales of existing products in existing markets. Firms can attempt to extend their penetration of markets in several ways. They may modify products, improve product quality, or promote new and different ways to use products. Packaged goods marketers often pursue this strategy to boost market share for mature products in mature markets. Product positioning often plays a major role in such a strategy.

Product positioning refers to consumers' perceptions of a product's attributes, uses, quality, and advantages and disadvantages relative to competing brands. Marketers often conduct marketing research studies to analyze consumer preferences and to construct product positioning maps that plot their products' positions in relation to those of competitors' offerings.

A *market development strategy* concentrates on finding new markets for existing products. Market segmentation, discussed in Chapter 8, provides useful support for such an effort. Bank of America has succeeded in developing a new market by targeting Asian residents in San Francisco with special television commercials aimed at Chinese, Koreans, and Vietnamese consumers. Mott's Inc. has focused on building loyal customers among Asian Americans, particularly for its Mott's Juice, Hawaiian Punch, and Clamato juice drinks.[21]

The strategy of *product development* refers to the introduction of new products into identifiable or established markets. A few years ago, Nike decided to enter the golf market by creating a new division called Nike Golf and introducing its first new golf products—branded golf balls. Although the company stumbled at first by targeting casual and budget-oriented players, the firm's marketers quickly changed gears and went after more skilled players who were willing to purchase premium balls. Today, Nike Golf lays claim to somewhere between 8 and 10 percent of the entire golf ball market of $800 million. With that success, the company decided to introduce its golf clubs, which it spent two years developing. Nike began by offering drivers, and later introduced a complete range of clubs.[22]

Firms may choose to introduce new products into markets in which they have already established positions to try to increase overall market share. These new offerings are called *flanker brands*. Smucker's flanks its famous jams and jellies with dessert products such as its Magic Shell toppings, illustrated in Figure 12.10.

Finally, a *product diversification strategy* focuses on developing entirely new products for new markets. Some firms look for new target markets that complement their existing markets; others look in completely new directions. The Sara Lee Corporation doesn't just sell pound cakes and other desserts. The company has grown so diversified that it offers a vast array of branded products, from Wonderbras to Kiwi shoe polish to Endust furniture polish and Chock Full O' Nuts coffee. However, the firm had become so fragmented over the years that one of the first moves CEO C. Steven McMillan made when he took over was to sell off disparate brands, vowing to concentrate on its core businesses: food, underwear, and household products.[23]

Marketers need to consider *cannibalization* in picking a new product strategy. Any firm wants to avoid investing resources in a new product introduction that will adversely affect sales of existing products. A product that takes sales from another offering in the same product line is said to cannibalize that line. A firm can accept some loss of sales from existing products if the new offering will generate sufficient additional sales to warrant the firm's investment in its development and market introduction.

**FIGURE 12.9
Alternative Product Development Strategies**

	Old Product	**New Product**
Old Market	Market Penetration	Product Development
New Market	Market Development	Product Diversification

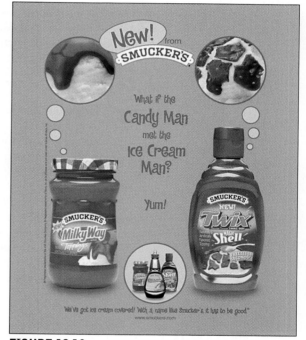

**FIGURE 12.10
From Jellies to Ice Cream Toppings: Smucker's Promotes Flanker Brands**

6

Describe the consumer adoption process.

The Consumer Adoption Process

Consumer purchases also influence decisions regarding a new product offering. In the **adoption process,** consumers go through a series of stages from learning about the new product to

Marketing Dictionary

adoption process   Stages that consumers go through in learning about a new product, trying it, and deciding whether to purchase it again.

trying it and deciding whether to purchase it regularly or to reject it. These stages in the consumer adoption process can be classified as the following:

1. *Awareness.* Individuals first learn of the new product, but they lack full information about it.
2. *Interest.* Potential buyers begin to seek information about it.
3. *Evaluation.* They consider the likely benefits of the product.
4. *Trial.* They make trial purchases to determine its usefulness.
5. *Adoption/Rejection.* If the trial purchase produces satisfactory results, they decide to use the product regularly.[24]

Marketers must understand the adoption process to move potential consumers to the adoption stage. Once marketers recognize a large number of consumers at the interest stage, they can take steps to stimulate sales by moving these buyers through the evaluation and trial stages. Johnson & Johnson enhanced the evaluation and trial of its disposable contact lenses by offering free trial pairs to consumers. Time Warner's America Online mails its Internet-access software and offers a free one-month membership to computer owners who are not AOL members. From time to time you may receive free samples of breakfast cereals, snack foods, cosmetics, or shampoos in the mail. These companies are encouraging you to try their products in the hope that you will eventually adopt these products.

Adopter Categories

Consumer innovators are people who purchase new products almost as soon as these products reach the market. Other adopters wait for additional information and rely on the experiences of initial buyers before making trial purchases. Consumer innovators welcome innovations in each product area. Some computer users, for instance, rush to install new software immediately after each update becomes available. Some physicians, as well, pioneered the uses of new pharmaceutical products for their AIDS patients. Some fans bought season tickets before the NFL Browns came back to Cleveland.

A number of studies about the adoption of new products have identified five categories of purchasers based on relative times of adoption. These categories, shown in Figure 12.11, are consumer innovators, early adopters, early majority, late majority, and laggards.

The *diffusion process* brings acceptance of new goods and services by the members of the community or social system. Figure 12.11 shows a normal distribution over the course of this process. A few people adopt at first, then the number of adopters increases rapidly as the value of the innovation

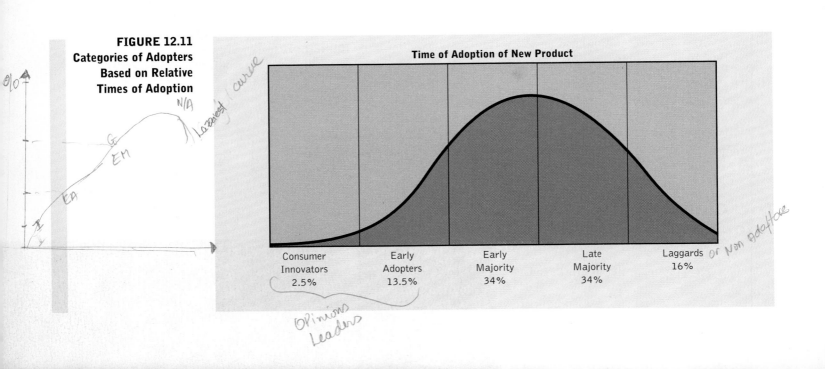

FIGURE 12.11
Categories of Adopters Based on Relative Times of Adoption

Time of Adoption of New Product

| Consumer Innovators 2.5% | Early Adopters 13.5% | Early Majority 34% | Late Majority 34% | Laggards 16% |

becomes apparent. The adoption rate finally diminishes as the number of potential consumers who have not adopted, or purchased, the product diminishes. Typically, innovators make up the first 2.5 percent of buyers who adopt the new product; laggards are the last 16 percent to do so. Figure 12.11 excludes those who never adopt the innovation.

Identifying Early Adopters

It's no surprise that identifying consumers or organizations who are most likely to try a new product can be vital to a product's success. By reaching these buyers early in the product's development or introduction, marketers can treat these adopters as a test market, evaluating the product and discovering suggestions for modifications. Since early purchasers often act as opinion leaders from whom others seek advice, their attitudes toward new products quickly spread to others. Acceptance or rejection of the innovation by these purchasers can help forecast its expected success. Several auto companies, including Honda and Ford, have developed gasoline-electric vehicles for the consumer market. These hybrid vehicles use a combination of gasoline and electric batteries to get superior gas mileage and send fewer exhaust emissions into the air. But although Honda and Ford got their vehicles to market first, Toyota tried an entirely different marketing approach in attempting to gain a competitive edge anyway. While Honda and Ford targeted environmentalists and consumers who are concerned about clean air, Toyota aimed its first promotional efforts at consumer innovators and early adopters. The ads for its new Prius mentioned its environmentally friendly features, but they focused on consumers who wanted to be the first on their block to have one of these unique cars.[25]

A large number of studies have established the general characteristics of first adopters. These pioneers tend to be younger, have higher social status, are better educated, and enjoy higher incomes than other consumers. They are more mobile than later adopters and change both their jobs and addresses more often. They also rely more heavily than later adopters on impersonal information sources; more hesitant buyers depend primarily on company-generated promotional information and word-of-mouth communications.

Rate of Adoption Determinants

Frisbees progressed from the product introduction stage to the market maturity stage in a period of six months. By contrast, the U.S. Department of Agriculture tried for 13 years to convince corn farmers to use hybrid seed corn, an innovation capable of doubling crop yields. Five characteristics of a product innovation influence its adoption rate:

1. *Relative advantage.* An innovation that appears far superior to previous ideas offers a greater relative advantage—reflected in terms of lower price, physical improvements, or ease of use—and increases the product's adoption rate.

2. *Compatibility.* An innovation consistent with the values and experiences of potential adopters attracts new buyers at a relatively rapid rate. Investors who are already comfortable with making transactions online would probably be attracted to Lycos's LiveCharts, which offers live, real-time streaming charts showing the activity of stocks.

3. *Complexity.* The relative difficulty of understanding the innovation influences the speed of acceptance. In most cases, consumers move slowly in adopting new products that they find difficult to understand or use. Farmers' cautious acceptance of hybrid seed corn illustrates how long an adoption can take.

4. *Possibility of trial use.* An initial free or discounted trial of a good or service means that adopters can reduce their risk of financial or social loss when they try the product. A coupon for a free item or a free night's stay at a hotel can accelerate the rate of adoption.

Marketing Dictionary

consumer innovators   People who purchase new products almost as soon as the products reach the market.

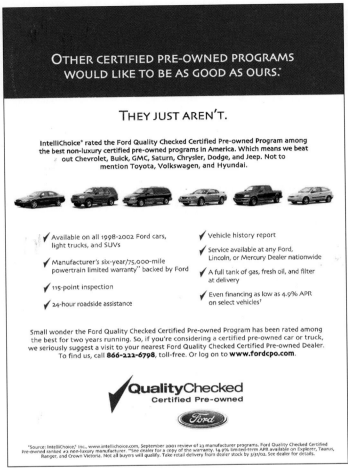

FIGURE 12.12
Ford: Focusing on Observability through a Quality Checklist

5. *Observability.* If potential buyers can observe an innovation's superiority in a tangible form, the adoption rate increases. In-store demonstrations or even advertisements that focus on the superiority of a product, like the one for Ford's Quality Checked Pre-owned Program in Figure 12.12, can encourage buyers to adopt a product.

Marketers who want to accelerate the rate of adoption can manipulate these five characteristics at least to some extent. An informative promotional message about a new allergy drug could help consumers overcome their hesitation in adopting this complex product. Effective product design can emphasize a product's advantages over the competition. Everyone likes to receive something for free, so giving away small samples of a new product lets consumers try it at little or no risk. In-home demonstrations or trial home placements of items such as furniture or carpeting can achieve similar results. Marketers must also make positive attempts in ensuring the innovation's compatibility with adopters' value systems.

Organizing for New Product Development

A firm needs to be organized in such a way that its personnel can stimulate and coordinate new product development. Some companies contract with independent design firms to develop new products. Many assign product-innovation functions to one or more of the following entities: new product committees, new product departments, product managers, and venture teams.

New Product Committees

The most common organizational arrangement for activities in developing a new product is to center these functions in a new product committee. This group typically brings together experts in such areas as marketing, finance, manufacturing, engineering, research, and accounting. Committee members spend less time conceiving and developing their own new product ideas than reviewing and approving new product plans that arise elsewhere in the organization. The committee might review ideas from the engineering and design staff, or perhaps from marketers and salespeople who are in constant contact with customers.

Since members of a new product committee hold important jobs in the firm's functional areas, their support for any new product plan likely foreshadows approval for further development. However, new product committees in large companies tend to reach decisions slowly and maintain conservative views. Sometimes members may compromise so they can return to their regular responsibilities.

New Product Departments

Many companies establish separate, formally organized departments to generate and refine new product ideas. The departmental structure overcomes the limitations of the new product committee system and encourages innovation as a permanent, full-time activity. The new product department is responsible for all phases of a development project within the firm, including screening decisions, developing product specifications, and coordinating product testing. The head of the department wields substantial authority and typically reports to the chief executive officer, chief operating officer, or a top marketing executive.

Product Managers

A *product manager* is another term for a brand manager, a function mentioned earlier in the chapter. This marketing professional supports the marketing strategies of an individual product or product line. Procter & Gamble, for instance, assigned its first product manager in 1927, when it made one person responsible for Camay soap.

Product managers set prices, develop advertising and sales promotion programs, and work with sales representatives in the field. In a company that markets multiple products, product managers fulfill key functions in the marketing department. They provide individual attention for each product and support and coordinate efforts of the firm's sales force, marketing research department, and advertising department. Product managers often lead new product development programs, including creation of new product ideas and recommendations for improving existing products.

However, as mentioned earlier in the chapter, companies such as Procter & Gamble and General Mills have either modified the product manager structure or done away with it altogether in favor of a category management structure, based on small teams. Category managers have profit and loss responsibility, which is not characteristic of the product management system. This change has largely come about because of customer preference, but it can also benefit a manufacturer by avoiding duplication of some jobs and competition among the company's own brands and its managers.

Venture Teams

A *venture team* gathers a group of specialists from different areas of an organization to work together in developing new products. The venture team must meet criteria for return on investment, uniqueness of product, serving a well-defined need, compatibility of the product with existing technology, and strength of patent protection. Although the organization sets up the venture team as a temporary entity, its flexible life span may extend over a number of years. When purchases confirm the commercial potential of a new product, an existing division may take responsibility for that product, or it may serve as the nucleus of a new division within the company or of an entirely new company.

Some marketing organizations differentiate between venture teams and task forces. A new-product task force assembles an interdisciplinary group working on temporary assignment through their functional departments. Its basic activities center on coordinating and integrating the work of the firm's functional departments on a specific project.

Unlike a new product committee, a venture team does not disband after every meeting. Team members accept project assignments as major responsibilities, and the team exercises the authority it needs to both plan and implement a course of action. To stimulate product innovation, the venture team typically communicates directly with top management, but it functions as an entity separate from the basic organization.

The New-Product Development Process

Once a firm is organized for new product development, it can establish procedures for moving new product ideas to the marketplace. Developing a new product is often time-consuming, risky, and expensive. Usually, firms must generate dozens of new product ideas to produce even one successful product. In fact, the failure rate of new products averages 80 percent. Products fail for a number of reasons, including inadequate market assessments, lack of market orientation, poor screening and project evaluation, product defects, and inadequate launch efforts. And these blunders cost a bundle: firms invest nearly half of the total resources devoted to product innovation on products that become commercial failures.

A new product is more likely to become successful if the firm follows a six-step development process: (1) idea generation, (2) screening, (3) business analysis, (4) development, (5) test marketing, and (6) commercialization. Of course, each step requires decisions about whether to proceed further or abandon the project. And each step involves a greater financial investment.

Traditionally, most companies have developed new products through phased development, which follows the six-step process in an orderly sequence. Responsibility for each phase passes first from product planners to designers and engineers, to manufacturers, and finally to marketers. The phased

7

List the stages in the process for developing new products.

development method can work well for firms that dominate mature markets and can develop variations on existing products. But with rapid changes in technology and markets, many companies feel pressured to speed up the development process.

After a decade of flops and near-successes, several competitors—large and small—are racing to get their version of the "smart box" to consumers' televisions as fast as possible. Satellite companies have been developing receivers with hard drives so that digital movies and programs can be beamed right into subscribers' TV sets. Cable companies are fighting back with their own style of smart box. But it's the Moxi Digital software that has industry watchers watching even more closely. With Moxi, TV watchers can use a single remote to surf through galaxies of digital media feeds and capture whatever they want. "It's one box and one remote control, and no cables," boasts Moxi founder Steve Perlman. "That's a revolution!"[26]

This time pressure has encouraged many firms to implement parallel product development programs. These programs generally consist of teams with experts from design, manufacturing, marketing, and sales who carry out development projects from idea generation to commercialization. Venture teams, discussed earlier, follow this parallel development model. This method can reduce the time needed to develop products because team members work on the six steps concurrently rather than in sequence. Wyeth was able to bring its antidepressant Effexor to market in just two years—half the usual time it takes to develop and launch such a drug—by using such a team.[27]

Whether a firm pursues phased development or parallel product development, all phases can benefit from planning tools and scheduling methods such as the program evaluation and review technique (PERT) and the critical path method (CPM). These techniques, originally developed by the U.S. Navy in connection with construction of the Polaris missile and submarine, map out the sequence of each step in a process and show the time allotments for each activity. Detailed PERT and CPM flowcharts help marketers to coordinate all activities entailed in the development and introduction of new products.

In introducing its golf clubs described earlier in the chapter, Nike followed its own patented business strategy that included a systematic product introduction, extensive endorsement by golf tour professionals—including phenom Tiger Woods—and a new product budget of up to $100 million, with a $35 million marketing budget. Those numbers illustrate the importance of planning.[28]

Idea Generation

New product development begins with ideas from many sources: the sales force, suggestions from customers, research-and-development specialists, competing products, suppliers, retailers, and independent inventors. Some top executives are beginning to recognize the value of keeping their eyes, ears, and minds open to ideas from employees at all levels of the firm. Susan Lyne, president of ABC Entertainment, says, "My top priority is getting the younger, creative people at the network to feel comfortable speaking up. . . . We need to find the gaps in our schedule, identify categories of viewers that we're missing, and force everyone to address those needs as we read the material coming in."[29]

Screening

Screening separates ideas with commercial potential from those that cannot meet company objectives. Some organizations maintain checklists of development standards in determining whether a project should be abandoned or considered further. These checklists typically include such factors as product uniqueness, availability of raw materials, and the proposed product's compatibility with current product offerings, existing facilities, and present capabilities. The screening stage may also allow for open discussions of new product ideas among different parts of the organization.

Business Analysis

A product idea that survives the initial screening must then pass a thorough business analysis. This stage consists of assessing the new product's potential market, growth rate, and likely competitive strengths. Marketers must evaluate the compatibility of the proposed product with organizational resources.

[Handwritten marginalia:]

developing opt.
this fall in the most planning art
100 ideas
ideal generats
IG
(BS) Rough Screen 50 Rejected 50 accepted
(BA) Bus Analysis 85 Rejected 15 Accepted
(PCT) Product Concept Test
(D) Development
(TM) Test Marketing
Roll out or Commercializit.

PCT = definitely will buy
Probably " " "
May or may not buy
Probably will not buy
Definitely will not buy.

Concept testing subjects the product idea to additional study prior to its actual development. This important aspect of a new product's business analysis represents a marketing research project that attempts to measure consumer attitudes and perceptions about the new product idea. Focus groups and in-store polling can contribute effectively to concept testing. When Kolcraft Enterprises learned that its customers wanted a more rugged mode of transporting babies than the traditional baby stroller it had been manufacturing, the company actually licensed the Jeep brand name from DaimlerChrysler and came out with a heavy-duty stroller modeled after the parents' SUVs.[30]

The screening and business analysis stages generate extremely important information for new product development because they (1) define the proposed product's target market and customers' needs and wants and (2) determine the product's financial and technical requirements. Firms that are willing to invest money and time during these stages tend to be more successful at generating viable ideas and at creating successful products.

Development

Financial outlays increase substantially as a firm converts an idea into a physical product. The conversion process is the joint responsibility of the firm's development engineers, who turn the original concept into a product, and of its marketers, who provide feedback on consumer reactions to the product design, package, color, and other physical features. Many firms implement computer-aided design systems to streamline the development stage, and prototypes may go through numerous changes before the original mock-up reaches the stage of a final product.

Test Marketing

In Mrtg concept the consumer is the King - Here they'll have some Focus group at this stage and they'll have - Definitely'll buy -

As discussed in Chapter 7, many firms test market their new product offerings to gauge consumer reaction. After a company has developed a prototype, it may decide to test market it to gauge consumer reactions under normal conditions. Test marketing's purpose is to verify that the product will perform well in a real-life business environment. If the product does well, the company can proceed to commercialization. If it flops, the company can decide to fine-tune certain features and reintroduce it or pull the plug on the project altogether. Industries that rely heavily on test marketing are snack foods, automobiles, and movies. Of course, even if a product tests well and reaches the commercialization stage, it may still take a while to catch on with the general public, as has been the case of inventor Dean Kamen's Segway Human Transporter, a gyroscopic scooter that Kamen hopes will change individual transportation.[31]

Definitely'll buy'll pass the concept test.

Commercialization

When a new product idea reaches the commercialization stage, it is ready for full-scale marketing. Commercialization of a major new product can expose the firm to substantial expenses. It must establish marketing strategies, fund outlays for production facilities, and acquaint the sales force, marketing intermediaries, and potential customers with the new product.

When Nike was ready to launch its drivers, wedges, and irons, the company unveiled them at the PGA Merchandise Show in Orlando, Florida. Several golf pros, including John Cook, Michael Campbell, and David Duval used the clubs in successful tournament play. And Nike signed a multimillion-dollar endorsement deal with golf star Tiger Woods.[32] All of this was part of the commercialization process.

Product Safety and Liability

A product can fulfill its mission of satisfying consumer needs only if it ensures safe operation. Manufacturers must design their products to protect users from harm. Products that lead to injuries, either directly or indirectly, can have disastrous consequences for their makers. *Product liability* refers to the responsibility of manufacturers and marketers for injuries and damages caused by their products.

8

Discuss the relationship between product safety and product liability.

Chapter 3 discussed some of the major consumer protection laws that affect product safety. These laws include the Flammable Fabrics Act of 1953, the Fair Packaging and Labeling Act of 1966, the Poison Prevention Packaging Act of 1970, and the Consumer Product Safety Act of 1972.

Federal and state legislation play a major role in regulating product safety. The Poison Prevention Packaging Act requires drug manufacturers to place their products in packaging that is child resistant yet accessible to all adults, even ones who have trouble opening containers. The Consumer Product Safety Act created a powerful regulatory agency—the Consumer Product Safety Commission (CPSC). This agency has assumed jurisdiction over every consumer product category except food, automobiles, and a few other products already regulated by other agencies. The CPSC has the authority to ban products without court hearings, order recalls or redesigns of products, and inspect production facilities. It can charge managers of negligent companies with criminal offenses. The CPSC is especially watchful of products aimed at babies and young children. In one unanimous vote, the agency resolved to warn parents about potential safety problems with infant bath seats made by such companies as Safety 1st that could slip into the water or topple over if a child were to be left unattended.[33] In another case, the CPSC fined Costco $1.3 million in civil penalties to settle charges that the retailer had violated a federal law by failing to report hundreds of injuries and even a death related to its Options 5 high chair as well as several other defective products.[34]

The federal Food and Drug Administration (FDA) must approve food, medications, and health-related devices such as wheelchairs. The FDA can also take products off the market if concerns arise about the safety of these products.

The number of product liability lawsuits filed against manufacturers has skyrocketed in recent years. Although many such claims reach settlements out of court, juries have decided on many claims, sometimes awarding multimillion-dollar settlements. This threat has led most companies to step up efforts to ensure product safety. Safety warnings appear prominently on the labels of such potentially hazardous products as cleaning fluids and drain cleaners to inform users of the dangers of these products, particularly to children. Changes in product design have reduced the hazards posed by such products as lawn mowers, hedge trimmers, and toys. Product liability insurance has become an essential element for any new or existing product strategy. Premiums for this insurance have risen alarmingly, however, and insurers have almost entirely abandoned some kinds of coverage.

Regulatory activities and the increased number of liability claims have prompted companies to sponsor voluntary improvements in safety standards. Safety planning is now a vital element of product strategy, and many companies now publicize the safety planning and testing that go into the development of their products, as illustrated by the ad for Toyota in Figure 12.13.

FIGURE 12.13
Publicizing Safety Planning and Testing at Toyota

Strategic Implications of Marketing in the 21st Century

Marketers who want to see their products reach the marketplace successfully have a number of options for developing them, branding them, and developing a strong brand identity among consumers and business customers. The key is to integrate all of the options so that they are compatible with a firm's overall business and marketing strategy, and ultimately the firm's mission. Thus, as marketers consider ideas for new products, they need to be careful not to send their companies in so many different directions as to dilute the identities of their brands, making it nearly impossible to keep track of what their companies do well, as in the case of the Sara Lee Corporation. Category management can help companies develop a consistent product mix with strong branding, while at the same time meeting the needs of customers. Looking for ways to extend a brand without diluting it or compromising brand equity is also an important marketing strategy. Even though Sara Lee CEO C. Steven McMillan sold off 15 of the corporation's unrelated businesses, he also purchased the breadmaker Earthgrains, which quadrupled the company's bakery operations and was compatible with Sara's Lee's core food operations.[35]

Finally, marketers must continue to work to produce high-quality products that are also safe for all users. Even though Costco has been plagued with safety problems in some of its products, the organization has made efforts to turn things around. Upon recommendation from the CPSC, the company hired safety expert Mark Evanko to oversee issues related to product hazard analysis, safety testing, and quality control. Evanko vowed to improve the system.[36]

Summary of Chapter Objectives

1. Explain the benefits of category and brand management.

Category management is beneficial to a business because it gives direct responsibility for creating profitable product lines to category managers and their product group. Consumers respond to branding by making repeat purchases of favored goods and services. Therefore, managing brands and categories of brands or product lines well can result in a direct response from consumers, increasing profits and revenues for companies and creating consumer satisfaction. Brand and category managers can also enhance relationships with business customers such as retailers.

2. Identify the different types of brands.

- Generic product—an item characterized by a plain label, no advertising, and no brand name.

- Manufacturer's brand—a brand name owned by a manufacturer or other producer.

- Private brand—a brand name placed on products marketed by a wholesaler or retailers.

- Family brand—a brand name that identifies several related products.

- Individual brand—a unique brand name that identifies a specific offering within a firm's product line to avoid grouping it under a family brand.

3. Explain the strategic value of brand equity.

Brand equity provides a competitive advantage for a firm because consumers are more likely to buy a product that carries a respected, well-known brand name. Brand equity also smoothes the path for global expansion.

4. Discuss how companies develop strong identities for their products and brands.

Effective brands communicate to a buyer an idea of the product's image. Trademarks, brand names, slogans, and brand icons create an association that satisfies the customer's expectation of the benefits that using or having the product will yield.

5. Describe the strategies for new product development.

The success of a new product can result from four product development strategies: (1) market penetration, in which a company seeks to increase sales of an existing product in an existing market; (2) market development, which concentrates on finding new markets for existing products; (3) product development, which is the introduction of new products into identifiable or established markets; and (4) product diversification, which focuses on developing entirely new products for new markets.

6. Describe the consumer adoption process.

In the adoption process, consumers go through a series of stages from learning about the new product to trying it and deciding whether to purchase it again. The stages are called awareness, interest, evaluation, trial, and adoption/rejection.

7. List the stages in the process for developing new products.

The six-step process follows the following sequence: (1) idea generation, (2) screening, (3) business analysis, (4) development, (5) test marketing, and (6) commercialization.

8. Discuss the relationship between product safety and product liability.

Product safety refers to the goal of manufacturers to create products that can be operated safely and will protect consumers from harm. Product liability is the responsibility of marketers and manufacturers for injuries and damages caused by their products. There are major consumer protection laws in place to protect consumers from faulty products.

Marketing Terms You Need to Know

brand 346
brand recognition 347
brand preference 347
brand insistence 347

generic products 348
manufacturer's brand 348
family brand 349
brand equity 351

category management 352
brand name 353
trademark 354
label 358

brand extension 359
adoption process 361
consumer innovator 362

Other Important Marketing Terms

private brand 349
captive brand 349
individual brand 350
brand manager 352
brand mark 353
trade dress 355

Universal Product Code
  (UPC) 358
line extension 359
brand licensing 359
market penetration
  strategy 360

product positioning 360
market development
  strategy 361
product development 361
product diversification
  strategy 361

cannibalization 361
diffusion process 362
product manager 365
venture team 365
concept testing 367
product liability 367

Review Questions

1. What are the stages that consumers go through in achieving the ultimate brand loyalty?
2. Identify and briefly describe the different types of brands.
3. Why is brand equity so important to companies?
4. What are the characteristics of an effective brand name? Describe a brand name, with its accompanying brand mark, that you think is especially effective and explain why.
5. What role does packaging play in helping to create brand loyalty and brand equity?
6. Describe the different product development strategies.
7. What are the five stages of the consumer adoption process? Describe an instance in which you went through those stages to reach a decision about whether to adopt or reject a product.
8. Describe the different ways companies can organize to develop new products. Which do you think would be most effective for a firm that is trying to create a brand extension? Why?
9. List the six steps in the new-product development process. Do you think this process accounts for products that come into being by chance or accident? Why or why not?
10. Do you think that strict regulations about product safety help or hurt marketers of products? Explain your answer.

Projects and Teamwork Exercises

1. Locate an advertisement for a product that illustrates an especially effective brand name, brand mark, packaging, and overall trade dress. Explain to the class why you think this product has a strong brand identity.
2. With a classmate, go shopping for a product in the grocery store that you think could benefit from updated or new package design. Then sketch out a new package design for your product, identifying and explaining your changes as well as your reasons for these changes. Bring the old package and your new package design to class to share with your classmates.
3. With a classmate, identify two companies whose products you think could benefit from a co-branding or co-market-ing effort. Go to the companies' Web sites to learn more about their products, and outline a plan describing how you would bring the products together under one marketing effort.
4. What type of consumer adopter are you? Do you follow the same adoption pattern for all products, or are you an early adopter for some and a laggard for others? Create a graph or chart showing your own consumer adoption patterns for different products.
5. With a classmate, choose a firm that interests you and together generate some ideas for new products that might be appropriate for the company. Test your ideas out on each other, then your classmates. Which ideas make it past the first stage? Which don't? Why?

'net Work

1. Brand loyalty. Visit the Web site listed and read how Born, a marketing consulting firm, used the Internet to help Frito-Lay build brand loyalty among children. Write a brief report summarizing what you read and include a paragraph on whether or not you agree with the approach used by Born.

http://www.born.com/case_studies/case_study_51.html

2. Brand equity. The Web site of international advertising agency Young and Rubicam contains information on the firm's Brand Equity Valuator (BAV). Visit the Web site and read the basic information on BAV. Next, examine several of the links that provide BAV applications. Examples include "Four Basic Pillars," "Interpreting Brand Patterns," the "Brand Development Cycle," and "Sample Brands" grids. Print out the application that interests you the most. Submit the printout as an attachment to a brief paper addressing any aspect of what you learned about BAV.

http://www.yr.com

3. Trademarks. Go to the Web site for the U.S. Patent and Trademark Office. Review the procedure for registering a trademark. Note how much it costs to register a trademark and the benefits of trademark registration. Bring the material to class to contribute to a discussion of trademarks.

http://www.uspto.gov

Note: Internet Web addresses change frequently. If you don't find the exact sites listed, you may need to access the organization or company's home page and search from there.

CASE 12.1

How Samsung Polished Its Global Brand

Back in the 1970s, Samsung Electronics was a new company making cheap black-and-white television sets under the Sanyo brand. People recognized the Sanyo brand as a lower-end product and didn't pay much attention to it other than price. Thirty years later, the Korean-based company is building not only brand recognition but brand loyalty and brand equity as one of the top technology companies in the world. While Samsung makes some components for other firms, such as Dell Computer and IBM, the company has become known for developing truly innovative products of its own, across several product lines—from combined cell phone and handheld devices to flat-screen TVs and ultrathin laptops. Samsung "can't be classified as a replicator of other people's technology anymore," notes the head of equity research for UBS Warburg in Seoul.

It helps that Korea's 47 million people have embraced wireless communications and broadband Internet access with gusto—so there is a market filled with consumer innovators and early adopters just waiting for Samsung to come up with the next new gadget. According to government figures, 56 percent of Koreans own a cell phone. More than 50 percent of Korean households subscribe to broadband, compared with 2.3 percent in Japan. So concept testing, as well as test marketing, come pretty easily in Korea, where people are willing to try anything new in the technology game. Samsung has already become the brand of choice for consumers in Russia and China. Its partnerships with Dell, Hewlett-Packard, and IBM have it poised to enter the U.S. market. In an effort to establish itself as a recognizable brand among U.S. consumers, Samsung spent $400 million on a high-profile advertising campaign, including playing a role at the Salt Lake City Winter Olympics. One new product that has recently been launched to U.S. consumers is the 1300 Smart Phone, which is being sold through Sprint PCS. The device costs $499 and is a combined PDA-cell phone with

capability for e-mail. Speaking of the $499 price tag, Samsung has decided to change where and how it sells its products by moving them away from discounters and into more upscale retail companies.

With strong positions in memory chips—the company is now the world leader in their manufacture—thin-film displays (also first), and wireless communications (fourth in the world in handset production) and $100 billion in revenues, the Samsung Group is the largest corporation in South Korea. Of the 25 companies that make up the group, Samsung Electronics is the strongest and, some would argue, the most important to the company's future growth. Samsung Electronics now manufactures in fourteen different countries, generating 70 percent of its revenues outside Korea. To manage these diverse operations, top-level executives leave much of the decision making to global brand managers.

Samsung's new—and expensive—ad campaign features an eerie, beautiful woman whom the company refers to as the "snow woman." According to company marketers, the snow woman evokes luxury, beauty, and class. Exactly how they want you to think about the Samsung brand.

Questions for Critical Thinking

1. In addition to new product development, which of the other product development strategies would be appropriate for Samsung? Why?

2. What steps can Samsung take to identify consumer innovators and early adopters outside Korea?

SOURCES: Brian Bremner, "Watch Out Japan, Korea Is Coming," *BusinessWeek Online*, May 9, 2002, http://www.businessweek.com; William J. Holstein, "Samsung's Golden Touch," *Fortune*, April 1, 2002, pp. 89–94; Moon Ihlwan, "A Nation of Guinea Pigs," *BusinessWeek*, February 4, 2002, p. 50.

VIDEO CASE 12.2   Stride Rite Keeps Its Brands in Step

The written case on Stride Rite appears on page VC-15. The recently filmed Stride Rite video is designed to expand and highlight the concepts in this chapter and the concepts and questions covered in the written video case.

Krispy Kreme Continuing Case for Part 4 appears on page KK-8.

Part 5 Pricing Strategy

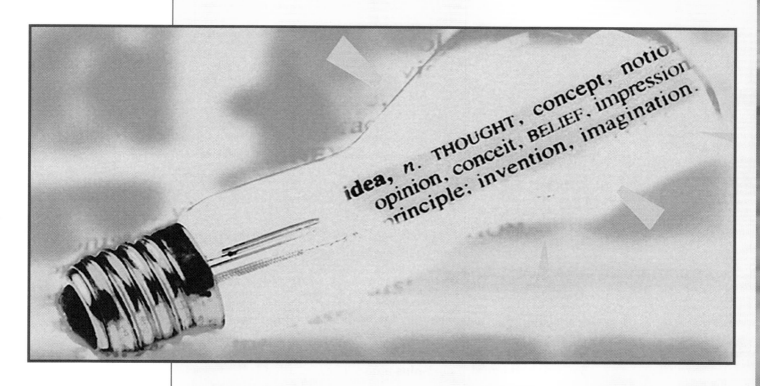

13 Price Determination

Chapter Objectives

1 Outline the legal constraints on pricing.

2 Identify the major categories of pricing objectives.

3 Explain price elasticity and its determinants.

4 List the practical problems involved in applying price theory concepts to actual pricing decisions.

5 Explain the major cost-plus approaches to price setting.

6 List the chief advantages and shortcomings of using breakeven analysis in pricing decisions.

7 Explain the superiority of modified breakeven analysis over the basic breakeven model and the role of yield management in pricing decisions.

8 Identify the major pricing challenges facing online and international marketers.

Airlines Fight for Their Lives

Perhaps no industry in the history of American commerce has been hit so hard by so many setbacks at once as the airline industry. In a period of less than two years, airlines suffered from terrorist attacks, a recession and slowly recovering economy, the war with Iraq, and the outbreak of SARS—all of which squashed flight plans by business travelers and vacationers. In addition, the increased security measures at airports created long lines at ticketing and boarding counters, discouraging many would-be travelers from flying. Fewer passengers meant empty planes, fewer flights, and decreased revenues. Yet airlines weren't going to lure passengers back by raising prices to cover losses. How could they survive?

Some airlines renegotiated contracts with union employees; some laid off hundreds of pilots and crew members; some, like U.S. Air and United, sought protection from creditors by filing for bankruptcy. Most dropped free meals and drinks except for international flights. Travelers now routinely grab sandwiches or snacks at the airport and eat them on the plane or purchase a meal once on board the flight. Delta—followed by other carriers—eliminated the commissions paid to travel agents and now offers discounts to travelers who purchase electronic tickets. Customers who want old-fashioned paper tickets pay a surcharge. This move, in addition to the increased popularity of online travel sites such as Orbitz, Travelocity, and Expedia, delivered a one-two punch to travel agencies, who now had to add customer surcharges to cover costs.

But the major airlines didn't start lowering their prices significantly until discount airlines such as JetBlue, Southwest, and AirTran Airways began to take hold of their markets. Previously, if travelers wanted to fly roundtrip from Atlanta to Los Angeles at the last minute, called a "walk-up" in the industry, Delta would be happy to take them there—for $2,221. Then

JetBlue and AirTran began offering the same walk-up roundtrip for about $400, naturally winning away Delta's customers. While the bigger airlines were still cutting back, discounters like Southwest, America West, Frontier, JetBlue, and AirTran were placing orders for more planes and securing new routes. JetBlue ordered 100 Brazilian-made, 100-seat jets in order to capture midsize markets. All of their other planes are the larger Airbus models. Still, marketers for the discounters empha-size that they won't bite off more than they can chew—they won't be flying to Tokyo or London. Instead, they plan to stay domestic because they believe they can provide better service at a lower price than the major airlines.

Meanwhile, the big carriers haven't given up. Walk-up customers and business travelers were once a major source of revenue because they made last-minute reservations and were unable to take advantage of traditional advance purchase and Saturday stay-over discounts. But with businesses cutting costs in general and air travel in particular, those revenues dropped significantly a few years ago. So, Delta tried an experiment—it cut business fares by over 20 percent on many of its routes, in the hope of encouraging business travelers to return. Continental and Northwest quietly followed suit. American announced a radical 40 percent price cut in business fares for 23 of its markets but raised its "leisure" fares at the same time. The goal was to stimulate more demand by welcoming back business travelers who might otherwise postpone their trips. Initial results were mixed, but some industry experts predicted that the trend would be here to stay. "Five years from now, instead of a pricing structure with business fares 5 or 6 times, on average, higher than discounted fares, I would expect it to be about 3-to-1," remarked one airline executive.

Gradually, travelers began to take to the skies again. Two years after the 9/11 terrorist attacks, several of the major airlines reported that their planes were again nearly full. That's partly due to cutbacks in the number of flights, but demand was genuinely beginning to increase. Some airlines began to introduce new in-flight services such as Internet access for a fee in an effort to gain more business travelers. United Airlines marketers conducted a survey that told them one of the biggest frustrations of business travelers was not being able to read their e-mail, so the company began offering two-way e-mail service through Verizon's Airfone subsidiary for $15.98 per flight. And the major airlines weren't rushing to increase fares again, perhaps understanding that the public—including business fliers—would reject higher prices in favor of the lower fares offered by discounters. "Even if the economy comes all the way back, business travelers who have been paying $600 coast-to-coast aren't going to say, 'Boy, I'm glad I can pay $2,300 again,'" said Scott Kirby, executive vice president of discount airline America West. That's a pretty safe bet.[1]

Chapter Overview

Briefly Speaking

Price is what you pay. Value is what you get.

Warren Buffett
(b. 1930)
American investor

As the airline industry's experience with discounts shows, price has a powerful impact on consumer spending behavior. One of the first questions shoppers ask is, "How much does it cost?" Marketers understand the critical role that price plays in the consumer's decision-making process. From lipstick and perfume to automobiles and gasoline to donuts and coffee, marketers must develop strategies that price products to achieve their firms' objectives.

As a starting point for examining pricing strategies, consider the meaning of the term *price*. A **price** is the exchange value of a good or service—in other words, it represents whatever that product can be exchanged for in the marketplace. Price does not necessarily involve money. In earlier times, the price of an acre of land might have been 20 bushels of wheat, three head of cattle, or one boat. Even though the barter process continues to be used in some transactions, in the 21st century price typically refers to the amount of funds required to purchase a product.

Prices are both difficult to set and dynamic; they shift in response to a number of variables. A higher-than-average price can convey an image of prestige, while a lower-than-average price may connote good value. Price can also powerfully affect a company's overall profitability and market share.

This chapter discusses the process of determining a profitable but justifiable (fair) price. The focus is on management of the pricing function, including pricing strategies, price-quality relationships, and pricing in various sectors of the economy. The chapter also looks at the effects of environmental conditions on price determination, including legal constraints, competitive pressures, and changes in global and online markets.

Pricing and the Law

1

Outline the legal constraints on pricing.

Pricing decisions are influenced by a variety of legal constraints imposed by federal and state governments. The next time you pull up to a gas station, consider where each dollar goes. Almost 50 percent is taken up in federal, state, local, and excise taxes. Tariffs—taxes levied on the sale of imported goods and services—often make it possible for firms to set prices on domestically produced goods well above world market levels. To shield the ailing U.S. steel industry and protect American jobs, the Bush administration imposed tariffs of up to 30 percent on steel imports, driving up the price of steel at home. The tariffs led to protests not only from foreign producers who were cut out of the U.S. market but from American manufacturers across a range of industries who are reliant on low-cost steel to make their products.[2] Tariffs on foodstuffs have a similar effect on price, resulting, for example, in higher prices for bananas in Europe than in the U.S.

An industry where the legal environment has a powerful impact on price is the firearms sector. Following a rash of public shootings—including several on school grounds by teenagers—antigun activists pressured Congress to pass tough restrictions regulating handgun ownership and sales. At the same time, survivors, families of victims, and even cities filed lawsuits against handgun manufacturers, which added to their costs. But consumer fears for personal safety following the terrorist attacks of September 11 led to increased handgun sales, and the added demand pushed retail prices up almost 10 percent.[3]

Pricing is also regulated by the general constraints of U.S. antitrust legislation, as outlined in Chapter 3. The following sections review some of the most important pricing laws for contemporary marketers.

Robinson-Patman Act Exam

The **Robinson-Patman Act** (1936) typifies Depression-era legislation. Known as the Anti-A&P Act, it was inspired by price competition triggered by the rise of grocery store chains—in fact, the original draft was prepared by the U.S. Wholesale Grocers Association. Enacted in the midst of the Great Depression, when legislators viewed chain stores as a threat to employment in the traditional retail sector, the act was intended primarily to save jobs.

The Robinson-Patman Act was technically an amendment to the Clayton Act, enacted 22 years earlier, that had applied only to price discrimination between geographic areas, which injured local sellers. Broader in scope, Robinson-Patman prohibits price discrimination in sales to wholesalers, retailers, and other producers. It rules that differences in price must reflect cost differentials and prohibits selling at unreasonably low prices in order to drive competitors out of business. Supporters justified the amendment by arguing that chain stores might secure substantial discounts from suppliers, while small, independent stores would continue to pay regular prices.

Price discrimination, where some customers pay more than others for the same product, dates back to the very beginnings of trade and commerce. Today, however, technology has added to the frequency and complexity of price discrimination, as well as the strategies marketers adopt to get around it. For example, marketers may encourage repeat business by inviting purchasers to become "preferred customers," entitling them to average discounts of 10 percent. As long as companies can demonstrate that their price discounts and promotional allowances do not restrict competition, they avoid penalties under the Robinson-Patman Act. Direct-mail marketers frequently send out catalogs of identical goods but with differing prices. Zip-code areas that traditionally consist of high spenders get the high-price catalogs, while price-sensitive zip-code customers get a low-price catalog. Victoria's Secret, Staples, and Simon & Schuster are among the hundreds of companies that employ legal price discrimination strategies. Amazon.com's recent experiments with so-called dynamic pricing—a method of using random price differentials to test the market—brought protests that the e-tailer was unfairly customizing its pricing according to consumer characteristics.[4]

Marketing Dictionary

price   Exchange value of a good or service.

Robinson-Patman Act   Federal legislation prohibiting price discrimination that is not based on a cost differential; also prohibits selling at an unreasonably low price to eliminate competition.

Marketing Hit

How Much Is Electricity Worth to You?

Background. During one recent summer, electricity costs in the U.S. hit a 20-year high, at 9 cents per kilowatt hour. Even though prices varied by region, the price increase meant that the average household paid more than $150 that year just for air conditioning alone. Several factors affected the price, including above-average temperatures and a jump in natural gas prices—the third-largest source of electricity, behind coal and nuclear power.

The Challenge. Marketers for utilities needed to find a way to keep costs reasonable for their customers without going bankrupt themselves. Old pricing structures just weren't working, and customers were upset by the rising costs.

The Strategy. Utilities in several states—Pennsylvania, Washington, Wisconsin, and Florida—tried a new rate structure, much like the old telephone rate structures. Customers would pay more for electricity during the peak hours in which demand also increased and less during off-peak hours. So, it would cost more for a customer to run the air conditioner at maximum power on a hot August afternoon than it would in the morning. Customers could save by cutting back on their power use or by using more electricity at other times of the day—for instance, by operating washing machines during the evening. The experimental rate structures were voluntary; customers could stay with traditional flat rates if they were more comfortable doing so.

The Outcome. Customers in these states seemed to like the idea of having some con-

continued on next page

Firms accused of price discrimination often argue that they set price differentials to meet competitors' prices and that cost differences justify variations in prices. When a firm asserts that it maintains price differentials as good-faith methods of competing with rivals, a logical question arises: What constitutes good-faith pricing behavior? The answer depends on the particular situation.

A defense based on cost differentials works only if the price differences do not exceed the cost differences resulting from selling to various classes of buyers. Marketers must then justify the cost differences; indeed many authorities consider this provision one of the most confusing areas in the Robinson-Patman Act. Courts handle most charges brought under the act as individual cases. Therefore, domestic marketers must continually evaluate their pricing actions to avoid potential Robinson-Patman violations.

Unfair-Trade Laws

More than 20 states supplement federal legislation with their own **unfair-trade laws,** which require sellers to maintain minimum prices for comparable merchandise. Enacted in the 1930s, these laws were intended to protect small specialty shops, such as dairy stores, from the loss-leader pricing tactics, in which chain stores might sell certain products below cost to attract customers. Typical state laws set retail price floors at cost plus some modest markup.

Although most unfair-trade laws have remained on the books for the past 70 years, marketers had all but forgotten them until recent years. Then in 1993, Wal-Mart, the nation's largest retailer, was found guilty of violating Arkansas's unfair-trade law for selling drugs and health-and-beauty aids below cost. The lawsuit filed by three independent drugstore owners accused the mass merchandiser of attempting to drive them out of business through predatory pricing practices. Wal-Mart appealed and the decision was overturned, but similar lawsuits have been filed in several other states, all seeking to end the chain's low-price marketing strategy.

Fair-Trade Laws

The concept of fair trade has affected pricing decisions for decades. **Fair-trade laws** allow manufacturers to stipulate minimum retail prices for their products and to require dealers to sign contracts agreeing to abide by these prices.

Fair-trade laws assert that a product's image, determined in part by its price, is a property right of the manufacturer. Therefore, the manufacturer should have the authority to protect its asset by requiring retailers to maintain a minimum price. Exclusivity is one method manufacturers use to achieve this. By severely restricting the number of retail outlets that carry their figurines, Lladro can coordinate the prices charged by retail partners and discourage price discounting, which might adversely affect the company's image. The Lladro collection, shown in Figure 13.1, is one example of the figurines available only through fine stores like Macy's, Burdines, and a few other premier outlets.

Like the Robinson-Patman Act, fair-trade legislation has its roots in the Depression era. In 1931, California became the first state to enact fair-trade legislation. Most other states soon followed; only Missouri, the District of Columbia, Vermont, and Texas failed to adopt such laws.

A U.S. Supreme Court decision invalidated fair-trade contracts in interstate commerce, and Congress responded by passing the Miller Tydings Resale Maintenance Act (1937). This law exempted interstate fair-trade contracts from compliance with antitrust requirements, thus freeing states to keep these laws on their books if they so desired.

Over the years, fair-trade laws declined in importance as discounters emerged and price competition gained strength in marketing strategy. These laws became invalid with the passage of the Consumer Goods Pricing Act (1975), which halted all interstate enforcement of resale price maintenance provisions, an objective long sought by consumer groups.

FIGURE 13.1
Protecting Brand Image by Avoiding Price Discounting

Pricing Objectives and the Marketing Mix

2

Identify the major categories of pricing objectives.

The extent to which any or all of the factors of production—natural resources, capital, human resources, and entrepreneurship—are employed depends on the prices those factors command. A firm's prices and the resulting purchases by its customers determine the company's revenue, influencing the profits it earns. Overall organizational objectives and more specific marketing objectives guide the development of pricing objectives, which in turn lead to development and implementation of more specific pricing policies and procedures, as the "Marketing Hit" box explains.

A firm might, for instance, set a major overall goal of becoming the dominant producer in its domestic market. It might then develop a marketing objective of achieving maximum sales penetration in each region, followed by a related pricing objective of setting prices at levels that maximize sales. These objectives might lead to the adoption of a low-price policy implemented by offering substantial price discounts to channel members.

Price affects and is affected by the other elements of the marketing mix. Product decisions, promotional plans, and distribution choices all impact the price of a good or service. For example, products distributed through complex channels involving several intermediaries must be priced high enough to cover the markups needed to compensate wholesalers and retailers for services they provide. Basic so-called "fighting brands" are intended to capture market share from higher-priced, options-laden

Marketing Hit

trol over their rates and did cut back on their electricity consumption during periods of high price—and high demand.

SOURCES: Ray Kopp, "Answers Needed Now on Natural Gas Problem," *The Boston Globe*, August 27, 2003, **http://www.boston.com/news/globe**; Barbara Hangenbaugh, "Electricity Costs Near 20-Year Highs," *USA Today*, June 10, 2003, p. A1; Robert Gavin, "Cut Your Electric Bill: Do Laundry at 3:00 A.M.," *The Wall Street Journal*, August 22, 2002, pp. D1, D3.

Marketing Dictionary

unfair-trade laws   State laws requiring sellers to maintain minimum prices for comparable merchandise.

fair-trade laws   Statutes enacted in most states that once permitted manufacturers to stipulate a minimum retail price for their product.

TABLE 13.1   **Pricing Objectives**

OBJECTIVE	PURPOSE	EXAMPLE
Profitability objectives	■ Profit maximization ■ Target return	Low introductory interest rates on credit cards with high standard rates after 6 months
Volume objectives	■ Sales maximization ■ Market share	Dell's low-priced PCs increase market share and sales of services
Meeting competition objectives	■ Value pricing	Price wars among major airlines
Prestige objectives	■ Lifestyle ■ Image	High-priced luxury autos such as Ferrari and watches by Rolex
Not-for-profit objectives	■ Profit maximization ■ Cost recovery ■ Market incentives ■ Market suppression	High prices for tobacco and alcohol to reduce consumption

competitors by offering relatively low prices to entice customers to give up some options in return for a cost savings.

While pricing objectives vary from firm to firm, they can be classified into four major groups: (1) profitability objectives, (2) volume objectives, (3) meeting competition objectives, and (4) prestige objectives. Not-for-profit organizations as well as for-profit companies must consider objectives of one kind or another when developing pricing strategies. Table 13.1 outlines the pricing objectives marketers rely on to meet their organization's overall goals.

Profitability Objectives Read Max ve π

Marketers at for-profit firms must set prices with profits in mind. Even not-for-profit organizations realize the importance of setting prices high enough to cover expenses and provide a financial cushion to cover unforeseen needs and expenses. As the Russian proverb goes, "There are two fools in every market: One asks too little, one asks too much." For consumers to pay prices that are either above average or below average, they must be convinced they are receiving fair value for money.

Economic theory is based on two major assumptions. It assumes, first, that firms will behave rationally and, second, that this rational behavior will result in an effort to maximize gains and minimize losses. Some marketers estimate profits by looking at historical sales data; others use elaborate calculations based on predicted future sales. It has been said that setting prices is an art, not a science. The talent lies in a marketer's ability to strike a balance between desired profits and the customer's perception of a product's value.

Marketers should evaluate and adjust prices continually to accommodate changes in the environment. The technological environment, for example, forces Internet marketers to respond quickly to competitors' pricing strategies. New search capabilities performed by shopping bots (described in Chapter 5) allow customers to compare prices locally, nationally, and globally in a matter of seconds.

Intense price competition—sometimes conducted even when it means forgoing profits altogether—often results when rival manufacturers battle for leadership positions in new product categories. Recently, Microsoft—which has yet to turn a profit on its Xbox video game—planned to disclose a deep price cut to revive flagging sales. Sony stole its thunder by announcing that the retail price of its PlayStation 2 would drop by a third, a move that Microsoft quickly matched. Meanwhile, Nintendo announced that it would undercut both products by pricing its Game Cube at $50 less than rival technologies.[5]

Profits are a function of revenue and expenses:

$$\text{Profits} = \text{Revenue} - \text{Expenses.}$$

Revenue is determined by the product's selling price and number of units sold:

$$\text{Total Revenue} = \text{Price} \times \text{Quantity Sold.}$$

Therefore, a profit maximizing price rises to the point at which further increases will cause disproportionate decreases in the number of units sold. A 10 percent price increase that results in only an 8 percent cut in volume will add to the firm's revenue. However, a 10 percent price hike that results in an 11 percent sales decline will reduce revenue.

Economists refer to this approach as *marginal analysis*. They identify **profit maximization** as the point at which the addition to total revenue is just balanced by the increase in total cost. Marketers must resolve a basic problem of how to achieve this delicate balance when they set prices. Relatively few firms actually hit this elusive target. A significantly larger number prefer to direct their effort toward more realistic goals.

Consequently, marketers commonly set **target-return objectives**—short-run or long-run goals usually stated as percentages of sales or investment. The practice has become particularly popular among large firms in which other pressures interfere with profit-maximization objectives. Target-return objectives offer several benefits for marketers in addition to resolving pricing questions. For example, these objectives serve as tools for evaluating performance. They also satisfy desires to generate "fair" profits as judged by management, stockholders, and the public.

Volume Objectives *Low Price ⟶ ↑ MKt share*

Some economists and business executives argue that pricing behavior actually seeks to maximize sales within a given profit constraint. In other words, they set a minimum acceptable profit level and then seek to maximize sales (subject to this profit constraint) in the belief that the increased sales are more important than immediate high profits to the long-run competitive picture. Such a company continues to expand sales as long as its total profits do not drop below the minimum return acceptable to management.

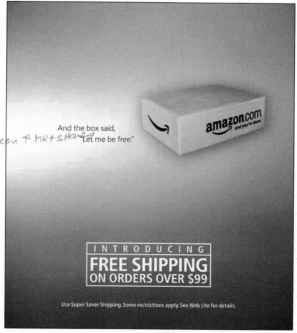

FIGURE 13.2
Absorbing Shipping Expenses as a Pricing Tool to Achieve Volume Objectives

In the continuing battle to maintain its online image as American's online store, Amazon.com decided to intensify the battle with smaller rivals with a special offer. Internet shoppers placing orders over $99 were provided with free shipping, a considerable savings particularly for bulky, heavy items. The promotion shown in Figure 13.2 describes the offer, an alternative to a price cut, that Amazon marketers anticipated would cover the cost of the upfront offer over time with increased sales volume.

Sales maximization can also result from non-price factors such as service and quality. Marketers increased sales for Dr. Scholl's new shoe insert, Dynastep, by advertising heavily in magazines. The ads explained how the Dynastep insert would help relieve leg and back pain. Priced around $14 per insert—twice as much as comparable offerings—Dynastep ran over its competitors to become number one in its category.

Marketing Dictionary

profit maximization   Point at which the additional revenue gained by increasing the price of a product equals the increase in total costs.

target-return objective   Short-run or long-run pricing objectives of achieving a specified return on either sales or investment.

In Mtg Percept= is Reality.

'net—x

Profit Impact of Market Strategies (PIMS) project. The Web site listed contains a report on *Creating Customer Value*. Read the report and review several case studies. Prepare a summary that you can contribute to a class discussion on the pricing implication of the PIMS studies.

http://www.naumann.com/outline.htm

Another volume-related pricing objective is the *market-share objective*—the goal set for controlling a portion of the market for a firm's good or service. Dr. Scholl's was able to increase its market share to 29 percent by focusing on the benefits of Dynastep. The company's specific goal may be to maintain its present share of a particular market, or to increase its share, for instance, from 10 percent to 20 percent. Volume-related objectives such as sales maximization and market share play an important role in most firms' pricing decisions.

Product Quality + Mkt Shares determine Mkt Profitability

The PIMS Studies *Read*

Exam

Mkt Share is Company Sales % of Industry Sales
Company w the most Mkt shares n the most Profitable.
Product Quality. #1. Mkt Share #2

Market-share objectives may prove critical to the achievement of other organizational objectives. High sales, for example, often mean more profits. The **Profit Impact of Market Strategies (PIMS) project,** an extensive study conducted by the Marketing Science Institute, analyzed more than 2,000 firms and revealed that two of the most important factors influencing profitability were product quality and market share. Marketing campaigns with ads like the one in Figure 13.3 help to enhance profitability for PepsiCo's Pepsi soft drinks. Battling industry leader Coca-Cola worldwide, Pepsi's second-place global ranking is currently approaching the market leader as a strong and growing competitor. As one of two leaders in the soft-drink industry, PepsiCo marketers do not focus on low price in their consumer promotions, but rather on emphasizing values such as the pleasure derived from consuming the product.

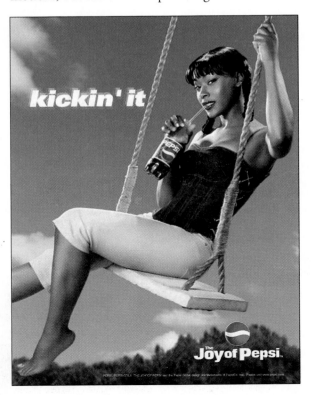

FIGURE 13.3
Increasing Market Share and Profitability by Emphasizing Product Quality and "The Joy of Pepsi"

Numerous studies confirm the link between market share and profitability.

The relationship between market share and profitability is evident in PIMS data that reveal an average 32 percent return on investment (ROI) for firms with market shares above 40 percent. In contrast, average ROI decreases to 24 percent for firms whose market shares are between 20 and 40 percent. Firms with a minor market share (less than 10 percent) generate average pretax investment returns of approximately 13 percent.[6]

The relationship also applies to a firm's individual brands. PIMS researchers compared the top four brands in each market segment they studied. Their data revealed that the leading brand typically generates after-tax ROI of 18 percent, considerably higher than the second-ranked brand. Weaker brands, on average, fail to earn adequate returns.

Marketers have developed an underlying explanation of the positive relationship between profitability and market share. Firms with large shares accumulate greater operating experience and lower overall costs relative to competitors with smaller market shares. Accordingly, effective segmentation strategies might focus on obtaining larger shares of smaller markets and on avoiding smaller shares of larger ones. A firm might achieve higher financial returns by becoming a major competitor in several smaller market segments than by remaining a relatively minor player in a larger market.

Meeting Competition Objectives

A third set of pricing objectives seeks simply to meet competitors' prices. In many lines of business, firms set their own prices to match those of established industry price leaders.

Price is a pivotal factor in the ongoing competition between long-distance telephone services and wireless carriers. When cellular companies began offering huge bundles of "use-anytime" minutes with free long-distance service, MCI rolled out its Select 200 program—offering customers 200 minutes of long-distance calling time, with no monthly fees, taxes, or surcharges attached. In its efforts to stem defections of customers to wireless services, AT&T recently offered unlimited long-distance calling at a flat rate of $19.95 a month—but only between households served by AT&T. Since, from the customer's perspective, long-distance companies and cellular companies offer a service that is in many respects interchangeable, neither class of carrier could continue operations unless they came close to matching each other's prices.[7]

Pricing objectives tied directly to meeting prices charged by major competitors deemphasize the price element of the marketing mix and focus more strongly on nonprice variables. Pricing is a highly visible component of a firm's marketing mix and an easy and effective tool for obtaining a differential advantage over competitors. It is, however, a tool that other firms can easily duplicate through price reductions of their own. Airline price competition of recent years exemplifies the actions and reactions of competitors in this marketplace. Rather than emphasizing the lowest fares of any carrier, most airlines choose to compete by offering convenient arrival and departure times, enhanced passenger comfort with more room between each row, an attractive frequent-flyer program, and customer-focused alliances with automobile rental, lodging, and other partners. Some airlines even returned to providing passenger meals on long flights, a practice that had previously been discontinued in a cost-cutting effort. Even when price increases are needed to remain profitable, an announced price hike by one airline will be implemented only if its major competitors match the new price. Because price changes directly affect overall profitability in an industry, many firms attempt to promote stable prices by meeting competitors' prices and competing for market share by focusing on product strategies, promotional decisions, and distribution—the non-price elements of the marketing mix.

Lands' End, a Sears catalog and online retail subsidiary, focuses on such nonprice elements. The copy-intensive ad in Figure 13.4 describes the benefits of the product, the range of colors and styles, the company's excellence in customer service, and its easy-ordering system, as well as price. While low

FIGURE 13.4
Lands' End: Implementing the Pricing Objective of Meeting Competition

---

Marketing Dictionary

Profit Impact of Market Strategies (PIMS) project   Research that discovered a strong positive relationship between a firm's market share and its return on investment.

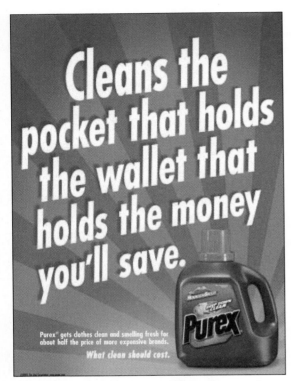

In the extremely price-competitive category of laundry products, Purex invites customers to make value comparisons—"Don't waste money on dirt."

Marketing Hit

How PepsiCo Is Making a Killing with Aquafina Bottled Water

Background. How do you persuade consumers to shell out as much for tap water as they pay for Mountain Dew? Unlike bottled beverages that are created from top-secret recipes or require added carbonation, pure water promises no additional ingredients or special preparation. It takes a leap of faith—or very clever marketing—to believe that Aquafina, plain old H_2O with nothing added, is worth paying for.

continued on next page

price is a key attraction, the emphasis on other product and customer-service benefits sets Lands' End apart.

Value Pricing

When discounts become normal elements of a competitive marketplace, other marketing-mix elements gain importance in purchase decisions. In such instances, overall product value, not just price, determines product choice. In recent years, a new strategy—**value pricing**—has emerged that emphasizes the benefits a product provides in comparison to the price and quality levels of competing offerings. This strategy typically works best for relatively low-priced goods and services.

Laundry detergents are a good example of value pricing. The label on Dash detergent proclaims *Value Price*, while Arm & Hammer's label assures customers that it *Cleans Great—Value Price, Too!* Yes detergent announces *Great Value!*, while Ultra Rinso claims *Super Value*, and the back label on Ultra Trend boasts that it offers *hard-working performance at a reasonable price*. The label on another detergent, All, simply advises customers to *Compare & Save*.

Value-priced products generally cost less than premium brands, but marketers point out that *value* does not necessarily mean *inexpensive*. The challenge for those who compete on value is to convince customers that low-priced brands offer quality comparable to that of a higher-priced product. An increasing number of alternative products and private-label brands has resulted in a more competitive marketplace in recent years. Pampers Premium baby diapers, like many Procter & Gamble brands, is premium priced, often selling at twice the price of rival store-brands. Luvs, a low-end P&G brand, costs 30 percent less. In a no-growth market marked with signs that shoppers are switching to lower-priced competition, P&G recently began to phase out Pampers Premium in favor of a product intended to deliver discernable extra value. Baby Stages—also priced at the high end of the market—is designed for specific stages during a child's first two years: extra absorbency for newborns, stretchy sides for crawlers, and pull-up pants for toddlers.[8]

Value pricing is perhaps best seen in the personal computer industry. In the past few years, PC prices have collapsed, reducing the effectiveness of traditional pricing strategies intended to meet competition. In fact, PCs priced at under $600 are now the fastest-growing segment of the market. This category now accounts for almost 20 percent of PCs sold in stores. Industry leaders like Dell, Hewlett-Packard/Compaq, and Gateway cannot continue to cut prices, so they are adding features such as increased memory and 3-D graphic accelerator cards that increase speed. Dell has even launched a home-installation plan to offset tumbling prices in the PC market.[9] The "Marketing Hits" box demonstrates how marketers are able to build a perception of value into a readily available resource: water.

Prestige Objectives

The final category of pricing objectives, unrelated to either profitability or sales volume, is prestige objectives. Prestige pricing establishes a relatively high price to develop and maintain an image of quality and exclusiveness that appeals to status-conscious consumers. Such objectives reflect marketers' recognition of the role of price in creating an overall image of the firm and its product offerings.

Prestige objectives affect the price tags of such products as Waterford crystal, Alfa Romeo sports cars, Omega watches, and Tiffany jewelry. When

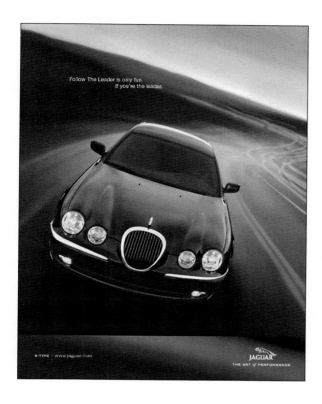

FIGURE 13.5
Emphasizing Exclusivity as Part of Jaguar's Prestige Pricing

a perfume marketer sets a price of $135 or more per ounce, this choice reflects an emphasis on image far more than the cost of ingredients. Analyses have shown that ingredients account for less than 5 percent of a perfume's cost. Thus, advertisements for Joy that promote the fragrance as the "costliest perfume in the world" use price to promote product prestige.

In contrast to low-price strategies used by marketers of economy cars, ads for Jaguar tout exclusivity and target wealthy clientele. Appearing in upscale magazines such as *Smithsonian,* the ad in Figure 13.5 states: "Follow the Leader is only fun if you're the leader."

In the business world, private jet ownership imparts an image of prestige, power, and high price tags—too high for most business travelers to consider. Recognizing that cost is the primary factor that makes jet ownership prohibitive, companies like Flight Options and NetJets have created an alternative—fractional ownership. The companies target firms whose executives travel periodically rather than year round. Instead of buying a preowned plane, they take a share in a new jet. Fractional ownership companies account for almost half the backlog of orders at the five major manufacturers of business jets.[10]

Pricing Objectives of Not-for-Profit Organizations

Pricing typically is a key element of the marketing mix for not-for-profit organizations. Pricing strategy can help these groups to achieve a variety of organizational goals:

1. *Profit maximization.* While not-for-profit organizations by definition do

Marketing Hit

The Challenge. PepsiCo twice tried to enter the bottled water business, first by buying a spring water company, then by offering a sparkling water to rival Perrier. Both attempts failed. In the ultimate back-to-basics strategy, the company finally hit on the idea of using an existing resource—its water treatment facilities—to filter everything it possibly could out of tap water.

The Strategy. While tap water is already free of harmful substances, PepsiCo stripped out any and all particles that might impart taste or smell. The result is the purest of the pure—Aquafina. A super-slick ad campaign featuring TV star Lisa Kudrow (Phoebe in *Friends*) gives gusto to Aquafina's purity claims. In a stroke of brilliance, the ad makes a virtue of the fact that Aquafina is nothing but water, plain and simple. Kudrow charmingly describes the brand as "Pure nothing." The tagline says it all: "We promise nothing."

The Outcome. PepsiCo is now the number two bottled-water company, behind Perrier. Aquafina, whose sales doubled within a year, leads the uncarbonated-water category. Leveraging its success, PepsiCo recently launched Aquafina Essentials, a flavor-enhanced brand.

SOURCES: Betsy McKay, "Liquid Assets," *The Wall Street Journal,* April 18, 2002, p. A1; Kenneth Hein, "Pour It On," *Brandweek,* April 1, 2002, p. 1; and Bob Garfield, "The Product Is Questionable, But Aquafina's Ads Hold Water," *Advertising Age,* July 9, 2001, p. 39.

Marketing Dictionary

value pricing   Pricing strategy emphasizing benefits derived from a product in comparison to the price and quality levels of competing offerings.

not cite profitability as a primary goal, there are numerous instances in which they do try to maximize their returns on single events or a series of events. A $1,000-a-plate political fundraiser is a classic example.

2. *Cost recovery.* Some not-for-profit organizations attempt to recover only the actual cost of operating the unit. Mass transit, toll roads and bridges, and publicly supported colleges are common examples. The amount of recovered costs is often dictated by tradition, competition, or public opinion.

3. *Market incentives.* Other not-for-profit groups follow a lower-than-average pricing policy or offer a free service to encourage increased usage of the good or service. Seattle's bus system offers free service in the downtown area in an attempt to reduce traffic congestion, encourage retail sales, and minimize the effort required to access downtown public services.

4. *Market suppression.* Price can also discourage consumption. High prices help to accomplish social objectives independent of the costs of providing goods or services. Illustrations include tobacco and alcohol taxes (the so-called "sin taxes"), parking fines, tolls, and gasoline excise taxes.

Briefly Speaking

A thing is worth whatever the buyer will pay for it.

*Publilius Syrus
(1st century B.C.)
Latin mimographer*

Methods for Determining Prices

Marketers determine prices in two basic ways—by applying the theoretical concepts of supply and demand and by completing cost-oriented analyses. During the first part of the previous century, most discussions for price determination emphasized the classical concepts of supply and demand. During the last half of the 20th century, however, the emphasis shifted to a cost-oriented approach. Hindsight reveals certain flaws in both concepts.

Treatments of this subject often overlook another concept of price determination—one based on the impact of custom and tradition. **Customary prices** are retail prices that consumers expect as a result of tradition and social habit. Candy makers have attempted to maintain traditional price levels by considerably reducing product size. Similar practices have prevailed in the marketing of soft drinks as bottlers attempt to balance consumer expectations of customary prices with the realities of rising costs.

Wm. Wrigley Jr. Co., manufacturer of such chewing gum standards as Juicy Fruit, Doublemint, and Big Red, took advantage of the weakness in the industry's customary pricing strategy by introducing a smaller-quantity pack at a lower price. While competitors continued to offer only seven-piece packs for 35 cents, Wrigley priced its five-piece packs at 25 cents. To spur impulse buying, the company prominently displayed the price on the package. The strategy was so successful that within two years of its inception, Wrigley discontinued selling seven-stick gum packs.

At some point, someone has to set initial prices for products. In addition, competitive moves and cost changes necessitate periodic reviews of price structures. The remaining sections delve into the issue of price determination. This section also considers how marketers can most effectively integrate the concepts to develop realistic pricing systems.

THERE'S MORE THAN ONE WAY TO GET 100 GALLONS OF DRINKING WATER INTO YOUR HOME.

PŪR
WATER FILTRATION SYSTEM
YOUR WATER SHOULD BE PŪR.

The problem with bottled water is the bottles. Get as much clean, healthy water as you need right from your tap. PŪR faucet mount filters attach easily and turn off and on with a simple twist. Nothing to lug home, nothing to store. Find out more at www.purwater.com

This message is intended to be a wake-up call to consumers who have become accustomed to buying bottled water—a reminder that water can be obtained practically free from a tap. PŪR offers healthy and great-tasting filtered water at one-tenth the cost of bottled water.

Price Determination in Economic Theory

Microeconomics suggests a way of determining prices that assumes a profit-maximization objective. This technique attempts to derive correct equilibrium prices in the marketplace by comparing supply and demand. It also requires more complete analysis than actual business firms typically conduct.

Demand refers to a schedule of the amounts of a firm's product that consumers will purchase at different prices during a specified period. *Supply* refers to a schedule of the amounts of a good or service that will be offered for sale at different prices during a specified time period. These schedules may vary for different types of market structures. Businesses operate and set prices in four types of market structures: pure competition, monopolistic competition, oligopoly, and monopoly.

Pure competition is a market structure with so many buyers and sellers that no single participant can significantly influence price. Pure competition presupposes other market conditions, as well: homogeneous products and ease of entry for sellers due to low start-up costs. The agricultural sector exhibits many characteristics of a purely competitive market, making it the closest actual example.

Monopolistic competition typifies most retailing and features large numbers of buyers and sellers. These diverse parties exchange heterogeneous, relatively well-differentiated products, giving marketers some control over prices.

Relatively few sellers compete in an *oligopoly*. Each seller may affect the market, but no single seller controls it. High start-up costs form significant barriers to entry for new competitors. Each firm's demand curve in an oligopolistic market displays a unique kink at the current market price. Because of the impact of a single competitor on total industry sales, competitors usually quickly match any attempt by one firm to generate additional sales by reducing prices. Price cutting in such industry structures is likely to reduce total industry revenues. Oligopolies operate in the petroleum refining, automobile, and tobacco industries.

The availability of alternative air transportation in the form of such discount carriers as Southwest Airlines and Frontier Airlines forces established air carriers to maintain competitive airfares—or risk losing business to the upstarts. For example, before JetBlue and Southwest launched their first coast-to-coast flights from Washington to Los Angeles, transcontinental flights were the domain of bigger, higher-fare airlines. If these alternatives disappear, prices will probably rise.[11]

A *monopoly* is a market structure where only one seller of a product exists and for which there are no close substitutes. Antitrust legislation has nearly eliminated all but temporary monopolies, such as those created through patent protection. The "Solving an Ethical Controversy" box explores how pharmaceutical companies protect their pricing policies through the exercise of patents. Regulated industries, such as utility companies, constitute another form of monopoly. The government allows regulated monopolies in markets in which competition would lead to an uneconomical duplication of services. In return for such a license, government reserves the right to regulate the monopoly's rate of return.

The four types of market structures are compared in Table 13.2 (on page 389) on the following bases: number of competitors, ease of entry into the industry by new firms, similarity of competing products, degree of control over price by individual firms, and the elasticity or inelasticity of the demand curve facing the individual firm. Elasticity—the degree of consumer responsiveness to changes in price—is discussed in more detail in a later section.

Cost and Revenue Curves

Marketers must set a price for a product that generates sufficient revenue to cover the costs of producing and marketing it. A product's total cost is composed of total variable costs and total fixed costs. *Variable costs* change with the level of production (such as human resource and raw materials costs), while *fixed costs* remain stable at any production level within a certain range (such as lease payments or insurance costs). *Average total costs* are calculated by dividing the sum of the variable and fixed costs by the number of units produced. Finally, *marginal cost* is the change in total cost that results from producing an additional unit of output.

The demand side of the pricing equation focuses on revenue curves. Average revenue is calculated by dividing total revenue by the quantity associated with these revenues. Average revenue is actually the demand curve facing the firm. Marginal revenue is the change in total revenue that results from selling an additional unit of output. Figure 13.6, on page 389, shows the relationships of various cost and revenue measures; the firm maximizes its profits when marginal costs equal marginal revenues.

Marketing Dictionary

customary prices   Traditional prices that customers expect to pay for certain goods and services.

right wrong   Solving an Ethical Controversy

What's a Fair Price for Prescription Drugs?

Americans spend more than $150 billion each year on prescription drugs, creating profits in excess of 30 percent for the big five pharmaceutical companies. Meanwhile, insurers and patients struggle to pick up the tab. Yet while drug makers rake in huge returns, they also spend millions in research and development, since the cost of bringing a blockbuster drug to market can top $880 million.

Even so, spiraling R&D costs do not fully explain why drug prices are soaring. Once a drug is approved for sale, it typically enjoys 12 to 14 years under patent. This monopoly position allows its maker to charge as much as the market will bear. Camptosar, Pharmacia's colon cancer medication, for example, prices out at more than $60,000 per patient per year, while Gleevec, a leukemia drug from Novartis, costs $28,000. As soon as a drug comes off patent, knockoffs take over the market and prices plummet. Four out of five sales are immediately lost to copycat companies. Since their profit margins on generics is more than four times that on brand drugs, some distributors and pharmacies push patients to make the switch as quickly as generic versions become available. In response, drug companies make incremental changes to their products—a "new" weekly dosage of Fosomax replaces a daily osteoporosis pill, allowing Merck to extend its patent and keep the price high. Setting a worrisome precedent for patent-protection supporters, the U.S. government—in the wake of terrorist attacks—threatened to strip Bayer of its patent-protected monopoly on Cipro, an antianthrax medication, if it did not lower the price.

Another factor that increases the nation's pill bill is the boom in direct-to-consumer advertising—ads that too often market drugs to people who don't need them. For instance, two out of three people taking Schering-Plough's pricey antiallergy medication, Claritin, reportedly don't even have allergies. Some ads steer patients toward drugs for conditions better tackled through prevention; others lead to overuse or misuse, as patients demand medications that clash.

Drug companies fight accusations of profiteering by offering evidence that high-priced drugs save billions each year by treating conditions that otherwise lead to chronic illnesses and costly hospitalizations. Moreover, the drug giants known as Big Pharma do their part to lower costs—Glaxo-Smith Kline offers discounts of up to 40 percent to elderly Americans, while Novartis provides Gleevec free to leukemia patients who can't afford it. Most drug companies now either give away or sell AIDS-related drugs in Africa at a fraction of their cost.

Considering the escalating costs of health care, should drug companies be allowed to set high prices for their patented products?

PRO

1. In a free market, marketing prescription drugs is a business—companies have a duty to shareholders to maximize profits.
2. If prices are squeezed, big pharmaceutical companies lose incentive to create better drugs.

CON

1. Taxpayers who pay for Medicaid stand to benefit from lower drug prices.
2. If prices are allowed to soar, it's possible that medicines will be available only to those able to pay—a possible death sentence for low-income Americans.

Summary

The aging population, the increase in drug use fueled by advertising, and the higher-than-ever costs of a new generation of gene-savvy medications threaten to bust the health-care budget. If Big Pharma, the government, and insurers are unable to control drug prices, the health-care industry is headed for a crash.

SOURCES: Vanessa Fuhrmans and Gautam Naik, "Drug Makers Fight to Fend Off Cuts in European Prices," *The Wall Street Journal*, June 7, 2002, pp. A1, A7; Ann Zimmerman and David Armstrong, "Swallow This: How Drug Makers Use Pharmacies to Push Pricey Pills," *The Wall Street Journal*, May 1, 2002, p. A1; Dyan Machan, "Doing Badly by Doing Good," *Forbes*, October 29, 2001, pp. 92–94; John Carey and Amy Barrett, "Drug Prices: What's Fair?" *BusinessWeek*, December 10, 2001, pp. 61–70.

Table 13.3, on page 390, illustrates why the intersection of the marginal cost and marginal revenue curves is the logical point at which to maximize revenue for the organization. Although the firm can earn a profit at several different prices, the price at which it earns maximum profits is $22. At a price of $24, $66 in profits are earned—$4 less than the $70 profit at the $22 price. If a price of $20 is set to attract additional sales, the marginal costs of the extra sales ($7) are greater than the marginal revenues received ($6), and total profits decline.

TABLE 13.2   Distinguishing Features of the Four Market Structures

	TYPE OF MARKET STRUCTURE			
CHARACTERISTICS	**PURE COMPETITION**	**MONOPOLISTIC COMPETITION**	**OLIGOPOLY**	**MONOPOLY**
Number of competitors	Many	Few to many	Few	No direct competitors
Ease of entry into industry by new firms	Easy	Somewhat difficult	Difficult	Regulated by government
Similarity of goods or services offered by competing firms	Similar	Different	Can be either similar or different	No directly competing goods or services
Control over prices by individual firms	None	Some	Some	Considerable
Demand curves facing individual firms	Totally elastic	Can be either elastic or inelastic	Kinked; inelastic below kink; more elastic above	Can be either elastic or inelastic
Examples	2000-acre ranch	Gap stores	Shell	Duke Energy

The Concept of Elasticity in Pricing Strategy

3

Explain price elasticity and its determinants.

Although the intersection of the marginal cost and marginal revenue curves determines the level of output, the impact of changes in price on sales varies greatly. In order to understand why it fluctuates, it is necessary to understand the concept of elasticity.

Elasticity is the measure of responsiveness of purchasers and suppliers to price changes. The price elasticity of demand (or elasticity of demand) is the percentage change in the quantity of a good or service demanded divided by the percentage change in its price. A 10 percent increase in the price of eggs that results in a 5 percent decrease in the quantity of eggs demanded yields a price elasticity of demand for eggs of 0.5. The price elasticity of supply of a product is the percentage change in the quantity of a good or service supplied divided by the percentage change in its price. A 10 percent increase in the price of shampoo that results in a 25 percent increase in the quantity supplied yields a price elasticity of supply for shampoo of 2.5.

Consider a case in which a 1 percent change in price causes more than a 1 percent change in the quantity supplied or demanded. Numerically, that means an elasticity greater than 1.0. When the elasticity of demand or supply is greater than 1.0, that demand or supply is said to be elastic. If a 1 percent change in price results in less than a

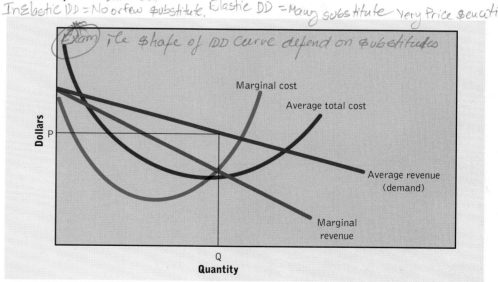

FIGURE 13.6
Determining Price by Relating Marginal Revenue to Marginal Cost

TABLE 13.3   **Price Determination Using Marginal Analysis**

PRICE	NUMBER SOLD	TOTAL REVENUE	MARGINAL REVENUE	TOTAL COSTS	MARGINAL COSTS	PROFITS (TOTAL REVENUE MINUS TOTAL COSTS)
—	—	—	—	—	—	($50)
$34	1	$34	$34	57	$7	(23)
32	2	64	30	62	5	2
30	3	90	26	66	4	24
28	4	112	22	69	3	43
26	5	130	18	73	4	57
24	6	144	14	78	5	66
22	7	154	10	84	6	70
20	8	160	6	91	7	69
18	9	162	2	100	9	62
16	10	160	(2)	110	11	50

1 percent change in quantity, a product's elasticity of demand or supply will be less than 1.0. In that case, the demand or supply is called *inelastic*. For example, the demand for cigarettes is relatively inelastic; research studies have shown that a 10 percent increase in cigarette prices results in only a 4 percent sales decline.

In countries such as Argentina or Brazil, where the annual inflation rate has been known to top 100 percent, prices on almost all products have risen accordingly. These higher prices have led to elastic demand for some items, such as houses and cars; many of the cars on Argentina's roads are over 10 years old, and the nation's housing market is severely depressed. For other products, demand has been inelastic; families continue to buy food because, after all, they need to eat. However, even if they do not affect demand, inflationary prices can alter consumers' buying patterns. Lower-income Brazilians, for instance, buy all the food items they can afford when they get each paycheck.

Determinants of Elasticity

Why is the elasticity of supply or demand high for some products and low for others? What determines demand elasticity? One major factor influencing the elasticity of demand is the availability of substitutes or complements. If consumers can easily find close substitutes for a good or service, the product's demand tends to be elastic. For example, the relatively inelastic demand for motor oil reflects its role as a complement to a more important product, gasoline. The end-of-chapter case explores pricing decisions at the U.S. Postal Service, including the effect of rate hikes on consumer demand.

As increasing numbers of buyers and sellers complete their business transactions online, the elasticity of a product's demand is drastically affected. Take large discounters, for example. Small businesses and individual do-it-yourselfers shop Home Depot for tools, such as wheelbarrows; parents look for birthday gifts at Toys "R" Us; and homeowners go

The next four years

brought to you by UNITED STATES POSTAL SERVICE

www.usps.com

The U.S. Postal Service, the subject of Case 13.1, uses promotional messages like this to rally support for policy changes—such as recent price increases—that affect users of its mail services.

to Circuit City for new refrigerators or stoves. Today, however, the Internet lets consumers contact product manufacturers and service providers directly, often giving them better selections and prices for their efforts. Wheelbarrows, for instance, were once sold at almost identical prices at a relatively small number of retail outlets (inelastic demand). Today's shoppers can pick up a wheelbarrow at dozens of different locations—traditional hardware stores, plant nurseries, home-improvement centers, discount stores, and even some department stores. No longer does one wheelbarrow fit all—the product comes in different sizes, colors, and materials to match the specific needs of different users. The availability of different models and different prices for each combine to create a market characterized by demand elasticity.

Elasticity of demand also depends on whether a product is perceived as a necessity or a luxury. The Four Seasons chain of luxury hotels and resorts enjoys such a strong reputation for service, comfort, and exclusiveness

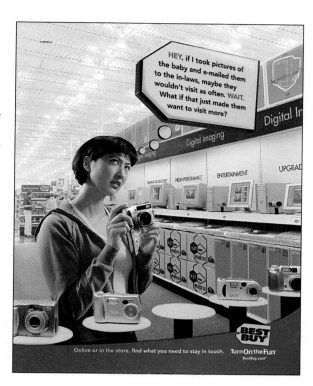

FIGURE 13.7
Promoting Digital Cameras as Necessities to Stimulate Demand and Lessen the Product's Price Elasticity

that it has become a favorite among affluent individual travelers and business professionals. The combination of personal service and exclusiveness attracts a select group of upscale travelers who consider reservations at Four Seasons hotels essential components of their trips to Atlanta or Tokyo. Because its accommodations are viewed as a necessity, not a luxury, sales remain strong despite rising room rates.

Most people regard high-fashion clothes, such as a $2,000 Armani suit, as luxuries. If prices for designer outfits increase, people can respond by purchasing lower-priced substitutes instead. In contrast, medical and dental care are considered necessities, so price changes have little effect on the frequency of medical or dental visits.

However, under the continuing influence of higher prices, some products once regarded as necessities may be dismissed as luxuries, leading to decreasing demand. Formerly booming personal computer sales have shown little or no growth in recent years. As home movies make the expensive conversion from VHS to DVD, many consumers choose to wait rather than spend the extra money for a DVD player and discs. In Figure 13.7, leading U.S. consumer electronics retailer Best Buy works hard to persuade potential buyers that a next-generation digital camera is a necessity rather than a luxury.

Elasticity also depends on the portion of a person's budget that he or she spends on a good or service. People no longer really need matches. They can easily find good substitutes. Nonetheless, the demand for matches remains very inelastic because people spend so little on them that they hardly notice a price change. In contrast, the demand for housing or transportation is not totally inelastic, even though they are necessities, because both consume large parts of a consumer's budget.

Elasticity of demand also responds to consumers' time perspectives. Demand often shows less elasticity in the short run than in the long run. Consider the demand for home air conditioning. In the short run, people pay rising energy prices because they find it difficult to cut back on the quantities they use. Accustomed to living with specific temperature settings and dressing in certain ways, they prefer to pay more during a few months out of the year than to explore other possibilities. Over time, though, with global warming becoming a real and present danger, they may find ways to economize. They can better insulate their homes, or plant shade trees.

Sometimes the usual patterns do not hold true, though. Alcohol and tobacco, which are not necessities but do occupy large shares of some personal budgets, are also subject to inelastic demand.

Elasticity and Revenue

The elasticity of demand exerts an important influence on variations in total revenue as a result of changes in the price of a good or service. Assume, for example, that San Francisco's Bay Area Rapid

Transit (BART) officials are considering alternative methods of raising more money for the city budget. One possible method for increasing revenues would be to change rail pass fares for BART commuters. But should the city raise or lower the price of a pass? The correct answer depends on the elasticity of demand for subway rides. A 10 percent decrease in fares should attract more riders, but unless it stimulates more than a 10 percent increase in riders, total revenue will fall. A 10 percent increase in fares will bring in more money per rider, but if more than 10 percent of the riders stop using the subway, total revenue will fall. A price cut will increase revenue only for a product with elastic demand, and a price increase will raise revenue only for a product with inelastic demand. BART officials seem to believe that the demand for rapid rail transit is inelastic; they raise fares when they need more money for the city budget.

4

List the practical problems involved in applying price theory concepts to actual pricing decisions.

Practical Problems of Price Theory

Marketers may thoroughly understand price theory concepts but still encounter difficulty applying them in practice. What practical limitations interfere with price setting?

First, many firms do not attempt to maximize profits. Economic analysis is subject to the same limitations as the assumptions on which it is based—for example, the proposition that all firms attempt to maximize profits. Second, it is difficult to estimate demand curves. Modern accounting procedures provide managers with a clear understanding of cost structures, so managers can readily comprehend the supply side of the pricing equation. But they find it difficult to estimate demand at various price levels. Demand curves must be based on marketing research estimates that may be less exact than cost figures. Although the demand element can be identified, it is often difficult to measure in real-world settings.

5

Explain the major cost-plus approaches to price setting.

Price Determination in Practice *Read*

The practical limitations inherent in price theory have forced practitioners to turn to other techniques. *No* *Cost-plus pricing*, the most popular method, uses a base-cost figure per unit and adds a markup to cover unassigned costs and to provide a profit. The only real difference among the multitude of cost-plus techniques is the relative sophistication of the costing procedures employed. For example, a local apparel shop may set prices by adding a 45 percent markup to the invoice price charged by the supplier. The markup is expected to cover all other expenses and permit the owner to earn a reasonable return on the sale of clothes.

In contrast to this rather simple pricing mechanism, a large manufacturer may employ a complex pricing formula requiring computer calculations. However, this method merely adds a more complicated procedure to the simpler, traditional method for calculating costs. In the end, someone still must make a decision about the markup. The apparel shop and the large manufacturer may figure costs differently, but they are remarkably similar in completing the markup side of the equation.

Cost-plus pricing often works well for a business that keeps its costs low, allowing it to set its prices lower than those of competitors and still make a profit. American discounter Wal-Mart keeps costs low by buying most of its inventory directly from manufacturers and relying on wholesalers and other intermediaries only in special instances like localized items. This strategy has helped the discounter in its rise to become the world's largest retailer.

Alternative Pricing Procedures

The two most common cost-oriented pricing procedures are the full-cost method and the incremental-cost method. *Full-cost pricing* uses all relevant variable costs in setting a product's price. In addition, it allocates those fixed costs that cannot be directly attributed to the production of the specific item being priced. Under the full-cost method, if job order 515 in a printing plant amounts to .000127 percent of the plant's total output, then .000127 percent of the firm's overhead expenses are charged to that job. This approach allows the marketer to recover all costs plus the amount added as a profit margin.

The full-cost approach has two basic deficiencies. First, there is no consideration of competition or demand for the item. Perhaps no one wants to pay the price the firm has calculated. Second, any method for allocating overhead (fixed expenses) is arbitrary and may be unrealistic. In manufacturing, overhead allocations often are tied to direct labor hours. In retailing, the square footage of each profit center is sometimes the factor used in computations. Regardless of the technique employed, it is difficult to show a cause-effect relationship between the allocated cost and most products.

One way to overcome the arbitrary allocation of fixed expenses is with *incremental-cost pricing*, which attempts to use only those costs directly attributable to a specific output in setting prices. Consider a small-scale manufacturer with the following income statement:

Sales (10,000 units at $10)		$100,000
Expenses:		
Variable	$50,000	
Fixed	40,000	90,000
Net Profit		$ 10,000

Suppose the firm is offered a contract for an additional 5,000 units. Since the peak season is over, these items can be produced at the same average variable cost. Assume that the labor force would otherwise be working on maintenance projects. How low should the firm price its product in order to get the contract?

Under the full-cost approach, the lowest price would be $9 per unit. This figure is obtained by dividing the $90,000 in expenses by an output of 10,000 units. The incremental approach, on the other hand, could permit any price above $5, which would significantly increase the possibility of securing the additional contract. This price would be composed of the $5 variable cost associated with each unit of production plus a $.10-per-unit contribution to fixed expenses and overhead. With a $5.10 proposed price, the income statement now looks like this:

Sales (10,000 at $10; 5,000 at $5.10)		$125,500
Expenses:		
Variable	$75,000	
Fixed	40,000	115,000
Net Profit		$ 10,500

Profits thus are increased under the incremental approach.

Admittedly, the illustration is based on two assumptions: (1) the ability to isolate markets such that selling at the lower price will not affect the price received in other markets, and (2) the absence of legal restrictions on the firm. The example, however, does illustrate that profits can sometimes be enhanced by using the incremental approach.

Breakeven Analysis *Read BEP where ur TC meets w/ ur (TR).*

Breakeven analysis is a means of determining the number of goods or services that must be sold at a given price to generate sufficient revenue to cover total costs. Figure 13.8 graphically depicts this process. The total cost curve includes both fixed and variable segments, and total fixed cost is represented by a horizontal line. Average variable cost is assumed to be constant per unit as it was in the example for incremental pricing.

The breakeven point is the point at which total revenue just equals total cost. In the example in Figure 13.8, a selling price of $10 and an average variable cost of $5 result in a per-unit contribution to fixed cost of $5. The breakeven point in terms of units is found by using the following formula, where the per-unit

Marketing Dictionary

breakeven analysis   Pricing technique used to determine the number of products that must be sold at a specified price in order to generate enough revenue to cover total cost.

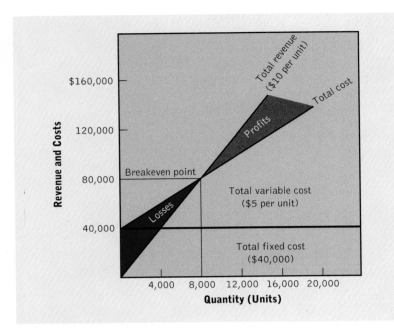

FIGURE 13.8
Breakeven Chart

contribution equals the product's price less the variable cost per unit:

$$\text{Breakeven Point (in units)} = \frac{\text{Total Fixed Cost}}{\text{Per-Unit Contribution to Fixed Cost}}$$

$$\text{Breakeven Point (in units)} = \frac{\$40,000}{\$5} = 8,000 \text{ units}$$

The breakeven point is found with the following formula:

$$\text{Breakeven Point (in dollars)} = \frac{\text{Total Fixed Cost}}{1 - \frac{\text{Variable Cost}}{\text{per Unit Price}}}$$

$$\text{Breakeven Point (in dollars)} = \frac{\$40,000}{1 - (\$5/\$10)} = \frac{\$40,000}{0.5} = \$80,000$$

Once the breakeven point has been reached, sufficient revenues will have been obtained from sales to cover all fixed costs. Any additional sales will generate per-unit profits equal to the difference between the product's selling price and the variable cost of each unit. As Figure 13.8 reveals, sales of 8,001 units (1 unit above the breakeven point) will produce net profits of $5 ($10 sales price less per-unit variable cost of $5). Once all fixed costs have been covered, the per-unit contribution will become the per-unit profit.

Thomas Lipsky knew enough about breakeven analysis to convince himself that he could start a record label—and make money. With limited financing and even less clout in the music business, the Raleigh, North Carolina–based concert promoter knew he would not be signing hot groups like the Backstreet Boys, who can sell 1.2 million copies of a new CD in a single week. So he signed the only acts he could afford: 1980s rock groups like Slaughter and Warrant that featured gaudy guitar solos and oversized stage theatrics. Even though Slaughter had sold 3 million albums in 1990, they quickly fell off the charts—and Lipsky had much more modest expectations for the Las Vegas–based group.

The key to making money was contained within the breakeven formula. Slaughter already owned a recording studio, so the $100,000 advance Lipsky shelled out went into the band members' pockets. Another $150,000 was spent on promotion, much of which went to retailers to persuade them to stock his product. Lipsky's record company makes a gross profit of $5 per disc, so he starts making money once an album sells more than 50,000 copies. Even though the advances are meager, the band goes along with it because (1) nobody else is beating down their doors to record them, and (2) the new albums make it easier to convince concert promoters to book them for tours. Lipsky is happy; the band rocks; and breakeven analysis shows how profits can be gleaned from modest sales by shrewd marketers who can control overhead.[12]

Target Returns

Although breakeven analysis indicates the sales level at which the firm will incur neither profits nor losses, most firms' managers include a targeted profit in their analyses. In some instances, management sets a desired dollar return when considering a proposed new product or other marketing action. A retailer may set a desired profit of $250,000 in considering whether to expand to a second location. In other instances, the target return may be expressed in percentages, such as a 15 percent return on sales. These target returns can be modified as follows:

$$\text{Breakeven Point (including specific dollar target return)} = \frac{\text{Total Fixed Cost + Profit Objective}}{\text{Per-Unit Contribution}}$$

Breakeven Point (in units) $= \dfrac{\$40,000\ +\ \$15,000}{\$5} = 11{,}000$ units

If the target return is expressed as a percentage of sales, it can be included in the breakeven formula as a variable cost. Suppose the marketer in the preceding example seeks a 10 percent return on sales. The desired return is $1 for each product sold (the $10 per-unit selling price multiplied by the 10 percent return on sales). In this case, the basic breakeven formula will remain unchanged, although the variable cost per unit will be increased to reflect the target return, and the per-unit contribution to fixed cost will be reduced to $4. As a result, the breakeven point will increase from 8,000 to 10,000 units:

Breakeven Point $= \dfrac{\$40,000}{\$4} = 10{,}000$ units

Evaluation of Breakeven Analysis

Breakeven analysis is an effective tool for marketers in assessing the sales required for covering costs and achieving specified profit levels. It is easily understood by both marketing and nonmarketing executives and may help them decide whether required sales levels for a certain price are in fact realistic goals. However, it has its shortcomings.

First, the model assumes that costs can be divided into fixed and variable categories. Some costs, such as salaries and advertising outlays, may be either fixed or variable depending on the particular situation. In addition, the model assumes that per-unit variable costs do not change at different levels of operation. However, these may vary because of quantity discounts, more efficient utilization of the workforce, or other economies resulting from increased levels of production and sales. Finally, the basic breakeven model does not consider demand. It is a cost-based model and does not directly address the crucial question of whether consumers will actually purchase the product at the specified price and in the quantities required for breaking even or generating profits. The marketer's challenge is to modify the breakeven analysis and the other cost-oriented pricing approaches to incorporate demand analysis. Pricing must be examined from the buyer's perspective. Such decisions cannot be made by considering only cost factors.

6

List the chief advantages and shortcomings of using breakeven analysis in pricing decisions.

Toward Realistic Pricing

Traditional economic theory considers both costs and demand in determining an equilibrium price. The dual elements of supply and demand are balanced at the point of equilibrium. In actual practice, however, most pricing approaches are largely cost oriented. Since purely cost-oriented approaches to pricing violate the marketing concept, modifications that will add demand analysis to the pricing decision are required.

Consumer research on such issues as degree of price elasticity, consumer price expectations, existence and size of specific market segments, and buyer perceptions of strengths and weaknesses of substitute products is necessary for developing sales estimates at different prices. Because much of the resulting data involves perceptions, attitudes, and future expectations of present and potential customers, such estimates are likely to be less precise than cost estimates.

The Modified Breakeven Concept No

The breakeven analysis method illustrated in Figure 13.8 assumes a constant $10 retail price regardless of quantity. But what happens at different retail prices? As Figure 13.9 shows, a more sophisticated approach called **modified breakeven analysis** combines the traditional breakeven analysis model with an evaluation of consumer demand.

Marketing Dictionary

modified breakeven analysis   Pricing technique used to evaluate consumer demand by comparing the number of products that must be sold at a variety of prices in order to cover total cost with estimates of expected sales at the various prices.

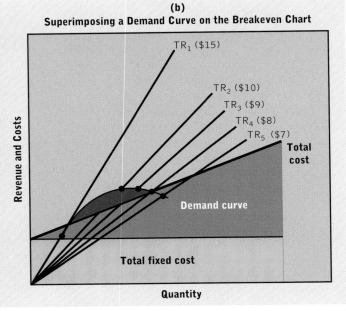

FIGURE 13.9
Modified Breakeven Chart: Parts A and B

7

Explain the superiority of modified breakeven analysis over the basic breakeven model and the role of yield management in pricing decisions.

Table 13.4 summarizes both the cost and revenue aspects of a number of alternative retail prices. The $5 unit variable cost and the $40,000 total fixed cost are based on the costs utilized in the basic breakeven model. The expected unit sales for each specified retail price are obtained from marketing research. The table contains the information necessary for calculating the breakeven point for each of the five retail price alternatives. These points are shown in Part A of Figure 13.9.

The data shown in the first two columns of Table 13.4 represent a demand schedule that indicates the number of units consumers are expected to purchase at each of a series of retail prices. As Part B of Figure 13.9 shows, these data can be superimposed onto a breakeven chart to identify the range of feasible prices for the marketer to charge.

TABLE 13.4   Revenue and Cost Data for Modified Breakeven Analysis

	REVENUES			COSTS			
PRICE	QUANTITY DEMANDED	TOTAL REVENUE	TOTAL FIXED COST	TOTAL VARIABLE COST	TOTAL COST	BREAKEVEN POINT (NUMBER OF SALES REQUIRED TO BREAK EVEN)	TOTAL PROFIT (OR LOSS)
$15	2,500	$37,500	$40,000	$12,500	$52,500	4,000	$(15,000)
10	10,000	100,000	40,000	50,000	90,000	8,000	10,000
9	13,000	117,000	40,000	65,000	105,000	10,000	12,000
8	14,000	112,000	40,000	70,000	110,000	13,334	2,000
7	15,000	105,000	40,000	75,000	115,000	20,000	(10,000)

Figure 13.9 reveals that the range of profitable prices exists from a low of approximately $8 (TR$_4$) to a high of $10 (TR$_2$), with a price of $9 (TR$_3$) generating the greatest projected profits. Changing the retail price produces a new breakeven point. At a relatively high $15 (TR$_1$) retail price, the breakeven point is 4,000 units; at a $10 retail price, it is 8,000 units; and at the lowest price considered, $7 (TR$_5$), it is 20,000 units.

The contribution of modified breakeven analysis is that it forces the marketer to consider whether the consumer is likely to purchase the number of units of a good or service required for achieving breakeven at a given price. It demonstrates that a large number of units sold does not necessarily produce added profits, since—other things equal—lower prices are necessary for stimulating additional sales. Consequently, it is important to consider both costs and consumer demand in determining the most appropriate price.

[handwritten: Not based on TT table - based on E of DD.]

Yield Management

[handwritten: Read when time is slow yield Mgt is worked very well (so for movies at noon, the price is cheaper)]

When most of a firm's costs are fixed over a wide range of outputs, the primary determinant of profitability will be the amount of revenue generated by sales. **Yield management** strategies allow marketers to vary prices based on such factors as demand, even though the cost of providing those goods or services remains the same. For example, sports teams like the San Francisco Giants charge more for weekend games, while the Colorado Rockies raise ticket prices based on the crowd-pleasing power of visiting teams. In the public sector, the Port Authority of New York and New Jersey recently experimented with variable pricing, charging more to cross the George Washington bridge at peak rush hours.[13]

Similar yield management strategies typify the marketing of such goods and services as the following:

- *Theater tickets*—lower prices in the afternoons to offset low demand and higher prices in the evening when demand rises

- *Lodging*—lower prices off season and higher prices during peak season periods; low-priced weekend rates (except in locations like Las Vegas, New Orleans, and Charleston with high weekend tourist visits)

- *Auto rental*—lower prices on weekends when business demand is low and higher prices during the week when business demand is higher

- *Airfares*—low prices on nonrefundable tickets with travel restrictions such as advance-purchase and Saturday-night stay requirements and penalties for flight changes; high prices on refundable tickets that can be changed without penalty

The following example from the airline industry demonstrates how yield management maximizes revenues in situations where costs are fixed.[14]

Airlines constantly monitor reservations on every flight. Beginning approximately 330 days before the flight, space is allocated between full-fare, discount-fare, and free tickets for frequent flyers who qualify for complimentary tickets. This allocation is monitored and adjusted at regular intervals until the actual departure.

Assume, for example, that Northwest Airlines has scheduled a 180-seat plane as Flight 1480 with an 8 A.M. departure from Memphis to Minneapolis on October 23. When Flight 1480 leaves its gate for departure, all costs associated with the flight (fuel, crew, and other operating expenses) are fixed. The pricing that maximizes revenues on this flight will also maximize profits. An examination of past sales indicates that Northwest could sell 40 to 60 round-trip, full-fare tickets at $600 per passenger and 100 to 150 round-trip restricted-fare tickets at $200 per passenger. Demand for frequent-flyer space should be at least 10 seats.

Marketing Dictionary

yield management   Pricing strategy that allows marketers to vary prices based on such factors as demand, even though the cost of providing those goods or services remains the same; designed to maximize revenues in situations such as airfares, lodging, auto rentals, and theater tickets, where costs are fixed.

In the intensively competitive, global marketplace for credit cards, American Express frequently features cardholding celebrities in its international promotions. This ad features two award-winning filmmakers—producer Brian Grazer and former child star and successful director Ron Howard—who frequently collaborate in such memorable pictures as Academy Award–winning *A Beautiful Mind*. Since foreign revenues from U.S.-made films often match or even exceed domestic revenues, American Express expects to recoup the endorsement fees paid through increased U.S. and international revenues.

If Northwest reserves 60 seats for full-fare passengers and accepts reservations for 110 restricted-fare tickets but sells only 40 full-fare tickets (leaving 20 vacant seats), total revenues will be:

$$\text{Revenues} = (40 \times \$600) + (110 \times \$200)$$
$$= \$46,000$$

On the other hand, if Northwest's pricing decision makers want to reduce vacancies, they might decide to reduce the number of full-fare tickets to 20 and increase the restricted-fare tickets to 150. If the plane leaves the gate at full capacity, the flight will generate the following total revenues:

$$\text{Revenues} = (20 \times \$600) + (150 \times \$200)$$
$$= \$42,000$$

Instead of rigidly maintaining the allocations established nearly a year before the flight, Northwest will use yield management to maximize the revenue per flight. In this example, the airline initially holds 60 full-fare seats and accepts reservations for up to 110 restricted-fare seats. Thirty days before the October 23 departure, updated computer projections indicate that 40 full-fare seats are likely to be sold. The allocation is now revised to 40 full-fare and 130 restricted-fare tickets. A full flight leaves the gate and revenues are:

$$\text{Revenues} = (40 \times \$600) + (130 \times \$200)$$
$$= \$50,000$$

Applying yield management for the Memphis–Minneapolis flight increases revenues by at least $4,000 over the inflexible approach of making advance allocations and failing to adjust them based on passenger reservations and other data.

Global Issues in Price Determination

8

Identify the major pricing challenges facing online and international marketers.

It is equally important for a firm engaging in global marketing to use a pricing strategy that reflects its overall marketing strategy. Prices must support the company's broader goals, including product development, advertising and sales, customer support, competitive plans, and financial objectives.

In general, there are five pricing objectives that firms can use to set prices in global marketing. Four of these are the same pricing objectives that we discussed earlier in the chapter: profitability, volume, meeting competition, and prestige. In addition, international marketers work to achieve a fifth objective: price stability.

In the global arena, marketers may choose profitability objectives if their company is a price leader that tends to establish international prices. Profitability objectives also make sense if a firm is a low-cost supplier that can make a good profit on sales.

Volume objectives become especially important in situations where nations lower their trade barriers to expose domestic markets to foreign competition. As the European Union lowered economic barriers between countries, for instance, competition for customers soared. A recent trend has been mergers of European firms to form larger companies that can achieve volume objectives. As one economist notes, "Merger activity [is] a way to get economies of scale." Carrefour, France's version of Wal-Mart, recently acquired a former European competitor to become the world's second-largest retailer behind the Arkansas-based discount giant.

Increased competition in Europe has also spurred firms to work toward the third pricing objective of meeting competitors' prices. Dutch corporation Philips Electronics offers U.S.-style coupons that give buyers 10 to 15 percent discounts off kitchen appliances. Aldi and Lidl, two German-owned food retailers, have opened discount outlets in France, forcing native French stores such as Carrefour to reduce prices. Automaker Fiat once boasted a 54 percent share of the Italian car market; its share has since dropped significantly due to inroads from competitively priced Ford of Europe, Inc. Fiat has fought back by offering $1,600 rebates and zero-interest financing on certain models.

Prestige is a valid pricing objective in international marketing when products are associated with intangible benefits, such as high quality, exclusiveness, or attractive design. The greater a product's perceived benefits, the higher its price can be. Marketers must be aware, however, that cultural perceptions of quality can differ from one country to the next. Sometimes items that command prestige prices in the U.S. are considered run-of-the-mill in other nations; sometimes products that are anything but prestigious in America seem exotic to overseas consumers. American patrons, for instance, view McDonald's restaurants as affordable fast-food eateries, but in China they are seen as fashionable and relatively expensive.

The fifth pricing objective, price stability, is desirable in international markets although it is difficult to achieve. Wars, terrorism, economic downturns, changing governments and political parties, and shifting trade policies can alter prices. An example is the computer industry. A few years ago, U.S. computer manufacturers sold their products in Europe for 30 to 50 percent more than U.S. prices. Today, greater competition within the European Union has forced computer prices down until they average only 10 percent higher than the U.S. prices, barely enough to cover manufacturers' costs in retooling machines for the local market. Falling prices have slashed profits for both American and European manufacturers, including IBM, Hewlett-Packard, and Olivetti.

Price stability can be especially important for producers of commodities—goods and services that have easily accessible substitutes that other nations can supply quickly. Countries that export international commodities, such as wood, chemicals, and agricultural crops, suffer economically when their prices fluctuate. A nation such as Nicaragua, which exports sugar cane, can find that its balance of payments changes drastically when the international price for sugar shifts. This makes it vulnerable to stiff price competition from other sugar cane producers.

In contrast, countries that export value-oriented products, rather than commodities, tend to enjoy more stable prices. Prices of electronic equipment and automobiles tend to fluctuate far less than prices of sugar cane or bananas.

Strategic Implications of Marketing in the 21st Century

This chapter has focused on traditional pricing concepts and methods—principles that are critical to all marketing strategies, especially in e-commerce. Consumers can now compare prices quickly, heightening the already intense competitive pricing environment. The Web allows for prices to be negotiated on the spot and anything can be auctioned. From airline tickets to automobiles, the Web allows consumers to name their price.

While Internet shopping has not resulted in massive price cutting, it has increased the options available for consumers. Online price comparison engines, known as shopping bots, promise to help consumers find the lowest price for any good or service. Reverse auctions offered by sites like priceline.com, which allows customers to submit the highest price they are willing to pay for airline tickets, could conceivably be extended to other types of goods.[15]

Electronic delivery of music, books, and other goods and services will only lead to further price reductions. E-commerce has smoothed out the friction of time, which kept pricing relatively static. Microsoft cofounder Bill Gates recently gave a futuristic view of what he sees as a "friction-free economy." The current obsession with time and the ability to measure it will change perceptions and pricing of tangible goods. Goods and services are no longer made before they are ordered and their prices will no longer be fixed; instead, prices will shift up and down.

While at least in the short term consumers are enjoying the benefits of competitive online pricing, retailers worry as they watch their profit margins disappearing. The giant discount warehouse Costco, for example, offers housewares, furniture, and even office supplies delivered to your door through its discounted Web site. Meanwhile, Buy.com goes a step further. The online superstore recently announced plans to price goods at wholesale—wiping out any profit margin and depending entirely on on-site advertising for revenues. [16] While there is no obvious blueprint for success, pricing strategies at Costco and Buy.com derive from a similar way of thinking: Spend generously to win new customers, offer the lowest prices possible, and then give them superior customer services to keep them loyal.

Summary of Chapter Objectives

1. Outline the legal constraints on pricing.

A variety of laws affect pricing decisions. Antitrust legislation provides a general set of constraints. The Robinson-Patman Act amended the Clayton Act to prohibit price discrimination in sales to other producers, wholesalers, or retailers that are not based on a cost differential. This law does not cover export markets. At the state level, unfair-trade laws require sellers to maintain minimum prices for comparable merchandise. These laws have become less frequently enforced in recent years. Fair-trade laws were one legal barrier to competition that was removed. These laws permitted manufacturers to set minimum retail prices for products and to require their dealers to sign contracts agreeing to abide by such prices. The Consumer Goods Pricing Act banned interstate use of fair-trade laws.

2. Identify the major categories of pricing objectives.

Pricing objectives should be the natural consequence of overall organizational goals and more specific marketing goals. They can be classified into four major groups: (1) profitability objectives, including profit maximization and target returns; (2) volume objectives, including sales maximization and market share; (3) meeting competition objectives; and (4) prestige objectives.

3. Explain price elasticity and its determinants.

Elasticity is an important element in price determination. The degree of consumer responsiveness to price changes is affected by such factors as (a) availability of substitute or complementary goods; (b) the classification of a good or service as a luxury or a necessity; (c) the portion of a person's budget spent on an item, and (d) the time perspective.

4. List the practical problems involved in applying price theory concepts to actual pricing decisions.

In practice, there are three problems in using price theory. First, many firms do not attempt to maximize profits, a basic assumption of price theory. Second, it is difficult to accurately estimate demand curves. Finally, inadequate training of managers and poor communication between economists and managers make it difficult to apply price theory in the real world.

5. Explain the major cost-plus approaches to price setting.

Cost-plus pricing uses a base-cost figure per unit and adds a markup to cover unassigned costs and to provide a profit. It is the most commonly used method of setting prices today. There are two primary cost-oriented pricing procedures. Full-cost pricing uses all relevant variable costs in setting a product's price and allocates those fixed costs that cannot be directly attributed to the production of the specific item being priced. Incremental-cost pricing attempts to use only those costs directly attributable to a specific output in setting prices to overcome the arbitrary allocation of fixed expenses. The basic limitation of cost-oriented pricing is that it does not adequately account for product demand.

6. List the chief advantages and shortcomings of using breakeven analysis in pricing decisions.

Breakeven analysis is a means of determining the number of goods or services that must be sold at a given price to generate revenue sufficient for covering total costs. It is easily understood by managers and may help them decide whether required sales levels for a certain price are realistic goals. Its shortcomings are as follows. First, the model assumes that cost can be divided into fixed and variable categories and ignores the problems of arbitrarily making some allocations. Second, it assumes that per-unit variable costs do not change at different levels of operation, ignoring the possibility of quantity discounts, more efficient utilization of the workforce, and other possible economies. Third, the basic breakeven model does not consider demand. It is a cost-based model and fails to directly address the crucial question of whether consumers will actually purchase the product at the specified price and in the quantities required for breaking even or generating profits.

7. Explain the superiority of modified breakeven analysis over the basic breakeven model and the role of yield management in pricing decisions.

Breakeven analysis is a means of determining the number of products that must be sold at a given price to generate sufficient revenue to cover total costs. The modified breakeven concept combines the traditional breakeven analysis with an evaluation of consumer demand. It directly addresses the key question of whether consumers will actually purchase the product at different prices and in what quantities. Yield management pricing strategies are designed to maximize revenues in situations where costs are fixed, such as airfares, auto rentals, and theater tickets.

8. Identify the major pricing challenges facing online and international marketers.

In general, firms can choose from among five pricing objectives to set prices in global marketing. Four of these objectives are the same pricing objectives discussed earlier: profitability, volume, meeting competition, and prestige. The fifth objective is price stability, which is difficult to achieve since wars, border conflicts, terrorism, economic trends, changing governments and political parties, and shifting trade policies can alter prices. The same types of changes can alter pricing in online marketing.

Marketing Terms You Need to Know

price 376	target-return objective 381	customary prices 386	yield management 397
Robinson-Patman Act 377	Profit Impact of Market	elasticity 389	
unfair-trade laws 378	Strategies (PIMS)	breakeven analysis 393	
fair-trade laws 378	project 382	modified breakeven	
profit maximization 381	value pricing 384	analysis 395	

Other Important Marketing Terms

marginal analysis 381	pure competition 387	variable costs 387	cost-plus pricing 392
market-share objective 382	monopolistic competition 387	fixed costs 387	full-cost pricing 392
demand 387	oligopoly 387	average total costs 387	incremental-cost pricing 393
supply 387	monopoly 387	marginal cost 387	

Review Questions

1. Distinguish between fair-trade laws and unfair-trade laws. As a consumer, would you support such laws? Would your answer change if you were the owner of a small retail store?
2. Identify the major categories of pricing objectives. Give an example of each.
3. What are the major price implications of the PIMS studies? Suggest possible explanations for the relationships they reveal.
4. Explain the concept of elasticity. Identify each factor influencing elasticity and give a specific example of how it affects the degree of elasticity in a good or service.
5. Explain the advantages of using incremental-cost pricing rather than full-cost pricing. What potential drawbacks exist?
6. Why do many firms choose to de-emphasize pricing as a marketing tool and instead concentrate on the other marketing mix variables in seeking to achieve a competitive advantage?
7. How can locating the breakeven point assist in price determination? What are the primary dangers in relying solely on breakeven analysis in pricing decisions?
8. What is the breakeven point for a product with a selling price of $40, average variable cost of $24, and related fixed cost of $37,500? What impact would a $4-per-unit profit requirement have on the breakeven point?
9. Explain how the use of yield management can result in greater revenue than other pricing strategies. Under what conditions is yield management a useful pricing strategy?
10. Identify the factors that can affect prices in international and online marketing.

Projects and Teamwork Exercises

1. In small teams, categorize each of the following as a specific type of pricing objective. Suggest a company or product likely to utilize each pricing objective. Compare your findings.
   a. a 5 percent increase in profits over the previous year
   b. prices no more than 6 percent higher than prices quoted by independent dealers
   c. a 5 percent increase in market share
   d. a 25 percent return on investment (before taxes)
   e. following the price set by the most important competitor in each market segment
   f. setting the highest prices in the product category to maintain favorable brand image

2. In pairs, discuss the market situations that exist for the following products. Defend your answers and present them to the class.
   a. local dry-cleaning service
   b. DVD players
   c. golf clubs
   d. platinum
   e. soybeans
   f. remote control car alarms
   g. razors
   h. personal watercraft

3. How are the following prices determined and what do they have in common?
   a. ticket to a local museum
   b. your college tuition
   c. local sales tax rate
   d. printing of business cards

4. WebTech Development of Nashville, Tennessee, is considering the possible introduction of a new product proposed by its research-and-development staff. The firm's marketing director estimates that the product can be marketed at a price of $70. Total fixed cost is $278,000, and average variable cost is calculated at $48.
   a. What is the breakeven point in units for the proposed product?
   b. The firm's president has suggested a target profit return of $214,000 for the proposed product. How many units must be sold in order to both break even and achieve this target return?

5. The marketing research staff at Cleveland-based Cyber Novelties has developed the following sales estimates for a proposed new item designed to be marketed through direct mail sales:

Proposed Selling Price	Sales Estimate (units)
$8	55,000
10	22,000
15	14,000
20	5,000
24	2,800

   The new product has a total fixed cost of $60,000 and a $7 variable cost per unit.
   a. Which of the proposed selling prices would generate a profit for Cyber Novelties?
   b. Cyber Novelties' director of marketing also estimates that an additional $.50 per-unit allocation for extra promotion will produce the following increases in sales estimates: 60,000 units at an $8 unit selling price, 28,000 units at $10, 17,000 units at $15, 6,000 units at $20, and 3,500 units at $24. Indicate the feasible range of prices if this proposal is implemented and results in the predicted sales increases.
   c. Indicate the feasible price or prices if the $.50 per-unit additional promotion proposal is not implemented but management insists on a $25,000 target return.

'net Work

http://www.google.com

http://www.expedia.com

http://www.orbitz.com

http://www.travelocity.com

http://www.quicken.com/shopping/

http://www.amazon.com

1. Predatory pricing practices. Use a search engine such as Google to find recent news on predatory pricing practices. Identify the company, or companies, involved in these industries and the basis for the predatory pricing charges.

2. Yield management. Theater tickets, lodging, rental cars, and airfares all illustrate the concept of yield management. For this exercise, assume you want to fly between Boston and Miami. Visit one of the travel-oriented Web sites, such as Expedia, Orbitz, or Travelocity, and search for airfares. Vary your travel dates and time. How much variation in pricing did you find? What factors explain the differences in price?

3. Strategic implications of pricing in the 21st Century. Go to http://www.quicken.com/shopping/. Download and install the Quicken Shopper program. Go through the steps of pricing a recent CD at a site such as http://www.amazon.com without actually making a purchase. Once you've selected an item, launch the Quicken Shopper and print out the results.

Note: Internet Web addresses change frequently. If you don't find the exact sites listed, you may need to access the organization or company's home page and search from there.

CASE 13.1 — U.S. Postal Service Fights Chronic Financial Losses by Raising Prices for First-Class Mail

"The Post Office was bleeding," says Robert Wientzen, president of the Direct Marketing Association, describing the lackluster performance of the U.S. Postal Service in the 1990s, "and now it's hemorrhaging." For the last ten years, the beleaguered U.S. Postal Service has struggled to withstand competition from private delivery services like FedEx and UPS that have slashed into its revenues. Neither incremental price increases on first-class mail and business rates nor value-added services such as priority mail succeeded in boosting performance. With deficits in excess of $1.6 billion a year, the writing was already on the wall for the Postal Service's outmoded business model.

Then, disaster—in the form of anthrax-laced mail—sent the Postal Service into an inescapable downward spiral. The huge and unexpected expenses involved in beefing up security sent costs spinning out of control. A $500 million bailout from Congress helped the Postal Service cope with the anthrax scare and plan for future letter-borne attacks, but it did little to get the service out of its tailspin. Worse still, rather than mail letters and bills, consumers greatly expanded their use of credit card and electronic bill payment. Marketers also scaled back their bulk mailing programs, slicing 10 percent off postal service volume.

Facing a deficit that was expected to soar to $5 billion a year by 2006, the Postal Service proposed an overhaul of operations to Congress in 2002. The first item in the proposal to be implemented was aimed at an immediate cash inflow. The price of a first-class postage stamp—already increased twice during 2001 by a penny each time—jumped 3 cents to 37 cents. Across-the-board increases in business rates and bulk mailing rates soon followed. Other components of the proposal that were not immediately implemented included possible post office closings and the end of Saturday deliveries. A new law converting the post office into a commercial government agency after 2006 would allow it even greater pricing flexibility.

While price increases may help contain losses in the short term, experts predict that rate hikes will lead to a long-term falloff in revenues. If costs get too high, marketers may decide to stop using USPS for volume mailings like credit-card applications or mail order catalogs. Magazine and newspaper publishers, too, may devise alternative delivery systems. Many are experimenting with joint-marketing deals and Internet channels. Robert Wientzen of the Direct Marketing Association predicts that over time more and more companies will desert the mail. "The Post Office," he says, "is slowly pricing themselves out of business."

Questions for Critical Thinking

1. In what ways is the U.S. Postal Service's business model—particularly its pricing strategies—outdated?
2. Does the Postal Service offer fair value for money to consumers and business customers? Why or why not?

SOURCES: Kathy Chen, "Postal Panel Set to Increase Rates," *The Wall Street Journal,* March 22, 2002, p. A6; Randolph E. Schmid, "Post Office May Cut Six-Day Delivery," *Mobile Register,* April 5, 2002, p. B6; "Belt Tightening at the Post Office," CBS News, April 5, 2002, http://www.cbsnews.com; Adam Bryant, "Pushing the Envelope," *Newsweek,* October 29, 2001, p. 8.

VIDEO CASE 13.2 — Cybex International Whips Pricing into Shape

The written case on Cybex International appears on page VC-16. The recently filmed Cybex International video is designed to expand and highlight the concepts in this chapter and the concepts and questions covered in the written video case.

14

Managing the Pricing Function

Chapter Objectives

1 Compare the alternative pricing strategies and explain when each strategy is most appropriate.

2 Describe how prices are quoted.

3 Identify the various pricing policy decisions that marketers must make.

4 Relate price to consumer perceptions of quality.

5 Contrast competitive bidding and negotiated prices.

6 Explain the importance of transfer pricing.

7 Compare the three alternative global pricing strategies.

8 Relate the concepts of cannibalization, bundle pricing, and bots to online pricing strategies.

When Consumers and Retailers Say "No" to Higher Prices

Suppose you walked into your local supermarket, picked up a box of name-brand cereal—maybe Cheerios or Wheaties—and said to the checkout clerk, "I'm not paying this high a price for a box of cereal." Sound far-fetched? Actually, consumers who are just like you do this every day, and so can you. You don't even need to say anything to the cashier or the store manager—just select a private label or store brand instead. Prices for store-brand products are usually lower than prices set by the major manufacturers, and if you believe the quality of what you are buying is equal to or better than that of the name-brand product, you're ahead of the game. That store-brand crunchy oat cereal not only costs less but tastes just as good.

Major food manufacturers such as Kraft Foods, General Mills, Quaker Oats, and Kellogg Co. face this consumer revolt as they try to manage the prices of the various products they stock on supermarket shelves. In one recent year, three of the four—General Mills, Kraft Foods, and Quaker Oats—experienced a decline in sales of their cereals; even Kellogg grew by less than 1 percent. But private-label cereal sales jumped more than 3 percent. Consumers were resisting paying $4 to $5 for a box of cereal. "Many consumers have reacted to the higher prices by trading down to private label [goods]," noted Dave Nelson, an analyst for Crédit Suisse First Boston. Brian Sharoff, president of the Private Label Manufacturers Association, acknowledged that price isn't always the main issue when consumers select between major brands and private-label goods. For instance, they are more apt to be loyal to a certain brand of laundry detergent or pet food. But when it comes to cereal, "there is price-point resistance . . . which forces consumers to look elsewhere for the product." To make matters tougher for food companies, when industry leaders like Kraft announced a price increase of 2 percent to 3 percent for boxed cereals—because

of a rise in the cost of ingredients—retailing giant Wal-Mart simply rejected the increase. "Everyday low prices continue to be our goal when working with our [suppliers]," explained a Wal-Mart spokesperson.

The price of cereal illustrates a shift in distribution channel power. Traditionally, producers, such as General Mills or Quaker Oats, were the most powerful members of the channel because they were larger, better financed, and capable of extending credit to other channel members. They also had fewer competitors, so they could command just about any price within reason. But times have changed. Retailers like Wal-Mart have proven to be stronger, and consumers have grown accustomed to bargains, discounts, and lower prices in general. How can the producers survive in this changing environment? Some employ innovation, creating an entirely new class of products. Others acquire smaller companies in order to grow in certain areas. Kellogg's bought Kashi Foods and General Mills bought Small Planet Foods—both of them small producers of health-conscious foods. Some companies increase the size or weight of the product, offering more content to coincide with a higher price.

Still, not all industries are experiencing a loss of pricing power. Services such as health care and insurance continue to command higher prices, and home prices increased a whopping 8 percent during one recent quarter (that's a $16,000 increase on a $200,000 house). The price of entertainment—from movie tickets to National Basketball Association games—keeps going up, as well. But if the old maxim that what goes up must come down holds true in the next decade, marketers in these industries will be looking for new ways to attract and keep their customers from looking for alternatives.[1]

Chapter Overview

As food manufacturers will attest, setting prices is not a one-time decision, nor is it a routine or standard practice. Considered as much an art as a calculated scientific process, pricing is a dynamic function of the marketing mix. While about half of all companies change prices once a year or less frequently, one in ten does so every month. Online companies, who face enormous price pressures, often adjust prices daily. Some even negotiate prices on the spot.

Companies translate pricing objectives into pricing decisions in two major steps. First, someone must accept responsibility for making pricing decisions and administering the resulting pricing structure. Second, someone must set the overall pricing structure—that is, basic prices and appropriate discounts for channel members, quantity purchases, and geographic and promotional considerations.

The decision to make price adjustments is directly related to demand. Most businesses slowly change the amounts they charge customers, even when they clearly recognize strong demand. Instead of raising prices, they may choose to scale down customer service or add fees to cover added costs. They may also wait to raise prices until they see what their competitors will do. (Few businesses want the distinction of being the first to charge higher prices.) Since many businesses base their prices on manufacturing costs rather than consumer demand, they may wait for increases in their own costs before responding with price changes. These increases generally emerge more slowly than changes in consumer demand. Finally, since many business executives believe that steady prices will help to preserve long-term relationships with customers, they are reluctant to raise prices even when strong demand probably justifies the change.

Chapter 13 introduced the concept of price and its role in the economic system and marketing strategy. This chapter examines various pricing strategies and price structures, such as reductions from list prices and geographic considerations. It then looks at the primary pricing policies, including psychological pricing, price flexibility, product-line pricing, and promotional pricing, as well as price/quality relationships. Competitive and negotiated prices are discussed, and one section focuses entirely on transfer pricing. Finally, the chapter concludes by describing important factors in pricing goods and services for online and global markets.

Pricing Strategies

Compare the alternative pricing strategies and explain when each strategy is most appropriate.

The specific strategies that firms use to price goods and services grow out of the marketing strategies they formulate to accomplish overall organizational objectives. One firm's marketers may price products to attract customers across a wide range; another group of marketers may set prices to appeal to a small segment of a larger market; still another group may simply try to match competitors' price tags. In general, firms can choose from three pricing strategies: skimming, penetration, and competitive pricing. The following sections look at these choices in more detail.

[handwritten annotations: highest Possible Price (Price is not the key consideratº. Exam. M Skiming Penetratº. If the DD is Inelastic u might want to use a Skiming Pricing strategy. But If the DD curve is Elastic u might want to use a penetratº strategy. Price is sensitive. When competition comes u come 2 the Growth stage]

Skimming Pricing Strategy *Read Exam*

Derived from the term "skimming the cream," **skimming pricing strategies** are also known as *market-plus pricing*. They involve the intentional setting of a relatively high price compared with the prices of competing products. Although some firms continue to utilize a skimming strategy throughout most stages of the product life cycle, it is more commonly used as a market entry price for distinctive goods or services with little or no initial competition. Such was the case with early Polaroid cameras, the first video-cassette recorders, and the introduction of electric toothbrushes. More recently, in the marketing of personal computers and DVD players, early high prices were followed by rapid declines as competitors flooded the marketplace.

A company may practice a skimming strategy in setting a market-entry price when it introduces a distinctive good or service with little or no competition. Canon released its new S600 bubble-jet printer with a clever "Out of the Blue" ad campaign focusing on an innovative product feature—individual ink tanks that let users replenish a single color without having to throw away an entire cartridge. This money-saving feature alone allowed Canon to price the printer at the top of the market.[2]

Improvements in existing products may allow firms to change from other pricing structures to a skimming strategy. Following a failed attempt to hike prices for its fleece apparel, Polartec modified its products by using fabrics to offer enhanced wind resistance. By bringing something new to the market for which consumers were willing to pay more, Polartec improved its chances that its new price structure would be successful.[3]

Skimming strategies are often used by marketers of high-end goods and services. For instance, the ad for the Weber gas grill and outdoor oven in Figure 14.1 makes no mention of price. While the product is backed by a warranty, the firm's marketers play up the notion that the Weber name is the only quality guarantee buyers will ever need.

In some cases, a firm may maintain a skimming strategy throughout most stages of a product's life cycle. The jewelry category is a good example. For example, even though relatively stable prices of gold bullion allow

don't let your kitchen stove see you reading this.

EVERYTHING YOU DO IN YOUR OVEN, YOU CAN DO IN A WEBER® GAS GRILL. BECAUSE IT PROVIDES PRECISE HEAT CONTROL. NOT TO MENTION, IT'S CONSTRUCTED FROM THE HIGHEST-QUALITY U.S. STEEL AND BACKED BY A WARRANTY YOU'LL PROBABLY NEVER NEED. LIFE'S NOT PERFECT. THAT'S WHY WE STRIVE TO MAKE PRODUCTS THAT ARE. **genesis® gas grill and outdoor oven**

weber®

www.weber.com

© 2002 Weber-Stephen Products Co. The Weber name, logo, url, and kettle grill configuration are registered U.S. trademarks.

FIGURE 14.1
Weber: Distinctive Grills Marketed with a Skimming Pricing Strategy

Marketing Dictionary

skimming pricing strategy   Pricing strategy involving the use of a high price relative to competitive offerings.

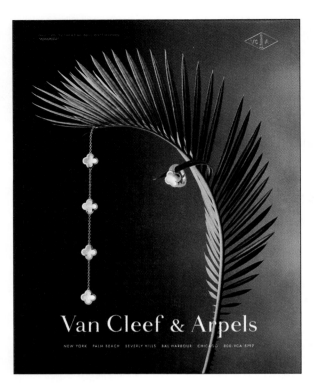

Van Cleef & Arpels

NEW YORK   PALM BEACH   BEVERLY HILLS   BAL HARBOUR   CHICAGO   800-VCA-5797

discounters such as Service Merchandise to offer high-karat jewelry for just a couple of hundred dollars, prestige brands like Tiffany or Cartier are able to command prices in excess of $5,000 for similar pieces. Exclusivity and craftsmanship justify the pricing—and the price, once set, never falls. Van Cleef & Arpels, featured in Figure 14.2, uses a skimming pricing strategy for its distinctive jewelry collections. Similarly, in the industrial sector, high-end Canadian steelmaker Dofasco Inc. was able to ride out an industry slump that dragged down rivals while keeping its prices up. The company focused on customized products for which price is not the main consideration.

Sometimes maintaining a high price through the product's life cycle works and sometimes it does not. Consider, for example, the entertainment industry. From Disney World to Six Flags and from Cirque du Soleil to movie theaters, admission prices for popular entertainment have soared in recent years. The cost of rock concert tickets has climbed by a third and the average ticket to an NBA game has gone up by almost 20 percent. Broadway attractions top $100 a seat, and fans can pay as much as $450 each for a VIP package to see Madonna, the Eagles, or the Rolling Stones in concert. Even a family outing to a nearby museum with a special exhibit can cost $20 or more per person—not including parking. Prices have, in fact, gone so high that many people have decided to stay home. As consumers reeled with sticker shock, concert grosses plummeted 35 percent in a single year. At Disney, attendance was off by 8 percent. Crowds at baseball parks, too, are steadily thinning out across the nation.

Despite the risk of backlash, a skimming strategy offers several benefits. First, it allows a manufacturer to quickly recover its research-and-development (R&D) costs. Pharmaceutical companies, who fiercely protect their patents on new drugs, justify high prices because of astronomical R&D costs—an average of 16 cents of every sales dollar, compared with 8 cents for computer makers and 4 cents in the aerospace industry. To protect their brand names from competition from lower-cost generics, drug makers frequently make small changes to their products, enabling them to extend their patents. Eli Lilly, for example, hopes to move patients to a newly patented weekly-dosage Prozac antidepressant, while Schering-Plough is seeking approval for a reformulation of its blockbuster antiallergy drug Claritin.[4]

A skimming strategy also offers a second benefit. It allows a firm to maximize revenue from a new product before competitors enter the field. In many industries, increasing competition eventually drives down initially high prices, as with television sets, digital watches, and pocket calculators.

A skimming pricing strategy is also a useful tool for segmenting a product's overall market on price. For a significant new product innovation, a relatively high price conveys an image of distinction, helping the product to appeal to buyers with low sensitivity to price. Over 50 years ago, the ballpoint pen was a dramatic breakthrough in writing instruments—and a highly visible one. Wealthy consumers with high discretionary incomes were willing to spend as much as $20 on the innovation. Today the best-selling ballpoint pens are priced at less than $1.

A final advantage of a skimming strategy is that it permits marketers to control demand in the introductory stages of a product's life cycle and then adjust productive capacity to match changing demand. A low initial price for a new product risks problems if demand outstrips the firm's production capacity, resulting in consumer and retailer complaints and possibly permanent damage to the product's image. Excess demand occasionally leads to poor-quality products, as the firm strives to satisfy consumer desires for the product with inadequate production facilities.

FIGURE 14.3
Price Reductions to Increase Market Share

During the late growth and early maturity stages of its life cycle, a product's price typically falls for two reasons: (1) the pressure of competition and (2) the desire to expand its market. Figure 14.3 shows that 10 percent of the market would buy Product X at $10.00, and another 20 percent would buy at a price of $8.75. Successive price declines expand the firm's market and meet challenges posed by new competitors.

A skimming strategy has one chief disadvantage: It attracts competition. Potential competitors see innovative firms reaping large financial returns and decide to enter the market. This new supply forces the price of the original product even lower than its eventual level under a sequential skimming procedure. However, if patent protection or some other unique proprietary ability allows a firm to exclude competitors from its market, it may continue a skimming strategy for a relatively long period. Gillette marketers took out 35 patents to stave off competition for its Mach3 shaving system. When the top-selling product had been on the market less than three years, Gillette was ready with a new and improved Mach3 Turbo.[5]

Penetration Pricing Strategy

A **penetration pricing strategy** sets a low price as a major marketing weapon. Marketers often price products noticeably lower than competing offerings when they enter new industries characterized by dozens of competing brands. Once the product achieves some market recognition through consumer trial purchases stimulated by its low price, marketers may increase the price to the level of competing products. Marketers of consumer products such as detergents often use this strategy. A penetration pricing strategy may also extend over several stages of the product life cycle as the firm seeks to maintain a reputation as a low-price competitor.

A penetration pricing strategy is sometimes called *market-minus pricing* when it implements the premise that a lower-than-market price will attract buyers and move a brand from an unknown newcomer to at least the brand-recognition stage or even to the brand-preference stage. Since many firms begin penetration pricing with the intention of increasing prices in the future, success depends on generating many trial purchases.

Should competitors view the new product as a threat, marketers attempting to use a penetration strategy often discover that rivals will simply match their prices. Even though about 40 percent of the population currently uses cell phones, the U.S. is five years behind Japan and many parts of Northern Europe, where usage tops 50 percent. And in at least one country—Finland—cell phone usage has hit the 75 percent mark. But even as U.S. cell phone usage has soared, worries that price cuts for cell phones will immediately be matched by the growing number of competing service providers have resulted in cell phone prices remaining fairly stable while competitors decided to focus on lower fees, increased time and geographic limits, and improved customer service.[6]

Discount air carriers like AirTran, America West, JetBlue, and Southwest continually face the problem of having their prices matched by larger competitors. As a result, they often compete with major carriers by offering not just low prices, but a combination of attractive airfares, high customer service levels, and routes

Marketing Dictionary

penetration pricing strategy   Pricing strategy involving the use of a relatively low entry price compared with competitive offerings; based on the theory that this initial low price will help secure market acceptance.

that are often underserved by the majors. Aided by flight purchase guarantees from local businesses seeking improved air service, AirTran has established routes to minor markets such as Myrtle Beach, SC, and Biloxi, MS.[7]

Retailers may use penetration pricing to lure shoppers to new stores. Strategies might take such forms as zero interest charges for credit purchases at a new furniture store, two-for-one offers for dinner at a new restaurant, or an extremely low price on a single product purchase for first-time customers to get them to come in and shop.

Penetration pricing works best for goods or services characterized by highly elastic demand. Large numbers of highly price-sensitive consumers pay close attention to this type of appeal. The strategy also suits situations in which large-scale operations and long production runs result in low production and marketing costs. Finally, penetration pricing may be appropriate in market situations in which introduction of a new product will likely attract strong competitors. Such a strategy may allow a new product to reach the mass market quickly and capture a large share prior to entry by competitors. Research shows that about 25 percent of companies use penetration pricing strategies on a regular basis.

Everyday Low Pricing

#1 Price strategy for retailer. Exple Home Depot - Wal-Mart.
Promotional Pricing #2 " " " " called also (Hi-Low-Pricing) They run sale every 2 weeks

Closely related to penetration pricing is *everyday low pricing (EDLP)*, a strategy devoted to continuous low prices as opposed to relying on short-term, price-cutting tactics such as cents-off coupons, rebates, and special sales. EDLP can take two forms. In the first, retailers like Wal-Mart compete by consistently offering consumers low prices on a broad range of items. Through its EDLP policy, Lowe's offers not only to match any price the consumer sees elsewhere but to take off an additional 10 percent. The Lowe's EDLP strategy is featured in the firm's promotion shown in Figure 14.4.

In many cases, the EDLP pricing strategy is used by the manufacturer in dealing with channel members. Manufacturers may seek to set stable wholesale prices that undercut offers that competitors make to retailers, offers that often rise and fall with the latest trade promotion deals. Many marketers reduce the list prices on a number of products while simultaneously reducing promotion allowances to retailers. While reductions in allowances mean that retailers may not fund in-store promotions, such as shelf merchandising and end-aisle displays, the manufacturers hope that stable low prices will stimulate sales instead. During the 1990s, Procter & Gamble initiated a program that led to many dramatic price cuts on some of its products such as detergents, paper towels, and disposable diapers. Recently, R. J. Reynolds used EDLP to fend off deeply discounted cigarette imports. Reynolds cut the prices of its own deep-discount brands, Monarch and Best Value. For other brands, retailers received an extra 70 cents per pack from RJR as an incentive to stock more of its higher-tier brands instead of cheaper cigarettes. In addition, participating retailers are encouraged to price RJR's deep-discount cigarettes below or on a par with rivals.[8]

Some retailers oppose EDLP strategies. Grocery stores, for instance, operate on "high-low" strategies that set profitable regular prices to offset losses of frequent specials and promotions. Other retailers believe that EDLP will ultimately benefit both sellers and buyers. Supporters of EDLP in the grocery industry point out that it already succeeds at two of the biggest competitors, Wal-Mart and warehouse clubs. Marketing theorists express differing opinions about the prospects of EDLP emerging as a dominant pricing strategy.

FIGURE 14.4
Lowe's: Succeeding with an Everyday Low Pricing Strategy

NEED A NEW APPLIANCE?
WE HAVE THE ONE YOU WANT.
(AND 249 MORE JUST IN CASE.)

Shopping at Lowe's for appliances definitely has its advantages. Our team of experts can help you choose from over 250 name brand appliances. They're in-stock and ready to go. So you get the appliance you want, when you want it. We'll also deliver your new appliance within 24 hours.* And we'll even haul your old one away for free. Stop by today or visit lowes.com for more information.

LOWE'S
Improving Home Improvement
EVERYDAY LOW PRICES. GUARANTEED!*

One popular myth of pricing is that a low price is a sure sell. Low prices are an easy means of distinguishing the offerings of one marketer from other sellers, but such moves are easy to counter by competitors. Unless overall demand is price elastic, overall price cuts will mean less revenue for all firms in the industry. In addition, low prices may generate an image of questionable quality. As 19th-century critic John Ruskin put it, "There is hardly anything in the world that some men can't make a little worse and sell a little cheaper, and the people who consider price only are this man's lawful prey." The astute marketer should evaluate both the benefits derived from low-price strategies and the costs involved before launching an EDLP strategy.

Competitive Pricing Strategy

Although many organizations rely heavily on price as a competitive weapon, even more implement **competitive pricing strategies.** These organizations try to reduce the emphasis on price competition by matching other firms' prices and concentrating their own marketing efforts on the product, distribution, and promotion elements of the marketing mix. As pointed out earlier, while price offers a dramatic means of achieving competitive advantage, it is also the easiest marketing variable for competitors to match. In fact, in industries with relatively homogeneous products, competitors must match each other's price reductions to maintain market share and remain competitive.

Retailers like Home Depot and Lowe's both use price-matching strategies, assuring consumers they will meet—and beat—competitors' prices. Grocery chains such as Safeway, Winn-Dixie, and Raley's often compete with seasonal items: watermelons, soft drinks, and hot dogs in the summer; apples, hot chocolate, and turkeys in the winter. As soon as one store lowers the price of an item like turkey, the rest follow suit.

Even when marketers sell relatively heterogeneous products, they continue to analyze the prices of major competing offerings and ensure their own prices do not markedly differ. When IBM entered the personal computer market, its marketing efforts emphasized the versatility and power of its machines. However, the firm's marketers also quickly pointed out to potential customers that each PC in the line carried a competitive price.

Under competitive pricing, a price reduction results in financial effects throughout an industry as other firms match the drop. Unless the lower prices can attract new customers and expand the overall market enough to offset the loss of per-unit revenue, the price cut will leave all competitors with less revenue. Research shows that nearly two-thirds of all firms set prices using competitive pricing as their primary pricing strategy.

Web marketing is typically associated with penetration pricing strategies due to the inroads that book, music, and air travel sales have made using low, negotiable prices with razor-thin profit margins. However, online marketers are discovering that such customer benefits as selection, quick order fulfillment, and easy returns are also important decision criteria. Customers drawn to a Web site with lots of perks and lavish customer service are likely to pay full price for more individualized, high-ticket items like brand-name apparel and accessories. Amazon.com, for example, frequently charges more than its cut-price competitors. Although now defunct e-discounter Books.com consistently charged less for the same commodity products, its market share never rose above 2.2 percent. Having gained not only brand awareness but the trust of online shoppers, Amazon stayed way ahead.[9]

By pricing products at the general levels of competitive offerings, marketers largely negate the price variable in their marketing strategies. They must then emphasize nonprice variables to develop areas of distinctive competence and attract customers. Consider the bottled water market. While some firms currently marketing bottled water to a thirsty public emphasize price as a primary component of their marketing mixes, when global bottlers Coca-Cola and PepsiCo decided to launch their Dasani and Aquafina brands, they chose to emphasize product quality, the brands' easy availability due to saturation coverage of the marketplace, and considerable promotion focusing on the products' attributes. Although their prices are higher than those of the smaller competitors, both companies chose to align their prices with well-known brands like Evian and Poland

Briefly Speaking

Cutting prices is usually insanity if the competition can go as low as you can.

Michael E. Porter
(b. 1947)
American educator

Marketing Dictionary

competitive pricing strategy   Pricing strategy designed to de-emphasize price as a competitive variable by pricing a good or service at the general level of comparable offerings.

FIGURE 14.5
The Coca-Cola
Company's Dasani
Bottled Water:
Building Market
Share by Emphasizing
Non-Price Marketing
Mix Elements

Springs. As Figure 14.5 illustrates, the Dasani ad emphasizes fresh taste, enjoyment, and high-quality fresh water. And even though both brands were latecomers to the competitive fray, both have enjoyed considerable sales success.

Price Quotations

The choice of the best method for quoting prices depends on many industry conditions, including competitive trends, cost structures, and traditional practices, along with the policies of individual firms. This section examines the reasoning and methodology behind price quotation practices.

Most price structures are built around *list prices*—the rates normally quoted to potential buyers. Marketers usually determine list prices by one or a combination of the methods discussed in Chapter 13. The sticker price on a new automobile is a good example: It shows the list price for the basic model and then adds the prices of options.

T-shirts offer another familiar example of list prices. About 1 billion of them are bought in the U.S. each year, generating sales revenues of $10 billion. Many of the most lucrative sales involve T-shirts sporting images of musical groups or sports stars and event dates. But where does the money go when you purchase a concert T-shirt at a list price of $25? Figure 14.6 supplies the answers. Although 54 percent of the $25 list price goes for production costs, the $7.50 licensing fee paid to the recording artist accounts for nearly half of the total. The remaining 46 percent is paid to the retailer (the concert arena) and to concert vendors.

2

Describe how prices are quoted.

Reductions from List Price

The amount that a consumer pays for a product—its *market price*—may or may not equal the list price. Discounts and allowances sometimes reduce list prices. A list price often defines a starting point

FIGURE 14.6
The Take on a
$25 T-Shirt

Production Costs 54%

Cost of T-Shirt $3.50

Silk-Screening, Processing, and Transportation $2.50

Licensing Fee Paid to Recording Artist $7.50

Marketing Costs 46%

Payment to Concert Vendor $4.00

Payment to Concert Arena $7.50

$25

from which discounts set a lower market price. Marketers offer discounts in several classifications: cash, trade, and quantity discounts.

Cash Discounts

Consumers, industrial purchasers, or channel members sometimes receive reductions in price in exchange for prompt payment of bills; these price cuts are known as *cash discounts*. Discount terms usually specify exact time periods, such as 2/10, net 30. This notation means that the customer must pay within 30 days, but payment within 10 days entitles the customer to subtract 2 percent from the amount due.

Cash discounts represent a traditional pricing practice in many industries. They fulfill legal requirements, provided that all customers can take the same reductions on the same terms. Sellers originally instituted such discount practices to improve their own liquidity positions, reduce their bad-debt losses, and cut collection expenses. Whether these advantages outweigh the relatively high cost of capital that sellers incur by offering cash discounts depends on the need for liquidity as well as alternative sources (and costs) of funds.

Trade Discounts

Payments to channel members for performing marketing functions are known as *trade discounts,* or functional discounts. Later chapters discuss the services performed by various channel members and the related costs. A manufacturer's list price must incorporate the costs incurred by channel members in performing required marketing functions and expected profit margins for each member.

Trade discounts initially reflected the operating expenses of each category, but they have become more or less customary practices in some industries. The Robinson-Patman Act allows trade discounts as long as all buyers in the same category, such as all wholesalers or all retailers, receive the same discount privileges.

Figure 14.7 shows how a chain of trade discounts works. In the first instance, the trade discount is "40 percent, 10 percent off list price" for wholesalers. In other words, the 40 percent discount on the $40 product is the trade discount the retailer receives to cover operating expenses and earn a profit. The wholesaler receives 10 percent of the $24 price to retailers to cover expenses and earn a profit. The manufacturer receives $21.60 from the wholesaler for each order.

In the second example, the manufacturer and retailer decide to bypass the wholesaler. The producer offers a trade discount of 45 percent to the retailer. In this instance, the retailer receives $18 for each product sold at its list price, and the manufacturer receives the remaining $22. Either the retailer or the manufacturer must assume responsibility for the services previously performed by the wholesaler, or they can share these duties between them.

Quantity Discounts

Price reductions granted for large-volume purchases are known as *quantity discounts*. Sellers justify these discounts on the grounds that large orders reduce selling expenses and may shift some costs for storage, transportation, and financing to buyers. The law allows quantity discounts, provided they are applied on the same basis to all customers.

Quantity discounts may specify either cumulative or noncumulative terms. *Cumulative quantity discounts* reduce prices in amounts determined by purchases over stated time periods. Annual purchases of at least $25,000

"40 PERCENT, 10 PERCENT OFF" TRADE DISCOUNT			
List Price	− Retail Trade Discount	− Wholesale Trade Discount	= Manufacturer Proceeds
$40	− $16 ($40 × 40%)	− $2.40 ($24 × 10%)	= $21.60 ($40 − $16 − $2.40)

"45 PERCENT" TRADE DISCOUNT		
List Price	− Retail Trade Discount =	Manufacturer Proceeds
$40	− $18 ($40 × 45%) =	$22 ($40 − $18)

FIGURE 14.7
Chain of Trade Discounts

might entitle a buyer to a 3 percent rebate, while purchases exceeding $50,000 would increase the refund to 5 percent. These reductions are really patronage discounts, since they tend to bind customers to a single supply source.

Noncumulative quantity discounts provide one-time reductions in the list price. For example, a firm might offer the following discount schedule for a product priced at $1,000 per unit:

1 unit	List: $1,000
2–5 units	List less 10 percent
6–10 units	List less 20 percent
Over 10 units	List less 25 percent

Many businesses have come to expect quantity discounts from suppliers. Ignoring these expectations can create competitive trouble for a firm. When United Parcel Service (UPS) balked at providing quantity discounts for large clients such as DuPont, it created an opportunity for competitors. One rival, Roadway Package System, lured several UPS customers by offering discounts to a wide range of organizational clients.

Marketers typically favor combinations of cash, trade, and volume discounts. For example, catalogers like Oriental Trading Co., specializing in novelty products, and Current, Inc., specializing in stationery supplies, offer customers discounts according to how much they purchase. They typically place time limits on when such discounts are applicable for each catalog. In addition, Current includes free samples of seasonally timed greeting cards for customers on their mailing list.

Allowances NO

Allowances resemble discounts by specifying deductions from list price. The major categories of allowances are trade-ins and promotional allowances. *Trade-ins* are often used in sales of durable goods such as automobiles. The new product's basic list price remains unchanged, but the seller accepts less money from the customer along with a used product—usually the same kind of product as the buyer purchases.

Promotional allowances reduce prices as part of attempts to integrate promotional strategies within distribution channels. Manufacturers often return part of the prices that buyers pay in the form of advertising and sales-support allowances for channel members. Automobile manufacturers frequently offer allowances to retail dealers to induce them to lower prices and stimulate sales. In an effort to alert consumers to the difference between a car's sticker price and the price the dealer actually pays to the manufacturer, *Consumer Reports* recently began selling car and truck buyers a breakdown on dealers' wholesale costs. The information discloses secret dealer profits such as manufacturers' "holdbacks"— amounts as high as 3 percent of the full sticker price, or $750 on a $25,000 car—that are refunded to dealers after sales are completed. The breakdown also reveals allowances for the dealers' advertising and other promotional costs. Once they are aware of the dealer's actual cost, car buyers are better able to negotiate a fair purchase price. Dealers dislike the move to reveal their markups, arguing that no other retail sector is forced to give consumers details of their promotional allowances.[10]

For years, the price of music CDs has been artificially high, partly as a result of promotional allowances. Major record companies paid fees to stores that agreed not to advertise their CDs below set prices. Known as *minimum advertised pricing (MAP)*, the policy, in effect, raised prices per CD by $1 to $2 across the board, eliminating competition. Under pressure from the Federal Trade Commission, major companies such as Bertelsmann, Sony, and EMI recently agreed to discontinue MAP allowances.[11]

Rebates NO

In still another way to reduce a consumer's cost, marketers may offer a *rebate*—a refund of a portion of the purchase price. Rebates have appeared most prominently in automobile promotions by manufacturers eager to move models during periods of slow sales. However, firms have also offered rebates for sales in product categories ranging from appliances and sports equipment to grocery products and toiletries. Bed manufacturer Sealy has successfully used rebates to move consumers up its product line, offering the biggest rebates for its top-priced mattresses.

Rebates. Assume you are in the market for a new car and want to use the Internet to find out what rebates are currently available. Use a search engine to find rebate information or visit one of the car-buying Web sites—such as Edmonds (http://www.edmonds.com) or Intellichoice (http://www.intellichoice.com). Select the best rebate offer based on a car you might like to purchase and the attractiveness of the rebate offer.

Internet companies like Upromise.com offer rebates that can be funneled into savings plans to pay for future college tuition. By purchasing products at participating retailers—including 15,000 grocery stores across the U.S., as well as major companies like ExxonMobil and AT&T, consumers can earn from 3 to 5 percent back for college when they buy any of the thousands of participating items, from Coca-Cola and Pop Tarts to Keebler cookies and Huggies diapers. Since the program is folded into existing loyalty card programs at grocery stores, consumers need to do nothing more than register, and Upromise keeps track of spending and credits their accounts.[12]

Geographic Considerations

Rare is the 21st-century business whose operations are not affected by geographic considerations. In industries dominated by catalog and online marketers, these factors weigh heavily on the firm's ability to deliver orders in a cost-effective manner at the right time and place. In other instances, geographic factors affect the marketer's ability to receive additional inventory quickly in response to demand fluctuations. And although geographic considerations strongly influence prices when costs include shipping heavy, bulky, low-unit-value products, they can also affect lightweight, lower-cost products. The "Marketing Misses" box explains the complexity of adjusting online pricing to cover shipping costs.

Buyers and sellers can handle transportation expenses in several ways: (1) The buyer pays all transportation charges, (2) the seller pays all transportation charges, or (3) the buyer and the seller share the charges. This decision has major effects on a firm's efforts to expand its geographic coverage to distant markets. How can marketers compete with local suppliers in distant markets who are able to avoid the considerable shipping costs that their firms must pay? Sellers can implement several alternatives for handling transportation costs in their pricing policies.

FOB Pricing

FOB (free on board) plant, or *FOB origin*, prices include no shipping charges. The buyer must pay all freight charges to transport the product from the manufacturer's dock. The seller pays only to load the merchandise aboard the carrier selected by the buyer. Legal title and responsibility pass to the buyer after the seller's employees load the purchase and get a receipt from the representative of the common carrier.

Many marketing intermediaries, such as Virginia-based General Medical Corp., sell only on FOB plant terms to downstream channel members. These distributors believe that their customers have more clout than they do in dealing with carriers. They prefer to assign transportation costs to the channel members in the best positions to negotiate the most cost-effective shipping terms.

Sellers may also quote prices as **FOB origin-freight allowed,** or **freight absorbed.** These terms permit buyers to subtract transportation expenses from their bills. The amount such a seller receives for its product varies with the freight charged against the invoice. This alternative is popular among firms with high fixed

Marketing Dictionary

FOB (free on board) plant   Price quotation that does not include shipping charges; also called FOB origin.

FOB origin-freight allowed or **freight absorbed**   Price quotation system that allows the buyer to deduct shipping expenses from the cost of purchases.

Marketing Miss

Who Pays to Get It There?

Background. In the frenzy to acquire customers, early Internet retailers regularly offered free shipping and handling with online purchases. This practice made it easy for shoppers to compare prices, adding to the convenience and price competitiveness of purchasing online.

The Marketing Problem. While free shipping was a boon to customers, it all but wiped out profits for struggling e-tailers. Startups like Urbanfetch.com—offering city dwellers free delivery on everything from videos to ice cream—drowned in shipping costs. The inability to absorb freight charges also factored into the failure of online stores like Toys "R" Us.

The Outcome. While some e-tailers charge by weight, others use the total value of the order to determine shipping costs. Neither method is without its drawbacks. Charging by weight to ship heavy items like exercise equipment can boost the final price above the customer's local fitness or sporting goods store, negating the convenience of ordering online. On the other hand, charging a standard freight fee of $4.95 on small, lightweight items like CDs adds significantly to the overall price. Companies like Outpost.com have revised their policies several times within a year, seeking formulas that neither damage the bottom line nor offend the customer's sense of fair play. Of course, frequent changes to shipping costs are a turnoff, too.

Lessons Learned. What the marketers learned is to look at shipping charges not as a profit center but as a breakeven proposition. It may be tempting to pass high shipping charges along to customers, but inflated prices can drive them away. Today, almost 7 of every 10 online shopping carts are aban-

continued on next page

costs because it helps them to expand their markets considerably by quoting the same prices regardless of shipping expenses.

Uniform-Delivered Pricing NO

When a firm quotes the same price, including transportation expenses, to all buyers, it adopts a **uniform-delivered price** policy. Such a pricing structure is the exact opposite of FOB origin pricing. This system resembles the pricing structure for mail service, so it is sometimes called *postage-stamp pricing*. The price quote includes a transportation charge averaged over all of the firm's customers, meaning that distant customers actually pay a smaller share of shipping costs while nearby customers pay what is known as phantom freight (the amount by which the average transportation charge exceeds the actual cost of shipping).

Zone Pricing NO

Zone pricing modifies a uniform-delivered pricing system by dividing an overall market into different zones and establishing a single price within each zone. This pricing structure incorporates average transportation costs for shipments within each zone as part of the delivered price of goods sold there; by narrowing distances, it reduces but does not eliminate phantom freight. The primary advantage of zone pricing comes from easy administration methods that help a seller to compete in distant markets. The U.S. Postal Service's parcel rates depend on zone pricing.

Zone pricing helps explain why gasoline can cost more in one suburb than it costs in a neighborhood just two or three miles down the road. One way in which refinery companies boost profits is by mapping out areas based on formulas that factor in location, affluence, or simply what the local market will bear. Dealers are then charged different wholesale prices, which are reflected in the prices paid at the pump by customers. In response to recent upswings in the price of gasoline, many dealers are now pushing to make zone pricing illegal or at least establish rules for fair use. As drivers shop around for cheaper gas, stations in high-price zones are unable to compete. Ironically, it is the local dealer, not just the oil company, that consumers suspect of price gouging.[13] The "Solving an Ethical Controversy" box on page 419 examines a legal loophole in Europe's trade laws that allows for a form of zone pricing from country to country.

Basing Point Pricing NO

In **basing-point pricing,** the price of a product includes the list price at the factory plus freight charges from the basing-point city nearest the buyer. The basing point specifies a location from which to calculate freight charges—not necessarily the point from which the goods are shipped. In either case, the actual shipping point does not affect the price quotation. Such a system seeks to equalize competition between distant marketers since all competitors quote identical transportation rates. Few buyers would accept a basing-point system today, however.

The best-known basing-point system for many years was the Pittsburgh-plus pricing structure common in the steel industry. Steel buyers paid freight charges from Pittsburgh regardless of where the steel was produced. As the industry matured, manufacturing centers emerged in Chicago; Gary, Indiana; Cleveland; and Birmingham, Alabama. Still, Pittsburgh remained the basing point for steel pricing, forcing a buyer in Atlanta that purchased steel from a Birmingham mill to pay phantom freight from Pittsburgh.

Pricing Policies *Read*

Pricing policies contribute important information to buyers as they assess the firm's total image. A coherent policy provides an overall framework and consistency that guides day-to-day pricing decisions. Formally, a *pricing policy* is a general guideline that reflects marketing objectives and influences specific pricing decisions.

Decisions concerning price structure generally tend to focus on technical, detailed questions, but decisions concerning pricing policies cover broader issues. Price structure decisions take the firm's pricing policy as a given, from which they specify applicable discounts. Pricing policies have important strategic effects, particularly in guiding competitive efforts. They form the basis for more practical price-structure decisions.

Firms implement variations of four basic types of pricing policies: psychological pricing, price flexibility, product-line pricing, and promotional pricing. Specific policies deal effectively with various competitive situations; the final choice depends on the environment within which marketers must make their pricing decisions.

Psychological Pricing *Read*

Psychological pricing applies the belief that certain prices or price ranges make products more appealing to buyers than others. No research offers a consistent foundation for such thinking, however, and studies often report mixed findings. Nevertheless, marketers practice several forms of psychological pricing. Chapter 13 discussed one—prestige pricing. Two more psychological pricing techniques include odd pricing and unit pricing.

In *odd pricing*, marketers set prices at odd numbers just under round numbers. Many people assume that a price of $4.95 appeals more strongly to consumers than $5.00, supposedly because buyers interpret it as $4.00 plus change. Odd pricing originated as a way to force clerks to make change, thus serving as a cash-control device. Odd pricing remains a common feature of contemporary price quotations.

Some producers and retailers practice odd pricing but avoid prices ending in 5, 9, or 0. These marketers believe that customers view price tags of $5.95, $5.99, or $6.00 as regular retail prices, but they think of an amount like $5.97 as a discount price.

Unit pricing states prices in terms of some recognized unit of measurement (such as grams and liters) or a standard numerical count. Unit pricing arose to improve convenience when consumer advocates complained about the difficulty of comparing the true prices of products packaged in different sizes. These advocates thought that posting prices in terms of standard units would help shoppers make better-informed purchases. Some supermarket chains have come to regard unit pricing as a competitive tool, and they feature it extensively in advertising. However, unit pricing has not improved consumers' shopping habits as much as supporters originally envisioned that it would. Instead, research shows that standard price quotes most often affect purchases only by relatively well-educated consumers with high earnings.

With gasoline prices soaring way above $1.60 per gallon in some states, it is interesting to compare its unit price with that of other products. As Table 14.1 demonstrates, most other products command far higher unit prices than gasoline!

3

Identify the various pricing policy decisions that marketers must make.

Marketing Miss

doned at the checkout, where consumers tack delivery costs on to prices. The best sites offer FAQs (frequently asked questions) explaining their shipping policies, while the worst make customers fill out endless screens of personal information before revealing freight charges.

SOURCES: David Geller, "The Seven Deadly Sins of E-Commerce," *E-Commerce Times*, http://www.ecommerce times.com, accessed January 15, 2003; Robert D. Hof and Monica Roman, "Jeffrey Bezos: The Shipping News," *BusinessWeek*, May 6, 2002, p. 42; Melissa Campanelli, "Who Pays to Get It There?" *Entrepreneur*, February 2002, pp. 34–35.

Marketing Dictionary

uniform-delivered pricing   Pricing system for handling transportation costs under which all buyers are quoted the same price, including transportation expenses. Sometimes known as *postage-stamp pricing*.

zone pricing   Pricing system for handling transportation costs under which the market is divided into geographic regions and a different price is set in each region.

basing-point pricing   System used in some industries during the early 20th century in which the buyer paid the factory price plus freight charges from the basing-point city nearest the buyer.

psychological pricing   Pricing policy based on the belief that certain prices or price ranges make a good or service more appealing than others to buyers.

TABLE 14.1	Unit Price of Gasoline Compared with Other Products	

Product	Price per Container	Price per Gallon
Gasoline	—	$1.50 and higher
Coors Light	$5.19 per six-pack	$9.23
Ozarka Natural Spring Water	69 cents for 8 oz.	$11.04
Crest toothpaste	$2.98 for 6.2 oz.	$62.00
OPI Nail Lacquer	$6 for 1/2 oz.	$1,536.00
Ralph Lauren's Romance fragrance	$60 for 3.4 oz.	$2,252.00
Estee Lauder Resilience Lift Eye Crème	$42.50 for 1/2 oz.	$10,880.00

Price Flexibility

Marketing executives must also set company policies that determine whether their firm will permit **price flexibility**—that is, the decision of whether to set one price that applies to every buyer or permit variable prices for different customers. Generally, one-price policies suit mass-selling marketing programs, whereas variable pricing is more likely to be applied in marketing programs based on individual bargaining. In a large department store, customers do not expect to haggle over prices with retail salespeople. Instead, they expect to pay the amounts shown on the price tags. Generally, customers pay less only when the retailer replaces regular prices with sale prices or offers discounts on damaged merchandise.

Traditionally, car buyers have come to expect variable pricing policies from dealers. During the 1990s, however, when Saturn marketers chose to stray from the norm with a nonnegotiable pricing policy on its vehicles, many other automakers such as Ford and Honda were attracted to its success and followed suit. While the trend toward nonnegotiable pricing did not last long, manufacturers have begun using the Internet to deliver pricing information to potential customers. Ford, GM, and Toyota offer Web sites that allow car buyers to price out models with the options they require, along with lists of actual cars on nearby lots. The sites also provide suggested retail prices—customers can e-mail dealerships to check how much they are charging. However, while checking out pricing online may allow customers a stronger negotiating position, the prices are not fixed.

The telecommunications industry, on the other hand, has moved toward flat-rate pricing strategies. Rather than charge different rates for different times of the day, AT&T and MCI offer a one-rate nationwide plan. Yet while flat rates may mean that customers pay as little as five cents a minute for long-distance calls, their phone bills are still rising. A grab bag of access fees and service charges ups the ante. Second-line charges, portability fees, rural service fees, and federal excise taxes are just a few of the mandatory monthly charges. In addition, customers may decide to pay more for options such as call waiting, caller ID, or call forwarding. As the whole package of service costs continues to rise, increasing numbers of customers are cutting the wire and going cellular.[14]

While variable pricing adds some flexibility to selling situations, it may conflict with provisions of the Robinson-Patman Act. It may also lead to retaliatory pricing by competitors, and it may stir complaints among customers who find that they paid higher prices than necessary.

Product-Line Pricing

Since most firms market multiple product lines, an effective pricing strategy must consider the relationships among all of these products instead of viewing each in isolation. **Product-line pricing** is the practice of setting a limited number of prices for a selection of merchandise. For example, a clothier might offer three lines of men's suits—one priced at $475, a second at $625, and the most expensive

right wrong
Solving an Ethical Controversy

Fair Play across Borders

In Germany, its country of manufacture, a Volkswagen Golf costs car buyers $11,040, excluding taxes. Take a train ride to France or Italy and you'll drive one home for about $500 less. Make it all the way to Finland and the same car is only $8,290. But if you go to the other side of the English Channel, you pay a whopping $13,040 for the identical car—and that doesn't even include Britain's high value-added taxes.

Volkswagen is not the only manufacturer to practice variable pricing. Pricing for identical models varies by up to 40 percent across the European marketplace. Why the massive disparity? Part of the explanation lies in a 16-year-old exemption to European antitrust law, meant to protect local manufacturers and dealers from a flood of cheap imported cars. The exemption allows carmakers to avoid price competition by selling only vehicles through selected dealerships, each with exclusive territories. Though it was intended to assure top-quality maintenance and high safety standards, a loophole in the law allows carmakers to vary prices from country to country. For example, manufacturers are allowed to discount their home-market prices in order to enter new markets or to compensate for higher taxes. In effect, since they control the dealerships, carmakers can legally fix prices to whatever the market will bear. Moreover, by excluding imports from their single-brand dealerships, they restrict the ability of foreign car makers to compete on price.

Should the EU end the auto industry's traditional practice of charging different prices for identical cars in different countries?

PRO

1. The present system restricts imports, thereby reducing consumer choice and driving up prices.
2. Consumers have a right to buy at the same prices as people in other member nations.

CON

1. Removing dealers' exclusivity will result in lower standards of after-sales service for motorists, leading to possible safety hazards.
2. European automakers already suffer from overcapacity and escalating costs, so price liberalization could put them out of business.

Summary

New regulations proposed by the European Commission seek to remove the block exemption, allowing not only for multibrand dealerships but for car sales through the Internet and through deep-discount supermarkets. The new rules will open the doors to lower-priced imports, making price competition a reality in the single market.

SOURCES: "Car Prices across Europe," *BBC News*, February 11, 2002, http://www.bbc.co.uk; "Driving a Hard Bargain," *The Economist*, January 26, 2002, p. 55.

---

at $795. These price points help the retailer define important product characteristics that differentiate the three product lines and contribute to customer choices to trade up or trade down.

Retailers practice extensive product-line pricing. In earlier days, five-and-dime variety stores exemplified this technique. It remains popular, however, because it offers advantages to both retailers and customers. Shoppers can choose desired price ranges and then concentrate on other product variables such as colors, styles, and materials. Retailers can purchase and offer specific lines in limited price categories instead of more general assortments with dozens of different prices.

Most airlines divide their seating areas on international flights according to product-line pricing. These flights offer a certain percentage of discount, business-class, first-class, and coach-price seats on each flight. On an overseas flight, for instance, the industry averages about 18 percent business-class seats. A round-trip, business-class ticket from Houston to Paris on Continental Airlines costs almost twice the regular coach fare and several times more than the discount fare.

A potential problem with product-line pricing is that once marketers decide on a limited

Marketing Dictionary

price flexibility Pricing policy permitting variable prices for goods and services.

product-line pricing Practice of setting a limited number of prices for a selection of merchandise and marketing different product lines in each of these price levels.

[handwritten: Cost pless pricing is used by Retailer. (w/ discount making even double)]

Marketing Hit

Dell's Low-Price Strategy Dominates PC Market

Background. For years, PC makers based their prices on unit cost estimates, with a markup to allow a lucrative profit. Dealers then added in their own margins, formulating a final retail price. Since computers were perceived as a high-end, proprietary technology, customers were willing to pay. Demand increased, the cost of components fell, and prices began to slide—yet manufacturers still had room for generous margins.

The Challenge. Along came Dell. The upstart company set PC pricing on its head. Figuring that it could make more money by reducing margins and moving computers in much higher volumes, Dell began a price-slashing frenzy unprecedented in the high-tech industry.

The Strategy. Since Dell PCs were sold directly to customers via telephone, the Internet, or catalogs, there was no middleman to raise prices to retail standards. Falling component costs meant Dell was able to pass even greater savings along to customers. Matching Dell's prices all but eliminated profits for competitors Compaq, Hewlett-Packard, and Gateway, whose price models did not allow for paper-thin margins.

The Outcome. Dell's pricing policy made commodities out of PCs, encouraging customers to bargain hunt, just as they would for airline tickets. Next, Dell has set its sights on two high-growth industry sectors—network switches and storage. But the computer giant then moved in a totally different

continued on next page

number of prices to use as their price lines, they may have difficulty making price changes on individual items. Rising costs, therefore, force sellers to either change the entire price-line structure, which results in confusion, or cut costs through production adjustments. The second option opens the firm to customer complaints that its merchandise is not what it used to be. Frito Lay, which competes in the highly price-sensitive snack foods category, recently responded to rising costs not by raising its prices but by shrinking the size of its packages. Such silent price hikes, achieved in the form of "package shrink," have also been implemented by marketers of candy, coffee, and diapers.

Promotional Pricing *[handwritten: is called Hi-Low Pricing one of the strategy for Retailer]*

In **promotional pricing,** a lower-than-normal price is used as a temporary ingredient in a firm's selling strategy. Some promotional pricing arrangements form part of recurrent marketing initiatives, such as a shoe store's annual "buy one pair, get the second pair for one cent" sale. Another example would be "7 CDs for 1 cent." This artificially low price attracts customers who must then agree to purchase a set number of CDs within a specified time limit. Another firm may introduce a promotional model or brand with a special price to begin competing in a new market.

Leader Pricing and Loss Leaders *[handwritten: ⇒ sale above cost / sell below cost / Read / b/c Traffic builder]*

Retailers rely most heavily on promotional pricing. In one type of technique, stores offer **loss leaders**—goods priced below cost to attract customers who, the retailer hopes, will also buy other, regularly priced merchandise. Loss leaders can form part of an effective marketing program, but—as pointed out in the previous chapter—states with unfair-trade laws prohibit the practice.

Retailers frequently use a variant of loss-leader pricing called *leader pricing.* To avoid violating minimum-markup regulations and to earn some return on promotional sales, they offer so-called leader merchandise at prices slightly above cost. Among the most frequent practitioners of this combination pricing/promotion strategy are supermarkets and mass merchandisers such as Wal-Mart and Target. Retailers sometimes treat private-label products (like Sam's Choice colas at Wal-Mart stores) as leader merchandise since prices of the store brands average 5 percent to 60 percent less than those of comparable national brands. While store brand goods generate lower per-unit revenues than national brands would produce, higher sales volume will probably offset some of the difference, as will related sales of high-margin products like toiletries and cosmetics.

The personal computer industry provides an excellent example of this trend in pricing. Just a decade ago, PCs cost up to $5,000. At first, prices tumbled because of production economies and high demand. But the industry became embroiled in a brutal price war that saw Dell not only slash PC prices to under $400 but also throw in free printers, free Internet access, and free delivery. Working on razor-thin profit margins, competitors struggled to match Dell's plunging prices. Apple Computer focused on product image and caught buyers' eyes with the attractive iMac design. Both Apple and IBM realigned their operations to provide services they could bundle along with the basic PC offerings. Compaq and Hewlett-Packard consolidated in order to compete. The economic slowdown at the beginning of this century, combined with a saturated U.S. market and consumer expectations of low prices, set the stage for long-term problems ahead.[15] The "Marketing Hits" box explains Dell's aggressive pricing strategy.

Marketers should anticipate two potential pitfalls when making a promotional pricing decision:

1. Some buyers are not attracted by promotional pricing.

2. By maintaining an artificially low price for a period of time, marketers may lead customers to expect it as a customary feature of the product. In the airline industry, for example, pervasive ticket discounting has taught consumers to expect to pay prices below full fare. As a result, airlines are losing money because many travelers will fly only if they can get discounted fares.

Price-Quality Relationships

Higher Price the better quality.   Read

One of the most thoroughly researched aspects of pricing is its relationship to consumer perceptions of product quality. In the absence of other cues, price serves as an important indicator of a product's quality to prospective purchasers. Many buyers interpret high prices as signals of high-quality products.

The relationship between price and perceived quality provides a widely used tool for contemporary marketers. Figure 14.8 shows the Land Rover, a vehicle known around the globe for its dependability, performance, and price. Instead of attempting to justify its price, Land Rover instead focuses on being the logical choice for a trek across Africa.

The recent recession obviously took its toll on upscale brand sales, but premium products have also proven they are able to withstand ups and downs. Wineries in the Pacific Northwest have discovered a growing market niche. In recent years, increasing numbers of consumers have traded up from cheaper California wines, priced from $3 to $6, weakening demand at the low end of the market. Although they are not ready to plunk down $80 for a top vintage wine, shoppers are willing to pay anything from $7 to $30 a bottle at wine shops or grocery stores. With a reputation for high-quality grapes, Washington State wineries continue to sell well, despite lackluster demand in the industry overall.[16]

Probably the best statement of the price-quality connection is the idea of price limits. Consumers define certain limits within which their product-quality perceptions vary directly with price. A potential buyer regards a price below the lower limit as too cheap, and a price above the higher limit seems too expensive. This perception holds true for both national brands and private-label products.

In some South American and Asian countries, hyperinflation occurring during the past 10 years has left consumers little relationship between price and quality. In Brazil during the mid-1990s, for example, a consumer could buy a deluxe ice cream sundae or two kitchen blenders for 950 cruzados ($15). Moreover, prices for a single product also varied tremendously from store to store. As a result, a consumer could end up paying anywhere from 2 cruzados ($.03) to 21 cruzados for a pencil eraser.

Marketing Hit

direction, marching into territory previously dominated by the likes of Sony, Matsushita, and Samsung, when it unveiled plans for a major push into consumer electronics. The company began producing and marketing flat-panel TVs and MP3 players on its popular Web site—and even opened an online music-downloading store. Two reasons were offered for the drastic move: first, the PC business isn't growing; and even more importantly, entertainment is increasingly digital. Music, movies, and photos are becoming an extension of the PC. As CEO Michael Dell explained, "The whole new ballgame is these worlds [computing and consumer electronics] converging, and that's a world we're comfortable in."

The move is likely to be dramatic. After all—like SouthWest Airlines and Wal-Mart moving into their new markets—Dell's super-efficient manufacturing and direct-selling economies could result in plummeting prices for music downloads, MP3 players, and even those dazzling plasma TVs.

SOURCES: Kevin Maney, "Dell to Dive into Consumer Electronics Market," *USA Today*, September 28, 2003, pp. B1, B2; Daniel Fisher, "Pulled in a New Direction," *Forbes*, June 10, 2002, pp. 102–112; and Andy Serwer, "Dell Does Domination," *Fortune*, January 21, 2002, pp. 71–75.

4

Relate price to consumer perceptions of quality.

Marketing Dictionary

promotional pricing   Pricing policy in which a lower-than-normal price is used as a temporary ingredient in a firm's marketing strategy.

loss leader   Product offered to consumers at less than cost to attract them to stores in the hope that they will buy other merchandise at regular prices.

FIGURE 14.8
Relationship between
Price and Perceived
Quality

5

Contrast competitive bidding and negotiated prices.

Competitive Bidding and Negotiated Prices   NO

Many government and organizational procurement departments do not pay set prices for their purchases, particularly for large purchases such as U.S. Department of Defense orders for MREs (Meals Ready to Eat) to replace those used by troops assigned to Afghanistan and other isolated areas. Instead, they determine the lowest prices available for items that meet specifications through *competitive bidding*. This process consists of inviting potential suppliers to quote prices on proposed purchases or contracts. Detailed specifications describe the good or service that the government agency or business organization wishes to acquire. One of the most important procurement tasks is to develop accurate descriptions of products that the organization seeks to buy. This process generally requires the assistance of the firm's technical personnel, such as engineers, designers, and chemists.

Ford Motor Co. has been particularly successful in supplying state and government agencies with auto models that meet their price and performance specifications. At present, 85 of every 100 U.S. police cars are Crown Victorias.

In some cases, business and government purchasers negotiate contracts with favored suppliers instead of inviting competitive bids from all interested parties. The terms of such a contract emerge through offers and counteroffers between the buyer and the seller.

Where only one supplier offers a desired product or where projects require extensive research and development, buyers and sellers often set purchase terms through negotiated contracts. In addition, some state and local governments permit their agencies to skip the formal bid process and negotiate purchases under certain dollar limits—say $500 or $1,000. This policy seeks to eliminate economic waste that would result from obtaining and processing bids for relatively minor purchases.

Negotiating Prices Online

Many people see today's cyberworld as one big auction site. Whether it is toys, art, or automobiles, there seems to be an online auction site to serve every person's needs—buyer and seller alike. Auctions are the purest form of negotiated pricing. As Figure 14.9 shows, buyers and sellers electronically communicate ask and bid prices until a mutually agreed-upon price is set.

Ticket sales are an online auction favorite. Whether it is a Broadway show, a NASCAR race, a trip to the zoo, or an OzzFest concert, you can find tickets online. Tickets.com catalogs the dates, times, and locations of everything from concerts to museum exhibits. It recently tied in with the Advantix ticketing system, opening up a sales site for sports venues. In addition, Tickets.com also functions as a reseller through its own online auctions.

The Transfer Pricing Dilemma

A pricing problem peculiar to large-scale enterprises is the determination of an internal **transfer price**—the price for moving goods between **profit centers,** which are any part of the organization to which revenue and controllable costs can be assigned, such as a department. As companies expand, they tend to decentralize management and set up profit centers as a control device in the newly decentralized operation.

In a large company, profit centers might secure many needed resources from sellers within their own organization. The pricing problem thus poses several questions: What rate should profit center A (maintenance department) charge profit center B (production department) for the cleaning compound used on B's floors? Should the price be the same as it would be if A did the work for an outside party? Should B receive a discount? The answers to these questions depend on the philosophy of the firm involved.

Transfer pricing can be complicated, especially for multinational organizations. The government closely monitors transfer pricing practices because these exchanges offer easy ways for companies to avoid paying taxes on profits. Recent Congressional investigations of the trend for U.S. firms to incorporate in Bermuda have focused on U.S. tax savings made possible by transfer pricing rates used between the firm's production location (U.S.) and its home country (Bermuda), even though no production takes place in Bermuda.

Figure 14.10 shows how this type of pricing manipulation might work. Suppose that a South Korean VCR manufacturer sells its machines to its U.S. subsidiary for distribution to dealers. Although each unit costs $50 to build, the manufacturer charges the distributor $150. In turn, the distributor sells the VCRs to retailers for $200 each. This arrangement gives the South Korean manufacturer a $100 profit on each machine, on which it pays taxes only in South Korea. Meanwhile, the American distributor writes off $50 for advertising and shipping costs, leaving it with no profits—and no tax liability.

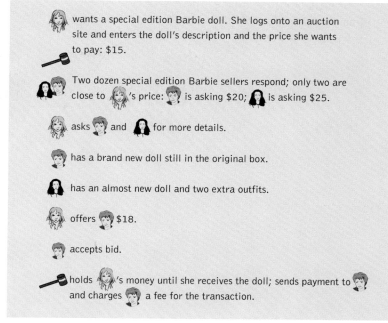

FIGURE 14.9
Online Auctions: Purest Form of Negotiated Pricing

6

Explain the importance of transfer pricing.

Global Considerations and Online Pricing

Throughout the text and especially in Chapter 5, we have seen the impact of the Internet on every component of the marketing mix. This chapter has touched on the outer edges of the Internet's influence on pricing practices. Remember that every online marketer is inherently a global marketer who must understand the wide variety of internal and external conditions that affect global pricing strategies. Internal influences include the firm's goals and marketing strategies; the costs of developing, producing, and marketing its products; the nature of the products; and the firm's competitive strengths.

Marketing Dictionary

transfer price   Cost assessed when a product is moved from one profit center in a firm to another.

profit center   Any part of an organization to which revenue and controllable costs can be assigned.

FIGURE 14.10
Transfer Pricing to Escape Taxation

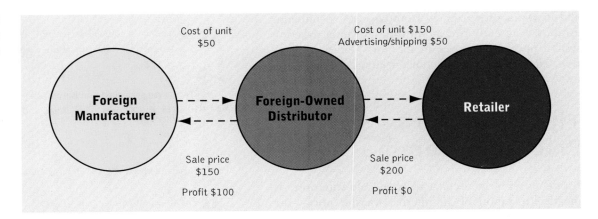

External influences include general conditions in international markets, especially those in the firm's target markets, regulatory limitations, trade restrictions, competitors' actions, economic events, and the global status of the industry.

Traditional Global Pricing Strategies

7

Compare the three alternative global pricing strategies.

In general, a company can implement one of three export pricing strategies: a standard worldwide price, dual pricing, or market-differentiated pricing. Exporters often set standard worldwide prices, regardless of their target markets. This strategy can succeed if foreign marketing costs remain low enough that they do not affect overall costs or if their prices reflect average unit costs. A company that implements a standard pricing program must monitor the international marketplace carefully, however, to make sure that domestic competitors do not undercut its prices.

The dual pricing strategy distinguishes prices for domestic and export sales. Some exporters practice cost-plus pricing to establish dual prices that fully allocate their true domestic and foreign costs to product sales in those markets. These prices ensure that an exporter makes a profit on any product it sells, but final prices may exceed those of competitors. Other companies opt for flexible cost-plus pricing schemes that allow marketers to grant discounts or change prices according to shifts in the competitive environment or fluctuations in the international exchange rate.

The third strategy, market-differentiated pricing, makes even more flexible arrangements to set prices according to local marketplace conditions. The dynamic global marketplace often requires frequent price changes by exporters who choose this approach. Effective market-differentiated pricing depends on access to quick, accurate market information.

Pharmaceutical marketers practice market-differentiated pricing in their global marketing strategies. While they cannot openly admit that they are levying a North American surcharge on the drug, marketers can set a high price on the treatment for wealthier patients in America while charging pennies for the same drug in needy areas of Africa. However, it is more difficult to understand why some drugs are priced as much as 60 percent less in Europe or Canada than in the U.S. A month's supply of Claritin, for example, costs $17 in Canada and $13 in Australia, where it is available over the counter. American consumers—who until recently needed a prescription to get it—typically paid $62.[17]

Characteristics of Online Pricing

To deal with the influences of the Internet on pricing policies and practices, marketers are applying old strategies in new ways and companies are updating operations to compete with new electronic technologies. Coldwater Creek's Web site offers time-strapped professional women who may not be able to visit its retail outlets frequently an easy shopping option. As the ad in Figure 14.11 shows, a limited-time cash discount is used to lure customers to the site, where it can be applied against purchases of quality apparel totaling $75 or more.

The Cannibalization Dilemma

However, by pricing the same products differently online, companies run the risk of **cannibalization.** The new twist to an old tactic is that companies are self-inflicting price cuts by creating competition among their own products. By building new e-businesses designed to compete head-on with the parent company, marketers are hoping to survive the transition from bricks-and-mortar to electronic storefronts on the Web. Online securities trading company e.Schwab cannibalized its parent Charles Schwab when it offered online investors a flat $29.95 transaction fee. Traditional clients, who were still being charged $65 per trade, demanded and received the same flat fee.[18]

Books-A-Million, the nation's third-largest bookstore chain, sells its Top 20 best-sellers at 40 percent below list price. But click on the company's Web site, and you can buy the same book at discounts of 46 percent or more. Why sell books online at a lower price than you charge at the store? Books-A-Million's head of online marketing supplies two reasons:

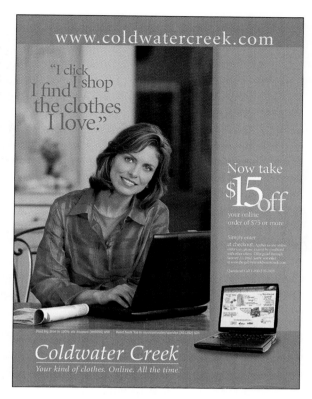

www.coldwatercreek.com

"I click I shop I find the clothes I love."

Now take $15 off your online order of $75 or more

Coldwater Creek
Your kind of clothes. Online. All the time.

FIGURE 14.11
Using Cash Discounts to Attract Shoppers as an Online Pricing Strategy

- It provides an additional channel to reach book buyers who do not regularly patronize their local Books-A-Million as well as those purchasers who live in areas with no BAM retail stores.

- It also represents a defensive move, since the company would rather have the business—even at extremely low margins—than lose it to Amazon.com.

8

Relate the concepts of cannibalization, bundle pricing, and bots to online pricing strategies.

Use of Shopping Bots

A second characteristic of online pricing is the use of search programs called *bots* or *shopbots*—derived from the word "robots"—that act as comparison shopping agents. As Chapter 5 explained, bots search the Web for a specific product, then print out a list of sites that offer the best prices. In online selling, bots force marketers to keep prices low. However, marketing researchers report that almost 4 of every 5 online shoppers will check out several sites before buying, and price is not the only variable they consider when making a purchase decision. For example, service quality and support information are powerful motivators in the decision process. Also, while price is an important factor with products such as books and CDs, it is not as important with complex or highly differentiated products, such as real estate or investment banking. Brand image and customer service often outweigh price in these purchase decisions. In an attempt to protect its proprietary server resources, the popular portal Google recently decided to wall off sections of its site from other search bots. As a result, a search for "L.L. Bean" performed through a link to Google from any other search engine will come up empty. The same search that goes directly through google.com will bring up 20 pages of references.[19]

McDonald & Burgerking w/ the supermal; *menu* season tickets; rent a car.

Bundle Pricing *Read*

As marketers have watched e-commerce weaken their control over prices, they have modified their use of the price variable in the marketing mix. Whenever possible, they have moved to an approach called **bundle pricing,** where customers acquire a host of goods and

Marketing Dictionary

cannibalization Securing additional sales through lower prices that take sales away from the marketer's other products.

bundle pricing Offering two or more complementary products and selling them for a single price.

services in addition to the tangible products they purchase. In Dallas, SBC Communications' customers can purchase a full-service bundle for $137 a month. This entitles the household to two telephone lines; DirectTV satellite television; discounted local toll calling, wireless calling, and dial-up Internet services; inside wire maintenance on both lines; and 13 add-on features such as voice mail and caller ID. The personal computer industry has proven the feasibility of almost giving away products that require installation, hookups, and ongoing maintenance. In the face of intense price competition for PCs, these firms generate earnings by supplying software, Internet access, e-mail, and downloaded pay-per-view entertainment. A full year's worth of America Online service is now bundled into the purchase of computers from Gateway, while Dell offers AOL free for six months. The bundling is part of a deliberate strategy to increase long-term use, since AOL is counting on the possibility that a high percentage of free users will become paying customers once the trial period is up.[20]

Strategic Implications of Marketing in the 21st Century

Over the years, price was arguably the marketing variable least likely to be used as a source of competitive advantage. Even in industries where the discounting phenomenon resulted in radical changes in customer service levels, marketers gradually moved away from this competitive weapon. In moves consistent with discussion of the wheel of retailing theory in upcoming Chapter 16, minimal-service, low-priced operations added services, and prices began to creep up. Some retailers—including giants like Wal-Mart, the world's largest retailer with major international expansion currently taking place in Brazil, China, Germany, and South Korea—continue to use price as a major (but not sole) feature. But firms who use price to attract and retain customers cannot be ignored, and the risk of dangerous, money-losing price wars in such industries is ever present. Not surprisingly, then, many marketers drift toward developing marketing mixes that feature nonprice competition.

But technology has forever changed these markets. The traditional geographic monopolies that permitted inefficient marketers to continue in business are being destroyed by lower-priced, big-selection mass merchandisers whose rapid expansion now places them within a few miles of most shoppers, and they operate in fields as diverse as office supplies and pet food, sporting goods and books, toys and pharmaceuticals.

In addition to the new breed of high-volume marketers featuring unsurpassed selection and major price savings, the Internet has delivered competition to the homes and offices of even the most geographically isolated shoppers. For example, a customer in Kansas might want to purchase an individually carved and painted walking cane from Kenya or an ornamental fan from Kyoto. Not a problem—the Web connects buyers and sellers around the globe. Similarly, the cost of shipping an overnight FedEx package from New York to California is no more than shipping it to a nearby city.

Not only is it possible to escape the boundaries of time and space on the Internet, but price is no longer a constant in the marketing process. With the increasing number of auction sites and new search technologies like bots, customers now have more power to control the prices of goods and services. Consumers can find the lowest prices on the market, and they can also negotiate prices for many of the products they buy.

What marketers must continue to do to remain successful in the 21st century is offer value—good prices for quality goods and services—and superior customer service. These factors are the critical success factors in marketing in the new millennium.

Summary of Chapter Objectives

1. Compare the alternative pricing strategies and explain when each is most appropriate.

The alternative pricing strategies are skimming pricing strategy, penetration pricing strategy, and competitive pricing strategy. Skimming pricing is commonly used as a market-entry price for distinctive products with little or no initial competition. Penetration pricing is used when there is a wide array of competing brands. Competitive pricing is employed when marketers wish to concentrate their competitive efforts on marketing variables other than price. More than two-thirds of the firms surveyed in a recent study used competitive pricing.

2. Describe how prices are quoted.

Methods for quoting prices depend on such factors as cost structures, traditional practices in the particular industry, and policies of individual firms. Price quotes can involve list prices, market prices, cash discounts, trade discounts, quantity discounts, and allowances such as trade-ins, promotional allowances, and rebates. Shipping costs often figure heavily into the pricing of goods. A number of alternatives for dealing with these costs exist: FOB plant pricing, in which the price includes no shipping charges; FOB origin-freight allowed, or freight absorbed, which allows the buyer to deduct transportation expenses from the bill; uniform-delivered price, in which the same price, including shipping expenses, is charged to all buyers; and zone pricing, in which a set price exists within each region.

3. Identify the various pricing policy decisions that marketers must make.

A pricing policy is a general guideline based on pricing objectives and is intended for use in specific pricing decisions. Pricing policies include psychological pricing, unit pricing, price flexibility, product line pricing, and promotional pricing.

4. Relate price to consumer perceptions of quality.

The relationship between price and consumer perceptions of quality has been the subject of considerable research. In the absence of other cues, price is an important influence on how the consumer perceives the product's quality. A well-known and accepted concept is that of *price limits*—limits within which the perception of product quality varies directly with price. The concept of price limits suggests that extremely low prices may be considered too cheap, thus indicating inferior quality.

5. Contrast competitive bidding and negotiated prices.

Competitive bidding and negotiated prices are pricing techniques used primarily in the industrial sector and in government and organizational markets. Sometimes prices are negotiated through competitive bidding, in which several buyers quote prices on the same service or good. Buyer specifications describe the item that the government or B2B firm wishes to acquire. Negotiated contracts are another possibility in many procurement situations. The terms of the contract are set through talks between buyer and seller.

6. Explain the importance of transfer pricing.

A phenomenon in large corporations is transfer pricing, in which a company sets prices for transferring goods or services from one company profit center to another. The term *profit center* refers to any part of the organization to which revenue and controllable costs can be assigned. In large companies whose profit centers acquire resources from other parts of the firm, the prices charged by one profit center to another will directly impact both the cost and profitability of the output of both profit centers.

7. Compare the three alternative global pricing strategies.

Companies can choose from three export pricing strategies: a standard worldwide price, dual pricing, or market-differentiated pricing. A standard worldwide price may be possible if foreign marketing costs are so low that they do not affect overall costs or if the price is based on an average unit cost. The dual pricing approach establishes separate domestic and export price strategies. Some exporters use cost-plus pricing methods to establish dual prices that fully allocate their true domestic and foreign cost to their product; others choose flexible cost-plus pricing. Market-differentiated pricing is the most flexible export pricing strategy, since it allows firms to price their products according to marketplace condition. It requires good access to quick, accurate market information.

8. Relate the concepts of cannibalization, bundle pricing, and bots to online pricing strategies.

To deal with the influences of the Internet on pricing policies and practices, marketers are applying old strategies in new ways, and companies are updating operations to compete with new electronic technologies. Cannibalization secures additional sales through lower prices that take sales away from the marketer's other products. Bots, also known as robots or shopbots, act as comparison shopping agents. Bundle pricing is offering two or more complementary products and selling them for a single price.

Marketing Terms You Need to Know

skimming pricing strategy 407
penetration pricing
strategy 409
competitive pricing
strategy 411

FOB (free on board) plant 415
FOB origin-freight allowed (or
freight absorbed) 415
uniform-delivered pricing 416
zone pricing 416

basing-point pricing 416
psychological pricing 417
price flexibility 419
product-line pricing 419
promotional pricing 420

loss leader 420
transfer price 423
profit center 423
cannibalization 425
bundle pricing 425

Other Important Marketing Terms

everyday low pricing
(EDLP) 410
list price 412
market price 412
cash discount 413
trade discount 413

quantity discount 413
cumulative quantity
discount 413
noncumulative quantity
discount 414
trade-in 414

promotional allowance 414
rebate 414
postage-stamp pricing 416
pricing policy 417
odd pricing 417
unit pricing 417

leader pricing 420

Review Questions

1. What is a skimming pricing strategy? What benefits does it offer for a firm?
2. What is penetration pricing? Under what circumstances do marketers prefer penetration pricing?
3. What is everyday low pricing? Explain why it stirs debate among marketers and retailers.
4. Contrast the freight absorption and uniform-delivery pricing systems. Cite examples of each. How does a basing-point system incorporate transportation costs?
5. Define the term *pricing policy*. List and discuss the reasons for establishing pricing policies.
6. When does a price become a promotional price? What pitfalls does a firm risk in promotional pricing?
7. How does price relate to consumer perceptions of quality? Give examples of your perception of an acceptable price range for a product such as toothpaste, a haircut, or mouthwash. How might a price outside this range affect your image of the product's quality?
8. What is a transfer price? How does it affect management of a large organization?
9. Describe three possible strategies that a company might follow to price exports.
10. Give examples of how marketers can benefit from using cannibalization, bundle pricing, and bots in their pricing strategies.

Projects and Teamwork Exercises

1. Skimming pricing, penetration pricing, and competitive pricing are the three alternative pricing strategies. Divide the class into three teams. Then assign each team one of the three strategies and ask them to prepare a brief argument discussing the merits of their assigned pricing strategy for the following five products. Share your findings with the rest of the class. Once all three presentations have been completed, ask the class to vote on the most appropriate strategy for the products.
   a. Nintendo video game
   b. digital television
   c. fuel additive that boosts automobile mileage
   d. remote-control burglar, smoke, and fire alarm
   e. new brand of men's cologne
2. Frequent-flyer programs are discount offers designed by airlines to secure and reward consumer loyalty. In what category of discount plans do these programs fit? Explain. What potential dangers may limit the effectiveness of such programs?
3. How do sellers quote prices for each of the following products? In four teams, select one item per team. Research pricing practices within the industry and come up with a draft price quote.
   a. American Airlines ticket to Buenos Aires
   b. installation of a flashing sign by a local contractor
   c. scuba-diving suit from a sportswear retailer
   d. new Ford Expedition sport-utility vehicle
4. Assume that a product sells for $100 per ton and that Pittsburgh is the basing-point city for calculating transportation charges. Shipping from Pittsburgh to a potential customer in Cincinnati costs $10 per ton. The actual shipping costs of suppliers in three other cities are $8 per ton for Supplier A, $11 per ton for Supplier B, and $10 per ton for Supplier C. Using this information, answer the following questions:
   a. What delivered price would a salesperson for Supplier A quote to the Cincinnati customer?
   b. What delivered price would a salesperson for Supplier B quote to the Cincinnati customer?
   c. What delivered price would a salesperson for Supplier C quote to the Cincinnati customer?
   d. How much would each supplier net (after subtracting actual shipping costs) per ton on the sale?

5. In teams, use the campus library or the Internet to find out as much as you can about the merger between Compaq and Hewlett-Packard. Determine the chain of events that led to the consolidation. Explain how the merger may change the dynamics of the personal computer industry and related sectors.

'net Work

1. Pricing strategies. The pricing philosophy of Wal-Mart, whose annual sales rank it as the world's largest corporation, can be summarized as "everyday low prices." Visit the Wal-Mart Web site and click on "about Wal-Mart" to read more details about the discount retailer's pricing philosophy. Prepare a brief report summarizing what you learned. Can you think of any other major retailers who have adopted all or part of Wal-Mart's approach to pricing?

http://www.walmart.com/cservice/aw_index.gsp

2. Price negotiations. Many consumers dislike buying automobiles because they are forced to negotiate prices with dealerships and frequently experience uncertainty about whether they are skilled enough about negotiating to obtain the lowest possible price. Visit the *Consumer Report* Web site and click on "Autos." Read the article on dealing with dealers. Next, visit the Web site of Auto By Tel and read about its approach to buying a new car. If you were in the market for a new auto, would you prefer to negotiate over price or to buy the car under some sort of fixed price arrangement?

http://www.consumerreports.org

http://www.autobytel.com

3. Auctions. The largest online auction site is eBay. Visit the firm's Web site and read about how it conducts its auctions, how bids are entered, and how sellers are paid. Choose a category that interests you and print out one or two pages of some of the items currently up for sale.

http://www.ebay.com

Note: Internet Web addresses change frequently. If you don't find the exact sites listed, you may need to access the organization or company's home page and search from there.

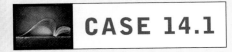

CASE 14.1   CQC Dental Makes a Price Increase Easier to Swallow

Robert Ingrassio, owner of CQC Dental Laboratory, pored over year-end sales figures, trying to figure out what had happened to his profits. Ingrassio's company makes prosthodontics, commonly known as dental implants, crowns, and cosmetic bridges. In an industry characterized by steady growth, sales revenues had enjoyed a satisfying upward sweep since its start-up days, back in 1986. The trouble was, while revenues fattened, profit margins grew slimmer and slimmer from year to year. Already facing increased competition from high-volume, lower-cost manufacturers overseas, Ingrassio knew that unless he took steps to improve his margins, profits would continue to slide. Since he was unwilling to step up production to achieve better economies of scale, Ingrassio made a radical move—he ratcheted up his prices.

Created from precious alloys, such as gold and gold/palladium, and from high-quality veneers, Ingrassio's product was top-notch, and he was confident it was worth top dollar. At his 50-employee lab in Rochester, New York, he also knew that his company delivered superior service. A committed new-product research team ensured that CQC not only kept abreast of new materials and technologies but was attuned to changes in dental procedures and practice. While Ingrassio believed in the link between quality and price, he also knew that the price hikes would lead to lost accounts and he braced himself for a downturn.

To explain the rate increases, Ingrassio altered his pricing model to make it as transparent as possible. Customers could easily see that CQC's cost basis included fixed charges (labor) and variable charges (materials). By clearly identifying the fluctuating costs of precious metals, for example, Ingrassio was able to justify higher charges to customers rather than absorb them himself.

The year the price increases were put into effect, CQC experienced its lowest-ever revenue growth—only 12 percent. The good news was profit margins leaped by 15 percent, more than making up for the shortfall in sales. While the company forfeited a few cost-sensitive accounts, 97 percent of its customer base remained loyal.

Questions for Critical Thinking

1. Is CQC likely to maintain profit margin increases in the long term? Why or why not? How might its pricing policy be adjusted to improve its chances of success?

2. In what other situations might price increases be considered a justifiable business strategy?

SOURCES: Web site for CQC Prosthodontics, http://www.cqcinc.com, accessed January 20, 2003; Mochari Ilan, "Taking the Bite Out of a Price Increase," *Inc.*, August, 2001, p. 75.

VIDEO CASE 14.2   Bombardier Lets Prices Soar

The written case on Bombardier appears on page VC-17. The recently filmed Bombardier video is designed to expand and highlight the concepts in this chapter and the concepts and questions covered in the written video case.

Krispy Kreme Continuing Case for Part 5 appears on page KK-10.

Part 6

Distribution Strategy

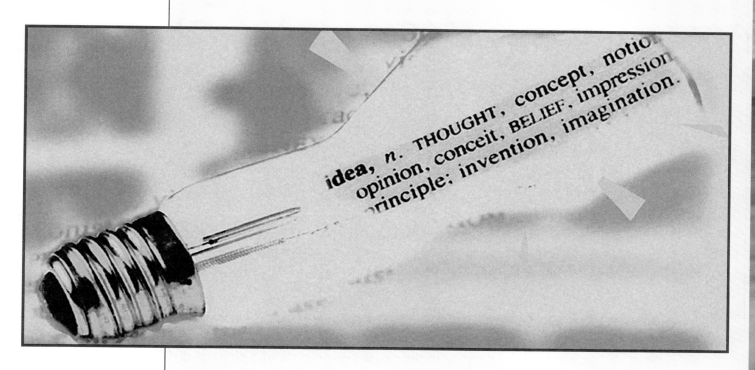

Chapter 15

13 pages

15

Marketing Channels, Logistics, and Supply Chain Management

Chapter Objectives

1 Describe the roles that marketing channels and logistics play in marketing strategy.

2 Describe the various types of distribution channels available to marketers.

3 Outline the major channel strategy decisions.

4 Describe the concepts of channel management, conflict, and cooperation within the marketing channel.

5 Identify and compare the major components of a physical distribution system.

6 Outline the suboptimization problem in logistics.

7 Compare the major transportation alternatives on the basis of speed, dependability, cost, frequency of shipments, availability in different locations, and flexibility in handling products.

8 Discuss how transportation intermediaries and combined transportation modes can improve physical distribution.

Blockbuster Faces Competition from Its Suppliers

Sometimes the logistics of just getting up in the morning and making it to class on time can seem overwhelming. But imagine getting up one morning and facing competition from the very people who are supposed to be your marketing partner. That's what happened to Blockbuster, whose own suppliers—movie studios—shortened the time between the theater release of a new movie and the outright sale of its DVDs directly to consumers through merchandisers such as Target, Circuit City, Wal-Mart, and Best Buy. Blockbuster, owned by Viacom, was then squeezed between giants—movie studios and large retailers.

The reduced time between a movie's release and the sale of its DVD to the public meant added sales for the studios and the retailers but decreased income from rentals for Blockbuster—especially for high-profile, easily-rentable films. Consumers were happy to buy their own copy of a particular movie instead of renting it, particularly if they hadn't made time to view it during the rental period. Since Blockbuster is responsible for about 40 percent of all video rentals, the decline represents a significant loss. In addition, the retailers were selling the DVDs below cost to attract more customers. A typical DVD might wholesale for $17, but Wal-Mart would sell it to the public for $15—a popular practice with consumers. During the past 12 months, consumers spent over $8 billion on DVDs—an increase of 54 percent from the previous year.

Now that Blockbuster is actually competing against its channel partners, company marketers have had to rethink how the firm does business. They've come up with some innovative programs to win back customers. Deciding that if it can't beat the competition, it might as well join them, Blockbuster has jumped into the business of selling DVDs in addition to renting them. Company spokespeople say that renting-which accounts for 80 percent of Blockbuster's revenues—will continue to be the core business, but including a sales effort makes sense. Many of Blockbuster's 8,000 stores have been revamped to consolidate retail space into one "Buy This" section, where consumers can browse through new and "pre-viewed" tapes and DVDs. Blockbuster has also begun a mail subscription service to compete against Netflix, charging a monthly fee to rent movies.

Customers select a movie online, which is sent by mail; after viewing, they return the movie by mail in a prepaid envelope. The effort involves some new channel members and a new set of logistics, including warehousing, scheduling, order fulfillment and packing, and delivery tailored to the program. But the company is well equipped to make the adjustments, since it already has a state-of-the-art distribution center in Texas. The 850,000-square-foot facility supports all company-operated stores in the U.S.

Blockbuster also now offers customers the opportunity to order new films and games online before they are released to the public. The retail giant reserves copies for these preferred customers and ships the disks as soon as they are available. Finally, there's the Blockbuster Freedom Pass, under which cus-

tomers can rent two DVDs for $20 a month or three for $25. The Freedom program is designed for customers who want to keep the films longer without paying late fees.

When competition occurs among channel members, there's bound to be some conflict—but innovation as well. Blockbuster illustrates how a company can respond positively to these types of changes. Although there's no guarantee of success, consumers are likely to benefit in the long run.[1]

u get rid of the W+R but u can't get of rid of their funct.

Chapter Overview

1

Describe the role that marketing channels and logistics play in marketing strategy.

Distribution—moving goods and services from producers to customers—is an important marketing concern. Although good design and creative promotion may motivate consumers to purchase a product, these practices are useless if consumers cannot actually buy the product when and where they want it. Distribution strategy has two critical components: marketing channels and logistics.

A **marketing,** or **distribution, channel** is an organized system of marketing institutions and their interrelationships that promote the physical flow and ownership of goods and services from producer to consumer or business user. The choice of marketing channels should support the firm's overall marketing strategy. By contrast, **logistics** refers to the process of coordinating the flow of information, goods, and services among members of the marketing channel. Efficient logistical systems support customer service, enhancing customer relationships—an important goal of any marketing strategy.

A key aspect of logistics is physical distribution, which covers a broad range of activities aimed at efficient movement of finished goods from the end of the production line to the consumer. Although some marketers use the terms *transportation* and *physical distribution* interchangeably, these terms do not carry the same meaning. Physical distribution extends beyond transportation to include such important decision areas as customer service, inventory control, materials handling, protective packaging, order processing, transportation, warehouse site selection, and warehousing.

Well-planned marketing channels and effective logistics provide ultimate users with convenient ways for obtaining the goods and services they desire. This chapter discusses the activities, decisions, and marketing intermediaries involved in managing marketing channels and logistics. Chapter 16 looks at other players in the marketing channel: retailers, direct marketers, and wholesalers.

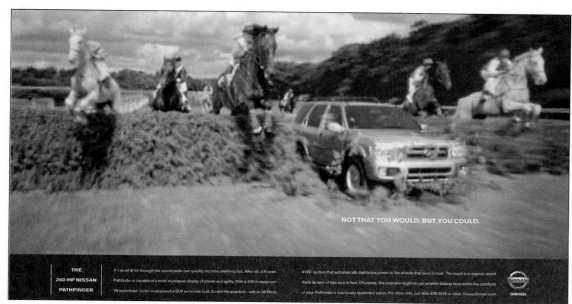

FIGURE 15.1
Marketing Channels: Linking Buyers and Sellers

RM is converted to Finished goods

The Role of Marketing Channels in Marketing Strategy

A firm's distribution channels play a key role in its marketing strategy because these channels provide the means by which the firm moves the goods and services it produces to ultimate users. Channels perform four important functions. First, they facilitate the exchange process by cutting the number of marketplace contacts necessary to make a sale. Suppose you want to buy a new SUV. You see an ad for the Nissan Pathfinder like the one in Figure 15.1. The ad prompts you to check Nissan's Web site, where you will be able to find out more about the car and connect with a local dealer. You can also call a toll-free number to make the same connection. The dealer forms part of the channel that brings you, a potential buyer, and Nissan, the seller, together to complete the exchange process.

Distributors adjust for discrepancies in the market's assortment of goods and services via a process known as sorting, the second channeling function. A single producer tends to maximize the quantity it makes of a limited line of goods, while a single buyer needs a limited quantity of a wide selection of merchandise. Sorting alleviates such discrepancies by channeling products to suit both the buyer's and the producer's needs.

The third function of marketing channels involves standardizing exchange transactions by setting expectations for products, and it involves the transfer process itself. Channel members tend to standardize payment terms, delivery schedules, prices, and purchase lots among other conditions.

Finally, marketing channels facilitate searches by both buyers and sellers. Buyers search for specific goods and services to fill their needs, while sellers attempt to learn what buyers want. Channels bring buyers and sellers together to complete the exchange process.

Literally hundreds of distribution channels carry products today, and no single channel best serves the needs of every company. Instead of searching for the best channel for all products, a marketing manager must analyze alternative channels in light of consumer needs to determine the most appropriate channel or channels for the firm's goods and services.

Marketers must remain flexible, however, since channels, like so many marketing variables, may change. Today's ideal channel may prove inappropriate in a few years. As an example, for many years flowers were sold exclusively through independent specialty shops.

Marketing Dictionary

marketing, or distribution, channel   System of marketing institutions that promotes the physical flow of goods and services, along with ownership title, from producer to consumer or business user.

logistics   Process of coordinating the flow of information, goods, and services among members of the distribution channel.

During the past decade, however, consumer shopping habits have changed as customers started to look for convenience and one-stop shopping. Increasingly, consumers decided to buy flowers in supermarkets, over the telephone, or through the Internet. Consequently, florist services are now available via a variety of marketing channels.

The following sections examine the diverse types of channels available to marketers. The chapter looks at the decisions marketers must make to develop an effective distribution strategy that supports their firm's marketing objectives.

Types of Marketing Channels

2

Describe the various types of distribution channels available to marketers.

The first step in selecting a marketing channel is determining which type of channel will best meet both the seller's objectives and the distribution needs of customers. Figure 15.2 depicts the major channels available to marketers of consumer and business goods and services.

Some channel options involve several different *marketing intermediaries*. A marketing intermediary (or *middleman*) is an organization that operates between producers and consumers or business users.

**FIGURE 15.2
Alternative Marketing
Channels**

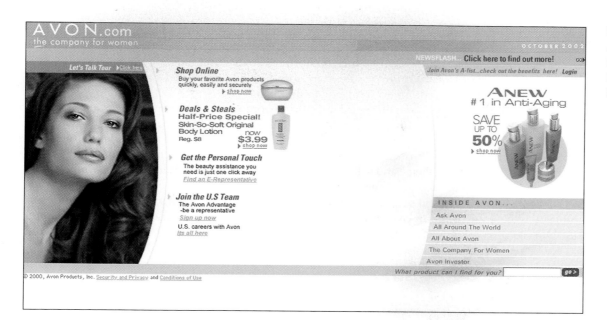

FIGURE 15.3
Avon's Web Site: Connecting Consumers Directly with Avon Representatives

Retailers and wholesalers are both marketing intermediaries. A retail store owned and operated by someone other than the manufacturer of the products it sells is one type of marketing intermediary. A *wholesaler* is an intermediary that takes title to the goods it handles and then distributes these goods to retailers, other distributors, or sometimes end consumers.

A short marketing channel involves few intermediaries. By contrast, a long marketing channel involves many intermediaries working in succession to move goods from producers to consumers. In general, business products tend to move through shorter channels than consumer products due to geographical concentrations and comparatively few business purchasers. Service firms market primarily through short channels because they sell intangible products and need to maintain personal relationships within their channels. Not-for-profit organizations also tend to work with short, simple, and direct channels. Any marketing intermediaries in such channels usually act as agents, such as independent ticket agencies or fund-raising specialists.

Direct Selling

buy directly from the manufacture
Exam. The shortest MKTg Mkt. B2C

The simplest and shortest marketing channel is a direct channel. A **direct channel** carries goods directly from a producer to the business purchaser or ultimate user. This channel forms part of *direct selling*, a marketing strategy in which a producer establishes direct sales contact with its product's final users. Direct selling is an important option for goods that require extensive demonstrations in convincing customers to buy.

Direct selling plays a significant role in business-to-business marketing. Most major installations, accessory equipment, and even component parts and raw materials are sold through direct contacts between producing firms and final buyers. Firms that market products to other businesses often develop and maintain large sales forces to call on potential customers.

Direct selling is also important in consumer goods markets. Direct sellers, such as Mary Kay, Amway, and Avon, sidestep competition in store aisles by developing networks of independent dealers that sell their products direct to consumers. Even the Avon Web site, shown in Figure 15.3, links customers to one of the company's 30,000 sales reps, operating in their own localities. Avon kiosks in shopping malls, too, are operated by local reps, maintaining a simple, direct channel between the "Avon lady" and her customers.[2]

A traditional direct selling strategy is the so-called party plan, popularized by Tupperware and others. Recent hits include candle parties,

Marketing Dictionary

direct channel Marketing channel that moves goods directly from a producer to the business purchaser or ultimate user.

cookware parties, and basket parties. The seller recruits someone to invite friends to her home, where the seller demonstrates goods and encourages guests to make purchases. Longaberger Basket, which started as a one-store operation in Dresden, Ohio, now markets products from more than 7,000 designers through basket parties run by 70,000 independent sales associates. Other direct sellers have used party plans to sell everything from lingerie to popcorn.[3]

Dell sells computers and computer parts directly to companies, government agencies, and consumers. Dell builds computers to customer specifications, configured for processor speed, hard drive size, and monitor type. Michael Dell founded the company as a 19-year-old college student when he realized how difficult it was to track down parts for his own computer system. By buying parts from manufacturers, assembling them, and selling directly to customers, Dell is able to cut overhead and save customers money at the same time. Today, Dell sells more than $31.2 billion worth of computers each year via telephone and the Internet. Recent expansions into network servers, storage, and communications equipment promise continued rapid growth. Case 15.1 at the end of the chapter features Dell Direct.[4]

Channels Using Marketing Intermediaries

Although direct channels allow simple and straightforward marketing, they do not always move goods from producers to consumers efficiently. Some products serve geographically dispersed markets or large numbers of potential end users. Other categories of goods rely heavily on repeat purchases. The producers of these goods may find more efficient, less expensive, and less time-consuming alternatives to direct channels by using marketing intermediaries. This section considers five channels that involve marketing intermediaries.

Producer to Wholesaler to Retailer to Consumer

The traditional channel for consumer goods proceeds from producer to wholesaler to retailer to user. This method carries goods between small retailers and literally thousands of small producers with limited lines. Small producers with limited financial resources rely on the services of wholesalers as immediate sources of funds and as marketers to hundreds of retailers that will stock their output. Small retailers draw on wholesalers' specialized buying skills, which ensure balanced inventories of goods produced in various regions of the world. The wholesaler's sales force promotes the producer's output to its customers. In addition, many manufacturers employ field sales representatives to service retail accounts. These representatives serve as sources of marketing information, but actual sales are typically handled by wholesalers.

Producer to Wholesaler to Business User

Similar characteristics in the organizational market often attract marketing intermediaries to operate between producers and business purchasers. The term *industrial distributor* commonly refers to intermediaries in the business market that take title to the goods.

Producer to Agent to Wholesaler to Retailer to Consumer

When many small companies serve a market, a unique intermediary—the agent—performs the basic function of bringing buyer and seller together. An agent may or may not take possession of the goods but never takes title. The agent merely represents a producer by seeking a market for its output or a wholesaler (which does take title to the goods) by locating a source of supply.

Producer to Agent to Wholesaler to Business User

Like agents, brokers are independent intermediaries who may or may not take possession of goods but never take title to these goods. Agents and brokers also serve the business market when small producers attempt to market their offerings through large wholesalers. Such an intermediary, often called a *manufacturers' representative*, provides an independent sales force to contact wholesale buyers.

Producer to Agent to Business User

For products sold in small units, only merchant wholesalers can economically cover the markets. A merchant wholesaler is an independently owned wholesaler that takes title to the goods. By maintaining regional inventories, this wholesaler achieves transportation economies, stockpiling goods and making small shipments over short distances. For a product with large unit sales, however, and for which transportation accounts for a small percentage of the total cost, the producer-agent-business user channel is usually employed. The agent in effect becomes the producer's sales force, but bulk shipments of the product reduce the intermediary's inventory management function.

Dual Distribution *(Exam) means more than one. e-commerce, catalog.*

Dual distribution refers to movement of products through more than one channel to reach the same target market. Talbot's, for instance, has a three-pronged distribution system, selling through stores, catalogs, and the Internet. Marketers usually adopt this distribution strategy either to maximize their firm's coverage in the marketplace or to increase the cost effectiveness of the firm's marketing effort. For instance, automobile parts manufacturers promote products through both direct sales forces and independent jobbers. The cost-effectiveness goal, on the other hand, might lead a manufacturer to assign its own sales force to sell in high-potential territories while relying on manufacturers' representatives (independent, commissioned salespeople) in lower volume areas.

Starbucks, which once relied on its franchised coffee-shop network, now offers its whole-bean coffees through grocery stores. The ad in Figure 15.4 invites coffee drinkers to take the distinctive taste of Starbucks home with them.

Reverse Channels *Exam is less efficient.*

While the traditional concept of marketing channels involves the movement of goods and services from producer to consumer or business user, marketers should not ignore *reverse channels*—channels designed to return goods to their producers. Reverse channels have gained increased importance with rising prices for raw materials, spreading availability of recycling facilities, and passage of additional conservation laws. For instance, consumers pay refundable deposits on bottled products in states like Maine, Michigan, and Oregon. New Jersey requires businesses and households to separate their trash to aid recycling.

Some reverse channels move through the facilities of traditional marketing intermediaries. In states that require bottle deposits, retailers and local bottlers perform these functions in the soft-drink industry. For other products, manufacturers establish redemption centers, develop systems for rechanneling products for recycling, and create specialized organizations to handle disposal and recycling. Other reverse channel participants include community groups that organize cleanup days and develop recycling and waste disposal systems.

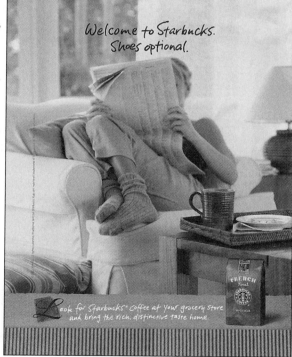

FIGURE 15.4 Starbucks' Dual Distribution Strategy

Marketing Dictionary

dual distribution   Network that moves products to a firm's target market through more than one marketing channel.

Reverse channels also handle product recalls and repairs. Registration of car owners allows manufacturers to send proper notification in the event of recalls. For example, an automobile recall notice might advise owners of potential problems that may need correcting at their dealerships. Similarly, reverse channels have carried some items to manufacturers' repair centers. The warranty for a small appliance might direct the owner to return a defective unit to the dealer for repairs within 90 days after the sale and to the factory after that period. Such reverse channels are a vital element of product recall and repair procedures.

Channel Strategy Decisions

3

Outline the major channel strategy decisions.

Marketers face several strategic decisions in choosing channels and marketing intermediaries for their products. Selecting a specific channel is the most basic of these decisions. Marketers must also resolve questions about the level of distribution intensity, the desirability of vertical marketing systems, and the performance of current intermediaries.

Selection of a Marketing Channel

Consider, for example, the following questions: What characteristics of a franchised dealer network make it the best channel option for a company? Why do operating supplies often go through both agents and merchant wholesalers before reaching their actual users? Why would a firm market a single product through multiple channels? Marketers must answer many such questions in choosing marketing channels.

A variety of factors impact the selection of a marketing channel. Some channel decisions are dictated by the marketplace in which the company operates. In other cases, the product itself may be a key variable in picking a marketing channel. Finally, the marketing organization may set limits or offer opportunities related to specific distribution channels.

Market Factors

Channel structure reflects a product's intended markets, either for consumers or business users. Business purchasers usually prefer to deal directly with manufacturers (except for routine supplies or small accessory items), but most consumers make their purchases from retailers. Marketers often sell products that serve both business users and consumers through more than one channel.

Other market factors also affect channel choice, including the market's needs, its geographical location, and its average order size. To serve a concentrated market with a small number of buyers, a direct channel offers a feasible alternative. To serve a geographically dispersed potential market in which customers purchase small amounts in individual transactions—the conditions in the consumer goods market—distribution through marketing intermediaries makes sense.

Product Factors

Product characteristics also guide the choice of an optimal marketing channel strategy. Perishable goods, such as fresh produce, beverages, and fashion products with short life cycles, typically move through short channels.

One way that the Coca-Cola Company sells its beverages is through vending machines, a relatively short channel. Vending machine sales account for 10 percent of the company's unit volume in the U.S. To maximize customer convenience, the firm is exploring radio-frequency identification in which office workers can swipe a key chain in front of a machine to buy a can of pop instead of using change. Meanwhile, United Artists, which operates 206 theaters, is testing vending machines that cook frozen pizzas from Kraft Foods in less than 90 seconds.[5]

Complex products, producers of custom-made installations, and computer equipment are often sold directly to ultimate buyers. In general, relatively standardized items pass through comparatively long channels. For another generalization, low product unit values, such as a pack of Post-it notes shown in Figure 15.5, call for long channels.

Organizational Factors

Companies with adequate financial, management, and marketing resources feel little need for help from intermediaries. A financially strong manufacturer can hire its own sales force, warehouse its own goods, and grant credit to retailers or consumers. A weaker firm must rely on marketing intermediaries for these services. In one exception, a large retail chain may purchase all of a manufacturer's output, bypassing independent wholesalers. A production-oriented firm may need the marketing expertise of intermediaries to offset its own lack of such skills.

A firm with a broad product line can usually market its products directly to retailers or business users since its own sales force can offer a variety of products. High sales volume spreads selling costs over a large number of items, allowing returns from direct sales. Single-product firms often view direct selling as unaffordable.

The manufacturer's desire for control over marketing of its product also influences channel selection. To ensure aggressive promotion by retailers, producers often choose the shortest available channels. To distribute a new product, the producer may have to implement an informative advertising campaign before independent wholesalers will agree to handle the campaign.

FIGURE 15.5
Post-it Notes: A Simple Product with a Long Distribution Channel

Businesses that explore new marketing channels must be careful to avoid antagonizing their channel intermediaries. Lids Corporation, a mall retailer of hats and caps, sought a means of offering 7,000 nonstore items to mall buyers without alienating sales associates. The company installed point-of-sale kiosks—with a Web site hook-up—inside its stores. Salespeople guide in-store customers around the site and earn commissions on purchases initiated inside the store.[6]

Competitive Factors

Some firms feel compelled to develop new marketing channels to remedy inadequate promotion of their products by independent marketing intermediaries. In one popular alternative, a manufacturer might add a direct sales force or set up its own retail distribution network (a move discussed later in the chapter). Table 15.1 summarizes the factors that affect the selection of a marketing channel and examines the effect of each on the channel's overall length.

Determining Distribution Intensity *(Exam)* ᵃ

Another key channel strategy decision is the intensity of distribution. *Distribution intensity* refers to the number of intermediaries through which a manufacturer distributes its goods. The decision about distribution intensity should ensure adequate market coverage for a product. Adequate market coverage varies depending on the goals of the individual firm, the type of product, and the consumer segments in its target market. In general, however, distribution intensity varies along a continuum with three general categories: intensive distribution, selective distribution, and exclusive distribution.

TABLE 15.1   Factors Influencing Marketing Channel Strategies

	CHARACTERISTICS OF SHORT CHANNELS	CHARACTERISTICS OF LONG CHANNELS
Market factors	Business users	Consumers
	Geographically concentrated	Geographically dispersed
	Extensive technical knowledge and regular servicing required	Little technical knowledge and regular servicing not required
	Large orders	Small orders
Product factors	Perishable	Durable
	Complex	Standardized
	Expensive	Inexpensive
Producer factors	Manufacturer has adequate resources to perform channel functions	Manufacturer lacks adequate resources to perform channel functions
	Broad product line	Limited product line
	Channel control important	Channel control not important
Competitive factors	Manufacturing feels satisfied with marketing intermediaries' performance in promoting products	Manufacturer feels dissatisfied with marketing intermediaries' performance in promoting products

Intensive Distribution

An **intensive distribution** strategy seeks to distribute a product through all available channels in a trade area. M&M Mars, for example, implements an intensive distribution strategy, placing its products in supermarkets, chain stores, vending machines, and drugstores. Producers of convenience goods try to saturate their markets, enabling purchasers to buy their products with minimum efforts. Usually, an intensive distribution strategy suits items with wide appeal across broad groups of consumers. Examples of goods distributed through this strategy include soft drinks, candy, gum, and cigarettes.

Selective Distribution

In another market coverage strategy, **selective distribution,** a firm chooses only a limited number of retailers in a market area to handle its line. This arrangement helps to control price cutting since relatively few dealers handle the firm's line. By limiting the number of retailers, marketers can reduce total marketing costs while establishing strong working relationships within the channel. Moreover, selected retailers often agree to comply with the company's strict rules for advertising, pricing, and displaying its products. *Cooperative advertising,* in which the manufacturer pays a percentage of the retailer's advertising expenditures and the retailer prominently displays the firm's products, can be utilized for mutual benefit, and marginal retailers can be avoided. Where service is important, the manufacturer usually provides training and assistance to dealers it chooses.

Exclusive Distribution

When a producer grants exclusive rights to a wholesaler or retailer to sell its products in a specific geographical region, it practices **exclusive distribution,** an extension of selective distribution. The automobile industry provides the best example of exclusive distribution. A city with a population of 40,000 may have a single Mazda or Ford dealer. Exclusive distribution agreements also govern marketing for some major appliance and apparel brands.

Marketers may sacrifice some market coverage by implementing a policy of exclusive distribution. As compensation, however, they often develop and maintain an image of quality and prestige for the product. In addition, exclusive distribution limits marketing costs since the firm deals with a smaller number of accounts. In exclusive distribution, producers and retailers cooperate closely in decisions concerning advertising and promotion, inventory carried by the retailers, and prices.

In recent years, carmakers have sought to gain tighter control over the sales process, traditionally the dealerships' domain. DaimlerChrysler initiated its Five Star program, through which it rewards dealers who meet its sales training, customer service, and relationship management objectives by sharing some marketing costs and awarding special recognition. Despite initial resistance from dealers who resented being told how to run their businesses, more than half of all Chrysler dealers are now certified. Ford's best practice system, Blue Oval, is similar but offers cash incentives in the form of an additional 1.25 percent discount off wholesale prices.[7]

Legal Problems of Exclusive Distribution   *Not in test*

Exclusive distribution presents potential legal problems in three main areas: exclusive dealing agreements, closed sales territories, and tying agreements. Although none of these practices is illegal per se, all may break the law if they reduce competition or tend to create monopolies.

As part of an exclusive distribution strategy, marketers may try to enforce an *exclusive dealing agreement,* which prohibits a marketing intermediary (a wholesaler or, more typically, a retailer) from handling competing products. Producers of high-priced shopping goods, specialty goods, and accessory equipment often require such agreements to assure total concentration on their own product lines. Such contracts violate the Clayton Act only if the producer's or dealer's sales volumes represent a substantial percentage of total sales in the market area. While exclusive dealing is legal for companies first entering a market, such agreements violate the Clayton Act if used by firms with a sizable market share seeking to bar competitors from the market.

Producers may also try to set up *closed sales territories* to restrict their distributors to certain geographical regions. Although the distributors gain protection from rival dealers in their exclusive territories, they sacrifice any opportunities in opening new facilities or marketing the manufacturers' products outside their assigned territories. The legality of a system of closed sales territories depends on whether the restriction decreases competition. If so, it violates the Federal Trade Commission Act and provisions of the Sherman Act and the Clayton Act.

The legality of closed sales territories also depends on whether the system imposes horizontal or vertical restrictions. Horizontal territorial restrictions result from agreements between retailers or wholesalers to avoid competition among sellers of products from the same producer. Such agreements consistently have been declared illegal. However, the U.S. Supreme Court has ruled that vertical territorial restrictions—those between producers and wholesalers or retailers—may meet legal criteria. The ruling gives no clear-cut answer, but such agreements likely satisfy the law in cases where manufacturers occupy relatively small parts of their markets. In such instances, the restrictions may actually increase competition among competing brands; the wholesaler or retailer faces no competition from other dealers carrying the manufacturer's brand, so it can concentrate on effectively competing with other brands.

The third legal question of exclusive dealing involves *tying agreements,* which allow channel members to become exclusive dealers only if they also carry products other than those that they want to sell. In the apparel industry, for example, an agreement might require a dealer to carry a comparatively unpopular line of clothing to get desirable, fast-moving items.

Tying agreements violate the Sherman Act and the Clayton Act when they reduce competition or create monopolies that keep competitors out of major markets. For this reason, the courts prohibited International Salt Company from selling salt as a tying product with leases of its patented salt-dispensing machines for snow and ice removal. The Supreme Court ruled that such an agreement unreasonably reduced competition among sellers of salt.

Marketing Dictionary

intensive distribution   Distribution of a product through all available channels.

selective distribution   Distribution of a product through only a limited number of channels.

exclusive distribution   Distribution of a product through one wholesaler or retailer in a specific geographical region.

BMW North America expanded its channels to include its Financial Services division. The company started with vehicle financing for its autos and motorcycles, and it has now branched into personal banking for the BMW driver, offering such services as credit cards, certificates of deposit, and money market accounts.

Who Should Perform Channel Functions?

A fundamental marketing principle governs channel decisions: Some member of the channel must perform certain central marketing functions; channel members can shift responsibility, but they cannot eliminate those functions. Although independent wholesalers perform many of these functions for manufacturers, retailers, and other wholesaler clients, other channel members could fulfill these roles instead. Manufacturers might, for example, bypass wholesalers by establishing regional warehouses, maintaining field sales forces, serving as sources of information for retail customers, or arranging details of financing. Carmakers, for example, who have long operated credit units that offer new-car financing, have even opened their own banks. Within a year of opening, BMW's bank signed up 25,000 customers.[8] Rather than fill the intermediary function themselves, manufacturers might push responsibility for some functions through the channel to retailers or ultimate purchasers. Large retailers face the same choices, but the principle remains the same: Channel members can eliminate an intermediary only when someone else performs its channel functions.

An independent intermediary earns a profit in exchange for providing services to manufacturers and retailers. This profit margin is low, however, ranging from 1 percent for food wholesalers to 5 percent for durable goods wholesalers. Manufacturers and retailers could reap these profits, or they could market directly and reduce retail prices—but only if they could perform the channel functions and match the efficiency of the independent intermediaries.

To grow profitably in a competitive environment, an intermediary must provide better service at lower costs than manufacturers or retailers can provide for themselves. In this case, consolidation of channel functions can represent a strategic opportunity for a company.

The $5 million pawnshop industry, at first suspicious that availability of used products over the Internet would damage sales, has discovered that the opposite is true. Pawnshops like California-based Desert Jewelry Mart use online auction site eBay as an intermediary in selling hard-to-move merchandise such as buffalo teeth, muskrat skulls, or some Native American jewelry. By selling online through eBay, Desert Jewelry has tripled its revenues.[9]

Channel Management and Leadership

4

Describe the concepts of channel management, conflict, and cooperation within the marketing channel.

Distribution strategy does not end with the choice of a channel. Manufacturers must also focus on channel management by developing and maintaining relationships with the intermediaries in their marketing channels. Positive channel relationships encourage channel members to remember their partners' goods and market them. Manufacturers also must carefully manage the incentives offered to induce channel members to promote their products. This effort includes weighing decisions about pricing, promotion, and other support efforts that the manufacturer performs.

Increasingly, marketers are managing channels in partnership with other channel members. Effective cooperation allows all channel members to achieve goals that they could not achieve on their own. Keys to successful management of channel relationships include the development of high levels of coordination, commitment, and trust between channel members.

Not all channel members wield equal power in the distribution chain, however. The dominant and controlling member of a marketing channel is called the **channel captain.** This firm's power to control a channel may result from its control over some type of reward or punishment to other channel members, such as granting an exclusive sales territory or taking away a dealership. Power might also result from contractual arrangements, specialized expert knowledge, or agreement among channel members about their mutual best interests. Central Steel & Wire Company controls the distribution of its products through its Performance Assured service system. The company provides on-time delivery by operating its own fleet of delivery trucks and helps customers reduce their inventory costs by offering just-in-time and distributor managed inventory programs.

Channel Conflict *Exam*

Channel captains often must work to resolve channel conflicts. Marketing channels work smoothly only when members cooperate in well-organized efforts to achieve maximum operating efficiencies, yet channel members often perform as separate, independent, and even competing forces. Too often, marketing institutions see only one step forward or backward along a channel. They think about their own suppliers and customers rather than about vital links throughout the channel. Two types of conflict—horizontal and vertical—may hinder the normal functioning of a marketing channel.

Horizontal Conflict *Ex*

Horizontal conflict sometimes results from disagreements among channel members at the same level, such as two or more wholesalers or two or more retailers, or among marketing intermediaries of the same type, such as two competing discount stores or several retail florists. With 1,675 dealerships nationwide, farm equipment manufacturer Deere & Company has run into conflicts with its dealer network. Dealers complain that high saturation—48 dealers in a 35-mile radius in Ohio, for example—along with a downturn in the farming industry has reduced their ability to achieve market share. Not only must they compete against other manufactures, but too many Deere dealers are chasing after the same customers.[10]

More often, horizontal conflict causes sparks between different types of marketing intermediaries that handle similar products. An independent retail druggist competes with discount houses, department stores, convenience stores, mail-order houses, and Internet sites, all of which may buy identical branded products from a single producer. Varied consumer preferences have drawn products into multiple channels and numerous rival outlets.

Consider the experiences of furniture manufacturer American Leather. One of its retailers set up a Web site offering Internet-only discounts to consumers outside its exclusive territories, sparking fury among rival dealers. At first, the company reacted by forbidding retail partners to use its brand name or image for e-commerce. But this solution was far from ideal because it closed off the company from sales and promotion opportunities through fast-growing Internet channels. It also frustrated dealers who had developed costly Web sites of their own. Instead, American Leather updated its own Web site with detailed product information and a "dealer locator" system that directed customers to local stores. The company also stepped up its advertising in consumer magazines and newspapers in an effort to drive customers first to the site and from there to retail outlets. Within a year, sales from the same dealer base were up by 40 percent.[11]

Vertical Conflict *Ex*

Vertical relationships also cause frequent and often severe conflict. Channel members at different levels find many reasons for disputes, as when retailers develop private brands to compete with producers' brands or when producers establish their own retail stores or create mail-order operations that compete with retailers. Producers may annoy wholesalers and retailers when they attempt to bypass these intermediaries and sell directly to consumers. In one well-publicized case, Levi Strauss suspended attempts to sell over its own Web site following complaints from enraged

Marketing Dictionary

channel captain   Dominant and controlling member of a marketing channel.

right wrong

Solving an Ethical Controversy

Secret Costs of Shelf Space

Entrepreneurial companies fighting for shelf space know how hard—and expensive—it is to get their tasty new chip dips or fruit drinks into supermarket chains. Not only must they cover development, manufacturing, and marketing costs, but there is a huge price to pay just to get stores to put products on their shelves. Through retail incentives called *slotting allowances*, chains charge thousands of dollars per item, per store—fees that few small companies can afford.

Recently, due to a Federal Accounting Standards Board ruling, consumers caught a glimpse of the real cost of fees paid by big manufacturers. Forced to subtract "give-backs" from reported sales, Kraft revealed it spent $4.6 billion—14 percent of revenues—on retail incentives in a single year. Other food companies, including General Mills and PepsiCo, were not far behind. Major manufacturers reported an astounding $60 billion a year in fees to retailers.

Are retail slotting allowances fair to channel members?

PRO
1. Slotting fees keep the risks associated with new products where they belong—with the manufacturer. Retailers shouldn't have to carry marginal products without assurance of compensation.

2. Slotting fees cover the costs of stocking, shelving, pricing, and promoting new brands. If they take up costly space and fail to sell, retailers lose revenue.

CON
1. Large manufacturers use slotting fees to stamp out competition. The FTC recently forced McCormick & Co., which produces 40 percent of the spices on grocery shelves, to desist payment of slotting fees to stores that agreed to limit space for competing brands.
2. Slotting fees discourage innovation. Small companies cannot afford huge fees to get their products into chains. This barrier, in turn, limits consumer choices.

Summary

The FDA is investigating whether slotting fees are anticompetitive. Recently, in closed hearings, small companies alleged that the big brands manipulate give-backs to block competitive products. Witnesses wore hoods and testified behind screens for fear of retaliation. While the FTC is looking more closely at the practice, slotting fees continue to extend beyond packaged foods and dry goods into the fresh produce category.

SOURCES: Julie Forster, "The Hidden Cost of Shelf-Space," *BusinessWeek*, April 15, 2002, p. 103; "Slotting Allowances in the Supermarket Industry," Food Marketing Institute, November 2001, http://www.fmi.org.

---

retailers. In another, a Chicago area carpet dealer attempted to set up a reverse auction site—Carpetshopping.com—that allowed customers to purchase any brand of carpet at discount prices. Customers fed their requirements into the site, and then dealers offered bids to fulfill the sales. The lowest bidder won the right to strike a deal with the customer. Fearful that Internet discounts would drive down prices at retail, the three largest carpet manufacturers—which account for 80 percent of the $26 billion market—demanded that Yahoo! close down the offending Web site. The biggest of the three revoked the dealer's exclusive license.[12]

In other instances, retailers may anger suppliers by requesting concessions suppliers believe are unfair. The "Solving an Ethical Controversy" box explains the practice of *slotting fees*, or *slotting allowances* (discussed in Chapter 11), in which retailers demand payment for granting new products coveted shelf space. In other instances, retailers take unexpected deductions from payments to manufacturers to cover damaged or defective goods. Although retailers allege deductions like these cover essential costs that belong with the producers, manufacturers claim retailers are using their power as channel captains to reduce the cost of goods.

The Grey Market Exam

Another type of channel conflict results from activities in the grey market. As U.S. manufacturers license their technology and brands abroad, they sometimes find themselves in competition in the U.S.

market against versions of their own brands produced by overseas affiliates. These *grey goods*, or *parallel goods*, enter U.S. channels through the actions of foreign distributors. While licensing agreements usually prohibit foreign licensees from selling in the U.S., no such rules inhibit their distributors.

A decade ago, the grey market became a problem for U.S. firms in the electronics field. It then spread to such products as flashlight batteries, photographic film, packaged goods, and the apparel industry. Some manufacturers have protested against this practice, but retailers can still legally buy goods through the grey market because the Supreme Court has ruled that products made under legitimate licenses can legally enter the market regardless of their countries of origin.

Because of the disproportionately high cost of medications in the U.S., many consumers turn to Canada to fill prescriptions. Internet sites like unitedhealthalliance.com forward a medical history along with a doctor's prescription to a Canadian pharmacy. Once a Canadian doctor reviews the order, the drugs are shipped directly to the patient's home in the U.S. Although it is technically illegal to import drugs, authorities have made exceptions for "personal use." Recently, the U.S. Senate backed a bill that would allow reimportation of U.S. drugs from Canada. Although the ultimate fate of the bill is uncertain, widespread support exists for this measure.[13]

Achieving Channel Cooperation

The basic antidote to channel conflict is effective cooperation among channel members. Cooperation is best achieved when all channel members regard themselves as components of the same organization. Achieving this kind of cooperation is the primary responsibility of the dominant member—the channel captain—which must provide the leadership necessary to ensure the channel's efficient functioning.

Vertical Marketing Systems

Efforts to reduce channel conflict and improve the effectiveness of distribution have led to the development of vertical marketing systems. A **vertical marketing system (VMS)** is a planned channel system designed to improve distribution efficiency and cost effectiveness by integrating various functions throughout the distribution chain.

A vertical marketing system can achieve this goal through either forward or backward integration. In *forward integration,* a firm attempts to control downstream distribution. For example, a manufacturer might buy a retail chain that sells its products. *Backward integration* occurs when a manufacturer attempts to gain greater control over inputs in its production process. A manufacturer might buy the supplier of a raw material the manufacturer uses in the production of its products. Backward integration can also extend the control of retailers and wholesalers over producers that supply them.

A VMS offers several benefits. First, it improves chances for controlling and coordinating the steps in the distribution or production process. It may lead to the development of economies of scale that ultimately saves money. A VMS may also let a manufacturer expand into profitable new businesses. However, a VMS also involves some costs. A manufacturer assumes increased risk when it takes control of an entire distribution chain. Manufacturers may also discover that they lose some flexibility in responding to market changes.

Marketers have developed three categories of VMSs: corporate systems, administered systems, and contractual systems. These categories are outlined in the sections that follow.

Corporate Systems

Where a single owner runs organizations at each stage of the marketing channel, it operates a **corporate marketing system.** The "Marketing Hits" box explains one company's success in marketing lifestyle products through company-owned stores and tightly controlled independent retailers. Phillips Auctioneers, shown in Figure 15.6, restricts

Marketing Dictionary

vertical marketing system (VMS)   Planned channel system designed to improve distribution efficiency and cost effectiveness by integrating various functions throughout the distribution chain.

corporate marketing system   A VMS in which a single owner operates the entire marketing channel.

FIGURE 15.6
Channel Leadership

Coach Builds a World-Class Accessory Business with a Corporate Marketing Channel

Background. Throughout its 60-year history, Coach has sold its classic leather goods to affluent clientele who stepped inside its dark, wood-paneled stores. But the company wanted to build on its success by extending its reach to younger customers while still maintaining its upscale image.

The Challenge. Many companies seek to diversify channels to maximize revenues, but Coach is bucking the trend to rejuvenate not just its brands but the outlets that sell them. With the launch of its Signature line of handbags, Coach reinvented itself—and its retail channels.

continued on next page

its channels to company-owned salesrooms in the U.S., the U.K., and Switzerland, supplemented by representatives in 15 countries. A Web site connects potential customers with sales representatives.

Administered Systems

An **administered marketing system** achieves channel coordination when a dominant channel member exercises its power. Even though Goodyear sells its tires through independently owned and operated dealerships, Goodyear controls the stock that these dealerships carry. Other examples of powerful channel captains leading administered channels include McKesson, Sears, and Wal-Mart.

Contractual Systems

Instead of common ownership of intermediaries within a corporate VMS or the exercising of power within an administered system, a **contractual marketing system** coordinates distribution through formal agreements among channel members. In practice, three types of agreements set up these systems: wholesaler-sponsored voluntary chains, retail cooperatives, and franchises.

Wholesaler-Sponsored Voluntary Chain

A wholesaler-sponsored voluntary chain represents an attempt by an independent wholesaler to preserve a market by strengthening its retail customers. To enable independent retailers to compete with outlets of rival chains, the wholesaler enters into a formal agreement with retailers to use a common name, maintain standardized facilities, and purchase the wholesaler's products. Often, the wholesaler develops a line of private brands to be stocked by the members of the voluntary chain.

IGA (Independent Grocers' Alliance) Food Stores is a good example of a voluntary chain. Other wholesaler-sponsored chains include Associated

Druggists, Sentry Hardware, and Western Auto. Since a single advertisement promotes all the retailers in the trading area, a common store name and similar inventories allow the retailers to save on advertising costs.

Retail Cooperative

In a second type of contractual VMS, a group of retailers establish a shared wholesaling operation to help them compete with chains. This is known as a retail cooperative. The retailers purchase ownership shares in the wholesaling operation and agree to buy a minimum percentage of their inventories from this operation. The members typically adopt a common store name and develop common private brands. Ace Hardware is an example of a retail cooperative.

Franchise

A third type of contractual vertical marketing system is the franchise, in which a wholesaler or dealer (the franchisee) agrees to meet the operating requirements of a manufacturer or other franchiser. Franchising is a huge and growing industry. Twenty years ago, Subway had 134 franchises and McDonald's had 5,749; today, Subway has almost 17,000 franchises and McDonald's boasts more than 30,000 outlets worldwide. Over 3,000 U.S. companies distribute goods and services through systems of franchised dealers, and numerous firms also offer franchises in international markets. The total number of franchise units tops 250,000, and it continues to rise. The five fastest growing franchise categories are photo processing, human resource training, children's businesses, computer services, and maintenance companies.

Franchise owners pay anywhere from several thousand dollars to hundreds of thousands of dollars to purchase their franchises. Typically, they also pay a royalty on sales to the franchising company. In exchange for these initial and ongoing fees, the franchise owner receives the right to use the company's brand name as well as services such as training, marketing, advertising, and volume discounts. Franchise fees for top brands are shown in Figure 15.7.

Major franchise chains justify the steep price of entry since it allows new businesses to hitch onto winning brands. But if the brand enters a slump or the corporation behind the franchise makes poor strategic decisions, franchisees feel the pain. In recent years, Burger King, the number two fast-food chain, made moves that negatively influenced the revenues of franchisees. Troubles began when the company withdrew its longstanding 99-cent Whopper promotion, depriving owners of a powerful tool for drawing diners into their restaurants. A series of movie tie-ins with some box-office busts exacerbated the problem. Plans to overhaul restaurant designs and kitchen operations—at a cost to owners of $250,000 per store—enraged franchisees. Recently, Burger King has scaled back remodeling plans and strengthened menu choices. Tie-ins with recent hit movies have improved the outlook for franchisees. Even so, a Los Angeles–based owner of 140 Burger King franchises claims to have lost millions of dollars because of corporate-mandated policies.[14]

Marketing Hit

The Strategy. Like the Signature brand, which is lighter and less pricey than the venerable Coach handbags of old, the company's retail stores have undergone a transformation. Bigger and brighter, with a design that appeals to younger customers, Coach stores stock an exciting mix of products, including shoes, watches, and jewelry. Although leather handbags still account for more than half of all sales, Coach is positioned as a lifestyle company—hip, affordable, and fun to shop.

Beyond its own outlets, Coach keeps tight control over a wholesale network of 1,400 department and specialty stores. Its products—typically priced as "affordable luxuries," with purses at around $300—are never allowed to go on sale.

The Outcome. Even in a bleak economy, Coach maintained its prices and met sales expectations. What's next? Eyeing Japan as a key growth market, the company recently opened a new flagship store in Tokyo's prestigious Ginza shopping district.

SOURCES: "Coach Hitches Up Earnings," *Forbes*, January 9, 2002, http://www.forbes.com; "Coach Opens First Japan Flagship Store in Ginza, Tokyo," Coach press release, May 28, 2002, http://www.corporate-ir.net; Melissa Phipps, "Growth in Store," *Worth*, December 2001, pp. 35–38.

Marketing Dictionary

administered marketing system VMS that achieves channel coordination when a dominant channel member exercises its power.

contractual marketing system VMS that coordinates channel activities through formal agreements among channel members.

FIGURE 15.7
Costs of Acquiring Top Franchise Brands

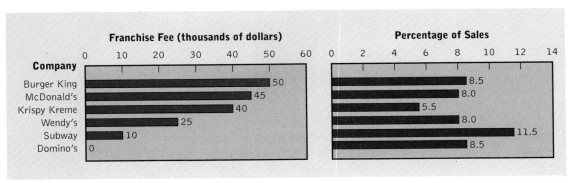

SOURCE: Data from companies; Kessev Finance, in Daniel Kruger, "Carrying the Flame," *Forbes*, December 24, 2001, p. 65.

The Role of Logistics *and Supply chain management*
in Distribution Strategy

Pier 1 imports its eclectic mix of items from 600 vendors in 55 countries, and more than 80 percent come from small companies. If high-demand items or seasonal products are late into its warehouses or are shipped in insufficient quantities, the company misses opportunities to deliver popular shopping choices at its 700 retail stores and risks losing ground to competitors such as Pottery Barn and Crate & Barrel.

This situation illustrates the importance of logistics. Careful coordination of Pier 1's supplier network, its shipping processes, and its inventory control is the key to its continuing success. Yet while rival merchandisers manage to sell through inventory at a rate of three times a year, Pier 1's turnover rate is not much better than two turns a year. In a recent year, this meant the company paid for $34 million worth of goods that—due to inventory logjams—did not make it onto retail shelves. To improve its processes, Pier 1's logistics team is implementing an electronic monitoring system that will track goods as they move from the point of origin into retail outlets. If sales of a particular product in a particular region move faster than anticipated, the company will be able to divert shipments of goods to undersupplied warehouses. The system will also improve storage-space allocation and labor assignments, making for better efficiencies in unpacking containers and moving goods out to retail stores while demand is still high.[15]

Effective logistics requires proper management of the supply chain (also known as the *value chain*). As discussed in Chapter 6, the *supply chain* is the complete sequence of suppliers that contribute to the creation and delivery of merchandise. The supply chain begins with the raw-material inputs for the manufacturing process of a product and then proceeds to the actual production activities. The final link in the supply chain is the movement of finished goods through the marketing channel to customers. Each link of the chain benefits the consumers as goods move from raw materials through manufacturing to distribution. The value chain encompasses all activities that enhance the value of the finished goods, including design, quality manufacturing, customer service, and delivery. Customer satisfaction results directly from the perceived value of a purchase to its buyer. To manage the supply chain, businesses must look for ways to add and maximize customer value in each activity they perform.

As Pier 1's experience makes clear, logistical management plays a major role in giving customers what they need when they need it. Therefore, logistical management plays a central role in the supply chain. Another important component of this chain, *value-added service*, adds some improved or supplemental service that customers do not normally receive or expect.

Upstream mngmt involves managing Raw materials, inbound logistics, and warehouse and storage facilities. Downstream mgt involves managing finished product storage, outbound logistics, mktg and sales, and customer service.

Enterprise Resource Planning

Software is an important aspect of logistics management and the supply chain. Consider the case of Mott's, the applesauce people. Their ideal production plan is developed from enterprise resource planning (ERP) software sold by SAP, the largest German software producer. An *enterprise resource planning system* is an integrated software system that consolidates data from among the firm's units. Roughly two-thirds of ERP system users are manufacturers that are concerned with production issues such as sequencing and scheduling.

As valuable as it is, ERP and its related software aren't always perfect. For example, ERP failures were blamed for Hershey's inability to fulfill all of its candy orders during a recent Halloween period, when a fall-off in sales was blamed on a combination of shipping delays, inability to fill orders, and partial shipments while candy stockpiled in warehouses. The nation's major retailers were forced to shift their purchases to other candy vendors.[16]

Logistical Cost Control

In addition to enhancing their products by providing value-added services to customers, many firms are focusing on logistics for another important reason: to cut costs. Distribution functions currently represent almost half of a typical firm's total marketing costs.

Historically, cost-cutting efforts have focused on economies in production. These attempts began with the Industrial Revolution, when the emerging science of management emphasized efficient production and a continual drive to decrease production costs and improve the output levels of factories and production workers. Managers, however, now recognize that production efficiency leaves few easy opportunities for further cost savings. Increasingly, managers are looking for possible cost savings in their logistical functions.

To reduce logistical costs, businesses are reexamining each link of their supply chains to identify activities that do not add value for customers. By eliminating, reducing, or redesigning these activities, they can often cut costs and boost efficiency.

Enterprise Resource Planning software has been a very valuable integrated software tool for many companies. Unfortunately, Hershey Foods had some difficulties fulfilling their orders during the time they were implementing their ERP system.

Third-Party Logistics

Some companies try to cut costs and offer value-added services by outsourcing some or all of their logistics functions to specialist firms. The *third-party (contract) logistics firms* specialize in handling logistical activities for their clients. The Wallace Company, whose W.I.N. total print management Web site is featured in Figure 15.8, is a leading provider of comprehensive print-related activities to Fortune 1,000 companies. Wallace's Total Print Management (TPM) strategy dramatically reduces customers' process costs for printing, shipping, distribution, storage, and payment of all printing needs.

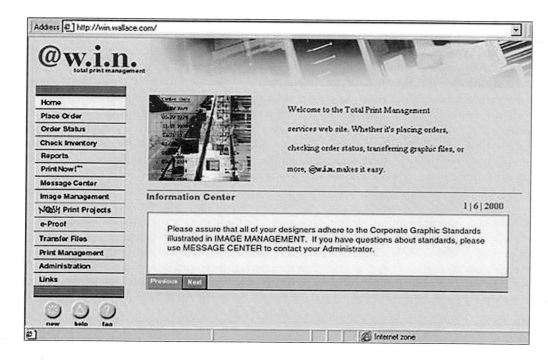

FIGURE 15.8
W.I.N.: Third-Party Print Management Firm

Recently, TRW Aeronautical Systems won a contract to provide supply chain management systems to South African Airways Technical. The third-party logistics firm will manage overhaul and repair of avionics and engine control parts for a fleet of Boeing jets.[17]

Through such outsourcing alliances, producers and logistical service suppliers cooperate in developing innovative, customized systems that speed goods through carefully constructed manufacturing and distribution pipelines. Although many companies have long outsourced transportation and warehousing functions, today's alliance partners use similar methods to combine their operations.

Physical Distribution

5

Identify and compare the major components of a physical distribution system.

A firm's physical distribution system is an organized group of components linked according to a plan for achieving specific distribution objectives. It contains the following elements:

1. *Customer service.* What level of customer service the distribution activities should support.
2. *Transportation.* How the firm should ship its products.
3. *Inventory control.* How much inventory the firm should maintain at each location.
4. *Protective packaging and materials handling.* How the firm can efficiently handle goods in the factory, warehouse, and transport terminals.
5. *Order processing.* How the firm should handle orders.
6. *Warehousing.* Where the distribution system will locate stocks of goods. The number of warehouses the firm should maintain.

All of these components function in interrelated ways. Decisions made in one area affect relative efficiency in others. The physical distribution manager must balance each component so that the system avoids stressing any single aspect to the detriment of overall functioning. For example, a firm might decide to reduce transportation costs by shipping its products by inexpensive—but slow—water transportation. However, slow deliveries would likely force the firm to maintain high inventory levels and to raise inventory holding costs, such as warehousing expenses. This mismatch between system elements often leads to increased production costs.

The Problem of Suboptimization

6

Outline the suboptimization problem in logistics.

Logistics managers seek to establish a specified level of customer service while minimizing the costs of physically moving and storing goods from their production point to their ultimate purchasers. Marketers must first agree on their customer service priorities and then seek to minimize the total costs of moving goods to buyers—all while meeting customer service goals. To meet customer service levels at minimum costs, marketers must mesh all physical distribution elements together rather than setting up independent arrangements. Marketers do not always achieve this goal, however.

Suboptimization results when the managers of individual physical distribution functions attempt to minimize costs, but the impact of one task on the others leads to less than optimal results. A frequently used analogy describes a football team composed of many talented players who hold individual records in different aspects of the game. Unfortunately, though, these personal accomplishments fail to result in a winning team if the players do not cooperate and score more points than their opponents.

Suboptimization may cause problems in physical distribution when marketers judge each logistics activity by its ability to achieve its own objectives, some of which may work at cross-purposes with other goals. Suboptimization becomes particularly likely when a firm introduces a new product that may not fit easily into its current physical distribution system. Businesspeople often focus on certain adjustments to their systems without anticipating related problems that eventually arise.

Effective management of the physical distribution function requires some cost trade-offs. By accepting relatively high costs in some functional areas in order to cut costs in others, managers can minimize their firm's total physical distribution costs. Of course, any reduction in logistical costs should support progress toward the goal of maintaining customer service standards.

Customer-driven production. General Motors has begun to experiment with a streamlined assembly line that will allow customers to place an online order and receive delivery of a tailor-made car within 10 days. Visit the two Web sites listed below and read about this new initiative. What are some of the benefits of customer-driven production for GM? Specifically, how will customer-driven production improve GM's distribution strategy?

http://www.salon.com/tech/view/1999/11/08/hogan/

http://gmbuypower.com

Customer Service Standards

Customer service standards state goals and define acceptable performance for the quality of service that a firm expects to deliver to its customers. For example, one firm might set a customer service standard that calls for the shipment of 95 percent of all orders within 48 hours after the receipt of the orders and the shipment of all orders within 72 hours. Many e-tailers survive through their ability to ship within hours of receiving an order.

Designers of a physical distribution system begin by establishing acceptable levels of customer service. These designers then assemble physical distribution components in a way that will achieve this standard at the lowest possible total cost. As shown in Figure 15.9, this overall cost breaks down into five components: (1) transportation, (2) warehousing, (3) customer service/order processing, (4) administrative costs, and (5) inventory control.

Transportation *Exam*

As noted in Table 3.1 in Chapter 3, the transportation industry has been largely deregulated. Deregulation has been particularly important for motor carriers, railroads, and air carriers. Many transporters are now free to develop unique solutions to shippers' needs. Before deregulation, no truck carrier served all 48 contiguous U.S. states. Today, more than 4,000 carriers have that authority. In addition, the trucking industry now operates far more efficiently than it did under government regulation; many carriers have reduced empty mileage by two-thirds.

Typically adding 10 percent to the cost of a product, transportation and delivery expenses represent the largest category of logistics-related costs for most firms.[18] Also, for many items—particularly perishable ones such as fresh fish—transportation makes a central contribution to satisfactory customer service.

Many logistics managers have found that the key to controlling their shipping costs is careful management of relationships with shipping firms. Freight carriers set two basic rates: class and commodity rates. A *class rate* is a standard rate for a specific commodity moving between any pair of destinations. A carrier may charge a lower *commodity rate,* sometimes called a *special rate,* to a

Briefly
Speaking

Timely service, like timely gifts, is doubled in value.

George MacDonald (1824–1905) Scottish novelist, poet, and clergyman

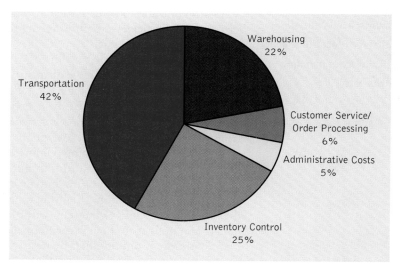

SOURCE: These 2003 estimates were provided by Dr. Julie Gentry, Logistics Faculty, University of Arkansas–Fayetteville.

FIGURE 15.9
Allocation of Physical Distribution Expenditures

favored shipper as a reward for either regular business or a large-quantity shipment. Railroads and inland water carriers frequently reward customers in this way.

In addition, the railroad and motor carrier industries sometimes supplement this rate structure with negotiated, or contract, rates. In other words, the two parties finalize terms of rates, services, and other variables in a contract.

Classes of Carriers

Freight carriers are classified as common, contract, and private carriers. Common carriers, often considered the backbone of the transportation industry, provide transportation services as for-hire carriers to the general public. The government still regulates their rates and services, and they cannot conduct their operations without permission from the appropriate regulatory authority. Common carriers move freight via all modes of transport.

Contract carriers are for-hire transporters that do not offer their services to the general public. Instead, they establish contracts with individual customers and operate exclusively for particular industries, most commonly the motor freight industry. These carriers operate under much looser regulations than common carriers.

Private carriers do not offer services for hire. These carriers provide transportation services solely for internally generated freight. As a result, they observe no rate or service regulations. The Interstate Commerce Commission (ICC), a federal regulatory agency, permits private carriers to operate as common or contract carriers as well. Many private carriers have taken advantage of this rule by operating their trucks fully loaded at all times.

Major Transportation Modes

7

Compare the major transportation alternatives on the basis of speed, dependability, cost, frequency of shipments, availability in different locations, and flexibility in handling products.

Logistics managers choose among five major transportation alternatives: railroads, motor carriers, water carriers, pipelines, and air freight. Each mode has its own unique characteristics. Logistics managers select the best options for their situations by matching the situation features to their specific transportation needs.

Railroads—The Nation's Leading Transporter

Railroads continue to control the largest share of the freight business as measured by ton-miles. The term *ton-mile* indicates shipping activity required to move 1 ton of freight 1 mile. Thus, a 3-ton shipment moving 8 miles equals 24 ton-miles. Rail shipments quickly rack up ton-miles because this mode provides the most efficient way for moving bulky commodities over long distances. For instance, rail carriers generally transport huge quantities of coal, chemicals, grain, nonmetallic minerals, lumber and wood products, and automobiles.

The railroads have improved their service standards through a number of innovative concepts, such as unit trains, run-through trains, *intermodal* (piggyback) operations, and double-stack container trains. Unit trains carry much of the coal, grain, and other high-volume commodities shipped, running back and forth between single loading points (such as a mine) and single destinations (such as a power plant) to deliver a single commodity. Run-through trains bypass intermediate terminals to speed up schedules. They work similar to unit trains, but a run-through train may carry a variety of commodities.

In piggyback operations, highway trailers and containers ride on railroad flatcars, thus combining the long haul capacity of the train with the door-to-door flexibility of the truck. A double-stack container train pulls special rail cars equipped with bathtub-shaped wells so they can carry two containers stacked on top of one another. By nearly doubling train capacity and slashing costs, this system offers enormous advantages to rail customers.

A recent alliance between GE Capital Rail Services and logistics software company IntelliTrans introduces tracking and tracing capabilities to rail operations. Through easy Web access, manufacturers can get instant information about commodities contained in rail cars en route and integrate the data into their management systems. The system allows for improved production planning, inventory control, and supply forecasting.[19]

Motor Carriers—Flexible and Growing

About 80 percent of all goods in the U.S. ride on trucks at some point. The trucking industry has grown dramatically over recent decades and is expected to grow by 25 percent in the next 10 years to keep up with demand.[20] Trucking offers some important advantages over the other transportation modes, including relatively fast shipments and consistent service for both large and small shipments. Motor carriers concentrate on shipping manufactured products, while railroads typically haul bulk shipments of raw materials. Motor carriers, therefore, receive greater revenue per ton shipped, since the cost for shipping raw materials is higher than for shipping manufactured products.

Technology has also improved the efficiency of trucking. Many trucking firms now track their fleets via satellite communications systems, and in-truck computer systems allow drivers and dispatchers to make last-minute changes in scheduling and delivery. The Internet is also adding new features to motor carrier services.

Some private fleets function as rolling assembly plants that pick up semifinished products from manufacturers, assemble them en route, and deliver the finished goods to customers, increasing overall service and customer satisfaction. Arizona-based distributor Pinacor, for example, partners with New Jersey–based Lucent Technologies to perform final testing and configuration of Lucent's telecommunications systems. Pinacor's ability to assume these final manufacturing steps reduces product lead time dramatically, from an average of 30 to 45 days to about 10 days. Other distribution companies, like Gates/Arrow, have broadened their roles to offer ordering, shipping, and tracking solutions for companies such as Hewlett-Packard and Intel Corp.[21]

Water Carriers—Slow but Inexpensive

Two basic types of transport methods move products over water: inland or barge lines and oceangoing, deep-water ships. Barge lines efficiently transport bulky, low unit value commodities such as grain, gravel, lumber, sand, and steel. A typical lower Mississippi River barge line may stretch more than a quarter-mile across.

Oceangoing container ships, such as the Carsten Maersk Sealand ship shown here, are behemoths. Rows of containers are piled 17 across and 14 deep—so many that if they were placed end to end they would reach 27 miles. Why so large? Their size helps cut shipping costs for customers.

Oceangoing ships carry a growing stream of containerized freight between ports around the world. Large ships also operate on the Great Lakes. New supertankers from global companies like Maersk Sealand are the size of three football fields, almost doubling the capacity of other vessels. At full capacity, the ships can cut the cost of shipping a container across the Pacific by a fifth.[22] Shippers that transport goods via water carriers incur very low costs compared with the rates for other transportation modes. Standardized modular shipping containers maximize savings by limiting loading, unloading, and other handling.

Pipelines—Specialized Transporters

Although the pipeline industry ranks third after railroads and motor carriers in ton-miles transported, many people scarcely recognize its existence. More than 214,000 miles of pipelines crisscross the U.S. in an extremely efficient network for transporting natural gas and oil products. Oil pipelines carry two types of commodities: crude (unprocessed) oil and refined products, such as gasoline, jet fuel, and kerosene. In addition, one so-called slurry pipeline carries coal in suspension after it has been ground up into a powder and mixed with water. The Black Mesa Pipeline, owned by Union Pacific, moves the coal 290 miles from northern Arizona into southern Nevada.

Although pipelines offer low maintenance and dependable methods of transportation, a number of characteristics limit their applications. They have fewer locations than water carriers, and they can accommodate shipments of only a small number of products. Finally, pipelines represent a relatively slow method of transportation; liquids travel through this method at an average speed of only 3 to 4 miles per hour.

Air Freight—Fast but Expensive

International water carriers still transport many low value products or heavy mass-market goods such as automobiles, but more and more international shipments travel by air. The significant growth in shipping volume handled by air carriers will probably continue as freight carriers seek to satisfy increased customer demand for fast delivery. Although 80 percent of the world's overnight air deliveries take place in the U.S., international demand for overnight air-freight service is soaring by 18 percent every year. Already more than 1.3 million 24-hour deliveries are made daily outside the U.S.[23]

The photo in Figure 15.10 was taken during the ceremony celebrating UPS's inaugural flight into China, the most recent member of the World Trade Organization. The company now offers express carrier service six days a week to mainland China.

Table 15.2 compares the five transportation modes on several operating characteristics. Although all shippers judge reliability, speed, and cost in choosing the most appropriate transportation methods, they assign varying importance to specific criteria when shipping different goods. For example, while motor carriers rank highest in availability in different locations, shippers of petroleum products frequently choose the lowest ranked alternative, pipelines, for their low cost. Examples of the types of goods most often handled by the various transport modes include the following:

■ *Railroads.* Lumber, iron and steel, coal, automobiles, grain, chemicals

■ *Motor carriers.* Clothing, furniture and fixtures, lumber and plastic products, food products, leather and leather products, machinery

FIGURE 15.10
UPS: Air Freight—Fast but Expensive

TABLE 15.2 **Comparison of Transport Modes**

MODE	SPEED	DEPENDABILITY IN MEETING SCHEDULES	FREQUENCY OF SHIPMENTS	AVAILABILITY IN DIFFERENT LOCATIONS	FLEXIBILITY IN HANDLING	COST
Rail	Average	Average	Low	Low	High	Average
Water	Very slow	Average	Very low	Limited	Very high	Very low
Truck	Fast	High	High	Very extensive	Average	High
Pipeline	Slow	High	High	Very limited	Very low	Low
Air	Very fast	High	Average	Average	Low	Very high

- *Water carriers.* Fuel, oil, coal, chemicals, minerals, petroleum products

- *Pipelines.* Oil, diesel fuel, jet fuel, kerosene, natural gas

- *Air carriers.* Flowers, technical instruments and machinery, high-priced specialty products, direct-to-consumer e-commerce goods

Freight Forwarders and Supplemental Carriers

Freight forwarders act as transportation intermediaries, consolidating shipments to gain lower rates for their customers. The transport rates on less-than-truckload (LTL) and less-than-carload (LCL) shipments often double the per-unit rates on truckload (TL) and carload (CL) shipments. Freight forwarders charge less than the highest rates but more than the lowest rates. They profit by consolidating shipments from multiple customers until they can ship at TL and CL rates. The customers gain two advantages from these services: lower costs on small shipments and faster delivery service than they could achieve with their own LTL and LCL shipments.

In addition to the transportation options reviewed so far, a logistics manager can also ship products via a number of auxiliary, or supplemental, carriers that specialize in small shipments. These carriers include bus freight services, United Parcel Service, FedEx, DHL International, and the U.S. Postal Service.

8

Discuss how transportation intermediaries and combined transportation modes can improve physical distribution.

Intermodal Coordination

Transportation companies emphasize specific modes and, as a result, serve certain kinds of customers, but they sometimes combine their services to give shippers the service and cost advantages of each. Piggyback service, mentioned in the section on rail transport, is the most widely used form of intermodal coordination. *Birdyback service,* another form of intermodal coordination, sends motor carriers to pick up a shipment locally and deliver that shipment to local destinations, while an air carrier takes it between airports near those locations. *Fishyback service* sets up a similar intermodal coordination system between motor carriers and water carriers.

Intermodal transportation generally gives shippers faster service and lower rates than either mode could match individually because each method carries freight in its most efficient way. However, intermodal arrangements require close coordination between all transportation providers.

Recognizing this need, multimodal transportation companies have formed to offer combined activities within single operations. Piggyback service generally joins two separate companies—a railroad and a trucking company. A multimodal firm provides intermodal service through its own internal transportation resources. Shippers benefit because the single service assumes responsibility from origin to destination. This unification prevents arguments over which carrier delayed or damaged a shipment.

Multimodal transportation options allowed DaimlerChrysler to avert a parts crisis following the terrorist attacks of September 11, which suspended air freight and brought mass disruptions to road transportation. Like other carmakers, the company relied on just-in-time supply of auto parts—an inventory control system that works only if trucks, trains, boats, and planes carrying assembly-line parts all run precisely on schedule. Following the attacks, DaimlerChrysler went into crisis mode, airlifting supplies from production points to assembly plants. When U.S. airspace closed, the company turned to two-person teams of truckdrivers for nonstop highway driving. The company persuaded U.S. customs to keep trucking open between Detroit and Windsor, Ontario, with more inspectors to ease congestion. Canadian Pacific Railroad Co. set up shuttle service to transport goods through road-traffic logjams.[24] The U.S. military has turned to the private sector for advice on transportation, warehousing, and other logistical issues (see the "Marketing Hit" box).

Warehousing

Products flow through two types of warehouses: storage and distribution warehouses. A storage warehouse holds goods for moderate to long periods in an attempt to balance supply and demand for producers and purchasers. For example, controlled atmosphere—also called *cold storage*—warehouses in Yakima and Wenatchee, Washington, serve nearby apple orchards. By contrast, a distribution warehouse assembles and redistributes goods, keeping them moving as much as possible. Many distribution warehouses or centers physically store goods for less than 24 hours before shipping them on to customers.

Logistics managers have attempted to save on transportation costs by developing central distribution centers. A manufacturer located in Philadelphia, for example, could send direct shipments to customers in the Illinois-Wisconsin-Indiana area, but if each customer placed small orders, the shipper would pay high transportation charges. Instead, it might send a single, large, consolidated shipment to a break-bulk center—a central distribution center that breaks down large shipments into several smaller ones and delivers them to individual customers in the area. Many Internet retailers use break-bulk distribution centers. UPS Logistics manages the entire fulfillment process for several companies, receiving and stocking inventory, picking, packing, and then shipping to customers. For Nike.com, UPS Logistics handles far more than shipping. Its employees provide customer service at Nike's 800 number, and the company maintains an inventory of shoes and clothing in its warehouses and exchanges or extends credit for returned goods.[25]

Automated Warehouse Technology

Logistics managers can cut distribution costs and improve customer service dramatically by automating their warehouse systems. Although automation technology represents an expensive investment, it can provide major labor savings for high-volume distributors such as grocery chains. A computerized system might store orders, choose the correct number of cases, and move those cases in the desired sequence to loading docks. This kind of warehouse system reduces labor costs, worker injuries, pilferage, fires, and breakage.

Mother's Work, a $366 million maternity-apparel company, uses a sophisticated warehouse-automation system to sort, pick, pack, label, ship, and replenish inventory of up to 140,000 items each day. Its assembly-line sorting process allows pickers to select from more than 12,000 products in a range of sizes, colors, and styles. The software checks and double-checks all orders before they are routed onto trucks and out to stores. Computer-generated inventories, integrated with retail point-of-sale terminals, allow for easy identification of fast- or slow-moving items at each outlet.[26]

Warehouse Locations

Every company must make a major logistics decision when it determines the number and locations of its storage facilities. Two categories of costs influence this choice: (1) warehousing and materials handling costs and (2) delivery costs from warehouses to customers. Large facilities offer economies of scale in facilities and materials handling systems; per-unit costs for these systems decrease as volume increases. Delivery costs, on the other hand, rise as the distance from warehouse to customer increases.

Marketing Hit

The U.S. Military Turns to Private-Sector Logistics

Background. Moving an army of a hundred thousand or more men and women, supplies, and equipment from one place to another is a logistical nightmare. Yet that is what the U.S. military does each time it engages in a major operation. Recently, the military turned to the business world for tips on how to accomplish this more efficiently.

The Challenge. Maneuvering people and equipment into position for the start of the war with Iraq was a huge challenge for the U.S. military. But military officials had learned some hard lessons from the fragmented way supplies were distributed during the Vietnam and 1991 Gulf wars.

continued on next page

Warehouse location also affects customer service. Businesses must place their storage and distribution facilities in locations from which they can meet customer demands for product availability and delivery times. They must also consider population and employment trends. For example, the rapid growth of metropolitan areas in the southern and western U.S. has caused some firms to open more distribution centers to these areas.

Inventory Control Systems

Inventory control captures a large share of a logistics manager's attention because companies need to maintain enough inventory to meet customer demand without incurring unneeded costs for carrying excess inventory. Some firms attempt to keep inventory levels under control by implementing just-in-time (JIT) production, discussed in Chapter 10.

Companies like Costco have shifted responsibility—and costs—for inventory control from retailers back to individual manufacturers. Costco gives Kimberly-Clark access to individual store sales data. Kimberly-Clark uses the information to track inventory levels of its diapers and other products and replenish stocks as needed. Vendor-managed inventory (VMI) systems like this are based on the assumption that suppliers are in the best position to spot understocks or surpluses, cutting costs along the supply chain that can be translated into lower prices at the checkout.[27]

Order Processing

Like inventory control, order processing directly affects the firm's ability to meet its customer service standards. A company may have to compensate for inefficiencies in its order processing system by shipping products via costly transportation modes or by maintaining large inventories at many expensive field warehouses.

Order processing typically consists of four major activities: (1) conducting a credit check; (2) keeping a record of the sale, which involves recordkeeping tasks such as crediting a sales representative's commission account; (3) making appropriate accounting entries; and (4) locating orders, shipping them, and adjusting inventory records. A *stockout* occurs when an order for an item is not available for shipment. A firm's order processing system must advise affected customers of a stockout and offer a choice of alternative actions.

As in other areas of physical distribution, technological innovations improve efficiency in order processing. Many firms are streamlining their order processing procedures by using e-mail and the Internet. Outdoor gear retailer REI, for example, pushes customers toward Web ordering, its least costly fulfillment channel, in its catalogs, store receipts, signs, mailers, and membership letters.[28]

Protective Packaging and Materials Handling

Logistics managers arrange and control activities for moving products within plants, warehouses, and transportation terminals, which together compose the *materials handling* system. Two important concepts influence many materials handling choices: unitizing and containerization.

Unitizing combines as many packages as possible into each load that moves within or outside a facility. Logistics managers prefer to handle materials on pallets (platforms, generally made of wood, on which goods are transported). Unitizing systems often lash materials in place with steel bands

Marketing Hit

The Strategy. Before the war with Iraq began, the military invested in information technology and cargo planes and studied the way companies such as FedEx manage their logistics. It consolidated the transportation divisions for all the military branches into one, called the U.S. Transportation Command, or Transcom. Officials at Transcom studied the distribution methods of Anheuser-Busch. "Given the complexity of Anheuser-Busch's product mix and regional shipping needs, it's a better fit for Transcom to study than Boeing," explained one expert. In addition, they reviewed the way General Motors and Caterpillar had reduced their warehousing needs by adopting just-in-time delivery of necessary equipment parts. Transcom then adopted a radio-frequency identification-tag (RFID) system—similar to the one used by shippers FedEx and CSX— and hired Bank of America to streamline its bill-paying and other financial systems.

The Outcome. By looking to the private sector for innovation, the U.S. military saved a lot of time and billions of dollars during the war with Iraq. The RFID system alone saved at least $3 million. Transcom streamlined its activities further with another business-world practice—teleconferencing. Managers all over the world now sit at their computers equipped with microphones each morning for a brief update. "Better productivity can make us better, not just more cost-efficient," says Transcom's commanding officer, Air Force Gen. John Handy.

SOURCE: "U.S. Marine Corps: Modernizing Military Logistics," Sapient Web site, **http://www.sapient.com**, accessed January 15, 2004; David Kiley, "Military Uses Private Sector Supply Tactics," *USA Today*, April 18, 2003, p. B5; Faith Keenan, "The Marines Learn New Tactics—from Wal-Mart," *BusinessWeek*, December 25, 2001, p. 74.

Strategic Implications of Marketing in the 21st Century

Several factors, not the least of which is today's burgeoning e-commerce environment, are driving changes in channel development, logistics, and supply chain management. As the Internet continues to revolutionize the ways in which manufacturers deliver goods to ultimate consumers, marketers must find ways to promote cooperation between existing dealer, retailer, and distributor networks while harnessing the power of the Web as an alternative channel. This system demands not only delivery of goods and services faster and more efficiently than ever before but also superior service to Web-based customers. Companies like Liveperson.com, featured in Figure 15.11, can provide personalized customer service to e-commerce operations.

In addition, increased product proliferation—grocery stores typically stock almost 50,000 different items—demands logistics systems that can manage multiple brands delivered through multiple channels. And those channels must be finely tuned to identify and rapidly rectify problems such as retail shortfalls or costly overstocks. The trend toward leaner retailing, in which the burden of product tracking and inventory control is switching from retailers to manufacturers, means that to be effective, logistics and supply chain systems must result in cost savings.[29]

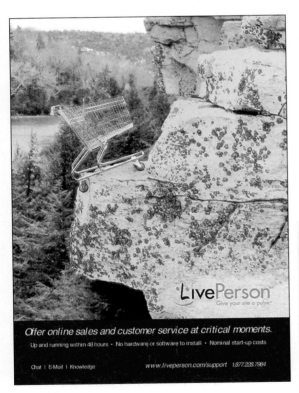

FIGURE 15.11
Providing Critical Customer Service for Online Sales

or shrink packaging. A shrink package surrounds a batch of materials with a sheet of plastic that shrinks after heating, securely holding individual pieces together. Unitizing promotes efficient materials handling because each package requires minimal labor to move. Securing the materials together also minimizes damage and pilferage.

Logistics managers extend the same concept through *containerization*—combining several unitized loads. A container of oil rig parts, for example, can be loaded in Tulsa and trucked to Kansas City, where rail facilities place the shipment on a high-speed, run-through train to New York City. There, the parts are loaded on a ship headed to Saudi Arabia.

In addition to the benefits outlined for unitizing, containerization also markedly reduces the time required to load and unload ships. Containers limit in-transit damage to freight because individual packages pass through few handling systems en route to purchasers.

Summary of Chapter Objectives

1. Describe the roles that marketing channels and logistics play in marketing strategy.

Marketing channels and logistics bridge the gap between producer or manufacturer and consumer. Effective distribution systems make goods and services available when and where the consumer wants to purchase.

2. Describe the various types of distribution channels available to marketers.

Distribution channels refer to the various marketing institutions and the interrelationships responsible for the physical and title flow of goods and services from producer to consumer or business user. Wholesalers and retailers are the marketing intermediaries in the distribution channel.

3. Outline the major channel strategy decisions.

Basic channel strategy decisions involve channel selection, level of distribution intensity, and use of vertical marketing systems. The selection of a distribution channel is based on market, product, producer, and competitive factors. The decision on distribution intensity involves choosing from among intensive distribution, selective distribution, and exclusive distribution.

4. Describe the concepts of channel management, conflict, and cooperation within the marketing channel.

Channel management focuses on developing and maintaining relationships with the intermediaries in their marketing channels. Increasingly, marketers are managing channels in partnership with other channel members. The marketing intermediary that makes the major decisions concerning the operation of a particular channel is called the *channel captain*. In some channels, the manufacturer or service provider is the channel captain. In others, powerful retailers, such as nationwide chains, may fill this role. In still others, wholesalers serve as channel captains. Channel conflict is a problem in distribution channels. There are two types of conflict: horizontal (occurring among channel members at the same level) and vertical (occurring among channel members at different levels). Marketers should work toward cooperation among all channel members to remedy channel conflict.

5. Identify and compare the major components of a physical distribution system.

Physical distribution involves a broad range of activities concerned with efficient movement of finished goods from the end of the production line to the consumer. As a system, physical distribution consists of six elements: (1) customer service,

(2) transportation, (3) inventory control, (4) protective packaging and materials handling, (5) order processing, and (6) warehousing. These elements are interrelated and must be balanced to create a smoothly functioning distribution system and to avoid suboptimization.

6. Outline the suboptimization problem in logistics.

Suboptimization refers to a situation in which each manager of a physical distribution activity attempts to minimize his or her costs, resulting in a negative impact on other physical distribution activities. The objective of the physical distribution function is to focus on total distribution costs to minimize the degree of suboptimization.

7. Compare the major transportation alternatives on the basis of speed, dependability, cost, frequency of shipments, availability of different locations, and flexibility in handling products.

Railroads rank high on flexibility in handling products and availability in different locations; average on speed, dependability in meeting schedules, and cost; and low on frequency of shipments. Motor carriers are relatively high in cost but rank high on speed, dependability, shipment frequency, and availability in different locations. Water carriers balance their slow speed, low shipment frequency, and limited availability with very low costs. The special nature of pipelines makes them rank relatively low on availability, flexibility, and speed, but they are also low in cost. Air transportation is high in cost but offers very fast and dependable delivery schedules.

8. Discuss how transportation intermediaries and combined transportation modes can improve physical distribution.

Transportation intermediaries facilitate transportation in a variety of ways, including piggyback, birdyback, and fishyback services—all forms of intermodal coordination. Methods such as unitization and containerization facilitate intermodal transfers.

Marketing Terms You Need to Know

marketing, or distribution,
   channel 434
logistics 434
direct channel 437
dual distribution 439

intensive distribution 442
selective distribution 442
exclusive distribution 442
channel captain 444

vertical marketing system
   (VMS) 447
corporate marketing
   system 447

administered marketing
   system 448
contractual marketing
   system 448

Other Important Marketing Terms

marketing intermediary
   (middleman) 436
wholesaler 437
direct selling 437
reverse channel 439

distribution intensity 441
exclusive dealing
   agreement 443
closed sales territory 443
tying agreement 443

grey good 447
enterprise resource planning
   (ERP) system 451
third-party (contract) logistics
   firm 451

suboptimization 452
customer service standard 453
intermodal service 454
materials handling 459
containerization 460

Review Questions

1. Outline the major categories of marketing channels. For each type of channel, cite an example of a firm that uses that channel.
2. Discuss the basic reasons for the increased attention to logistics management. How has this focus been influenced by the emergence of a global marketplace?
3. How do marketing channels create utility? What specific functions do marketing channels perform?
4. Outline the major categories of channel decisions. How might the grey market affect a firm's channel decision?
5. Who should perform the various marketing channel functions? How have these arrangements changed over time?
6. Explain the concept of power in the marketing channel. Under what conditions do producers, wholesalers, and retailers act as channel captains?
7. Outline the basic strengths and weaknesses of each transportation mode. What types of shipments suit the strengths of each mode?
8. Identify the major forms of intermodal coordination, and give an example of a good for which each offers special advantages. Why have piggyback railcars become so popular?
9. What considerations should influence the location decision for a new distribution warehouse? What cost trade-offs must a company consider in its location decision?
10. Explain the advantages and potential problems of the just-in-time system of inventory control. Relate your answer to the need to control inventory carrying costs.

Projects and Teamwork Exercises

1. Imagine a vending machine that would charge more for soft drinks during hot weather. The Coca-Cola Company has tested such a device. What is your opinion of a temperature-sensitive vending machine? How do you think customers would react? Is this a logical distribution strategy for The Coca-Cola Company to pursue? Discuss in teams.
2. In small teams, outline the marketing channel used by a firm in your area. Why did the company select this particular channel?
3. How might e-commerce lead to channel conflict? What type of channel conflict could result from e-commerce? Suggest a resolution to this conflict. Divide the class into two teams and discuss channel conflict from the perspectives of the different channel members.
4. One recent Halloween, children were disappointed because Hershey was unable to stock retailer's shelves with supplies of chocolate candy. In small groups, research this distribution and logistics failure. What went wrong? What lessons does this offer for future distribution strategies?
5. Suggest the most appropriate method for transporting the products listed here. Defend your choices.
   a. iron ore
   b. oil field equipment
   c. crude oil
   d. cherries
   e. lumber

'net Work

http://www.dell.com/us/en/ gen/corporate/ factpack_000.htm

1. Distribution channels. The world's largest maker of personal computers is Dell, a start-up launched in 1984 by former University of Texas student Michael Dell. The company uses a direct approach to the distribution of its products to consumer and business purchasers. Visit the Web site listed and prepare a report on the distribution approach used by Dell and how it differs from the approach used by other PC manufacturers, such as Hewlett-Packard. Be sure to consider the advantages and disadvantages of the direct approach to distribution in your report.

http://www.bts.gov/ntda/ cfs

2. Transportation modes. As noted in the chapter, two of the major transportation modes are railroads and trucks. The *Commodity Flow Survey* is a regular publication of the Bureau of Transportation Statistics and the U.S. Census Bureau. It provides detailed information on the transportation of goods. Go to the Web site listed and access the most recent *Commodity Flow Survey* you can find. Answer the following questions:
   a. Did railroads or trucks grow the fastest over the most recent 12-month period?
   b. What types of goods are most commonly transported by truck? By rail?
   c. What is the average distance of goods shipped by truck? By rail?
   d. What is the average cost per mile for goods shipped by truck? By rail?

http://www.accenture.com

3. Inventory control systems. Visit the Web site of business consulting firm Accenture. Click on "Case Studies" and review several of the inventory controls systems Accenture has designed for clients. What do all of these systems have in common? Prepare a list and take it to class to contribute to a discussion on inventory control systems.

Note: Internet Web addresses change frequently. If you don't find the exact sites listed, you may need to access the organization or company's home page and search from there.

CASE 15.1   Dell Direct? Well, Not Always

From selling PCs out of a college dorm in Texas, entrepreneur-extraordinaire Michael Dell developed a dynamic, immensely profitable business model by marketing computers directly to businesses via phone and the Internet. Selling directly not only eliminated the costs of operating in the retail environment but allowed Dell to create unique relationships with customers. By offering PCs configured to match each customer's precise needs, Dell achieved unparalleled success in delivering products attuned to demand. Through just-in-time manufacturing and tight control over supplier networks, Dell carried practically no inventory—and was able to pass huge savings along to customers. No slave to channels, Dell gave customers exactly what they wanted—not the plain-vanilla packaged PCs they could buy at retail.

Dell's radical business model allowed the company to stay profitable during a depressed high-tech market that wore down its major rivals. Dell even managed to wage a price war, cutting PC prices to the bone, and it still came out on top.

Recently, branching out for the first time from its direct-selling roots, Dell has tiptoed into the retail sector. At shopping malls in Franklin, Tennessee, and Frisco, Texas, the company is testing Dell Direct retail kiosks, offering PCs, hand-held computers, and digital cameras. The experiments are part of a push into the home-PC market that currently represents only 15 percent of Dell's annual revenues. Moreover, with Michael Dell as pitchman, the company is advertising on cable shopping network QVC, promoting a $599 ready-made computer package.

It remains to be seen whether Dell's mass-market efforts will produce the volume of sales it takes to cover costs. At present, the company claims it has no plans to compete on its rival's turf by opening company-owned stores or entering mainstream retail channels.

Meanwhile, in Europe, where small businesses tend to purchase computers in stores, recent retail sales increased while the overall PC market contracted. In Japan, where corporate computer sales are slow, Dell is losing ground. As the only major PC maker without a retail presence, the company lacks access to home-PC channels.

Questions for Critical Thinking

1. Can Dell succeed in the home-PC market with no retail outlets?
2. Dell is known to have its finger on the pulse of consumer needs. Could sales of Dell PCs through retail outlets negatively impact the company's relationship with customers?

SOURCES: John G. Spooner, "Toshiba Sprints Past Dell in Notebooks," *ZDNet*, June 3, 2002, http://www.techupdate.com/techupdate/filters/main/; "PC Sales in Europe Take a Beating," *CNET News*, February 12, 2002, http://www.news.com .com; Gary McWilliams, "Dell Tries Selling in Kiosks, on TV as PC Sales Drop," *The Wall Street Journal*, December 20, 2001, pp. B1–B2.

VIDEO CASE 15.2   Ipswich Shellfish Delivers Fresh Lobster

The written case on Ipswich Shellfish appears on page VC-18. The recently filmed Ipswich Shellfish video is designed to expand and highlight the concepts in this chapter and the concepts and questions covered in the written video case.

16

Direct Marketing and Marketing Resellers: Retailers and Wholesalers

Chapter Objectives

1 Explain the wheel of retailing.

2 Explain how retailers select target markets.

3 Show how the elements of the marketing mix apply to retailing strategy.

4 Explain the concepts of retail convergence and scrambled merchandising.

5 Identify the functions performed by wholesaling intermediaries.

6 Identify the major types of independent wholesaling intermediaries and the situations appropriate for each.

7 Compare the basic types of direct marketing and nonstore retailing.

8 Explain ways in which the Internet has altered the wholesaling, retailing, and direct marketing environments.

Lowe's Knows Women

A couple of generations ago, men populated hardware and home-improvement stores. You'd rarely see a woman in one of these stores unless she was shopping for her husband with a very specific list. All that has changed. Now women are far more involved in do-it-yourself home projects than they were; in fact, they outnumber men when it comes to swinging the proverbial hammer. According to marketing research, women currently initiate 80 percent of all home-improvement projects, especially the big ones like remodeling a kitchen or adding a bathroom. This means women need a place to shop for everything from kitchen cabinets to whirlpool tubs. They also want a selection of premium brands. For projects they plan to undertake themselves—and there are plenty—they need a store in which to buy tools and supplies, as well as guidance on how to select and use them. While retail giant Home Depot has made its fortune catering to remodeling professionals and men, Lowe's—based in Northboro, NC—has found its own target market: women. "We [focus] on a customer nobody in home improvement has focused on," explains Lowe's CEO Robert Tillman. "Don't get me wrong, but women are far more discriminating than men."

To attract more female customers, Lowe's marketers have used a number of strategies. First, they've made Lowe's a comfortable place to browse. The stores are bright and open, with wide aisles and supermarket signs listing what's on each aisle. Those big pallets stacked with merchandise are gone—they obstruct the view of the aisle and make the store feel cluttered and crowded, which women don't like. Lowe's now stocks more appliances like refrigerators and stoves. Home décor displays let customers see and touch items such as ready-made draperies and valances that can be purchased on the spot. As holiday shoppers enter the front doors of one new Lowe's, they are

greeted by a huge display of Christmas ornaments and decorations for the winter season. Another Lowe's recently installed an in-store waterfall with gurgling fountains near bags of topsoil that were on sale. Second, Lowe's has pushed to become the seller of prestige brands such as Laura Ashley paints, Pella windows, Pergo laminate floors, Jacuzzi tubs, and Husqvarna chain saws. In addition, its sales staff is trained to offer the best product in each category. While Larry Stone, chief

of store operations, admits that they are unlikely to sell a lot of Sottini Fairhaven pedestal sinks at $1,800 each, "The point is to show that if it's made, Lowe's has it."

Lowe's also emphasizes customer service. Instead of forcing consumers to search aisle after aisle for someone to answer a question, Lowe's has installed call buttons in its aisles that shoppers can use to summon a salesperson to help. The goal is for someone to respond within 60 seconds—important to busy women who may be shopping on their lunch hour or trying to squeeze in an errand before heading home to fix dinner. Finally, the Lowe's Web site is chock full of ideas, advice, and information about products and projects. Consumers can find out when to plant bulbs in the garden, how to install indoor/outdoor carpeting, or how to repair damaged wood. They can get ideas for inexpensive makeovers such as faux marble painting or wood-graining on the bedroom wall. The site also offers tips on how to do this type of painting. Or they can go all out in the "Design Your Dream Bathroom" section. And they can browse through Lowe's online magazine, *Creative Ideas*.

Once considered to be headed to the junkyard as Home Depot's early success drove dozens of home-improvement retailers out of business, Lowe's has rebuilt itself into a serious competitor in the home-improvement retail business. Many people believe this is because the company has focused on its women customers. And who knows, maybe these loyal shoppers will bring their spouses along for the ride.[1]

Chapter Overview

In exploring how today's retailing sector operates, this chapter introduces many examples that explain the combination of activities involved in selling goods to ultimate consumers, as Lowe's does in its efforts to attract women who are interested in home improvements. Then the chapter discusses the role of wholesalers and other intermediaries who deliver goods from the manufacturers into the hands of retailers. Finally, the chapter looks at nonstore retailing. Direct marketing, a channel consisting of direct communication to consumers or business users, is a major form of nonstore retailing. It includes not just direct mail and telemarketing but direct-response advertising, infomercials, and Internet marketing. The chapter concludes by looking at a less pervasive but growing aspect of nonstore retailing, automatic merchandising.

Briefly Speaking

When I walk into a grocery store and look at all the products you can choose, I say, "My God! No king ever had anything like I have in my grocery store today."

Bill Gates (b. 1954) founder, Microsoft Corp.

Retailing

Retailers are the marketing intermediaries who are in direct contact with ultimate consumers. **Retailing** describes the activities involved in selling merchandise to ultimate consumers. Retail outlets serve as contact points between channel members and ultimate consumers. In a very real sense, retailers represent the distribution channel to most consumers since a typical shopper has little contact with manufacturers and virtually no contact with wholesaling intermediaries. Retailers determine locations, store hours, quality and quantity of salespeople, store layouts, merchandise selections, and return policies—factors that often influence the consumers' images of the offerings more strongly than consumers' images of the products themselves. Both large and small retailers perform the major channel activities: creating time, place, and ownership utilities.

Retailers act as both customers and marketers in their channels. They sell products to ultimate consumers, and at the same time they buy from wholesalers and manufacturers. Because of their critical location in their channels, retailers often perform a vital feedback role. They obtain information from customers and transmit that information to manufacturers and other channel members.

Evolution of Retailing

The development of retailing illustrates the marketing concept in operation. Retailing continues to satisfy changing consumer wants and needs.

Early retailing in the U.S. can be traced to the establishment of trading posts, such as the Hudson Bay Company, and to pack peddlers who carried their wares to outlying settlements. The first type of retail institution, the general store, stocked a wide range of merchandise that met the needs of an isolated community or rural area. Supermarkets appeared in the early 1930s in response to consumers' desire for lower prices. In the 1950s, discount stores delivered lower prices in exchange for reduced services. The emergence of convenience food stores in the 1960s satisfied consumer demand for fast service, convenient locations, and expanded hours of operation. The development of off-price retailers in the 1980s and 1990s reflected consumer demand for brand-name merchandise at prices considerably lower than those of traditional retailers. In recent years, Internet-enabled retailing has increased in influence and importance.

A key concept, known as the **wheel of retailing,** attempts to explain the patterns of change in retailing. According to the wheel of retailing, a new type of retailer gains a competitive foothold by offering customers lower prices than current outlets charge and maintains profits by reducing or eliminating services. Once established, however, the innovator adds more services, and its prices gradually rise. It then becomes vulnerable to new low-price retailers that enter with minimum services—and so the wheel turns. The retail graveyard is littered with former giants like W.T. Grant and Montgomery Ward, as well as such merchandisers as the original Sears catalog and catalog retailers such as Service Merchandise.

Many major developments in the history of retailing appear to fit the wheel's pattern. Early department stores, chain stores, supermarkets, discount stores, hypermarkets, and catalog retailers all emphasized limited service and low prices. Most of these retailers gradually increased prices as they added services.

Some exceptions disrupt this pattern, however. Suburban shopping centers, convenience food stores, and vending machines never built their appeals around low prices. However, the wheel pattern has been a good indicator enough times in the past to make it an accurate indicator of future retailing developments.

1

Explain the wheel of retailing.

Retailing Strategy

Like manufacturers and wholesalers, a retailer develops a marketing strategy based on the firm's goals and strategic plans. The organization monitors environmental influences and assesses its own strengths and weaknesses in identifying marketing opportunities and constraints. A retailer bases its key decisions on two fundamental steps in the marketing strategy process: (1) selecting a target market and (2) developing a retailing mix to satisfy the chosen market. The retailing mix specifies merchandise strategy, customer service standards, pricing guidelines, target market analysis, promotion goals, location/distribution decisions, and store atmosphere choices. The combination of these elements projects a desired *retail image*—consumers' perceptions of the store and the shopping experience it provides. Retail image communicates the store's identity to consumers as, say, an economical, a high-value, or a prestigious outlet. Crate & Barrel, for instance, featured in Figure 16.1, counts on its trendy, contemporary image to draw affluent, style-conscious consumers. All components of retailing strategy must work together to create an image that appeals to the store's target market.

Once unbeatable for snappy, casual fashions at reasonable prices, Gap Inc. has recently floundered. In an attempt to appeal to younger customers, the retailer replaced its popular basic jeans and khakis with hip, gimmicky apparel. Following a drop-off in same-store sales, Gap switched back to its old formula—but not before losing market share to rivals like Target.[2]

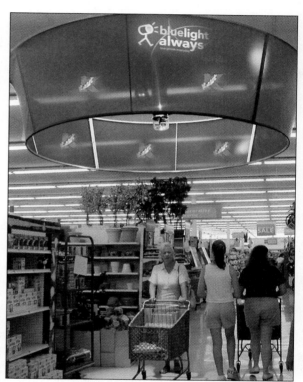

Kmart's failed attempt to match Wal-Mart's low pricing strategy head on by reviving its Blue Light Special contributed to the bankruptcy of one of the nation's largest retailers.

**FIGURE 16.1
Crate & Barrel:
Creating a
Contemporary
Retail Image**

Marketing Miss

JCPenney Wants to Be Where the Girls Are

Background. Teen and preteen girls are picky shoppers. They know what they want. And what they want today, they may sneer at tomorrow. JCPenney has been struggling to hit the right note with these fickle consumers, who represent hundreds of millions of retail dollars each year.

The Marketing Problem. Girls just want to be cool, and most of them don't think JCPenney is cool at all. They wouldn't be caught dead wearing anything with a Penney's label in it—even its supposedly hip Arizona label. Penney's image has been cultivated over decades. "Customers see us as the store from their childhood that their grandma dragged them to when the family had no money," explains CEO Allen Questrom ruefully. Not only were the clothes unstylish, the stores themselves weren't fun to shop in. Merchandise was jammed into racks with a huge sign advertising "Girls

continued on next page

Selecting a Target Market

2

Explain how retailers select target markets.

A retailer starts to define its strategy by selecting a target market. The size and profit potential of a target and the level of competition for its business influence this decision. Retailers pore over demographic, geographic, and psychographic profiles to segment markets. In the end, most retailers identify their target markets in terms of certain demographics.

The importance of identifying and targeting the right market is dramatically illustrated by the erosion of department store retailing. While mall anchor stores like Sears and JCPenney fight to hold on to customers (see the "Marketing Miss" box), stand-alone store Target, known for its chic but cheap casual clothes, has solidified its niche. The store attracts style-conscious consumers with fashionable lines under its own designer labels, like cosmetics from Kashuk, apparel from Mossimo Giannulli, and sleek kitchenware from Michael Graves. The trendy but affordable lines draw shoppers with conservative tastes away from traditional department stores.[3]

Deep-discount chains like Family Dollar Stores or Dollar General, with their so-so locations and low-price merchandise crammed into narrow aisles, target low-income shoppers. Attracted by cents-off basics like shampoo, cereal, or laundry detergent, customers typically pick up higher margin goods—toys or chocolates—on their way to the checkout.[4]

By appealing to women, hardware chain Lowe's hopes to hammer archrival Home Depot, as described in the opening vignette. Wide aisles, clean presentation, friendly service, and a broad selection of high-end merchandise, such as Laura Ashley paints, have boosted the store's popularity with female shoppers, who now account for half of all customers.[5]

After identifying a target market, a retailer must then develop marketing strategies to attract these chosen customers to its stores. The following sections discuss tactics for implementing different strategies.

Merchandising Strategy *Read*

3

Show how the elements of the marketing mix apply to retailing strategy.

A retailer's merchandising strategy guides decisions regarding the items it will offer. A retailer must decide on general merchandise categories, product lines, specific items within lines, and the depth and width of its assortment. Target stores, for example, offer customers a wide variety of merchandise, from apparel to personal care, home décor, and automotive products. But to compete as the upscale alternative to Wal-Mart, Target has rolled out a chain of combination food and general merchandise stores called SuperTarget. Bringing fashion to food, the retailer has expanded its categories. Its *planogram*—a computerized diagram of how to exhibit selections of merchandise within each store—now includes gourmet brand pastas and sauces, produce, and fresh-baked goods.[6]

Exam

To develop a successful merchandise mix, a retailer must weigh several priorities. First, it must consider the preferences and needs of its previously defined target market, keeping in mind that the competitive environment influences these choices. The retailer must also consider the overall profitability of each product line and product category.

Category Management

As mentioned in Chapter 12, a popular merchandising strategy is *category management,* in which a category manager oversees an entire product line and is responsible for the profitability of the product group. Category management seeks to improve the retailer's product category performance through more coordinated buying, merchandising, and pricing.[7] Rather than focusing on the performance of individual brands, such as Flex shampoo or Kleenex tissue, category management evaluates performance according to each product category. Laundry detergent, skin-care, and paper goods, for example, are each viewed as individual profit centers, and the category manager supervises the performance and growth of the entire group. Those that underperform are at risk, regardless of the strength of individual brands. To improve their profitability, for example, some department stores have narrowed their traditionally broad product categories to eliminate high-overhead, low-profit lines like toys, appliances, and furniture.

Ateeco Inc., a family-owned business specializing in ethnic foods such as the Polish pierogi, targets tiny categories that the giant food marketers leave unserved. To win freezer space, the company presents marketing research that proves its products are profitable. In-store demonstrations and samplings introduce pierogies—a child-friendly food as well as a mainstay of Polish cuisine—to customers. While Ateeco virtually owns the category, its success may tempt companies with deeper pockets—such as Kraft, Nestlé, or ConAgra Foods—to introduce new brands, forcing Ateeco to devise new strategies to keep its market share.[8]

The Battle for Shelf Space *Read*

As discussed in Chapter 15, large-scale retailers are increasingly taking on the role of channel captain within many distribution networks. Some have assumed traditional wholesaling functions, while others dictate product design and specifications to manufacturers. The result is a shift in power from the manufacturers of top-selling brands to the retailer who makes them available to customers.

Marketing Miss

size 7-14" above it. Who would want to shop there instead of trendy Limited Too's boutique just a few doors down the mall corridor? Penney's image was so bad that it teetered on the brink of bankruptcy just a few years ago.

The Outcome. Honest about Penney's poor image, Questrom got to work. He courted upscale, hip designers like Michele Bohbot of Bisou Bisou and got her to sign an exclusive deal. He's currently jazzing up the store décor in the girls' department and is chasing several other runway fashion designers as well. He's not trying to turn Penney's into Saks or Neiman Marcus, but he wants to offer the latest styles at the lowest prices.

Lessons Learned. Allowing its stores to fall hopelessly out of style was a dangerous slip by Penney's previous marketers and executives. But Questrom is determined to get the girls to come back—without being dragged by their mothers and grandmothers. "We're not your granny's store anymore," he insists.

SOURCES: Company Web site, http://www.jcpenney.net, accessed January 11, 2004; Cora Daniels, "JCPenney Dresses Up," *Fortune*, June 9, 2003, pp. 127-130; Debbie Howell, "JCPenney Rebounds as Turnaround Efforts Take Off," *DSN Retailing Today*, May 6, 2002, accessed at http://www.findarticles.com.

Exam.
Radio Frequency strategy

Adding to the pressure is the increase in the number of new products and variations on existing products. To identify the varying items within a product line, retailers refer to a specific product offering as a **stockkeeping unit (SKU).** Within the skin-care category, for example, each facial cream, body moisturizer, and sunscreen in each of a variety of sizes and formulations is a separate SKU. The proliferation of new SKUs has resulted in a fierce battle for space on store shelves.

Increasingly, major retailers, such as Wal-Mart, Sears, and JCPenney, make demands in return for shelf space. They may, for example, seek pricing and promotional concessions from manufacturers as conditions for selling their products. Retailers also routinely require that manufacturers participate in their electronic data interchange (EDI) and quick-response systems. Manufacturers unable to comply may find themselves unable to penetrate the marketplace.

Slotting allowances, described in Chapter 11, are just one of the range of nonrefundable fees retailers receive from manufacturers to secure shelf space for new products. A manufacturer can pay a retailer as much as $25,000 per item just to get its new products displayed on store shelves.[9] Other fees include failure fees (imposed if a new product does not meet sales projections), annual renewal fees (a "pay to stay" inducement for retailers to continue carrying brands), trade allowances, discounts on high-volume purchases, survey fees for research done by the retailers, and even fees to allow salespeople to present new items.

Customer Service Strategy

Some stores build their retailing strategy around heightened customer services for shoppers. Gift wrapping, alterations, return privileges, bridal registries, consultants, interior design services, delivery and installation, and perhaps even electronic shopping via gift-ordering machines in airports are all examples of services that add value to the shopping experience. A retailer's customer service strategy must specify which services the firm will offer and whether it will charge customers for these services. Those decisions depend on several conditions: store size, type, and location; merchandise assortment; services offered by competitors; customer expectations; and financial resources.

The basic objective of all customer services focuses on attracting and retaining target customers, thus increasing sales and profits. Some services—such as convenient rest rooms, lounges, and complimentary coffee—enhance shoppers' comfort. Other services are intended to attract customers by making shopping easier and faster than it would be without the services. Some retailers, for example, offer child-care services for customers to ease the burden of shopping. At Kroger's supermarket chain, featured in Figure 16.2, a self-scanning device allows customers to avoid the cashier's line, and the wait involved, by checking out their own groceries.

FIGURE 16.2
Self-Scanners:
Avoiding the Wait in
the Checkout Line

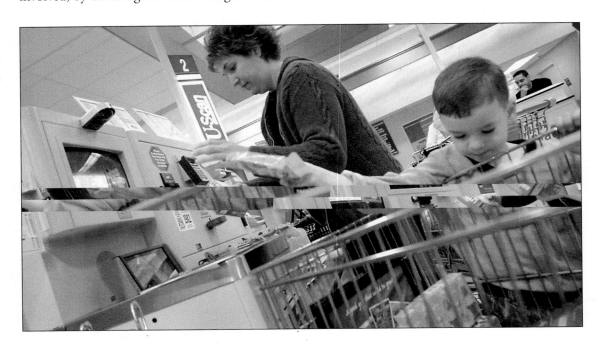

A customer service strategy can also support efforts in building demand for a line of merchandise. Debra's Natural Gourmet, a Concord, Massachusetts, healthful-food-and-lifestyle store, employs a personal touch to entice customers. The store solicits advice and referrals from 35 health practitioners and shares its findings with its customers. Through in-store workshops and a monthly newsletter with tips on everything from healthful diets to antiaging treatments, the store nurtures an ongoing relationship with its customers. It even employs a registered nurse to make sure its natural remedies will not interfere with customers' routine medications.[10]

Pricing Strategy

As we discussed in Chapters 13 and 14, prices reflect a retailer's marketing objectives and policies. They also play a major role in consumers' perceptions of a retailer. Consumers realize, for example, that when they enter a Gucci boutique in Milan, New York, or Tokyo, they will find such expensive products as $275 suede pumps and $1,500 boar-hide briefcases. Customers of the retail chain Everything's $1.00 expect a totally different line of merchandise; true to the name, every product in the store bears the same low price.

Wal-Mart, described in Chapter 13 as a major user of everyday low pricing, also employs price reductions to eliminate slow-moving items and leftover seasonal merchandise such as these shoes available during the spring selling season.

Markups and Markdowns

The amount that a retailer adds to a product's cost to set the final selling price is the **markup.** The amount of the markup typically results from two marketing decisions:

1. *The services performed by the retailer.* Other things being equal, stores that offer more services charge larger markups to cover their costs.

2. *The inventory turnover rate.* Other things being equal, stores with a higher turnover rate can cover their costs and earn a profit while charging a smaller markup.

A retailer's markup exerts an important influence on its image among present and potential customers. In addition, the markup affects the retailer's ability to attract shoppers. An excessive markup may drive away customers; an inadequate markup may not generate sufficient income to cover costs and return a profit. Retailers typically state markups as percentages of either the selling prices or the costs of the products.

Marketers determine markups based partly on their judgments of the amounts that consumers will pay for a given product. When buyers refuse to pay a product's stated price, however, or when improvements in other products or fashion changes reduce the appeal of current merchandise, a retailer must take a **markdown.** The amount by which a retailer reduces the original selling price—the discount typically advertised for a sale item—is the markdown. Markdowns are sometimes used to evaluate merchandisers. For example, a department store might base its evaluations of buyers partly on the average markdown percentages for the product lines for which they are responsible.

The formulas for calculating markups and markdowns are provided on pages B-3–B-4 in Appendix B on financial analysis in marketing.

Marketing Dictionary

stockkeeping unit (SKU) Specific offering within a product line such as a specific size of liquid detergent.

markup Amount that a retailer adds to the cost of a product to determine its selling price.

markdown Amount by which a retailer reduces the original selling price of a product.

right wrong

Solving an Ethical Controversy

Wal-Mart on the March

When national grocery chain Kroger's announced a fall-off in profits of more than a third in a single quarter, industry analysts pointed the finger at Wal-Mart. Sprawling suburban Wal-Mart Supercenters now devote a third of their hangar-like space to food and sundries, making huge inroads into traditional grocery markets. With more than 1,100 megastores, Wal-Mart has grabbed an astounding 16 percent market share—or $80 billion in food sales—to become the nation's No. 1 grocery retailer. Rivals like Safeway, Food Lion, and Albertson's have all fought back by aggressively cutting costs to match Wal-Mart's prices, but the casualties are high. For instance, Albertson's announced plans to shutter 116 stores in four major markets.

The best strategy to fend off Wal-Mart may be to offer smaller, easy-to-shop stores. But here, a more intense battle is looming. Wal-Mart has opened 33 small-format Neighborhood Markets. With easy parking, fast checkout, *and* low prices, these Markets are, as one analyst says, "the traditional food retailer's worst nightmare."

It's not just supermarkets that are out to protect their turf. For instance, in apparel, specialty stores, too, have seen financially weary customers gravitate toward the ever-hungry big-box retailers.

Should something be done to reign in Wal-Mart's retail dominance?

PRO

1. Wal-Mart is waging a price war to drive competitors out, limiting customers' choices of places to shop.
2. Wal-Mart uses its low-price strategy to lure shoppers with big deals on high-turnover items.

CON

1. Kroger and Albertson's are not mom-and-pop stores. They can fend for themselves.
2. Wal-Mart's low-price, high-volume strategies deliver value to customers. It should not be penalized for being smarter, better, and faster than competitors.

Summary

With the number of Supercenters set to double by 2005 and the early success of Neighborhood Markets, there is no end in sight to the battle for the consumer's food dollars. Wal-Mart's low prices will force grocery chains to reevaluate their supply chains, profit formulas, and merchandising mix.

SOURCES: Lorrie Grant, "Wal-Mart Bagging Success as Grocer," *USA Today*, June 6, 2002, p. B3; Daniel McGinn, "Honey, I Shrunk the Store," *Newsweek*, June 3, 2002, pp. 36–38; James McNair, "Wal-Mart Is Closing In on Kroger," *The Cincinnati Enquirer*, April 22, 2002, http://www.enquirer.com; Robert Berner and Stephanie Anderson, "Wal-Mart Is Eating Everybody's Lunch," *BusinessWeek*, April 15, 2002, p. 43.

Location-Distribution Strategy *Read*

Retail experts often cite location as a potential determining factor in the success or failure of a retail business. A retailer may choose to locate at an isolated site, in a central business district, or in a planned shopping center. The location decision depends on many conditions, including the type of merchandise, the retailer's financial resources, characteristics of the target market, and site availability.

In recent years, many localities have become saturated with stores. As a result, some retailers have reevaluated their location strategies. A chain may close individual stores that do not meet sales and profit goals. Kmart, for example, plans to close hundreds of its suburban locations to focus on better performing, high-density, urban populations.[11]

Other retailers have experimented with nontraditional location strategies. McDonald's now operates stores in hospitals, military bases, amusement parks, train stations, and gasoline stations. As described in the "Solving an Ethical Controversy" box, even the world's largest big-box retailer is diverging from its suburban megastore formula by testing small-format outlets in urban markets.

Locations in Planned Shopping Centers *Read*

Over the past several decades, retail trade has shifted away from traditional downtown retailing districts and toward suburban shopping centers. A **planned shopping center** is a group of retail stores designed, coordinated, and marketed as a unit to shoppers in a geographical trade area. Together, the stores provide a single convenient location for shoppers as well as free parking. They facilitate shopping by maintaining uniform hours of operation, including evening and weekend hours.

There are four main types of planned shopping centers. The smallest, the *neighborhood shopping center*, most often consists of a supermarket and a group of smaller stores, such as a drugstore, a dry cleaner, a small appliance store, and perhaps a hair-styling salon. This kind of center provides convenient shopping for 5,000 to 50,000 shoppers who live within a few minutes' commute. It contains 5 to 15 stores, and the product mix is usually confined to convenience goods and some shopping goods.

A *community shopping center* serves 20,000 to 100,000 people in a trade area extending a few miles from its location. It contains anywhere from 10 to 30 retail stores, with a branch of a local department store or some other large store as the primary tenant. In addition to the stores found in a neighborhood center, a community center probably encompasses more stores featuring shopping goods, some professional offices, a branch bank, and maybe a movie theater or supermarket. Community shopping centers typically offer ample parking, and tenants often share some promotion costs. With the advent of stand-alone big-box retailers, some community shopping centers have declined in popularity.

A *regional shopping center* is a large facility with at least 400,000 square feet of shopping space. Its marketing appeal usually emphasizes one or more major department stores with the power to draw customers, supplemented by as many as 200 smaller stores. A successful regional center needs a location within 30 minutes' driving time of at least 250,000 people. A regional center—or a superregional center like Minnesota's Mall of America—provides a wide assortment of convenience, shopping, and specialty goods, plus many professional and personal service facilities.

A *power center,* usually located near a regional or superregional mall, brings together several huge specialty stores, such as Toys "R" Us, Home Depot, or Bed, Bath, and Beyond, as stand-alone stores in a single trading area. Rising in popularity during the 1990s, power centers offered value because they were able to underprice department stores while providing a huge selection of specialty merchandise. Heated competition from cost-cutter Wal-Mart and inroads from more upscale discounters like Target and Kohl's have now reduced the drawing power of these centers.

Recently, a fifth type of planned center has emerged, known as a *lifestyle center*. This retailing format seeks to offer a combination of shopping, entertainment, and restaurants in an attractive environment. At 300,000 square feet, the centers are large, but they seek to offer the intimacy and easy access of neighborhood retailing with a fashionable cachet. Here, there are no big anchor stores but rather a mix of just the right upscale tenants—Williams-Sonoma, Eddie Bauer, or Restoration Hardware, for instance. Movie theaters and fine dining complete the mix. About 50 lifestyle centers are currently operating around the nation.[12]

Retail analysts believe that the "malling of America" has reached the saturation point. There are 20 square feet of retail space per capita, up by more than a third over a 15-year period. As upscale shoppers migrate to newer lifestyle centers or to the Internet, the malls have begun to shift away from traditional department store anchors. Some are turning to high-traffic draws like Target or Kohl's, but this puts specialty retailers like Gap or Banana Republic in a tough spot. Taking their lead from the popularity of lifestyle centers, others seek to combine shopping with entertainment; malls are adding carousels, rock-climbing walls, movie theaters, and large food courts. For example, Mall of America promotes its shopping center as a "shopping and fun destination," complete with an amusement park, a spa, an aquarium, and nightclubs and restaurants. Still others, such as the Market Place Mall in Champaign-Urbana,

In some instances, major malls can even become tourist destinations. Mall of America attracts more than 40 million people a year, making it Minnesota's top tourist attraction. The mall has 520-plus stores, 86 restaurants and food shops, 9 nightclubs, 15 movie screens, and more—like this Camp Snoopy amusement park.

Marketing Dictionary

planned shopping center Group of retail stores planned, coordinated, and marketed as a unit.

Illinois, emphasize customer service: well-padded playgrounds for toddlers, comfortable lounges for their parents, and luxurious restrooms equipped with infant changing rooms and nursing rooms with rocking chairs. Some malls hire concierges to help customers locate hard-to-find gifts and order theater tickets; others may offer valet parking, gift-wrap services, and parking-lot shuttle buses.[13]

Promotional Strategy

To establish store images that entice more shoppers, retailers use a variety of promotional techniques. Through its promotional strategy, a retailer seeks to communicate to consumers information about its stores—locations, merchandise selections, hours of operation, and prices. If merchandise selection changes frequently to follow fashion trends, advertising is typically used to promote current styles effectively. In addition, promotions help retailers to attract shoppers and build customer loyalty.

Innovative promotions can pay off in unexpected ways. Consider the opening of a new flagship store in New York's Times Square by Toys "R" Us. The store opened its door prior to the Christmas shopping season. An estimated 25 percent of retail revenue comes from the holiday shopping season, and for toys, the number is even greater. Bigger-than-life attractions, like the 60-foot indoor Ferris wheel, make this a "must-see" store with huge word-of-mouth advertising potential. Timed to coincide with the rejuvenation of Toys "R" Us outlets—remodeled stores, branded merchandise, and a customer service training initiative—the flagship helped reposition the retailer away from its discount roots.[14]

National retail chains often purchase advertising space in newspapers, on radio, and on television. Like many retail chains, Best Buy promotes its stores through advertising circulars in local and regional Sunday newspapers, as shown in Figure 16.3. Other retailers are experimenting with promoting over the Internet. Sometimes a well-chosen store location aids promotion; this is why dollar stores like California-based 99¢ Only Stores tend to locate on major streets leading to a large competitor, such as a Wal-Mart.

Retailers also try to combine advertising with in-store merchandising techniques that influence decisions at the point of purchase. 7-Eleven's drive to recast itself as a popular stop for teens on the go led to choice placement for trendy new products like its Slurpees and prepaid cellular phones. In-store point-of-purchase displays feature the latest hot teen products.[15]

A retail salesperson plays a vital role in conveying a store image to consumers and in persuading shoppers to buy. To serve as a source of information, a salesperson must possess extensive knowledge regarding credit policies, discounts, special sales, delivery terms, layaways, and returns. To increase store sales, the salesperson must persuade customers that the store sells what those customers need. To this end, salespeople should receive training in selling up and suggestion selling.

FIGURE 16.3
Best Buy's Advertising Circulars in Sunday Newspapers

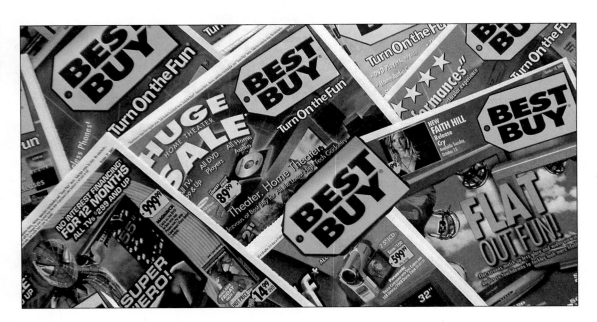

By *selling up*, salespeople try to persuade customers to buy higher priced items than originally intended. For example, an automobile salesperson might convince a customer to buy a more expensive model than the car that the buyer had initially considered. Of course, the practice of selling up must always respect the constraints of a customer's real needs. If a salesperson sells customers something that they really do not need, the potential for repeat sales dramatically diminishes.

Another technique, *suggestion selling*, seeks to broaden a customer's original purchase by adding related items, special promotional products, or holiday or seasonal merchandise. Here, too, the salesperson tries to help a customer recognize true needs rather than unwanted merchandise. Beauty advisors in upscale department stores are masters of suggestion selling. Estee Lauder's 8,800 beauty advisors receive 100 hours of training in their first year and annual follow-up classes. A 150-page training guide covers everything from icebreakers to "link selling"—a lip-liner pencil to go with that new lipstick?—to follow-up calls.[16]

Just as knowledgeable and helpful sales personnel can both boost sales and set retailers apart from competitors, poor service influences customers' attitudes toward a retailer. Increasing customer complaints about unfriendly, inattentive, and uninformed salespeople have prompted many retailers to intensify their attention to training and motivating salespeople.

Store Atmospherics *Read*

While store location, merchandise selection, customer service, pricing, and promotional activities all contribute to a store's consumer awareness, stores also project their personalities through *atmospherics*—physical characteristics and amenities that attract customers and satisfy their shopping needs. Atmospherics include both a store's exterior and interior décor.

A store's exterior appearance, including architectural design, window displays, signs, and entryways, helps to identify the retailer and attract its target market. The Saks Fifth Avenue script logo on a storefront and McDonald's golden arches are exterior elements that readily identify these retailers. Other retailers design eye-catching exterior elements aimed at getting customers' attention. Life-size cartoon figures seem poised in midflight over the entrance to the Warner Brothers outlet in the Horton Plaza Shopping Center in San Diego, drawing customer interest.

The interior décor of a store should also complement the retailer's image, respond to customers' interests, and most important, induce shoppers to buy. Interior atmospheric elements include store layout, merchandise presentation, lighting, color, sounds, scents, and cleanliness. At Sam's Club or Costco, for instance, merchandise is stacked high on pallets to emphasize the chains' rock-bottom pricing and no-frills approach and to encourage customers to buy in bulk. Low, low prices and unexpected deals on selected upscale merchandise draw customers in.[17]

When designing the interior and exterior of a store, the fact that many people shop for reasons other than just purchasing needed products must be taken into account. Other common reasons for shopping include escaping the routine of daily life, avoiding weather extremes, fulfilling fantasies, and socializing with family and friends. Retailers expand beyond interior design to create welcoming and entertaining environments that draw shoppers. To cater to teens, Nordstrom needed to rethink multiple aspects of the store environment and product placement. New, hip fashions are located right by the doors and are visible from the mall; music summons teen shoppers inside, where they no longer need to pass through housewares to get to their stuff.[18]

Types of Retailers *Read*

Since new types of retailers continue to evolve in response to changes in consumer demand, a universal classification system for retailers has yet to be devised. Certain differences do, however, define several categories of retailers: (1) forms of ownership, (2) shopping effort expended by customers, (3) services provided to customers, (4) product lines, and (5) locations of retail transactions.

Most retailing operations fit in different categories. A 7-Eleven outlet may be classified as a convenience store (category 2) with self-service (category 3) and a relatively broad product line (category 4). It is both a store-type retailer (category 5) and a member of a chain (category 1).

Classification of Retailers by Form of Ownership

Perhaps the easiest method for categorizing retailers divides retailers by ownership structure, distinguishing between chain stores and independent retailers. In addition, independent retailers may join wholesaler-sponsored voluntary chains, band together to form retail cooperatives, or enter into franchise agreements with manufacturers, wholesalers, or service-provider organizations. Each type of ownership has its own unique advantages and strategies.

Chain Stores cvs

Chain stores are groups of retail outlets that operate under central ownership and management and handle the same product lines. Chains have a major advantage over independent retailers in economies of scale. Volume purchases allow chains to pay lower prices than their independent rivals must pay. Since a chain may encompass hundreds of retail stores, it can afford advertising layout specialists, sales training, and sophisticated computerized systems for merchandise ordering, inventory management, forecasting, and accounting. Also, the large sales volume and wide geographical reach of a chain may enable it to advertise in a variety of media, including television and national magazines.

Independent Retailers

The U.S. retailing structure supports a large number of small stores, many medium-size stores, and a small number of large stores. Even though only 12 percent of the almost 2.7 million retail establishments earn annual sales of $1 million or more, those large operators account for almost three-quarters of all retail sales in the U.S. On the other hand, over half of all stores generate yearly sales below $500,000. According to the Department of Commerce, independent retailers account for about 43 percent of all retail sales.

Independent retailers compete with chains in a number of ways. The traditional advantage of independent stores is friendly, personalized service. Cooperatives offer another strategy for independents. For instance, cooperatives like Ace Hardware and Valu-Rite Pharmacies help independents compete with chains by providing volume buying power as well as advertising and marketing programs.

Classification by Shopping Effort

Another classification system is based on the reasons consumers shop at particular retail outlets. This approach categorizes stores as convenience, shopping, or specialty retailers.

Convenience retailers focus their marketing appeals on accessible locations, long store hours, rapid checkout service, and adequate parking facilities. Local food stores, gasoline stations, and dry cleaners fit in this category.

Shopping stores typically include furniture stores, appliance retailers, clothing outlets, and sporting goods stores. Consumers usually compare prices, assortments, and quality levels at competing outlets before making purchase decisions. Consequently, managers of shopping stores attempt to differentiate their outlets through advertising, window displays, in-store layouts, well-trained and knowledgeable salespeople, and appropriate merchandise assortments.

Specialty retailers combine carefully defined product lines, services, and reputations in attempts to convince consumers to expend considerable effort to shop at their stores. Examples include Neiman-Marcus, Lord & Taylor, and Nordstrom.

Classification by Services Provided

Another category differentiates retailers by the services they provide to customers. This classification system consists of three retailer types: self-service, self-selection, or full-service retailers.

Target illustrates a self-service store, while Kroger grocery stores and A&P Future Stores are examples of self-selection stores. Both categories sell convenience goods that people can purchase frequently with little assistance. By contrast, full-service retailers, like Saks Fifth Avenue,

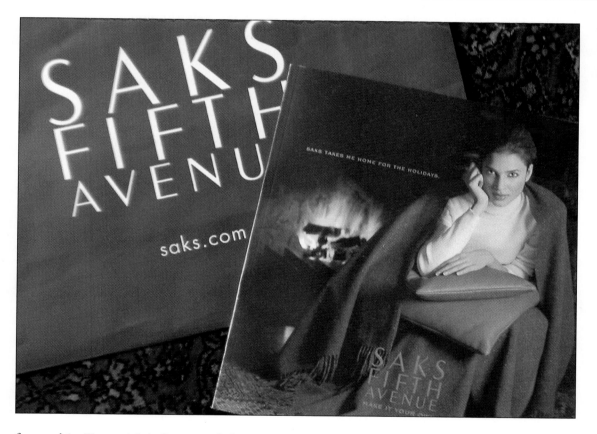

FIGURE 16.4
Saks Fifth Avenue: Providing a Full-Service Environment for Its Stylish Offerings

featured in Figure 16.4, focus on fashion-oriented merchandise, backed by a complete array of customer services.

Classification by Product Lines

Product lines also define a set of retail categories and the marketing strategies appropriate for firms within those categories. Grouping retailers by product lines produces three major categories: specialty stores, limited-line retailers, and general merchandise retailers.

Specialty Stores   Read Stores in middle of the mall

A *specialty store* typically handles only part of a single product line. However, it stocks this portion in considerable depth or variety. Specialty stores include a wide range of retail outlets: Examples include fish markets, grocery stores, men's and women's shoe stores, and bakeries. Although some specialty stores are chain outlets, most are independent small-scale operations. They represent perhaps the greatest concentration of independent retailers who develop expertise in one product area and provide narrow lines of products for their local markets.

Specialty stores should not be confused with specialty products. Specialty stores typically carry convenience and shopping goods. The label *specialty* reflects the practice of handling a specific, narrow line of merchandise. For example, Lady Foot Locker is a specialty store that offers a wide selection of name-brand athletic footwear, apparel, and accessories made specifically for women.

Limited-Line Retailers /

Customers find a large assortment of products within one product line or a few related lines in a *limited-line store*. This type of retail operation typically develops in areas with a large enough population to sufficiently support it. Examples of limited-line stores are IKEA (home furnishings and housewares) and Levitz (furniture). These retailers cater to the needs of people who want to select from complete lines in purchasing particular products.

A unique type of limited-line retailer is known as a *category killer*. These stores offer huge selections and low prices in single product lines. Stores within this category—for example, Borders Books; Bed, Bath, and Beyond; and Home Depot—are among the most successful retailers in the nation. Popular in the 1990s, category killers at first took business away from general merchandise discounters, which were not able to compete in selection or price. Recently, however, expanded merchandise and aggressive cost cutting by warehouse clubs and by Wal-Mart have turned the tables. Competition from Internet companies that are able to offer unlimited selection and speedy delivery has also taken customers away. While they still remain a powerful force in retailing, category killers are not invulnerable.[19]

General Merchandise Retailers Read

General merchandise retailers, which carry a wide variety of product lines that are all stocked in some depth, distinguish themselves from limited-line and specialty retailers by the large number of product lines they carry. The general store described earlier in this chapter is a primitive form of a general merchandise retailer. This category includes variety stores, department stores, and mass merchandisers such as catalog retailers, discount stores, off-price retailers, and hypermarkets.

Variety Stores

A retail outlet that offers an extensive range and assortment of low-price merchandise is called a *variety store*. Less popular today than they once were, many of these stores have evolved into or given way to other types of retailers such as discount stores. The nation's variety stores now account for less than 1 percent of all retail sales. However, variety stores remain popular in other parts of the world. Many retail outlets in Spain and Mexico are family-owned variety stores.

Department Stores

A *department store* gathers a series of limited-line and specialty stores under one roof. By definition, this large retailer handles a variety of merchandise, including men's, women's, and children's clothing and accessories; household linens and dry goods; home furnishings; and furniture. It serves as a one-stop shopping destination for almost all personal and household products. Chicago's Marshall Field's is a classic example.

Department stores built their reputations by offering wide varieties of services, such as charge accounts, delivery, gift wrapping, and liberal return privileges. As a result, they incur relatively high operating costs, averaging about 45 to 60 percent of sales.

Department stores have faced intense new competition over the past several years. Relatively high operating costs have left them vulnerable to retailing innovations such as discount stores, catalog merchandisers, and hypermarkets. In addition, department stores' traditional locations in downtown business districts suffered from problems associated with limited parking, traffic congestion, and population migration to the suburbs.

Department stores have fought back in a variety of ways. Many have closed certain sections, such as electronics, in which high costs kept them from competing with discount houses and category killers. They have added bargain outlets, expanded parking facilities, and opened major branches in regional shopping centers. They have attempted to revitalize downtown retailing in many cities by modernizing their stores, expanding store hours, making special efforts to attract the tourist and convention trade, and serving the needs of urban residents.

Retailers like Macy's constantly try to stop the slide by reinventing the department store, experimenting with different layouts, store-branded merchandise, and adding amenities like child care, day spas, and e-mail stations for customers. Sears recently stated that it no longer wanted to be classified as a department store at all, but it has yet to find a profitable niche of its own.[20]

Mass Merchandisers

Mass merchandising has made major inroads into department stores' sales by emphasizing lower prices for well-known brand-name products, high product turnover, and limited services. A *mass merchandiser* often stocks a wider line of items than a department store but usually without the same depth of assortment within each line. Discount houses, off-price retailers, hypermarkets, and catalog retailers are all examples of mass merchandisers.

Discount Houses
A *discount house* charges low prices and offers fewer services. Early discount stores sold mostly appliances. Today, they offer soft goods, drugs, food, and furniture.

By eliminating many of the "free" services provided by traditional retailers, these operations can keep their markups 10 to 25 percent below those of their competitors. Some of the early discounters have since added services, stocked increasingly prestigious name brands, and boosted their prices. In fact, many now resemble department stores. Kohl's, for instance, defies classification. The store offers centralized checkouts at more than one entrance and distinctive black mesh shopping carts. Departments are staffed by knowledgeable personnel—jewelry and cosmetics counters offer personal assistance, for example. The widespread success of Kohl's—with sales up by 10 percent when rival retailers reported losses—has inspired mall-based department stores like JCPenney to experiment by cutting back on some aspects of one-on-one customer service.[21]

A discount format that is gaining strength is the warehouse club. Costco and Wal-Mart's Sam's Club are the largest warehouse clubs in the U.S. These no-frills, cash-and-carry outlets offer consumers access to name-brand products at deeply discounted prices. Selection at warehouse clubs includes everything from gourmet popcorn to fax machines to peanut butter to luggage and sunglasses, sold in vast warehouselike settings. Attracting business away from almost every retailing segment, warehouse clubs now even offer fresh food and gasoline. Customers must be members to shop at warehouse clubs.[22]

Off-Price Retailers
Another version of a discount house is an *off-price retailer*. This kind of store stocks only designer labels or well-known brand-name clothing at prices equal to or below regular wholesale prices and then passes the cost savings along to consumers. While many off-price retailers are located in outlets in downtown areas or in freestanding buildings, a growing number are concentrating in *outlet malls*—shopping centers that house only off-price merchandise by many retailers.

Inventory at off-price retailers changes frequently as buyers take advantage of special price offers from manufacturers selling excess merchandise. Off-price retailers such as Loehmann's, Marshall's, Stein Mart, and T.J. Maxx also keep their prices below those of traditional retailers by offering fewer services. Off-price retailing has been well received by today's shoppers.

Hypermarkets and Supercenters
Another innovation in discount retailing is the creation of *hypermarkets*—giant one-stop shopping facilities that offer wide selections of grocery and general merchandise products at discount prices. Store size determines the major difference between hypermarkets and supercenters. Hypermarkets typically fill up 200,000 or more square feet of selling space, about a third larger than most *supercenters*. At Meijer stores, for example, Michigan, Ohio, and Indiana consumers can buy food, hardware, soft goods, building materials, auto supplies, appliances, and prescription drugs in locations averaging 245,000 square feet. When consumers finish shopping, Meijer customers can visit a restaurant, beauty salon, barber shop, bank branch, or bakery within the facility. Fred Meyer on the West Coast is another hypermarket approach. By contrast, the supercenter format is used by Wal-Mart, Kmart, and Target.

Showroom and Warehouse Retailers   Showroom retailers send direct mail to their customers and sell the advertised goods from showrooms that display samples. Back-room warehouses fill orders for the displayed products. Low prices are important to catalog store customers. To keep prices low, these retailers offer few services, store most inventory in inexpensive warehouse space, limit shoplifting losses, and handle long-lived products such as luggage, small appliances, gift items, sporting equipment, toys, and jewelry.

Classification of Retail Transactions by Location   Although most retail transactions occur in stores, nonstore retailing serves as an important marketing channel for many products. In addition, both consumer and business-to-business marketers rely on nonstore retailing to generate orders or requests for more information that may result in future orders.

Direct marketing is a broad concept that includes direct mail, direct selling, direct response retailing, telemarketing, Internet retailing, and automatic merchandising. The last sections of this chapter will consider each type of nonstore retailing.

Retail Convergence and Scrambled Merchandising

4

Explain the concepts of retail convergence and scrambled merchandising.

Many traditional differences no longer distinguish familiar types of retailers, rendering any set of classifications less useful. **Retail convergence,** whereby similar merchandise is available from multiple retail outlets distinguished by price more than any other factor, is blurring distinctions between types of retailers and the merchandise mix they offer. A few years ago, a customer looking for a fashionable coffeepot might have headed straight for Williams-Sonoma or Starbucks. Today, she's just as likely to pick one up at Target or Wal-Mart, where she can check out new spring fashions and stock up on paper goods. Gap is no longer pitted only against Eddie Bauer or American Eagle Outfitters but against designer-label brands at department stores and Kohl's, too. Grocery stores compete with Wal-Mart.[23]

Scrambled merchandising—in which a retailer combines dissimilar product lines in an attempt to boost sales volume—has also muddied the waters. Drugstores not only fill prescriptions but offer cameras, cards, housewares, magazines, and even small appliances. Convenience retailer 7-Eleven recently began offering such services as bill payment, payroll check cashing, money wiring, and ticket purchasing through in-store terminals hooked up to the Web. Goods ordered through the system are delivered to the store for later pick-up.[24]

Wholesaling Intermediaries

Recall from Chapter 15 that several distribution channels involve marketing intermediaries called **wholesalers.** These firms take title to the goods they handle and sell those products primarily to retailers or to other wholesalers or business users. They sell to ultimate consumers only in insignificant quantities if at all. **Wholesaling intermediaries,** a broader category, includes not only wholesalers but also agents and brokers, who perform important wholesaling activities without taking title to goods.

Functions of Wholesaling Intermediaries

5

Identify the functions performed by wholesaling intermediaries.

As specialists in certain marketing functions, as opposed to production or manufacturing functions, wholesaling intermediaries can perform these functions more efficiently than producers or consumers. The importance of these functions results from the utility they create, the services they provide, and the cost reductions they allow.

Creating Utility

Wholesaling intermediaries create three types of utility for consumers. They enhance time utility by making products available for sale when consumers want to purchase them. They create place utility by helping to deliver goods and services for purchase at convenient locations. They create ownership (or possession) utility when a smooth exchange of title to the products from producers or intermedi-

TABLE 16.1   Wholesaling Services for Customers and Producer-Suppliers

SERVICE	BENEFICIARIES OF SERVICE	
	Customers	**Producer-Suppliers**
Buying Anticipates customer demands and applies knowledge of alternative sources of supply; acts as purchasing agent for customers.	✓	
Selling Provides a sales force to call on customers, creating a low-cost method for servicing smaller retailers and business users.		✓
Storing Maintains warehouse facilities at lower costs than most individual producers or retailers could achieve. Reduces risk and cost of maintaining inventory for producers.	✓	✓
Transporting Customers receive prompt delivery in response to their demands, reducing their inventory investments. Wholesalers also break bulk by purchasing in economical carload or truckload lots, then reselling in smaller quantities, thereby reducing overall transportation costs.	✓	✓
Providing Marketing Information Offers important marketing research input for producers through regular contacts with retail and business buyers. Provides customers with information about new products, technical information about product lines, reports on competitors' activities and industry trends, and advisory information concerning pricing changes, legal changes, and so forth.	✓	✓
Financing Grants credit that might be unavailable for purchases directly from manufacturers. Provides financing assistance to producers by purchasing products in advance of sale and by promptly paying bills.	✓	✓
Risk Taking Evaluates credit risks of numerous, distant retail customers and small business users. Extends credit to customers that qualify. By transporting and stocking products in inventory, the wholesaler assumes risk of spoilage, theft, or obsolescence.	✓	✓

aries to final purchasers is complete. Possession utility can also result from transactions in which actual title does not pass to purchasers, as in rental-car services.

Providing Services

Table 16.1 lists a number of services provided by wholesaling intermediaries. The list clearly indicates the marketing utilities—time, place, and possession utility—that wholesaling intermediaries create or enhance. These services also reflect the basic marketing functions of buying, selling, storing, transporting, providing market information, financing, and risk taking.

Marketing Dictionary

retail convergence   The coming together of shoppers, goods, and prices, resulting in the blurring of distinctions between types of retailer and the merchandise mix they offer.

scrambled merchandising   Retailing practice of combining dissimilar product lines to boost sales volume.

wholesaler   Channel intermediary that takes title to goods it handles and then distributes these goods to retailers, other distributors, or B2B customers.

wholesaling intermediary   Comprehensive term that describes wholesalers as well as agents and brokers.

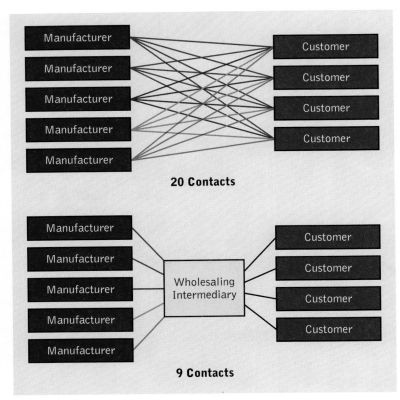

FIGURE 16.5
Transaction Economies through Wholesaling Intermediaries

Of course, many types of wholesaling intermediaries provide varying services, and not all of them perform every service listed in the table. Producer-suppliers rely on wholesaling intermediaries for distribution, which also entails the selection of firms that offer the desired combinations of services. In general, however, the critical marketing functions listed in the table form the basis for any evaluation of a marketing intermediary's efficiency. The risk-taking function affects each service of the intermediary.

Synnex Information Technologies of Fremont, California, markets computer-related products and peripherals, and it also offers warehousing and trucking capabilities that help lower overhead for retail customers. Inventory management, next-day delivery, financing, and technical service support are among the menu of services the company offers.[25]

Lowering Costs by Limiting Contacts

When an intermediary represents numerous producers, it often cuts the costs of buying and selling. The transaction economies are illustrated in Figure 16.5, which shows five manufacturers marketing their outputs to four different retail outlets. Without an intermediary, these exchanges create a total of 20 transactions. Adding a wholesaling intermediary reduces the number of transactions to 9.

For example, United Stationers is a wholesaler of everything from paper clips to fax machines to discount chains, independent stores, and Internet resellers. While big-box retailers buy in bulk directly from manufacturers, they are able to order low-volume specialty goods faster and more efficiently from United Stationers. Through Web-enabled ordering, mom-and-pop stores have access to more than 35,000 items, delivered either to the store or directly to customers overnight. Positioning itself as a one-stop warehousing, logistics, and distribution network, the company recently expanded beyond its office-products roots by establishing a new janitorial supply unit.[26]

Types of Wholesaling Intermediaries

6

Identify the major types of independent wholesaling intermediaries and the situations appropriate for each.

Various types of wholesaling intermediaries operate in different distribution channels. Some provide wide ranges of services or handle broad lines of goods, while others specialize in individual services, goods, or industries. Figure 16.6 classifies wholesaling intermediaries by two characteristics: ownership and *title flows* (whether title passes from manufacturer to wholesaling intermediary). The three basic ownership structures are as follows: (1) manufacturer-owned facilities, (2) independent wholesaling intermediaries, and (3) retailer-owned cooperatives and buying offices. The two types of independent wholesaling intermediaries are merchant wholesalers, which take title of the goods, and agents and brokers, which do not.

Manufacturer-Owned Facilities

Several reasons lead manufacturers to distribute their goods directly through company-owned facilities. Some perishable goods need rigid control of distribution to avoid spoilage; other goods require complex installation or servicing. Some goods need aggressive promotion. Goods with high-unit values allow profitable sales by manufacturers directly to ultimate purchasers. Manufacturer-owned facilities include sales branches, sales offices, trade fairs, and merchandise marts.

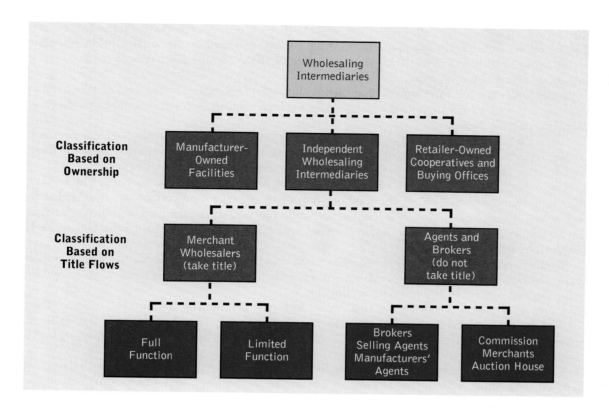

FIGURE 16.6
Major Types of Wholesaling Intermediaries

A *sales branch* carries inventory and processes orders for customers from available stock. Branches provide a storage function like independent wholesalers and serve as offices for sales representatives in their territories. They are prevalent in marketing channels for chemicals, commercial machinery and equipment, motor vehicles, and petroleum products.

A *sales office*, in contrast, does not carry inventory, but it does serve as a regional office for a manufacturer's sales personnel. Locations close to the firm's customers help limit selling costs and support active customer service. For example, numerous sales offices in the Detroit suburbs serve the area's automobile industry.

A *trade fair* (or trade exhibition) is a periodic show at which manufacturers in a particular industry display their wares for visiting retail and wholesale buyers. For example, the Internet World Conference sponsors an enormous trade exhibition that brings together over 600 companies to demonstrate their latest Internet technology.

A *merchandise mart* provides space for permanent showrooms and exhibits, which manufacturers rent to market their goods. One of the world's largest merchandise marts is Chicago's Mart Center, a 7-million-square-foot complex that hosts more than 30 seasonal buying markets each year.

Independent Wholesaling Intermediaries

Many wholesaling intermediaries are independently owned. These firms fall into two categories: merchant wholesalers and agents and brokers.

Merchant Wholesalers

A *merchant wholesaler* takes title to the goods it handles. Merchant wholesalers account for roughly 60 percent of all sales at the wholesale level. Further classifications divide these wholesalers into full-function or limited-function wholesalers, as indicated in Figure 16.6. Synnex, mentioned in the previous section, is a merchant wholesaler.

A full-function merchant wholesaler provides a complete assortment of services for retailers and business purchasers. Such a wholesaler stores merchandise in a convenient location, allowing customers to make purchases on short notice and minimizing inventory requirements. The firm typically maintains a sales force that calls on retailers, makes deliveries, and extends credit to qualified buyers. Full-function wholesalers are common in the drug, grocery, and hardware industries. In the business-goods market, full-function merchant wholesalers (often called *industrial distributors*) sell machinery, inexpensive accessory equipment, and supplies.

A *rack jobber* is a full-function merchant wholesaler who markets specialized lines of merchandise to retailers. A rack jobber supplies the racks, stocks the merchandise, prices the goods, and makes regular visits to refill shelves.

Limited-function merchant wholesalers fit into four categories: cash-and-carry wholesalers, truck wholesalers, drop shippers, and mail-order wholesalers. Limited-function wholesalers serve the food, coal, lumber, cosmetics, jewelry, sporting goods, and general merchandise industries.

A *cash-and-carry wholesaler* performs most wholesaling functions except for financing and delivery. Although feasible for small stores, this kind of wholesaling generally is unworkable for large-scale grocery stores. Today, cash-and-carry operations typically function as departments within regular full-service wholesale operations. Cash-and-carry wholesalers are commonplace outside the U.S., such as in the United Kingdom.

A *truck wholesaler*, or *truck jobber*, markets perishable food items such as bread, tobacco, potato chips, candy, and dairy products. Truck wholesalers make regular deliveries to retailers, perform sales and collection functions, and promote product lines.

A *drop shipper* accepts orders from customers and forwards these orders to producers, which then ship the desired products directly to customers. Although drop shippers take title to goods, they never physically handle or even see the merchandise. These intermediaries operate in industries selling bulky goods that customers buy in carload lots, such as coal and lumber.

A *mail-order wholesaler* is a limited-function merchant wholesaler who distributes catalogs as opposed to sending sales representatives to contact retail, business, and institutional customers. Customers then make purchases by mail or phone. Such a wholesaler often serves relatively small customers in outlying areas. Mail-order operations mainly exist in the hardware, cosmetics, jewelry, sporting goods, and specialty food lines as well as in general merchandise.

Table 16.2 compares the various types of merchant wholesalers and the services they provide. Full-function merchant wholesalers and truck wholesalers rank as relatively high-cost intermediaries due to the number of services they perform, while cash-and-carry wholesalers, drop shippers, and mail-order wholesalers provide fewer services and set lower prices since they incur lower operating costs.

Agents and Brokers

A second group of independent wholesaling intermediaries, agents and brokers, may or may not take possession of the goods they handle, but they never take title. They normally perform fewer services than merchant wholesalers, typically working mainly to bring together buyers and sellers. Agents and

TABLE 16.2   **Comparison of the Types of Merchant Wholesalers and Their Services**

SERVICE	Full-Function	Cash-and-Carry	Truck	Drop Shipper	Mail-Order
		LIMITED-FUNCTION WHOLESALER			
Anticipates customer needs	✓	✓	✓	—	✓
Carries inventory	✓	✓	✓	—	✓
Delivers	✓	—	✓	—	—
Provides market information	✓	Rarely	✓	✓	—
Provides credit	✓	—	—	✓	Sometimes
Assumes ownership risk by taking title	✓	✓	✓	✓	✓

brokers fall into five categories: commission merchants, auction houses, brokers, selling agents, and manufacturers' agents.

Commission merchants, who predominate in the markets for agricultural products, take possession when producers ship goods such as grain, produce, and livestock to central markets for sale. Commission merchants act as producers' agents and receive agreed-upon fees when they make sales. Since customers inspect the products and prices fluctuate, commission merchants receive considerable latitude in marketing decisions. The owners of the goods may specify minimum prices, but the commission merchants sell these goods at the best possible prices. The commission merchants then deduct their fees from the sales proceeds.

An auction house gathers buyers and sellers in one location and allows potential buyers to inspect merchandise before submitting competing purchase offers. Auction house commissions typically reflect specified percentages of the sales prices of the auctioned items. Auctions are common in the distribution of tobacco, used cars, artworks, livestock, furs, and fruit. The Internet has led to a new type of auction house that connects customers and sellers in the online world. A well-known example is eBay, which auctions a wide variety of products in all price ranges. Another example, Sotheby's, featured in Figure 16.7, offers high-end items such as jewelry, paintings, and furniture to Internet bidders.

FIGURE 16.7
An Internet-based Auction Site

Brokers work mainly to bring together buyers and sellers. A broker represents either the buyer or the seller, but not both, in a given transaction, and the broker receives a fee from the client when the transaction is completed. Intermediaries that specialize in arranging buying and selling transactions between domestic producers and foreign buyers are called *export brokers.* Brokers operate in industries characterized by large numbers of small suppliers and purchasers, such as real estate, frozen foods, and used machinery. Since they provide one-time services for sellers or buyers, they cannot serve as effective channels for manufacturers seeking regular, continuing service. A firm that seeks to develop a more permanent channel might choose instead to use a selling agent or manufacturer's agent.

A *selling agent* typically exerts full authority over pricing decisions and promotional outlays, and it often provides financial assistance for the manufacturer. Selling agents act as independent marketing departments because they can assume responsibility for the total marketing programs of client firms' product lines. Selling agents mainly operate in the coal, lumber, and textiles industries. For a small, poorly financed, production-oriented firm, such an intermediary might prove the ideal marketing channel.

While a manufacturer may deal with only one selling agent, a firm that hires **manufacturers' agents,** commonly known as manufacturers' reps, often delegates marketing tasks to many of these agents. Such an independent salesperson may work for a number of firms that produce related, noncompeting products. Manufacturers' reps are paid on a commission basis, such as 6 percent of sales. Unlike selling agents, who may contract for exclusive rights to market a product, manufacturers' agents operate in specific territories. They may develop new sales territories or represent relatively small firms and those firms with unrelated lines.

Marketing Dictionary

broker Agent wholesaling intermediary who does not take title to or possession of goods in the course of its primary function, which is to bring together buyers and sellers.

manufacturers' agent Agent wholesaling intermediary who represents a number of manufacturers of related but noncompeting products and who receives a commission on each sale.

TABLE 16.3   Services Provided by Agents and Brokers

SERVICE	Commission Merchant	Auction House	Broker	Manufacturers' Agent	Selling Agent
Anticipates customer needs	✓	Sometimes	Sometimes	✓	✓
Carries inventory	✓	✓	—	—	—
Delivers	✓	—	—	Sometimes	—
Provides market information	✓	✓	✓	✓	✓
Provides credit	Sometimes	—	—	—	Sometimes
Assumes ownership risk by taking title	—	—	—	—	—

When inventor Jane McKittrick first launched Earth Bud-Eze, an innovative range of tools that eased the strains of many gardening tasks, the products—sold largely at state fairs—were modestly successful. But when McKittrick enlisted the expertise of Marshall Associates, a manufacturers' rep group with extensive contacts in the hardware and gardening markets, sales skyrocketed. The start-up product line was even able to penetrate mass merchants nationwide.[27]

The importance of selling agents in many markets has declined because manufacturers want better control of their marketing programs than these intermediaries allow. In contrast, the volume of sales by manufacturers' agents has more than doubled and now accounts for 37 percent of all sales by agents and brokers. Table 16.3 compares the major types of agents and brokers on the basis of the services they perform.

Retailer-Owned Cooperatives and Buying Offices

Retailers may assume numerous wholesaling functions in an attempt to reduce costs or provide special services. Independent retailers sometimes band together to form buying groups that can achieve cost savings through quantity purchases. Other groups of retailers establish retailer-owned wholesale facilities by forming cooperative chains. Large chain retailers often establish centralized buying offices to negotiate large-scale purchases directly with manufacturers.

Direct Marketing and Other *Read* Nonstore Retailing

7

Compare the basic types of direct marketing and nonstore retailing.

Although most retail transactions occur in stores, nonstore retailing is an important marketing channel for many products. As well as sales, both consumer and business-to-business marketers rely on nonstore retailing to generate leads or requests for more information that may result in future orders.

Direct marketing is a broad concept that includes direct mail, direct selling, direct-response retailing, telemarketing, Internet retailing, and automatic merchandising. Direct and interactive marketing expenditures top $190 billion a year, a figure that is expected to rise at the rate of 6.5 percent a year until 2006.[28] The last sections of this chapter will consider each type of nonstore retailing.

Direct Mail *Read*

Direct mail is a major component of direct marketing. It comes in many forms, ranging from sales letters, postcards, brochures, booklets, catalogs, and house organs (periodicals issued by organizations) to video and audio cassettes. Both not-for-profit and profit-seeking organizations make extensive use of this distribution channel.

Direct mail offers several advantages such as the ability to select a narrow target market, achieve intensive coverage, send messages quickly, choose from various formats, provide complete information, and personalize each mailing piece. Response rates are measurable and higher than other types of advertising. In addition, direct mailings stand alone and do not compete for attention with magazine articles and television programs. On the other hand, the per-reader cost of direct mail is high, effectiveness depends on the quality of the mailing list, and some consumers object strongly to direct mail, considering it to be "junk mail."

Direct mail marketing relies heavily on database technology in managing lists of names and in segmenting these lists according to the objectives of the campaign. Recipients get targeted materials, often personalized with their names within the ad's content. The "Marketing Misses" box shows what can happen when personalized pitches like these misfire.

Catalogs are a popular form of direct mail, with more than 10,000 different consumer specialty mail-order catalogs—and thousands more for business-to-business sales—finding their way to almost every mailbox in the U.S. In a typical year, mail-order catalogs generate almost $40 billion in consumer sales and $24 billion in business-to-business sales. Catalogs can be a company's only or primary sales method. Spiegel, L.L. Bean, Lands' End, Eddie Bauer, and Patagonia are well-known examples. Brick-and-mortar retailers like Bloomingdale's and Macy's also distribute catalogs. Web retailers, too, have discovered that catalogs stimulate sales. Exotic goods e-tailer eZiba.com used a catalog to expand its customer base beyond young, Web-savvy clientele to older shoppers. Amazon has recently mailed a catalog of home and garden products, while Yahoo! is testing direct-mail offers for its range of premium pay services.[29]

New technologies are changing catalog marketing. Today's catalogs can be updated quickly, providing consumers with the latest information and prices. CD-ROM catalogs allow marketers to display products in three-dimensional views and can include video sequences of product demonstrations. Following terrorist scares in which letters laced with anthrax were sent through the mail, direct marketers responded by combining e-mail marketing and direct mail. E-mails alerted customers that catalogs or direct mail packages were coming through the postal service, easing concerns over mail from unknown sources.[30]

Direct Selling

Through direct selling, manufacturers completely bypass retailers and wholesalers. Instead, they set up their own channels to sell their products directly to consumers. Avon, the Fuller Brush Company, Dell, and party-plan marketers like Tupperware are all direct sellers. This channel was discussed in detail in Chapter 15.

Direct-Response Retailing

Customers of a direct-response retailer can order merchandise by mail or telephone, by visiting a mail-order desk in a retail store, or by computer or fax machine. The retailer then ships the merchandise to the customer's home or to a local retail store for pickup. Shown in

Marketing Miss

Prozac by Mail

Background. The big pharmaceutical companies regularly come under fire for their aggressive marketing practices. While their unstoppable deluge of consumer-directed ads may be considered questionable practices, Eli Lilly's latest direct marketing pitch clearly steps over ethical and even legal boundaries.

The Marketing Problem. For years, pharmaceutical companies have maintained sophisticated databases of patients with prescriptions for their own and rival drugs. Through cooperation with local pharmacies and prescribing doctors, it's not unusual for patients to receive solicitations for new drugs through the mail or even over the Internet. Then a Florida woman opened her mailbox to find a package from Walgreen's containing a free monthly trial of Eli Lilly's antidepressant Prozac Weekly.

The Outcome. The woman filed a class-action lawsuit against the drug company, the pharmacy, and her doctor. The suit charged that the three parties had colluded to misuse patients' medical records and invade their privacy. It is not yet clear how many hundreds or thousands of patients received the mailings, but the campaign was initiated at a time when Prozac sales were plummeting due to the release of generic alternatives in the market.

continued on next page

Marketing Dictionary

direct marketing Distribution channel consisting of direct communication with a consumer or business user.

Marketing Miss

Lessons Learned. Eli Lilly's pills-in-the-mail campaign raises not just privacy issues but concerns over public safety—the colorful capsules could easily be mistaken for candy by curious children. Since the patient who filed the suit claims she did not have a current prescription for Prozac or any other antidepressant, Eli Lilly is also open to charges of illegally dispensing prescription drugs.

SOURCES: Adam Liptak, "Free Prozac in the Junk Mail Draws a Lawsuit," *The New York Times*, July 6, 2002, p. 1; Bruce Japsen, "Florida Prozac Case Raises Issues of Privacy, Health," *Chicago Tribune*, June 11, 2002, Section 1, pp. 1, 5; Vanessa O'Connell and Rachel Zimmerman, "Drug Pitches Resonate with Edgy Public," *The Wall Street Journal*, January 14, 2002, p. B5.

Enjoy dairy, not the discomfort.
Try *Lactaid* for
FREE.

If dairy foods cause you cramps, gas and bloating, take LACTAID® Supplements with your first bite of dairy and help prevent the symptoms before they start.

Call 1-800-LACTAID for your FREE 6-count pack of LACTAID® Ultra, to help you enjoy dairy without the consequences.

Enjoy dairy again.   www.lactaid.com

Call
1-800-LACTAID for a
FREE 6-count pack of
Lactaid Ultra

Lactaid Ultra

FIGURE 16.8
A Direct Response Marketer

Figure 16.8, Lactaid offers free samples via direct response by telephone or to its Web site.

Many direct-response retailers rely on direct mail, such as catalogs, to create telephone and mail-order sales and to promote in-store purchases of products featured in the catalogs. Additionally, some firms, such as Lillian Vernon, make almost all of their sales through catalog orders. Mail-order sales have grown about 10 percent a year in recent years, about twice the rate of retail store sales.

Direct-response retailers are increasingly reaching buyers through the Internet and through unique catalogs. Lillian Vernon supplements its general merchandise catalogs with specialty catalogs of children's products and personalized gifts. Jackson and Perkins holiday season catalogs offer a variety of plants for gift giving. Signals advertises merchandise with tie-ins to Public Broadcasting Service programs.

Direct-response retailing also includes home shopping, which runs promotions on cable television networks to sell merchandise through telephone orders. One form of home shopping has existed for years—the late-night commercials that run for at least 30 minutes. Such products as K-Tel Records and Veg-O-Matic vegetable slicers have been featured on these commercials. More recently, TV networks like Home Shopping Network have successfully focused exclusively on providing shopping opportunities. Programming ranges from extended commercials to call-in shows to game-show formats. Shoppers call a toll-free number to buy featured products, and the retailer ships ordered goods directly to their homes.

Telemarketing

Telemarketing refers to direct marketing conducted entirely by telephone. It is the most frequently used form of direct marketing. It provides marketers with a high return on their expenditures, an immediate response, and the opportunity for personalized two-way conversations. Telemarketing is discussed in further detail in Chapter 19.

Internet Retailing

Internet-based retailers sell directly to customers via virtual storefronts on the Web. They usually maintain little or no inventory, ordering directly from vendors to fill customer orders received via their Web sites. In recent years, conventional retailers have anxiously watched the rise—and then the demise—of Internet-based retailers. During the dot.com bust, 130 e-tailers failed. Even early successes like Ezshop, an online home furnishings retailer, eventually ran aground. Traditional retailers, using the Web to support brick-and-mortar stores, have had much better staying power. Gap, Best Buy, and Lands' End, for example, have succeeded in extending their expertise to the Web. Office Depot credits its success to its solid brand name, its low-cost buying strategies, and most important, its extensive distribution network—customers can pick up purchases they initiate on the Web at local Office Depot outlets.[31] Chapter 5 discussed Internet retailing and other forms of e-commerce in more detail.

Automatic Merchandising

The world's first vending machines dispensed holy water for five-drachma coins in Egyptian temples around 215 B.C. This retailing method has grown rapidly ever since; today, about 4.7 million vending machines sell approximately $25 billion in convenience goods to Americans.

While in the past U.S. vending machines have been limited to snacks, soft drinks, and lottery tickets, Japanese consumers use automatic merchandising for everything from fresh sushi to new underwear. Recently, U.S. marketers have begun to realize the potential of this underused marketing tool. As technological advances and credit-card payments make it easier to sell high-cost items, vending machines offering $15 movie soundtracks are popping up in movie-theater lobbies, while Underwear to Go offers boxer shorts in pop-up aluminum cans.[32] The end-of-chapter case explains that automated merchandising is just one way in which marketers seek to keep pace with today's 24/7 society.

8

Explain ways in which the Internet has altered the wholesaling, retailing, and direct marketing environments.

Strategic Implications of Marketing in the 21st Century

As the Internet revolution steadily becomes a way of life—both for consumers and for the businesses marketing goods and services to them—technology will continue to transform the ways in which retailers, wholesalers, and direct marketers connect with customers.

In the retail sector, the unstoppable march toward lower and lower prices has forced retailers from Saks Fifth Avenue to dollar stores to reevaluate everything from their logistics and supply networks to their profit margins. Many have used the power of the Internet to strengthen such factors as store image, the merchandising mix, customer service, and the development of long-term relationships with customers.

Though manufacturers first anticipated that Internet technology would enable them to bypass such intermediaries as wholesalers and agents, bringing them closer to the customer, the reality is quite different. Successful wholesalers have been able to establish themselves as essential links in the supply, distribution, and customer service network. By leveraging technology, they have been able to carve out new roles, providing such expert services as warehousing or fulfillment to multiple retail clients.

The Internet has empowered direct marketers by facilitating ever more sophisticated database segmentation. Traditional catalog and direct mail marketers have integrated Internet sites, Web advertising, and e-mailing programs into a cohesive targeting, distribution, and repeat-buying strategy.

Briefly Speaking

If you're not doing Internet business, then you're in the Dark Ages, and you're going to be left behind.

John Chambers
(b. 1948)
CEO, Cisco Systems

Summary of Chapter Objectives

1. Explain the wheel of retailing.

The wheel of retailing is the hypothesis that each new type of retailer gains a competitive foothold by offering lower prices than current suppliers and maintains profits by reducing or eliminating services. The most recent example is the bankruptcy of Kmart, which is struggling to compete on price against cost-cutter Wal-Mart and is having difficulty finding an alternate niche.

2. Explain how retailers select target markets.

A retailer starts to define its strategy by selecting a target market. The target market dictates, among other things, the prod-

uct mix, pricing strategy, and location strategy. Retailers deal with consumer behavior at the most complicated level, and a clear understanding of the target market is critical. Strategies for selecting target markets include merchandising, customer services, pricing, location-distribution, and promotional strategies.

3. Show how the elements of the marketing mix apply to retailing strategy.

A retailer must first identify a target market and then develop a product strategy. Next, it must establish a customer service strategy. Retail pricing strategy involves decisions on markups and markdowns. Location is often the determining factor in a retailer's success or failure. A retailer's promotional strategy and store atmosphere play important roles in establishing a store's image.

4. Explain the concepts of retail convergence and scrambled merchandising.

Retail convergence is the coming together of shoppers, goods, and prices, resulting in the blurring of distinctions between types of retailers and the merchandise mix they offer. Similar selections are available from multiple sources and are differentiated mainly by price. Scrambled merchandising refers to retailers' practice of carrying dissimilar product lines in an attempt to generate additional sales volume. Retail convergence and scrambled merchandising have made it increasingly difficult to classify retailers.

5. Identify the functions performed by wholesaling intermediaries.

The functions of wholesaling intermediaries include creating utility, providing services, and lowering costs by limiting contacts.

6. Identify the major types of independent wholesaling intermediaries and the situations appropriate for each.

Independent wholesaling intermediaries can be divided into two categories: merchant wholesalers and agents and brokers. The two major types of merchant wholesalers are full-function merchant wholesalers, such as rack jobbers, and limited-function merchant wholesalers, including cash-and-carry wholesalers, truck wholesalers, drop shippers, and mail-order wholesalers. Full-function wholesalers are common in the drug, grocery, and hardware industries.

  Limited-function wholesalers are sometimes used in the food, coal, lumber, cosmetics, jewelry, sporting goods, and general merchandise industries. Agents and brokers do not take title to the products they sell; this category includes commission merchants, auction houses, brokers, selling agents, and manufacturers' agents. Commission merchants are common in the marketing of agricultural products. Auction houses are used to sell tobacco, used cars, livestock, furs, and fruit. Brokers are prevalent in the real estate, frozen foods, and used machinery industries. Finally, companies seeking to develop new sales territories, firms with unrelated lines, and smaller firms use manufacturers' agents.

7. Compare the basic types of direct marketing and nonstore retailing.

Direct marketing is a distribution channel consisting of direct communication to a consumer or business recipient. It generates orders and sales leads that may result in future orders. Since direct marketing responds to fragmented media markets and audiences, growth of customized products, and shrinking network broadcast audiences, marketers consider it an important part of their planning efforts. While most U.S. retail sales take place in stores, such nonstore retailing activities as direct mail, direct selling, direct-response retailing, telemarketing, Internet retailing, and automatic merchandising are important in marketing many types of goods and services.

8. Explain the ways in which the Internet has altered the wholesaling, retailing, and direct marketing environments.

The Internet has affected everything from how supply networks operate to how relationships are formed with customers. Successful wholesalers have carved out a niche as a source of expertise offering faster, more efficient, Web-enabled distribution and fulfillment. The Internet has allowed retailers to enhance their merchandising mix and their customer service by, among other things, giving them access to much broader selections of goods. Direct marketers have merged their traditional catalog or direct mail programs with an Internet interface that allows for faster, more efficient, and more frequent contact with customers and prospects.

Marketing Terms You Need to Know

retailing 466	markdown 471	wholesaler 480	direct marketing 486
wheel of retailing 467	planned shopping center 472	wholesaling intermediary 480	
stockkeeping unit (SKU) 470	retail convergence 480	broker 485	
markup 471	scrambled merchandising 480	manufacturers' agent 485	

Other Important Marketing Terms

atmospherics 475	general merchandise	supercenter 479	drop shipper 484
convenience retailer 476	retailer 478	merchant wholesaler 483	mail-order wholesaler 484
specialty retailer 476	department store 478	rack jobber 484	commission merchant 485
limited-line store 478	mass merchandiser 479	truck wholesaler	selling agent 485
category killer 478	discount house 479	(truck jobber) 484	

Review Questions

1. How do retailers identify target markets? Explain the major strategies by which retailers reach their target markets.
2. What is the current status of shopping center development in the U.S.? Describe the major types of shopping centers.
3. Outline the five bases for categorizing retailers. Cite examples of each subclassification.
4. Identify the major types of general merchandise retailers. Cite examples of each type.
5. Define the term *scrambled merchandising*. Why has this practice become so common in retailing?
6. What is a wholesaling intermediary? Describe its function(s) in a marketing strategy.
7. Distinguish among the different types of manufacturer-owned wholesaling intermediaries. What conditions might suit each one?
8. What is a broker's main function? How are they paid for their work?
9. Differentiate between direct selling and direct-response retailing. Cite examples of both.
10. Define automatic merchandising. Explain its role in U.S. retailing today and in the future.

Projects and Teamwork Exercises

1. Research and then classify each of the following retailers:
   a. Circuit City
   b. Petite Sophisticates
   c. Limited
   d. Ethan Allen Galleries
   e. Macy's

2. In small groups, visit a local Wal-Mart store and observe such aspects as product placement, shelf placement, inventory levels on shelves, traffic patterns, customer service, and checkout efficiency. Discuss what makes Wal-Mart the world's most successful retailer.
3. Target has become known for trendy clothes and stylish housewares, all readily available in spacious stores at reasonable prices. With your team, visit a local Target store or the company's Web site and compare its product selection to your local hardware store and/or a department store. Make a list of each store's advantages and disadvantages, including convenience, location, selection, service, and general prices. Do any of their product lines overlap? How are they different from each other? Which would your team members visit most often?
4. In pairs, match each industry with the most appropriate type of wholesaling intermediary.
   _____ hardware
   _____ perishable foods
   _____ lumber
   _____ wheat
   _____ used cars
   a. drop shipper
   b. truck wholesaler
   c. auction house
   d. full-function merchant wholesaler
   e. commission merchant
5. In teams, develop a retailing strategy for an Internet retailer. Identify a target market and then suggest a mix of merchandise, promotion, service, and pricing strategies that would help a retailer to reach that market via the Internet. What issues must Internet retailers address that do not affect traditional store retailers?

'net Work

1. Retailing strategy. Go to http://www.bn.com and answer the following questions regarding the retailing strategy at this site:
   a. Describe the target market.
   b. Describe several elements that combine to establish the site's retail image—such factors as merchandising strategy, customer service standards, and "store atmospherics."
http://www.bn.com

2. Location strategy. Alberta's West Edmonton Mall promotes itself as the largest enclosed shopping center in the world. Visit the mall's Web site and list the factors that make this mall's location a desirable one. Does a mall in your area share any of these three factors?
http://www.westedmall.com

3. Slotting allowances. Visit the FTC's Web site and conduct a search for information on slotting allowances. Read two or three articles, print the article you found to be the most insightful, and bring it to class to contribute to a discussion on the topic.
http://www.ftc.gov

Note: Internet Web addresses change frequently. If you don't find the exact sites listed, you may need to access the organization or company's home page and search from there.

CASE 16.1   Retail Rocks around the Clock

Sometimes ordering within minutes online for express next-day delivery is simply not fast enough. In today's 24/7 society, it's no longer considered unreasonable to demand a must-have video at midnight or a deli-fresh sandwich at 3 A.M. The consumer's desire for instant gratification—regardless of the time of day or the price to pay—is changing the way we live and turning business operations inside out.

Round-the-clock retailing has its roots in the Internet. Consumers quickly adapted to browsing, chatting, and buying at all hours and gradually became impatient with stores that shut their doors at 9:00 or 10:00 P.M. In particular, dual working parents, people working off-shifts, and young adults ready to party the night away sought greater flexibility.

As a result, 24/7 has become marketing chic. In urban populations, everything from beauty salons to health clubs to golf practice ranges to bookstores remains open from dusk to dawn. During a recent Van Gogh exhibit, the Los Angeles County Museum of Modern Art cashed in by staying open 64 hours straight. While the costs of operating are slightly higher, many businesses are realizing 10 to 15 percent of sales during the wee hours. And some ask a surcharge for the convenience of all-night service.

Besides convenience stores like 7-Eleven, grocery chains and big-box retailers like Wal-Mart and Home Depot were among the first to open 24 hours. Houston's Woodforest National Bank, with branches inside Wal-Mart staffed by a night manager and a teller, credits the extended hours with bringing in 15 percent of new business. Health club chain 24 Hour Fitness esti-mates that all-night service brings in $50 million in revenue each year—at the extra cost of only $5 million.

All-night shopping does not pan out everywhere, however. For instance, tests in low-density populations like Ottawa, Canada, where night work is not common, have failed even for Home Depot. Contrast this with Japan's crowded cities where 24-hour stores are fast becoming the norm, easing congestion in aisles and in parking lots.

Round-the-clock cravings have also led to a revival of automated merchandising. Zoom Systems Inc. has reengineered traditional vending machines to offer a wide range of gifts, flowers, books, and even cameras. Located at airports and in hotel lobbies, the machines advertise their merchandise on animated commercials on computer screens. Since payments are by credit card and locations are secure, high-priced items are not a problem.

Questions for Critical Thinking

1. Discuss the impact of 24-hour retailing on wholesaling and traditional retailing.
2. How might round-the-clock retailers leverage the Internet to maximize revenues and control costs?

SOURCES: Cheryl Rosen, *InformationWeek,* http://www.informationweek.com, accessed March 15, 2003; "24-Hour Stores Becoming Norm," http://www.japanupdate.com, April 16, 2002; Courtney Prieur, "Shopping Around the Clock in Ottawa," http://www.ottawainsight.com, March 2002; Bruce Horowitz, "24/7 Almost a Way of Life," *USA Today,* August 1, 2001, p. 1B.

VIDEO CASE 16.2   Neiman Marcus Takes Care of Its Customers

The written case on Neiman Marcus appears on page VC-19. The recently filmed Neiman Marcus video is designed to expand and highlight the concepts in this chapter and the concepts and questions covered in the written video case.

Krispy Kreme Continuing Case for Part 6 appears on page KK-12.

Part 7

Promotional Strategy

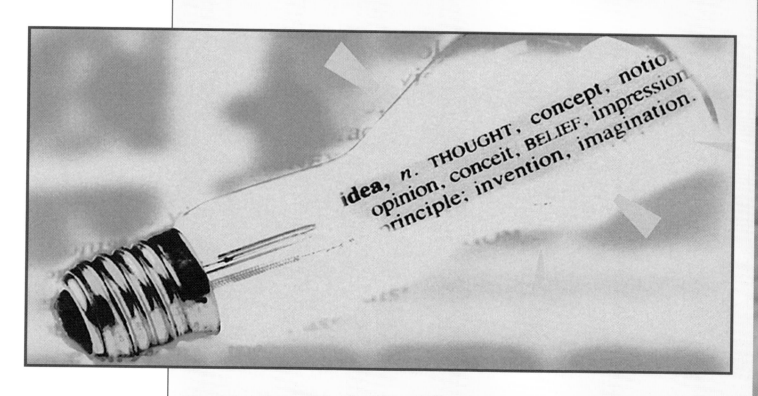

17
Integrated Marketing Communications

[handwritten: Chapt 15]

*[handwritten: Promo Mix
— Advertising
— Public Relations
— Sales Promotion
— Personal Sales]*

Chapter Objectives

1 Discuss how integrated marketing communications relates to the development of an optimal promotional mix.

2 Describe the communication process and how it relates to the AIDA concept.

3 Discuss how the promotional mix relates to the objectives of promotion.

4 Identify the different elements of the promotional mix and explain how marketers develop an optimal promotional mix.

5 Discuss the role of sponsorships and direct marketing in integrated marketing communications.

6 Contrast the two major alternative promotional strategies.

7 Explain how marketers budget for and measure the effectiveness of promotion.

8 Discuss the value of marketing communications.

How Marketers Plan to Reach You

Just in case you aren't already aware of it, marketers want you. Unless you returned to school at a later age, as a "traditional" college student you most likely fall between the ages of 18 and 24, an age group that marketers are eager to reach. According to research, people in this age group spend more than $200 billion a year on consumer goods and services. "There is heavy competition among marketers for those consumer dollars," says Derek White of research firm Alloy, Inc.

Although you've already had considerable experience in purchasing various products, you haven't necessarily developed long-term loyalty to particular brands. You might be more willing to try a new or interesting product than older consumers. And although you haven't yet bought many big-ticket items, except maybe your first car, within a few years you'll be earning serious money and looking for furniture, appliances, electronics, clothing, vacations, a more expensive car—and eventually your own home. Marketers want to capture your attention now—while you are still open to new ideas. "College is the place that you adopt spending habits that you keep for the rest of your life," explains Dennis Roche, chief operating officer for YouthStream Media Networks.

The challenge is, even though there are millions of you around the country, you aren't so easy to reach through traditional advertising media. As a group, you don't watch much network TV, you don't read many newspapers, and you are skeptical of traditional advertising anyway. So marketers are adapting their strategies in the hunt for your attention. They are changing their mix of promotional activities and devising innovative ways to get their messages to you. For one thing, they are packing up and taking their messages—and products—on the road to you. Spring break is the one time of the year when the most college students—about 500,000—gather in concentrated areas, so

marketers eagerly engage in their special brand of guerilla marketing during this time. They head to the beach and ski slopes to tell you and show you about their products. "Wherever [college students] are having fun, marketers are all asking themselves: How can we play with our customers today?" says Janine Lopiano of Sputnik, a youth culture marketing firm. During one recent spring break in Panama City Beach, Florida, Panasonic set up tents where students could try out its new SD-AV10 recorder. Sony took its newest video game, Hot Shots Golf 3, to the same beach, where it hosted video tournaments. Old Spice handed out its disposable Old Spice Cool Contact Towels to students who were baking in the hot sand. And the WB promoted its new TV show, "My Guide to Becoming a Rock Star," by hosting a pretend-to-be-a-rock-star contest on the beach.

Next time you go on spring break—even if you hang around campus—take note of the efforts that marketers make to reach you. "Let's go to the nerve center of it all," says Ryan Bowling of Sony Computer Entertainment. As a college student, you happen to be that nerve center.[1]

Chapter Overview

Three of the four components of the marketing mix—product, pricing, and distribution strategies—were discussed in previous chapters. The following three chapters in Part 7 analyze the fourth marketing mix variable—promotion. **Promotion** is the function of informing, persuading, and influencing the consumer's purchase decision.

This chapter introduces the concept of integrated marketing communications, briefly describes the elements of a firm's promotional mix—personal and nonpersonal selling—and explains the characteristics that determine the success of the mix. Next, the chapter identifies the objectives of promotion and describes the importance of developing promotional budgets and measuring the effectiveness of promotion. Finally, the chapter discusses the importance of the business, economic, and social aspects of promotion. Chapter 18 covers advertising, sales promotion, and the other nonpersonal selling elements of the promotional mix. Chapter 19 completes this part of the book by focusing on personal selling.

Throughout this book, special emphasis has been given to new information that focuses on how technology is changing the way marketers approach communication, the transmission of a message from a sender to a receiver. Consumers receive **marketing communications**—messages that deal with buyer-seller relationships—from a variety of media, including television, magazines, and the Internet. Marketers can broadcast an ad on the Web to mass markets or design a customized appeal targeted to a small market segment. Each message the customer receives from any source represents the brand, company, or organization. A company needs to coordinate all these messages so the consumer doesn't completely tune them out.

To prevent this loss of attention, marketers are turning to **integrated marketing communications (IMC),** which coordinate all promotional activities—media advertising, direct mail, personal selling, sales promotion, and public relations—to produce a unified, customer-focused promotional message. IMC is a broader concept than marketing communications and promotional strategy. It uses database technology to refine the marketer's understanding of the target audience, segment this audience, and select the best type of media for each segment.

This chapter shows that IMC involves not only the marketer but also all other organizational units that interact with the consumer. Marketing managers set the goals and objectives of the firm's promotional strategy in accordance with overall organizational objectives and marketing goals. Based on these objectives, the various elements of the promotional strategy—personal selling, advertising, sales promotion, direct marketing, publicity, and public relations—are formulated into an integrated communications plan. This plan becomes a central part of the firm's total marketing strategy to reach its selected market segments. The feedback mechanism, including marketing research and field reports, completes the system by identifying any deviations from the plan and suggesting improvements.

1

Discuss how integrated marketing communications relates to the development of an optimal promotional mix.

Integrated Marketing Communications

Stop and think for a moment about all the marketing messages you receive in a single day. You click on the television for the morning news, and you see plenty of commercials. Listen to the car radio on the way to work or school, and you can sing along with the jingles. You get catalogs, coupons, and flyers in the mail. People even leave promotional flyers stuck under your car's windshield wiper while it sits in the parking lot. When you log on to your computer, you're deluged with banner and pop-up ads and even e-mail from marketers. Even an annoying phone call during dinner from a telemarketer is a message. Marketers know that you are receiving many types of communication. They know they need to compete for your attention. So they look for ways to reach you in a coordinated manner through integrated marketing communications.

Successful marketers use the marketing concept and relationship marketing to develop customer-oriented marketing programs. The customer is also at the heart of integrated marketing communications. An IMC strategy begins not with the organization's goods and services but with consumer wants or needs and then works in reverse to the product, brand, or organization. It sends receiver-focused rather than product-focused messages.

Rather than separating the parts of the promotional mix, IMC looks at these elements from the consumer's viewpoint: as information about the brand, company, or organization. Even though the messages come from different sources—sales presentations, TV, radio, newspaper, billboards, direct mail, coupons, public relations, the Internet, and online services—consumers may perceive them as "advertising" or a "sales pitch." IMC broadens promotion to include all the ways a customer has contact with an organization, adding to traditional media and direct mail such sources as packaging, store displays, sales literature, and online and interactive media. Unless the organization takes an integrated approach to present a unified, consistent message, it may send conflicting information that confuses consumers. Figure 17.1 illustrates how several organizations—including a television network, a manufacturer, and a major retailer—joined together to create a unified marketing message about family first aid and products that can help consumers have a safe summer.

Today's marketing environment is characterized by many diverse markets and media, creating both opportunities and challenges. The success of any IMC program depends on identifying the members of an audience and understanding what they want. Without good current information about existing and potential customers, their purchase histories, needs, and wants, marketers may send the wrong message. But they cannot succeed simply by improving the quality of the messages or by sending more of them. IMC must not only deliver messages to intended audiences but also gather responses from them. Databases and interactive marketing are important IMC tools that help marketers collect information from customers and then segment markets according to demographics and preferences. Marketers can then design specialized communications programs to meet the needs of particular segments.

Art museums often face an uphill battle when it comes to attracting more visitors. It's even harder, sometimes, for television networks to get viewers to sit down and watch programming about art. But A&E Network met the challenge in promoting its special "Biography" series, *The Impressionists,* with a successful IMC campaign. Working in conjunction with the Civic Entertainment Group in New York, A&E contacted dozens of art museums around the country, whose regular customers matched the demographic profiles of A&E's viewers. A&E then supplied the museums with a "Fundraiser in a Box" promotional kit, complete with a 20-minute preview of the series, a customized press release and invitations, a handbook for producing fund-raising events (with special tips on French catering and music), a coupon for purchasing cheese and crackers, and two cases of Turning Leaf wine supplied by Gallo Wines. The museums loved it—and so did their visitors, who then tuned in to watch *The Impressionists.* A&E reported a viewing audience of 2.7 million households, which was 32 percent higher than its prime time average for that month.[2]

The increase in media options provides more ways to give consumers product information; however, it can also create information overload. Marketers have to spread available dollars across fragmented media markets and a wider range of promotional activities to achieve their communication goals. Mass media such as TV ads, while still useful, are no longer the mainstays of marketing campaigns. In 1960, a company could reach about 90 percent of U.S. consumers by advertising on the three major TV networks. Today, these network ads reach fewer than 60 percent. Audiences are also more fragmented. So to reach desired groups, organizations are turning to niche marketing by advertising in special-interest magazines; by purchasing time on cable TV channels to target consumers with

Marketing Dictionary

promotion Function of informing, persuading, and influencing a consumer's purchase decision.

marketing communications Messages that deal with buyer-seller relationships.

integrated marketing communications (IMC) Coordination of all promotional activities to produce a unified, customer-focused promotional message.

FIGURE 17.1
Joint Integrated Marketing Promotion by ABC's *Good Morning America,* **Band-Aid, and Target.**

sports, family, science, history, comedy, and women's interests; by reaching out through telecommunications like the Internet; and by sponsoring events and activities. Without an IMC program, marketers frequently encounter problems within their own organizations because separate departments have authority and responsibility for planning and implementing specific promotional mix elements.

The coordination of an IMC program frequently produces a competitive advantage based on synergy and interdependence among the various elements of the promotional mix. With an IMC strategy, marketers can create a unified personality for the product or brand by choosing the right elements from the promotional mix to send the message. At the same time, they can develop more narrowly focused plans to reach specific market segments and choose the best form of communication to send a particular message to a specific target audience. IMC provides a more effective way to reach and serve target markets than less coordinated strategies.

Importance of Teamwork

IMC requires a big-picture view of promotion planning, a total strategy including all marketing activities, not just promotion. Successful implementation of IMC requires that everyone involved in every aspect of promotion—public relations, advertising, personal selling, and sales promotion—function as a team. They must present a consistent, coordinated promotional effort at every point of customer contact with the organization. This way, they save time, money, and effort. They avoid duplication of efforts, increasing marketing effectiveness and reducing costs.

Teamwork involves both in-house resources and outside vendors. It involves marketing personnel; members of the sales force who deal with wholesalers, retailers, and organizational buyers; and customer service representatives. A firm gains nothing from a terrific advertisement featuring a toll-free telephone number that has unhelpful, surly operators on the other end. The company must train its representatives to send a single positive message to consumers and also to solicit information for the firm's customer database. Excedrin Migraine, featured in Figure 17.2, will have a successful promotional message if consumers can quickly receive the free sample offered and can easily access information at the Web site or via the toll-free number.

IMC also challenges the traditional role of the advertising agency. A single agency may no longer fulfill all of a client's communications requirements, including traditional advertising and sales promotions, interactive marketing, database development, direct marketing, and public relations. To best serve client needs, an agency must often assemble a team with members from other companies.

Role of Databases in Effective IMC Programs

With the growth of the Internet during the last 10 years, marketers have been given the power to gather more information faster and to organize it more easily than ever before in history. By sharing this detailed knowledge appropriately among all relative parties, a company can lay the foundation for a successful IMC program.

The move from mass marketing to a customer-specific marketing strategy—a characteristic of online marketing—requires not only a means of identifying and communicating with the firm's target market but also information regarding important characteristics of each prospective customer. As discussed in Chapter 6, organizations can compile different kinds of data into complete databases with customer information, including names and addresses, demographic data, lifestyle considerations, brand preferences, and buying behavior. This information provides critical guidance in designing an effective IMC strategy that achieves organizational goals and finds new opportunities for increased sales and profits.

Direct sampling is another method frequently used to quickly obtain customer opinions regarding a particular firm's goods and services. If you've ever received a free sample of bath soap, aspirin, or even a newspaper in your mailbox, you've been the recipient of direct sampling. Companies such as Illinois-based Snyder Communications use databases to target these promotions to certain consumers for companies. They might target a particular ethnic audience, such as Hispanic consumers, or they might target a particular age group, such as aging baby boomers.

FIGURE 17.2
Excedrin Migraine: Using Free Samples, a Web Site, and a Toll-free Number in an IMC Effort

The Communications Process

When you have a conversation with someone, do you wonder whether the person understood your message? Do you worry that you might not have heard the person correctly? Marketers have the same concerns—when they send a message to an intended audience or market, they want to make sure it gets through clearly and persuasively. That is why the communications process is so important to marketing. The top portion of Table 17.1 shows a general model of the communications process and its application to promotional strategy. The *sender* acts as the source in the communications system as he or she seeks to convey a *message* (a communication of information, advice, or a request) to a receiver. An effective message accomplishes three tasks:

2

Describe the communication process and how it relates to the AIDA concept.

1. It gains the receiver's attention.
2. It achieves understanding by both receiver and sender.
3. It stimulates the receiver's needs and suggests an appropriate method of satisfying them.

The table also provides several examples of promotional messages. Although the types of promotion may vary from a highly personalized sales presentation to such nonpersonal promotions as television advertising and dollar-off coupons, each goes through every stage in the communications process.

The three tasks just listed are related to the **AIDA concept** (attention-interest-desire-action), the steps consumers take in reaching a purchase decision. First, the promotional message must gain the potential consumer's attention. It then seeks to arouse interest in the good or service. At the next stage, it stimulates desire by convincing the would-be buyer of the product's ability to satisfy his or her needs. Finally, the sales presentation, advertisement, or sales promotion technique attempts to produce action in the form of a purchase or a more favorable attitude that may lead to future purchases.

The message must be *encoded,* or translated into understandable terms, and transmitted through a communications channel. *Decoding* is the receiver's interpretation of the message.

Marketing Dictionary

AIDA concept   Explanation of steps through which an individual reaches a purchase decision: attention, interest, desire, and action.

TABLE 17.1   **Relating Promotion to the Communications Process**

TYPE OF PROMOTION	SENDER	ENCODING BY SENDER	CHANNEL	DECODING BY RECEIVER	RESPONSE	FEEDBACK
Personal selling	IBM e-solutions networking system	Sales presentation on new applications of system	IBM sales representative	Office manager and employees discuss sales presentation and those of competing suppliers.	Order is placed for IBM e-solutions system installation.	Customer asks about a second system for subsidiary company.
Dollar-off coupon (sales promotion)	Kellogg's Special K cereal	Coupons prepared by Kellogg's marketing department and advertising agency	Coupon insert in Sunday newspaper	Newspaper reader sees coupon for Special K cereal and saves it.	Special K is purchased by consumer using coupon.	Kellogg researchers see increase in market share.
Television advertising	Styx River Water World	Advertisement developed by Styx River's advertising agency featuring the new park rides	Network television ads during program with high percentages of viewers under 20 years old	Teens and young adults see ad and decide to try out the new park.	Water World tickets are purchased.	Customers purchase season ticket packages for Water World.

The receiver's response, known as *feedback,* completes the system. Throughout the process, *noise* can interfere with the transmission of the message and reduce its effectiveness.

The marketing manager is the message sender in Table 17.1. He or she encodes the message in the form of sales presentations, advertising, displays, or publicity releases. The *channel* for delivering the message may be a salesperson, a public relations outlet, or an advertising medium. Decoding is often the most troublesome step in marketing communications because consumers do not always interpret promotional messages in the same way that senders do. Since receivers usually decode messages according to their own frames of reference or experiences, a sender must carefully encode a message in a way that matches the frame of reference of the target audience. Consumers today receive many sales messages through many media channels. This communications traffic can create confusion as noise in the channel increases. Consumers choose to process only a few messages each, and ignored messages waste communications budgets. Marketers for Sharp, a leading producer of copiers and electronics products, wanted to convey the message that their new wireless device delivers clear communication and computing capabilities to users—wherever they happen to be. So they juxtaposed an image of the source of a creative idea—the sandcastle—with the tagline "be brilliant" above the business message being sent on the device and the words "be sharp." A simple glance at the ad, shown in Figure 17.3, tells consumers that the Zaurus mobile tool delivers accurate, unrestricted communication, allowing people to maintain their wireless connections, even at the beach.

The AIDA concept is also vital to online marketers. It is not enough to say a Web site has effective content or high response rates. Marketers must know just how many "eyeballs" are looking at the site, how often they come to view a message, and what they are examining. Most important, they must find out what consumers do besides just look. The bottom line is that if nobody is responding to a Web site, it might as well not exist. According to Bill White, vice president of sales for financial services site

The Motley Fool, "A few years ago, advertisers just wanted to get on the Internet. Today it's all about return on investment (ROI)."[3] Experts advise attracting users' attention by including people in advertisements and other communications in addition to new content and formats. Marketers at iwon.com alternate the sizes of their customers' ads, as well as balancing the types of ads that appear on the site. Ad sales increased 37 percent during the following year as a result of greater response to varying messages.[4]

Feedback, the receiver's response to the message, provides a way for marketers to evaluate the effectiveness of the message and tailor their responses accordingly. Feedback may take the form of attitude changes, purchases, or nonpurchases. In some instances, organizations use promotion to create favorable attitudes toward their goods or services in the hope of future purchases. Other promotional communications have the objective of directly stimulating consumer purchases. Marketers using infomercials that urge the viewer to call a toll-free number to place orders for music

FIGURE 17.3
Sending a Clear Marketing Message

collections, the latest fitness fad, or other products can easily measure the success of their objective by counting the number of calls they receive that result in orders.

A few years ago, marketers at Mars Inc., one of the nation's largest candy makers, launched a novel promotional campaign inviting consumers to vote on a new color to include in packages of M&M® chocolate candies. Even though colors on each candy shell are flavorless, maintaining purchaser interest of the brand (first introduced in 1941) was essential in maintaining high sales levels—and extensive promotions were used to urge consumers to participate in a series of color-naming contests. The ad shown in Figure 17.4 illustrates a recent contest in which global participants were asked to choose from among pink, purple, and aqua. (Purple won.) Comparisons of participation rates over time assisted marketers in assessing the effectiveness of each promotion.

Even nonpurchases may serve as feedback to the sender. Failure to purchase may result from ineffective communication in which the receivers do not believe or remember the message. Alternatively, the message may have failed to persuade the receiver that the firm's goods or services are superior to those of its competitors. Marketers frequently gather feedback through such techniques as marketing research studies and field sales reports.

Noise represents interference at some stage in the communications process. It may result from disruptions such as transmissions of competing promotional messages over the same communications channel, misinterpretation of a sales presentation or advertising message, receipt of the promotional message by the wrong person, or random events such as people conversing or leaving the room during a television commercial. Noise can also result from distractions within an advertising message itself.

Noise can be especially problematic in international communications. Disruption often results from too many competing messages. Italian television channels, for instance, broadcast all advertisements during a single half-hour slot each night. Noise might stem from differences in technology, such as a bad telephone connection, or from poor translations into other languages. Nonverbal cues, such as body language and tone of voice, are important parts of the communication process, and cultural differences may lead to noise and misunderstandings. For example, in the U.S., the round o sign made with the thumb and first finger means "okay." However, in Mediterranean countries, it means "zero" or "the worst." A Tunisian interprets this same sign as "I'll kill you," and to a Japanese it means "money."

Perhaps the most misunderstood language for U.S. marketers is English. It is often said that the 74 English-speaking nations are separated by a common language. The following examples illustrate how

**FIGURE 17.4
Collecting Feedback
on Promotional
Effectiveness by
Using Contests**

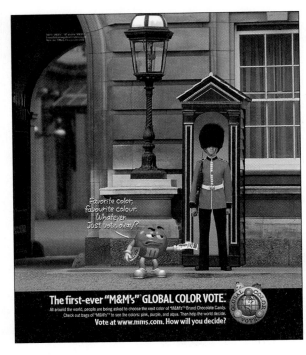

easy it can be for marketers to make mistakes in English-language promotional messages:

- *Underpants:* pants (Britain), underdaks (Australia)
- *Police:* bobby (Britain), garda (Ireland), Mountie (Canada), police wallah (South Asia)
- *Porch:* stoep (South Africa), gallery (Caribbean)
- *Bar:* pub (Britain), hotel (Australia), boozer (Australia, Britain, New Zealand)
- *Bathroom:* loo (Britain), dunny (Australia), lav (Britain, South Africa)
- *Ghost or monster:* wendigo (Canada), duppy (Caribbean), taniwha (New Zealand)
- *Barbecue:* braai (South Africa), barbie (Australia)
- *Pickup truck:* bakkie (South Africa), ute (Australia), utility vehicle (New Zealand)

Faulty communications can be especially risky on a global level, where noise can lead to some interesting misinterpretations. Here are three recent international examples:

- *On a sign in a Bucharest hotel lobby:* The lift is being fixed for the next day. During that time, we regret that you will be unbearable.
- *From a Japanese information booklet about using a hotel air conditioner:* Cooles and Heates: If you want just condition of warm in your room, please control yourself.
- *In an Acapulco hotel:* The manager has personally passed all the water served here.

3

**Discuss how the pro-
motional mix relates to
the objectives of pro-
motion.**

Objectives of Promotion Read

What specific tasks should promotion accomplish? The answers to this question seem to vary as much as the sources consulted. Generally, however, marketers identify the following objectives for promotion:

1. Provide information to consumers and others.
2. Increase demand.
3. Differentiate a product.
4. Accentuate a product's value.
5. Stabilize sales.

Provide Information

The traditional function of promotion was to inform the market about the availability of a particular good or service, as described in the "Marketing Hits" box about JetBlue Airways. In fact, marketers still direct much of their current promotional efforts at providing product information for potential customers. An advertisement for a musical performance typically provides information about the performer, time, and place. A commercial for a theme park offers information about rides, location, and admission price. Information can also help differentiate a product from its competitors by focusing on its features or benefits.

In addition to traditional print and broadcast advertising, marketers often distribute a number of high-tech, low-cost tools to give consumers product information. One such tool, the information-packed videocassette, is currently used for products ranging from cosmetics to automobiles to exercise equipment. In fact, one college recently sent videos to alumni in an attempt to increase attendance at their upcoming reunion. A 10-minute video costs about $1.50 to duplicate and send (not including production costs), compared with $8 or more for a full-color brochure. Consumers are more likely to regard the video as a novelty that stands out from other promotions, so they are less likely to throw out the cassette. In fact, 9 of every 10 recipients take the time to view them. In some cases, response rates are as high as 49 percent and returns on investment exceed 1,000 percent. These figures translate into substantial profits for companies involved in video promotions.

Many companies also send CDs containing software that provides information about or sampling of a product or service. Music companies and Internet service providers such as AOL are regular users of this promotional technique.

Increase Demand

Most promotions pursue the objective of increasing demand for a good or service. Some promotions are aimed at increasing *primary demand,* the desire for a general product category such as HDTVs or DVD players. This type of promotion is more typical for marketers who decide to expand overseas, creating new markets for their products in other parts of the world. When Procter & Gamble first introduced its Pampers disposable diapers in Hungary, most parents were using overpants with paper inserts to diaper their babies. So early Pampers television ads focused on generating interest in the novel product.

More promotions, however, are aimed at increasing *selective demand,* the desire for a specific brand. Denny's restaurant chain decided to stimulate selective demand for its food and service by offering free kids' meals every night. During the promotion, two children under the age of 10 years received a free dinner with each adult entree purchased. The kids' meals cost the restaurant only about 50 cents to give away but could bring in about $14 worth of business when the parents each ordered a meal. In addition, Denny's tailored to kids' tastes by offering mini–corn dogs and dinosaur-shaped chicken nuggets in an effort to create a preference for Denny's among children.[5]

Differentiate the Product

A frequent objective of the firm's promotional efforts is *product differentiation.* Homogeneous demand for many products results when consumers regard the firm's output as virtually identical to its competitors' products. In these cases, the individual firm has almost no control over marketing variables such as price. A differentiated demand schedule, in contrast, permits more flexibility in marketing strategy, such as price changes.

Marketing Hit

Up, Up, and Away with JetBlue

Background. In some respects, JetBlue Airways couldn't have taken off at a worse time. The airline's first flights took to the skies from its New York base in 2000, serving smaller airports outside major cities, such as the Los Angeles suburb of Long Beach.

The Challenge. Then came September 11, 2001—and the airline industry nearly tumbled from the sky. How could JetBlue possibly win passengers who not only didn't want to fly but most of whom still didn't even know the company existed?

The Strategy. Even before the disaster, JetBlue was committed to unorthodox marketing strategies. Instead of plastering the airwaves and print media with traditional commercials, JetBlue sent college interns out to the beaches, boardwalks, hotels, restaurants, and bars to hand out bumper stickers, Frisbees, buttons, and tote bags with the airline's logo printed on them. These barefoot beachcombers were backed by Volkswagen Beetles painted in JetBlue colors. The word began to spread—JetBlue would offer cheaper fares than the big carriers but throw in luxury features such as leather seats and individual passenger access to DirectTV satellite television. Cutting expenses like in-flight meals and paper tickets helped hold the costs down.

The Outcome. Within six months, the company had 23 Airbus planes flying to 19

continued on next page

Marketing Hit

cities, including Tampa and Rochester, New York, with plans to add 60 more planes by the end of 2007. Perhaps because the company didn't have much to lose in September 2001, JetBlue was one of only three carriers to post profits for that year, and it did not lay off a single employee. Industry watchers liked what they saw, even if the marketing tactics were a bit unusual.

SOURCES: JetBlue Airways Web site, **http://www.jet blue.com**, accessed January 24, 2003; Amy Tsao, "Thinking of Taking Off with JetBlue?" *BusinessWeek Online,* April 5, 2002, **http://www.businessweek.com**; Chris Woodyard, "JetBlue Turns to Beetles, Beaches, Bars," *USA Today,* August 22, 2001, p. 3B.

FIGURE 17.5
EarthLink: Focusing on Increased Market Share by Differentiating Its Service

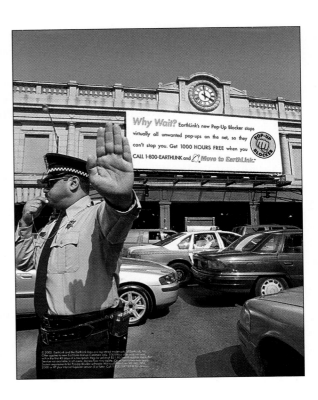

Surveys focusing on the Internet experience often list pop-up ads as the most annoying online experience. So marketers at Atlanta-based EarthLink came up with an idea: offer subscribers software to block them. Although the 4.9 million subscribers to the USA's No. 3 Internet service provider sound like small change in an industry dominated by industry giant AOL, EarthLink based its recent market growth strategy on offering a solution to the estimated 4.8 billion ads that pop up on computer screens worldwide every month. As Figure 17.5 shows, EarthLink combines its Pop-Up Blocker feature with 1,000 hours free to new subscribers.[6]

Accentuate the Product's Value

Promotion can explain the greater ownership utility of a product to buyers, thereby accentuating its value and justifying a higher price in the marketplace. This objective benefits both consumer and business products. A firm's promotional messages must build brand image and equity and at the same time deliver a "call to action." Advertising typically offers reasons why a good or service fits into the consumer's lifestyle. Today, consumers everywhere value their time; the challenge for marketers is to demonstrate how their products will make their life better.

Best Western and Shell recently teamed up in a "Sleep and Win" promotion in which Best Western hotel guests received a scratch-and-win card offering one of 15 Jaguars and Ford Explorers, free or discounted room nights, or gas redeemable at more than 10,000 Shell stations. Ramada countered with a "Getaway for Life Sweepstakes" in which guests staying at Ramada Inns had a chance to win an annual week-long vacation at any Ramada for life.[7]

Stabilize Sales

For the typical firm, sales are not uniform throughout the year. Sales fluctuations may result from cyclical, seasonal, or irregular demand. Stabilizing these variations is often an objective of promotional strategy. Coffee sales, for example, follow a seasonal pattern, with purchases and consumption increasing during the winter months. To stimulate summer sales of Sanka brand decaffeinated coffee, General

'net =x

Promotional mix. Visit three or four prominent e-commerce retailers, including at least one that has brick-and-mortar stores in addition to its Web-based store, such as Old Navy or Eddie Bauer. Write a brief report comparing and contrasting the promotional mix used by each retailer.

Foods created ads that include a recipe for instant iced coffee, promoting it as a refreshing, caffeine-free summer beverage. Hotels and motels often seek to supplement high occupancy during the week from business travelers by promoting special weekend packages with lower room rates. Some firms sponsor sales contests during slack periods that offer prizes to sales personnel who meet goals.

Elements of the Promotional Mix

Like the marketing mix, the **promotional mix** requires a carefully designed blend of variables to satisfy the needs of a company's customers and achieve organizational objectives. The promotional mix works like a subset of the marketing mix, with its product, pricing, distribution, and promotion elements. With the promotional mix, the marketers attempt to blend various elements optimally to achieve promotional objectives. The components of the promotional mix are personal selling and nonpersonal selling, including advertising, sales promotion, direct marketing, public relations, and guerilla marketing.

Personal selling, advertising, and sales promotion usually account for the bulk of a firm's promotional expenditures. However, direct marketing, guerilla marketing, sponsorships, and public relations also contribute to integrated marketing communications. Later sections of this chapter examine the use of guerilla marketing, sponsorships, and direct marketing, and Chapters 18 and 19 present a detailed discussion of the other elements. This section defines the elements and discusses their advantages and disadvantages.

4

Identify the different elements of the promotional mix and explain how marketers develop an optimal promotional mix.

Personal Selling

Personal selling is the oldest form of promotion, dating back as far as the beginning of trading and commerce. Traders vastly expanded both market sizes and product varieties as they led horses and camels along the Silk Road from China to Europe roughly between 300 B.C. and A.D. 1600, conducting personal selling at both ends. Personal selling may be defined as a seller's promotional presentation conducted on a person-to-person basis with the buyer. This direct form of promotion may be conducted face to face, over the telephone, through videoconferencing, or through interactive computer links between the buyer and seller. Today, about 14 million people in the U.S. are employed in personal selling, and the average sales call costs about $300.

Nonpersonal Selling

Nonpersonal selling includes advertising, sales promotion, direct marketing, and public relations. Advertising and sales promotion are usually regarded as the most important forms of nonpersonal selling. About one-third of marketing dollars pay for media advertising, and two-thirds fund trade and consumer sales promotions.

Marketing Dictionary

promotional mix   Subset of the marketing mix in which marketers attempt to achieve the optimal blending of the elements of personal and nonpersonal selling to achieve promotional objectives.

personal selling   Seller's promotional presentation conducted on a person-to-person basis with the buyer.

nonpersonal selling   Promotion that includes advertising, sales promotion, direct marketing, and public relations—all conducted without being face-to-face with the buyer.

Advertising

Advertising is any paid, nonpersonal communication through various media about a business firm, not-for-profit organization, product, or idea by a sponsor identified in a message that is intended to inform or persuade members of a particular audience. It is a major promotional mix component for thousands of organizations. Mass consumption and geographically dispersed markets make advertising particularly appropriate for marketing goods and services using the same promotional messages to large audiences.

Advertising primarily involves the mass media, such as newspapers, television, radio, magazines, and billboards, but also includes electronic and computerized forms of promotion such as Web commercials, videotapes, and video screens in supermarkets. The rich potential of the Internet as an advertising channel to reach millions of people one at a time has attracted the attention of companies large and small, local and international.

Product Placement *when Ed is driving the new Lexus*

Product placement is a form of nonpersonal selling in which the marketer pays a motion picture or television program owner a fee to display his or her product prominently in the film or show. The practice gained attention more than two decades ago in the movie *E.T.: The Extraterrestrial* when E.T. dropped Reese's Pieces behind himself to mark a path. Product sales for Reese's Pieces candies went through the roof. (Interestingly, this was not the moviemakers' first choice of candy; Mars turned down the opportunity to have its M&Ms appear in the film.) Fees charged to marketers for such placements have grown significantly since then, and most studios employ specialists to market them to relevant product suppliers.

Sales Promotion *⇒ Anything the company is paying; not advertising. (Coupon sales)*

Sales promotion consists of marketing activities other than personal selling, advertising, and public relations that stimulate consumer purchasing and dealer effectiveness. This broad category includes displays, trade shows, coupons, contests, samples, premiums, product demonstrations, and various nonrecurring, irregular selling efforts. Sales promotion provides a short-term incentive, usually in combination with other forms of promotion, to emphasize, assist, supplement, or otherwise support the objectives of the promotional program. Restaurants, including those that serve fast food, often place certain items on the menu at a lower price "for a limited time only." Advertisements may contain coupons for free or discounted items for a specified period of time. Or companies may conduct sweepstakes for prizes such as new cars or vacations, which may even be completely unrelated to the products the companies are selling.

Movies are famous for sales promotions and tie-ins, which combine such products and toys and games with characters and themes from hit films. Disney's recent animated hit *Monsters, Inc.,* shown in Figure 17.6, attracted $80 million in promotional tie-ins from PepsiCo, McDonald's, and Kellogg. PepsiCo ran advertisements featuring the *Monsters, Inc.* characters, McDonald's ran promotions offering action

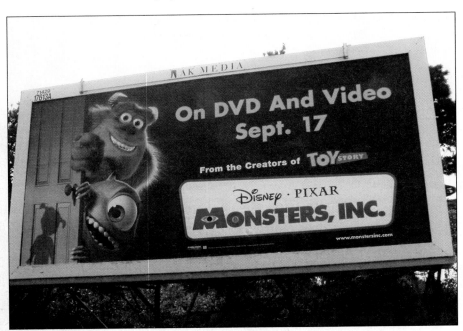

FIGURE 17.6
Sales Promotions Tied to Movies

figures and puzzles for Happy Meal customers, and Kellogg included a movie-branded spoon inside its cereal boxes.[8]

However, many companies that used to be involved with sales promotions, advertising, and tie-ins with movies are finding that they no longer get the return they were hoping for. Taco Bell, which lost money on promotions tied to recent releases in the six-film *Star Wars* movies, recently decided to abandon movie characters and focus its promotion on featuring expanded menu offerings. "It's less risky than tying in with a movie that may or may not be a hit—or might not help your product, even if it is," explains vice president Amy Sherwood.[9]

Sales promotion geared to marketing intermediaries is called *trade promotion*. Companies actually spend about as much on trade promotion as on advertising and consumer-oriented sales promotion combined. Trade promotion strategies include offering free merchandise, buyback allowances, and merchandise allowances along with sponsorship of sales contests to encourage wholesalers and retailers to sell more of certain products or product lines.

Direct Marketing no retailer

Another element in a firm's integrated promotional mix is **direct marketing,** the use of direct communication to a consumer or business recipient designed to generate a response in the form of an order (direct order), a request for further information (lead generation), or a visit to a place of business to purchase specific goods or services (traffic generation). While many people equate direct marketing with direct mail, this promotional category also includes telephone marketing (telemarketing), direct-response advertising and infomercials on television and radio, direct-response print advertising, and electronic media.

Public Relations and Publicity Free advertising (seems on show)

Public relations refer to a firm's communications and relationships with its various publics. These publics include customers, suppliers, stockholders, employees, the government, the general public, and the society in which the organization operates. Public relations programs can conduct either formal or informal contacts. The critical point is that every organization, whether or not it has a formally organized program, must be concerned about its public relations.

Publicity is an important part of an effective public relations effort. It can be defined as nonpersonal stimulation of demand for a good, service, person, cause, or organization through unpaid placement of significant news about it in a published medium or through a favorable presentation of it through radio, television, or the stage. Compared with personal selling, advertising, and even sales promotion, expenditures for public relations are usually low in most firms. Since companies do not pay for publicity, they have less control over the publication by the press or electronic media of good or bad company news. But this often means that consumers find this type of news source more believable than if the information were disseminated directly by the company. Of course, bad publicity can damage a company's reputation and diminish brand equity. Continental Tire, aware of the severe damage to the Bridgestone/Firestone brands following a series of accidents involving Ford Explorers when the tread separated from the tire and alerted to a heightened risk of tread separation, recently spent little time deciding to recall half a million tires installed as original equipment on Ford SUVs.[10]

Sometimes bad publicity is just a matter of bad luck, as happened to Major League Baseball's Houston Astros and the city of Houston. When the team and city needed to

Marketing Dictionary

advertising Any paid, nonpersonal communication through various media about a business firm, not-for-profit organization, product, or idea by a sponsor identified in a message that is intended to inform or persuade members of a particular audience.

sales promotion Marketing activities other than personal selling, advertising, and public relations that stimulate consumer purchasing and dealer effectiveness.

direct marketing Direct communications, other than personal sales contacts, between buyer and seller, designed to generate sales, information requests, or store or Web site visits.

public relations Firm's communications and relationships with its various publics.

Marketing Hit

Guerilla Marketing: PepsiCo's Code Red

Background. Sometimes a sneak attack works best. That's what Cie Nicholson, Mountain Dew's vice president, and her team of marketers discovered when they launched Code Red, a cherry-flavored extension of PepsiCo's Mountain Dew line.

The Challenge. Cracking the already saturated soft drink market is a tough assignment. Before Code Red, beverage sales in general were flat. So, when the sugar- and caffeine-laden Code Red hit convenience store shelves and vending machines in urban areas, marketers had to find a way to grab consumers' attention.

The Strategy. Based on research, PepsiCo's marketing team learned that Hispanic consumers preferred cherry-flavored beverages. They also found out from focus groups that young, urban, and ethnic consumers liked the name Code Red more than alternatives like Wild Cherry Mountain Dew. Ad agency UniWorld Group came up with a rap radio jingle called "Crack the Code" and placed ads in hip-hop magazines *Vibe* and the *Source*. But they avoided mass marketing. Instead, they stuck to guerilla marketing. Then two California computer programmers began staying up nights trying to crack a new computer virus. They drank Code Red to keep awake. And they liked the drink so much they named the virus "Code Red."

The Outcome. Soon Code Red became the fifth most popular soft drink sold in convenience stores. "With the urban youth audience, you really have to gain street credibility first, and you can't do that with a typical mass-marketing campaign," says Charles Taylor-Hines, PepsiCo's director of urban

continued on next page

raise additional funds for their state-of-the-art, gleaming new ballpark, they offered the naming rights to another company—an increasingly common practice. So when one of Houston's largest employers agreed to write a check for $30 million for the naming rights for a 30-year period, MLB and Houston fans breathed a sigh of relief. The glitch? The newly named field would be called Enron Field. The agreement was canceled by all parties following the Enron bankruptcy, and the Astros signed a $100 million, 28-year deal with Minute Maid (a unit of Coca-Cola) to rename the field Minute Maid Park.[11]

Guerilla Marketing Read

Guerilla marketing is a relatively new approach used by marketers whose firms are underfunded for a full marketing program. Many of these firms can't afford the huge costs involved in the orthodox media of print and broadcasting, so they need to find an innovative, low-cost way to reach their market. But some large companies, like PepsiCo, engage in guerilla marketing as well, as described in the "Marketing Hits" box. The results can be funny and outrageous—even offensive to some people. But they almost always get consumers' attention. Some guerilla marketers stencil their company and product names anywhere graffiti might appear. Marketers for Yoo-hoo, the chocolate milk drink (whose parent companies didn't want to spend valuable dollars on promoting the product) served Yoo-hoo in consumers' own shoes at their booth during a rock concert. The American Legacy Foundation decided to circulate its antismoking message—which it refers to as a "brand" called Truth—with a mobile program. Trucks outfitted with DJ decks, computer games, and Web access stopped at beaches, concerts, and skate parks, where they sent out teams armed with "Infect Truth" viral kits containing T-shirts, stickers, and bandannas. Truth teams weren't clean-cut geeks or baby boomers, either. They were rappers, boarders, skaters, and musicians—all of them ex-smokers delivering the harsh message of smoking's damage to the body. During the tour, Truth trucks reached more than 4 million teens, 850,000 of whom actually interacted with team members.[12]

As Table 17.2 indicates, each type of promotion has both advantages and shortcomings. Although personal selling entails a relatively high per-contact cost, it wastes less effort than do nonpersonal forms of promotion such as advertising. Personal selling often provides more flexible promotion than the other forms because the salesperson can tailor the sales message to meet the unique needs—or objections—of each potential customer.

The major advantages of advertising come from its ability to create instant awareness of a good, service, or idea; build brand equity; and deliver the marketer's message to mass audiences for a relatively low cost per contact. Major disadvantages of advertising include the difficulty in measuring its effectiveness and high media costs. Sales promotions, by contrast, can be more accurately monitored and measured than advertising, produce immediate consumer responses, and provide short-term sales increases. Direct marketing gives an action-oriented choice, permits narrow audience segmentation and customization of communications, and produces measurable results. Public relations efforts such as publicity frequently offer substantially higher credibility than other promotional techniques. Guerilla marketing efforts can be innovative—and highly effective—at a low cost to a company, as long as the tactics are not too outrageous, but it is more difficult to reach people. The marketer must determine the appropriate blend of these promotional mix elements to effectively market the firm's goods and services.

TABLE 17.2   Comparison of the Six Promotional Mix Elements

	PERSONAL SELLING	ADVERTISING	SALES PROMOTION	DIRECT MARKETING	PUBLIC RELATIONS	GUERILLA MARKETING
Advantages	Permits measurement of effectiveness Elicits an immediate response Tailors the message to fit the customer	Reaches a large group of potential consumers for a relatively low price per exposure Allows strict control over the final message Can be adapted to either mass audiences or specific audience segments	Produces an immediate consumer response Attracts attention and creates product awareness Allows easy measurement of results Provides short-term sales increases	Generates an immediate response Covers a wide audience with targeted advertising Allows complete, customized, personal message Produces measurable results	Creates a positive attitude toward a product or company Enhances credibility of a product or company	Is low cost Attracts attention because it is innovative Is less cluttered with competitors trying the same thing
Disadvantages	Relies almost exclusively upon the ability of the salesperson Involves high cost per contact	Does not permit totally accurate measurement of results Usually cannot close sales	Is nonpersonal in nature Is difficult to differentiate from competitors' efforts	Suffers from image problem Involves a high cost per reader Depends on quality and accuracy of mailing lists May annoy consumers	May not permit accurate measurement of effect on sales Involves much effort directed toward non-marketing-oriented goals	May not reach as many people If the tactics are too outrageous, they may offend some people

My autograph will be after this time   Jesus loves U. 03/28/07

Sponsorships *Read*

5

Discuss the role of sponsorships and direct marketing in integrated marketing communications.

One of the hottest trends in promotion during the past 10 years offers marketers the ability to integrate several elements of the promotional mix. Commercial sponsorships of an event or activity apply personal selling, advertising, sales promotion, and public relations in achieving specific promotional goals. These sponsorships link events with sponsors and with media ranging from TV and radio to print and the Internet, billions of dollars in business worldwide.

Sponsorship occurs when an organization provides cash or in-kind resources to an event or activity in exchange for a direct association with that event or activity. The sponsor purchases two things: (1) access to the activity's audience and (2) the image associated with the activity. Sponsorships typically involve advertising that includes direct mail, sales promotion, and personal selling at the event itself. They also involve relationship marketing, bringing together the event, its participants, and the sponsoring firms. Marketers underwrite varying levels of sponsorships depending on the amount their companies wish to spend and the types of events.

Sponsorship Spending

Global marketers have flocked to sponsorships as a means of reaching an increasingly segmented audience to leverage the equity of

Marketing Hit

and ethnic marketing. Code Red started a trend—since its launch, the beverage market has been flooded with other flavored drinks like Dr. Pepper Red Fusion. But none have lived up to Code Red.

SOURCES: Kenneth Hein, "Cracking the Code for Pepsi," *Brandweek*, October 14, 2002, pp. M13-M16; Theresa Howard, "Marketers of Colorful Drinks Dye for Big Sales," *USA Today*, May 5, 2002, http://www.usatoday.com.

Marketing Dictionary

guerilla marketing   Innovative, low-cost marketing schemes designed to get consumers' attention in unusual ways.

sponsorship   When an organization provides cash or in-kind resources to an event or activity in exchange for a direct association with that event or activity.

sports and entertainment properties. In addition, an army of e-commerce firms found sponsorships to be a quick way to enhance—and in many cases, initiate—brand awareness. Sponsorships also provide a platform through which sports and entertainment properties can expand their programs and attract new partners. Even utilities and pharmaceutical firms that sell over-the-counter medication and prescription drugs are also increasing their activities. In a recent year, more than 60 companies spent more than $10 million on sponsorships. Altria is the largest sponsor with over $145 million in sponsorship commitments. Anheuser-Busch is second and General Motors is third, followed by The Coca-Cola Company and rival PepsiCo. Total sponsorship spending more than tripled over the past 10 years to almost $10 billion.[13]

Nowhere is sponsorship more prevalent than at sports events. Total spending for sports marketing in one recent year was $35 billion; about $6.4 billion of that was devoted to sponsorships. One of the biggest deals of the year was among CBS, the National Collegiate Athletic Association, and The Coca-Cola Company. In the $500 million agreement, the Coca-Cola brand appeared on everything from the NCAA championships to CBS broadcasts of the "March Madness" basketball finals.

Growth of Sponsorships

Commercial sponsorship of sporting and cultural events is not a new phenomenon. Aristocrats in ancient Rome sponsored gladiator competitions and chariot races featuring teams that were often supported financially by competing businesses. Over 2,000 years ago, wealthy Athenians underwrote drama, musical, and sporting festivals. Craft guilds in 14th-century England sponsored plays (occasionally insisting that the playwrights insert "plugs" for their lines of work in the scripts). In the U.S. during the 1880s, streetcar companies commonly sponsored local baseball teams.

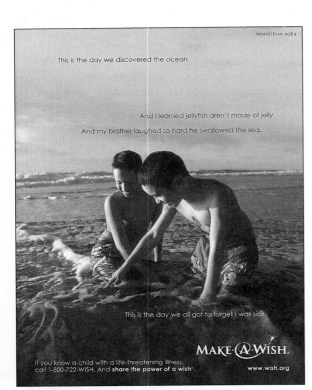

The Make-A-Wish Foundation® grants the wishes of children with life-threatening illnesses to enrich their lives with hope, strength, and joy. The Foundation is funded by numerous corporate sponsorships, which are described on the Foundation's Web site at http://www.wish.org.

Sponsorship as a promotional alternative has grown rapidly over the past three decades. During this period, corporate sponsorship spending has increased faster than promotional outlays for advertising and sales promotion. Several factors have influenced the growth of commercial sponsorships:

- Government restrictions on tobacco and alcohol advertising and the growing reluctance of newspaper and magazine publishers to accept print ads for alcoholic beverages and tobacco products have led marketers to seek alternative promotional media.

- Escalating costs of traditional advertising media make commercial sponsorships cost-effective marketing tools.

- Additional opportunities resulting from diverse leisure activities, as well as the increasing array of sporting events featured on television and in newspapers and magazines, allow marketers to target specific audiences.

- Greater media coverage of sponsored events allows sponsors to gain greater exposure for their money.

- Global marketers recognize sponsorship as an effective way to reach an international audience in a manner that is universally understood.

- The proven effectiveness of a sponsorship that is properly planned and executed can buy productive marketing contacts. Sponsorships also represent alternatives to the increased clutter associated with advertising and direct mail.

It is important to note that today's sponsorships cover a broad base, including events and programs that fall into the category of social responsibility. Companies and nonprofit organizations may sponsor reading programs, child-care programs, programs to help small or minority-owned businesses get started, as well as humanitarian programs like the Make-A-Wish Foundation® and cultural events such as free classical concerts.

How Sponsorship Differs from Advertising

Even though sponsorship spending and traditional advertising spending represent forms of nonpersonal selling, their differences outnumber their similarities. Chief among these differences are the sponsor's degree of control versus that of advertising, the nature of the message, audience reaction, and measurements of effectiveness.

Marketers have considerable control over the quantity and quality of market coverage when they advertise. Sponsors, on the other hand, must rely on signs to present their messages. Also, they have little control of sponsored events beyond matching the audiences to profiles of their own target markets. In addition, sponsorship is a mute, nonverbal medium since the message is delivered in association with an activity possessing its own personality in the eyes of its audience. By contrast, a traditional advertisement allows the marketer to create an individual message containing an introduction, a theme, and a conclusion.

Audiences react differently to sponsorship as a communications medium than to other media. The sponsor's investment provides a recognizable benefit to the sponsored activity that the audience can appreciate. As a result, sponsorship is often viewed more positively than traditional advertising. Some marketers have tried to take advantage of this fact by practicing *ambush marketing*, in which a firm that is not an official sponsor tries to link itself to a major international event, such as the Olympics or a concert tour by a musical group. While it might be tempting to assume that smaller firms with limited marketing budgets would be most likely to engage in this type of marketing, this is not always the case. At a recent World Cup soccer match, television cameras panned hordes of cheering spectators wearing caps bearing the Samsung logo. Samsung was not the official sponsor for the match; its competitor Philips Electronics was.[14] While passing out logo-bearing hats is not illegal, some ambush practices clearly are. If a nonsponsor used the Olympic rings in an advertisement, the ad would be illegal. Famed guerilla marketer Schirf Brewing Co. of Park City, Utah, was priced out of any sponsorship possibilities at the Salt Lake City winter games, so it adorned its sales manager's Chevy Blazer with signs advertising its Wasatch beer as "The *Unofficial* Beer of the 2002 Winter Games." Although the unamused U.S. Olympic Committee and official beer sponsor, Anheuser-Busch, quickly responded with a cease-and-desist order, Wasatch generated millions in free publicity from the stunt.[15]

Dedication

brought to you by Lance Armstrong and ▱ UNITED STATES POSTAL SERVICE.

www.usps.com

Faced with growing competition from UPS and overnight delivery companies like DHL and FedEx, the U.S. Postal Service decided to sponsor the start-up U.S. cycling team almost a decade ago to deliver the theme that the former monopoly should be everyone's first choice as a source of fast, dependable service. Then along came team member and cancer survivor Lance Armstrong. With five Tour de France victories, Armstrong gives USPS steady but silent publicity with the postal service logo emblazoned on his jersey.

Assessing Sponsorship Results

To assess the results of sponsorships, marketers utilize some of the same techniques by which they measure advertising effectiveness. However, the differences between the two promotional alternatives often necessitate some unique research techniques as well. A few corporate sponsors attempt to link expenditures to sales. Kraft General Foods, for example, evaluates the effectiveness of its NASCAR sponsorship by comparing Country Time lemonade sales in the races' primary southeastern U.S. markets with sales in other markets. Other sponsors measure improved brand awareness and image as effectiveness indicators; they conduct traditional surveys before and after the events to secure this information. Still other sponsors measure the impact of their event marketing in public relations terms. Typically, a researcher will count press clippings featuring a sponsor's name or logo and then translate this number into equivalent advertising costs.

Despite the impressive visibility of special events like soccer's World Cup and football's Super Bowl, these events do not necessarily lead directly to increased sales. Marketers want their brands to be associated with characteristics of the sporting event such as speed, accuracy, precision, and teamwork.

Direct Marketing *no Retail.*

Few promotional mix elements are growing as fast as direct marketing. Overall media spending for direct marketing initiatives such as interactive electronic media, direct mail, telemarketing, infomercials, and direct-response advertising totals more than $1.7 trillion a year.[16] Both consumers and business-to-business marketers rely on this promotional mix element to generate orders or sales leads (requests for more information) that may result in future orders. Direct marketing also helps to increase store traffic (visits to the store or office to evaluate and perhaps purchase the advertised goods or services).

Direct marketing opens new international markets of unprecedented size. Electronic marketing channels have become the focus of direct marketers, and Web marketing is international marketing. Even direct mail and telemarketing will grow outside the U.S. as commerce becomes more global. Consumers in Europe and Japan are proving to be responsive to direct marketing. But most global marketing systems remain undeveloped, and many are almost dormant. The growth of international direct marketing is being spurred by marketing operations born in the U.S.

Direct marketing communications pursue goals beyond creating product awareness. Marketers want direct marketing to persuade people to place an order, request more information, visit a store, call a toll-free number, or respond to an e-mail message. In other words, successful direct marketing should prompt consumers to take action. Since direct marketing is interactive, marketers can tailor individual responses to meet consumers' needs. They can also measure the effectiveness of their efforts more easily than with advertising and other forms of promotion. Direct marketing is a very powerful tool that helps organizations to win new customers and enhance relationships with existing ones.

The growth of direct marketing parallels the move toward integrated marketing communications in many ways. Both respond to fragmented media markets and audiences, growth in customized products, shrinking network broadcast audiences, and the increasing use of databases to target specific markets. Lifestyles also play a role because today's busy consumers want convenience and time savings.

Databases are an important part of direct marketing. Using the latest technology to create sophisticated databases, a company can select a narrow market segment and find good prospects within that segment based on desired characteristics. Marketers can cut costs and improve returns on dollars spent by identifying those customers who are most likely to respond to messages and by eliminating others from their lists who are not likely to respond. In fact, mining information about customers is a trend boosted by the growth of e-commerce. DNA software from Austin, Texas–based Smart Technologies can create profiles of customers, suppliers, and business partners by analyzing their movements on a Web site.

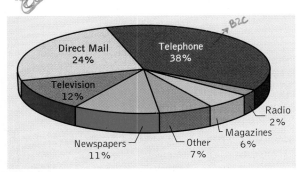

FIGURE 17.7
Direct Marketing Sales by Media Category

Direct Marketing Communications Channels

As Figure 17.7 indicates, direct marketing uses many different media forms. Each works best for certain purposes, although marketers often combine two or more media in one direct marketing program. A company can start with telemarketing to screen potential customers and then follow up by sending more material by direct mail to interested consumers.

Direct Mail *Replace telephone for B2C*

As the amount of information about consumer lifestyles, buying habits, and wants continues to mount, direct mail has become a viable channel for identifying a firm's best prospects. Marketers gather information from internal and external databases, surveys, personalized coupons, and rebates that require responses. **Direct mail** is a critical tool in creating effective direct-marketing campaigns. It comes in many forms, ranging from sales letters, postcards, brochures, booklets, catalogs, and house organs (periodicals issued by organizations) to video and audio cassettes.

Direct mail offers advantages such as the ability to select a narrow target market, achieve intensive coverage, send messages quickly, choose from various formats, provide complete information, and personalize each mailing piece. Figure 17.8 shows the power of direct mail to "target new customers and their wallets and keep existing ones coming back for more."

Response rates are measurable and higher than other types of advertising. In addition, direct mailings stand alone and do not compete for attention with magazine articles and television programs. On the other hand, the per-reader cost of direct mail is high, effectiveness depends on the quality of the mailing list, and some consumers object strongly to what they consider "junk mail."

**FIGURE 17.8
Promoting the Benefits of Direct Mail**

The recent anthrax scare caused a real disruption in many direct mail marketing efforts. According to a survey conducted by the Direct Marketing Association, one-third of all consumers were now treating their mail with at least some suspicion. Some companies, such as the B2B software maker Commerce One, decided to abandon its traditional direct mail programs in favor of e-mail and telemarketing. "Normally we would have used direct mail," explained vice president Bill Fraine. "But I don't think people are opening their mail." Although the anthrax scare that followed the September 11 terrorist attacks disrupted the direct mail portion of the Nissan Altima IMC campaign because the firm sent unsolicited packages to prospective customers, marketers at Foot-Smart turned the problem into an opportunity. With the assistance of Caroline Ernst, director of e-commerce at the health-care products firm, they contacted customers in advance to alert them that the new Foot-Smart catalog was in the mail. As a result of this advance message, Foot-Smart saw a 20 percent increase in sales.[17]

Catalogs

Catalogs have been a popular form of direct mail in the U.S. for more than 100 years. More than 10,000 different consumer, specialty, mail-order catalogs—and thousands more for business-to-business sales—find their way into almost every U.S. mailbox. In a typical year, they generate over $57 billion in consumer sales and $36 billion in business-to-business sales. On any given day, you might find a catalog from Patagonia, Crate & Barrel, Office Depot, Title IX, or Birkenstock in your mailbox. Catalogs fill so many segments that you could probably order just about anything you need for any facet of your life from a catalog.

Many companies, such as Sears and its new Lands' End subsidiary, built their businesses and created a well-known image through their catalogs. More recently, however, catalog companies have expanded into Web sites, and some have even opened retail stores to increase sales and market share. (Sears discontinued its catalog in favor of its retail stores but continued to use specialty catalogs and later bought Wisconsin-based catalog retailer Lands' End.) Sophisticated electronic technologies are changing catalog marketing.

Marketing Dictionary

direct mail Communications in the form of sales letters, postcards, brochures, catalogs, and the like conveying messages directly from the marketer to the customer.

Today's catalogs can be updated quickly, providing consumers with the latest information and prices. CD-ROM catalogs allow marketers to display products in three-dimensional views and include video sequences of product demonstrations.

Many Americans still refuse to purchase from a catalog, but others—such as those who live in rural areas with little or no access to retail stores or busy professionals who do not have time to spend wandering store aisles—depend on them for their shopping needs. Although many consumers like to receive direct mail, others object to unsolicited communications. Many catalog companies do not understand their customers' needs and wants but, instead, send loads of catalogs to millions of people whether or not they want them. The 21st-century consumer is time-pressed and overloaded with information. To help consumers escape the barrage of mail stuffed into their boxes, the Direct Marketing Association established its Mail Preference Service. This consumer service sends name removal forms to people who do not wish to receive direct-mail advertising.[18]

Telemarketing

Any person whose dinner has been interrupted by a sales call can attest that telemarketing is the most frequently used form of direct marketing. It provides marketers with a high return on their expenditures, an immediate response, and the opportunity for personalized two-way conversations. *Telemarketing* refers to direct marketing conducted entirely by telephone. It can be classified as either outbound or inbound contacts. Outbound telemarketing involves a sales force that uses only the telephone to contact customers, reducing the cost of making personal visits. The customer initiates inbound telemarketing, which typically provides a toll-free number for customers to use at their convenience to obtain information and/or make purchases. Like direct mail, telemarketing taps into databases to target calls based on customer characteristics like family income, number of children, and home ownership. For example, income is an important criterion for banks that use telemarketing to solicit new credit-card customers.

Telemarketing is gaining importance in the marketing strategies of many firms; revenues from phone sales, now at $600 billion annually, are expected to grow about 9 percent per year. New predictive dialer devices improve telemarketing's efficiency and reduce costs by automating the dialing process to skip busy signals and answering machines. When the dialer reaches a human voice, it instantaneously puts the call through to a salesperson. This technology is often combined with a print advertising campaign that features a toll-free number for inbound telemarketing.

Business-to-business telemarketing is on the rise as well. Marketers at Xerox and long-distance telephone companies use telemarketing to develop sales leads. Because recipients of both consumer and business-to-business telemarketing calls often find them annoying, the Federal Trade Commission passed a Telemarketing Sales Rule in 1996. The rule cracks down on abusive telemarketing practices by establishing allowed calling hours and regulating call content. Companies must clearly disclose details of any exchange policies, maintain lists of people who do not want to receive calls, and keep records of telemarketing scripts, prize winners, customers, and employees for two years. While designed to protect customers against fraud—with losses estimated in excess of $40 billion, almost 10 percent of telemarketing-generated revenues—the rule also helps improve the image of telemarketers. Consumers can cut down on undesirable sales calls by requesting that the DMA Telephone Preference Service put them on the "do not call" list.[19]

Direct Marketing via Broadcast Channels

Broadcast direct marketing can take three basic forms: brief direct-response ads on television or radio, home shopping channels, and infomercials. Direct-response spots typically run 30, 60, or 90 seconds and include product descriptions and toll-free telephone numbers for ordering. Often shown on cable television and independent stations and tied to special-interest programs, broadcast direct marketing usually encourages viewers to respond immediately by saying that they will receive a special price or a gift if they call within a few minutes of an ad's airing. Radio direct-response ads also provide product descriptions and addresses or phone numbers to contact the sellers. Radio actually proves expensive compared with other direct marketing media, and listeners may not pay close enough attention to catch the number or may not be able to write it down because they are driving a car, which accounts for a major portion of radio listening time.

Home shopping channels like Quality Value Convenience (QVC), Home Shopping Network (HSN), and ShopNBC represent another type of television direct marketing. Broadcasting around the clock, these channels offer consumers a variety of products, including jewelry, clothing, skincare, home furnishings, computers, cameras, kitchen appliances, and toys. In essence, home shopping channels function like on-air catalogs. The channels also have Web sites that consumers can browse through to make purchases. In both cases, customers place orders via toll-free telephone numbers and pay for their purchases by credit card.

Infomercials are 30-minute or longer product commercials that resemble regular television programs. Because of their length, infomercials do not get lost as easily as 30-second commercials can, and they permit marketers to present their products in more detail. But they are usually shown at odd hours, and people often watch only portions of them—think of how many times you have channel-surfed past an infomercial for Bow-flex, Victoria Principal's skincare line, or Ronco's rotisserie. Infomercials do provide toll-free telephone numbers so viewers can order products or request more information. Although infomercials incur higher production costs than prime-time 30-second ads on national network TV, they generally air on less expensive cable channels and in late-night time slots on broadcast stations.

Electronic Direct Marketing Channels

Anyone who has ever logged on to the Web is abundantly aware of the growing number of commercial advertisements that now clutter their computer screen. Web advertising is a recurring theme throughout this text, alluding to its importance as a component of the promotional mix. In fact, Chapter 5 explained the vital role e-commerce now plays in contemporary marketing practices. In one recent year, Web companies sold $1 billion in advertising, and that number grows with each new application of electronic technology.

Web advertising, however, is only one component of electronic direct marketing. E-mail direct marketers have found that traditional practices used in print and broadcast media are easily adapted to electronic messaging. Experts agree that the basic rules for online direct marketing mirror those of traditional practices. Any successful offline direct marketing campaign can be applied to e-mail promotions.

Electronic media deliver data instantly to direct marketers and help them to track customer buying cycles quickly. As a result, they can place customer acquisition programs online for about 50 to 80 percent less than the cost of traditional programs. In the early years of the Internet, the most predominant products for direct marketers were books, music CDs, wine, and gourmet foods. Today, however, there seems to be no limit to the variety of goods and services available to online shoppers. In fact, consumer-to-consumer sales through auction sites are becoming the most popular avenue for direct online sales.

Other Direct Marketing Channels

Print media like newspapers and magazines do not support direct marketing as effectively as do Web marketing and telemarketing. However, print media and other traditional direct marketing channels are still critical to the success of all electronic media channels. Magazine ads with toll-free telephone numbers enhance inbound telemarketing campaigns. Companies can place ads in magazines or newspapers, include reader-response cards, or place special inserts targeted for certain market segments within the publications.

Kiosks provide another outlet for electronic sales. Dell the nation's largest PC marketer, recently began placing kiosks at malls so consumers could touch, see, and try out different configurations of its computers. However, because the company builds customized computers to order, until recently consumers had to place their orders by phone or online. In an about-face from its traditional exclusive direct sales approach, Dell recently decided to expand its market share by selling to dealers. In addition to marching directly onto the turf long dominated by Hewlett-Packard and IBM, Dell hopes to capture a sizable share of the $3 billion-a-year so-called "white box" market, the no-name computers put together with parts from various suppliers and tailored to a customer's specific needs.[20]

Developing an Optimal Promotional Mix

By blending advertising, personal selling, sales promotion, and public relations to achieve marketing objectives, marketers create a promotional mix. Since they can refer to no quantitative measures to determine the effectiveness of each mix component in a given market segment, the choice of an effective mix of promotional elements presents one of marketers' most difficult tasks. Several factors influence the effectiveness of a promotional mix: (1) the nature of the market, (2) the nature of the product, (3) the stage in the product life cycle, (4) the price, and (5) the funds available for promotion.

Nature of the Market

The marketer's target audience has a major impact on the choice of a promotion method. When a market includes a limited number of buyers, personal selling may prove a highly effective technique. However, markets characterized by large numbers of potential customers scattered over sizable geographical areas may make the cost of contact by personal salespeople prohibitive. In such instances, extensive use of advertising often makes sense. The type of customer also affects the promotional mix. Personal selling works better in a target market made up of industrial purchasers or retail and wholesale buyers than in a target market consisting of ultimate consumers. Similarly, pharmaceutical firms use large sales forces to sell prescription drugs directly to physicians and hospitals, but they advertise to promote over-the-counter drugs for the consumer market. When a prescription drug receives FDA approval to be sold over the counter, the drug firm must switch its promotional strategy from personal selling to consumer advertising.

As people have grown tired of cola drinks over the last few years, the Coca-Cola Co. and PepsiCo have had to come up with new ways to appeal to consumers. Both companies are still big media spenders—in one recent year, Coca-Cola spent $194 million, and PepsiCo came in at $125 million. PepsiCo has run a highly successful series of splashy ads with pop star Britney Spears and Austin Powers creator Mike Myers and did promotional tie-ins with the hit movie *Monsters Inc.* Its Atlanta-based rival poured out ads to support its sponsorships at the Olympics and created nostalgic ads for the holiday season. Still, baby boomers and seniors aren't drinking the amount of cola they once did, so the cola giants are focusing on younger target markets. Both companies are now focusing on their bottled water brands Aquafina and Dasani, and both have a stable of noncarbonated drinks that are doing well. PepsiCo has created a 100-person sales force to sell its noncarbonated drinks, such as Gatorade and Lipton iced teas.[21]

Nature of the Product

A second important factor in determining an effective promotional mix is the product itself. Highly standardized products with minimal servicing requirements usually depend less on personal selling than do custom products with technically complex features and/or requirements for frequent maintenance. Consumer products are more likely to rely heavily on advertising than are business products. Ralston Purina has launched a $34 million television and print advertising campaign to promote its new Beneful dry dog food. Nestlé, Purina's parent company, wants to establish Beneful as a premium line of pet food priced between the value brands and the highest priced brands such as Procter & Gamble's Iams.[22]

With its "Healthful. Flavorful. Beneful" ad, Ralston Purina develops advertising based on the nature of the product—promoting its healthy ingredients.

Promotional mixes vary within each product category. In the B2B market, for example, installations typically rely more heavily on personal selling than does marketing of operating supplies. In contrast, the promotional mix for a convenience product is likely to involve more emphasis on manufacturer advertising and less on personal selling. On the other hand, personal selling plays an important role in the promotion of shopping products, and both personal and nonpersonal selling are important in the promotion of specialty goods. A personal-selling emphasis is also likely to prove more effective than other alternatives in promotions for products involving trade-ins.

Stage in the Product Life Cycle

The promotional mix must be tailored to the product's stage in the product life cycle. In the introductory stage, heavy emphasis on personal selling helps to inform the marketplace of the merits of the new good or service. Salespeople contact marketing intermediaries to secure interest in and commitment to handling the offering. Trade shows frequently inform and educate prospective dealers and ultimate consumers.

Marketers of new products may need to work closely with customers to answer questions and adjust promotional mixes as needed. Advertising and sales promotion at this stage create awareness and stimulate initial purchases. As the good or service moves into the growth and maturity stages, advertising gains relative importance in persuading consumers to make purchases. Marketers continue to direct personal-selling efforts at marketing intermediaries in an attempt to expand distribution. As more competitors enter the marketplace, advertising begins to stress product differences to persuade consumers to purchase the firm's brand. In the maturity and early decline stages, firms frequently reduce advertising and sales promotion expenditures.

Mature products often require creative promotions to keep the product in the mind of the consumer. That's the case with Coke and Pepsi, as described earlier. During the fall and winter before PepsiCo launched its Britney Spears ads, the company conducted one of the most successful advertising campaigns in its 103-year existence. Run in partnership with Yahoo!, the company set up a Web site called Pepsistuff.com, where consumers could log on and enter a code found under the caps of 1.5 billion Pepsi bottles. Each code was worth 100 points, redeemable for prizes such as sporting apparel and DVDs. The only requirement was that participants provide their name, e-mail address, zip code, and date of birth—all to be used in future marketing efforts. The Web site greeted 3.5 million registered visitors, and national sales of Pepsi's single-serve bottles rose 5 percent during the promotion. And at the end, Pepsi marketers had a database to use in further efforts.[23]

Price

The price of the good or service is the fourth factor that affects the choice of a promotional mix. Advertising dominates the promotional mixes for low-unit-value products due to the high per-contact costs in personal selling. These costs make the sales call an unprofitable tool in promoting lower value goods and services. Advertising, in contrast, permits a low promotional expenditure per sales unit because it reaches mass audiences. For low-value consumer goods, such as chewing gum, soft drinks, and snack foods, advertising is the most feasible means of promotion. Even shopping products like the Westinghouse ceiling fan advertised in Figure 17.9 can be sold at least partly on the basis of price—in this case,

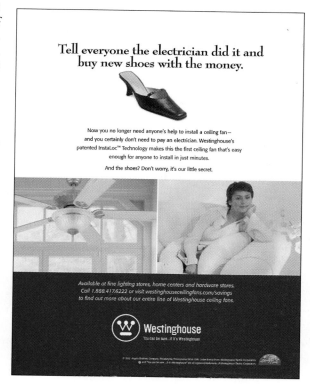

FIGURE 17.9
Promotion Based on Price

Tell everyone the electrician did it and buy new shoes with the money.

Now you no longer need anyone's help to install a ceiling fan—and you certainly don't need to pay an electrician. Westinghouse's patented InstaLoc™ Technology makes this the first ceiling fan that's easy enough for anyone to install in just minutes.

And the shoes? Don't worry, it's our little secret.

Available at fine lighting stores, home centers and hardware stores. Call 1.888.417.6222 or visit westinghouseceilingfans.com/savings to find out more about our entire line of Westinghouse ceiling fans.

Westinghouse
You can be sure...if it's Westinghouse

TABLE 17.3   **Factors Influencing Choice of Promotional Mix**

	EMPHASIS	
	PERSONAL SELLING	**ADVERTISING**
Nature of the market		
Number of buyers	Limited number	Large number
Geographic concentration	Concentrated	Dispersed
Type of customer	Business purchaser	Ultimate consumer
Nature of the product		
Complexity	Custom-made, complex	Standardized
Service requirements	Considerable	Minimal
Type of good or service	Business	Consumer
Use of trade-ins	Trade-ins common	Trade-ins uncommon
Stage in the product life cycle	Often emphasized at every stage; heavy emphasis in the introductory and early growth stages in acquainting marketing intermediaries and potential consumers with the new good or service	Often emphasized at every stage; heavy emphasis in the latter part of the growth stage, as well as the maturity and early decline stages, to persuade consumers to select specific brands
Price	High unit value	Low unit value

the money saved by purchasing and installing the fan without having to hire an electrician. On the other hand, consumers of high-priced items like luxury cars expect lots of well-presented information. High-tech direct marketing promotions like videocassettes, CD-ROMs, fancy brochures, and personal selling appeal to these potential customers.

Funds Available for Promotion

A real barrier in implementing any promotional strategy is the size of the promotional budget. A single 30-second television commercial during the Super Bowl telecast costs an advertiser $2 million. While millions of viewers may see the commercial, making the cost per contact relatively low, such an expenditure exceeds the entire promotional budgets of thousands of firms, which is how guerilla marketing got its start. And if a company wants to hire a celebrity to advertise its goods and services, try these numbers: Basketball star Michael Jordan earns about $45 million a year in endorsement deals, and singer Ricky Martin gets at least $3 million to perform at private corporate parties (which are designed to promote company products).[24] Table 17.3 summarizes the factors that influence the determination of an appropriate promotional mix: nature of the market, nature of the product, stage in the product life cycle, and price.

Pulling and Pushing Promotional Strategies

6

Contrast the two major alternative promotional strategies.

Marketers may implement essentially two promotional alternatives: a pulling strategy and a pushing strategy. A **pulling strategy** is a promotional effort by the seller to stimulate final-user demand, which then exerts pressure on the distribution channel. When marketing intermediaries stock a large number of competing products and exhibit little interest in any one of them, a firm may have to implement a pulling strategy to motivate them to handle the product. In such instances, this strategy is implemented with the objective of building consumer demand so that consumers will request the product from retail stores. Advertising and sales promotion often contribute to a company's pulling strategy.

In contrast, a **pushing strategy** relies more heavily on personal selling. Here the objective is promoting the product to the members of the marketing channel rather than to final users. To achieve this goal, marketers employ cooperative advertising allowances, trade discounts, personal selling efforts by salespeople, and other dealer supports. Such a strategy is designed to gain marketing success for the firm's products by motivating representatives of wholesalers and/or retailers to spend extra time and effort promoting the products to customers. About half of manufacturers' promotional budgets—$30 million a year—pays for cash incentives to get retailers to stock their products.

While pulling and pushing strategies are presented here as alternative methods, few companies depend entirely on either one. Most firms combine the two methods. Skechers' IMC strategy combines pushing and pulling strategies aimed at both retailers who purchase the company's trendy shoes for their stores and the ultimate consumers. Consumers can see television commercials and print ads in many magazines. To push its products, the company once spent $5 million on a lavish display at a national footwear trade show, including lasers, dancers, and a 30-foot-high transparent wall that displayed tens of thousands of shoes.[25]

Timing also affects the choice of promotional strategies. The relative importance of advertising and selling changes during the various phases of the purchase process. Prior to the actual sale, advertising usually is more important than personal selling. However, one of the primary advantages of a successful advertising program is the support it gives the salesperson who approaches the prospect for the first time. Selling activities are more important than advertising at the time of purchase. Personal selling provides the actual mechanism for closing most sales. In the postpurchase period, advertising regains primacy in the promotional effort. It affirms the customer's decision to buy a particular good or service and reminds him or her of the product's favorable qualities by reducing any cognitive dissonance that might occur.

The promotional strategies used by auto marketers illustrate this timing factor. Car, truck, and SUV makers spend heavily on consumer advertising to create awareness before consumers begin the purchase process. At the time of their purchase decisions, however, the personal-selling skills of dealer salespeople provide the most important tools for closing sales. Finally, advertising frequently maintains postpurchase satisfaction by citing awards such as *Motor Trend's* Car of the Year and results of J.D. Power's customer-satisfaction surveys to affirm buyer decisions.

Budgeting for Promotional Strategy

Promotional budgets may differ not only in amount but also in composition. Business-to-business marketers generally invest larger proportions of their budgets in personal selling than in advertising, while the reverse is usually true of most producers of consumer goods. Cannondale Associates, a leading U.S. sales and marketing consulting firm, conducts an annual survey of trade promotion spending in different industries. Figure 17.10 provides an estimate of how consumer packaged goods manufacturers will allocate their promotional budgets in 2005.

7

Explain how marketers budget for and measure the effectiveness of promotion.

Marketing Dictionary

pulling strategy Promotional effort by the seller to stimulate final-user demand, which then exerts pressure on the distribution channel.

pushing strategy Promotional effort by the seller directed to members of the marketing channel rather than final users.

SOURCE: Data from Donnelley Marketing and Accenture Analysis, "Capturing and Sustaining Value Opportunities in Trade Promotion," accessed at the Accenture Web site, September 6, 2002, http://www.accenture.com.

FIGURE 17.10
Allocation of Promotional Budgets for Consumer Packaged Goods

Evidence suggests that sales initially lag behind promotional expenses for structural reasons—funds spent filling up retail shelves, boosting low initial production, and supplying buyer knowledge. This fact produces a threshold effect in which few sales may result from substantial initial investments in promotion. A second phase might produce sales proportionate to promotional expenditures—the most predictable range. Finally, promotion reaches the area of diminishing returns where an increase in promotional spending fails to produce a corresponding increase in sales.

For example, an initial expenditure of $40,000 may result in sales of 100,000 product units for a consumer goods manufacturer. An additional $10,000 expenditure may generate sales of 30,000 more units, and another $10,000 may produce sales of an additional 35,000 units. The cumulative effect of the expenditures and repeat sales will have generated increasing returns from the promotional outlays. However, as the advertising budget moves from $60,000 to $70,000, the marginal productivity of the additional expenditure may fall to 28,000 units. At some later point, the return may actually become zero or negative as competition intensifies, markets become saturated, and marketers employ less expensive advertising media.

The ideal method of allocating promotional funds would increase the budget until the cost of each additional increment equals the additional incremental revenue received. In other words, the most effective allocation procedure increases promotional expenditures until each dollar of promotional expense is matched by an additional dollar of profit. This procedure—referred to as marginal analysis—maximizes the input's productivity. The difficulty arises in identifying the optimal point, which requires a precise balance between marginal expenses for promotion and the resulting marginal receipts. Traditional methods for creating a promotional budget include the percentage-of-sales and fixed-sum-per-unit methods, along with techniques for meeting the competition and achieving task objectives. Each method is briefly examined in Table 17.4.

TABLE 17.4   Promotional Budget Determination

METHOD	DESCRIPTION	EXAMPLE
Percentage-of-sales method 10%	Promotional budget is set as a specified percentage of either past or forecasted sales.	"Last year we spent $10,500 on promotion and had sales of $420,000. Next year we expect sales to grow to $480,000, and we are allocating $12,000 for promotion."
Fixed-sum-per-unit method	Promotional budget is set as a predetermined dollar amount for each unit sold or produced.	"Our forecast calls for sales of 14,000 units, and we allocate promotion at the rate of $65 per unit."
Meeting competition method	Promotional budget is set to match competitor's promotional outlays on either an absolute or relative basis.	"Promotional outlays average 4 percent of sales in our industry."
Task-objective method	Once marketers determine their specific promotional objectives, the amount (and type) of promotional spending needed to achieve them is determined.	"By the end of next year, we want 75 percent of the area high-school students to be aware of our new, highly automated fast-food prototype outlet. How many promotional dollars will it take, and how should they be spent?"

The *percentage-of-sales method* is perhaps the most common way of establishing promotional budgets. The percentage can be based on sales either from some past period (such as the previous year) or forecasted for a future period (the current year). While this plan is appealingly simple, it does not effectively support the achievement of basic promotional objectives. Arbitrary percentage allocations can't provide needed flexibility. In addition, sales should depend on promotional allocation rather than vice versa.

The *fixed-sum-per-unit method* differs from budgeting based on a percentage of sales in only one respect: It allocates a predetermined amount to each sales or production unit. This amount can also reflect either historical or forecasted figures. Producers of high-value consumer durable goods, such as automobiles, often use this budgeting method.

Another traditional budgeting approach, *meeting competition,* simply matches competitors' outlays, either in absolute amounts or relative to the firms' market shares. But this method doesn't help a company gain a competitive edge. A budget that is appropriate for one company may not be appropriate for another.

The *task-objective method* develops a promotional budget based on a sound evaluation of the firm's promotional objectives. As a result, it attunes its allocation of funds to modern marketing practices. The method involves two steps:

1. The firm's marketers must define realistic communication goals that they want the promotional mix to achieve. Say that a firm wants to achieve a 25 percent increase in brand awareness. This step quantifies the objectives that promotion should attain. These objectives in turn become integral parts of the promotional plan.

2. Then the company's marketers determine the amount and type of promotional activity required for each objective that they have set. Combined, these units become the firm's promotional budget.

A crucial assumption underlies the task-objective approach: Marketers can measure the productivity of each promotional dollar. That assumption explains why the objectives must be carefully chosen, quantified, and accomplished through promotional efforts. Generally, budgeters should avoid general marketing objectives such as, "We want to achieve a 5 percent increase in sales." A sale is a culmination of the effects of all elements of the marketing mix. A more appropriate promotional objective might be, "We want to achieve an 8 percent response rate from a targeted direct-mail advertisement."

Promotional budgeting always requires difficult decisions. Still, recent research studies and the spread of computer-based models have made it a more manageable problem than it used to be.

Measuring the Effectiveness of Promotion *Not in Test*

It is widely recognized that part of a firm's promotional effort is ineffective. John Wanamaker, a successful 19th-century retailer, observed the following: "I know half the money I spend on advertising is wasted, but I can never find out which half."

Evaluating the effectiveness of a promotion today is a far different exercise in marketing research than it was even a few decades ago. For years, marketers depended on store audits conducted by large organizations like A.C. Nielsen. Other research groups conducted warehouse withdrawal surveys. These research studies were designed to determine whether sales had risen as a direct result of a particular promotional campaign. In the 1980s, the introduction of scanners and automated checkout lanes completely changed marketing research. For the first time, retailers and manufacturers had a tool to obtain sales data quickly and efficiently. The problem was that the collected data was used for little else than determining how much of which product was bought at what price and at what time.

By the 1990s, marketing research entered another evolutionary period with the advent of the Internet. Now marketing researchers can delve into each customer's purchase behavior, lifestyle, preferences, opinions, and habits. All of this information can also be obtained in a matter of seconds. The next section explains the impact of electronic technologies on measuring promotional effectiveness. However, marketers today still depend on two basic measurement tools: direct sales results tests and indirect evaluations.

Most marketers would prefer to use a *direct sales results test* to measure the effectiveness of promotion. Such an approach would reveal the specific impact on sales revenues for each dollar of promotional spending. This type of technique has always eluded marketers, however, due to their inability to control other variables operating in the marketplace. A firm may receive $20 million in additional sales orders following a new $1.5 million advertising campaign, but the market success may really have resulted from price increases for competing products rather than from the advertising outlays.

Marketers often encounter difficulty isolating the effects of promotion from those of other market elements and outside environmental variables. *Indirect evaluation* helps researchers to concentrate on quantifiable indicators of effectiveness, such as recall (how much members of the target market remember about specific products or advertisements) and readership (size and composition of a message's audience). The basic problem with indirect measurement is the difficulty of relating these variables to sales. Will the fact that many people read an ad lead directly to increased sales?

Marketers need to ask the right questions and understand what they are measuring. Promotion to build sales volume produces measurable results in the form of short-term returns; brand-building programs, however, and efforts to generate or enhance consumers' perceptions of value in a product, brand, or organization cannot be measured over the short term.

Measuring Online Promotions

The latest challenge facing marketers is how to measure the effectiveness of electronic media. Early attempts at measuring online promotional effectiveness involved counting hits (user requests for a file) and visits (pages downloaded or read in one session). But as Chapter 5 explained, it is not how many times a Web site is visited, but how many people actually buy something. Traditional numbers that work for other media forms are not necessarily relevant indicators of effectiveness for a Web site. For one thing, the Web combines both advertising and direct marketing. Web pages effectively integrate advertising and other content, such as product information, that may be the page's main feature. For another consideration, consumers generally choose the advertisements they want to see on the Net, whereas traditional broadcast or print media automatically expose consumers to ads.

One way that marketers measure performance is by incorporating some form of direct response into their promotions. This technique also helps them to compare different promotions for effectiveness and rely on facts rather than opinions. Consumers may say they will try a product in response to a survey question yet not actually buy it. A firm may send out three different direct mail offers in the same promotion and compare response rates. An offer to send for a sample may generate a 75 percent response rate, coupons might show a 50 percent redemption rate, and rebates might appeal to only 10 percent of the targeted group.

The two major techniques for setting Internet advertising rates are *cost per impression* and *cost per response (click-throughs)*. Cost per impression is a measurement technique that relates the cost of an ad to every thousand people who view it. In other words, anyone who sees the page containing the banner or other form of ad creates one impression. This measure assumes that the site's principal purpose is to display the advertising message. Cost per response is a direct marketing technique that relates the cost of an ad to the number of people who click on it. Measurement based on click-throughs assumes that those who actually click on an ad want more information and, therefore, consider the ad valuable. Both rating techniques have merit. Site publishers point out that click-through rates are influenced by the creativity of the ad's message. Advertisers, on the other hand, point out that the Web ad has value to those who click on it for additional information.

The Value of Marketing Communications

The nature of marketing communications is changing as new formats transform the traditional idea of an advertisement or sales promotion. Sales messages are now placed subtly, or not so subtly, in movies and television shows, blurring the lines between promotion and entertainment and changing the traditional definition of advertising. Messages show up on stadium turnstiles, buses, and even police cars.

right wrong — Solving an Ethical Controversy

Should Marketing Promotions Target Children?

Every day, consumers are bombarded with marketing messages through television and radio commercials, ads in newspapers and magazines, telemarketing, and direct mail communications. It's one thing for adults to receive these messages and make choices about which they want to accept and which they prefer to reject. But a growing number of people are concerned about marketing promotions that target children, particularly those that take place in schools and those that employ psychologists to help marketers find new ways to attract children to their products. "Advertising is a massive, multi-million dollar project that's having an enormous impact on child development," says psychologist Allen D. Kanner.

Are promotional messages aimed at children an ethical marketing practice?

PRO

1. Today's children are sophisticated enough to make their own product purchase decisions and should be offered the same range of selection that adults receive.
2. It is the parents' responsibility to help children interpret marketing messages and make good purchasing choices.

CON

1. According to some experts, children who are exposed to massive amounts of advertising become "convinced that they're inferior if they don't have an endless array of new products."
2. Consumers Union reports that marketing activity within schools further blurs the line between school as a place to learn and school as a place to make purchasing choices.

Summary

No one argues that children will receive marketing messages their entire lives. Perhaps it's the intent of those messages as well as how they are delivered that is the problem. Recently, psychologists have been hired by some companies to direct marketers in how to reach children. Test marketing as well as advertising has been taking place in some schools from Massachusetts to New Jersey to California. Marketers need to understand the impact they have on children and be responsible about the messages they convey.

SOURCES: "Online Marketing: Targeting Children and Youth," downloaded from http://www.cme.org/children/marketing/index_mktg.html, accessed January 23, 2002; "The ABCs at the FTC: Marketing and Advertising to Children," http://www.ftc.gov/speeches/starek/minnfin.htm, downloaded January 23, 2002; "Should Schools Allow Companies into the Classroom to Collect Personal Information from Children?" downloaded from Consumers Union Web site, http://www.consumersunion.org, accessed January 23, 2003.

Despite new tactics by advertisers, promotion has often been the target of criticism. Some people complain that it offers nothing of value to society and simply wastes resources. Others criticize that promotion encourages consumers to buy unnecessary products that they cannot afford. Many ads seem to insult people's intelligence or offend their sensibilities, and they criticize the ethics—or lack thereof—displayed by advertisers and salespeople. Many consumers would agree that the value of cigarette advertising is limited at best; in fact, many would consider it unethical to promote smoking in this way.

New forms of promotion are considered even more insidious because marketers make pitches that do not look like paid advertisements. Many of these complaints cite true problems. Some salespeople use unethical sales tactics. Some product advertising hides its promotional nature or targets consumer groups that can least afford the advertised goods or services. Many television commercials do, in fact, contribute to the growing problem of cultural pollution. One area that has sparked both criticism and debate is promotion aimed at children, as discussed in the "Solving an Ethical Controversy" box.

While promotion can certainly be criticized on many counts, it also plays a crucial role in modern society. This point is best understood by examining the social, business, and economic importance of promotion. The AARP message in Figure 17.11 provides valuable information to seniors who are taking prescription drugs.

FIGURE 17.11
Using Promotion to Provide Valuable Information for Product Users

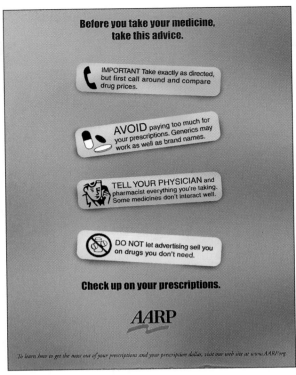

Social Importance ~Read~

Criticisms of promotional messages as tasteless and lacking any contribution to society sometimes ignore the fact that our social framework provides no commonly accepted set of standards or priorities for these judgments. We live in a varied economy characterized by consumer segments with differing needs, wants, and aspirations. What one group finds tasteless may be quite appealing to another. But diversity is one of the benefits of living in our society because it offers us many choices and opportunities. Promotional strategy faces an averaging problem that escapes many of its critics. The one generally accepted standard in a market society is freedom of choice for the consumer. Consumer buying decisions eventually determine acceptable practices in the marketplace, which is why consumers who criticize cigarette ads may also agree that it is acceptable for them to appear.

Promotion has also become an important factor in campaigns aimed at achieving social objectives, such as stopping drug abuse or supporting national parks. Advertising agencies donate their expertise to creating *public service announcements (PSAs)* aimed at promoting these causes, as illustrated by the Ad Council message in Figure 17.12 on afterschool programs.

PSA they r not identify the sponsor.

FIGURE 17.12
Promotional Message Addressing an Important Social Concern

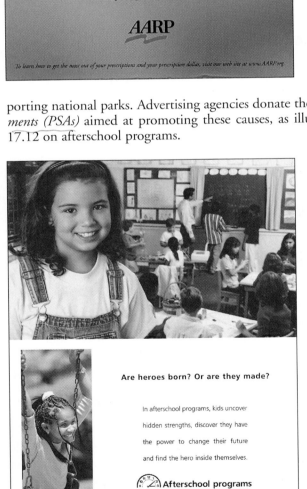

Promotion performs an informative and educational task crucial to the functioning of modern society. As with everything else in life, what is important is how promotion is used rather than whether it is used.

Business Importance ~Read~

Promotional strategy has become increasingly important to both large and small business enterprises. The well-documented, long-term increase in funds spent on promotion certainly attests to management's faith in the ability of promotional efforts to encourage attitude changes, brand loyalty, and additional sales. It is difficult to conceive of an enterprise that would not attempt to promote its good or service in some manner. Most modern institutions simply cannot survive in the long run without promotion. Business must communicate with its publics.

Nonbusiness enterprises also recognize the importance of promotional efforts. The U.S. government spends about $300 million a year on advertising and ranks 36th among all U.S. advertisers. The Canadian government is the leading advertiser in Canada, promoting many concepts and programs. Religious organizations have acknowledged the importance of promotional channels to make their viewpoints known to the public at large.

Economic Importance   *Read How many is spent on advertising + Promotion.*

Promotion has assumed a degree of economic importance, if for no other reason than because it provides employment for thousands of people. More important, however, effective promotion has allowed society to derive benefits not otherwise available. For example, the criticism that promotion costs too much isolates an individual expense item and fails to consider its possible beneficial effects on other categories of expenditures.

Promotional strategies increase the number of units sold and permit economies of scale in the production process, thereby lowering the production costs for each unit of output. Lower unit costs allow lower consumer prices, which in turn make products available to more people. Similarly, researchers have found that advertising subsidizes the information contents of newspapers and the broadcast media. In short, promotion pays for many of the enjoyable entertainment and educational opportunities in contemporary life as it lowers product costs.

Strategic Implications of Marketing in the 21st Century

With the incredible proliferation of marketing messages in the media, today's marketers—who are also consumers themselves—must find new ways to reach customers without overloading them with unnecessary or unwanted communications. Guerilla marketing has emerged as an effective strategy for large and small companies, but ambush marketing has raised ethical concerns. Product placement has gained in popularity, but if movies and television shows become jammed with brands, marketers will have to find yet another venue for their messages. In addition, it is difficult to overstate the impact of the Internet on the promotional mix of 21st-century marketers. Small companies are on the Web, and big businesses are there as well. Even individual entrepreneurs have found a lucrative new launch pad for their enterprises. But even though cyberspace marketing has been effective in business-to-business transactions and, to a lesser extent, for some types of consumer purchases, a major source of Internet revenues is advertising. The Net has ads for almost every good or service imaginable. In fact, Web companies sell over $1 billion in advertising each year.

Integrating marketing communications into an overall consumer-focused strategy that meets a company's promotional and business objectives has become more and more critical in the busy global marketplace. Chapter 18 will examine specific ways marketers can use advertising, sales promotion, and public relations to convey their messages; then Chapter 19 will discuss personal selling and sales-force management in the same manner.

Summary of Chapter Objectives

1. Discuss how integrated marketing communications relates to the development of an optimal promotional mix.

Integrated marketing communications (IMC) refers to the coordination of all promotional activities to produce a unified, customer-focused promotional message. Developing an optimal promotional mix involves selecting the personal and non-personal selling strategies that will work best to deliver the overall marketing message as defined by IMC.

2. Describe the communication process and how it relates to the AIDA concept.

In the communication process, a message is encoded and transmitted through a communications channel; then it is decoded, or interpreted by the receiver; finally, the receiver provides feedback, which completes the system. The AIDA concept (attention-interest-desire-action) explains the steps through which a person reaches a purchase decision after being exposed to a promotional message. The marketer sends the promotional message, and the consumer receives and responds to it via the communication process.

3. Discuss how the promotional mix relates to the objectives of promotion.

The objectives of promotion are to provide information, stimulate demand, differentiate a product, accentuate the value of a product, and stabilize sales. The promotional mix, which is the blend of numerous variables intended to satisfy the target market, must fulfill the overall objectives of promotion.

4. Identify the different elements of the promotional mix and explain how marketers develop an optimal promotional mix.

The different elements of the promotional mix are personal selling and nonpersonal selling (advertising, sales promotion, direct marketing, and public relations). Guerilla marketing is frequently used by marketers with limited funds and those firms attempting to attract attention for new products with innovative promotional approaches. Marketers develop the optimal mix by considering the nature of the market, the nature of the product, the stage in the product life cycle, price, and funds available for promotion.

5. Discuss the role of sponsorship and direct marketing in integrated marketing communications.

Sponsorship, which occurs when an organization provides cash or in-kind resources to an event or activity in exchange for a direct association with the event or activity, has become a hot trend in promotion. The sponsor purchases access to an activity's audience and the image associated with the activity, both of which contribute to the overall promotional message being delivered by a firm. Direct marketing involves direct communication between a seller and a B2B or final customer. It includes such promotional methods as telemarketing, direct mail, direct-response advertising and infomercials on TV and radio, direct-response print advertising, and electronic media.

6. Contrast the two major alternative promotional strategies.

The two major strategies are pushing and pulling. In a pulling strategy, marketers attempt to stimulate final-user demand, which then exerts pressure on the distribution channel. In a pushing strategy, marketers attempt to promote the product to channel members rather than final users. To do this, they rely heavily on personal selling.

7. Explain how marketers budget for and then measure the effectiveness of promotion.

Marketers may choose among several methods for determining promotional budgets, including percentage-of-sales, fixed-sum-per-unit, meeting competition, or task-objective, which is considered the most flexible and most effective. Today, marketers use either direct sales results tests or indirect evaluation to measure effectiveness. Both methods have their benefits and drawbacks because of the difficulty of controlling variables.

8. Discuss the value of marketing communications.

Despite valid criticism, marketing communications provide socially important messages, are important to businesses, and contain economic importance. As with every communication in society, it is important to consider how promotion is used rather than whether it is used at all.

Marketing Terms You Need to Know

promotion 496
marketing
   communications 496
integrated marketing
   communications (IMC) 496

AIDA concept 499
promotional mix 505
personal selling 505
nonpersonal selling 505
advertising 506

sales promotion 506
direct marketing 507
public relations 507
guerilla marketing 508
sponsorship 509

direct mail 513
pulling strategy 518
pushing strategy 519

Other Important Marketing Terms

sender 499
message 499
encoding 499
decoding 499
feedback 500
noise 500
channel 500
primary demand 503

selective demand 503
product differentiation 503
product placement 506
trade promotion 507
publicity 507
ambush marketing 511
telemarketing 514
home shopping channel 515

infomercial 515
percentage-of-sales
   method 521
fixed-sum-per-unit method 521
meeting competition 521
task-objective method 521
direct sales results test 522
indirect evaluation 522

cost per impression 522
cost per response (click-
   throughs) 522
public service announcements
   (PSAs) 524

Review Questions

1. Define integrated marketing communications (IMC) and discuss the importance of teamwork in achieving a successful IMC effort.
2. Describe the three tasks an effective promotional message accomplishes. How are these tasks related to the AIDA concept?
3. Identify and describe briefly the five objectives of promotion.
4. State whether you think each of the following would benefit most from personal or nonpersonal selling and explain why. If you think a product would benefit from both, explain your answer:
   a. a new juice drink
   b. a home security system designed for small homes and apartments
   c. a complete skincare system
   d. exercise equipment
5. In what ways does sponsorship differ from advertising?
6. What are the goals of direct marketing? Why do you think it has gained in popularity among marketers?
7. What are the six major factors that influence the effectiveness of a promotional mix?
8. What is the most effective method for developing a promotional budget? Why?
9. Identify and describe briefly the two methods marketers use today for measuring the effectiveness of promotion. What are the benefits and drawbacks of each?
10. Describe your own criticisms of some marketing communications. Then discuss the ways in which *you* think marketing communications are valuable.

Projects and Teamwork Exercises

1. Select a print advertisement that catches your attention and analyze it according to the AIDA concept (attention-interest-desire-action). Describe what features about the ad catch your attention, pique your interest, make you desire the product, and spur you toward a purchase. Present your findings to the class.
2. With a classmate, locate up to five print ads that illustrate each of the five objectives of promotion (an ad might fulfill more than one objective). Present the ads to class, identifying the objectives fulfilled in each.
3. With a classmate, choose a product—good or service—that you feel could benefit from guerilla marketing. Imagine that you have a limited promotional budget and come up with a plan for a guerilla approach. Outline several ideas and explain how you plan to carry them out. Present your plan to class.
4. Evaluate two or three pieces of direct mail that you have received lately. Which items caught your attention and at least made you save the mailing? Which items did you toss in the trash without even opening or considering beyond an initial glance? Why?
5. With a classmate, choose one of the products listed here or select another that interests you. Then, keeping in mind your objectives for promotion, write an outline for an infomercial for the product. Present your infomercial to the class.
   a. a piece of exercise equipment
   b. a line of cosmetics
   c. a top-of-the-line backyard grill
   d. a personal shopping service

'net Work

http://www.amazon.com

1. AIDA. Go to an e-commerce Web site, such as http://www.amazon.com, and explain how the site has applied the AIDA concept (attention-interest-desire-action).

http://www.letour.fr/
indexus.html

2. Sponsorships. Visit the English Web site of the 2003 Tour de France and review the sponsor list. Identify the sponsor levels; the costs, benefits, and expectations at each level; and the companies that are sponsors at each level.

http://www.realtime
media.com

3. Measuring online performance. Go to Real Time Media's Web site. Read three or four of the case studies explaining what Real Time has done for some of its clients. Print out the case study you found most interesting and discuss it in class.

Note: Internet Web addresses change frequently. If you don't find the exact sites listed, you may need to access the organization or company's home page and search from there.

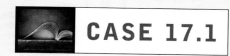

CASE 17.1   Elvis Is Alive and Well— in Graceland

The year 2004 marks the 27th anniversary of the death of rock 'n' roll legend Elvis Presley. He performed on stage for 23 years. Yet his legacy is alive and well more than a quarter of a century after his death at age 42. How could the managers of Elvis Presley Enterprises (EPE), which controls everything from Graceland to the licensing of Elvis music boxes, fan the flame for so long?

Jack Soden, CEO of Elvis Presley Enterprises, was personally appointed to the job by Elvis's widow, Priscilla Presley, in 1981 and has been at the helm for almost a quarter-century. Under his leadership, marketers for EPE have used a wide range of communications techniques to keep the fans who actually remember Elvis coming back for more—while building a whole new generation of Elvis followers around the world. In fact, although nearly 60 percent of Elvis's fan base is made up of working-class baby boom–generation women (the former teenyboppers who swooned over Elvis in the flesh), it's also true that 53 percent of the 500,000 visitors who pay $16 to tour Graceland each year are under age 35. And the fastest growing number of visitors weren't even born when he died. "The median age of visitors at Graceland had steadily declined for the past decade," says Soden. "We worked very hard to get Elvis to those young eyes and ears."

Here's how they do it. First, EPE controls closely every brand license that bears the Elvis name. Candy maker Russell Stover produces Elvis tins of chocolate; the Bradford Group offers 25 Elvis ornaments, music boxes, and commemorative plates. EPE even maintains fan interest with a touring Elvis show, in which surviving members of Elvis's band play alongside a Jumbotron of old footage. In addition, the U.S. Postal Service issued a highly publicized Elvis stamp in the mid-1990s, and the Franklin Mint has an entire line of music boxes, prints, and other collectibles.

And EPE worked with companies such as Northwest Airlines and Fuji Film in 2002 for the "celebration" of the 25th anniversary of Elvis's death. (EPE director of media and creative development Todd Morgan says that the August 16th anniversary of Elvis's death is always a busier time at Graceland than his January birthday.) Perhaps the most successful recent move at renewing interest in the singer was to grant first-ever permission to remix a little-known Elvis recording from 1968. The song, "A Little Less Conversation," used as the theme for Nike's extensive ads during the World Cup, sold 1.6 million copies, topped 20-plus music charts, and moved Elvis out of a long-term tie with the Beatles as the artist with the greatest number of No. 1 hits.

Just as important as the message EPE conveys through its integrated marketing communications is the message it conveys by *not* licensing, selling, or sponsoring certain events or products. It's true that 6,000 types of Elvis merchandise are available, including plush jumpsuited dolls, dancing-Elvis watches, and BBQ seasoning. But here are some of the items EPE won't get involved with: black-velvet paintings (those on the market come from Mexico, not EPE), flags, Bibles, or caskets (a casketmaker requested a license for Elvis's image, and EPE declined).

While it is sometimes difficult to measure the effectiveness of promotion, no one would dispute that the 25-year efforts by those at EPE have resulted in a global fan base for the Elvis brand that shows no signs of diminishing; in fact, it is growing. "In every nook and cranny of the earth, Elvis is recognizable," says CEO Jack Soden. Todd Morgan agrees that EPE's marketing efforts have been instrumental in keeping Elvis alive—at least in spirit. "Elvis's career in death became longer than his career," he says. "If some of us who have been here for a long time stay, there's going to be a point where some of us have been in the Elvis business longer than Elvis."

Questions for Critical Thinking

1. Do you think that EPE needs to develop a different promotional mix for its new generation of Elvis followers? Why or why not?

2. Try to define the nature of the Elvis product. How does this affect the way EPE marketers make choices about their marketing communications?

SOURCES: Elvis Presley Enterprises Web site, http://www.elvis.com, accessed January 24, 2003; David J. Jefferson, "Elvis Lives," *Newsweek*, August 19, 2002, pp. 54–56; "BMG Celebrates Elvis Presley during 25th Anniversary Year of World's Best-Selling Artist," BMG press release, March 26, 2002.

VIDEO CASE 17.2   Cherry Capital Airport Keeps People Flying

The written case on Cherry Capital Airport appears on page VC-21. The recently filmed Cherry Capital Airport video is designed to expand and highlight the concepts in this chapter and the concepts and questions covered in the written video case.

18

Advertising, Sales Promotion, and Public Relations

Chapter Objectives

1 Identify the three major advertising objectives and the two basic categories of advertising.

2 List the major advertising strategies.

3 Describe the process of creating an advertisement.

4 List and compare the major advertising media.

5 Outline the organization of the advertising function and the role of an advertising agency.

6 Identify the principal methods of sales promotion.

7 Explain the roles of cross promotions, public relations, publicity, and ethics in an organization's promotional strategy.

8 Explain how marketers assess promotional effectiveness.

George Foreman and His Lean Mean Grilling Machine

George Foreman's boxing career was a huge success. In fact, he won the heavyweight title twice—20 years apart—a feat at which boxing enthusiasts still marvel. Yet he is better known to a new generation of consumers as the man who sells the Lean Mean Grilling Machine.

Celebrities play a big part in the advertising campaigns of many products. Just about every time you turn on the television or flip through a magazine, you'll see a celeb selling something. Actor James Earl Jones delivers Verizon's message in sonorous tones. Celebrated chef Emeril Lagasse brightens his teeth with Crest. But George Foreman was an unlikely candidate for the celebrity sell, even though he made modest pitches for several companies before the grill manufactured by Salton landed on his own countertop. He was perceived as unsocial, unfriendly. "He was a guy who never smiled," recalls his friend and attorney Henry Holmes. "He feared and rejected the public." Then he had a personal revelation and underwent a major change. Today, he growls with a warm twinkle in his eye, and consumers eat it up. They also like eating food cooked on the specially designed grill he began promoting in the 1990s. That's because they believe what Foreman has to say. "You feel like he really likes the grill and believes in it," explains Michael Schiferl, a media relations expert. "The personality he projects is what's driving this." Holmes agrees. "Now, when [George] walks into a room, he lights it up. He is successful because he transcends age and race."

Since their relationship began, grill manufacturer Salton and celebrity spokesperson Foreman have created their own gold mine. After several years together, Salton simply gave Foreman a lump sum of $137.5 million instead of continuing to pay royalties on sales of the grill, which have climbed steadily over the last decade. Foreman is now the third highest-paid sports celebrity product endorser. He trails only Tiger Woods and Michael Jordan.

While some celebrities advertise a product for a short time, others like Foreman stay with it for so long that consumers eventually cannot separate the product from the name or face of the celebrity. That is certainly true of the Lean Mean Grilling Machine. We couldn't quite imagine buying it from anyone else. Meanwhile, Foreman has expanded his domain to include his own line of grill-ready foods—the perfect complement to the grill. Consumers can go online to Foreman's Web site to order a range of foods including bacon-wrapped filets, marinated chicken breasts, tuna steaks, and even the original "Knock Out" burger—all with George's name attached to them. They can also pick up a copy of *George Foreman's Guide to Life*, which offers tips on "how to get up off the canvas when life knocks you down." In addition, Foreman signed a deal to launch a clothing line for Casual Male Retail Group, which offers clothes for big and tall men.

A well-known face like George Foreman's can often mean the difference between an ignored message and one that attracts the viewer's attention. Foreman is now recognized by a broader audience than he was as a fighter—but he can still use his former career to build on his image as a health-conscious athlete. His career as a celebrity spokesperson may last even longer than his boxing career. So far, it's a total knockout.[1]

Chapter Overview

From the last chapter, you already know that the nonpersonal elements of promotion include advertising, sales promotion, and public relations. Thousands of organizations rely on nonpersonal selling in developing their promotional mixes and integrated marketing communications strategies. While advertising is the most visible form of nonpersonal promotion, marketers spend three times as much on sales promotion, and they often use them together to create effective promotional campaigns. Television is probably the most obvious medium for nonpersonal selling dollars. But theater advertising is a major ad component in Europe, and Regal Entertainment, the large U.S. movie theater chain, took in $70 million in on-screen advertising in just one year during a recent test.[2]

Marketers seeking excitement for new-product launches have recently paid as much as $3 million to have the Rolling Stones perform at a single event. Kraft Foods recently moved away from its traditional TV advertising for its back-to-school sales push in favor of sponsoring 'tween idol Aaron Carter's 30-city summer tour. The singer, a favorite of older children and preteens, was recently voted No. 1 Pop Star in a *Tiger Beat* poll. The marketer of such popular snacks as Oreos, Post cereals, Ritz crackers, Cheese Nips, and Kraft Cheese Singles mined kids' obsession with music and fame with an instant-win "Be a Pop Star" game with five grand prize trips to Los Angeles to meet Carter and make a demo CD.[3]

This chapter begins with a discussion of the types of advertising and explains how advertising is used to achieve a firm's objectives. It then considers alternative advertising strategies and the process of creating an advertisement. Next, we provide a detailed look at various advertising media channels, from television and radio to print advertising and direct mail to outdoor and interactive media. Sales promotion, the second major type of nonpersonal advertising, is explained with detailed discussions of both consumer-oriented and trade promotions. The chapter then focuses on the importance of public relations, publicity, and cross promotions in e-commerce. Alternative methods of measuring the effectiveness of both online and offline nonpersonal selling are examined. We conclude the chapter by exploring current ethical issues relating to nonpersonal selling.

Advertising

Twenty-first century advertising is closely related to integrated marketing communications (IMC) in many respects. While IMC involves a message dealing with buyer-seller relationships, **advertising** involves paid nonpersonal communication through various media with the purpose of informing or persuading members of a particular audience. Advertising is used by marketers to reach target markets such as business firms, not-for-profit organizations, or individuals identified in the message.

While the ability of the Internet to make every marketer a global marketer has become a truism, America remains home to most of the world's leading advertisers. General Motors, Procter & Gamble, Time Warner, Altria, and DaimlerChrysler are five of the top advertisers in the world, each spending more than $1 billion—an average of almost $3 million a day—on advertising. Although advertising spending totals over $200 billion each year, belt tightening by businesses facing declining revenues during the recent recession resulted in a 6.5 percent drop in ad spending during a recent 12-month period. But spending flattened the following year and, by 2003, was once again on the increase.[4]

Advertising spending varies among industries as well as companies. The cosmetic industry is widely known for pouring dollars into advertising, as is the auto manufacturing industry. In fact, total auto ad spending amounts to nearly $15 billion a year. Other industries, such as aviation manufacturing, spend far less—a mere $48 million annually.

As previous chapters have discussed, the emergence of the marketing concept, with its emphasis on a companywide consumer orientation, boosted the importance of integrated marketing communications. This change, in turn, expanded the role of advertising. Today, a typical consumer is exposed to hundreds of advertising messages each day. Advertising provides an efficient, inexpensive, and fast method of reaching the ever-elusive, increasingly segmented consumer market. Its current role rivals those of sales promotion and personal selling. In fact, advertising has become a key ingredient in the effective implementation of the marketing concept.

FIGURE 18.1
An Example of Institutional Advertising

Types of Advertising

1
Identify the three major advertising objectives and the two basic categories of advertising.

Advertisements fall into two broad categories: product advertising and institutional advertising. **Product advertising** is nonpersonal selling of a particular good or service. This is the type of advertising the average person usually thinks of when talking about most promotional activities. **Institutional advertising,** in contrast, promotes a concept, an idea, a philosophy, or the goodwill of an industry, company, organization, person, geographical location, or government agency. This term has a broader meaning than *corporate advertising,* which is typically limited to nonproduct advertising sponsored by a specific profit-seeking firm.

Institutional advertising is often closely related to the public-relations function of the enterprise. The ad in Figure 18.1 featuring the Statue of Liberty attempts to encourage visitors to return to the beauty and excitement of New York. Its ultimate objective is to increase overall spending by visitors to the state rather than increase market share for a specific brand.

Objectives of Advertising

Marketers use advertising messages to accomplish three primary objectives: to inform, to persuade, and to remind. These objectives may be used individually or, more typically, in conjunction with each other. For example, an ad for a not-for-profit agency may inform the

Briefly Speaking

In good times people want to advertise; in bad times they have to.

Bruce Barton (1886–1967) American advertising executive

Marketing Dictionary

advertising Paid nonpersonal communication through various media with the purpose of informing or persuading members of a particular audience.

product advertising Nonpersonal selling of a particular good or service.

institutional advertising Promotion of a concept, idea, philosophy, or goodwill of an industry, company, organization, person, geographical location, or government agency.

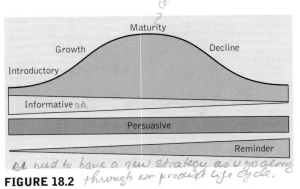

FIGURE 18.2
Advertising Objectives in Relation to Stage in the Product Life Cycle

public of the existence of the organization and at the same time persuade the audience to make a donation, join the organization, or attend a function.

Informative advertising seeks to develop initial demand for a good, service, organization, person, place, idea, or cause. The promotion of any new market entry tends to pursue this objective because marketing success at this stage often depends simply on announcing availability. Therefore, informative advertising is common in the introductory stage of the product life cycle.

Persuasive advertising attempts to increase demand for an existing good, service, organization, person, place, idea, or cause. Persuasive advertising is a competitive type of promotion suited to the growth stage and the early part of the maturity stage of the product life cycle.

Reminder advertising strives to reinforce previous promotional activity by keeping the name of a good, service, organization, person, place, idea, or cause before the public. It is common in the latter part of the maturity stage and throughout the decline stage of the product life cycle. Nabisco's Triscuits have been around for a long time; the packaged-good company's marketers continue to advertise as a means of reminding consumers of the heartiness of the crackers.

Figure 18.2 illustrates the relationship between advertising objectives and the stages of the product life cycle. Informative advertising tends to work best during the early stages, while reminder advertising is effective later on. Persuasive advertising, if done well, can be effective through the entire life cycle.

Traditionally, marketers stated their advertising objectives as direct sales goals. A more current and realistic standard, however, views advertising as a way to achieve communications objectives, including informing, persuading, and reminding potential customers of the product. Advertising attempts to condition consumers to adopt favorable viewpoints toward a promotional message. The goal of an ad is to improve the likelihood that a customer will buy a particular good or service. In this sense, advertising illustrates the close relationship between marketing communications and promotional strategy.

To get the best value for a firm's advertising investment, marketers must first determine what that firm's advertising objectives are. Effective advertising can enhance consumer perceptions of quality in a good or service, leading to increased customer loyalty, repeat purchases, and protection against price wars. In addition, perceptions of superiority pay off in the firm's ability to raise prices without losing market share.

Advertising Strategies

2

List the major advertising strategies.

If the primary function of marketing is to bring buyers and sellers together, then advertising is the means to an end. Effective advertising strategies accomplish at least one of three tasks: informing, persuading, or reminding consumers. The secret to success in choosing the best strategy is developing a message that best positions a firm's product in the audience's mind. Among the advertising strategies available for use by 21st century marketers are comparative advertising and celebrity advertising, as well as decisions about global and interactive ads. Channel-oriented decisions such as retail and cooperative advertising must also be devised.

Marketers often combine several of these advertising strategies to ensure that the advertisement accomplishes set objectives. As markets become more segmented, the need for personalized advertising increases. The next sections describe strategies that contemporary marketers develop to reach their target markets.

Comparative Advertising

Firms whose goods and services are not the leaders in their markets often favor **comparative advertising,** a promotional strategy that emphasizes advertising messages with direct or indirect comparisons to dominant brands in the industry. By contrast, market leaders seldom acknowledge in their advertising that competing products even exist, and when they do, they usually do not point out any benefits of the competing brand.

Struggling desktop computer maker Gateway recently launched an advertising campaign for its new Profile PC by showing it alongside Apple Computer's iMac to demonstrate their similar appearance and then touting Gateway's advantage in price, performance, and software selection. Print ads and TV commercials urged consumers to "Think Smarter," a phrase borrowed from Apple's long-running "Think Different" tag line.[5]

A generation ago, comparative advertising was not the norm; in fact, it was frowned on. But the Federal Trade Commission now encourages comparative advertising. Regulators believe such ads keep marketers competitive and consumers better informed about their choices. Generally speaking, where there is competition through advertising, prices tend to go down because people can shop around. This benefit has proved increasingly true for online consumers, who now use bots to help find the best prices on goods and services.

Celebrity Testimonials *Tiger Woods, Serena Williams*

A popular technique for increasing advertising readership in a cluttered promotional environment and improving overall effectiveness of a marketing message involves the use of celebrity spokespeople. About one of every five U.S. ads currently includes celebrities. This type of advertising is also popular in foreign countries. In Japan, 80 percent of all ads use celebrities, both local and international stars. U.S. celebrities featured in Japanese ads include actors Harrison Ford for Kirin Beer, Jodie Foster for Keri Cosmetics and Latte Coffee, and Paul Newman for Evance watch stores. Japanese consumers view foreign stars as images more than actual people, which helps marketers to sell products. They also associate American stars with quality.

Both the number of celebrity ads and the dollars spent on those ads have increased in recent years. Professional athletes are among the highest paid product endorsers, raking in millions per year. They appear in advertisements for a wide variety of products, many having little or nothing to do with sports. Basketball great Michael Jordan earns more than $30 million annually as a spokesperson for underwear maker Hanes and for his MJ clothing line. Practically everyone has seen former boxer George Foreman in ads for Salton's Lean Mean Fat-Reducing Grilling Machine, as the opening vignette discussed. And golfing phenom Tiger Woods has lucrative deals with dozens of products, ranging from telecommunications and credit card giants to Buick automobiles, in addition to his $40 million agreement with Nike Golf.

One advantage of associations with big-name personalities is improved product recognition in a promotional environment filled with hundreds of competing 15- and 30-second commercials. Advertisers use the term *clutter* to describe this situation. As e-commerce continues to soar, one inevitable result has been the increase in advertising clutter as companies rush to sell their goods and services online. But marketers need to remember that an effective online site must have meaningful content and helpful service.

Another advantage to using celebrities occurs when marketers are trying to reach consumers of another culture. Blockbuster

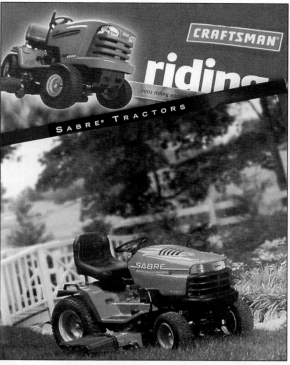

Marketers at tractor and lawn-equipment giant John Deere chose a strong comparative advertising campaign to position its little-known Sabre entry-level lawn tractor against the popular Sears Craftsman tractor. In addition to detailed copy emphasizing Sabre's advantages over its rival at Sears, the comparative ad included the John Deere Web address, toll-free number for additional information, and a comparison chart for the two models.

Marketing Dictionary

informative advertising Promotion that seeks to develop initial demand for a good, service, organization, person, place, idea, or cause.

persuasive advertising Promotion that attempts to increase demand for an existing good, service, organization, person, place, idea, or cause.

reminder advertising Advertising that reinforces previous promotional activity by keeping the name of a good, service, organization, person, place, idea, or cause before the public.

comparative advertising Advertising strategy that emphasizes messages with direct or indirect promotional comparisons between competing brands.

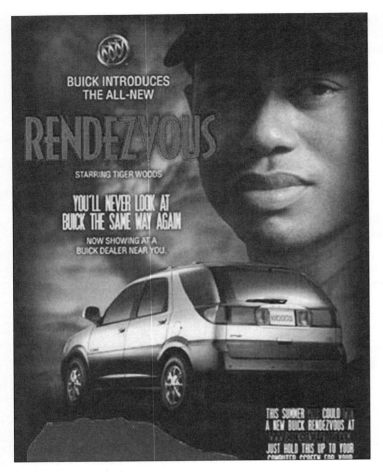

Tiger Woods, easily the most recognizable golfer in the PGA, has numerous endorsement deals. One of his most successful campaigns has been for Buick.

Video and McDonald's have hired Hispanic stars to attract Hispanic consumers to their stores. Actress Daisy Fuentes appears in ads for McDonald's, while John Leguizamo and Hector Elizondo advertise for Blockbuster. "We see lots of new companies going into the Hispanic market who have never advertised before, and one way is hiring celebrities," explains Raul Mateu, a vice president at the William Morris talent agency. "It seems like an easy way of getting instant credibility in the marketplace is using [the celebrity's] equity."[6]

A celebrity testimonial generally succeeds when the celebrity is a credible source of information for the product being promoted. The most effective ads of this type establish relevant links between the celebrities and the advertised goods or services, such as the models and actresses who endorse Revlon cosmetics, as described in the "Marketing Hits" box. Note that in the examples listed earlier, even though many of the products are not sports related, they do make a link to the celebrity—likable boxing champion George Foreman seems like a person who enjoys eating. Several studies of consumer responses show that celebrities improve the product's believability, recall of the product, and brand recognition. Celebrity endorsements also create positive attitudes, leading to greater brand equity.

However, a celebrity who endorses too many products may create marketplace confusion. Customers may remember the celebrity but not the product or brand; worse, they might connect the celebrity to a competing brand. Another problem can arise if a celebrity is involved in a scandal or has trouble with the law, as marketers do not want their products associated with a negative image. Kmart merchandisers worried about a shopper backlash harming sales of their highly successful Martha Stewart product line when allegations of insider stock trading by the nation's decorating diva became the subject of a congressional investigation.[7]

Some advertisers try to avoid such problems by using cartoon characters as endorsers. Snoopy, a character in the popular *Peanuts* comic strip and long-running TV animated programs, has appeared in MetLife ads for years. Some advertisers may actually prefer cartoon characters because the characters can never say anything negative about the product, they do exactly what the marketers want them to do, and they cannot get involved in scandals. The only drawback is high licensing fees; popular animated characters often cost more than live celebrities. Companies may create their own cartoon characters, which eventually become celebrities in their own right as a result of many appearances in advertisements, as is the case with the Keebler elves.

In recent years, marketers have begun to consider celebrities as marketing partners rather than pretty or famous faces who can sell goods and services. Tiger Woods has been active in developing Nike's golf gear and apparel. Former supermodel Claudia Schiffer not only agreed to endorse a signature line of PalmPilots, but she also assisted in positioning the hand-held com-

Marketing Hit

Revlon Wants to Be Unforgettable

Background. What do Julianne Moore, James King, Halle Berry, and Ellen Barkin have in common? They are all celebrities hired recently to appear in Revlon ads. Why the sudden rush? Revlon made a mistake a couple of years ago by firing long-time model Cindy Crawford in what proved to be an ill-fated decision to focus on unknown models to promote its cosmetics.

continued on next page

puters in the electronics market by selecting fashionable colors and her own favorite software programs. Of course, George Foreman actually uses the grills he advertises. "George has been very active in the marketing of his grills and genuinely believes in them," says Jake Fuller, an equity research analyst at Credit Suisse First Boston in New York. The grills served up $375 million in sales for Salton in one year.[8]

Retail Advertising

Most consumers are confronted daily with **retail advertising,** which includes all advertising by retail stores that sell goods or services directly to the consuming public. While this activity accounts for a sizable portion of total annual advertising expenditures, retail advertising varies widely in its effectiveness. One study showed that consumers often respond with suspicion to retail price advertisements. Source, message, and shopping experience seem to affect consumer attitudes toward these advertisements.

Many retail stores view advertising as a secondary activity, although that is changing. Except for the giants like electronics retailer Best Buy, illustrated in Figure 18.3, retailers rarely use independent advertising agencies, perhaps because of the expense associated with agencies. Instead, store managers may accept responsibility for advertising in addition to their other duties. Management can begin to correct this problem by assigning one individual the sole responsibility and authority for developing an effective retail advertising program.

A retailer often shares advertising costs with a manufacturer or wholesaler in a technique called **cooperative advertising.** For example, an apparel marketer may pay a percentage of the cost of a retail store's newspaper advertisement featuring its product lines. Cooperative advertising campaigns originated to take advantage of the media's practice of offering lower rates to local advertisers than to national ones. Later, cooperative advertising became part of programs to improve dealer relations. The retailer likes the chance to secure advertising that it could not run otherwise. Cooperative advertising can create vertical links, as when a manufacturer and retailer coordinate their resources. It can also involve firms at the same level of the supply chain. In a horizontal arrangement, a group of retailers—for example, all the Ford dealers in the northeastern U.S.—might pool their resources.

Interactive Advertising

Millions of advertising messages float across idle—and active—computer screens in homes and offices around the country every day. Net surfers play games that are embedded with ads from the site sponsors. Companies offer free e-mail service to people willing to receive ads with their personal messages. Video screens on grocery carts display ads for shoppers to see as they wheel down the aisles of grocery stores.

Since marketers realize that two-way communications provide more effective methods for achieving promotional objectives, they are interested in interactive media. *Interactive advertising* involves two-way promotional messages transmitted through communication channels that induce message recipients to participate actively in the promotional effort. Achieving this involvement is the difficult task facing contemporary marketers. Although interactive advertising has become nearly synonymous with e-commerce and the Web, it also includes other

Marketing Dictionary

retail advertising All advertising by retail stores that sell goods or services directly to the consuming public.

cooperative advertising Strategy in which a retailer shares advertising costs with a manufacturer or wholesaler.

FIGURE 18.3
Retail Advertising Used to Inform and Persuade Shoppers to Patronize Electronics Retailer Best Buy

formats such as kiosks in shopping malls. Multimedia technology, the Internet, and commercial online services are changing the nature of advertising from a one-way, passive communication technique to more effective, two-way marketing communications. Interactive advertising creates dialogue between marketers and individual shoppers, providing more materials as the user asks. The advertiser's challenge is to gain and hold consumer interest in an environment where these individuals control what they want to see.

Interactive advertising changes the balance between marketers and consumers. Unlike the traditional role of advertising—providing brief, entertaining, attention-catching messages—interactive media provide information to help consumers throughout the purchase and consumption processes. In a sense, it becomes closer to personal selling as consumers receive immediate responses to questions or requests for more information about goods and services. Interactive advertising provides consumers with more information in less time to help them make necessary comparisons between available products.

Successful interactive advertising adds value by offering the viewer more than just product-related information. An ad on the Web can do more than promote a brand; it can create a company store, provide customer service, and offer additional content.

Most firms deliver their interactive advertising messages through proprietary online services and through the Web. In fact, online ad spending is estimated at $6 billion per year. Top high-tech Internet spenders include Microsoft and IBM. Of the eight largest Internet spenders not based in information technologies, four are auto firms—General Motors, Ford, Toyota, and Honda. The other four include CBS Sportsline, Disney, Visa, and Amazon.[9]

Creating an Advertisement

3

Describe the process of creating an advertisement.

Marketers spend about $200 billion a year on advertising campaigns in the U.S. alone. With so much money at stake, they must create effective, memorable ads that increase sales and enhance their organizations' images. They cannot afford to waste resources on poor ads that fail to capture consumers' attention, communicate a message effectively, and lead to a purchase, donation, or other positive action for the organization.

Research helps marketers create better ads by pinpointing goals that an ad needs to accomplish, such as educating consumers about product features, enhancing brand loyalty, or improving consumer perception of the brand. These objectives should guide the design of the ad. Marketers can also discover what appeals to consumers and can test ads with potential buyers before committing funds for a campaign.

Marketers sometimes face specific challenges as they develop advertising objectives for services. They must find a creative way to fill out the intangible images of most services and successfully convey the benefits that consumers receive. Also, they may have to find a strategy for advertising in a way that turns a negative event into a positive one, as in the case of life insurance.

Translating Advertising Objectives into Advertising Plans

Once a company defines its objectives for an advertising campaign, it can develop its advertising plan. Marketing research assists managers in making strategic decisions that guide choices in technical areas

FIGURE 18.4
Elements of the Advertising Planning Process

such as budgeting, copywriting, scheduling, and media selection. Posttests, which will be discussed in greater detail later in the chapter, measure the effectiveness of advertising and form the basis for feedback concerning possible adjustments. The elements of advertising planning are shown in Figure 18.4. The most experienced marketers know the importance of following even the most basic steps in the process, such as market analysis.

As Chapter 8 explained, positioning involves developing a marketing strategy that aims to achieve a desired position in a prospective buyer's mind. Marketers use a positioning strategy that distinguishes their good or service from those of competitors. Effective advertising then communicates the desired position by emphasizing certain product characteristics, such as performance attributes, price/quality, competitors' shortcomings, applications, user needs, and product classes.

Advertising Messages

The strategy for creating a message starts with the customer benefits a product offers and moves to the creative concept phase, in which marketers strive to bring an appropriate message to consumers using both visual and verbal components. Marketers work to create an ad with meaningful, believable, and distinctive appeals—one that stands out from the clutter and escapes "zapping" by the television remote control.

Usually, ads are not created individually but as part of specific campaigns. An **advertising campaign** is a series of different but related ads that use a single theme and appear in different media within a specified time period. The series of Gateway Computer ads, aimed at capturing market share from the Apple iMac, represents an advertising campaign.

In developing a creative strategy, advertisers must decide how to communicate their marketing message. They must balance message characteristics, such as the tone of the appeal, the extent of information provided and the conclusion to which it leads the consumer, the side of the story the ad tells, and its emphasis on verbal or visual primary elements.

Should the tone of the advertisement focus on a practical appeal such as price, or should it evoke an emotional response of, say, fear, humor, or fantasy? In recent years, marketers have relied increasingly on fear appeals. Ads for insurance, cars, health-care products, and even certain foods imply that incorrect buying decisions could lead to illness, injury, or other bad consequences. Even ads for business services imply that if a company doesn't purchase the advertised services, its competitors will move ahead or valuable information may be lost.

Pharmaceutical companies spend nearly $2 billion a year on advertising, much of which is directed toward consumers' fears—whether fear of hair loss, fear of allergies, or fear of heart attacks. These drug advertisements have flourished in both print and broadcast media after the Food and Drug Administration lifted a ban on prescription drug advertising on television. Such ads have become a key component of marketers' pulling channel strategies.

Marketing Dictionary

advertising campaign   Series of different but related ads that use a single theme and appear in different media within a specified time period.

Typical ads encourage readers and viewers to ask their doctors whether the medication should be prescribed for their medical needs.

Fear appeals can backfire, however. Viewers are likely to practice selective perception and tune out statements they perceive as too strong or not credible. Some analysts believe that viewer/reader backlash will eventually occur due to the amount of prescription drug advertising based on fear appeals.

A humorous ad seeks to create a positive mood related to a product. Humor can improve audience awareness and recall and enhance the consumer's favorable image of the brand. After all, if the ad makes the consumer feel good, then the product may as well. But advertising professionals differ in their opinions of the effectiveness of humorous ads. Some believe that humor distracts attention from brand and product features; consumers remember the humor but not the product. Humorous ads, because they are so memorable, may lose their effectiveness sooner than ads with other kinds of appeals. In addition, humor can be tricky because what one group of consumers finds funny may not be funny at all to another group. Men and women sometimes have a different sense of humor, as do people of different ages. This distinction may become even greater across cultures.

Developing and Preparing Ads

The final step in the advertising process—the development and preparation of an advertisement—should flow logically from the promotional theme selected. This process should create an ad that becomes a complementary part of the marketing mix with a carefully determined role in the total marketing strategy. Preparation of an advertisement should emphasize features like its creativity, its continuity with past advertisements, and possibly its association with other company products.

What immediate tasks should an advertisement accomplish? Regardless of the chosen target, an advertisement should (1) gain attention and interest, (2) inform and/or persuade, and (3) eventually lead to a purchase or other desired action. It should gain attention in a productive way; that is, it should instill some recall of the good or service. Otherwise, it will not lead to buying action.

Gaining attention and generating interest—cutting through the clutter—can be a formidable task. Stimulating buying action is often difficult because an advertisement cannot actually close a sale. Nevertheless, if an ad gains attention and informs or persuades, it probably represents a worthwhile investment of marketing resources. Too many advertisers fail to suggest how audience members can purchase their products if they desire to do so. Creative design should eliminate this shortcoming.

**FIGURE 18.5
Elements of a
Typical Ad**

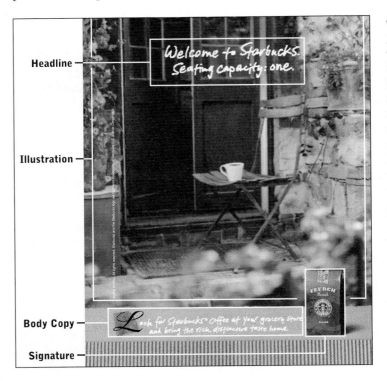

When Starbucks decided to expand its market by offering its premium coffee in retail stores, it developed a series of ads to inform customers of its availability in non-Starbucks outlets. The ad in Figure 18.5 shows the four major elements of this print advertisement: headline, illustration, body copy, and signature. Headlines and illustrations (photographs, drawings, or other artwork) should work together to generate interest and attention. Body copy serves to inform, persuade, and stimulate buying action. The signature, which may include the company name, address, phone number, Web address, slogan, trademark, or simply a product photo, names the sponsoring organization. An ad may also have one or more subheads—headings subordinate to the main headline that either link the main headline to the body copy or subdivide sections of the body copy.

After advertisers conceive an idea for an ad that gains attention, informs and persuades, and stimulates purchases, their next step involves refining the thought sketch into a rough layout. Continued refinements of the rough layout eventually produce the final version of the advertisement design that is ready to be executed, printed, or recorded.

The creation of each advertisement in a campaign requires an evolutionary process that begins with an idea and ultimately results in a finished ad that is ready for distribution through print or electronic media. The idea itself must first be converted into a thought sketch, which is a tangible summary of the intended message.

Advances in technology allow advertisers to create novel, eye-catching advertisements. Innovative computer software packages now allow artists to merge multiple images to create a single image with a natural, seamless appearance. Computer-generated images appeal to younger, computer-literate consumers.

Creating Interactive Ads

Web surfers want engaging, lively content that takes advantage of the medium's capabilities and goes beyond what they find elsewhere. Increasingly, Web ads are competing with television ads by enhancing their content with video and audio clips. But this orientation overlooks the Web's major advantages: offering speed, providing information, exchanging input through two-way communications, offering self-directed entertainment, and allowing personal choice.

The growing number of new ways to advertise on the Web attest to the rapidly changing environment marketers encounter on the Internet and in e-commerce in general. Web ads have grown from information-based home pages to innovative, interactive channels for transmitting messages to cyberaudiences, including banners, pop-ups, keyword ads, advertorials, and interstitials. In fact, many online ads now closely resemble television commercials.

Advertising banners were the trendsetters in online advertising, allowing customers to quickly access a company's goods and services through other Web site links. *Banners,* advertisements on a Web page that link to an advertiser's site, are the most common type of advertising on the Web. They can be free of charge or cost thousands of dollars per month depending on the amount of hits the site receives. Online advertisers often describe their Internet ads in terms of "richness," referring to the degree to which new technologies—such as streaming video, 3-D animation, Java script, and interactive capabilities—are implemented in the banners.

Banners have evolved into a more target-specific technique for Internet advertising with the advent of missiles, which are messages that appear on the screen at exactly the right moment. When a customer visits the site of Company A's competitor, a missile can be programmed to appear on the customer's monitor that allows the customer to click on a direct link to Company A's site, which many people may feel is a questionable practice.

Keyword ads are an outcropping of banner ads. Used in search engines, keyword ads appear on the results page of a search, specific to the term being searched. Advertisers pay search engines to target their ads and only display the banners when users search for relevant keywords, allowing marketers to target specific audiences. For example, if a user searched on the term "digital camera," keyword ads might appear for electronic boutiques or camera shops that sell digital cameras and film.

Banner designs that have also evolved into larger advertising squares that closely resemble advertisements in the telephone Yellow Pages are called *advertorials.* An advertorial on the *Forbes* Web site costs about $25,000 a month. Advertisers quickly expanded on these advertorials with *interstitials*— ads that appear in between Web pages of related content. Interstitials appear in a separate browser window while the user waits for a Web page to download. Then there are pop-ups, as described in the "Solving an Ethical Controversy" box, which are little advertising windows that appear in front of the top window of a user's computer screen, and "pop-unders," which appear under the top window. All of these ads are more aggressive than banners, forcing consumers to take action to eliminate them from their screens, which is the source of controversy discussed in the box.[10] Many users complain that interstitials, like pop-ups and missiles, are intrusive and unwanted. Interstitials are more likely to contain large graphics and streaming presentations than banner ads and therefore are more difficult to

right wrong

Solving an Ethical Controversy

What to Do about Pop-Up Ads?

If dinnertime telemarketing calls were the bane of consumers' existence during the 1990s, pop-up ads must be the new generation of unwanted communication. Pop-ups—those pesky little advertising windows that appear, unsolicited, on your computer screen—are increasing in number and thus becoming a widespread problem for PC users who do not want to view them. Still, online advertisers have a right to show you their wares and give you the opportunity to buy them, don't they?

Should pop-up advertising be subject to some regulation?

PRO

1. It is difficult to "turn off" a pop-up ad. Consumers have to install special software to do so. "At least when I watch TV I can switch channels when the commercial starts," complains one consumer. "Pop-ups leave us with no options. They're annoying and intrusive."

2. Pop-ups can lead to links that are inappropriate or undesirable for children. "Schools have a real problem with that," explains Matina Fresenius, CEO of Panicware Software.

CON

1. People who do not want to view pop-ups can install programs such as http://www.panicware.com to eliminate them.

2. Not all pop-ups are unsavory; some provide additional services. "The sites that use pop-ups to view a new window in a smaller screen or to sign up for a newsletter are OK," notes Panicware Software CEO Matina Fresenius.

Summary

Online advertising is still navigating new territory, and disagreements over what is acceptable and what is not are bound to surface. Perhaps the most important consideration for marketers is whether their practices may cause distress or even harm to the very people they are trying to reach. Certainly, pop-ups are noticeable—a goal of every marketer. But if some companies use them indiscriminately, they may be inviting regulation—or even rejection—of what could have been a powerful, positive advertising medium. America Online, the number one ISP, has already decided to stop selling those pesky pop-up ads.

SOURCES: Paul Davidson, "AOL Takes Aim at Pop-Up Ads," *USA Today*, October 15, 2002, p. B1; Tobi Elkin, "'Intrusive' Pop-Ups Get Closer Scrutiny after iVillage Block," *Advertising Age*, August 5, 2002, p. 6; Jefferson Graham, "Software Blocks That Deluge of Pop-Ups," *USA Today*, January 29, 2002, p. D4.

---

ignore than typical banner ads. And despite complaints, some studies show that users are more likely to click on interstitials than banners.

Web site developers can now add 3-D effects to their sites, a capability that provides new opportunities for advertisers. For example, graphics can show products in lifelike representations. Retailers can create 3-D stores where visitors can take a stroll through the virtual aisles viewing merchandise on display; Web sites need no longer provide their information in cataloglike formats.

Media Selection

4

List and compare the major advertising media.

One of the most important decisions in developing an advertising strategy is the selection of appropriate media to carry a firm's message to its audience. The media selected must be capable of accomplishing the communications objectives of informing, persuading, and reminding potential customers of the good, service, person, or idea being advertised.

Research identifies the ad's target market to determine its size and characteristics. Advertisers then match the target characteristics with the media best able to reach that particular audience. The objective of media selection is to achieve adequate media coverage without advertising beyond the identifiable limits of the potential market. Finally, cost comparisons between alternatives should determine the best possible media purchase.

TABLE 18.1   **Comparison of Advertising Media Alternatives**

MEDIA OUTLET	PERCENTAGE OF TOTAL*	ADVANTAGES	DISADVANTAGES
Broadcast			
Network television	17	Mass coverage; repetition; flexibility; prestige	High cost; temporary message; public distrust; lack of selectivity
Cable television	8	Same strengths as network TV; less market coverage since not every viewer is a cable subscriber	Same disadvantages as network TV, although cable TV ads are considerably more targeted to specific viewer segments
Radio	8	Immediacy; low cost; flexibility; targeted audience; mobility	Short life span; highly fragmented audience
Print			
Newspapers	19	Tailored to individual communities; ability to refer back to ads	Short life span
Direct mail	19	Selectivity; intense coverage; speed; flexibility; opportunity to convey complete information; personalization	High cost; consumer resistance; dependence on effective mailing list
Magazines	5	Selectivity; quality image reproduction; long life; prestige	Lack of flexibility
Outdoor	2	Quick, visual communication of simple ideas; link to local goods and services; repetition	Brief exposure; environmental concerns
Electronic			
Internet	3	Two-way communications; flexibility; link to self-directed entertainment	Poor image reproduction; limited scheduling options; difficult to measure effectiveness

*An estimated 20 percent is spent on a variety of miscellaneous media, including Yellow Pages listings, business papers, transit displays, point-of-purchase displays, cinema advertising, and regional farm papers.

SOURCE: Data from "Advertising Boom in U.S. Ended in '01," *Advertising Age*, May 13, 2002, p. 24.

Table 18.1 compares the major advertising media by noting their shares of overall advertising expenditures. It also compares the advantages and disadvantages of each media alternative. *Broadcast media* include television (network and cable) and radio. Newspapers, magazines, outdoor advertising, and direct mail represent the major types of print media. Electronic media include the Internet and kiosks.

Television

Television—network and cable combined—accounts for almost one of every four advertising dollars spent in the U.S. The attractiveness of television advertising is that marketers can reach local and national markets. Whereas most newspaper advertising revenues come from local advertisers, the greatest share of television advertising revenues comes from companies that advertise nationally. The newest trend in television advertising is virtual ads—banner-type logos and brief messages that are superimposed onto television coverage of sporting events so that they seem to be a part of the arena's signage but cannot be seen by anyone attending the game. Then there are streaming headlines run by some news stations, which are paid for by corporate sponsors whose names and logos appear within the news stream. Another trend in television advertising is the abbreviated spot—15- and 30-second spots— that costs less to make and buy and is too quick for most viewers to zap with their remote controls.

Marketing Hit

Monster.com Does a Good Job Advertising

Background. Just a few years ago, about one in four television commercials aired during the Super Bowl was sponsored by a then-high-flying dot.com company at about $2 million for a 30-second spot. But most of the advertising presented by the Internet firms was about as uninspiring as their earnings prospects or—worse yet—confusing to the viewer. One striking exception was job services site Monster.com.

The Challenge. Catching viewers' attention, especially during a hyped event like the Super Bowl, is a challenge. Yet for the last five years or so, Monster.com has been praised for its clever, creative ads. How do they keep it up?

The Strategy. Monster.com has a huge advertising budget for a company its size. It spent $4 million on one recent Super Bowl and another $10 million on Olympics ads. Heavy-hitters such as Anheuser-Busch and Visa are also prominent advertisers during these events, which places Monster in prestigious company. Monster's long-running "Never Settle" campaign is aimed at both employers and job seekers instead of just one segment of the employment market. And the job-search dot.com doesn't only focus on one or two major events for its advertising; in fact, its advertising budget is spread over a range of venues.

The Outcome. Monster continues to be the Web's largest job site (HotJobs is second). The firm reports that job searches have doubled and even quadrupled in the days following several Super Bowls, hitting 8.1 million after one recent game. "This is a company that spends a lot of money on marketing,"

continued on next page

In the past decade, cable television's share of ad spending and revenues has grown tremendously. Satellite television has contributed to increased cable penetration, which almost three-fourths of all Americans now have installed in their homes. In response to declining ratings and soaring costs, network television companies like NBC, CBS, ABC, Fox, and Warner Bros. (WB) are refocusing their advertising strategies with a heavy emphasis on moving onto the Net to capture younger audiences.

As cable audiences grow, programming improves, and ratings rise, advertisers are compelled to earmark more of their advertising budgets to this medium. In fact, cable was the only advertising medium—other than direct mail—to actually grow in the advertising downturn that accompanied the recent recession.[11] Cable advertising offers marketers access to more narrowly defined target audiences than other broadcast media can provide. The great variety of special-interest channels devoted to subjects such as cooking, history, home and garden, health, and golf attract specialized audiences and permit niche marketing.

Television advertising offers the advantages of powerful impact, mass coverage, repetition of messages, flexibility, and prestige, as described in the "Marketing Hits" box about Monster.com. Its disadvantages include loss of control of the promotional message to the telecaster (which can influence its impact), high costs, high mortality rates for commercials, and some public distrust. Compared with other media, television can suffer from lack of selectivity since specific TV programs may not reach consumers in a precisely defined target market without a significant degree of wasted coverage. However, the growing specialization of cable TV channels can help to resolve the problem.

Finally, it is important to note that some types of products are actually banned from television advertising. Tobacco goods, such as cigarettes, cigars, and smokeless tobacco, fall into this category. Ads for alcoholic beverages are not allowed on network television, but companies such as Anheuser-Busch have done very well with their commercials on cable channels and independent stations permitting them.

Radio

Radio advertising has always been a popular media choice for up-to-the-minute newscasts and for targeting advertising messages to local audiences. But in recent years, radio has become one of the fastest growing media alternatives. As more and more people find they have less and less time, radio provides immediate information and entertainment at work, at play, and in the car. In addition, as e-commerce continues to push the growth in global business, more people are traveling abroad to seek out new markets. For these travelers, radio, because many radio stations are airing over the Internet, is a means of staying in touch with home—wherever that may be. Marketers frequently use radio advertising to reach local audiences. But in recent years, it plays an increasingly important role as a national—and even global—listening favorite. Thousands of online listeners use the Internet to beam in on radio stations from almost every city—tuning in on an easy-listening station in London, a top-40 Hong Kong broadcaster, or a chat show from Toronto. Other listeners equip their vehicles with satellite radio to maintain contact with hometown or destination stations during long trips.

Radio ad revenues in the U.S. are slightly larger than those for cable television. Advertisers like the chance to reach people while they drive because they are a captive audience. With an increase in commuters, this market is growing. Stations can adapt to local preferences by changing format, such as going from country and western to an all-news or rock-and-talk radio. The variety of stations allows advertisers to easily target audiences and to tailor their messages to those listeners. Other benefits include low cost, flexibility, and mobility. Disadvantages include fragmentation, the temporary nature of messages, and a lack of research information as compared with television.

While most radio listening is done at home, in cars, or with headset-equipped portables, technology has given birth to Net radio. Web-cast radio allows customers to widen their listening times and choices through their computers. The potential for selling on this new channel is great. A listener can simply "click here to purchase the song you're hearing." Other goods are easily adapted to click-and-sell possibilities.

Newspapers

Newspaper advertising continues to dominate local markets, accounting for $44 billion of annual advertising expenditures. In addition to retail advertisements, classified advertising is an important part of newspaper revenues.

Newspapers' primary advantages start with flexibility because advertising can vary from one locality to the next. Newspapers offer community prestige since readers recognize they have deep impacts on their communities. "Newspapers provide the kind of touch points for people to get the depth behind the broad premise laid out in other media," says Chris Wall, creative director for ad agency Ogilvy & Mather. "Creative people have always liked newspapers. And newspapers have gotten much better technology in the past fifteen years."[12] Newspapers allow intensive coverage for ads. In a typical location, a single newspaper reaches 90 percent of the homes. "One thing we know is that media you can target geographically should do better," observes Jon Mandel, comanaging director of MediaCom. "The closer you can get to the point of sale, especially in a recessionary environment, the better off you're going to be."[13] Readers control their exposure to the advertising message, unlike television or radio advertising messages, and can refer back to newspaper ads.

According to a survey by the Newspaper Association of America and the American Society of Newspapers, consumers rely on newspapers as their primary source of advertising information for a variety of goods and services. Survey participants reported referring to newspapers for information on new cars 52 percent of the time (compared with television 15 percent of the time). Consumers shopping for home appliances also favor newspapers over television (53 percent versus 10 percent), as well as those looking for personal computers (37 percent versus 8 percent).[14]

Newspaper advertising does have some disadvantages: a short life span, hasty reading (the typical reader spends about 40 minutes reading the newspaper), and relatively poor reproduction quality, although that is changing as technology improves.

Magazines

Advertisers divide magazines into two broad categories: consumer magazines and business magazines. These categories are also subdivided into monthly and weekly publications. The four top magazines in the U.S. in order of their ad revenue ranking are *TV Guide, People, Sports Illustrated,* and *Time.* Of these four, only *TV Guide* is not owned by Time Warner.

The primary advantages of magazine advertising include the following: selectivity in reaching precise target markets, quality reproduction, long life, the prestige associated with some magazines, and the extra services that many publications offer. The primary disadvantage is that magazines lack the flexibility of newspapers, radio, and television.

Media buyers study circulation numbers and demographics information for various publications to choose placement opportunities and to negotiate rates. The same advertising categories have claimed the title for big spenders for several years running. Automotive, retail, and movies and media advertising have held their first, second, and third places, respectively, each year and have continued to show

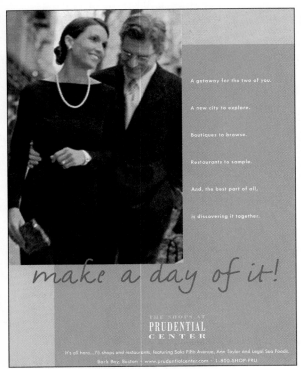

Marketers for **The Shops at Prudential Center,**
Boston's upscale high-fashion group of 75 shops and
restaurants, pooled their advertising media dollars and
selected *Yankee Magazine* for their advertisement.
The magazine, widely circulated in New England,
enjoys a readership of affluent consumers residing in
the Northeast.

strong growth percentages. Advertisers seeking to promote their products
to target markets can reach them by advertising in the appropriate magazines.

Direct Mail

As discussed in Chapter 16, direct mail advertising consists of sales letters,
postcards, leaflets, folders, booklets, catalogs, and house organs (periodicals published by organizations to cover internal issues). Its advantages
come from direct mail's selectivity, intensive coverage, speed, formal flexibility, completeness of information, and personalization. Disadvantages
of direct mail include high cost per reader, dependence on the quality of
mailing lists, and some consumers' resistance to it.

The advantages of direct mail explain its widespread use. Although
nearly half of the direct mail sent to consumers is discarded immediately,
Americans spend about $200 billion each year from these promotions.
Data are available on previous purchase patterns and preferred payment
methods, as well as household characteristics such as number of children
or seniors. Direct mail accounts for about 19 percent of total advertising
expenditures.[15]

The downside to direct mail is clutter, otherwise known as junk mail.
So much advertising material is stuffed into people's mailboxes every day
that the task of grabbing consumers' attention and evoking some interest
is daunting to direct mail advertisers. Three of every five respondents to
a survey about "things most likely to get on consumers' nerves" rated junk
mail at the top—above telemarketing, credit-card fees, and the fine print
on billing statements.

Outdoor Advertising

Outdoor advertising, perhaps the oldest and simplest media business
around, represents just over 2 percent of total advertising spending.[16] Traditional outdoor advertising
takes the form of billboards, painted bulletins or displays (such as those that appear on the walls of
buildings), and electric spectaculars (large, illuminated, and sometimes animated signs and displays).
But advertisers are finding new places to put their messages outdoors. You might find an advertising
message stenciled guerilla-style on the base of a traffic light or the back of a park bench. A section of
highway might be mowed and cleaned up by a local real estate company or restaurant, with a sign
implanted where passersby can easily see it. All of these are outgrowths of outdoor advertising.
Ironically, the Internet has breathed new life into outdoor advertising. "All the clutter online has actually created a huge push for more and more billboards," comments Diane Cimini, executive vice president for marketing at the Outdoor Advertising Association of America.[17]

This form of advertising has the advantages of immediate communication of quick and simple
ideas, repeated exposure to a message, and strong promotion for locally available products. Outdoor
advertising is particularly effective along metropolitan streets and in other high-traffic areas.

But outdoor advertising, just like every other type, is subject to clutter.[18] It also suffers from the
brevity of exposure to its messages by passing motorists. Driver concerns about rush-hour safety and
limited time also combine to limit the length of exposure to outdoor messages. As a result, most such
ads use striking, simple illustrations, short selling points, and humor to attract people interested in
products like beer, vacations, local entertainment, and lodging. As Figure 18.6 shows, Diamond
Trading Companies marketers decided the affluent New York commuter market represented a good
target market for their firm's diamonds and used billboards to deliver this message.

A third problem involves public concern over aesthetics. The Highway Beautification Act of 1965,
for example, regulates the placement of outdoor advertising near interstate highways. In addition,

FIGURE 18.6
Outdoor Advertising for a Luxury Product

many cities have local ordinances that set regulations on the size and placement of outdoor advertising messages. Critics have even labeled billboard advertising as "pollution on a stick."

New technologies are helping to revive outdoor advertising, offsetting the huge drop that resulted from limitations on ads for tobacco and alcohol products. Technology livens up the billboards themselves with animation, large sculptures, and laser images. Digital message signboards can display winning lottery numbers or other timely messages like weather and traffic reports. The best-known digital signboard in the U.S. is in New York's Times Square. And very soon, certain billboards will be able to "beam" messages to consumers' cell phones as they drive past.

France spends the greatest amount on outdoor advertising—nearly 12 percent of total ad spending, compared with 6 percent for Europe as a whole and 4 percent for the U.S. But recent changes in advertising policy brought about by the European Union may disallow France's ban on TV advertising, which could shift revenues away from outdoor advertising. Retailers in France are eagerly awaiting the outcome.[19]

Interactive Media

Interactive media—especially the Internet—are growing up. A recent survey conducted by the Online Publishers Association revealed that 57 percent of consumers prefer to find out about new products online, 43 percent report that the Internet contains advertising that is rich in information, and 42 percent feel that online advertising helps them decide what products to buy.[20] Not surprisingly, interactive advertising budgets are being beefed up at a growing number of companies. Five years ago, Adidas America viewed online advertising as nothing more than static banner ads, allocating a mere 2 percent of its total marketing budget to online ads. Today, however, Adidas is changing its strategy to increase its customer base via the Internet. Competing shoemaker Reebok is currently spending 10 to 15 percent more on online advertising than it did two years ago. At AT&T, online advertising spending has reached nearly 10 percent of the company's total advertising budget. "We've learned how to better use the medium," says Jeff Bauer, media director for AT&T Business. "We're moving beyond the banner and placing greater emphasis on interactivity with the creative message." By 2005, total online advertising is expected to hit $14 billion.[21]

Other Advertising Media

As consumers filter out appeals from traditional as well as Internet ads, marketers need new ways to catch their attention. In addition to the major media, firms use a vast number of other vehicles to communicate their messages. Transit advertising includes ads placed both inside and outside buses, subway trains and stations, and commuter trains. Some firms place ads on the roofs of taxicabs, on bus stop shelters and benches, on entertainment and sporting event turnstiles, in public restrooms, and even on parking meters. About half of the 23,000 U.S. movie theaters accept commercials. Movie-theater ads have proved especially effective for targeting young people aged 12 to 24 years.

Ads also appear on T-shirts, inlaid in store flooring, in printed programs of live-theater productions, and as previews on movie videocassettes. Directory advertising includes the familiar Yellow Pages in telephone books, along with thousands of business and industry directories. Some firms pay to have their advertising messages placed on hot-air balloons, blimps, banners behind airplanes, and on scoreboards at sporting events. Other companies have their own advertising vehicles, called mobile marketing squads. Yahoo! and Dreyer's Grand Ice Cream pay to have their logos placed on autos via a San Francisco–based company called Autowraps. Autowraps then hires drivers based on their regular driving routes and occupations, paying them a monthly fee for the use of the outside of their vehicles as advertising space. Shopping bags have long been great spots for advertising retail stores, but now the space is for sale. "With bagvertising, we place your company name, logo or Web address on minimum orders of 100,000 paper bags that we give away to about 500 stores," explains Moses Abughosh, president of Smart Bags.[22]

Media Scheduling

Once advertisers have selected the media that best match their advertising objectives and promotional budget, attention shifts to *media scheduling*—setting the timing and sequence for a series of advertisements. A variety of factors influence this decision as well. Sales patterns, repurchase cycles, and competitors' activities are the most important variables.

Seasonal sales patterns are common in many industries. An airline might reduce advertising during peak travel periods and boost its media schedule during low travel months. Repurchase cycles may also play a role in media scheduling—products with shorter repurchase cycles will more likely require consistent media schedules throughout the year. Competitors' activities are still other influences on media scheduling. A small firm may avoid advertising during periods of heavy advertising by its rivals.

Advertisers use the concepts of reach, frequency, and gross rating points to measure the effectiveness of media scheduling plans. *Reach* refers to the number of different people or households exposed to an advertisement at least once during a certain time period, typically four weeks. *Frequency* refers to the number of times an individual person is exposed to an advertisement during a certain time period. By multiplying reach times frequency, advertisers quantitatively describe the total weight of a media effort, which is called the campaign's *gross rating point.*

Recently, marketers have questioned the effectiveness of reach and frequency to measure ad success online. The theory behind frequency is that the average advertising viewer needs a minimum of three exposures to a message to get it. For Web surfers, the "wear-out" is much quicker, hence the greater importance of building customer relationships through advertisements.

A media schedule is typically created in the following way. Say an auto manufacturer wants to advertise a new model designed primarily to appeal to professional consumers in their 30s. The model would be introduced in November with a direct mail piece offering test drives. Outdoor, newspaper, and magazine advertising would support the direct mail campaign but also follow through the winter and into the spring and summer. The newspaper ads might actually be cooperative, for both the manufacturer and local dealers. Early television commercials might air during a holiday television special in mid-December, and then one or more expensively produced, highly creative spots would be first aired during the Super Bowl in late January. Another television commercial—along with new print ads—might be scheduled for fall clearance sales as the manufacturer gets ready to introduce next year's models. This example illustrates how marketers might plan their advertising year for just one product.

Organization of the Advertising Function

5

Outline the organization of the advertising function and the role of an advertising agency.

Although the ultimate responsibility for advertising decision making often rests with top marketing management, organizational arrangements for the advertising function vary among companies. A producer of a technical industrial product may interact with one person within the company, who works primarily to write copy for submission to trade publications. A consumer goods company, on the other hand, may staff a large department with advertising specialists.

The advertising function is usually organized as a staff department reporting to the vice president (or director) of marketing. The director of advertising is an executive position with the responsibility for the

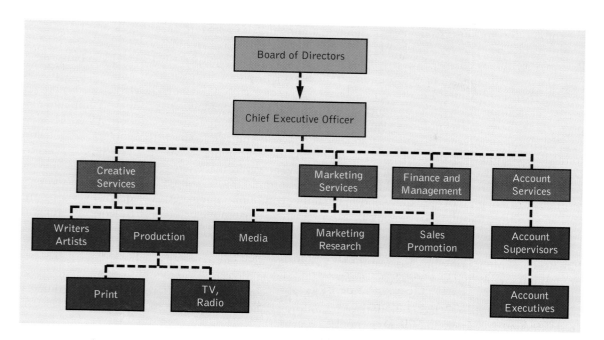

FIGURE 18.7
Advertising Agency Organizational Chart

functional activity of advertising. This position requires not only a skilled and experienced advertiser but also an individual who communicates effectively within the organization. The success of a firm's promotional strategy depends on the advertising director's willingness and ability to communicate both vertically and horizontally. The major tasks typically organized under advertising include advertising research, design, copywriting, media analysis, and in some cases, sales and trade promotion.

Advertising Agencies

Most large companies in industries characterized by large advertising expenditures will hire an independent **advertising agency,** a firm whose marketing specialists assist advertisers in planning and preparing advertisements. Advertising is a huge, global industry. Ranked by worldwide gross income, Japan's Dentsu is the world's largest advertising agency. McCann-Erickson Worldwide, based in New York, is second largest.[23]

Most large advertisers cite several reasons for relying on agencies for at least some portion of their advertising. Agencies typically employ highly qualified specialists who provide a degree of creativity and objectivity that is difficult to sustain in a corporate advertising department. Some also manage to reduce the cost of advertising by allowing the advertiser to avoid many of the fixed expenses associated with maintaining an internal advertising department.

Figure 18.7 shows a hypothetical organization chart for a large advertising agency. Although job titles may vary among agencies, the major functions may be classified as creative services; account services; marketing services, including media services, marketing research, and sales promotion; and finance and management.

6

Identify the principal methods of sales promotion.

Sales Promotion

Sales promotion, those marketing activities other than personal selling, advertising, and publicity that enhance consumer purchasing and dealer effectiveness, accounts for double the promotional dollar outlays of advertising. Like advertising, these activities trace their roots to the far reaches of antiquity. Examples of both

Marketing Dictionary

advertising agency   Firm whose marketing specialists assist advertisers in planning and preparing advertisements.

sales promotion   Marketing activities other than personal selling, advertising, and publicity that enhance consumer purchasing and dealer effectiveness.

sales promotion and advertising have been found among the ruins of Pompeii and Ephesus. In the U.S., Adolphus Busch gave away samples of his beer and a pocket knife as a premium in 1880. Ten years later, Procter & Gamble exchanged watch-chain charms for Ivory soap wrappers. In 1895, Grape Nuts cereal marketers were the first to offer a coupon on the box (for a one-cent discount off the purchase price), and in 1914, Ford Motor Co. offered a rebate of $50 for each $490 Model T. Marketers spend over $250 billion annually on such consumer and trade sales promotion activities as coupons, sampling, displays, trade shows and exhibitions, demonstrations, and various nonrecurrent promotional efforts.

Sales promotion techniques were originally intended as short-term incentives aimed at producing immediate consumer buying responses. Traditionally, these techniques were viewed as supplements to other elements of the firm's promotional mix. Today, however, marketers recognize them as integral parts of many marketing plans, and the focus of sales promotion has shifted from short-term to long-term goals of building brand equity and maintaining continuing purchases. A frequent-flyer program enables an airline to build a base of loyal customers where it had none before. A frequent-stay program allows a chain of hotels to attract regular guests.

Both retailers and manufacturers use sales promotions to offer consumers extra incentives to buy. Rather than emphasizing product features to make consumers feel good about their purchases, these promotions are likely to stress price advantages. The general objectives of sales promotion are to speed up the sales process and increase sales volume. Through a consumer promotion, a marketer encourages consumers to try the product, use more of it, and buy it again. The firm also hopes to foster sales of complementary products and increase impulse purchases.

Because sales promotion is so important to a marketing effort, an entire promotion industry exists to offer expert assistance in its use, just as an entire advertising industry offers similar services for advertisers. These companies, like advertising agencies, provide other firms with assistance in promoting their goods and services.

Sales promotion complements advertising, and marketers often produce their best results when they combine the two. Ads create awareness, while sales promotions lead to trial or purchase. Promotions encourage immediate action because they impose limited time frames. For example, cents-off coupons and rebates have expiration dates. In addition, sales promotions produce measurable results, making it relatively easy for marketers to evaluate their effectiveness.

It is important to understand what sales promotions can and cannot do. They can encourage interest from salespeople and consumers for both new and mature products, help introduce new products, encourage trial and repeat purchases, increase usage, neutralize competition, and reinforce advertising. On the other hand, sales promotions cannot overcome poor brand images, product deficiencies, or poor training for salespeople. While sales promotions increase volume in the short term, they often lead to lower profits.

Sales promotion techniques may serve all members of a marketing channel. In addition, manufacturers may use trade promotion methods to promote their products to resellers. A single promotional strategy may combine more than one option, but probably no promotional strategy has ever used all of them in a single program. While the different types are not mutually exclusive, promotions generally are employed selectively. Sales promotion techniques include the following consumer-oriented promotions: samples, bonus packs, premiums, coupons, price-off deals, refunds, contests, sweepstakes, and specialty advertising. Trade-oriented promotions include trade allowances, point-of-purchase advertising, trade shows, dealer incentives, and training programs.

Consumer-Oriented Sales Promotions

In the $85 billion promotion industry, marketers use all types of sales promotions, including games, contests, sweepstakes, and coupons to persuade new and existing customers to try their products. Consumer-oriented sales promotions encourage repurchases by rewarding current users, boosting sales of complementary products, and increasing impulse purchases. These promotions also attract consumer attention in the midst of advertising clutter. Table 18.2 lists the most popular consumer promotion techniques for firms using this element of the promotional mix.

It's important for marketers to use sales promotions selectively because if they are overused, consumers begin to expect price discounts, which ultimately diminish brand equity. The following sections briefly describe the various forms of consumer-oriented sales promotions.

Coupons and Refunds

Coupons, the most widely used form of sales promotion, offer discounts on the purchase price of goods and services. Consumers can redeem the coupons at retail outlets, which receive a handling fee from the manufacturer. The $5 billion coupon industry has been somewhat clipped in recent years due to more complex accounting rules that make couponing less attractive to some marketers, as well as the growing clout of retailers. But coupons are still popular among consumers and many marketers, who allocate roughly 15 percent of their marketing budgets to the practice. Although nearly 300 billion coupons are issued in a typical year, fewer than 5 billion are actually redeemed.[24]

TABLE 18.2	Seven Most Popular Consumer Promotion Techniques
TECHNIQUE	**PERCENTAGE OF MARKETERS WHO USE IT**
Coupons in retail ads	90
In-store coupons	88
Refunds	85
Electronic in-store displays	83
Samples of established products	78
Premiums	75
Sweepstakes	70

Mail, magazines, newspapers, package insertions, and increasingly, the Internet are the standard methods of distributing coupons. Free-standing inserts (FSIs) in certain magazines and Sunday newspapers account for nearly 75 percent of all coupons distributed. In one recent year, Kraft Foods launched a magazine-style FSI, called *Food and Family,* distributed by NewsAmerica and Meredith Publishing. The insert was dropped in nationally to newspapers each month and contained eight pages of recipes, tips on food storage and serving, and family-friendly tips or other information that featured Kraft brands such as Oscar Mayer, Kraft Macaroni & Cheese, and Post cereals. The first insert carried six coupons from such brands as Tombstone pizza, DiGiorno pasta, and Minute Rice. "We wanted to do something that stands out [and carries] our equity message of helping families connect over food," explained Wendy Kritt, director of corporate and consumer promotions.[25]

Refunds, or rebates, offer cash back to consumers who send in proof of purchasing one or more products. Refunds help packaged goods companies to increase purchase rates, promote multiple purchases, and reward product users. Although many consumers find the refund forms too bothersome to complete, plenty still take the time and energy to do so. "Rebates are tried and true," says Roy Spencer, general manager of the Promotion Fulfillment Center. Computer hardware, software, and sporting goods companies have been increasing their rebate programs in recent years.[26]

Samples, Bonus Packs, and Premiums

Marketers are increasingly adopting the "try it, you'll like it" approach as an effective means of getting consumers to try and then purchase their goods and services. *Sampling* refers to the free distribution of a product in an attempt to obtain future sales. Samples may be distributed door-to-door, by mail, via demonstrations in stores or at events, or by including them in packages with other products.

Sampling produces a higher response rate than most other promotions. About three-quarters of the consumers who receive samples try them, and total annual spending on this sales promotion technique has reached $1.12 billion.[27] A recent survey showed that 92 percent of consumers preferred receiving free samples rather than coupons. With sampling, marketers can target potential customers and be certain that the product reaches them. Sampling provides an especially useful way to promote new or unusual products because it gives the consumer a direct product experience.

One of the disadvantages of sampling is the high cost. Not only must the marketer give away small quantities of a product that might otherwise have generated revenues through regular sales, but the market is

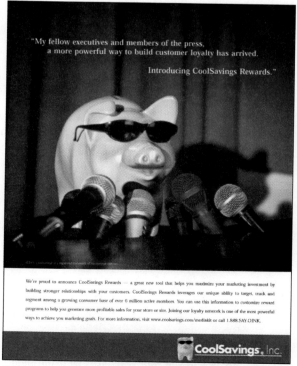

Shoppers seeking coupons can turn to such Web sites as CoolSavings.com, where they can access and print out coupons and be linked to sites of the manufacturer or retailer.

also, in effect, closed for the time it takes consumers to use up the samples. In addition, the marketer may encounter problems in distributing the samples. Hellman's marketers annoyed consumers instead of pleasing them when the firm distributed sample packets of Italian and French salad dressing in home-delivered copies of *The New York Times.* Many of the packets burst when the papers hit the driveways.

A *bonus pack* is a specially packaged item that gives the purchaser a larger quantity at the regular price. For instance, Camay soap offered three bars for the price of two, and Salon Selectives often increases the size of its shampoos and conditioners for the same price as regular sizes.

Premiums are items given free or at reduced cost with purchases of other products. For example, Pantene frequently attaches a purse-size bottle of hairspray to the sides of its other hair-care products. Premiums have proven effective in motivating consumers to try new products or different brands. A premium should have some relationship with the product or brand it accompanies, though. A home-improvement center might offer free nail aprons to its customers, for example.

Contests and Sweepstakes

Firms often sponsor contests and sweepstakes to introduce new goods and services and to attract additional customers. *Contests* require entrants to solve problems or write essays, and they may also require proofs of purchase. A recent contest by Irish brewer Guinness gave a pub in Ireland to the author of a winning essay. *Sweepstakes,* on the other hand, choose winners by chance, so no product purchase is necessary. They are more popular with consumers than contests because they do not take as much effort for consumers to enter. Marketers like them, too, because they are inexpensive to run and the number of winners is predetermined. With some contests, the sponsors cannot predict the number of people who will correctly complete the puzzles or gather the right number of symbols from scratch-off cards.

A recent Visa sales promotion contest offering cardholders a chance to win free purchases by using their Visa cards. Every time cardholders used their Visa cards for a purchase, they were automatically entered in the contest.

Not surprisingly, contests and sweepstakes have become more sophisticated and creative with the advent of the Internet. The mall-based hat retailer Lids came up with a promotion in which customers received a special game piece with their receipts each time they bought a hat. Then they went home to their computers, logged on to lids.com, and held the game piece up to the computer screen to see if they'd won a prize.[28] With the recent rash of court rulings and legal restrictions, the use of contests requires careful administration. Any firm contemplating using this promotional technique should engage the services of online promotion specialists such as WebStakes or NetStakes.

Specialty Advertising [having or name on a pen- key chain.]

The origin of specialty advertising has been traced to the Middle Ages, when artisans gave wooden pegs bearing their names to prospects, who drove them into the walls at home to serve as convenient hangers for armor. In more modern times, corporations began putting their names on a variety of products in the late 1800s, as newspapers and print shops looked for ways to make more money from their presses.

Specialty advertising is a sales promotion technique that places the advertiser's name, address, and advertising message on useful articles that are then distributed to target consumers. Marketers give out more than $8 billion worth of specialty advertising items each year. Wearable products, including T-shirts, baseball caps, and jackets, are the most popular products, accounting for nearly a third of distributor sales. Writing instruments, glassware, and calendars are other popular forms of specialty advertising.

Advertising specialties help to reinforce previous or future advertising and sales messages. Consumers like these giveaways, which generate stronger responses to direct mail, resulting in three times the dollar volume of sales compared with direct mail alone. Companies use this form of promotion to highlight store openings and new products, motivate salespeople, increase visits to trade show booths, and improve customer relationships.

Trade-Oriented Promotions

Sales promotion techniques can also contribute effectively to campaigns aimed at such channel members as retailers and wholesalers. *Trade promotion* is sales promotion that appeals to marketing intermediaries rather than to consumers. Marketers use trade promotion in push strategies by encouraging resellers to stock new products, continue to carry existing ones, and promote both effectively to consumers. As discussed earlier, the typical firm actually spends half of its promotional budget on trade promotion—as much money as it spends on advertising and consumer-oriented sales promotions combined. Successful trade promotions offer financial incentives. They require careful timing and attention to costs and are easy to implement by retailers. These promotions should bring quick results and improve retail sales.

Trade Allowances

Among the most common trade promotion methods are *trade allowances*—special financial incentives offered to wholesalers and retailers that purchase or promote specific products. These offers take various forms. A *buying allowance* gives retailers a discount on goods. They include *off-invoice allowances* through which retailers deduct specified amounts from their invoices or receive free goods, such as one free case for every ten ordered, when they order certain quantities. When a manufacturer offers a *promotional allowance,* it agrees to pay the reseller a certain amount to cover the costs of special promotional displays or extensive advertising that features the manufacturer's product. The goal is to increase sales to consumers by encouraging resellers to promote effectively.

As mentioned in previous chapters, some retailers require vendors to pay a special slotting allowance before they agree to take on new products. These fees guarantee so-called slots, or shelf space, in the stores for new items. This practice is common in large supermarket chains. Retailers defend these fees as essential to cover the added costs of carrying the products, such as redesigning display space and shelves, setting up and administering control systems, managing inventory, and taking the risks inherent in stocking new products. The fees can be sizable, from several hundred dollars per store to many thousands of dollars for a retail chain and millions of dollars for nationally distributed products. Naturally, this puts smaller food manufacturers at a disadvantage. The controversy has resulted in recent congressional inquiries to determine whether they constitute unfair methods of competition.

Point-of-Purchase Advertising

A display or other promotion located near the site of the actual buying decision is known as **point-of-purchase (POP) advertising.** This method of sales promotion capitalizes on the fact that buyers make many purchase decisions within the store, so it encourages retailers to improve on-site merchandising. They directly benefit the retailer by creating special displays designed to stimulate sales of the item being promoted.

Free-standing POP promotions often appear at the ends of shopping aisles. On a typical trip to the supermarket, you might see a POP display for Disney videos, sunscreen, or Kodak film. Warehouse-style retailers such as Home Depot and Sam's Club, along with Staples and Wal-Mart, all use POP advertising displays frequently. Electronic kiosks, which allow consumers to place orders for items not available

Marketing Dictionary

specialty advertising Sales promotion technique that places the advertiser's name, address, and advertising message on useful articles that are then distributed to target consumers.

point-of-purchase (POP) advertising Display or other promotion located near the site of an actual buying decision.

in the store, have begun to transform the POP display industry, as creators of these displays look for ways to involve consumers more actively as well as entertain them.[29]

Trade Shows

To influence resellers and other members of the distribution channel, many marketers participate in *trade shows*. These shows are often organized by industry trade associations, perhaps as part of these associations' annual meetings or conventions. Vendors who serve the industries are invited to appear at the shows to display and demonstrate their products for members. Every year, over 4,300 different shows in the U.S. and Canada draw more than 1.3 million exhibitors and 85 million attendees. One of the biggest trade shows is Comdex, the information technology show held in Las Vegas each November. Roughly 220,000 people attend the show. Each year, workers arrange 7,000 chairs, lay enough carpet to cover 21 football fields, and hang 2,500 banners around town advertising Comdex. At the opening gala, Microsoft CEO Bill Gates delivers his "state of the industry" speech. The following day, corporate executives, electronics manufacturers, and computer resellers pour through the display aisles evaluating 10,000 new products offered by the show's 2,100 exhibitors.

Because of the expense involved in trade shows like Comdex, a company must assess the value of such a show on several criteria, such as direct sales, any increase in product awareness, image building, and any contribution to the firm's marketing communications efforts. Trade shows give especially effective opportunities to introduce new products and to generate sales leads. Some types of shows reach ultimate consumers as well as channel members. Home, recreation, and automobile shows, for instance, allow businesses to display and demonstrate home improvement, recreation, and other consumer products to entire communities.

Dealer Incentives, Contests, and Training Programs

Manufacturers run dealer incentive programs and contests to induce retailers and their salespeople to increase sales and to promote products. These channel members receive incentives for performing promotion-related tasks and can win contests by reaching sales goals. Manufacturers may offer major prizes to resellers such as trips to exotic places. *Push money* is another incentive that gives retail salespeople cash rewards for every unit of a product they sell. This benefit increases the likelihood that the salesperson will try to convince a customer to buy the product rather than a competing brand.

For more expensive and highly complex products, manufacturers often provide specialized training for retail salespeople. This background helps salespeople explain features, competitive advantages, and other information to consumers. Training can be provided in several ways: A manufacturer's sales representative can conduct training sessions during regular sales calls, or the firm can distribute sales literature and videocassettes.

Public Relations

7

Explain the roles of cross promotions, public relations, publicity, and ethics in an organization's promotional strategy.

Chapter 17 defined public relations as the firm's communications and relationships with its various publics, including customers, employees, stockholders, suppliers, government agencies, and the society in which it operates. Organizational public relations efforts date back to 1889, when George Westinghouse hired two people to publicize the advantages of alternating-current electricity and to refute arguments for direct-current systems.

Public relations is an efficient, indirect communications channel through which a firm can promote products, although it serves broader objectives than those of other components of promotional strategy. It is concerned with the prestige and image of all parts of the organization. Today, public relations plays a larger role than ever within the promotional mix, and it may emphasize more marketing-oriented information. In addition to its traditional activities, such as surveying public attitudes and creating a good corporate image, PR also supports advertising in promoting the organization's goods and services.

Approximately 160,000 people work in public relations in both the not-for-profit and profit-oriented sectors. Some 1,800 public relations firms currently operate in the U.S. In addition, thousands of smaller firms and one-person operations compete to offer these services.

Public relations is in a period of major growth as a result of increased public pressure on industries regarding corporate ethical conduct and environmental and international issues. International expenditures on public relations are growing more rapidly than those for advertising and sales promotion. Many top executives are becoming more involved in public relations as well. The public expects top managers to take greater responsibility for company actions than they have accepted in the past. Those who refuse are widely criticized, censured, and even arrested. Tobacco manufacturer Altria has long been the target of criticism for allegedly creating advertisements that appeal to young people. While strongly denying these allegations, the company decided to create its Youth Smoking Prevention campaign, designed to be aired in school classrooms through Primedia. The tag line of one of the ads read, "Reflect confidence—think don't smoke." But antitobacco activists continued to blast these efforts as "one more attempt to get kids when they say they're not trying to reach kids."[30]

The PR department is the link between the firm and the media. It provides press releases and holds news conferences to announce new products, the formation of strategic alliances, management changes, financial results, or similar developments. The PR department may issue its own publications as well, including newsletters, brochures, and reports. Such new innovations as the Segway personal transporter and Crest's WhiteStrips received tremendous boosts when their PR managers placed them on popular TV shows. The Segway transporter was demonstrated on *Good Morning America* and WhiteStrips on Rosie O'Donnell's former syndicated TV talk show.[31]

A PR plan begins much like an advertising plan, with research to define the role and scope of the firm's overall public relations and current challenges. Next come strategic decisions on short-term and long-term goals and markets, analysis of product features, and choices of messages and media channels—or other PR strategies such as speaking engagements or contests—for each market. Plan execution involves developing messages highlighting the benefits that the firm brings to each market. The final step is to measure results.

The Internet has actually changed some PR planning, as PR representatives now have more direct access to the public instead of having their messages filtered through journalists and the news media. This direct access gives them greater control over their messages.[32]

Marketing and Nonmarketing Public Relations

Nonmarketing public relations refers to a company's messages about general management issues. When a company makes a decision that affects any of its publics, input from public relations specialists can help to smooth its dealings with those publics. A company that decides to close a plant would need advice on how to deal with the local community. Other examples include a company's attempts to gain favorable public opinion during a long strike or an open letter to Congress published in a newspaper during congressional debates on a bill that would affect a particular industry. Although some companies organize their public relations departments separately from their marketing divisions, PR activities invariably affect promotional strategies.

In contrast, *marketing public relations (MPR)* refers to narrowly focused public relations activities that directly support marketing goals. MPR involves an organization's relationships with consumers or other groups about marketing concerns and can be either proactive or reactive.

With proactive MPR, the marketer takes the initiative and seeks out opportunities for promoting the firm's products, often including distribution of press releases and feature articles. For example, companies send press releases about new products to newspapers, television stations, and relevant consumer, business, and trade publications. It is a powerful marketing tool since it adds news coverage that reinforces direct promotion activities.

Reactive MPR responds to an external situation that has potential negative consequences for the organization. Examples of reactive MPR are responses to product tamperings, such as the deaths caused by cyanide in Tylenol (1982) and Sudafed (1991) capsules. Prompt corrective action and strong PR campaigns from Johnson & Johnson and Burroughs Wellcome, respectively, prevented these situations from becoming disasters. On the other hand, both Ford and Bridgestone/Firestone fumbled in their attempts to blame each other for injuries and deaths caused by defective tires. More recently, several major airlines have used MPR to try to attract more flying customers after the tragedies of September 11, 2001.

Publicity

The aspect of public relations that is most directly related to promoting a firm's products is **publicity,** nonpersonal stimulation of demand for a good, service, place, idea, person, or organization by unpaid placement of significant news regarding the product in a print or broadcast medium. It has been said that if advertising is the hammer, publicity is the nail. It creates credibility for the advertising to follow. Firms generate publicity by creating special events, holding press conferences, and preparing news releases and media kits. Many firms, such as Starbucks and Wal-Mart's Sam's Club, have built their brands with virtually no advertising. Pharmaceutical products including Viagra and Prozac became worldwide brands with relatively little advertising, although advertising now supports them.

While publicity generates minimal costs compared with other forms of promotion, it does not deliver its message entirely free of cost. Publicity-related expenses include the costs of employing marketing personnel assigned to create and submit publicity releases, printing and mailing costs, and related expenses.

Firms often pursue some publicity to promote their images or viewpoints. Other publicity efforts involve organizational activities such as plant expansions, mergers and acquisitions, management changes, and research-and-development programs. A significant amount of publicity, however, provides information about goods and services, particularly new goods and services.

Because many consumers consider news stories to be more credible than advertisements as sources of information, publicity releases are often sent to media editors for possible inclusion in news stories. The media audiences perceive the news as coming from the communications media, not the sponsors. The information in a publicity release about a new good or service can provide valuable assistance for a television, newspaper, or magazine writer, leading to eventual broadcast or publication. Publicity releases sometimes fill voids in publications, and at other times, they become part of regular features. In either case, they offer firms valuable supplements to paid advertising messages.

Cross Promotion

In recent years, marketers have begun to combine their promotional efforts for related products using a technique called *cross promotion,* in which marketing partners share the cost of a promotional campaign that meets their mutual needs—an important benefit in an environment of rising media costs. Relationship marketing strategies like comarketing and cobranding, discussed in earlier chapters, are forms of cross promotion. Marketers realize that these joint efforts between established brands provide greater benefits in return for both companies; investments of time and money on such promotions will become increasingly important to many partners' growth prospects.

The entertainment industry is one of the most prominent users of cross promotion. Movie studios frequently partner with fast-food chains. Consider a cartoon show called *SpongeBob SquarePants,* which has achieved a loyal following among fans of all ages— and brand equity—with very little advertising. Aired by Nickelodeon, the show quickly became the No.1 children's show on television. Now Nickelodeon has a variety of cross promotional deals, from license agreements with toy manufacturers to a deal with Kraft Foods to place SpongeBob on the

FIGURE 18.8 SpongeBob SquarePants and Macaroni & Cheese: Cross Promotion between Nickelodeon and Kraft Foods

cover of its macaroni and cheese boxes and to offer "ocean blue" colored cheese sauce inside, as shown in Figure 18.8.[33]

Measuring Promotional Effectiveness

Each element of the promotional mix represents a major expenditure for a firm. Although promotional prices vary widely, advertisers typically pay a fee based on cost to deliver the message to viewers, listeners, or readers—the so-called *cost per thousand (CPM)*. Billboards are the cheapest way to spend advertising dollars, with television and some newspapers the most expensive. So while price is an important factor in media selection, it is by no means the only one—or all ads would appear on billboards!

Because promotion represents such a major expenditure for many firms, they need to determine whether their campaigns accomplish appropriate promotional objectives. Companies want their advertising agencies and in-house marketing personnel to demonstrate how promotional programs contribute to increased sales and profits. Marketers are well aware of the number of advertising messages and sales promotions that consumers encounter daily, and they know that these people practice selective perception and simply screen out many messages.

By measuring promotional effectiveness, organizations can evaluate different strategies, prevent mistakes before spending money on specific programs, and improve their promotional programs. As the earlier discussion of promotional planning explained, any evaluation program starts with objectives and goals; otherwise, marketers have no yardstick against which to measure effectiveness. However, determining whether an advertising message has achieved its intended objective is one of the most difficult undertakings in marketing. Sales promotions and direct marketing are somewhat easier to evaluate because they evoke measurable consumer responses. Like advertising, public relations is also difficult to assess on purely objective terms.

Measuring Advertising Effectiveness

Measures to evaluate the effectiveness of advertising, while difficult and costly, are essential parts of any marketing plan. Without an assessment strategy, marketers will not know whether their advertising achieves the objectives of the marketing plan or whether the dollars in the advertising budget are well spent. To answer these questions, marketers can conduct two types of research. *Media research* assesses how well a particular medium delivers the advertiser's message, where and when to place the advertisement, and the size of the audience. Buyers of broadcast time base their purchases on estimated Nielsen rating points, and the networks have to make good if ratings do not reach promised levels. Buyers of print advertising space pay fees based on circulation. Circulation figures are independently certified by specialized research firms.

The other major category, *message research,* tests consumer reactions to an advertisement's creative message. Pretesting and posttesting, the two methods for performing message research, are discussed in the following sections.

Pretesting

To assess an advertisement's likely effectiveness before it actually appears in the chosen medium, marketers often conduct *pretesting*. The obvious advantage of this technique is the opportunity to evaluate ads when they are being developed. Marketers can conduct a number of different pretests, beginning during the concept phase in the campaign's earliest stages when they have only rough copy of the ad and continuing until the ad layout and design are almost completed.

Pretesting employs a variety of evaluation methods. Focus groups can discuss their reactions to mock-ups of ads using different themes, headlines, or illustrations. To test magazine advertisements, the Batten, Barton, Durstine & Osborn ad agency cuts ads out of

8

Explain how marketers assess promotional effectiveness.

Marketing Dictionary

publicity Nonpersonal stimulation of demand for a good, service, place, idea, person, or organization by unpaid placement of significant news regarding the product in a print or broadcast medium.

advance copies of magazines and then inserts the ads it wants to test. Interviewers later check the impact of the advertisements on readers who receive free copies of the revised magazines. Another ad agency, McCann-Erickson, uses a *sales conviction test* to evaluate magazine advertisements. Interviewers ask heavy users of a particular item to pick one of two alternative advertisements that would convince them to purchase it.

To screen potential radio and television advertisements, marketers often recruit consumers to sit in a studio and indicate their preferences by pressing two buttons, one for a positive reaction to the commercial and the other for a negative reaction. Sometimes, proposed ad copy is printed on a postcard that also offers a free product; the number of cards returned represents an indication of the copy's effectiveness. *Blind product tests* are also frequently used. In these tests, people are asked to select unidentified products on the basis of available advertising copy.

Mechanical devices offer yet another method of assessing how people read advertising copy. One mechanical test uses a hidden camera to photograph eye movements of readers. The results help advertisers to determine headline placement and copy length. Another mechanical approach measures the galvanic skin response—changes in the electrical resistance of the skin produced by emotional reactions.

Posttesting

Posttesting assesses advertising copy after it has appeared in the appropriate medium. Pretesting generally is a more desirable measurement method than posttesting because it can save the cost of placing ineffective ads. However, posttesting can be helpful in planning future advertisements and in adjusting current advertising programs.

In one of the most popular posttests, the *Starch Readership Report* interviews people who have read selected magazines to determine whether they observed various ads in them. A copy of the magazine is used as an interviewing aid, and each interviewer starts at a different point in the magazine. For larger ads, respondents are also asked about specifics, such as headlines and copy. All such *readership tests,* also called recognition tests, assume that future sales are related to advertising readership.

Unaided recall tests are another method of posttesting the effectiveness of advertisements. Respondents do not see copies of the magazine after their initial reading but must recall the ads from memory. Burke Research Corp. conducts telephone interviews the day after a commercial has aired on television to test brand recognition and the advertisement's effectiveness. Another unaided recall test is adWatch, a joint project of *Advertising Age* magazine and the Gallup Organization. It measures ad awareness by telephone polling that asks each consumer to name the advertisement that first comes to mind of all the ads he or she has seen, heard, or read in the previous 30 days.

Inquiry tests are another popular form of posttest. Advertisements sometimes offer gifts—generally product samples—to people who respond to them. The number of inquiries relative to the advertisement's cost forms a measure of its effectiveness.

Split runs allow advertisers to test two or more ads at the same time. Although advertisers traditionally place different versions in newspapers and magazines, split runs on cable television systems frequently test the effectiveness of TV ads. With this method, advertisers divide the cable TV audience or a publication's subscribers in two: Half view advertisement A and the other half view advertisement B. The relative effectiveness of the alternatives is then determined through inquiries or recall and recognition tests.

Regardless of the exact method they choose, marketers must realize that pretesting and posttesting are expensive efforts. As a result, they must plan to use these techniques as effectively as possible.

Measuring Sales Promotion Effectiveness

Because many sales promotions, especially consumer-oriented techniques, result in direct consumer responses, marketers can relatively easily track their effectiveness. As with other elements in the promotional mix, marketers must weigh the cost of the promotion against the benefits. They can measure the redemption rate of cents-off coupons, for example, and coupons often carry printed codes indicating their sources to let manufacturers and retailers know which media provide the highest redemption rates. To evaluate sampling, one of the most popular types of consumer promotions, marketers want to know how effectively it induces consumers to actually buy the product once they try the sample. Studies have shown that sampling does promote trial purchases. Newspaper samples seem to do particularly well at generating brand awareness and trial. "It breaks through the clutter, because it reaches people when they have time on their hands," explains Tom Butler of the Sunflower Group.[34] Still, marketers have found no definitive answers about whether sampling helps the rate of repurchase. Sweepstakes and contest entries can also be tracked.

Some trade promotions—allowances, contests, and dealer incentives, for example—give easily measurable results like sales increases or heavier customer traffic. Other promotions, however, like trade shows and training programs, may require more subjective judgments of the first results, such as greater product awareness and knowledge, while sales gains will take longer to show up.

Measuring Public Relations Effectiveness

As with other forms of marketing communications, organizations must measure PR results based on their objectives both for the PR program as a whole and for specific activities. In the next step, marketers must decide what they want to measure. This choice includes determining whether the message was heard by the target audience and whether it had the desired influence on public opinion.

The simplest and least costly level of assessment involves outputs of the PR program: whether the target audience received, paid attention to, understood, and retained the messages directed to them. To make this judgment, the staff could count the number of media placements and gauge the extent of media coverage. They could count attendees at any press conference, evaluate the quality of brochures and other materials, and pursue similar activities. Formal techniques include tracking publicity placements, analyzing how favorably their contents portrayed the company, and conducting public opinion polls.

To analyze PR effectiveness more deeply, a firm could conduct focus groups, interviews with opinion leaders, and more detailed and extensive opinion polls. The highest level of effectiveness measurement looks at outcomes: Did the PR program change people's opinions, attitudes, and behavior? PR professionals measure these outcomes through before-and-after polls (similar to pretesting and posttesting) and more advanced techniques like psychographic analysis, cluster analysis, and communicants audits.

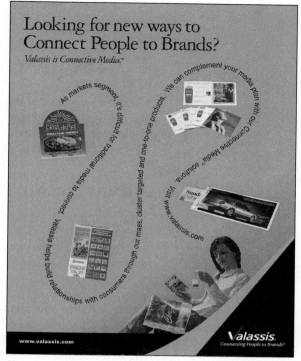

Newspaper sampling is often effective because consumers take time to read the paper and examine its contents. Inclusion of samples may result in additional attention from recipients than would be the case for other sampling delivery systems.

Evaluating Interactive Media

Marketers employ several methods to measure how many users view Web advertisements: hits (user requests for a file), impressions (the number of times a viewer sees an ad), and clickthroughs (when the user clicks on the ad to get more information). However, some of these measures can be misleading. Because each page, graphic, or multimedia file equals one hit, simple interactions can easily inflate the hit count, making it less accurate. To increase effectiveness, advertisers must give viewers who do click through their site something good to see. Successful Web campaigns use demonstrations, promotions, coupons, and interactive features.

Internet marketers price ad banners based on cost per thousand (CPM). Web sites that sell advertising typically guarantee a certain number of impressions—the number of times an ad banner is downloaded and presumably seen by visitors. Marketers then set a rate based on that guarantee times the CPM rate.

Although the Web does not yet have a standard measurement system, a number of companies like I/Pro, NetCount, and Interse offer different Web tracking and counting systems. At least two auditing services, Audit Bureau of Verification Services and BPA International, are currently in operation. Nielsen NetRatings rates Internet sites based on the number of different visitors they receive.

Ethics in Nonpersonal Selling

Chapter 3 introduced the topic of marketing ethics and noted that promotion is the element in the marketing mix that raises the most ethical questions. People actively debate the question of whether marketing communications contribute to better lives. The final section of this chapter takes a closer look at ethical concerns in advertising, sales promotion, and public relations.

Advertising Ethics

Even though laws allow certain types of advertising, many promotions still may involve ethical issues. One area of controversy is advertising aimed at children. To woo younger consumers, especially teens and those in their twenties, advertisers make messages as different from advertisements as possible; they design ads that seem more like entertainment.

Liquor advertising on television is another controversial area. Beer marketers advertise heavily on television and spend far more on advertising in print and outdoor media than do marketers of hard-liquor brands. Some members of Congress want much stricter regulation of all forms of liquor advertising on television and other media. This change would restrict ads in magazines with a 15 percent or more youth readership to black-and-white text only. Critics decry advertisements with messages implying that drinking the right beer will improve a person's personal life or help to win a sports contest. Many state and local authorities are considering more restrictive proposals on both alcohol and tobacco advertising.

In cyberspace ads, it is often difficult to separate advertising from editorial content since many sites resemble magazine and newspaper ads or television infomercials. Another ethical issue surrounding advertising online is the use of *cookies*, small text files that are automatically downloaded to a user's computer whenever a site is visited. Each time the user returns to that site, the site's server accesses the cookie and gathers information: What site was visited last? How long did the user stay? What was the next site visited? Marketers claim that this device helps them determine consumer preferences and argue that cookies are stored in the user's PC, not the company's Web site. The problem is that cookies can and do collect personal information without the user's knowledge. Lawsuits were recently filed by several consumers against Netscape for use of its SmartDownload program. In another case, Mattel apologized for adding a data-gathering program to more than 100 titles of its educational programs for children.[35]

Puffery and Deception

Puffery refers to exaggerated claims of a product's superiority or the use of subjective or vague statements that may not be literally true. A company might advertise the "most advanced system" or claim that its product is "most effective" in accomplishing its purpose.

Exaggeration in ads is not new. Consumers seem to accept advertisers' tendencies to stretch the truth in their efforts to distinguish their products and get consumers to buy. This inclination may provide one reason that advertising does not encourage purchase behavior as successfully as sales promotions do. A tendency toward puffery does raise some ethical questions, though: Where is the line between claims that attract attention and those that provide implied guarantees? To what degree do advertisers deliberately make misleading statements?

The Uniform Commercial Code standardizes sales and business practices throughout the U.S. It makes a distinction between puffery and any specific or quantifiable statement about product quality or performance that constitutes an "express warranty," which obligates the company to stand behind its claim. General boasts of product superiority and vague claims are puffery, not warranties. They are considered so self-praising or exaggerated that the average consumer would not rely on them to make a buying decision.

A quantifiable statement, on the other hand, implies a certain level of performance. For example, tests can establish the validity of a claim that a brand of long-life light bulbs outlasts three regular light bulbs.

Ethics in Sales Promotion and Public Relations

Both consumer and trade promotions can also raise ethical issues. Sales promotions provide opportunities for unscrupulous companies to take advantage of consumers. Companies may not fulfill rebate and premium offers or may mislead consumers by inaccurately stating the odds of winning sweepstakes or contests. Trade allowances, particularly slotting allowances, have been criticized for years as a form of bribery.

Several public relations issues open organizations to criticism. Various PR firms perform services for the tobacco industry; publicity campaigns defend unsafe products. Also, marketers must weigh ethics before they respond to negative publicity. For example, do firms admit to problems or product deficiencies, or do they try to cover them up? It should be noted that PR practitioners violate the Public Relations Society of America's Code of Professional Standards if they promote products or causes widely known to be harmful to others.

Strategic Implications of Marketing in the 21st Century

Greater portions of corporate ad budgets will migrate to the Web in the near future. In the five years since consumer Web advertising began, Web ad expenditures have seen a 753 percent increase.[36] Currently, North America leads the world in Internet advertising by a wide margin: nearly $20 billion, as opposed to nearly $2 billion by European advertisers.[37] This trend means that marketers must be increasingly aware of the benefits and pitfalls of Internet advertising. But they should not forget the benefits of other types of advertising as well.

Promotion industry experts agree that e-commerce broadens marketers' job tasks, though many promotional objectives still remain the same. Today, advertisers need 75 different ways to market their products in 75 countries in the world and innumerable market segments. In years to come, advertisers also agree that channels will become more homogeneous while markets become more fragmented.

Summary of Chapter Objectives

1. Identify the three major advertising objectives and the two basic categories of advertising.

The three major objectives of advertising are to inform, to persuade, and to remind. The two major categories of advertising are product advertising and institutional advertising. Product advertising involves the nonpersonal selling of a good or service. Institutional advertising is the nonpersonal promotion of a concept, idea, or philosophy of a company or organization.

2. List the major advertising strategies.

The major advertising strategies are comparative, which makes extensive use of messages with direct comparisons between competing brands; celebrity, which uses famous spokespeople to boost an advertising message; and interactive, which encourages two-way communication either via the Internet or kiosks.

3. Describe the process of creating an advertisement.

An advertisement evolves from pinpointing goals, creating a plan, developing a message, developing and preparing the ad, and selecting the appropriate medium (or media).

4. List and compare the major advertising media.

The major media include broadcast (television and radio), newspapers and magazines, direct mail, outdoor, and interactive. Each medium has benefits and drawbacks. Newspapers are flexible and dominate local markets. Magazines can target niche markets. Interactive media encourage two-way communication. Outdoor advertising reaches many people at once, as does television and radio. Direct mail allows selective and intensive coverage.

5. Outline the organization of the advertising function and the role of an advertising agency.

Within a firm, the advertising department is usually a staff group that reports to a marketing executive. Advertising departments usually include research, art and design, copywriting, and media analysis. Outside advertising agencies assist and support firms that do not have their own advertising departments. These specialists are usually organized by creative services, account services, marketing services, and finance.

6. Identify the principal methods of sales promotion.

Sales promotions are divided into two major categories: consumer oriented and trade oriented. Consumer-oriented promotions take the form of coupons and refunds, samples, contests and sweepstakes, and specialty advertising. Trade promotions include trade allowances, point-of-purchase advertising, trade shows, and dealer incentives, contests, and training programs.

7. Explain the roles of cross promotions, public relations, publicity, and ethics in an organization's promotional strategy.

Cross promotions, illustrated by tie-ins between popular movies and fast-food restaurants, permit the marketing partners to share the cost of a promotional campaign that meets their mutual needs. Public relations consists of the firm's communications and relationships with its various publics, including customers, employees, stockholders, suppliers, government, and the society in which it operates. Publicity is the dissemination of newsworthy information about a product or organization. This information activity is frequently used in new product introductions. Although publicity is welcomed by firms, negative publicity is easily created when a company enters a gray ethical area with the use of its promotional efforts. Therefore, marketers should be careful to construct ethically sound promotional campaigns, avoiding such practices as puffery and deceit.

8. Explain how marketers assess promotional effectiveness.

The effectiveness of advertising can be measured by both pretesting and posttesting. Pretesting is the assessment of an ad's effectiveness before it is actually used. It includes such methods as sales conviction tests and blind product tests. Posttesting is the assessment of the ad's effectiveness after it has been used. Commonly used posttests include readership test, unaided recall tests, inquiry tests, and split runs.

Marketing Terms You Need to Know

advertising 532
product advertising 533
institutional advertising 533
informative advertising 534

persuasive advertising 534
reminder advertising 534
comparative advertising 534
retail advertising 537

cooperative advertising 537
advertising campaign 539
advertising agency 549
sales promotion 549

specialty advertising 552
point-of-purchase (POP)
   advertising 553
publicity 556

Other Important Marketing Terms

interactive advertising 537	contest 552	nonmarketing public relations 555	pretesting 557
banners 541	sweepstakes 552	marketing public relations (MPR) 555	posttesting 558
media scheduling 548	trade promotion 553	cross promotion 556	split runs 558
coupon 551	trade allowances 553	media research 557	cookies 560
refund 551	trade show 554	message research 557	puffery 560
sampling 551	push money 554		
premium 552			

Review Questions

1. Identify and define the two broad categories of advertising. Give an example of each.
2. What are the three primary objectives of advertising messages? At what stage of the product life cycle is each most commonly used?
3. Describe each of the four major advertising strategies.
4. What variables might marketers consider in creating an advertising message for a firm that offers financial services, including retirement accounts, credit cards, and other investments?
5. Identify and describe the different advertising media. Then give an example of one type of product that could best be advertised via each.
6. How is advertising through interactive media different from advertising in traditional media? Describe how you think a chain of resorts could use interactive advertising effectively.
7. Under what circumstances are celebrity spokespersons in advertising likely to be effective? Give recent examples of effective and ineffective uses of spokespersons in advertisements.
8. Distinguish between advertising and sales promotion. Describe the different types of consumer-oriented sales promotions and give an example of each.
9. How can firms use marketing public relations (MPR) to their advantage? Do you agree with the statement that publicity is free advertising?
10. Describe the ways in which marketers assess promotional effectiveness. Identify the major ethical issues affecting advertising, sales promotion, and public relations.

Projects and Teamwork Exercises

1. With a classmate, review a number of advertising messages across several media and identify two effective messages and two you think are ineffective. Describe why you think each is effective or ineffective. Bring at least two of the ads to class to discuss with classmates.
2. Choose a magazine that interests you and analyze the advertisements in one issue. Describe whom you think the magazine's readers are by reviewing the ads.
3. With a classmate, find at least two examples of cross promotion. If possible, bring them in to class to discuss their effectiveness. Then create your own plan for cross promoting two products that you think would be a good combination.
4. Take a trip to the supermarket or to a large retailer like Wal-Mart, Kohl's, or Home Depot. Identify as many consumer-oriented sales promotions as you can and log them in a journal. Which type of promotion appeared the most often? Why do you think that is?
5. Access the Internet and surf around to some sites that interest you. How many banner ads or pop-ups do you see? Do you like to view these ads, or do you find them intrusive? Which are most appealing? Which are least?

'net Work

http://www.adage.com/
century

1. Advertising. Go to *Advertising Age's* Web site to access information on "The Advertising Century" issue with its analysis of advertising in the 20th century. Complete the following:

   a. Using the "Timeline," list several interesting historical facts.

   b. List the top two in each of the following categories:

      (1) Top 100 Campaigns

      (2) Top 10 Jingles

      (3) Top 10 Slogans

      (4) Top 10 Ad Icons

2. Outdoor advertising. Visit the Web site for an outdoor advertising firm. Identify the primary products in the firm's line and print a copy of your favorite ad featured on the site.

http://www.aaaa.org

3. Advertising ethics. The American Association of Advertising Agencies (AAAA) is a professional organization whose members include many of the nation's largest ad agencies. Visit the association's Web site and prepare a report citing the association's mission, its standards of practice, and its creative code. Select an ad from a recent newspaper or magazine that you believe adheres to the association's creative code.

Note: Internet Web addresses change frequently. If you don't find the exact sites listed, you may need to access the organization or company's home page and search from there.

CASE 18.1 JCPenney Learns Some Tough Advertising Lessons

As you've learned throughout this chapter—in fact, throughout this book—marketing can walk a fine line between what is acceptable to some consumers and what is not, between what is in good taste and what is not, and between what is offensive and what is not. You've read about the controversy over pop-up ads on the Internet. You've watched the soaring success of George Foreman. Undoubtedly, some people out there must actually like to view pop-ups, and others must think George is not cute or endearing. But the general consensus is that marketers need to restrain themselves in the use of pop-ups and that George is a pretty effective character when it comes to selling grills. Reading consumers' attitudes is a tricky assignment, though.

Sometimes well-intentioned marketers make mistakes. That was the case when retailer JCPenney aired a television commercial called "Attitude Adjustment," in which a teenage girl was trying on hiphugger jeans when her mom stopped her, demanding, "You're not going to school dressed like *that*, are you?" Then the mom yanked the jeans even lower on her daughter's hips. Parents who saw the ads were outraged, complaining that they encouraged teenagers to dress provocatively. "It's certainly not what I would do with my daughter, and I bet it's not what the CEO of JCPenney would do with his daughter or granddaughter," said Joe Kelly, executive director of the advocacy group Dads & Daughters. Penney spokesperson Stephanie Brown countered that the retailer was "trying to be fashion-forward in our message, but unfortunately our customers thought it was too forward."

In any case, Penney pulled the ad after only four days on the air, after listening to what its customers wanted—and didn't want. Although the ads were well intentioned, and perhaps meant to be humorous, they went over poorly with the very people the company was trying to reach. So it made sense to return to the drawing board. Ironically, JCPenney sells more conservative clothing than most of its direct competitors, so it is likely that the firm was trying to attract a broader market by illustrating how stylish its clothes really could be. But the attempt bombed, and marketers were wise to heed the warning.

Unfortunately, that wasn't the only marketing gaffe the retailer made. For a brief period, Penney sold a T-shirt in its stores that showed a broken-down mobile home with the slogan "Home Skooled" scrawled across the front. Many customers considered the shirt offensive, and Penney removed it quickly from store shelves. Both of these errors point out that marketers need to pay attention to the message they are sending and how it is being received by their market. Advertising is a powerful vehicle, and it can have a powerful effect on its audience—and ultimately, the success or failure of a company's marketing efforts.

Questions for Critical Thinking

1. What steps could JCPenney marketers have taken in the planning stage of their advertising campaign to avoid these mistakes?
2. How could Penney use public relations strategies to counteract the bad publicity it received as a result of the ad and the T-shirts?

SOURCES: "JCPenney Corporation Capsule," downloaded from http://www.hoovers.com, January 14, 2003; Michael McCarthy, "Oops!" *USA Today*, August 28, 2001, p. 3B; Cindy Moorehead, "Who's Wearing Those Tiny Tops, Anyway?" *The Courier.com*, August 20, 2001, http://www.thecourier.com.

VIDEO CASE 18.2 Oxygen Media and Mullen Advertising Team Up for Women's Programming

The written case on Oxygen Media and Mullen Advertising appears on page VC-22. The recently filmed Oxygen Media/Mullen Advertising video is designed to expand and highlight the concepts in this chapter and the concepts and questions covered in the written video case.

19

Personal Selling and Sales-Force Management

Chapter Objectives

1 Explain the conditions that determine the relative importance of personal selling in the promotional mix.

2 Contrast over-the-counter selling, field selling, telemarketing, and inside selling.

3 Describe each of the four major trends in personal selling.

4 Identify the three basic sales tasks.

5 Outline the steps in the sales process.

6 Describe the sales manager's boundary-spanning role.

7 List and discuss the functions of sales-force management.

8 Discuss the role of ethics in personal selling and sales-force management.

Transforming the Sales Force at IBM

I t's difficult to imagine a company that's nearly a century old and employs 325,000 workers undergoing any kind of fundamental change. It may be even harder to imagine that company being IBM, which for decades has had a reputation of being bogged down in bureaucracy so sluggish that it actually missed major opportunities in the marketplace. But IBM is making huge changes in the way it sells both its computer hardware and its software solutions to businesses around the world. Big Blue, as the company is often called, is reengineering its sales force into a rapid-response team that's 35,000 strong.

Personal selling is probably the most important component of IBM's business-to-business marketing, because businesses of all sizes make significant investments in computer technology. But in previous years, IBM's business customers rarely saw a sales rep in person. That's because IBM reps were often stuck in office meetings, discussing strategies and sales numbers with their managers. This might be all right if IBM were selling mechanical pencils, but it doesn't work in a business environment where computer technology changes so fast. All of that—and a lot more—is changing under recently appointed CEO Sam Palmisano, who took over the top executive spot when IBM legend Lou Gerstner stepped down.

Before reorganizing the sales force, IBM managers asked their customers what the company lacked in service. The response was expertise. Although sales reps knew a little about a lot of things, they simply couldn't answer more complex, in-depth questions from customers. So salespeople are now trained to be industry experts. They also work in tactical teams, so they can support each other and their customers on the spot without having to take the time to climb the chain of command to find the answers and obtain the authority they need to implement them.

IBM sales reps now spend far more time in the field, calling and visiting customers. One sales rep says that her customers have been surprised at the amount of time she now spends with them. "They want to know if I have fewer customers. I'm more accessible and more visible to them," she explains. In fact, this visibility has won her more accounts. "Sales can be a matter of being in the right place at the right time," she says. "If an executive comes out of a meeting with a problem that I can help him solve, it is

Samuel J. Palmisano, current Chairman of the Board and Chief Executive Officer, IBM; Louis V. Gerstner, Jr., Former Chief Executive Officer.

better if I'm already there in his office rather than giving him time to call someone else."

Change requires overall vision for the company. What is the big picture for Big Blue? Sam Palmisano and his management team are busy positioning IBM to become single-stop shopping outlets for big and small business customers. By reorganizing and retraining the sales staff, IBM can fulfill its customers' technological needs as well as their needs for support and expertise. IBM has the potential to wield considerable clout in the marketplace as a large product company and a large professional services company. "The challenge is leveraging the combination of the two and getting the sales force comfortable with selling solutions that involve the mix of products and services," says Jim Shepherd, senior vice president of AMR Research in Boston. By all accounts, Big Blue intends to win big.[1]

Chapter Overview

Personal selling at IBM focuses on the customer, on building a relationship that will in time lead to ongoing sales. Chapters 17 and 18 explained how increased emphasis on customer relationships has transformed traditional concepts of promotion and the promotional mix in achieving marketing objectives. In exploring personal selling strategies, this chapter gives special attention to the relationship-building opportunities that the selling situation presents.

Personal selling is the process of a seller's person-to-person promotional presentation to a buyer. The sales process is essentially interpersonal, and it is basic to any enterprise. Accounting, engineering, human resource management, production, and other organizational activities produce no benefits unless a seller matches the needs of a client or customer. The 15 million people employed in sales occupations in the U.S. testify to the importance of selling. While the average firm's advertising expenses may represent from 1 to 3 percent of total sales, personal selling expenses are likely to equal 10 to 15 percent. This makes personal selling the single largest marketing expense in many firms.

Personal selling is a primary component of a firm's promotional mix in certain well-defined conditions:

1 Explain the conditions that determine the relative importance of personal selling in the promotional mix.

1. Customers are geographically concentrated.

2. Individual orders account for large amounts of revenue.

3. The firm markets goods and services that are expensive, technically complex, or require special handling.

4. Trade-ins are involved.

5. Products move through short channels.

6. The firm markets to relatively few potential customers.

Table 19.1 summarizes the factors that influence the importance of personal selling in the overall promotional mix based on four variables: consumer, product, price, and marketing channels.

The Evolution of Personal Selling ⟵ *training a sales force*

Selling has been a standard business activity for thousands of years. The earliest peddlers sold goods in which they had some type of ownership interest after manufacturing or importing them. They viewed selling as a secondary activity. Selling later became a business function in its own right. In 18th-century

TABLE 19.1   **Factors Affecting the Importance of Personal Selling in the Promotional Mix**

VARIABLE	CONDITIONS THAT FAVOR PERSONAL SELLING	CONDITIONS THAT FAVOR ADVERTISING
Consumer	Geographically concentrated	Geographically dispersed
	Relatively low numbers	Relatively high numbers
Product	Expensive	Inexpensive
	Technically complex	Simple to understand
	Custom made	Standardized
	Special handling requirements	No special handling requirements
	Transactions frequently involve trade-ins	Transactions seldom involve trade-ins
Price	Relatively high	Relatively low
Channels	Relatively short	Relatively long

America, peddlers sold directly to farmers and settlers of the vast territories to the west. In the 19th century, salespeople called drummers sold to both consumers and marketing intermediaries. These early sellers sometimes used questionable sales practices and techniques and earned undesirable reputations for themselves and their firms. Negative stereotypes persist today. To some people, the term *salesperson* conjures up unpleasant visions of Arthur Miller's antihero Willy Loman in the classic American play *Death of a Salesman*:

> Willy is a salesman. . . . He don't put a bolt to a nut. He don't tell you the law or give you medicine. He's a man way out there in the blue, riding on a smile and a shoe shine. And when they start not smiling back—that's an earthquake.

But selling is far different today than in its early years. Far from the fast-talking, joke-telling, back-slapping caricatures in some novels and comic strips, today's salesperson is highly trained. Sales professionalism has been aptly defined as "a customer-oriented approach that employs truthful, nonmanipulative tactics to satisfy the long-term needs of both the customer and the selling firm."[2] Professional salespeople are problem solvers who focus on satisfying the needs of customers before, during, and after sales are made. Armed with knowledge about their firm's goods or services, those of competitors, and their customers' business needs, salespeople pursue a common goal of creating long-term relationships with customers.

Personal selling is a vital, vibrant, dynamic process. As domestic and foreign competition increases emphasis on productivity, personal selling is taking on a more prominent role in the corporate marketing mix. Salespeople must communicate the subtle advantages of their firms' goods and services over those of competitors. The salesperson's role has changed from persuader to consultant and problem solver. In addition, mergers and acquisitions, along with a host of new products and promotions, have expanded the scope and complexity of many selling jobs.

As discussed in Chapter 6, relationship marketing affects all aspects of an organization's marketing function, including personal selling and sales-force management. This transition involves marketers in both internal and external relationships and forces them to develop different sales skills. Instead of working alone, many salespeople now unite their efforts in sales teams. The customer-focused firm wants its salespeople to form long-lasting relationships with buyers by providing high levels of customer service, rather than going for quick sales. Even the way salespeople perform their jobs is changing. Growing numbers of companies are integrating communications

Briefly Speaking

A salesperson is someone who sells goods that won't come back to customers who will.

Anonymous

Marketing Dictionary

personal selling Interpersonal influence process involving a seller's promotional presentation conducted on a person-to-person basis with the buyer.

and computer technologies into the sales routine. These trends are covered in more detail later in the chapter.

Personal selling is an attractive career choice for today's college and university students. Approximately 60 percent of all marketing graduates choose sales jobs as their first marketing positions, in part because they see attractive salaries and career potentials. The Bureau of Labor Statistics projects that jobs in selling and marketing occupations requiring a college degree will show faster than average rates of growth compared with all occupations during the next 10 years. A sales background provides visibility for the individual and serves as an excellent route to the top of the corporate hierarchy. Many corporations are headed by executives who began their careers in sales.

The Four Sales Channels

2

Contrast over-the-counter selling, field selling, telemarketing, and inside selling.

Personal selling occurs through several types of communication channels: over-the-counter selling, field selling, telemarketing, and inside selling. Each of these channels includes both business-to-business and direct-to-customer selling. Although telemarketing and online selling are lower cost alternatives, their lack of personal interaction with prospective customers often makes them less effective than personalized, one-to-one field selling and over-the-counter channels. In fact, many organizations use a number of different channels. The ad in Figure 19.1, for example, invites T. Rowe Price customers to receive personalized investment information by meeting one-on-one with an investment advisor, talking with a trained phone representative, or going online.

Over-the-Counter Selling

The most frequently used sales channel, **over-the-counter selling,** typically describes selling in retail and some wholesale locations. Most over-the-counter sales are direct-to-customer, although wholesalers

FIGURE 19.1
Multiple Sales, Service, and Information Options Offered to T. Rowe Price Clients

serve business customers. Customers typically visit the seller's location on their own initiative to purchase desired items. Some visit their favorite stores because they enjoy shopping and consider it a type of leisure activity. Others come in response to many kinds of invitations, including direct mail appeals, personal letters of invitation from store personnel, and advertisements for sales, special events, and new-product introductions. From the electronics-product salesperson at Circuit City to the diamond purveyor at Tiffany's, this type of selling typically involves providing product information and arranging for completion of sales transactions.

Before the advent of big chain retailers and discount stores, it was not unusual for local retailers to know their customers by name or to be familiar with their tastes and preferences. Today, in a back-to-the-future trend, similar one-on-one sales tactics are paying off for astute marketers. Top direct marketers like Lands' End, for example, use sophisticated database technology to identify callers and any recent purchases made. This customer recognition helps build strong relationships in over-the-counter sales as well. Starbucks is a successful model of how over-the-counter selling builds relationships by creating an enjoyable

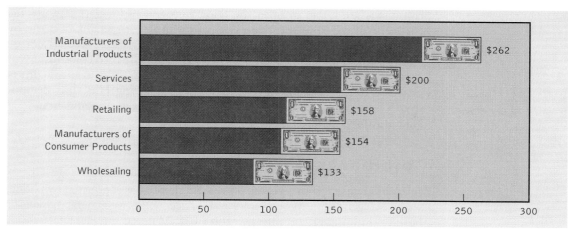

FIGURE 19.2 Cost of a Sales Call by Industry

Industry	Cost
Manufacturers of Industrial Products	$262
Services	$200
Retailing	$158
Manufacturers of Consumer Products	$154
Wholesaling	$133

SOURCE: Sales data reported in "Cost of a Call Survey," *Sales & Marketing Management*, September 2000, p. 82.

and satisfying experience for customers. Starbucks emphasizes "one customer, one partner, one cup at a time." Customers are willing to pay premium prices for Starbucks coffee because they are buying more than just coffee—it's the personal touch that keeps them coming back.

Other marketers are trying to re-create the personalized, one-to-one experience of over-the-counter selling on the Internet, but for most, success remains elusive. Though many have experimented with Web-driven sales, most banks, for instance, still rely heavily on face-to-face selling for insurance sales. Customer referral, followed by one-on-one meetings between insurance reps and potential customers, is the method most likely to result in a sale. Banks use their Web sites mainly to educate customers about insurance, not to close sales.[3]

Field Selling

Field selling involves making sales calls on prospective and existing customers at their businesses or homes. Some situations involve considerable creative effort, such as in-home sales of encyclopedias and insurance or industrial sales of major computer installations. Often the salesperson must convince customers first that they need the good or service and then that they need the particular brand the salesperson is selling. Field sales of large industrial installations also often require considerable technical expertise.

Largely because it involves travel, field selling is considerably more expensive than other selling options. Figure 19.2 shows the average cost of sales calls across a range of industries. B2B sales calls, because of the sophistication or technical nature of products and the level of expertise needed to communicate to potential buyers, top the list.

In fairly routine field selling situations, such as calling on established customers in industries like food, textiles, or wholesaling, the salesperson may basically act as an order taker who processes regular customers' orders. Field selling may involve regular visits to local stores or businesses, or it may involve many days and nights of travel, by car or plane, every month. Salespeople who travel a great deal are frequently labeled *road warriors*. A recent study found that it costs an average of $215 per day to keep a salesperson on the road. More than half the money is eaten up in hotel costs.[4] As technology seeps into every modern business transaction, marketers have adapted their personal selling techniques to take advantage of electronic communications channels, including voice mail, e-mail, and the Internet.

Avon, whose 3 million independent sales reps worldwide built a business on door-to-door selling, has explored several alternative sales methods to counter the fact that changes in consumer lifestyles—two-career couples, for example—means that fewer and fewer

Marketing Dictionary

over-the-counter selling Personal selling conducted in retail and some wholesale locations in which customers come to the seller's place of business.

field selling Sales presentations made at prospective customers' homes or businesses on a face-to-face basis.

Marketing Hit

Sales Pro Bounces Back

Background. After 19 years at Black & Decker, Joe Galli's career took a few curves. The 45-year-old sales pro, described in the press as a "driven huckster," hooked up with Amazon.com, touted to become the world's biggest retailer. Falling profits sent him out the door to VerticalNet, where he lasted only 167 days as CEO.

The Challenge. Galli signed on with Newell Rubbermaid, and he was back in his old stomping ground. But could even Galli's brand of salesmanship rescue the floundering home-products manufacturer? Newell's brands included the once-unbeatable Rubbermaid and Paper-Mate, both on the verge of being ousted from Wal-Mart.

The Strategy. Galli's turnaround plan called for a combination of jazzed-up products, sizzling prime-time ads, and lean financial management. But to get Rubbermaid and other high-profile brands into the customer's hands, Galli hired a 500-strong team of high-energy college grads to hit every Wal-Mart, Home Depot, and Lowe's nationwide. Each recruit got a new Ford Explorer emblazoned with the Rubbermaid name. Fuel and lease payments were part of the package. As well as making sure Newell products were in stock and priced right, Galli's troops would pile them high in prominent spots, take over checkout areas, and chat up customers and store staff. In-store demonstrations, scavenger hunts for Newell products, and good old-fashioned salesmanship brought back a sense of excitement that had been missing for years.

The Outcome. If all goes according to plan, Newell Rubbermaid will soon report sales growth at 10 percent a year—up from zero. With its stock trading 18 times higher than analysts' estimates, Rubbermaid shows every sign of bouncing back—and Galli, too.

SOURCES: Bruce Upbin, "Rebirth of a Salesman," *Forbes*, October 1, 2002, pp. 95–104; Tara Murphy, "Newell Rubbermaid Bounces Back," February 2, 2002, http://www.forbes.com; "Magazine Survey Ranks Rubbermaid Most Powerful Brand in Home Products," Newell Rubbermaid press release, October 24, 2001, http://www.newellco.com.

consumers are home to open the door. Recognizing that its reps are the backbone of the company, Avon is experimenting with retail kiosks run by local Avon representatives in shopping malls. A Web site, focused on the "eRepresentative," allows salespeople who sell online to earn commissions of up to 25 percent for orders shipped direct or up to 50 percent for orders delivered to the customer in person.[5] The "Marketing Hits" box demonstrates how high-energy field selling helped revitalize flagging brands at Newell Rubbermaid.

Telemarketing

Telemarketing, a channel in which the selling process is conducted by phone, serves two general purposes—sales and service—and two general markets—business-to-business and direct-to-customer. As noted in Chapter 16, both inbound and outbound telemarketing are forms of direct marketing.

Outbound telemarketing involves a sales force that relies on the telephone to contact customers, reducing the substantial costs of personal visits to customers' homes or businesses. Technologies such as predictive dialers, autodialing, and random-digit dialing increase chances that telemarketers will reach customers at home. Predictive dialers weed out busy signals and answering machines, nearly doubling the number of calls made per hour. Autodialing allows telemarketers to dial numbers continually; when a customer answers the phone, the call is automatically routed to a live sales agent. Random-digit dialing allows telemarketers to reach unlisted numbers and blocks caller ID.[6] The effectiveness of telemarketers is evaluated on various bases, including total calls made per hour or per shift, revenue per sale or per hour, and profitability. In general, outbound telemarketing calls geared toward men get the best responses between 7 P.M. and 9 P.M., whereas women tend to respond more favorably to telemarketers between 10 A.M. and 4 P.M.

As demonstrated in the "Solving an Ethical Controversy" box, a major drawback of telemarketing is that 32 of every 33 consumers detest the practice. The interruption of dinners by a ringing telephone solicitation was so offensive that a do-not-call registry was made law in 2003. When 50 million people signed up, an estimated 2 million phone solicitation jobs disappeared. But some inbound messages are still allowed. Here's who can still call:

- Charities, politicians, pollsters, and market researchers
- Companies you do business with
- Companies that have sold you something, billed you, or made a delivery to you in the past 18 months
- Businesses you've contacted in the past three months
- Companies that obtain your permission[7]

Why, then, is outbound telemarketing such a popular sales technique? Companies like it because it is cost-effective and it works. An average telemarketing call costs $5, compared with hundreds of dollars for a field sales call. Despite the annoyance of receiving unsolicited calls, some people do respond. In a recent year, 185 million U.S. consumers made a purchase via outbound telephone calls. The effectiveness of outbound telemarketing as a sales technique is further evidenced by the size of the industry. Generating sales of more than $660 billion a year, consumer and business-to-business telemarketing accounts for 6 percent of GDP. Consumer sales alone are expected to grow by 8 percent a year, exceeding $400 billion in 2006. The industry also employs close to 6 million people, mainly entry-level and minority jobs.[8]

Solving an Ethical Controversy

right / wrong

The National Do Not Call List: Friend or Foe?

By now, nearly everyone has heard of the Federal Trade Commission's "Do Not Call" list prohibiting telemarketers from making unsolicited calls to consumers who do not want to hear from them. It's likely that you or your parents were among the 50 million people who signed up to be on the list. The list itself met with some initial controversy. Telemarketers naturally have fought it, citing their Constitutional right to free speech. Judges in Colorado and Oklahoma—at least one of whom was reportedly on the "do not call" list—tried to block the registry by ruling that the FTC lacked authority to establish it. However, President Bush swiftly signed the registry into law, and it took effect in the fall of 2003.

Is the FTC "Do Not Call" registry a necessary tool to curb the telemarketing industry?

PRO

1. Without the list—and its fines of up to $11,000 per call—telemarketers would continue to call, probably at dinner time. According to recent polls, 97 percent of American consumers oppose these calls.

2. The registry actually benefits the telemarketing industry by weeding out those consumers who do not want to receive unsolicited calls. (Those who want to receive calls simply didn't sign up for the list.) This way, telemarketers don't waste time and money on calls that will not result in an inquiry or sale.

CON

1. The list will cost many telemarketers their jobs.
2. Many companies have actually used telemarketing successfully, and the restrictions may cause them to lose business.

SUMMARY

Despite the arguments on both sides, which are likely to continue for some time, consumers who registered their phone numbers on the list began to see an immediate decline in calls after October 1, 2003. "Consumers want more control over their telephones—today we give it to them," said Michael K. Powell, chairman of the Federal Communications Commission.

SOURCES: Geoffrey Colvin, "America Hangs Up on Telemarketers," *Fortune*, October 13, 2003, p. 58; Ryan J. Foley, "The Bad News: Telemarketers Will Still Call," *The Wall Street Journal*, October 9, 2003, pp. D1, D2; James Toedtman, "Do Not Call Registry Finally Up and Running," *Newsday.com*, October 2, 2003, http://www.newsday.com; Michael C. Dorf, "Legal Status of the Do-Not-Call Registry," *CNN.com*, October 2, 2003, http://www.cnn.com.

Inbound telemarketing typically involves a toll-free number that customers can call to obtain information, make reservations, and purchase goods and services. When a customer calls in on a toll-free line, the caller can be identified and routed to the sales agents with whom he or she has done business before, creating a human touch not possible before. This form of selling provides maximum convenience for customers who initiate the sales process. Many large catalog merchants, like The Sharper Image, Lillian Vernon, and Lands' End, keep their inbound telemarketing lines open 24 hours a day, 7 days a week. In fact, you can even call L.L. Bean on Christmas Day to place an order! Other catalog retailers maintain reputations for superior customer service and marketing ideas. Williams-Sonoma, a kitchen and culinary cataloguer, for instance, satisfies its customers by guaranteeing that any product defect will be corrected or repaired using genuine parts from the manufacturer or with a new product.

Inside Selling

The role of many of today's telemarketers is a combination of field selling techniques applied through inbound and outbound telemarketing channels with a strong customer orientation, called **inside selling.** Inside sales reps perform two primary jobs: They turn opportunities into actual sales, and they support technicians and

Marketing Dictionary

telemarketing Promotional presentation involving the use of the telephone on an outbound basis by salespeople or on an inbound basis by customers who initiate calls to obtain information and place orders.

inside selling Performing the functions of field selling but avoiding travel-related expenses by relying on phone, mail, and electronic commerce to provide sales and product service for customers on a continuing basis.

FIGURE 19.3 Alternative Sales Channels for Serving Customers

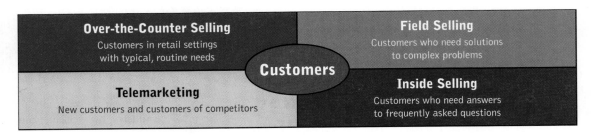

purchasers with current solutions. Inside sales reps do far more than read a canned script to unwilling prospects. They perform a dynamic selling function that goes beyond taking orders to solving problems, providing customer service, and selling. eTapestry.com, an Indianapolis-based application service provider for nonprofit organizations, is one of many companies that successfully combines selling approaches. eTapestry's inside salespeople do far more than run down leads; they close major deals over the phone—some worth more than a quarter-million dollars. The team is made up of former outside sales pros. With revenues that exceed $3 million a year, eTapestry finds its inside reps more cost effective and easier to manage than an outside sales force.[9]

A successful inside sales force relies on close working relationships with field representatives to solidify customer relationships. In the printing industry, for example, the increasing complexity of the printing process has led to a need for more detailed coordination and internal management than in the past. Across the industry, the traditional role of customer service has evolved to incorporate account development and resource management responsibilities. Increasingly, sales reps and customer service personnel work together in teams, providing the inside backup that allows the salesperson to spend more time focusing on new business.[10]

Integrating the Various Selling Channels

Figure 19.3 illustrates how firms are likely to blend alternative sales channels—from over-the-counter selling and field selling to telemarketing and inside selling—to create a successful cost-effective sales organization. Existing customers whose business problems require complex solutions are likely to be best served by the traditional field sales force. Other current customers who need answers but not the same handholding as the first group can be served by inside sales reps who call on them as needed. Over-the-counter sales reps serve existing customers by supplying information and advice and completing sales transactions. Telemarketers are often used to contact prospective customers and to attempt to win back previous clients who are currently purchasing from competitors. In some instances, telemarketers attempt to complete the sale; in other, more complex selling situations, they turn promising sales leads over to the field sales force for follow-up.

Georgia-based Omnibus Solutions, a $120 million company that provides new and refurbished computer servers, employs 15 inside and 25 outside sales reps. Cost-effective inside salespeople handle specific customer needs, and the outside team concentrates on building long-term relationships. The ability of outside reps to cross-sell multiple products due to the customer intelligence they glean from face-to-face selling situations is vital to the company's success.[11]

Recent Trends in Personal Selling

In today's complex business environment, effective personal selling requires different strategies than salespeople used in the past. Rather than selling one-on-one, it is now the norm to sell to teams of corporate representatives who make up the client firm's decision-making units. In particular, in business-to-business sales situations involving technical products, customers expect salespeople to answer technical questions—or bring along someone who can. They also want representatives who understand technical jargon and can communicate using sophisticated technological tools. Patience is also a requirement for personal selling because the sales cycle, from initial contact to closing, may take years. The average industrial sale takes at least four sales calls to close, and the larger and more expensive the equipment, the longer it takes.

TABLE 19.2   What Buyers Expect from Salespeople

Buyers prefer to do business with salespeople who:

- Orchestrate events and bring to bear whatever resources are necessary to satisfy the customer
- Provide counseling to the customer based on in-depth knowledge of the product, the market, and the customer's needs
- Solve problems extremely proficiently to ensure satisfactory customer service over extended time periods
- Demonstrate high ethical standards and communicate honestly at all times
- Willingly advocate the customer's cause within the selling organization
- Create imaginative arrangements to meet buyers' needs
- Arrive well-prepared for sales calls

3

Describe each of the four major trends in personal selling.

To address these concerns, companies rely on four major personal selling approaches: relationship selling, consultative selling, team selling, and sales-force automation. Together, these methods are changing the sales function at companies of all sizes.

Relationship Selling

As competitive pressures mount, more firms are emphasizing **relationship selling,** a technique for building a mutually beneficial relationship with a customer through regular contacts over an extended period. Such buyer-seller bonds become increasingly important as companies cut back on the number of suppliers and look for companies that provide high levels of customer service and satisfaction. Salespeople must also find ways to distinguish themselves and their products from competitors. To create strong, long-lasting relationships with customers, salespeople must meet buyers' expectations. Table 19.2 summarizes the results of several surveys that indicate what buyers expect of professional salespeople.

The success of tomorrow's marketers depends on the relationships they build today, in both the business-to-customer and business-to-business markets. Merrill Lynch recently refocused its 10,000-plus U.S. brokers on a relationship selling approach. For years, the company had tried to compete with low-cost brokerages like Charles Schwab by matching their cheap trading fees. Recently, the company redirected its brokers to concentrate only on wealthy clients with $1 million or more to invest. Investors with more modest assets are now handled by call centers. The firm's expert salespeople work only with its best customers. The change not only has cut costs but positions Merrill Lynch for faster growth, as brokers are able to offer more sophisticated advice to fewer but more profitable clients.[12] While it is far from abandoning its low-cost trade positioning, Charles Schwab also seeks a personal relationship between its sales professionals and top investors.

Relationship selling is equally important in business-to-business sales. ProSlide Technology sells water rides to amusement parks, but a closer look reveals that the company's success is centered on the ability of its sales force to customize each customer's order. New attractions like the CanonBOWL, an exhilarating water ride that allows parents to ride with children, are created by asking customers what they want and delivering both quality products and premium customer service. Rather than depend on repeat sales from established customers, ProSlide works to shape and reshape relationships with each order a customer places. As a result, over 70 percent of ProSlide's business comes from the same customers.[13]

Consultative Selling

The once-popular "good-old boy" sales style—getting chummy with customers,

Marketing Dictionary

relationship selling   Regular contacts over an extended period to establish a sustained seller-buyer relationship.

buying them a meal or a drink, giving the standard sales presentation, applying pressure, and expecting to get the sale on that basis—is rapidly going the way of the dinosaur. Field representatives and inside sales reps require sales methods that satisfy today's cost-conscious, knowledgeable buyers. One such method, **consultative selling,** involves meeting customer needs by listening to customers, understanding—and caring about—their problems, paying attention to details, and following through after the sale. It works hand in hand with relationship selling in building customer loyalty. Anne M. Mulcahey, president of Xerox Corp., is an advocate of consultative selling. A 25-year veteran saleswoman, Mulcahey insists on putting the company's resources and expertise behind its sales force. A hugely popular, high-energy manager, she promises to fly anywhere, anytime to help salespeople close tough deals.[14]

As rapid technological changes drive business at an unprecedented pace, selling has become more complex, often changing the role of salespeople. At Zeks Compressed Air Solutions, for instance, sales representatives have a background in engineering. With the job title Application Engineer, they bring technical proficiency to the sales situation. The change in title has helped the company overcome resistance to sales calls, since the expertise offered brings extra value to the customer-seller relationship.[15]

Online companies have instituted consultative selling models to create long-term customers. Particularly for complicated, high-priced products that require installation or specialized service, Web sellers must be able to quickly communicate the benefits and features of their products. They accomplish this through consultative selling. In its ad featured in Figure 19.4, software vendor SAP uses a consultative selling approach to promote its sophisticated customer relationship management software mySAP—after all, customer service should concern more than one department.

Similar to consultative selling, *cross-selling*—offering multiple products or services to the same customer—is another technique that capitalizes on a firm's strengths. It costs a bank five times more to acquire a new customer than to cross-sell to an existing one. Moreover, research shows that the more a customer buys from an institution, the less likely that person is to leave.

Wells Fargo uses cross-selling to sell twice as many financial products to its clients than its competing institutions are able to achieve. As well as training in cross-selling, bank staff receive generous incentives for sending checking-account customers, for example, to the credit-card department.[16]

MAYBE "CUSTOMER SERVICE" SHOULD BE MORE THAN ONE DEPARTMENT.

When everyone focuses on customers, something amazing happens: departments communicate, questions get answered, and products keep moving. That's why the mySAP™ Customer Relationship Management solution links customers with your complete organization. It keeps data consistent across all touch points and it's the only CRM solution that integrates with all other business processes, so it shortens sales cycles and lowers costs. Which means your customers won't be waiting around for good service, they'll be too busy getting it. For more info, visit www.sap.com

THE BEST-RUN E-BUSINESSES RUN SAP

FIGURE 19.4
SAP: Consultative Selling for Sophisticated Products

Team Selling

One of the latest developments in the evolution of personal selling is **team selling,** in which the salesperson joins with specialists from other functional areas of the firm to complete the selling process. Teams can be formal and ongoing or created for a specific short-term selling situation. Some salespeople have hesitated to embrace the idea of team selling. Although some salespeople prefer working alone, others believe that team selling brings better results. Customers often prefer the team approach, which makes them feel well served. Another advantage of team selling is the formation of relationships between companies rather than between individuals.

In sales situations that call for detailed knowledge of new, complex, and ever-changing technologies, team selling offers a distinct competitive edge in meeting customers' needs. In most computer software B2B departments, up to a third of the sales force is composed of technically trained, nonmarketing experts such as engineers or programmers. A salesperson continues to play the lead role in most sales situations, but technical experts bring extra value to the sales process. Some companies establish permanent sales-and-tech teams that conduct all sales presentations together; others, like software vendor ClientSoft, have a pool of engineers or other professionals who are on call for different client visits.[17]

CDW Computer Centers, the largest direct seller of Hewlett-Packard, IBM, Microsoft, Toshiba, and other top-name computer industry brands, relies on team selling to serve its 600,000 consumer and business customers. Each customer is provided with a highly trained account manager who serves as the team leader of a group of specialists dedicated to finding solutions to buyers' needs. In a typical day, more than 700 systems are custom configured for CDW customers. Customers can receive continuing lifetime technical support by visiting the CDW extranet or by calling a toll-free telephone number to speak with factory-trained technicians.[18]

In some cases, team selling brings in help from outside the company. AT&T, for example, works with PeoplePC to form a team-selling partnership to serve Delta Airlines. Through their Wired Workplace Program, the two companies provide free Internet access and free PCs for home-based Delta employees. This unique solution helps AT&T create a competitive advantage.

In any team-selling situation, preparation is the key to performing well. At Sun Microsystems, team members gather frequently in any way they can to share information—via e-mail, conference calls, and face-to-face meetings. Each team member reaches out to insiders at the client company to gather insights that can help them leapfrog over the competition. Good preparation, along with a clear designation of team leader, helps avoid in-team conflicts that can hamper the overall sales efforts.[19]

Sales-Force Automation

A major trend in personal selling is **sales-force automation (SFA)**—the application of new technologies to the sales process. Broadly used, the term refers to the use of everything from pagers and Web-browsing cell phones, to voice and electronic mail, to laptops and notebook computers. More narrowly used, it refers to the use of computers by salespeople for activities beyond the use of word processors, spreadsheets, and connections to order-entry systems.

With SFA tools, both large and small companies can increase their efficiency and spend more time on client acquisition and retention. The benefits of SFA include improvements in the quality and effectiveness of sales calls because of improved access to information; low selling, printing, and training costs; improved product launches; and attentive customer service. Sales reps at Old World Christmas, a supplier of Christmas ornaments, now use

Marketing Dictionary

consultative selling   Meeting customer needs by listening to them, understanding—and caring about—their problems, paying attention to details, and following through after the sale.

team selling   Combination of salespeople with specialists from other functional areas to promote a product.

sales-force automation (SFA)   Applications of computer and other technologies to make the sales function more efficient and competitive.

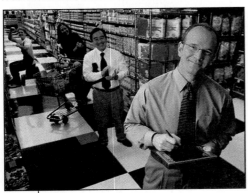
Fujitsu puts technology into sales reps' hands. Its touch-screen PC displays product lines, places orders, checks inventory, and more.

hand-held devices to speed order processing. The devices scan UPC bar codes on products and e-mail orders to headquarters. The scanner can then be hooked to a printer to give the customer instant, accurate written confirmation of pricing. The company's old, cumbersome order processing system has been reduced to just seconds using the new electronic sales aid.[20]

Other companies have integrated telephony with the Internet to provide both team selling and consultative selling online. Wrigley, the Chicago chewing-gum company, for example, uses software created by SAP to operate in real time online. Sales representatives can collaborate on sales projects, bringing in experts as needed to strengthen their sales presentations. They can also use the software to get instant access to marketing or customer data, receive detailed product information, or download competitive data—all of which can be incorporated into customized sales presentations.[21]

SFA usage differs sharply by industry: Food, beverage, and pharmaceutical industries are using sophisticated third-generation systems, whereas many apparel companies have not yet moved to SFA. Software for sales-force automation also falls into several categories depending on its intended use. Most salespeople use basic productivity and general-purpose programs such as word processors, e-mail, and spreadsheets. Some programs help to organize prospect lists and to remind salespeople to make follow-up calls. More expensive systems may integrate order processing and other types of information.

Sales Tasks *Read*

Today's salesperson is more concerned with establishing long-term buyer-seller relationships and with helping customers select the correct products for meeting their needs than with simply selling whatever is available. Where repeat purchases are common, the salesperson must be certain that the buyer's purchases are in his or her best interest; otherwise, no future sales will be made. The seller's interests are tied to the buyer's in a symbiotic relationship.

4

Identify the three basic sales tasks.

Not all selling activities are alike. While all sales activities assist the customer in some manner, the exact tasks that are performed vary from one position to another. Three basic sales tasks can be identified: (1) order processing, (2) creative selling, and (3) missionary sales. These tasks form the basis for a sales classification system.

Most sales personnel do not fall into a single category. Instead, they often perform all three tasks to some extent. A sales engineer for a computer firm may be doing 50 percent missionary sales, 45 percent creative selling, and 5 percent order processing. Most selling jobs, however, are classified on the basis of the primary selling task performed.

A major consideration for most businesses is improving productivity throughout their operations, and sales-force productivity is no exception. With the climbing costs of travel and compensation for experienced salespeople, each sales rep must spend time efficiently and effectively to raise productivity.

Order Processing

Order processing, which can involve both field selling and telemarketing, is most often typified by selling at the wholesale and retail levels. For instance, a Pepsi-Cola route salesperson who performs this task must take the following steps:

1. *Identify customer needs.* The route salesperson determines that a store has only 7 cases left in stock when it normally carries an inventory of 40 cases.

2. *Point out the need to the customer.* The route salesperson informs the store manager of the inventory situation.

3. *Complete (write up) the order.* The store manager acknowledges the need for more of the product. The driver unloads 33 cases, and the manager signs the delivery slip.

Order processing is part of most selling positions. It becomes the primary task in situations where needs can be readily identified and are acknowledged by the customer. Even in such instances, however, salespeople whose primary responsibility involves order processing will devote some time convincing their wholesale or retail customers to carry more complete inventories of their firms' products or to handle additional product lines. They also are likely to try to motivate purchasers to feature some of their firms' products, increase the amount of shelf space devoted to their products, and improve product location in the stores.

Sales-force automation is easing order-processing tasks. In the past, salespeople would write up an order on the customer's premises but spend much time later, after the sales visit, completing the order and transmitting it to headquarters. Today, many companies have automated order processing. With portable computers and state-of-the-art software, the salesperson can place an order on the spot, directly to headquarters, thus freeing up valuable time and energy. Computers have even eliminated the need for some of the traditional face-to-face contacts for routine reorders.

Creative Selling

When a considerable amount of analytical decision making is involved in purchasing a good or service, the salesperson must use **creative selling** techniques to solicit an order. In contrast to the order-processing task, which deals mainly with maintaining existing business, creative selling generally is used to develop new business either by adding new customers or by introducing new goods and services. New products often require a high degree of creative selling. The salesperson must first identify the customer's problems and needs and then propose a solution in the form of the good or service being offered. Creative selling techniques are used in over-the-counter selling, field selling, telemarketing, and inside selling.

As more and more companies consolidate and the number of buyers for a product or service shrinks, creative selling approaches are increasingly necessary to win the sale. Take the case of Blue Barn Interactive, a New York–based online community developer. Blue Barn inked a $250,000-a-year deal to deliver online solutions to a Web division representing three major cable television brands. To get close to a sale, Blue Barn offered to begin work on a trial basis. Before the contract was final, the cooperative Web division disappeared in a cost-cutting move, and each of the three cable companies took control of its own Web content. Blue Barn had invested heavily in a deal—and a buyer—that vanished overnight into thin air. Rather than walk away, Blue Barn reinvented its sales approach. Representatives courted each of the three cable companies to start building relationships and find out where the eventual buy-in would be. Blue Barn also went directly to the CEO overseeing all three brands' Web content. A renewed presentation explained how the product fit in with the new overall initiative

Marketing Dictionary

order processing   Selling, mostly at the wholesale and retail levels, that involves identifying customer needs, pointing them out to customers, and completing orders.

creative selling   Personal selling involving situations in which a considerable degree of analytical decision making on the buyer's part results in the need for skillful proposals of solutions for the customer's needs.

Marketing Hit

Selling SAP Software in a Rotten Economy

Background. A top rep at software maker SAP, Sudha Shah recently closed deals worth $40 million, four times her quota. But now, in a soft economy, as the software sector reels from budget cuts at client firms, customers are unwilling to take sales calls, never mind sign a check.

The Challenge. Take AMD, a leader in the semiconductor industry. Despite weeks of networking and constant dialing, no one would pick up the phone. Undeterred, Shah shifted gears, asking a colleague who had done business with AMD to help her get her foot in the door.

The Strategy. That one introduction was all she needed. The client—who had already decided to buy from Oracle—signed a $20 million deal with Shah. The reasons? He liked the way she listened and took notes. He liked her willingness to create custom solutions and her detailed follow-up. Most of all, her liked her enthusiasm.

Clients like AMD are why Sudha spends 70 hours a week gathering information, reworking her contacts, and making constant calls. She's willing to end vacations early to structure deals. When clients insist that the budget is not there, she'll work out creative solutions: Try out the product for free before signing. Install your system now, and once the economy picks up, you'll be way ahead. Buy now, she insists, and slash thousands of dollars off the cost.

continued on next page

5

Outline the steps in the sales process.

and with each company's specific needs. The multilevel approach paid off, and Blue Barn was at last able to make a deal. Later, the company found that the three brand managers—with whom they could have pursued contracts individually—were laid off or transferred due to further consolidations.[22] The "Marketing Hits" box describes some of the ways top reps craft creative selling solutions for their clients.

Missionary Selling

Missionary selling is an indirect approach to sales. Salespeople sell the firm's goodwill and provide their customers with information and technical or operational assistance. For example, a toiletries company salesperson may call on retailers to check on special promotions and overall product movement, even though a wholesaler takes orders and delivers merchandise. Large pharmaceutical companies are the most aggressive of missionary sales operations. Through extensive gift-giving, wining and dining, free seminars, and other incentives, teams of sales reps typically court doctors (the indirect customer) in the hope of persuading them to prescribe a particular brand to patients. They also inundate doctors with glossy product literature. Here, the doctor is clearly the decision maker, even though the transaction is not complete until the patient hands the prescription over to a pharmacist.[23] And increasingly, they rely on a flurry of direct-to-consumer ads for new medications like Allegra that can be purchased only with a prescription. The pharmaceutical marketers urge consumers to consult their doctors as a first step in a diagnosis—and to request a free sample of the product.

Missionary sales may involve both field selling and telemarketing. Many aspects of team selling can also be seen as missionary sales, as when technical support salespeople help design, install, and maintain equipment; when they train customers' employees; and when they provide information or operational assistance. For example, Harris InfoSource, a Cleveland-based corporate communications company, compiles and markets databases profiling U.S. manufacturers and their decision makers. Recently, the firm has branched into services research, too. Harris's salespeople gather leads from such sources as trade shows and field sales activities and follow up with missionary sales strategies. After each trade show, between two and three people from Harris's internal sales staff call on the leads, looking for customers who need accurate, in-depth sales lead information. The Harris selling approach begins at the trade show booth and continues with follow-up letters, phone calls, and sales calls.[24]

The Sales Process Read

If you have worked in a retail store or simply sold candy or wrapping paper to raise money for your band, swim team, or other organization, you will recognize some of the activities involved in the sales process, even if you did not think of them as such. Personal selling encompasses the following sequence of activities: (1) prospecting and qualifying, (2) approach, (3) presentation, (4) demonstration, (5) handling objections, (6) closing, and (7) follow-up.

As Figure 19.5 indicates, these steps follow the attention-interest-desire-action concept (AIDA) discussed in Chapter 17. Once a sales prospect has been qualified, an attempt is made to secure his or her attention. The presentation and demonstration steps are designed to generate interest and desire. Successful handling of buyer objections should arouse further desire. Action occurs at the close of the sale.

Salespeople modify the steps in this process to match their customers' buying processes. For instance, the Girl Scout whose Aunt Ada buys boxes and boxes of Girl Scout Thin Mint cookies every year probably needs no presentation. She could just call her aunt and tell her that cookies are on sale. She might also remind her aunt how grateful she is for her order each year and highlight the new cookies in the hope that she will also order some of those. If every other house has a girl selling the cookies, the scout may need to join with other members of her troop to find new customers in different locations, such as the lobby of local grocery stores.

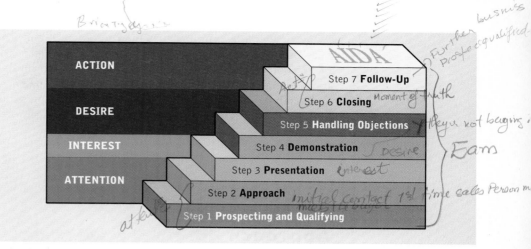

FIGURE 19.5
The AIDA Concept and the Personal Selling Process

Prospecting and Qualifying

Prospecting, the process of identifying potential customers, is difficult work involving many hours of diligent effort. Leads about prospects may come from many sources: computerized databases, trade show exhibits, previous customers, friends and neighbors, other vendors, nonsales employees in the firm, suppliers, and social and professional contacts. Although a firm may emphasize personal selling as the primary component of its overall promotional strategy, direct mail and advertising campaigns are also effective in identifying prospective customers. Technology consulting firm The Meta Group credits a prospecting initiative with boosting revenues by $1.5 million. The company ran a series of real-time informational teleconferences for potential customers. Participants were invited to complete a poll, providing details on their organizations and their consulting needs. The conferences increased sales lead flow by 600 percent.[25]

New sales personnel may find prospecting frustrating because they usually receive no immediate payback. But selling is frequently a numbers game, and for many salespeople, sales numbers start with prospecting. Without successful prospecting, future sales growth is limited to current accounts. Prospecting is a continuous process because of the inevitable loss of some customers over time, as well as the emergence of new potential customers or first-time prospects.

Recently, salespeople have turned to the Internet in their efforts to identify prospective customers. Auto marketers, for instance, offer Internet shoppers an array of promotional incentives, including coupons off the purchase price, gift certificates, savings bonds, sweepstakes, and games. Once consumers sign up for the incentives, they are often asked for information about themselves and their preferences. Auto marketers use this information to track and communicate with customers in ways they could not do offline. Some companies report successes in turning respondents to Web giveaways into real customers, but others are less enthusiastic about prospecting on the Internet. In a recent survey of auto dealers, more than half rated the quality of Internet leads as poor or very poor.[26]

Marketing Hit

The Outcome. SAP continues to ride out a slow economy, adjusting annual sales growth downward. Undaunted, the company recently expanded into the public sector, as well as into small business. These are challenging times, but with a cell phone, a thick skin, and sheer optimism, reps like Sudha Shah will see SAP through.

SOURCES: James McKenzie and Siobhan Kennedy, "SAP Cuts Forecast, Shares Plunge," Reuters Company News, July 11, 2002, **http://biz.yahoo.com**; "SAP Lowers Forecast, Implements Hiring Freeze," *Infoworld*, January 11, 2002, **http://www.infoworld.com**; "Blind Optimism, Thick Skin, and a Cell Phone," *Fortune*, August 13, 2001, pp. 134–140.

Marketing Dictionary

missionary selling   Indirect type of selling in which specialized salespeople promote the firm's goodwill among indirect customers, often by assisting customers in product use.

Qualifying—determining that the prospect really is a potential customer—is another important sales task. Not all prospects are qualified to make purchase decisions. A person with an annual income of $25,000 may wish to own a $200,000 house, but his or her ability to actually become a customer is questionable.

Qualifying can be a two-way street. The sales representative determines that the prospect has the authority and the resources to make the purchase decision. Likewise, prospects must agree that they are candidates for the goods or services being offered. If either of those conditions is not met, then further contact is not likely to lead to a sale and will be a waste of time for both salesperson and prospect. To keep costs under control, many firms engage in telemarketing for both prospecting and qualifying. Telemarketers and inside sales reps pass on qualified leads to field salespeople, who can concentrate on prospects most likely to buy.

Approach

Once the salesperson has identified a qualified prospect, he or she collects all available, relevant information and plans an *approach*—the salesperson's initial contact with the prospective customer. Information about the prospect can provide invaluable help to ease the initial contact for telemarketers, inside sales reps, and field salespeople. Salespeople can gather information from secondary sources—magazine or newspaper articles—or from the prospect's own published literature—annual reports, press releases, and even Internet sites. In collecting information, the salesperson must be sensitive to the issue of invading the prospect's privacy. A sales professional does not use unethical tactics to obtain personal information about a prospect.

Information gathering makes *precall planning* possible. A salesperson who has gathered relevant information about a prospect can make an initial contact armed with knowledge about the prospect's purchasing habits; his or her attitudes, activities, and opinions; and common interests between the salesperson and the prospect. This preparation often provides key help for winning an account.

Retail salespeople usually cannot conduct precall planning, but they can compensate by asking leading questions to learn more about the purchase preferences of buyers. Business marketers have access to far more data than retail sellers, and they should review it before scheduling the first sales contact. Marketing research studies often provide invaluable information that serves as the basis of a sales approach. Answering the following questions can help salespeople complete effective precall planning:

- Who are the audience members and what jobs do they perform each day?

- What is their level of knowledge? Are they already informed about the idea you are going to present?

- What do they want to hear? Do they want detailed, technical jargon or general information?

- What do they need to hear? Do they need to know more about your company or more about the good or service your company provides? Do they need to know more about the availability and cost of your product or more about how your product actually works?

Presentation

The salesperson gives the sales message to a prospective customer in a *presentation*. The seller describes the product's major features, points out its strengths, and concludes by citing illustrative successes. One popular form of presentation is a "features-benefits" framework wherein the seller's objective is to talk about the good or service in terms that are meaningful to the buyer. The salesperson relates product features to customer needs and explains benefits of those features, rather than relating technical specifications.

The presentation should be well organized, clear, and concise, and it should emphasize the positive. Printed sales support materials (charts, product literature, market research, product reviews), charts designed on a laptop computer, and audiovisual aids such as videotapes enhance the clarity and effectiveness of presentations. The level of preparation depends on the type of call. For a routine sales call, up-to-date product knowledge and information about the prospect may be sufficient. When the sales-

'net **Ex**

Improving your sales presentations. Many salespeople find that ordinary PowerPoint presentations are no longer adequate. Some clients want presentations containing more multimedia material and high-tech graphics. Consequently, a number of software publishers offer PowerPoint add-in tools so users can add these materials to existing PowerPoint presentations. One add-in can be found at **http://www .crystalgraphics.com**. Go to the site and download the free trial. Try it with one of your existing PowerPoint presentations. Be prepared to comment in class on what you liked or disliked about its ability to add multimedia and high-tech graphics to your PowerPoint presentations.

person is competing with several other companies for an account, a major presentation requires in-depth preparation and rehearsals to ensure that everything goes perfectly. Flexible presentations are nearly always needed to match the unique circumstances of each purchase decision. Proper planning and sensitivity to the customer's reactions are an important part of tailoring a presentation to each prospective customer.

Increasingly, presentations are going high-tech. Computer-based multimedia presentations are considered the next wave in sales-force automation. With a multimedia-ready laptop or a larger PC or LCD projection computer, salespeople can bring color, animation, video, audio, and interactivity—as well as the latest product and pricing information—to their presentations. CNN Headline News salespeople previously used ordinary PowerPoint presentations to sell ads to cable operators. But when the company recently decided to change the look and feel of the Atlanta-based 24-hour cable news network, executives knew their sales force would need multimedia presentation materials that matched the network's more modern cutting-edge look. Presentations now include audio and video clips and high-tech graphics.[27]

Demonstration

One important advantage of personal selling over most advertising is the ability of salespeople to provide a *demonstration* of the good or service to the potential buyer. As shown in Figure 19.6,

**FIGURE 19.6
Demonstration—
Critical Step for
Buyers Purchasing a
New Color Copier**

Canon's new ink jet printers have individual ink tank systems, allowing customers to replace a single color rather than an entire cartridge when they are "out of blue." The ad for this new product invited customers to check out the Canon ink jet Web site at http://www.usa.canon.com or to call a toll-free number for further information.

But a static magazine advertisement or even a quasi-demonstration of a product in action on a television screen is a far cry from the real thing. A demonstration ride in a new automobile, for example, allows the prospect to become involved in the presentation. It awakens customer interest in a way that no amount of verbal presentation can.

More firms use new technologies to make their demonstrations more effective. Multimedia interactive demonstrations are now common. Sales representatives for magazines such as *Forbes* and *Newsweek*, for instance, use data stored on CD-ROM or interactive laser discs to demonstrate the magazine's demographics and circulation patterns. These presentations use full-color video and sound, along with animation, statistics, and text, to demonstrate how a prospective client's ad will appear.

The key to a good demonstration—one that gains the customer's attention, keeps his or her interest, is convincing, and stays in the customer's memory—is planning. The salesperson should check and recheck all aspects of the demonstration prior to its delivery.

Handling Objections

A vital part of selling involves handling objections. *Objections* are expressions of sales resistance by the prospect, and it is reasonable to expect them: "Well, I really should check with my spouse." "Perhaps I'll stop by next week." "I like everything except the color." Objections typically involve the product's features, its price, and services to be provided by the selling firm. A sales professional uses each objection as a cue for providing additional information for the prospect. In most cases, an objection such as "I don't like the color of the interior" is really the prospect's way of asking what other choices or product features are available. A customer's question reveals an interest in the product and gives the seller an opportunity to expand a presentation by supplying additional information. For instance, testimonials from satisfied customers may be effective in responding to product objections. Also, providing a copy of the warranty and the dealer's service contract may resolve the buyer's doubts about customer service.

During this stage of the selling process, salespeople often are confronted with objections concerning competitors' products. Professional salespeople avoid criticizing the competition. Instead, they view objections as an opportunity to provide more information about the good or service. Often this requires conducting extra behind-the-scenes research. Sales-force automation can help sales representatives handle certain objections by making needed information immediately available. In just a few moments, the salesperson can confirm for the customer that the amount and type of a certain product are in stock and can be quickly shipped, for example.

Overcoming objections in the marketplace starts with a "we can do it" attitude. When Marshall Maguire, national sales manager for New Jersey–based RMB Miniature Bearings, heard that more and more customers were using price as an objection to purchase, he refused to let reps negotiate. RMB produced a commodity-type product—foreign-made bearings could be bought at a fraction of the price. To avoid reducing margins, Maguire insists that reps emphasize the value of the product to the customer—RMB offers vastly superior customer service and customization to the client's needs. Overcoming objections by offering value rather than low price allows the company to keep a reasonable profit margin and stay in business.[28]

Closing

The moment of truth in selling is the *closing*—the point at which the salesperson asks the prospect for an order. If the sales representative has made an effective presentation based on applying the product to the customer's needs, the closing should be the natural conclusion. However, a surprising number of sales personnel find it difficult to actually ask for an order. Nearly 80 percent of salespeople fail to close when the buyer is ready, and many customers are ready to close much earlier than the salesperson is.

To be effective, salespeople must learn when and how to close a sale. Commonly used methods of closing a sale include the following:

1. The "if I can show you . . ." technique first identifies the prospect's major concern in purchasing the good or service and then offers convincing evidence of the offering's ability to resolve it. ("If I can show you how the new heating system will reduce your energy costs by 25 percent, would you be willing to let us install it?")

2. The alternative-decision technique poses choices for the prospect in which either alternative is favorable to the salesperson. ("Will you take this sweater or that one?")

3. The SRO (standing-room-only) technique warns the prospect that a sales agreement should be concluded now because the product may not be available later or an important feature, such as price, will soon be changed.

FIGURE 19.7
Low-Pressure Closing Phrases

I need your approval to proceed.
To confirm delivery date, all you need to do is OK this tentative order.
When do you want to have this up and running?
Tell me where we stand.
You won't regret this decision.
That's quite a return, isn't it?
Can we confirm your order now and start planning the installation schedule?
When would you like to start seeing these benefits?
What else do I need to do to earn your business?
If we've covered all the bases, will you authorize an order?
Do you have any concerns that I haven't addressed? If not . . .
Which papers should we look at: the lease or the order form?

SOURCE: "Hot Closing Phrases," *The Competitive Advantage*, 2001, p. 3, adapted from Terry L. Booton, *Cracking New Accounts*.

4. Silence can be used as a closing technique, since a discontinuance of a sales presentation forces the prospect to take some type of action (either positive or negative).

5. An extra-inducement close offers special incentives designed to motivate a favorable buyer response. Extra inducements may include quantity discounts, special servicing arrangements, or layaway options.

Figure 19.7 suggests several low-pressure phrases salespeople may use to move smoothly from the presentation to the close, wrapping up a deal.

Follow-Up

The word *close* can be misleading, since the point at which the prospect accepts the seller's offer is where much of the real work of selling begins. In today's increasingly competitive sales environment, the successful salesperson seeks to ensure that today's customers will be future purchasers. It is not enough to close the sale and move on. Relationship selling requires the salesperson to reinforce the customer's purchase decision and make sure that the company delivers high-quality goods or services on schedule. Salespeople must also ensure that customer service needs are met and that satisfaction results from all of a customer's dealings with the company. Otherwise, another company may get the next order.

These postsale activities, which often determine whether a person will become a repeat customer, constitute the sales *follow-up*. Whenever possible, the sales representative should contact customers to find out whether they are satisfied with their purchases. This step allows the salesperson to psychologically reinforce the customer's original decision to buy. It also gives the seller an opportunity to correct any sources of discontent with the purchase and to secure important market information and make additional sales, as well.

Follow-up helps to strengthen the bond salespeople try to build with customers in relationship selling. Automobile dealers, for example, often keep elaborate records of their previous customers so that they can promote new models to individuals who already have shown a willingness to buy from them.

Some auto dealers assign representatives from their service departments to call several days after a customer's appointment to make sure the customer is satisfied with the work. Proper follow-up is a logical part of the selling sequence.

Managing the Sales Effort

The overall direction and control of the personal selling effort are in the hands of sales managers, who are organized on a hierarchical basis. For example, in a typical geographical sales structure, a district or divisional sales manager might report to a regional or zone manager, and these people, in turn, may report to a national sales manager or vice president of sales.

6

Describe the sales manager's boundary-spanning role.

Sales managers perform a **boundary-spanning role** in that they link the sales force to other elements of the internal and external environments. The internal organizational environment consists of top management, other functional areas in the firm, and other internal information sources. The external environment includes trade groups, competitors, customers, suppliers, and regulatory agencies.

The sales manager's job requires a unique blend of administrative and sales skills depending on the specific level in the sales hierarchy. Sales skills are very important for first-level sales managers since these managers must train and directly lead the sales force. But as people rise in the sales management structure, they require more managerial skills and fewer sales skills to perform well. Over 60 percent of a typical salesperson's time is devoted to prospecting, face-to-face selling, and travel. The typical time allocations for a salesperson are shown in Figure 19.8.

As with other promotional activities, personal selling requires effective planning and strategic objectives, including such strategies as selling existing products to new customers, selling new products, servicing customer accounts to enhance retention and satisfaction, and expanding customer relationships by selling more products to existing customers.

7

List and discuss the functions of sales-force management.

Sales-force management is the administrative channel for sales personnel; it links individual salespeople to general management. The sales manager performs seven basic managerial functions: (1) recruitment and selection, (2) training, (3) organization, (4) supervision, (5) motivation, (6) compensation, and (7) evaluation and control. Sales managers perform these tasks in a demanding and complex environment. They must manage an increasingly diverse sales force that includes more women and minorities. Women account for almost half of U.S. professional salespeople, and their numbers are growing at a faster rate than that for men. The fastest growth rate is among salespeople of Hispanic and Asian descent.

However, women account for only one of every four business-to-business salespeople. As the workforce composition continues to change, more people will be needed to fill a growing number of sell-

FIGURE 19.8
How Salespeople and Sales Managers Spend Their Time

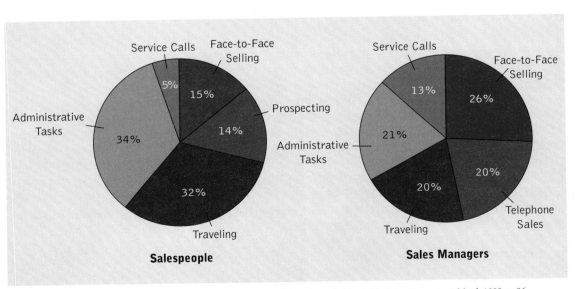

SOURCE: Salesperson time allocations reported in "How Salespeople Spend Their Time," *Sales & Marketing Management*, March 1998, p. 96.

ing positions such as product specialists, sales consultants, telemarketers, and customer service and sales support representatives.

Recruitment and Selection

Recruiting and selecting successful salespeople are one of the sales manager's greatest challenges. The turnover rate of salespeople is the highest of all white-collar professions. Sources of new salespeople include colleges and universities, trade and business schools, sales and nonsales personnel in other firms, and the firm's current nonsales employees. A growing number of companies are offering bonuses and perks for employees who help find recruits.

Not all of these methods are equally productive. One problem area involves the reluctance of some high-school guidance counselors and college instructors to promote the advantages of a selling career to students. But in fact, a successful sales career offers satisfaction in all of the following five areas that a person generally considers when deciding on a profession:

1. *Opportunity for advancement.* Studies have shown that successful sales representatives advance rapidly in most companies. Advancement can come either from within the sales organization or laterally to a more responsible position in some other functional area of the firm.

2. *High earnings.* The earnings of successful salespeople compare favorably with those of successful people in other professions. The average top-level consumer goods salesperson can earn more than $75,000 per year.

3. *Personal satisfaction.* A salesperson derives satisfaction from achieving success in a competitive environment and from helping customers satisfy their wants and needs.

4. *Job security.* Contrary to what many students believe, selling provides a high degree of job security. Experience has shown that economic downturns affect personnel in sales less than they do people in most other employment areas. In addition, there is a continuing need for good sales personnel.

5. *Independence and variety.* Salespeople most often operate as "independent" businesspeople or as managers of sales territories. Their work is quite varied and provides an opportunity for involvement in numerous business functions.

Careful selection of salespeople is important for two reasons. First, the selection process involves substantial amounts of money and management time. Second, selection mistakes are detrimental to customer relations and sales-force performance and are costly to correct, as well.

A seven-step process typically is used in selecting sales personnel: application, screening interview, in-depth interview, testing, reference checks, physical examination, and analysis and hiring decision. An application screening is followed by an initial interview. If the applicant looks promising, an in-depth interview is conducted. During the interview, sales managers look for personal characteristics like enthusiasm, good organizational skills, ambition, persuasiveness, the ability to follow instructions, and sociability.

Next, the company may use testing in its selection procedure, including aptitude, intelligence, interest, knowledge, and personality tests. One testing approach gaining in popularity is the assessment center. This technique, which uses situational exercises, group discussions, and various job simulations, allows the sales manager to measure a candidate's skills, knowledge, and ability. Assessment centers enable managers to see what potential salespeople can do rather than what they say they can do. After testing applicants, companies check their references to ensure that job candidates have represented themselves accurately. A physical examination is usually included before the final analysis and hiring decision.

Training

To shape new sales recruits into an efficient sales organization, managers must conduct an

> **Briefly Speaking**
>
> I couldn't believe that God meant a woman's brain to bring 50 cents on the dollar.
>
> *Mary Kay Ash (1918–2001) Founder, Mary Kay Cosmetics (on her 1963 decision to start her own company after her male assistant at a direct-sales company was promoted at twice her salary)*

Marketing Dictionary

boundary-spanning role Role performed by a sales manager in linking the sales force to other elements of the organization's internal and external environments.

effective training program. The principal methods used in sales training are on-the-job training, individual instruction, in-house classes, and external seminars.

Popular training techniques include instructional videotapes, lectures, role-playing exercises, slides, films, and interactive computer programs. Simulations can help salespeople improve their selling techniques. Another key area for training is sales-force automation (SFA). However, salespeople who are not very computer literate can balk when presented with SFA tools. Many firms supplement their training by enrolling salespeople in executive development programs at local colleges and by hiring specialists to teach customized training programs. In other instances, sales reps attend courses and workshops developed by outside companies.

Construction Information Systems, a company that provides building contractors with information on jobs sent out to bid via the Internet, is a fast-growing business that credits its success to its sales-training process. Concentrated sessions at regular intervals focus on precall planning, through which reps learn to set goals for every call they make, prospecting skills, questioning skills that encourage customers to express their business needs, and role playing, in which reps work through difficult sales challenges.[29]

Ongoing sales training is also important for veteran salespeople. Much of this type of training is conducted by sales managers informally. A standard format is for the sales manager to travel with a field sales representative periodically and then critique the person's work. Sales meetings, training tapes, classes, and seminars are other important forms of training for experienced personnel.

Mentoring is a key training tool at many organizations. Sealed Air Corporation, a New Jersey company, offers a sales mentoring program that cuts training costs, fosters loyalty, and helps groom future managers. Top sales performers spend three years coaching new or underperforming salespeople in their territories. While the trainee sets up calls and takes the lead in sales pitches, the mentor provides help and encouragement along the way. Microsoft uses mentoring as a means of helping women and minority personnel develop their careers, and communications and electronics designer Agilent Technologies' mentor program—open only to those who excel—mixes people from different functions in the company to give future managers a broader view of operations.[30]

Organization

Sales managers are responsible for the organization of the field sales force. General organizational alignments, which are usually made by top marketing management, may be based on geography, products, types of customers, or some combination of these factors. Figure 19.9 presents a simplified organizational chart illustrating each of these alignments.

A product sales organization should have specialized sales forces for each major category of the firm's products. This approach is common among industrial product companies that market large numbers of similar but separate products of a very technical or complex nature that are sold through different marketing channels.

Firms that market similar products throughout large territories often use geographical specialization. For example, multinational corporations may have different sales divisions in different continents. Geographical organization may be combined with one of the other organizational methods. However, companies are moving away from using territorial sales reps as they adopt

FIGURE 19.9
Basic Approaches to Organizing the Sales Force

customer-focused sales forces. When confronted with a sales territory problem, Stephen Wald, CEO of apparel manufacturer Naturally Knits, had to devise a plan that would settle a dispute between two of his salespeople. The problem arose when one sales rep lost a lucrative account when the territories in his district were reconfigured. Wald knew the importance of maintaining positive relationships between the salesperson and the customer—even though the customer was now located in another sales rep's territory. The company, therefore, added a "cherry-picking clause" that spells out exceptions to the home-territory rule. This reorganization saved two multimillion-dollar accounts that came to the company through relationships developed long-distance by reps outside their territories.[31]

Customer-oriented organizations use different sales-force strategies for each major type of customer served. Some firms assign separate sales forces for their consumer and organizational customers. Others have sales forces for specific industries, such as financial services, educational, and automotive. Sales forces can also be organized by customer size, with a separate sales force assigned to large, medium, and small accounts.

A growing trend among firms using a customer-oriented organizational structure is the **national accounts organization.** This structure, designed to strengthen a firm's relationship with large and important customers, assigns senior sales managers or sales teams to major accounts in each market. Organizing by national accounts helps sales representatives develop cooperation between departments to meet customer needs. The classic example of a national account selling situation is the relationship between Wal-Mart and its major vendors. Clorox, Colgate, Coleman, H.J. Heinz, Johnson & Johnson, Kraft, and Nestlé are just seven of the growing number of companies that have set up sales offices near Wal-Mart's Bentonville, Arkansas, headquarters. Doing so places dedicated sales resources close to this key account.

A decade ago, the Boise Cascade office products sales force had a regional organization, and large customers were required to deal with a different sales representative in each region. The system was inefficient, resulting in additional selling expenses for Boise Cascade and complicating the purchasing process for buyers. "Our corporate customers were telling us that we were a very good provider on a regional basis, but they wanted us to meet their strategic needs," says Tom VanHootegem, director of national accounts. In response, Boise created a formal national account management program that today includes 23 national account managers who call on approximately 600 accounts worth $250,000 in annual revenues. This reorganization has boosted total revenues to over $1 billion in just six years.[32]

As companies expand their market coverage across national borders, they may use a variant of national account sales teams. These global account teams may be staffed by local sales representatives in the countries in which a company is operating. In other instances, the firm selects highly trained sales executives from its domestic operations. In both instances, training is critical to the success of a company's global sales force. End-of-chapter Case 19.1 explains some of the challenges presented by the international marketplace.

The individual sales manager also has the task of organizing the sales territories within his or her area of responsibility. Factors such as sales potential, strengths and weaknesses of available personnel, and workloads are considered in territory allocation decisions.

Supervision

A source of constant debate among sales managers concerns the supervision of the sales force. It is impossible to pinpoint the exact amount of supervision that is correct in each situation since the individuals involved and the environments in which they operate vary. However, a concept known as *span of control* helps provide some general guidelines. Span of control refers to the number of sales representatives who report to first-level sales managers. The optimal span of control is affected by such factors as complexity of work activities being performed, ability of the individual sales manager, degree of interdependence among individual salespeople, and the extent of training each salesperson receives. A 6-to-1 ratio has been suggested as the optimal span of control for first-level sales managers supervising technical or industrial salespeople. In contrast, a 10-to-1 ratio is recommended if sales representatives are calling on wholesale and retail accounts.

Marketing Dictionary

national accounts organization Organizational arrangement that assigns sales teams to a firm's largest accounts.

Motivation *charging us own battery.*

The sales manager's responsibility for motivating the sales force cannot be taken lightly. Because the sales process involves problem solving, it often leads to considerable mental pressures and frustrations. Sales often result only after repeated calls on customers and may involve a long completion period, especially with new customers and complex technical products. Efforts to motivate salespeople usually take the form of debriefings, information sharing, and both psychological and financial encouragement. Appeals to emotional needs, such as ego needs, recognition, and peer acceptance, are examples of psychological encouragement. Monetary rewards and special benefits, such as club memberships, are types of financial incentives. Well-managed incentive programs can motivate salespeople and improve customer service. They typically include leisure trips or travel, gifts, recognition dinners, plaques and awards, and cash.[33] Figure 19.10 illustrates a range of gifts from Sharper Image, positioned as rewards to motivate salespeople.

However, not all incentive programs are effective in motivating employees. Poorly planned programs—for example, those that have targets set too high, are poorly publicized, allow only the top performers to participate, or feature trips that do not include spouses—can actually have an adverse effect. Companies should not expect these programs to solve all their sales problems.

Sales managers can improve sales-force productivity by understanding what motivates individual salespeople. They can gain insight into the subject of motivation by studying the various theories of motivation developed over the years. One theory that has been applied effectively to sales-force motivation is **expectancy theory,** which states that motivation depends on the expectations an individual has of his or her ability to perform the job and on how performance relates to attaining rewards that the individual values.

Sales managers can apply the expectancy theory of motivation by following a five-step process:

1. Let each salesperson know in detail what is expected in terms of selling goals, service standards, and other areas of performance. Rather than setting goals just once a year, many firms do so on a semiannual, quarterly, or even monthly basis.

2. Make the work valuable by assessing the needs, values, and abilities of each salesperson and then assigning appropriate tasks.

3. Make the work achievable. As leaders, they must inspire self-confidence in their salespeople and offer training and coaching to reassure them.

FIGURE 19.10
Sales Incentives from the Sharper Image

Work Hard + Smart

4. Provide immediate and specific feedback, guiding those who need improvement and giving positive feedback to those doing well.

5. Offer rewards that each salesperson values. JD Edwards, an e-business solutions provider, runs a twice-yearly customer satisfaction survey. Questions include ratings for employee integrity and overall satisfaction. Salespeople must score at a certain level or forfeit compensation amounting to between 75 and 125 percent of total bonuses earned that year.[34]

Compensation *don't get a straight salary.*

Because monetary rewards are an important factor in motivating subordinates, compensating sales personnel is a critical matter for managers. Sales compensation can be based on a commission plan, a straight-salary plan, or some combination of these options. Bonuses based on end-of-year results are another popular form of compensation. The increasing popularity of team selling has also impelled companies to set up reward programs to recognize performance of business units and teams. Today, about one in four companies reward business-unit performance.

A *commission* is a payment tied directly to the sales or profits that a salesperson achieves. For example, a salesperson might receive a 5 percent commission on all sales up to a specified quota and a 7 percent commission on sales beyond that point. This approach to sales compensation is increasingly popular. But while commissions reinforce selling incentives, they may cause some sales-force members to shortchange nonselling activities, such as completing sales reports, delivering sales promotion materials, and performing normal account servicing. Commission programs can also backfire. Some retailers, such as Sears and electronics chain Highland Superstores, modified their compensation systems after discovering that salespeople were being too aggressive or recommending unnecessary services.

A salary is a fixed payment made periodically to an employee. A firm that bases compensation on salaries rather than commissions might pay a salesperson a set amount every week. A company must balance benefits and disadvantages in paying predetermined salaries to compensate managers and sales personnel. A straight salary plan gives management more control over how sales personnel allocate their efforts, but it reduces the incentive to expand sales. As a result, many firms develop compensation programs that combine features of both salary and commission plans.

Because good salespeople are both hard to find and expensive to train, sales managers want to do what they can to encourage productive workers to stay with their firms. Incentive plans that favor experienced sales representatives tend to provide fewer benefits for new representatives who are not yet fully productive. Some companies, therefore, have developed interim compensation plans for new recruits, such as a straight salary for a given period of time or a commitment that the salesperson will not earn less than a certain amount but can earn more during his or her training period.

The typical U.S. sales representative earns $54,000 in salary with average bonuses and commission of a further $26,000. Figure 19.11 shows total sales compensation figures for various levels of sales personnel. Total compensation packages vary according to industry, with the finance, insurance, and real estate industries coming out on top, followed closely by general services. They also vary according to years of experience in sales.[35]

Evaluation and Control

Perhaps the most difficult tasks required of sales managers are evaluation and control. Sales managers are responsible for setting standards and choosing the best methods for measuring sales performance. Sales volume, profitability, and investment return are the usual means of evaluating sales effectiveness. They typically involve the use of **sales quotas**—specified sales or profit targets that the firm expects salespeople to achieve. For example, a particular sales representative might be expected to sell

Marketing Dictionary

expectancy theory   Theory developed by management author Victor Vroom stating that motivation depends on an individual's expectations of his or her ability to perform a job and how that performance relates to attaining a desired reward.

sales quota   Level of expected sales for a territory, product, customer, or salesperson against which actual results are compared.

**FIGURE 19.11
Annual Pay for Sales
Representatives and
Sales Managers**

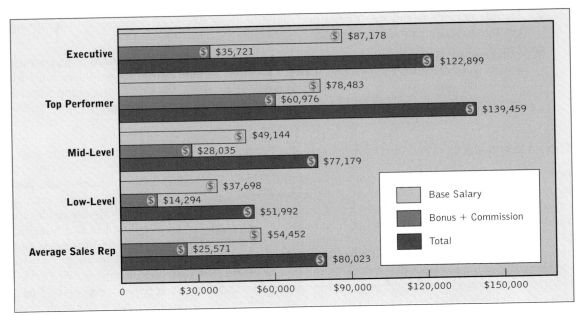

SOURCE: Christine Galea, "2002 Salary Survey," *Sales & Marketing Management*, May 2002, p. 32.

$720,000 in territory 27 during a given year. In many cases, the quota is tied to the compensation system. SFA has greatly improved the ability of sales managers to monitor the effectiveness of their sales staffs. Databases enable sales managers to break out revenue by salesperson, by account, and by geographical area.

In addition to sales quotas, other measures such as customer satisfaction, profit contribution, share of product-category sales, and customer retention are also coming into play. The changes are the result of three factors:

1. An increasingly long-term orientation that results from greater use of total quality management and customer relationship building efforts.

2. The realization that evaluations based on sales volume alone can lead to overselling and excessive inventory problems that work against customer relationship building

3. The need to encourage sales representatives to develop new accounts, provide customer service, and emphasize new products. A concentration on sales quotas tends to focus salespeople's attention on short-term selling from which they can generate the most sales today.

Regardless of the key elements in the evaluation program, the sales manager must follow a formal system of decision rules. Such a system supplies information to the sales manager for action. This input helps the sales manager to answer three general questions.

First, where does each salesperson's performance rank relative to the predetermined standards? This comparison should fully consider the effect of uncontrollable variables on sales performance. Preferably, each adjusted rank should be stated as a percentage of the standard. This system simplifies evaluation and facilitates converting various ranks into a single composite index of performance.

The second evaluation question asks about the salesperson's strong points. One way to answer this question is to list areas of the salesperson's performance in which he or she has surpassed the respective standard. Another way is to categorize a salesperson's strong points in three areas of the work environment:

1. *Task, or technical ability.* This strength appears in knowledge of the products (end uses), customers, and company, as well as selling skills.

2. *Process, or sequence of work flow.* This strength pertains to actual sales transactions—the salesperson's application of technical ability and interaction with customers. Managers frequently

measure process performance based on personal observation. Other measures are sales calls and expense reports.

3. *Goal, or end results (output) of sales performance.* Sales managers usually state this aspect of the salesperson's work environment in terms of sales volume and profits.

The third evaluation question asks about the weaknesses or negatives in the salesperson's performance. The manager should categorize these faults as carefully as the salesperson's strong points. The sales manager should explain candidly, but kindly, the employee's weak areas. Because few people like to hear this part of an evaluation and consequently tend to listen with only "half an ear," the manager should make sure the employee understands any performance problems that he or she needs to correct and ways the manager will measure progress. The manager and employee should then establish specific objectives for improvement and set a timetable for judging the employee's improvement.

In completing the evaluation summary, the sales manager should follow a set procedure:

1. Each aspect of sales performance for which a standard exists should be measured separately. This helps prevent the halo effect, in which the rating given on one factor influences those on other performance variables.

2. Each salesperson should be judged on the basis of actual sales performance rather than potential ability. This emphasizes the importance of rankings in the evaluation.

3. Sales managers should judge each salesperson on the basis of sales performance for the entire period under consideration rather than for the particular incidents. As an evaluator, the sales manager should avoid reliance on isolated examples of the salesperson's success or failure.

4. Each salesperson's evaluation should be reviewed for completeness and evidence of possible bias. Ideally, this review would be made by the sales manager's immediate superior.

Although evaluation includes both revision and correction, the sales manager must focus attention on correction. This priority translates into a drive to adjust actual performance to conform with predetermined standards. Corrective action, with its obviously negative connotations, typically poses a substantial challenge for the sales manager.

Ethical Issues in Sales

As the previous chapter discussed, promotional activities raise many ethical questions, and personal selling is no exception. The pervasiveness of personal selling in our daily lives and the vast differences in the training, experience, and professionalism of different types of salespeople combine to produce a negative image of the profession for many. Plays like *Death of a Salesman,* television shows, and movies reinforce this poor image.

Today's highly paid, highly professional salesperson knows that long-term success is based on building and maintaining mutually satisfying relationships with clients. Still, the stereotype lingers. A recent Gallup poll offered still more evidence of how much people dislike certain types of salespeople. Car salespeople ranked at the bottom of a list of professionals with high levels of honesty and ethics. Advertising execs and insurance reps ranked below average, too.[36]

Some people believe that ethical problems are inevitable because of the very nature of the sales function. They simply do not trust someone who by making a sale will personally benefit from the interaction. Responding to the high level of distrust among car buyers, some dealerships have initiated a videotape strategy that involves taping all final sales transactions. There are four main objectives: to make sure that customers fully understand what they are buying, to prevent finance and insurance staff from overselling extras or misleading customers, to ensure all extras are offered with every purchase, and to handle customer claims of dishonesty or mistreatment. While videotaping customers has raised issues of consumer privacy, dealers consider that the tapes benefit car buyers by providing an accurate record of transactions.[37]

Thousands of companies are working to overcome the stigma associated with sales careers and to educate the general public about the contributions of today's sales professionals. It is to their advantage

8

Discuss the role of ethics in personal selling and sales-force management.

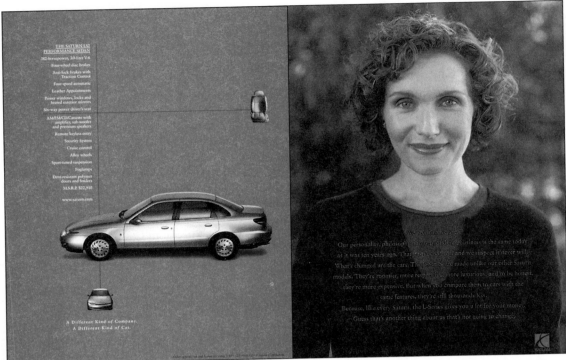

Saturn built a business on improving the car buyer's perceptions of the new-car purchase experience. Its no-hassle pricing policies sought to attract buyers who might not quite trust other dealerships.

to do so because salespeople generate the firm's revenue, link the company to the customer, and provide valuable product information to customers and members of the marketing channel as well as supplying feedback for the producer. By recruiting highly ethical, educated individuals and by training them in relationship selling techniques, companies develop sales forces able to win the customer's respect and trust. By stressing consultative selling techniques, sales professionals meet customer needs without resorting to unethical behavior. In addition, sales managers create an ethical sales environment by doing the following:

- Promoting ethical awareness during training programs, sales meetings, and sales calls
- Making sure that all employees—salespeople and other company personnel—know that the firm opposes unethical conduct
- Establishing control systems to monitor ethical conduct

Ethical Dilemmas

Despite management efforts to foster ethical behavior, from time to time, salespeople may find themselves in situations with their employers, fellow employees, and customers that involve ethical dilemmas. Among the ethical breaches that occur between salespeople and their employers are improper use of company assets and cheating. Use of a company car for personal purposes is one such possibility; padding expense reports is another. A salesperson might resort to deception in an attempt to win a sales contest, such as holding on to orders until a contest begins or shipping unordered merchandise to customers, which will not be returned until after the contest ends.

Sexual harassment is another problem faced by many sales representatives. An Ohio State University study reported that about 30 percent of business-to-business saleswomen—and about 20 percent of salesmen—have experienced unwanted sexual advances from customers.

Another type of unethical conduct involves using bribes to secure a sale. While gifts such as pens and tickets to sporting events are accepted business practices, they can be misused. Since expensive gifts may be considered a form of bribery, many firms prohibit their employees from accepting any gift from a sales representative.

Customer demand for cash kickbacks represents another ethical dilemma. Suppose, for example, a copy-machine salesperson calls on an important business customer who is planning to order new copiers for most of his company's departments. The purchasing manager offers her the account if she will share half of her commission with him. Although she knows this is illegal and she has signed her company's strong code of ethical conduct, she also wants the sale.

In cases like this, possible options include going along with the unethical request, ignoring the request, confronting the person, or reporting the behavior. Experts recommend telling the purchasing manager that the representative wants to gain the buyer's business without resorting to such tactics. If the purchasing agent refuses to move forward on these terms, the salesperson should report the incident to a manager, who should then speak to the customer representative's supervisor. Companywide codes of ethics should help guide salespeople with such situations and should aim to protect all parties.

Strategic Implications of Marketing in the 21st Century

Today's sales forces are a new breed of businesspeople. Richly nourished in a tradition of sales, their roles are strengthened even further through technology. However, as many companies are discovering, nothing can replace the power of personal selling in generating sales and in building strong, loyal customer relationships.

Selling has experienced a series of evolutionary stages, each building on the strengths of previous ones. Whereas salespeople of the early 1900s were familiar with customers' lifestyles as well as their occupational needs, the mid-1900s moved selling from a one-to-one environment to a process of providing goods and services to massive numbers of people who remained largely anonymous. In the past decade, however, database technology and the Internet have again enabled salespeople to satisfy the needs of individual customers, often through teamwork and partnerships. Instead of eliminating many of the processes performed by a salesperson, electronic technologies enhance the ability to sell the right product to the right consumer at the right time.

Salespeople today are a critical link in developing relationships between the customer and the company. They communicate customer needs and wants to coworkers in various departments and divisions within an organization, enabling a cooperative, companywide effort in improving product offerings and in better satisfying individuals within the target market. For salespeople, the greatest benefit of electronic technologies is the ability to share knowledge when it is needed with those who need to know, including customers, suppliers, and employees.

A number of environmental pressures have led to changes in personal selling and sales-force management:

- Buyers are more sophisticated, demanding more rapid, low-cost transactions.
- Customer and supplier data are linked via computerized data warehousing systems that identify optimal consumer characteristics.
- New technology makes alternative, low-cost distribution methods possible.
- Automatic inventory reorder processes reduce the need for face-to-face meetings with buyers.

- Computer databases, telecommunication sales, catalogs, and the Internet provide transaction mediums at much lower costs per transaction than the traditional field-selling channel.
- Product life cycles are accelerating, with products moving more rapidly into and out of the marketplace.
- Customers in some market segments are less loyal and more prone to switch suppliers.

Recognizing the long-term impact of keeping satisfied buyers—those who make repeat and cross-purchases and provide referrals—versus dissatisfied buyers—who generally tell about 11 other people of their dissatisfaction—organizations are increasingly training their sales forces to provide superior customer service and rewarding them for increasing satisfaction levels.

Where skills of the last century's salesperson were likely to include persuasion, selling ability, and product knowledge, the 21st-century sales professional is more likely to possess communication skills, problem-solving skills, and knowledge of products, customers, industries, and applications. Last century's salesperson tended to be self-driven; today's sales professional is more likely to be a team player as well as a customer advocate who serves his or her buyers by solving problems.

Summary of Chapter Objectives

1. Explain the conditions that determine the relative importance of personal selling in the promotional mix.

Personal selling is likely to be relatively more important in the following instances: (1) when consumers are concentrated geographically and relatively few in number; (2) when a good or service is expensive or technically complex, when it requires special handling, or when a transaction typically involves a trade-in; (3) when the channel is relatively short; and (4) when the price of the product is relatively high.

2. Contrast over-the-counter selling, field selling, telemarketing, and inside selling.

Over-the-counter (retail) selling involves providing product information and arranging for completion of the sales transaction when customers come to the retail location. Field selling involves sales calls to customers at their homes or businesses for the purpose of providing demonstrations or information about the good or service. Telemarketing is used to reduce the substantial cost involved in maintaining a sales force that makes personal calls at customers' homes or businesses. It involves personal selling conducted entirely by telephone, either outbound (when salespeople contact customers) or inbound (when customers call to obtain information and make purchases). Inside selling involves performing the functions of field selling but

avoiding travel-related expenses by relying on phone, mail, and e-commerce to provides sales and product services for customers on a continuing basis.

3. Describe each of the four major trends in personal selling.

To address new challenges, companies are turning to relationship selling, consultative selling, team selling, and sales-force automation. Relationship selling occurs when a salesperson builds a mutually beneficial relationship with a customer on a regular basis over an extended period. Consultative selling involves meeting customer needs by listening to customers, understanding and caring about their problems, paying attention to the details, and following through after the sale. Team selling occurs when the salesperson joins with specialists from other functional areas of the firm to complete the selling process. Sales-force automation (SFA) is the use of various technologies to make the sales function more efficient and competitive.

4. Identify the three basic sales tasks.

Order processing is the routine handling of an order. It characterizes a sales setting in which the need is made known to and is acknowledged by the customer. Creative selling is persuasion aimed at making the prospect see the value of the good or service being presented. Missionary selling is indirect selling, such as making goodwill calls and providing technical or operational assistance.

5. Outline the steps in the sales process.

The basic steps in the sales process are prospecting and qualifying, approach, presentation, demonstration, handling objections, closing, and follow-up.

6. Describe the sales manager's boundary-spanning role.

A sales manager links the sales force to other aspects of the internal and external environments. The internal environment consists of top management, other functional units in the firm, such as advertising, and other internal information sources. The external environment includes trade groups, customers, competitors, suppliers, and regulatory agencies.

7. List and discuss the functions of sales-force management.

Sales-force management involves seven basic functions: recruitment and selection, training, organization, supervision, motivation, compensation, and evaluation and control.

8. Discuss the role of ethics in personal selling and sales-force management.

Despite management efforts to foster ethical behavior, from time to time, salespeople may find themselves in situations with their employers, fellow employees, and customers that involve ethical dilemmas posed by such opportunities as bribes, cash kickbacks, improper use of company assets, and sexual harassment. It is crucial for a sales-management team to minimize the occurrence of such undesired situations and to create positive stereotypes associated with selling and with the entire company. Today, most sales managers find themselves dealing with additional tasks such as encouraging an ethical sales environment by promoting ethical awareness during training, operations, and control systems.

Marketing Terms You Need to Know

personal selling 568
over-the-counter selling 570
field selling 571
telemarketing 572
inside selling 573

relationship selling 575
consultative selling 576
team selling 577
sales-force automation
   (SFA) 577

order processing 579
creative selling 579
missionary selling 580
boundary-spanning role 586

national accounts
   organization 589
expectancy theory 590
sales quota 591

Other Important Marketing Terms

outbound telemarketing 572
inbound telemarketing 572
cross-selling 577
prospecting 581

qualifying 582
approach 582
precall planning 582
presentation 582

demonstration 583
objection 584
closing 584
follow-up 585

span of control 589
commission 591

Review Questions

1. How does personal selling differ among the four major selling channels? Give examples of local firms that operate in each channel.
2. What is meant by relationship selling? Why is it becoming such a factor in personal selling?
3. What is meant by team selling? Why is it important?
4. Explain how sales-force automation can improve the sales function in a company.
5. Cite two local examples of each of the three basic sales tasks.
6. Under what conditions is the so-called *canned approach* of using memorized sales presentations likely to be used? What are the major problems with this method?
7. Give an example of each function performed by sales managers in an organization.
8. Compare the alternative sales compensation plans. Point out the advantages and disadvantages of each.

9. Explain how a sales manager's problems and areas of emphasis might change in dealing with each of the following:
   a. telephone salespeople
   b. over-the-counter retail salespeople
   c. field sales representatives
   d. missionary salespeople
10. Give three examples of situations that present ethical dilemmas for salespeople.

Projects and Teamwork Exercises

1. In pairs or small groups, explain and offer examples of how the following factors affect the decision to emphasize personal selling or advertising.
   a. geographical market concentration
   b. length of marketing channels
   c. degree of product technical complexity
   d. price
   e. number of customers
   f. prevalence of trade-ins
2. What sales tasks are involved in selling the following products? Have each team prepare a summary of one or more situations.
   a. Lexmark laser printers
   b. American Heart Association (to an employee group)
   c. used Honda Accord
   d. fast food from Broadway Bagels
   e. janitorial supplies for use in plant maintenance
3. Describe the job of each of the following salespeople. In a group, discuss the differences and similarities.
   a. salesperson in a Blockbuster Video store
   b. Coldwell Banker real-estate sales representative
   c. route driver for Keebler snack foods (sells and delivers to local food retailers)
   d. sales engineer for Dell
4. As mixed-skill representatives at a large paper company, your team is invited to make a sales presentation to a national warehouse and shipping company. List the five most important messages you wish to relate and then role-play the sales presentation.
5. Suppose you are the local sales manager for the telephone company's Yellow Pages and you employ six representatives who call on local firms to solicit advertising space sales. What type of compensation system would you use? What types of sales-force automation would be effective in presenting the benefits of advertising in the Yellow Pages? How would you suggest that your sales personnel be evaluated?

'net Work

http://www.hotjobs.com

http://www.monster.com

1. Job opportunities in sales. Go to one of the major online job search sites, such as Hot Jobs or Monster.com, and search for job opportunities in sales. Print the job description for a sales position in the location and at a company that would appeal to you if you were in the job market.

http://www.smei.org

2. Professional certification. Sales and Marketing Executives International offers a number of programs that lead to several certifications for sales and marketing professionals. Visit the organization's Web site and read about these certifications. Prepare a report answering the following questions:
   a. What professional certifications are available for sales professionals?
   b. What are the objectives of professional certification?
   c. What are the benefits?

http://www.cathcart.org

3. Relationship selling. Jim Cathcart, author of *Relationship Selling: The Key to Getting and Keeping Customers,* is a leading expert on relationship selling. Go to the Cathcart Institute's Web site. Several links provide information on relationship selling. Watch the video clip on relationship selling and service, and read the summary of his book. Write a brief report on what you learned about relationship selling by visiting this Web site.

Note: Internet Web addresses change frequently. If you don't find the exact sites listed, you may need to access the organization or company's home page and search from there.

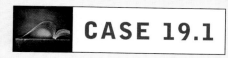

CASE 19.1

The Complex World of Overseas Sales

When an Internet wine seller decided to save on packaging by shipping an order for a single bottle of wine in a carton designed for two, the confused Japanese customer demanded the other bottle. The salesperson failed to realize that in Japan people consider the packaging an intrinsic part of a prestige product. Gaffes like this one, along with the intricacies of currency conversion, import regulations, and international business ethics too often crimp the expansion ambitions of sellers that see the Web as a conduit to massive new markets overseas.

Yet while the global marketplace has melded business practices and even some aspects of culture around the world, key differences still affect successful salesmanship, whether over the Internet or out in the field. Take the sales cycle, for instance. Sales typically take a good deal longer to close in almost every other country than in the U.S. Some cultures, Germany included, devote extended periods of time to detailed research on prospective partner companies. In southern Mediterranean countries, on the other hand, it's important for suppliers and customers to get to know each other on a social level, which can hold up the proceedings for weeks or even months. In China, it can take years to build the relationships that drive business decisions. In places like Turkey, where the economy is unstable, it takes time to structure deals—and payment schedules—in a mutually beneficial way. Since few sales opportunities move quickly toward closure, international salespeople find they need to juggle several deals at one time to meet their quotas. Only by having several irons simultaneously in the fire can they earn regular commissions.

Selling overseas not only takes careful long-term planning but also requires expertise in aspects of the business that are not even on the radar of national reps. The international salesperson, for example, needs to know about import-export tariffs and quotas, the logistics of delivery, duties, taxes, and a host of other import-export issues on which a deal may hinge.

On the upside, a stint in international sales can fast-track a rep's career. As one overseas pro explains it, "Selling in an international context exposes you to more varied and complex sales situations, which accelerates your sales experiences."

Questions for Critical Thinking

1. International sales is one area in which it pays to team up with local experts. Explain why this is so.
2. Despite differences in culture, the fundamentals of selling are the same the world over. Do you agree with this statement? Why or why not?

SOURCES: Lisa Bertagnoli, "Research the Marketing Environment," Small Business Administration, http://www.sba.gov, accessed January 15, 2003; "20 Tips to Succeed in Latin America's DRTV Market," *Response,* Feburary 2002, http://www.findarticles.com; Lisa Bertagnoli, "Selling Overseas Complex Endeavor," *Marketing News,* June 30, 2001, p. 4.

VIDEO CASE 19.2   Concept2 Rows to Success

The written case on Concept2 appears on page VC-23. The recently filmed Concept2 video is designed to expand and highlight the concepts in this chapter and the concepts and questions covered in the written video case.

Krispy Kreme Continuing Case for Part 7 appears on page KK-14.

Video Case Contents

VIDEO CASE 1.2

How Burton Snowboards Built a Sport—and a Customer Base

No one would deny that Jake Burton is an innovative guy. But he's quick to dispel the myth that he invented snowboarding or snowboards. He points out that the snowboard—a single board that looks and operates like a cross between a skateboard and a surfboard that athletes ride down snow-covered mountains—has been around since the 1920s. And Jake himself experimented with the Snurfer, a precursor to the snowboard, as a kid. But the Snurfer—a short, fat ski with a rope tied to the tip that the rider would hold like a rein in one hand—was marketed more like a toy, on the order of a snow tube or one-person toboggan. Certainly, no one thought of Snurfing as a full-blown sport.

No one, that is, except Jake Burton. Burton had grown up skiing and, after graduating from college in 1977 with a degree in economics, he moved from New York to Vermont to follow a hunch. "I felt like [snowboarding] could be a sport, but it wasn't a sport for the company that was manufacturing [Snurfers]," he recalls. So he set out to do two things simultaneously: build the boards and the market. "I was blindly optimistic," he says. In addition to developing a new product, he needed to develop the market for that product. He had to find a way to show people how snowboards would create utility. Then he had to build a relationship with these new customers. "I became more concerned with hyping the sport to make sure it happened so that I was right," says Burton. But at the time, most ski resorts viewed snowboarding as a fringe activity—and didn't allow it on their slopes. So the few pioneers that Burton recruited to his new sport and product had to climb hills, carrying the heavy boards, each time they wanted a single ride down. Meanwhile, skiers were whisked to the tops of the country's best winter resorts on high-speed lifts, warmed up in heated lodges, and skied down groomed slopes. It rapidly became clear that Burton not only had to build relationships with potential boarders but had to forge alliances with ski resorts as well—or there would be no future for snowboarding.

So he knocked on the doors of ski resorts until Stratton Mountain in Vermont opened up, becoming the first major resort to allow snowboarders to ride its lifts and slopes. At this time, Burton was manufacturing and selling only 700 of his Burton Snowboards a year—hardly enough to make a living. But snowboarding was beginning to catch on as more ski mountains followed Stratton's example and not only allowed snowboarders on their slopes but launched their own advertising campaigns to attract them. The timing was perfect, as the number of new skiers was gradually declining and people were looking for a different kind of winter sport. As more and more people tried—and enjoyed—snowboarding, Burton found he had to develop a third type of marketing relationship, one with distributors and dealers.

Today, Burton Snowboards, which is still based in Burlington, Vermont, is both the pioneer and the world leader in the development and sale of snowboards and related products. Burton markets its snowboards and accessory gear through a network of about 3,000 dealers around the world. The company continues to develop relationships with consumers by staging promotions featuring demonstrations at ski resorts—about 400 demos around the world per year, according to vice president and director of sales, Dave Schmidt. These events are conducted by Burton representatives who show up at a resort, unload Burton products, and let people try them for free. In addition, for the past 20 years the firm has sponsored a number of snowboarding competitions—including the U.S. Open for snowboarding—as another effective technique for developing relationships with its customers. Finally, Burton's Learn-to-Ride (LTR) program teaches snowboarding to anyone who wants to learn from instructors. The program includes lessons taught by certified American Association of Snowboard Instructors on Burton equipment specifically designed for beginners. All of these events and programs enhance Burton's relationships with its consumers and participating ski resorts by creating utility for both.

Burton's print catalog has proved to be a key contact with young consumers. According to Schmidt, teenagers read "every word" of each new Burton catalog, memorizing product names and specs. And recently, technology has helped the company keep in touch with ski resorts, its distribution network, and consumers. Burton has a Web-based e-commerce application that provides its dealers with access to real-time manufacturing, delivery, and account data they need to serve their customers efficiently. The company's Web site provides consumers with information about products as well as special programs and events.

In just a couple of decades, snowboarding reached what many consider to be the pinnacle of sport—it debuted as a medal event at the recent Winter Olympics. Perhaps to no one's surprise, the top medalists at the premier were American. Jake Burton may not have been on the podium, but his boards were.

Questions

1. In what ways does Burton Snowboards create utility for its different types of customers?
2. How can event marketing help Burton expand the customer base for its products?

3. Suggest additional ways Burton Snowboards marketers can use the Internet to more effectively build relationships and market their products.

4. Relationship marketing is key to Burton's success. Suggest two or three steps that the firm should consider taking during the next five years to further enhance its relationships with consumers and ski resorts.

SOURCES: Burton Snowboards Web site, http://www.burton.com, accessed January 3, 2003; Helena Kimball, Greenough Communications, "Burton Snowboards Teams with Mirror Image to Boost Global Site Performance," June 25, 2002, http://www.mirror-image.com; Josh Reid, "Burton Snowboards Establishes Learn to Ride Program," http://www.boarding.com, January 17, 2001.

VIDEO CASE 2.2   Caribou Coffee Brews Up a Fine Cup of Strategy

People who love finely brewed coffee produced from high-quality beans have their favorites, from certain flavors to specific brands to just the right spot to sit and sip their daily cup (or cups) of java. Such gathering places filled with distinctive touches are what retailers like to call "atmospherics." When Kim and John Puckett opened their first coffee shop in Minneapolis back in 1992, they hoped it would become a local favorite. Just before launching the new business, the couple had been hiking Sable Mountain in Alaska. When the Pucketts reached the peak, they were enthralled by the view surrounding them, including a distant herd of caribou galloping through the valley below. When they returned to Minneapolis, Kim and John decided that they would design their coffee shop in such a way that customers could share some of the wilderness experience they had enjoyed so much—without leaving the Twin Cities. So they combined their two loves—coffee and the outdoors—into one, creating a coffee shop decorated to resemble an Alaskan lodge, with knotty-pine cabinets, a rustic fireplace, and comfortable seating.

Minneapolis coffee buffs loved it. The new venture was hotter than the roaring fire in the Caribou Coffee fireplace, but the Pucketts knew they needed a real marketing plan if they were going to take the idea further. They already had a clear mission (which they later posted on the firm's Web site):

> Our mission is to be the best neighborhood gathering place; fast and friendly service is at the heart of this goal.

They knew, too, that the strategic, tactical, and marketing plans they needed—to deal with issues ranging from how fast, and where, to grow; sources of funds to finance any expansion; deciding whether to franchise the operation or remain company owned; recruiting, training, and motivating employees to provide the high-quality coffee and unparalleled customer service they promised; and community involvement—had to support Caribou's overall mission.

In addition to agreeing on their mission, Kim and John also knew from the beginning both the style they wanted in their coffee shop and the overall image Caribou Coffee should convey: rustic, hearty, outdoorsy, relaxed. They had set about bringing this image to life by employing specific tactics like creating coffee shops to look and feel exactly like ski lodges and hunting cabins in the great Northwest. With the assistance of a local advertising agency, Caribou came up with taglines designed to capture the Caribou experience for its customers: "Outdoorsy. Leave smiling. Hand-made. Down to Earth. Clever. Transformational." And they decided to grow their little business by expanding into new locations.

As Caribou expanded, adding shops in new locations, consumers seemed to become loyal customers as soon as the doors opened. The Pucketts began experimenting with additional coffee flavors and new brewing methods, a practice their "800 pound gorilla" competitor Starbucks later implemented as well. While each of these marketing efforts proved successful, Kim and John remained uneasy about the trouble they were having with creating an overall strategic plan.

Even without a strategic plan in place, by 1997, 125 Caribou Coffee shops were operating in cities around the country. By then, Caribou had moved up the sales ladder to become the second-largest specialty coffee company in the U.S. Although then–company president Jay Willoughby announced, "Our intent is to be a national player," the plan for accomplishing this intent left much to be desired. Lacking a clear strategic plan, Caribou let industry leader Starbucks drive its growth by simply placing shops in locations where Starbucks wasn't. Instead of relying on marketing research to guide expansion and developing its own strategy, Caribou continued to react to what its largest competitor was doing. And in the meantime, another threat was looming in the background: The company was running out of money to finance its growth.

In 1999, Don Dempsey, the former head of McDonalds' China division, joined Caribou as its new CEO. Although he had stated from the outset that his goal for Caribou was to "reliably and consistently grow profits," Dempsey quickly learned that major inflows of additional funds would be required. So he began calling on potential investors with a newly devised strategic plan calling for the firm to continue to operate profitably by remaining in locations in which Caribou already had shops and to build the brand within these locations. Not surprisingly, Caribou's largest market was its hometown of

Minneapolis–St. Paul, but other large markets existed in the midwestern cities of Chicago, Cleveland, Columbus, and Detroit, as well as southeast locations in Georgia, North Carolina, and Washington, D.C. Eventually, the Crescent Capital group of Atlanta agreed to purchase an ownership share in the company, giving Dempsey the dollars he needed to proceed with his original plan. "We have to increase penetration and increase brand awareness in order to improve our economics," he stated.

In addition, it was vital that Caribou maintain its high standards of quality and the atmosphere for which it had become so well-known as it embarked on further expansion. So far, the company has managed to achieve this. One tactic employed in the shops is to wait until customers place an order for coffee beans before roasting them, to ensure absolute freshness. Another involves educating consumers about everything from the names of different types of beans to how best to store them. Visitors to the Caribou Web site (http://www.cariboucoffee.com) discover a virtual encyclopedia of coffee information. Finally, Caribou maintains total control over quality and marketing messages by restricting expansion to company-owned stores; no franchises are sold.

Today, the number-two company in the specialty coffee business serves up cups of java in more than 185 "lodges" in Georgia, Illinois, Maryland, Michigan, Minnesota, North Carolina, Ohio, Washington, D.C., and Wisconsin. Coffee lovers residing outside these locations can order their favorite Caribou flavors from the company Web site, and company executives are currently considering teaming up with other, compatible retailers in new shopping centers under construction in the Rocky Mountain states, the Upper Midwest, and Texas. All of these decisions are part of a grand plan to serve the heartiest coffee in the best mug in the most comfortable spot anyone could imagine.

Questions

1. Why is a marketing plan so important to Caribou's future?
2. Industry leader Starbucks has decided to pursue further sales growth by distributing its branded coffee through retail stores and expanding into the Latin American market, beginning with several outlets in San Juan, Puerto Rico. Should Caribou Coffee implement a similar growth strategy? Do you think that opening a drive-through window or putting a Caribou shop inside upscale food stores and SuperTarget outlets would be good strategies for Caribou marketers to consider?
3. What do you think are two of Caribou's internal strengths and weaknesses? Also, identify two opportunities for and two threats to the company's success. Explain your answers.
4. What types of environmental characteristics might influence Caribou's strategic decisions during the next five years?

SOURCES: Caribou Coffee Web site, http://www.cariboucoffee.com, accessed January 3, 2003; Hoover's Online, http://www.hoovers.com, accessed January 3, 2003; "The Return of the Griswolds," *Business Wire Features*, May 29, 2002, http://hoovnews.hoovers.com; Jessica Griffith, "Caribou Coffee Brewing a Caffeine-Fueled Expansion," *Finance and Commerce*, December 26, 2001, http://www.finance-commerce.com.

 VIDEO CASE 3.2   Equal Exchange: Fair Pay Is Fair Play

When you sip your morning cup of coffee, you might think about what type of beans were used to give it the rich flavor you love; you might even consider where those beans came from, say Costa Rica or Colombia. But you probably aren't thinking about the farmers who grow the beans a long way from your breakfast table or favorite coffee shop. In fact, coffee is big business—the world's second-most popular commodity next to oil, according to Virginia Berman, organizing director of Equal Exchange, the gourmet coffee company founded almost two decades ago in Canton, Massachusetts. And the economic environment in which the coffee industry operates is both fragile and volatile. Until Equal Exchange came along, the people who consistently wound up at the bottom of the economic hill of beans were the coffee farmers themselves.

Traditionally, small coffee farmers in poor countries such as Nicaragua, Peru, Bolivia, Costa Rica, Mexico, El Salvador, Sumatra, and Tanzania sell their crops through foreign distributors and other marketing intermediaries. They receive only a tiny fraction of the final purchase price, which keeps them in poverty with a lack of access to credit, market information, education, and buyers within their own countries. Poverty often forces the farmers to flee the land to become part of the urban poor or to plant more profitable short-term—and illegal—drug-related crops just to raise enough cash to plant the next coffee crop.

Equal Exchange cofounders Rink Dickinson, Michael Rozyne, and Jonathan Rosenthal have been trying to change this environment for coffee farmers by adopting a concept first introduced in Europe called *fair trade*. Fair trade embraces the philosophy that businesses are responsible and accountable to other groups in addition to company stockholders. These additional constituencies consist of their employees, their customers, and the general public in areas where they purchase beans and also where they market Equal Exchange. So the coffee growers that Equal Exchange now deals with—about 20 cooperatives in Bolivia, Colombia, Costa Rica, El Salvador, Guatemala, Mexico, Nicaragua, Peru, Sumatra, and Tanzania—receive better prices under exclusive agreements. According to Dickinson, farmers are paid a minimum price for their crops even if the outside market price is lower. Equal Exchange also arranges preharvest financing so farmers know the price they will receive for their beans in advance of production, a price that is honored even if the going price in the global market should plummet. As a result, consumers are guaranteed high-quality coffee at fair prices, and the general public in the growers' regions benefit from projects such as new schools, day care, and carpentry workshops that the cooperatives have been able to undertake with the additional income they earn.

Dickinson is quick to note that Equal Exchange has prospered in a large way because he and his partners started their company in the mid-1980s social-cultural environment, which meshed with their product—and their ideals. Back then, American consumers were just beginning to develop their taste for high-quality, specialty coffees. And they were more interested in ethical practices and in marketers who not only would "talk the talk" about social responsibilities but, more importantly, were willing to "walk the walk." Today, purchasing Equal Exchange products offers an opportunity for consumers to enjoy the coffee they like while having an impact on the lives of people in poorer nations. "Consumers can help farmers succeed," observes Dickinson.

Equal Exchange's marketing messages reflect its mission:

- to build long-term trade partnerships that are economically just and environmentally sound;
- to foster mutually beneficial relations between farmers and consumers;
- to demonstrate through its success the viability of worker-owned cooperatives and fair trade.

Visitors to Equal Exchange's Web site find such messages as, "Coffee is a leading source of income for the Developing World. Through fair trade, it can be a delicious and powerful tool to bring about positive change for small farmers and their families." So far, American coffee lovers have been drinking it up. "We've been profitable every year but one," points out Virginia Berman. And she refers to a key aspect of her company's success: "It's about relationships." Those relationships include farmers, communities, and consumers.

Questions

1. Explain the ways in which the competitive environment affects Equal Exchange and its marketing strategy.
2. How can Equal Exchange use the consumer buying power of Americans to make marketing decisions?
3. How might changes in the current social-cultural environment influence marketing decisions made by Equal Exchange?
4. Does Equal Exchange fulfill all levels of the social responsibility pyramid discussed in Chapter 3? Why or why not?

SOURCES: Equal Exchange Web site, http://www.equalexchange.com, accessed January 14, 2003; Dick Sherman, "Equal Exchange: Good Coffee and a Fair Deal," *The Business Journal of Southeastern Massachusetts,* June 2002, http://www.thebizjournal.com; Marjorie Kelly, "Leading the Way to Fairer Trade Practices," *Business Ethics,* accessed at http://www.inc.com, January 10, 2001.

VIDEO CASE 4.2

Fallon Worldwide: Going Global, Targeting Local

Right from the start, Minneapolis-based advertising agency Fallon Worldwide set its sights on the global marketplace. In fact, company founders Pat Fallon and Fred Senn recruited employees from as far away as Australia, Europe, and South America. Fallon, Senn, and their associates built an agency with a reputation for creativity and innovations, winning praise—and major industry awards—for many of their ads. Then in 1999, with an impressive portfolio of successful home-grown advertising campaigns already making his company (then called Fallon McElligott) the talk of the industry, Fallon met business executive Robert Senior in London. Fallon had been searching for his first foreign partners in Britain, and Senior and his colleagues were quick to jump on board. Within a year, the Fallon London office had a dozen top clients and billings of $40 million.

A year later, French media giant Publicis proposed a merger with the American firm. Although some worried that Fallon's reputation for highly innovative campaigns might be compromised by the presence of a new parent company, Fallon's founders knew that the only way to serve their clients on a global basis was to partner with a larger organization. In addition, rapid changes in the technological environment meant that ad agencies had to now search for new ways to serve their clients rapidly—yet with a personal touch. "It will take a new kind of branding communications company to succeed in the emerging worldwide digital economy," noted Fallon at the time, "and with Publicis' support, we intend to be that company."

In 2001, the ad agency now known as Fallon Worldwide announced the formation of three new "creativity centers" located on two continents, with six internationally known partners. The company would open new agencies in Hong Kong, São Paulo, and Singapore. These centers would allow Fallon marketers to deal with distinct cultural, economic, and legal-political differences present in each region. The centers would also give them the ability to maintain a local focus on the needs of clients and consumers in the area. The structure fit perfectly with the flexible, innovative way Fallon had always operated. "We believe there are clients who will get excited by the idea of a lean, agile network built around the power of creativity, not mass," observed Pat Fallon.

The locations for the new creativity centers were chosen carefully to cover certain economic regions. Equally important was the selection of partners who would manage these centers. Top managers had to be experienced in both global and local marketing. "Our network will be highly intimate—with people who know each other, respect each other, and share a passion for work that drives business success," explained John Gerzema, Fallon's managing partner for international expansion.

This philosophy appears to have played out as planned. For example, Calvin Soh, a creative partner for Fallon Singapore and Fallon Hong Kong, had worked in both New York and Singapore before taking the post, giving him personal perspective on Asian and American cultural beliefs and values.

Meanwhile, advances in technology have been fueling Fallon's Internet strategies. A new division, Fallon Interactive, makes innovative use of current and emerging technologies to boost its clients' brands and create stronger—and ultimately more profitable—relationships between clients and their customers. Fallon Interactive offers such services as online advertising and marketing, rapid prototype creation, Web site design and development, and product design and development, all aimed at creating a bond between products and consumers. Clients currently using the services of Fallon Interactive include BMW of North America, Citigroup, Lee Jeans, Microsoft, Nikon, Public Broadcasting Service (PBS), Timberland, and United Airlines.

Recently, Fallon Worldwide landed global marketing responsibilities for four Nestlé Purina pet food brands: Purina Dog Chow, Puppy Chow, O.N.E., and Pro Plan. In addition, it received a New York–based assignment for cosmetics company L'Oréal. Fallon's Minneapolis office was hired by PBS to head its new brand campaign, titled *Be More*. "People tell us . . . that PBS inspires them to grow, to stretch, to simply be more," says Lesli Rotenberg, head of brand management at PBS. So Fallon has created several new spots with a quirky, cinematic feel just right for PBS. In one spot, a lonely composer receives inspiration from pigeons chirping outside his window. In another, a goldfish is watching a PBS nature program from inside his bowl, when suddenly he leaps out of the bowl and joins a group of salmon swimming upstream.

Today, Fallon Worldwide reports billings of over $700 million, with diverse clients around the globe. Yet despite its global reach, Fallon has not lost sight of its local perspective. Around the world, the company fosters creativity in its approach to each client and each project in each region. In a way, Fallon is like the goldfish watching television: It is willing to jump out of the bowl and join a different group, just to understand them better.

Questions

1. Explain how Fallon has benefited from going global.
2. How might multinational economic integration affect some of Fallon's strategies for its clients?
3. Why is it important for Fallon marketers to "think globally, but act locally" when it comes to the international marketing environment?
4. Fallon executives consider the Publicis merger an important ingredient in their international growth plans. Why do you think the combination was an important acquisition for Publicis?

SOURCES: Fallon Worldwide Web site, http://www.fallon.com, accessed January 6, 2003; "Fallon Worldwide," Hoover's Online, http://www.hoovers.com, accessed January 6, 2003; "Sun Could Be on Fallon's Horizon," *Minneapolis Star-Tribune*, July 27, 2002, http://www.startribune.com; "PBS Launches Brand Campaign Urging Viewers to Be More," June 26, 2002, http://www.pbs.org/insidepbs/news/bemore.html.

VIDEO CASE 5.2   Tower Records Uses Bricks—and Clicks—to Survive Troubled Times

Hard times are visiting the music industry. The troubles are so many that they conjure up memories of *Hydra*, the multiheaded serpent of Greek mythology that would grow two new heads for each one that was cut off. Here are a few of those deadly heads.

First of all, music buffs have taken to the Internet in ways no one could have imagined only a few years ago. Their expectations are well-known: high-quality sound, endless selection, immediate delivery, and the lowest prices they can find. And a growing number of them are discovering that they can satisfy these expectations on Internet music sites such as CDNow, as well as through online purchases from Amazon, Buy.com, and Web sites operated by the major brick-and-mortar bookstores. Only six years ago, just over 50 percent of all the recordings sold in the U.S. were through brick-and-mortar music retailers. Today, these traditional outlets account for only two of every five dollars spent on recordings.

A second problem involves turf battles between record companies and the retailers. The Big Five record companies, fresh from their court victories over the now-defunct music-sharing site Napster, are making a big push to market digital music. And this new channel promises to be huge. Forrester Research predicts that digital downloads will surpass online CD sales by 2005. And if the producers can go direct, they can pocket the retailers' share of the proceeds. As National Association of Recording Merchandisers president Pamela Horovitz puts it, "The record company content owners see digital music as an opportunity to sell direct to the consumers as well. . . . [They] have squeezed them on the margins of CDs in the physical-goods world, and they're trying to squeeze them out of business altogether in the digital world."

But the worst current bogeymen of both the retailers and the record companies are the music-sharing sites set up following the demise of Napster. The largest of this new crop is Kazaa, a site whose location is more difficult to pinpoint because there is no central repository of downloadable music, as there was on Napster. Instead, users can download the music they want from thousands of participants who are willing to allow visitors to access their personal collections—a type of peer-to-peer cooperative, albeit one that the music industry strongly believes violates copyright law.

And we're not talking pocket change here. A recent Recording Industry Association of America (RIAA) report revealed a 10 percent drop in sales of music products over the previous year. An RIAA survey of music consumers aged 12 to 54 with Internet access showed that 63 percent had acquired at least one home-recorded, or "burned," compact disc during the past year, and one in four acquired eleven or more.

These are the major problems currently facing the industry, including Tower Records, a pillar of the music retail business. Tower and its competitors such as Sam Goody and HMV are currently doing their best to become major players in the Internet music business. On Tower's Web site, music lovers can find an array of CDs, DVDs, issues of *Pulse* magazine, music videos, and other music-related products. They can browse through 500,000 music samples and try a number of free downloads, as well as some paid downloads. And as Tower marketing director, Russ Eisenmann, stresses, the site is as current as they get, with as many as 6,000 new CDs added every day. If a consumer isn't quite sure what titles or artists to look for, he or she will soon be able to type in key words like "electronic music," "beach music," or "wedding music," and the site will do an intuitive search for appropriate pieces.

Eisenmann credits Tower's brick-and-mortar success with helping the retail music chain build a strong Internet presence.

He realizes the success of this traditional music channel has been achieved by focusing on what it does best: providing shoppers with easy access to a wide range of titles and an enjoyable shopping experience. He knows that Tower has been able to build a successful online presence by promoting it to current customers as an occasional alternative to store visits. This way Tower doesn't have to spend extra marketing dollars in acquiring new customers, as Amazon.com or CDNow does. The customers already exist and usually have visited at least one Tower store to make a purchase before going online. In addition, tracking consumers' behavior online is much easier than following people around its stores. Tower can track the music selections people listen to and ultimately purchase, giving marketers valuable information about what its customers want.

But the industrywide sales decline also affects Tower—and the changes in distribution methods and sales losses from the music-sharing sites have cost them as well. But Tower has ways of fighting back. First, it has a strong base in its brick-and-mortar operations with more than 200 stores, including nearly 40 franchise locations, and 7,400 employees worldwide. Tower has taken steps into the Internet slowly, being careful not to undermine the physical presence of its major outlets. In addition to its push into online music retailing, the firm has launched self-service Music Discovery Center kiosks in several of its Los Angeles, New York, and San Francisco stores. The kiosks are designed to help music buffs navigate the huge Tower music catalog, and each contains a "scan and listen" component in which listeners can preview song clips of more than 250,000 CDs without opening—and purchasing—the CD package. "With self-service kiosks, retailers can provide their customers an interactive way to explore in-store music catalogs," explains Nelson Gomez, vice president of NCR EasyPoint, which developed the kiosks.

Marketing director Eisenmann emphasizes that a vital component of Tower's future success is its strategic alliances—such as the one with NCR EasyPoint. In addition, Tower has agreements with AOL.com and flooz.com, among others. (At flooz.com, people can purchase online currency to buy Tower products as gifts.) Tower also has an agreement with Alliance Entertainment for fulfillment and distribution services. Alliance provides CDs, cassettes, DVDs, and VHS tapes to Tower's online site. So Tower continues to search for ways to remain competitive, both online and offline. "You've got to be on edge all the time," says company founder Russ Solomon. "We're never satisfied and complacent," adds Michael Solomon, Tower's president. If the Solomons have anything to say about it, this tower isn't going to topple for a long time.

Questions

1. Analyze the strengths and weaknesses of Tower Records. What opportunities and threats do you see in its marketing environment, particularly regarding e-commerce? (Hint: Refer back to the discussion of SWOT analysis in Chapter 2.)

2. In what ways does Tower use the Internet to achieve its marketing objectives?

3. Why are interactive tools so important in Tower's online marketing strategy?
4. In what ways can Tower measure the effectiveness of its online marketing efforts?

SOURCES: Tower Records Web site, http://www.towerrecords.com, accessed January 21, 2003; "MTS, Incorporated," Hoover's Online, http://www.hoovers.com, accessed January 21, 2003; Jennifer Ordonez, "Sales of Recorded Music Decline," *The Wall Street Journal,* August 27, 2002, p. D3; "Tower Records First to Deploy Music Discovery Center Kiosk from NCR, Savage Beast," *Business Wire,* June 10, 2002; Liz Borod, "A Tower of Trouble?" *Fortune,* June 8, 2001, http://www.fortune.com.

VIDEO CASE 6.2

Dunkin' Donuts and Hill, Holliday: A Recipe for Good Relationships

Most of the hype in the donut business lately has been focused on Krispy Kreme, the North Carolina–based firm whose product has achieved cult status as it expands into new cities in the U.S. and Canada with plans aimed at making it a national player in the donut industry. Even though its marketing strategy has been so successful that Krispy Kreme was selected as the subject of the *Contemporary Marketing* continuing case, its size is dwarfed by its larger competitor from New England. Dunkin' Donuts, which celebrates its 60th birthday in 2008, is the world's largest donut chain. Its 5,000 retail shops that operate in 37 countries combine to sell about 20 cups of coffee every second and six million donuts each day.

But Dunkin' Donuts isn't content to rest on its laurels. Instead, it has chosen not only to meet competition head on but also to aggressively strengthen existing relationships with customers and business partners as well as build new ones. One of the first steps taken by the firm's marketing team was to meet with its counterparts at advertising agency Hill, Holliday to find ways to make Dunkin' Donuts feel new again. And the result was an entirely new promotional campaign.

"Loosen up a little." By now, the phrase has become synonymous with Dunkin' Donuts. It's actually the tagline from an advertising campaign dreamed up by a creative team at Hill, Holliday for their client Dunkin' Donuts. For years, Dunkin' Donuts ran ads featuring Fred the Baker—who woke before dawn each morning saying, "It's time to make the donuts." But Dunkin' Donuts marketers knew they had to come up with something new to keep the product fresh in customers' minds—and competitive in the marketplace. They wanted to make Dunkin' Donuts fun again. So, the Hill, Holliday team came up with a series of commercials and print ads featuring average people in all kinds of stressful situations—stuck in commuter traffic, chaperoning a children's Halloween party, even being chased by a police car. Then they made the situations funny, ending with the tagline "Loosen up a little."

The ads were a hit—both with the public and with Dunkin' Donuts—and a relationship was born. Now Hill, Holliday must look for ways to nurture that relationship, just as Dunkin'

Donuts continues to search for ways to find and retain loyal customers. At Hill, Holliday the Dunkin' Donuts account has grown into numerous creative teams headed by creative directors Marty Smith and Tim Jones. The entire account team is focused on satisfying marketers and executives at Dunkin' Donuts. Within the overall account team, smaller creative teams are focused on coming up with ideas to satisfy the standards set by the creative directors. Both Smith and Jones point out that they like to give their creative teams as much autonomy as possible so they can come up with the best ideas for new ads. "Brilliant ideas can come out of the seed of a really bad idea," says Jones. Smith concurs. "The only thing that matters is the strength of the idea."

Technology can play an important part in forging customer and client relationships. Recently, Hill, Holliday acquired interactive agency SF Interactive (SFI) to enhance its relationships with clients such as Dunkin' Donuts. Hill, Holliday wants to offer clients an integrated package of options to reach customers, including online marketing, advertising, and customer relationship management tools, as well as interactive television, wireless, and broadband technologies. "The acquisition of SFI will allow us to service clients more effectively with a broad menu of marketing and communications offerings," notes ad agency executive Jack Connors.

While Hill, Holliday is working hard to reinvigorate Dunkin' Donuts' relationship with consumers, Dunkin' Donuts is developing relationships with other companies. One is AirIQ, a wireless application service provider that specializes in fleet management. AirIQ will help simplify and streamline the purchase and distribution of product ingredients for Dunkin' Donuts franchises in the southeastern U.S. Another partner is Captivate Network, which airs company advertisements on its screens placed in building elevators, thus providing riders with something to concentrate on—besides the backs of fellow passengers' heads—during those awkward silences. And in a recent move, Dunkin' Donuts has forged an agreement with Home Depot, the nation's largest home improvement retailer. Dunkin' Donuts is placing its own full-service bakeries inside several Home Depot stores in a trial run. "We did some survey research and found that a lot of professional builders and contractors visit our stores, particularly in the early hours, to collect materials," explains John Simley of Home Depot. "On their way to the work site, they stop off at a Dunkin' Donuts for coffee, bagels, and doughnuts for their crews, so this just makes it a little more convenient for them." Coincidentally, the tagline for some of Hill, Holliday's more recent ads reads, "There's always time for Dunkin' Donuts." Even if you're shopping at Home Depot first thing in the morning.

Questions

1. What types of strategies can Dunkin' Donuts use to build a relationship with consumers and keep them coming back?

2. Describe the ways that Hill, Holliday uses CRM in its relationship with Dunkin' Donuts.

3. Dunkin' Donuts is currently building a relationship with Home Depot. Describe at least one other company with which you think Dunkin' Donuts could develop a relationship, and explain why.

4. Why do you think Hill, Holliday is interested in online and interactive technologies?

SOURCES: Dunkin' Donuts Web site, http://www.dunkindonuts.com, accessed January 15, 2003; Hill, Holliday Web site, http://www.hillholliday.com, accessed January 15, 2003; "Dunkin' Donuts Opens Stores Inside Home Depot," *The Boston Globe*, August 20, 2002, http://www.boston.com; "AirIQ Helps Keep Dunkin' Donuts Rolling," *10 Meters News Service*, http://www.10meters.com; Brendan Gibbon, "Elevated Ideas," *Business Forward*, August 8, 2001, http://www.bizforward.com.

VIDEO CASE 7.2

Fisher-Price: Marketing Research Is More than Child's Play

Who wouldn't love a job doing marketing research on toys? That's what Shelly Glick Gryfe does for toy maker Fisher-Price, as director of marketing research. But she is quick to make you realize that marketing research in the highly competitive 21st century toy market is more than child's play—although it does include inviting children to play with toys. Gryfe describes how her group at Fisher-Price, a subsidiary of Mattel, Inc., used primary data collected through different sampling techniques to ensure that the company's new line of Rescue Heroes figures would be a hit with kids.

Fisher-Price marketers used exploratory research to discover that a gap existed between toys available for toddler boys and those available for school-age boys. Preschoolers—roughly ages three to five—liked the idea of their older siblings' action figures, but they didn't understand how to use the toys. And they certainly weren't going to pay attention to toys they viewed as "for babies." In addition, the moms of these youngsters felt a growing need to shield their young children from a world scarred by terrorism, suicide bombers, and other threats so real and so prevalent that they required troop commitments from the U.S. and its allies. As they worked to screen their impressionable small children from ever-present news coverage of these events, they certainly didn't want to introduce toys with violent overtones in their kids' play areas.

This research caused Fisher-Price marketers to coin the term KAGOY, or Kids Are Getting Older Younger. Gryfe explains that the term refers to the fact that although younger children aren't necessarily more sophisticated than they used to be, they are aware of options and begin searching for them sooner. But those options need to be tailored to the needs of younger children. "We saw an opportunity for Fisher-Price," says Gryfe, "to offer toys that weren't already being offered."

So the idea of Rescue Heroes—originally dubbed Everyday Heroes—was born. These heroes had to appeal to young boys—with active roles like firefighters or police officers—and they had to be easy to understand and play with. They needed to evoke excitement and adventure at a preschooler's level. To learn more about what parents and kids wanted, Fisher-Price used a combination of in-house and outside research to obtain primary data on their concept and later build prototypes of the toys.

Fisher-Price marketers don't begin the new-product development process by conducting expensive, full-blown research. The first step typically consists of a number of focus groups. Then they regroup and discuss what was learned from these give-and-take information-gathering sessions with mothers of preschool children. Additional research frequently occurs as a result of these discussions. In the case of Rescue Heroes, marketers first conducted in-house "mom talks," or focus groups in which mothers discussed what they wanted—and didn't want—in a new toy for their sons. The moms confirmed quickly that, although they liked the idea of imaginative play with action figures, they didn't want their sons playing with toys that had violent themes. Gryfe is well aware of the presence of sampling bias in many of these focus groups: People who participate in these sessions want to say positive things about the product or idea. Still, she says, "people do want to have an impact" on what types of toys are developed for their children. But Gryfe has this warning for users of this qualitative research technique: "Focus groups should never be used to determine if a product is or isn't going to be a strong market seller. [Focus groups] should always be for directional information to provide insights into how to make that product better." Instead, Fisher-Price uses other types of research in its efforts to forecast potential sales.

Initial research told Fisher-Price marketers that Rescue Heroes could fill a niche for young boys. "We knew we had something very strong," comments Gryfe. "We developed models and did a viability test, which tested our prototypes against the competitors." Some of these tests were conducted in the company play lab, where kids are free to color, do arts and crafts, have snacks—and play with toys. In the Rescue Heroes test, children were shown a video about Rescue Heroes, then a photo board describing them further. Then the boys were given a choice of Rescue Heroes or competing action figures. Later, the mothers were asked some questions about what they liked or didn't like about the toys. According to Gryfe, Rescue Heroes actually tested better with the moms until marketers discovered why: The original name for the figures, Everyday Heroes, was confusing to the kids. So Fisher-Price changed the name to Rescue Heroes, which pinpointed the idea more precisely—and sounded more adventurous and fun.

Later, Fisher-Price conducted more studies away from the company, including one at Canada's Simon Fraser University, involving 28 families with boys aged three to six. In another study, Fisher-Price sent the figures home with children to play with for a week, with follow-up interviews. By now, the Rescue Heroes had names, occupations, and stories to back them up. Billy Blazes and Wendy Waters fought fires fearlessly; Perry Medic saved many lives; and alpine guide Cliff Hanger and scuba diver Gil Gripper were ready to leap or dive to the rescue.

Still, Fisher-Price learned that children wanted more stories about their heroes. So the company developed stories that were included directly on the box containing the Rescue Hero and also developed videos to provide children with interesting depictions of the character in action. And when CBS decided that a *Rescue Heroes* series would fit perfectly into its Saturday morning cartoon lineup, the new heroes became stars.

Questions

1. What problem was identified through the exploratory research conducted by Fisher-Price? What role did this step play in the development of a new product?
2. How might Fisher-Price supplement its primary data with secondary data? In what ways might secondary data be beneficial?
3. Do you think that Fisher-Price's sampling techniques were effective? Why or why not?
4. In what ways might Fisher-Price use computer technology to enhance its research?

SOURCES: Fisher-Price Web site, http://www.fisher-price.com, accessed January 13, 2003; Diane Rezendes Khirallah, "Fisher-Price Toys with Modeling Software," *InformationWeek.com,* April 1, 2002, http://www.informationweek.com.

VIDEO CASE 8.2

Annie's Homegrown: A Natural Success

If you're a student trying to survive on a tight grocery budget, or if you have any younger brothers or sisters, chances are you've had a meal or two featuring macaroni and cheese. Ann Withey, founder of Connecticut-based Annie's Homegrown, hopes you've tried at least one of her company's natural macaroni-and-cheese products. You may have sampled her original shells and cheddar (made with real aged Wisconsin cheddar), or branched out to the alfredo sauce flavor or the Mexican flavor. If you've become hooked on the taste of Annie's Homegrown products, you probably have sampled several of her organically grown line of pasta products. Withey is counting on at least one of two factors to attract you as a customer: Either you are interested in a healthful diet, or you are a parent who wants more healthful choices for your children. She's also counting on the fact that you like macaroni and cheese—or, at least, pasta. All of these factors are linked directly to the company's market segmentation strategy.

Withey launched Annie's Homegrown in 1989 with her former husband, Andrew Martin. The couple were still basking in the huge success of their previous food product innovation: Smartfood, the cheese-flavored popcorn snack that has become

a fixture in the lunchbox menus of both children and adults. As Withey recalls, the timing for introducing Smartfood couldn't have been better. "People were getting interested in healthy foods . . . and the only flavored popcorn out there was bright orange." Smartfood became so successful that PepsiCo was willing to pay $15 million to acquire the company and add it to its salty-snacks FritoLay division.

In addition to being well on their way to becoming two rich marketers, Withey and Martin came away from the Smartfood introduction with years of marketing experience. And they began almost immediately to apply this experience, especially that related to product development. They knew that their experience in developing a cheese coating for Smartfood popcorn could also be applied to prepackaged macaroni-and-cheese products—if they could come up with the right recipe. And as long as the new recipe didn't involve a bright orange color, they were convinced they could attract the same people who earlier had flocked to Smartfood to try their new macaroni-and-cheese products.

The result of a series of trial-and-error attempts was Annie's Homegrown original shells and white cheddar, a product that sold well during its first two years. Then Withey began to experiment with other flavors and product variations. But perhaps the most innovative addition to the original Annie's Homegrown product line was the microwavable, single-serve version, which doesn't even require adding milk or butter to the cheese mix: Hungry consumers simply pop it in the microwave.

Why is this important? It is a highly visible solution to the needs of two key Annie's Homegrown market segments: kids and busy adults. Annie's Homegrown is as simple for a 10-year-old to fix as a bag of microwave popcorn, so it's a perfect after-school snack. And it makes a great on-the-run lunch or snack for the busy adult who wants something substantial—and healthful—to eat.

Right from the start, Withey and Martin were clear about the needs and wants of their customers, and they set about creating a product line capable of meeting them. Their previous experience with Smartfood also taught them that competition in the grocery industry is perhaps the toughest there is. Even today, Annie's Homegrown would be thought of as a pebble in the macaroni-and-cheese food category, compared with giant boulders such as Kraft Foods and FritoLay, either of whom could swallow the tiny company in a single gulp.

Withey has also demonstrated her products' customer-satisfaction might against Kraft's prepared macaroni-and-cheese products (in the famous blue box that every kid knows). In instances where grocers stocked her brand in shelf locations where it would compete directly with the blue boxes of Kraft, Annie's held its own.

But although the product competes in the same product space as competitors like FritoLay and Kraft, Withey's marketing plan does not call for it to go head to head against the giants. Instead, Annie's Homegrown products are carefully positioned on the basis of several factors:

- *Attributes*—Healthy, all-natural ingredients.
- *Competitors*—More nutritious than the bright orange cheese sauce of Kraft Foods.
- *Price/quality*—Although Annie's products cost about 20 percent more than conventional boxed macaroni-and-cheese dinners, Annie's ingredients are all natural.
- *Product user*—Consumers who want food that is nutritious, tastes good, and is convenient to prepare.

Annie's has remained so focused on communicating this simple message—that its food is not only the most convenient to prepare but, more importantly, is of the highest quality—that its name has become synonymous with the quest of consumers for a healthful alternative to the products offered by its competitors.

A visitor to the Annie's Homegrown Web site (http://www .annies.com) will be greeted at the home page by a *Welcome* sign hung above a vegetable patch where bunnies and gardeners happily coexist. Bernie the Bunny, whose picture graces every box of Annie's Homegrown food products, has become the company's mascot. And yes, just as a real Annie actually exists, so also is there a real Bernie. The site has something for everyone: adults who want to learn more about the new organic pastas and meals, as well as kids who might want to play games or download pictures of Bernie to color. And even though Solera Capital, a large investment firm, recently purchased an ownership share in the firm (as well as supplying a needed infusion of additional funds to finance expansion of both products and distribution), Annie's Homegrown remains committed to serving its market with high-quality, all-natural foods. Food shoppers are likely to continue to reach for the box with the bunny as loyally as they have in the past. According to some estimates, organic food sales will grow at double-digit rates each year for the next several years. That's welcome news to the folks at Annie's.

Questions

1. Why is market segmentation crucial to Annie's success?
2. Do Annie's markets fulfill the criteria necessary for effective segmentation? Why or why not?
3. Which of the four alternative strategies for reaching a target market do you think would work best for Annie's Homegrown? Why?
4. Why is positioning so important to Annie's? What conditions might cause Annie's marketers to reposition their products?

SOURCES: Annie's Homegrown Inc. Web site, http://www.annies.com, accessed January 13, 2003; Chris Reidy, "NY Firm Acquires Majority Stake in Annie's Homegrown," *The Boston Globe,* August 13, 2002, http://www.boston.com; Healthy Foods Newsletter, "Healthy Food News: Annie's Homegrown," February 26, 2002, http://www.care2.com.

VIDEO CASE 9.2 WBRU Sounds Good to Listeners

You probably have a favorite radio station, whether it's rock, folk, classical, talk, or news. You might tune in when you're driving, studying, or even working. Believe it or not, your radio station cares about you as a consumer— from what kind of music you like to listen to, including your favorite artists and songs, to what local restaurants you prefer, where you shop for clothes, and even what kind of car you drive. That's because your radio station is a business, and to remain successful, its marketers need to understand your behavior as a consumer.

WBRU, which broadcasts from Brown University in Providence, Rhode Island, is a typical college radio station in many ways. Billing itself as "Southern New England's only modern rock station," it serves a local market across Rhode Island and southeastern Massachusetts. It employs a combination of student and professional staff. Its DJs are mostly students. And its core listeners are in their late teens to late twenties. In addition, says general sales manager Randy Hershoff, WBRU's listeners tend to be well educated, planning to work or already working in professional careers, and affluent for their age group. About 28 percent own their own home, and one in nine drives a luxury car such as a Lexus, BMW, or Saab. The station's listeners are loyal, notes Hershoff, and they like the idea that WBRU isn't a large corporate station. They appreciate the fact that the DJs "talk just like they talk to their friends."

All of this information is important for WBRU marketers because it paints a picture of its listeners as consumers. The station can then tailor its programming to their preferences. Based on the desires of its listeners, the station calls itself "music intensive," keeping chitchat by DJs to a minimum. It also keeps commercial breaks to a minimum, airing only nine commercials per hour. Following its modern rock format, the station specializes in playing songs that are not often played by the larger, more mainstream radio stations. WBRU has a history of offering the unusual to listeners who want something apart from the mainstream. The station was founded in the late 1960s and claims to be the "first rock station to break from a Top 40 format." Today, the station offers programs that fill different niches. One such program, called "360 Degree Black Experience in Sound," is an urban contemporary program that airs all day Sunday and covers a variety of music from gospel to rap.

Not only is it important for WBRU to understand the behavior of its consumers in terms of listening preferences, but it is also vital for the station to match its listeners with the right advertisers. If advertisers are successful at attracting customers via WBRU, then they will continue advertising with the station, which puts more revenue dollars in the WBRU coffers. So, WBRU needs to understand the purchasing habits of the folks who regularly listen to its programming. Based on the data, say, about what kinds of cars listeners choose to drive, WBRU marketers can determine the influences at work on consumer

behavior and approach the right companies as potential advertisers. In WBRU's case, a regional luxury-car dealership might be very happy to advertise with it. The station often teams up with advertisers such as Budweiser and Cingular in promotional efforts to attract consumers. In one recent campaign, listeners were invited to a local Cingular store on a Saturday afternoon, when they could meet the "BRU Crew" and view Cingular wireless products. The first five people to sign up for Cingular wireless service received a free Motorola personal organizer.

WBRU likes to be known for excellence—not just in the quality of its music programming but also in the way it covers news and produces its shows. For several years running, the station has been named News Station of the Year by the Associated Press, which recognizes college radio stations around the country. WBRU has also received awards from *Rolling Stone*, along with other music industry publications.

All of this points to a radio station that is in tune with its customers, both listeners and advertisers. If you want the latest music news, like to win free CDs and other prizes, or want to stay in touch with other music buffs, you can tune in to WBRU—or visit the station's Web site. Need to stay awake while you write that big report? Check out "WBRU LOUD" on Thursday night, and you won't be catching any Zs. Your parents may not like your consumer behavior, but WBRU sure will.

Questions

1. What types of influences might be at work on consumers who choose to listen to WBRU?
2. Where does WBRU—and most of its advertisers—fit into Maslow's Hierarchy of Needs? How can WBRU use this information to its benefit?
3. What steps can WBRU take in creating a favorable attitude toward its station among potential listeners?
4. Tune in to your favorite radio station. What types of advertisements—and how many—are aired during an hour of play? What do those ads tell you about the consumer behavior of your station's listeners?

SOURCES: WBRU Web site, http://www.wbru.com, accessed January 16, 2003; Brown University Web site, http://www.brown.edu, accessed January 16, 2003; Gabrielle Johnson, "WBRU Wins AP Award for Third Straight Year," *The Brown Daily Herald*, April 19, 2000, http://www.browndailyherald.com.

 # VIDEO CASE 10.2   UPS Delivers for Its Business Customers

When the UPS driver comes to your door, you probably don't think about the giant delivery firm's relationship with the company that sent you your package. Even if you've seen the UPS ads asking, "What can Brown do for you?" you probably haven't thought about its impact on you as a consumer. Instead, you're more interested in ripping open the package to see what's inside. But although each of those brisk, friendly delivery people in the big brown trucks makes contact with dozens of consumers every day, behind-the-scenes UPS marketers are building relationships with companies that need to ship packages, letters, and even electronic documents. "It's a very competitive industry," explains Ed Buckley, vice president of UPS marketing in Europe. "There's only a limited quantity of big companies who will ship thousands of packages every day. We love those customers and build relationships through personal contact." But what about the thousands and thousands of medium-sized and small firms that have shipping needs as well? That's where segmentation comes in.

Buckley admits that UPS simply can't afford to sit down for one-on-one, personal conferences with the heads of the "masses of smaller firms." So UPS marketers set out to find an effective method for segmenting its business markets that would allow it to continue to serve its smaller customers competitively. But this quest proved to be one of the most challenging they had faced. At first, recalls Buckley, UPS experimented with what seemed to be a simple, straightforward approach: segmentation by industry. But marketers quickly learned that "just because you happen to be in the same line of business doesn't mean your shipping needs are the same," says Buckley. This method clearly didn't work.

Then they tried to apply segmentation by traditional categories such as demographic, customer based, end-use application, and purchasing situation, but this just wasn't commercially viable, according to Buckley. "There's no way to classify businesses into these academic or idealistic segments," he observes. In addition, in both cases UPS had relied on outside marketing research firms for assistance, and while they were somewhat helpful, Buckley and his associates were disappointed at what they believed was the researchers' overemphasis on data collection and statistical analysis rather than zeroing in on industry needs and UPS capabilities. So, company management decided to move much of this research back home, calling on in-house marketers to use their own knowledge and experience to devise a segmentation scheme that would work. Buckley recalls being somewhat overwhelmed by the assignment, but in the long run he believes it was a crucial move because UPS marketers understood "the full picture." In the end, they bridged the two previous segmentation attempts and devised methods that allowed UPS marketers to predict the needs of business customers and offer appropriate solutions.

Today, Buckley explains, UPS marketers try to accomplish two objectives through segmentation: (1) identify groups of business customers who have common needs and fulfill them and (2) promote and develop markets for some of UPS's most profitable services. To boost interest in the company's Overnight Express service, UPS sent out direct mail pieces to hundreds of small firms and got a terrific response. As a result of that single mailing, UPS experienced a 28 percent increase in the use of Overnight Express by small businesses.

Buckley notes that organizational buying situations are often very fluid. He explains that organizations are dynamic, with people changing jobs and moving around. As a result, it's a mistake to try to peg a single decision maker into a single segment over a long period of time. In fact, he says, "the decision maker" is a mythical being. Instead, several decision makers usually exist within an organization, and they change over time. So UPS must be flexible and change its offerings to appeal to the different styles and types of decisions that customers make throughout the relationship.

This adaptability while maintaining continuity requires "working deeper in our customers' organizations," explains Buckley. That means developing a relationship with the CEO of an organization, the engineering department, the purchasing department, and others, as well as the shipping department, so that as many people within an organization as possible understand their role in shipping. Of course, UPS can't personally visit every company, but through different marketing efforts, including the Business Solutions link on its Web site and direct mail, customers can learn more about the wide range of products UPS offers.

And the variety of UPS products is nearly endless—there's a lot more behind the big brown truck than meets the eye, although the small-package delivery business is roughly a $60-billion-a-year market in the U.S. alone. UPS offers such services as tracking information via wireless phone or PDA; Web-enabled pager notification; customs and brokerage services; strategic business solutions, including distribution strategies, engineering, and package design; and assistance with supply chain management. And that's just a small sampling of UPS products. Ultimately, says Buckley, UPS marketers ask themselves the same question every day: "How can we make our customers more successful and in turn make UPS more successful?" In other words, what can Brown do for you today?

Questions

1. Why do you think the first two attempts at segmentation didn't work for UPS?

2. How might derived demand and inventory policy among its customers affect UPS? Describe how UPS might help its customers find solutions to changes in these two types of demand.

3. How is UPS's relationship with its business customers different from its relationship with final consumers?

4. Ed Buckley observes that organizational purchasing decisions are usually made by more than one person. How does this relate to the buying center concept?

SOURCES: UPS Web site, http://www.ups.com, accessed January 17, 2003; Charlotte Jane Dyson, "UPS Delivers," *Brandchannel.com*, August 22, 2002, http://www.brandchannel.com; "Q&A: The Man Who's Repackaging UPS," *BusinessWeek Online*, May 28, 2002, http://www.businessweek.com.

VIDEO CASE 11.2

Fossil Is a Reminder of Good Times

Twenty million dollars for a one-week vacation on the U.S.–Russian space station? If you had $20 million to burn—and someone had just perfected time travel—you might put your money down on a quick trip back 50 years ago. What a trip: seeing your grandparents as youngsters and raving at all those retro fashions. And if you checked out the watches they wore then, you'd notice that watches were considered jewelry. They were expensive, often jewel bedecked, and usually sold at retail jewelry stores.

But then along came Timex—and market segmentation came to visit the watch industry and never left. Timex was inexpensive, highly utilitarian, almost disposable, and possessed an image of quality resulting from decades of TV and print ads hammering away at the tagline "Takes a licking and keeps on ticking." Timex was followed by other relatively low-priced watches like Swatch and Guess, but the newcomers were careful to emphasize fashion as well as practicality. In fact, the different colors and designs of these new brands permitted their marketers to emphasize the wisdom of purchasing different colors and designs to go with different clothes.

The image of the timepiece as jewelry continued to be featured in expensive, high-fashion brands such as Cartier, Movado, Patek Philippe, Piaget, Raymond Weil, and Rolex. Such watches carried price tags as high as $20,000 and were marketed through exclusive specialty retailers.

Two decades ago, two brothers, Tom and Kosta Kartsotis, decided to enter the watch market with a completely new line of watches designed to combine the advantages of the moderately priced and high-fashion segments. The result was Fossil, Inc., headquartered in the Dallas suburb of Richardson and recognized today as an emerging leader in the fashion watch industry.

But the Kartsotis brothers were an unlikely pair to found a soon-to-be market leader. Prior to the launch, Tom was selling hard-to-get tickets for sporting events and concerts. Tom's older brother, Kosta, at the time a merchandise executive for a large Dallas department store chain, told him about the large profit margins being earned by importing retail goods from the Far East—in particular, the increasing trend toward moderately priced watches pioneered by Swiss-owned Swatch. Taking Kosta's suggestion, Tom went to Hong Kong, where he hired a manufacturer to make 1,500 watches, which he brought back and sold to local department stores and boutiques. Fossil was born.

To carve their own niche in the fashion watch industry, Tom and Kosta came up with a retro theme to differentiate their watches from Swatch or Guess. Inspiration for the watch designs came largely from old magazines of the 1940s and 1950s. Within that nostalgic Americana theme, says Fossil executive vice president Richard Gundy, "We made the decision to be a world-class brand."

But Fossil wasn't content to make and sell just one watch. Instead, the company wanted to create and market watches of different designs to match the different tastes of everyone, all at affordable prices. So the firm developed several lines of Fossil watches. Among the more than 500 styles of Fossil watches available today you can find watches for men, women, and children—even watches for collectors. If you're an Elvis fan, you're in luck: You can pick up a Fossil watch commemorating the 25th anniversary of his death for about $95. If you're hung up on Batman, a *Batman Dark Knight* model will set you back $125 (but hurry; it's part of a limited edition of 2,000). You can even join the Fossil Collectors' Club to get monthly updates on new and upcoming Fossil collectible items.

Fossil also offers specialty watches like the Kaleido, which comes in several models at prices ranging from $65 to $75. With the touch of a button, the Kaleido dial changes colors just like a kaleidoscope. Of course, conservative customers can set the dial color to remain constant as well. If you want the dial numbers in Chinese characters, you can purchase the Chinese Tic for about $65. And for the more technologically advanced watch buyers, Fossil offers two new high-tech models: the Wrist PDA and the Wrist PDA-PC. The Wrist PDA, used as a companion to the Palm OS, can store personal data from your handheld computer using infrared beaming. The Wrist PDA-PC has a memory capacity, allowing you to store pocket PC handheld information such as personal contacts, a calendar, upcoming tasks, and notes. All of these watches—even the Wrist PDAs—convey the Americana image (although Fossil marketers do concede that they didn't have PDAs back in the 1950s).

Fossil currently has sales and distribution centers in the U.S., Canada, Germany, Hong Kong, Italy, Mexico, and Spain. This network of distributors offers Fossil products to over 70 countries.

But Tom and Kosta Kartsotis have not been content to limit Fossil to watches. They expanded the length, width, and depth of their mix, gradually becoming an accessories company in addition to a watch company. They believed that a natural progression existed from watches to sunglasses, then to small leather goods and apparel. Today, you can pick up a hip pair of sunglasses—with such models as the Capricorn, Flute, Soprano, and Oboe—from the firm's eyewear line, each priced between $28 and $35. Students and busy parents can do their back-to-school shopping at Fossil's Web site, where they can buy jeans (with names like Bandit, Scout, Starfire, and Tempest), as well as T-shirts, bags, and, of course, watches.

As Fossil diversified its product offerings, it remained close to its Americana theme, which continues to be particularly popular in the U.S. market. Also, each new addition has to fall into the category of fashion accessories and be related to the other items in the existing product lines. A few years ago, Fossil paired up with London Fog for the production and marketing of Fossil outerwear in the U.S. More recently, it was awarded a license from Giorgio Armani SpA to make and sell a line of Emporio Armani jewelry. Although this move represents a departure from the Americana theme, the Armani brand is popular worldwide, and Fossil prides itself in offering "something for everyone." Regardless of the style you choose, Fossil wants its watches and fashion accessories to remind you of the good times.

Questions

1. How would you classify Fossil products as consumer goods?
2. How might Fossil use quality as a product strategy?

3. What steps has Fossil already taken to extend the product life cycle of its watches?
4. Do you think it is a good idea for Fossil to enter into licensing agreements with foreign companies like Armani and London Fog? Why or why not?

SOURCES: Fossil Web site, http://www.fossil.com, accessed January 9, 2003; "Fossil Reaches Agreement for EMPORIO ARMANI Jewelry," *AP Online*, August 12, 2002, http://hoovnews.hoovers.com; Tischelle George, "The Fossil PDA You Wear," *InformationWeek.com*, November 9, 2001, http://www.information week.com.

VIDEO CASE 12.2   Stride Rite Keeps Its Brands in Step

Do you have a favorite pair of shoes? Maybe they're sneakers, sandals, hiking boots, clogs, platforms, mules, loafers. Did you have a favorite pair as a kid? Stride Rite hopes you did—and still do. The Stride Rite Corporation is a leading U.S. marketer of high-quality shoes for children and adults. And although the company was founded and built on the Stride Rite brand of children's shoes, Stride Rite also markets several other well-known brands, either under its ownership or through license agreements: Keds, Sperry, Tommy Hilfiger, and Grasshoppers. Even if you don't own a pair of one of these brands, you've probably at least heard of them.

That's the strength of a good brand—providing instant recognition and connection with customers. And Stride Rite is deeply ingrained in the U.S. business culture, since it has been making children's shoes since 1918. During the 1970s, the company purchased another top brand, Keds, known for decades for their canvas sneakers with the little blue label on the heel. More recently, Stride Rite acquired Grasshoppers, casual shoes for women over age 50, and Sperry Top-Siders, a line of boat shoes that's been around since 1935. The company also partners with Tommy Hilfiger, a high-profile marketer of fashion apparel, accessories, and home products, to license its shoe line. Managing all of these brands under one umbrella is a challenge that Stride Rite marketers believe they can handle well by remaining focused on the quality of their products and the needs of their customers. As CFO John Kelliher puts it, "Product is king." In other words, Stride Rite is committed to developing and marketing high-quality products that continue to generate brand equity. The Stride Rite brand certainly enjoys strong brand equity, since parents have been purchasing Stride Rite shoes for their children for more than 80 years.

Keds and Sperry are two other brands that have enjoyed decades of brand equity. "Keds is a lifestyle brand that provides fresh, honest, spirited footwear for every woman, everywhere," says the company Web site. Although Keds adds new designs to its line each year, the designers are careful not to stray too far

from the original Keds canvas sneaker design. Consumers can buy mule-style or platform Keds, but the shoes retain the distinctive Keds style and blue label. The same goes for Sperry Top-Siders, a line of marine shoes that landlubbers and boating enthusiasts alike have been wearing since the mid-1930s. Technology has advanced the design of boat shoes, which now contain the trademarked Full Active Comfort System, but when a customer asks for a pair of boat shoes, he or she expects the traditional look—and gets it.

The Tommy Hilfiger brand holds the record for the greatest variety of products under a single designer name. This family brand includes clothing, shoes, accessories, fragrances, and home products for men, women, and children. Stride Rite calls its Tommy Hilfiger shoe brand a "global lifestyle brand" with every product carrying the recognizable Tommy Hilfiger logo—and the brand's signature red, white, and blue colors.

When it comes to children's shoes, "we know little feet and are committed to providing shoes for a wide range of consumer needs," says Stride Rite CEO David Chamberlain. Recently, the company launched two new trademarked brands of children's shoes: Kid Smart and Baby Smart, which are available at Target stores throughout the U.S. "We are excited to expand our brand lineup to fill the needs of Target guests looking for stylish, value-priced children's shoes," continued Chamberlain. The partnership with Target is an important part of Stride Rite's brand strategy. In order to develop new footwear products successfully, says Stride Rite CFO John Kelliher, "you have to run your business with the eye of a retailer." In other words, Stride Rite shoes are designed and developed with a strong link to the retailers who will be marketing them to consumers.

The same goes for its clothing. Recently, Stride Rite's licensing agency, The Beanstalk Group, forged a licensing partnership with the Heyman Corporation, a leading manufacturer of quality children's clothing and accessories. Heyman will use the Stride Rite brand on a new line of newborn clothing and accessories, playwear, sleepwear, and other clothing items for boys and girls from infancy to size 7. The Stride Rite clothing lines will be sold in upscale department stores and specialty stores. "This is an important next step in our strategy to develop the Stride Rite brand into a lifestyle brand by partnering with companies that excel in our product categories," says Chamberlain. There's no doubt that for nearly a century, Stride Rite has taken all the right steps with a truly American brand.

Questions

1. What are some of the benefits of brand equity to Stride Rite?

2. An effective brand communicates to buyers an idea of a product's image. What image or images do any of Stride Rite's brands convey to you? If you have never heard of them before, how might Stride Rite reach you as a new customer?

3. What steps might Stride Rite take to develop loyalty for its new brands, such as Kid Smart and Baby Smart?

4. Choose one of the product development strategies and describe briefly how Stride Rite might use it for introducing a new product under any one of its brand names.

SOURCES: Stride Rite Corporation Web site, http://www.strideritecorp.com, accessed January 11, 2003; Tom Smith, "Stride Rite Chain Plots Retail Systems Upgrade," *InternetWeek.com,* March 29, 2002, http://www.internetweek.com; "Stride Rite Signs Licensing Agreement with Heyman Corporation for Children's Apparel," *Business Wire,* February 4, 2002, http://www.corporate-ir.net; "New Children's Footwear Brands from Stride Rite Introduced at Target Stores in the U.S.," *Business Wire,* http://www.corporate-ir.net.

 VIDEO CASE 13.2

Cybex International Whips Pricing into Shape

Are you the classic gym rat, visiting your local health club, Y, or school gym five or six times a week to work out? Maybe you prefer to get your exercise by running, walking, or playing outdoor sports. Even if you've only poked your head into a gym during a tour of your school, you'd probably recognize the giant treadmills, stationary bikes, steppers, and hikers, along with resistance machines and weights. If you ask a trainer for the name of the company that makes all of this equipment, you will often get a one-word answer: Cybex. Cybex International manufactures and markets premium fitness equipment—cardiovascular systems, strength systems, and personal systems—mostly for health clubs, schools, and hotels. Only about 20 cents of every Cybex sales dollar is generated from individual consumers. These purchasers buy from independent retailers who carry the Cybex product lines.

Steve Suchanek, director of product management for Cybex, explains that the company focuses on high-end customers. "What we want to be is a premium supplier," says Suchanek. This means that Cybex equipment is expensive. "We know, right out of the gate, that we'll be at the top of the price tier." If paying a premium to get fit makes you nervous, you might want to slip on your running shoes and go for a jog or walk outdoors instead. But consumers in the market for durable, high-quality exercise equipment comparable to the machines found in a gym can purchase a personal gym system for just under $4,200. If that's a bit too much for the budget, they can pick up a Personal Climber 400s Stepper for about $2,400. Strength systems come in components that run anywhere from $500 to $1,000 each. But all of this is peanuts compared with the outlay a fitness club makes for a complete line of Cybex equipment, which often tops $60,000.

Suchanek notes that Cybex uses a cost-plus approach as the starting point in pricing its equipment. Cost figures that include everything from raw materials, components, human resource expenses, and other production-related inputs to the costs of different distribution methods used and packaging and shipping costs to expected markups are combined to arrive at an approximation of the final price. For products sold in the international marketplace, additional considerations—such as exchange rate fluctuations—can affect prices.

Even though Cybex pricing objectives might be characterized as prestige pricing, the firm maintains some price elasticity in its offerings. If a 20-percent reduction in price results in a 40-percent increase in the number of units sold, Cybex is likely to be flexible in the case of such large orders, Suchanek reports. However, the impact of a price reduction on the Cybex product image as well as its potential to damage working relations with long-time customers are also carefully examined prior to agreeing to such price cuts.

Cybex marketers realize that adopting a prestige pricing objective means that lower-priced personal gym systems marketed by competitors are likely to take large bites out of the overall market through their appeal to shoppers seeking systems providing adequate performance at lower prices. But volume isn't the company's objective. Instead, says Suchanek, Cybex knows that "the affluent consumer is looking for something like the commercial product," and Cybex can provide it. Cybex also markets its products as part of a total "good life" lifestyle. "To say Cybex International is an exercise equipment company is like saying filet mignon is just food. Or that German luxury automobiles are simply transportation," says the company's Web site. "Fitness reaches into every motion and emotion in our daily lives, whether at work, at home, or at play. The pursuit of fitness is about nothing less than the quality of our lives." However, Cybex has to be careful not to price itself out of sales. "Your pricing has to make sense to the dealer," notes Suchanek. Otherwise, those treadmills and steppers will remain in inventory—or won't be stocked at all by retail fitness stores. But Cybex doesn't seem to be in any such danger.

With fitness clubs, hotels, and schools, Cybex often adopts a value pricing approach because the company is more likely to sell an entire line of equipment at once. "Clubs want to be able to shop from one vendor," explains Suchanek. The only time they'll purchase items from different vendors is when they can get a significantly better price. "So if we provide the right product at a reasonable price, it makes sense to bundle it," he says. In other words, Cybex can afford to offer a club or school a slightly lower price for premium equipment if the customer orders a number of items at the same time. The customer is getting the best products available but at a better price than would be possible if the items were purchased individually. When it comes to calculating costs and prices, Cybex looks for the right balance—which is right in step with the company's philosophy that "life is about finding the perfect balance."

Questions

1. Do you think Cybex would be more successful if the company began producing a lower-priced line of equipment and adopted a volume pricing objective for that line? Why or why not?
2. How might Cybex account for demand in its cost-plus approach to pricing?
3. Identify several pricing challenges that Cybex is likely to be facing in international markets.
4. As a consumer, how do you respond to prestige pricing? Are you attracted to items priced this way or are you a bargain hunter?

SOURCES: Cybex International Web site, http://www.cybexintl.com, accessed January 16, 2003; "Cybex International, Inc.," Hoover's Online, http://www.hoovers.com, accessed January 16, 2003; Sam Greengard, "Make for Midsize," *Industry Week*, July 1, 2002, http://www.industryweek.com.

VIDEO CASE 14.2   Bombardier Lets Prices Soar

Are you one of those rare people with literally too much cash? You realize that your bank is paying you next to nothing in interest on your excess deposits and want to take your passion for flying to another level by buying your own plane. If those excess dollars add up to several million dollars, Bombardier Aerospace may be able to make your dream come true. Montreal-based Bombardier has a global workforce of 33,000 people and includes three major categories of aircraft in its product lines: commercial jets, business jets, and amphibious aircraft. Its commercial jets are purchased by airlines around the world, including China's Shandong Airlines, which recently purchased two 70-seat regional jets. Business jets are purchased by wealthy individuals, large- and medium-sized businesses, and government agencies, as well as heads of state. They range in price from the $5 million Learjet to the $40 million Bombardier Global Express. The company's amphibious aircraft are purchased primarily to be used in putting out forest fires.

Claude Chidiac, Bombardier's director of planning and strategy for business aircraft, explains how his company arrives at and manages its prices for different aircraft. "This is a highly differentiated, low-volume industry with a highly educated buyer, and pricing is pretty much diametrically opposed to the pricing of commodities," he says. Features and capabilities of the different aircraft play an enormous part in how each plane is priced. The $5 million Learjet can carry four to five passengers in a relatively small cabin and is capable of traveling about 1,500 miles without refueling. At the other end of the scale, the $40 million Global Express has room for up to 20 passengers and can fly nonstop from New York to Tokyo.

Although Bombardier marketers maintain standard pricing procedures worldwide, price flexibility exists as a result of numerous variables that come into play in establishing, quoting, and finalizing actual prices. "Different buyers value different things and will be prepared to pay different amounts of money [for them]," notes Chidiac. Typically, a private purchaser is interested in buying a single plane. By contrast, a government agency or a business purchaser might want to replace its entire fleet of 10 to 20 aircraft. In the latter situations, the final price is much more likely to be the result of extensive negotiations. And when a business buyer is considering similar aircraft from a competitor, competitive bidding may become the method of finalizing the purchase decision. On the other hand, Chidiac points out that the buyer may decide to pay a higher price for Bombardiers because they better meet the unique needs of the company or government agency. For example, sometimes a company already owns a Bombardier jet, and its staff is trained to maintain and fly it. In this case, top management may limit its choices to Bombardier planes to avoid the expenses involved in retraining staff on aircraft available from competitors.

Chidiac refers to his company's pricing strategy as either *price leader* or *features leader.* He explains, "We see where the biggest profit potential is and try to fill the gaps [between the traditional aircraft offerings]." During the development of its new super-midsized Continental jet, Bombardier waited until several competitors announced their entries into the new market—and then quoted features and prices for its new Continental plane. Then Bombardier executives carefully studied their overall costs and decided to offer the new Continental jet at about $11 million, an attention-getting 21 percent below the $14 million price tag on competing jets. Not surprisingly, the new jet has proven to be an extremely successful addition to the Bombardier product offerings. By implementing a penetration pricing strategy for the new aircraft, Bombardier became the price leader, forcing competitors to follow suit or risk pricing themselves out of the market.

Bombardier's *features leader* pricing strategy applies to the company's top-of-the-line models like the Global Express. "Pricing does not need to be lower or even on par with the competition because [the plane's] features and capabilities are leaders [in the industry]," explains Chidiac.

Bombardier marketers pay special attention to managing the price structure of their aircraft as they move through each stage of the product life cycle. Chidiac notes that the company typically increases prices by one percent to three percent each year, rather than making radical changes at later PLC stages. "One reason that a customer selects one plane over another is residual value," he explains. So a consistent small increase helps an older aircraft maintain its value without discouraging new customers from making a purchase. Although Chidiac believes that Bombardier might be able to justify as much as a four-percent price increase in a few cases, he also feels that a price hike of five percent or greater would probably drive customers away.

Last—but certainly not least—Chidiac emphasizes the fact that "selling business jets is primarily a relationship. Face it; it's a purchase of $5 million to $40 million." So Bombardier's sales directors know their territories and they know their customers. They build and continue to strengthen relationships not only with the flight staff of their clients but also with the CEO and others involved in making aircraft purchase decisions.

But once a customer decides to buy a Bombardier jet, what about delivery? Is it flown directly to the buyer's door (or specified location) as part of the purchase price? No, explains Chidiac, shipping is not usually included. The customer travels to Montreal to take ownership of the aircraft and then flies it home. "It's kind of romantic that way," adds Chidiac with a smile.

Questions

1. Do you think that a competitive pricing strategy would be effective for Bombardier? Why or why not?
2. Why is it possible for Bombardier to adopt a policy of price flexibility?
3. When might psychological pricing come into play for Bombardier products?
4. What challenges might Bombardier face in establishing prices worldwide?

SOURCES: Bombardier Aerospace Web site, http://www.bombardier.com, accessed January 18, 2003; "Bombardier Sells CRJ700 Aircraft to Shandong Airlines of China," press release, September 6, 2002, http://www.bombardier.com.

 VIDEO CASE 15.2   Ipswich Shellfish Delivers Fresh Lobster

From Maine to Rhode Island, the New England coast is famous for its fresh seafood. Seven days a week, area restaurants serve a variety of fish, scallops, shrimp, crab, and the king of shellfish: the lobster. At premium prices, lobster is considered a delicacy, even by locals who scoop them out of saltwater tanks at the supermarket. It's hard to believe that 300 years ago, when the first European settlers arrived at Cape Cod, thousands of lobsters floated in the waves and rolled ashore each day. In fact, they were often used as bait by fishermen and were considered "junk" seafood by colonists.

Today, restaurants steam, boil, broil, and bake these creatures for customers who enjoy dipping the sweet meat in bowls of melted butter or clam juice and don't mind paying top dollar to do so. Granted, New Englanders can enjoy this treat for a lot less money than those who live in other areas of the country because distribution channels are shorter. People who live

close enough to the ocean can often go right down to the dock to buy their lobsters directly from locals who tend the lobster traps in area waters. Even if they buy them at the supermarket or order them at a restaurant, the lobsters haven't traveled very far. But it's the job of companies like Ipswich Shellfish to get the lobsters wherever they are going within 24 hours—fresh, alive, and healthy. And the destination might be local, across the country, Europe, or even Japan.

Ipswich Shellfish Co., headquartered in the coastal town of Ipswich, Massachusetts, was started in 1935 by Alexis Pappas's father. "It's a crazy business," says Pappas, who is now the company's general manager. That's because the price and availability of lobster change every day, which is why you often see "Market Price" listed for lobster on a typical restaurant menu. In addition, Ipswich Shellfish must negotiate purchase prices with each fisherman, then turn around and negotiate selling prices with each customer, usually a restaurant buyer. Then there is the time crunch. Lobsters have to be delivered fresh and on time, regardless of the destination. Unlike other types of seafood, lobsters must be delivered alive to be cooked and eaten safely. "Every hour is essential because no one wants dead lobsters," explains Pappas.

Although some lobstermen engage in direct selling to individual household shoppers or to restaurant food purchasers, many sell their catch to companies like Ipswich Shellfish, who then resell them to restaurants and supermarkets. Because it is a small company, Ipswich concentrates on the restaurant industry as its core business. "We stick to what we do best," says Pappas. Ipswich occasionally purchases an order of lobster from a broker in Canada, but the company does most of its business with local fishermen. Once the lobsters come off the boat, they are placed in a holding tank at Ipswich Shellfish's facility, where they are weighed so that Pappas knows what to charge his customers. Then the lobsters are packed in specially insulated boxes and loaded onto one of the firm's 100 trucks, which can transport 45,000 pounds of seafood at a time—either en route elsewhere in New England, or to Boston's Logan Airport, where they are flown to U.S. destinations or to England, Italy, or Japan. Ipswich maintains vital relations with air carriers such as FedEx and several major airlines transporting both freight and passengers, as well as with highway carriers Common Carrier Refrigerated and Freezer Trucks.

But international distribution of Ipswich's crustaceans is a different matter. Ipswich relies on independent distributors to market its seafood in both Europe and Japan. The reason: Pappas believes that the distributors in those regions know their markets better and can do a better job at marketing their products—and getting them delivered efficiently.

Why doesn't Ipswich purchase and maintain its own fleet of lobster boats? Pappas explains that buying directly from independent fishermen provides his company with more flexibility and choice. If one boat doesn't have a good catch on a given day, he can always go to another, thus ensuring both quality

and adequate supplies to meet the needs of Ipswich customers. On the other hand, he prefers to maintain his own fleet of delivery trucks because, he says, "I can't count on anyone else to deliver our lobsters on time."

Ipswich has recently expanded to include the Internet as part of its marketing and distribution channels. The company now has two Web sites—one for final consumers and another for business customers. Consumers can visit http://www.ipswichfishmarket.com to order a traditional New England clambake complete with lobsters and steamer clams for an entire family, delivered right to their door. Business customers can log on to http://www.ipswichshellfish.com to order lobsters, sweet Ipswich clams, and other products in bulk. Customers who are lucky enough to live nearby can visit the company's gourmet seafood takeout shop in Ipswich. That evening they can sit down in their own homes to enjoy a delicious dinner caught fresh that morning—sweet, tender, and dipped in warm melted butter.

Questions

1. What product characteristics dictate Ipswich Shellfish's optimal marketing channel strategy?
2. What kinds of channel conflict might Ipswich Shellfish have to deal with?
3. Ipswich Shellfish has decided not to engage in backward or forward integration (other than operating its own fleet of delivery trucks). Do you think this will hinder or help the company's growth in the future?
4. Transportation is a key element in Ipswich Shellfish's physical distribution system. Why is intermodal coordination so important to this company?

SOURCES: Ipswich Shellfish Web sites, http://www.ipswichshellfish.com and http://www.ipswichfishmarket.com, accessed January 9, 2003; "Ipswich Fishmarket Case Study," Integrated Information Systems, http://www.iisweb.com, accessed January 9, 2003; Tonia Noell Molinski, "Ipswich Shellfish Keeps It Fresh," Pulse 2001, Essex County Newspapers, April 6, 2001, http://www.northshoreonline.com.

VIDEO CASE 16.2   Neiman Marcus Takes Care of Its Customers

Would you drive several hours just to shop at your favorite store? Can you imagine spending $3,000 a year at that store, just to earn frequent-shopping points? Some loyal Neiman Marcus customers do just that. Neiman Marcus is part of their lifestyle, which is exactly what the retailer wants to be. Even if you have never set foot in a

Neiman Marcus store or browsed through *The Book*—the store's famous catalog—you have probably heard the name. Neiman Marcus is known around the world as a specialty retailer offering high-end fashion, designer jewelry, home furnishings, and gifts to die for. Neiman Marcus is based in Dallas, where it's rumored that everything is bigger, better, pricier, and more glamorous. The first store opened during the early years of the 20th century, and the company has gradually expanded across the country to 15 states and more than 30 locations from Boston to Southern California.

Neiman Marcus targets a market that includes "households with an income of $150,000 a year or more," says Billy Payton, vice president of marketing and customer programs. Most of the customers are women between the ages of 35 and 55, but men feel just as comfortable walking through the doors of any Neiman Marcus store, whether they are shopping for themselves or for their wives. Payton notes that the Neiman's customer "appreciates fashion and appreciates quality in merchandise and gifts and apparel."

To serve its target market, Neiman Marcus adopts several fundamental retail strategies. One is merchandising. Neiman's, as it is affectionately called by its customers, carries luxury goods from around the world. Quality and style are a vital part of the lineup, notes Pam Ames, sales associate in the gift gallery. Apparel must be chic; home furnishings must be unique. Price is another component of the strategy. Neiman's customers expect to pay top dollar—it's part of the cachet of shopping there—but they also expect value in their purchases. Ames observes that part of her job is educating customers about why certain goods are priced the way they are: Perhaps one item is an antique, or another is one of a kind. But beyond the exclusive merchandise, perhaps the most important part of Neiman's strategy is customer service.

"Salespeople have great relationships with the clientele," says Ames. Each salesperson keeps detailed information about the preferences of his or her customers on file, including a favored designer line of clothes or a cherished type of Christmas ornament. They all go out of their way to accommodate customers in any way they can. Ames says she thinks nothing of dropping a dress off at a customer's home during her lunch break or calling a customer when an item comes in that she thinks the customer would like to see. And Neiman's customers expect this special treatment. "Customers at Neiman Marcus are very sophisticated and have a high taste level. We match that," says Ames. Sales associates at Neiman's often act as personal shoppers because their customers are so busy. The extra effort pays off, as the relationships built between Neiman's and its customers often last across generations. "This is about building a family relationship, and generations of a family continuing to find Neiman Marcus the store that takes care of their fashion needs and lifestyle needs," says Billy Payton.

One special way that Neiman's cements this relationship for its preferred customers is with the InCircle Program, a purchase reward program in which customers earn one point for each dollar spent at the store during the year. If they reach 3,000 points, they are automatically part of the InCircle Program. They can then redeem those points for shopping rewards—but the rewards aren't cell phones or magazine subscriptions. Instead, they may include trips to special events such as the Kentucky Derby or the Super Bowl, vacations to Paris or London, or gifts such as a new Jaguar. Of course, the more the customer spends, the larger the reward. The InCircle Program was a novel idea when it was introduced back in 1984, but its success—not to mention imitation by other retailers—has stood the test of time. Payton observes that, over the years, the InCircle Program has helped identify the store's best customers as well as create branding for Neiman Marcus.

Although Neiman's has traditionally focused on loyal, long-term customers, marketers have begun to recognize that many consumers visit Neiman's only occasionally, often in search of a special item, so the company is beginning to cultivate them as well. Payton comments that *The Book* is a good way for newer, occasional shoppers to get to know the store better. "It's about the lifestyle branding of Neiman Marcus and the goods we carry," he explains. The store is also making greater use of the Internet to attract younger consumers. "We're constantly trying to stay in tune with customers' needs from goods to services," he says. That means allowing them to shop from the comfort of home or meeting their needs the minute they set foot in the door until they leave. And it includes gift packaging, clean restrooms, good food in the store's restaurant, and smooth transactions. Not to mention, of course, the shopping.

Questions

1. Describe other retail strategies that Neiman's could use to attract the occasional shopper to its stores.
2. If Neiman's decided to carry some slightly less expensive merchandise as a strategy for attracting younger or less affluent customers, do you think it would hurt or help the business? Why?
3. How would you classify Neiman's by the service it provides? Why is this classification an important part of the store's marketing strategy?
4. Briefly describe your idea for a Neiman's sales promotion—say, for a new line of clothing, for a holiday event, or for a special selection of rewards for InCircle customers.

SOURCES: Neiman Marcus Web site, http://www.neimanmarcus.com, accessed January 12, 2003; "Business Summary," Yahoo!, September 12, 2002, http://biz.yahoo.com; "Neiman Marcus Tops Forecasts," *Smart Money*, September 10, 2002, http://www.smartmoney.com; "Neiman Marcus Sows Seeds for a Turnaround," September 10, 2002, http://www.forbes.com.

VIDEO CASE 17.2 Cherry Capital Airport Keeps People Flying

On September 11, 2001, air travel as we know it changed forever. After four commercial jets were crashed by terrorists, U.S. air space was closed for several days, thousands of air travelers were stranded far from their destinations, and airports remained silent. When jet engines around the country finally started up again, airlines flew empty seats back and forth across the nation. No one wanted to fly, and no one blamed anyone who didn't want to set foot on a plane. All kinds of businesses suffered as a result, including hotels and restaurants, travel agencies, and airports and their retail tenants. Cherry Capital Airport, located outside Traverse City in northwestern Michigan, was no exception. Some airlines cut back on service to the airport despite the fact that the facility had recently won $1.7 million in federal grants to construct a new terminal building and provide aircraft parking gates. There just seemed to be no point in building new buildings if people weren't going to use them.

It's difficult to believe that the terrorist attacks weren't the first devastating blow dealt to the airline industry, but they weren't. Back in the mid-1980s, federal deregulation of the industry sent many carriers spiraling out of control. There is no question that the events of 2001 were far more tragic and had a much greater effect on the American public, but it is helpful to examine how one airport pulled through the last crisis in order to find answers to how it may pull through this one.

The airline deregulation of 15 years ago left small airports like Cherry Capital in disarray when they lost their government subsidies. Losing these funds forced airport managers to struggle to provide the kind of service that their airline customers and travelers had come to expect. As airlines reduced the number of flights into and out of Cherry Capital, this began to spill over to companies considering relocating to the Traverse City area. Concerns about access to good air service resulted in several relocation decisions being put on hold, and the local economy began to slow down. Managers at Cherry Capital Airport knew they had to do something to revitalize their facility and its operations.

Airport director Steve Cassens, along with other marketers, developed an integrated marketing communications strategy based on the goal of improving service and increasing passenger and airline traffic. First, they targeted their audiences: passengers, businesses, airlines, and travel agents. Although travel agents now play a smaller role in the air travel industry as more and more air travelers choose to book trips through the Internet, at the time they were an important part of the communications loop. Cassens and his team discovered that many potential passengers were people who had relocated to the

area for a more relaxed lifestyle, but they were still sophisticated enough to want the top-notch air service they had become accustomed to in Chicago or Detroit. Marketers also confirmed that business travelers were the lifeblood of the airlines and the airport because they would fly regularly and pay full fare. Then they conducted marketing research aimed at identifying travel patterns, customer preferences, and travel priorities. Through the research, they learned that travelers were most concerned with frequency of flights, fares, and the type of equipment provided (i.e., jets).

To get the message out that Cherry Capital Airport was a great place to fly to and from, Cassens and his marketers used a combination of personal selling, public relations, sales promotion, and advertising. "The way that you inform people is to get out there and talk to them," explains Cassens. "Those people can pass that [information] along." In this case, airport representatives made calls on travel agents to discuss ways to increase business—both for the travel agents and the airports. Eventually, they conducted sales promotions through some travel agencies. Marketers worked hard to improve air service to three nearby hubs: Chicago, Detroit, and Minneapolis. Cherry Capital also sponsored special events such as air shows to bring people to the airport and get them accustomed to the environment. In this way, prospective customers became familiar with the parking, the layout of the airport, and the people who worked in and around the facility. Cherry Capital has always enjoyed good relations with the media, then and now. Cassens explains that it just makes sense to help the media with news stories, try to understand their deadlines, and cooperate whenever possible. "It doesn't mean we always get a good story," he says. But at least the airport has a positive relationship with journalists. Finally, Cassens worked with advertising agency Brauer Productions to come up with a memorable, award-winning commercial featuring a goose that decided he'd rather fly than walk.

Today, Cherry Capital Airport, like other small airports, is feeling the harsh effects of September 2001. But it is surviving. Air activity in the year following the tragedy declined, then remained flat with hopes of increasing again. In 2001, about 400,000 travelers flew from Cherry Capital, and with the completion of the new terminal building, more should begin to pass through the gates on their way to and from the skies.

Questions

1. As travelers increasingly use the Internet for their travel plans, how might Cherry Capital incorporate this trend into its IMC strategy?

2. How could Cherry Capital use a pulling strategy? How could the airport use a pushing strategy?

3. Describe your idea for a direct marketing piece that Cherry Capital might target to either airlines or potential passengers.

4. In the current environment, what kinds of marketing messages might Cherry Capital be able to convey to the public that could be socially or economically important?

SOURCES: Cherry Capital Airport Web site, http://www.tvcairport.com, accessed January 13, 2003; "Saginaw and Traverse City Airports to Receive Funding," press release, May 2, 2001, http://levin.senate.gov.

 VIDEO CASE 18.2

Oxygen Media and Mullen Advertising Team Up for Women's Programming

Launching a new cable television channel is a long shot. Not only do start-up costs quickly climb into the millions, but success will ultimately be calculated based on the number of viewers the new channel attracts—and the money spent on advertising by marketers who want to communicate with these viewers. Although as many as 20 to 25 new channels enter the competitive fray each year, most of them fail before their fifth birthday. So far, however, Oxygen Media has proven to be a survivor. Founded in 1998 by media moguls Oprah Winfrey, Marcy Carsey, Geraldine Laybourne, Tom Werner, and Caryn Mandabach, Oxygen's focus was on providing programming, information, and entertainment for its target market: women. In addition, it would take a 21st century approach to communications, offering viewers the combined channels of TV and Oxygen's Internet site. "Oxygen is predominantly a television concept. . . . It's a TV network with an Internet attitude," explains Paul Silverman, founding creative director of Mullen Advertising, Oxygen's advertising agency.

Oxygen marketers knew the importance of attracting viewers and advertisers even before launching the channel— and that meant a heavy dose of promotion designed to increase awareness and interest. The firm's founders turned to Massachusetts-based Mullen Advertising, known for its creative, memorable ads, to perform its magic for the new channel. Although the target audience consists of women, that designation needed to be further refined since females make up more than half of the TV viewing audience. The Oxygen woman can be viewed in terms of psychographics. As Christine Hamilton, head of Oxygen brand planning at Mullen, puts it, "We describe our market in a psychographic sense. The Oxygen woman is someone who is adventurous." Which explains how Mullen came up with the now-famous ad for Oxygen that first aired during the Super Bowl. Often referred to as the "clenched-fist ad," the commercial is set in the newborn nursery at a hospital, where a nurse carefully places a pink knitted cap on the head of a baby girl. Within seconds, the cap is on the floor. In the next few seconds, more caps are on the floor, and pink booties are flying out of other bassinets in the nursery, with accompanying clenched baby girl fists in the air. "A new voice," declares the tagline. "For women, by women."

This wasn't the only component in Oxygen's promotional mix—nor did it spring to the screen fully formed. An entire team of Mullen specialists, working with Oxygen employees, brought the idea to fruition. All of Mullen's communications about Oxygen have focused on developing a brand. "A brand is a personality," notes Paul Silverman. From the beginning, Mullen set out to give life to Oxygen's personality. "We have a strategic branding approach for every piece of communication we do," says Christine Hamilton. "It's really critical to have a united message." So every component of the Oxygen promotional mix, from TV ads to special promotional events, sends the same message about Oxygen as a brand.

To develop a united message, Mullen staff went out and talked to women about their views of the media. What types of programming did they want? How did they want to see women portrayed on television? What kind of information was important to them? Women the nation over were eager to see programming that featured women in stronger, more active roles. Oxygen was ready to deliver. "It was an opportunity to celebrate a woman being a woman instead of a victim," recalls Bruce Gold, senior vice president and Oxygen account director at Mullen. "But it's man-friendly," says Christine Hamilton.

Mullen had to convince both cable operators and viewers that Oxygen would be a viable station. So, they took Oxygen's message on tour—a special promotional tour called the *Oxygen Tank Tour*. An Airstream trailer toured a number of cities and states, setting up in town centers and village squares, to offer consumers a peek at the new Web site, recruiting young reporters who could ultimately contribute content, and generally "making a lot of noise" in local markets. In addition, they hooked up with radio stations in every market they toured and visited universities to deliver their message among college students, faculty, and staff. Meanwhile, Mullen marketers knocked on the doors of cable operators, trying to persuade them to carry the new station for their subscribers.

Six years after its founding, the Oxygen network offers original programming that includes comedy series such as *O2Be* and *Girls Behaving Badly;* documentaries such as *Women of Rockaway,* which commemorates several widows of September 11, 2001; newsmagazine shows such as *Candice Checks It Out,* starring Candice Bergen; interview shows such as *Eavesdropping with Alan Cumming;* and original movies. Oxygen also airs several health and lifestyle programs. By 2003, the station had captured more than 41 million subscribers, climbing by over a million in one 30-day period. During that period, large cable operators such as AT&T Broadband, Time Warner Cable, Cablevision, Cox, and Charter Communications jumped on the bandwagon to distribute the station in markets such as Boston; Houston; Bakersfield, California; and Lehigh Valley, Pennsylvania. In addition, Oxygen recently received the National Affiliate Sales Award from the Cable Television Advertising Bureau.

While the Oxygen network seems to be breathing well on its own, the Web portal has been struggling somewhat for air. "We are doing extremely well on the television side of our business," notes Oxygen CEO Geraldine Laybourne. "However, the online side is simply not structured in a way that it can sustain itself economically," which means that Oxygen and Mullen marketers will refocus the site and its message. For a while, they report, Oxygen.com will serve as a tool to promote the cable network instead of producing its own content. This doesn't mean that the Internet site can't be resuscitated in the future. But Oxygen marketers are focusing on the component that their markets seem to want most—television programming. When you think of television, they hope you'll think of Oxygen because, as the commercial says, "It's in you."

Questions

1. In what ways do Mullen's promotional efforts satisfy the three major advertising objectives?
2. Suggest methods with which Mullen might use comparative advertising in promoting the Oxygen channel.
3. Describe the key points that should be included in a celebrity ad that might be used in the Oxygen promotional campaign. Explain why your choice of celebrity advertising—as well as the celebrity you suggested—are sound.
4. After reviewing Oxygen.com, outline the steps you feel that Oxygen and its advertising agency need to take to revitalize the site.

SOURCES: Oxygen Media Web site, http://www.oxygen.com, accessed January 29, 2003; "The Women-Focused Web Portal Loses Most of Its Staff, Will Undergo a Drastic Change in Mission," *INT Media Group,* August 29, 2002; "Oxygen Receives National Affiliate Sales Award," *Entertainment Wire,* June 25, 2002, http://hoovnews.hoovers.com; "Oxygen Bypasses 41 Million Subscribers," *Entertainment Wire,* June 18, 2002, http://hoovnews.hoovers.com.

VIDEO CASE 19.2   Concept2 Rows to Success

In 1976, brothers Pete and Dick Dreissigacker decided to try out for the U.S. Olympic Rowing Team. During their training for the trials, they started tinkering with new designs for a better oar. Pete is a design engineer; Dick is a mechanical engineer. In the end, the brothers didn't make the final cut for the team, but they did come up with an oar design that is now a standard for rowers around the world. Made from synthetic materials instead of wood, the oars are stronger, lighter, and cheaper than their traditional counterparts.

The brothers moved to Vermont, where they continued to row but discovered that the cold winters in northern Vermont make for a pretty short rowing season. The winters there aren't just cold—the lakes and rivers tend to freeze over. And while they continued to produce and sell their oars, Pete and Dick also began to devote time to their ideas about how to improve existing designs for rowing machines. That way, the Dreissigackers and their friends could train year-round. To build the first rowing machine, they turned Pete's old bicycle upside down, nailed it to the floor, and added a handle and sliding seat.

Twenty-eight years later, the Concept2 rower, which comes in several models priced at about $1,000, is still sold directly to business and other organizational customers as well as final purchasers, directly from the Dreissigackers' factory in Morrisville, Vermont. Organizational customers fall into one of three categories: health and fitness clubs (including private fitness centers, family Ys, and hospital rehabilitation centers), fitness centers in hotels and resorts, and high schools and universities. In addition, final customers also make direct purchases through telephone orders or by using the firm's Web site. Outside the U.S. and Canada, Concept2 markets its oars and rowers and provides customer service in 47 countries through authorized worldwide dealers.

Judy Geer, wife of cofounder Dick Dreissigacker, believes that the firm's direct channel is the most important component of its sales success. That's because selling directly to the customer—whether it's a health club or an individual rower—offers so many advantages for both Concept2 and the customer. The original decision to rely on direct selling resulted from the fact that retail networks for rowing gear didn't exist in 1976. Over time, however, Pete and Dick learned that this direct channel not only keeps the price of goods lower for customers but also offers benefits for Concept2. First, it keeps the price of the firm's products lower for customers. Second, it helps the firm develop a sense of community among its customers. Third, it gives Concept2 marketers more control over what is being said about its products during sales efforts. The big drawback, says Geer, is that many potential customers remain unaware of the company and its products because they are unable to be introduced to, learn about, try out, and purchase them from retail specialty fitness stores nearby.

Geer explains that the approach Concept2 takes to personal selling is considerably different from that of firms in other industries. "Our most effective selling is our own customers selling the machine to their friends," she says. "Early on, word of mouth was our biggest and most effective sales technique." This has remained the case today. "We prefer not to induce or convince someone to buy [our products]. We'd rather educate someone about the sport of rowing and our machine." Often, says Geer, people call the company because they have already tried the machine—at a health club or at a friend's house. In fact, she estimates that roughly one customer in three finds Concept2 this way. A potential customer might locate the firm's Web site, then send an e-mail or call the firm's toll-free telephone number to request brochures, ask questions about the product, or make a purchase. If he or she hasn't tried the machine yet, a member of the Concept2 sales staff will locate a nearby club to arrange a trial run. Of course, says Geer, some people just call up and purchase the machine because they are already convinced of its quality and benefits.

Concept2 sales representatives are trained to understand not only who the company's customers are but also how to use the machines themselves. "Everybody gets a chance to row," notes Geer. Concept2 customers tend to fall into two categories: serious rowers and recreational rowers. Serious rowers are those who use the Concept2 rower as a training vehicle for actual outdoor rowing events. Recreational rowers are those who use the machine for fitness. So Concept2 has developed a range of customer service programs to meet the needs of both types of customers. The company produces a semiannual newsletter for customers, containing stories about other rowers, rowing tips, and results of the 1 million meter rowing club. (Rowing clubs also exist for 5 million, 10 million, and 15 million meters.) Customers keep an online log recording the number of meters they have rowed on their machines and receive a T-shirt, patch, and certificate upon completion of each distance. They can also compare their results with other rowers' results on the Concept2 Web site. Geer observes that recreational rowers really respond to these marketing efforts because they need more motivation and sense of community than do competitive rowers, who are already part of the rowing community.

Geer believes that Concept2 has been able to achieve "a desirable level of success," growing at 5 to 15 percent a year, by maintaining a low-key, no-pressure sales strategy. "Our approach to personal selling is information, honesty, and enthusiasm," she says. "It's definitely not a hard sell."

Questions

1. What conditions make personal selling so important to Concept2's promotional mix?
2. How would you categorize Concept2's approach to personal selling based on the four major trends? Which of the four alternative channels for serving customers shown in Figure 19.3 best describes the firm?
3. Is the demonstration phase of the personal selling process important at Concept2? Why or why not?
4. Every company needs to be aware of ethical issues in selling. How does Concept2's approach to selling help the company avoid ethical problems?

SOURCES: Concept2 Web site, http://www.concept2.com, accessed January 30, 2003; Peter Dreissigacker, "Reflections on 25 Years at Concept2," *The Concept 2 Update*, Fall 2001.

Krispy Kreme Continuing Case Contents

Part 1   KRISPY KREME Continuing Case

Consumers Are Sweet on Krispy Kreme

When it comes to doughnuts, America is a nation of Homer Simpsons. Despite knowing that each pastry isn't the healthiest of foods, we still love them. Add a cup of coffee or a carbonated soft drink and millions of time-pressed people on the go consider it breakfast. Millions more list doughnuts as one of their favorite snack foods. In a typical year, Americans will eat about 10 billion doughnuts, or roughly 40 for every man, woman, and child. Among the typical favorites are glazed, chocolate covered, jelly stuffed, spicy cinnamon, rich cream filled, or simple frosted.

Blame this infatuation on the Dutch settlers who brought their *olie-kochen,* or fried cakes, with them to these shores back in the 1640s. The cakes contained nuts embedded in the center, so colonists combined the words *dough* and *nut* to create the name that stuck: *doughnuts.* Two hundred years later, Hanson Gregory, a Rockport, Maine, sea captain, began the practice of punching a hole in each cake. In the 1920s, when the first doughnut-making machines were perfected, the kitchen craft of doughnut making turned into a growing industry.

Several decades later, a young man named Vernon Carver Rudolph bought a doughnut shop in Kentucky from a French chef. As part of the deal, Rudolph received the secret recipe for a yeast-raised doughnut. A few years later, he moved the business to Winston-Salem, North Carolina, where he opened a bakery called Krispy Kreme Doughnuts and began selling his output to area grocery stores and local eateries. As word of mouth spread about the tasty doughnuts, a growing number of consumers began to trek to the bakery to ask if they could buy the hot doughnuts. Seeing a new marketing opportunity, Rudolph responded by cutting a hole in one wall of the bakery for a convenient entry and began selling his freshly made doughnuts directly to consumers.

Today, Krispy Kreme has grown far beyond its roots in the southeast states of the U.S. to become one of the nation's most popular doughnuts. Although the 5,000 retail outlets of industry leader Dunkin' Donuts far exceed Krispy Kreme's 240-plus shops in 34 states, Krispy Kreme is in the midst of implementing its strategic plan to grow and market its products in every region of the U.S. and Canada and to begin an international expansion designed to make Krispy Kreme the favorite of pastry lovers on every continent. Shops have already opened in Canada, and Krispy Kreme is beginning international expansion into Mexico and South America, Japan, South Korea, Australia, Spain, and the United Kingdom. To improve consumer access to fresh doughnuts—and to expand sales opportunities—Krispy Kreme marketers have agreements with a growing number of grocery chains, convenience stores, and gas stations to stock their fresh doughnuts in kiosk-type areas every morning. Approximately five million Krispy Kreme doughnuts are freshly baked every day—or a total of almost two billion a year.

The recent economic downturn witnessed industry after industry postponing outlays for high-cost investments in technology and market expansion until an economic recovery takes place. How has Krispy Kreme managed to succeed in its aggressive market expansion strategy in the midst of such a shaky economy and so much economic uncertainty? A fundamental requirement for success in this mature industry filled with thousands of competitors ranging from giants like Dunkin' Donuts to the many regional and local producers is a high-quality, good-tasting product. And consumers love Krispy Kreme doughnuts. In a recent taste test conducted by *Good Housekeeping,* Krispy Kreme came out on top in two major categories: glazed and cake. So the product continues to be high quality and just what consumers crave. Another factor is that, at a price of about 60 cents for each doughnut, they're a bargain compared with other snack foods. Still another is the fact that once consumers try Krispy Kreme, they tend to become fiercely loyal, make repeat purchases, and communicate this loyalty to coworkers, family, and friends.

The company's expansion from its southeast U.S. roots has been aided enormously by the so-called "Krispy Kreme phenomenon." As word spread about each initial store in a new market, it became a media event complete with live radio and TV coverage, informal taste tests, and volumes of publicity. Krispy Kreme's entry into the New York City market was the talk of the town, encouraged by company marketers who delivered fresh "hot doughnuts" directly to network TV and radio morning programs and to the casts of financial news cable broadcasts. People waited in line for 15 hours to be first to sample the sweets. In Denver, the line stretched around the block despite a foot of snow on the ground. Some of these enthusiasts had savored Krispy Kreme doughnuts elsewhere in the country; others came because of word of mouth.

Krispy Kreme builds on this relationship in a variety of ways, from presenting special sales promotions to offering memorabilia such as Krispy Kreme T-shirts and hats on its Web site. Fans can also become members of Friends of Krispy Kreme via the Web site, through which they receive a monthly e-mailed newsletter about the company, its special events, and new varieties of doughnuts. Web site visitors are asked to complete an online survey, which gives them an opportunity to express their level of satisfaction with the company and its products—this supplies marketers with valuable information with which to make needed adjustments to their marketing plans.

Competition is one environmental threat that Krispy Kreme faces daily. When the company announced its plans to open its first outlet in Chicago's Loop, competitors such as Dunkin' Donuts—which already had shops nearby—didn't stand by idly. Opening day at the new Krispy Kreme saw Dunkin' Donuts representatives outside handing out free doughnuts. Other competitors were also there to offer discount coupons for their brands. But even though major competitors may offer more varieties of doughnuts, none has been able to match Krispy Kreme's signature: the Hot Original Glazed doughnut.

Krispy Kreme doughnuts have also proved to be an ideal product for charity giveaways and fundraisers. They are inexpensive and easy to transport, and everyone loves them. So the company often donates the doughnuts outright or charges wholesale prices to charitable organizations that keep the profits for their causes. "We helped raise over $27 million for various non-profit organizations in fiscal year 2002," says Stan Parker, senior vice president of marketing. "We get e-mails all the time from people who sold our doughnuts as kids, years ago, to raise money for baseball uniforms or to go on a field trip." Parker notes that the company wants "to be involved in the community."

Visit a Krispy Kreme shop and you won't go away thirsty either. You can sip specially roasted coffee or espresso, guzzle one of the frozen drinks, or down a cold glass of milk on a hot day. In fact, some Krispy Kreme franchisees report that coffee sales account for up to 15 percent of their revenues. You can also relax in a nostalgic atmosphere—with all the modern-day comforts—where, for just a few moments, you can forget about your diet and your fitness class and simply enjoy some true comfort food.

Questions

1. Free promotion resulting from "the Krispy Kreme phenomenon" generates consumer interest in a way that paid ads could never duplicate. What other examples of similar phenomena have you observed with other products or retail outlets? Why does the phenomenon appear to apply to these examples and not to others?

2. In what ways might Krispy Kreme use relationship marketing to gain an edge over a larger competitor such as Dunkin' Donuts?

3. Identify what you think might be some of Krispy Kreme's strengths, weaknesses, opportunities, and threats over the next few years.

4. Krispy Kreme fulfills the philanthropic level of the social responsibility pyramid. In what ways might marketers use this as part of the company's marketing strategy?

5. What types of challenges might Krispy Kreme face as it prepares to enter markets in regions like Asia and South America?

SOURCES: Company Web site, http://www.krispykreme.com, accessed January 26, 2003; Benedict Carey, "Doughnuts Are Heavy Hitters in U.S. Diet," *Mobile Register,* September 30, 2002, pp. D1, D3; Rob Kaiser, "Krispy Kreme Incursion Sweetens Rivalry," *The Chicago Tribune,* September 24, 2002, http://www.chicagotribune.com; "Convenience Stores to Begin Selling Krispy Kreme Doughnuts," Hoover's Online, September 13, 2002, http://hoovnews.hoovers.com; Sid Smith, "The Selling of a Doughnut," *The Chicago Tribune,* May 2, 2002, http://www.chicagotribune.com.

Part 2   KRISPY KREME Continuing Case

Technology Helps Krispy Kreme Serve Up Treats

Say you're taking a road trip and you know it's a fact that, somewhere down the line, you're going to start craving your favorite treats. What if you could actually plan your route to include stops along the way at Krispy Kreme doughnut shops? You could drive so many miles and then stop for a doughnut break—whether you're touring Washington, D.C., or passing through Scottsdale, Arizona. The good news is that you *can* plan a doughnut-filled trip with the help of MapQuest—it's called the *Great American Doughnut Road Trip*. All you have to do is log on to **http://doughnuts .mapquest.com** and use the Krispy Kreme Store Locator menu to find the spots you want to visit. You'll get complete street-by-street directions and an easy-to-read map that you can print out. "Over the years, we've had many different road trip requests," says Tommy McGloin, senior vice president and general manager of MapQuest at AOL. "But the *Great American Doughnut Road Trip* definitely hits the sweet spot as a fun way to celebrate the new agreement between Krispy Kreme and MapQuest."

This is just one example of the creative ways in which Krispy Kreme is using technology to help build relationships with its customers while producing as many hot glazed doughnuts as consumers demand. Krispy Kreme, which is widely known for its Hot Original Glazed doughnuts and the homey atmosphere in its shops, is up to date in its pursuit of technology as a tool for customer-driven marketing. To help its franchisees, vendors, and corporate employees stay in touch with each other as well as exchange marketing and business information, Krispy Kreme opened an information portal called MyKrispyKreme. "As Krispy Kreme grows internationally, more employees will need remote access," notes Frank Hood, vice president of information services. "For that reason and others, we were motivated to set up a portal." With this extranet, approved users can view financial reports, access daily cash balances, and order supplies online from the company's distribution center. The exchange of information and increased efficiency translate to better service for Krispy Kreme doughnut customers.

Naturally, Krispy Kreme fans can't get enough of a good thing, so they flock to the company's Web site at **http://www.krispy kreme.com**, where they can purchase commemorative hats, mugs, sweatshirts, and collectibles—in fact, just about everything but the doughnuts themselves. They can order a vintage Krispy Kreme toy truck or a replica of an original Krispy Kreme store produced by Dept. 56 for its Original Snow Village line of collectibles. They can view the currently featured doughnut and enjoy tidbits of information about their favorites in the 25-variety lineup. They can find the shops located closest to their homes, join a fan club called Friends of Krispy Kreme—which will send them a monthly e-newsletter—and participate in a consumer survey conducted by Krispy Kreme marketers. E-mails from consumers, responses to the consumer survey, and feedback from those who participate in the Friends of Krispy Kreme club all supply marketers with valuable information about their loyal customers.

The survey, in particular, provides information about consumers' most recent experiences at Krispy Kreme shops. It is short, to the point, and easy to complete. Participants rate their most recent visit on a scale of 1 to 7 for nine categories, ranging from the taste of the doughnuts and the friendliness of employees to the accuracy of the order. The survey then asks the respondent to identify the store visited, the type of visit they made (drive through, carry out, or dine in), and the time of day. Customers then have the option to make other suggestions or comments about their Krispy Kreme experiences. The information is simple and straightforward, giving marketers a snapshot of how Krispy Kreme is doing in the eyes—and taste buds—of consumers.

Krispy Kreme has also turned to technology for the training and education of franchisees and corporate employees. The company hired Charlotte-based training systems specialist

Handshaw & Associates to help update its management training materials, including the development of a Web-based training system that uses graphics, videos, and animation. The training system is available to franchisees through their store-based computers via the MyKrispyKreme extranet and to other chain employees through their home computers when they register for training courses. When the courses are completed, computer-based test results are transferred directly to Krispy Kreme's human resource department via the extranet. Trainees needing more training in a certain area are referred back to the parts of the curriculum for which test results indicate that review or reinforcement is desirable.

All this Web-based technology is great, but you can't taste or smell it. So Krispy Kreme has continued to update its doughnut production technology, as well. Recently, the company unveiled its "Hot Doughnut Machine," which takes up less space, reduces labor, and costs less than the previous doughnut-making machines. This allows Krispy Kreme to open shops in smaller spaces such as airports, malls, and downtown urban areas, where its customers are. You can grab a Krispy Kreme on your way to catch a plane or between shops at the mall. Now that's technology that tastes great.

Questions

1. Access the Krispy Kreme Web site at **http://www.krispy kreme.com** and look at the ways the company already uses its site to enhance customer relationships. Then write a memo describing two or three more ways Krispy Kreme could use interactive tools and other Internet strategies to further strengthen these relationships.

2. Krispy Kreme must develop and maintain business-to-business relationships with its vendors and its franchisees. How might the company expand its MyKrispyKreme extranet or use other technologies to develop these relationships?

3. The customer satisfaction survey on Krispy Kreme's Web site is very short and covers a few key issues about consumers' visits to their nearby Krispy Kreme shops. As a marketer for Krispy Kreme, how would you expand the survey? Decide what your goal would be and add questions to the survey designed to accomplish your goal.

4. If Krispy Kreme marketers decided to use sampling in order to gather information about new markets, which technique do you think would be most effective? Why?

SOURCES: Company Web site, http://www.krispykreme.com, accessed January 26, 2003; "How Companies Use Coreport," Corechange Web site, http://www.corechange.com, accessed January 26, 2003; "MapQuest Creates the Great American Doughnut Road Trip," *Business Wire,* July 1, 2002; Maureen Licata, "Krispy Kreme Serves Up Piping Hot Information Portal for Far-flung Operations," *National Retail Federation,* November 2001, p. 1; "Krispy Kreme Eyes New Gear as Expansion Aid," *Nation's Restaurant News,* October 8, 2001, http://www.findarticles.com; Jennifer Disabatino, "New Krispy Kreme Intranet a Recipe for Success," *ComputerWorld,* July 26, 2001, http://www.computerworld.com; C. Dickinson Waters, "Krispy Kreme's Hood Has Taste for High Tech," *Nation's Restaurant News,* March 12, 2001, http://www.findarticles.com.

Who Is Eating All Those Krispy Kreme Doughnuts?

Would you wait in line all night just for the sweet, gooey taste of a doughnut the next morning? Would you fly to another country to satisfy your doughnut craving? Maybe not, but whenever Krispy Kreme opens a new shop, doughnut fanatics appear in droves, waiting with facial expressions reminiscent of kids staring at Grandma's cookie jar. The night before the grand opening of a new Krispy Kreme outlet in Wichita, onlookers might have thought they were viewing music fans determined to get front-row seats to a Beck

concert. About 75 customers camped all night outside the store just to be first to taste the rewards. "We love Krispy Kreme doughnuts," declared Darin Dredge, who was the first person in line. Dredge and his friends brought blankets, games, a portable TV, and plenty of food for their sidewalk expedition. The overnight wait didn't seem to bother them at all. When a Krispy Kreme shop opened in Denver, Cornelia Scherle and her friend Nicole Balle cut classes from school in Stuttgart, Germany, and flew to the opening on a bargain fare. "They're so creamy and tasty," explained Scherle. "They don't compare to those in Germany." The Denver store was so mobbed that a highway traffic sign flashed a caution to motorists in the area: "Grand Opening Traffic." A similar scene played out several months later in Seattle. One young man standing in the Seattle line had never even sampled a Krispy Kreme doughnut before committing himself to the wait. When someone handed him a doughnut while in line, he said, "It was like eating sweet air." Naturally, he stuck it out until his turn came.

Perhaps these cases are a bit extreme, but it's obvious that doughnut lovers will go to great lengths to score their favorite Krispy Kreme treats, whether it's the signature Hot Original Glazed doughnut or one of the chocolate-covered or filled varieties. In an era when we are constantly being reminded by health and nutrition specialists that we're supposed to be watching our fat and calorie intakes, people appear willing to give up other indulgences—but not their Krispy Kremes. "I eat about two dozen a week," says one consumer who points to his tummy. "Can't you tell? Usually two in the morning and four in the afternoon. I have that wonderful smell of doughnuts on me all the time." Okay, so not everyone eats that many. But thousands would sure like to if they could.

Krispy Kreme fans are fervent about their product. The company receives as many as 10,000 e-mails each month from its doughnut-loving customers, suggesting everything from new doughnut varieties to possible locations for new stores (usually near the e-mail sender's home or work). They join the Friends of Krispy Kreme fan club at the company's Web site and purchase Krispy Kreme hats, mugs, and sweatshirts. All of these behaviors provide Krispy Kreme marketers with valuable information. Most importantly, these behaviors tell them that their company is doing something right: offering a product that consumers want, at a price they are willing to pay (around 60 cents for a doughnut, $5.59 for a dozen). Doughnuts are a low-involvement purchase, which means that the purchase poses little social or economic risk to the consumer. People who become loyal to their Krispy Kremes are likely to engage in routinized response behavior—they buy the doughnuts over and over again.

It might be tempting to say that everyone who tries a Krispy Kreme becomes a fan, but in order to market the product successfully and expand sensibly, Krispy Kreme marketers do need to employ market segmentation. In addition to assessing such personal determinants of consumer behavior as motives, perception, and attitudes, they need to understand such interpersonal influences as culture, family, and reference groups on the buying behavior of those segments. Not surprisingly, Krispy Kremes are a big hit with college students. In fact, a group of UCLA students made a formal request for an outlet near their campus. "We've had an overwhelming number of requests from UCLA students, staff, and faculty to bring Krispy Kreme doughnuts to campus," says director of food service Bob Williams. "We listened to our customers and went out and found a way to make it happen. It's important that the [campus food service] Association stay current with the most popular trends in the marketplace. Krispy Kreme is something fresh and exciting that we can offer the campus." A similar shop is now located in Reno, near the University of Nevada campus, where students can munch and study at the same time.

Another loyal consumer segment is the auto-racing crowd—both participants and spectators. "Like the high-octane gas that fuels engines, [Krispy Kreme] doughnuts often fuel the mechanics," writes one racing journalist. Still another segment that Krispy Kreme has recently targeted is made up of consumers who require kosher foods. The company operates more than twenty kosher shops, including two in Florida, in response to requests from local Jewish communities. "Both our mix plants and our doughnut mix are certified kosher. In addition, we certify individual stores when there is demand in a particular market," says Stan Parker, senior vice president of marketing for Krispy Kreme. Then there are the opinion leaders—public figures as well as local and national journalists—who feel compelled to rave, or rant, about Krispy Kremes, from novelist and screenwriter Nora Ephron to humorist and writer Roy Blount Jr. (both of whom love them).

Building relationships with these target markets also means building relationships with other businesses and organizations, such as universities. When Krispy Kreme begins to plan moving to a market such as one dominated by a nearby college or university, company marketers work to tailor their marketing efforts to the needs of the educational institution and its students, faculty, and community. The company has strengthened its relationships with franchisees and vendors by offering access to its MyKrispyKreme portal, which provides data, online ordering, and other services. Each of these efforts is aimed at the goal of reaching every consumer who might become the next Krispy Kreme fan.

Questions

1. Which of the four alternative strategies for reaching a target market do you think would be the most effective for Krispy Kreme? Why? What changes might the company have to make in order to satisfy certain markets?
2. Describe what you think would be the best positioning strategy or strategies for Krispy Kreme. Explain why.
3. What are some of the social influences on consumers' decisions to purchase—or not purchase—Krispy Kreme products?
4. Would you like to see a Krispy Kreme shop open near your college or university? Would you visit it? Why or why not?

SOURCES: "Krispy and Kosher," *Cahners Business Information*, April 1, 2002, http://www.findarticles.com; Cindy Petterson, "Krispy Kreme Provides Sugar Fix and Clean Study Spot," *Zephyr*, March 14, 2002, http://zephyr.unr.edu; "Talk About Your Sugar High," *Money*, March 2002, p. 32; Dan Voorhis, "Krispy Kremes Roll into Town," *The Wichita Eagle*, December 2001, pp. 4B, 7B; Kathy Mulady, "Debut Is One of Krispy Kreme's Busiest Ever," *Seattle Post-Intelligencer*, October 2001, pp. D1, D2; Danielle Giovannelli, "The Sweet Smell of Excess," *Kiplinger's*, September 2001, p. 93; Dennis Pollock, "Krispy Crazy," *The Fresno Bee*, August 2001, pp. A1, A12.

Part 4   KRISPY KREME Continuing Case

The Krispy Kreme Brand

Krispy Kreme. Just say the name and think of the images it conjures up: airy doughnuts served warm, the retro logo, nostalgic-looking shops, the sweet sugary smell, and the color of the Krispy Kreme employee uniforms. This isn't a psychological test; it's a closer examination of the impact a brand has on you and other consumers. For some people, it's the smell of fresh-baked doughnuts. For others, it's a reaction to the flashing neon "Hot Doughnuts Now" sign or the feeling they get when they walk into the shop. For still others, it's the simple pleasure of pulling a warm doughnut out of the bag—instead of a cold one. It's no accident that Krispy Kreme has built a huge reputation—and a significant amount of its brand awareness and loyalty—on its signature warm glazed doughnut. "You can eat them hot," says Stan Parker, Krispy Kreme's senior vice president of marketing. "That's a huge branding asset for us." But Krispy Kreme doesn't just roll out the warm doughnuts and leave them on a rack to sell themselves. "We look at every touch point with consumers as an opportunity to brand," says Parker, which includes everything from the neon sign to the retro shops.

Today's Krispy Kreme marketers know the value of brand equity—but so did company founder Vernon Rudolph. He kept his recipe for glazed, yeast-raised doughnuts a secret but gave his customers the opportunity to buy the doughnuts hot. They became loyal Krispy Kreme lovers just as their children and grandchildren are today. Wherever Krispy Kreme fans travel, they know the "Hot Doughnuts Now" sign means that the Hot Original Glazed doughnuts are currently being made. And although they can't get the secret recipe, they can actually see the doughnuts emerge from the doughnut machine through the "doughnut theater"—a window inside the shop that allows viewers to watch the process. Who could possibly resist a dozen of these treats after seeing them made fresh? Joseph "Mac" MacAleer Jr., former CEO of the company and current franchisee, observes that these hot, fresh doughnuts are

the central topic of the thousands of e-mails Krispy Kreme receives from consumers. "In the minds of our customers, that is the essence of what Krispy Kreme is about as a brand," he notes. "There's no question these people have done a masterful job at creating a mindset of an unusually tasty product," says Neil Morgan, assistant professor of marketing at the University of North Carolina, near where Krispy Kreme is headquartered. "They set out to create a brand mythology, and they've been remarkably successful."

Even the fact that there *isn't* a Krispy Kreme shop on every corner is a strategy that helps strengthen the brand. "We're convenient, but not commonplace, and we want to keep it that say," explains Eric Sigurdson, a Canadian who owns several franchises in Illinois and Missouri. Professional industry analysts agree. "You have to go out of your way to get them, and it has kind of developed a mystique about it," explains Len Kubas, a retail consultant in Canada. Still, Krispy Kreme marketers want their product to continue to reach new customers. In addition to opening new stores around the country, in Canada, and overseas, the company sends its Krispy Kreme mobile store—contained entirely inside a custom-designed, 18-wheel truck—on the road. The mobile store can produce up to 1,200 of the original glazed doughnuts in an hour, serves additional varieties, and offers coffee, cold drinks, and even a selection of collectibles for the diehards. The truck appears at state fairs and other events to help develop brand awareness—and, of course, serve those consumers who already can't live without their Krispy Kremes.

Although many people are aware of the Krispy Kreme signature Hot Original Glazed doughnut, they may not be aware that each store actually produces 25 varieties of doughnuts, plus specialty or seasonal items such as the caramel-apple doughnut for a limited time during autumn. Since it's pretty hard to down a dozen doughnuts without something to quench the thirst, Krispy Kreme also sells both cold and hot beverages. A few years ago, Krispy Kreme acquired Digital Java

Inc., a Chicago-based coffee company that produces premium, microroasted coffees as well as coffee-making equipment. This way, Krispy Kreme could maintain control over the quality of its beverages just as it does the doughnut. But make no mistake: Although the coffee is positioned as a quality brew, it will not be upstaging the doughnuts. The company is building equity by ensuring its coffee is on par with its doughnuts, not trying to become another Starbucks. In addition to its food products, the firm offers its line of Krispy Kreme memorabilia. But Krispy Kreme hasn't strayed from what it does well—offering fresh, hot doughnuts. So the product mix is narrow—there's a line of doughnuts, a line of beverages, and a line of collectibles. It's also fairly short. It's fairly deep if you consider the 25 varieties of doughnuts, but larger competitors certainly produce more varieties.

Like any product, even one that spans generations of loyal customers, the doughnut does have a life cycle, so Krispy Kreme has come up with some new ways to extend the product life cycle. Want an unusual wedding cake? Have one made from Krispy Kreme doughnuts. Brides and grooms have been buying the doughnuts by the dozen, then having local grocery stores or bakeries transform them into cakes. Sometimes the loving couple even makes the cake themselves. Krispy Kreme can supply templates—plans—for building several tiers out of doughnuts. If the couple wants a traditional cake instead but would love their guests to sample a Krispy Kreme treat, they can order as many doughnuts as necessary to be delivered to the reception as favors for departing guests. "We have had people coming who buy dozens as parting gifts," says one franchisee. At less than a dollar each, the doughnuts are a bargain compared with other types of party favors.

Perhaps the Krispy Kreme mystique is best expressed by college students. "They're more than doughnuts," gushes one Wichita State University student. "They taste like heaven," says another.

Questions

1. Imagine that you are a Krispy Kreme marketer charged with expanding the product mix. Would you lengthen, widen, or deepen it? What type(s) of products would you add? Describe your strategy.
2. What further steps could Krispy Kreme take to extend the life cycle of its product?
3. Describe all the ways you can think of in which Krispy Kreme develops a strong identity for its product. To help, you can visit the company's Web site at http://www.krispy kreme.com.
4. Why is brand equity vital to Krispy Kreme?

SOURCES: Company Web site, http://www.krispykreme.com, accessed January 27, 2003; Elise Christenson and Geoffrey Gagnon, "Coffee Brew Ha Ha," *Newsweek*, October 7, 2002, p. 9; "Krispy Kreme Brings Mobile Store to Fair St. Louis," *St. Louis Business Journal*, June 28, 2002, http://www.bizjournals.com; Sid Smith, "The Selling of a Doughnut," *The Chicago Tribune*, May 2, 2002, http://www.chicagotribune.com; Don Fernandez, "Krispy Kreme Doughnuts Take the Cake at Weddings," *The Atlanta Journal-Constitution*, March 31, 2002, http://www.accessatlanta .com; Hollie Shaw, "Krispy Kreme Puts on a Show," *National Post*, December 2001; Chris Penttila, "Brand Awareness," *Entrepreneur*, September 2001, pp. 48–51; Maura Webber, "More than Dough Rises at Krispy Kreme," *Chicago Sun-Times*, August 2001, http://www.suntimes.com; Scott Hume, "Model Behavior," *Restaurants & Institutions*, July 1, 2001, http://www.findarticles .com; Emily Fromm, "Marketers of the Next Generation," *Brandweek*, March 26, 2001, p. 23.

Part 5   KRISPY KREME Continuing Case

Krispy Kreme: Value in Every Bite

In today's economy, consumers and business owners alike are looking for value in every product they buy or sell. Price is part of value, but so is quality. Consumers want to know they are getting the best possible product for their money, and merchants want to know they are selling the best product at a competitive price. Krispy Kreme marketers, along with franchise partners, seem to have struck the right balance between price and quality.

How much would you pay for a doughnut? Your answer will probably depend on where you live, since the price range from the Atlantic to the Pacific is 30 to 80 cents and, occasionally, even a bit more. Your answer may also depend on the purchase location: a restaurant, a supermarket or convenience food store, a gas station, or a Krispy Kreme outlet. Franchisees set their own prices, and, in general, the final price depends on costs and geographic locations. Each franchisee calculates his or her costs, then adds an expected profit using the basic cost-plus method of pricing.

Each franchisee pays an initial franchising fee of about $40,000 to Krispy Kreme and an additional 4.5 percent of the shop's sales revenue. However, total start-up costs typically run from $1 to $2 million. Here's why. Franchisees are responsible for constructing their shops based on specifications from company headquarters. In addition, they purchase their doughnut mix and equipment from Krispy Kreme—and a single doughnut machine can cost more than $325,000. Since Krispy Kreme does not offer financing for these costs, franchisees must have either good credit or lots of ready cash—and they must be able to demonstrate a net worth of $5 million to even apply for a franchise. That's why franchisees tend to be development corporations that can raise funds more easily than a single business owner. The flip side of these initial costs is the success of Krispy Kreme—shops do very well, even in their first year of operation. On average, each new Krispy Kreme store achieves a mind-boggling 100 percent return on investment within a year. That's four times the 25 percent return on investment for new—and successful—restaurants in general. The average Krispy Kreme shop posts sales of $2.5 million a year, which is about five times that of a Dunkin' Donuts shop, despite the fact that the Dunkin' Donuts company is larger. "It's a good deal for everybody," says Andrew Wolf, an analyst with BB&T Capital Markets. "The developers are doing very [well] and can afford to spend a little more."

Back to the single doughnut. If you—or more likely your great-grandparents—had bought one of the original Krispy Kreme doughnuts from Vernon Rudolph back in 1937, you could have bought a dozen for 25 cents. Almost 80 years later, the average price a customer pays for a single doughnut is about 70 cents. With a dozen doughnuts going for $5.29, a purchase of this quantity would reduce the per-unit price to about 44 cents. And Krispy Kreme lovers in some locations report local prices as low as 60 cents, with a dozen going for $4.50. But even at today's prices, most consumers see Krispy Kreme as a good value, especially when compared with alternatives like gourmet cookies that can run more than a dollar each. "Our doughnuts are an affordable indulgence," explains Krispy Kreme CEO Scott Livengood. "Instead of buying an expensive dessert, people can just buy a doughnut for less than a dollar." In addition, loyal consumers expect the highest quality—and get it—when they purchase Krispy Kreme products, which keeps them from drifting to slightly less expensive competitors. And Krispy Kreme's reputation for quality precedes it into new markets. "Our customers' expectations are higher than ever," says Stan Parker, senior vice president of marketing. "They've heard so much about us, and when we arrive [in a new market], we have to execute flawlessly."

Product pricing for charitable organizations and special causes is less than retail so that they can generate earnings from fund-raising efforts. They purchase the doughnuts from Krispy Kreme at half price, sell them to consumers at full price, and keep the profits, which may be used to purchase books, field trips, uniforms, and anything else the organization needs. Over the years, Krispy Kreme has helped organizations raise millions of dollars.

For fans who just can't get enough Krispy Kremes, or who want to tell the world they love them without adding more calories to their diets, the company Web site and the mobile doughnut shop offer plenty of collectibles to buy. You can pick up a Krispy Kreme sweatshirt for $29.95 or a T-shirt for $11.95. A variety of mugs and tumblers is available from which to enjoy your Krispy Kreme coffee. For instance, try a stainless-steel travel mug for $19.95 or a plastic tumbler for $9.95. Diehard nostalgia buffs can pick up a set of two ceramic Krispy Kreme mugs for $14.95. If you're a toy collector—or want to pass your passion along to the next generation—you can buy a small die-cast metal Krispy Kreme toy truck for $10.95. The larger version, which doubles as a bank, goes for $24.95.

The success of Krispy Kreme demonstrates that consumers believe they are paying a fair price for a product they love. In fact, most Krispy Kreme customers feel they are getting a bargain for an experience they enjoy so much. "I don't think of them as doughnuts; they melt in your mouth, like warm cotton candy," raves one customer who never even liked doughnuts until he tried a Krispy Kreme. That's a sweet experience, especially for less than a buck.

Questions

1. How do you think the price of Krispy Kreme doughnuts relates to consumers' perceptions of quality?
2. How does Krispy Kreme's pricing strategy relate to its policy of *not* opening a store on every corner?
3. Do you think the cost-plus method of pricing Krispy Kreme products is effective? Why or why not?
4. What kinds of pricing challenges does Krispy Kreme face as it expands into other countries?

SOURCES: Company Web site, http://www.krispykreme.com, accessed January 15, 2003; Randall E. Stross, "A Hot Glazed Don't," *U.S. News & World Report,* June 10, 2002, p. 37; Lisa Gibbs, "Talk About Your Sugar High," *Money,* March 2002, p. 32; Kathy Mulady, *Seattle Post-Intelligencer,* October 2001, pp. D1, D2; Danielle Giovanni, "The Sweet Smell of Excess," *Kiplinger's,* September 2001, p. 93; Maura Webber, "More than Dough Rises at Krispy Kreme," *Chicago Sun-Times,* August 2001, http://www.suntimes.com; Brian O'Keefe, "Kreme of the Crop," *Fortune,* July 23, 2001, pp. 247–248; Scott Hume, "Model Behavior," *Restaurants and Institutions,* July 1, 2001, pp. 30–38; Chris Sieroty, "Filling a Hole in the Market," *Los Angeles Business Journal,* June 11, 2001, http://www.findarticles.com; Nichola Groom, "Krispy Kreme Marks NYSE Move with Free Doughnuts," *The Chicago Tribune,* May 17, 2002, http://www.chicagotribune.com.

Part 6   KRISPY KREME Continuing Case

Krispy Kreme's Distribution Strategy

If Krispy Kreme's most important relationship is with its adoring fans, then perhaps its second-most important relationship is with its franchisees, who purchase the rights to develop and operate Krispy Kreme stores in a particular market. Without those dedicated entrepreneurs, Krispy Kreme doughnuts might be served cold. Eric Sigurdson, president of Sweet Traditions, a licensed Krispy Kreme franchisee, is one of the largest independent developers of Krispy Kreme stores. Currently, he has the exclusive rights to own and operate Krispy Kreme stores in Illinois and Missouri, with a goal of opening 25 shops in the Chicago area during the next five years. Sigurdson, a former executive for a Canadian company, moved to the U.S. in the mid-1990s and happened to visit a Krispy Kreme shop in Indianapolis. He loved the doughnuts, and he loved watching them come out of the doughnut maker fresh. In fact, he loved them so much he visited Krispy Kreme headquarters in North Carolina to negotiate a franchise agreement. He hasn't looked back since. "If I had a dollar for everybody who thought I had lost my mind for leaving the corporate world and going into doughnuts, I'd be on a beach somewhere," Sigurdson says with a laugh.

To maintain consistency of its products, Krispy Kreme requires its franchisees to purchase their doughnut mix and doughnut-making equipment from the company. In addition, Krispy Kreme maintains close contact with its franchisees in a variety of ways, including its extranet portal, MyKrispyKreme. With MyKrispyKreme, store managers can access enterprise applications such as the order-entry system, and they can have immediate access to their own daily sales figures. In addition, they can use the extranet to communicate with corporate headquarters and share information with other franchisees. This ease of communication helps Krispy Kreme manage its marketing and supply chain channels, aids franchise owners in solving problems and operating more efficiently, and helps ensure consistency throughout the retail stores—an ever-increasing issue as the company expands into new markets.

Although the Krispy Kreme distribution strategy is based primarily on its retail and wholesale operations, the company has recently been exploring other channels. Recognizing that college students are doughnut lovers, the company has already begun to open stores both on and near campuses such as UCLA and the University of Nevada at Reno. Through an agreement with ASUCLA Catering, UCLA students can get their doughnuts on campus at the Cafe Synapse. Or they can phone in orders for their Krispy Kremes and single-serve coffee carafes. ASUCLA employees attend special Krispy Kreme training in order to maintain quality. "Managers and employees [go] to Krispy Kreme Training School to learn the history of the Krispy Kreme doughnut and to learn the proper serving techniques," notes Dave Nirenberg, associate director of UCLA restaurants. At the University of Nevada at Reno, students buy their doughnuts at a nearby Krispy Kreme shop equipped with tables on which to spread out their books for studying.

In addition, Krispy Kreme has a long history of distributing doughnuts at select grocery stores and convenience stores. Fifty Loaf 'N Jug convenience stores in Pueblo and Colorado Springs, Colorado, receive dozens of doughnuts every morning, well in time for rush-hour commuters. The doughnuts are made at the Krispy Kreme outlet in Colorado Springs between 1:00 and 4:00 each morning and then trucked to the Loaf 'N Jug shops. Supermarket chain Kroger, which owns Loaf 'N Jug, also receives the doughnuts at some of its stores. In Ann Arbor, Michigan—home to the University of Michigan—Kroger markets have replaced their own in-house pastries with Krispy Kremes.

Then there's the Krispy Kreme mobile unit—a rolling Krispy Kreme store housed in a 78,000-pound, 18-wheel truck that can go anywhere, anytime. The truck shows up at all kinds of public events, from state fairs to the homecomings of military personnel. Paired with the truck is a chase vehicle—equipped, of course, with Krispy Kreme collectibles. This mobile Krispy Kreme unit is the real thing. Powered by a generator, the doughnut maker inside the truck can produce up to 1,200 fresh doughnuts an hour. It takes employees an entire day to set up the truck and begin making doughnuts and another day to disassemble the works, so the truck usually stays put for at least a day or two. Sometimes the doughnuts are sold to the public; at other occasions, such as the homecoming of the *USS Theodore Roosevelt,* service personnel and their families are treated to Krispy Kremes at no cost.

Krispy Kreme's distribution strategy—through retail stores, colleges, grocery markets, businesses, and the Krispy Kreme mobile store—is closely tied to its overall marketing strategy as described by Stan Parker, the company's senior vice president of marketing: "We strive to be a valuable community partner everywhere we operate stores."

Questions

1. Krispy Kreme uses dual distribution to reach its target markets. In addition to those discussed in the case, can you list any other channels that might be successful for the company? Explain your choices.

2. What product factors determine Krispy Kreme's marketing channel strategy?

3. How do store atmospherics play a part in the Krispy Kreme retailing strategy?

4. Describe Krispy Kreme's location-distribution strategy as part of an overall marketing strategy.

SOURCES: Company Web site, http://www.krispykreme.com, accessed January 27, 2003; "Krispy Kreme Integrates B2B Extranet with Coreport Enterprise Portal," Corechange, http://www.corechange.com, accessed September 26, 2002; "Convenience Stores to Begin Selling Krispy Kreme Doughnuts," Hoover's Online, September 13, 2002, http://hoovnews .hoovers.com; "Krispy Kreme Brings Mobile Store to Fair St. Louis," *St. Louis Business Journal,* June 28, 2002, http://www.bizjournals.com; Cindy Petterson, "Krispy Kreme Provides Sugar Fix and Clean Study Spot," *Zephyr,* March 14, 2002, http://zephyr.unr.edu; Maura Webber, "More than Dough Rises at Krispy Kreme," *Chicago Sun-Times,* August 2001, http://www.sun times.com; Laura McReynolds, "Krispy Kreme Doughnuts Finally Hit Ann Arbor," *Ann Arbor Observer,* June 2001, http://www.arborfood .com; Emily Fromm, "Marketers of the Next Generation," *Brandweek,* March 26, 2001, p. 23.

Part 7   KRISPY KREME Continuing Case

Krispy Kreme Communicates Sweet Nothings

How did Krispy Kreme develop such a loyal following for a simple product that many describe as "like eating sweet air"? Promoting this warm, gooey confection is a bit like handling a delicate movie star. It requires a combination of skill and belief in the product on the part of Krispy Kreme marketers. Overexposure to the public could result in consumer burnout or boredom. Underexposure could result in dozens of doughnuts cooling on bakery racks instead of sliding into the mouths of consumers. So, developing the right promotional mix through integrated marketing communications is vital to keeping the doughnuts rolling.

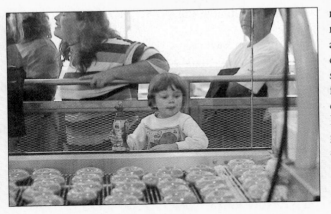

From the very beginning, Vernon Rudolph relied on satisfied customers to sell the doughnuts. Once they tried a Krispy Kreme fresh from the doughnut machine, they'd never go back to a competitor. Furthermore, they'd tell their friends about Krispy Kreme. Today, Krispy Kreme's marketers adopt much the same philosophy. "Once someone's had a hot Krispy Kreme," says director of marketing Steve Bumgarner, "it's done the job for us." Industry observers approve of this approach. "Relying on word of mouth is infinitely more credible than paid advertising," says Neil Morgan, a University of North Carolina at Chapel Hill marketing professor. "They don't just cultivate people who say Krispy Kreme is a better doughnut. They cultivate people who eulogize over it." But it doesn't stop there. Krispy Kreme targets its most enthusiastic followers and recruits them as ambassadors through the company Web site and mailings. When Krispy Kreme is getting ready to enter a market near these consumers, marketers send packets of memorabilia such as T-shirts and hats to their so-called ambassadors to help build anticipation for the opening.

Krispy Kreme also relies heavily on both public relations and publicity to get the word out about their product. "We don't do a lot of traditional things, like advertising," says Stan Parker, senior vice president of marketing. "We want to be involved in the community." So the company participates in fundraisers in which Krispy Kreme gives away doughnuts or supplies them at wholesale prices to charities, youth sports, and school groups, who sell them and keep the profits. Its "Good Grades" program gives out free doughnuts to students who achieve As on their report cards. In addition, the mobile doughnut shop shows up at military bases for the homecomings of overseas service personnel, and at state fairs, music festivals, and other community events. And celebrities who are Krispy Kreme lovers pass on the good word—writers Nora Ephron and Roy Blount Jr., actress Nicole Kidman, and baseball legend Henry "Hank" Aaron, to name a few. Krispy Kremes have even appeared on the HBO hit *Sex in the City* starring Sarah Jessica Parker.

The buzz surrounding every opening of a new Krispy Kreme shop is loud enough to make marketers at other companies envious. People wait in line for hours, often wearing those Krispy Kreme shirts and hats, just to be first to sample the doughnuts. Traffic may get snarled, as it did on a Denver highway during a new-store opening, but Krispy Kreme lovers don't seem bothered at all. Of course, local news media cover the openings with gusto. "When people stand in line 15 hours for something, that's news," explains *Chicago Tribune* reporter Delma Francis. But perhaps the biggest publicity blitz came from Fresno, which officially proclaimed the opening of a new shop "Krispy Kreme Day." Radio stations did live broadcasts from the site, television crews jockeyed for the best position, and the ribbon cutting was accompanied by a Dixieland jazz band. The new shop received immediate praise from Foster Friends, a charity that works with foster children who have special needs, for donating part of its proceeds from the first day's sales to the organization. The fact is, marketers just couldn't buy advertising as good as this. "We are extremely fortunate to have passionate and loyal customers who like to share their Krispy Kreme experiences with others. This strong word-of-mouth endorsement helps us build awareness as we enter new markets, both in the U.S. and internationally," explains Stan Parker.

Naturally, Krispy Kreme had to celebrate its 65th birthday by doing something newsworthy, so company volunteers created the world's largest doughnut cake. Measuring 18 feet wide and 12 feet tall and weighing in at 2,413 pounds, the doughnut cake was an attempt to establish a new Guinness World Record. Krispy Kreme staff used 14,832 Krispy Kreme Hot Original Glazed and Chocolate Iced Sprinkled doughnuts and more than 1,000 pounds of icing and 330 pounds of candy for decoration. The cake was displayed in the historic district of Winston-Salem, North Carolina, where the first Krispy Kreme store was located, and the event was accompanied by a variety of activities and entertainment for the public.

Sponsorship has also become part of the Krispy Kreme promotional mix. Auto racing is the number one U.S. spectator sport, so Krispy Kreme is at the races. The Krispy Kreme Road Racing Team, sponsored by the Krispy Kreme shops in Daytona Beach and Melbourne, Florida, is a multicar race team that competes in the southeastern division of the Sports Car Club of America. Of course, the main goal of the team is to promote Krispy Kreme doughnuts so that race fans will associate Krispy Kremes with their favorite sport.

None of these promotional activities could take place successfully without communication between Krispy Kreme headquarters and its franchise owners, who play a huge role in making these events happen. The MyKrispyKreme extranet helps provide communication among all interested parties—corporate headquarters, franchisees, and suppliers—so promotional activities can be planned and carried out smoothly. In addition, communication with the media is crucial. But so far, even media skeptics seem to soften when they get near the action. "You pick out a doughnut after it comes out hot from the glazed waterfall," says Stan Parker. Who could resist?

Questions

1. If you were a marketer for Krispy Kreme, how would you define the company's overall marketing message?
2. In what ways does Krispy Kreme's promotional mix fulfill its overall objectives of promotion?
3. Identify two types of consumer-oriented sales promotions that might be effective for Krispy Kreme and explain their objectives.
4. At what point in the product life cycle do you think Krispy Kreme marketers might begin to employ advertising? Why?

SOURCES: Krispy Kreme Road Racing Team Web site, http://www.kkrr.net, accessed January 29, 2003; "Krispy Kreme to Celebrate 65th Birthday by Creating Record-Breaking Cake," Newstream.com, July 2002, http://www.newstream.com; "Krispy Kreme Inks 1st Offshore Deal, Signs Hank Aaron," *Nation's Restaurant News,* June 17, 2002, http://www.findarticles.com; "Krispy Kreme's Movable Feast," *Restaurants & Institutions,* June 1, 2002, http://www.findarticles.com; Sid Smith, "The Selling of a Doughnut," *The Chicago Tribune,* May 2, 2002, http://www.chicagotribune.com; Dennis Pollack, "Krispy Crazy," *The Fresno Bee,* August 2001; Chris Sieroty, "Filling a Hole in the Market," *Los Angeles Business Journal,* June 11, 2001, http://www.findarticles.com; Theresa Howard, "Who Needs Ads When You've Got Hot Doughnuts Now?" *USA Today,* May 31, 2001, p. 3B.

FUBU Integrated Case

FUBU: A Hip Urban Fairy Tale

It's a Cinderella story, in a way, the rags-to-riches-to-fashion-empire tale of FUBU. Even the four friends who founded the company call it "an urban fairy tale come true."

FUBU was born of a simple desire. Daymond John, waiting tables in his early twenties and still living in the middle-class New York City neighborhood where he'd grown up, wanted a hat. Not just any hat, but a particular type of knitted tie-top stocking cap he'd begun to see in MTV videos. He had to travel to the city's trendy downtown area to find what he wanted, and once he did, he realized he could easily make the same hat at home. With a couple of his boyhood friends, he quickly put together 40 hats in his mother's basement and set out to sell them on the streets of Queens for $20 each. They were gone in a day.

John convinced his mother that he was on to something, and she took a second mortgage on her home to provide him with the $100,000 he needed to fill the flood of orders he'd quickly collected. Scarcely anyone realized it at the time, but that's when FUBU was born.

Targeting—and Riding—the Hip-Hop Wave

The name FUBU is an acronym of "for us, by us," and the four young founders who oversee the multinational lifestyle brand still proudly echo that sentiment. "If it doesn't fit us or we don't feel it," they say, "then we don't make it." The company's hot clothing styles for men, women, boys, and girls have expanded to a host of other items: shoes, jewelry, watches, bags, eyeglasses, fragrance, swimwear, formalwear, and towels and bedding. FUBU products retain their urban edge, however. Their original hip-hop, ethnic appeal long ago crossed racial, urban, and national borders along with the music style that inspires them, and it just keeps on going. "It's important that we diversify," says John. "The hip-hop business is growing, so we are expanding."

Licensing deals with the NBA and FUBU's deal to produce Harlem Globetrotters "Dream Team" sportswear—and to serve as the official uniform outfitter for the team—have helped solidify the company's lock on streetwise cool. Its latest line expansion is the Platinum collection, which celebrates the Harlem Globetrotters and Muhammad Ali, as well as the beloved cartoon character Fat Albert. The firm's sales are now estimated at almost $400 million a year, and its plans for the future include expansion into music, videos, and film under the auspices of its FB Entertainment division, which already

produces and promotes several musical artists within the hip-hop, R&B, and soul genres. There's even a line of furniture on the drawing board.

Distribution Online and Around the Globe

Daymond John, Alexander Martin, Carl Brown, and Keith Perrin are the company's owners. They still make all its fashion decisions together, relying on their instinct for spotting trends, their carefully maintained ties with the streets where they met and grew up, and Martin's stint at New York's Fashion Institute of Technology. Of course they now have several dozen employees to help them run the business side of the firm; manage the manufacturing, selling, and distribution processes; and market new items at fashion industry showcases around the world.

FUBU maintains a retail store locator at its Web site, http://www .fubu.com. Its products are also sold at several independent retail Web sites like http://www.urbanclothing.net. And in addition to boutiques in more than 5,000 retail stores, including giants like Macy's, Nordstrom, and Sears, it has about 45 franchised stores, many of which stock the entire line of FUBU products. Wherever its customers like to shop, FUBU is there. There are already several FUBU stores in China, and FUBU products are sold in a total of 26 countries in Central and South America, the Middle East, and Asia, including a Web site in Russia.

The four partners have come a long way since the day that a surprise overseas phone call brought them their first small international order. Now every distribution move, at home, abroad, and on the Internet, is carefully planned. Among the advantages John sees in FUBU's Internet presence are the abilities to reach customers worldwide, to develop a mailing list of all the company's customers, to direct shoppers to retail outlets quickly and accurately, and to sell merchandise that buyers might not be able to find anywhere else.

Promotion as Innovative as Hip-Hop Itself

FUBU's road to success was a little slow at first. After its inspired beginning in 1992, FUBU operated out of John's mother's home for several months, with the founders doing all the designing, manufacturing, and selling themselves. The friends sewed hats during

the day and closed up shop to sleep in the same rooms at night. They couldn't afford advertising, but another old friend of theirs was beginning a successful career as a rap artist. LL Cool J agreed to wear a FUBU logo shirt in a Gap commercial, and the exposure that brought to the tiny company's target market couldn't have been better timed. "They arrived just as hip-hop went from being a musical genre into becoming an overall lifestyle," according to Michael Wood, vice president of a consulting and research firm that monitors teen buying habits.

In another year or two, after crashing a major apparel trade show in Las Vegas and racking up a big order from a Chicago retailer, John knew he needed to expand. He took out a tiny ad in a couple of New York newspapers that read, "Have $300,000 in orders; need financing." Samsung's textile division became the company's initial distribution partner, and the company was on its way to the top. With headquarters in New York's Empire State Building, it is now the city's largest minority-owned firm.

Product placement on television, in movies, and in lifestyle consumer magazines, similar to LL Cool J's original promotion of that early FUBU shirt, makes up a big part of the marketing strategy for FUBU's home product lines, which are also gathered into a big catalog. Scent strips in national magazines support a print campaign to promote the company's fragrances. More of FUBU's nontraditional marketing strategies such as staging splashy happenings and events—complete with product giveaways—are always in the works.

Product and Pricing Decisions

FUBU remains a team operation for the owners. Perrin oversees promotion, Brown handles licensing, and Perrin and Brown together manage FB Entertainment. On the fashion side, Martin supervises design, and John sets the company's overall vision. According to John, the four founders place a high value on "honesty and respect of others on the team . . . to make everybody's vote count." Decisions on how to select the right products for entry into a new market such as home furnishings, for instance, are made by the founders. Says John of the company's motivation for entry into the home linens market, "There really weren't manufacturers out there that were making products we were attracted to. The colors weren't wet enough and rich enough, and there wasn't enough styling."

With sexier appeal, sharp colors, and carefully selected fabrics, all reminiscent of the company's hottest clothing lines, FUBU's new home collection is targeted at customers 18 to 35, male and female alike, with a few items for younger children and teens. There are three price levels—luxury, young adult, and bed-in-a-bag—and the prices range from about $130 down to $25. "We already know fabrics and clothing textiles," John explains. "We already are purchasers of stuff for the home. It was really a pretty easy decision for us once we put it down on paper." Expansion into other categories such as tableware may follow the planned launch of bath products—towels, shower curtains, and bath accessories. "If you look at bath accessories, you can see we're already thinking about the plate collection," says the company's president of marketing and advertising. "But the timing has to be right."

The timing was right for the introduction of FUBU's fragrance collection for men and women. Sleek and elegant bottles hold men's after-shave sprays and balms, shampoo, and body wash. Women's products include fragrance mist, lotion, shower gel, and body cream. The products range from about $38 to $48 retail.

Price must be attractive for a product's success. "Consumers are price conscious," says Martin, and the company tries to price just below the competition to make sure its products are affordable. But quality is still critical, because competition for young consumers' discretionary dollars is fierce. "Everyone's our competitor, but no one is our competitor," says John. Tanks, tees, and jerseys range from $20 to about $70, with prices slightly higher for the Harlem Globetrotters line. Jeans, shorts, and pants are in the $50 to $70 range; velour track suits can run to $100; and baseball hats are about $20. The eyewear collection was designed in Italy using the highest quality materials, and the sunglasses offer 100 percent UV protection. The price for eyewear ranges from $110 to $150.

In 2001 FUBU released its first CD, *The Goodlife*, and it has also released 54th Platoon's "Holdin It Down" music video for television. John would like the firm to achieve the status of a media and fashion conglomerate. "That is where we are aiming."

FUBU Stays Close to Its Target Market

Although its target market has expanded to include customers "from 5 to 50," as John says, FUBU's founders still periodically go home to Queens to meet and talk with young consumers; they also visit urban communities in other cities where their products are popular. They enjoy meeting people who love their brand, whether they are celebrities like Boys II Men and Phat Farm or middle-class urban kids. The concept of "street promotion" lives on in the company's newest marketing concept. The FUBU Riders are 20 bike riders bearing logos from all the FUBU brands and collections. An earlier promotion used a van to drive up and down the East Coast offering FUBU fans tickets to a party on the island of St. Martin in the Caribbean, and in its earliest days the firm painted its logo on antitheft gates that stores rolled down after closing hours. When FUBU briefly sponsored a youth-oriented Internet portal, Macy's created an interactive window display to promote it. New ways to market the brand remain a critical part of the company's marketing strategy, heavily mixed with ever-varied print and television ads. "We still look for the next vein . . . not the normal channels," says John. "We're always looking for something different."

That's important when your market has expanded. "Those people 18 to 35 also have kids," says John, "so you make children's clothes that appeal to a 5-year-old. Sometimes you make the classier garments that appeal to people 25 to 50 who have to work every day. It's not that I'm trying to expand, it's just that we're naturally expanding."

FUBU's Tomorrow

FUBU has received two Congressional achievement awards and two entrepreneurship awards from the NAACP, as well as the Black Alumni of Pratt Institute's Creative Spirit Award, the Christopher Wallace Award, the Online Hiphop Award, and more. FUBU was also the first company to receive the Essence Enterprise award. John recently created the FUBU Foundation, which uses its $1 million annual budget to refurbish neighborhood basketball courts in Queens and Harlem and makes donations to various charities, including funds to benefit families of victims of 9/11. FUBU's expansion plans—and its success—seem to grow and grow.

Is the sky the limit? "Hip-hop is a multicultural movement as opposed to a minority one," says Xochil Arkin, president of the research and business development group Urban Media. "So the platform provides far more opportunities for businesses to grow." And that suits FUBU just fine. Even though its products are available in the mainstream, it still embodies a particular urban lifestyle that Daymond John is ready to admit is not for everyone. "I don't mind being a mainstream brand. You can still be mainstream as long as you keep the aggressive marketing, the imaging, the aggressive designing. It doesn't mean that it's for everybody, but it means it's available in the mainstream, so I don't have a problem with that." FUBU has found that its niche is exceptionally wide. And longevity is the goal. "We are in this for the long run," says John.

Questions

1. Do you think it was inevitable that FUBU's product line expanded from clothing and shoes into jewelry, fragrances, bath and bedding products, and CDs and videos? Why or why not? How do you think the decision was made to expand the product line so broadly? What impact on FUBU's growth and success do you think the growth of hip-hop, from a music style to a fashion style to a lifestyle, has had? Why?

2. What advantage do you think a youth-oriented company like FUBU gains by selling its merchandise in two kinds of retail outlets—its own freestanding stores and boutiques in other stores like Macy's? What advantages does it gain by allowing Internet retailers also to stock its products? Are there any risks in distributing products through more than one supply chain in this way? If so, what are they and how do you think a company could protect itself from those risks?

3. What does FUBU need to do to succeed and grow as it broadens its target market? Can it become mainstream and still stay ahead of fashion trends? How can it ensure that it retains its core buyers (teens and young adults), and that they don't perceive the company as one that targets older customers? Conversely, what (if anything) does FUBU need to do to make sure its products are attractive to 35- to 50-year-olds?

4. How does a company benefit from marketing several different lines of similar products, like FUBU's luxury, young adult, and bed-in-a-bag collections, at various price levels? To which of FUBU's product lines does this product-line pricing best lend itself?

SOURCES: Company Web site, http://ww.fubu.com, accessed October 22, 2003; Urban Clothing Net Web site, http://www.urbanclothing.net/fubu-clothing.htm, accessed October 22, 2003; "The Secrets of Success of Wealthy African Americans," *The Black Collegian Magazine*, 2003, http://www.black-collegian.com, accessed October 22, 2003; "100 Most Influential Leaders in Business," *Crain's New York Business*, http://www.crainsny.com, accessed October 22, 2003; "Daymond John," http://www.thehistorymakers.com/biography/, accessed October 22, 2003; "FUBU The Collection Inks New Deal for Eyewear," FUBU press release, October 11, 2003, http://www.prweb.com; Erik Spanberg, "FUBU Eyes Charlotte," *Charlotte Business Journal*, September 23, 2003, http://www.bizjournals.com/charlotte; Tania Padgett, "Minority Businesses Grow, Diversity," *Newsday*, September 22, 2003, http://www.newsday.com; "FUBU Home Line on the Horizon," *Home Textiles Today*, April 21, 2003, http://www.findarticles.com; "Start Me Up—Online Chats," *SmartMoney Magazine*, December 27, 2002, http://www.smartmoney.com; "Fabulous FUBU," *Global Cosmetic Industry*, June 2002, http://www.findarticles.com; "Hip Hop Home," *Home Textiles Today*, April 1, 2002, http://www.findarticles.com; "FUBU Interactive Profile," *CNN Online*, accessed October 22, 2003, http://www.cnn.com; "FUBU Records/Universal Records Prepare to Release First Album under Joint Venture," *PR Newswire*, May 21, 2001; Sloane Lucas, "For Us, Forever," *Brandweek*, October 11, 1999, http://www.brandweek.com.

Developing a Marketing Plan

Marketing plans are detailed descriptions of the sources and actions needed to achieve stated marketing objectives. They are an integrated—and essential—component of the organization's overall business plan.

The marketing plan component of an overall business plan is needed for a variety of reasons:

- to obtain financing, because banks and most private investors require a detailed business plan before they will even consider a loan application or a venture capital investment;
- to provide direction for the firm's overall business and marketing strategies;
- to support the development of long-term and short-term organizational objectives;
- to guide employees in achieving these objectives;
- to serve as a standard against which the firm's progress can be measured and evaluated.

After creating and implementing this plan, marketers should reevaluate it periodically to gauge its success in moving the organization toward its goals. If necessary, changes should be implemented promptly.

Components of a Business Plan

Business plans vary in length and format. However, most contain the following components:

- An *executive summary* briefly answers the who, what, when, where, and how questions for the plan. Although the summary appears early in the plan, it should be written last.

- A *competitive analysis* section focuses on the environment in which the marketing plan is to be implemented. Although this section is more closely associated with the comprehensive business plan, factors specifically influencing marketing are likely to be inserted here.

- The *mission statement* summarizes the organization's purpose, vision, and overall goals. This statement provides the foundation upon which further planning is based.

- The overall business plan includes a series of *component* plans that present goals and strategies for each functional area of the enterprise. They typically include the following:

  - *Marketing plan.* Describes strategies for informing potential customers about goods and services that are offered, and strategies to be employed in obtaining repeat business.

  - *Financing plan.* Lays out a realistic approach for securing needed funds and managing debt and cash flows.

  - *Production plan.* Describes how the organization will go about producing its products in the most efficient, cost-effective manner possible.

> **Briefly Speaking**
>
> Turn your face to the sun and the shadows fall behind you.
>
> *Anonymous*

■ *Facilities plan.* Describes the physical environment and equipment required to implement the production plan.

■ *Human resources plan.* Estimates employment needs and the skills necessary to achieve organizational goals; includes comparison of current employees with needs and establishes processes for securing adequately trained personnel should a gap exist between current employee skills and future needs.

Briefly Speaking

Make no little plans; they have no magic to stir men's blood and probably themselves will not be realized. Make big plans; aim high in hope and work, remembering that a noble, logical diagram once recorded will not die.

Daniel H. Burnham (1846–1912)

This basic format applies to the planning process of any firm. Whether a company operates in the manufacturing, wholesaling, retailing, or service sector, the plan components described here will appear in the overall business plan of the organization. It is also important to remember that the marketing plan must be developed in conjunction with other components of the business plan. Now, let's examine what a marketing plan would look like in practice.

The Executive Summary and Competitive Analysis

The executive summary of a recent Hewlett-Packard marketing plan would concentrate on its $19 billion acquisition of Compaq Computer Corp. and the improved product offerings from merging the two companies' product lines: enterprise systems (servers, storage, networking technology, and related software); consulting services; printing and imaging; and personal systems (PCs, notebooks, handheld devices, personal storage, mobile technologies, and emerging Internet-access devices). In addition, the executive summary would address the firm's improved pricing competitiveness resulting from the expected $3 to $4 billion savings from the merger of the two electronic giants. By contrast, the executive summary of the Target Stores marketing plan would probably outline the rollout of its Super-Target stores, which combine groceries with the retailer's traditional merchandise.

The competitive analysis section for the new Hewlett-Packard plan might outline expectations of increased market share at the expense of competitors such as IBM Corp. and Dell as a result of product line improvements resulting from its $4 billion annual R&D budget and its ability to combine the best of the technology breakthroughs from both product lines.[1] Target's analysis could examine how it is positioned price-wise relative to competitors such as Wal-Mart and Kohl's.

Creating the Mission Statement and Determining Organizational Objectives

The mission statement presents the organization's broad objectives—its overall purpose and reason for existing. Consider the following two mission statements. The first is from John Deere & Co.:[2]

JOHN DEERE

The company is guided today, as it has been since 1837, by John Deere's original values: a commitment to product quality, customer service, business integrity, and a high regard for individual contribution. The company strives to create shareholder value through its pursuit of continuous improvement and profitable growth.

The second mission statement comes from Amgen, a leading biotechnology company. It is brief and to the point:[3]

Amgen

We aspire to be the best human therapeutics company. We will live the Amgen values and use science and innovation to dramatically improve people's lives.

These broad mission statements can then be used to develop more specific objectives that state a course of action to be followed. These objectives should be both quantifiable and measurable so they can be evaluated objectively and adjusted as necessary.

Based on the mission statement, John Deere & Co.'s organizational objectives include:

- to grow and pursue leadership positions in each of the company's businesses;

- to extend its preeminent leadership position in the agricultural equipment market worldwide;

- to create new opportunities to leverage the Deere brand globally.

Similarly, Amgen developed a number of organizational objectives based on its mission statement:

- to launch a stream of products that will dramatically improve patients' lives;

- to create an environment where the best people choose to work;

- to deliver superior shareholder returns compared with peer companies;

- to be a good corporate citizen in communities where the firm's staff live and work.

Formulating a Marketing Strategy

As discussed in the text's early chapters, a marketing strategy begins with the analysis and evaluation of potential markets in light of the firm's specific strengths and weaknesses. This evaluation ultimately leads to the selection of a target market. For example, executives at Foot Locker, an athletic shoe and apparel retailer, realized that its stores were more appealing to men than to women. As a result, the firm created a separate line of stores, called Lady Foot Locker, with active women in mind. Lady Foot Locker defines its target market as active women aged 20 years or older who participate in sports.

After selecting the target market, the marketer develops a marketing mix to reach the chosen consumer segments:

- *Product strategy.* Which goods and services should the firm offer to meet customers' needs? Drug giant Johnson & Johnson is divided into three main business segments: consumer products, medical products, and pharmaceuticals. Each segment consists of a number of operating units. Each operating unit concentrates on developing new products to meet its specific customer needs.

- *Pricing strategy.* At what general level should the firm set prices? The concept of everyday low prices is the foundation of Wal-Mart's pricing strategy. But most retailers rely on periodic sales as a component of their pricing strategies, believing that shoppers expect—and are drawn to the store by—such price discounts. The pricing strategies of upscale retailers such as Saks Fifth Avenue are even more complicated. The New York–based fashion retail chain features both higher-priced designer apparel and more modestly priced private labels such as 5/48 and Real Clothes.[4]

- *Distribution strategy.* Through which channel(s) and physical facilities will the firm distribute its products? Sherwin-Williams bases its distribution strategy on company-owned stores. By contrast, for decades Avon has used a direct channel based on its network of independent contractors.

- *Promotional strategy.* What mix of personal selling, advertising, and sales promotion activities should the firm pursue? Safeco, the Seattle-based insurance company, decided that naming the Seattle Mariners' new ballpark Safeco Field should be part of its promotional strategy.

Sample Marketing Plan

We conclude this appendix by considering what a sample marketing plan would look like. Consider the hypothetical Chainlink Cycles, a large bicycle retailer located in Naperville, Illinois. The firm's owners have prepared the following marketing plan for part of their annual loan review with First Commercial Bank. The plan is also designed to clarify how the firm's managers are planning to market this business.

CHAINLINK CYCLES

Target market. The Chainlink Cycles target market consists of physically active adults with above-average household incomes. These men and women restrict their purchases of bicycles and accessories, both for themselves and their children, to professional bicycle shops where they are confident they will receive excellent products at fair prices, and the ultimate in personal service.

Product strategy. The Chainlink Cycles inventory consists of products from several well-known, highly respected manufacturers. Its product line extends from serious entry-level bicycles—starting at around $300—to high-end models selling for

$1,500 or more. The retailer also stocks a wide range of bicycling-related accessories and maintains a large service department. Excellent after-sale service is an important component of the Chainlink Cycles product strategy.

Pricing. Chainlink Cycles sells at list price, a common retail pricing strategy among high-end bicycling retailers. To attract new customers and keep current customers and to maintain inventory "freshness" by clearing out older products, it also has several clearance sales during the year.

Distribution. The key distribution choice for a retailer is location. Chainlink Cycles is located in a neighborhood mall adjacent to a large regional park. Customers have a convenient location for test rides.

Promotion. Strong personal selling efforts by a retail staff made up of experienced cyclists is a key element of the firm's promotion strategy. The business maintains a Web site with information and links to cycling-related sites. Chainlink Cycles also advertises on cable television sports channels. Store manager Susan Donahue hosts a weekly 30-minute cycling/fitness program on a local cable channel.

Assignment

Follow the format described in this appendix to prepare a marketing plan for one of the following organizations:

- The NFL's Baltimore Ravens, the NBA's San Antonio Spurs, or the NHL's Colorado Avalanche
- A Mail Boxes Etc. franchise
- A San Antonio microbrewery
- Eastern Illinois University

Financial and New-Product Analysis

A number of basic concepts from accounting and finance offer invaluable tools to marketers. Understanding the contributions made by these concepts can improve the quality of marketing decisions. In addition, marketers often must be able to explain and defend their decisions in financial terms. These accounting and financial tools can be used to supply quantitative data to justify decisions made by marketing managers. In this appendix we describe the major accounting and finance concepts that have marketing implications and explain how they assist in making informed marketing decisions.

Financial Statements

All companies prepare a set of financial statements on a regular basis. Two of the most important financial statements are the income statement and balance sheet. The analogy of a motion picture is often used to describe an *income statement,* since it presents a financial record of a company's revenues, expenses, and profits over a period of time, such as a month, quarter, or year. By contrast, the *balance sheet* is a snapshot of what a company owns—called *assets*—and what it owes—called *liabilities*—at a point in time, such as at the end of the month, quarter, or year. The difference between assets and liabilities is referred to as *owner's, partners',* or *shareholders' equity*—the amount of funds the firm's owners have invested in its formation and continued operations. Of the two financial statements, the income statement contains more marketing-related information.

A sample income statement for Composite Technology is shown in Figure B.1. Headquartered in a Boston suburb, Composite Technology is a B2B producer and marketer. The firm designs and manufactures composite panels for defense contractors who have been awarded government contracts to supply a series of military products. Total sales revenues for 2004 amounted to $300 million. Total expenses, including taxes, for the year were $268.8 million. 2004 proved to be a profitable year for Composite Technology—the firm reported a profit, referred to as net income, of $31.2 million. While total revenue is a fairly straightforward number, several of the expenses shown on the income statement require additional explanation.

For any company that makes its own products (a manufacturer) or simply markets one or more items produced by others (an importer, retailer, or wholesaler), the largest single expense is usually a category called *cost of goods sold.* This reflects the cost, to the firm, of the goods that it markets to its customers. In the case of Composite Technology, the cost of goods sold represents the cost of components and raw materials as well as the cost of designing and manufacturing the composite panels the firm produces and markets to its business customers.

The income statement illustrates how cost of goods sold is calculated. The calculation begins with the value of the firm's inventory at the beginning of 2004. Inventory is the value of unsold products held by the firm. The cost of materials Composite Technology purchased during the year and the direct cost of manufacturing the finished goods are then added to the beginning inventory figure. The result is cost of goods the firm has available for sale during the year. Once the firm's accountants subtract the value of inventory held by the firm at the end of 2004, they know the cost of goods sold. By simply subtracting cost of goods sold from total sales revenues generated during the year, they determine that Composite achieved gross profits of $105 million in 2004.

Composite Technology
2893 Fitzgerald Parkway
Southhampton, MA 02349

INCOME STATEMENT
For the Year Ended December 31, 2004
(in $millions)

Revenues		$300
Beginning Inventory	$70	
Materials Purchases	75	
Direct Design and Manufacturing Costs	120	
Cost of Goods Available for Sale	$265	
Less: Ending Inventory	70	
Cost of Goods Sold	195	
Gross Profit		105
Less: Operating Expenses	39	
Operating Profit		66
Less: Depreciation	12	
Interest Expense	6	
Taxable Income		48
Less: Taxes	16.8	
Net Income		31.2

Operating expenses are another significant cost for most firms. This broad category includes such marketing outlays as sales compensation and expenses, advertising and other promotions, and the expenses involved in implementing marketing plans. Accountants typically combine these financial outlays into a single category with the label *selling expenses*.

Other expense items included in the operating expenses section of the income statement are administrative salaries, utilities, and insurance. Subtracting operating expenses from the gross profit equals the firm's operating profit. For 2004, Composite's operating expenses totaled $39 million, resulting in an operating profit of $66 million.

Depreciation represents the systematic reduction over time in the value of certain company assets, such as production machinery, office furniture, or laptops provided for the firm's sales representatives. Depreciation is an unusual expense in that it does not involve an actual cash expense. However, it does reflect the reality that equipment owned by the company

is physically wearing out over time from use and/or from technological obsolescence. Also, charging a portion of the total cost of these long-lived items to each of the years in which they are used results in a more accurate determination of the total costs involved in the firm's operation each year.

Net interest expense is the difference between what a firm paid in interest on various loans and what it collected in interest on investments it might have made during the time period involved. Subtracting depreciation and net interest expense from the firm's operating profit reveals the firm's taxable income. Composite had depreciation of $12 million and a net interest expense of $6 million for the year, so its 2004 taxable income was $48 million.

Profit-seeking firms pay taxes calculated as a percentage of their taxable income to the federal government, as well as state income taxes in most states. Composite's tax rate is 35 percent, so, given taxable income of $48 million, the company paid $16.8 million in taxes. The company's 2004 *net income* of $31.2 million was determined by subtracting its $16.8 million tax payment from its $48 million before-tax income.

Performance Ratios

Managers often compute a variety of financial ratios to assess the performance of their firm. These ratios are calculated using data found on both the income statement and the balance sheet. Ratios are then compared with industry standards and with data from previous years. Several ratios are of particular interest to marketers.

A number of commonly used financial ratios focus on *profitability measures*. They are used to assess the firm's ability to generate revenues in excess of expenses and earn an adequate rate of return. Profitability measures include gross profit margin, net profit margin, and return on investment (or sales).

Gross Profit Margin

The gross profit margin equals the firm's gross profit divided by its sales revenues. In 2004, Composite had a gross profit margin of:

$$\frac{\text{Gross Profit}}{\text{Sales}} = \frac{\$105 \text{ million}}{\$300 \text{ million}} = 35\%$$

The gross profit margin is the percentage of each sales dollar that can be used to pay other expenses and meet the firm's profit objectives. Ideally, businesses would like to see gross profit margins that are equal to or higher than those of other firms in their industry. A declining gross profit margin may indicate that the firm is under some competitive price pressure.

Net Profit Margin

The net profit margin equals net income divided by sales. For 2004, Composite had a net profit margin of:

$$\frac{\text{Net Income}}{\text{Sales}} = \frac{\$31.2 \text{ million}}{\$300 \text{ million}} = 10.4\%$$

The net profit margin is the percentage of each sales dollar that the firm earns in profit, or keeps after all expenses have been paid. Companies generally want to see rising, or at least stable, net profit margins.

Return on Investment (ROI) (or Assets)

A third profitability ratio, return on investment, measures the firm's efficiency in generating sales and profits from the total amount invested in the company. A variation of ROI, return on assets, focuses more narrowly on the firm's assets. As the following calculation shows, ROI for Composite Technology during 2004 was 16 percent:

$$\frac{\text{Sales}}{\text{Average Assets}} \times \frac{\text{Net Income}}{\text{Sales}} \times \frac{\text{Net Income}}{\text{Average Assets}}$$

$$\frac{\$300 \text{ million}}{\$200 \text{ million}} \times \frac{\$31.2 \text{ million}}{\$300 \text{ million}} \times \frac{\$31.2 \text{ million}}{\$200 \text{ million}} = 16\%$$

The ROI ratio actually consists of two components. The first component, called *asset turnover,* is the amount of sales generated for each dollar invested. The second component is *net profit margin.* Data for total assets are found on the firm's balance sheet.

Assume that Composite began 2004 with $190 million in assets and ended the year with $210 million in assets. Its average assets for the year would be $200 million.

As was the case for the other profitability ratios, Composite's ROI should be compared with that of other firms in the industry and with its own previous performance to be meaningful.

Inventory Turnover

Inventory turnover is typically categorized as an *activity* ratio because it evaluates the effectiveness of the firm's resource use. Specifically, it measures the number of times a firm "turns" its inventory each year. The ratio can help answer the question of whether the firm has the appropriate level of inventory. Inventory turnover equals cost of goods sold divided by average inventory. From the income statement we see that Composite Technology began 2004 with $70 million in inventory and also ended the year with $70 million in inventory. Therefore, the firm's average inventory was also $70 million. The firm's inventory turnover ratio equals:

$$\frac{\text{Cost of Goods Sold}}{\text{Average Inventory}} = \frac{\$195 \text{ million}}{\$70 \text{ million}} = 2.8 \text{ times per year}$$

For 2004, Composite Technology turned its inventory almost three times a year. While a faster inventory turn is usually a sign of greater efficiency, to be really meaningful the inventory turnover ratio must be compared with historical data and appropriate peer firm averages. Different organizations can have very different inventory turnover ratios, depending on the types of products they sell. For instance, a supermarket such as Safeway might turn its inventory every two weeks for an annual rate of 26 times per year. By contrast, a large furniture retailer is likely to average only about 2 turns per year. Again, the determination of a "good" or "inadequate" inventory turnover rate depends on typical rates in the industry and the firm's performance in previous years.

Markups and Markdowns

In earlier chapters we discussed the importance of pricing decisions for firms. This section expands on our prior discussion by introducing two important pricing concepts: markups and markdowns. They can help to establish selling prices and evaluate various pricing strategies, and are closely tied to a firm's income statement.

Markups

The amount that a marketer adds to a product's cost to set the final selling price is the *markup.* The amount of the markup typically results from two marketing decisions:

1. *The services performed by the marketer.* Other things being equal, retailers who offer more services charge larger markups to cover their costs.

2. *The inventory turnover rate.* Other things being equal, retailers with a higher turnover rate can cover their costs and earn a profit while charging a smaller markup.

A marketer's markup exerts an important influence on its image among present and potential customers. In addition, the markup affects the retailer's ability to attract shoppers. An excessive markup may drive away customers; an inadequate markup may fail to generate sufficient income to cover costs and return a profit.

Markups are typically stated as percentages of either the selling prices or the costs of the products. The formulas for calculating markups are as follows:

$$\text{Markup Percentage on Selling Price} = \frac{\text{Amount Added to Cost (Markup)}}{\text{Selling Price}}$$

$$\text{Markup Percentage on Cost} = \frac{\text{Amount Added to Cost (Markup)}}{\text{Cost}}$$

Consider a product with an invoice of 60 cents and a selling price of $1. The total markup (selling price less cost) is 40 cents. The two markup percentages are calculated as follows:

$$\text{Markup Percentage on Selling Price} = \frac{\$0.40}{\$1.00} = 40\%$$

$$\text{Markup Percentage on Cost} = \frac{\$0.40}{\$0.60} = 66.7\%$$

To determine the selling price knowing only the cost and markup percentage on selling price, a marketer applies the following formula:

$$\text{Price} = \frac{\text{Cost in Dollars}}{100\% - \text{Markup Percentage on Selling Price}}$$

In the previous example, to determine the correct selling price of $1, the marketer would calculate as follows:

$$\text{Price} = \frac{\$0.60}{100\% - 40\%} = \frac{\$0.60}{60\%} = \$1.00$$

Similarly, you can convert the markup percentage from a specific item based on the selling price to one based on cost and the reverse using the following formulas:

$$\text{Markup Percentage on Selling Price} = \frac{\text{Markup \% on Cost}}{100\% + \text{Markup \% Based on Cost}}$$

$$\text{Markup Percentage on Cost} = \frac{\text{Markup Percentage on Selling Price}}{100\% - \text{Markup \% on Selling Price}}$$

Again, data from the previous example give the following conversions:

$$\text{Markup Percentage on Selling Price} = \frac{6.7\%}{100\% + 66.7\%} = \frac{66.7\%}{166.7\%} = 40\%$$

$$\text{Markup Percentage on Cost} = \frac{40\%}{100\% - 40\%} = \frac{40\%}{60\%} = 66.7\%$$

Marketers determine markups based partly on their judgments of the amounts that consumers will pay for a given product. When buyers refuse to pay a product's stated price, however, or when improvements in other products or fashion changes reduce the appeal of the current merchandise, a producer or retailer must take a markdown.

Markdowns

A markdown is a price reduction a firm makes on an item. Reasons for markdowns include sales promotions featuring price reductions or a decision that the initial price was too high. Unlike markups, markdowns cannot be determined from the income statement since the price reduction takes place before the sale occurs. The markdown percentage equals dollar markdowns divided by sales. For example, a retailer may decide to reduce the price of an item by $10, from $50 to $40, and sells 1,000 units. The markdown percentage equals:

$$(1,000 \times \$10)/(\$1,000 \times \$40)$$
$$\$10,000/\$40,000 = 25\%$$

New-Product Analysis

Throughout *Contemporary Marketing* we discussed the steps involved in the development and marketing of new products. The following section deals with how marketers can determine whether a new product will be profitable. Marketers do this by comparing the benefits of a new product to its cost. If the benefits exceed the cost, then the product is profitable.

When you take a course in finance you will learn about a concept called capital investment analysis, or capital budgeting, and the net present value technique. While often used to analyze the purchase of expensive, long-lived assets, such as machines, the net present value technique can also be used to analyze the profit potential of a new product.

Net present value compares the present value of cash inflows produced over a specific time period by an investment, such as a new product, with the present value of cash outflows associated with the investment. Future cash flows are discounted because money has time value—that is, the value of a dollar received at some point in the future is worth less than a dollar today. Only cash flows directly or indirectly linked to the investment are relevant. In other words, consider only cash flows that would occur if the new product is introduced. Let's work through an example.

Assume that during 2003 Composite Technology was offered a contract to produce a new type of composite panel. The contract calls for the production and delivery of 5,000 panels per year for five years beginning in 2004 at a price of $5,000 per panel. Composite estimates that the variable cost of each panel is $3,000 and fixed production costs are $6 million per year. To produce the panels, Composite will have to invest $10 million immediately in plant and equipment and $1 million in working capital (such as inventory and accounts receivable). The working capital will be released at the end of five years. The plant and equipment will be depreciated over the five-year life of the product. At the end of five years, it will be worthless. Composite's tax rate is 35 percent, and its required return on capital is 10 percent. Is the new product profitable?

Data for Calculating New-Product Profitability

Number of units sold (per year)	5,000
Price per unit	$5,000
Variable cost per unit	$3,000
Fixed costs per year	$6,000,000
Capital investments	$10,000,000
Working capital investments	$1,000,000
Tax rate	35%
Required rate of return	10%

		Year				
	2003	2004	2005	2006	2007	2008
Revenues		$25,000,000	$25,000,000	$25,000,000	$25,000,000	$25,000,000
Variable costs		($15,000,000)	($15,000,000)	($15,000,000)	($15,000,000)	($15,000,000)
Fixed costs		($6,000,000)	($6,000,000)	($6,000,000)	($6,000,000)	($6,000,000)
Depreciation		($2,000,000)	($2,000,000)	($2,000,000)	($2,000,000)	($2,000,000)
Before-tax profits		$2,000,000	$2,000,000	$2,000,000	$2,000,000	$2,000,000
Taxes		($700,000)	($700,000)	($700,000)	($700,000)	($700,000)
After-tax profits		$1,300,000	$1,300,000	$1,300,000	$1,300,000	$1,300,000
Depreciation		$2,000,000	$2,000,000	$2,000,000	$2,000,000	$2,000,000
Capital investment	($10,000,000)					
Working capital investment	($1,000,000)					$1,000,000
After-tax case flows	($11,000,000)	$3,300,000	$3,300,000	$3,300,000	$3,300,000	$4,300,000
Present value	($11,000,000)	$3,000,000	$2,727,273	$2,479,339	$2,253,944	$2,669,962
Net present value	$2,130,518					

Table B.1 shows the relevant cash flows from the new product. Cash outflows during 2003 were $11 million ($10 million for plant and equipment and $1 million for working capital). Note that working capital will be a positive cash flow in 2008 when it is released. Starting in 2004, revenues are $25 million ($5,000 x 5,000 units) and variable costs are $15 million ($3,000 x 5,000 units). Fixed costs are $6 million, and the depreciation charge is $2 million ($10 million divided by five). Subtracting costs from revenues gives us before-tax profits. Subtracting taxes of $700,000 gives us annual after-tax profits of $1.3 million. To calculate the actual after-tax cash flow produced by the new product, we need to add the depreciation charge to after-tax profits. Keep in mind that depreciation is a noncash expense. The product's after-tax cash flow equals $3.3 million per year in 2004 through 2007 and $4.3 million in 2008.

Because money has time value, we discount each of the annual after-tax cash flows by 10 percent, the required return on capital specified by Composite's top management. Adding up the present value of all cash flows, including the initial cash outlay of $11 million, gives us our net present value: about $2.13 million. Because the product's net present value is positive, the product is profitable for Composite Technology—the present value of benefits (cash inflows) exceeds the present value of costs (cash outflows). Even though this example is simplified, in the real world firms use the same basic procedure when analyzing the financial aspects of new products.

Assignments

1. Obtain a recent income statement and balance sheet for a business of your choosing whose stock is publicly traded. (A good source of recent financial statements is the MSN Investor Web site, **http://investor.msn.com**.) Use the relevant data included on the income statement to calculate each of the following ratios:
   a. gross profit margin
   b. net profit margin
   c. inventory turnover
   d. return on assets
   e. price markup

2. Choose a new product you've heard about recently and are interested in learning more about. Prepare a list of all the items the firm had to estimate when first evaluating the profitability of the product.

PROLOGUE

1. Julie Rawe, "Young & Jobless," *Time*, June 6, 2002, pp. 36–39; Stephanie Armour, "Young Job Seekers Get Squeezed Out," *USA Today*, January 29, 2002, p. B1.
2. Joanne Gordon, "Battle of the Boards," *Forbes*, August 12, 2002, p. 50.
3. Diya Gullapalli, "Who Says Interns No Longer Get Any Perks?" *The Wall Street Journal*, July 30, 2002, pp. B1, B8.
4. Reported in Louis E. Boone, *Quotable Business, 2nd ed.* New York: Random House, 1999, p. 103.
5. Daniel Eisenberg, "The Coming Job Boom," *Time*, May 6, 2002, p. 41.
6. Christine Galea, "2002 Salary Survey," *Sales & Marketing Management*, May 2002, p. 34.

CHAPTER 1

1. Steven Levy, "Pirates of The Internet," *Newsweek*, August 4, 2003, p. 48; Chris Taylor, "Downloader Dragnet," *Time*, August 4, 2003, p. 42; Jenny Eliscu, "Downloaders Beware," *Rolling Stone*, July 24, 2003, p. 22; Jefferson Graham, "Unlimited Downloads Are Now PC," *USA Today*, July 22, 2003, p. D3; Megan Johnston, "Say, Ya Want a Revolution?" *Money*, July 2003, p. 114; Michelle Kessler, "Lawsuits May Help Net Song Sellers," *USA Today*, June 30, 2003, p. 2B; "Artists Flee Labels," *Rolling Stone*, June 26, 2003, p. 16; May Wong, "Apple Computer's Chief Pulls Off Coup in Music Industry," *Mobile Register*, May 10, 2003, p. B1.
2. David M. Szymanski and David H. Henard, "Customer Satisfaction: A Meta-Analysis of the Empirical Evidence," *Journal of the Academy of Marketing Science*, Winter 2001, vol. 29, no. 1, pp. 16–35.
3. Erik Hedegaard, "The Osbournes—America's First Family," *Rolling Stone*, May 9, 2002, pp. 33–36; Edna Gundersen, Bill Kennedy, and Ann Oldenburg, "'The Osbournes' Find a Home in America's Living Rooms," *USA Today*, April 19, 2002, pp. A1, A2.
4. David Finnigan, "Toy Kingpins Find Reluctant Buyers with Showroom Virtually Quiet," *Brandweek*, February 18, 2002, pp. 11–12; Seth M. Siegel, "The Quietest Toy Fair," *Brandweek*, February 11, 2002, pp. 23–24.
5. Joseph P. Guiltinan and Gordon W. Paul, *Marketing Management*, 6th ed. (New York: McGraw-Hill, 1996), pp. 3–4.
6. Betsy McKay, "In a Water Fight, Coke and Pepsi Try Opposite Tacks," *Wall Street Journal*, April 18, 2002, pp. A1, A8.
7. Advertisement, copyright 2001, New York Stock Exchange.
8. Zachary Schiller, "Make It Simple," *Business Week*, September 9, 1996, p. 102.
9. Paul A. Herbig, *Handbook of Cross-Cultural Marketing* (New York: The International Business Press, 1998), pp. 96–100.
10. Robert J. Keith, "The Marketing Revolution," *Journal of Marketing*, January 1960, p. 60.
11. Laura Hillenbrand, *Seabiscuit: An American Legend* (New York: Random House, 2001), pp. 3–6.
12. Robert J. Keith, "The Marketing Revolution," *Journal of Marketing*, January 1960, p. 60.
13. Theodore Levitt, *Innovations in Marketing* (New York: McGraw-Hill, 1962), p. 7.
14. Steven Rosenbush, "Armstrong's Last Stand," *BusinessWeek*, February 25, 2001, pp. 88–96.
15. Ann Marsh, "Ryder System," *Forbes*, May 21, 2001, p. 106.
16. Steve Rosenbush, "Armstrong's Last Stand," *Business Week*, February 25, 2001, pp. 88–96.
17. Jacquelyn Lynn, "Hidden Resources," *Entrepreneur*, January 2000, p. 102.
18. Betsy Spethmann, "Charity Begins at the Home Page," *Promo*, February 2000, p. 52.
19. Ibid., p. 50.
20. Michael M. Phillips, "Taking Stock: Top Sports Pros Find a New Way to Score: Getting Equity Stakes," *Wall Street Journal*, April 18, 1997, pp. A1, A8.
21. Roy Hoffman, "A Conversation with Jimmy Buffett," *Mobile Register*, April 21, 2002, pp. E1, E5; James Brady, "In Step with Jimmy Buffett," *Parade*, April 28, 2002, p. 22.
22. John Rofe, "Giants Take Pauses for Causes," *Sports Business Journal*, April 23–29, 2001, p. 10.
23. Andy Brumer, "Coca-Cola Steps up for Woods' Charity," *Sports Business Journal*, April 29, 2001, p. 10.
24. "Consumers Care About Causes," *Sales & Marketing Management*, June 1999, p. 74; and Linda I. Nowak, "Cause Marketing Alliances: Corporate Associations and Consumer Responses," *Proceedings of the Winter Educators Conference*, St. Petersburg, FL: American Marketing Association, February 1999.
25. Hilary Cassidy, "An Olympic Moment," *Brandweek*, October 29, 2001, pp. 1, 8.
26. Anne Marie Chaker, "Red Cross Will Use the Entire $564 Million of Liberty Fund for September 11 Victims, Relief," *The Wall Street Journal*, November 15, 2001, http://wsjclassroomedition.com.
27. Louis E. Boone and David L. Kurtz, *Recession and the Terrorist Attacks on America* (Mason, OH: South-Western Publishing, 2002).
28. Gene D. Cohen, "c=me," *Modern Maturity*, March–April 2000, p. 43.
29. Mylene Mangalindan, "Yahoo Says Its Online Sales Volume Jumped 86 %," *The Wall Street Journal*, December 27, 2001, p. B2; Chris Pentila, "Wholesell Changes," *Entrepreneur*, May 2002, pp. 48–49.
30. Laura Bly, "Budget Car Rental Joins Online Name-Your-Price Fray," *USA Today*, June 4, 1999, p. A1.
31. Steve Jarvis, "A Whirlwind of Technologies May Sweep up Marketers," *Outlook 2002*, January 7, 2002, p. 8.
32. Ibid.
33. Ibid.
34. Scott McCartney, "Flight of Fancy," *The Wall Street Journal*, February 4, 2002, p. A1.
35. "Forbes Magnetic 40," *Forbes*, May 21, 2001, p. 100.
36. Michael McCarthy, "Anti-Smoking Ad Stirs Up Super Bowl," *USA Today*, January 25, 2002, p. B7.
37. Alan Byrd, "Where NFL Leads, Many Sports Follow," *Street & Smith's Sports Business Journal*, January 4–10, 1999, p. 21.
38. "Shell Gives Students a Head Start," from a special report of the Shell Oil Company, *Fortune*, November 9, 1998, pp. S7–S8.

CHAPTER 2

1. Company Web site, http://www.curvesinternational.com, accessed January 21, 2004; Loryli Nicolaisen, "Curves Simplifies Workouts," *Appeal-Democrat.com*, June 23, 2002; Heather Won Tesoriero, "A Slim Gym's Fat Success," *Time*, May 5, 2003; Molly Martin, "A Few Curves," *The Seattle Times*, January 19, 2003, http://seattletimes.newsource.com.
2. Kathy Mulady, "Nordstrom Way Is Legendary in Shopping," *Seattle P-1.com*, June 26, 2001, http://seattlep-i.nwsource.com; Ron Lieber, "She Reads Customers' Minds," *Fast Company*, February 2001, http://www.fastcompany.com.
3. Louise Lee and Nanette Byrnes, "More Than Just a Bad Patch at the Gap," *Business Week*, February 11, 2002, p. 36.
4. "Office Depot's E-Diva," *Business Week Online*, August 6, 2001, http://www.businessweek.com.
5. Bass Pro Shops promotional brochure, Bass Pro Shops, Springfield, Missouri.
6. Company Web site, http://www.maldenmills.com, accessed March 8, 2002.
7. Darrell Rigby, "Smart Managing/Best Practices, Careers, and Ideas: What's Today's Special at the Consultant's Cafe?" *Fortune*, September 7, 1998, p. 162.
8. Derek F. Abell, "Strategic Window," *Journal of Marketing*, July 1978, pp. 21–26; and John K. Ryans and William L. Shanklin, *Strategic Planning: Concepts and Implementation* (New York: Random House, 1985), p. 11.
9. Stephanie N. Mehta, "Cisco Fractures Its Own Fairy Tale," *Fortune.com*, May 14, 2001, http://www.fortune.com.
10. Presentation by Maxine Clark, St. Louis, March 2002.
11. Genaro C. Armas, "Black, Hispanic Populations Nearly Equal," *Mobile Register*, March 8, 2001, p. A9.
12. Bob Woods, "Hispanic Marketing Can Be Eventful," *Promo*, May 2000, pp. 25–26.
13. "Women on Their Way," Wyndham Hotels Web site, http://www.wyndham.com, accessed January 3, 2003; Katherine Conrad, "Hoteliers Cashing in with Women Business Travelers," *East Bay Business Times*, March 8, 2002, http://eastbay.bizjournals.com.
14. Gary Hamel, "Smart Mover, Dumb Mover," *Fortune*, September 3, 2001, pp. 191–192.
15. Peter Newcomb, "Sony," and Jody Yen, "Georgia-Pacific Group," in "Forbes Magnetic 40," *Forbes*, May 21, 2001, pp. 84, 86.
16. John G. Spooner, "EMachines Shows Off Latest PC Fashions," *C/Net News.com*, April 10, 2002, http://news.com.com.
17. Kathryn Kranhold, "Sotheby's Chief Is Convicted of Price-Fixing," *The Wall Street Journal*, December 6, 2001, p. B1; Noelle Knox, "Former Chairman of Sotheby's Convicted," *USA Today*, December 6, 2001, p. B1.
18. Emily Thornton, "Enviro-Cars: The Race Is On," *Business Week*, February 8, 1999, pp. 74–76.
19. Andrew Gillies, "General Mills," in "Forbes Magnetic 40," *Forbes*, May 21, 2001, p. 86.
20. Scott Thurm, "The Ultimate Weapon," *The Wall Street Journal*, April 17, 2000, p. R18.
21. L.L. Bean Web site, http://www.llbean.com, accessed May 10, 2002; William Symonds, "Paddling Harder at L. L. Bean," *Business Week*, December 7, 1998, pp. 48–49.
22. Eryn Brown, "Just Another Product Launch," *Fortune*, November 12, 2001, p. 104.
23. Alex Taylor III, "Eat Our Dust," *Fortune*, June 11, 2001, p. 151.
24. John Bissell, "Top of the Mind: No. 1 Means Little in Fast Times," *Brandweek*, March 22, 1999, p. 28.
25. A meta-analysis of 48 studies revealed a positive relationship between market share and profitability. See David M. Szymanski, Sundarwaj G. Bharadgaj, and P. Rajan Varadarajan, "An Analysis of the Market Share-Profitability Relationship," *Journal of Marketing*, July 1993, pp. 1–18.

CHAPTER 3

1. Lawrence Ulrich, "The New Green Machines," *Money*, July 2003, pp. 117–119; Stuart F. Brown, "Dude, Where's My Hybrid?" *Fortune*, April 28, 2003, pp. 112–118; Sholnn Freeman, "Hybrid Cars Attract More Buyers," *The Wall Street Journal*, March 13, 2003, p. D3.

2. "Top 10 Scams on the Information Highway," *U.S. News & World Report,* November 13, 2000, p. 16; Paul Keegan, "Online Auctions: From Seedy Flea Markets to Big Business," *Upside,* July 1999, pp. 70–80; Kip Cheng, "eBay: Best Virtual Marketing," *Adweek,* June 28, 1999, p. 42.

3. Larry Margasak, "UPS Flexed Political Muscle to Win First Flights to China," *Mobile Register,* April 11, 2001, p. B6; Charles Haddad, "How UPS Delivered through the Disaster," *BusinessWeek,* October 1, 2001, p. 66.

4. "MasterCard and Hotel Reservations Announce Strategic Alliance," *Card News,* February 20, 2002; "Love at First Site," *Art & Auction,* July/August 1999, p. 7.

5. "Go to Jail," *Forbes,* May 29, 2000, p. 62.

6. G. Pascal Zachary, "Let's Play Oligopoly!" *The Wall Street Journal,* March 8, 1999, p. B1.

7. David Pringle, "Motorola Hopes Early Push in 3G Market Yields Gains," *The Wall Street Journal,* March 28, 2002, p. B4; Jennifer Tanaka, "Design: The Coolest Cell Phone Wins," *Newsweek,* February 25, 2002, p. 9; Maureen Tkacik, "Hey Dude, This Sure Isn't the Gap—Pink Fur Pants, Tongue Rings Draw 'Alternative' Teens to Hot Topic's Mall Stores," *The Wall Street Journal,* February 12, 2002, p. B1.

8. Paulo Prada and Bruce Orwall, "A Certain 'Je Ne Sais Quoi' at Disney's New Park," *The Wall Street Journal,* March 12, 2002, p. B1.

9. Gardiner Harris, "Back to the Lab," *The Wall Street Journal,* January 29, 2002, p. A1.

10. Amy Tsao, "Fiorina's Stereotype-Smashing Performance," *BusinessWeek,* April 3, 2002, http://www .businessweek.com; Kristine Ellis, "Sharing Best Practices Globally," *Training,* July 2001.

11. Faith Keenan and Spencer E. Ante, "The New Teamwork," *BusinessWeek,* February 18, 2002, http://www.businessweek.com.

12. Dori Jones Yang, "Leaving Moore's Law in the Dust," *U.S. News & World Report,* July 10, 2000, p. 37.

13. Michael Gartenburg, "Enough Is Enough with Microsoft Case," *Computerworld,* March 25, 2002, p. 25; Joseph Nocera, "Witnesses in Wonderland," *Fortune,* March 1, 1999, pp. 168–180.

14. "DotCons," *Entrepreneur,* March 2001, p. 24; John Rendleman, "FTC Steers Clear of Internet Regulation—For Now," *Informationweek,* October 9, 2000. See also http://www.ftc.gov/bcp/ conline/edcams/dotcon.

15. Elizabeth Crowley and Glenn R. Simpson, "Citicorp Joins Up with Secret Service to Fight E-Fraud," *The Wall Street Journal,* March 16, 2000, p. A12.

16. Dana James, "Deregulation Growing by Fits and Starts," *Marketing News,* June 5, 2000, p. 10.

17. Bryan Gruly and Rebecca Smith, "Anatomy of a Fall: Keys to Success Left Kenneth Lay Open to Disaster," *The Wall Street Journal,* April 26, 2002, pp. A1, A5; "AGL Chief Sees Deregulation Reform in Georgia," *Reuters Limited,* January 28, 2002.

18. William Glanz, "Bankruptcies Climb to Record Levels in 2001," *The Washington Times,* February 20, 2002.

19. Tully, "From Bad to Worse."

20. Jeannine Aversa, "Unemployment Rate Hits 6 Percent," Associated Press, downloaded from AOL.com, May 3, 2002.

21. Joan Raymond, "The Jaws of Victory," *Newsweek,* March 18, 2002, p. 38P.

22. Betsy Shiffman, "Still Want to Teach the World to Sing?" *Forbes,* January 16, 2002; Brian Zajac, "Yankee Travelers," *Forbes,* July 27, 1998, p. 162.

23. "High Powered Alliance Demonstrates Wireless Internet Services in China," *Direct Marketing,* August 2000, p. 12.

24. Marc L. Songini, "Phillips Gives Petroleum Blending Software the Gas," *Computerworld,* March 18, 2002, p. 19.

25. Anita Hamilton, "Why Hybrids Are Hot," *Time,* April 29, 2002, pp. 52–53.

26. Daniel Fisher, "When the National Nanny Does Your Laundry," *Forbes,* July 9, 2001, p. 64.

27. Kerry A. Dolan and Quentin Hardy, "The Challenge from China," *Forbes,* May 13, 2002, pp. 73–76.

28. Gaston F. Ceron, "Online Brokerage Firms Face Pinched Earnings," *The Wall Street Journal,* July 16, 2001, p. B8; Charles Gasparino and Rebecca Buckman, "Facing Internet Threat, Merrill to Offer Trading Online for Low Fees," *The Wall Street Journal,* June 1, 1999, pp. A1, A10.

29. Scott Woolley, "Steal This Movie," *Forbes,* February 18, 2002, p. 66.

30. "Dieste Multicultural Shop of Year," *Advertising Age,* January 14, 2002, p. S-8.

31. Leslie E. Royal, "Make 'Lemon Law' Lemonade," *Black Enterprise,* May 2001, p. 150; Lawrence Lindner, "Whole Grains, Half Truths; You Must Know the Code to Tell the Whole Wheat from the Chaff," *The Washington Post,* July 31, 2001, p. F1.

32. O. C. Ferrell, John Fraedrich, and Linda Ferrell, *Business Ethics* (Boston, MA: Houghton Mifflin Company, 2002), pp. 85–86; David Barboza, "Tyson Fosters Ties to Officials but Is Unable to Avoid Scrutiny," *The New York Times,* January 1, 2002, p. C1.

33. Jim Carroll, "Significant Drop in Teen Smoking Is Recorded in U.S.," *The Wall Street Journal,* December 20, 2001, http://www.wsj.com; Corinne Economaki, "Still Smokin' at the Track," *Brandweek,* March 22, 1999, pp. 20–22; Robert D. Deutsch, "A Eulogy for Joe Camel," *Brandweek,* May 3, 1999, pp. 29, 32.

34. Larry Dobrow, "Tread Carefully on Privacy," *Advertising Age,* October 29, 2001, http://www .adage.com; Megan Santosus, "The Price Is Right," *CIO Enterprise,* June 15, 1999, p. 24.

35. "DoubleClick Settles Online-Privacy Suits, Plans to Ensure Protections, Pay Legal Fees," *The Wall Street Journal,* April 1, 2002, p. B8.

36. Eilene Hu, "What That Seal of 'Approval' Really Means," *McCall's,* November 1998, p. 152.

37. Brandon Copple, "Bake Off," *Forbes,* April 16, 2001, p. 305.

38. Cindy Starr, "Pharmaceutical Advertising Barrage Lures Consumers, Worries Doctors," Scripps Howard News Service, February 2, 2002; Devika Sennik, "Influence of Direct to Consumer Pharmaceutical Advertising and Patients' Requests on Prescribing Decision," *British Medical Journal,* February 2, 2002.

39. Laura Johannes and David Armstrong, "Why Some Dialysis Patients Take $12-a-Day Drug Instead of Tums," *The Wall Street Journal,* June 26, 2001, p. B1.

40. Donna Rosato, "New Travel Sites under Scrutiny on Ticket Costs," *USA Today,* May 24, 2000, p. 1B; Ira Teinowitz, "Web Ad Disclosures Examined," *Advertising Age,* May 24, 1999, p. 48.

41. "Schering-Plough Corp.: U.S. Attorney Begins Issuing Subpoenas in Pricing Probe," *The Wall Street Journal,* April 1, 2002, p. C5.

42. Karen Lowry Miller, "The Pill Machine," *Newsweek,* November 19, 2001, p. 46.

43. Joel Dreyfuss, "Planned Obsolescence Is Alive and Well," *Fortune,* February 15, 1999, p. 192.

44. Bob Garfield, "Inspiration and Urge-to-Serve Mark the Best of Ad Council," *Advertising Age,* April 29, 2002, p. C2.

45. Michelle Kessler, "PC Makers Soon May Be Forced to Recycle," *USA Today,* February 26, 2002, p. B1.

46. Christopher Tkaczyk, "Recycling," *Fortune,* April 1, 2002, p. 36; Laura Cohn, "The Nuclear Waste Debate: All Over but the Shouting?" *BusinessWeek,* December 10, 2001, p. 43; John T. Maybury, "Your Wedding Band May Have Once Lived in a Computer," *Forbes ASAP,* February 22, 1999, p. 20.

47. Arlene Weintraub and Laura Cohn, "A Thousand-Year Plan for Nuclear Waste," *BusinessWeek,* May 6, 2002, pp. 94, 96.

48. Geoffrey A. Fowler, "Green Sales Pitch Isn't Moving Many Products," *The Wall Street Journal,* March 6, 2001, p. B1.

49. "The Nation's CEOs Look to the Future," National Institute of Science and Technology, http:// www .quality.nist.gov, June 16, 1999.

CHAPTER 4

1. European Union Web site, http://europa.eu.int, accessed January 23, 2004; "U.S., EU Must Work Together, Powell Says," *U.S. Department of State,* April 16, 2003, http://usinfo.state.gov; Brandon Mitchener, "Ten New Members to Weigh in on Future of EU," *The Wall Street Journal,* April 16, 2003, p. A16; "EU Sets Financial Terms of Growth," *CBS.MarketWatch,* December 13, 2002, http://www.CBS.MarketWatch.com; "EU Reaches Landmark Expansion Deal," *BBC News,* October 9, 2002, http://news.bbc.co.uk.

2. Margret Johnson, "Report: U.S. Hi-Tech Exports Now Largest Segment," IDG News Service, March 13, 2000, http://www.idg.net; Eric S. Hardy, "An Almost Perfect World," *Forbes,* July 26, 1999, pp. 160–161.

3. Wendy Zellner et al., "How Well Does Wal-Mart Travel?" *Business Week,* September 3, 2001, pp. 82, 84.

4. "About New York Metro Weddings," company Web site, http://www.NewYorkMetroWeddings .com, accessed January 13, 2003; Scott S. Smith, "The Vow Factor," *Entrepreneur,* February 2001, http://www.entrepreneur.com.

5. Ad for Hilton HHonors Worldwide, copyright 2002 Hilton HHonors Worldwide.

6. "IDC Predicts Worldwide Internet Services Revenues Will Surge Past $78 million in 2003," *NetScorecard,* http://www.netscorecard.com, accessed June 9, 1999.

7. "Finance Site the Stickiest Online," http://cyberatlas.internet.com, February 28, 2002; Michael Pastore, "Branches Still Rule Banking in Europe," http://cyberatlas.internet.com, November 19, 2001.

8. "REI Opens First International Store in Tokyo," *Sports Trend,* June 2000, p. 6.

9. Business Latin America, "Two U.S. Fast Food Chains Expand Locally," Yahoo Finance, biz.yahoo.com, February 25, 2002; "Arby's to Open 102 Restaurants in Britain," *Mobile Register,* July 11, 1999, p. 6B.

10. Mark Tatge, "Burgertory," *Forbes,* June 11, 2001, p. 76; and Jonathan Asher, "Global Branding: Same, but Different," *Brandweek,* April 9, 2001, p. 25.

11. Jack Neff, "Test in Paris, France, Launch It in Paris, Texas," *Advertising Age,* May 31, 1999, p. 26; and Jack Neff, "P&G Marks First with U.S. Test of Swiffer," *Advertising Age,* July 12, 1998, p. 32.

12. "World Population Profile: 1998 Highlights," U.S. Census Bureau, http://www.census.gov, accessed April 11, 2002.

13. Daniel Fisher, "Gone Flat," *Forbes,* October 15, 2001, p. 79.

14. Betsy McKay, "Pepsi and Coke Roll Out Flavors to Boost Sales," *The Wall Street Journal,* May 7, 2002, pp. B1, B4; "The Coca-Cola Co.," *Hoover's Online* company capsule, http://www.hoovers .com, accessed April 26, 2002.

15. John A. Byrne, "Today, Mexico. Tomorrow . . . ," *BusinessWeek,* April 10, 2000, p. 184.

16. Mercedes M. Cardona, "J&J Readies U.S. Intro of Leading French Brand," *Advertising Age,* July 12, 1999, p. 57.

17. David Woodruff, "For French Retailers, a Weapon against Wal-Mart," *The Wall Street Journal,* September 27, 1999, p. B1.

18. Miriam Jordan, "Marketing Gurus Say: In India, Think Cheap, Lose the Cold Cereal," *The Wall Street Journal,* October 11, 1996, p. A7.

19. Reuters Limited, "Nokia Looks to Dominate Sales in China," *CNet Asia,* February 26, 2002, asia.cnet.com; Andrew Tanzer, "China Goes Wireless," *Forbes,* July 26, 1999, pp. 60–63.

20. Geri Smith et al., "A Wrong Turn?" *BusinessWeek,* January 21, 2002, pp. 42–44; Tony Smith, "Argentina Devalues Peso, Drops Peg to Dollar," *Mobile Register,* January 7, 2002, p. A7.

21. Colleen Barry, "Euro Currency Begins in Europe," *Mobile Register,* January 1, 2002, p. A11; and "Europeans Make Change to Euro," *USA Today,* December 26, 2001, p. 3B.

22. Lalita Khosla, "You Say Tomato," *Forbes,* May 21, 2001, p. 36.

23. Desa Philadelphia, "And What Does It Mean in Farsi?" *Time Global Business,* November 2001, pp. B16–17; David Lieberman, "I'd Like to Buy a Vowel, Drivers Say," *USA Today,* August 9, 2001, p. B3; Sally McGrane, "Cultural Web Faux Pas," *Forbes ASAP,* February 21, 2000, p. 28.

24. *Marketing News,* July 3, 2000, p. 15; "Projected Growth of Online Population," *Mobile Register,* June 25, 2000, p. 6A; "The Web Is Truly Worldwide," *Global Insights,* June 1999, pp. 1–2.

25. "Europe to Demand Strict Molecular Characterisation for GMOs?" the Institute of Science in Society press release, May 21, 2002, http://www.biotech-info.net; Amy Bowdler and Emily Felt, "GMO's Exporters Should Follow the Debate," *Insight,* Summer 1999, pp. 1–2.

26. Anne Neville, "France's Shopping Frenzy: All's Well That Sells Well," *Mobile Register,* February 25, 1999, p. 3D.

27. Dexter Roberts et al., "Days of Rage," *Business Week,* April 8, 2002, pp. 50–51.

28. Lisa Bertagnoli, "E-Marketing Tricky in Europe," *Marketing News,* July 16, 2001, p. 19.

29. Michael Plogell and Felix Hofer, "No-Nos in Europe," *Promo,* April 2000, p. 23.

30. Antoaneta Bezlova, "McDonald's Arches Outlawed in Beijing," *USA Today,* March 5, 2002, p. 7B.

31. "Landmark Trade Agreement Sets Vietnam on Course Toward Reform," *Mobile Register,* July 15, 2000, p. 6B.

32. Martin Crutsinger, "Canadian Timber Slapped with Tariff," *USA Today,* August 13, 2001, p. B3.

33. James Cox, "Tariffs Shield Some U.S. Products," *USA Today,* May 6, 1999, pp. B1, B2.

34. Andrew Tanzer, "The Great Quota Hustle," *Forbes,* March 6, 2000, p. 124.

35. James Bennett, "To Clear the Air with Europe, U.S. Waives Some Sanctions," *The New York Times,* May 19, 1998, http://www.nytimes.com, accessed July 27, 1999.

36. Aaron Bernstein, "Backlash," *Business Week,* April 24, 2000, pp. 38–48.

37. Paul Geitner, "World Trade Organization Hands Major Loss to U.S.," *Mobile Register,* January 15, 2002, p. B5.

38. "USWA Challenging NAFTA Constitutionality in Lawsuit," *Fair Trade Watch,* http://www.fairtradewatch.org, accessed July 27, 1999; David C. Datelle, "NAFTA's Effect on U.S. Jobs," *Progressive Policy Institute,* http://www.ppionline.org, accessed July 28, 1999.

39. Jim Rogers, "Running on Empty," *Worth,* January/February 2002, pp. 55–56; Traci Carl, "Mexican Stand-off on Trade," *The Morning News,* August 22, 2001, p. 3C; Geri Smith, "Is the Magic Starting to Fade?" *Business Week,* August 6, 2001, pp. 42–43; Charles J. Whalen et al., "NAFTA's Scorecard: So Far, So Good," *Business Week,* July 9, 2001, p. 54.

40. Geri Smith et al., "Betting on Free Trade," *Business Week,* April 23, 2001, pp. 60, 62.

41. Geri Smith et al., "Mexico Pulls Off Another Trade Coup," *Business Week,* February 7, 2000, p. 56.

42. Lambeth Hochwald, "Are You Smart Enough to Sell Globally?" *Sales & Marketing Management,* July 1998, pp. 53–55.

43. Jay Green and Ken Belson, "The Mariners Catch a Tsunami," *Business Week,* June 25, 2001, pp. 98–99.

44. "Foreign Direct Investment Is on the Rise around the World," *The New Economy Index,* accessed April 26, 2002, http://www.neweconomyindex.org; Russell B. Scholl, "The International Investment Position of the United States at Year-end 1998," *Survey of Current Business,* U.S. Bureau of Economic Analysis, July 1999, pp. 4, 7.

45. Stephen Baker, "Why Europe Keeps Gobbling Up U.S. Companies," *Business Week,* June 18, 2001.

46. Lisa Bertagnoli, "Middle East Muddle," *Marketing News,* July 16, 2001, pp. 1, 9.

47. Herb Greenberg, "Does Tyco Play Accounting Games?" *Fortune,* May 6, 2002, pp. 83–86; Peter Marsh, "Tyco Searches for Directors in Europe and Asia," *Financial Times,* July 16, 2001, http://news.ft.com.

48. Jonathan Asher, "Global Branding: Same, but Different," *Brandweek,* April 9, 2001, p. 25.

49. William Echikson and Dean Foust, "For Coke, Local Is It," *Business Week,* July 3, 2000, p. 122.

50. Ibid.

51. "The Best Global Brands," *Business Week,* August 5, 2002, pp. 92–96.

52. Juliana Korentang, "SonicNet Tunes into Youth Music Worldwide," *Ad Age International,* June 1999, p. 29.

53. Venture Safenet Inc. Web site, http://www.vsnet.com, accessed January 12, 2003.

54. Stephen Baker, "Why Europe Keeps Gobbling up U.S. Companies," *Business Week,* June 18, 2001, p. 56.

CHAPTER 5

1. Robyn Greenspan, "Net-Driven Sales to Surge," *CyberAtlas,* May 29, 2003, http://cyberatlas.internet.com; Timothy J. Mullaney et al., "E-Biz Surprise," *Business Week,* May 12, 2003, pp. 60–68; Thomas Mucha, "The Minimart," *Business 2.0,* May 2003, p. 89; Mark Athitakis, "How to Make Money on the Net," *Business 2.0,* May 2003, pp. 83–87.

2. CyberAtlas, accessed from the CyberAtlas Web Site, http://cyberatlas.internet.com, April 15, 2002.

3. Robert Hof, "Don't Cut Back Now," *Business Week,* accessed at the *Business Week* Web site, http://www.businessweek.com, March 30, 2002.

4. Neoforma, accessed from the Neoforma Web site, http://www.neoforma.com, April 8, 2002.

5. CyberAtlas, accessed from the CyberAtlas Web site, http://cyberatlas.internet.com, April 8, 2002.

6. Lisa Bowman, "Disney Wins Round in Movie-Trailer Case," CNET News, accessed from the CNET Web site, http://www.cnet.com, April 9, 2002.

7. "Top of the Week," *U.S. News & World Report,* April 15, 2002, p. 15.

8. CyberAtlas, accessed from the CyberAtlas Web site, http://cyberatlas.internet.com, April 9, 2002.

9. CIO Web Business, accessed from the CIO Web site, http://www.cio.com, March 29, 2002.

10. CIO Web Business, accessed from the CIO Web site, http://www.cio.com, March 30, 2002.

11. Lands' End, accessed from the Lands' End Web site, http://www.landsend.com, April 12, 2002; Dell Computer, accessed from the Dell Computer Web site, http://www.dell.com, April 12, 2002; *USA Today,* accessed from the *USA Today* Web site, http://www.usatoday.com, April 12, 2002; Farm.com, accessed from the Farm.com Web site, http://www.farm.com, April 12, 2002.

12. http://cyberatlas.internet.com, accessed April 22, 2002.

13. "H.J. Heinz Company Case Study," http://www.freemarkets.com, accessed March 27, 2002.

14. http://cyberatlas.internet.com, accessed April 22, 2002.

15. Alex Salkever and Olga Kharif, "Business' Killer App: The Web," *Business Week,* http://www.businessweek.com, accessed April 15, 2002.

16. IBM, accessed from the IBM Web site, http://www.ibm.com, April 15, 2002.

17. Robert Hof et al., "The 'Click Here' Economy," *Business Week,* http://www.businessweek.com, accessed April 15, 2002.

18. Alex Salkever and Olga Kharif, "Business' Killer App: The Web."

19. "Falling in Gov," *Entrepreneur,* March 2002, pp. 58–63.

20. Anne D'Innocenzio, "2nd Chance for Customizing," Associated Press, http://www.ap.org, accessed April 15, 2002.

21. HistoryBuff.com, http://www.historybuff.com, accessed April 17, 2002.

22. Robyn Greenspan, "Customer Service Is Key to Travelers," http://cyberatlas.internet.com, accessed April 17, 2002.

23. Amy Tsao, "Where Retailers Shop for Savings," *Business Week,* http://www.businessweek.com, accessed April 17, 2002.

24. AutoNetwork.com, http://www.autonetwork.com, accessed April 17, 2002.

25. http://cyberatlas.internet.com, accessed April 22, 2002.

26. Ibid.

27. Ibid.

28. Marcia Stepanek, "None of Your Business," *Business Week,* http://www.businessweek.com, accessed March 28, 2002.

29. Ibid.

30. "Privacy Groups Ask for Investigation of Amazon.com," ZDNet News, http://www.zdnet.com, accessed March 29, 2002; Nick Wingfield, "Amazon Clarifies Customer Info Policy," *Wall Street Journal,* http://www.zdnet.com, accessed March 29, 2002.

31. Nick Wingfield, "Amazon Clarifies Customer Info Policy."

32. "PrivaSeek E-Wallet Protects Privacy," *PC World,* http://www.pcworld.com, accessed March 21, 2002.

33. http://www.cyberatlas.com, accessed April 22, 2002.

34. Source: U.S. Department of Commerce, http://www.doc.gov, accessed April 17, 2002.

35. "Irrelevance through Constant Consumer Analysis," Jupiter Media Metrix, http://www.jmm.com, accessed April 17, 2002.

36. Ibid.

37. About Dell Computer, accessed at the Dell Web site, http://www.dell.com, April 22, 2002.

38. http://cyberatlas.internet.com, accessed April 22, 2002.

39. J. William Gurley, "The One Internet Metric that Really Matters," Fortune, http://www.fortune.com, accessed March 29, 2002.

40. "Success Story: Lexmark International," WebCriteria, http://www.webcriteria.com, accessed March 18, 2002.

CHAPTER 6

1. Company Web site, http://www.dylanscandybar.com, accessed January 12, 2004; Donna Fenn, "A Knack for Sweet Deals," *Inc.,* April 2003, pp. 25–26; Devlin Smith, "Candy Heaven," *Entrepreneur,* December 2002, http://www.entrepreneur.com.

2. Lawrence A. Crosby and Sheree L. Johnston, "CRM and Management," *Marketing Management,* January/February 2002, p. 10.

3. Cara B. DiPasquale, "CRM: Navigate the Maze," *Advertising Age,* October 29, 2001, p. s1.

4. Wendy Cole, "Suddenly Loyalty Is Back in Business," *Time* Bonus Section: Your Business, December 2001, pp. Y13–16.

5. Veronica Agosta, "Nat City Takes Customer Focus to the Airwaves," *American Banker,* March 19, 2002, p. 1.

6. Karen Norman Kennedy, Felicia G. Lask, and Jerry R. Goolsby, "Customer Mind-Set of Employees throughout the Organization," *Journal of the Academy of Marketing Science,* Spring 2002, Vol. 30, No. 2, pp. 159–71; and Cole, "Suddenly Loyalty Is Back in Business."

7. Alan J. Liddle, "Internal Marketing As Important to Success at Pleasing Customers," *Restaurant News,* October 29, 2001, p. 60; and Jennifer Koch Laabs, "Optimas 2001—General Excellence: Thinking Outside the Box At The Container Store," *Workforce,* March 2001, pp. 35–38.

8. Mary Naylor and Susan Greco, *How to Keep the Customers You Want—and Say "Good-bye" to the Ones You Don't* (New York: McGraw-Hill, 2002).

9. Andy Cohen, "Look Who's Cooking Now," *Sales & Marketing Management,* December 2001, pp. 31–35.

10. Mary Jo Bitner, "Building Service Relationships: It's All About Promises," *Journal of the Academy of Marketing Science,* Fall 1995, pp. 246–251.

11. Cynthia Crossen, "The Big Power Crunch—Hot Selling Point: Guaranteed Cost of Utility Bills," *The Wall Street Journal,* May 9, 2001, p. B1.

12. Ron Zemke, "Training Top 100: FedEx," *Training,* March 2002, p. 67.

13. Leonard L. Berry, "Relationship Marketing of Service-Growing Internet, Emerging Perspectives," *Journal of the Academy of Marketing Science,* Fall 1995, p. 240.

14. "Deals and Discounts," *The New York Times,* March 17, 2002, p. 3.
15. Edmund O. Lawler, "Fine Line Between Added Value, Spam," *Advertising Age,* October 29, 2001, p. s4.
16. Bernard Stamler, "The Web Doesn't Sell Cars, But Lets Buyers Build Their Own," *The New York Times,* September 26, 2001, p. H10.
17. Lawler, "Fine Line between Added Value, Spam."
18. Richard Levey, "Tracking May Avoid Customer Defections," *Direct,* September 1, 1998, p. 50.
19. "Marriott Rewards Introduces Elite Membership and Benefits," Marriott News Release, April 27, 2000, **http://www.marriott.com.**
20. Mike Koller, "Harrah's Rewards Gamblers," *Internetweek,* October 8, 2001, pp. 10–11.
21. Greenberg, "Chrysler Group Maps Out Tactical Ventures into Alternative Marketing"; and Kate Fitzgerald, "Events a Big 1st Step," *Advertising Age,* October 29, 2001, p. s4.
22. Jeff Howe, "Ready for Prime Time," *Adweek,* September 10, 2001, p. Q10.
23. Steve Jarvis, "Net to the Rescue," *Marketing News,* February 18, 2002, p. 9.
24. Lawrence A. Crosby and Sheree L. Johnson, "CRM and Management," *Marketing Management,* January/February, 2002, p. 10; and Cara B. DiPasquale, "CRM: Navigate the Maze," *Advertising Age,* October 29, 2001, pp. s1–2.
25. Carleen Hawn, "The Man Who Sees Around Corners," *Forbes,* January 21, 2002, p. 72.
26. Ibid.
27. Kathleen Cholewka, "CRM: The Failures Are Your Fault," *emanager,* January 2002, pp. 23–24.
28. Hawn, "The Man Who Sees Around Corners."
29. David Finnigan, "The Biz," *Brandweek,* April 8, 2002.
30. Henry Canaday, "Is Bigger Better?" *Selling Power,* April 1999, pp. 64–65.
31. Joanne Cleaver, "Subtle Net Pitch Works for Seniors," *Marketing News,* July 19, 1999, pp. 1, 7.
32. Howard Millman, "Easy EDI for Everyone," *InfoWorld,* August 17, 1998, pp. 38–39.
33. Heather Harreld, "Supply Chain Collaboration," *InfoWorld,* December 24, 2001, pp. 22–25.
34. Harreld, "Supply Chain Collaboration."
35. Howard Millman, "Easy EDI for Everyone," *InfoWorld,* August 17, 1998, pp. 38–39.
36. "SkyTeam Gets on Board with $18 M Effort," *Brandweek,* April 11, 2002.

CHAPTER 7

1. Justin Hunt, "Don't Make Us Angry," *Guardian Unlimited Online,* July 17, 2003, **http://www.guardian.co.uk/online;** Scott Bowles, "Fans Use Their Muscle to Shape the Movie," *USA Today,* June 20–22, 2003, p. 4D; Tom King, "Hollywood Previews Go Private," *The Wall Street Journal,* April 26, 2002, p. W9.
2. Gilbert A. Churchill, Jr., *Basic Marketing Research,* 4th Ed. (Fort Worth, TX: Harcourt, Inc., 2001), pp. 12–13.
3. Jack Honomichl, "Colossal Changes," *Marketing News,* August 13, 2001, p. H2.
4. Sandra Yin, "The Nose Knows," *American Demographics,* February 2002, p. 14.
5. "Spies Like Us," *Inc.,* August 1998, p. 45.
6. Ibid.
7. Stephanie Thompson, "Wal-Mart Tops List for New Food Lines," *Advertising Age,* April 29, 2002, pp. 4, 61.
8. Jerry W. Thomas, "Skipping MR a Major Error," *Marketing News,* March 4, 2002, p. 50.
9. Bob Edwards, "Analysis: Businesses Eagerly Anticipating the Release of U.S. Census Numbers," interview with Ross DeVal, Milken Institute, *Morning Edition* (National Public Radio), March 7, 2001.
10. "Census Bureau Breaks New Ground with Release of DVD Products," *US Newswire,* February 6, 2001.
11. Jack Neff, "Rivals Shut Out Wal-Mart," *Advertising Age,* August 27, 2001, p. 8; and Kevin Murphy, "Opening the Gates," *Executive Edge,* February–March 1999, p. 13.
12. Matt Michell, "The Internet as a Market Research Tool," *Public Relations Tactics,* March 2002, p. 6; Theano Nikitas, "Your Customers Are Talking. Are You Listening?" *Ziff Davis Smart Business,* February 2002, p. 50.
13. Deborah Szynal, "Big Bytes," *Marketing News,* March 18, 2002, p. 3.
14. Steve Jarvis, "Sum of the Parts," *Marketing News,* January 21, 2002, p. 1.
15. Theano Nikitas, "Your Customers Are Talking. Are You Listening?" *Ziff Davis Smart Business,* February 2002, p. 50; Claire Tristram, "Mining for Meaning," *Technology Review,* July/August 2001, p. 3.
16. Linda Moss, "A Constant Companion," *Broadcasting & Cable,* February 11, 2002.
17. Melanie Wells, "New Ways to Get into Our Heads," *USA Today,* March 2, 1999, pp. 1B–2B.
18. Michael McCarthy, "Stalking the Elusive Teenage Trendsetter," *The Wall Street Journal,* November 18, 1998, pp. B1, B10.
19. Alicia Clegg, "Seen and Heard," *Marketing Week,* April 19, 2001, p. 53; Stephen B. Wilcox, "Ethnography as a Product Development Tool," *Appliance Manufacturer,* July 2001, p. 58.
20. Steve Jarvis, "CMOR Finds Survey Refusal Rate Still Rising," *Marketing News,* February 4, 2002, p. 4.
21. "TRU Announces Launch of First Teen Online Offer," Teenage Research Unlimited Press Release, April 19, 2001; and McCarthy, "Stalking the Elusive Teenage Trendsetter."
22. Kenneth Wade, "Focus Groups' Research Role Is Shifting," *Marketing News,* March 4, 2002, p. 47.
23. Sylvia Marino, "Survey Says!" *Econtent,* April 2002, pp. 32–36.
24. Tedra Meyer, "Circuit City Seeks Customer Feedback Online," *Twice,* August 6, 2001, p. 17.
25. Dana James, "This Bulletin Just In," *Marketing News,* March 4, 2002, p. 45.
26. Anni Layne Rodgers, "More Than a Game," *Fast Company,* May 2002, p. 46; Heather Green, "Tracking Who Surfs Where," *Business Week,* April 27, 1998, p. 78.

27. Richard Natale, "Audiences Return to Movies," *Los Angeles Times,* October 1, 2001, **http://www.latimes.com.**
28. Jim Kirk, "Wait Nearly Over for U.S. Rollout of Low-Carb Beer," *Chicago Tribune,* May 2, 2002, S3, p. 3.
29. Carol Power, "Citi Wireless Test to Go Global," *American Banker,* January 6, 2000, p. 1.
30. Wesley Sprinkle, "In Sync with Customers," *Bests Review,* April 2002.
31. Gary H. Anthes, "The Search Is On," *ComputerWorld,* April 15, 2002, pp. 54–56.
32. Carol Krol, "Data Warehouse Generates Surprises, Leads for Camelot," *Advertising Age,* January 4, 1999, p. 20.
33. Peter J. Howe, "Verizon to Test 10-Cent Pay Phones in the Boston Area," *The Boston Globe,* January 31, 2001, **http://www.boston.com/globe.**
34. Thomas, "Skipping MR a Major Error."

CHAPTER 8

1. Company Web site, **http://www.ateenmall.com/torrid,** accessed January 13, 2004; Galina Espinoza and Amy Baumgartner, "Next Big Thing," *People,* May 26, 2003, pp. 153–154; Tracie Rozhon, "The Race to Think Like a Teenager," *The New York Times,* February 9, 2003, **http://www.hottopic.com;** Becky Ebenkamp, "What a Teen Wants," *Brandweek,* June 24, 2002, pp. 21–28.
2. Jean Halliday, "Toyota Leads in Hispanic Niche," *Advertising Age,* July 3, 2000, p. 16.
3. Samar Farah, "What Women Want," *Metro,* February 14, 2002, p. 11 [originally published in the *Christian Science Monitor*].
4. Ibid.
5. John Henry, "State, Area Demographics Give Marketing Clues," *Northwest Arkansas Business Journal,* January 21, 2002, p. 18.
6. Sonia Reyes, "Betty Crocker Says *Hola!* in TV Ads, Twin Entries, Seeking Authenticity," *Brandweek,* May 22, 2000, p. 4.
7. "The Customization Bandwagon," *Sporting Goods Business,* April 16, 2001, p. 12.
8. Roger Simon and Angie Cannon, "An Amazing Journey," *U.S News & World Report,* August 6, 2001, p. 13.
9. U.S. Census Bureau Web site, **http://www.census.gov/population/www/pop-profile/stproj .html,** May 2, 2002.
10. "Metropolitan Areas and Primary Metropolitan Statistical Areas," **http://www.itl.nist.gov/fipspubs/ fip8-6-3.htm,** accessed April 19, 2002.
11. Ibid.
12. Ibid.
13. Haya El Nasser, "Out-of-State Moves Are Up for Second Year," *USA Today,* May 31, 2001, p. 3A.
14. "Domino's," company capsule, *Hoover's Online,* **http://www.hoovers.com,** accessed May 2, 2002; Mark Hammond, "GIS Lands on the Map," *PC Week,* January 4, 1999, p. 1.
15. Samar Farah, "What Women Want."
16. "Do Gender-Specific Razors Differ?" *Fortune,* November 12, 2001, p. 48.
17. Ibid.
18. Sally Beatty, "Oxygen Media, After Long Lag, Shows New Life," *The Wall Street Journal,* December 21, 2001, p. B1.
19. Roger Simon and Angie Cannon, "An Amazing Journey."
20. Ibid.
21. Robert N. Anderson, "United States Life Tables," *National Vital Statistics Reports,* Vol. 47, No. 28, Centers for Disease Control and Prevention, December 13, 1999, **http://www.cdc.gov.**
22. "Longer Life for 50-Plus Americans," *AARP Bulletin,* November 2001, p. 4.
23. "Done Deals," *mm,* January/February 2002, p. 13.
24. Paul Campbell, "State Population Projections," U.S. Census Bureau, **http://www.census.gov/ population/www/pop-profile/stproj.html,** accessed May 26, 2002.
25. Ibid; and Roger Simon and Angie Cannon, "Amazing Journey."
26. Bob Woods, "Hispanic Marketing Can Be Eventful," *Promo,* May 2000, pp. 25–26, 35–36.
27. Wilfred Masumura, "Money Income," U.S. Census Bureau, **http://www.census.gov/population/ www-pop-profile/moninc.html,** March 9, 2000.
28. "Work," *Advertising Age,* March 4, 2002, p. 28.
29. Foxwoods Resort & Casino Web site, **http://www.foxwoods.com,** accessed May 8, 2002.
30. Roger Simon and Angie Cannon, "Amazing Journey."
31. Ibid.
32. Ibid.
33. Jean Halliday, "GayRide," *Advertising Age,* February 25, 2002, p. 18.
34. **http://www.sric-bi.com/vals,** March 9, 2000.
35. **http://www.yankelovich.com,** March 9, 2000.
36. Roper ASW, **http://www.roper.com,** accessed May 7, 2002; Tom Miller, "Global Segments from Strivers to Creatives," *Marketing News,* July 20, 1998, p. 11.
37. Scott Kirsner, in "Best of the Best 2002," *Fast Company,* May 2002, pp. 92–100.
38. Alison Overholt, "New Leaders, New Agenda," *Fast Company,* May 2002, p. 52.
39. *Chronicle,* WCVB-TV, May 7, 2002.
40. Tony Case, "Triumph of the Niche," *Spring Magazines,* March 4, 2002, pp. SR4–SR8.
41. Laurie Freeman, "Small, Smaller, Smallest," *Marketing News,* September 24, 2001, p. 17.
42. Ibid.
43. Ibid.

CHAPTER 9

1. Company Web site, http://www.phatfarmstore.com, accessed January 22, 2004; Johnnie L. Roberts, "Beyond Definition," *Newsweek*, July 28, 2003, pp. 40–43; "Music, Fashion . . . and Now Beverage," *BevNet*, July 24, 2003, http://www.bevnet.com.
2. Robert Sharoff, "Diversity in the Mainstream," *Marketing News*, May 21, 2001, p. 14.
3. Tobi Elkin, "Sony Marketing Aims at Lifestyle Segments," *Advertising Age*, March 18, 2002, p. 72.
4. John U. Bacon, "A Yen for Pork," *Time Global Business*, October 2001, p. B18.
5. Nancy Coltun Webster, "Teens Under Watchful Eye," *Advertising Age*, September 18, 2000, p. s23.
6. Charles Schwab & Co., http://www.schwab.com, accessed May 16, 2002; Jennifer Gore, "Ethnic Marketing May Become the Norm," *Bank Marketing*, September 1998, p. 12.
7. Patricia Sellers, "The Business of Being Oprah," *Fortune*, April 1, 2002, pp. 52–53.
8. John Henry, "State, Area Demographics Give Marketing Clues," *Northwest Arkansas Business Journal*, January 21, 2002, p. 18; Laurie Freeman, "Fast-Food's Battleground," *Advertising Age*, September 18, 2000, p. s20.
9. Robert Sharoff, "Diversity in the Mainstream," *Marketing News*, May 21, 2001, p. 13.
10. Sharoff, "Diversity in the Mainstream."
11. Roger Simon and Angie Cannon, "An Amazing Journey," *U.S. News & World Report*, August 6, 2001, pp. 15, 18.
12. Carole Paquette, "Drive-Throughs," *Mobile Register*, April 22, 2001, p. 2J.
13. Marci McDonald, "Call It Kid-fluence," *U.S. News & World Report*, July 30, 2001, pp. 32–34.
14. Ibid.
15. Ibid.
16. Gregory L. White, "Battling the Inferior-Interior Complex," *The Wall Street Journal*, December 3, 2001, p. B1.
17. These categories were originally suggested in John A. Howard, *Marketing Management: Analysis and Planning* (Homewood, IL: Richard D. Irwin, 1963).
18. Robert Sharoff, "Diversity in the Mainstream," *Marketing News*, May 21, 2001, p. 1.
19. Marci McDonald, "Call it 'Kid-fluence,'" *U.S. News & World Report*, July 30, 2001, p. 34.

CHAPTER 10

1. Parija Bhatnagar, "Halfway to Christmas," *CNN Money*, June 24, 2003, http://money.cnn.com; Gabriel Kahn and Ann Zimmerman, "In Age of SARS, Wal-Mart Adjusts Global Buying Machine," *The Wall Street Journal*, May 28, 2003, pp. B1, B4; "Wal-Mart Donated RMB One Million to Combat SARS," company press release, May 2003, http://www.wal-martchina.com; "Wal-Mart Halts Travel to SARS Nations," *Twincities.com*, April 9, 2003, http://www.twincities.com.
2. Robert A. Hamilton, "Budget Plan Has Billions for the State," *The New York Times*, February 10, 2002, p. 4.
3. Frederick E. Webster Jr. and Yoram Wind, "A General Model for Understanding Organizational Buying Behavior," *Marketing Management*, Winter/Spring 1996, pp. 52–57.
4. The market orientation of resellers is discussed in Thomas L. Baker, Penny M. Simpson, and Judy A. Siguaw, "The Impact of Suppliers' Perceptions of Reseller Market Orientation on Key Relationship Constructs," *Journal of the Academy of Marketing Science*, 27, Winter 1999, pp. 50–57.
5. B2B E-Commerce Headed for Trillions," http://www.cyberatlas.internet.com, March 6, 2002.
6. Michael D. Hutt and Thomas W. Speh, *Business Marketing Management*, 8th Edition (Mason, OH: South-Western Publishing, 2004).
7. "Small Business 2001," *Inc. Magazine*, May 29, 2001, p. 16.
8. http://www.census.gov/epcd/www/naics.html; and http://www.census.gov/naics, downloaded February 1, 2003.
9. Gordon A. Wyner, "Segmentation Architecture," and Gerald E. Smith, "Segmenting B2B Markets with Economic Value Analysis," *Marketing Management*, March/April 2002, pp. 6 and p. 35.
10. Spencer S. Hsu, "Federal Spending in Region Surged," *The Washington Post*, April 21, 2001, p. E1.
11. Jim Mateja, "Ford Suppliers Coming to First-of-Kind Campus," *Chicago Tribune*, May 16, 2002, S3, p.1.
12. Sean Callahan, "China Calling," *BtoBonline*, March 11, 2002, http://www.btobonline.com.
13. Jon E. Hilsenrath, "Globalizations Persists in Precarious New Age," *The Wall Street Journal*, December 31, 2001, p. A1.
14. John Pletz and Kirk Ladendorf, "Quick Fix Unlikely for PC Chip Producers, Research Firm Finds," *Knight/Ridder, Tribune Business News*, August 9, 2001.
15. "MasterCard Rolls Out Interoperable API for Storing Personal Data on Smart Cards," *Card News*, May 1, 2002, p. 1.
16. Patrick Burnson, "Just Too Critical," *World Trade*, April 2002, p. 8.
17. Diane Rezendes Khirallah, "Affiliated Computer Near Outsourcing Deal with P&G," *InformationWeek*, July 8, 2002, http://www.informationweek.com; Elliot Spagat, "P&G Narrows Outsourcing Candidates," *The Wall Street Journal*, May 14, 2002, p. B16.
18. Robyn Greenspan, "Companies Look Outside Themselves," May 3, 2002, http://www.cyberatlas.internet.com.
19. Desiree De Myer, "Combat the Downside of Outsourcing Sprint," *Ziff Davis Smart Business*, May 1, 2002, p. 47.
20. Bob Frances, "Gold Winner: Color My World, Boise," *Brandweek*, March 18, 2002, p. R17.
21. References for the organizational buying process incorporate several stages. Arthur Hughes, "Building Profits with Relationship Marketing," *Direct*, January 1999, pp. 49–52, reflects use in stages 1, 2, 3, 4.
22. Betsy McKay, "Pepsi Is Set to Become the Cola of Choice for United Airlines, *The Wall Street Journal*, March 25, 2002, p. A3.

23. Hughes, "Building Profits with Relationship Marketing."
24. Hutt and Speh, Business Marketing Management.
25. Don Green, "Count on Strong Relationships," *Paperboard Packaging*, November 2001, p. 8.
26. Hsu, "Federal Spending in Region Surged."
27. Shane Harris, "The Only Game in Town," *Government Executive*, December 2001, pp. 16–26; and Edward Robinson, "The Pentagon Finally Learns How to Shop," *Fortune*, December 21, 1998, pp. 174–182.
28. Allan V. Burman, "Buying Better All the Time," *Government Executive*, December 2001, p. 72.
29. John H. Cushman, "The Government Shops on the Web, Too," *The New York Times*, March 29, 2000, p. H31.
30. Harris, "The Only Game in Town."
31. Matt Forney, "Cultural Revolution: Taiwan Breaks Free of China Syndrome," *The Wall Street Journal*, July 27, 1999, pp. A1, A12.

CHAPTER 11

1. Dan Neil, "Porsche Cayenne Turbo," *Car and Driver*, August 2003, pp. 62–67; Matt Nauman, "Porsche Dives into SUV Market with the Sleek Cayenne," *Mobile Register*, May 26, 2003, p. 24F; David Kiley, "Porsche Hopes Cayenne Spices Sales," *USA Today*, April 30, 2003, pp. B1, B2; "Sporty Spice," *Newsweek*, April 7, 2003, p. 68; James R. Healey, "Cayenne Has True Off-Road Grit," *USA Today*, March 28, 2003, p. 7D.
2. Concept first introduced by G. Lynn Shostack, "Breaking Free from Product Marketing," *Journal of Marketing*, April 1977, p. 77; and John M. Rathmell, "What Is Meant by Services?" *Journal of Marketing*, October 1980, pp. 32–36.
3. "How Marriott Never Forgets a Guest," *Business Week*, February 21, 2000, p. 74.
4. U.S. Census Bureau, *1997 Economic Census: Advance Summary Statistics for the United States*, http://www.census.gov/epcd/www/advanc1a.htm, accessed June 3, 2002.
5. Catharine P. Taylor, "Buck Stops Here; Doctors, and Their Rx Pads, at the Forefront of DTC," *Advertising Age Special Report on Direct-to-Consumer Marketing*, May 27, 2002, pp. S-2, S-8.
6. Melissa Campanelli, "Gotta Have It!" *Entrepreneur*, April 2001, p. 49.
7. Brandon Copple, "Shelf-Determination," *Forbes*, April 15, 2002, pp. 131–142.
8. Michael D. Hutt and Thomas W. Speh, *Business Marketing Management*, Eighth Edition (Mason, OH: South-Western, 2004).
9. Ben Berentson, "Johnson Controls," *Forbes*, May 21, 2001, p. 70.
10. Karen Bannon, "Akamai Technologies," *Forbes*, May 21, 2001, p. 94.
11. Katherine Bruce, "Equity Office Properties," *Forbes*, May 21, 2001, p. 100.
12. Diane Brady, "Why Service Stinks," *Business Week*, October 23, 2000, p. 119.
13. Alex Taylor III, "Finally GM Is Looking Good," *Fortune*, April 1, 2002, pp. 69–74.
14. *The Clorox Company 2001 Annual Report*, p. 21, accessed at Clorox Web site, http://www.clorox.com, June 11, 2002.
15. *L.L. Bean Catalog*, Summer 2002, p. 4.
16. Lorrie Grant, "Coach Bags Old Ideas," *USA Today*, April 24, 2001, p. B5.
17. Ibid.
18. Dori Jones Yang, "Wireless but Useless," *U.S. News & World Report*, May 7, 2001, pp. 32–33.
19. Cara Beardi, "Zippo's Eternal Flame," *Advertising Age*, August 13, 2001, p. 4.
20. Ibid.
21. William Erickson et al., "Wine War," *Business Week*, September 3, 2001, p. 57.
22. Devon Spurgeon, "The Hard Life of Orphan Brands," *The Wall Street Journal*, April 13, 2001, p. B1.
23. Ibid.
24. Bill Shepherd, "Wizards of Light," *Worth*, July/August 2001, pp. 61–64.

CHAPTER 12

1. "Fat Profits," *Business Week*, August 25, 2003, p. 12; Bruce Horovitz, "Applebee's Plans to Slim Down Menu," *USA Today*, July 25, 2003, p. B1; Leila Abboud, "The Truth about Trans Fats: Coming to a Label Near You," *The Wall Street Journal*, July 10, 2003, p. D1; Melanie Wells, "Pepsi's New Challenge," *Forbes*, January 20, 2003, pp. 68–74.
2. Joseph Agnese, "Tyson Rules the Roost," *Business Week Online*, July 1, 2002, http://www.businessweek.com; Stephanie Thompson, "Meat Gets Branded," *Advertising Age*, September 24, 2001, p. 6.
3. Jack Neff, "Private Party at Wal-Mart," *Advertising Age*, October 29, 2001, p. 8.
4. Gary McWilliams, "Retailers Create Own-Label PCs as Brand Names Dwindle," *The Wall Street Journal*, May 3, 2002, p. B1.
5. Gerry Khermouch, Stanley Holmes, and Moon Ihlwan, "The Best Global Brands," *Business Week*, August 6, 2001, p. 50.
6. Ibid.
7. "What Is Brand Asset Valuator? Brand Development Findings," http://www.yr.com/knowledge/what2.php, March 22, 2000.
8. "The Good Housekeeping Seal," *Good Housekeeping*, May 2002, p. 14.
9. Gerry Khermouch, Holmes and Ihlwan, "The Best Global Brands," p. 53.
10. David Welch, "GM Brand Managers Get the Boot," *Business Week*, April 22, 2002, p. 14.
11. Brandon Copple, "Shelf-Determination," *Forbes*, April 15, 2002, pp. 131–142.
12. The concept of trade dress is examined in Michael Harvey, James T. Rothe, and Laurie A. Lucas, "The 'Trade Dress' Controversy: A Case of Strategic Cross-Brand Cannibalization," *Journal of Marketing Theory and Practice*, 6, Spring 1998, pp. 1–15. The *Kendall-Jackson v. Gallo* case is

discussed in "Jury Clears E&J Gallo-Winery in Lawsuit Over Bottle Design," *The Wall Street Journal*, April 7, 1997.

13. Paxan Company Web site, **http://www.iran-export.com/exporter/company/PAXAN**, accessed July 9, 2002.

14. Deborah Ball, "Osama Relative Fashions Apparel Bin Ladin Line," *The Wall Street Journal*, June 17, 2002, p. B1.

15. Olga Kharif, "Getting a Grip on Consumer Tastes," *BusinessWeek*, July 16, 2001, p. 12.

16. Steve Jarvis, "French Fried," *Marketing News*, June 4, 2001, p. 3.

17. Anita Lienert, "Wheels Sport New Labels," The Detroit News, April 25, 2001, **http://detnews.com**; Jean Halliday, "L.L. Bean, Subaru Pair for Co-Branding," Advertising Age, February 21, 2000, p. 21.

18. James Martin and James E. Samuels, "Campus Scoreboards Tell Us More Than the Score," *Boston Business Journal*, Spring 2002.

19. "Ballpoint Perfume," *Forbes*, July 3, 2000, p. 154.

20. "Uniforms, New Ball MLB's Big Stories," *Sports Trend*, June 2000, p. 30.

21. Gerry Kermouch, "An Almost Invisible $1 Trillion Market," *BusinessWeek*, June 11, 2001, p. 151.

22. Chuck Stogel, "It's Easier Being Green," *Brandweek*, January 28, 2002, pp. 16, 18, 20.

23. Julie Forster, "Sara Lee: Changing the Recipe—Again," *BusinessWeek*, September 10, 2001, pp. 125–126.

24. Everett M. Rogers and F. Floyd Shoemaker, *Communication of Innovation* (New York: Free Press, 1971), pp. 135–157. Rogers later relabeled his model as an innovation-decision process. He called the five steps knowledge, persuasion, decision, implementation, and information. See Everett M. Rogers, *Diffusion of Innovations*, 3rd ed. (New York: Free Press, 1983), pp. 164–165.

25. Reuters Limited, "Toyota's Prius First to Get $2,000 Tax Deduction OK," *Forbes*, August 12, 2002, **http://www.forbes.com**; Jeff Green, "Attention Techies and Assorted Geniuses: Toyota Prius Wants You," *Brandweek*, May 15, 2000, p. 113.

26. Devin Leonard, "The Most Valuable Square Foot in America," *Fortune*, April 1, 2002, pp. 118, 120, 124.

27. Wyeth Web site, **http://www.wyeth.com**, accessed August 14, 2002; Rob Wherry, "No Worries," *Forbes*, July 23, 2001, p. 168.

28. Chuck Stoge, "It's Easier Being Green," *Brandweek*, January 28, 2002, p. 16.

29. Alison Overholt, "New Leaders, New Agenda," *Fast Company*, May 2002, p. 54.

30. Wendy Cole, "SUV Strollers," *Time*, January 29, 2001.

31. John Heilimann, "Reinventing the Wheel," *Time.com*, December 2, 2001, **http://www.time.com**.

32. E. Michael Johnson, "The Swoosh Swoops In," *Golf Digest*, January 25, 2002, **http://www.golf digest.com**.

33. Amanda Spake, "Bath Seats Demand a Watchful Eye," *U.S. News & World Report*, June 11, 2001, p. 67.

34. Jayne O'Donnell, "Costco's History Reads Like Recipe for Recalls," *USA Today*, April 4, 2001, p. B1.

35. Julie Forster, "Sara Lee: Changing the Recipe—Again," *BusinessWeek*, September 10, 2001, pp. 125–126.

36. Jayne O'Donnell, "New Safety VP Plans Quality Improvements," *USA Today*, April 4, 2001, p. B1.

CHAPTER 13

1. Marilyn Adams, "Discounters' Determination to Grow Is Likely to Shrink Fares," *USA Today*, August 8, 2003, p. B1; Dan Reed, "Fewer Flights Mean Really, Really Full Planes," *USA Today*, August 6, 2003, p. B1; Dan Reed, "Cost of Flying for Business Gets Cheaper," *USA Today*, July 18, 2003, **http://www.usatoday.com**; Wendy Zellner, "Strafing the Big Boys—Again," *BusinessWeek*, June 23, 2003, p. 36; Susan Carey, "United to Install In-Flight E-Mail by End of Year," *The Wall Street Journal*, June 17, 2003, p. D1; Scott McCartney, "Airlines Cut Fares for Business Travelers," *Mobile Register*, November 23, 2002, pp. A1, B1, B2.

2. Richard S. Dunham and Paul Magnusson, "Those Steel Tariffs Look Anything But Ironclad," *BusinessWeek*, May 6, 2001, p. 45.

3. Al Baker, "Steep Rise in Gun Sales Reflects Post-Attack Fears," *The New York Times*, December 16, 2001, p. A1.

4. Paul Krugman, "What Price Fairness?" *The New York Times*, October 4, 2000, p. A35.

5. Byron Acohido, "Will Microsoft's Xbox Hit the Spot?" *USA Today*, June 4, 2002, pp. B1, B2; Todd Wasserman, "Playing to Win," *Brandweek*, May 20, 2002, pp. 1, 8; Tobi Elkin, "Video-Game Makers Heat Up Competition," *Advertising Age*, May 20, 2002, pp. 3, 157.

6. Robert D. Buzzell and Frederick D. Wiersema, "Successful Share Building Strategies," *Harvard Business Review* (January–February 1981), pp. 135–144.

7. Jon Van, "AT&T to Offer Unlimited Long Distance Calling Plan with Certain Limits," *Chicago Tribune*, February 7, 2002.

8. Emily Nelson, "Bottom Line," *The Wall Street Journal*, December 27, 2001, p. A1.

9. Michelle Kessler, "PC Makers Jump into House Call Business," *USA Today*, May 10, 2002, p. B1.

10. Joe Sharkey, "Life Can Be Pretty Good Five Miles Up," *The New York Times*, May 14, 2002, p. C7.

11. Barbara De Lollis, Chris Woodyard, and Marilyn Adams, "Savvy Travelers Fly for Less," *USA Today*, April 21, 2002.

12. Peter Kafka, "Rock On," *Forbes*, September 20, 1999, p. 142.

13. David Leonhardt, "Tiptoeing Toward Variable Pricing," *The New York Times*, May 12, 2002.

14. See James L. McKenney, *Stouffer Yield Management System*, Harvard Business School Case 9-190-193 (Boston: Harvard Business School, 1994); and Anirudh Dhebar and Adam Brandenburger,

American Airlines, Inc: Revenue Management, Harvard Business School Case 9-190-029 (Boston: Harvard Business School, 1992).

15. David P. Hamilton, "E-Commerce: The Price Isn't Right," *The Wall Street Journal*, February 12, 2001, p. B1.

16. Ibid.

CHAPTER 14

1. Kathleen Madigan, "It Sure Doesn't Feel Like Low Inflation," *BusinessWeek*, May 19, 2003, p. 39; Jon E. Hilsenrath, "America's Pricing Paradox," *The Wall Street Journal*, May 16, 2003, p. B1; Stephanie N. Mehta, "How to Thrive When Prices Fall," *Fortune*, May 12, 2003, pp. 131–133; Stephanie Thompson, "Retailers Thwart Food-Price Hikes," *Advertising Age*, May 5, 2003, pp. 3, 25; Dean Foust et al., "Raising Prices Won't Fly," *BusinessWeek*, June 3, 2002, pp. 34–36.

2. "Canon News," downloaded from **http://www.canon.com**, January 22, 2003; see also Karl Greenberg, "Canon Fires Off $20M in Colorful Launch for Money-Saving Printer," *Brandweek*, April 9, 2001, p. 6.

3. "Polartec Windbloc Series," downloaded from **http://www.polartec.com**, January 22, 2003.

4. "Prescription Drug Pricing, Utilization, and Spending," downloaded from **http://aspe.os.dhhs.gov/ health/reports/drugstudy**, January 22, 2003; "Court Agrees to Review State Regulation of Drug Pricing," downloaded from **http://www.washingtonpost.com**, June 28, 2002.

5. Jack Neff, "$100 Million-Plus Push Seen for Gillette Razors," *Advertising Age*, February 25, 2002, p. 1.

6. Nara Schoenberg, "Cell Phone Use Expected to Grow, Mature in America," *Mobile Register*, July 29, 2002, p. D1.

7. Marilyn Adams, "Airlines' Balance of Power Shifts," *USA Today*, July 30, 2002, pp. B1, B2.

8. "Domestic Tobacco Pricing," downloaded from **http://www.tobacco.org/news**, January 23, 2003.

9. "Amazon.com and Dynamic Pricing on the Internet," downloaded from **http://faculty-gsb.stan ford.edu/groseclose/Papers/amazon.pdf**, January 24, 2003; see also Kevin Newman, "Amazon.com Admits to Variable Pricing," downloaded from **http://abcnews.go.com/onair/ worldnewstonight/wnt000927_amazonpricing_feature.html**, January 24, 2003.

10. "Dealer Holdbacks: What Are They and What Do They Do?" downloaded from **http://www.car buytip.com/dealer-holdbacks.html**, January 23, 2003.

11. "The New 'Digital Economics' of the Music Industry," downloaded from **http://64.33.34.112/ .WWW/digecon.html**, January 24, 2003.

12. Justin Pope, "Tuition from Grocery Rebates," *Chicago Sun Times*, May 5, 2002, p. 41.

13. "A Primer on Gasoline Prices," downloaded from **http://www.eia.doe.gov/pub/oil_gas/petroleum/ analysis_publications/primer_on_gasoline_prices/html/petbro.html**, January 25, 2003; "How Gas Prices Work," downloaded from **http://www.howstuffworks.com/gas-price.html**, January 24, 2003.

14. "Telephone Service Pricing," downloaded from **http://indian.vinu.edu/telecomm/links.htm**, January 25, 2003.

15. "PC Makers Ready for Price War," downloaded from **http://www.newsfactor.com/perl/story/ 7591.html**, January 25, 2003.

16. Frank Vinlaun, "Washington State Wineries Thrive in 'Premium' Niche," *The Seattle Times*, April 19, 2002, p. B7.

17. "AIDS Drug Makers Slash Prices for Third World," downloaded from **http://abcnews.go.com/ sections/living/DailyNews/aidsdrugs_africa0511.html**, January 26, 2003.

18. "Product Preannouncement, Market Cannibalization, and Price Competition," downloaded from **http://netec.mcc.ac.uk/BibEc/data/Papers/fthecsucp98-136.html**, January 25, 2003.

19. Brian McWilliams, "Google Turns Away Robots from Its Front Door," *News Bytes*, March 28, 2002.

20. Julia Angwin, "More Subscribers to AOL Get Online Free," *The Wall Street Journal*, March 14, 2002.

CHAPTER 15

1. Blockbuster Web site, **http://www.blockbuster.com**, accessed January 14, 2004; Martin Peers, "After Living on Rented Time, Blockbuster Plunges into Sales," *The Wall Street Journal*, February 13, 2003, p. A1; David Lieberman, "DVD Sales Surge Puts Crimp in Blockbuster's Profits," *USA Today*, December 19, 2002, p. 4B; Michael Liedtke, "Renting DVDs by Mail Popular," *Mobile Register*, October 4, 2002, p. B6; Holly J. Morris, "You've Got DVD Mail," *U.S. News & World Report*, September 9, 2002, p. 71.

2. Ann D'Innocenzio, "Avon Calling on a New Retail Plan," *Mobile Register*, May 13, 2001, p. 3F.

3. Richard Roeper, "Oh for the Simpler Days of Tupperware Parties," *Chicago Sun Times*, May 1, 2002.

4. Michael Schrage, "The Dell Curve," *Wired*, October 7, 2001, **http://www.wired.com**.

5. Cathleen Egan, "Vending Machine Technology Matures, Offering Branded Foods, Convenience," *The Wall Street Journal*, December 13, 2001, p. B13.

6. Dan Hanover, "Channel Conflict? Put a Lid on It," *Sales & Marketing Management*, March 2000, p. 86.

7. Mark McMaster, "Shifting Gears," *Sales & Marketing Management*, August 2001, pp. 43–48.

8. Pallavi Gogoi, "What's Next—The Bank of Burger King?" *BusinessWeek*, June 18, 2001, p. 150.

9. Dean Foust, "Ebay, A Hock Shop's Best Friend," *BusinessWeek*, July 30, 2001, p. 10.

10. Brandon Copple, "Plowed Under," *Forbes*, February 21, 2000, p. 56.

11. Bob Duncan, "First, Do No Harm," *Inc Tech*, accessed at the *Inc.* Web site, **http://www.inc.com**, August 4, 2002.

12. Ann Stuart, "Not Dead Yet," *Inc Tech*, accessed at the *Inc.* Web site, http://www.inc.com, August 4, 2002; Mark Tatge, "Rug Burns," *Forbes*, March 5, 2001, pp. 58–60.

13. "U.S. Senate Backs Canada Drug Reimports," Reuters Limited, July 17, 2002, http://ca.news .yahoo.com; Debra Rosenberg, "Getting Their Fill," *Newsweek*, June 24, 2002, p. 25.

14. Josh Kosman, "TPG, Goldman Sachs Want Burger King Their Way," *TheDeal.com*, April 9, 2002, http://tdnycprodwww01.thedeal.com; Daniel Kruger, "Carrying the Flame," *Forbes*, December 24, 2001, pp. 64–65.

15. Victoria Murphy, "The Logistics of a Dinner Plate," *Forbes*, January 21, 2002, pp. 96–97.

16. Ed Pasahow, "How Can You Improve the Odds for Successful ERP Implementation," *Digital Systems Report*, Spring 2000, pp. 24–26.

17. John Gorsuch, "Examining the Links," *Overhaul & Maintenance*, April 20, 2002, p. 38.

18. Special Advertising Section, *BusinessWeek*, June 26, 2000.

19. "Partnerships," GE Capital rail services Web sites, http://www.ge.com/capital/rail, accessed August 28, 2002; "GE Pursues e-Fulfillment from All Angles," *BusinessWeek*, June 26, 2000.

20. "The Lifelong Lure of the Open Road," *US News & World Report*, February 18, 2002, p. 48.

21. Warren S. Hersch, "Midrange Distributors' Role Broadens in E-Commerce World," *Computer Reseller News*, accessed at the CRN Web site, http://www.crn.com, August 4, 2002.

22. "The New Wave in Giant Ships," *Fortune*, November 12, 2001, p. I182 I-P.

23. Andrew Tanzer, "Warehouses That Fly," *Forbes*, accessed at the *Forbes* Web site, http://www. forbes.com, August 4, 2002.

24. Jeffrey Ball, "Chrysler Averts a Parts Crisis," *The Wall Street Journal*, September 24, 2001, p. B1.

25. Philip Siekman, "New Victories in the Supply-Chain Revolution," *Fortune*, accessed at the *Fortune* Web site, http://www.fortune.com, August 4, 2002.

26. Siekman, "New Victories."

27. Emily Nelson and Ann Zimmerman, "Kimberly-Clark Keeps Costco in Diapers, Absorbing Costs Itself," *The Wall Street Journal*, September 7, 2000, p. A1.

28. "Web Trails," *Forbes Best of the Web*, December 3, 2001, p. 15.

29. Mark Henricks, "No Long-Term Parking," *Entrepreneur*, January 2002, pp. 83–85.

CHAPTER 16

1. Company Web site, http://www.lowes.com, accessed January 10, 2004; Bruce Upbin, "Merchant Princes," *Forbes*, January 20, 2003, pp. 52–56; "Robert Tillman," *BusinessWeek*, January 13, 2003, p. 63.

2. Jean Scheidnes, "Retailers Woo Youth Dollars with Discount Denim," *Forbes*, August 23, 2002, http://www.forbes.com; and Louise Lee, "Can Gap Put It All Together Again?" *BusinessWeek*, August 14, 2000, pp. 58–60.

3. Anne D'Innocenzio, "Designer Names Helping Target Offer Cheap Chic," *Mobile Register*, March 16, 2002, p. B7; and Teri Agins, "Todd Does Target," *The Wall Street Journal*, April 11, 2002, p. B1.

4. "Family Dollar Reports Record Third Quarter and First Three Quarters Sales and Earnings; and Announces Plans to Open 575 New Stores in Fiscal 2003," Family Dollar Stores press release, *PR Newswire*, June 25, 2002; and Chad Terhune, "In Modest Times, Dollar Stores Remain Upbeat," *The Wall Street Journal*, December 22, 2000, pp. B1, B4.

5. Aixa M. Pascual, "Lowe's Is Sprucing Up Its House," *BusinessWeek*, June 3, 2002, pp. 56–58.

6. SuperTarget Web site, accessed January 4, 2003, http://www.target.com; and Calmetta Y. Coleman, "Target's Aim: 'Bring Fashion to Food' on a National Scale," *The Wall Street Journal*, March 1, 2000, p. 4.

7. Kristof De Wulf, "Retail Category Strategy Varies by the Store," *Marketing News*, September 10, 2001, p. 22.

8. Donna Fenn, "Leveraging Local Intelligence," *Inc.*, August 2001, pp. 54–56.

9. Chana R. Schoenberger, "Ca-Ching!" *Forbes*, June 12, 2000, pp. 84–85.

10. D. M. Osborne, "The Store That Stark Built," *Inc.*, August 2001, p. 46.

11. Alexander R. Moses, "Analysts: Rivals Hold Key to Kmart Closures," *Mobile Register*, January 24, 2002, p. B6.

12. Dean Starkman, "The Mall, Without the Haul," *The Wall Street Journal*, July 25, 2001, p. B1.

13. Alice Z. Cuneo, "What's in Store?" *Advertising Age*, February 25, 2002, pp. 30–31.

14. Nanette Byrnes and Christopher Palmeri, "A Showstopper on Broadway," *BusinessWeek*, December 24, 2001, p. 54; "NetWorth Datebook," *Worth*, December 2001, p. 50; and Steven T. Goldberg, "Retailing's Comeback Kid," *Kiplinger's*, November 2001, p. 60.

15. "7-Eleven to Cast Itself as New Teen Heaven," *Brandweek*, April 2, 2001, pp. 1, 8.

16. Emily Nelson, "The Art of the Sale," *The Wall Street Journal*, January 11, 2001, p. B1.

17. Wendy Zellner, "Warehouse Clubs: When the Going Gets Tough," *BusinessWeek*, July 16, 2001.

18. Katherine Hobson, "Miracle on 34th Street," *U.S. News & World Report*, November 26, 2001, pp. 44–45.

19. William M. Bulkeley, "Cut Down to Size: Category Killers Go from Lethal to Lame in Less Than a Decade," *The Wall Street Journal*, March 9, 2000, p. B1.

20. Hobson, "Miracle on 34th Street."

21. Lorrie Grant, "Department Stores Ring Up Centralized Checkouts," *USA Today*, June 6, 2002, p. 5B.

22. Zellner, "Warehouse Clubs: When the Going Gets Tough."

23. Cuneo, "What's in Store?"

24. "Products & Services," 7-Eleven Web site, http://www.7-Eleven.com/products, accessed September 4, 2002; and Benjamin Fulford, "I Got It @ 7-Eleven," *Forbes*, April 3, 2000, p. 53.

25. Russell Flannery, "Happy in the Middle," *Forbes*, April 1, 2002, p. 62.

26. "United Stationers Opens New State-of-the-Art Distribution Center in Denver," United Stationers' press release, June 25, 2001; and Ashlea Ebeling, "Paper Tiger," *Forbes*, February 21, 2000, pp. 71–74.

27. Don Debelak, "Farmers' Market," *Entrepreneur*, February 2002, p. 104.

28. Cara B. Dipasquale, "Direct Marketing Rose 3.6% in '01," *Advertising Age*, June 10, 2002, p. 8.

29. Tobi Elkin, "Yahoo! Increases Direct Marketing," *Advertising Age*, April 22, 2002, p. 20; and Ellen Neuborne, "Coaxing with Catalogs," *BusinessWeek e.biz*, August 6, 2001, p. EB6.

30. Deborah Szynal, "Anthrax and You," *Marketing News*, April 29, 2002, pp. 1, 4.

31. Office Depot Web site, http://www.officedepot.com, accessed January 5, 2003; Jon Swartz, "E-Tailers Turn Net Profits," *USA Today*, December 13, 2000, pp. 1B–2B; and David Rocks, "Why Office Depot Loves the Net," *BusinessWeek e.biz*, September 27, 1999, pp. EB66–68.

32. JapanScan Market Report, "Automatic Vending Machines in Japan," January 2002, http://www .foodindustryjapan.com/automatic_vending.htm; Tim Sanford, "Vending and Beyond," *Vending Times*, March 25–April 24, 2001, http://www.vendingtimes.com.

CHAPTER 17

1. Robyn Greenspan, "College Students Surf, Spend," *CyberAtlas*, February 13, 2003, http:// www.cyberatlas.internet.com; Olivia Barker, "Dude, the Spring Break Beach Scene Is So Over," *USA Today*, March 22, 2002, p. 8D; Bruce Horovitz, "Marketers Revel with Spring Breakers," *USA Today*, March 12, 2002, p. B3.

2. Dale Buss, "Art of Gaining Impressions," *Brandweek*, March 18, 2002, p. R14 ("Reggie Awards").

3. Betsy Cummings, "Making It Click," *Sales & Marketing Management*, April 2002, p. 21.

4. Ibid., p. 22.

5. Bruce Horovitz, "Kids Eat Free as Chains Vie for Business," *USA Today*, April 9, 2001, p. B2.

6. Jon Swartz, "EarthLink Joins Movement to Kill Pop-Up Ads," *USA Today*, August 20, 2002, p. B1; "EarthLink Will Offer Subscribers Software to Block Pop-Up Ads," *The Wall Street Journal*, August 20, 2002, p. B6.

7. Mike Beirne, "Hoteliers Take Different Roads to Travelers," *Brandweek*, June 10, 2002, p. 4.

8. David Finnigan, "Disney's Search for Treasure," *Brandweek*, August 12, 2002, pp. 1, 8.

9. Ronald Grover and Gerry Khermouch, "The Trouble with Tie-ins," *BusinessWeek*, June 3, 2002, p. 63.

10. David Kiley, "Half a Million Tires Recalled, Most on Ford SUVs," *USA Today*, August 20, 2002, p. B2.

11. Kenneth Hein, "Here's Chocolate in Your Eye," *Brandweek*, Nov. 12, 2001, p. 26.

12. Kenneth Hein, "Here's Chocolate in Your Eye," and Mike Beirne, "Butt-Kicking Big Tobacco," *Brandweek*, Nov. 12, 2001, pp. 26, 28.

13. Lisa M. Keefe, "*Still* Brought to You by . . . ," *Marketing News*, October 22, 2001, p. 3; data from IEG Inc., Chicago.

14. Gabriel Kahn, "Soccer's FIFA Cries Foul as Ambushers Crash World Cup," *The Wall Street Journal*, June 20, 2002, p. B1.

15. Donna Fenn, "Honeys, Hand Me a Polygamy Porter," *Inc.*, August 2002, pp. 94–97.

16. Direct Marketing Association, http://www.the-dma.org, accessed January 27, 2003.

17. Laird Harrison, "You've Got Ads!" *Time Bonus Section—Inside Business*, January 2002, p. Y7.

18. Direct Marketing Association, http://www.the-dma.org, accessed January 28, 2003.

19. Ibid.

20. Gary McWilliams, "In About-Face, Dell Will Sell PCs to Dealers," *The Wall Street Journal*, August 20, 2002, pp. B1, B4.

21. Kenneth Hein, "Memo from the Front," *Brandweek*, February 11, 2002, p. 38.

22. Sonia Reyes, "Purina Plots Poaching Protective Pooch Pals," *Brandweek*, August 27, 2001, p. 7.

23. John Gaffney, "Case Study: Corn Syrup, Britney, the Web, and Thou," *Business 2.0*, August 2001, http://www.business2.com.

24. Mark Hyman, "Betting That His Airness Will Soar Again," *BusinessWeek*, October 1, 2001, p. 72; "Rent-a-Celeb," *BusinessWeek*, July 9, 2001, p. 10.

25. Melanie Wells, "Sole Survivors," *Forbes*, August 6, 2001, pp. 62–68.

CHAPTER 18

1. Company Web site, http://www.georgeforeman.com, accessed January 12, 2004; Richard Hoffer, "Born Again and Again and Again," *Sports Illustrated*, December 1, 2003, pp. 70–77. "George Foreman Signs Exclusive Deal to Launch New Clothing Line with Casual Male Retail Group Inc.," *Yahoo!*, July 8, 2003, http://biz.yahoo.com; "Buy George!" *People*, April 28, 2003, pp. 115–116ff.

2. Dorothy Pomerantz, "Coming Distractions," *Forbes*, June 10, 2002, p. 50.

3. Stephanie Thompson, "Kraft Eschews TV for Pop Star Promo," *Advertising Age*, August 12, 2002, p. 11.

4. Anna Bernasek, "Is This Where the Economy Is Headed?" *Fortune*, September 2, 2002, pp. 85–90; William Spain, "Ad Spending Almost Flat in First Half," downloaded from http://www.CBS .MarketWatch.com, August 26, 2002; Robert J. Coen, "Advertising Boom in U.S. Ended in '01," *Advertising Age*, May 13, 2002, p. 24.

5. Gary McWilliams, "Gateway Barks Right Up Apple's Tree in New Ad Campaign," *The Wall Street Journal*, August 26, 2002, pp. B1, B4.

6. Laurel Wentz, "Marketers Turn to Celebrities to Lure Hispanic Consumers," *Advertising Age*, May 13, 2002, p. 20.

7. Christopher H. Schmitt, "Earth to Martha: Forget the Doilies. You're in Big Trouble," *U.S. News & World Report*, July 1, 2002, pp. 26–27.

8. Betsy Cummings, "Star Power," *Sales & Marketing Management*, April 2001, pp. 52–56.
9. Coen, "Advertising Boom in U.S. Ended in '01."
10. Jon Swartz, "EarthLink Joins Movement to Kill Pop-Up Ads," *USA Today*, August 20, 2002, p. B1; Tobi Elkin, "'Intrusive' Pop-Ups Get Closer Scrutiny after iVillage Block," *Advertising Age*, August 5, 2002, p. 6.
11. Coen, "Advertising Boom in U.S. Ended in '01."
12. Tony Case, "The Last Mass Medium?" *Newspapers*, April 30, 2001, pp. SR13–SR14.
13. Ibid.
14. Ibid.
15. Coen, "Advertising Boom in U.S. Ended in '01."
16. Ibid.
17. Charles Pappas, "Ad Nauseum," *Advertising Age*, July 10, 2000, p. 16.
18. Ibid.
19. Erin White, "Outdoor Ads May Get Indoor Rival," *The Wall Street Journal*, July 17, 2002, p. B10.
20. Scott Hays, "Has Online Advertising Finally Grown Up?" *Advertising Age*, April 1, 2002, p. C1.
21. Ibid.
22. Charles Pappas, "Ad Nauseum."
23. "Agency Report," *Advertising Age*, April 22, 2002, p. S-2.
24. Jack Neff, "Coupons Get Clipped," *Advertising Age*, November 5, 2001, p. 1.
25. "Back to Basics," *Industry Report—Promo Magazine*, May 2000, p. A20.
26. "Virtual Satisfaction," *Industry Report—Promo Magazine*, May 2000, p. A26.
27. "Give and Take," *Industry Report—Promo Magazine*, May 2000, p. A36.
28. "Getting Labeled," *Industry Report—Promo Magazine*, May 2000, p. A8.
29. "Retailment Today," *Industry Report—Promo Magazine*, May 2000, p. A16.
30. Bonnie Tsui, "Philip Morris Coverup: No-Smoke Ads Hit Books," *Advertising Age*, September 4, 2000, p. 12.
31. Jack Neff, "Ries' Thesis: Ads Don't Build Brands, PR Does," *Advertising Age*, July 15, 2002, pp. 14–15.
32. Steve Jarvis, "How the Internet Is Changing the Fundamentals of Publicity," *Marketing News*, July 17, 2000, p. 6.
33. Suzanne C. Ryan, "Soak Up the Fun!" *Boston Sunday Globe*, July 7, 2002, p. L1.
34. "Give and Take," *Industry Report—Promo Magazine*.
35. Maxine Lans Resky, "Just Posting Cookie Agreement Not Enough," *Marketing News*, September 24, 2001, p. 12.
36. "U.S. Ad Expenditures by Type of Media, 1997–2001," *Marketing News*, July 2, 2001, p. 11.
37. "Worldwide Internet Advertising Spending, by Region," *Marketing News*, July 2, 2001, p. 13.

CHAPTER 19

1. Michele Marchetti, "Cold Feet," *Sales & Marketing Management*, October 2003, http://www.salesandmarketing.com; Clint Boulton, "Siebel, IBM Take CRM on Demand," *Internet News.com*, October 2, 2003, http://www.internetnews.com; Erin Stout, "Blue Skies Ahead?" *Sales & Marketing Management*, March 2003, pp. 25–29.
2. Thomas N. Ingram, Raymond W. LaForge, Charles H. Schwepker, Jr., Ramaon A. Avila, and Michael R. Williams, *Sales Management: Analysis and Decision Making*, 5th ed. (Mason, OH: South-Western, 2004).
3. Trevor Thomas, "FIIA Study Finds Banks Favor One-on-One Selling for Insurance," *National Underwriter*, May 6, 2002, p. 41.
4. Andy Cohen, "Costs on the Road," *Sales & Marketing Management*, April 2001, p. 11.
5. "Welcome to Avon's Home Page," http://avon.avon.com/, accessed January 16, 2003.
6. John J. Miller, *National Review online*, May 30, 2002, http://www.nationalreview.com.
7. Lorraine Woellert, "The Do-Not-Call Law Won't Stop the Calls," *BusinessWeek*, September 29, 2003, p. 89.

8. "The Direct Marketing Association Responds to the Federal Trade Commission's Proposed Changes to the Telemarketing Sales Rule," Direct Marketing Association press release, April 19, 2002, http://www.the-dma.org.
9. Kimberly L. McCall, "The Ins and Outs," *Sales & Marketing Management*, March 2002, pp. 87–88.
10. Dick Gorelick, "The Changing Sales Rep-CSR Relationship," *American Printer*, June 2001, p. 108.
11. McCall, "The Ins and Outs."
12. Emily Thornton, "'Reengineering' at Merrill Lynch," *BusinessWeek*, August 6, 2001, p. 31.
13. Tim O'Brien, "Kahuna Lagoon Makes a Splash at Camelbeach," *Amusement Business*, May 20, 2002, p. 6.
14. Pamela L. Moore, "She's Here to Fix the Xerox," *BusinessWeek*, August 6, 2001, p. 47.
15. Gabrielle Birkner, "Who Says Titles Don't Matter?" *Sales & Marketing Management*, July 2001, p. 14.
16. Nick Pachetti, "A Tough Sell," *Money*, June 2002, p. 138.
17. Steve Jarvis, "Double Teamed," *Marketing News*, March 18, 2002, pp. 1, 7.
18. L. Biff, "Customers Still Want Expert Advice," *Bank Marketing*, May 2002, p. 41.
19. Ellen Neuborne, "Tag Team Pitches," *Sales & Marketing Management*, March 2002, p. 57.
20. Gabrielle Birkner, "In the Field: Closing Deals Quickly," *Sales & Marketing Management*, September 2002, p. 22.
21. Jennifer Maselli, "Wrigley Sales Rep Pitch in Real Time," *InformationWeek*, January 14, 2002, p. 51.
22. Mark McMaster, "The Incredible Shrinking Customer Base," *Sales & Marketing Management*, July 2001, pp. 65–66.
23. Scott Hensley, "More Than Ads, Drug Makers Rely on Sales Reps," *The Wall Street Journal*, March 14, 2002, pp. B1, B6.
24. "Harris InfoSource: The Gold Standard in Sales & Marketing for over 30 Years," http://www.hoovers.com/store/reports, accessed January 17, 2003.
25. Kathleen Cholewka, "What's Old Is New Again," *Sales & Marketing Management*, June 2002, p. 20.
26. Julie Cantwell, "Dealers Unhappy with Internet Sales Leads," *Automotive News*, March 25, 2002, p. 37.
27. "Multimedia Information Services," http://viswiz.gmd.de/MultimediaInfo/, accessed January 18, 2003.
28. Mark McMaster, "Ask S&M," *Sales & Marketing Management*, May 2001, p. 74.
29. Ian Gelenter, "Train Sales Reps to Reach the Next Sales Plateau," *Selling*, November 2001, p. 9.
30. Kathleen Cholewka, "Motivating Mentors," *Sales & Marketing Management*, June 2002, p. 61.
31. "Back to the Future Naturally with Hemp Clothing," http://www.hemp-sisters.com/, accessed January 18, 2003.
32. "Boise," http://www.endgame.org/boise.html, accessed January 18, 2003.
33. "2001 Salary Survey," *Sales & Marketing Management*, May 2001, p. 50.
34. "IBM and JD Edwards," downloaded from http://www.ibm-jdedwards.com, January 18, 2003.
35. Christine Galea, "2002 Salary Survey," *Sales & Marketing Management*, May 2002, p. 32.
36. Kathleen Cholewka, "Survey Says: Some Sales Execs Are Liars," *Sales & Marketing Management*, February 2001, p. 18.
37. Earle Eldridge, "More Car Dealers Now Videotape Sales," *USA Today*, July 3, 2001, p. B1.

APPENDIX A

1. "The New HP," downloaded from http://www.hp.com, August 14, 2002.
2. John Deere and Co. mission statement downloaded from http://www.deere.com, January 15, 2003.
3. Amgen mission statement downloaded from http://www.amgen.com, January 15, 2003.
4. Melanie Wells, "He Stoops to Conquer," *Forbes*, January 21, 2002, pp. 46–48.

A

accelerator principle Disproportionate impact of changes in consumer demand on business market demand.

accessory equipment Capital items that typically cost less and last for shorter periods of time than installations.

acculturation Degree to which newcomers adapt to a culture.

administered marketing system VMS that achieves channel coordination when a dominant channel member exercises its power.

adoption process Stages that consumers go through in learning about a new product, trying it, and deciding whether to purchase it again.

advertising Any paid, nonpersonal communication through various media about a business firm, not-for-profit organization, product, or idea by a sponsor identified in a message that is intended to inform or persuade members of a particular audience.

advertising agency Firm whose marketing specialists assist advertisers in planning and preparing advertisements.

advertising campaign Series of different but related ads that use a single theme and appear in different media within a specified time period.

advertorial Large advertising square on Web pages, which resembles an ad seen in the Yellow Pages.

affinity marketing Marketing effort sponsored by an organization that solicits responses from individuals who share common interests and activities.

AIDA concept Explanation of steps through which an individual reaches a purchase decision: attention, interest, desire, and action.

AIO statements Items on lifestyle surveys that describe various activities, interests, and opinions of respondents.

ambush marketing Attempt by a firm that is not an official sponsor of an event or activity to link itself to the event or activity.

application service providers (ASPs) Outside companies that specialize in providing both the computers and the application support for managing information systems of business clients.

approach Salesperson's initial contact with a prospective customer.

Asch phenomenon Impact of groups and group norms on individual behavior, as described by S. E. Asch. People often conform to majority rule, even when majority rule goes against their beliefs.

atmospherics Combination of physical characteristics and amenities that contribute to a store's image.

attitudes Person's enduring favorable or unfavorable evaluations, emotions, or action tendencies toward some object or idea.

average total costs Costs calculated by dividing the sum of the variable and fixed costs by the number of units produced.

B

banner Advertisement on a Web page that links to an advertiser's site.

basing-point pricing System used in some industries during the early 20th century in which the buyer paid the factory price plus freight charges from the basing-point city nearest the buyer.

benchmarking Method of measuring quality by comparing performance against industry leaders.

blind product test Test of advertising effectiveness in which participants are asked to select unidentified products on the basis of available advertising copy.

bonus pack Sales promotion technique consisting of a specially packaged item that gives the purchaser a larger quantity at the regular price.

boomers People born between the years of 1946 and 1965.

bot Search program that checks hundreds of Web sites, gathers and assembles information, and brings it back to the sender.

bottom line Business jargon referring to the overall profitability of an organization.

boundary-spanning role Role performed by a sales manager in linking the sales force to other elements of the organization's internal and external environments.

brand Name, term, sign, symbol, design, or some combination that identifies the products of one firm while differentiating them from the competition's.

brand equity Added value that a brand name gives to a product in the marketplace.

brand extension Strategy of attaching a popular brand name to a new product in an unrelated product category.

brand insistence Consumer refusals of alternatives and extensive search for desired merchandise.

brand licensing Firm's authorization of other companies to use its brand names.

brand manager Marketer who supports a specific brand.

brand mark Symbol or pictorial design that distinguishes a product.

brand name Part of a brand consisting of words or letters that form a name that identifies and distinguishes a firm's offerings from those of its competitors.

brand preference Consumer reliance on previous experiences with a product to choose that product again.

brand recognition Consumer awareness and identification of a brand.

breakeven analysis Pricing technique used to determine the number of products that must be sold at a specified price in order to generate enough revenue to cover total cost.

broadband technology Extremely high speed, always-on Internet connection.

broadcast media Television (network and cable) and radio.

broker Agent wholesaling intermediary who does not take title to or possession of goods in the course of its primary function, which is to bring together buyers and sellers.

bundle pricing Offering two or more complementary products and selling them for a single price.

business cycle Pattern of differing stages in the level of economic activity of a nation or region. Although the traditional cycle includes the four stages of prosperity, recession, depression, and recovery, most economists believe that future depressions can be prevented through effective economic policies.

business products Goods and services purchased for use either directly or indirectly in the production of other goods and services for resale.

business services Intangible products that firms buy to facilitate their production and operating processes.

business-to-business marketing (B2B) Organizational purchases of goods and services to support production of other products, for daily company operations, or for resale.

buyer Person who has the formal authority to select a supplier and to implement the procedures for securing a good or service.

buyer partnership Relationship in which a firm purchases goods or services from one or more providers.

buyer's market Market in which there are more goods and services than people willing to buy them.

buying allowance Promotional incentive that gives retailers a discount on goods.

buying center Participants in an organizational buying action.

C

cannibalization Loss of sales of an existing product due to competition from a new product in the same line.

captive brand National brands that are sold exclusively by a retail chain.

cash discount Price reduction offered to a consumer, business user, or marketing intermediary in return for prompt payment of a bill.

category killer Store that offers huge selections and low prices in single product lines.

category management Product management system in which a category manager—with profit and loss responsibility—oversees a product line.

cause marketing Identification and marketing of a social issue, cause, or idea to selected target markets.

channel Medium through which a message is delivered.

channel captain Dominant and controlling member of a marketing channel.

click-through rate The percentage of people presented with a Web banner ad who click on it.

closed sales territory Exclusive geographic selling region of a distributor.

closing Stage of personal selling where the salesperson asks the customer to make a purchase decision.

cluster sample Probability sample in which researchers select geographic areas or clusters, and all of the chosen individuals within this area become respondents.

cognitive dissonance Imbalance among a person's knowledge, beliefs, and attitudes.

cohort effect Tendency of members of a generation to be influenced and bound together by events occurring during their key formative years—roughly 17 to 22 years of age.

commercial market Individuals and firms that acquire products to support, directly or indirectly, production of other goods and services.

commission Incentive compensation directly related to the sales or profits achieved by a salesperson.

commission merchant Agent wholesaling intermediary who takes possession of goods shipped to a central market for sale, acts as the producer's agent, and collects an agreed-upon fee at the time of the sale.

common market Extension of a customs union by seeking to reconcile all government regulations affecting trade.

comparative advertising Advertising strategy that emphasizes messages with direct or indirect promotional comparisons between competing brands.

competitive environment Interactive process that occurs in the marketplace among marketers of directly competitive products, marketers of products that can be substituted for one another, and marketers competing for the consumer's purchasing power.

competitive pricing strategy Pricing strategy designed to de-emphasize price as a competitive variable by pricing a good or service at the general level of comparable offerings.

competitive strategy Methods through which a firm deals with its competitive environment.

component parts and materials Finished business products of one producer that actually become part of the final products of another producer.

concentrated marketing Focusing marketing efforts on satisfying only one market segment; also called *niche marketing*.

concept testing Method for subjecting a product idea to additional study before actual development, by involving consumers through focus groups, surveys, in-store polling, and the like.

consolidated metropolitan statistical area (CMSA) Urban area that includes two or more PMSAs.

consultative selling Meeting customer needs by listening to them, understanding—and caring about—their problems, paying attention to details, and following through after the sale.

consumer behavior Buying behavior of individuals who will use the goods and services they purchase.

consumer innovator People who purchase new products almost as soon as the products reach the market.

consumer orientation Business philosophy incorporating the marketing concept that emphasizes first determining unmet consumer needs and then designing a system for satisfying them.

consumer products Products bought by ultimate consumers for personal use.

consumer rights As stated by President Kennedy in 1962, the consumer's right to choose freely, to be informed, to be heard, and to be safe.

consumerism Social force within the environment designed to aid and protect the consumer by exerting legal, moral, and economic pressures on business and government.

containerization Process of combining several unitized loads into a single, well-protected load for shipment.

contest Sales promotion technique using games that require entrants to solve problems or write essays to win prizes.

contractual marketing system VMS that coordinates channel activities through formal agreements among channel members.

controlled experiment Scientific investigation in which a researcher manipulates a test group (or groups) and compares the results with those of a control group that did not receive the experimental controls or manipulations.

convenience products Goods and services that consumers want to purchase frequently, immediately, and with minimal effort.

convenience retailer Store that appeals to customers on accessible location, long hours, rapid checkout, and adequate parking.

convenience sample Nonprobability sample selected from among readily available respondents.

conversion rate The percentage of visitors to a Web site who make a purchase.

cookie Controversial technique for collecting information about online Web site visitors in which a small text file is automatically downloaded to a user's computer to gather such data as length of visit and the site visited next.

cooperative advertising Strategy in which a retailer shares advertising costs with a manufacturer or wholesaler.

core competencies Activities that a company performs well, and that customers value and competitors find difficult to duplicate.

corporate marketing system A VMS in which a single owner operates the entire marketing channel.

corporate Web site Web site that seeks to build customer goodwill and supplement other sales channels rather than to sell goods and services.

cost per impression (CPM) Measurement technique that relates the cost of an ad to every thousand people who view it.

cost per response (also called *click-throughs*) Direct marketing technique that relates the cost of an ad to the number of people who click on it.

cost per thousand (CPM) Calculation of the cost to deliver a message to each 1,000 viewers, listeners, or readers.

cost-plus pricing Practice of adding a percentage of specified dollar amount (markup) to the base cost of a product to cover unassigned costs and to provide a profit.

countertrade Form of exporting whereby goods and services are bartered rather than sold for cash.

coupons Form of sales promotion that offers discounts on the purchase price of goods and services.

creative selling Personal selling involving situations in which a considerable degree of analytical decision making on the buyer's part results in the need for skillful proposals of solutions for the customer's needs.

creativity Human activity that produces original ideas or knowledge, frequently by testing combinations of ideas or data to produce unique results.

critical thinking Process of determining the authenticity, accuracy, and worth of information, knowledge, claims, and arguments.

cross promotion Promotional technique in which marketing partners share the cost of a promotional campaign that meets their mutual needs.

cross-selling Selling of multiple, often unrelated products and services to the same customer, based on knowledge of that customer's needs.

cue Any object in the environment that determines the nature of a consumer's response to a drive.

culture Values, beliefs, preferences, and tastes handed down from one generation to the next in a society.

cumulative quantity discount Price discount determined by amounts of purchases over stated time periods.

customary prices Traditional prices that customers expect to pay for certain goods and services.

customer-based segmentation Dividing a business-to-business market into homogeneous groups based on buyers' product specifications.

customer behavior Buying behavior of individual consumers as well as organizational buyers.

customer relationship management (CRM) Combination of strategies and tools that drive relationship programs, reorienting the entire organization to a concentrated focus on satisfying customers. Leveraging technology, CRM integrates all stakeholders into a company's product design and development, manufacturing, marketing, sales, and customer service processes.

customer satisfaction Extent to which customers are satisfied with their purchased goods or services.

customer service standard Statement of goals and acceptable performance for the quality of service that a firm expects to deliver to its customers.

customs union Establishment of a free-trade area plus a uniform tariff for trade with nonmember unions.

cybermall Group of virtual stores planned, coordinated, and operated as a unit for online shoppers.

D

data mining Process of searching through customer databases to detect patterns that guide marketing decision making.

database marketing Use of software to analyze marketing information, identifying and targeting messages toward specific groups of potential customers.

decider Person who chooses a good or service, although another person may have the formal authority to do so.

decoding Receiver's interpretation of a message.

Delphi technique Qualitative sales forecasting method that gathers and redistributes several rounds of anonymous forecasts until the participants reach a consensus.

demand Schedule of the amounts of a firm's product that consumers will purchase at different prices during a specified time period.

demarketing Process of reducing consumer demand for a good or service to a level that the firm can supply.

demographic segmentation Dividing an overall market into homogeneous groups based on variables such as gender, age, and income.

demonstration Opportunity for the customer to try out or otherwise see how a product or service works before purchase.

department store Large store that handles a variety of merchandise, including clothing, household goods, appliances, and furniture.

deregulation movement Opening of markets previously subject to government control.

derived demand Demand for a business product that results from demand for a consumer product.

differentiated marketing Marketing strategy to produce several products and promote them with different marketing mixes designed to satisfy smaller segments.

diffusion process Process by which new goods or services are accepted in the marketplace.

digital tools Electronic technologies used in e-commerce, including fax machines, computer modems, telephones, and CD-ROMS.

direct channel Marketing channel that moves goods directly from a producer to the business purchaser or ultimate user.

direct mail Communications in the form of sales letters, postcards, brochures, catalogs, and the like conveying messages directly from the marketer to the customer.

direct marketing Direct communications, other than personal sales contacts, between buyer and seller, designed to generate sales, information requests, or store or Web site visits.

direct sales results test Method for measuring the effectiveness of promotion based on the specific impact on sales revenues for each dollar of promotional spending.

direct selling Strategy designed to establish direct sales contact between producer and final user.

discount house Store that charges low prices but may not offer services such as credit.

discretionary income Money people have available to spend after buying necessities such as food, clothing, and housing.

distribution intensity Number of intermediaries through which a manufacturer distributes its goods.

distribution strategies Planning that ensures that consumers find their products in the proper quantities at the right times and places.

drive Any strong stimulus that impels a person to act.

drop shipper Limited-function merchant wholesaler who accepts orders from customers and forwards these orders to producers, which then ship directly to the customers who place the orders.

dual distribution Network that moves products to a firm's target market through more than one marketing channel.

dumping Controversial practice of selling a product in foreign market at a price lower than what it receives in the producer's domestic market.

E

economic environment Factors that influence consumer buying power and marketing strategies, including stage of the business cycle, inflation, unemployment, income, and resource availability.

80/20 principle Principle stating that 80 percent of a product's revenues come from 20 percent of its total customers.

elasticity Measure of responsiveness of purchasers and suppliers to a change in price.

electronic bulletin board Specialized online service that provides information on a specific topic or area of interest.

electronic commerce (e-commerce) Targeting customers by collecting and analyzing business information, conducting customer transactions, and maintaining online relationships with customers by means of computer networks.

electronic data interchange (EDI) Computer-to-computer exchanges of invoices, orders, and other business documents.

electronic exchanges Online marketplaces that bring buyers and sellers together.

electronic marketing (e-marketing) Strategic process of creating, distributing, promoting, and pricing goods and services to a target market over the Internet or through digital tools.

electronic signature Electronic approval of a document that has the same status as a written signature.

electronic storefront Online store where customers can view and order merchandise much like window shopping at traditional retail establishments.

embargo Complete ban on the import of specified products.

employee satisfaction Employee's level of satisfaction for his or her company and the extent to which that loyalty or lack of loyalty is communicated to external customers.

encoding Translating a message into understandable terms.

end-use application segmentation Segmenting a business-to-business market based on how industrial purchasers will use the product.

Engel's laws Three general statements based on Engel's studies of the impact of household income changes on consumer spending behavior.

enterprise resource planning (ERP) system Software system that consolidates data from among a firm's units.

environmental management Attainment of organizational objectives by predicting and influencing the competitive, political-legal, economic, technological, and social-cultural environments.

environmental scanning Process of collecting information about the external marketing environment in order to identify and interpret potential trends.

ethnocentrism Tendency to view one's own culture as the norm.

ethnography Observational research method developed by social anthropologists; also known as interpretive research or "going native."

European Union (EU) Customs union that is moving in the direction of an economic union by adopting a common currency, removing trade restrictions, and permitting free flow of goods and workers throughout the member nations.

evaluative criteria Features that a consumer considers in choosing among alternatives.

event marketing Marketing of sporting, cultural, and charitable activities to selected target markets.

everyday low pricing (EDLP) Pricing strategy of continuously offering low prices rather than relying on such short-term price cuts as cents-off coupons, rebates, and special sales.

evoked set Number of alternatives that a consumer actually considers in making a purchase decision.

exchange control Method used to regulate the privilege of international trade among importing organizations by controlling access to foreign currencies.

exchange function Buying and selling functions of marketing.

exchange process Activity in which two or more parties give something of value to each other to satisfy perceived needs.

exchange rate Price of one nation's currency in terms of other countries' currencies.

exclusive dealing agreement Arrangement between a manufacturer and a marketing intermediary that prohibits the intermediary from handling competing product lines.

exclusive distribution Distribution of a product through one wholesaler or retailer in a specific geographical region.

expectancy theory Theory developed by management author Victor Vroom stating that motivation depends on an individual's expectations of his or her ability to perform a job and how that performance relates to attaining a desired reward.

exploratory research Process of discussing a marketing problem with informed sources both within and outside the firm and examining information from secondary sources.

exponential smoothing Quantitative forecasting technique that assigns weights to historical sales data, giving the greatest weight to the most recent data.

exporting Marketing domestically produced goods and services in foreign countries.

extended problem solving Situation that results when brands are difficult to categorize or evaluate, and usually involves lengthy external searches.

external customer People or organizations that buy or use another firm's goods or services.

external marketing Marketing efforts that a company directs toward customers, suppliers, and other parties outside the organization.

extranet Secure network accessible through a Web site by external customers or organizations for electronic commerce. It provides more customer-specific information than a public site.

F

facilitating functions Functions that assist the marketer in performing the exchange and physical distribution functions.

fads Fashions with abbreviated life cycles.

fair-trade laws Statutes enacted in most states that once permitted manufacturers to stipulate a minimum retail price for their product.

family brand Single brand name that identifies several related products.

family life cycle Process of family formation and dissolution.

fashions Currently popular products that tend to follow recurring life cycles.

feedback Receiver's response to a message.

field selling Sales presentations made at prospective customers' homes or businesses on a face-to-face basis.

first-mover strategy Concept that advocates that the company that is first to offer a product in a marketplace will be the long-term winner.

fixed costs Costs that remain stable at any production level within a certain range (such as lease payments or insurance costs).

fixed-sum-per-unit method Method of promotional budgeting in which a predetermined amount is allocated to each sales or production unit.

FOB (free on board) plant Price quotation that does not include shipping charges; also called FOB origin.

FOB origin-freight allowed or **freight absorbed** Price quotation system that allows the buyer to deduct shipping expenses from the cost of purchases.

focus group Marketing research procedure that typically brings together 8 to 12 individuals to discuss a given subject.

follow-up Post sales activities that often determine whether an individual who has made a recent purchase will become a repeat customer.

foreign licensing Agreement that grants foreign marketers the right to distribute a firm's merchandise or to use its trademark, patent, or process in a specified geographic area.

franchise Contractual arrangement in which a wholesaler or retailer agrees to meet the operating requirements of a manufacturer or other franchiser.

free-trade area Region in which participating nations agree to the free trade of goods among themselves, abolishing tariffs and trade restrictions.

Free Trade Area of the Americas (FTAA) Proposed free trade area stretching the length of the entire Western hemisphere and designed to extend free trade benefits to additional nations in North, Central, and South America.

frequency Number of times an individual is exposed to an advertisement during a certain time period.

frequency marketing Frequent buyer or user marketing programs that reward customers with cash, rebates, merchandise, or other premiums.

friendship, commerce, and navigation (FCN) treaties International agreements that deal with many aspects of commercial relations among nations.

full-cost pricing Pricing method that uses all relevant variable costs in setting a product's price and also allocates those fixed costs that cannot be directly attributed to the production of the specific item being priced.

full-service research supplier Customized service that provides all the steps in the marketing research process.

G

gatekeeper Person who controls the information that all buying center members will review.

General Agreement on Tariffs and Trade (GATT) International trade accord that has helped reduce world tariffs.

general merchandise retailer Store that carries a wide variety of product lines, stocking all of them in some depth.

generic products Products characterized by plain labels, no advertising, and no brand names.

geographic information system (GIS) System that places data in a spatial format, on a map.

geographic segmentation Dividing an overall market into homogeneous groups based on their locations.

global marketing strategy Standardized marketing mix with minimal modifications that a firm uses in all of its domestic and foreign markets.

global sourcing Contracting to purchase goods and services from suppliers worldwide.

good Tangible product that customers can see, hear, smell, taste, or touch.

goods-services continuum Spectrum along which goods and services fall according to their attributes, from pure good to pure service.

green marketing Production, promotion, and reclamation of environmentally sensitive products.

grey good Product manufactured abroad under license from a U.S. firm and then sold in the U.S. market in competition with that firm's own domestic output.

gross rating point Total weight of a media effort, which is determined by multiplying reach times frequency.

guerilla marketing Innovative, low-cost marketing schemes designed to get consumers' attention in unusual ways.

H

high-involvement purchase decision Buying decision that evokes high levels of potential social or economic consequence.

home shopping channel Television direct marketing in which a variety of products are offered and consumers can order them directly by phone or online.

hypothesis Tentative explanation for some specific event.

I

import quotas Trade restriction that limits the number of units of certain goods that can enter a country for resale.

importing Purchasing foreign goods, services, and raw materials.

inbound telemarketing Sales method in which prospects call a toll-free number to obtain information, make reservations, and purchase goods and services.

incremental-cost pricing Pricing method that attempts to use only those costs directly attributable to a specific output in setting prices.

indirect evaluation Method for measuring promotional effectiveness by concentrating on quantifiable indicators of effectiveness such as recall and readership.

individual brand Single brand that uniquely identifies a product itself.

inflation Rising prices caused by some combination of excess consumer demand and increases in the costs of one or more factors of production.

influencer Typically technical staff such as engineers who affect the buying decision by supplying information to guide evaluation of alternatives or by setting buying specifications

infomercial Paid 30-minute product commercial that resembles a regular television program.

informative advertising Promotion that seeks to develop initial demand for a good, service, organization, person, place, idea, or cause.

infrastructure A nation's basic system of transportation networks, communication systems, and energy facilities.

inquiry tests Posttests that measure the number of inquiries relative to an advertisement's cost.

inside selling Performing the functions of field selling but avoiding travel-related expenses by relying on phone, mail, and electronic commerce to provide sales and product service for customers on a continuing basis.

installations Business products that are major capital investments.

instant messaging E-mail service that allows for the immediate exchange of short messages between online users.

institutional advertising Promotion of a concept, idea, philosophy, or goodwill of an industry, company, organization, person, geographical location, or government agency.

integrated marketing communications (IMC) Coordination of all promotional activities to produce a unified, customer-focused promotional message.

intensive distribution Distribution of a product through all available channels.

interactive advertising Two-way promotional messages transmitted through communication channels that induce message recipients to participate actively in the promotional effort.

interactive marketing Buyer-seller communications in which the customer controls the amount and type of information received from a marketer through such channels as the Internet, CD-ROMS, interactive toll-free telephone numbers, and virtual reality kiosks.

interactive television (iTV) Television service package that includes a return path for viewers to interact with programs or commercials by clicking their remote controls.

intermodal service Combination of transport modes such as rail and highway carriers (piggyback), air and highway carriers (birdyback), and water and air carriers (fishyback) to improve customer service and achieve cost advantages.

internal customer Employees or departments within an organization that depend on the work of another employee or department to perform tasks.

internal marketing Managerial actions that help all members of the organization understand and accept their respective roles in implementing a marketing strategy.

Internet (or Net) Worldwide network of interconnected computers that lets anyone with access to a personal computer send and receive images and data anywhere.

Internet service provider (ISP) Organization that provides access to the Internet via a telephone or cable television network.

interstitial Ad that appears between Web pages of related content.

intranet Internal corporate network that allows employees within an organization to communicate with each other and gain access to corporate information.

ISO (International Standards Organization) 9000 certification Internationally recognized standards that ensure a company's goods and services meet established quality levels.

ISO 9002 International quality standards developed by the International Standards Organization in Switzerland to ensure consistent quality among products manufactured and sold throughout the nations of the European Union (EU).

J

joint demand Demand for a business product that depends on the demand for another business product used in combination with the first item.

jury of executive opinion Qualitative sales forecasting method that considers the sales expectations of various executives.

just-in-time (JIT)/just-in-time II (JIT II) Inventory practices that seek to boost efficiency by cutting inventories to absolute minimum levels. With JIT II, suppliers' representatives work at the customer's facility.

K

keyword ad Web advertisement that appears on the results page of a search, specific to the term being searched.

L

label Branding component that carries an item's brand name or symbol, the name and address of the manufacturer or distributor, information about the product, and recommended uses.

lateral partnership Strategic relationships that extend to external entities but involve no direct buyer-seller interactions.

leader pricing Variant of loss-leader pricing in which marketers offer prices slightly above cost to avoid violating minimum-markup regulations and earn a minimal return on promotional sales.

learning Immediate or expected changes in consumer behavior as a result of experience.

lifetime value of a customer Revenues and intangible benefits, such as referrals and customer feedback, that a customer brings to the seller over an average lifetime, less the amount the company must spend to acquire, market to, and service the customer.

limited-line store Retailer that offers a large assortment within a single product line or within a few related product lines.

limited problem-solving Situation in which the consumer knows the evaluative criteria for a product, but has not applied the criteria to assess a new brand.

line extension Development of individual offerings that appeal to different market segments while remaining closely related to the existing product line.

list price Established price normally quoted to potential buyers.

logistics Process of coordinating the flow of information, goods, and services among members of the distribution channel.

loss leader Product offered to consumers at less than cost to attract them to stores in the hope that they will buy other merchandise at regular prices.

low-involvement purchase decision Routine purchase that poses little risk to the consumer, either socially or economically.

M

mail-order wholesaler Limited-function merchant wholesaler who distributes catalogs instead of sending sales representatives to contact customers.

mall intercept Interviews conducted randomly in shopping centers.

manufacturers' agent Agent wholesaling intermediary who represents a number of manufacturers of related but noncompeting products and who receives a commission on each sale.

manufacturer's brand Brand name owned by a manufacturer or other producer.

marginal analysis Method of analyzing the relationship between costs, sales price, and increased sales volume.

marginal cost Change in total cost that results from producing an additional unit of output.

markdown Amount by which a retailer reduces the original selling price of a product.

market Group of people or institutions with sufficient purchasing power, authority, and willingness to buy.

market attractiveness/business strength Portfolio analysis technique that rates SBUs according to the attractiveness of their markets and their organizational strengths.

market development strategy Strategy that concentrates on finding new markets for existing products.

market penetration strategy Strategy that seeks to increase sales of existing products in existing markets.

market price Price that a consumer or marketing intermediary actually pays for a product after subtracting any discounts, allowances, or rebates from the list price.

market segmentation Division of the total market into smaller, relatively homogeneous groups.

market share/market growth matrix Framework that places SBUs in a chart that plots market share against market growth potential.

market-share objective Volume-related pricing objective in which the goal is to achieve control of a portion of the market for a firm's good or service.

market test Quantitative forecasting method that introduces a new product, price, promotional campaign, or other marketing variable in a relatively small test-market location in order to assess consumer reactions.

marketing Process of planning and executing the conception, pricing, and distribution of ideas, goods, services, organizations, and events to create and maintain relationships that will satisfy individual and organizational objectives.

marketing communications Messages that deal with buyer-seller relationships.

marketing concept Company-wide consumer orientation with the objective of achieving long-run success.

marketing decision support system (MDSS) Marketing information system component that links a decision maker with relevant databases and analysis tools.

marketing distribution channel System of marketing institutions that promotes the physical flow of goods and services, along with ownership title, from producer to consumer or business user.

marketing ethics Marketers' standards of conduct and moral values.

marketing information system (MIS) Planned, computer-based system designed to provide managers with a continuous flow of information relevant to their specific decisions and areas of responsibility.

marketing intermediary (middleman) Wholesaler or retailer that operates between producers and consumers or business users.

marketing mix Blending of the four strategy elements—product, pricing, distribution, and promotion—to fit the needs and preferences of a specific target market.

marketing myopia Management's failure to recognize the scope of its business.

marketing planning Implementing planning activities devoted to achieving marketing objectives.

marketing public relations (MPR) Narrowly focused public relations activities that directly support marketing goals.

marketing research Process of collecting and using information for marketing decision making.

markup Amount that a retailer adds to the cost of a product to determine its selling price.

mass merchandiser Store that stocks a wider line of goods than a department store, usually without the same depth of assortment within each line.

materials handling Set of activities that move production inputs and other goods within plants, warehouses, and transportation terminals.

media research Advertising research that assesses how well a particular medium delivers an advertiser's message, where and when to place the advertisement, and the size of the audience.

media scheduling Setting the timing and sequence for a series of advertisements.

meeting competition Method of promotional budgeting that simply matches competitors' outlays.

merchant wholesaler Independently owned wholesaling intermediary who takes title to the goods that it handles; also known as an industrial distributor in the business-goods market.

message Communication of information, advice, or a request by the sender to the receiver.

message research Advertising research that tests consumer reactions to an advertisement's creative message.

metropolitan statistical area (MSA) Freestanding urban area with a population in the urban center of at least 50,000, and a total MSA population of 100,000 or more.

micromarketing Targeting potential customers at a basic level, such as zip code.

mission Essential purpose that differentiates one company from others.

missionary selling Indirect type of selling in which specialized salespeople promote the firm's goodwill among indirect customers, often by assisting customers in product use.

modified breakeven analysis Pricing technique used to evaluate consumer demand by comparing the number of products that must be sold at a variety of prices in order to cover total cost with estimates of expected sales at the various prices.

modified rebuy Situation in which a purchaser is willing to reevaluate available options for repurchasing a good or service.

monopolistic competition Market structure involving a heterogeneous product and product differentiation among competing suppliers, allowing the marketer some degree of control over prices.

monopoly Market structure in which a single seller dominates trade in a good or service for which buyers can find no close substitutes.

motive Inner state that directs a person toward the goal of satisfying a need.

MRO items Business supplies that include maintenance items, repair items, and operating supplies.

multidomestic marketing strategy Application of market segmentation to foreign markets by tailoring the firm's marketing mix to match specific target markets in each nation.

multinational corporation Firm with significant operations and marketing activities outside its home country.

multiple sourcing Spreading purchases among several vendors.

N

national account selling Promotional effort in which a dedicated sales team is assigned to a firm's major customers to provide sales and service needs.

national accounts organization Organizational arrangement that assigns sales teams to a firm's largest accounts.

need Imbalance between a consumer's actual and desired states.

new-task buying First-time or unique purchase situation that requires considerable effort by the decision makers.

9/11 Generation People in their formative years at the time of the September 11 terrorist attacks.

noise Any stimulus that distracts a receiver from receiving a message.

noncumulative quantity discount Price reduction granted on a one-time-only basis.

nonmarketing public relations Organizational messages about general management issues.

nonpersonal selling Promotion that includes advertising, sales promotion, direct marketing, and public relations—all conducted without being face-to-face with the buyer.

nonprobability sample Arbitrary grouping that produces data unsuited for most standard statistical tests.

norms Values, attitudes, and behaviors that a group deems appropriate for its members.

North American Free-Trade Agreement (NAFTA) Accord removing trade barriers among Canada, Mexico, and the United States.

North American Industrial Classification System (NAICS) Classification used by NAFTA countries to categorize the business marketplace into detailed market segments.

O

objection Expression of sales resistance by the prospect.

odd pricing Pricing policy based on the belief that a price ending with an odd number just under a round number is more appealing—for instance, $9.97 rather than $10.

off-invoice allowance Promotional incentive through which retailers deduct specified amounts from their invoices or receive free goods.

oligopoly Market structure, like those in the steel and telecommunications industries, in which relatively few sellers compete, and where high start-up costs form barriers to keep out new competitors

opinion leaders Trendsetters who are likely to purchase new products before others in a group and then share their experiences and opinions via word of mouth.

order processing Selling, mostly at the wholesale and retail levels, that involves identifying customer needs, pointing them out to customers, and completing orders.

organization marketing Marketing by mutual-benefit organizations, service organizations, and government organizations intended to influence others to accept their goals, receive their services, or contribute to them in some way.

outbound telemarketing Sales method in which sales representatives place phone calls to prospects and try to conclude the sale over the phone.

outsourcing Using outside vendors to produce goods and services formerly produced in-house.

over-the-counter selling Personal selling conducted in retail and some wholesale locations in which customers come to the seller's place of business.

P

partnership Affiliation of two or more companies that assist each other in the achievement of common goals.

penetration pricing strategy Pricing strategy involving the use of a relatively low entry price compared with competitive offerings; based on the theory that this initial low price will help secure market acceptance.

percentage-of-sales method Way of establishing a promotional budget in which a dollar amount is based on a percentage of past or projected sales.

perception Meaning that a person attributes to incoming stimuli gathered through the five senses.

perceptual screen Filtering process through which all inputs must pass in a person's mind.

person marketing Marketing efforts designed to cultivate the attention, interest, and preference of a target market toward a person (typically a political candidate or celebrity).

personal selling Interpersonal influence process involving a seller's promotional presentation conducted on a person-to-person basis with the buyer.

persuasive advertising Promotion that attempts to increase demand for an existing good, service, organization, person, place, idea, or cause.

physical distribution function Transportation and distribution of goods and services.

place marketing Marketing efforts to attract people and organizations to a particular geographic area.

planned obsolescence Intentional design, manufacture, and marketing of products with limited durability.

planned shopping center Group of retail stores planned, coordinated, and marketed as a unit.

planning Process of anticipating future events and conditions, and of determining the best way to achieve organizational goals.

point-of-purchase (POP) advertising Display or other promotion located near the site of an actual buying decision.

political-legal environment Component of the marketing environment consisting of laws and interpretations of laws that require firms to operate under competitive conditions and to protect consumer rights.

political risk assessment (PRA) Units within a firm that evaluate the political risks of the marketplaces in which they operate as well as proposed new marketplaces.

population (universe) Total group that researchers want to study.

pop-up ads Advertising messages that appear unsolicited as windows on a computer screen.

positioning map Graphic depiction of consumers' perceptions of competing products within an industry.

POSSLQ Abbreviation for unmarried "people of the opposite sex in the same living quarters."

postage-stamp pricing System for handling transportation costs under which all buyers are quoted the same price, including transportation expenses. Also known as *uniform-delivered price*.

posttesting Research that assesses advertising effectiveness after it has appeared in the appropriate medium.

precall planning Use of information collected during the prospecting and qualifying stages of the sales process and during previous contacts with the prospect to tailor the approach and presentation to match the customer's needs.

premium Sales promotion technique in which an item is provided free or at a reduced cost with the purchase of other products.

presentation Describing a product's major features and relating them to a customer's problems or needs.

pretesting Research that evaluates an ad during its development stage.

price Exchange value of a good or service.

price flexibility Pricing policy permitting variable prices for goods and services.

pricing policy General guidelines based on pricing objectives and intended for use in specific pricing decisions.

pricing strategy Methods of setting profitable and justifiable prices.

primary data Information collected for the first time.

primary demand Desire for a general product category.

primary metropolitan statistical area (PMSA) Urbanized county or set of counties with social and economic ties to nearby areas.

private brand Brand offered by a wholesaler or retailer.

probability sample Sample that gives every member of the population a chance of being selected.

product Bundle of physical, service, and symbolic attributes designed to satisfy a customer's wants and needs.

product advertising Nonpersonal selling of a particular good or service.

product development Introduction of new products into identifiable or established markets.

product differentiation When consumers regard a firm's products as different in some way from those of competitors.

product diversification strategy Developing entirely new products for new markets.

product liability Responsibility of manufacturers and marketers for injuries and damages caused by their products.

product life cycle Progression of a product through introduction, growth, maturity, and decline.

product line Series of related products offered by one company.

product-line pricing Practice of setting a limited number of prices for a selection of merchandise and marketing different product lines in each of these price levels.

product manager Marketers who support an individual product or product line; also called a brand manager.

product mix Assortment of product lines and individual product offerings that a company sells.

product placement Form of promotion in which a marketer pays a motion picture or television program owner a fee to display a product prominently in the film or show.

product positioning Consumers' perceptions of a product's attributes, uses, quality, and advantages and disadvantages relative to competing brands.

product-related segmentation Division of a population into homogeneous groups based on characteristics of their relationships to the product.

product strategy Decisions about what goods or services a firm will offer its customers; also includes decisions about customer service, packaging, brand names, and the like.

production orientation Business philosophy stressing efficiency in producing a quality product, with the attitude toward marketing that "a good product will sell itself."

profit center Any part of an organization to which revenue and controllable costs can be assigned.

Profit Impact of Market Strategies (PIMS) project Research that discovered a strong positive relationship between a firm's market share and its return on investment.

profit maximization Point at which the additional revenue gained by increasing the price of a product equals the increase in total costs.

promotion Communication link between buyers and sellers. Function of informing, persuading, and influencing a consumer's purchase decision.

promotional allowance Promotional incentive in which the manufacturer agrees to pay the reseller a certain amount to cover the costs of special promotional displays or extensive advertising.

promotional mix Subset of the marketing mix in which marketers attempt to achieve the optimal blending of the elements of personal and nonpersonal selling to achieve promotional objectives.

promotional pricing Pricing policy in which a lower-than-normal price is used as a temporary ingredient in a firm's marketing strategy.

prospecting Personal selling function of identifying potential customers.

protective tariff Taxes designed to raise the retail price of an imported product to match or exceed that of a similar domestic tariff.

psychographic segmentation Division of a population into groups that have similar psychological characteristics, values, and lifestyles.

psychological pricing Pricing policy based on the belief that certain prices or price ranges make a good or service more appealing than others to buyers.

public relations Firm's communications and relationships with its various publics.

public service announcements (PSAs) Advertisements aimed at achieving socially oriented objectives by focusing on causes and charitable organizations.

publicity Nonpersonal stimulation of demand for a good, service, place, idea, person, or organization by unpaid placement of significant news regarding the product in a print or broadcast medium.

puffery Exaggerated claims of a product's superiority, or the use of subjective or vague statements that may not be literally true.

pulling strategy Promotional effort by the seller to stimulate final-user demand, which then exerts pressure on the distribution channel.

pure competition Market structure characterized by homogeneous products in which there are so many buyers and sellers that none has a significant influence on price.

push money Promotional incentive that gives retail salespeople cash rewards for products they sell.

pushing strategy Promotional effort by the seller directed to members of the marketing channel rather than final users.

Q

qualifying Determining that a prospect has the needs, income, and purchase authority necessary for being a potential customer.

qualitative forecasting Use of subjective techniques to forecast sales.

quantitative forecasting Use of techniques based on numerical data developed through statistical analysis.

quantity discount Price reduction granted for a large-volume purchase.

quick response merchandising Just-in-time strategy that reduces the time a retailer must hold merchandise in inventory, resulting in substantial cost savings.

quota sample Nonprobability sample divided to ensure representation of different segments or groups in the total sample.

R

rack jobber Full-function merchant wholesaler who markets specialized lines of merchandise to retail stores.

raw materials Natural resources such as farm products, coal, copper, or lumber, which become part of a final product.

reach Number of different individuals or households exposed to an advertisement at least once during a certain time period.

readership test Test of advertising effectiveness based on the assumption that future sales are related to advertising readership; also called *recognition test*.

rebate Refund of a portion of the purchase price, usually granted by the product's manufacturer.

reciprocity Policy to extend purchasing preference to suppliers that are also customers.

reference groups Groups whose value structures and standards influence a person's behavior.

refund Sales promotion technique in which consumers who send in proof of purchasing one or more products are offered cash to reduce the total price paid; also called a *rebate*.

reinforcement Reduction in drive that results from a proper response.

relationship marketing Development and maintenance of long-term, cost-effective relationships with individual customers, suppliers, employees, and other partners for mutual benefit.

relationship selling Regular contacts over an extended period to establish a sustained seller-buyer relationship.

reminder advertising Advertising that reinforces previous promotional activity by keeping the name of a good, service, organization, person, place, idea, or cause before the public.

repositioning Changing the position of a product within the minds of prospective buyers relative to the positions of competing products.

research design Master plan for conducting marketing research.

reseller Marketing intermediaries that operate in the trade sector.

response Individual's reaction to a set of cues and drives.

retail advertising All advertising by retail stores that sell goods or services directly to the consuming public.

retail convergence The coming together of shoppers, goods, and prices, resulting in the blurring of distinctions between types of retailer and the merchandise mix they offer.

retailing Activities involved in selling merchandise to ultimate consumers.

revenue tariff Taxes designed to raise funds for the importing government.

reverse channel Channel designed to return goods to their producers.

Robinson-Patman Act Federal legislation prohibiting price discrimination that is not based on a cost differential; also prohibits selling at an unreasonably low price to eliminate competition.

role Behavior that members of a group expect of individuals who hold specific positions within that group.

routinized response behavior Type of rapid consumer problem solving in which the consumer has already set evaluative criteria and identified available options.

S

sales analysis In-depth evaluation of a firm's sales.

sales conviction test Test of advertising effectiveness in which participants evaluate two alternative ads and choose the one that best convinces them to make a purchase.

sales-force automation (SFA) Applications of computer and other technologies to make the sales function more efficient and competitive.

sales force composite Qualitative sales forecasting method based on the combined sales estimates of the firm's salespeople.

sales forecast Estimate of company revenue for a specified future period.

sales orientation Business assumption that consumers will resist purchasing nonessential goods and services with the attitude toward marketing that only creative advertising and personal selling can overcome consumers' resistance and convince them to buy.

sales promotion Marketing activities other than personal selling, advertising, and public relations that stimulate consumer purchasing and dealer effectiveness.

sales quota Level of expected sales for a territory, product, customer, or salesperson against which actual results are compared.

sampling Sales promotion technique in which a product is distributed at no cost in an attempt to encourage trial use by potential customers to stimulate future sales.

scrambled merchandising Retailing practice of combining dissimilar product lines to boost sales volume.

search engine A tool to help online users find specific Web sites and pages.

secondary data Previously published information.

selective demand Desire for a specific brand.

selective distribution Distribution of a product through only a limited number of channels.

self-concept Person's multifaceted picture of himself or herself.

seller partnership Relationship involving long-term exchanges of goods or services in return for cash or other valuable consideration.

seller's market Market in which there are more buyers for fewer goods and services.

selling agent Agent wholesaling intermediary responsible for the entire marketing program of a firm's product line.

sender Source of the message communicated to the receiver.

service Intangible task that satisfies the needs of consumer and business users.

shaping Process of applying a series of rewards and reinforcements to permit more complex behavior to evolve over time.

shopping products Products that consumers purchase after comparing competing offerings.

simple random sample Basic type of probability sample in which every individual in the relevant universe has an equal opportunity of selection.

skimming pricing strategy Pricing strategy involving the use of a high price relative to competitive offerings.

slotting allowances Money paid to retailers to guarantee prominent display.

slotting fee See *slotting allowances.*

smart card Multipurpose card embedded with computer chips that store personal and financial information, such as credit card data, health records, and driver's license number.

social-cultural environment Component of the marketing environment consisting of the relationship between the marketer and society and its culture.

social responsibility Marketing philosophies, policies, procedures, and actions that have the enhancement of society's welfare as a primary objective.

sole sourcing Purchasing a firm's entire stock of a product from just one vendor.

span of control Approach to supervision of sales personnel based on the number of representatives who report to first-level sales managers.

specialty advertising Sales promotion technique that places the advertiser's name, address, and advertising message on useful articles that are then distributed to target consumers.

specialty products Products that offer unique characteristics that cause buyers to prize those particular brands.

specialty retailer Store that combines carefully defined product lines, services, and reputation to convince shoppers to spend considerable shopping effort there.

split run Method of testing alternate ads by dividing a cable TV audience or a publication's subscribers in two, using two different ads, and then evaluating the relative effectiveness of each.

sponsorship When an organization provides cash or in-kind resources to an event or activity in exchange for a direct association with that event or activity.

spreadsheet analysis Analysis that lays out a rigid grid of columns and rows that organize numerical information in a standardized, easily understandable format.

status Relative position of any individual member in a group.

stockkeeping unit (SKU) Specific offering within a product line such as a specific size of liquid detergent.

straight rebuy Recurring purchase decision in which a customer repurchases a good or service that has performed satisfactorily in the past.

strategic alliance Partnerships in which two or more companies combine resources and capital to create competitive advantages in a new market

strategic business units (SBUs) Key business units within diversified firms.

strategic planning Process of determining an organization's primary objectives and adopting courses of action that will achieve these objectives.

strategic window Limited periods during which the key requirements of a market and the particular competencies of a firm best fit together.

stratified sample Probability sample constructed to represent randomly selected subsamples of different groups within the total sample.

subcontracting Contractual agreements that assign the production of goods or services to local or smaller firms.

subcultures Groups with their own distinct modes of behavior.

subliminal perception Subconscious receipt of incoming information.

suboptimization Condition that results when individual operations achieve their objectives but interfere with progress toward broader organizational goals.

subsidy Government financial support of a private industry.

supercenter Large store, smaller than a hypermarket, that combines groceries with discount store merchandise.

supplies Regular expenses that a firm incurs in its daily operations.

supply Schedule of the amounts of a good or service that firms will offer for sale at different prices during a specified time period.

supply (value) chain Sequence of suppliers that contribute to the creation and delivery of a good or service.

survey of buyer intentions Qualitative sales forecasting method that samples opinions among groups of present and potential customers concerning their purchase intentions.

sweepstakes Sales promotion technique using games in which prize winners are chosen by chance.

switchless reseller Telecommunications company with no lines or equipment that buys blocks of long-distance time from major carriers and resells it by the minute at a discount.

SWOT analysis Analysis that helps planners compare internal organizational strengths and weaknesses with external opportunities and threats.

syndicated service Organization that regularly provides standardized data to all customers.

systems integration Centralization of the procurement function within an internal division or as a service of an external supplier.

T

tactical planning Planning that guides the implementation of activities specified in the strategic plan.

target market Group of people toward whom the firm decides to direct its marketing efforts, and ultimately its goods and services.

target-return objective Short-run or long-run pricing objectives of achieving a specified return on either sales or investment.

tariff Tax levied against imported goods.

task-objective method Development of a promotional budget based on evaluation of the firm's promotional objectives.

team selling Selling situation in which several sales associates or other members of the organization are recruited to assist the lead sales representative in reaching all those who influence the purchase decision.

technological environment Applications to marketing of knowledge based on discoveries in science, inventions, and innovations.

telemarketing Promotional presentation involving the use of the telephone on an outbound basis by salespeople or on an inbound basis by customers who initiate calls to obtain information and place orders.

test-marketing Method that involves introducing a new product in a specific area and then observing its degree of success.

third-party (contract) logistics firm Company that specializes in handling logistics activities for other firms.

time-based competition Strategy of developing and distributing goods and services more quickly than competitors.

total quality management (TQM) Movement that asks all employees in a firm to continually improve products and work processes with the goal of achieving customer satisfaction and world-class performance.

trade allowance Promotional incentive offered to wholesalers and retailers who purchase specific products.

trade discount Payment to a channel member or buyer for performing marketing functions; also known as a functional discount.

trade dress Visual components that contribute to the overall look of a brand.

trade-in Credit allowance given for a used item when a customer purchases a new item.

trade industry Retailers or wholesalers that purchase products for resale to others.

trade promotion Sales promotion that appeals to marketing intermediaries rather than consumers.

trade show Show organized by industry trade associations in which vendors are invited to appear in order to display and demonstrate their products for association members.

trademark Brand for which the owner claims exclusive legal protection.

transaction-based marketing Buyer and seller exchanges characterized by limited communications and little or no ongoing relationship between the parties.

transfer price Cost assessed when a product is moved from one profit center in a firm to another.

trend analysis Quantitative sales forecasting method that estimates future sales through statistical analyses of historical sales patterns.

truck wholesaler Limited-function merchant wholesaler who markets perishable food items; also called a truck jobber.

tying agreement Arrangement that requires a marketing intermediary to carry items other than those they want to sell.

U

unaided recall tests Posttests in which respondents do not see copies of an ad after its original reading, but must recall it from memory.

undifferentiated marketing Marketing strategy to produce a single product and market it to all customers; also called *mass marketing*.

unemployment Proportion of people in the economy who are actively seeking work but do not have jobs.

unfair-trade laws State laws requiring sellers to maintain minimum prices for comparable merchandise.

uniform-delivered price Pricing system for handling transportation costs under which all buyers are quoted the same price, including transportation expenses. Sometimes known as *postage-stamp pricing*.

unit pricing Pricing policy in which prices are stated in terms of a recognized unit of measurement or a standard numerical count.

unitizing Process of combining individual materials into large loads for easy handling.

Universal Product Code (UPC) Numerical bar code system used to record product and price information.

unsought products Products marketed to consumers who may not yet recognize any need for them.

utility Want-satisfying power of a good or service.

V

VALS2 System that divides consumers into eight psychographic categories: actualizers, fulfilleds, believers, achievers, strivers, experiencers, makers, and strugglers.

value analysis Systematic study of the components of a purchase to determine the most cost-effective approach.

value pricing Pricing strategy emphasizing benefits derived from a product in comparison to the price and quality levels of competing offerings.

variable costs Costs that change with the level of production (such as labor and raw materials costs).

vendor analysis Assessment of supplier performance in areas such as price, back orders, timely delivery, and attention to special requests.

vendor-managed inventory (VMI) Inventory management system in which the seller—based on an existing agreement with a buyer—determines how much of a product is needed.

venture team Group of specialists from different areas of an organization who work together in developing new products.

vertical marketing system (VMS) Planned channel system designed to improve distribution efficiency and cost effectiveness by integrating various functions throughout the distribution chain.

W

Web kiosk Small, free-standing computer, often located in a store, that provides consumers with Internet connections to a firm and its goods and services.

wheel of retailing Hypothesis that each new type of retailer gains a competitive foothold by offering lower prices than current suppliers charge, and maintains profits by reducing or eliminating services.

wholesaler Channel intermediary that takes title to goods it handles and then distributes these goods to retailers, other distributors, or B2B customers.

wholesaling intermediary Comprehensive term that describes wholesalers as well as agents and brokers.

wireless technology Technology that allows communications connections without wires.

World Trade Organization (WTO) Organization that replaces GATT, overseeing GATT agreements, making binding decisions in mediating disputes, and reducing trade barriers.

World Wide Web Collection of resources on the Internet that offers easy access to text, graphics, sound, and other multimedia resources.

Y

yield management Pricing strategy that allows marketers to vary prices based on such factors as demand, even though the cost of providing those goods or services remains the same; designed to maximize revenues in situations such as airfares, lodging, auto rentals, and theater tickets, where costs are fixed.

Z

zone pricing Pricing system for handling transportation costs under which the market is divided into geographic regions and a different price is set in each region.

Prologue 1　AP Topic Gallery

Prologue 2　"©2002 Principal Financial Services, Inc. Used with permission. Depicted are trademarks and registered trademarks of Principal Financial Services, Inc."

Prologue 3　"Courtesy, 6FigureJobs, a Workstream, Inc. Company"

Prologue 4　©Giry Daniel/CORBIS Sygma

Prologue 5　©Susan Van Etten

Opening Vignette 1　©AP/Wide World Photos

Figure 1.1　"©Reuters NewMedia, Inc./CORBIS"

Figure 1.2　Image used with permission of the New York Stock Exchange.

Figure 1.4　©Susan Van Etten

Figure 1.5　"©2002 City Harvest. Special thanks to the NY Giants. Photo: David Leach. Agency: Foote, Cone & Belding."

Unnumbered 1.1　©Susan Van Etten

Unnumbered 1.2　Source: San Antonio Convention & Visitors Bureau

Unnumbered 1.3　©2002 Corporate Angel Network

Unnumbered 1.4　©Athens 2004; Photo by Allsport

Figure 1.6　"Courtesy, General Motors"

Figure 1.7　Reprinted by permission of Duke Energy Corporation. All rights reserved.

Unnumbered 1.5　Courtesy of Sirius Satellite Radio

Unnumbered 1.8　©Roy Zipstein. Courtesy of Expedia Inc.

Figure 1.9　"Courtesy, Stride Rite Shoes"

Figure 1.11　Reprinted with permission of The Timberland Company. Timberland and 🌳 are trademarks or registered trademarks of The Timberland Company. ©2001 The Timberland Company. All rights reserved.

Opening Vignette 2　©Nancy Newberry

Figure 2.1　"©2002 Nordstrom, Inc."

Unnumbered 2.1　©2002 Bass Pro Shops

Figure 2.2　©Susan Van Etten

Figure 2.4　©Mark Laita. Used by permission of Apple.

Unnumbered 2.3　"Courtesy, Latina Magazine"

Figure 2.6　"Courtesy of Nestle USA, Inc."

Figure 2.7　AP Topic Gallery

Figure 2.8　©Susan Van Etten

Opening Vignette 3　Courtesy of Honda

Figure 3.2　©Susan Van Etten

Figure 3.3　©Susan Van Etten

Figure 3.4　Courtesy of Toyota Motor Sales, U.S.A., Inc.

Figure 3.5　©AP/Wide World Photos

Figure 3.6　"Courtesy, Council for Biotechnical Information"

Figure 3.7　"©2002, Quaker Oats Company. Used by permission."

Figure 3.12　"Photo appears courtesy of Keep America Beautiful, Inc."

Unnumbered 3.1　"Courtesy, United Parcel Service."

Unnumbered 3.2　"Courtesy, Boca Foods Company"

Unnumbered 3.3　©AP/Wide World Photos

Unnumbered 3.4　©Peter Turnley/CORBIS

Unnumbered 3.5　©Susan Van Etten

Unnumbered 3.6　"©2002. Used by permission of HotJobs.com, Ltd."

Unnumbered 3.7　©Susan Van Etten

Unnumbered 3.8　©2002 Scott Lowden Photography for Home Depot

Unnumbered 3.9　©AP/Wide World Photos

Opening Vignette 4　"©2002. Lands' End, Inc. Used with permission."

Unnumbered 14.1　©Susan Van Etten

Figure 4.2　"Courtesy, ©United States Postal Service"

Figure 4.3　"The creative part of Hitachi's Global Brand Campaign is courtesy of Hitachi America, Ltd."

Figure 4.4　"Courtesy, Korean Investment Service Center"

Unnumbered 4.2　AP Topic Gallery

Unnumbered 4.3　Used with permission from McDonald's Corporation.

Unnumbered 4.4　©2002 Rolex

Unnumbered 4.5　©Leo Burnett USA

Opening Vignette 5　©Royalty-Free/CORBIS

Figure 5.3　"Courtesy, Bank of America"

Figure 5.5　©Susan Van Etten

Figure 5.9　©TRUSTe

Figure 5.13A　Courtesy of Amazon.com

Figure 5.13B　©2002 Nokia.

Opening Vignette 6　©Erin Patrice O'Brien

Figure 6.3A　AP Topic Gallery

Figure 6.3B　AP Topic Gallery

Figure 6.4　Courtesy Toyota and Team One Advertising

Figure 6.6　Courtesy of L.L.Bean

Figure 6.7　"Courtesy, Marriott Rewards"

Unnumbered 6.1　"Priority Club is a registered trademark of Six Continents Hotels, Inc. Used by permission."

Unnumbered 6.2　©Jack Gruber/USA TODAY

Unnumbered 6.3　"Courtesy, PeopleSoft, Inc."

Unnumbered 6.4　"The advertisement within this book is reprinted by arrangement with Sears, Roebuck and Co. and is protected under copyright. No duplication is permitted"

Unnumbered 6.5　©2002 Bax Global

Opening Vignette 7　©AP/Wide World Photos

Figure 7.1　"Courtesy, Roper Starch"

Figure 7.2　Courtesy Cunningham Research

Figure 7.5　"Courtesy, Ipsos-ASL, Inc."

Figure 7.6　"©2002 C & R Research Services, Inc."

Figure 7.7　"Used by permission, FocusVision Worldwide, Inc."

Figure 7.8　"Courtesy, NOP World"

Unnumbered 7.1　©Susan Van Etten

Unnumbered 7.2　Courtesy of U.S. Navy Recruiting Command

Unnumbered 7.3　"©Decision Analyst, Inc."

Opening Vignette 8　©Courtesy of Torrid

Figure 8.1　©General Motors Corp. Used with permission

Figure 8.2　©Susan Van Etten

Unnumbered 8.1　©Lowe's Companies Inc.

Unnumbered 8.2　©Mitchell Gerber/CORBIS

Unnumbered 8.4　"©Wendy's International, Inc."

Unnumbered 8.3　©Susan Van Etten

Figure 8.5　©Unilever Bestfoods North America. Used with permission.

Unnumbered 8.5　©Dave G. Houser/CORBIS

Unnumbered 8.6　Image courtesy of Dodge

Figure 8.6　©2002 Cessna Aircraft Company. Used by permission.

Figure 8.8　Courtesy of Mastercard and McCann-Erickson.

Unnumbered 8.7　©Susan Van Etten

Figure 8.9　©Susan Van Etten

Figure 8.11　"The advertisement within this book is reprinted by arrangement with Sears, Roebuck and Co. and is protected under copyright. No duplication is permitted"

Unnumbered 8.8　Used by permission of Old Sturbridge Village.

Unnumbered 8.9　©Susan Van Etten

Opening Vignette 9　©Joseph Rodriguez/Black Star

Figure 9.1　"Courtesy of Nestle USA, Inc."

Figure 9.2　©Susan Van Etten

Unnumbered 9.1　"©2002 Charles Schwab & Co., Inc. All rights reserved."

Unnumbered 9.2　"Courtesy, Sears/Kang & Lee Advertising"

Unnumbered 9.3　"The Phoenix Companies, Inc."

Figure 9.4　"©Daren Rees, Photographer; Virginia Museum of Transportation. Used by permission of Mercedes-Benz©2002"

Figure 9.6　©Susan Van Etten

Unnumbered 9.4　"Courtesy, Quaker Oats Company"

Figure 9.7　©Susan Van Etten

Figure 9.8　©2002 Olive Garden. Used by permission.

Unnumbered 9.5　©Whirlpool

Name and Company Index

Subject Index

International Index